W. B. Yeats
A Classified Bibliography of Criticism

Including Additions to Allan Wade's
Bibliography of the Writings of W. B. Yeats and
a Section on the Irish Literary and Dramatic Revival

K. P. S. JOCHUM

DAWSON

First published in 1978

© 1978 by the Board of Trustees of the University of Illinois

British Library Cataloguing in Publication Data

Jochum, K P S
  W. B. Yeats.
  1. Yeats, William Butler — Bibliography
  016.821′8   Z8992

ISBN 0-7129-0862-5

ℓ

Manufactured in the United States of America

W. B. Yeats
A Classified Bibliography of Criticism

for R. E. G. M. J. H. J.,
the bibliographer's wife

Contents

Introduction and Acknowledgments

Among twentieth-century English and American writers, only T. S. Eliot and William Faulkner have received as much critical attention as W. B. Yeats. The bibliography that follows contains more than 7,900 items; this number includes about 350 additions to Allan Wade's bibliography of Yeats's own writings. Given the great amount of material, it is not surprising that several bibliographies of Yeats criticism were published from 1903 onward, including three book-length compilations. Arranged chronologically, the first of the three was my own *W. B. Yeats's Plays: An Annotated Checklist of Criticism* (1966). It contains several mistakes and numerous omissions and is now completely superseded. Next came John E. Stoll's *The Great Deluge* (1971), which is of little value (see also the annotation to item 362, below). The most comprehensive and substantial publication to date is *A Bibliography of Yeats Criticism, 1887-1965* by K. G. W. Cross and R. T. Dunlop, which was published late in 1971. In order to characterize this bibliography, it is necessary to say something about my own efforts in the field.

I started to collect material in 1961, not with a view of compiling a bibliography but as a preparation for my doctoral dissertation on Yeats's plays. By 1965 I had so much material that I thought it worthwhile to publish it independently of the thesis. Then, in November 1965, I came across *In Excited Reverie*, the centenary tribute to Yeats edited by A. Norman Jeffares and K. G. W. Cross, in which Professor Cross stated that a complete bibliography of Yeats criticism, compiled by himself and R. T. Dunlop, was "with the publishers." I wrote to him at once, asking for more information, and received a very courteous reply in which he suggested two possibilities: send him my material, which he would use with suitable acknowledgment, or publish as soon as possible so that he could make use of my printed bibliography. I preferred publication, and for the next three months I was busy getting my manuscript into shape and typing it on stencils. With the help of a student I printed the pages on a machine kindly provided by the English Department of the University of Saarbrücken, had them bound, and sold the book with a minimum of publicity. There were 215 copies in all; they are all gone with the exception of a few I have kept for reference. One copy went to Professor Cross together with a list of material I had not used, but there was no reply. I did not know that he was seriously ill.

Professor Cross's bibliography continued to be listed in some booksellers' catalogues as forthcoming until 1967. In early 1968 I wrote a letter to Macmillan's of London, his publisher, asking for the approximate date of publication. In reply, Mr. T. M. Farmiloe informed me of Professor Cross's death and indicated that publication plans were uncertain. Through Mr. Farmiloe I tried to get into contact with R. T. Dunlop, Professor Cross's collaborator, but had no success. In the meantime I had continued to collect further material, and in September 1968 I took up a two-year position at the University of Illinois and added a considerable amount of material from the splendid collection of the University of Illinois Library at Urbana-Champaign. In 1969 I finally managed to locate Mr. Dunlop at the University of New South Wales, and eventually he came to see me in Urbana on his way to London. We had many friendly conversations and discussed collaboration, but he was in effect all set to deliver his manuscript to the publisher. I gathered from what he showed me that there would be room for yet another bibliography, so each of us went ahead with his own plans.

A Bibliography of Yeats Criticism, 1887-1965 by K. G. W. Cross and R. T. Dunlop lists in six parts (1) bibliographies, concordances, and descriptions of Yeatsiana; (2) reviews of writings by W. B. Yeats; (3) books and pamphlets wholly or partly about Yeats; (4) commemorative and special issues of periodicals; (5) articles wholly or partly about Yeats; and (6) dissertations and theses. There is a list of periodicals and newspapers cited and an index of names, selected subjects, and book titles. The standard of accuracy is fairly high, and the book is altogether very useful. I am indebted to it in several ways. First, it provided me with a unique opportunity to check the accuracy of my own items. Whenever I found discrepancies, I made a second check of the material itself to ensure correct entries. Second, there were in it quite a few items that had eluded me. Third, the structure of the bibliography suggested to me some opportunities for improvement:

(1) The classification used by Cross and Dunlop is very mechanical; a subject arrangement would be of more help for the Yeats scholar. (2) Volume numbers of periodicals are better given in arabic, not roman, numerals; it saves space and eliminates many possible errors. (3) Entries should be numbered to ensure a good cross-referencing system, which again would save space by disposing of a number of multiple listings. (4) Cross and Dunlop give very little annotation; the subject index is no real substitute. (5) A complete checking against my own files revealed that many more items should have been marked with a dagger (for "not seen"). Mr. Dunlop admits as much in his introduction, the reason for not marking being mainly Professor Cross's untimely death. (6) More than 500 items of the period 1887-1965 are missing in Cross and Dunlop. Only very few items appear from East European countries, from Italy, France, the Netherlands, and, surprisingly, Ireland. There are no entries from *The Leader* and *United Ireland* and only a few from *Sinn Féin* and *United Irishman*. The Irish daily press has not been checked with any degree of thoroughness. Perhaps this is demanding too much, and I myself have not had the time and opportunity to see the entire sets of the *Irish Times, Freeman's Journal, Irish Independent,* and so on. However, Mr. Dunlop might have included an introductory note to that effect. (7) The following subjects are not or only sporadically represented: (a) poems about Yeats, (b) parodies, (c) recordings, (d) films, (e) musical renderings and operas, (f) interviews with Yeats, reports of his speeches and lectures, and reviews of first performances of his plays (admittedly very elusive material, but plenty of it exists).

These, then, are the more important points in which my bibliography differs from Cross and Dunlop's. My classification scheme is outlined in the table of contents; further explanations will be found in the headnotes to some sections. All the entries have been numbered consecutively. References to Allan Wade's *Bibliography of the Writings of W. B. Yeats* (3rd edition, 1968) are by W plus number (e.g., W211) for numbered entries, or by Wp. plus number (e.g., Wp. 396) for page numbers of unnumbered entries. Cross-references in the present bibliography are indicated by numbers prefixed by J (e.g., J304).

Many items are annotated, particularly in parts A-F, less so in parts K-M. Annotations indicate, as a rule, the contents, main argument, subject(s), or approach of the item concerned (often in the form of an appropriate quotation). The reference "(see index)" refers to the index of that particular book. Sometimes I have taken the liberty to make value judgments. Items marked with an asterisk (*) are, in my opinion, essential reading for any extended research on Yeats. I do not annotate items with self-explanatory titles, publications of a general, introductory, or survey character, or short notes. I have seen most of the items in my bibliography; those that I could not inspect personally are marked °. In multiple-title entries the sign precedes that part of the entry that I have not seen.

The bibliography is reasonably complete through 1971 and includes material from 1972 and 1973. I did not decide on a rigorous cut-off date, although I stopped systematic searching in November 1972. Omissions are possible in several areas and for a number of reasons. (1) For some countries, most notably France and Italy but also East European countries before 1945, there is no adequate bibliography of articles in periodicals. (2) There is always the odd periodical or book that is at the binder's or missing from the shelves or temporarily unavailable from the bookseller. (3) M.A. theses that came to my attention are included, but nothing short of on-the-spot research at the major American university libraries would produce anything like completeness. B.A. theses have not been included, with the exception of Harvard Honors theses. I have not searched for theses from countries other than Great Britain, Ireland, the United States, Canada, France, Germany, Austria, and Switzerland. Theses are listed in the sections to which they belong, not separately. (4) I have mentioned the problem of newspaper articles. Very few newspapers have ever been indexed. The Henderson, Holloway, and Horniman collections of press cuttings (listed in section AH) are invaluable but somewhat irritating. Important dates are frequently missing, illegible, or misleading. As a matter of fact, I do not think it necessary to trace every item in these collections, because the energy put into the search often exceeds the actual value of the results. I have tried to locate at least one review of first performances of most plays, particularly in Dublin papers. Only a few reviews exist for the first performances of *The Resurrection* and *The King of the Great Clock Tower* (30 July 1934) because of a newspaper strike in Ireland. I have also tried to include some newspaper reviews of books by and about Yeats. In my search I have greatly benefited from the help of several newspaper librarians, especially of the *Irish Independent, Irish Times, (Manchester) Guardian,* and *Sunday Times.* I have included at least one report or summary of a number of important Yeats lectures and speeches, particularly those mentioned by Donald T. Torchiana (J1147). Other possible omissions are noted in the headnotes to the respective sections.

There are, however, some deliberate omissions. (1) Routine articles in encyclopedias are not included, whereas more extended discussions are. The dividing line here and elsewhere is of course hard to draw. (2) Perfunctory treatments in some histories of literature are not mentioned. (3) The same applies to anthologies. (4) I have included reviews of the important monographs, but not as extensively as do Cross and Dunlop, since I see no point in listing reviews in out-of-the-way papers. I suspect from the incompleteness of data in the Cross-Dunlop entries (frequently no volume, issue, and page numbers are given) that these items were not actually seen by the compilers. (5) I have excluded short reviews, such as the notices in *Library Journal* and *Kirkus*. (6) Some of the entries in Cross-Dunlop are either erroneous (e.g., Arthur J. M. Smith, p. 141) or more in the nature of background literature and do not go beyond the mere mentioning of Yeats's name (e.g., John Symonds, *Madame Blavatsky*, p. 146). These items will therefore not be found in my bibliography. (7) In parts K-M I have not tried to cover the literature on the Gaelic Language Revival. (8) I include some Arabic and Japanese items, but I have made no systematic search in these and other non-European languages. Most of the Japanese Yeats criticism published until 1965 is listed in the bibliography to Shotaro Oshima's *W. B. Yeats and Japan* (J2282). I saw no point in copying Professor Oshima's list and restricted myself to include only those of his items that are written in English and that were available to me. For Japanese and Arabic items I have used the transcriptions of my sources; Cyrillic characters are transcribed according to the Library of Congress system. (9) With a few exceptions I do not include unpublished material.

I have tried to avoid multiple listings as much as possible. Theses and articles that were worked into, or became part of, books are referred to in the book entry only. Multiple listings occur regularly only with those items of section AB that are also relevant to other sections. In book publications I have cited the latest edition or reprint that I have seen (although I found it impossible to keep up with the production speed of the reprint business). The date of the first edition is added in square brackets. Different publishers for American and British editions of the same book are not noted, unless the book was issued under different titles (a wicked practice, not only from the bibliographer's point of view). I am aware of the possibility that I may not have traced several articles and reviews (particularly those published anonymously) to their final book publications.

Since there are few multiple listings, I would direct the reader's attention to the cross-references appended to most sections, and to the index of selected subjects. With a little patience he will, I hope, find all the material he needs.

Books are cited as follows:

AUTHOR: *Title*. Place: Publisher, Date [Date of first publication]. Pages. (Series. No.).

Theses appear thus:

AUTHOR: "Title," Degree, University, Date. Pages. (Abstract.);

articles, thus:

AUTHOR: "Title," *Periodical*, Volume: Issue (Date), Pages.

Issue numbers of periodicals without volume numbering are indicated by #. In the case of some periodicals with unusual numbering (especially French ones), I have added explanations like series, period, or year. Abbreviations for certain periodicals are explained in the index of periodicals; generally, Journal, Quarterly, Review, and University appear as J, Q, R, and U. UP stands for University Press.

Anonymous books or books without apparent editor are listed under title, unless an author or editor could be ascertained from reliable sources. Anonymous articles in periodicals are listed under Anon., unless an author could be identified (generally from reprints). I have no uniform policy in the handling of pseudonyms and gaelicized names, but I attempted to be consistent with respect to individuals. Thus Frank O'Connor, John Eglinton, and Andrew E. Malone appear under these names rather than under Michael O'Donovan, William Kirkpatrick Magee, and Lawrence P. Byrne, whereas AE (or A. E. or Y. O.) is always found under Russell. I have retained the maiden names of Maud Gonne and Katharine Tynan. Roibeárd O Faracháin and P. S. Ó h-Éigeartaigh will be found under their English names, Farren and O'Hegarty (which they used just as frequently as the Gaelic equivalents). Ford Madox Hueffer appears under Ford; there are separate entries, however, for that unique phenomenon Fiona Macleod / William Sharp. A reader in doubt about where to look for a certain author is referred to the index of names.

I have decided on an alphabetical order in each section with the exception of sections AB, BF, and BG and parts G and H, since I felt that a chronological arrangement (which I am sure has many advantages) would upset the cross-reference system and necessitate a host of multiple listings. Two and more items of the same author in any given section are arranged chronologically.

A compiler of a bibliography of such dimensions becomes, after a while, a very humble person, particularly when he feels that he can be taken to task for numerous inconsistencies, omissions, and mistakes. Since I intend to continue to collect material and to publish the results, I would be grateful if every error and omission were pointed out to me. Another lesson to be learned from reading or seeing so much literature on Yeats is that he himself was ever so much cleverer than most if not all of his critics, adulators, detractors, and just plain readers. It is something of a relief to return to a Yeats poem or play or essay (especially a less glamorous one) and simply enjoy it. I would like to warn the budding Yeats scholar not to read too much of the material assembled here; I would be very sorry indeed if the bibliography should serve only to produce more confusion.

Although the compilation of this bibliography has been, in effect, a single-handed effort, I have nevertheless accumulated numerous and deep obligations. First of all, I am grateful to the many Yeats scholars who identified their sources and out-of-the-way material (and my wrath on those who didn't). More instrumental, however, have been some persons who nursed the project along its way: Professor Willi Erzgräber of the University of Freiburg, who started my Yeats studies; Professors George Hendrick and A. Lynn Altenbernd of the University of Illinois at Urbana-Champaign, who gave me time and opportunity to collect the bulk of the material; Professor John P. Frayne, also at the University of Illinois, for reasons that he himself knows best; and Professor Armin Paul Frank and Mrs. Barbara Frank of the University of Göttingen, who contributed significantly and read the manuscript in its entirety.

Many libraries and librarians throughout the world have granted me reader's privileges, have answered numerous inquiries, or have been helpful in other ways. I am particularly indebted to the University of Illinois Library at Urbana-Champaign, its very fine Reference Department, and Miss Eva F. Benton of the English Library; the Yale University Library; the Harvard University Library; Mr. Michael J. Durkan and the Wesleyan University Library, Middletown, Connecticut; the Newberry Library, Chicago; the University of Chicago Library; Mr. R. Russell Maylone and the Northwestern University Library, Evanston, Illinois; Southern Illinois University Library; Kenyon College Library; the Library of Congress; the New York Public Library; Colby College Library, Waterville, Maine; the University of Kansas Library; the Humanities Research Center at the University of Texas; the Henry E. Huntington Library, San Marino, California; the University of Toronto Library; the Library of the University of Victoria, British Columbia; Dr. Wolfgang Kehr, Dr. Gerd Schmidt, and the Universitätsbibliothek Freiburg in Germany; almost all the other German university libraries; the Bayerische Staatsbibliothek, München; the Staatsbibliothek der Stiftung Preussischer Kulturbesitz; Mr. Alf MacLochlainn and the National Library of Ireland; the Library of Trinity College, Dublin; the British Library, Reference Division (especially Mr. Richard Bancroft) and Newpaper Library; the university libraries of London, Cambridge, Reading, and Manchester; the Bodleian Library, Oxford; the Bibliothèque Nationale, Paris; the National Library of Australia; the National Széchényi Library, Budapest; the Narodna in Universitetna Knjižnica, Ljubljana, Yugoslavia; the University Library, Prague; the All-Union State Library of Foreign Literature, Moscow; and many others that lack of space forbids to mention.

I should like to thank the Graduate College and the Department of English of the University of Illinois at Urbana-Champaign, the University of Freiburg, and the Deutsche Forschungsgemeinschaft for financial help, and the Deutsche Akademische Austauschdienst, particularly Mr. Martin L. Mruck and the staff of his London office, for its hospitality. I am greatly indebted to Miss Linda Glass, copy editor, and Miss Frances Warner, typist, for their care and diligence.

I am grateful for the help of many individuals who answered my inquiries or supplied urgently required material, especially Professor Winfried Herget and Mrs. Doris Herget (Saarbrücken), Dr. S. C. Sen (Santiniketan), and Professors Shotaro Oshima (Tokyo), René Fréchet (Paris), Richard J. Finneran (New Orleans), Dan H. Laurence (San Antonio, Texas), James L. Allen (Hilo, Hawaii), and David R. Clark (Amherst, Massachusetts). I should also like to thank the editor of the *Bulletin of Bibliography* for permission to reprint material originally published in its pages.

And finally there are my wife, who shook her head in despair more than once; some friends whose hospitality on a second trip to the United States is gratefully remembered: Gebhard and Gisela Dörmer and Dinu and Mirela Susan (especially Mirela, who died before she could see this); Jeannie, Jerry, Larry, and Lex, who marveled; and S. A. L., who listened once in a while.

W. B. Yeats: A Classified Bibliography of Criticism

A BIBLIOGRAPHIES, CONCORDANCES, AND CATALOGUES

AA Bibliographies of Yeats's Writings

1. ANON.: "Bibliographies of Modern Authors: William Butler Yeats," *London Mercury*, 2:8 (June 1920), 220-21.

2. JOCHUM, K. P. S.: "Additions to the Yeats Bibliography," *Bulletin of Bibliography*, 28:4 (Oct-Dec 1971), 129-35.
   Additions to Wade, 3rd edition (J12), now incorporated in section AB of this bibliography.

3. Ó HAODHA, MICHEÁL: "Unrecorded Yeats Contributions to Periodicals," *Irish Book*, 2:3/4 (Autumn 1963), 129.
   Now included in Wade, 3rd edition (J12).

4. ————: "When Was Yeats First Published?" *Irish Times*, #34207 (5 June 1965), 10.
   A sonnet, "I saw a shepherd youth . . . ," signed "Y." and first published in *Hibernia*, 1 Apr 1882 (J129), is presumed to be by Yeats. Reprints the poem.

5. ————: "When Was Yeats First Published?" *Éire-Ireland*, 2:2 (Summer 1967), 67-71.
   Eleven poems, published in *Hibernia* between Apr 1882 and June 1883 over the initial "Y," may have been written by Yeats.

6. O'HEGARTY, P. S.: "Notes on the Bibliography of W. B. Yeats," *Dublin Mag*, 14:4 (Oct-Dec 1939), 61-65; 15:1 (Jan-Mar 1940), 37-42.

7. ROTH, WILLIAM MATSON: *A Catalogue of English and American First Editions of William Butler Yeats.* Prepared for an exhibition of his works held in the Yale University Library beginning May 15, 1939. New Haven, 1939. 104 p.

8. SAUL, GEORGE BRANDON: *Prolegomena to the Study of Yeats's Poems.* Philadelphia: U of Pennsylvania Press, 1957. 196 p. Reprinted, °NY: Octagon Books, 1971.
   "This book . . . purports to give an accurate commentary on the divisions of the relatively definitive . . . *Collected Poems* . . . ; and for individual poems (1) a full record of publication and of title changes . . . , (2) a statement of recorded dates and other significant facts of composition, and (3) an attempted resolution of else unclarified obscurities . . . as well as indication of parallel or closely related passages and recording of available important references and glosses" (p. 7). Eccentricities of judgment and insufficient bibliographical descriptions mar what may have been, in its time, a good handbook on Yeats's poetry. Today the book is largely out of date. See also J10.
   Reviews:
   1. Denis Donoghue, *Studies,* 48:[] (Spring 1959), 106-8.
   2. Thomas Parkinson, "The Respect of Monuments," *Sewanee R*, 68:1 (Jan-Mar 1960), 143-49.
   3. T. J. B. Spencer, *MLR*, 53:4 (Oct 1958), 626-27.
   4. Peter Ure, *RES*, 11:41 (Feb 1960), 113-14.

9. ————: *Prolegomena to the Study of Yeats's Plays.* Philadelphia: U of Pennsylvania Press, 1958. 106 p. Reprinted, °NY: Octagon Books, 1971.
   Corresponds to the preceding item. See also J10.

3

Reviews:
1. Anon., "Yeats's Drama," *TLS*, 58:2982 (24 Apr 1959), 239.
2. William C. Burto, *ETJ*, 12:3 (Oct 1960), 233-34.
3. Thomas Parkinson, "The Respect of Monuments," *Sewanee R*, 68:1 (Jan-Mar 1960), 143-49.

10. ———: "W. B. Yeats: Corrigenda," *N&Q*, os 205 / ns 7:8 (Aug 1960), 302-3.
Corrections in J8 and 9.

10a. SMYTHE, COLIN: "Allan Wade's *Bibliography of the Writings of W. B. Yeats:* Some *Errata* and *Addenda*," *Long Room*, #8 (Autumn/Winter 1973), 41-42.

11. SYMONS, ALPHONSE JAMES ALBERT: *A Bibliography of the First Editions of Books by William Butler Yeats*. London: First Editions Club, 1924. viii, 46 p.
Reviews:
1. Anon., *TLS*, 23:1180 (28 Aug 1924), 526.

12. *WADE, ALLAN: *A Bibliography of the Writings of W. B. Yeats*. 3rd edition, revised and edited by Russell K. Alspach. London: Hart-Davis, 1968 [1951]. 514 p. (Soho Bibliographies. 1.)
Based on a compilation made in 1908 (see J4195). Incorporates Alspach's "Additions to Allan Wade's Bibliography of W. B. Yeats," *Irish Book*, 2:3/4 (Autumn 1963), 91-114.
Includes "The Cuala Press, First Called the Dun Emer Press," 451-57 (a list of publications); "Some Books about Yeats and His Work," 458-66; George Whalley, "Yeats and Broadcasting," 467-77 (an annotated list of broadcasts in which Yeats participated and of some broadcasts concerning Yeats made between 1939 and 1957).
For additions see section AB of the present bibliography.
Reviews:
1. Anon., *Book Collector*, 1:1 (Spring 1952), 62-63.
2. Anon., "The Writings of W. B. Yeats," *TLS*, 51:2608 (25 Jan 1952), 84. Correspondence by Marion Witt, :2619 (11 Apr 1952), 251.
3. Anon., "Yeats in Youth and Maturity," *TLS*, 57:2923 (7 Mar 1958), 126.
4. John Hayward, *Library*, ser 5 / 7:1 (Mar 1952), 66-68.
5. T. R. Henn, "Towards the Study of Yeats," *NSt*, 43:1088 (12 Jan 1952), 43.
6. W. P. M., *Dublin Mag*, 27:2 (Apr-June 1952), 38-40.
7. Donagh MacDonagh, "Two Hundred Books by W. B. Yeats," *Irish Press*, 22:7 (8 Jan 1952), 6.
8. Gerald D. McDonald, *PBSA*, 52:4 (1958), 322-26.

See also J133a, 177a, 1132, 2282, 2373, 4195.

AB   Additions to Allan Wade's *Bibliography*
of the Writings of W. B. Yeats (1968)

This section lists more than 350 items that will have to be incorporated in a future fourth edition of Wade's bibliography. I suspect that more items can be found with a little bit of luck, particularly translations in periodicals that have never been indexed. The additions are principally of four kinds: (1) reprints of existing titles (e.g., the Shannon reprints of Cuala Press books), (2) new material published after 1965/66 (Alspach's cut-off date for the third edition of Wade), (3) contributions to books and articles in periodicals overlooked by both Wade and Alspach, and (4) translations published both before and after 1965. My entry style does not reproduce the niceties of bibliographical description employed by Wade and

Alspach; the order of entries, however, corresponds to that in Wade.
Numbers in parentheses preceding my entries indicate the page in the third
edition of Wade where the additions should be made. These numbers are
provided for first entries of any given page in Wade; they are not repeated
in entries belonging to the same page.

There is one curious item, "Under the Moon," mentioned by Allan Wade
in his edition of Yeats's *Letters* and thought to be at least "inspired"
by Yeats (pp. 243-44), which I have not included here; its correct bibliographical data (Wade misquotes) will be found under J4312.

Books by W. B. Yeats

13. (63) *Ideas of Good and Evil*. NY: Russell & Russell, 1967. vii, 341 p.
    Reprint of W46.

14. (66) °*In the Seven Woods: Being Poems Chiefly of the Irish Heroic Age*.
Shannon: Irish UP, 1970. iv, 64 p.
    Reprint of W49.

15. (74) °*Stories of Red Hanrahan*. Shannon: Irish UP, 1971. vi, 57 p.
    Reprint of W59.

16. (82) °*Discoveries: A Volume of Essays*. Shannon: Irish UP, 1970. vi,
45 p.
    Reprint of W72.

17. (96) YEATS, W. B., and LADY ISABELLA AUGUSTA GREGORY: *The Irish National
Theatre: Its Work and Its Needs*. [London: Haycock, 1910]. 8 p.
    Contents: "The Irish National Theatre," 2-4, signed W. B. Yeats and
    Lady Gregory (see also the letter to the *Times*, 16 June 1910 [Wp. 372]);
    "A Record of Work: Plays Produced by the Abbey Theatre Co. and Its
    Predecessors, with Dates of First Performances," 5-7, unsigned. There
    is a copy of the pamphlet in the New York Public Library, Berg Collec-
    tion. Reprinted in J6703.

18. [————]: *Abbey Theatre Endowment Fund*. Dublin: Corrigan & Wilson,
1910. 8 p.
    A copy of the pamphlet is in the New York Public Library, Berg Collec-
    tion.

19. °*The Green Helmet and Other Poems*. Shannon: Irish UP, 1970. viii, 33 p.
    Reprint of W84.

20. (99) °*Synge and the Ireland of His Time*. With a note concerning a walk
through Connemara with him by Jack Butler Yeats. Shannon: Irish UP, 1970.
vii, 45 p.
    Reprint of W88.

21. (103) *The Land of Heart's Desire*. Girard, Kans.: Haldeman-Julius, [ca.
1923]. 32 p. (Little Blue Book. 335.)
    A copy of this edition is in the Southern Illinois University Library,
    Carbondale.

22. *The Land of Heart's Desire*. NY: Little Leather Library Corporation,
n.d. 80 p. (Little Leather Series. 84.)
    It seems to me that this was published around the same time as the
    preceding item. Again, the Southern Illinois University Library owns
    a copy.

23. (107) °*The Green Helmet and Other Poems*. Folcroft, Pa.: Folçroft Press,
1969. 91 p.
    Reprint of W101.

24. (113) °*A Selection from the Love Poetry*. Shannon: Irish UP, 1970. viii, 30 p.
     Reprint of W106.

25. (114) °*The Hour Glass*. Shannon: Irish UP, 1970. ii, 35 p.
     Reprint of W108.

26. (115) °*Responsibilities: Poems and a Play*. Shannon: Irish UP, 1971. viii, 83 p.
     Reprint of W110.

27. (119) °*Reveries over Childhood and Youth*. Shannon: Irish UP, 1971. vii, 128 p.
     Reprint of W111.

28. (124) °*The Wild Swans at Coole, Other Verses and a Play in Verse*. Shannon: Irish UP, 1970. vi, 48 p.
     Reprint of W118.

29. (128) °*Two Plays for Dancers*. Shannon: Irish UP, 1970. iii, 39 p.
     Reprint of W123.

30. (132) °*Michael Robartes and the Dancer*. Shannon: Irish UP, 1970. viii, 35 p.
     Reprint of W127.

31. (135) °*Four Years*. Shannon: Irish UP, 1971. ii, 92 p.
     Reprint of W131.

32. (136) °*Seven Poems and a Fragment*. Shannon: Irish UP, 1970. iv, 25 p.
     Reprint of W132.

33. (146) °*The Cat and the Moon and Certain Poems*. Shannon: Irish UP, 1970. vi, 43 p.
     Reprint of W145.

34. (149) °*The Bounty of Sweden: A Meditation and a Lecture Delivered before the Royal Swedish Academy and Certain Notes*. Shannon: Irish UP, 1971. iv, 55 p.
     Reprint of W146.

35. (153) °*Estrangement: Being Some Fifty Thoughts from a Diary Kept by William Butler Yeats in the Year Nineteen Hundred and Nine*. Shannon: Irish UP, 1970. ii, 40 p.
     Reprint of W150.

36. (158) °*The Lake Isle of Innisfree*. Pasadena: Grey Bow Press, 1927. 4 p.
     According to Will Ransom, *Private Presses and Their Books* (NY: Bowker, 1929), p. 307, only 15 copies were printed.

37. °*October Blast*. Shannon: Irish UP, 1970. iv, 27 p.
     Reprint of W156.

38. (163) °*The Death of Synge and Other Passages from an Old Diary*. Shannon: Irish UP, 1970. iv, 37 p.
     Reprint of W162.

39. (164) °*A Packet for Ezra Pound*. Shannon: Irish UP, 1970. ii, 39 p.
     Reprint of W163.

40. (168) °*Stories of Michael Robartes and His Friends: An Extract from a Record Made by His Pupils: And a Play in Prose*. Shannon: Irish UP, 1970. iv, 46 p.
     Reprint of W167.

41. (169) °*Words for Music Perhaps and Other Poems*. Shannon: Irish UP, 1970. vi, 43 p.
    Reprint of W168.

42. (176) *Letters to the New Island*. Edited with an Introduction by Horace Reynolds. London: Oxford UP, 1970. xiii, 222 p.
    Reprint of W173.

43. (178) °*The Words upon the Window-Pane: A Play in One Act, with Notes upon the Play and Its Subject*. Shannon: Irish UP, 1970. viii, 59 p.
    Reprint of W174.

44. (182) °*The King of the Great Clock Tower, Commentaries and Poems*. Shannon: Irish UP, 1970. viii, 47 p.
    Reprint of W179.

45. (186) °*Dramatis Personae*. Shannon: Irish UP, 1971. ii, 89 p.
    Reprint of W183.

46. (193) °*Essays: 1931 to 1936*. Shannon: Irish UP, 1971. iv, 133 p.
    Reprint of W194.

47. (195) °*New Poems*. Shannon: Irish UP, 1970. iv, 47 p.
    Reprint of W197.

48. (199) °*Last Poems and Two Plays*. Shannon: Irish UP, 1970. iv, 61 p.
    Reprint of W200.

49. °*The Lake Isle of Innisfree*. [San Francisco: Grabhorn Press, 1939]. 2 leaves.
    150 copies printed "For Albert M. Bender's St. Patrick's Day Party from Francis P. Farquhar." The Stanford University Library owns a copy.

50. (202) °*The Autobiography of William Butler Yeats, Consisting of Reveries over Childhood and Youth, The Trembling of the Veil and Dramatis Personae*. Louisville, Ky.: American Printing House for the Blind, 1939. 4 v.
    In Braille. According to the *National Union Catalog*, there is a copy in the Cleveland Public Library.

51. (203) °*If I Were Four-and-Twenty*. Shannon: Irish UP, 1971. iv, 69 p.
    Reprint of W205.

52. (204) °*Mosada*. Shannon: Irish UP, 1970. iv, 21 p.
    Reprint of W206.

53. °*Pages from a Diary Written in Nineteen Hundred and Thirty*. Shannon: Irish UP, 1971. iv, 59 p.
    Reprint of W207.

54. (205) °*Tribute to Thomas Davis* [. . .]. Cork: Cork UP, 1965. 22 p.
    Reprint of W208.

55. (210) *A Selection of Poetry by W. B. Yeats (1865-1939)*. Cambridge: Metcalfe, 1951. 16 p. (*Oasis*, No. 4 [Nov 1951].)
    Contains "Yeats, a Sketch," 4 (unsigned), and eleven poems. Presumably printed as a program for a poetry reading by Siobhan McKenna on 25 Nov 1951. The British Museum owns a copy (X.909/10852).

56. (212) °*Some Letters from W. B. Yeats to John O'Leary and His Sister from Originals in the Berg Collection*. Edited by Allan Wade. Folcroft, Pa.: Folcroft Press, 1969. 25 p.
    Reprint of W211F.

57. (216) YEATS, W. B., and GEORGE MOORE: "A Critical Edition of *Diarmuid and Grania* by William Butler Yeats and George Moore." Edited by Ray Small. Editor's Ph.D. thesis, U of Texas, 1958. vi, 324 p. (*DA*, 19:5 [Nov 1958], 1073-74.)
Contains a hitherto unpublished version of the play.

57a. (222) *Poems of W. B. Yeats*. Selected with an introduction and notes by A. Norman Jeffares. London: Macmillan, 1962. xxii, 261 p. (The Scholar's Library.)
This is nearly identical with W211X.

57b. (227) *Eleven Plays of William Butler Yeats*. Edited with an introduction and notes by A. Norman Jeffares. NY: Collier Books, 1973 [1964]. v, 250 p.
Textually the same as W211BB with only minor alterations.

57c. (228) °*The Autobiography of William Butler Yeats, Consisting of Reveries over Childhood and Youth, The Trembling of the Veil, and Dramatis Personae*. NY: Collier Books, 1965. 404 p.
Not identical with W211B.

58. (229) *Running to Paradise*. An introductory selection by Kevin Crossley-Holland. Illustrated by Judith Valpy. NY: Macmillan, 1968. 94 p.
Contains 47 poems or parts of poems.

59. *John Sherman & Dhoya*. Edited with an introduction, collation of the texts, and notes by Richard J. Finneran. Detroit: Wayne State UP, 1969. 138 p.

60. *The Poems*. Selected, edited, and introduced by William York Tindall. Illustrated with drawings by Robin Jacques. NY: Printed at the Thistle Press for the Members of the Limited Editions Club, 1970. xviii, 135 p.

61. *Uncollected Prose*. Collected and edited by John P. Frayne. NY: Columbia UP, 1970-. 2 v.
Volume 1: *First Reviews and Articles, 1886-1896*. 437 p. This includes the material on pp. 329-51 of Wade, 3rd edition. Frayne adds a review of Edward Garnett's *An Imaged World*, which appeared anonymously in the *Speaker* of 8 Sept 1894 and which is attributed to Yeats on strong evidence. Quotes from an unpublished letter to Horace Reynolds, dated 24 Dec 1932 (p. 34). For an omission see J4104.

62. *Reflections*. Transcribed and edited by Curtis Bradford from the Journals. Dublin: Cuala Press, 1970. iii, 63 p.
The Journals of 1908-14. Now contained in J67.

63. *A Tower of Polished Black Stones: Early Versions of "The Shadowy Waters."* Arranged and edited by David Ridgley Clark and George Mayhew with five illustrations by Leonard Baskin and drawings by the poet. Dublin: Dolmen Press, 1971. xvi, 71 p. (Dolmen Editions. 11.)
The text is reprinted in J64. For details see J3895.

64. *Druid Craft: The Writing of "The Shadowy Waters."* Manuscripts of W. B. Yeats transcribed, edited & with a commentary by Michael J. Sidnell, George P. Mayhew, and David R. Clark. Amherst: U of Massachusetts Press, 1971. xxiii, 349 p. (Manuscripts of W. B. Yeats. 1.)
For details see J3896.

65. DOMVILLE, ERIC: *A Concordance to the Plays of W. B. Yeats*. Based on *The Variorum Edition of the Plays*, edited by Russell K. Alspach. Ithaca: Cornell UP, 1972. xxi, 1559 p. in 2 v.

66. *W. B. Yeats and the Designing of Ireland's Coinage.* Dublin: Dolmen Press, 1972. 76 p. (New Yeats Papers. 3.)
For details see J4231.

67. *Memoirs: Autobiography--First Draft. Journal.* Transcribed and edited by Denis Donoghue. London: Macmillan, 1972. 318 p.

67a. *A Prayer on Going into My House.* With drawings by Rigby Graham. Gort, County Galway: Published for the Friends of Thoor Ballylee, 1973. [7 p.]

67b. *The Speckled Bird.* Edited by William H. O'Donnell. Dublin: Cuala Press, 1973-74. 2 v.
Volume 1: 1973. xi, 88 p. Contains a preface by the editor and Book I of the novel.
Volume 2: 1974. iii, 100 p. Contains Books II-IV and some notes.

67c. MOORE, GEORGE, and W. B. YEATS: *Diarmuid and Grania: A Three Act Tragedy.* Introduction by Anthony Farrow. Chicago: De Paul U, 1974. i, 59 p. (Irish Drama Series. 10.)
Reprints, "with only cosmetic changes," the text in the *Variorum Edition of the Plays.*

Books and Periodicals Edited by W. B. Yeats

68. (240) °BLAKE, WILLIAM: *The Works of William Blake: Poetic, Symbolic, and Critical.* Edited [. . .]. NY: AMS Press, 1973. 3 v.
Reprint of W218.

69. (242) ————: *Poems.* Edited by W. B. Yeats. Cambridge, Mass.: Harvard UP, 1969. xlix, 277 p.
Reprint of W221.

70. (245-47) *Beltaine: The Organ of the Irish Literary Theatre.* Number one to number three, May 1899-April 1900. Edited by W. B. Yeats. Reprinted in one volume with an introductory note by B. C. Bloomfield. London: Cass, 1970.
Reprint of W226.

71. (247-56) *Samhain, October 1901-November 1908.* Edited by W. B. Yeats. Numbers one to seven reprinted in one volume together with paragraphs from the unpublished number 1909. With an introduction by B. C. Bloomfield. London: Cass, 1970.
Reprint of W227-30, 233, 237, 241, 244A. For a different version of "Paragraphs from the Forthcoming Number of *Samhain*" see J71a and 125, as well as J2402.

71a. (256) °*Paragraphs from Samhain 1909.* N.p., [1909]. 8 p.
Described, not quite correctly, in J2402, reprinted in J125. Roger McHugh argues in J125 (p. 196) that this should come between W244A and W244B.

72. (249) °JOHNSON, LIONEL: *Twenty One Poems.* Selected by William Butler Yeats. Shannon: Irish UP, 1971. xvi, 40 p.
Reprint of W231.

73. (250) °ALLINGHAM, WILLIAM: *Sixteen Poems.* Selected by William Butler Yeats. Shannon: Irish UP, 1971. xvi, 48 p.
Reprint of W234.

74. (252) °TYNAN, KATHARINE: *Twenty One Poems.* Selected by W. B. Yeats. Shannon: Irish UP, 1971. xvi, 48 p.
Reprint of W238.

75. (254) °YEATS, W. B., and LIONEL JOHNSON: *Poetry and Ireland: Essays*.
Shannon: Irish UP, 1970. 53 p.
    Reprint of W242.

76. (255) °SYNGE, JOHN MILLINGTON: *Poems and Translations*. Shannon: Irish
UP, 1970. xiii, 45 p.
    Reprint of W243.

76a. (262) *Fairy and Folk Tales of Ireland*. Edited by W. B. Yeats with a
foreword by Kathleen Raine. Gerrards Cross: Smythe, 1973. xix, 389 p.
    Combines *Fairy and Folk Tales of the Irish Peasantry*, 1888 (W212),
    and *Irish Fairy Tales*, 1892 (W216/217).

76b. °*Irish Folk Tales*. Illustrated by Rowel Friers. Avon, Conn.: Printed
for the Members of the Limited Editions Club, 1973. xix, 409 p.

Books with a Preface or Introduction by W. B. Yeats

77. (264) GREGORY, LADY ISABELLA AUGUSTA: *Cuchulain of Muirthemne: The
Story of the Men of the Red Branch of Ulster*. Arranged and put into English
by Lady Gregory. With a preface by W. B. Yeats and a foreword by Daniel
Murphy. Gerrards Cross: Smythe, 1970. 272 p. (Coole Edition of the Works
of Lady Gregory. 2.)
    New edition of W256.

78. (265) ─────: *Gods and Fighting Men: The Story of the Tuatha de Danaan
and of the Fianna of Ireland*. Arranged and put into English by Lady Gregory.
With a preface by W. B. Yeats and a foreword by Daniel Murphy. Gerrards
Cross: Smythe, 1970. 367 p. (Coole Edition of the Works of Lady Gregory.
3.)
    New edition of W258.

79. (267) TAGORE, SIR RABINDRANATH: *Gitanjali (Song Offerings)*. A collection
of prose translations made by the author from the original Bengali. With
an introduction by W. B. Yeats. London: Macmillan, 1965. xxii, 101 p.
(Unesco Collection of Representative Works. Indian Series.)
    Reprint of W264.

80. (272) BUSHRUI, SUHEIL BADI (ed): *Sunshine and the Moon's Delight: A
Centenary Tribute to John Millington Synge, 1871-1909* [. . .]. Gerrards
Cross: Smythe / Beirut: American U of Beirut, 1972. 356 p.
    Shotaro Oshima: "Synge in Japan," 253-63; reprints on pp. 262-63 a
    preface written by Yeats, dated Dec 1921, for a Japanese edition of
    Synge's plays, °*Shingu Gikyoku Zenshu* (1924).

81. (278) VILLIERS DE L'ISLE ADAM, [JEAN MARIE MATHIAS PHILIPPE AUGUSTE,
COMTE DE]: *Axel*. Translated by Marilyn Gaddis Rose. Dublin: Dolmen Press,
1970. xv, 175 p.
    Reprints Yeats's preface from W275, pp. xiii-xv.

Books Containing Contributions by W. B. Yeats, Including Letters from Him

82. (288) NATIONAL THEATRE SOCIETY: *Rules of the National Theatre Society
Limited*. Dublin: Cahill, [1903]. 19 p.
    Signed by F. J. Fay (secretary), Augusta Gregory, W. B. Yeats, W. G.
    Fay, Vera Esposito, J. M. Synge, Sara Allgood, U. Wright.

83. ROYAL HIBERNIAN ACADEMY AND METROPOLITAN SCHOOL OF ART, DUBLIN: *Report
by Committee of Inquiry into the Work Carried On by the Royal Hibernian
Academy and the Metropolitan School of Art, Dublin, Together with Minutes
of Evidence, Appendices and Index*. Presented to both Houses of Parliament
by command of His Majesty. Dublin: HMSO, 1906. xxv, 98 p.

Yeats's evidence, given on 13 Oct 1905, appears on pp. 60-61. See *passim* for reactions to this evidence.

84. (293) GREGORY, LADY ISABELLA AUGUSTA: *Visions and Beliefs in the West of Ireland*. Collected and arranged by Lady Gregory. With two essays and notes by W. B. Yeats. With a foreword by Elizabeth Coxhead. Gerrards Cross: Smythe, 1970. 365 p. (Coole Edition of the Works of Lady Gregory. 1.)
   New edition of W312.

85. WESTON, JESSIE LAIDLAY: *From Ritual to Romance*. Garden City: Doubleday, 1957 [1920]. xvii, 217 p. (Doubleday Anchor Book. A215.)
   A quotation from a letter appears on p. 79.

86. (299) BEDDINGTON, FRANCES ETHEL: *All That I Have Met*. By Mrs. Claude Beddington. London: Cassell, 1929. xiii, 287 p.
   For details see J588.

87. (301) DRINKWATER, JOHN: *Discovery: Being the Second Book of an Autobiography, 1897-1913*. London: Benn, 1932. 235 p.
   Quotations from letters appear on pp. 170-78.

88. (305) GWYNN, STEPHEN (ed): *William Butler Yeats: Essays in Tribute*. Port Washington, N.Y.: Kennikat Press, 1965 [1940]. viii, 229 p.
   For details see J1089 (#3).

89. °SHAW, [GEORGE] BERNARD, and W. B. YEATS: *Florence Farr, Bernard Shaw and W. B. Yeats*. Edited by Clifford Bax. Shannon: Irish UP, 1971. xvi, 96 p.
   Reprint of W327.

90. (312) LEWIS, WYNDHAM: *Rude Assignment: A Narrative of My Career Up-to-Date*. London: Hutchinson, [1950]. 231 p.
   A letter to Lewis, n.p., n.d. (1928?), appears on pp. 126-27. Reprinted in *Letters* (W211J/K), pp. 762-63.

91. (315) GOGARTY, OLIVER ST. JOHN: *Start from Somewhere Else: An Exposition of Wit and Humor Polite and Perilous*. Garden City: Doubleday, 1955. 189 p.
   Prints, from memory, an unpublished poem, "Crazy Jane and the King," pp. 126-27. See also J161 for a somewhat different version, and J3009 for details. The poem was mentioned by Gogarty in Feb 1937 (cf. *Dolmen Press Yeats Centenary Papers* [J1076], p. 398) and appears as "Cracked Mary's Vision" in Ellmann's *Identity of Yeats* (J1081), pp. 101-2.

92. CRAIG, EDWARD GORDON: *Index to the Story of My Days: Some Memoirs, 1872-1907*. London: Hulton Press, 1957. vii, 308 p.
   Contains a letter from Yeats to Craig, dated 2 Apr 1901 (p. 239), and an extract from another letter, dated 13 Mar 1902 (p. 242).

93. LYTTON, NOEL ANTHONY SCAWEN LYTTON, EARL OF: *The Desert and the Green*. London: Macdonald, 1957. 350 p.
   Contains "Salutation to Wilfrid Scawen Blunt" (1914), signed by Yeats, F. S. Flint, Richard Aldington, Victor Plarr, T. Sturge Moore, and Ezra Pound (p. 36).

94. SCHUTTE, WILLIAM METCALF: *Joyce and Shakespeare: A Study in the Meaning of "Ulysses."* New Haven: Yale UP, 1957. xiv, 197 p. (Yale Studies in English. 134.)
   Quotes a remark on John Eglinton, p. 40.

95. (316) EGERTON, GEORGE: *A Leaf from the Yellow Book: The Correspondence of George Egerton*. Edited by Terence de Vere White. London: Richards Press, 1958. 184 p.
> For details see J635.

96. JOYCE, STANISLAUS: *My Brother's Keeper*. Edited with an introduction by Richard Ellmann [. . .]. London: Faber and Faber, 1958. 258 p.
> Contains two letters from Yeats to James Joyce: (1) Nassau Hotel, Dublin, n.d. (p. 185); (2) 41 Montague Mansions, London, 18 Dec 1902 (pp. 207-9). See also J97.

97. (317) ELLMANN, RICHARD: *James Joyce*. NY: Oxford UP, 1965 [1959]. xvi, 842 p. (Galaxy Book. GB149.)
> Contains the following Yeats material: (1) part of a letter to JJ, n.p., ca. 1902 (p. 108), reprinted from J96; (2) a letter to JJ, London, ca. 1902 (p. 112), no source given; (3) a letter to JJ, n.p., 18 Dec 1902 (p. 118), reprinted from J96; (4) a letter to JJ, Coole Park, 2 Oct [1904] (pp. 183-84), from the Slocum collection, Yale U; (5) a letter to JJ, n.p., [1915] (p. 414), from the Joyce collection at Cornell U; a letter to Ezra Pound, n.p., 11 Feb 1917 (p. 414), no source given.

98. (319) LAWRENCE, ARNOLD WALTER (ed): *Letters to T. E. Lawrence*. 2nd impression. London: Cape, 1964. 216 p.
> Contains one letter to T. E. Lawrence and one to Mrs. G. B. Shaw, pp. 213-14.

99. LESLIE, SEYMOUR: *The Jerome Connexion*. London: Murray, 1964. x, 220 p.
> For details see J711.

100. *1913: Jim Larkin and the Dublin Lock-out*. Dublin: Worker's Union of Ireland, 1964. 124 p.
> "Dublin Fanaticism," 71-72; reprinted from *Irish Worker*, 1 Nov 1913 (Wp. 375).

101. (322) BRADFORD, CURTIS BAKER: *Yeats at Work*. Carbondale: Southern Illinois UP, 1965. xix, 407 p.
> For details see J1073.

102. DAS GUPTA, R. K. (ed): *Rabindranath Tagore and William Butler Yeats* [. . .]. Delhi: Department of Modern Indian Languages, U of Delhi, 1965. iv, 36 p.
> For details see J2177.

103. JEFFARES, ALEXANDER NORMAN, and KENNETH GUSTAV WALTER CROSS (eds): *In Excited Reverie: A Centenary Tribute to William Butler Yeats, 1865-1939*. London: Macmillan, 1965. viii, 354 p.
> For details see J1101 (#9, 12).

104. (323) JOYCE, JAMES: *Letters*. Edited by Stuart Gilbert and Richard Ellmann. NY: Viking Press, 1957-66. 3 v.
> For details see J843.

105. (324) MOKASHI-PUNEKAR, SHANKAR: *The Later Phase in the Development of W. B. Yeats. (A Study in the Stream of Yeats's Later Thought and Creativity)*. Dharwar: Karnatak U, 1966. xv, 285 p. (Karnatak U Research Series. 8 [i.e., 9].)
> Contains excerpts from 30 letters to Shri Purohit Swami, 29 Mar 1932 to 22 Dec 1938, pp. 259-67.

106. NOWELL-SMITH, SIMON (ed): *Letters to Macmillan.* London: Macmillan, 1967. 384 p.

Contains four letters from Yeats (pp. 290-94): (1) c/o Mme. Gonne, Colleville, Calvados, 9 July 1916; (2) 18 Woburn Buildings, 28 Jan 1917; (3) 63 James Street, 14 Sept 1916; (4) Hôtel St. Georges, Route de Fréjus, Cannes, 12 Jan 1928.

106a. POUND, EZRA: *Pound/Joyce: The Letters of Ezra Pound to James Joyce, with Pound's Essays on Joyce.* Edited and with commentary by Forrest Read. NY: New Directions, [1967]. vi, 314 p.

Contains two short letters to Pound and an extract from a letter to Joyce, pp. 37, 40, 93.

107. HOLLOWAY, JOSEPH: *Joseph Holloway's Abbey Theatre: A Selection from His Unpublished Journal "Impressions of a Dublin Playgoer."* Edited by Robert Hogan and Michael J. O'Neill. With a preface by Harry T. Moore. Carbondale: Southern Illinois UP, 1967. xxiii, 296 p.

Contains the following letters by Yeats: (1) to John O'Leary, Irish Literary Society, London, [28 Mar 1894] (p. 106); (2) to John Guinan, Coole Park, 28 Aug [1908] (pp. 117-18); (3) to Guinan, Coole Park, 23 Aug 1914 (pp. 164-65); (4) to Guinan, Stephen's Green Club, Dublin, 3 Oct 1914 (p. 166); (5) to Guinan, 18 Woburn Buildings, 23 Oct 1914 (pp. 166-67); (6) to Holloway, 82 Merrion Square, 28 Nov 1923 (p. 223).

108. ————: *Joseph Holloway's Irish Theatre.* Edited by Robert Hogan and Michael J. O'Neill. Dixon, Calif.: Proscenium Press, 1968-70. 3 v.

Contains a letter to Holloway, Riverside, Rathfarnham, [ca. 29 July 1935], 2:45.

109. JEFFARES, ALEXANDER NORMAN: *A Commentary on the Collected Poems of W. B. Yeats.* Stanford: Stanford UP, 1968. xxxiv, 563 p.

Quotations from unpublished material appear *passim.*

110. OREL, HAROLD: *The Development of William Butler Yeats: 1885-1900.* Lawrence: U of Kansas Publications, 1968. vii, 104 p. (Humanistic Studies. 39.)

Quotes unpublished material on pp. 37-38.

111. RONSLEY, JOSEPH: *Yeats's Autobiography: Life as Symbolic Pattern.* Cambridge, Mass.: Harvard UP, 1968. xii, 172 p.

Quotes from unpublished material *passim.*

111a. REID, BENJAMIN LAWRENCE: *The Man from New York: John Quinn and His Friends.* NY: Oxford UP, 1968. xviii, 708 p.

Includes numerous short quotations from unpublished Yeats letters, 1903-23; cf. pp. 13-14, 19, 36, 48-49, 70-71, 179, 184, 194-95 (on Aleister Crowley), 197, 215-16, 241-42, 243, 306, 307, 388, 420, 424, 493-94, 584-85; also a satiric quatrain on George Moore (p. 177, not in the *Variorum Edition of the Poems*). See also J768.

112. STURM, FRANK PEARCE: *His Life, Letters, and Collected Works.* Edited and with an introductory essay by Richard Taylor. Urbana: U of Illinois Press, 1969. viii, 382 p.

For details see J814.

113. FRENZ, HORST (ed): *Nobel Lectures Including Presentation Speeches and Laureates' Biographies: Literature, 1901-1967.* Amsterdam: Elsevier, 1969. xxi, 640 p.

For details see J1358.

114. SOPHOCLES: *King Oedipus in the Translation of W. B. Yeats* [. . .].
Edited and with an introduction by Balachandra Rajan. Toronto: Macmillan
of Canada, 1969. vii, 99 p.
    For details see J2155.

115. STALLWORTHY, JON: *Vision and Revision in Yeats's "Last Poems."*
Oxford: Clarendon Press, 1969. xi, 182 p.
    Manuscript drafts are quoted *passim*. See also J2440.

116. MARCUS, PHILLIP LEDUC: *Yeats and the Beginning of the Irish Renaissance*. Ithaca, N.Y.: Cornell UP, 1970. xvii, 299 p.
    Unpublished material is quoted on pp. 75, 78, 148, 150-51.

117. THATCHER, DAVID S.: *Nietzsche in England, 1890-1914: The Growth of a
Reputation*. Toronto: U of Toronto Press, 1970. xi, 331 p.
    Quotes all of the 16 annotations that Yeats made in a copy of the
    Thomas Common edition of *Nietzsche as Critic, Philosopher, Poet, and
    Prophet* (London, 1901) (pp. 45ff.).

118. YEATS, W. B., and MARGOT RUDDOCK: *Ah, Sweet Dancer: A Correspondence*.
Edited by Roger McHugh. London: Macmillan, 1970. 142 p.
    Contains 31 letters from Yeats to Margot Ruddock, 35 from her to him,
    Yeats's poem "Margot" (pp. 33-34), his emendations to some of her
    poems (pp. 130-32), her essay "Almost I Tasted Ecstasy" (reprinted
    from W284), and various odds and ends. McHugh provides notes and an
    introduction, pp. 9-15, which explains the biographical background and
    the value of the letters to Yeats scholarship.

119. YEATS, W. B., and THOMAS KINSELLA: *Davis, Mangan, Ferguson? Tradition
& the Irish Writer*. Dublin: Dolmen Press, 1970. 72 p. (Tower Series of
Anglo-Irish Studies. 2.)
    Contains the following Yeats items: (1) "Thomas Davis: Speech at the
    Davis Centenary," 15-20 (reprinted from Wp. 377); (2) "Clarence Mangan,
    1803-1849," 21-26 (Wp. 330); (3) extracts from "Clarence Mangan's Love
    Affair," 26-27 (Wp. 336); (4) "The Poetry of Sir Samuel Ferguson," 29-
    53 (Wp. 329). See also J4235.

120. GREGORY, LADY ISABELLA AUGUSTA: *The Wonder and Supernatural Plays,
Being the Third Volume of the Collected Plays*. Edited and with a foreword
by Ann Saddlemyer. Gerrards Cross: Smythe, 1970. xviii, 434 p. (Coole
Edition of the Works of Lady Gregory. 7.)
    Contains a letter to Lady Gregory, 18 Woburn Buildings, 27 Apr 1915
    (pp. 413-16).

121. ———: *The Translations and Adaptations and Her Collaborations with
Douglas Hyde and W. B. Yeats, Being the Fourth Volume of the Collected
Plays*. Edited and with a foreword by Ann Saddlemyer. Gerrards Cross:
Smythe, 1970. xix, 376 p. (Coole Edition of the Works of Lady Gregory. 8.)
    "The Unicorn from the Stars," 303-39; "Heads or Harps," 341-50 and
    373-76 (a political satire written by Yeats and Lady Gregory, printed
    from the two manuscript drafts in the possession of the New York
    Public Library, Berg Collection. Both drafts are undated.)

122. JEFFARES, ALEXANDER NORMAN: *The Circus Animals: Essays on W. B. Yeats*.
London: Macmillan, 1970. x, 183 p.
    Unpublished material is quoted on pp. 7, 8, 9, 10, 11, 13, 26, 100.
    See also J1102.

123. MURPHY, WILLIAM M.: *The Yeats Family and the Pollexfens of Sligo*.
With drawings by John Butler Yeats. Dublin: Dolmen Press, 1971. 88 p. (New
Yeats Papers. 1.)

Quotes from an unpublished journal on p. 83, from a letter to Lily
Yeats on p. 88. See also J923.

124. O'DRISCOLL, ROBERT (ed): *Theatre and Nationalism in Twentieth-Century
Ireland.* Toronto: U of Toronto Press, 1971. 216 p.
For details see J6321 (#4, 9).

124a. °*Aleksandr Solzhenitsyn, Rabindranath Tagore, Sigrid Undset, William
Butler Yeats.* NY: Gregory, 1971. vi, 360 p. (Nobel Prize Library.)

125. GREGORY, LADY ISABELLA AUGUSTA: *Our Irish Theatre: A Chapter of
Autobiography.* With a foreword by Roger McHugh. Gerrards Cross: Smythe,
1972. 279 p. (Coole Edition of the Works of Lady Gregory. 4.)
A new edition of W307. Contains *Paragraphs from Samhain 1909* (J71a),
pp. 196-99, a somewhat different version of W244B. The text from
W244B is collated in the footnotes. See also J2402 and 6703.

126. BRIDGWATER, PATRICK: *Nietzsche in Anglosaxony: A Study of Nietzsche's
Impact on English and American Literature.* Leicester: Leicester UP, 1972.
236 p.
For details see J2142.

127. ROTHENSTEIN, WILLIAM: *Imperfect Encounter: Letters of William Rothenstein and Rabindranath Tagore, 1911-1941.* Edited with introduction and
notes by Mary M. Lago. Cambridge, Mass.: Harvard UP, 1972. xx, 402 p.
Contains extracts from the following letters by W. B. Yeats: (1) to
Rothenstein, Coole Park, 7 Sept [1912] (p. 41); (2) to Rothenstein,
14 Nov [1912] (p. 42); (3) to Tagore, 25 Apr [1913] (p. 46); (4) to
Tagore, 31 July [1915] (pp. 212, 216); (5) to Rothenstein, [Aug ? 1915]
(p. 226).

128. SHAW, [GEORGE] BERNARD: *Collected Letters, 1898-1910.* Edited by Dan H.
Laurence. London: Reinhardt, 1972. xxiv, 1017 p.
Quotations from letters to Shaw appear on pp. 452-53.

128a. RAFROIDI, PATRICK, RAYMONDE POPOT, and WILLIAM PARKER (eds): *Aspects
of the Irish Theatre.* Lille: P. U. L. / Paris: Editions universitaires,
[1972]. 300 p.
For details see J6327 (Thilliez).

128b. GREGORY, LADY ISABELLA AUGUSTA: *Sir Hugh Lane: His Life and Legacy.*
With a foreword by James White. Gerrards Cross: Smythe, 1973. 324 p. (Coole
Edition of the Works of Lady Gregory. 10.)
Contents: 1. "Hugh Lane's Life and Achievement, with Some Account of
the Dublin Galleries," first published in 1921 (see W313).
2. "Case for the Return of Sir Hugh Lane's Pictures to Dublin," first
published in 1926.
3. "Sir Hugh Lane as a Pioneer of Taste," reprinted from W314A.
4. "Hugh Lane's Desire," reprinted from *Irish Statesman*, 31 May 1924.
5. W. B. Yeats: "The Clairvoyant Search for Hugh Lane's Will," 209-15;
previously unpublished.
6. "Letters to the Press from Lady Gregory and W. B. Yeats," 216-47.
Contains the following Yeats material:
a. The interview in J955 (but not the reply).
b. Letter to the *Spectator*, 23 Dec 1916 (Wp. 377).
c. Letter to the *Observer*, 24 Dec 1916 (Wp. 378).
d. Letter to the *Times*, 28 Dec 1916 (Wp. 378).
e. Letter to the *Observer*, 21 Jan 1917 (Wp. 378); galley proof
version.
f. Letter to the *Observer*, 3 Feb 1918 (Wp. 379).

g. Letter to the *TLS*, 31 Mar 1921 (Wp. 381).

h. Letter to the *Times*, 29 July 1926 (Wp. 383).

7. "The Senate Speeches of W. B. Yeats," 248-56; those relevant to the case.

8. Appendices. They contain a message by Yeats to a public meeting at Mansion House, Dublin, 25 Jan 1918 (p. 287), and a letter to Lloyd George, 29 Jan 1917, signed by Yeats and many others (pp. 306-9, not in *Letters*).

128c. FINNERAN, RICHARD J.: *The Prose Fiction of W. B. Yeats: The Search for "Those Simple Forms."* Dublin: Dolmen Press, 1973. 42 p. (New Yeats Papers. 4.)

Quotes from *The Speckled Bird*, *passim*.

128d. WEBSTER, BRENDA SCHWABACHER: *Yeats: A Psychoanalytic Study.* Stanford: Stanford UP, 1973. ix, 246 p.

Quotations from unpublished letters to Mabel Dickinson appear on pp. 45, 116, 117, 118, 121. Also scattered quotations from unpublished play drafts, *passim*.

128e. CROFT, P. J. (ed): *Autograph Poetry in the English Language: Facsimiles of Original Manuscripts from the Fourteenth to the Twentieth Century.* London: Cassell, 1973. 2 v.

Contains a facsimile and a transcript of a late draft of "The Wild Swans at Coole," together with a note, 2:152-53.

Contributions to Periodicals

129. (327) Y.: "Sonnet" ["I saw a shepherd youth . . ."], *Hibernia*, 1:4 (1 Apr 1882), 55.

Reprinted in *Irish Times*, #34207 (5 June 1965), 10; cf. J4. For further poems published under this initial see J5.

130. (339) "A Proposed National Literary Society," *Daily Express*, #12489 (2 June 1892), 6.

See also J5958.

131. "When You Are Old," *Independent*, 44:2287 (29 Sept 1892), 1351.

For details see J3246.

132. "The Sorrow of the World," *Independent*, 44:2290 (20 Oct 1892), 1469.

For details see J3246.

133. (346) [YEATS, W. B.]: "An Imaged World," *Speaker*, 10:245 (8 Sept 1894), 273-74.

Identified by John P. Frayne and reprinted in J61, pp. 341-43.

133a. (350) "William Carleton," *Bookman* [NY], 3:6 (Aug 1896), 549-50.

A review of Carleton's *The Traits and Stories of the Irish Peasantry*, first noted by George Monteiro; see his "An Unrecorded Review by Yeats," *N&Q*, os 219 / ns 21:1 (Jan 1974), 28.

134. (356) Annotations to an article by Bryan J. Jones, "Traditions and Superstitions Collected at Kilcurry, County Louth, Ireland," *Folk-Lore*, 10:1 (Mar 1899), 122-23.

Jones's article is on pp. 119-22. See also J2322.

135. (357) "Irish Literary Theatre: Lecture by Mr. W. B. Yeats," *Irish Literary Society Gazette*, 1:4 (June 1899), 5-7.

136. (359) Y.: "The Great Enchantment," *All Ireland R*, 1:38 (22 Sept 1900), 4.

John P. Frayne thinks that this short note was written by Yeats. In it, the editor Standish O'Grady is asked to "give us more and more of your opinions. What we want from you is a kind of Irish *Fors Clavigera*." See O'Grady's answer, *ibid.*, 4-5 (reprinted in J5918) and J2373.

136a. (360) "Mr. W. B. Yeats and the *Daily Mail*," *Irish Daily Independent and Daily Nation*, #2879 (2 May 1901), 6.
About the interview in J928.

137. "A Correction," *Daily Express*, #15312 (5 Aug 1901), 5.
Letter to the editor about the *Free Lance* interview (J929). See J2373.

137a. (362) "An Ancient Conversation," *All Ireland R*, 3:6 (12 Apr 1902), 87.
An introduction to extracts from Lady Gregory's *Cuchulain of Muirthemne*, not identical with the introduction in W256/257.

137b. (370) °"A Dirge over Dierdre e Naisi," *Poesia*, 2:9-10-11-12 (Oct 1906-Jan 1907), 12.
See also J3696a.

137c. "Irish National Theatre: Extraordinary Scenes in Dublin," *Aberdeen Free Press*, #11869 (31 Jan 1907), 6.
Includes a verbatim statement made by Yeats to a press representative about the *Playboy* row.

137d. "Mr. Boyle's Plays," *Evening Telegraph*, #7955 (6 Feb 1907), 3.
Letter to the editor.

138. Letter to John O'Byrne, *Freeman's J*, 140:[] (25 Mar 1907), 5.
For details see J6352.

139. "Mr. W. B. Yeats on *The Piper*," *Abbey Theatre Programme*, 20 Feb 1908, [3].
On the play by Norreys Connell, reprinted from an unspecified issue of *Freeman's J*, which I have not been able to identify. See also J1002.

140. (372) Letter to the editor about an interview, *Pall Mall Gazette*, #14392 (10 June 1911), 7.
For the interview see J943.

140a. (373) "Mr. Yeats on the Abbey Theatre," *Irish Times*, 53:16910 (9 Sept 1911), 8.
Statement about the projected American tour of the Abbey Company.

141. "Statement by Mr. W. B. Yeats," *Irish Times*, 54:17023 (20 Jan 1912), 8.
For details see J6598.

142. YEATS, W. B., and others: "Dublin Protestants and Mr. Redmond: Confidence in Home Rule [. . .]," *Irish Times*, 54:17093 (11 Apr 1912), 6.
A letter to John Redmond, stating that Dublin Protestants do not live in fear of their Catholic neighbors.

142a. (377) "'Revolt Due to Fear of Loss of Home Rule.' By W. B. Yeats. The Famous Irish Poet," *NY American*, 28 Apr 1916, 1.
A statement on the Easter Rising.

143. (380) "To ——," *NY Evening Post*, 120:63 (31 Jan 1921), 6.
Reprinted in *N&Q*, os 216 / ns 18:11 (Nov 1971), 420-21. See also J3163.

144. (382) COULTER, GEOFFREY: "Litir o Eirinn," *Transatlantic R*, 2:5 [1924], 537-46.
Contains Yeats's speech made at the occasion of the Royal Irish Academy award at the Tailteann Festival, pp. 539-42.

145. (383) "Letter from Senator Yeats," *Irish Times*, 68:21471 (9 Feb 1926),
5.
For details see J4046.

146. (384) "Sympathy with Mrs. O'Higgins: Messages from W. B. Yeats and
'AE,'" *Irish Times*, 69:21914 (14 July 1927), 4.
Two paragraphs from a letter to Mrs. O'Higgins, written after the
assassination of Kevin O'Higgins.

147. (386) "The Story of *Oedipus the King* as Told by W. B. Yeats," *Irish
Weekly and Ulster Examiner*, 64:3217 (12 Sept 1931), 9.
This is the text of the radio program referred to in Wp. 468.

148. (387) "Irish Ban on *The Puritan*: Mr. O'Flaherty's Novel. Mr. W. B.
Yeats's Protest. 'Grotesque' Charge," *Manchester Guardian*, #26666 (24 Feb
1932), 9.

149. "'No Question of Disloyalty': Mr. Yeats on Objection to the Oath,"
Times, #46098 (4 Apr 1932), 14.
"Mr. W. B. Yeats . : . made a statement to a Press representative in
London on Saturday with reference to the Oath of Allegiance. He
said. . . ."

150. (390) ANON.: "Mohini Mohan Chatterji," *Calcutta Municipal Gazette*,
23:12 (22 Feb 1936), 470-71.
Contains a letter from Yeats to Chatterji, Riversdale, 29 Sept 1935.
Reprinted in J2162.

151. Letter to the editor, *Spectator*, 157:5658 (4 Dec 1936), 995.
For details see J5337.

152. (393) CLEMENS, CYRIL: "The Passing of W. B. Yeats," *Canadian Bookman*,
22 [i.e., 21]:2 (June/July 1939), 21-25.
Quotes from letters that Yeats wrote to Clemens in connection with the
award of the Mark Twain Medal by the Mark Twain Society.

153. Facsimile of a short letter to Lennox Robinson, dated 14 Nov [1912],
Arrow: W. B. Yeats Commemoration Number, Summer 1939, facing p. 13.
See also J1068.

154. (396) HINKSON, PAMELA: "The Friendship of Yeats and Katharine Tynan,"
Fortnightly R, os 180 / ns 174:1032 (Oct 1953), 253-64; :1033 (Nov 1953),
323-36.
For details see J690.

155. KIERNAN, T. J.: "Lady Gregory and W. B. Yeats," *Southerly*, 14:4
(1953), 239-51.
Reprinted in *Dalhousie R*, 38:3 (Autumn 1958), 295-306. Quotes from a
letter Yeats wrote to him on 22 Jan 1939. See also Wp. 393 and J864.

156. Facsimile of a short letter to Mr. [J. G.] Wilson, Athenaeum Club,
Pall Mall, 12 Apr [19-], *Tribüne: Halbmonatsschrift der Bühnen der Stadt
Köln*, 25:9 (1955/56), 79.

157. (397) RYAN, STEPHEN P.: "W. B. Yeats and Thomas MacDonagh," *MLN*, 76:8
(Dec 1961), 715-19.
Contains a letter to MacDonagh, 18 Woburn Buildings, 3 Dec 1907.

158. JEFFARES, A. NORMAN: "Yeats's Byzantine Poems and the Critics," *ESA*,
5:1 (Mar 1962), 11-28.
Quotes from unpublished drafts.

159. (398) AYLING, R.: "Seven Letters of W. B. Yeats," *Theoria*, #20 (15 June 1963), 60-70.
    (1) to Christina Walshe Broughton, 18 Woburn Buildings, 27 Jan [1917?]; (2) to Cherry Hobart Houghton, 82 Merrion Square, 5 Apr [1924]; (3) to the same, 82 Merrion Square, [June 1924?]; (4) to Joseph Holloway, [July 1935?], copied from Holloway's diary and referring to *The Player Queen*; (5) to the *Irish Times*, printed in its issue of 19 Jan 1924; (6) to *Time and Tide*, printed in its issue of 27 May 1933; (7) to the *Irish Times*, printed in its issue of 3 Sept 1935. Letters 1-3 and 5-7 are reprinted in *Threshold* of Autumn 1965 (Wp. 400), letters 5-7 in *Modern Drama* of May 1966 (Wp. 401), in each case without indication of previous publication in *Theoria*. (The Wade entry for the *Threshold* reprint is inaccurate.) Ayling's comments on the letters have been incorporated in the *Threshold* reprint. See also J4193 and 4194.

160. Letter to Eva Gore-Booth, edited with a note by Ian Fletcher, *REL*, 4:3 (July 1963), between pp. 24 and 25.
    A letter written from c/o Mme. Gonne, Colleville, Calvados, 23 July [19-].

161. (399) "Crazy Jane on the King," *Amherst Literary Mag*, 10:2 (Summer 1964), 4-5.
    See also J91 and 3009.

162. (400) "Letters of W. B. Yeats," *Visva-Bharati Q*, 30:3 (1964-65), 159-76.
    Fifteen letters to Rabindranath Tagore, written between [July 1912?] and 1935. Reprinted in J2162.

163. (401) EDWARDS, PHILIP: "Yeats and the Trinity Chair," *Hermathena*, 101 (Autumn 1965), 5-12.
    Includes two letters to J. P. Mahaffy, (1) Nassau Hotel, [late Feb-early Mar 1911], and (2) 18 Woburn Buildings, 14 May [1913].

164. FISHER, JONATHAN: "Unpublished Letters of W. B. Yeats for Auction," *Irish Times*, #34563 (10 Oct 1966), 8.
    Letters to one Mr. Pollock; one of them is reprinted by Fisher (dated Gort, [ca. Summer 1933]).

165. WATTS, C. T.: "A Letter from W. B. Yeats to R. B. Cunninghame Graham," *RES*, 18:71 (Aug 1967), 292-93.
    Undated letter from Stone Cottage, Coleman's Hatch [ca. 1913-16].

166. SIDNELL, MICHAEL J.: "John Bull's Other Island: Yeats and Shaw," *MD*, 11:3 (Dec 1968), 245-61.
    Contains a letter to Shaw, Coole Park, 5 Oct 1904.

167. YEATS, MICHAEL: "Yeats: The Public Man," *Southern R*, 5:3 (July 1969), 872-85.
    Quotes from unpublished parts of the autobiography.

168. "W. B. Yeats to John Masefield: Two Letters." Edited by Paul Delany, *MassR*, 11:1 (Winter 1970), 159-62.
    Printed from manuscripts now in the Columbia U Library, dated by the editor 7 Mar 1930 and Mar-Apr 1932.

169. MURPHY, WILLIAM M.: "'In Memory of Alfred Pollexfen': W. B. Yeats and the Theme of Family," *Irish UR*, 1:1 (Autumn 1970), 31-47.
    Includes a previously unpublished manuscript version.

170. ATKINSON, F. G.: "W. B. Yeats: A Biographical Note," *N&Q*, os 216 / ns 18:3 (Mar 1971), 106-9.

Contains three letters to Arthur Quiller-Couch, (1) 18 Woburn Buildings, 11 Aug [1898?], (2) Thornhill, Sligo, 10 Nov [1898?], and (3) Nassau Hotel, Dublin, Saturday [6 Oct 1900?].

171. *"The Tables of the Law*: A Critical Text." Edited by Robert O'Driscoll, *Yeats Studies*, #1 (Bealtaine 1971), 87-118.
> Reprints the texts together with variants, prefaced by a lengthy interpretation (pp. 87-101). The relationship between the texts is as follows: (1) *Savoy*, Nov 1896, revised in W24 (1897), again slightly revised in W25 (1904), considerably revised in W81 (1908). This revision was reprinted in W26 (1914). (2) However, Yeats made another revision of W25 in 1925 (W147/148), which was reprinted with minor changes in *Mythologies* (W211P/Q). There are, then, two different final versions of the text.

172. "Versions of the Stories of Red Hanrahan." Edited by Michael J. Sidnell, *Yeats Studies*, #1 (Bealtaine 1971), 119-74.
> Reprints the early versions of the six stories of Red Hanrahan (O'Sullivan the Red, as he was called then) and collates their revisions in *The Secret Rose* of 1897 (W21). Lists the variants 'of the post-1903 versions, which were written with the help of Lady Gregory. Editor's comments on pp. 119-22 and 166-68.

173. "Letters to Herbert Horne, Ernest Radford, and Elkin Mathews." Edited by Ian Fletcher, *Yeats Studies*, #1 (Bealtaine 1971), 203-8.
> (1) to Horne, 3 Blenheim Road, [Jan 1891?], from a private collection; (2) to Radford, 56 North Circular Road, Dublin, [1893], from a private collection; (3) to Mathews, Thornhill, Sligo, 7 Apr 1895, from the U of Reading Library; (4) to the same, 3 Blenheim Road, 6/4 [?] July [1895?], from the same collection; (5) to the same, 18 Woburn Buildings, [Feb 1896?], from the same collection; (6) to the same, Coole Park, 4 Aug 1901, from the same collection.

174. "Letter to M. Clifford Harrison." Edited by George Mills Harper, *Yeats Studies*, #1 (Bealtaine 1971), 209-10.
> Letter to a U of Virginia graduate student, dated On Board R.M.S. *Adriatic*, 1 Apr 1914, from the U of Virginia Library.

175. STALLWORTHY, JON: "'The Second Coming,'" *Agenda*, 9:4-10:1 (Autumn-Winter 1971/72), 24-33.
> Quotes from manuscript versions.

176. FLETCHER, IAN: "The Ellis-Yeats-Blake Manuscript Cluster," *Book Collector*, 21:1 (Spring 1972), 72-94.
> For details see J1957.

177. LONDRAVILLE, RICHARD: "The Manuscript of 'The Queen and the Jester,'" *Ariel*, 3:3 (July 1972), 67-68 and plates I-IV.
> An early version of "The Cap and Bells."

177a. "The London Irregulars," *Times*, #58674 (6 Jan 1973), 8.
> A full-page extract from J67.

177b. FUROMOTO, TAKETOSH: "W. B. Yeats's Missing Review," *TLS*, 73:3748 (4 Jan 1974), 12.
> Contains a quotation from an article on Katharine Tynan (*Irish Monthly*, 15:169 [July 1887], 416-17), originally published in a review written by Yeats for the elusive periodical *The Gael* (Dublin), of which no copy seems to have survived (see Wp. 11).

Translations into Other Languages: Separate Translations

178. (409) *Tajemná růže.* Translated by Antonín L. Stříž. Stará Říše na
Moravě: Florianová, 1915. 97 p. (Dobré dílo. 22.)

179. *Objevy: Essaye.* Translated by Jaroslav Skalický. Praha: Jílovská,
1920. 72 p. (Dobré dílo. 65.)

179a. *Z knihy "Vítr v síti."* Translated by Bohuslav Reynek. Stará Říše:
Florianová, 1920. 8 p.

180. *Rosa Alchemica. Desky zákona. Klanění Králů.* Translated by Jaroslav
Skalický. Stará Říše na Moravě: Florianová, 1921. 78 p. (Nova et vetera.
41.)

181. *Cathleen ni Houlihan. Zlatá přilba. Přesýpací hodiny.* Translated by
Jaroslav Skalický. Stará Říše na Moravě: Florian, 1921. 82 p. (Nova et
vetera. 45.)

182. (410) *Drømmerier over barneår og ungdom.* Translated by Valdemar
Rørdam. København: Haase, 1924 [1923]. 180 p.

183. (412) *Per amica silentia lunae.* Translated by Jaroslav Skalický.
Brno: Pojer, 1925. 82 p. (Atlantis. 4.)

184. *Opowiadania o Hanrahanie rudym. Tajemnicza róża. Rosa alchemica.*
Translated by Józef Birkenmajer. Lwów: Nakładem Wydawnictwa Polskiego,
1925. xx, 222 p. (Bibljoteka Laureatów Nobla. 41.)

185. *Příběhy Ryšavého Hanrahana.* Translated by Jaroslav Skalický. Praha:
Štorch-Marien, 1926. 45 p. (Knihy dněsku. 13.)

186. (413) *Tři hry (Temné vody. Na Bailové břehu. Deirdre).* Translated by
Jaroslav Skalický, preface by Eva Jurčinová. Praha: Otto, 1928. 103 p.
(Sborník Světové Poesie. 155.)

187. *Přesýpací hodiny: Hra o jednom dějstvi.* Translated by Otto F. Babler.
Olomouc: Lidové závody tiskařske a nakladatelské v Olomouci, 1928. 43 p.

188. (414) *Ystoriya umnogo chelovieka (Moral'naya p'esa so spievamy).*
Translated by A. Fylyppovski. Wilkes-Barre, Pa.: Izdanie gazety "Sviet,"
1931. 40 p.
   A Ukrainian adaptation, rather than a translation, of *The Hour-Glass.*

189. (415) °*Dous folk-dramas.* Translated by Plácido R. Castro and the
brothers Vilar Ponte. Santiago de Compostela, 1935. 30 p. (Teatro irlandés.)

190. °*La rosa nel vento.* Translated by F. Gargàro. Città di Castello, 1935.

191. (417) *Růže světa: Poesie.* Translated by Bohdan Chudoba. Praha: Vilímek,
1941. 56 p.

192. *Básně.* Translated by Jaroslav Skalický. Brno: Pojer, 1944. 144 p.
(Atlantis. 61.)

193. (418) *Essaye.* Translated by Jaroslav Skalický. Brno: Pojer, 1946.
252 p. (Atlantis. 62.)

194. *Objevy: Essaye.* Translated by Jaroslav Skalický. Brno: Pojer, 1946.
125 p. (Atlantis. 68.)

195. (419) *Tajemná růže: Povídky.* Translated by Jaroslav Skalický. Brno:
Pojer, 1947. 179 p. (Atlantis. 70.)

196. (421) *De tre tiggere: Digt af W. B. Yeats.* Translated by Otto Gelsted, illustrated by Mads Stage. København: Scripta, 1949. [32 p.] (Scripta Publikation. 1.)

197. (428) *Teatro completo y otras obras: Teatro, poesía, ensayo.* Translated by Amando Lázaro Ros, preface by G. S. Fraser. Madrid: Aguilar, 1956. liv, 1381 p. (Biblioteca Premios Nobel.)
     A third edition was published in 1962. Fraser's preface is a translation of J1085.

198. (431) *Enkele gedichten. Gevolgd door "De Gravin Catelene" (een drama).* Translated by A. Roland Holst. 's Gravenhage: Boucher, 1958. 96 p.

199. *Gedichte.* Selection, translation, and postscript by Herberth E. Herlitschka. Zürich: Verlag der Arche, 1958. 84 p. (Kleine Bücher der Arche. 222-23.)

200. *Calvario.* Translated by Roberto Sanesi. Varese: Editrice Magenta, 1960. 55 p. (Oggetti e simbolo. 8.)

201. *Versek.* Edited with introduction and notes by Tamás Ungvari. Budapest: Európa Könyvkiadó, 1960. 244 p.
     Hungarian translations of 114 poems by various translators.

202. *A húsleves* [and three plays by other authors]. Budapest: Gondolat, 1961. 95 p. (Játékszín. 32.)
     Cover title: *Kezedben a sorsod: Válogatott egyfelvonásosok.* Contains "*A húsleves (The Pot of Broth)*: Egyfelvonásos komédia," 3-16; translated by Geyza Bányay. V[ilmos] D[obai]: "Rendezoi utószó" [Producer's postscript], 17-18.

203. *Poesie.* Translation, introduction, and notes by Roberto Sanesi. Milano: Lerici, 1961. 513 p. (Poeti europei. 8.)

204. *Slova snad pro hudbu: Výbor z poezie.* Translated by Jiří Valja, preface and explanatory notes by Jiří Levý. Praha: SNKLU, 1961. 144 p. (Světová četba. 265.)

205. *Théâtre.* Translated by Madeleine Gibert, illustrated by Keogh. Paris: Rombaldi, 1962. 277 p. (Collection des Prix Nobel de la littérature.)
     Contains: Gunnar Ahlström: "La 'petite histoire' de la attribution du Prix Nobel à William Butler Yeats," 7-14; translated by Malou Höjer.
     Per Hallström: "Discours de réception prononcé lors de la remise du Prix Nobel de littérature à William Butler Yeats le 10 décembre 1923," 15-22; first published in J1378.
     Franck [*sic*] Kermode: "La vie et l'oeuvre de William Butler Yeats," 23-56.
     Translations of six plays.
     Pierre Barkan: "Bibliographie," 263-74.

205a. °*Teatro.* Translated by Paulo Memdes Campos, critical introduction by Franck Kermode, illustrated by Keogh. Rio de Janeiro: Editôra Delta, 1963. 229 p. (Colleção dos Prêmios Nobel de literatura. Prêmio de 1923.)
     Evidently based on J205.

206. *Drammi celtici.* Introduction by Roberto Sanesi, translation by Francesco Vizioli. Parma: Guanda, 1963. xxxiii, 325 p. (Fenice ns. Sezione poeti. 2.)

207. YEATS, W. B., [GEORGE] BERNARD SHAW, and EUGENE O' NEILL: *Gedichten / Toneel.* With introductions by W. H. Stenfert Kroese, A. C. Ward, and David

Koning. Haarlem: De Toorts, 1964. 419 p. (Pantheon der winnaars van de Nobelprijs voor literatuur.)
Contains translations of 16 poems and of *The Countess Cathleen* by A. Roland Holst.

208. *Enfance et jeunesse resongées.* Translated by Pierre Leyris. Paris: Mercure de France, 1965. 211 p.

209. *Marakata dvīpa kā svara; arthāt, Viliĝama Batalara Iṭsa kī kavitāem.* Translated by Harbans Rai Bachchan. Delhi: Rājapāla, 1965. 146 p.

210. *Quaranta poesie.* Preface and translation by Giorgio Melchiori. Torino: Einaudi, 1965. 104 p. (Collezione di poesia. 15.)

211. *Versuri.* Translated by Aurel Covaci. Bucureşti: Editura pentru literatură universală, 1965. 288 p.

212. *Runoja.* Translation, introduction, and notes by Aale Tynni. Porvoo, Helsinki: Söderström, 1966. 212 p.

213. *William Butler Yeats: Premio Nobel per la letteratura, 1923.* Milano: Fabbri, 1966. iii, 508 p. (Collana Premi Nobel di Letteratura. 24.)
Contains: Gunnar Ahlström: "Il conferimento del Premio Nobel a William Butler Yeats," 5-13; translated from J205.
Per Hallström: "Discorso uffiziale per il conferimento del Premio Nobel a William Butler Yeats," 15-23; translated from J205.
Roberto Sanesi: "La vita e l'opera di William Butler Yeats," 25-65.
Translations by Giuseppe Sardelli, 67-245; includes prose, plays, and poetry.
"Bibliografia," 491-508. Selective.

214. LUNARI, GIGI (ed): *Teatro irlandese moderno.* Roma: Casini, 1967. 96 p. (Tutto il teatro. 18.)
For details see J6316.

215. MALORY, THOMAS, THOMAS SACKVILLE, and W. B. YEATS: *Testi.* Translation and commentary by Gabriele Baldini. Roma: De Santis, [1967]. 239 p. (Università degli studi di Roma. Facoltà di magistero. Anno accademico 1966-67.)
"W. B. Yeats," 173-208; contains a short general introduction (175-79) and 13 poems or parts of poems in English and Italian.

216. °*Shishsha maḥazot ufroza.* Translated by M. Er'el. Ramat-Gan (Israel): Massada, 1968. 220 p.

217. CROSSE, GORDON: *Purgatory.* Opera in 1 act, op. 18. German translation by Ernst Roth. London: Oxford UP, 1968. iv, 75 p.
For details see J5623.

218. °*Bara. Ashima no kaze.* Translated by Shotaro Oshima. Tokyo: Heibonsha, 1969. 228 p. (Sekai meishishū. 3.)

219. *Le opere: Poesia, teatro, prosa.* Edited by Salvatore Rosati. Torino: UTET, 1969. xxviii, 690 p. (Scrittori del mondo: i Nobel. [22].)
Contains: Salvatore Rosati: "William Butler Yeats," ix-xxviii.
Translations by Roberto Sanesi, Giorgio Melchiori, Carlo Linati, Francesco Vizioli, Agar Pampanini, and Giuseppe Sardelli.

220. *Racconti, liriche.* Edited, translated, and introduced by Giuseppe Sardelli. Milano: Fabbri, 1969. 256 p. (I grandi della letteratura. 61.)

220a. *Shi'un min Yaits: Shi'r, nathir, masrah.* Translated by S. B. Bushrui. Beirut: Matabi' Dar al-Nadwa, 1969. xix, 242 p.
See also J4254.

23

221. *Le fremissement du voile*. Translation and introduction by Pierre Leyris. Paris: Mercure de France, 1970. 301 p.

222. °*Yeh Tz'ŭ Hsi Chü Hsüan Chi*. Taipei: Ching Shen (Tamkang College of Arts and Sciences), 1970. 272 p.

223. *Werke*. Edited by Werner Vordtriede. Neuwied: Luchterhand, 1970-73. 6 v.

(1) *Ausgewählte Gedichte*. 1970. 315 p. Contents: (a) an introduction by the editor, "William Butler Yeats--Urbild und Gegenwart," 7-29, reprinted from *Neue deutsche Hefte*, 16:4 (1969), 61-82; (b) translations of 154 poems by Stefan Andres, Ursula Clemen, Wilhelm Deinert, Richard Exner, Herberth E. Herlitschka, Ernst Jandl, Gerschon Jarecki, Erich von Kahler, Heinz Piontek, Susanne Schaup, Georg von der Vring, and the editor; (c) notes to the poems; (d) chronology.
(2) *Erzählungen*. 1971. 225 p. Contains translations from the prose fiction by Susanne Schaup, Ernst E. Stein, Herberth E. Herlitschka, and the editor.
(3) *Dramen I*. 1972. 247 p. Contains translations of nine plays by Ernst E. Stein, the editor, Wilhelm Deinert, Henry von Heiseler, Ursula Clemen and Konrad Bayer, and notes by Susanne Schaup, 230-41.
(4) *Dramen II*. 1972. 223 p. Contains translations of nine plays by Herberth E. Herlitschka, Ernst E. Stein, Ursula Clemen, the editor, Elisabeth Schnack, and Richard Exner, and notes by Susanne Schaup, 202-16.
(5) *Essays und Einführungen*. 1972. 344 p. Translated by Elizabeth Gilbert.
(6) *Autobiographie*. 1973. 539 p. Translated by Susanne Schaup. Includes a short introduction (pp. 7-8) and "Anmerkungen" (pp. 508-17) by the translator, as well as a loosely inserted corrigenda sheet for volume 5 (pp. 349-52).

223a. °*Viljem Batler Jeits*. Translated by Ranka Kuić. Beograd: Mlado pokolenje, 1971. 67 p.

224. *Ausgewählte Werke*. Zürich: Coron-Verlag, [1971]. 365 p. (Nobelpreis für Literatur. 23.)
Contains the first three items of J205 in German translation and excerpts from the translations in J223.

224a. °*Le vent parmi les roseaux. The Wind among the Reeds: 16 poèmes et 2 notes*. Translated by André Pieyre de Mandiargues, illustrated by Joan Miró. Paris: Lazar-Vernet, 1971. [43 p.] (Collection Paroles peintes. 3.)

224b. °*Dix-sept poèmes*. Translated by Fouad El-Etr. Paris: La Délirante, 1973. 41 p.

224c. *Una visione*. Translated by Adriana Motti. Milano: Adelphi, 1973. 344 p. (Biblioteca Adelphi. 44.)

Books with Introductions by Yeats

225. (431) TAGORE, SIR RABINDRANATH: *Gitanjali (Sångoffer): En samling dikter, af författare öfverförda till engelsk prosa från original-dikterna på bengali*. Med inledning af W. B. Yeats. Translated by Andrea Butenschön. Stockholm: Norstedt, 1913. 77 p.

226. (432) °————: *Kītāñcali tamirākkam* [103 poems translated into Tamil verse by Cō. Naṭarācan, preceded by a Tamil translation of W. B. Yeats's introduction to the English translation]. Chunnakam, 1950. xxxii, 92 p.
There is a copy in the British Museum (14172.a.120).

227. [MOTOKIYO]: *Nishikigi.* Edited by Ernest Fenollosa and Ezra Pound. Introduction to the Nō by W. B. Yeats. Translation by Mary de Rachewiltz. Milano: All' insegna de Pesce d'oro, 1957. 46 p. (Serie oltremare. 12.)

228. °POUND, EZRA, and ERNEST FENOLLOSA: *Il teatro giapponese Nō.* Translated by Mary de Rachewiltz. Firenze: Vallecchi, 1966. 250 p.
Includes Yeats's introduction.

Translations in Periodicals

229. (433) "Les errances d'Oisin: Chanson de jeune fille: Ephemera, une idylle d'automne; Chanson indienne; Kanva, l'indien, sur dieu; Le crépuscule celte: Les inlassables," translated by René Philipson. "Innisfree," translated by Laurence Jerrold, *Magazine international*, #6 (May 1896), 158-63.
Corrected entry.

229a. "Das Binden des Haares," translated by Anie Dauthendey, *Insel*, vol 1 / 1st quarter / #12 (Sept 1900), 322-30.

229b. "Serce wiosny," *Nowe słowo*, #6 (1902), 153-56.
Translator's name not given.

230. "Gräfin Kathlin: Irisches Drama in drei Aufzügen," translated by Eduard Engel, *Bühne und Welt*, 6:2 (15 Oct 1903), 46-60.

230a. "Księżniczka Kasia (The Countess Cathleen)," translated by Jan Kasprowicz, *Chimera* [Warszawa], 7:20/21 (May-June 1904), 217-86.

230b. (434) "Der Liebe Erbarmen," translated by Irene Forbes-Mosse, *Insel Almanach*, 1906, 62.

231. "Das Stundenglas: Ein geistliches Spiel," translated by Marie Freudenthal, *Bühne und Welt*, yr 10 / 19:8 (Jan 1908), 320-28.

232. "Das Land der Sehnsucht (The Land of Heart's Desire): Ein dramatisches Märchen in einem Aufzug," translated by Frieda Weekly and Ernst Leopold Stahl, *Masken: Wochenschrift des Düsseldorfer Schauspielhauses*, 6:10 (7 Nov 1910), 145-60.
This translation is presumably identical with the one published in book form in 1911 and listed in Wp. 406. No copy of the book seems to have survived in public libraries.

232a. (435) "Die Anbetung der Könige," *Neue Blätter*, 1:6 (1912), 42-45.
Translator's name not given. Reprinted with slight changes in *Aktion*, 6:3/4 (22 Jan 1916), 29-34.

232b. "Aus dem Zwielicht. Die da nie müde werden. Erde, Feuer und Wasser," *Neue Blätter*, 1:12 (1912), 100-102.
Translator's name not given. Reprinted in *Aktion* 5:47/48 (20 Nov 1915), 581-83.

232c. (437) "Ein Besuch bei Verlaine," *Aktion*, 6:26 (24 June 1916), 356-58.
Translator's name not given.

232d. "Serce wiosny," translated by M. J., *Romans i Powieść*, 8:34 (19 Aug 1916), 3-5. (*Świat*, 11:34, supplement.)

233. (438) "Les songes celtiques," translated by Jeanne Lichnerowicz, *Douce France*, 4:36 (Nov 1921), 66-70.
Two extracts from *The Celtic Twilight*.

234. "Poems of Yeats / Poèmes de Yeats," translated by Jeanne Lichnerowicz, *Douce France*, 4:38 (Jan 1922), 214-21.

235. "Le sablier," translated by Jeanne Lichenerowiez [sic], Ecrits
nouveaux, 9:2 (Feb 1922), 26-48.

236. "W. B. Yeats et Oscar Wilde," translated by Cecil Georges-Bazile,
Comoedia, 16:3528 (23 Aug 1922), 3.
    Extracts from Yeats's autobiographical articles in the London Mercury.

237. "L'Irlande et J. M. Synge," translated by Jeanne Lichnérowicz [sic],
Revue européenne, 2:9 (Nov 1923), 1-9.

238. "Surgi de la rose," translated by Jeanne Lichnecowicz [sic], Figaro,
ser 3 / yr 69 / #363 (29 Dec 1923), Supplement Litt., 1-2.

239. "La pièce de moeurs modernes. Louange des contes de vieilles femmes.
Le drame de la vie contemporaine possède-t-il une racine à soi?" [trans-
lated by Jeanne Lichnerowicz], Revue critique des idées et des livres,
36:220 (Jan 1924), 58-61.

240. "La clavicule du lièvre. L'aurore. A Irlande des temps futurs. A la
mémoire du Major Robert Gregory," [translated by Jeanne Fournier-
Pargoire?], Revue de Genève, 9:43 (Jan 1924), 6-12.

241. "De la poésie populaire," translated by Jeanne Lichnerowicz,
Comoedia, 17:4032 (1 Jan 1924), 4.

242. (439) "Cathleen ni Houlihan," translated by Jeanne Lichnerowicz,
Revue belge, [1]:5 (1 Mar 1924), 418-28.

243. "Le pot de bouillon," translated by Jeanne Lichnerowicz, Alsace
française, yr 4 / 8:52 (27 Dec 1924), 1229-33.

244. "Le club des rimeurs (1): Fragment de Le voile tremble. Mémoires--
1887-1891," translated by Jeanne Lichnerowicz, Navire d'argent, yr 1 /
2:6 (1 Nov 1925), 227-36.
    No more published.

245. "Oscar Wilde," translated by Jeanne Lichnerowicz, Revue européenne,
yr 3 / 6:36 (1 Feb 1926), 18-27.
    An extract from The Trembling of the Veil.

246. "Théâtre: Préface des pièces pour un théâtre irlandais," translated
by Jeanne Lichnerowicz, Revue du siècle, 6:1 (15 Jan 1927), 150-57.

247. (440) "Szerelmesét halottnak kiránja," translated by Mihály Babits,
Nyugat, 23:14 (16 July 1930), 140.

248. "La poussière a clos les yeux d'Hélène. Fantômes de village," translated by Claude Dravaine, Revue européenne, ns #12 (Dec 1930), 993-1009.
    There is a note indicating that the two pieces are taken from La
    crépuscule celtique, to be published by Stock (Paris). The project
    does not seem to have materialized.

249. "Poèmes," translated by Claude Dravaine, Europe, 25:17 (15 Jan 1931),
69-70.

250. PERSILES [pseudonym]: "Persiflage: Concepto de las ánimas," Repertorio
americano, yr 13 / 23:561 (7 Nov 1931), 262-63.
    Contains a translation of "All Souls' Night."

251. "Deux traductions de Yeats (L'aube; Un hindou parle à son aimée),"
[translated by Georges Cattaui?], Journal des poètes, 2:3 (29 Nov 1931),
[4].

251a. "L'isola del lago di Innisfree. La meditazione del vecchio pescatore.
Il pastor triste. Ephemera. Sol che tu fossi. . . . La valle degli amanti.
I magi. Le voci sempiterne. Taci mio cuor . . . ," translated by F.
Gargàro, *Rassegna italiana*, #176 (Jan 1933), 2-5.

252. "Aus den Essays," translated by Herberth E. Herlitschka, *Deutsche
Zeitschrift*, 47:9 (June 1934), 557-59.

253. "Wie das Seil gedreht wurde," translated by Herberth E. Herlitschka,
Deutsche Zeitschrift, 47:9 (June 1934), 559-64.
    Reprinted from *Die chymische Rose* (Wp. 412).

254. "Die Heerfahrt der Sidhe. Die Wehen der Leidenschaft. Im Tal des
schwarzen Ebers," translated by Herberth E. Herlitschka, *Deutsche Zeitschrift*, 47:9 (June 1934), 564-65.

255. "Deirdre," translated by Henry von Heiseler, *Deutsche Zeitschrift*,
47:9 (June 1934), 565-76.
    An excerpt reprinted from *Irische Schaubühne* (Wp. 414).

256. (441) "Le dormeur qui rêva de faeryland," translated by Bertrand
d'Astorg. "Un Hindou parle à son aimée," translated by Georges Cattaui,
Yggdrasill, 3:3 (25 June 1938), 45-46.

257. "Olio e sangue. I cigni selvaggi a Coole. Bizanzio. L'isola del lago
d'Innisfree," translated by Leone Traverso, *Frontespizio*, 10:10 (Oct 1938),
646-49.

257a. "Die Maske," translated by Ludwig Wagner, *Blätter der Städtischen
Bühnen Frankfurt am Main*, 6:19 (1939), 218.

258. "Quatre poèmes," translated by P. J. Couster, *Echanges et recherches*,
2:5 (Mar 1939), 300-303.

259. "Die Stimmungen," *Bücherwurm*, 24:7 (Mar 1939), 161.
    Translator's name not given.

259a. OSCHILEWSKI, WALTHER G. (ed): *Festschrift des Bücherwurms zu Beginn
seines 25. Jahrgangs dem Herausgeber gewidmet von Freunden und Mitarbeitern.*
Markkleeberg-Leipzig: Rauch, 1939. 84 p.
    "Liebe ist ein masslos Ding," 25. Translated by Henry von Heiseler.

260. "Le parole sui vetri della finestra (Dramma in un atto)," translated
by Luigi Berti, *Letteratura*, 3:12 (Oct 1939), 108-22.

261. "Die Rose des Friedens," translated by Franz Josef Sailer, *Westermanns
Monatshefte*, yr 84 / 167:1000 (Dec 1939), 242.

262. "Irland nach der Revolution," *Auslese: Internationale Zeitschriften-
schau*, 14:1 (Jan 1940), 12-13.
    An extract from *On the Boiler*; translator's name not given.

263. "Guslač iz Dooneya," translated by Ivan Goran Kovačič, *Savremenik*,
yr 28 / 1:5 (1 Mar 1940), 147.

264. °"Geen tweede Troje," translated by S. I. M., *Brandwag*, 5:240 (13 Mar
1942), 17.

265. (442) "Wanneer ge oud zult zijn," translated by E. Ro, *Faun*, 2:3
(Feb 1946), 32.

266. "Het lied van de oude moeder," translated by Hans van Straten,
Litterair paspoort, Mar 1946, 4.

267. "De oude man," translated by E. Ro, *Faun*, 2:5 (Apr 1946), 120.

268. "La pietra del miracolo: Un atto," translated by Micaela de Pastrovich, *Dramma*, 22:10 (1 Apr 1946), 47-50.

269. "Koningin Maeve. Bij een strijd in de geestenwereld," translated by A. A. M. Horsting-Boerma, *Criterium*, #12 (Sept 1946), 597-602.

270. "Les rameaux flétris. Le poète invoque les puissances élémentaires. Les oiseaux blancs. Les deux arbres. Ne donnez jamais tout votre coeur. Les cygnes sauvages de Coole," translated by Alliette Audra, *Carte du ciel: Cahiers de poésie*, 4 (1947), 57-64.

271. "Ir repülő halálát jósolja," translated by Lőrinc Szabó, *Diarium*, 17:4 (1947), 155.

272. "Verlangend naar het kleed des hemels," translated by Johan de Molenaar, *Linie*, 2:47 (21 Feb 1947), 10.

272a. "Die chymische Rose," translated by Herberth E. Herlitschka, *Story*, 1:10 (May 1947), 17-23.

273. "Dialogo dell'anima e di se stesso," translated by Leone Traverso, *Letteratura*, 9:35 (July-Oct 1947), 152-53.

274. "Genkomsten," translated by Thorkild Bjørnvig, *Heretica*, 1:3 (1948), 180.

275. "Hoe de takken verdorden," translated by A. Roland Holst, *Ad interim*, 5:7/8 (July-Aug 1948), 245.

276. "Ein irischer Flieger sieht seinen Tod voraus," translated by Hans Feist, *Monat*, 1:4 (Jan 1949), 121.

277. "Tre poesie," translated by Leone Traverso, *Rassegna d'Italia*, 4:5 (May 1949), 476-77.

278. "Seis fersen fan Yeats yn Fryske oersetting," translated by D. Kalma, *Tsjerne*, 4:6 (June 1949), 167-70.

278a. "Gedichte," translated by Herberth E. Herlitschka, *Neue Rundschau*, 60:16 (1949), 483-86.

279. "Otok na jezeru Innisfree," [translated by Božo Pahor], *Mladinska revija*, 5:9-10 (1949/50), 422.

280. YAETS [*sic*], W. B.: "Wanneer je oud bent . . . ," translated by A. van Elslander, *Roeping*, 27:6 (Sept 1950), 275.

281. "L'ost de l'air," translated by Helen Mackay, *Bayou*, 15:46 (Summer 1951), 437-38.

282. "La rose secrète," translated by Helen Mackay, *Bayou*, 15:47 (Autumn 1951), 500.

283. "Ha megöregszel . . . ," translated by József Reményi, *Hid*, 15:12 (12 Oct 1951), 775.

284. "Chanson de Red Hanrahan," translated by Helen Mackay, *Bayou*, 15:48 (Winter 1951), 550.

285. "Tam doli na aleji . . . ," translated by Janez Menart, *Beseda*, 1:8 (1951-52), 360.

286. "Lied des wandernden Aengus. In den sieben Wäldern. Er denkt seiner vergangenen Grösse, da er ein Teil der himmlischen Sternbilder war. Der

Liebende spricht zu denen, die in kommenden Tagen seine Lieder hören
werden. Lebendige Schönheit. Nach langem Schweigen. Meerfahrt nach Byzanz.
Unter Ben Bulben (V, VI). Der Fluch Cromwells," translated by Werner
Vordtriede, *Castrum Peregrini*, #9 (1952), 68-75.

287. "A tada? Kraj vrbovih vrtova. Pjesma Aengusa Lutalice. Kaput.
Ljubavnik se zalaže kod svoje prijateljice. Riječi. Pjesma jedne lude.
Ludo ko magla i snijeg," translated by Goran Kovačić, *Radio Zagreb*, 8:1
(1952), 8-9.

288. JITS, VILJEM BATLER: "Kad budete stari," translated by Ivan Goran
Kovačić, *Omladinska riječ*, 9:389 (20 Jan 1952), 5.

289. "Rose de bataille. Mémoire," translated by Helen Mackay, *Bayou*, 16:
49 (Spring 1952), 60.

290. "La mère de dieu," translated by Helen Mackay, *Bayou*, 16:50 (Summer
1952), 123.

291. "Katell, merc'h Houlihan," translated by Jord Ar Mee, *Liamm--Tir na
n-òg*, #39 (July-Aug 1953), 31-45.

292. JITS, VILJEM BATLER: "Jezersko ostrvo Inisfri," translated by
Tomislav Ladan, *Naši dani*, 1:1 (15 Dec 1953), 4.

293. "De ouderdom van Koningin Meve," translated by A. Roland Holst,
Maatstaf, 2:3 (June 1954), 139-43.

293a. YEATS, WILLIAM BUTTLER [*sic*]: "Ein irischer Flieger sieht seinen
Tod voraus," translated by Gisbert Kranz, *Besinnung*, 9:6 (Nov-Dec 1954),
333.

294. "Der Kater und der Mond: Ein Spiel für Tänzer in 1 Akt," translated
by Herbert E. Herlitschka, *Merkur*, 9:12 (Dec 1955), 1134-43.

294a. "Sailing to Byzantium," English and German, translated by Hans
Hennecke, *Deutsche Akademie für Sprache und Dichtung Jahrbuch*, 1956, 78-79.

295. JEITS, V. B.: "Leda i labud," translated by Slobodan Selenić, *Student*,
19:9 (1 June 1956), page not available.

296. "Ego Dominus Tuus," translated by Hans Hennecke, *Jahresring*, [3]
([19]56/57), 49-55.

297. ÏEÏTS, VIL'ÏAM: "Staraia pesnia, proletaia vnov'," translated by S.
Marshak, *Ogonek*, 35:25 (1957), 24.
     Reprinted, together with a translation of "The Fiddler of Dooney,"
     in Samuil Ïakovlevich Marshak, *Sobranie sochinenii v vos'mi tomakh*.
     T. 3: *Perevody iz angliiskikh i shotlandskikh poétov*. Moskva:
     Khudozhestvennaia literatura, 1969. 832 p. (pp. 700-701).

298. "Vágyódás a menny vászna után," translated by Mihály Baki, *Kiskunság*,
3 (Aug 1957), 49.

299. "Życzył sobie chusty. Nakazuje odwagę swemu sercu," translated by
Bolesław Lubosz, *Przemiany*, 2:41 (2 Oct 1957), 8.

300. "Cathleen, córka Houlihana," translated by Zofia and Lucjan Porembscy,
Dialog, 2:11 (Nov 1957), 57-83.

301. "Ha enyém volna. Ha ősz leszel. Ki a hajnalba. Ott lenn a füzes
árnyán. Aki tündérországról álmodott. A tündérek. Tünderdal," translated
by Imre Gombos, *Nagyvilág*, 3:1 (Jan 1958), 19-21.

302. "Innisfree," translated by Lőrinc Szabó, *Dolgozók*, 12:13 (29 Mar 1958), 8.

303. "Fahrt nach Byzanz," translated by Hans Hennecke, *Englische Rundschau*, 8:13 (20 June 1958), 200.

304. "Dix poèmes," translated by Yvonne Feron and Harry Goldgar, *Bayou*, 22 [i.e., 21]:72 (Winter 1958), 553-6.

305. "Ridjokosi Hanrahan," *Subotičke novine*, 14:49 (5 Dec 1958), 6-7. Translator's name not given.

306. "Fegefeuer: Ein Einakter," translated by Herberth E. Herlitschka, *Neue deutsche Hefte*, 5:54 (Jan 1959), 898-904.

307. "Canções de uma peça de teatro. Os magos. Os intelectuais," translated by Soares Martins, *Tempo presente*, #7 (Nov 1959), 37-38.

308. "Die Gesetzestafeln," translated by Herberth E. Herlitschka, *Antaios*, 1:4 (Nov 1959), 367-78.

309. "Un inedito Poundiano: A un poeta che voleva indurmi a dir bene di certi cattive poeti, emuli suoi e miei," translated by Ezra Pound, *Almanacco del Pesce d'oro*, [1] (1960), 16.

310. (443) JEJTS, VILJEM BATLER: "Kad ostariš," translated by Saša Lengold, *Bagdala*, 2:11 (1960), 10.

311. JEJTS, VILIJEM BATLER: "Vrtlozi. Lapis Lazuli. Dugonoga muha," translated by Tomislav Ladan, *Književne novine*, 11:129 (7 Oct 1960), 5.

312. "Die Komödiantenkönigin: Eine Posse in zwei Akten," translated by Herberth E. Herlitschka, *Theatrum Mundi*, 1961, 55-85.

313. JETS, V. B.: "Simbolika poezije," translated by Dušan Puvačić, *Susreti*, 9:11-12 (Nov-Dec 1961), 913-17.

314. JEJTS, VILJEM BATLER: "Luda devojka," [translated by Gordana Mihajlova], *Studentski zbor*, 8:16-17 (30 Dec 1961), 11.

315. "Leda," translated by Yves Bonnefoy, *Cahiers de la Compagnie Madeleine Renaud--Jean-Louis Barrault*, #37 (1962), 68.

315a. "Des Himmels Tücher," translated by Josef Mühlberger, *Hochland*, 54:6 (1962), 547.

316. "Vtoroto doaďanje. Plovejći kon Vizant. Vizant." translated by Bogomil Ðuzel, *Razgledi*, ser 3 / 4:8 (1962), 763-65.

317. "După o lungă tăcere," translated by Lucian Blaga, *Viaţa romînească*, 16:5 (May 1963), 62.

318. "Lapis Lazuli," translated by Johannes Kleinstück, *Du*, 23:269 (July 1963), 52.

319. "Magie," translated by Herberth E. Herlitschka, *Antaios*, 5:2 (July 1963), 101-21.

320. "Een klein veldje gras," translated by F. W. van Heerikhuizen, *Ontmoeting*, 16:12 (Sept 1963), 357.

321. "Madrość króla," translated by Józef Birkenmajer, *Odgłosy*, 6:51/52 (22-29 Dec 1963), 1, 4.

322. "Gravskrift över Swift," translated by Johannes Edfelt, *Bokvännen*, 19:4 (1964), 74.

323. "Kiedy już siwa twa głowa . . . ," translated by Z. Kubiak, *Tygodnik powszechny*, 18:16 (19 Apr 1964), 3.

324. "Mina böckers väg," translated by Eric Bladh, *Bokvännen*, 19:6 (1964), 122.

325. "Otok na jezeru Innisfree," translated by Goran Kovačić, *15* [i.e., *Petnaest*] *dana*, 7:8 (1964), 26.

326. "Kada budeš stara," translated by [Antun] Šoljan and [Ivan] Slamnig, *15 dana*, 8:3-4 (1965), 32.

327. "Enfance et jeunesse resongées," translated by Pierre Leyris, *Mercure de France*, 353:1216 (Feb 1965), 257-72.

328. "El viaje a Bizancio," translated by J[aime] García Terrés, *Revista de la Universidad de México*, 19:9 (May 1965), 4.

329. "Alegerea. În zori. 16 morti," translated by Aurel Covaci, *Tribuna*, 9:25 (24 June 1965), 12.

330. "Căruntă, azi . . . ," translated by Aurel Covaci, *Steaua*, 16:7 (July 1965), 65.

331. "Cuando seas vieja. Aedh clama por los bordados del cielo. Las voces eternas," translated by Enrique Díez-Canedo, *Revista de bellas artes*, 1:4 (July-Aug 1965), 5-6.

332. "Trzy krzaki," translated by Ludmiła Marjańska, *Zwierciadło*, 9:35 (1965), 3.

333. "Wielkanoc 1916 r," translated by Adam Czerniawski, *Kultura*, #10 (Oct 1965), 66-67.

334. "Poemas," translated by Hernando Valencia Goelkel, *Eco*, 12:1 (Nov 1965), 76-83.

335. °"Un om tînăr şi bătrîn . . . ," *Familia*, 1:3 (Nov 1965), 21. Translator's name not known.

336. "Leda şi lebăda," translated by Marcel Breslaşu. "Irlandei în vremea ce va să vină," translated by Aurel Covaci. "Vîrtejurile. Lapis Lazuli," translated by Dan Constantinescu. A fragment from *Autobiographies*, translated by Alexandru Bucur, *Secolul 20*, 5:12 (1965), 129-39.

337. "El se tînguie pentru schimbarea sa şi a iubitei sale şi doreşte sfîrşitul lumii," translated by Lucian Blaga, *Steaua*, 17:1 (Jan 1966), 25.

338. "Cuatro poemas," translated by Juan Tovar and Alejandro Aura, *Palabra y el hombre*, #37 (Jan-Mar 1966), 5-8.

339. "Biserica şi statul," translated by Marcel Breslaşu, *Secolul 20*, 6:4 (Apr 1966), 8.

340. "Kad budeš ostarjela. Bez druge Troje. Mudraci. Bizantija," translated by Mario Suško, *Republika*, 22:5 (May 1966), 209.

341. "Ephemera. Żałość miłości. Smutek miłości," translated by Zygmunt Kubiak, *Tygodnik powszechny*, 20:21 (22 May 1966), 4.

342. "Despre o detinută politică," *Săteanca*, #26 (June 1966), 14. Translator's name not given.

343. "Souvenirs sur Wilde," translated by Pierre Leyris, *Nouvelle revue française*, 14:163 (1 July 1966), 72-85.

31

344. "När du bliv gammal . . . ," translated by Gösta Berggren, *Studie-kamraten*, 48:8 (1966), 150.

345. "Yeats despre Wilde," *Ramuri*, 3:9 (15 Aug 1966), 22. Translator's name not given.

346. JEJTS, V. B.: "Labud što leti u samotno nebo: Bijele ptice. Hladino nebo. Divilji labudovi u Kul Parku. Drugi dolazak. Jedrenje u Bizantiju. Leda i labud. Kul Park i Belili 1931. Utješeni kukalen," translated by Mario Suško, *Život*, 16:1-2 (Jan-Feb 1967), 53-57.

347. "Innisfree, wyspa na jeziorze. Dolina czarnej świni. Do cienia. Coole i Ballylee, 1931. Po długim milczeniu. Głowa z brązu. Dwie pieśni ze sztuki. Trzej królowie," translated by Jarosław Marek Rymkiewicz. "Wielkanoc 1916 r," translated by Adam Czerniawski, *Poezja*, 3:3 (Mar 1967), 62-68.

348. "Prière pour ma fille," translated by René Fréchet, *Langues modernes*, 61:2 (Mar-Apr 1967), 192-95.

349. "Quando sarai vecchio. Al crepuscolo. Tre momenti. Quando i vecchi si riconoscono nell'acqua. Olio e sangue. Innisfree l'isola del lago," translated by Vivalda Brancati, *Persona*, 8:3 (1967), 12-13.

350. "Opodal ogrodów Salley," translated by Ludmiła Marjańska, *Zwierciadło*, 11:29 (1967), 4.

351. "Auf einer Insel im Wasser," translated by Alfred Margul-Sperber, *Neuer Weg*, 20:5814 (13 Jan 1968), 3.

352. "Tărîna şi răsăritul soarelui," [translated by Zoe Dumitrescu-Buşulenga?], *Secolul 20*, 8:2 (Feb 1968), 76-79.

353. "Şi ce-i?" translated by Constantin Crişan, *Viaţa românească*, 21:12 (Dec 1968), caietul poeţii si meditaţia, xxvi.

354. "Róża bitwy. Róża pokoju," translated by Bohdan Zadura, *Kultura*, 7:5 (2 Feb 1969), 3.

354a. "Gedichte," translated by Werner Vordtriede, *Neue deutsche Hefte*, 16:4 (1969), 80-82.

355. "Plovidba u Bizant," translated by Antun Šoljan, *Književna smotra*, 1:2 (Winter 1969-70), 54.

355a. "Zwei Gedichte: Die Gelehrten. Die tolle Hanne wird zurechtgewiesen," translated by Werner Vordtriede, *Akzente*, 17:1 (1970), 72.

356. "Bland ängens pilar," translated by Karl Asplund, *Tidsspegel*, #2 (1970), 51.

357. "Segling till Byzantium," translated by Anders Österling, *Böckernas värld*, 5:8 (Dec 1970), 82-83.

357a. °"Gdy będziesz stara," translated by M. Hemar, *Tydzień Polski*, 31:45 (1970), 4.

358. "Din poezia celtică contemporană: Trandafirul lumii. Nebunia regelui Goll," translated by Margareta Sterian, *Luceafărul*, 14:12 (20 Mar 1971), 7.

358a. "És Rényi Ferenc hallgatott," translated by Ágnes Gergely, *Nagyvilág*, 16:11 (Nov 1971), 1730-32.

358b. "La mort de Cuchulain," translated by Serge Fauchereau, *Lettres nouvelles*, #1 (Mar 1973), 53-64.

358c. °"Poezija i tradicija," translated by Aleksandar I. Spasić, *Radio Sarajevo--Treći Program*, 2:2 (1973), 23-31.

358d. °"Medj školskom decom," translated by D. Marković and B. Horvat, *Naše stvaranje*, 20:5 (1973), 36-37.

AC Bibliographies of Yeats Criticism

359. CROSS, KENNETH GUSTAV WALTER, and RONALD T. DUNLOP: *A Bibliography of Yeats Criticism, 1887-1965*. With a foreword by A. Norman Jeffares. London: Macmillan, 1971. xxvi, 341 p.
   Reviews:
   1. Anon., "Yeats as an Adolescent Dreamer," *TLS*, 71:3655 (17 Mar 1972), 311.
   2. John Bryson, "Yeatsiana," *Books and Bookmen*, 17:199 (Apr 1972), 24.
   3. Richard J. Finneran, "Progress Report on the Yeats Industry," *JML*, 3:1 (Feb 1973), 129-33.
   4. John Kelly, "Yeats Industry Booming," *Times Higher Education Supplement*, #15 (21 Jan 1972), 17.
   5. Robert Kent, *Éire-Ireland*, 7:4 (Winter 1972), 145-46.

360. GERSTENBERGER, DONNA: "Yeats and the Theater: A Selected Bibliography," *MD*, 6:1 (Summer 1963), 64-71.

361. JOCHUM, K. P. S.: *W. B. Yeats's Plays: An Annotated Checklist of Criticism*. Saarbrücken: Anglistisches Institut der Universität des Saarlandes, 1966. 180 p.

362. STOLL, JOHN E.: *The Great Deluge: A Yeats Bibliography*. Troy, N.Y.: Whitston, 1971. vii, 100 p.
   A checklist of criticism, containing about a thousand items. No index, no annotations, no cross-references, riddled with errors and mistakes. Some of the items are not on Yeats at all, some simply do not exist, some are virtually unidentifiable. Practically worthless.
   Reviews:
   1. Richard J. Finneran, "Progress Report on the Yeats Industry," *JML*, 3:1 (Feb 1973), 129-33.

See also J8, 9, 12, 402, 1090, 1112, 1132, 2282, 2970a.

AD Bibliographies concerning Yeats in Part

363. ADELMAN, IRVING, and RITA DWORKIN: *Modern Drama: A Checklist of Critical Literature on 20th Century Plays*. Metuchen: Scarecrow Press, 1967. 370 p.
   Lady Gregory, pp. 132-33; Martyn, 192-93; Murray, 205; O'Casey,206-10; Synge, 306-9; Yeats, 332-40. Lists only titles in English; selective.

363a. BREED, PAUL F., and FLORENCE M. SNIDERMAN: *Dramatic Criticism Index: A Bibliography of Commentaries on Playwrights from Ibsen to the Avant-Garde*. Detroit: Gale Research Company, 1972. ix, 1022 p.
   On Yeats, pp. 762-76. Lists only criticism in English and omits many standard monographs.

363b. CLINE, GLORIA STARK, and JEFFREY A. BAKER: *An Index to Criticisms of British and American Poetry*. Metuchen: Scarecrow Press, 1972. x, 307 p.
   Criticism of Yeats's poems is indexed on pp. 145-48. Highly selective.

364. COLEMAN, ARTHUR, and GARY R. TYLER: *Drama Criticism*. Volume 1: A checklist of interpretation since 1940 of English and American plays. Denver: Swallow, 1966. 457 p.

"Sean O'Casey," 154-56; "John Synge," 202-5; "William Butler Yeats," 232-35. Selective.

365. CUTLER, BRADLEY DWYANE, and VILLA STILES: *Modern British Authors: Their First Editions*. NY: Greenberg, 1930. xi, 171 p.
"William Butler Yeats," 164-67.

366. DYSON, ANTHONY EDWARD (ed): *English Poetry: Select Bibliographical Guides*. London: Oxford UP, 1971. xi, 378 p.
Jon Stallworthy: "Yeats," 345-59. A review of research and a list of 89 entries, both of which are rather selective.

366a. HOWARD, PATSY C.: *Theses in English Literature, 1894-1970*. Ann Arbor: Pierian Press, 1973. xix, 387 p.
Lists only M.A. and B.A. theses. On Lady Gregory, #3674-78; Moore, 5632-44; O'Casey, 5753-74; Stephens, 7938-41; Synge, 8156-96; Yeats, 8939-9000 (incomplete; authors A-N only). I saw this book too late to be able to incorporate some of its material into my bibliography.

367. JUCHHOFF, RUDOLF, and HILDEGARD FÖHL: *Sammelkatalog der biographischen und literarkritischen Werke zu englischen Schriftstellern des 19. und 20. Jahrhunderts (1830-1958). Verzeichnis der Bestände in deutschen Bibliotheken*. Krefeld: Scherpe, [1959]. 272 p.
Yeats, pp. 267-72. Lists books and theses only, but is generally very useful because it contains many out-of-the-way items and analyzes collections.

367a. KRAWITZ, HENRY: *A Post-Symbolist Bibliography*. Metuchen: Scarecrow Press, 1973. 284 p.
"Yeats," 234-48. See also "Comparative Studies," 51-95, which, unaccountably, is not indexed properly anywhere in the book.

368. KUNTZ, JOSEPH MARSHALL: *Poetry Explication: A Checklist of Interpretation since 1925 of British and American Poems Past and Present*. Revised edition. Denver: Swallow, 1962 [1950]. 352 p.
Yeats, pp. 298-316.

369. MANLY, JOHN MATTHEWS, and EDITH RICKERT: *Contemporary British Literature: A Critical Survey and 232 Author-Bibliographies*. Revised by Fred B. Millett. NY: Harcourt Brace, 1935 [1921]. xi, 556 p.
Yeats, pp. 518-22. The list of periodical articles on Yeats, included in the 1928 edition (p. 318), is not in the 1935 edition.

370. *The New Cambridge Bibliography of English Literature*. Edited by George Watson. Cambridge: University Press, 1969—.
Volume 3, 1800-1900, contains D[avid] H. G[reene]: "Anglo-Irish Literature," 1885-1948; on Yeats, pp. 1915-34. Includes material through 1965.
In *The Cambridge Bibliography of English Literature*, edited by F. W. Bateson (1940, 1957), the Yeats material was compiled by Sean O'Faolain, Peter Allt, and T. R. Henn (3:1059-62; 5:700-704).
Volume 4, 1900-1950, edited by I. R. Willison, contains sections on Austin Clarke, Gogarty, Higgins, MacDonagh, Seumas O'Sullivan, Stephens, the theater in Ireland, O'Casey, Johnston, and Brinsley Macnamara.

371. NORTON, CLARA MULLIKEN, and others (comps): *Modern Drama and Opera: A Reading List*. Boston: Boston Book Company, 1911-15. 2 v. (Useful Reference Series. 4. 13.)
Alice Thurston McGirr: "Synge," 2:131-36; "Yeats," 2:148-54. The last item is a revision of "Reading List on William Butler Yeats," *Bulletin of Bibliography*, 7:4 (Jan 1913), 82-83.

372. ØKSNEVAD, REIDAR: *Det Britiske Samvelde og Eire i norsk litteratur: En bibliografi / The British Commonwealth of Nations and Eire in Norwegian Literature: A Bibliography.* Oslo: Gyldendal, 1949. 187 p.
Yeats, pp. 74-75.

373. PALMER, HELEN H., and ANNE JANE DYSON (comps): *European Drama Criticism.* Hamden, Conn.: Shoe String Press, 1968. vii, 460 p.
"William Butler Yeats," 433-39. Supplement I: 1970. vii, 243 p. (Yeats, 185-88). Supplement II: 1974. vii, 209 p. (Yeats, 172-74).

374. SCHLÖSSER, ANSELM: *Die englische Literatur in Deutschland von 1895 bis 1934 mit einer vollständigen Bibliographie der deutschen Übersetzungen und der im deutschen Sprachgebiet erschienenen englischen Ausgaben.* Jena: Biedermann, 1937. vii, 535 p. (Forschungen zur englischen Philologie. 5.)
Scattered notes on the German Yeats reception (see index), including a list of translations in anthologies.

375. SCHWARTZ, JACOB: *1100 Obscure Points: The Bibliographies of 25 English and 21 American Authors.* London: Ulysses Bookshop, 1931. xiii, 95 p.
Yeats, pp. 41-42. The listing of Yeats items is best described in the foreword: "This is the first bibliography ever written in which the author will not make any apologies for missing items therein" (p. vii).

376. ULLRICH, KURT: *Who Wrote about Whom: A Bibliography of Books on Contemporary British Authors.* Berlin: Collignon, 1932. 60 p.
Lists only titles published between 1920 and 1931. Yeats, *passim* (see index).

See also J379, 380, 389, 390, 399.

AE   Bibliographies of Anglo-Irish Literature and Drama,
Including Checklists of Plays and Performances

376a. ALDUS, JUDITH BUTLER: "Anglo-Irish Dialects: A Bibliography," *Regional Language Studies*, #2 (15 Sept 1969), 1-17.

377. ANON.: "List of Works in the New York Public Library Relating to Ireland, the Irish Language and Literature, etc," *BNYPL*, 9:3 (Mar 1905), 90-104; :4 (Apr 1905), 122-44; :5 (May 1905), 159-84; :6 (June 1905), 201-29; :7 (July 1905), 249-80.

378. ANON.: "Ulster Books and Authors, 1900-1953," *Rann*, #20 (1953), 55-73.

379. BAKER, BLANCH MERRITT: *Theatre and Allied Arts: A Guide to Books Dealing with the History, Criticism, and Technic of the Drama and Theatre and Related Arts and Crafts.* NY: Wilson, 1952. xiv, 536 p.
"Ireland," 113-20; Yeats, pp. 118-20.

380. BROWN, STEPHEN JAMES (ed): *A Guide to Books on Ireland.* Part 1: Prose literature, poetry, music, and plays. Dublin: Hodges Figgis / London: Longmans Green, 1912. xviii, 371 p.
No more published. An annotated bibliography, arranged as follows: (1) general collections and selections (prose and poetry); (2) prose literature, including a section "Books about the Theatre in Ireland," compiled by Joseph Holloway; (3) poetry; (4) music; (5) Irish plays, arranged chronologically, compiled by Holloway (Yeats, 244-51). Contains several indexes; on Yeats, *passim*.

381. ———: *The Press in Ireland: A Survey and a Guide*. Dublin: Browne & Nolan, 1937. xi, 304 p.
A historical sketch and a bibliography.

382. [BURGOYNE, F. J. P. (comp)]: *Belfast Library and Society for Promoting Knowledge: Catalogue of the Books in the Irish Section*. Belfast: MacBride, 1917. vi, 268 p.

383. CARTY, JAMES: *Bibliography of Irish History, 1912-1921*. Dublin: Stationery Office for Department of Education, 1936. xxxix, 177 p.

384. ———: *Bibliography of Irish History, 1870-1911*. Dublin: Stationery Office, 1940. xviii, 319 p.
"Literary and Dramatic Movements," 262-82; and *passim*.

385. CLEEVE, BRIAN: *Dictionary of Irish Writers*. Cork: Mercier Press, 1967-71. 3 v.
First series: Fiction, novelists, playwrights, poets, short-story writers in English. 1967. 143 p. Second series: Nonfiction. 1969. 111 p. Volume 3: Writers in the Irish language. 1971. 144 p. On Yeats, 1:142-43.

386. EAGER, ALAN ROBERT: *A Guide to Irish Bibliographical Material: Being a Bibliography of Irish Bibliographies and Some Sources of Information*. London: Library Association, 1964. xiii, 392 p.

387. FRENCH, FRANCES-JANE: *The Abbey Theatre Series of Plays: A Bibliography*. Dublin: Dolmen Press, 1969. 53 p.

388. HARMON, MAURICE: *Modern Irish Literature, 1800-1967: A Reader's Guide*. Dublin: Dolmen Press, 1967. 71 p.
A selective bibliography in three sections, Irish literature 1800-1890, 1890-1920, and postrevolutionary; each section is headed by an introductory survey.
Reviews:
1. Anon., *TLS*, 67:3453 (2 May 1968), 465. The book is "not as useful as it might have been."

389. *HAYES, RICHARD JAMES (ed): *Manuscript Sources for the History of Irish Civilization*. Boston: Hall, 1965. 11 v.
See particularly under: Abbey Theatre, 1:1-2; Fay (Brigit, Frank J., Gerard, William George), 2:95-96; Gregory (Isabella Augusta), 2:328-29; Henderson (William A.), 2:451; Holloway (Joseph), 2:496-97; Hone (Joseph M.), 2:503; Horniman (Annie E. F.), 2:512; Hyde, 2:547-48; MacBride (Maud Gonne), 3:169-70; Martyn, 3:326; Moore (George), 3: 420-21; Roberts (George), 4:238-39; Robinson (Lennox), 4:244; Russell (George William), 4:292-93; Synge, 4:581-82; Tynan (Katharine), 4: 704-5; Yeats (family, Elizabeth Corbet, Jack B., John B., Lily, W. B.), 4:926-29.
For a continuation see: NATIONAL LIBRARY OF IRELAND: *Shelf-List of Additional Mss. Catalogued since Publication of "Manuscript Sources for the History of Irish Civilization."* With index of names. [Dublin: National Library of Ireland], 1970. (Additions through June 1970.)

390. *———: *Sources for the History of Irish Civilization: Articles in Irish Periodicals*. Boston: Hall, 1970. 9 v.
Volumes 1-5: Persons; volumes 6-8: Subjects; volume 9: Places and Dates.

391. °HOLLOWAY, JOSEPH: A copybook containing an alphabetical list of Irish plays, and a volume containing lists of plays performed at the

Abbey Theatre, Dublin, 1909-44. 2 v.
In the National Library of Ireland, MSS. 4438-39.

392. HOLZAPFEL, RUDI: "A Survey of Irish Literary Periodicals from 1900 to the Present Day," M.Litt. thesis, Trinity College, Dublin, 1964. xix, 668 p.
A valuable but rather poorly organized thesis in two parts: (1) a list of various periodicals with more or less complete information about publication dates, editors, contributors, and library holdings; (2) an author index to some of these periodicals.

393. INTERNATIONAL ASSOCIATION FOR THE STUDY OF ANGLO-IRISH LITERATURE: "Bibliography Bulletin," *Irish UR*, 2:1 (Spring 1972), 79-110.
Lists publications in various countries through 1970. Selective.

394. ———: "Bibliography Bulletin 1971," *Irish UR*, 2:2 (Autumn 1972), 209-36.

394a. ———: "Bibliography Bulletin 1972," *Irish UR*, 3:2 (Autumn 1973), 194-240.

395. LOEWENBERG, ALFRED: *The Theatre of the British Isles Excluding London: A Bibliography*. London: Printed for the Society of Theatre Research, 1950 (for 1949). ix, 75 p. (Society for Theatre Research: First Annual Publication, 1948-49.)
"Dublin," 19-27; "Ireland," 38-39.

396. MIKHAIL, EDWARD HALIM: *A Bibliography of Modern Irish Drama, 1899-1970*. With a foreword by William A. Armstrong. London: Macmillan, 1972. xi, 51 p.
About 650 items. Valuable, but not annotated and not classified. No indication is given whether the items were seen or not. Particularly deficient in Irish and continental European material.
Reviews:
1. Anon., "The Pagan Roots," *TLS*, 71:3681 (22 Sept 1972), 1112.

396a. ———: *Dissertations on Anglo-Irish Drama: A Bibliography of Studies, 1870-1970*. London: Macmillan, 1973. x, 73 p.
Contains a number of printing mistakes, especially in the Yeats section. Not annotated; no indication is given whether the items were seen or not. Not exhaustive.

397. NATIONAL LIBRARY OF IRELAND: *Leabhra ar Éirinn: Liosta ar na ullmhú ag leabharlann náisiúnta na h-Éireann / Books on Ireland: List Compiled by National Library of Ireland*. Dublin: At the Sign of the Three Candles, 1953. 47 p.

398. [O'BRIEN, MAURICE NEILL]: *Irish Plays*. NY: National Service Bureau, Federal Theatre Project, 1938. xii, 110 p. (Publication #47-L.)
Includes synopses of the following Yeats plays: *The Countess Cathleen, Cathleen ni Houlihan, The King's Threshold, On Baile's Strand, The Words upon the Window-Pane, The Pot of Broth, Fighting the Waves, The Land of Heart's Desire.*

399. O'DONOGHUE, DAVID JAMES: *The Poets of Ireland: A Biographical and Bibliographical Dictionary of Irish Writers of English Verse*. Dublin: Hodges Figgis / London: Oxford UP, 1912 [1892-93]. iv, 504 p.
Yeats, p. 492.

400. O'NEILL, JAMES J.: *A Bibliographical Account of Irish Theatrical Literature*. Part 1: General theatrical history, players, and theatrical periodicals. Dublin: Falconer, 1920. Pp. 57-88. (Publications of the

Bibliographical Society of Ireland. 1:6.)
   No more published.

401. ROYAL IRISH ACADEMY. COMMITTEE FOR THE STUDY OF ANGLO-IRISH LANGUAGE
AND LITERATURE: *Handlist*. [Dublin, 1969—].
   A list of work in progress. So far, the following installments have
   been published: #1 (June 1969); #2 (July 1971); Supplement to #2
   (n.d.); #3 (Aug 1973); #4 (Sept 1974).

401a. ————: *Handlist of Theses Completed but Not Published*. [Dublin,
1973 —].
   Mimeographed list. #1 (Aug 1973).

402. SAUL, GEORGE BRANDON: *Stephens, Yeats, and Other Irish Concerns*. NY:
New York Public Library, 1954. 45 p.
   Partial contents: 1. "An Introductory Bibliography in Anglo-Irish
   Literature," 12-18; reprinted from *BNYPL*, 58:9 (Sept 1954), 429-35.
   2. "Thread to a Labyrinth: A Selective Bibliography in Yeats," 19-22;
   reprinted from *BNYPL*, 58:7 (July 1954), 344-47. Lists only books,
   some of which are irrelevant.
   3. "The Winged Image: A Note on Birds in Yeats's Poems," 23-29; reprinted from *BNYPL*, 58:6 (June 1954), 267-73, and reprinted in J1076.

403. STEWART, MARY ISABEL HELEN: "The Abbey Theatre, Dublin: A Bibliography," [Diploma in Librarianship thesis, U of London, 1939]. ix, 51 p.

404. [TAYLOR, LUCIEN EDWARD]: *A List of Books on Modern Ireland in the
Public Library of the City of Boston*. Boston: The Trustees, 1921. vii,
90 p.

405. WEITENKAMPF, FRANK: "The Irish Literary Revival: A Contribution to
Literary Bibliography," *Lamp*, [ser 3] / 29:3 (Oct 1904), 238-40.
   Lists and comments upon 29 items.

See also J363, 364, 370, 501, 517-20, 523, 532, 533, 538, 540, 547,
5917a, 6324, 6583, 6744, 6841, 6895, 7223, 7472.

AF   Other Bibliographies Used

The items listed in this section represent only a small part of the
reference tools I have used. There are numerous other bibliographies
and indexes that list a Yeats item here and there (at the rate of perhaps
one per ten volumes) but that do not warrant inclusion because of their
limited usefulness.

406. *Abstracts of English Studies*, 1 (1958) —.

407. ALTICK, RICHARD DANIEL, and WILLIAM R. MATTHEWS: *Guide to Doctoral
Dissertations in Victorian Literature, 1886-1958*. Urbana: U of Illinois
Press, 1960. vii, 119 p.

408. *Annual Bibliography of English Language and Literature*, 1 (1920)—.

409. *Annual Literary Index*, 1892-1904. Continued as *Annual Library Index*,
1905-10.

410. *Bibliografia republicii populare romîne. Articole din publicaţii
periodice şi seriale* [title varies], 1 (1953)—.

411. *Bibliografia zawartosci czasopism*, 1 (1947)—.

412. *Bibliografie van de Vlaamse Tijdschriften*. Hasselt: Heideland, 1960—.

413. *Bibliografija jugoslavije: Članci i prilozi u časopisima i listovima.*
Serija C, 3 (1952)—.

414. *Bibliographic Index*, 1937—.

415. *Bibliographie der deutschen Zeitschriftenliteratur (Internationale
Bibliographie der Zeitschriftenliteratur, Abteilung A)*, 1 (1896)— 128
(1964).

416. *Bibliographie der fremdsprachigen Zeitschriftenliteratur (Internationale Bibliographie der Zeitschriftenliteratur, Abteilung B)*, 1
(1911)— 22 (1921/25); ns 1 (1925/26)— 51 (1962/64).

417. *Bibliographie der Rezensionen (Internationale Bibliographie der
Zeitschriftenliteratur, Abteilung C)*, 1 (1900)— 77 (1943).

418. *Biography Index*, 1946— .

419. BOOKS ABROAD: "Periodicals at Large," *BA*, 24:2 (Spring 1950)— 34:4
(Autumn 1960).
    An unsystematic, unclassified, and unindexed checklist of articles
    in periodicals in various languages. With enough patience, one detects
    numerous out-of-the-way items, which are not indexed elsewhere.

420. *British Humanities Index*, 1962— .

421. *Bulletin signalétique*, section 19 (Sciences humaines), 1961-66;
section 23 (Littérature et arts du spectacle), 1967—.

422. *Canadian Graduate Theses in the Humanities and Social Sciences, 1921-
1946*. Ottawa: Cloutier, 1951. 194 p.

423. *Canadian Index to Periodicals and Documentary Films* [title varies],
1948— .

424. *Canadian Periodical Index*, 1938-47.

425. *Canadian Theses / Thèses canadiennes*, 1960/61—.

426. *Catholic Periodical Index* [title varies], 1 (1930)—.

427. *Cumulated Dramatic Index, 1909-1949: A Cumulation of the F. W. Faxon
Company's Dramatic Index* [etc.]. Boston: Hall, 1965. 2 v.

428. *Cumulated Magazine Subject Index, 1907-1949*. Boston: Hall, 1964. 2 v.
    A cumulation of *Magazine Subject Index* (1907) and *Annual Magazine
    Subject Index* (1908-49).

429. DENSON, ALAN: *Thomas Bodkin: A Bio-Bibliographical Survey with a
Bibliographical Survey of His Family*. Dublin: Bodkin Trustees, 1966. ii,
236 p.
    See also J6879.

430. *Education Index*, 1 (1929)— .

431. *Essay and General Literature Index*, 1900— .

432. GROVE, SIR GEORGE: *Grove's Dictionary of Music and Musicians*. 5th
edition, edited by Eric Blom. London: Macmillan, 1954-61. 10 v.
    See especially 9:381.

433. *Guide to Indian Periodical Literature*, 1 (1964)— .

434. HEFLING, HELEN, and JESSIE W. DYDE: *Hefling and Richards' Index to
Contemporary Biography and Criticism*. Boston: Faxon, 1934 [1929]. 229 p.
(Useful Reference Series. 50.)

435. HOFFMAN, FREDERICK J., CHARLES ALLEN, and CAROLYN F. ULLRICH: *The Little Magazine: A History and a Bibliography*. NY: Kraus, 1967 [1946]. xiii, 450 p.

436. *Index to Latin American Periodical Literature*, 1929— .

437. *Index to Little Magazines*, 1940— .

438. *Index to Theses Accepted for Higher Degrees in the Universities of Great Britain and Ireland*, 1 (1950/51)—.

439. *Index translationum*, 1 (1932)— .

440. *International Index to Periodicals*, 1907-64; continued as *Social Sciences & Humanities Index*, 1965—.

441. *Internationale Bibliographie der Zeitschriftenliteratur aus allen Gebieten des Wissens*, 1 (1963/64)—.

442. LITTO, FREDRIC M.: *American Dissertations on the Drama and Theatre: A Bibliography*. Kent, Ohio: Kent State UP, 1969. ix, 519 p.

443. *MLA International Bibliography of Books and Articles on Modern Languages and Literatures* [title varies], 1921—.

444. MACLOCHLAINN, ALF: "Towards National Bibliography: Irish Books Reviewed, 1969," *Leabharlann*, 28:1 (Mar 1970), 4-19.
    Continued as "Irish Books Reviewed, 1970," *Leabharlann*, 29:1 (Apr 1971), 11-13, 15-17, 19-20, 22-23. No list for 1971 has been published so far. Indexes reviews in *Hibernia*, *Irish Independent*, *Irish Press*, and *Irish Times*.

445. MCNAMEE, LAWRENCE F.: *Dissertations in English and American Literature: Theses Accepted by American, British, and German Universities, 1865-1964*. NY: Bowker, 1968. xi, 1124 p.
    Supplement 1, 1964-68. 1969. x, 450 p.

446. *Nijhoff's Index*, 1 (1909)—.

447. *Nineteenth Century Reader's Guide to Periodical Literature, 1890-1899, with Supplementary Indexing, 1900-1922*. NY: Wilson, 1944. 2 v.

448. PONDROM, CYRENA NORMAN: "English Literary Periodicals, 1885-1918," Ph.D. thesis, Columbia U, 1965. vii, 370 p. (*DA*, 26:10 [Apr 1966], 6026.)

449. *Poole's Index to Periodical Literature*, 1802-1907.

450. *Reader's Guide to Periodical Literature*, 1 (1900)—.

451. *Review of Review Index*, 1 (1890)— 13 (1902).

452. *Revue de la Société d'histoire du théâtre*, 1 (1948)— .
    Contains an annual international bibliography.

453. SMITH, EDWARD DOYLE: "A Survey and Index of *The Irish Statesman* (1923-1930)," Ph.D. thesis, U of Washington, 1966. v, 699 p. (*DA*, 27:6 [Dec 1966], 1794A-95A.)

454. SPRUG, JOSEPH W. (ed): *An Index to G. K. Chesterton*. Washington, D.C.: Catholic U of America Press, 1966. xx, 427 p.
    Yeats, p. 426. Only the more substantial Yeats references have been incorporated in this bibliography.

455. *Subject Index to Periodicals*, 1915/16— 1961.

456. TEMPLEMAN, WILLIAM DARBY (ed): *Bibliographies of Studies in Victorian Literature for the Thirteen Years 1932-1944*. Urbana: U of Illinois Press, 1945. ix, 450 p. Reprinted from *MP*.
    Continued as: WRIGHT, AUSTIN (ed): *Bibliographies of Studies in Victorian Literature for the Ten Years 1945-1954*. Urbana: U of Illinois Press, 1956. vii, 310 p. Reprinted from *MP*.
    Continued as: SLACK, ROBERT C. (ed): *Bibliographies of Studies in Victorian Literature for the Ten Years 1955-64*. Urbana: U of Illinois Press, 1967. xvii, 461 p. Reprinted from *MP* (1956-57) and *VS* (1958-65). Continued in *VS*, 9 (1965-66)—.

457. WOODBRIDGE, HENSLEY C.: "Thomas Kinsella: A Bibliography," *Éire-Ireland*, 2:2 (Summer 1967), 122-33.

458. *Year's Work in English Studies*, 1 (1919/20)—.

AG Reviews of Research and Extended Review-Articles

Items listed in section AG are not further analyzed in this bibliography.

459. ADAMS, HAZARD: "Yeats Scholarship and Criticism: A Review of Research," *TSLL*, 3:4 (Winter 1962), 439-51.

459a. ————: "Scholarship and the Idea of Criticism: Recent Writing on Yeats," *Georgia R*, 26:3 (Fall 1972), 249-78.

460. ALLEN, JAMES L.: "Recent Yeatsiana: The Failed Quest for Unity of Being," *JML*, 2:1 (Sept 1971), 148-54.

461. ANON.: "Surveying Yeats from China to Peru," *TLS*, 65:3337 (10 Feb 1966), 99.

462. ANON.: "Saving Yeats from the Critics," *TLS*, 70:3602 (12 Mar 1971), 292.

463. BERGSTEN, STAFFAN: "Nyare Yeatslitteratur," *Samlaren*, 90 (1969), 198-201.

464. BINNI, FRANCESCO: "Yeats e i critici," *Letteratura*, 31 / ns 15:88-90 (July-Dec 1967), 305-8.

465. BLOOM, HAROLD: "Recent Studies in the Nineteenth Century," *SEL 1500-1900*, 10:4 (Autumn 1970), 817-29.
    Yeats, pp. 828-29.

466. CAREW, RIVERS: Omnibus review, *Dublin Mag*, 6:2 (Summer 1967), 92-94.

467. DAICHES, DAVID: *English Literature*. Englewood Cliffs: Prentice-Hall, 1964. xv, 174 p.
    See pp. 10-18 for comments on American Yeats scholarship with particular condemnation of Delmore Schwartz (J1603).

468. DUNLOP, RONALD: "W. B. Yeats, 1865-1939: What *Would* Susan Yeats Have Thought?" *Poetry Australia*, #6 (Oct 1965), 36-39.

469. FLETCHER, IAN: "The Present State of Yeats Criticism," *Literary Half-Yearly*, 2:2 (July 1961), 22-26.

470. HARPER, GEORGE MILLS: "'All the Instruments Agree': Some Observations on Recent Yeats Criticism," *Sewanee R*, 74:3 (July-Sept 1966), 739-54.

471. ————: "'Sing Whatever Is Well Made': Recent Books about Yeats," *CEA Critic*, 33:3 (Mar 1971), 29-35.

472. JEFFARES, A. NORMAN: "An Account of Recent Yeatsiana," *Hermathena*, 72 (Nov 1948), 21-43.
　　To be used with caution; contains numerous inaccuracies.

473. ————: "The Last Twelve Years' Yeatsiana," *Levende talen*, #149 (Apr 1949), 109-13.

473a. JOCHUM, K. P. S.: "W. B. Yeats: A Survey of Book Publications, 1966-1972," *Anglia*, 92:1/2 (1974), 143-71.

474. KAIN, RICHARD M.: "W. B. Yeats: Centenary Studies and Tributes," *Southern R*, 3:3 (July 1967), 742-56.

475. ————: "The Status of Yeats Scholarship," *Éire-Ireland*, 2:3 (Autumn 1967), 102-10.

476. KIRSCHNER, ALLEN ROGER: "The Critical Reputation of William Butler Yeats, 1889-1928," M.A. thesis, New York U, 1955. ii, 90 p.

477. LEARY, LEWIS (ed): *Contemporary Literary Scholarship: A Critical Review*. NY: Appleton-Century-Crofts, 1958. x, 474 p.
　　Notes on American Yeats scholarship appear *passim* (see index).

478. LIGHTCAP, JANE STREATOR: "William Butler Yeats' Reputation in Selected American Periodicals: 1895-1940," M.A. thesis, U of Florida, 1964. iii, 129 p.
　　The periodicals are *Atlantic Monthly*, *Bookman*, *Dial*, *Nation*, *New Republic*, and *Poetry*.

479. MACKENZIE, NORMAN H.: "The Yeats Canon and Recent Scholarship," *QQ*, 78:3 (Autumn 1971), 462-64.

480. M[ALONE], A. E.: "The 'Abbey' Shelf: Books about the Theatre, Biographies and Autobiographies," *Irish Times*, 80:25300 (13 Aug 1938), 7.

481. ORACKI, TADEUSZ: "Twórczość W. B. Yeatsa w Polsce," *Kultura*, 7:8 (23 Feb 1969), 9.
　　Yeats's work in Poland and in Polish.

482. PATTINSON, JOHN PATRICK: "A Study of British Poetic Criticism between 1930 and 1965 as Exemplified in the Critics of Yeats, Pound, and Eliot," Ph.D. thesis, New York U, 1968. iv, 261 p. (*DA*, 30:10 [Apr 1970], 4460A-61A.)
　　"Yeats's British Critics," 48-129.

483. [QUINN, JOHN (comp)]: *Some Critical Appreciations of William Butler Yeats as Poet, Orator, and Dramatist*. N.p., [1903?]. 23 p.

484. RAFROIDI, PATRICK: "Yeats and Co.," *Langues modernes*, 61:2 (Mar-Apr 1967), 196-206.

485. REYNOLDS, HORACE: "'To Follow Yeats down All the Diverse Paths,'" *CSM*, 44:168 (12 June 1952), 13.

486. RODGERS, W. R.: Omnibus review, *Listener*, 74:1913 (25 Nov 1965), 867-68.

487. SERGEANT, HOWARD: Omnibus review, *English*, 20:106 (Spring 1971), 26-27.

488. SETURAMAN, V. S.: "Yeats and His Modern Critics," *Aryan Path*, 30:10 (Oct 1959), 457-61.
　　Mainly on what the critics did with "Among School Children."

489. SHAW, PRISCILLA W.: "The Yeats Centenary: Part of the Harvest," *VQR*, 42:1 (Winter 1966), 173-76.

490. SIDNELL, MICHAEL: "Yeats: Editions and Commentaries," *UTQ*, 41:3 (Spring 1972), 263-74.

491. STALLWORTHY, JON: "A Short Guide to Yeats Studies," *Critical Survey*, 3:1 (Winter 1966), 17-22.

492. STAMM, RUDOLF: *Englische Literatur.* Bern: Francke, 1957. 422 p. (Wissenschaftliche Forschungsberichte. Geisteswissenschaftliche Reihe. 11.)
Yeats, pp. 386-88.

493. STAUB, AUGUST W.: "Yeats: The Hundredth Year," *QJS*, 52:1 (Feb 1966), 81-85.

494. URE, PETER: Omnibus review, *ES*, 48:3 (June 1967), 264-68.

495. VALLETTE, JACQUES: "La marque de Yeats," *Mercure de France*, 322:1096 (1 Dec 1954), 705-9.

496. WATSON, THOMAS L.: "The French Reputation of W. B. Yeats," *Comparative Literature*, 12:3 (Summer 1960), 256-62.
Far from being exhaustive.

497. WITT, MARION: "Yeats: 1865-1939," *PMLA*, 80:4 (Sept 1965), 311-20.
On the present state of Yeats editions and texts, collected and uncollected.

See also J366, 1101, 1125, 1152, 2282, 2970a, 3169a, 4004, 4045.

AH Catalogues and Collections

There are three kinds of omission in this section. (1) With one or two exceptions I have not checked the catalogues of booksellers and auctioneers. The catalogues of Sotheby's in particular might yield some interesting material.

(2) Although I had planned to do so, I do not list manuscript holdings in public libraries, but I include published information about these collections. The manuscript material held by the National Library of Ireland and a few other libraries is recorded by Hayes (J389). Some other libraries known to possess unpublished Yeats manuscripts (letters, drafts of published works, and so on) are the British Museum (letters to William Archer, May Morris, Ernest Rhys, George Bernard Shaw, C. K. Shorter, and Dora Sigerson Shorter); the Bodleian Library (letters to John Masefield and Charles Ricketts as well as letters from Robert Bridges to Yeats); the Cambridge University Library (several letters); the Liverpool University Library (the Birrell papers include a letter from Yeats); the National Library of Scotland (letters, particularly to Sir Herbert Grierson); the Boston University Library (the Frank O'Connor papers and the Ethel Mannin papers); the Koopman papers at Brown University Library, Providence, Rhode Island (several letters); the Ellen Clark Bertrand Library, Bucknell University, Lewisburg, Pennsylvania (letters to Oliver St. John Gogarty); the William Andrews Clark Memorial Library at the University of California, Los Angeles (several letters); the Bancroft Library of the University of California at Berkeley (letters to Mabel Dickinson); the University of Chicago Library (the *Poetry* records include the Yeats correspondence); the Special Collections at Columbia University, New York (material relating to the Yeats family and the Cuala Press as well as a transcript of Robert Lowell's Yeats memorial lecture, 4 May 1965); the New York Public Library (the Lady Gregory papers, the John Quinn Memorial Collection); the Olin Library at Cornell University

(several letters); the Henry E. Huntington Library, San Marino, California (a 17-page manuscript on "The Bishop of Toronto on Emigration" and several letters, particularly to Alexandra Schepeler); the Lilly Library, Indiana University, Bloomington (letters to AE); the Kenneth Spencer Research Library at the University of Kansas, Lawrence (letters to A. H. Bullen); Mills College Library, Oakland, California (several letters, particularly to Albert Maurice Bender); the Special Collections Department, Northwestern University, Evanston, Illinois (letters, particularly to Lady Gregory and Robert Lynd); Princeton University Library (Yeats's corrections and notes to Arthur Symons's *Knave of Hearts*, 1913); the Southern Illinois University Library at Carbondale (letters to Conal O'Riordan, Lennox Robinson, and Katharine Tynan); the Academic Center Library at the University of Texas, Austin (several manuscripts and letters); and the Wellesley College Library, Wellesley, Massachusetts (notes on a lecture "The Irish Fairy Kingdom" and some letters).

(3) There are, I am sure, numerous Yeats manuscripts and letters in private collections, about which little information has surfaced so far. One such collection is alluded to, although not quite accurately, by Roger McHugh in his edition of the Margot Ruddock correspondence (J118), p. 134.

498. ADAMS, HAZARD: "The William Butler Yeats Collection at Texas," *Library Chronicle of the U of Texas*, 6:1 (Spring 1957), 33-38.
>   For more information about this collection see *ibid.*, 5:4 (Spring 1956), 49, and 6:3 (Spring 1959), 34.

499. ANON.: "Exhibitions in Retrospect: The Indomitable Irishry," *Gazette of the Grolier Club*, ns #2 (Oct 1966), 4-37.
>   An exhibition held from October through December 1962.

500. ANON.: "The Charles Riker Collection of William Butler Yeats," *Kenyon College Library, Gambier, Ohio: Acquisitions Bulletin*, #83 (Feb 1959), 1-6; #109 (Nov 1961), 1-4.
>   The collection includes 13 unpublished letters.

501. ASH, LEE, and DENIS LORENZ: *Subject Collections: A Guide to Special Book Collections and Subject Emphases as Reported by University, College, Public, and Special Libraries in the United States and Canada.* 3rd edition, revised and enlarged. NY: Bowker, 1967. ix, 1221 p.
>   Ireland and Irish literature, pp. 558-60; Yeats, 1216-17.

502. BANDLER, SAMUEL WYLLIS: *Selections from the Library of the Late Dr. Samuel Wyllis Bandler of New York City.* NY: Boesen, [194-]. 4 v.
>   Lists 64 letters to T. Fisher Unwin ([Feb 1892] to May 1901) and three other pieces, 4:61-62, #446.

503. BIBLIOTHÈQUE NATIONALE: *Gordon Craig et le renouvellement du théâtre.* Paris: Bibliothèque nationale, 1962. 101 p.
>   Catalogue of an exhibition. A list of items concerning Craig and Yeats appears on pp. 59-61.

504. BLACK, HESTER MARY: *William Butler Yeats: A Catalog of an Exhibition from the P. S. O'Hegarty Collection in the University of Kansas Library.* Lawrence, 1958. 41 p.
>   Items are listed and commented upon with appropriate quotations from letters, autobiographical writings, and so on. See also J528, 532, and 6781.
>   *Reviews:*
>   1. Anon., "American Libraries," *TLS*, 58:2976 (13 Mar 1959), 152.

504a. BLAKE-HILL, PHILIP V.: "The Macmillan Archive," *British Museum Q*, 36:3-4 (Autumn 1972), 74-80.
Includes letters from Yeats.

505. [BRITISH MUSEUM. DEPARTMENT OF PRINTED BOOKS. KING'S LIBRARY]: *Yeats and His Contemporaries*. [London, 1965]. 10 p.
Mimeographed guide to the Yeats centenary exhibition at the British Museum. See also "Yeats and His Contemporaries," *British Museum Q*, 28:3-4 (Oct 1964), News Supplement, 1.

506. BUSHEE, RALPH: "Morris Library Houses Extensive Yeats Collection," *Daily Egyptian*, 47:89 (12 Feb 1966), 3.
The library of Southern Illinois University at Carbondale. See also J525.

507. COX, E. M. H.: *The Library of Edmund Gosse, Being a Descriptive and Bibliographical Catalogue of a Portion of His Collection*. With an introductory essay by Mr. Gosse. London: Dulau, 1924. 300 p.
Yeats, pp. 297-99. See also J515.

508. DOUGAN, ROBERT ORMES (comp): *W. B. Yeats: Manuscripts and Printed Books Exhibited in the Library of Trinity College, Dublin, 1956. Catalogue.*
Dublin: Colm O Lochlainn at the Sign of the Three Candles for the Friends of the Library of Trinity College, Dublin, [1956]. 50 p.
Reprinted: [Darby, Pa.]: Folcroft Press, 1970.
Reviews:
1. Anon., "Books and Manuscripts of W. B. Yeats," *TLS*, 55:2827 (4 May 1956), 276.

509. DURKAN, MICHAEL J.: *William Butler Yeats, 1865-1965*. A catalogue of his works and associated items in Olin Library, Wesleyan University, together with an essay by David R. Clark. Middletown, Conn. [i.e., Dublin: Dolmen Press], 1965. 92 p.
Contents: (1) Wyman W. Parker: "Preface," 7-9. (2) David R. Clark: "Key Attitudes in Yeats," 11-21 (Irish nationalism, religion, mysticism, and the preoccupation with the aristocratic). (3) Catalogue, 23-92.

510. [FRENCH, HANNAH DUSTIN]: "William Butler Yeats at Wellesley," *Friends of the Wellesley College Library Bulletin*, #10 (July 1952), 3-19.
A description of the Yeats collection at Wellesley and some reminiscences of Yeats's visits.

511. GORDAN, JOHN D.: "New in the Berg Collection: 1952-1956," *BNYPL*, 61: 7 (July 1957), 353-63.

512. ———: "New in the Berg Collection: 1957-1958," *BNYPL*, 63:3 (Mar 1959), 134-47; :4 (Apr 1959), 205-15.
Includes material by AE, Lady Gregory, George Moore, James Stephens, and Yeats.

513. GORDON, DONALD JAMES, IAN FLETCHER, and FRANK KERMODE: *I, the Poet William Yeats: A Descriptive Guide*. The exhibition was assembled by D. J. Gordon and designed by Margaret Fuller. 21 May— 7 June 1957. [Reading: U of Reading, 1957]. i, 31 p.
A mimeographed guide. See also J514.
Reviews:
1. Anon., "Visual Aids," *TLS*, 56:2884 (7 June 1957), 349.
2. G. S. F[raser], "Yeats Exhibition at Reading University," *NSt*, 53: 1368 (1 June 1957), 706.

45

514. *[GORDON, DONALD JAMES, and IAN FLETCHER]: *W. B. Yeats: Images of a Poet. My Permanent or Impermanent Images. Exhibition Catalogue.* [Manchester: U of Manchester, 1961]. 151 p.

> The exhibition was held in Manchester (3 May—3 June 1961) and Dublin (17 June—1 July 1961) and was based on the Reading exhibition (J513). Contents: "The Image of the Poet," "Persons and Places" (Thoor Ballylee, Coole Park and Lady Gregory, Robert Gregory, Lionel Johnson, Synge, George Pollexfen, Maud Gonne, John O'Leary, John B. Yeats, Eva Gore-Booth, Constance Markievicz, Sligo), "The Poet and the Theatre," "Byzantium," "Symbolic Art and Visionary Landscape," "The Dancer" (by Frank Kermode), and "Books and Manuscripts" (by Robin Skelton).
>
> *Reviews:*
> 1. Anon., "Important Exhibition of Yeatsiana," *Irish Times*, #32969 (20 June 1961), 9. Correspondence by J. de Courcy, #32971 (22 June 1961), 7.
> 2. Anon., "Images of a Poet," *TLS*, 60:3089 (12 May 1961), 293. Correspondence by Frank Kermode, :3090 (19 May 1961), 309.
> 3. Richard Ellmann, "Heard and Seen," *NSt*, 62:1604 (8 Dec 1961), 887–88.
> 4. G. S. Fraser, "Images of Yeats," *NSt*, 61:1574 (19 May 1961), 763.
> 5. Robin Skelton, "Images of a Poet: W. B. Yeats," *Irish Book*, 1:4 (Spring 1962), 89–97.
> 6. W. L. Webb, "Images of a Poet," *Guardian*, #35716 (3 May 1961), 7.
> 7. Margaret Willy, *English*, 14:79 (Spring 1962), 29–30.

515. GOSSE, SIR EDMUND: *A Catalogue of the Gosse Correspondence in the Brotherton Collection, Consisting Mainly of Letters Written to Sir Edmund Gosse from 1867 to 1928* [. . .]. Leeds: U of Leeds, 1950. xiv, 80 p. (Library Publications. 3.)

> Lists 25 letters from Yeats to Gosse, 23 July 1903—28 Feb 1917, p. 80. The Wade edition contains only 12 letters to Gosse.

516. HASTINGS, HENRY C.: *Spoken Poetry on Records and Tapes: An Index of Currently Available Recordings.* Chicago: Association of College and Reference Libraries, 1957. iv, 52 p. (ACRL Monographs. 18.)

> Yeats, p. 32.

517. HENDERSON, WILLIAM ARTHUR: Newspaper cuttings, programmes, and photographs relating to the Irish Literary Theatre, 1899-1901, with manuscript notes and an index. 1 v.

> In the National Library of Ireland, MS. 1729.

518. ————: The Irish national theatre movement: Three years' work at the Abbey Theatre told in press cuttings. With manuscript notes and indexes. 1904-7. 1 v.

> In the National Library of Ireland, MS. 1730.

519. ————: The Irish national theatre movement: A year's work at the Abbey Theatre told in press cuttings; also programmes, photographs, and letters. With manuscript notes and indexes. 1908-11. 4 v.

> In the National Library of Ireland, MSS. 1731-34.

520. ————: Press cuttings and theatre programmes relating to literary movements in Ireland. 1909-10. 1 v.

> In the National Library of Ireland, MS. 1736.

521. HODGES, FIGGIS AND CO., LTD.: *William Butler Yeats: 13 June 1865-13 June 1965.* Dublin: Dolmen Press for Hodges Figgis, 1965. viii p.

> Annotated catalogue of an exhibition.

522. °HOLLOWAY, JOSEPH: Diaries containing entries on business and social arrangements and including some newspaper cuttings relating to the theatre. 1894-1911. 12 v.
    In the National Library of Ireland, MSS. 4861-72. For other collections made by Holloway see J389.

523. HORNIMAN, ANNIE ELIZABETH FREDERICKA: A collection of newspaper cuttings, etc., concerning the Abbey Theatre, Dublin. 1903-30. 10 v.
    In the John Rylands Library, Manchester, shelfmark R.44272. After 1913 the collection becomes exceedingly selective and seems to have been made by somebody else. Nevertheless, it is noteworthy that Miss Horniman retained her interest in Abbey affairs after she had severed her connections with the Irish National Theatre. The cuttings were collected by herself, sent by friends, or supplied by a press cutting agency, Woolgar & Roberts, telegram address "Mutilating London."

524. HUSS, ROY: "Max Beerbohm's Drawings of Theatrical Figures (II)," *Theatre Notebook*, 21:2 (Spring 1967), 102-19.
    Max's caricatures of Yeats are listed on p. 119. N.B.: This is now superseded by Rupert Hart-Davis: *A Catalogue of the Caricatures of Max Beerbohm*. London: Macmillan, 1972. 258 p. (Yeats, #144, 616, 748, 1046, 1650, 1825-29).

525. [JACKSON, THOMAS J.]: *The Irish Collection: Rare Book Room / Morris Library*. Carbondale: Southern Illinois U, [1970]. i, 11 p.
    See also J506.

526. KAIN, RICHARD M.: "The Curran Library," *Éire-Ireland*, 7:4 (Winter 1972), 135-36.
    Short description of the Curran collection at University College, Dublin, which includes some Yeats letters.

527. KANSAS UNIVERSITY LIBRARIES. DEPARTMENT OF SPECIAL COLLECTIONS: *A Guide to the Collection*, Lawrence: University of Kansas Libraries, 1964. iv, 31 p.
    "The W. B. Yeats Collection," 11-12.

528. KANSAS UNIVERSITY LIBRARIES. P. S. O'HEGARTY COLLECTION: *A Catalog of Books in the Library of P. S. O'Hegarty*. Baile Átha Cliath: Teach na hÁrdphÁirce, 1958. 4 v.
    Yeats is listed *passim*, especially 1:1-5 (manuscript material) and 4:76. See also J504, 532, and 6781.

529. LIBRARY OF CONGRESS: *Literary Recordings: A Checklist of the Archive of Recorded Poetry and Literature in the Library of Congress*. Washington, D.C.: Library of Congress, General Reference and Bibliography Division, Reference Department, 1966. iv, 190 p.
    Includes Yeats recordings made by George Barker, Denis Carey, Padraic Colum, Denis Devlin, Liam Redmond, Theodore Roethke, and David Ross (see index).

530. ———: *National Union Catalog of Manuscript Collections*, 1959/61—.

531. NATIONAL GALLERY OF IRELAND: *W. B. Yeats: A Centenary Exhibition*. Dublin: Dolmen Press, 1965. 102 p.
    Contents: Yeats the man; the heritage; the early years; the family; pictures as inspiration; the poet as painter; the Abbey Theatre; the Abbey Theatre: playwrights; the Abbey Theatre: actors; the public life.

532. NELICK, FRANK C.: "Yeats, Bullen, and the Irish Drama," *MD*, 1:3 (Dec 1958), 196-202.
     Partial description of the P. S. O'Hegarty collection at Kansas University Libraries, which includes letters to A. H. Bullen. See also J504, 528, and 6781.

533. NEW YORK PUBLIC LIBRARY: *Dictionary Catalog of the Albert A. and Henry W. Berg Collection of English and American Literature*. Boston: Hall, 1969. 5 v.
     Includes printed and manuscript material as well as letters. See particularly under Abbey Theatre, 1:1-4; Gregory, 2:266-317 and 4:684-760; O'Casey, 3:394-95; Russell, 3:657-64 and 5:284-85; Synge, 4:133-37; Yeats, 4:469-503 and 5:411-18.

534. ————. LINCOLN CENTER FOR THE PERFORMING ARTS LIBRARY. THEATRE COLLECTION: Collection of clippings, reviews, etc., concerning W. B. Yeats.
     Shelfmark MWEZ / + / N.C. / 20,030. Very brittle material.

535. NEWCASTLE-UPON-TYNE. UNIVERSITY LIBRARY: *William Butler Yeats, 1865-1939: Catalogue of an Exhibition, 13th—22nd May 1965.* [Newcastle-upon-Tyne, 1965. 18 p.]

536. NILAND, NORA: "The Yeats Memorial Museum, Sligo," *Irish Book*, 2:3/4 (Autumn 1963), 122-26.
     Description of the Yeats collection and related material. See also J544.

537. PARKE-BERNET GALLERIES, INC.: *The Important Collection of First Editions of William Butler Yeats*. Property of C. Walter Buhler, Westport, Conn., sold by his order [. . .]. NY: Parke-Bernet Galleries, 1941. iv, 56 p. (Sale Number 281.)
     The Yeats items appear on pp. 21-33 (#121-82); they include first editions, manuscripts, and letters.

538. PRINCETON UNIVERSITY LIBRARY. THEATER COLLECTION: Irish theater. 6 v.
     Six scrapbooks containing clippings from daily and weekly papers, most of them from New York, concerning the Abbey Theatre performances in the United States; also book reviews, interviews, sketches, and similar material.

539. QUINN, JOHN: *Complete Catalogue of the Library of John Quinn, Sold by Auction in Five Parts (With Printed Prices)*. NY: Anderson Galleries, 1924. 2 v.
     Yeats, 2:1128-60, 1204-5 (#11338-610, 12082-94).

540. RONDEL, AUGUSTE: Inventaire de la collection théâtrale Auguste Rondel: Théâtre irlandais.
     A collection of press cuttings in the Bibliothèque de l'Arsenal, Paris, shelfmark Re. 10.993-11.061.

541. SCHOLES, ROBERT EDWARD: *The Cornell Joyce Collection: A Catalogue*. Ithaca: Cornell UP, 1961. xvii, 225 p.
     Letters from Yeats and concerning Yeats are mentioned *passim* (see index).

542. SCHULZ, H. C.: "English Literary Manuscripts in the Huntington Library," *HLQ*, 31:3 (May 1968), 251-302.
     Yeats, p. 302.

543. SIMMONDS, HARVEY: "John Quinn: An Exhibition to Mark the Gift of the John Quinn Memorial Collection," *BNYPL*, 72:9 (Nov 1968), 569-83.
     Includes numerous Yeats items.

544. SLIGO COUNTY LIBRARY AND MUSEUM: *Jack B. Yeats and His Family: An Exhibition of the Works of Jack B. Yeats and His Family at the Sligo County Library and Museum, Sligo, 29th October to 29th December 1971.* Dublin: Irish Printers, [1971]. 91 p.
   Nora Niland: "Foreword," 5-6; Hilary Pyle: "Introduction," 9-10 (to Jack B. Yeats); Roger McHugh: "Introduction to W. B. Yeats," 47-48. Includes a list of WBY items. See also J536.

545. SMYTHE, COLIN: "Collecting Yeats and Publishing Lady Gregory," *Private Library*, ser 2 / 4:1 (Spring 1971), 4-24.

546. SZLADITS, LOLA L.: "New in the Berg Collection, 1962-1964," *BNYPL*, 73:4 (Apr 1969), 227-52.
   "Lady Gregory and W. B. Yeats," 243-52.

547. ————: "New in the Berg Collection, 1965-1969," *BNYPL*, 75:1 (Jan 1971), 9-29.
   "Ireland," 18-24; includes material concerning the Abbey, Sara Allgood, Lennox Robinson, Austin Clarke, O'Casey, Lady Gregory, Brinsley MacNamara, and Yeats (among others, the typescript of a poem, "Hills of Mourne," attributed to him, and a letter to Sara Allgood, 5 Oct 1935).

548. YEATS, W. B.: Two albums of cuttings of reviews and articles referring to W. B. Yeats. ca. 1897-1904 and 1904-9.
   In the National Library of Ireland, MSS. 12145-46. According to a note I found in these albums, Yeats seems to have subscribed to a press cutting agency (General Press Cutting Association, Ltd., Lennox House, Norfolk Street, London, W.C.).

549. YEATS SOCIETY OF JAPAN: [in Japanese] *Catalogue of the Centenary Exhibition of the Birth of William Butler Yeats, 19 May—21 May 1966.* Edited by the Library of Waseda University and the Yeats Society of Japan. Tokyo: Waseda U, 1966. 32 p.

See also J7, 389, 1136, 1161 (#2), 2041, 3949, 6309, 6310, 6781, 6812, 7436.

AI   Concordances

550. CONNER, LESTER IRVIN: "A Yeats Dictionary: Names of the Persons and Places in the Poetry of W. B. Yeats," Ph.D. thesis, Columbia U, 1964. iv, 210 p. (*DA*, 28:4 [Oct 1967], 1429A.)
   An annotated list with only a few attempts at interpretation.

551. COPELAND, TOM W.: "The Proper Names in William Butler Yeats's Non-Dramatic Poetry: An Annotated Index," Ph.D. thesis, Texas Tech, 1957. xxii, 786 p.

552. DOMVILLE, ERIC: *A Concordance to the Plays of W. B. Yeats.* Based on *The Variorum Edition of the Plays of W. B. Yeats* edited by Russell K. Alspach. Ithaca: Cornell UP, 1972. xxi, 1559 p. in 2 v.
   Reviews:
   1. R. D[erolez], *ES*, 54:4 (Aug 1973), 405.
   2. M. J. Sidnell, *QQ*, 80:2 (Summer 1973), 298-99.

553. PARRISH, STEPHEN MAXFIELD (ed): *A Concordance to the Poems of W. B. Yeats.* Programmed by James Allan Painter. Ithaca: Cornell UP, 1963. xxxix, 967 p.
   "Editor's Preface," v-xxvii, contains some remarks on Yeats's poetic vocabulary. "Programmer's Preface," xxix-xxxvii, explains the

technical process of feeding poetry into computers.
Reviews:
1. Anon., "Computer and Concordancer," *TLS*, 63:3230 (23 Jan 1964), 69.
2. Robert B. Davis, *MP*, 63:1 (Aug 1965), 87-88.
3. T. R. Henn, *MLR*, 59:2 (Apr 1964), 285-86.
4. Josephine Miles, *VS*, 8:3 (Mar 1965), 290-92.
5. Peter Ure, *RES*, 16:62 (Apr 1965), 221-22.

See also J1719, 3991a.

B BIOGRAPHIES AND BIOGRAPHICAL MATERIAL

BA Books and Pamphlets Exclusively on Yeats

554. BUSHRUI, SUHEIL BADI, and JOHN MURCHISON MUNRO (eds): *Images and Memories: A Pictorial Record of the Life and Work of W. B. Yeats*. Designed by Z. N. Khuri. Beirut: Dar el-Mashreq, 1970. xvi, 164 p.
   Based on an exhibition held in the Jafet Memorial Library of the American University of Beirut, 6-20 Jan 1969. Contains fewer pictures than J562 but a better text.

555. CLARK, DAVID RIDGLEY, and NOEL KAVANAGH (comps): *Yeats and Sandymount*. Dublin: Yeats Association, 1966. 16 p.
   Compiled from previously published material.

556. *ELLMANN, RICHARD: *Yeats: The Man and the Masks*. NY: Dutton, [1958] [1948]. xi, 331 p. (Dutton Paperback. D24.)
   Based on "William Butler Yeats: The Fountain Years," B.Litt. thesis, Trinity College, Dublin, 1947. ii, 107 p.; and on "Triton among the Streams: A Study of the Life and Writings of William Butler Yeats," Ph.D. thesis, Yale U, 1947. v, 404 p.
   Incorporates: "W. B. Yeats: The End of Youth," *Furioso*, 3:3 (Spring 1948), 25-31; "Robartes and Aherne: Two Sides of a Penny," *Kenyon R*, 10:2 (Spring 1948), 177-86; "W. B. Yeats, Magician," *Western R*, 12:4 (Summer 1948), 232-40.
   The development of Yeats's mind and work in biographical progression with special reference to the influence of John Butler Yeats.
   Reviews:
   1. Anon., *Listener*, 43:1095 (19 Jan 1950), 124, 126. Correspondence by Joseph Hone, :1102 (9 Mar 1950), 435.
   2. Anon., "The Dream and the Analyst," *TLS*, 48:2492 (4 Nov 1949), 716.
   3. A. W. J. Becker, "In Search of Yeats," *Isis*, #1105 (19 May 1949), 16.
   4. Thomas Bodkin, "Yeats Interpreted," *Birmingham Post*, #28477 (15 Nov 1949), 2.
   5. H[ayden] C[arruth], "Cherchez l'homme," *Poetry*, 74:4 (July 1949), 244-45.
   6. Mary M. Colum, *Tomorrow*, 8:6 (Feb 1949), 58-59.
   7. John Cournos, *Commonweal*, 49:12 (31 Dec 1948), 308.
   8. David Daiches, *MLN*, 65:4 (Apr 1950), 267-69.
   9. Babette Deutsch, "No Longer a Matter of Literature," *New Republic*, 120:1790 (21 Mar 1949), 22-23.
   10. St. John Ervine, "Unmasking Yeats," *Spectator*, 183:6333 (11 Nov 1949), 640, 642.
   11. Horace Gregory, "Paradoxical Destiny of Yeats as Poet and Man: Scholarly, Tactful, Intelligent Study of His Personality, Sources, and Crucial Years of Development," *NYHTB*, 25:13 (14 Nov 1948), 5.
   12. James Hall, "Essence and Accidents," *VQR*, 25:3 (Summer 1949), 456-58.
   13. Lawrence Haward, "Ruskin and Yeats," *Manchester Guardian Weekly*, 62:1 (5 Jan 1950), 11.
   14. J. V. Healy, "On Understanding Yeats," *Western R*, 13:3 (Spring 1949), 182-84.
   15. F. W. van Heerikhuizen, "Gedreven door angst," *Litterair paspoort*, 7:53 (Jan 1952), 10-11.
   16. Joseph Hone, *Cambridge R*, 72:1752 (2 Dec 1950), 212.
   17. Brian Inglis, "'I, the Poet . . . ,'" *Spectator*, 206:6940 (30 June 1961), 956.

18. Leo Kennedy, "Behind Yeat's [sic] Many Masks," *Chicago Sun-Times*, 1:259 (29 Nov 1948), 56.
19. A. M. Klein, "The Masked Yeats," *Northern R*, 3:5 (June–July 1950), 43–45.
20. R[oger] McH[ugh], *Studies*, 39:155 (Sept 1950), 345–46.
21. Seán O'Faoláin, "Yeats Divested," *Britain To-day*, #165 (Jan 1950), 38–39.
22. John Pick, "Irishman without Priest," *America*, 80:2071 (22 Jan 1949), 437.
23. M. A. R., "American Professor's Study of Yeats and His Work," *Irish Independent*, 58:310 (31 Dec 1949), 4.
24. Kathleen Raine, "Yeats's Gazebo," *NSt*, 38:979 (10 Dec 1949), 700, 702.
25. Horace Reynolds, "Clearing Mist & Haze from a Shy Man," *SatR*, 31:46 (13 Nov 1948), 11–12.
26. ————, "Reflections on a Poet and His World," *CSM*, 41:18 (16 Dec 1948), 15.
27. Lorna Reynolds, *Dublin Mag*, 26:4 (Oct–Dec 1951), 58–60.
28. A. Rivoallan, *EA*, 5:1 (Feb 1952), 80–81
29. Peter Russell, "Yeats," *Time and Tide*, 31:22 (3 June 1950), 560.
30. Cecil ffrench Salkeld, "Hooded Hawk," *Irish Writing*, #10 (Jan 1950), 72–74.
31. Elizabeth Schneider, "Two Studies of Yeats," *Nation*, 171:5 (29 July 1950), 112–13.
32. Donald A. Stauffer, "Artist Shining through His Vehicles," *Kenyon R*, 11:2 (Spring 1949), 330, 332–34, 336.
33. James Johnson Sweeney, "The Development of the Poet Yeats," *NYTBR*, [53:] (19 Dec 1948), 5.
34. William Troy, "Poet and Mystifier," *Partisan R*, 16:2 (Feb 1949), 196–98.
35. Jacques Vallette, "Un mot sur Yeats," *Mercure de France*, 310:1047 (1 Nov 1950), 566–68.
36. Charles Weir, *Furioso*, 4:2 (Spring 1949), 61–63.
37. George Whalley, "Yeats's Mind," *Yale R*, 39:1 (Sept 1949), 165–67.
38. Margaret Willy, *English*, 8:43 (Spring 1950), 37–38.
39. Edmund Wilson, "New Light on W. B. Yeats [. . .]," *New Yorker*, 24:43 (18 Dec 1948), 103–7.

557. GIBBON, MONK: *The Masterpiece and the Man: Yeats as I Knew Him*. London: Hart-Davis, 1959. 226 p.
An unorthodox book. Gibbon is a distant relation of the Yeats family and describes his encounters with, and opinions of, WBY, occasionally with somewhat less than reverence. At the same time, he is fully appreciative of Yeats's work, especially his poetry. Includes reminiscences of Lily and Elizabeth C. Yeats, AE, Maud Gonne, and other figures of the Irish Literary Revival; also two poems, "Yeats's Earlier Poems" (p. 146; see also J5758) and "On Re-reading Yeats" (pp. 221–22). Contains some notes on the Yeats-Hopkins, Yeats-Moore, and Yeats-AE relationships.
Reviews:
1. Anon., "Yeats: Portrait by a Critical Cousin," *Scotsman*, #36165 (25 Apr 1959), 13.
2. Anon., "Farewell to Irish Fairies but Not to Playboys," *Times*, #54478 (4 June 1959), 15.
3. Anon., "A Partial View," *TLS*, 58:2984 (8 May 1959), 274.
4. A[erol] A[rnold], *Personalist*, 42:2 (Spring 1961), 254–55.

5. Thomas Bodkin, "Yeats: An Unfriendly Poet," *Birmingham Post*, #31412 (5 May 1959), 3.
6. Donald Davie, "Maker and Breaker," *NSt*, 57:1470 (16 May 1959), 695.
7. Richard Ellman[n], "Out of Date Objections to W. B. Yeats," *Chicago Sunday Tribune*, 119:11 (13 Mar 1960), pt 4, p. 2.
8. DeLancey Ferguson, "Memories of Yeats," *NYHTB*, 37:5 (4 Sept 1960), 6.
9. Eric Forbes-Boyd, "Listening to Mr. Gibbon," *CSM*, 51:201 (23 July 1959), 11.
10. René Fréchet, "L'étude de Yeats: Textes, jugements et éclairissements," *EA*, 14:1 (Jan-Mar 1961), 36-47.
11. Eric Gillett, "Some Uncommon People," *National and English R*, 152: 916 (June 1959), 231-35.
12. Vivienne Koch, "Three Lives," *Poetry*, 98:1 (Apr 1961), 59-62.
13. Louis MacNeice, *London Mag*, 7:8 (Aug 1960), 70-73.
14. Donat O'Donnell [i.e., Conor Cruise O'Brien], "The Great Conger," *Spectator*, 202:6830 (22 May 1959), 736. Reprinted in O'Brien, *Writers and Politics*, NY: Pantheon Books, 1965. xxii, 259 p. (pp. 119-20).
15. Frank O'Connor, "A Man with a Grievance," *Nation*, 190:9 (27 Feb 1960), 190-91.
16. Ulick O'Connor, "Ripe Dublin Talk," *Sunday Independent*, 54:27 (5 July 1959), 10.
17. Risteárd Ó Glaisne, *Focus*, 2:6 (June 1959), 27.
18. P. P., "The Man Yeats," *Irish Independent*, 68:116 (16 May 1959), 8.
19. Charles Poore, "Books of the Times," *NYT*, 109:37285 (23 Feb 1960), 29.
20. W. R. Rodgers, "Seeing Yeats Plain," *Sunday Times*, #7094 (3 May 1959), 17.
21. John Unterecker, "In Yeats' Shadow," *NYTBR*, 65:16 (17 Apr 1960), 20.
22. Jacques Vallette, "Vous que j'aimais éperdument," *Mercure de France*, 338:1160 (Apr 1960), 738-39.
23. W. L. Webb, "Flattening Young Men," *Manchester Guardian*, #35112 (22 May 1959), 4.

558. GOGARTY, OLIVER ST. JOHN: *William Butler Yeats: A Memoir*. With a preface by Myles Dillon. Dublin: Dolmen Press, 1963. 27 p.
Many of the anecdotes contained in this memoir appear in other books and articles by Gogarty (listed separately).
Reviews:
1. R[ivers] C[arew], *Dubliner*, 3:1 (Spring 1964), 82-83.
2. Richard Ellmann, "Deadly Merits," *NSt*, 67:1723 (20 Mar 1964), 461.
3. Stephen Fanning, *Kilkenny Mag*, #10 (Autumn-Winter 1963), 127, 129, 131.
4. Robert Greacen, *Listener*, 71:1817 (23 Jan 1964), 162.
5. T. R. Henn, *MLR*, 59:4 (Oct 1964), 655.

559. HANLEY, MARY: *Thoor Ballylee—Home of William Butler Yeats*. Edited by Liam Miller from a paper given to the Kiltartan Society in 1961. With a foreword by T. R. Henn. Dublin: Dolmen Press, 1965. 32 p.
An illustrated history of Yeats's tower, which was restored in 1963-65. Some quotations from Yeats's poetry and letters supplement the story.
Reviews:
1. Giorgio Melchiori, *N&Q*, os 211 / ns 13:11 (Nov 1966), 430-31.

560. HARPER, GEORGE MILLS: *"Go Back to Where You Belong": Yeats's Return from Exile.* Dublin: Dolmen Press, 1973. 43 p. (New Yeats Papers. 6.)
    Discusses Yeats's "life-long odyssey" and his views on exile.

561. *HONE, JOSEPH: *W. B. Yeats, 1865-1939.* London: Macmillan, 1962 [1942, i.e., 1943]. ix, 504 p.
    The "official" biography, authorized by Mrs. Yeats. Although this is a pleasant book to read, and in some respects still indispensable, it is far from perfect: (1) Since Hone wrote close after Yeats's death, many names and incidents had to be omitted. (2) There is no critical distance to the man and his work. (3) Hone simplifies Yeats's complex personality. (4) He is not very enlightening on Yeats's work. (5) The documentation is singularly poor.
    Reviews:
    1. Peter Allt, *Hermathena*, 62 (Nov 1943), 115-17.
    2. Anon., *DUJ*, os 35 / ns 4:3 (June 1943), 102-4.
    3. Anon., *Listener*, 29:744 (15 Apr 1943), 457.
    4. Anon., "W. B. Yeats and Symbolism," *Poetry R*, 34:2 (Mar-Apr 1943), 126-28. Makes the curious statement that Yeats's "life outside his poetry was not particularly interesting."
    5. Anon., "1865-1939," *Time*, 41:5 (8 Feb 1943), 88, 91.
    6. Anon., "William Butler Yeats: The Dual Anglo-Irish Heritage," *TLS*, 42:2141 (13 Feb 1943), 78.
    7. Joan Bennett, *RES*, 20:77 (Jan 1944), 90-91.
    8. Thomas Bodkin, "Poet and Autocrat," *Birmingham Post*, #26385 (16 Feb 1943), 2.
    9. Louise Bogan, "Yeats and His Ireland," *Partisan R*, 10:2 (Mar-Apr 1943), 198-201.
    10. Elizabeth Bowen, "With Silent Friends," *Tatler and Bystander*, 167: 2174 (24 Feb 1943), 246, 248.
    11. Ernest A. Boyd, "Romantic Ireland's Dead and Gone," *New Leader*, 26:10 (6 Mar 1943), 3.
    12. W. Bardsley Brash, *London Q and Holborn R*, 168 / ser 6, 12:3 (July 1943), 273-74.
    13. Paul Vincent Carroll, "Democracy Hater, He Fanned Revolution," *Daily Record and Mail*, #29991 (8 Mar 1943), 2.
    14. Sydney W. Carroll, "The Theatre as a Poet's Workshop," *Daily Sketch*, #10530 (11 Feb 1943), 6.
    15. S. C. Chew, "A Biography of Yeats," *CSM*, 35:84 (6 Mar 1943), Weekly Mag Section, 11.
    16. A. Choudhuri, *Visva-Bharati Q*, 27:3&4 (1961/62), 285-87.
    17. Richard Church, "A Poet's Design for Living," *Fortnightly R*, os 159 / ns 153:916 (Apr 1943), 258-62.
    18. Mary M. Colum, "Yeats: He Lived a Full Life [. . .]," *NYTBR*, [48:] (7 Feb 1943), 1, 22.
    19. Cyril Connolly, "The Last of the Magi," *Observer*, 152:7916 (14 Feb 1943), 3.
    20. Malcolm Cowley, "The Hosting of the Shee," *New Republic*, 108:1471 (8 Feb 1943), 185-86.
    21. Gustav Cross, "Yeats: Angry Old Poet," *Sydney Morning Herald*, 132: 38975 (17 Nov 1962), 16.
    22. M. D., *Dublin Mag*, 18:2 (Apr-June 1943), 60-63.
    23. Howell Daniels, *Anglo-Welsh R*, 13:31 (1962), 94-96.
    24. J[ames] D[elehanty], *Kilkenny Mag*, #8 (Autumn-Winter 1962), 56-58.
    25. Babette Deutsch, "W. B. Yeats, the Greatest Poet of Our Time: A Lifetime of Intellectual Excitement and Personal Passion," *NYHTB*, 19:24 (7 Feb 1943), 1; :27 (28 Feb 1943), 26.

26. Myles Dillon, *JEGP*, 42:4 (Oct 1943), 610-14

27. Clifton Fadiman, "The Magician," *New Yorker*, 18:51 (6 Feb 1943), 53-55.

28. H[ugh] I'A[nson] F[ausset], "A Poet's Life," *Manchester Guardian*, #30097 (17 Mar 1943), 3.

29. P. J. Gannon, *Studies*, 32:125 (Mar 1943), 130-31.

30. Oliver St. John Gogarty, "Ireland's Great Poet," *Gazette*, 172:98 (24 Apr 1943), 9.

31. Horace Gregory, "Yeats as Dublin Saw Him," *Yale R*, 32:3 (Mar 1943), 599-602.

32. ———, *Chimera*, 1:4 (Spring 1943), 45-46, 48.

33. Joseph P. Hackett, "Shaw and Yeats," *Studies*, 32:127 (Sept 1943), 369-78. Involves a Shaw-Yeats comparison.

34. J. V. Healy, "Ancient Lineaments," *Poetry*, 62:4 (July 1943), 223-28.

35. Richard Jennings, "Poetry and Occultism," *Nineteenth Century and After*, 133:794 (Apr 1943), 180-81.

36. F. J. K., "A Yeats Biography," *Irish Independent*, 52:75 (29 Mar 1943), 2.

37. Patrick Kavanagh, "W. B. Yeats," *Standard*, 15:9 (26 Feb 1943), 2.

38. Charlotte Kohler, "A Faithful Chronicle," *VQR*, 19:3 (Summer 1943), 472-75.

39. Lewis Leary, "An Authorized Biography of W. B. Yeats," *SAQ*, 42:3 (July 1943), 303-4.

40. T. McAlindon, *CQ*, 5:2 (Summer 1963), 183-85.

41. Desmond MacCarthy, "A Life of Yeats," *Sunday Times*, #6253 (14 Feb 1943), 3. "What I find lacking is a balanced interpretation of his character."

42. M. J. MacM[anus], "Mr. Joseph Hone's Life of Yeats," *Irish Press*, 13:58 (9 Mar 1943), 2.

43. Samuel Mathai, *Cultural Forum*, 5:2 (Dec 1962 / Jan 1963), 103-4.

44. M[argaret] M[eagher], *Catholic World*, 157:937 (Apr 1943), 99-100.

45. E. H. W. Meyerstein, "The Music of Death and Change," *English*, 4:23 (Summer 1943), 161-63.

46. John Montague, "Responsibilities," *Guardian*, #36069 (22 June 1962), 7. Correspondence by Lovatt Dickson, #36077 (2 July), 8; John Montague and Geoffrey de C. Parmiter, #36081 (6 July), 10; Ronald Dunlop, #36087 (13 July), 10; Lovatt Dickson, #36090 (17 July), 8.

47. Raymond Mortimer, "Books in General," *NSt*, 25:625 (13 Feb 1943), 111-12.

48. Kate O'Brien, *Life and Letters To-day*, 39:1 (Oct 1943), 59-60, 62.

49. Hermann Peschmann, "W. B. Yeats (1865-1939)," *New English Weekly*, 23:5 (20 May 1943), 41-43.

50. Una Pope-Hennessy, *Dublin R*, 213:427 (Dec 1943), 180-82.

51. James Reaney, "Yeats Unconquered," *Canadian Forum*, 42:504 (Jan 1963), 235-36.

52. Cecil Roberts, "The Majesty of Yeats," *SatR*, 26:7 (13 Feb 1943), 5. Correspondence by Mary M. Colum, :8 (20 Feb 1943), 15.

53. R. A. Scott-James, "The Life of Yeats," *Britain To-day*, #84 (Apr 1943), 23-24.

54. Edward Shanks, "W. B. Yeats—Poet and Practical Man," *Daily Dispatch*, #13387 (13 Feb 1943), 2.

55. Naomi Royde Smith, "W. B. Yeats," *Time and Tide*, 24:11 (13 Mar 1943), 201-2.

56. Robert Speaight, "Light on the Celtic Twilight," *Tablet*, 181:5371 (17 Apr 1943), 188-89.

57. Theodore Spencer, "Our Greatest Poet-Statesman," *Atlantic Monthly*, 171:3 (Mar 1943), 148.
58. Sir John Squire, "A Great Poet of the English-Speaking World," *Illustrated London News*, 202:5420 (6 Mar 1943), 258.
59. L. A. G. Strong, "The Eagle Mind of Yeats," *John o' London's Weekly*, 48:1203 (26 Mar 1943), 241-42.
60. P. C. T., *Irish Book Lover*, 29:2 (Mar 1944), 47-48.
61. Geoffrey Taylor, *Bell*, 6:1 (Apr 1943), 59-62.
62. W. J. Turner, "Poet and Patriot," *Spectator*, 170:5982 (19 Feb 1943), 176.
63. Richard Weber, *Dubliner*, #5 (Sept-Oct 1962), 54-56.
64. E. V. R. Wyatt, "The Dail and the Druids," *Commonweal*, 37:26 (16 Apr 1943), 637-40.
65. Morton Dauwen Zabel, "Yeats: The Image and the Book," *Nation*, 156: 10 (6 Mar 1943), 348-50. A revised version of this review is included in J1090.

562. MACLIAMMÓIR, MICHEÁL, and EAVAN BOLAND: *W. B. Yeats and His World*. London: Thames & Hudson, 1971. 144 p.

About 140 pictures and an undistinguished text.

Reviews:
1. Anon., "Poet in Pictures," *TLS*, 70:3638 (19 Nov 1971), 1438.
2. Peter Faulkner, *DUJ*, os 65 / ns 34:1 (Dec 1972), 122.
3. Brian H. Finney, "Yeats Gallery," *Irish Press*, 41:279 (27 Nov 1971), 12.
4. Geoffrey Grigson, "Vision, Faith, and Murder," *Country Life*, 150: 3881 (28 Oct 1971), 1168.
5. Michael Hartnett, "Yeats, Warts and All," *Irish Times*, #36004 (30 Oct 1971), 10.
6. John Jordan, "Presenting Yeats," *Irish Independent*, 80:246 (16 Oct 1971), 8.
7. Mary Lappin, "Yeats Surveyed," *Hibernia*, 36 [i.e., 35]:20 (5 Nov 1971), 16.
8. D[iane] R[oman], *J of Irish Literature*, 1:3 (Sept 1972), 95.

563. MACMANUS, FRANCIS (ed): *The Yeats We Knew*. Memoirs by Pádraic Colum, Francis Stuart, Monk Gibbon, Earnán de Blaghd [i.e., Ernest Blythe], and Austin Clarke. Cork: Mercier Press, 1965. 94 p. (Thomas Davis Lectures.)

Colum's recollections are largely concerned with Yeats's theatrical career (pp. 13-24); Stuart (27-40) usually found Yeats's presence a strain and thinks that Yeats's "life and his poetry never merged" and that the poetry "lacks an inherent unifying vision of man"; Gibbon (43-57) "never penetrated—as others claim to have done—behind the poetic mask to the human individual"; Blythe (61-75) recollects Abbey Theatre business and comments on Yeats's involvement in politics; and Clarke (79-94) tells of three occasions on which he saw Yeats, at the Abbey, at the Thomas Davis Centenary, and at Coole.

Reviews:
1. Anon., "Aghaidh fidil," *Comhar*, 24:7 (July 1965), 23, 25.
2. W. R. Grey, *Focus*, 8:8 (Aug 1965), 187.

564. MASEFIELD, JOHN: *Some Memories of W. B. Yeats*. NY: Macmillan, 1940. vi, 31 p.

Includes three poems on Yeats.

Reviews:
1. Anon., "Mr. Masefield on Yeats," *TLS*, 40:2036 (8 Feb 1941), 68.
2. R. O'F. [Robert Farren], *Bell*, 2:1 (Apr 1941), 96.

3. G[arland] G[reever], "Puzzle-Map Reminiscences," *Personalist*, 22:
3 (Summer 1941), 310-11.

4. Louis MacNeice, "Through Stained Glass," *Spectator*, 166:5876 (7 Feb
1941), 152.

5. Horace Reynolds, "Yeats as Portrayed by Masefield," *CSM*, 33:28 (28
Dec 1940), Weekly Mag Section, 10.

6. Winfield Townley Scott, "The Foolish, Passionate Man," *Accent*, 1:4
(Summer 1941), 247-50.

7. William Soutar, "William Butler Yeats," *Adelphi*, 17:12 (Sept 1941),
425-27.

565. MOORE, VIRGINIA: *The Unicorn: William Butler Yeats' Search for Reality.*
NY: Macmillan, 1954. xxi, 519 p.
Based on °"Religion and William Butler Yeats," Ph.D. thesis, Columbia
U, 1952. 619 p. (*DA*, 12:4 [1952], 427.)
Author's summary of what this book tries to give: "1. Some new
light [biographically] from talks with George Yeats, Maud Gonne, Ezra
Pound, and others. 2. Heretofore unused . . . material from unpublished
manuscripts, including the rituals of the Irish 'mysteries' . . . ;
also epistolary evidence which alters the accepted view of his relation
to Maud Gonne; also . . . the 'Seven Propositions' of 1937 which set
forth . . . his mature philosophy. 3. Full biographical and doctrinal
use . . . of the rituals and teachings of the 'Christian-cabalistic'
secret Order to which Yeats belonged for more than twenty-five years.
4. A detailed study . . . of Yeats' doctrinal sources: Hermetism,
Druidism, Cabalism, Neoplatonism, Gnosticism, Rosicrucianism, Blake,
and so forth. . . . 5. A painstaking study . . . of Yeats' long pursuit of philosophy, both Western and Eastern. . . . 6. A re-evaluation
of . . . *A Vision.* 7. A reassessment of Yeats' relation to Christianity . . ." (p. xvi). The book has been severely criticized for its
lack of organization and its gossipy and vulgar style.
Reviews:

1. Hazard Adams, "Where All Ladders Start," *Western R*, 19:3 (Winter
1955), 229-34.

2. Anon., "Yeats's Religious Beliefs," *Nation*, 179:5 (31 July 1954),
96-97.

3. S. Appleton, *Thought*, 29:115 (Winter 1954/55), 615-16.

4. Mary P. Brody, *Catholic World*, 179:1072 (July 1954), 317-18.

5. Reuben A. Brower, "The Incarnation of Yeats," *Yale R*, 44:2 (Dec
1954), 290-92.

6. Babette Deutsch, "Yeats, with Many Footnotes," *NYHTB*, 30:49 (18
July 1954), 5.

7. René Fréchet, *EA*, 12:4 (Oct-Dec 1959), 365-66.

8. Horace Gregory, "Yeats' Golden Dawn," *NYTBR*, [59:] (30 May 1954),
6.

9. Hugh Kenner, "Unpurged Images," *Hudson R*, 8:4 (Winter 1956), 609-
17.

10. Russell Krauss, *Educational Forum*, 19:2, pt 1 (Jan 1955), 250-51.

11. Irving David Suss, *SAQ*, 54:1 (Jan 1955), 151-53.

12. W. D. T[empleman], *Personalist*, 36:4 (Autumn 1955), 424-25.

13. Charles Child Walcutt, *Arizona Q*, 11:2 (Summer 1955), 170-73.

14. George Whalley, *QQ*, 62:4 (Winter 1956), 617-21.

566. STRONG, LEONARD ALFRED GEORGE: *A Letter to W. B. Yeats.* London:
Hogarth Press, 1932. 31 p. (Hogarth Letters. 6.)
Some rather adulatory reminiscences. Includes a parody of Mrs. Leo
Hunter's "Ode to an Expiring Frog" (p. 18), done in the style of Yeats.

See also J513, 514, 923, 1093, 1100, 4202.

BB   Articles and Parts of Books

567. ADLARD, JOHN: *Stenbock, Yeats and the Nineties.* London: Woolf, 1969. xi, 113 p.
    Incorporates "Yeats's Stenbock," *Aylesford R*, 8:1 (Summer 1966), 37-41.
    The book is a misnomer and one cannot help noticing that it tries to cash in on the Yeats industry. The only important passage on Yeats is the following: "It must have been through [Lionel] Johnson that Eric [Stenbock] met Yeats and invited him to at least one supper. But here I am frustrated. I have been told that 'in an unpublished note-book of the 'twenties' Yeats left an account of a meeting with Eric. But Mrs. Yeats declined to allow my informant to send me this extract" (p. 60). WBY mentions Stenbock in the preface to the *Oxford Book of Modern Verse* and in *Autobiographies.*

568. ALDINGTON, RICHARD: *Life for Life's Sake: A Book of Reminiscences.* London: Cassell, 1968 [1941]. 374 p.
    Reminiscences of Yeats, pp. 95, 97-99, 306-7 (Tagore "hit Yeats bang in the Blavatsky").

569. ALFORD, NORMAN WILLIAM: "The Rhymers' Club (Founded 1891): A Study of Its Activities and Their Significance," Ph.D. thesis, U of Texas, 1966. x, 266 p. (*DA*, 27:2 [Aug 1966], 451A.)
    On Yeats, *passim* and 45-88. Does not seem to have seen Beckson's earlier thesis on the same subject (J587). Beckson seems to me more thorough, although Alford has the better documentation.

570. ANDREWS, IRENE DWEN: "A Glimpse of Yeats," *Reading and Collecting*, 2:3 (Feb-Mar 1938), 8-9.
    In Gogarty's house sometime in the thirties.

571. ANON.: "A Poet at Home: A Pen Portrait of Mr. Yeats," *Gael*, 20:1 (Jan 1901), 27.
    Yeats at Woburn Place.

572. ANON.: "A Pen Picture of Dr. Douglas Hyde and Mr. Yeats," *Gael*, 21: 12 (Dec 1902), 378-79.
    An interview with Hyde, who was constantly pestered by a nervous Yeats.

573. ANON.: "Mr. William Butler Yeats to Lecture in the United States This Autumn," *Gael*, 22:11 (Nov 1903), 387.

574. ANON.: "Moore Memorial to Yeats Unveiled: Juncture of Great Talents," *Irish Times*, #34887 (27 Oct 1967), 13.
    Includes the text of the speech made by the Taoiseach, Jack Lynch. Illustrated.

575. ANON.: "Yeats, 70, Is Feted by Irish Notables: 200 at Dublin Dinner in First Public Tribute Ever Paid to Him in Own Country [. . .]," *NYT*, 84:28279 (28 June 1935), 19.

576. ANON.: "All Fresh and Wide-Eyed," *New Yorker*, 39:37 (2 Nov 1963), 40-41.
    Interview with Anne Yeats reminiscing about her father.

577. ANON.: "W. B. Yeats in America," *T. P.'s Weekly* , 9:231 (12 Apr 1907), 452.
    Negligible anecdotes.

578. ANON.: "W. B. Yeats at School: Interesting Reminiscences of the Irish Poet's Schooldays by a Classmate," *T. P.'s Weekly*, 19:500 (7 June 1912), 709.

579. Entry canceled.

580. ANON.: "Mr. W. B. Yeats's Estate," *Times*, #48443 (23 Oct 1939), 11. Yeats left a personal estate valued at £8,329.

581. ANTHEIL, GEORGE: *Bad Boy of Music*. Garden City: Doubleday, Doran, 1945. vi, 378 p.
   Reminiscences of Yeats, for whose *Fighting of the Waves* he wrote the incidental music, pp. 228-29. Says that Yeats, Eliot, Pound, and others corrected the MS. of his detective story *Death in the Dark* (published under the pseudonym Stacey Bishop).

582. ATKINSON, F. G.: "W. B. Yeats: A Biographical Note," *N&Q*, os 216 / ns 18:3 (Mar 1971), 106-9.
   For details see J170.

583. BANGS, FRANCIS H.: "Julia Ellsworth Ford: An Appreciation," *Yale U Library Gazette*, 26:4 (Apr 1952), 153-92.
   On Mrs. Ford's contacts with Yeats during his first American lecture tour, pp. 153-57.

584. BARKER, DUDLEY: *Prominent Edwardians*. NY: Atheneum, 1969. iii, 257 p.
   "An Episode in the Life of William Butler Yeats," 100-136. Simply a retelling of Yeats's biography from his first meeting with Maud Gonne until her marriage.

585. BAX, CLIFFORD: *Inland Far: A Book of Thoughts and Impressions*. London: Heinemann, 1925. 332 p.
   Records a visit in Woburn Buildings, where Yeats somehow bewildered him, pp. 36-38.

586. BEARDSLEY, AUBREY: *The Letters*. Edited by Henry Maas, J. L. Duncan, and W. G. Wood. Rutherford, N.J.: Fairleigh Dickinson UP, 1970. ix, 472 p.
   Yeats is referred to *passim* (see index). Incorporates *Letters from Aubrey Beardsley to Leonard Smithers*. Edited with introduction and notes by R. A. Walker. London: First Edition Club, 1937. xvi, 240 p.

587. BECKSON, KARL E.: "The Rhymers' Club," Ph.D. thesis, Columbia U, 1959. vi, 200 p. (*DA*, 20:3 [Sept 1959], 1021-22.)
   On Yeats and the Rhymers' Club, *passim*; on his poetry, pp. 148-55; on the Irish Literary Society, whose foundation gave the fatal blow to the Rhymers' Club, 165-85. See also Alford (J569).

588. BEDDINGTON, FRANCES ETHEL: *All That I Have Met*. By Mrs. Claude Beddington. London: Cassell, 1929. xiii, 287 p.
   "Yeats and Shaw," 178-82. She met Yeats in 1916. Includes a letter from Yeats, dated 82 Merrion Sq., 9 Feb 1924.

589. BEERBOHM, SIR MAX: *Mainly on the Air*. Enlarged edition. London: Heinemann, 1957 [1946]. x, 192 p.
   "First Meetings with W. B. Yeats," 95-101 (not in 1946 edition). Written in 1914, broadcast on 26 Dec 1954, B.B.C. third programme. Reprinted from *Listener*, 53:1349 (6 Jan 1955), 15-16, and from *Atlantic Monthly*, 200:3 (Sept 1957), 70-72. Also in John Morris (ed): *From the Third Programme: A Ten Years' Anthology*. London: Nonesuch Press, 1956. x, 339 p. (pp. 154-61).
   Reviews of the broadcast:
   1. Anon., "W. B. Yeats, by Max," *Times*, #53124 (28 Dec 1954), 9.

2. Martin Armstrong, "The Spoken Word: The Detached Observer,"
Listener, 53:1349 (6 Jan 1955), 39.

590. BEHAN, BRENDAN: *Brendan Behan's Island: An Irish Sketchbook*. With
drawings by Paul Hogarth. [NY]: Geis, 1962. 192 p.
Behan's mother was maid in Maud Gonne's house and observed Yeats mis-
taking parsnips for pudding. Behan told the story to an American
professor who asked for Yeats's attitude to Stephen's greens (pp. 27-
28).

591. BENSON, SIR FRANK: *My Memoirs*. London: Benn, 1930. ix, 332 p.
Reminiscences of Yeats and of a performance of *Diarmuid and Grania*,
pp. 310-11.

592. BLUNT, WILFRID SCAWEN: *My Diaries: Being a Personal Narrative of
Events, 1888-1914*. London: Secker, [1921]. 2 v.
Yeats visits Blunt on 1 Apr 1898 and experiments magically with him:
"The performance was very imperfect, not to say null" (1:290-91).
Further meetings with Yeats on 26 Apr 1902 (2:22); 10 and 15 June 1902
(2:28); 2 May 1903 (2:53): Blunt attends a performance of *The Hour-
Glass* and finds it a "terrible infliction"; 10 May 1904 (2:100): Blunt
detects a trace of the charlatan in Yeats.

593. BOLSTERLI, MARGARET JONES: "Bedford Park: A Practical Experiment in
Aesthetics," °Ph.D. thesis, U of Minnesota, 1967. 141 p. (*DA*, 28:12 [June
1968], 5007A.)

594. BOOTH, JOHN R.: "Yeats as Reviewer," *Listener*, 20:501 (18 Aug 1938),
352.
Reminiscences of Yeats when he was a reviewer for the Dublin *Daily
Express*.

595. BOSE, ABINASH CHANDRA: "W. B. Yeats: His Last Indian Visitor,"
Shakti, 3:6 (June 1966), 6-11.
A fuller account than the one given in DasGupta (J2177). Correspond-
ence by Richard Ellmann and Bose, :11 (Nov 1966), 40.

596. BOWRA, SIR CECIL MAURICE: *Memoirs, 1898-1939*. Cambridge, Mass.:
Harvard UP, 1967 [1966]. xii, 369 p.
"W. B. Yeats," 230-42. Reminiscences and an appreciation of Yeats's
work, also two letters and a poem that Yeats addressed to Bowra by
way of apology when he missed an appointment with him.

597. BOYD, ERNEST: *Portraits Real and Imaginary: Being Memories and
Impressions of Friends and Contemporaries, with Appreciations of Divers
Singularities and Characteristics of Certain Phases of Life and Letters
among the North Americans as Seen, Heard and Divined*. London: Cape, 1924.
265 p.
"William Butler Yeats," 236-45.

598. BRADFORD, CURTIS B.: "George Yeats: Poet's Wife," *Sewanee R*, 77:3
(July-Sept 1969), 385-404.

599. BRENNAN, DIARMUID: "As Yeats Was Going Down Grafton Street,"
Listener, 71:1819 (6 Feb 1964), 236-38.
Recalls a meeting in the 1930s.

600. BROOKE, RUPERT: *The Letters*. Chosen and edited by Geoffrey Keynes.
London: Faber & Faber, 1968. xv, 709 p.
Several references to Yeats (see index), whose work, especially
Deirdre, Brooke seems to have liked very much. He met Yeats once in
Mar 1913.

601. BROOKS, VAN WYCK: *Emerson and Others*. London: Cape, [1927]. vi, 250 p.
"John Butler Yeats," 109-20; a memoir referring to WBY *passim*. See also *A Chilmark Miscellany*. NY: Dutton, 1948. ix, 315 p. (pp. 273-81).

602. ————: *Opinions of Oliver Allston*. NY: Dutton, 1941. 309 p.
Contains a few references to WBY (see index).

603. ————: *An Autobiography*. Foreword by John Hall Wheelock, introduction by Malcolm Cowley. NY: Dutton, 1965. xxxvi, 667 p.
Includes *Scenes and Portraits* (1954), which contains a memoir of John Butler Yeats, "Yeats at Petitpas'," 173-92.

604. BROWNE, MAURICE: *Too Late to Lament: An Autobiography*. London: Gollancz, 1955. 403 p.
Reminiscences of Yeats meeting Vachel Lindsay, pp. 138-39.

604a. BUCKLEY, TOM: "Yeats's Son Finds Poetry Leaves Him Cold," *NYT*, 122: 41916 (28 Oct 1972), 33.
Michael Yeats reminisces about his father.

605. D., D. [VACHER BURCH ?]: "Talking with Yeats, the Poet: A Memorable First Meeting," *Manchester Guardian*, #28820 (2 Feb 1939), 18.
Long letter to the editor about an undated meeting "in a Midland town [Liverpool?]." Says that Yeats refers to him in his autobiography as "my learned man." I assume that this is the man "learned in East Mediterranean antiquities," who supplied Yeats with the annotations to the archer vision. See R. F. Rattray, "Yeats and Vacher Burch," *TLS*, 54:2795 (23 Sept 1955), 557.

606. CARY, RICHARD: "William Butler Yeats at Colby College," *Colby Library Q*, 6:8 (Dec 1963), 360-69.
Yeats's visit and lecture in Oct 1932.

607. CHETTUR, GOVINDA KRISHNA: *The Last Enchantment: Recollections of Oxford*. Mangalore: B. M. Bookshop, 1934. xiv, 200 p.
"W. B. Yeats," 33-45, reprinted from °*Madras Mail*. Meetings in 1919-21. See also pp. 30-32.

608. CHRISTY, M. A.: "Yeats's Teacher," *TLS*, 64:3299 (20 May 1965), 397.
Quotes from a letter written by John McNeill, Yeats's teacher at the High School, Dublin.

609. CHUTE, DESMOND: "Poets in Paradise: Recollections of W. B. Yeats and Ezra Pound in Rapallo," *Listener*, 55:1401 (5 Jan 1956), 14-15.

610. CLARKE, AUSTIN: *First Visit to England and Other Memories*. Dublin: Bridge Press / London: Williams & Norgate, 1945. 82 p.
"First Visit to the Abbey Theatre," 37-40; "The Seven Woods," 49-53, a visit with Yeats ca. 1924.

611. ————: *A Penny in the Clouds: More Memories of Ireland and England*. London: Routledge & Kegan Paul, 1968. vii, 216 p.
Incorporates "Glimpses of W. B. Yeats," *Shenandoah*, 16:4 (Summer 1965), 25-36; and "Some Memories of W. B. Yeats," *Guardian*, #36991 (12 June 1965), 7.
Reminiscences of Yeats, AE, George Moore, James Stephens, Maud Gonne, other celebrities of the Irish literary revival, and the Abbey Theatre (see index).

612. CLARKE, LIA: "W. B. Yeats," *Leader*, 77:23 (11 Feb 1939), 592.
Reminiscences.

613. COCKERELL, SYDNEY CARLYLE: *Friends of a Lifetime: Letters to Sydney Carlyle Cockerell.* Edited by Viola Meynell. London: Cape, 1940. 384 p.
    See pp. 268-73. Not all the letters in this collection are reprinted in Wade's edition, and vice versa.

614. COLUM, MARY [MAGUIRE]: *Life and the Dream.* Dublin: Dolmen Press, 1966 [1947]. vii, 378 p.
    Incorporates "Memories of Yeats," *SatR*, 19:18 (25 Feb 1939), 3-4, 14; "Lady Gregory and the Abbey Theatre," *Tomorrow*, 4:6 (Feb 1945), 20-24; "The Yeats I Knew," *Tomorrow*, 4:8 (Apr 1945), 38-43; "The Dublin Scene: George Moore, Padraic Pearse and Other Figures in the Celtic Revival," *Tomorrow*, 4:10 (June 1945), 58-62; "The Dublin Sages," *Tomorrow*, 4:12 (Aug 1945), 52-56 (AE, Sarah Purser, George Sigerson, and others).
    Reminiscences of Yeats, *passim*, especially pp. 78-80, 83-102, and 110-23.

615. COLUM, PADRAIC: *Ourselves Alone! The Story of Arthur Griffith and the Origin of the Irish Free State.* NY: Crown, 1959. xvi, 400 p.
    Also published as °*Arthur Griffith*, Dublin: Browne & Nolan, 1959. On Yeats, *passim* (see index).

616. ————: "Reminiscences of Yeats," *Tri-Q*, #4 [Fall 1965], 71-76.
    Includes Colum's poem on Yeats, here entitled "The Arch Poet: William Butler Yeats." See also J1275.

617. CONNELY, WILLARD: "Two Irish Poets," *John o' London's Weekly*, 63:1543 (5 Feb 1954), 113-14.
    Meetings with Yeats and AE.

618. ————: *Adventures in Biography: A Chronicle of Encounters and Findings.* London: Laurie, 1956. 198 p.
    "Poets in Ireland," 39-51; contains an account of a railway journey with Yeats ca 1929.

619. [CRONE, JOHN S.]: "Editor's Gossip," *Irish Book Lover*, 7:11 & 12 (June & July 1916), 181-84.
    A short Yeats reminiscence is found on p. 184.

620. ————: "Willie Yeats and John O'Leary," *Irish Book Lover*, 27:5 (Nov 1940), 245-49.
    Yeats's letters to O'Leary, reprinted more accurately in Wade's edition.

621. CRONIN, COLM: "Ria Mooney Tells of That 'Likeable Person' W. B. Yeats in an Interview with Colm Cronin," *Irish Press*, 35:139 (12 June 1965), 10.

622. CROWLEY, ALEISTER: *The Spirit of Solitude: An Autohagiography Subsequently Re-Antichristened The Confessions of Aleister Crowley.* London: Mandrake Press, 1929. 2 v.
    Records a visit to Yeats ca. 1899 to show him some poems. They did not like each other very much (1:232). Mentions Yeats in connection with an account of the Golden Dawn (1:251, 283): "a lank dishevelled Demonologist who might have taken more pains with his personal appearance without incurring the reproach of dandyism." Identifies Yeats as one of the characters in his short story "At the Fork of the Roads" (1:259; see J5848).

623. CURRAN, CONSTANTINE PETER: *Under the Receding Wave.* Dublin: Gill & Macmillan, 1970. 149 p.

Recollections of Yeats, pp. 93-94; "University College and *The Countess Cathleen*," 96-110 (on the circumstances of the first performance and on the *Playboy* riots). Also on some background figures (George Sigerson, Arthur Clery, T. M. Kettle, and others). See letter by C. C. S. O'Mahony, "High Days at the Abbey Theatre," *TLS*, 69:3576 (11 Sept 1970), 999, on the *Countess Cathleen* performance.

624. DAUTHENDEY, MAX: *Gesammelte Werke*. München: Langen, 1925. 6 v.
"Gedankengut aus meinen Wanderjahren" reports Dauthendey's meeting with Yeats (1:584-86) in spring 1894 where Yeats tried to explain his theory of spirits. Dauthendey also attended the first performance of *The Land of Heart's Desire*, but did not understand it and slept soundly. Incidentally, he does not record the meeting in a Paris café that Yeats notes in *Autobiographies*.

625. DE BLACAM, AODH: "Memories of the Mighty," *Irish Bookman*, 1:6 (Jan 1947), 15-18.
Yeats, Lady Gregory, and others.

626. DEVAS, NICOLETTE: *Two Flamboyant Fathers*. London: Collins, 1966. 287 p.
Reminiscences of Yeats and Lady Gregory, pp. 126-31.

627. DICKINSON, PAGE LAWRENCE: *The Dublin of Yesterday*. London: Methuen, 1929. xi, 206 p.
Memories of Yeats at the Arts Club (ca. 1906), pp. 49-55; of the early days of the Abbey Theatre, 82-98, *Passim* on the Irish literary revival.

628. *The Dictionary of National Biography, 1931-1940*. Edited by L. G. Wickham Legg. London: Oxford UP, 1949. xvi, 968 p.
Joseph Hone: Yeats, pp. 928-32.

629. DOLMETSCH, MABEL: *Personal Recollections of Arnold Dolmetsch*. London: Routledge & Kegan Paul, 1957 [i.e., 1958]. viii, 198 p.
Records a meeting with Yeats in 1914, at which occasion Yeats "lilted" some of his poems. Dolmetsch, however, thought that "he was really only droning it on one note" (pp. 110-11).

630. DONOGHUE, DENIS: "Viewpoint," *TLS*, 72:3702 (16 Feb 1973), 178.
Donoghue's reasons for abandoning the project of writing the new authorized Yeats biography (which had been announced in *TLS*, 70:3642 [17 Dec 1971], 1578). Correspondence by Michael Yeats, :3703 (23 Feb 1973), 211; G. S. Fraser and John Whitehead, :3704 (2 Mar 1973), 240. See also Donoghue's letter in :3701 (9 Feb 1973), 153, and comment by the Oxford University Press, *ibid.*, 152. The biography will now be written by F. S. L. Lyons (see "Commentary," 73:3749 [11 Jan 1974], 33).

631. DRINKWATER, JOHN: *Discovery: Being the Second Book of an Autobiography, 1897-1913*. London: Benn, 1932. 235 p.
See pp. 170-78 for Drinkwater's impressions of Yeats, an account of a production of *The King's Threshold* by the Pilgrim Players, and Yeats's opinion of it.

632. DRUMMOND, ANN: "Florence Farr Emery," *Discourse*, 4:2 (Spring 1961), 97-100.

633. DULAC, EDMUND: "Yeats, as I Knew Him," *Irish Writing*, #8 (July 1949), 77-87.
Discusses Yeats's occult interests.

634. EBERHART, RICHARD: "Memory of Meeting Yeats, AE, Gogarty, James Stephens," *Literary R*, 1:1 (Autumn 1957), 51-56.
Saw Yeats in Oct 1928 and heard him discuss politics.

635. EGERTON, GEORGE: *A Leaf from the Yellow Book: The Correspondence of George Egerton*. Edited by Terence de Vere White. London: Richards Press, 1958. 184 p.
Two undated letters from Yeats, pp. 34-35; reminiscences of Yeats, 165-66. She did not like him very much, calls him "fat Willy" (146).

636. EGLINTON, JOHN: "Dublin Letter," *Dial*, 72:3 (Mar 1922), 298-301.
Reminiscences.

637. ———: "Yeats at the High School," *Erasmian*, ns 30:1 (June 1939), 11-12.

638. ———: "Early Memories of Yeats," *Dublin Mag*, 29 [i.e., 28]:3 (July-Sept 1953), 22-26.

639. ELLMANN, RICHARD: "Black Magic against White: Aleister Crowley versus W. B. Yeats," *Partisan R*, 15:9 (Sept 1948), 1049-51.
The Crowley—Althea Gyles—Yeats triangle, as told by Crowley to Ellmann. See also J5848.

640. ELTON, OLIVER: *Frederick York Powell: A Life and a Selection from His Letters and Occasional Writings*. Oxford: Clarendon Press, 1906. 2 v.
Some references to Yeats (see index).

641. ERVINE, ST. JOHN GREER: *Some Impressions of My Elders*. NY: Macmillan, 1922. vii, 305 p.
"William Butler Yeats," 264-305; reprinted from *NAR*, 211:771 (Feb 1920), 225-37, and :772 (Mar 1920), 402-10.

642. ———: "Edwardian Authors—III: Portrait of W. B. Yeats," *Listener*, 54:1383 (1 Sept 1955), 331-32.
Correspondence by C. S. Lewis, :1385 (15 Sept 1955), 427.

643: ———: *Bernard Shaw: His Life, Work, and Friends*. London: Constable, 1956. xii, 628 p.
Contains some not very flattering remarks on Yeats (see index).

644. ESSON, LOUIS: "Irish Memories and Australian Hopes," *Union Recorder*, 18:29 (24 Nov 1938), 281-82.
Reminiscences of Yeats and other celebrities of the Irish literary revival.

645. ———: "Portrait of W. B. Yeats: Poet and Mystic. The Man I Knew," *Sydney Morning Herald*, 108:31543 (4 Feb 1939), 21.
Recalls two meetings ca. 1904 and 1918. See also J753.

646. FALLON, GABRIEL: "Profiles of a Poet," *MD*, 7:3 (Dec 1964), 329-44.
Reminiscences of Yeats, Lady Gregory, and the Abbey Theatre.

647. FAY, GERARD: *Passenger to London*. NY: Macmillan, 1961. 222 p.
"Dublin of the Books," 92-97, contains some Yeats memories.

648. FIELD, MICHAEL [i.e., Katherine Harris Bradley and Edith Emma Cooper]: *Works and Days: From the Journals of Michael Field*. Edited by T. and D. C. Sturge Moore. London: Murray, 1933. xxii, 338 p.
Edith Cooper's recollection of a Yeats visit ca. 1901, pp. 261-63.

649. FINCH, EDITH: *Wilfrid Scawen Blunt: 1840-1922*. London: Cape, 1938. 415 p.
On Yeats and Blunt, *passim* (see index). See also J592 and J666.

650. FLANAGAN, GERALD: "Yeats' Sussex Haven," *Irish Press*, 35:210 (13 Nov 1965), 10.
Edith Shackleton Heald's Chantry House in Steyning. Illustrated.

651. FLETCHER, IAN: "Poet and Designer: W. B. Yeats and Althea Gyles," *Yeats Studies*, #1 (Bealtaine 1971), 42-79.
The biographical connections set against a discussion of Yeats's theories of art.

652. FREEMAN, JOHN: *Literature and Locality: The Literary Topography of Britain and Ireland*. London: Cassell, 1963. xiii, 402 p.
On Yeats and some of the places associated with his life, pp. 44, 313-14, 323-25.

653. FREMANTLE, ANNE: *Three-Cornered Heart*. NY: Viking Press, 1971. xi, 316 p.
Some reminiscences of Lady Gregory and Yeats, *passim* (see index).

654. FROST, ROBERT: *Selected Letters*. Edited by Lawrance Thompson. NY: Holt, Rinehart & Winston, 1964. lxiv, 645 p.
Some notes containing Frost's impression of Yeats and favorable comments on his poetry, *passim* (see index). See also J817.

655. GARRETT, EILEEN J.: *Many Voices: The Autobiography of a Medium*. With an introduction by Allan Angoff. London: Allen & Unwin, 1969. 254 p.
Reminiscences of Yeats, pp. 20, 27-28, 32, 60-61.

656. GIBBON, MONK: "The Advice of an Old Man," *Irish Times*, #28980 (24 June 1950), 6.
Recalls a meeting with Yeats, who expressed his cautious opinion of Gurdjieff's school at Fontainebleau.

657. GIBBS, PHILIP: *The Pageant of the Years: An Autobiography*. London: Heinemann, 1946. viii, 530 p.
"Victorian Flirtation," 15-16; a short Yeats reminiscence.

658. GOGARTY, OLIVER ST. JOHN: *As I Was Going Down Sackville Street: A Fantasy in Fact*. NY: Reynal & Hitchcock, 1937. x, 342 p.
Memories of Yeats at Rathfarnham, pp. 105-14; of Yeats and the ghost at Renvyle House, 179-89 (see also Gogarty's "Laying a Galway Ghost," *Irish Digest*, 2:3 [Jan 1939], 102-4); of the Abbey Theatre, 287-301. It might be useful to heed Gogarty's warning: "The names in this book are real, the characters fictitious."

659. ———: *Going Native*. London: Constable, 1941. ix, 294 p.
"How Ouseley Came to the Island of Friday-to-Tuesday," 3-22; a more or less fictitious account of a Yeats-Gogarty meeting (Ouseley being Gogarty).

660. ———: *Mourning Became Mrs. Spendlove and Other Portraits, Grave and Gay*. NY: Creative Age Press, 1948. v, 250 p.
"Reminiscences of Yeats," 209-24; reprinted from *Tomorrow*, 7 [i.e., 6]:9 (May 1947), 16-20.

661. ———: *Intimations*. NY: Abelard Press, 1950. vi, 271 p.
"George Moore's Blackbird," 18-24; the anecdote of a blackbird in Ely Place and Yeats's comments on it. "American Patrons and Irish Poets," 253-68; on Yeats and his American patrons John Quinn and Patrick McCartan.

662. ———: *Rolling Down the Lea*. London: Constable, 1950. vii, 278 p.

Contains an anecdote about Yeats and Seumas O'Sullivan, pp. 108-11; also some nasty remarks about the "Abbey Theatre coterie," 210-14.

663. ————: *It Isn't This Time of Year at All! An Unpremeditated Auto-biography.* Garden City: Doubleday, 1954. 256 p.
 Recollections of Yeats, *passim*, especially pp. 154-56 on Yeats and Moore and 242-47 on a private performance of *At the Hawk's Well.*

664. ————: *Start from Somewhere Else: An Exposition of Wit and Humor Polite and Perilous.* Garden City: Doubleday, 1955. 189 p.
 "Augustus John and Yeats," 121-27.

665. ————: *Many Lines to Thee: Letters to G. K. A. Bell from the Martello Tower at Sandycove, Rutland Square and Trinity College Dublin, 1904-1907.* Edited with a commentary by James F. Carens. Dublin: Dolmen Press, 1971. vii, 168 p. (Dolmen Editions. 14.)
 Yeats and other figures of the Irish literary revival mentioned *passim* in the letters; notes on the Yeats-Gogarty relationship in the commentaries.

666. GOING, WILLIAM T.: "A Peacock Dinner: The Homage of Pound and Yeats to Wilfrid Scawen Blunt," *JML*, 1:3 (Mar 1971), 303-10.
 See also J592 and J649.

667. GOLDRING, DOUGLAS: *Odd Man Out: The Autobiography of a "Propaganda Novelist."* London: Chapman & Hall, 1935. xii, 342 p.
 Scattered references to Yeats (see index).

668. ————: *South Lodge: Reminiscences of Violet Hunt, Ford Madox Ford and the English Review Circle.* London: Constable, 1943. xix, 240 p.
 Yeats is mentioned on pp. xvii, 48-49, 55, 123-24, 125, 160.

669. ————: *The Nineteen Twenties: A General Survey and Some Personal Memories.* London: Nicholson & Watson, 1945. xxiii, 266 p.
 Memories of Yeats and AE, pp. 115-18.

670. GONNE MACBRIDE, MAUD: *A Servant of the Queen: Reminiscences.* London: Gollancz, 1938. 350 p.
 Yeats is mentioned on pp. 90, 92-93, 98, 125, 147-48, 170, 172, 176-78, 250, 254-60 (concerning the Golden Dawn), 274-76, 282, 284, 308, 317-18, 328-35 (one of his marriage proposals), 339. The general impression is that Yeats seems to have thought more about Maud Gonne than she about him; most of the above references are not very important. The autobiography ends in 1903 with Maud Gonne's marriage.
 Reviews:
 1. J. M. Hone, "Irish Joan of Arc," *London Mercury*, 39:230 (Dec 1938), 209-10.

671. GOODWIN, K. L.: "Some Corrections to Standard Biographies of Yeats," *N&Q*, os 210 / ns 12:7 (July 1965), 260-62.
 Anent Yeats's relations with Pound.

672. GRANT, JOY: *Harold Monro and the Poetry Bookshop.* Berkeley: U of California Press, 1967. x, 286 p.
 Yeats reading at the Poetry Bookshop, pp. 77-78 and *passim* (see index).

673. GREGG, FREDERICK JAMES: "Going to School with the Poet Yeats," *NY Herald*, 88:94 (2 Dec 1923), section 9 (Magazine Section), 3.
 Yeats at the Anglican High School, Harcourt Street.

674. GREGORY, ANNE: *Me and Nu: Childhood at Coole.* Illustrated by Joyce Dennys with a prefatory note by Maurice Collis. Gerrards Cross: Smythe, 1971. 128 p.

Written by Lady Gregory's granddaughter; reminiscences of Lady Gregory, *passim*; of Yeats, 29-33, 89-90, 117, 128; of O'Casey, *passim*; all from a juvenile perspective.

674a. GREGORY, HORACE: *The House on Jefferson Street: A Cycle of Memories.* NY: Holt, Rinehart & Winston, 1971. xi, 276 p.
See pp. 252-54; notes on Yeats's works, *passim* (see index).

675. GREGORY, LADY ISABELLA AUGUSTA: *Coole.* Churchtown, Dundrum: Cuala Press, 1931. iv, 51 p.
Yeats is mentioned on pp. 24, 30, 32, 36-37 (with reference to "The Wild Swans at Coole"), 38, 42, 44, 45, 46.
Reedited as *Coole*. Completed from the manuscript and edited by Colin Smythe. With a foreword by Edward Malins. Dublin: Dolmen Press, 1971. 107 p. (Dolmen Editions. 10.). The foreword comments on the Yeats-Lady Gregory relationship (7-14).

676. GRIFFIN, GERALD: *The Wild Geese: Pen Portraits of Famous Irish Exiles.* London: Jarrolds, [1938]. 288 p.
"William Butler Yeats," 151-63; reminiscences and some notes on the poetry. Also on Shaw, Joyce, Moore, Stephens, Colum, Austin Clarke, O'Flaherty, Gogarty, Conal O'Riordan, O'Casey, and others.

677. GWYNN, FREDERICK LANDIS: *Sturge Moore and the Life of Art.* Lawrence: U of Kansas Press, 1951. xii, 159 p.
Numerous references to Yeats (see index) with occasional comparisons of Yeats's and Sturge Moore's poetry.

678. GWYNN, STEPHEN: *Garden Wisdom or From One Generation to Another.* Dublin: Talbot Press / London: Unwin, 1921. x, 149 p.
"The Ageing of a Poet," 1-19; recollections of Yeats and of the first performance of *Cathleen ni Houlihan*, as well as comments on *Responsibilities.*

679. ———: *Experiences of a Literary Man.* NY: Holt, 1927 [1926]. 312 p.
Some reminiscences of Yeats (see index) and of the beginnings of the Irish literary revival (see especially "Dublin of the 'Eighties," 55-75).

680. HACKETT, FRANCIS: *The Invisible Censor.* NY: Huebsch, 1921. vii, 167 p.
"William Butler Yeats," 114-18; reprint of "Books and Things," *New Republic*, 13:160 (24 Nov 1917), 100. Recalls a meeting with Yeats in the Pennsylvania Railroad Station.

681. HARVEY, ARNOLD: "Memories of Coole," *Irish Times*, #32496 (23 Nov 1959), 5; #32497 (24 Nov 1959), 7.
Reminiscences of AE, John Butler Yeats, Jack Yeats, and WBY.

682. HAWARD, LAWRENCE: "W. B. Yeats: A Visit to Manchester Recalled," *Manchester Guardian*, #28818 (31 Jan 1939), 5.

683. HEADLAM, MAURICE: *Irish Reminiscences.* London: Hale, 1947. 244 p.
On Yeats, pp. 36-37, 48, 223-24.

684. HELD, GEORGE M. C.: "The Second Book of the Rhymers' Club," *J of the Rutgers U Library*, 28:2 (June 1965), 15-21.

685. ———: "1. The Rhymers' Club, 1891-1894 [. . .]," Ph.D. thesis, Rutgers U, 1967. vi, 170 p. (*DA*, 28:10 [Apr 1968], 4176A-77A.)
"The Rhymers' Club," 1-69. Yeats mentioned *passim*.

686. [HEMINGWAY, ERNEST]: "W. B. Yeats a Night Hawk Kept Toronto Host Up: Also Forgot His Hair Brush and Pyjamas—Room Looked Like Premier Nitti's

Wrecked House," *Toronto Star Weekly*, 14:[] (22 Dec 1923), 35.

687. HIND, CHARLES LEWIS: *Authors and I*. London: Lane, 1921. 336 p.
"W. B. Yeats," 318-24.

688. HINE, REGINALD LESLIE: *Confessions of an Uncommon Attorney*. London:
Dent, 1946 [1945]. xix, 268 p.
Visited Yeats in 1908, pp. 151-53.

689. HINKSON, PAMELA: "Letters from W. B. Yeats," *Yale R*, 29:2 (Dec 1939),
307-20.
Letters to Katharine Tynan and reminiscences.

690. ————: "The Friendship of Yeats and Katharine Tynan," *Fortnightly R*,
os 180 / ns 174: 1032 (Oct 1953), 253-64; :1033 (Nov 1953), 323-36.
All the letters on pp. 253-64 are in McHugh's edition (W211H/I), sometimes markedly different. The letters on pp. 323-36 are published for
the first time.

691. HONE, JOSEPH: "A Scattered Fair: From a Diary in a Neutral Country,"
Wind and the Rain, 3:3 (Autumn 1946), 110-15.
Quotes from a diary kept by Elizabeth Corbet Yeats in 1888-89; also
reminiscences of Yeats and Maud Gonne.

692. [————]: "W. B. Yeats—A Bio-Bibliography: A Succinct Table of Events
and Works," *Irish Library Bulletin*, 9:[10] (Oct 1948), 167-72.

693. HORGAN, JOHN JOSEPH: *Parnell to Pearse: Some Recollections and
Reflections*. Dublin: Browne & Nolan, 1948. viii, 359 p.
Reminiscences of Yeats, pp. 82, 117-18; on the effect of *Cathleen ni
Houlihan*, pp. 93-94 ("This powerful allegory . . . did more than
hundreds of political speeches to influence the rising generation").

694. JOHN, AUGUSTUS: *Chiaroscuro: Fragments of Autobiography*. First series.
London: Cape, 1952. 285 p.
See pp. 100-101.

694a. °JOHNSON, J. A.: "Florence Farr: Biography of a New Woman," Ph.D.
thesis, U of Leeds, 1971/72.

695. JOHNSTON, CHARLES: "Personal Impressions of W. B. Yeats," *Harper's
Weekly*, 48:2461 (20 Feb 1904), 291.
Yeats's early interest in science and in Darwin.

696. ————: "Yeats in the Making," *Poet Lore*, 17:2 (Summer 1906), 102-12.
Reminiscences and an appreciation of the early work.

697. JONES, E. AYKROYD: "The Sincerity of Yeats," *Focus*, 3 [i.e., 8]:6
(June 1965), 127-28.
Reminiscences and an appraisal.

698. JOYCE, STANISLAUS: *The Complete Dublin Diary*. Edited by George H.
Healey. Ithaca: Cornell UP, 1971. xv, 189 p.
References to Yeats on pp. 25, 26, 63.

698a. KASSNER, RUDOLF: *Umgang der Jahre: Gleichnis—Gespräch—Essay—
Erinnerung*. Erlenbach-Zürich: Rentsch, 1949. 398 p.
See pp. 324-25.

699. KELLEHER, DANIEL LAWRENCE: *The Glamour of Dublin*. Dublin: Talbot
Press, 1928 [1918]. 108 p.
The first edition was published under the pseudonym D. L. Kay. "The
Abbey Theatre," 17; "The High School: W. B. Yeats," 64.

700. KELLNER, L[EON]: "Yeats," *Nation* [Berlin], 20:45 (8 Aug 1903), 713-15.
Describes a meeting with Yeats and discusses him as an "otherworldly poet."

701. KEYSERLING, HERMANN, COUNT: "W. B. Yeats: Recollections," *New English Weekly and New Age*, 15:16-20 (31 Aug 1939), 256.

701a. ————: *Reise durch die Zeit. II: Abenteuer der Seele.* Darmstadt: Holle, 1958. 428 p. (Gesammelte Werke. 2.)
See p. 182 for a Yeats reminiscence (ca. 1903/4).

702. KIERNAN, T. J.: "Lady Gregory and W. B. Yeats," *Southerly*, 14:4 (1953), 239-51.
Reprinted in *Dalhousie R*, 38:3 (Autumn 1958), 295-306.

703. KILDARE, PETER: "The Day I Met W. B. Yeats," *Sunday Press*, #787 (13 June 1965), 17.

704. KINGSMILL, HUGH: *The Best of Hugh Kingsmill.* Selections from his writings edited and introduced by Michael Holroyd. London: Gollancz, 1970. 399 p.
"Meetings with W. B. Yeats," 273-76. Reprinted from *NSt*, 21:515 (4 Jan 1941), 10-11, and *The Progress of a Biographer*, London: Methuen, 1949. viii, 194 p. (pp. 91-94). One meeting took place in 1912 and produced the *Hearth and Home* interview (see J947), the others in 1924.

705. Tante, Dilly [i.e., STANLEY JASSPON KUNITZ] (ed): *Living Authors: A Book of Biographies.* NY: Wilson, 1931. vii, 466 p.
"William Butler Yeats," 451-54.

706. KUNITZ, STANLEY JASSPON, and HOWARD HAYCRAFT (eds): *Twentieth Century Authors: A Biographical Dictionary of Modern Literature.* Complete in one volume with 1,850 biographies and 1,700 portraits. NY: Wilson, 1942. vii, 1577 p.
Lady Gregory, pp. 575-76; Lennox Robinson, 1187-88; J. M. Synge, 1378-80; W. B. Yeats, 1560-62.

707. LAWRENCE, SIR ALEXANDER: "W. B. Yeats," *Times*, #48220 (3 Feb 1939), 14.
An anecdote on Yeats's belief in fairies.

708. LEACOCK, STEPHEN: *Too Much College or Education Eating Up Life: With Kindred Essays in Education and Humour.* NY: Dodd, Mead, 1940 [1939]. xi, 255 p.
"Thinking of Tomorrow," 200. A supper party for Yeats when he lectured in Montreal. Yeats, thinking of the next day, wondered "if there is breakfast on the Boston train."

709. LEEMING, A. EMID: "Yeats and the Fairies," *Irish Times*, #34143 (22 Mar 1965), 8.
Recollection of a Yeats lecture.

710. LEGGE, M. DOMINICA: "Yeats and J. G. Legge," *TLS*, 55:2810 (6 Jan 1956), 7.
Identifies the J. G. Legge referred to in letters to Katharine Tynan.

711. LESLIE, SEYMOUR: *The Jerome Connexion.* London: Murray, 1964. x, 220 p.
Yeats and the ghost at Gogarty's house, pp. 142-44. Contains a letter about Lady Gregory to Leonie Jerome Leslie, undated, from Coole Park (p. 204).

712. LESLIE, SHANE. "How William Butler Yeats Became a Poet and Made Poets," *Ireland-American R*, [1]:4 [1940?], 86-90.
Discusses neither the first nor the second question but gives a sketchy biography with emphasis on Irish scenes.

713. LEWIS, CLIVE STAPLES: *Letters*. Edited with a memoir by W. H. Lewis. London: Bles, 1966. v, 308 p.
Met Yeats in Oxford in 1921, pp. 56-58.

714. LEWIS, WYNDHAM: *The Letters*. Edited by W. K. Rose. London: Methuen, 1963. xxxi, 580 p.
Yeats is mentioned *passim* (see index). Includes two letters from Lewis to Yeats, pp. 181-83.

715. L[INATI], C[ARLO]: Reminiscences of Yeats in 1902, *Convegno*, 4:4-5-6 (Apr-May-June 1923), 269-70.

716. LYNCH, ARTHUR: *My Life Story*. London: Long, 1924. 319 p.
Reminiscences of Yeats, whom he does not like, pp. 101-2; of Maud Gonne and Synge in Paris, 143-50.

717. MACDIARMID, HUGH: *The Company I've Kept*. Berkeley: U of California Press, 1967. 288 p.
Passim (see index).

718. MCGARRY, JAMES P.: *The Castle of Heroes*. Boyle: Roscommon Herald, 1965. vi, 41 p.
A description of Carraig Mhic Diarmada on Loch Key near Boyle, the Castle of Heroes of which Yeats and Maud Gonne dreamed and talked.

719. MCGRATH, JOHN: "W. B. Yeats and Ireland," *Westminster R*, 176:1 (July 1911), 1-11.
Reminiscences and on Yeats's concern with Irish literature.

720. MACGREEVY, THOMAS: "Uileachán dubh Ó," *Capuchin Annual*, 21 (1952), 211-45.
A tour of the Yeats country, County Sligo, and some reminiscences, pp. 222-30, 236-39. (In English.)

721. ———: "W. B. Yeats—A Generation Later," *University R* [Dublin], 3:8 [1966?], 3-14.
Mostly reminiscences.

722. MACKEN, MARY M.: "W. B. Yeats, John O'Leary and the Contemporary Club," *Studies*, 28:109 (Mar 1939), 136-42.

723. MACKENNA, STEPHEN: "Notes on the Celtic Renaissance: The Personality of W. B. Yeats," *Gael*, 18:5 (Aug 1899), 132-34.
Gossip, mainly concerned with the way Yeats walks on the street (he does not really walk, "he propels himself").

724. MACKENZIE, COMPTON: *My Life and Times*. London: Chatto & Windus, 1963-71. 10 v.
Yeats talking on astrology in 1921, 5:207-8. See also 6:41.

725. MACLIAMMÓIR, MICHEÁL: *All for Hecuba: An Irish Theatrical Autobiography*. Boston: Branden Press, 1967 [1946]. viii, 367 p.
Incorporates "Yeats, Lady Gregory, Denis Johnston," *Bell*, 6:1 (Apr 1943), 33-42. Reminiscences of Yeats, pp. 68-71 and *passim* (see index). On the Gate Theatre and the Abbey Theatre, *passim*.
Reviews:
1. Robert Hogan, *MD*, 11:3 (Dec 1968), 339-41.

726. MACNEICE, LOUIS: *The Strings Are False: An Unfinished Autobiography.*
London: Faber & Faber, 1965. 288 p.
    Records a visit with Yeats in Rathfarnham in 1935 ("his manner was
hierophantic"), pp. 147-48.

727. MANNIN, ETHEL: *Privileged Spectator: A Sequel to "Confessions and
Impressions."* Revised edition. London: Jarrolds, [1948] [1939]. 256 p.
    Reminiscences of Yeats, pp. 60-65: Ethel Mannin and Ernst Toller tried
to enlist Yeats's support of Ossietzky's nomination for the Nobel
Peace Prize (Yeats refused); Yeats declared that setting his poems to
music was an outrage (he was played a record of Peter Warlock's music
for "He Reproves the Curlew" and thought it was terrible and ridiculous). For Warlock's score see J5709.

728. ———: *Young in the Twenties: A Chapter of Autobiography.* London:
Hutchinson, 1971. 192 p.
    Note on Yeats, pp. 67-68. See also J770.

729. MONROE, HARRIET: *A Poet's Life: Seventy Years in a Changing World.*
NY: AMS Press, 1969 [1938]. xi, 488 p.
    "A Banquet: Yeats and Lindsay," 329-39 (incorporates "Poetry's Banquet,"
Poetry, 4:1 [Apr 1914], 25-29), and *passim* (see index). The *Poetry*
version includes an untitled poem by Arthur Davison Ficke, introducing
Yeats.

729a. MOORE, GEORGE: *Letters of George Moore.* With an introduction by
John Eglinton, to whom they were written. Bournemouth: Sydenham, 1942.
88 p.
    Yeats is referred to on pp. 35, 51, 52, 53, 59, 60, 64, 68. Also
passim on AE and James Stephens.

730. MOSES, MONTROSE J.: "With William Butler Yeats," *TAM*, 8:6 (June 1924),
382-88.
    Reminiscences and an interview.

731. MOYNIHAN, MICHAEL: "A Poet and His Daughter," *Sunday Times*, #7473
(14 Aug 1966), 32.
    Reprinted in *Irish Digest*, 87:4 (Oct 1966), 29-32. Anne Yeats's
recollections of her father.

732. MULCAHY, Mrs. J. B.: "A Pen Picture of Mr. Yeats," *Gael*, 22:12 (Dec
1903), 425.
    Yeats on his American lecture tour. With two rather unusual photo-
graphs.

733. NASH, PAUL: *Outline: An Autobiography and Other Writings.* London:
Faber & Faber, 1949. 271 p.
    Visited Yeats ca. 1913 because he wanted to illustrate a book of his
poems, but was glad he did not get the job (p. 88).

734. NEVINSON, HENRY WOODD: *Changes and Chances.* London: Nisbet, 1923.
xv, 360 p.
    See pp. 209, 301-3.

735. ———: *Last Changes, Last Chances.* NY: Harcourt, Brace, 1929. xvii,
361 p.
    Visited Yeats on 30 Oct 1916 and heard him talk about spiritism, pp.
122-23.

736. ———: *Visions and Memories.* Collected and arranged by Evelyn Sharp.
London: Oxford UP, 1944. viii, 199 p.

"W. B. Yeats: Poet of Vision," 52-60; reprinted from *London Mercury*, 39:233 (Mar 1939), 485-91. Rambling reminiscences and some general remarks on the early poetry.

737. NEWBOLT, SIR HENRY: *My World as in My Time: Memoirs, 1862-1932*. London: Faber & Faber, 1932. xvi, 321 p.
Yeats and Newbolt visit Bridges in 1897, pp. 189, 192-94.

738. ————: *The Later Life and Letters*. Edited by his wife, Margaret Newbolt. London: Faber & Faber, 1942. xi, 426 p.
Reminiscences of Yeats, pp. 4-6, 166-68 (Yeats and Newbolt present Hardy with a medal).

739. NICHOLLS, HARRY: "Memories of the Contemporary Club," *Irish Times*, #34315 (20 Dec 1965), 10; #34316 (21 Dec 1965), 8.

740. NICOLSON, HAROLD: *Diaries and Letters, 1930-1939*. Edited by Nigel Nicolson. London: Collins, 1966. 448 p.
A letter from Victoria Sackville-West to Nicolson, dated 9 Nov 1934, contains the following paragraph: "Then I went to luncheon with Virginia [Woolf], who gave me an imitation of Yeats telling her why he was occult. He has been confirmed in this theory because he saw a coat-hanger emerge from his cupboard and travel across the foot of his bed; next night, it emerged again, clothed in one of his jackets; the third night, a hand emerged from one of his cuffs; the fourth night—'Ah! Mrs Woolf, that would be a long story; enough to say, I finally recovered my potency'" (p. 188). See Yeats's poem "The Apparitions."

741. NOWELL-SMITH, SIMON (ed): *Letters to Macmillan*. London: Macmillan, 1967. 384 p.
Passim (see index); cf. J106.

742. O'BRIEN, SEUMAS: "Leaves from a Notebook," *Blarney Mag*, #10 (Summer 1956), 26-32.
Reminiscences of Padraic Colum, the Abbey Theatre, and Yeats, who came to see him in his sculptor's studio sometime before 1912.

743. O'CASEY, SEAN: *Autobiographies*. London: Macmillan, 1963 [1939-54]. 2 v.
The following chapters contain important references to Yeats and other figures of the Irish literary revival:
"At the Sign of the Pick and Shovel," 1:406-22 (defends Yeats against charges made by Irish nationalists).
"Song of a Shift," 1:506-20 (the *Playboy* riots).
"Blessed Bridget O'Coole," 2:102-13 (first Abbey experiences and visit to Lady Gregory).
"Where Wild Swans Nest," 2:114-25 (the visit continued).
"The Temple Entered," 2:139-57 (further Abbey experiences with *The Plough and the Stars*).
"Dublin's Gods and Half-Gods," 2:157-66 (a visit to Yeats).
"Dublin's Glittering Guy," 2:167-86 (AE).
"Inishfallen, Fare Thee Well," 2:231-47 (more Abbey experiences and a note on *At the Hawk's Well*).
"London Apprentice," 2:251-68 (Yeats's theories of literature).
"The Silver Tassie," 2:268-80.
"The Friggin Frogs," 2:281-91 (a visit to Yeats and later relations with the Abbey).
"Feathering His Nest," 2:291-310 (more comments on Yeats).

"Black Oxen Passing By," 2:334-47 (refusal to see Lady Gregory and another visit to Yeats where they talked about communism).
"Childermess," 2:470-90 (reminiscences of Lady Gregory).

744. O'CONNOR, FRANK: "The Old Age of a Poet," *Bell*, 1:5 (Feb 1941), 7-18.

745. ————: "What Made Yeats a Great Poet?" *Listener*, 37:955 (15 May 1947), 761-62.
Rambling reminiscences; does not attempt to answer his own question. See also "Yeats—the Man and the Poet. Condensed from a B.B.C. Broadcast," *Irish Digest*, 28:2 (Sept 1947), 19-23; and "Listening to Yeats. Condensed from a Broadcast," *Literary Digest*, 3:4 (Winter 1948), 27-30.

746.————: *Leinster, Munster and Connaught*. London: Hale, [1950]. 296 p.
Recollections of Yeats, pp. 256-61 and *passim* (see index); of Lady Gregory ("a holy terror"), 236-39; of the Abbey Theatre, 34-43.

747. ————: "Quarreling with Yeats: A Friendly Recollection," *Esquire*, 62:6 (Dec 1964), 157, 221, 224-25, 232.
About Abbey Theatre politics and the production of *The Herne's Egg*.

748. ————: "The Scholar," *Kenyon R*, 27:2 (Spring 1965), 336-43.
Osborn Bergin and what he thought of Yeats.

749. ————: *My Father's Son*. London: Macmillan, 1968. 200 p.
The second part of O'Connor's autobiography; contains numerous stories about Yeats and the Abbey, partly contained in J744-48.
Reviews:
1. Anon., "Up from Cork," *TLS*, 67:3477 (17 Oct 1968), 1173.
   ("Yeats's death seemed the end of the world; for O'Connor it was, in fact, a release.")

750. [O'CONNOR, T. P. (?)]: "A Poet at Home. W. B. Yeats's Eyrie. Tea under Difficulties. A Pen Portrait of Mr. Yeats," *M. A. P.*, 5:123 (20 Oct 1900), 369.
See the ironical note by "Seang Siúir," "Mr. Yeats's Jug," *Leader*, 1:10 (3 Nov 1900), 155; and Yeats's letter, :11 (10 Nov 1900), 173 (Wp. 359), denying that the meeting took place.

751. O'SULLIVAN, DONAL: *The Spice of Life and Other Essays*. Dublin: Browne & Nolan, 1948. ix, 126 p.
See pp. 3-5.

752. P., M.: "The Yeats—Father and Son" [*sic*], *Theatre*, 19:158 (Apr 1914), 176, 211.
Small talk.

753. PALMER, VANCE: *Louis Esson and the Australian Theatre*. Melbourne: Meanjin Press, 1948. viii, 114 p.
Esson's reminiscences of Yeats, pp. 3-4, 25-28, and *passim* (see index). Cf. J644-45.

754. PATMORE, BRIGIT: *My Friends When Young*. Edited with an introduction by Derek Patmore. London: Heinemann, 1968. xii, 159 p.
Incorporates "Some Memories of W. B. Yeats," *Texas Q*, 8:4 (Winter 1965), 152-59. On Yeats, *passim*, especially 92-93, 100-101, 109-19.

755. PATMORE, DEREK: "Memories of W. B. Yeats," *Irish Times*, #35245 (21 Dec 1968), 12.

756. PEARCE, DONALD: "Dublin's 'National Literary Society,' 1892," *N&Q*, 196:10 (12 May 1951), 213–14.
  Edward Leamy's and Yeats's share in the founding of the society.

757. POUND, EZRA: *The Letters, 1907–1941.* Edited by D. D. Paige. London: Faber & Faber, 1951. 464 p.
  Yeats is mentioned *passim* (see index); no letter to him is included.

758. POWER, ARTHUR: "A Contact with Yeats," *Irish Tatler and Sketch*, 74:3 (Dec 1964), 34, 61.

759. PRITCHETT, V[ICTOR] S[AWDON]: "Encounters with Yeats," *NSt*, 69:1786 (4 June 1965), 879–80.

760. ————: *Dublin: A Portrait.* Photographs by Evelyn Hofer. NY: Harper & Row, 1967. 99 p.
  Memories of the Abbey Theatre and of Yeats, pp. 13–18.

761. ————: *Midnight Oil.* NY: Random House, 1972. ix, 273 p.
  See pp. 130–33.

762. PYLE, HILARY: *Jack B. Yeats: A Biography.* London: Routledge & Kegan Paul, 1970. xii, 228 p.
  Notes on WBY, *passim* (see index).

763. PYPER, STANTON: "Chosen Vues," *Dublin Mag*, 1:6 (Jan 1924), 520–26.

764. QUINN, JOHN: "Lady Gregory and the Abbey Theater," *Outlook*, 99:16 (16 Dec 1911), 916–19.
  Reminiscences of Yeats, Lady Gregory, Hyde, and Synge.

765. RASCOE, BURTON: "Contemporary Reminiscences: Notes on [. . .] W. B. Yeates [*sic*], the Nobel Prize Winner," *Arts & Decoration*, 21:1 (May 1924), 31, 62, 68.

766. ————: *A Bookman's Daybook.* Edited with an introduction by C. Hartley Grattan. NY: Liveright, 1929. xx, 305 p.
  "Two Meetings with W. B. Yeats," 233–35.

767. RATTRAY, ROBERT FLEMING: *Poets in the Flesh: Tagore, Yeats, Dunsany, Stephens, Drinkwater.* Cambridge: Golden Head Press, 1961. v, 13 p.
  "A Day with Yeats," 5–8; in Leicester in 1922.

768. REID, BENJAMIN LAWRENCE: *The Man from New York: John Quinn and His Friends.* NY: Oxford UP, 1968. xviii, 708 p.
  On Yeats and other figures of the Irish literary revival, *passim*.
  Includes quotations of letters to and from Yeats (see also J111a).

769. REID, FORREST: *Private Road.* London: Faber & Faber, 1940. 243 p.
  Reminiscences of Yeats, pp. 76–77; of AE, pp. 126–42.

770. REYNOLDS, REGINALD: *My Life and Crimes.* London: Jarrolds, 1956. 260 p.
  Ethel Mannin's husband's reminiscences of Yeats, pp. 159–61. See also J727–28.

771. RHYS, ERNEST: *Everyman Remembers.* London: Dent, 1931. xi, 320 p.
  See pp. 105–14 on the Rhymers' Club and W. B. Yeats; pp. 251–57 on a poetry reading in which Yeats took part; and *passim* (see index).

772. ————: "W. B. Yeats: Early Recollections," *Fortnightly R*, os 144 / ns 138:823 (July 1935), 52–57.
  Yeats at the Rhymers' Club and at Madame Blavatsky's.

773. ————: *Letters from Limbo.* London: Dent, 1936. xvii, 289 p.
  See pp. 155–59.

774. ─────: *Wales England Wed: An Autobiography*. London: Dent, 1940. ix, 295 p.

> Memories of Yeats, *passim*, especially pp. 91-93, 104-7 (Yeats and Madame Blavatsky), 172-75 (Yeats and Maud Gonne).

775. RICHARDSON, DOROTHY M[ILLER]: "Yeats of Bloomsbury," *Life and Letters To-day*, 21:20 (Apr 1939), 60-66.

> A meeting with Yeats on a street in Bloomsbury and the view from the apartment opposite Yeats's in Woburn Buildings. Reprinted as "Yeats and Bloomsbury," *St. Pancras J*, 12:5 (Oct 1958), 67-70, together with a note on the plaque that marks the house in which Yeats lived. For a slightly fictionalized account of the meeting see the novel *The Trap*, included in *Pilgrimage III*, London: Dent, 1967. 509 p. (pp. 437-39, 502). See also J2061.

776. RICKETTS, CHARLES: *Self-Portrait Taken from the Letters & Journals*. Collected and compiled by T. Sturge Moore, edited by Cecil Lewis. London: Davies, 1939. xix, 442 p.

> On Yeats, *passim* (see index). Includes two letters from Ricketts to Yeats, pp. 341-43.

777. RITTENHOUSE, JESSIE BELLE: *My House of Life: An Autobiography*. Boston: Houghton Mifflin, 1934. ix, 335 p.

> Recalls two meetings with Yeats, pp. 230-33.

778. ROBERTSON, OLIVIA: *Dublin Phoenix*. London: Cape, 1957. 224 p.

> Memories of Yeats, pp. 27-29; "Surrounded by Footlights," 168-82 (on Irish theatrical life); note on *The Dreaming of the Bones*, pp. 189-90.

779. ROBINSON, LENNOX, TOM ROBINSON, and NORA DORMAN: *Three Homes*. London: Joseph, 1938. 261 p.

> Lennox Robinson's reminiscences of the Abbey Theatre and of Yeats, pp. 218-34.

780. ROBINSON, LENNOX: *Curtain Up: An Autobiography*. London: Joseph, 1942. 224 p.

> Reminiscences of Yeats and the Abbey Theatre, *passim*. Part of the material on Yeats's plays (especially pp. 44-72) is also contained in J1089.

780a. RODGERS, W. R.: "Speak and Span," *Listener*, 57:1469 (23 May 1957), 829-30.

781. ROGERS, WILLIAM GARLAND: *Ladies Bountiful*. London: Gollancz, 1968. xiv, 236 p.

> Note on Yeats and Miss Horniman, pp. 10-12.

782. ROSE, MARILYN GADDIS: "A Visit with Anne Yeats," *MD*, 7:3 (Dec 1964), 299-307.

> Anne Yeats talks about her father.

783. ROSS, MARGERY (ed): *Robert Ross, Friend of Friends: Letters to Robert Ross, Art Critic and Writer, Together with Extracts from His Published Articles*. London: Cape, 1952. 367 p.

> See pp. 278-79.

784. ROTHENSTEIN, SIR WILLIAM: *Men and Memories: Recollections*. London: Faber & Faber, 1931-39. 3 v.

> Volume 3 bears the title *Since Fifty.* Memories of Yeats, *passim* (see index); especially 1:282-83; 2:20 (a letter from Yeats); 144-45 and 266-67 (letters from Yeats, both in Wade's edition); 300-301 (Tagore and Rothenstein on Yeats's revisions of *Gitanjali*); 3:111-12 (a letter

on Aurobindo Ghose and Toru Dutt); 178-79 (a letter on *The Golden Book of Tagore*); 241-42 (Yeats on Berkeley, Swift, and sexual intercourse); 249-52 (Yeats and Dorothy Wellesley on folksong); 305-7 (a letter).

785.————: *Imperfect Encounter: Letters of William Rothenstein and Rabindranath Tagore, 1911-1941*. Edited with an introduction and notes by Mary M. Lago. Cambridge, Mass.: Harvard UP, 1972. xx, 402 p.
Numerous references to Yeats (see index).

786. RUDDOCK, MARGOT: *The Lemon Tree*. With an introduction by W. B. Yeats. London: Dent, 1938. xiv, 29 p.
"Almost I Tasted Ecstasy," 1-9, contains Margot Ruddock's account of her meeting with Yeats. Reprinted in J118.

787. RUGGLES, ELEANOR: *The West-Going Heart: A Life of Vachel Lindsay*. NY: Norton, 1959. 448 p.
Lindsay's encounter with Yeats in Chicago, 1 Mar 1914, pp. 216-18.

788. [RUSSELL, GEORGE WILLIAM]: *Letters from AE*. Selected and edited by Alan Denson with a foreword by Monk Gibbon. NY: Abelard-Schuman, 1961. xliii, 288 p.
Reprints some of the letters from J847. Gibbon's preface, pp. vii-xvi, compares Yeats and AE. Numerous letters are addressed to Yeats, who is also mentioned *passim* (see index). Extended comments on *The Hour-Glass* in a letter of [2 Mar 1903 (?)], 44-45.

789. [————]: "Unpublished Letters from AE to John Eglinton. Edited by H[enry] Summerfield," *Malahat R*, #14 (Apr 1970), 84-107.
Yeats is mentioned *passim*.

790. RUTENBERG, DANIEL: "A New Date for the Rhymers' Club," *ELT*, 12:3 (1969), 155-57.
See also Karl Beckson, 13:1 (1970), 37-38; R. K. R. Thornton, 14:1 (1971), 49-53.

791. RYAN, DESMOND: *Remembering Sion: A Chronicle of Storm and Quiet*. London: Barker, 1934. 308 p.
Reminiscences of the Abbey Theatre and of Yeats at the Thomas Davis Centenary, pp. 86-87, 164-65.

792. RYAN, MARK FRANCIS: *Fenian Memories*. Edited with an introduction by T. F. O'Sullivan. Dublin: Gill, 1945. xxiv, 226 p.
"'98 Centenary—Mr. W. B. Yeats a Prominent Figure in the Celebrations," 184-89.

793. SANDERS, DORA: "Man of Ireland," *Saturday Night*, 48:2 (19 Nov 1932), 5.
Visited Yeats in Dublin.

794. SHARE, BERNARD: *Irish Lives: Biographies of Fifty Famous Irish Men and Women*. Dublin: Figgis, 1971. Unpaged.
Contains short biographies of Lady Gregory, Yeats, and Synge.

795. SHARP, ELIZABETH AMELIA: *William Sharp (Fiona Macleod): A Memoir*. London: Heinemann, 1910. vii, 433 p.
Contains several letters from Yeats to Sharp and to Fiona Macleod and vice versa; also some reminiscences (see index).

796. SHAW, [GEORGE] BERNARD: *Collected Letters, 1898-1910*. Edited by Dan H. Laurence. London: Reinhardt, 1972. xxiv, 1017 p.

A letter to Yeats, pp. 452, 859-61. Yeats and Lady Gregory are mentioned *passim* (see index).

797. SIME, GEORGINA, and FRANK NICHOLSON: *Brave Spirits*. [London]: Privately Printed, [1952]. vii, 165 p.
"A Triple View of W. B. Yeats," 59-83. Recollections of Yeats in Chiswick, where he talked about Madame Blavatsky and tried psychic experiments, and of two Yeats lectures in Montreal.

798. SINCLAIR, FREDERICK: "A Poet's World in Woburn Walk," *St. Pancras J*, 2:7 (Dec 1948), 124-27.

799. SITWELL, EDITH: *Selected Letters*. Edited by John Lehmann and Derek Parker. London: Macmillan, 1970. 264 p.
Some references to Yeats, *passim* (see index).

800. SKELTON, ROBIN: "Thoor Ballylee," *Ireland of the Welcomes*, 15:1 (May-June 1966), 29-31.

801. SOUFFRIN-LE BRETON, EILEEN: "W. B. Yeats to Mallarmé," *TLS*, 53:2756 (26 Nov 1954), 759.
Yeats was to be introduced to Mallarmé by Verlaine and Henley, but the meeting did not take place.

802. SPEAIGHT, ROBERT: *William Rothenstein: The Portrait of an Artist in His Time*. London: Eyre & Spottiswoode, 1962. xv, 443 p.
Yeats is mentioned *passim* (see index).

803. ———: "W. B. Yeats and Some Later Friendships," *Greyfriar*, 8 (1965), 14-32.
Yeats's friendships with W. J. Turner, Lady Ottoline Morrell, L. A. G. Strong, Wyndham Lewis, Olivia Shakespear, Margot Ruddock, and Dorothy Wellesley; also personal reminiscences.

804. ———: *The Property Basket: Recollections of a Divided Life*. London: Collins & Harvill Press, 1970. 416 p.
A few references to Yeats, *passim* (see index).

805. SPEAKMAN, HAROLD: *Here's Ireland*. MY: McBride, 1931 [1925]. xiii, 353 p.
"Mr. Yeats and Others," 302-17; describes a meeting with Yeats, 302-8.

806. SPENDER, STEPHEN: *World within World: The Autobiography*. London: Hamilton, 1964 [1951]. ix, 349 p.
Reminiscences of Yeats, pp. 163-66.

807. STARKIE, WALTER: "Yeats and Company," *NYTBR*, [70:] (14 Nov 1965), 90-92.
Recollections of Yeats and the Abbey Theatre.

808. STEWART, DOUGLAS: *The Flesh and the Spirit: An Outlook on Literature*. Sydney: Angus & Robertson, 1948. viii, 281 p.
"The Heroic Dream," 10-16, on Yeats and Maud Gonne as described by Hone.

809. STRINGER, ALFRED: "W. B. Yeats," *Saturday Night*, 56:48 (9 Aug 1941), 25, 32.
Part of a series "Wild Poets I Have Known." Recalls a Yeats lecture.

810. [STRONG, LEONARD ALFRED GEORGE]: "A Memory of Yeats," *Listener*, 34: 884 (20 Dec 1945), 725.

811. ———: "Reminiscences of W. B. Yeats," *Listener*, 51:1312 (22 Apr 1954), 689-90.

812. ————: "Yeats at His Ease," *London Mag*, 2:3 (Mar 1955), 56-65.
Yeats in his Oxford years.

813. ————: *Green Memory*. London: Methuen, 1961. 313 p.
"Memories of Yeats from 1919 to 1924: The conversations were always
recorded the morning after they took place, and are as nearly accurate
as a faithful ear could make them," 242-63. See also 303-6 and a note
on the Abbey Theatre, 144-46.

814. STURM, FRANK PEARCE: *His Life, Letters, and Collected Works*. Edited
and with an introductory essay by Richard Taylor. Urbana: U of Illinois
Press, 1969. viii, 382 p.
On the Yeats-Sturm relationship (mutual influences and biographical
connections), *passim* (see index). Prints the entire Yeats-Sturm correspondence, which is mainly concerned with *A Vision*, 73-110.

815. SYNGE, JOHN MILLINGTON: *Letters to Molly: John Millington Synge to
Maire O'Neill, 1906-1909*. Edited by Ann Saddlemyer. Cambridge, Mass.:
Belknap Press of Harvard UP, 1971. xxxiv, 330 p.
Numerous references to Yeats (see index), some of them not very
flattering (see, e.g., pp. 113-14 for Synge's unmitigated jealousy).
Reviews:
1. Anon., "The Tramp and the Changeling," *TLS*, 71:3655 (17 Mar 1972),
306.
2. John P. Frayne, *Drama & Theatre*, 10:2 (Winter 1971-72), 120-21.
3. Milton Levin, *Éire-Ireland*, 7:4 (Winter 1972), 140-43.
4. Harold Orel, *MD*, 15:2 (Sept 1972), 213-15.

816. TÉRY, SIMONE: "Visite à W.-B. Yeats, lauréat du Prix Nobel," *Nouvelles littéraires*, 2:58 (24 Nov 1923), 6.

817. THOMPSON, LAWRANCE: *Robert Frost: The Early Years, 1874-1915*. London:
Cape, 1967. xvii, 641 p.
Frost meets Yeats, pp. 412-14, and some other references (see index).
See also J654.

818. TIETJENS, EUNICE: *The World at My Shoulder*. NY: Macmillan, 1938.
xiii, 341 p.
Meetings with Yeats, pp. 59-61.

819. TOBIN, RICHARD MONTGOMERY: "Personal Memoirs of William Butler Yeats,"
Oriel R, 1:[1 (1943)], 72-76.

820. TURNER, W. J.: "The Yeats I Knew," *Listener*, 36:925 (3 Oct 1946),
443-44.

821. TYLER, DOROTHY: "Carl Milles, Yeats, and the Irish Coinage," *Michigan
QR*, 22:4 (Autumn 1963), 273-80.
Describes two meetings between Milles and Yeats in London and Detroit.
It seems that Yeats encouraged Milles, the Swedish sculptor and one
of the artists in the coinage competition, to such an extent that
Milles regarded the invitation to participate as an order. Hence his
disappointment when somebody else's designs were chosen.

822. T[YNAN], K[ATHARINE]: "William Butler Yeats," *Sketch*, 4:44 (29 Nov
1893), 256.
A visit and an interview.

823. ————: *Twenty-five Years: Reminiscences*. London: Smith, Elder, 1913.
viii, 355 p.
The first volume of Katharine Tynan's autobiography. On Yeats, *passim*
(see index).

824. ———: *The Middle Years*. London: Constable, 1916. viii, 415 p.
The second volume of Katharine Tynan's autobiography. See J823.

825. ———: "Personal Memories of John Butler Yeats," *Double Dealer*, 4:19 (July 1922), 8–15.

825a. TYNAN, KATHERINE [*sic*]: "Letters: 1884–5." *Apex One*, #1 (Sept 1973), 1–27.
Letters to one Mrs. Pritchard of London. KT notes her first meeting with WBY in the letter of 30 June 1885 (p. 23).

826. UNDERWOOD, VERNON PHILIP: *Verlaine et l'Angleterre*. Paris: Nizet, 1956. 511 p.
A note on Yeats's visit, pp. 463–64.

827. UNTERECKER, JOHN: "An Interview with Anne Yeats," *Shenandoah*, 16:4 (Summer 1965), 7–20.
Contains some reminiscences of her father; also notes on her designs for *Purgatory*.

828. VALOIS, NINETTE DE: *Come Dance with Me: A Memoir, 1898–1956*. London: Hamilton, 1957. xvi, 234 p.
Reminiscences of Yeats and the Abbey, pp. 88–98.

829. W[ALSH], E. R.: "Reminiscences of 'W. B.': South Frederick Street Days," *Irish Times*, 82:25767 (10 Feb 1940), 13.
In 1907.

830. WELLESLEY, DOROTHY: *Far Have I Travelled*. London: Barrie, 1952. 240 p.
See pp. 162–70.

831. WEYGANDT, CORNELIUS: *Tuesdays at Ten: A Garnering from the Talks of Thirty Years on Poets, Dramatists, and Essayists*. Philadelphia: U of Pennsylvania Press, 1928. 325 p.
"With Yeats in the Woods of Coole," 176–85; reprinted from *Lippincott's Mag*, 73:436 (Apr 1904), 484–87. Further notes on Yeats, *passim* (see index).

832. ———: *On the Edge of Evening: The Autobiography of a Teacher and Writer Who Holds to the Old Ways*. NY: Putnam's, 1946. xi, 217 p.
Reminiscences of Yeats, *passim* (see index).

833. WHITTINGTON-EGAN, RICHARD, and GEOFFREY SMERDON: *The Quest of the Golden Boy: The Life and Letters of Richard Le Gallienne*. London: Unicorn Press, 1960. xxiii, 580 p.
The activities of the Rhymers' Club, pp. 167–76.

834. WILKINSON, MARGUERITE: "A Talk with John Butler Yeats about His Son, William Butler Yeats," *Touchstone*, 6:1 (Oct 1919), 10–17.
Illustrated.

835. WILLIAMS, WILLIAM CARLOS: *The Autobiography*. NY: New Directions, 1967 [1951]. xii, 402 p.
See pp. 114–15.

836. WOOLF, LEONARD: *Beginning Again: An Autobiography of the Years 1911–1918*. London: Hogarth Press, 1964. 260 p.
Yeats trying a psychic experiment and failing, pp. 142–43. A photograph of Yeats and Lytton Strachey, 145.

837. YEATS, W. B.: "Letters to Matthew Russell, S.J. Edited by Roger Mc-Hugh," *Irish Monthly*, 82 [i.e., 81]:954 (Feb 1953), 60–63; :955 (Mar 1953), 111–15; :956 (Apr 1953), 148–51.

838. ————: "An Unpublished Letter. Edited by C. G. Martin," *N&Q*, os 203 / ns 5:6 (June 1958), 260-61.
Yeats's answer to an admirer (dated 20 Mar 1906) who had asked for a book on prosody.

839. YOUNG, EDITH: *Inside Out*. London: Routledge & Kegan Paul, 1971. vii, 167 p.
AE, Yeats, and Joyce as remembered by Mrs. Young's father (D. N. Dunlop), pp. 6-9.

840. YOUNG, ELLA: *Flowering Dusk: Things Remembered Accurately and Inaccurately*. NY: Longmans Green, 1945. xvi, 356 p.
Memories of Yeats, *passim* (see index), especially 63-65, 90-93. Also on other figures of the Irish literary revival.

841. ZWEIG, STEFAN: *Die Welt von Gestern: Erinnerungen eines Europäers*. Frankfurt: Suhrkamp, 1949 [1944]. 485 p.
A recollection of Yeats reading his own poetry, pp. 181-82.

See also J510, 843, 845, 851, 926a, 1089, 1097, 1101, 1115, 1140, 1324, 1327, 1348, 1505, 1528, 1581, 1605, 1634, 1902, 1904, 2038, 2183, 2239, 2274, 2447, 4212, 4234, 5082, 5188, 5208, 5532-41 and note, 5573, 5592-95, 5751, 5760, 5854a, 5932, 5935, 5945, 5949, 5962, 5999, 6024, 6119, 6120, 6172, 6193, 6213, 6307, 6308, 6354, 6464, 6696, 6704, 6789, 6805, 6824, 6873, 6891, 6910, 6948, 6951, 6967, 6978, 7026, 7027, 7119, 7235, 7244, 7270, 7294, 7412, 7446, 7475.

BC   Letters to Yeats

841a. FOX, MICHAEL, and T. J. BRENNAN: "The New York Gaelic Society Denounce 'The Play Boy,'" *Irish World and American Industrial Liberator*, 41:2147 (21 Oct 1911), 7.
Letter addressed to Yeats. More denunciations of Yeats and of Synge's plays can be found in preceding and subsequent issues.

842. JOHNSON, LIONEL: "Some Letters." Edited by Raymond Roseliep, Editor's Ph.D. thesis, U of Notre Dame, 1954. 221 p. (*DA*, 15:3 [1955], 418.)
Contains three letters to Yeats: 26 Oct 1892 (pp. 127-28), 8 May 1894 (p. 147), 23 Oct 1894 (pp. 154-57).

843. JOYCE, JAMES: *Letters*. Edited by Stuart Gilbert and Richard Ellmann. NY: Viking Press, 1957-66. 3 v.
Letters from Joyce to Yeats, 1:71-72, 83-84, 94-95, 325; 2:321-22, 363; 3:100, 380-81, 384. Letters from Yeats to Joyce, 2:13-14, 17, 23-24, 58, 363, 405; 3:77. Letters from Yeats to Pound, 2:352, 388. Letter from Pound to Yeats, 2:354. Letter from Yeats to Edward Marsh, 2:381. Numerous other references to Yeats (see index in vols. 1 and 3).

844. LAWRENCE, THOMAS EDWARD: *The Letters*. Edited by David Garnett. London: Cape, 1938. 896 p.
See pp. 743-44 for the letter, signed T. E. Shaw, in which Lawrence rejects his nomination to the Irish Academy of Letters.

845. MOORE, GEORGE: "The Letters of George Moore to Edmund Gosse, W. B. Yeats, R. I. Best, Miss Nancy Cunard, and Mrs. Mary Hutchinson. Edited by Charles Joseph Burkhart," Editor's Ph.D. thesis, U of Maryland, 1958. xxvi, 410 p. (*DA*, 19:1 [July 1958], 131.)
Moore's letters to Yeats (1897-1901) are on pp. 254-74. They are mostly concerned with work on *Diarmuid and Grania*, also with *The*

Countess Cathleen and *Where There Is Nothing*. Other references to Yeats, *passim* (see index), particularly 196, where Moore condemns *Four Plays for Dancers* as "nonsense."

846. POUND, EZRA: "Two Incidents," *Shenandoah*, 4:2/3 (Summer–Autumn 1953), 112-16.
Three letters to Yeats, 1931-32.

847. [RUSSELL, GEORGE WILLIAM]: *Some Passages from the Letters of AE to W. B. Yeats*. Dublin: Cuala Press, 1936. iii, 64 p.
Reprinted °Shannon: Irish UP, 1971. Some of the letters appear, newly transcribed, in J788.
Reviews:
1. J. M. Hone, "An Irish Idealist," *Spectator*, 157:5648 (25 Sept 1936), 508.

848. STEVENSON, ROBERT LOUIS: *The Letters to His Family and Friends*. Selected and edited with notes and introduction by Sidney Colvin. NY: Scribner's, 1899. 2 v.
Letter to Yeats from Vailima, Samoa, dated 14 Apr 1894, praising "Lake Isle of Innisfrae" [*sic*], 2:387-88.

849. SYNGE, JOHN MILLINGTON: *Some Letters of John M. Synge to Lady Gregory and W. B. Yeats*. Selected by Ann Saddlemyer. Dublin: Cuala Press, 1971. vii, 87 p.
Part of a larger project, to be published by the New York Public Library. Mostly concerned with Abbey affairs.
Reviews:
1. Anon., "The Angel of the Abbey," *TLS*, 70:3632 (8 Oct 1971), 1222.

850. WELLESLEY, DOROTHY: *Beyond the Grave: Letters on Poetry to W. B. Yeats from Dorothy Wellesley*. Tunbridge Wells: Baldwin, [1949?]. 63 p.
Letters written to Yeats after his death. Very often they are only marginally concerned with his life and work.

851. WILDE, OSCAR: *The Letters*. Edited by Rupert Hart-Davis. London: Hart-Davis, 1962. xxv, 958 p.
Contains a letter to Yeats [Aug-Sept 1894] re Yeats's *A Book of Irish Verse* (p. 365), also scattered references to Yeats (see index).

852. YEATS, JOHN BUTLER: *Passages from the Letters of John Butler Yeats*. Selected by Ezra Pound. Churchtown, Dundrum: Cuala Press, 1917. viii, 61 p.
Reprinted °Shannon: Irish UP, 1971. Excerpts from letters to WBY, written 1911-16.
  Continued as *Further Letters of John Butler Yeats*. Selected by Lennox Robinson. Churchtown, Dundrum: Cuala Press, 1920. v, 83 p. Reprinted °Shannon: Irish UP, 1971. Extracts from letters written to WBY, 1916-20. See also next item.

853. ————: *Letters to His Son W. B. Yeats and Others, 1869-1922*. Edited with a memoir by Joseph Hone and a preface by Oliver Elton. NY: Dutton, 1946 [1944]. 304 p.
Includes an appendix with extracts from Elizabeth C. Yeats's diary, 1888-89, about family life at Bedford Park. For reviews see J5439-55.

854.————: "Death Exultant: A Poem by John B. Yeats. Commentary by Oliver Edwards," *Rann*, #13 (Oct 1951), 8-10.
A letter from JBY to WBY, which contains the poem.

See also J714, 768, 776, 788, 795, 796, 814, 926a, 1018, 1020, 2092, 4011, 4212, 4214, 4234, 6579, 6703.

BD   Obituaries

This section includes only routine articles; short notes are omitted. More substantial appraisals written on the occasion of Yeats's death are listed in the sections to which they belong (mainly in section CB). Accounts of the burial in Drumcliffe will be found in section CE.

855. ANON.: *Annual Register*, 181 (1939), 425-26.

856. ANON.: "William Butler Yeats, Poet and Patriot," *Christian Century*, 56:7 (15 Feb 1939), 205.

857. ANON.: "William Butler Yeats," *Church of Ireland Gazette*, 84:[] (3 Feb 1939), 72-73.

858. ANON.: "Scoffed at Fairies, but They Made His Living. Wrote 'Innisfree.' Won £7,000 Prize," *Daily Express* [London], #12073 (30 Jan 1939), 5.
    The penny press obituary: "Yeats . . . made a fortune out of fairies. His poems and plays were about places existing only in his mind."

859. ANON.: "W. B. Yeats: Poet, Playwright and Politician. Death at Mentone," *Daily Telegraph*, #26103 (30 Jan 1939), 13.

860. ANON.: "William Butler Yeats," *Deutsche Rundschau*, yr 65 / 258:3 (Mar 1939), 210-11.

861. ANON.: "W. B. Yeats," *Evening Mail*, #28646 (30 Jan 1939), 4.

862. ANON.: "W. B. Yeats Dead in Mentone," *Irish Press*, 9:25 (30 Jan 1939), 1, 7.
    With an unknown photograph of Yeats in a rose garden. See also editorial, "A Great Poet Passes," 8.

863. ANON.: "De mortuis . . . ," *Irish Rosary*, 43:3 (Mar 1939), 161-65.
    Yeats's work does not express the "truth" (because he was not Catholic), only "the effulgence of the fanciful and the fantastic."

864. ANON.: "Death of Mr. Yeats: Poet of European Reputation [. . .]," *Irish Times*, 81:25444 (30 Jan 1939), 7-8.
    See also editorial, p. 6; "Burial of W. B. Yeats [. . .]," :25445 (31 Jan 1939), 7; Desmond Fitzgerald, "W. B. Yeats: An Appreciation," :25446 (1 Feb 1939), 5; Kitty Clive, "Echoes of the Town: W. B. Yeats' Last Letter," :25448 (3 Feb 1939), 4 (to T. J. Kiernan; cf. J155).

865. ANON.: "William Butler Yeats, 73, Dies; Led Irish Literary Renaissance," *NYHT*, 98:33678 (30 Jan 1939), 8.

866. ANON.: "W. B. Yeats Dead; Famous Irish Poet [. . .]," *NYT*, 88:29591 (30 Jan 1939), 13.
    See also editorial, "William Butler Yeats," :29592 (31 Jan 1939), 20; and a report, "Yeats Is Mourned All over Ireland," 21.

867. ANON.: "William Butler Yeats," *Listener*, 21:525 (2 Feb 1939), 247.
    Text of a broadcast in the B.B.C. News Bulletin.

868. ANON.: "W. B. Yeats"; "W. B. Yeats: A Great Figure in Letters"; "Death of W. B. Yeats: A Great Irish Poet and Dramatist," *Manchester Guardian*, #28817 (30 Jan 1939), 8, 9, 13.

869. ANON., *Nation*, 148:6 (4 Feb 1939), 135.

870. ANON.: "William Butler Yeats," *Publishers' Weekly*, 135:5 (4 Feb 1939), 597.

871. ANON.: "William Butler Yeats," *Round Table*, 29:115 (June 1939), 597.

872. ANON.: "W. B. Yeats," *Saturday Night*, 54:14 (4 Feb 1939), 1.

873. ANON.: "William Butler Yeats: Famous Irish Poet Dies on Riviera," *Scotsman*, #29851 (30 Jan 1939), 11.

874. ANON., *TAM*, 23:3 (Mar 1939), 160-61.

875. ANON.: "Mr. W. B. Yeats: A Great Irish Poet and Dramatist," *Times*, #48216 (30 Jan 1939), 14.

876. B[ENÉT], W. R.: "William Butler Yeats, 1865-1939," *SatR*, 19:15 (4 Feb 1939), 8.

877. B[ODKIN], T[HOMAS]: "Obituary: Mr. W. B. Yeats," *Birmingham Post*, #25130 (30 Jan 1939), 14.

878. CALVERTON, V. F., *Current History*, 50:292 (Mar 1939), 46.

879. CATTAUI, GEORGES: "Rencontres avec Yeats: Un grand poète celtique vient de mourir à Menton," *Nouvelles littéraires*, #851 (4 Feb 1939), 1, 9.

880. CAZAMIAN, M.-L.: "William Butler Yeats, 1865-1939," *EA*, 3:2 (Apr-June 1939), 127-31.

881. CHAKRAVARTY, AMIYA: "William Butler Yeats," *Modern R*, 65:387 (Mar 1939), 326-29.

882. CHAUVIRÉ, ROGER: "Yeats: Avec Yeats a disparu un grand poète," *Journal des débats politiques et littéraires*, 151:85 (9 Apr 1939), 4.

883. CLEMENS, CYRIL: "The Passing of W. B. Yeats," *Canadian Bookman*, 22 [i.e., 21]:2 (June-July 1939), 21-25.
    See J152.

884. COLUM, PADRAIC: "The Greatness of W. B. Yeats: With His Passing Goes the Foremost Poet of His Time," *NYTBR*, 44:7 (12 Feb 1939), 1, 17.

885. COUSINS, J. H.: "Yeats—the Immortal," *Madras Mail*, 72:36 (5 Feb 1939), 6.

886. [COWLEY, MALCOLM]: "Yeats," *New Republic*, 98:1262 (8 Feb 1939), 4.

887. DREUX, ROBERT: "W. B. Yeats, prix Nobel de littérature, est mort: Ecrivain de langue anglaise, il avait l'inspiration strictement irlandaise," *Ordre*, 11:3277 (31 Jan 1939), 5.

888. ERVINE, ST. JOHN: "Mr. Yeats," *Observer*, 148:7706 (5 Feb 1939), 13.

889. GARNETT, DAVID: "W. B. Yeats," *NSt*, 17:415 (4 Feb 1939), 174.
    Correspondence by Sean O'Faolain, :416 (11 Feb 1939), 209, corroborating Garnett's contention that Yeats had a powerful political influence on his generation.

890. GILLET, LOUIS: "W. B. Yeats (1865-1939)," *Revue des deux mondes*, per 8 / yr 109 / 50:1 (1 Mar 1939), 219-23.

891. GLENDINNING, ALEX: "Commentary," *Nineteenth Century and After*, 125: 745 (Mar 1939), 352-55.

892. GOGARTY, OLIVER ST. JOHN: "Yeats," *Evening Standard*, #35697 (30 Jan 1939), 3.

893. GRAY, HUGH: "The Spoken Word: W. B. Yeats," *Listener*, 21:528 (23 Feb 1939), 439.

How the B.B.C. failed to present an adequate appreciation of Yeats's life and work when he died.

894. GRUBB, H. T. HUNT: "A Poet Passes," *Poetry R*, 30:2 (Mar-Apr 1939), 149-51.

895. GWYNN, STEPHEN: "W. B. Yeats: A Great Personality. The Man and His Measure," *Observer*, 148:7706 (5 Feb 1939), 8.

896. ————: "The Passing of W. B. Yeats," *Fortnightly R*, os 151 / ns 145: 867 (Mar 1939), 347-49.

897. LO DUCA, [GIUSEPPE]: "Yeats," *Larousse mensuel illustré*, 11:389 (July 1939), 460.

898. LYND, ROBERT: "The Greatest Poet Is Dead," *News Chronicle*, #28937 (30 Jan 1939), 6.

899. MACCARTHY, DESMOND: "W. B. Yeats," *Sunday Times*, #6043 (5 Feb 1939), 6.

900. *The New International Year Book: A Compendium of the World's Progress for the Year 1939*. NY: Funk & Wagnalls, 1940. xv, 822 p.
    See pp. 813-14.

901. NOYES, HENRY: "William Butler Yeats," *Canadian Poetry Mag*, 3:4 (Apr 1939), 5-10.

902. O'FAOLÁIN, SEÁN: "William Butler Yeats," *Spectator*, 162:5771 (3 Feb 1939), 183.

903. O'NEILL, DERMOT: "William Butler Yeats," *New Northman*, 7:1 (Spring 1939), 3-4.

904. O'NEILL, SEAMUS: "W. B. Yeats," *Leader*, 77:25 (25 Feb 1939), 639.

905. PFISTER, KURT: "William Yeats †," *Fränkischer Kurier*, 106:37 (6 Feb 1939), 11.

906. PRATI, RAFFAELLO: "William Butler Yeats," *Circoli*, yr 8 / ser 4 / #2 (Feb 1939), 207-8.

907. S., E.: "Der Dichter der irischen Wiedergeburt: Zum Tode von William Butler Yeats," *Berliner Börsenzeitung*, 84:55 (2 Feb 1939), Beilage Volk und Kultur, #28, p. 1.

908. SPEAIGHT, ROBERT: "William Butler Yeats," *Commonweal*, 29:23 (31 Mar 1939), 623-24.

909. ST[AMM], R[UDOLF]: "William Butler Yeats," *National-Zeitung*, 97:52 (1 Feb 1939), 2.

910. STARKIE, WALTER: "Poet Immortalized Celtic Lore: Tributes to the Late Dr. W. B. Yeats," *Irish Independent*, 48:25 (30 Jan 1939), 9.
    See also the anonymous obituary, p. 10.

911. STRONG, L. A. G.: "Yeats," *Time and Tide*, 20:5 (4 Feb 1939), 130-31.

912. SWIFT, GEORGE: "In Memoriam: William Butler Yeats," *America*, 60:1533 (25 Feb 1939), 498-99.
    Lame attempt at a satirical evaluation of Yeats's work.

913. WAGNER, LUDWIG: "Ein grosser Dichter ist gestorben: Zum Tode von W. B. Yeats," *Münchener Neueste Nachrichten*, 92:37 (6 Feb 1939), 4.
    Reprinted with slight revisions in *Blätter der Städtischen Bühnen Frankfurt am Main*, 6:19 (1939), 219-21, 224.

BE   The Yeats Family

For the purpose of this bibliography, the Yeats family is defined by its three most illustrious members, John Butler Yeats, WBY, and Jack Yeats, and by WBY's sisters Elizabeth Corbet (Lolly) and Susan Mary (Lily) Yeats. I also include material on WBY's ancestors, his wife, and his children. The listing is highly selective. Only those items will be found that have some bearing on WBY; hence discussions exclusively concerned with, e.g., Jack Yeats's paintings are excluded.

914. ANON.: "Where W. B. Yeats Will Lie [. . .] Associations of Drumcliffe," *Irish Times*, 81:25450 (6 Feb 1939), 8.
   On WBY's ancestors.

915. ARNOLD, BRUCE: *A Concise History of Irish Art*. London: Thames & Hudson, 1969. 216 p.
   Some notes on John BY and WBY, more extended remarks on Jack Yeats, *passim* (see index).

916. COLUM, PADRAIC: "John Butler Yeats," *Atlantic Monthly*, 172:1 (July 1943), 81-85.

917. ————: "My Memories of John Butler Yeats," *Dublin Mag*, 32:4 (Oct-Dec 1957), 8-16.

918. GILL, W. W.: "Pollexfen in W. B. Yeats' Ancestry," *N&Q*, 187:[] (30 Dec 1944), 294-95.

919. GREHAN, IDA: "Miss Yeats, and the Problem of Living in a Poet's Shadow," *Daily Telegraph*, #35985 (15 Jan 1971), 15.

919a. KENNY ART GALLERY, GALWAY: *An Exhibition of Paintings and Drawings by Jack B. Yeats*. Official opening on Friday 23rd of April [1971] by Anne Yeats. [Galway: Kenny, 1971]. 13 p.
   See pp. 1-3 for Anne Yeats's reminiscences of her uncle.

920. LETSKY, NAOMI M.: "John Butler Yeats," M.A. thesis, Columbia U, 1941. i, 117 p.
   Attempts "to give a complete account of the life and work of John Butler Yeats" (p. 1).

921. MCHUGH, ROGER (ed): *Jack B. Yeats: A Centenary Gathering*. Dublin: Dolmen Press, 1971. 114 p. (Tower Series of Anglo-Irish Studies. 3.)
   References to WBY appear *passim*.

922. MURPHY, WILLIAM M.: "The Ancestry of William Butler Yeats," *Yeats Studies*, #1 (Bealtaine 1971), 1-19.

923. *————: *The Yeats Family and the Pollexfens of Sligo*. With drawings by John Butler Yeats. Dublin: Dolmen Press, 1971. 88 p. (New Yeats Papers. 1.)
   A short biography of the Pollexfen family from about the middle of the 19th century down to WBY (whose mother was born Susan Mary Pollexfen). Includes a genealogical table and 14 drawings by John Butler Yeats. See also J123.
   Reviews:
   1. Mary Lappin, "J.B., Jack B., W.B.," *Irish Press*, 42:43 (19 Feb 1972), 12.
   2. Eilean Ni Chuilleanain, "Yeats, Gogarty and Others," *Irish Times*, #36079 (29 Jan 1972), 10.

924. RASCOE, BURTON: *Before I Forget*. Garden City: Doubleday, Doran, 1937. xix, 442 p.
   "John Butler Yeats on His Son and on Various Matters," 413-14.

924a. SHEEHY, JEANNE: "John Butler Yeats," *Hibernia*, 36:21 (17 Nov 1972), 18.

925. TYNAN, KATHARINE: *Memories*. London: Nash & Grayson, 1924. v, 432 p.
   "Artist and Philosopher—John Butler Yeats," 273-87.

926. WHITE, JAMES: *John Butler Yeats and the Irish Renaissance*. With pictures from the collection of Michael Butler Yeats and from the National Gallery of Ireland. Dublin: Dolmen Press, 1972. 72 p. (New Yeats Papers. 5.)
   An appreciation of JBY as a portrait painter; reproductions of 32 paintings (black and white), including some of leading figures of the Irish literary revival; and a catalogue of the anniversary exhibition in the National Gallery of Ireland, 1972.

926a. YEATS, JOHN BUTLER: *Letters from Bedford Park*. A selection from the correspondence (1890-1901) of John Butler Yeats, edited with introduction and notes by William M. Murphy. Dublin: Cuala Press, 1972. x, 79 p.
   Contains some letters to WBY (pp. 6-7, 49, 53-58, 63, 66-68), who is also mentioned *passim*.

See also J531, 544, 576, 598, 601, 603, 604a, 681, 691, 731, 752, 762, 782, 825, 827, 834, 852-54, 1101, 1181, 1185, 1208, 1581, 1813a, 1995a, 2272-75, 2391, 3068, 4076a, 5439-55, 5940 (#21), 5948, 6067, 6213, 6364, 7441, 7442, 7460-83.

BF   Interviews with Yeats

Items in this and the following section BG are not listed alphabetically but chronologically. The reason for this deviation from my general policy is that interviews and reported lectures can almost be considered primary material. Moreover, nothing is gained by accumulating the material under many ANON.s; most interviewers and reporters remain unknown. In all these cases, I merely give the headlines or titles without an added ANON.
   I am afraid that both sections are rather incomplete; I confess that I did not have the time and the opportunity to go systematically through the newspapers of all the places Yeats visited in his life. With his striking figure, pronounced habits, and unusual convictions, he must have been an easy and rewarding target for any reporter with a fair knowledge of modern literature.

927. D[UNLOP], D. N.: "Interview with Mr. W. B. Yeats," *Irish Theosophist*, 2:2 (15 Nov 1893), 147-49 [i.e., 15-17].
   Reprinted and misdated in J61, pp. 298-302.

928. "The New Irish Literary Movement," *Daily Mail*, #1565 (26 Apr 1901), 3.
   Interview in which Yeats expresses the optimistic opinion that Ireland will be bilingual in 50 years. See Yeats's letter, J136a.

929. "Mr. W. B. Yeats and the Irish Revival," *Free Lance*, 2:42 (20 July 1901), 363.
   Yeats predicts a dominant role for the Irish language among the intelligent and maintains that the average Irishman is more intelligent than the average Englishman. See Yeats's disclaimer in J137; the interviewer's correspondence, :48 (31 Aug 1901), 508; Yeats's answer,

:51 (21 Sept 1901), 578-79 (Wp. 360); and the interviewer's comment, *ibid.*

930. A., P.: "Views and Interviews: Mr. W. B. Yeats Talks about the Gaelic Movement and the Parliamentary Party," *Echo*, #10378 (25 Apr 1902), 1.
See also J2373.

931. "A Poet's Discovery: Speaking to the Psaltery. Mr. Yeats Interviewed," *Irish Daily Independent and Daily Nation*, #3336 (31 Oct 1902), 5.
A short report of Yeats's speech appears as "Celtic Literary Society: Speaking to Musical Notes," #3338 (3 Nov 1902), 2.

932. CAREW, KATE: "'I Find New York Like Paris, the Buoyancy--the Grace-- the Atmosphere!' Says William Butler Yeats, the Irish Poet," *World*, 44: 15433 (22 Nov 1903), Magazine Section, M3.

933. "Did Not Find Barbarians: William Butler Yeats, Leaving America, Expresses Astonishment," *NYT*, 53:16905 (10 Mar 1904), 1.

934. "A Poet's Lecture Tour: Mr. W. B. Yeats on America's 'Intellectual Curiosity,'" *Pall Mall Gazette*, 78:12160 (25 Mar 1904), 6.
An interview on American literature.

935. M., R.: "The National Theatre Society: Its Work and Ambitions. A Chat with Mr. W. B. Yeats," *Dublin Evening Mail*, #21200 (31 Dec 1904), 4.

936. "Mr. Yeats Interviewed," *Cambridge Daily News*, 17:5331 (25 Nov 1905), [3].
Yeats's views of the theater. The same page carries a review of the "Irish National Actors" and of a performance of *On Baile's Strand*.

937. "Art and Agriculture: The Academy Report. Views of Mr. W. B. Yeats: 'Committees Make Bad Galleries,'" *Evening Telegraph*, ns #7905 (8 Dec 1906), 5.
Yeats's views on a proposal that the Hibernian Academy be administered by the Agricultural and Technical Department.

938. "Abbey Theatre Scene: Interview with Mr. W. B. Yeats," *Evening Telegraph*, ns #7948 (29 Jan 1907), 3-4.
Re Synge's *Playboy*. See also p. 2, containing W. G. Fay's speech, and of course the preceding and following issues of this and other papers; e.g., letter by "A Commonplace Person," *Freeman's J*, 140:[] (30 Jan 1907), 8; interview in *Irish Independent*, 16:26 (30 Jan 1907), 5; in *Dublin Evening Mail*, #22850 (1 Feb 1907), 5; in *Evening Herald*, 16:28 (1 Feb 1907), 5; in *Evening Telegraph*, ns #7952 (2 Feb 1907), 5.

939. "Mr. Shaw's Play," *Times*, #39047 (25 Aug 1909), 5.
Quotes Yeats's defense of *The Shewing-Up of Blanco Posnet* in "the course of a conversation to-day."

940. UA FHLOINN, RIOBÁRD: Interview with Yeats on politics and the drama, *Irish Nation*, 2:76 (11 June 1910), 5.

941. "Irish Drama. Interview with Mr. W. B. Yeats: Politics and Plays. £5000 Wanted," *Observer*, 119:6213 (19 June 1910), 10.

942. "Abbey Theatre: New System of Stage Scenery Invented by Famous Theatrical Manager to Be Tried on Thursday. Interesting Interview with Mr. Yeats," *Evening Telegraph*, ns #9182 (9 Jan 1911), 3.
The Craig screens. A review of the performance of *The Hour Glass* by M. M. O'H. appears in #9186 (12 Jan 1911), 3-4.

943. "The Irish National Theatre: A Chat with Mr. W. B. Yeats," *Pall Mall Gazette*, #14391 (9 June 1911), 5.
See also the letter in which Yeats corrects the statement that he had "acquired" Gordon Craig's stage sets (J140).

944. "The Abbey Theatre. Mr. Yeats Interviewed: A Successful Year [. . .]," *Evening Telegraph*, ns #9313 (10 June 1911), 5.
Yeats on realistic drama.

945. "The Irish Plays," *Outlook*, 99:8 (21 Oct 1911), 397-98.
A report of a Yeats interview with the New York *Evening Sun* (which I have been unable to find).

945a. "Interview with Mr. W. B. Yeats," *Freeman's J*, 145:[] (19 Jan 1912), 7.
On the arrest of the Abbey Players in Philadelphia because of the *Playboy* performance.

945b. "Meaning of *The Playboy*: Mr. W. B. Yeats Interviewed," *Irish Independent*, 21:18 (20 Jan 1912), 5.

946. "Abbey Players in America: Some Reflections on the Visit [. . .]," *Irish Times*, 54:17071 (16 Mar 1912), 7.
An interview with Yeats and Lennox Robinson.

947. Lunn, Hugh [later HUGH KINGSMILL]: "An Interview with Mr. W. B. Yeats," *Hearth and Home*, 44:1124 (28 Nov 1912, Christmas Number), 229.
Yeats on Shaw, Synge, and Irish politics. See also J704.

948. B., M. M.: "The Poet and Modern Life: Mr. W. B. Yeats in Praise of the Medieval," *Daily News and Leader*, #20848 (3 Jan 1913), 12.
Interview on the function of poetry and art in general. Reprinted in *Freeman's J*, 146:[] (4 Jan 1913), 8, and in *REL*, 4:3 (July 1963), 12-13.

949. "The Gordon Craig Exhibition in Dublin: An Interview with Mr. Yeats," *Irish Times*, 55:17376 (8 Mar 1913), 7-8.

950. O'B., F. C.: "Stage Setting: Mr. G. Craig's Exhibition," *Freeman's J*, 146:[] (19 Mar 1913), 8.

951. BRISTOWE, SYBIL: "Mr. W. B. Yeats: Poet and Mystic. An Interview," *T. P.'s Weekly*, 21:543 (4 Apr 1913), 421.
Correspondence by Raymond Crompton Rhodes and F. Sheehy Skeffington, "The Irish National Theatre," :545 (18 Apr 1913), 504, and :547 (2 May 1913), 566, correcting statements concerning the Fay brothers and Fred Ryan. The interview was reprinted, together with an introductory note by G[regor] Sarrazin, in *Neueren Sprachen*, 21:4 (July 1913), 242-47.

952. MARSHALL, MARGUERITE MOOERS: "Reaction from the 'Sugar-Candy' Drama, Says Poet Yeats, Has Produced the Vice Play. Great Drama of the Future, He Predicts, Will Come from This Country and Not England, Where a Few Stale Themes Are in Control," *Evening World* [NY], 7 Feb 1914, 3.

953. "'American Literature Still in Victorian Era'--Yeats. Irish Poet and Dramatist Says Our Pet Phrase, 'Moral Uplift,' Proves This, and Laments That Erin, While It Is Now Turning Out a Big Crop of Tragedies, Is Producing No Comedies," *NYT*, 63:20483 (22 Feb 1914), Section V, 10.

954. NOGUCHI, YONE: "A Japanese Poet on W. B. Yeats," *Bookman* [NY], 43:4 (June 1916), 431-33.

955. "Dispute about a Picture Gallery: Sir Hugh Lane's Unsigned Codicil. England or Ireland? Appeal to the National Gallery. Interview with Mr. W. B. Yeats," *Observer*, 125:6551 (10 Dec 1916), 6.
>Reprinted in J128b. See also "Sir Hugh Lane's Pictures: Mr. W. B. Yeats's Reply," :6552 (17 Dec 1916), 12 (another interview); correspondence by Lady Gregory and W. B. Yeats, :6553 (24 Dec 1916), 12; by Robert C. Witt, D. S. MacColl, and Charles Aitken, :6554 (31 Dec 1916), 14; by D. S. MacColl, 126:6556 (14 Jan 1917), 14. A further reply by Yeats was published in :6557 (21 Jan 1917), 12. There are also other letters during this period not directly concerned with Yeats's position.

956. "Irish Poet Tells of Storms at Home: William Butler Yeats Says Self-Government to Suit the People Must Come. Is Opposed to Coercion," *NYT*, 69:22646 (25 Jan 1920), Section II, 3.

957. WILKINSON, MARGUERITE: "Irish Literature Discussed by William Butler Yeats in an Interview," *Touchstone*, 8:2 (Nov 1920), 81-85.

958. "The Pillar: Question of Its Removal. Various Viewpoints," *Evening Telegraph*, ns #12378 (25 Aug 1923), 4.
>Part of an interview with Yeats, who is in favor of removal for aesthetic reasons.

959. "Irish Poet Honoured: Nobel Prize Awarded Senator Yeats. Tribute to Synge [. . .]," *Freeman's J*, 156:[] (15 Nov 1923), 5.
>An interview. On the same page: "Inspired in Sligo. Senator Yeats Tells of Early Impressions" (report of a lecture). See also the editorial on p. 4, "Poet and Patriot."

960. "Irish Poet Honoured: Nobel Prize for Mr. Yeats. Our Special Interview," *Irish Times*, 65:20778 (15 Nov 1923), 7.
>An interview on the Irish literary revival. See also the editorial on p. 6, "The Poet's Crown."

961. CUMBERLAND, GERALD: *Written in Friendship: A Book of Reminiscences*. NY: Brentano's, 1924. 308 p.
>An interview with Yeats in Maud Gonne's drawing room, pp. 15-18.

962. "How to Restore the Arts: Mr. Yeats's Views [. . .]," *Irish Times*, 66:20838 (26 Jan 1924), 7.
>On the possibility of appointing a fine arts committee by the state.

963. "From Democracy to Authority: Paul Claudel and Mussolini—A New School of Thought," *Irish Times*, 66:20856 (16 Feb 1924), 9.

964. "Censorship in Ireland. The Free State Bill: Senator W. B. Yeats's Views," *Manchester Guardian*, #25579 (22 Aug 1928), 5.
>See also the comment in *Irish Independent*, 37:201 (23 Aug 1928), 5, "Censorship Bill: Mr. Yeats's Peculiar Views. Sneers at 'Zealots.'"

965. "As a Bee--Not as a Wasp: Senator Yeats in His Old Age," *Irish Independent*, 37:252 (22 Oct 1928), 6.
>Part of an interview published in the *Observer* (which I have been unable to find).

966. MORGAN, LOUISE: *Writers at Work*. London: Chatto & Windus, 1931. viii, 71 p. (Dolphin Books. 11.)
>"W. B. Yeats," 1-9; based on an interview, "How Writers Work: W. B. Yeats on the Future of Poetry," *Everyman*, 5:126 (25 June 1931), 683-84.

967. "A Poet Broadcasts: W. B. Yeats in Belfast. His First Experience in Front of a Microphone. An Interview on the Drama," *Belfast News-Letter*, 195:[] (9 Sept 1931), 6.
See also a photograph on p. 7.

968. "Greek Play over Radio: Abbey Players in Belfast. Mr. Yeats Explains the Broadcast," *Irish Times*, 73:23204 (9 Sept 1931), 4.
The Greek play was Yeats's version of Sophocles's *King Oedipus*.

969. "Yeats's 'Hello to Everybody!' Famous Irish Poet 'on the Air' for the First Time," *Northern Whig and Belfast Post*, #38384 (9 Sept 1931), 3.
An interview and a photograph.

970. "Joyce Rejects Bid of Irish Academy [. . .]," *NYT*, 82:27306 (28 Oct 1932), 17.
The same page carries a note that Yeats was elected an honorary member of the New York Authors Club.

971. SUGRUE, THOMAS: "Irish Writers Ignorant Lot, Yeats Asserts. Only Read Dante, Homer, Shakespeare and Such, Playwright-Poet Says. Evades Politics Deftly. Expects U.S. to Believe O'Neill Is Its Best Writer," *NYHT*, 92:31393 (28 Oct 1932), 19.

972. GILBERT, DOUGLAS: "Yeats, Who Once Spun Erin's Gossamer Dreams, Now Grows Eloquent on Irish Taxation Problem. At 67, Poet and Mystic Dismisses the Past, Discusses Economics and Politics—Calls Machine Age 'a Period of Terror' for the Artist," *NY World-Telegram*, 65:114 (12 Nov 1932), 4.

973. WOOLF, S. J.: "Yeats Foresees an Ireland of Reality: The Poet Describes the Turning of the Country from Romance to the Stern Task of Building," *NYT*, 82:27322 (13 Nov 1932), Section VI, 7, 19.

974. "Yeats, Sailing, Pays Tribute to Moore: Praises Realistic Force and Courage of the Writing of the Late Irish Novelist [. . .]," *NYT*, 82:27393 (23 Jan 1933), 11.

975. "Abbey Theatre Changes: Proposed Advisory Committee. Interview with Dr. W. B. Yeats," *Irish Times*, 77:24222 (23 Feb 1935), 5.
Correspondence by Frank O'Connor and Sean O'Faolain, :24224 (26 Feb 1935), 4; further correspondence in subsequent issues.

976. "W. B. Yeats Looks Back: Poet Celebrates His Seventieth Birthday [. . .]," *Irish Press*, 5:141 (14 June 1935), 7.

977. "W. B. Yeats Looks Back: Ireland in the Early Days of the Abbey Theatre," *Irish Press*, 5:245 (14 Oct 1935), 9.
A radio interview.

See also J730, 822, 2282, 3838, 3859, 3874, 6104, 7287, 7359.

BG Reports and Summaries of Speeches and Lectures

See the headnote to the preceding section BF for an explanation of structure and contents of this section.

978. "The Young Ireland League: Lecture by Mr. W. B. Yeats," *United Ireland*, 13:635 (4 Nov 1893), 3.
A lecture on "Irish Fairy Tales."

979. "Mr. W. B. Yeats in Belfast—Irish Fairy Lore," *United Ireland*, 13:639 (2 Dec 1893), 3.

980. "The Delegates Dinner," *Irish Homestead*, 3:36 (6 Nov 1897), 741-42.
Summary of a lecture on the new Irish literature.

980a. O'DONNELL, F. HUGH: "'The Celtic Movement' at the London Irish
Literary Society," *United Ireland*, 17:849 (11 Dec 1897), 5.
Report of a Yeats lecture of that title. "Mr. Yeats illustrated his
weirdly witching theories by several apposite readings from soulful
bards . . . [he] did not often transgress into the region of facts.
. . ." A more objective report can be found on p. 2 of the same issue
("The Celtic Movement: Interesting Lecture by Mr. Yeats").

981. "National Literary Society 'at Home,'" *Daily Express*, #14515 (10 Jan
1899), 6.
Résumé of a speech on the inauguration of the Irish Literary Theatre.
See also a commentary on p. 5; Yeats's letter "Irish Literary Theatre,"
#14517 (12 Jan 1899), 5 (Wp. 356); a commentary on this letter, p. 4;
and Yeats's article "The Irish Literary Theatre," #14519 (14 Jan 1899),
3 (Wp. 356).

982. "Dramatic Ideals and the Irish Literary Theatre," *Freeman's J*, 133:
[] (8 May 1899), 6.

983. "Ideal of Irish Drama: An Interesting Lecture. Mr. W. B. Yeats and
His Critics," *Irish Daily Independent*, 8:109 (8 May 1899), 8.

984. "Trinity College and the Literary Theatre: Speech of Mr. W. B. Yeats,"
Daily Express, #14636 (1 June 1899), 5.
A debate on the subject "That any attempt to further an Irish Literary
Movement would result in Provincialism."

985. Summary of Yeats's lecture on the Irish literary movement, *Claidheamh
Soluis*, 1:13 (10 June 1899), 200.
See a letter in defense of Yeats by Thomas C. Murray, :15 (24 June
1899), 229, and the editorial, 233; a leader in :16 (1 July 1899),
248-49, and in :17 (8 July 1899), 264-65; Murray's answer, :18 (15
July 1899), 277-78; further letters by C. J. Murphy, :22 (12 Aug 1899),
344-45, :23 (19 Aug 1899), 362, and :27 (16 Sept 1899), 422-23.

986. "Dr. Douglas Hyde on the Irish Language Movement: Speech by Mr. W. B.
Yeats," *Daily Express*, #14687 (31 July 1899), 6.
A speech on Hyde and the Gaelic League.

987. "Irish Literary Theatre: Yesterday's Luncheon. Mr. George Moore on
the Celtic Revival," *Daily Express*, #14863 (23 Feb 1900), 6.
Speeches by Hyde, Moore, Yeats, and others. See editorial in the
same issue, p. 4.

988. "The Irish Literary Theatre: Speech by Mr. George Moore," *Freeman's
J*, 134:[] (23 Feb 1900), 6.
Also speeches by Hyde and Yeats. See J987.

989. "Central Branch Sgoruigheacht: Address by Mr. W. B. Yeats," *Claidheamh Soluis*, 2:33 (27 Oct 1900), 516-17.
A speech on the Irish language.

990. O'NEILL, EAMONN: "An Interesting Meeting," *Claidheamh Soluis*, 3:35
(9 Nov 1901), 555.
Summary of a speech on the "nationalisation of art" and comment.

991. "The Irish Fairy Kingdom: Lecture by Mr. W. B. Yeats," *South Wales
Daily News*, #9556 (20 Feb 1903), 6.

992. "An Irish Poet Speaks," *NYT*, 53:16848 (4 Jan 1904), 16.
On "The Intellectual Revival in Ireland."

993. "Plays and Players: Irish National Theatre [. . .]. Speech of Mr.
W. B. Yeats," *Freeman's J*, 138:[] (2 Feb 1905), 6.

993a. [PEARSE, P. H.]: "About Literature," *Claidheamh Soluis*, 7:6 (22 Apr
1905), 7.
On a Yeats speech about "Nationality in Literature."

994. O'DRISCOLL, ROBERT: "Letters and Lectures of W. B. Yeats," *University
R* [Dublin], 3:8 [1966?], 29-55.
Apart from the letters (see Wp. 400), the following items are reprinted: a report of a lecture on "Literature and the Living Voice,"
°*Alma Mater* [Aberdeen], 23 (17 Jan 1906), 136; material on the *Playboy*
controversy from *Freeman's J*, 5 Feb 1907 (see also J7359); a summary
of a lecture preceding a poetry reading from the *Sheffield Daily Telegraph*, #20015 (23 Nov 1922), 8; and two items listed below (J997-98).

995. "The Watts Pictures: Lecture by Mr. W. B. Yeats," *Daily Express*,
#16696 (26 Jan 1906), 7.
A lecture on "The Ideal in Art."

996. "National Theatre Society [. . .]. Mr. Yeats and the Training of the
Actors," *Daily Express*, #16920 (15 Oct 1906), 7.

997. "Mr. W. B. Yeats in Aberdeen. Lecture to Franco Scottish Society:
'The Heroic Poetry of Ireland,'" *Aberdeen Free Press*, #11865 (26 Jan 1907),
3.
See also J994, 998-99.

998. "The Celtic Renaissance," *Bon Accord*, 41:5 (31 Jan 1907), 20.
See J994, 997.

999. "Resumé of a Lecture Given by Mr. W. B. Yeats on Friday, 25th January
1907," *Transactions of the Franco-Scottish Society*, 5:1 (1909), 12-14.
See J997.

1000. "*Playboy*: Abbey Theatre Debate. Some Vigorous Views Expressed by
Citizens. Mr. W. B. Yeats on His Defence," *Irish Independent*, 16:31 (5
Feb 1907), 5-6.
For more material on the *Playboy* affair see index NE (s.v. *Playboy*).
Yeats's various speeches are also summarized in *Evening Telegraph*,
ns #7949 (30 Jan 1907), 2-3; #7954 (5 Feb 1907), 2 (includes a report
of J. B. Yeats's sneer "An island of plaster saints"); and in other
papers.

1000a. "Mr. Yeats Unbosoms Himself on Literature & the Stage. 'The Living
Voice' Poetry in the Aran Isles. Poetic Drama Impossible. Taste of the
People Debased [. . .]. Scarcely Any Intellect in Ireland," *Evening Tele-
graph*, ns #7962 (14 Feb 1907), 2.
The same page carries a report of a discussion on "That decadence is
the prevailing characteristic of the modern stage" at the College
Historical Society, Trinity College, over which Yeats presided.

1001. "Mr. W. B. Yeats on Art. Remarkable Speech: 'The Immoral Irish
Bourgeoisie,'" *Irish Times*, 50:15792 (11 Feb 1908), 7.
Yeats's attack on the bourgeoisie and his views of art for art's sake.
Correspondence by A. Lloyd and R. B. A., :15793 (12 Feb 1908), 5.

1002. "Mr. W. B. Yeats and *The Piper*," *Daily Express*, #19135 (17 Feb 1908),
9.

Yeats's speech on Norreys Connell's play. See also J139.

1002a. [PEARSE, P. H.]: "The Gael in Trinity," *Claidheamh Soluis*, 10:38 (28 Nov 1908), 9.
   The inaugural meeting of the Dublin University Gaelic Society with speeches by Eoin MacNeill, Yeats, Sigerson, and J. P. Mahaffy [!] on "A Plea for Irish Studies."

1003. "Feis Ceoil Association: Address by Mr. W. B. Yeats," *Irish Times*, 51:16104 (10 Feb 1909), 5.

1004. "The Theatre in Ireland: Views of Mr. W. B. Yeats. The Business of Art. 'The Exposition of Human Nature.' A Connacht Story. Mr. Yeats on Newspapers and Politics. English Influence in Gaelic," *Evening Telegraph*, ns #8915 (4 Mar 1910), 2.
   The Connacht story is about Colonel Martin, whose wife was unfaithful to him (see Yeats's poem "Colonel Martin"). See also the next three items.

1005. "Lecture by Mr. W. B. Yeats: English Influence in Gaelic," *Freeman's J*, 143:[] (4 Mar 1910), 10.

1006. "The Theatre and Ireland: Lecture by Mr. W. B. Yeats," *Irish Times*, 52:16435 (4 Mar 1910), 9.
   See also the editorial, :16436 (5 Mar 1910), 6.

1007. "Ireland and the Theatre: Mr. W. B. Yeats at the Ard Chraobh of the Gaelic League," *Irish Nation*, 2:63 (12 Mar 1910), 8.

1008. "Lady Gregory 'at Home' at the Abbey Theatre," *Irish Times*, 52: 16660 (22 Nov 1910), 8.
   Includes a report of a Yeats speech on the Irish theater.

1009. "Spoken Literature," *Times*, #39511 (17 Feb 1911), 10.
   A lecture on "Ireland and the Arts of Speech."

1010. "Yeats upon Irish Drama: His Speech before the Drama League," *BET*, 82:228 (29 Sept 1911), 4.

1011. "A New Theory of Apparitions: Lecture by Mr. W. B. Yeats," *Irish Times*, 54:17017 (13 Jan 1912), 9.
   See also the editorial on p. 6.

1012. "Dinner to Mr. Rabindra Nath Tagore," *Times*, #39950 (13 July 1912), 5.
   Quotes extensively from Yeats's speech.

1013. "Home Rule and Religion: A 'Protest Meeting.' Mr. Yeats and Persecution," *Irish Times*, 55:17340 (25 Jan 1913), 9.
   Reprinted in *REL*, 4:3 (July 1963), 23.

1014. "'The Theatre and Beauty': Lecture by Mr. W. B. Yeats," *Irish Times*, 55:17385 (19 Mar 1913), 5.

1015. "Mr. Yeats's Ideals: Why He Left Politics. An Indian Parallel," *Freeman's J*, 146:[] (24 Mar 1913), 2.
   A lecture on "The Poetry of Rabindranath Tagore."

1016. "The Poetry of Rabindranath Tagore: Lecture by Mr. W. B. Yeats," *Irish Times*, 55:17389 (24 Mar 1913), 11.

1017. "Municipal Art Gallery [. . .]. Mr. Yeats and the 'Audience of the Unborn,'" *Irish Times*, 55:17430 (10 May 1913), 7-8.
   See also the editorial on p. 6.

1018. "Mr. G. B. Shaw and the Cup Finals: One Way to Get a Shakspere Theatre. A Letter Read at a Performance of *Blanco Posnet*," *Manchester Guardian*, #20885 (15 July 1913), 10.
   A letter from GBS to WBY and a summary of Yeats's speech. Reprinted in *REL*, 4:3 (July 1963), 34-35.

1019. "Ghosts and Dreams: Lecture by Mr. W. B. Yeats," *Irish Times*, 55: 17580 (1 Nov 1913), 7.
   A lecture at the Dublin branch of the Psychical Research Society. See also the editorial in the same issue, p. 6, and Yeats's letter, "Mr. W. B. Yeats and Ghosts," :17581 (3 Nov 1913), 6 (Wp. 375).

1020. "Yeats Believes in Ghosts: Poet Tells of Conversations with the Dead in Five Languages," *NYT*, 63:20385 (16 Nov 1913), Section III, 4.

1021. "Award of the Polignac Prize," *Times*, #40382 (29 Nov 1913), 11.
   Yeats's laudatio of James Stephens.

1022. "Mr. Yeats on the New Drama," *Times*, #40416 (9 Jan 1914), 8.
   A lecture on "The Tragic Theatre," in which Yeats favors an aristo-cratic theater of suggestion that is superior to the democratic drama of realism.

1023. ALDINGTON, RICHARD: "Presentation to Mr. W. S. Blunt," *Egoist*, 1:3 (2 Feb 1914), 56-57.
   Blunt, who was given a Gaudier Brzeska sculpture, made a speech in which he criticized Yeats's assumption that plays must be written in blank verse. Part of Yeats's reply follows.

1024. "Says America Will Produce Great Poets and Artists," *Chicago Daily Tribune*, 73:47 (24 Feb 1914), 10.

1025. "Mr. Yeats on Ghosts and Dreams: The Pros and Cons of Spiritism," *Times*, #40506 (24 Apr 1914), 13.

1026. "Ghosts and Dreams: Lecture by Mr. W. B. Yeats," *Christian Common-wealth*, 34:1698 (29 Apr 1914), 527.

1027. "Thomas Davis Centenary: Address by Mr. W. B. Yeats," *Irish Times*, 56:17925 (21 Nov 1914), 9.
   Cf. W208.

1028. "The Irish Theatre," *Times*, #41031 (7 Dec 1915), 5.
   A lecture chaired by Sir Thomas Beecham. Yeats obviously believed even at that time that the Irish theater movement would produce a "real national culture."

1029. "William Blake and His School: Lecture by Mr. W. B. Yeats," *Irish Times*, 60:19056 (15 Apr 1918), 3.
   Also on Calvert and Palmer.

1030. "Psychical Phenomena: Mr. W. B. Yeats and Spiritualism. Advice to the Church and the Press," *Irish Times*, 61:19299 (27 Jan 1919), 6.
   The advice was to stop treating the subject with derision.

1031. "College Historical Society: Socialism and the War [. . .]," *Irish Times*, 61:19302 (30 Jan 1919), 5-6.

1032. "Psychical Research: Debate at the Abbey Theatre," *Irish Times*, 61: 19305 (3 Feb 1919), 6.

1033. "Mr. Yeats's Stories of the Abbey Theatre," *Times*, #42713 (6 May 1921), 8.
   Summary of a fund-raising lecture.

1034. WHELDON, F. W.: "Maddermarket Theatre: Norwich Players in *As You Like It*. A Distinguished Guest," *Eastern Daily Press*, #15605 (27 Sept 1921), 7.
The guest was Yeats, who made a speech comparing Shakespearean and modern theater.

1035. "Mr. W. B. Yeats in Edinburgh," *Scotsman*, #24949 (16 May 1923), 8.
Lecture on "My Own Poetry." See also J1036.

1036. "Senator Yeats on His Poetry," *Irish Independent*, 32:117 (17 May 1923), 6.

1037. "Mr. W. B. Yeats's Secrets: How His Poems Were Inspired," *Irish Times*, 65:20660 (30 June 1923), 8.

1038. "Major Cooper's Candidature [. . .]," *Irish Times*, 65:20708 (25 Aug 1923), 7-8.
Including Yeats's speech of endorsement.

1039. "The Modern Novel: An Irish Author Discussed. Mr. Yeats Admires Good Breeding," *Irish Times*, 65:20773 (9 Nov 1923), 9.
In Jane Austen and Henry James; but does not find it in Dickens. Admires Joyce.

1040. "'The Supernatural': Mr. Yeats and His Poems," *Irish Times*, 65:20778 (15 Nov 1923), 7.
A lecture entitled "Reading and Comments," at the Central Catholic Library. "The audience consisted for the greater part of ladies."

1041. "Abbey's Growth: Senator Yeats Speaks on Irish Drama. Lady Gregory's Art," *Freeman's J*, 156:[] (17 Nov 1923), 8.

1042. "A Poet's Memoirs: Senator Yeats' Advice to Those in Love. Patriotism Defined," *Freeman's J*, 157:[] (26 Jan 1924), 10.
A lecture on his own poetry, especially the love poetry. See J1043.

1043. "My Own Poetry: Mr. Yeats's Reading," *Irish Times*, 66:20838 (26 Jan 1924), 6.
Notes a capacity-plus audience.

1044. "The Old House: Magnificent Building Worthy of Great Country," *Irish Independent*, 33:56 (5 Mar 1924), 7.

1045. "World-Famed Men at the Banquet [. . .]. A Victor at Last. Independent Nation," *Irish Independent*, 33:185 (4 Aug 1924), 4.
Yeats's speech at the Aonach Tailteann Council banquet.

1046. "Laurel Crowns: Tailteann Honours for Irish Men of Letters [. . .]," *Freeman's J*, 157:[] (11 Aug 1924), 6.

1047. "Abbey Theatre: A Government Grant. Act of Intelligent Generosity," *Irish Times*, 67:21315 (10 Aug 1925), 5.
Summary of Yeats's speech in which he thanked the government. See also editorial, "The Irish Drama," 4, and J1048.

1048. "The Abbey Theatre: Mr. W. B. Yeats on Decline of Modern Oratory," *Times*, #44036 (10 Aug 1925), 12.

1049. "Civilization: Mr. W. B. Yeats and France," *Irish Times*, 67:21396 (12 Nov 1925), 8.
A debate at the College Historical Society, "That civilization has progressed since this society first met." Yeats expresses his views about morals and divorce with reference to Ireland and France.

1050. "The Sphere of Woman: Influence in Literature and Politics. Mr. Yeats on Writing a Masterpiece," *Irish Times*, 67:21400 (17 Nov 1925), 8.

1051. "Abbey Theatre Scene [. . .]," *Irish Times*, 68:21474 (12 Feb 1926), 7-8.
  Yeats's speech in defense of O'Casey's *The Plough and the Stars*. See also the editorial, "Cant and Fact," :21475 (13 Feb 1926), 6, and J1052.

1052. "Abbey Theatre Uproar: Impassioned Speech by Mr. Yeats. Audience in Panic. Actors Fight with Republicans," *Manchester Guardian*, #24797 (13 Feb 1926), 11.
  See J1051.

1053. "National Theatre: Senator Yeats Defends Abbey," *Irish Independent*, 35:47 (24 Feb 1926), 8.
  In an answer to the criticism of Norman Reddin. See also J1054.

1054. "What Is a National Theatre. Mr. Reddin and the Abbey. Mr. Yeats on Drama and the Artist," *Irish Times*, 68:21484 (24 Feb 1926), 7-8.

1055. "My Own Poetry: Mr. Yeats Talks and Recites," *Irish Times*, 68:21485 (25 Feb 1926), 6.

1056. "The Lane Pictures: Free State Senate Demands Their Return [. . .]. Mr. W. B. Yeats and the King," *Irish Times*, 68:21604 (15 July 1926), 7.
  Yeats's speech in the Senate. See also the editorial on p. 6, deploring Yeats's "attempt . . . to drag the King into this controversy."

1057. "The Lane Pictures," *Times*, #44325 (16 July 1926), 16.
  See J1056.

1058. "Irish Literature's Position: Senator Yeats on the Bad Past," *Irish Times*, 68:21704 (9 Nov 1926), 6.

1059. "Irish Authors: An Academy of Belles Lettres," *Irish Independent*, 41:224 (19 Sept 1932), 10.
  Yeats's speech at the founding of the Irish Academy of Letters.

1060. "Modern Irish Literature: Four Epochs of Development. Mr. Yeats's Lecture at Ballsbridge," *Irish Times*, 75:23654 (18 Feb 1933), 8.

1061. "Homage to Dr. Yeats: P.E.N. Club's Dinner. Tribute by John Masefield [. . .]," *Irish Times*, 77:24328 (28 June 1935), 7-8.
  Includes a summary of a speech made by Yeats himself.

1062. PATMORE, DEREK: *Private History: An Autobiography*. London: Cape, 1960. 294 p.
  Yeats reading his own poetry in Oxford sometime in 1935, pp. 214-18.

1063. "New Demand for Art Treasures. Government to Press British for Lane Pictures [. . .]," *Irish Independent*, 46:196 (18 Aug 1937), 10.
  Yeats's speech at a dinner given in honor of Patrick McCartan. See also J1064.

1064. "Dinner to Dr. MacCartan [sic]: His Service to Irish Letters. Mr. Yeats to Write a Poem [. . .]," *Irish Times*, 79:24993 (18 Aug 1937), 7-8.
  Yeats's speech on the Lane pictures. The poem is "The Municipal Gallery Revisited."

See also J606, 959, 1178, 1371, 3357, 3623, 3624, 3775, 3785, 3946, 3949, 4143, 4144, 6307, 6594, 7287, 7359.

C THE WORKS (GENERAL SECTION)

CA Books, Pamphlets, and Special Issues of Periodicals Exclusively on Yeats

1065. AGENDA: [Yeats issue], *Agenda*, 9:4-10:1 (Autumn-Winter 1971/72). See the individual contributions by Dale (J2496), Hill (2836), Stallworthy (3233), Sisson (2264), Clothier (3157), and Cox (2903).

1066. AMHERST LITERARY MAGAZINE: "W. B. Yeats Commemorative Issue," *Amherst Literary Mag*, 10:2 (Summer 1964).
"This issue commemorates the fiftieth anniversary of William Butler Yeats' visit to Amherst College" (p. 1). See the individual contributions by Yeats (J161, 3009) and MacLeish (2820).

1067. ARIEL: "A Yeats Number," *Ariel*, 3:3 (July 1972).
A. N. J[effares]: "Editorial," 3-4. See the individual contributions by Elliott (J1994), Huxley (2201), Tomlinson (1984), Clarke (3628), Londraville (2992), Milne (2994), Fullwood (2764), and Martin (3963).

1068. ARROW: "W. B. Yeats Commemoration Number," *Arrow*, Summer 1939.
Contents: 1. L[ennox] R[obinson]: "Foreword," 5.
2. John Masefield: "William Butler Yeats," 5-6; reprinted from *Author, Playwright, and Composer*, 49:3 (Spring 1939), 86-87.
3. F. R. Higgins: "As Irish Poet," 6-8.
4. Austin Clarke: "Poet and Artist," 8-9; reprinted from *Observer*, 148:7706 (5 Feb 1939), 8.
5. Richard Hayes: "His Nationalism," 10-11.
6. Gordon Bottomley: "His Legacy to the Theatre," 11-14; reprinted in J1974.
7. Edmund Dulac: "Without the Twilight," 14-16.
8. William Rothenstein, W. J. Turner, and Oliver St. John Gogarty: "Three Impressions," 16-20.
9. Lennox Robinson: "As Man of the Theatre," 20-21.
Portraits by John B. Yeats, Charles Shannon, Sean O'Sullivan; caricatures by Sir Max Beerbohm and Edmund Dulac. See also J153.
Reviews:
1. Anon., "A Tribute to Yeats," *TAM*, 23:11 (Nov 1939), 837.
2. Stephen Spender, "Honey-Bubblings of the Boilers," *NSt*, 18:455 (11 Nov 1939), 686-87.

1069. BERRYMAN, CHARLES BEECHER: *W. B. Yeats: Design of Opposites. A Critical Study*. NY: Exposition Press, 1967. 149 p.
Based on "W. B. Yeats: Design of Opposites," °Ph.D. thesis, Yale U, 1965. 261 p. (*DA*, 26:8 [Feb 1966], 4624.)
A rather narrow and rigid study, beset with frequent misunderstandings. Discusses *A Vision*, *The Island of Statues*, *The Player Queen*, *The Resurrection*, *John Sherman*, and other prose fiction, "The Song of the Happy Shepherd," "The Sad Shepherd," *The Wanderings of Oisin*, and "Under Ben Bulben."
Reviews:
1. Anon., "Lore of Opposites," *TLS*, 66:3422 (28 Sept 1967), 890.
2. Paul H. Stacy, "Yeats's Dualities: Two Restatements," *Hartford Studies in Literature*, 2:1 (1970), 68-69.

1070. BITHELL, JETHRO: *W. B. Yeats*. Translated [into French] by Franz Hellens. Bruxelles: Lamertin / Paris: Librairie Générale des Sciences, Arts et Lettres, [1913]. 49 p.

Reprinted from *Masque*, ser 2 / #1 (1912), 2-16; #2 (1912), 69-77.
An essay on Yeats's life and work, including French translations
of some of his poems (cf. Wp. 406).
Reviews:
1. Anon., *Academy*, 83:2106 (14 Sept 1912), 340.

1071. BJERSBY, BIRGIT: *The Interpretation of the Cuchulain Legend in the
Works of W. B. Yeats*. Upsala: Lundequist, 1950. 189 p. (Upsala Irish
Studies. 1.)
On "The Death of Cuchulain" (later "Cuchulain's Fight with the Sea"),
On Baile's Strand, *The Golden Helmet* and *The Green Helmet*, *At the
Hawk's Well*, *The Only Jealousy of Emer* and *Fighting the Waves*, "Cuchulain Comforted," and *The Death of Cuchulain*. "In this study, we have
tried to show how the Cuchulain writings present W. B. Yeats in three
aspects, as Poet, as Man and as Interpreter of life. We have tried to
prove that the Cuchulain works occupy a central place in Yeats' writings, that they mirror important events in his own life and that they
are also closely associated with the problems of his outlook upon
life [i.e., with *A Vision*]" (p. 164).
Reviews:
1. Peter Allt, *ES*, 35:1 (Feb 1954), 31-33.
2. Anon., "Aspects of Yeats's Poetry," *TLS*, 50:2574 (1 June 1951), 339.
3. William Becker, *Dublin Mag*, 27:1 (Jan-Mar 1952), 46-48.
4. ————, "On the Margin of Yeats," *Poetry*, 81:5 (Feb 1953), 331-34.
5. Friedrich Biens, *Studia Neophilologica*, 24:1&2 (1952), 155-57.
6. Austin Clarke, "Footlights for Poetry," *Irish Times*, #29223 (7 Apr
1951), 6.
7. A. Norman Jeffares, *RES*, 4:13 (Jan 1953), 86-88.
8. A. Koszul, *EA*, 5:3 (Aug 1952), 263-64.
9. Roger McHugh, "Yeats, Synge, and the Abbey Theatre," *Studies*, 41:
163-64 (Sept-Dec 1952), 333-40.
10. W. H. Stenfert Kroese, "Yeats, gedetailleerd," *Litterair paspoort*,
7:53 (Jan 1952), 11.

1071a. BLÄTTER DER STÄDTISCHEN BÜHNEN FRANKFURT AM MAIN: "Gedenkheft zum
Tode von William Butler Yeats," *Blätter der Städtischen Bühnen Frankfurt
am Main*, 6:19 (1939).
For individual contributions see Yeats (J257a), Wagner (913), Lindemann (3639a).

1072. *BLOOM, HAROLD: *Yeats*. NY: Oxford UP, 1970. xii, 500 p.
A study based on two convictions: (1) Yeats was a Romantic and the
last representative, but also the betrayer, of a tradition that began
with Blake and Shelley; his achievement has to be judged against
theirs; (2) Yeats's achievement has been overrated. On these tenets,
Bloom attempts a revaluation of the entire work, which succeeds on
its own terms but hardly on any others. Bloom also discusses the
influence of Wordsworth, Browning, and Pater, and invokes the parallel
case of Wallace Stevens. For a particularly scathing review of the
book see Torchiana, below.
Reviews:
1. Eavan Boland, *Critic*, 29:3 (Jan 1971), 80-82.
2. James D. Boulger, *Thought*, 45:179 (Winter 1970), 620-23.
3. W. Bronzwaer, *Dutch QR*, 1:1 (1971), 42-43.
4. Gerald L. Bruns, *Spirit*, 38:4 (Winter 1972), 41-45.
5. Kenneth Connelly, "Yeats," *Yale R*, 60:3 (June 1971), 394-403.
6. Allen Grossman, "Harold Bloom's Yeats," *VQR*, 46:3 (Summer 1970),
520-25.

7. John Hollander, "Let a Thousand Blooms . . . ," *Poetry*, 117:1 (Oct 1970), 43-45.
8. A. Norman Jeffares, *RES*, 22:88 (Nov 1971), 514-17.
9. Augustine Martin, *Studies*, 60:237 (Spring 1971), 98-102.
10. George P. Mayhew, *BA*, 45:2 (Spring 1971), 321-22.
11. John Montague, "The Young and the Old Campaigner," *Guardian*, 3 Sept 1970, 7.
12. Harry T. Moore, *SatR*, 53:25 (20 June 1970), 37-39.
13. Thomas Parkinson, *ELN*, 9:3 (Mar 1972), 234-35.
14. Marjorie Perloff, "Yeats as Gnostic," *Contemporary Literature*, 12:4 (Autumn 1971), 554-61.
15. John Pick, *America*, 122:3169 (30 May 1970), 597-98.
16. William H. Pritchard, "Mr. Bloom in Yeatsville," *Partisan R*, 38:1 (Spring 1971), 107-12.
17. John Raymond, "In Yeats' Shadow," *Sunday Times*, #7682 (23 Aug 1970), 26.
18. Sandra Siegel, "Prolegomena to Bloom: The Opposing Virtue," *Diacritics*, 1:2 (Winter 1971), 35-38.
19. Donald T. Torchiana, *MP*, 70:2 (Nov 1972), 168-74.
20. Helen Vendler, *JEGP*, 70:4 (Oct 1971), 691-96.
21. Ann Wordsworth, "Wrestling with the Dead," *Spectator*, 225:7413 (25 July 1970), 74.

1073. *BRADFORD, CURTIS BAKER: *Yeats at Work*. Carbondale: Southern Illinois UP, 1965. xix, 407 p.
Prints, and comments upon, the early drafts of the following poems, plays, and prose pieces: "The Hosting of the Sidhe," "The Host of the Air," "The Lover Asks Forgiveness," "Words," "The Wild Swans at Coole," "Nineteen Hundred and Nineteen," "The Tower" (section 3), "Lullaby," "The Mother of God," "Vacillation" (section 8), "Ribh Considers Christian Love Insufficient," "The Gyres," "The Circus Animals' Desertion," *At the Hawk's Well*, *The Words upon the Window-Pane*, *The Resurrection*, *A Full Moon in March*, *Purgatory*, "The Religion of a Sailor" (from *The Celtic Twilight*), "The Rose of Shadow" and other material from *The Secret Rose*, sections from *Discoveries*, sections from *Autobiographies*, and extracts from *On the Boiler*.
Reviews:
1. Brian John, "Hurt into Poetry: Some Recent Yeats Studies," *J of General Education*, 18:4 (Jan 1967), 299-306.
2. Walther Martin, *ZAA*, 14:3 (1966), 308-12.
3. Giorgio Melchiori, *N&Q*, os 211 / ns 13:11 (Nov 1966), 430-31.
4. J. R. Mulryne, *MLR*, 63:3 (July 1968), 692-93.
5. Thomas Parkinson, *ELN*, 4:2 (Dec 1966), 154-56.
6. George Brandon Saul, *Éire-Ireland*, 4:3 (Autumn 1969), 127-29.
7. Robert E. Scholes, *JEGP*, 66:2 (Apr 1967), 280-82.
8. Jon Stallworthy, *RES*, 18:70 (May 1967), 225-27.
9. Donald T. Torchiana, "Three Books on Yeats," *PQ*, 46:4 (Oct 1967), 536-56.
10. Gertrude M. White, *Criticism*, 9:4 (Fall 1967), 392-93.

1074. COLWELL, FREDERIC STEWART: "W. B. Yeats: The Dimensions of Poetic Vision," Ph.D. thesis, Michigan State U, 1966. v, 220 p. (*DA*, 27:4 [Oct 1966], 1053A.)
Discusses dualism in *The Shadowy Waters*, Heraclitus and Plato as Yeats's sources; Yeats's departure from the Platonic tradition in the figure of the Daimon; Unity of Being; primary and antithetical experience in the hero, the artist, the saint, and the fool; and "the linea-

ments of the Yeatsian myth as it unfolds from an operative dualism to paradoxical resolution" (p. 8) in *A Vision*.

1075. COWELL, RAYMOND (ed): *Critics on Yeats: Readings in Literary Criticism*. London: Allen & Unwin, 1971. ix, 114 p. (Readings in Literary Criticism. 10.)
Contains "Introduction," vi–vii, and 33 snippets from previously published criticism (not analyzed in this bibliography). The selection is one-sided; almost all the material is on the poetry.
Reviews:
1. Peter Faulkner, *DUJ*, os 64 / ns 33:2 (Mar 1972), 171–72.
2. Phillip L. Marcus, "Approaching W. B.," *Irish Press*, 41:229 (25 Sept 1971), 12.

1076. *The Dolmen Press Yeats Centenary Papers MCMLXV*. Edited by Liam Miller with a preface by Jon Stallworthy. Dublin: Dolmen Press, 1965–68. xvi, 523 p.
Contents: Jon Stallworthy: "Preface," ix–xi; on the Cuala Press as predecessor of the Dolmen Press.
Liam Miller: "Introduction," xiii–xvi.
1. Edward Malins: "Yeats and the Easter Rising," 1–28; also in *MassR*, 7:2 (Spring 1966), 271–84. Discusses the effect of the Easter Rising on Yeats's political convictions and on his poetry.
2. Raymond Lister: "Beulah to Byzantium: A Study of Parallels in the Works of W. B. Yeats, William Blake, Samuel Palmer & Edward Calvert," 29–68; an expanded version of "W. B. Yeats and Edward Calvert," *Irish Book*, 2:3/4 (Autumn 1963), 72–80.
3. Russell K. Alspach: "Yeats and Innisfree," 69–83. On the genesis of the poem and the reverberations of its imagery and symbolism in the later work.
4. Giles W. L. Telfer: "Yeats's Idea of the Gael," 85–108. Yeats's idea of the Gael is peculiarly his own and very different from the originals. He comes closest to his Gaelic sources in *The Wanderings of Oisin*.
5. Peter Faulkner: "Yeats & the Irish Eighteenth Century," 109–24. The importance of Berkeley, Burke, and Swift.
6. Hiro Ishibashi: "Yeats and the Noh: Types of Japanese Beauty and Their Reflection in Yeats's Plays," edited by Anthony Kerrigan, 125–96. Includes a note on "Yeats and Zen."
7. George Brandon Saul: "In . . . Luminous Wind," 197–256; a collection of the following essays:
"The Short Stories of William Butler Yeats," 199–204; reprinted from *Poet Lore*, 57:3 (July 1962), 371–74; reprinted in J6287.
"Yeats's Verse before *Responsibilities*," 205–16; reprinted from *Arizona Q*, 16:2 (Summer 1960), 158–67.
"A Frenzy of Concentration: Yeats's Verse from *Responsibilities* to *The King of the Great Clock Tower*," 217–36; reprinted from *Arizona Q*, 20:2 (Summer 1964), 101–16.
"Coda: The Verse of Yeats's Last Five Years," 237–44; reprinted from *Arizona Q*, 17:1 (Spring 1961), 63–68.
"The Winged Image: A Note on Birds in Yeats's Poems," 245–56; reprinted from J402.
8. Curtis Bradford: "Yeats's *Last Poems* Again," 257–88; includes a reprint of "The Order of Yeats's *Last Poems*," *MLN*, 76:6 (June 1961), 515–16. Argues for the validity of the order in which Yeats arranged his poems in *Last Poems and Two Plays* (W200) and which is obscured in the *Collected Poems*.

9. George Mills Harper: "Yeats's Quest for Eden," 289-331. The development of the pastoral Eden—Golden Age symbolism in Yeats's works with particular reference to the influence of Blake.

10. "Yeats and Patrick McCartan: A Fenian Friendship. Letters with a Commentary by John Unterecker & an Address on Yeats the Fenian by Patrick McCartan," 333-443. Chronicles Yeats's friendship with Mc-Cartan, 1932-39, and provides material on some of the matters that interested Yeats during this period, e.g., the Irish Academy of Letters, the Casement affair, the fund set up for him by an American committee (including the role played by Gogarty), and the dinner in his honor. Reprints, with slight omissions and changes, McCartan's article (see J4071) and includes an appendix on the principal activities of the Irish Academy of Letters until spring 1965.

11. Richard Ellmann: "Yeats and Joyce," 445-79; reprinted, slightly revised, in J1874.

12. Edward Malins: "Yeats and Music," 481-508; incorporates "Yeats and the Bell-Branch," *Consort*, #21 (Summer 1964), 287-98. On Florence Farr's "Speaking to the Psaltery" experiments and on the music in Yeats's plays, particularly that specifically written for them.

Reviews:

1. Anon., "No Plays Like Noh Plays," *TLS*, 66:3396 (30 Mar 1967), 263. (#6, 8, 9.) Correspondence by G. S. Fraser, :3397 (6 Apr 1967), 296.

2. Anon., "Lore of Opposites," *TLS*, 66:3422 (28 Sept 1967), 890. (#10, 11)

3. T. P. Dunning, "Innisfree Onwards," *Irish Independent*, 78:201 (23 Aug 1969), 6.

4. William Empson, "A Time of Troubles," *NSt*, 70:1793 (23 July 1965), 123-24. (#1)

5. R. Fréchet, *EA*, 24:2 (Apr-June 1971), 211-12.

6. T. R. Henn, *RES*, 20:79 (Aug 1969), 373-75.

7. Gerhard Hoffmann, *Anglia*, 90:1/2 (1972), 266-70. (#12)

8. Augustine Martin, *Studies*, 57:225 (Spring 1968), 108-10. (#1, 2, 6, 8, 9, 10, 11)

9. Austin Martin, "Yeats the 'Fenian in Practice,'" *Irish Press*, 37: 221 (3 June 1967), 10. (#10)

10. George P. Mayhew, *BA*, 43:3 (Summer 1969), 420-21.

1077. DONOGHUE, DENIS (ed): *The Integrity of Yeats*. Cork: Mercier Press, 1964. 70 p. (Thomas Davis Lectures.)
Contents: 1. Denis Donoghue: "Yeats and Modern Poetry: An Introduction," 9-20.
2. A. Norman Jeffares: "Yeats the Public Man," 21-32; mainly as reflected in his poetry. See also J1102.
3. T. R. Henn: "Yeats's Symbolism," 33-46; particularly the tower and swan symbolism.
4. Frank Kermode: "Players and Painted Stage," 47-57; on the dramatic theories.
5. Donald Davie: "Yeats, the Master of a Trade," 59-70; i.e., the master of technical skill in writing poetry.

1078. *———, and JAMES RONALD MULRYNE (eds): *An Honoured Guest: New Essays on W. B. Yeats*. London: Arnold, 1965. viii, 196 p.
Contents: 1. Charles Tomlinson: "Yeats and the Practising Poet," 1-7. "Yeats gives us the sense of liberating scale, scale generated by—what remains for the practitioner the central and necessary miracle—the ability to remake himself and his verse" (p. 7).

2. Northrop Frye, "The Rising of the Moon: A Study of *A Vision*," 8-33.
3. T. R. Henn: *"The Green Helmet and Responsibilities,"* 34-53. On the poems in these volumes; mostly concerned with background and sources.
4. Graham Martin: *"The Wild Swans at Coole,"* 54-72. Discusses the inner coherence of the two volumes published under this title.
5. Donald Davie: *"Michael Robartes and the Dancer,"* 73-87. Again concerned with the inner structure of the volume. Discusses its prominent theme, "the matter of woman's role in society," and syntactical aspects.
6. John Holloway: "Style and World in *The Tower*," 88-105. Yeats's "common idiom" is by no means "colloquial" but rather a private language, through which Yeats creates his own world. This is an interesting article, unfortunately marred by unnecessarily obscure writing and atrocious mutilations of quotations from Yeats (see the *Samhain* quote on p. 89) and from Kant's *Kritik der reinen Vernunft*.
7. Denis Donoghue: "On *The Winding Stair*," 106-23. "The question which storms and cries through the entire book: in a world of mutability, what remains, what is possible, where does Value reside? The answer, but not the whole story, is: in the imagination of Man" (p. 107).
8. J. R. Mulryne: "The *Last Poems*," 124-42.
9. Peter Ure: "The Plays," 143-64.
10. Ian Fletcher: "Rhythm and Pattern in *Autobiographies*," 165-89.
Reviews:
1. A. Norman Jeffares, *RES*, 18:69 (Feb 1967), 93-94.
2. L. F. McNamara, *Michigan QR*, 7:1 (Jan 1968), 68-69.
3. John Montague, *CQ*, 8:4 (Winter 1966), 381-83.
4. Hermann Peschmann, *English*, 16:92 (Summer 1966), 67-69.
5. Christopher Ricks, "Yeats & Facts," *Encounter*, 27:1 (July 1966), 50-54.
6. V. K. Titlestad, *ESA*, 9:2 (Sept 1966), 215-17.

1079. *DONOGHUE, DENIS: *Yeats*. London: Fontana / Collins, 1971. 140 p. (Fontana Modern Masters.)
Not a new biography or work-by-work analysis but an exposé of "Yeats's sensibility," developed through a consideration of some key concepts. Yeats is seen first and foremost as a poet who judges imagination superior to experience on which it thrives, as a man who wants to exert power through his work and whose most important article of faith is a "sense of consciousness as conflict," hence as drama.
Reviews:
1. Anon., *Times*, #58171 (13 May 1971), 9.
2. Anon., "Yeats as a Modern Master," *TLS*, 71:3655 (17 Mar 1972), 311.
3. Gulliver Boyle, "Beautiful Women v. the Furies," *Teacher*, 18:6 (6 Aug 1971), 7.
4. Anthony Cronin, "Yeats Seminar," *Irish Press*, 41:151 (26 June 1971), 12.
5. Roy Fuller, "Trumpets?" *Listener*, 86:2217 (23 Sept 1971), 416-17.
6. Claire Hahn, *Commonweal*, 96:8 (28 Apr 1972), 196-97.
7. Christopher Lehmann-Haupt, "Sigmund Freud and W. B. Yeats," *NYT*, 121:41571 (18 Nov 1971), 45.
8. Laurence Lerner, "The Circus Animals," *Spectator*, 228:7489 (8 Jan 1972), 45-46.
9. John P. White, "Conceptions of the Self," *Tablet*, 225:6834 (29 May 1971), 527.

10. Terence de Vere White," In the Bee-Loud Glade," *Irish Times*,
    #35915 (17 July 1971), 10. Correspondence by Jeananne Crowley,
    #35919 (22 July 1971), 11.

1080. DUBLIN MAGAZINE: "W. B. Yeats Centenary Edition," *Dublin Mag*, 4:2
(Summer 1965).
    See the individual contributions by Harper (J4064), Carew (5736),
    Bradbrook (2724), and Henn (2244).

1081. *ELLMANN, RICHARD: *The Identity of Yeats*. NY: Oxford UP, 1964
[1954]. xxv, 342 p. (Galaxy Books. GB126.)
    Incorporates: "The Art of Yeats: Affirmative Capability," *Kenyon R*,
    15:3 (Summer 1953), 357-85; "Yeats without Analogue," *Kenyon R*, 26:1
    (Winter 1964), 30-47 (appears as preface to the 1964 edition only).
    One of the basic Yeats studies; a description of the development of
    Yeats's work, particularly of the poetry.
    Reviews:
    1. Hazard Adams, "Yeats the Stylist and Yeats the Irishman," *Accent*,
       15:3 (Summer 1955), 234-37.
    2. Anon., *Adelphi*, 31:1 (1954), 93-94.
    3. Anon., "Yeats Set in Place," *TLS*, 53:2744 (3 Sept 1954), 554.
       Correspondence by J. M. Hone, :2745 (10 Sept 1954), 573, confirm-
       ing that Yeats read Leibniz.
    4. Anon., *USQBR*, 10:4 (Dec 1954), 499-500.
    5. Sally Appleton, *Thought*, 30:117 (Summer 1955), 319-20.
    6. Reuben A. Brower, "The Incarnation of Yeats," *Yale R*, 44:2 (Dec
       1954), 290-92.
    7. Rivers Carew, *Dublin Mag*, 4:3/4 (Autumn-Winter 1965), 106-7.
    8. C. Day Lewis, *London Mag*, 1:10 (Nov 1954), 85-88.
    9. Denis Donoghue, *Studies*, 43:[] (Winter 1954), 482-84.
    10. J. A. Dowling, *Dublin Mag*, 30 [i.e., 29]:4 (Oct-Dec 1954), 56-58.
    11. Johannes Edfelt, *Utblick*, Stockholm: Bonnier, 1958. 218 p. ("Nytt
        ljus över Yeats," 93-100).
    12. H. I'A. F[ausset], "Yeats," *Manchester Guardian*, #33642 (24 Aug
        1954), 4.
    13. Iain Hamilton, "All Metaphor," *Spectator*, 193:6580 (6 Aug 1954),
        176-77.
    14. T. R. Henn, "When That Story's Finished, What's the News?" *NSt*,
        48:1231 (9 Oct 1954), 447-48.
    15. Hugh Kenner, "Unpurged Images," *Hudson R*, 8:4 (Winter 1956), 609-
        17.
    16. Vivian Mercier, "W. B. Yeats," *Commonweal*, 61:16 (21 Jan 1955),
        435-36.
    17. Raymond Mortimer, "The Progress of a Poet," *Sunday Times*, #6852
        (15 Aug 1954), 3.
    18. Herbert Read, "W. B. Yeats," *Listener*, 52:1336 (7 Oct 1954), 582,
        585.
    19. T[erence] S[mith], *Irish Writing*, #28 (Sept 1954), 67-68.
    20. G. T., "A Study of Yeats," *Irish Independent*, 63:277 (20 Nov 1954),
        6.
    21. George Whalley, *QQ*, 62:4 (Winter 1956), 617-21.

1082. *ENGELBERG, EDWARD: *The Vast Design: Patterns in W. B. Yeats's
Aesthetic*. Toronto: U of Toronto Press, 1965 [1964]. xxxi, 224 p.
    Based on "The Herald of Art: A Study of W. B. Yeats' Criticism and
    Aesthetic," °Ph.D. thesis, U of Wisconsin, 1958. 528 p. (*DA*, 18:6
    [June 1958], 2140.)

Incorporates "Picture and Gesture in the Yeatsian Aesthetic," *Criticism*, 3:2 (Spring 1961), 101-20; and "Passionate Reverie: W. B. Yeats's Tragic Correlative," *UTQ*, 31:2 (Jan 1962), 201-22. Includes a long interpretation of "The Statues" (180-204).
Reviews:
1. Hazard Adams, *JEGP*, 64:3 (July 1965), 596-98.
2. James L. Allen, *MP*, 62:4 (May 1965), 369-70.
3. Anon., "From Sligo to Byzantium," *TLS*, 64:3304 (24 June 1965), 529-30.
4. Harold Bloom, "Myth, Vision, Allegory," *Yale R*, 54:1 (Oct 1964), 143-49.
5. Frederic S. Colwell, *QQ*, 71:3 (Autumn 1964), 446-47.
6. David Fitzgerald, *Dubliner*, 3:3 (Autumn 1964), 56-57.
7. Paul J. Hurley, *CE*, 26:2 (Nov 1964), 170-71.
8. Thomas Parkinson, *Michigan QR*, 4:2 (Spring 1965), 146-47.
9. Robert L. Peters, *Criticism*, 6:4 (Fall 1964), 386-87.
10. B. Rajan, "Conflict, More Conflict!" *UTQ*, 35:3 (Apr 1966), 315-20.
11. A. G. Stock, *British J of Aesthetics*, 4:4 (Oct 1964), 373-75.
12. Peter Ure, *ES*, 47:2 (Apr 1966), 154-57.
13. George T. Wright, *JAAC*, 23:3 (Spring 1965), 392-93.
14. Dudley Young, *Cambridge R*, 88:2113 (15 Jan 1966), 185-86.

1083. ENGLISH: "W. B. Yeats: 1865-1939," *English*, 15:89 (Summer 1965). See individual contributions by Anon. (J2450), Stallworthy (5825), Ure (3466), Jeffares (1102), Brooks (3155), Peschmann (2052), and Willy (review of J1101).

1084. °FLYNN, JOHN: "'For There's More Enterprise in Walking Naked'--A Coat: W. B. Yeats," M.A. thesis, University College, Dublin, 1966.
I do not know whether this item is classified correctly.

1085. FRASER, GEORGE SUTHERLAND: *W. B. Yeats*. London: Longmans, Green, for British Council and the National Book League, 1968 [1954]. 44 p. (Writers and Their Work. 50.)
Mostly on the poetry, of which the later work is preferred to the earlier. Underrates the plays and the prose. Reprinted in J1356.
Reviews:
1. Kathleen Raine, "Master of Ideas," *NSt*, 47:1214 (12 June 1954), 764-65.

1086. GILBERT, SANDRA: *The Poetry of William Butler Yeats*. NY: Monarch Press, 1965. 133 p. (Monarch Notes and Study Guides. 00738.)
Introduction to the poetry and plays on the undergraduate level.

1087. °GILVARY, MICHAEL T.: "The Work of W. B. Yeats," M.A. thesis, University College, Dublin, 1920.

1088. GREEN, HENRY MACKENZIE: *The Poetry of W. B. Yeats*. An address delivered before the Australian English Association, Sydney, on November 19, 1931. Sydney: Australasian Medical Publishing Company, 1931. 61 p. (Australian English Association. Leaflet December 1931. No. 13.)
A sensible, though not very deep, introduction to Yeats's life and poetical work; discusses his biography, his place in the history of English poetry (comparing him with Blake, Shelley, Keats, Milton, and others), the four phases of his poetical development, his verse structures, and the question of whether he is a poet of escape. Does not pretend to understand the later poetry.

1089. GWYNN, STEPHEN (ed): *William Butler Yeats: Essays in Tribute*. Port Washington: Kennikat Press, 1965 [1940]. viii, 229 p.

The first edition was entitled *Scattering Branches: Tributes to the Memory of W. B. Yeats*.
Contents: 1. Stephen Gwynn: "Scattering Branches," 1-14; i.e., paying homage.
2. Maud Gonne: "Yeats and Ireland," 15-33. Reminiscences and MG's personal view of what WBY did and did not do for Ireland.
3. Sir William Rothenstein: "Yeats as a Painter Saw Him," 35-54. Reminiscences, including notes on the Yeats-Tagore and the Yeats-Dorothy Wellesley relationship. Quotes from several Yeats letters and reprints one of them (dated Mentone, 29 Dec 1938).
4. Lennox Robinson: "The Man and the Dramatist," 55-114. See also J780.
5. W. G. Fay: "The Poet and the Actor," 115-34.
6. Edmund Dulac: "Without the Twilight," 135-44.
7. F. R. Higgins: "Yeats as Irish Poet," 145-55.
8. C. Day Lewis: "A Note on W. B. Yeats and the Aristocratic Tradition," 157-82.
9. L. A. G. Strong: "William Butler Yeats," 183-229.
Reviews:
1. Anon., "To the Memory of W. B. Yeats: 'The Greatest Poet of His Time,'" *Irish Times*, 82:25922 (10 Aug 1940), 5.
2. Anon., "A Garland of Tributes to Yeats," *NYTBR*, 46:20 (18 May 1941), 2.
3. Anon., "Tributes to Yeats: Poetry and the Theatre," *TLS*, 39:2009 (3 Aug 1940), 376.
4. G. M. Brady, *Dublin Mag*, 16:3 (July-Sept 1941), 64-65.
5. James Burnham, "Yeats," *Commonweal*, 34:4 (16 May 1941), 88-89.
6. Thomas Quinn Curtiss, "Yeats and the Irish Drama," *Decision*, 1:6 (June 1941), 78-80.
7. Babette Deutsch, "Living Memories of W. B. Yeats," *NYHTB*, 17:37 (11 May 1941), 2.
8. J. J. H[ogan], *Studies*, 29:116 (Dec 1940), 650-53.
9. Winfield Townley Scott, "The Foolish, Passionate Man," *Accent*, 1:4 (Summer 1941), 247-50.
10. Stephen Spender, "Wise Man and Fool," *NSt*, 20:497 (31 Aug 1940), 214-15.
11. James Stephens, "Homage to W. B. Yeats," *Spectator*, 165:5846 (12 July 1940), 40.

1090. *HALL, JAMES, and MARTIN STEINMANN (eds): *The Permanence of Yeats*. NY: Collier Books, 1961 [1950]. ix, 371 p. (Collier Book. BS11.)
Perhaps the best collection of previously published criticism, although it neglects the early work. See the individual contributions by Murry (J4543), Wilson (1696), Blackmur (2460), Brooks (1241), Ransom (2613), Tate (1839), Daiches (2493), Mizener (2591), Leavis (2566), Spender (2640), Savage (1596), Beach (1288), Warren (1830), Bentley (3559), Burke (2742), Tindall (1288), Davidson (1299), Olson (3197), Jeffares (2553), Schwartz (1603), Eliot (2512), Auden (2454), Zabel (561 and 5031), Houghton (2699).
Also contained: [The editors]: "The Seven Sacred Trances," 1-8; discusses the problem of belief in Yeats's poetry and concludes that "Yeats habitually translates from his private system to public symbols: (p. 5). "A Select Bibliography of Articles and Books, in Whole or in Part, on Yeats," 349-71; about 460 pre-1950 items.
Reviews:
1. Anon., "Yeats and His Critics," *TLS*, 49:2534 (25 Aug 1950), 525-26.
2. M. C. Bradbrook, *MLR*, 46:3-4 (July-Sept 1951), 498-99.

3. Malcolm Brown, *MLQ*, 13:4 (Dec 1952), 413-15.
4. Babette Deutsch, "'High-Powered Exegesis' of William Butler Yeats, His Plays and Poems: A Critical Symposium Finds Authorities Disagreeing on Almost Every Aspect of Him Except His Greatness," *NYHTB*, 26:25 (5 Feb 1950), 3.
5. Richard Ellmann, "Philandering with the Sixth Sense," *SatR*, 33:15 (15 Apr 1950), 49.
6. Dudley Fitts, "Yeats Meets the Critics," *NYTBR*, 55:6 (5 Feb 1950), 5.
7. John M. Flynn, "Yeats Weathers the Test of Literary Permanence," *Chicago Sunday Tribune*, 109:10 (5 Mar 1950), part 4, 10.
8. James Gallagher, "W. B. Yeats's Permanence," *Spirit*, 17:2 (May 1950), 51-55.
9. Isabel Gamble, *Poetry*, 76:4 (July 1950), 227-29.
10. A. M. Klein, "The Masked Yeats," *Northern R*, 3:5 (June-July 1950), 43-45.
11. Robin Mayhead, "American Criticism," *Scrutiny*, 19:1 (Oct 1952), 65-75. (See 69-71.)
12. Vivian Mercier, *Commonweal*, 52:8 (2 June 1950), 204-5.
13. Thomas Riggs, *MLN*, 66:4 (Apr 1951), 280-81.
14. G. S., *San Francisco Chronicle*, 170:98 (23 Apr 1950), This World section, 27.
15. Donald A. Stauffer, "Measure of a Poet," *New Republic*, 122:1842 (20 Mar 1950), 20-21.
16. W. D. T[empleman], *Personalist*, 32:2 (Apr 1951), 214.

1091. *HENN, THOMAS RICE: *The Lonely Tower: Studies in the Poetry of W. B. Yeats*. London: Methuen, 1965 [1950]. xxiv, 375 p. (University Paperbacks. UP126.)

Contains chapters on the Irish background, the theory of the mask and of self and anti-self, women in Yeats's poetry and the love poetry, Yeats and Synge, Yeats's style, imagery and symbols, myth and magic, *A Vision*, the Byzantium motif, the influence of painting, the poetry of the plays, and other subjects. A somewhat loosely organized study.
Reviews:
1. Anon., *Adelphi*, 27:2 (1951), 184, 187.
2. Anon., *Listener*, 45:1143 (25 Jan 1951), 152-53.
3. Anon., "Studies in the Poetry of Yeats," *TLS*, 50:2559 (16 Feb 1951), 104.
4. A. C. Boyd, "Commentary on Yeats," *Britain To-day*, #180 (Apr 1951), 46.
5. M. C. Bradbrook, "The Country of Yeats and the Countries of His Mind," *Cambridge R*, 72:1761 (21 Apr 1951), 428, 430.
6. M.-L. Cazamian, "L'évolution de W. B. Yeats après ses dernières oeuvres," *EA*, 5:1 (Feb 1952), 50-54.
7. Austin Clarke, "The Mind's Eye," *Irish Times*, #29164 (27 Jan 1951), 6.
8. ———, "Yeats: A Centenary Tribute," *Irish Press*, 35:139 (12 June 1965), 12.
9. Mary Colum, "This Poet Was Quite Often 'Fighting Mad': A New Study of the Many Influences That Shaped the Ideas of W. B. Yeats," *NYTBR*, [57:] (10 Feb 1952), 1.
10. Babette Deutsch, "Some Backgrounds of the Art of Yeats: A New Study Centers on the Inter-relation of His Work and His Life," *NYHTB*, 28:26 (10 Feb 1952), 4.
11. Richard Eberhart, "New Looks at Yeats," *VQR*, 28:4 (Autumn 1952), 618-21.

12. Richard Ellmann, "Three Ways of Looking at a Triton," *Sewanee R*, 61:1 (Jan-Mar 1953), 149-56.
13. Gareth Lloyd Evans, "Yeats: Mirror of His Age," *Birmingham Post*, #33261 (5 June 1965), II.
14. K. F., *Irish Book Lover*, 31:6 (Nov 1951), 143.
15. Kimon Friar, "Contrapuntal Serpent," *New Republic*, 126:1952 (28 Apr 1952), 17-18.
16. Charles Graves, "Consistency in Yeats," *Scotsman*, #38079 (12 June 1965), Weekend Mag, 2.
17. P[atrick] K[avanagh], *Bell*, 16:5 (Feb 1951), 69-70, 72.
18. Roy McFadden, *Irish Writing*, #14 (Mar 1951), 63-65.
19. Francis MacManus, "Yeats: The Tree Still Flourishes," *Sunday Press*, #787 (13 June 1965), 21.
20. Giorgio Melchiori, *N&Q*, os 211 / ns 13:3 (Mar 1966), 114-17.
21. Edwin Muir, "Yeats and His Mask," *Observer*, #8323 (10 Dec 1950), 7.
22. Richard Murphy, "Footnotes to Yeats," *Spectator*, 186:6404 (23 Mar 1951), 390, 392.
23. John Frederick Nims, "On the Trifles of W. B. Yeats' Perfection," *Chicago Sunday Tribune*, 111:7 (17 Feb 1952), part 4, 8.
24. Lennox Robinson, *Irish Library Bulletin*, 12:[2-3] (Feb-Mar 1951), 22.
25. W. R. Rodgers, "The Poetry of Contraries," *NSt*, 41:1035 (6 Jan 1951), 18.
26. Grover Smith, *New Mexico Q*, 23:3 (Autumn 1953), 325-26.
27. K. R. Srinivasa Iyengar, *Aryan Path*, 22:5 (May 1951), 219-20.
28. W. D. T[empleman], *Personalist*, 34:2 (Spring 1953), 205-6.
29. Peter Ure, *Cambridge J*, 4:12 (Sept 1951), 762-66.

1092. HERMATHENA: "Yeats Number," *Hermathena*, #101 (Autumn 1965). See the individual contributions by Edwards (J1324), Kennelly (3482), Shields (3027), and Kennelly (review of J2571).

1093. HIRTH, MARY MARTHA: "A Study in the Works of W. B. Yeats," M.A. thesis, U of Texas, 1956. iv, 485 p.
Yeats, man and poet, explaining himself by numerous quotations from letters and autobiographical writings, arranged by subject matter.

1094. HONE, JOSEPH MAUNSELL: *William Butler Yeats: The Poet in Contemporary Ireland*. Dublin: Maunsel, [1916]. vii, 134 p. (Irishmen of To-day.)
A study in three parts: early life and work; Irish and other influences; theatre and later work. No index. In many ways this book is more satisfactory than Hone's later biography.
Reviews:
1. Anon., "The Irish Renaissance," *Athenaeum*, #4601 (Jan 1916), 24-25.
2. Anon., "Two Irishmen," *Spectator*, 115:4565 (25 Dec 1915), 921-22.
3. Anon., "W. B. Yeats," *TLS*, 15:730 (13 Jan 1916), 17. Attacks the alleged superficiality of Yeats's public rhetoric.
4. [T. W. H. Crosland (?)], "Irishmen of To-day," *Academy*, 90:2267 (12 May 1916), 10-11. "Yeats, as we all know, is a lesser poet than AE might have been. . . ."
5. Crawford Neil, "W. B. Yeats," *New Ireland*, 2:32 (18 Dec 1915), 98-100.
6. R. Ellis Roberts, "W. B. Yeats," *Bookman*, 50:299 (Aug 1916), 139-40.

1095. IRISH BOOK: "Special Yeats Issue," *Irish Book*, 2:3/4 (Autumn 1963). See individual contributions by Lister (J1076, #2), Miller (7473), Alspach (12), Faulkner (4102), Niland (536), Saddlemyer (2402),

Ó hAodha (3), Skelton (3288), and Miller and Saddlemyer (7034).

1096. IRISH TIMES: *William Butler Yeats Aetat. 70.* [Dublin: Irish Times, 1935]. 16 p.
Reprinted from *Irish Times*, 77:24315 (13 June 1935), 6-8.
Contents: 1. Anon.: "Ad Multos Annos," 3-4.
2. Francis Hackett: "Place in World Letters: 'A Crucible of an Art,'" 5-6.
3. Sean O Faolain: "Philosophy of W. B. Yeats: Two Elements at War," 7-8. Mystery and intellect, self and anti-self.
4. F. R. Higgins: "The Poet of a Dream: Where 'Beauty Is Taut, Passion Precise,'" 8-9.
5. Denis Johnston: "Yeats as Dramatist: Tenacity of Purpose through Thirty Years," 10-11.
6. Aodh de Blacam: "Yeats and the Nation: A Surrender to Subjectivity. Why the Abbey Ideal Failed," 11-14. The Abbey failed because its dramatists came from the Ascendancy and were out of touch with the Irish people.
7. Andrew E. Malone: "Yeats and the Abbey: School of Dramatists and School of Acting," 15-16.
    See also correspondence by Florence Lynch, :24316 (14 June 1935), 4; and Anon., "World-Wide Greetings: Mr. Yeats's Birthday Mail. Plans for the Future," :24317 (15 June 1935), 6.

1097. ————: *W. B. Yeats, 1865-1965: A Centenary Tribute.* [Dublin: Irish Times, 1965]. viii p.
A supplement to the *Irish Times*, 10 June 1965, with photographs by Jack MacManus and drawings by Ruth Brandt.
Contents: 1. Stephen Spender: "The Poet and the Legend: An Evaluation," i-ii. Yeats's impact on the leftist poets of the thirties, his influence compared with that of Eliot, and his importance for the modern reader.
2. Patrick Kavanagh: "George Moore's Yeats," ii. Rather Kavanagh's Yeats, and what a curious figure that is.
3. T. R. Henn: "The Poetry: A Stone with Many Facets," ii.
4. Richard Ellmann: "Gazebos and Gashouses: Yeats and Auden," iii. Incorporated in J1874.
5. Terence de Vere White: "The Social Mask of the Poet," iii-iv. His aristocratic ideals and political vagaries.
6. Conor Cruise O'Brien: "Passion and Cunning," iv. An extract from J1101.
7. V. C. Clinton-Baddeley: "Reciting the Poems," iv. A producer's reminiscences of the broadcasts that Yeats made for the B.B.C.
8. Eavan Boland: "A Young Writer's Reaction," iv. Love and gratitude, especially for Yeats the master craftsman.
9. Norman Jeffares: "The Literary Influence," vi.
10. Elizabeth Coxhead: "The Lifelong Friendship: Yeats and Lady Gregory," vi.
11. Sean Brooks, "The Ties with Sligo," vi.
12. Brendan Kennelly: "The Gaelic Epic," vi-vii. Yeats's Cuchulain.
13. Norah McGuinness: "Young Painter and Elderly Genius," vi. Reminiscences. Miss McGuinness made masks and costumes for a performance of *The Only Jealousy of Emer* and played the part of the Woman of the Sidhe.
14. A. J. Leventhal: "Yeats and the Abbey Theatre," vii.
15. Rachel Burrows: "The Yeats Theatre," vii. How to stage Yeats's later plays. Emphasizes that actors should know in detail the meaning

of the plays and of their symbolism.
16. "*The Silver Tassie*: An Abbey Controversy," vii-viii. Reprint of
J2250.
17. Padraic Fallon: "Yeats at Athenry Perhaps," viii. Poem.
18. John Horgan: "May Craig Recalls the Abbey Days: An Interview with
John Horgan," viii.

1098. IRISH WRITING: "W. B. Yeats: A Special Number," *Irish Writing*, #31
(Summer 1955).
See individual contributions by White (J5180), Yeats (3697), Allt
(2810), Kenner (2561), Davie (2198), Ure (3018), Iremonger (3408).
Reviews:
1. Denis Donoghue, "Mummy Truths to Tell," *Irish Times*, #30577 (24
Sept 1955), 6.
2. Anthony Hartley, *Spectator*, 195:6649 (2 Dec 1955), 778.
3. John Jordan, "Yeats and Irish Writing," *Irish Press*, 35:222 (17
Sept 1955), 4.

1099. JAMES JOYCE QUARTERLY: "Yeats Issue," *JJQ*, 3:2 (Winter 1966).
See individual contributions by Alspach (J1833), Parkinson (2733),
Levine (2429), Kain (2374), Friend (2315).

1100. JEFFARES, ALEXANDER NORMAN: *W. B. Yeats: Man and Poet*. NY: Barnes
& Noble, 1966 [1949]. ix, 365 p. (Barnes & Noble Paperback. 421.)
Based on °"The Sources & Symbolism of the Later Poems of William
Butler Yeats," Ph.D. thesis, Trinity College, Dublin, 1945; and on
°"W. B. Yeats: Man and Poet," D.Phil. thesis, Oxford U, 1947. ix,
204, 243 p. As the title indicates, a biography-cum-criticism type
of study. Valuable for much background and firsthand information
about the Yeats family and friends; the interpretations, however, do
not go very deep. Contains numerous small inaccuracies.
Reviews:
1. Anon., *Dublin Mag*, 25:5 [i.e., 1] (Jan-Mar 1950), 54-56.
2. Anon., "An Interpreter of Yeats," *TLS*, 48:2470 (3 June 1949), 363.
3. A. W. J. Becker, "In Search of Yeats," *Isis*, #1105 (19 May 1949),
16.
4. Thomas Bodkin, "W. B. Yeats," *Birmingham Post*, #28321 (17 May
1949), 2.
5. Austin Clarke, "A Poet's Progress," *Irish Times*, #28635 (14 May
1949), 6.
6. Mary Colum, "To a Yeatsian Urn," *SatR*, 33:4 (28 Jan 1950), 14-16.
7. Bruce Cutler, "Introductions and Conclusions," *Poetry*, 112:1 (Apr
1968), 52-56.
8. Richard Ellmann, *MLN*, 66:5 (May 1951), 335-36.
9. Isabel Gamble, "Two Views of Yeats," *Hopkins R*, 3:2 (Winter 1950),
52-54.
10. Robert Greacen, "Masks and the Man," *Poetry Q*, 11:2 (Summer 1949),
115-17.
11. Horace Gregory, "Yeats: A Self-Made Poet," *NYTBR*, 54:52 (25 Dec
1949), 4, 14.
12. H. W. Häusermann, *ES*, 30:5 (Oct 1949), 278-79.
13. Lawrence Haward, "W. B. Yeats," *Manchester Guardian*, #32022 (3
June 1949), 4.
14. F. W. van Heerikhuizen, "Gedreven door angst," *Litterair paspoort*,
7:53 (Jan 1952), 10-11.
15. B. P. Howell, *Aryan Path*, 20:10 (Oct 1949), 462-63.
16. John o' London, "More about W. B. Yeats," *John o' London's Weekly*,
58:1365 (24 June 1949), 375.

17. Patrick Kavanagh, "A Running Commentary on Yeats," *Spectator*, 182:6307 (13 May 1949), 650.
18. John Lehmann, "W. B. Yeats," *Time and Tide*, 30:27 (2 July 1949), 679-80.
19. J. B. Leishman, *RES*, 1:4 (Oct 1950), 375-77.
20. R[oger] McH[ugh], *Studies*, 39:155 (Sept 1950), 345-46.
21. M. J. MacM[anus], "Yeats: A New Study," *Irish Press*, 19:160 (7 July 1949), 6.
22. Vivian Mercier, *Commonweal*, 51:2 (21 Oct 1949), 48-49.
23. J. B. Morton, "William Butler Yeats," *Tablet*, 193:5690 (11 June 1949), 384-85.
24. Hermann Peschmann, "Portrait in a Mirror," *Student*, 47:5 (18 Jan 1951), 241-43.
25. R. G. G. Price, *New English R*, 3:2 (Aug 1949), 142-43.
26. Horace Reynolds, "Poet of Our Time," *CSM*, 42:29 (29 Dec 1949), 11.
27. A. Rivoallan, *EA*, 5:1 (Feb 1952), 80-81.
28. Mario M. Rossi, "Yeats nella sua torre incantata," *Nazione*, 92:86 (18 Mar 1950), 3.
29. Cecil ffrench Salkeld, "The Growth of Genius," *Irish Writing*, #9 (Oct 1949), 68-69.
30. George Brandon Saul, "Jeffares on Yeats," *MLN*, 66:4 (Apr 1951), 246-49. Corrects numerous inaccuracies. See also Jeffares's reply, "Saul on Jeffares," *MLN*, 67:7 (Nov 1952), 501-2.
31. Elizabeth Schneider, "Two Studies of Yeats," *Nation*, 171:5 (29 July 1950), 112-13.
32. Edith Shackleton, "New Books," *Lady*, 129:3352 (19 May 1949), 454.
33. George N. Shuster, "A Dutch Monument to a Great Irish Poet," *NYHTB*, 26:16 (4 Dec 1949), 36.
34. Rex Warner, "Man and Poet," *Books of the Month*, Aug 1949, 17.
35. Neil Weiss, "The Material of Yeats' Poetry," *New Leader*, 32:45 (5 Nov 1949), 9.
36. H. O. W[hite], *Hermathena*, #74 (Nov 1949), 76-77.

1101. *————, and KENNETH GUSTAV WALTER CROSS (eds): *In Excited Reverie: A Centenary Tribute to William Butler Yeats, 1865-1939*. London: Macmillan, 1965. viii, 354 p.
Contents: 1. W. R. Rodgers, "W. B. Yeats: A Dublin Portrait," 1-13. Reprinted from Laurence Gilliam (ed): *B.B.C. Features*. London: Evans, 1950. 208 p., pp. 176-86; and from *Books and Bookmen*, 10:9 (June 1965), 16, 18-20. Reprinted in J5945. A program evoking the personality of Yeats through numerous anecdotes and reminiscences by those who knew him. Participants are Frank O'Connor, Sean O'Faolain, Brinsley Macnamara, R. I. Best, Austin Clarke, Lennox Robinson, Maud Gonne, Iseult Gonne Stuart, Udolphus Wright, Anne Yeats, R. M. Smyllie, Arthur Hanna, Isa MacNie, and Mrs. Yeats.
2. Lennox Robinson: "William Butler Yeats: Personality," 14-23. Reminiscences and a character sketch.
3. A. Norman Jeffares: "John Butler Yeats," 24-47; reprinted in part in *Dublin Mag*, 4:2 (Summer 1965), 30-37; and completely in J1102. Comments on the JBY-WBY relationship.
4. David Daiches: "The Early Poems: Some Themes and Patterns," 48-67; reprinted in J1792.
5. Hugh MacDiarmid: "Ingenium Omnia Vincit," 68. Poem.
6. Edward Engelberg: "'He Too Was in Arcadia': Yeats and the Paradox of the Fortunate Fall," 69-92. Yeats's Arcadia as fallen Eden in *The Island of Statues* and some other poems; also on the influence of Pater.

7. A. G. Stock: "Yeats on Spenser," 93-101. Includes comments on *The Island of Statues*.
8. T. R. Henn: "The Rhetoric of Yeats," 102-22. In the poetry.
9. Donald T. Torchiana: "'Among School Children' and the Education of the Irish Spirit," 123-50. A reading of the poem against Yeats's ideas of education, as derived from Maria Montessori and Gentile. Includes a note on Maud Gonne and some previously unpublished material.
10. A. D. Hope: "William Butler Yeats," 151. Poem, reprinted from J5770.
11. Hazard Adams: "Some Yeatsian Versions of Comedy," 152-70. Comedy in *Autobiographies* and *A Vision*.
12. Jon Stallworthy: "Yeats as Anthologist," 171-92. The making of the *Oxford Book of Modern Verse*, including previously unpublished memos from the publisher's files and Yeats letters.
13. Brendan Kennelly: "Yeats," 193. Poem, reprinted in *Acorn*, #10 (Spring 1966), 4.
14. Russell K. Alspach: "The Variorum Edition of Yeats's Plays," 194-206. An outline of the work that went into the edition.
15. Conor Cruise O'Brien: "Passion and Cunning: An Essay on the Politics of W. B. Yeats," 207-78. Incorporates "Yeats and Fascism: What Rough Beast," *NSt*, 69:1772 (26 Feb 1965), 319-22; material from J1097; "Yeats and Irish Politics" *Tri-Q*, #4 [Fall 1965], 91-98. Reprinted in *Tri-Q*, #23/24 (Winter/Spring 1972), 142-203. The most controversial piece in the volume; O'Brien argues that there is no break between Yeats's poetry and politics, which became increasingly authoritarian and fascist in later years.
16. Randolph Stow: "Anarchy: For W. B. Yeats in Mid-Winter," 279. Poem.
17. S. B. Bushrui: "Yeats's Arabic Interests," 280-314. Particularly in *A Vision* and "The Gift of Harun Al-Rashid."
18. K. G. W. Cross: "The Fascination of What's Difficult: A Survey of Yeats Criticism and Research," 315-37.

Reviews:
1. Anon., "Poet's Centenary," *Economist*, 215:6354 (5 June 1965), 1179.
2. Anon., *Quarterly R*, 303:646 (Oct 1965), 464-65.
3. Anon., "From Sligo to Byzantium," *TLS*, 64:3304 (24 June 1965), 529-30. Correspondence by Owen Sheehy Skeffington re Hanna Sheehy Skeffington and what she thought about Yeats and his "fascism," and the reviewer's answer, :3306 (8 July 1965), 579; by Anthony Comerford on Yeats and fascism, :3307 (15 July 1965), 597.
4. Rivers Carew, "Bread That Tastes Sour," *Dublin Mag*, 4:3/4 (Autumn-Winter 1965), 91-93.
5. Austin Clarke, "Yeats: A Centenary Tribute," *Irish Press*, 35:139 (12 June 1965), 12.
6. Cyril Connolly, "Notes Towards an Understanding of Yeats," *Sunday Times*, #7413 (13 June 1965), 43. Reprinted in *The Evening Colonnade*. London: Bruce & Watson, 1973, 519 p. (pp. 244-49).
7. Patrick Cosgrave, "Yeats, Fascism and Conor O'Brien," *London Mag*, 7:4 (July 1967), 22-41. Accuses O'Brien of garbling the facts and of lack of evidence.
8. Donald Davie, "Bardolators and Blasphemers," *Guardian*, #36991 (12 June 1965), 7.
9. Denis Donoghue, "Bend Sinister," *Irish Times*, #34207 (5 June 1965), 8. Correspondence by Anthony Cronin, #34211 (10 June 1965), 9; Grattan Freyer and Arland Ussher, #34216 (16 June 1965), 7; Dermot MacManus, #34217 (17 June 1965), 9; and others.

10. William Empson, "A Time of Troubles," *NSt*, 70:1793 (23 July 1965), 123-24. Correspondence by Conor Cruise O'Brien, "Yeats's Politics," :1798 (27 Aug 1965), 284-85; Empson, :1800 (10 Sept 1965), 354.

11. Gareth Lloyd Evans, "Yeats: Mirror of His Age," *Birmingham Post*, #33261 (5 June 1965), II.

12. Michael P. Gallagher, *Studies*, 54:214-15 (Summer-Autumn 1965), 284-88.

13. Charles Graves, "Consistency in Yeats," *Scotsman*, #38079 (12 June 1965), Weekend Mag, 2.

14. Hilton Kramer, "The Politics of Yeats," *New Leader*, 48:23 (22 Nov 1965), 22-23. Particularly on O'Brien's essay, which he endorses wholeheartedly.

15. Francis MacManus, "Yeats: The Tree Still Flourishes," *Sunday Press,* #787 (13 June 1965), 21.

16. Giorgio Manganelli, "Un simposio per Yeats: Il mago astuto," *Mondo*, 17:33 (17 Aug 1965), 9.

17. John Montague, *CQ*, 8:4 (Winter 1966), 381-83.

18. Harry T. Moore, "Time Pardons Him for Writing Well," *SatR*, 48:50 (11 Dec 1965), 39, 81.

19. Frank O'Connor, "Yeats," *Sunday Independent*, 60:24 (13 June 1965), 10.

20. Sir Charles Petrie, "Recalling a Great Irish Poet," *Illustrated London News*, 246:6567 (12 June 1965), 24.

21. Martin Seymour-Smith, "The Honoured Guest," *Spectator*, 214:7146 (11 June 1965), 760.

22. John Unterecker, *CE*, 27:7 (Apr 1966), 580-81.

23. Peter Ure, *RES*, 17:66 (May 1966), 224-27.

24. Donald Weeks, *JAAC*, 25:4 (Summer 1967), 471-72.

25. M[argaret] W[illy], *English*, 15:89 (Summer 1965), 185-86.

1102. JEFFARES, ALEXANDER NORMAN: *The Circus Animals: Essays on W. B. Yeats*. London: Macmillan, 1970. x, 183 p.

Reprinted and revised essays (first publications in parentheses):

1. "Yeats's Mask," 3-14 (*ES*, 30:6 [Dec 1949], 289-98). The theory of the mask and the mask symbol in Yeats's works.

2. "Yeats, Public Man," 15-28 ("Yeats as Public Man," *Poetry*, 98:4 [July 1961], 253-63; "Yeats the Public Man," in J1077). Originally a review of *Senate Speeches* (W211R/S); comments on politics in Yeats's poetry.

3. "Poet's Tower," 29-46 ("Thoor, Ballylee," *ES*, 28:6 [Dec 1947], 161-68; "Poet's Tower," *Envoy*, 5:20 [July 1951], 45-55). The tower symbol in Yeats's poetry and the influence of Milton and Shelley.

4. "Yeats, Critic," 47-77 ("Yeats as Critic," *English*, 15:89 [Summer 1965], 173-76; "The Criticism of Yeats," *Phoenix*, #10 [Summer 1965], 27-45).

5. "Women in Yeats's Poetry," 78-102 (J1140, q.v.).

6. "Gyres in Yeats's Poetry," 103-14 ("'Gyres' in the Poetry of W. B. Yeats," *ES*, 27:3 [June 1946], 65-74). Includes comments on *A Vision*.

7. "John Butler Yeats, Anglo-Irishman," 117-46 (J1101, q.v.).

8. "Oliver St. John Gogarty, Irishman," 147-74 (*Proceedings of the British Academy*, 46 [1960], 73-98). Includes some remarks on the Yeats-Gogarty relationship.

Reviews:

1. Terence Brown, "Life as Art," *Irish Times*, #35674 (3 Oct 1970), 8.

2. Robert Greacen, "Aspects of Yeats," *Tribune*, 34:48 (27 Nov 1970), 10.

3. John S. Kelly, "Pathways," *Irish Press*, 40:278 (21 Nov 1970), 12.
4. Brendan Kennelly, "Yeats Ltd.," *Hibernia*, 34:19 (9 Oct 1970), 13.
5. Frank Lentricchia, "Yeats and Stevens," *Contemporary Literature*, 14:2 (Spring 1973), 247-52.
6. Norman H. MacKenzie, "The Yeats Canon and Recent Scholarship," *QQ*, 78:3 (Autumn 1971), 462-64.
7. Laurence Perrine, "Latest from a One-Man Yeats-Factory," *Southwest R*, 56:2 (Spring 1971), 211-12.
8. Hilary Pyle, *RES*, 23:89 (Feb 1972), 101-3.

1102a. KEANE, PATRICK J. (ed): *William Butler Yeats: A Collection of Criticism*. NY: McGraw-Hill, 1973. v, 151 p.

An eccentric collection. Contains 10 extracts from previously published criticism, mostly concerned with the later poetry, plus an introduction in which the editor justifies his selection, and a previously unpublished essay by the editor, "Embodied Song," which is concerned with antinomies in Yeats's poetry (the essay is overwritten and really a pastiche of quotations from the poems). Also a selected bibliography and a poem by M. L. Rosenthal, "Visiting Yeats's Tower" (reprinted from *The View from the Peacock's Tail: Poems*. NY: Oxford UP, 1972. viii, 52 p. [pp. 48-49]), answered by the editor's poem "Reconciliation."

1103. KEEP, WILLIAM CORBIN: "Yeats and the Public," Ph.D. thesis, U of Washington, 1965. vi, 212 p. (*DA*, 27:1 [July 1966], 209A.)

Discusses the influence of John B. Yeats, Morris, O'Leary, Mitchel, the Rhymers, and Arnold.

1104. KLEINSTÜCK, JOHANNES: *W. B. Yeats oder: Der Dichter in der modernen Welt*. Hamburg: Leibniz, 1963. 288 p.

Not much concerned with the problem announced in the subtitle (the poet in the modern world); mainly interested in Yeats's symbols, which he does not wish to link to the "system." An uneven book that contains numerous inaccuracies.

Reviews:
1. J. Blondel, *EA*, 18:3 (July-Sept 1965), 320-21.
2. Karl August Horst, "Ein vorbildlicher Interpret," *FAZ*, #189 (17 Aug 1963), Bilder und Zeiten, [7].
3. K. P. S. Jochum, *Neueren Sprachen*, 14:3 (Mar 1965), 147-48.
4. Christoph Kuhn, "Zu William Butler Yeats," *Du*, 23:7 (July 1963), 53.
5. Walther Martin, *ZAA*, 14:1 (1966), 87-91.

1105. KRANS, HORATIO SHEAFE: *William Butler Yeats and the Irish Literary Revival*. NY: Haskell House, 1966 [1904]. xi, 196 p.

Incorporates "Mr. Yeats and the Irish Literary Revival," *Outlook*, 76:1 (2 Jan 1904), 57-61. As the first monograph on Yeats, the book contains numerous small inaccuracies and hagiographical enthusiasms. Krans discusses the Irish literary revival, Yeats's poems based upon Irish myth, legend, and romance, as well as the entire output to date. Considering the little information available to Krans, his interpretations are fairly sound. Although he emphasizes Yeats's supposed mysticism and otherworldliness, he recognizes his ability as a leader of a literary and theatrical movement. Mainly of historical value.

Reviews:
1. Anon., *Bookman*, 28:164 (May 1905), 70.
2. Anon., "The Modern Irish Literary Revival and Its Leader," *Dial*, 37:439 (1 Oct 1904), 213.

3. Anon., "The 'Celtic Renascence,'" *Outlook* [London], 16:390 (22 July 1905), 97-98.
4. Treadwell Cleveland, *NYTBR*, [9:] (21 May 1904), 346. A letter referring to a review that I have not been able to locate.
5. [Wilmer Cave France Wright], *Nation*, 78:2027 (5 May 1904), 351.

1106. LONDON MERCURY: [Yeats issue], *London Mercury*, 39:233 (Mar 1939). See individual contributions by Scott-James (J1605), Nevinson (736), and Hone (4066).

1107. MACLEISH, ARCHIBALD: *Yeats and the Belief in Life*. An address at the University of New Hampshire, January 17, 1957. [Durham]: U of New Hampshire, 1958. 20 p.
    Reprinted in *A Continuing Journey*. Boston: Houghton Mifflin, 1967. x, 374 p., pp. 12-25. The modern mind wishes "to know" and believes that knowledge is possible. This applies particularly to Yeats's life and work.

1108. *MACNEICE, LOUIS: *The Poetry of W. B. Yeats*. With a foreword by Richard Ellmann. NY: Oxford UP, 1969 [1941]. 207 p. (Galaxy Book. GB269.)
    This is still one of the sanest books written about Yeats. MacNeice discusses, among other things, Yeats's nineties and Irish background, the early poems, the style in the prose and the plays, the later ballad technique, and Yeats's politics. He defines Yeats's place in the poetry and thought of the 20th century, frequently invoking comparisons with Housman, D. H. Lawrence, Rilke, Eliot, and Auden.
    Reviews:
    1. Anon., *Listener*, 26:661 (11 Sept 1941), 383.
    2. Anon., *N&Q*, 180:9 (1 Mar 1941), 161-62.
    3. Cleanth Brooks, *MLN*, 58:4 (Apr 1943), 319-20.
    4. James Burnham, "Yeats," *Commonweal*, 34:4 (16 May 1941), 88-89.
    5. S. C. C[hew], "Yeats as Seen by Mr. MacNeice," *CSM*, 33:134 (3 May 1941), Weekly Mag Section, 10.
    6. [Harold Child], "The Mystery of Yeats: Stages in a Poet's Search for Himself," *TLS*, 40:2043 (29 Mar 1941), 150. Reprinted in *Essays and Reflections*. Edited with a memoir by S. C. Roberts. Cambridge: UP, 1948. xii, 185 p., pp. 12-19.
    7. A[ustin] C[larke], *Dublin Mag*, 16:2 (Apr-June 1941), 75-77.
    8. Maurice James Craig, *Life and Letters*, 29:[1] (Apr 1941), 83-86.
    9. Babette Deutsch, "His Poetry Unique in Our Time," *NYHTB*, 17:40 (1 June 1941), 10.
    10. E[lizabeth] D[rew], *Atlantic Monthly*, 167:5 (May 1941), Atlantic Bookshelf section, unpaged.
    11. Roibeárd O Faracháin [Robert Farren], *Bell*, 2:2 (May 1941), 93-95.
    12. Dudley Fitts, "MacNeice on Yeats," *SatR*, 24:2 (3 May 1941), 6.
    13. F. W. van Heerikhuizen, "Een interessant boek over Yeats," *Litterair paspoort*, 2:12 (Nov 1947), 14-15.
    14. A. Norman Jeffares, *ES*, 27:1 (Feb 1946), 29-31.
    15. W. H. M[ellers], "A Book on Yeats," *Scrutiny*, 9:4 (Mar 1941), 381-83.
    16. E. H. W. Meyerstein, "Yeats, the Old and the New," *English*, 3:17 (Summer 1941), 223-25.
    17. Edwin Muir, "Yeats," *NSt*, 21:531 (26 Apr 1941), 440.
    18. F. T. Prince, *Dublin R*, 209:418 (July 1941), 101-3.
    19. Kathleen J. Raine, *Horizon*, 4:19 (July 1941), 66-71.
    20. Michael Roberts, "Mr. MacNeice on Yeats," *Spectator*, 166:5879 (28 Feb 1941), 234.

21. Winfield Townley Scott, "The Foolish, Passionate Man," *Accent*, 1:4 (Summer 1941), 247-50.
22. William Soutar, "William Butler Yeats," *Adelphi*, 17:12 (Sept 1941), 425-27.
23. George Woodcock, *Now*, #4 (Easter 1941), 28-30.

1109. MANVELL, ROGER: "W. B. Yeats: A Study of W. B. Yeats's Poetic Career with Special Reference to His Lyrical Poems," Ph.D. thesis, U of London, 1939. x, 323 p.

1110. MARCUS, PHILLIP LEDUC: *Yeats and the Beginning of the Irish Renaissance.* Ithaca: Cornell UP, 1970. xvii, 299 p.
Based on "The Beginnings of the 'Irish Literary Renaissance,' 1885-1899," Ph.D. thesis, Harvard U, 1967. xiv, 315 p. Incorporates "Old Irish Myth and Modern Irish Literature," *Irish UR*, 1:1 (Autumn 1970), 67-85. Describes Yeats's activities between 1885 and 1899. Discusses the literary theories as related to Irish literature, the prose fiction, and the controversies with Duffy, Dowden, and Eglinton. Also on Yeats's relationship to Katharine Tynan, Nora Hopper, Todhunter, Rolleston, Savage-Armstrong, Lionel Johnson, AE, Hyde, O'Grady, and Larminie, and on the beginnings of the Irish dramatic revival.
Reviews:
1. Anon., "Young Irishman," *TLS*, 70:3620 (16 July 1971), 836.
2. Anthony Cronin, "Poet above All," *Irish Press*, 41:56 (6 Mar 1971), 12.
3. J. P. Frayne, *JEGP*, 71:2 (Apr 1972), 280-82.
4. James MacKillop, "Yeats and the Gaelic Muse," *Antigonish R*, #11 (Autumn 1972), 97-109.
5. George P. Mayhew, *BA*, 45:4 (Autumn 1971), 699-700.
6. Michael O hAodha, "Poems and Ballads of Young Ireland," *Hibernia*, 36:15 (6 Aug 1971), 16.

1111. [MASEFIELD, JOHN]: *Words Spoken at the Music Room, Boar's Hill, in the Afternoon of November 5th, 1930 at a Festival Designed in the Honour of William Butler Yeats, Poet.* [Oxford, 1931. 10 p.]
Reprinted in *Recent Prose*. NY: Macmillan, 1933. ix, 294 p., pp. 193-97. "I suppose that any simpler age would have canonised him; of course, after first burning him at the stake."

1112. *MAXWELL, DESMOND ERNEST STEWART, and SUHEIL BADI BUSHRUI (eds): *W. B. Yeats, 1865-1965: Centenary Essays on the Art of W. B. Yeats.* Ibadan: Ibadan UP, 1965. xvi, 252 p. (Illustrated)
Contents: 1. A. Norman Jeffares: "Foreword," ix-x.
2. Christopher Okigbo: "Lament of the Masks. For W. B. Yeats: 1865-1939," xiii-xv. Poem.
3. Laurence D. Lerner: "The Shirt," xvi. Poem.
4. Johannes Kleinstück: "Yeats and Shakespeare," 1-17. Links Yeats's uneasy and complex attitude toward Ireland and things Irish to his equally ambiguous use of Shakespeare. Considers Yeats's conception of Shakespeare in terms of art and reality. Lengthy comment on "Lapis Lazuli."
5. D. E. S. Maxwell: "Swift's Dark Grove: Yeats and the Anglo-Irish Tradition," 18-32. Discusses Yeats's efforts to grasp the Anglo-Irish 18th century from the insecure standpoint of the 20th, Yeats's view of Swift, and Swift's influence on Yeats's verse.
6. F. F. Farag: "Oriental and Celtic Elements in the Poetry of W. B. Yeats," 33-53. Yeats adapted Celtic lore to suit traditions that he came to know through the influence of Mohini Chatterjee.

7. Richard M. Kain: "Yeats and Irish Nationalism," 54-61. Yeats's politics were personal.
8. Ian Fletcher: "Yeats and Lissadell," 62-78. "In Memory of Eva Gore-Booth and Constance Markiewicz" and its historical background.
9. Donna Gerstenberger: "Yeats and Synge: 'A Young Man's Ghost,'" 79-87.
10. Edward Engelberg: "The New Generation and the Acceptance of Yeats," 88-101. Yeats is popular with undergraduates, because his poetry lends itself to an extrinsic approach, especially to a political approach.
11. MacDonald Emslie: "Gestures in Scorn of an Audience," 102-26. Arrogance in Yeats's poetry.
12. Bruce A. King: "Yeats's Irishry Prose," 127-35.
13. George Brandon Saul: "Yeats's Dramatic Accomplishment," 137-53. A rather uneven appreciation and, at times, nasty depreciation. Does not consider any criticism of the plays written after 1953, and bewails Yeats's departures from the original legends and myths as unpardonable instead of trying to understand them.
14. John Rees Moore: "The Idea of a Yeats Play," 154-66. "The plays, then, are for our time whether we will or no."
15. Michael J. Sidnell: "Yeats's First Work for the Stage: The Earliest Versions of *The Countess Cathleen*," 167-88. A discussion of the pre-1892 MS. versions.
16. S. B. Bushrui: "*The Hour-Glass*: Yeats's Revisions, 1903-1922," 189-216.
17. René Fréchet: "Yeats's 'Sailing to Byzantium' and Keats's 'Ode to a Nightingale,'" 217-19.
18. W. H. Stevenson: "Yeats and Blake: The Use of Symbols," 219-25. Blake and Yeats differ significantly in their symbolism and imagery.
19. James Simmons: "A Famous Poet," 226. Poem.
20. "A Select Bibliography," 227-41. About 350 items.
Reviews:
1. Timothy Brownlow, *Dublin Mag*, 5:1 (Spring 1966), 90-93.
2. Sean Lucy, "Yeatsiana," *Irish Independent*, 75:49 (26 Feb 1966), 10.
3. Christopher Ricks, "Yeats & Facts," *Encounter*, 21:1 (July 1966), 50-54.
4. William Kean Seymour, "Reflections and Recollections," *Contemporary R*, 208:1202 (Mar 1966), 165-66.

1113. [MAYHEW, JOYCE]: *Ad Multos Annos: William Butler Yeats in His Seventieth Year*. [Oakland: Mills College, Eucalyptus Press], 1935. [4 p.]

1114. *MELCHIORI, GIORGIO: *The Whole Mystery of Art: Pattern into Poetry in the Work of W. B. Yeats*. London: Routledge & Kegan Paul, 1960. xiv, 306 p.

Incorporates: "Yeats, simbolismo e magia," *Spettatore italiano*, 8:11 (Nov 1955), 453-65; "Leda and the Swan: The Genesis of Yeats' Poem," *English Miscellany*, 7 (1956), 147-239; "Yeats' Beast and the Unicorn," *DUJ*, os 51 / ns 20:1 (Dec 1958), 10-23; "La cupola di Bisanzio," *Paragone*, 11:128 (Aug 1960), 41-70.

Investigates the sources and shaping of Yeats's symbolism, more precisely the transformation of visual into poetic patterns. Discusses the unicorn symbolism in *Where There Is Nothing, The Unicorn from the Stars*, and *The Player Queen*; "Leda and the Swan"; the imagery of swan, Helen of Troy, and tower; *A Vision*; the Byzantine poems; and other Yeats symbols.

Reviews:
1. Anon., "Tame Swan at Coole," *TLS*, 60:3077 (17 Feb 1961), 97-98.
2. Robert Armstrong, "Threads of the Tapestry," *Poetry R*, 52:1 (Apr-June 1961), 99-100.
3. Thomas Bodkin, "Yeats Re-examined," *Birmingham Post*, #31890 (3 Jan 1961), 3. "He [Melchiori] does not seem to suspect that Yeats, though indisputably a great poet at his best, was at his worst an ill-educated and pretentious man. . . ."
4. Donald Davie, "The Poet as Orator," *Guardian*, #35653 (17 Feb 1961), 6.
5. T. R. Henn, "The Unity of Yeats," *NSt*, 61:1557 (13 Jan 1961), 60.
6. A. Norman Jeffares, *RES*, 12:48 (Nov 1961), 437-39.
7. Frank Kermode, "The Spider and the Bee," *Spectator*, 206:6927 (31 Mar 1961), 448-49.
8. J. B. Morton, "Yeats under the Microscope," *Tablet*, 215:6307 (8 Apr 1961), 330-31.
9. R. F. Rattray, *Hibbert J*, 59:235 (July 1961), 373-74.
10. W. D. T[empleman], *Personalist*, 44:1 (Winter 1963), 123-24.

1115. MENON, VATAKKE KURUPATH NARAYANA: *The Development of William Butler Yeats*. With a preface by Sir Herbert J. C. Grierson. Edinburgh: Oliver & Boyd, 1960 [1942]. xiv, 92 p.
Based on °"The Development of the Poetry of William Butler Yeats," Ph.D. thesis, U of Edinburgh, 1940. Grierson's preface recalls some meetings with Yeats. The book itself is a fairly straightforward account of Yeats's development, which skips over the more complex features of his life and work. Menon criticizes the earlier work and prefers the later. A short conclusion raises the question of Yeats's political and social prejudice, but does not go very deep.
Reviews:
1. Mulk Raj Anand, *Life and Letters To-day*, 36:[2] (Feb 1943), 130, 132.
2. Anon., "Yeats Early and Late," *TLS*, 42:2135 (2 Jan 1943), 9.
3. Anon., "The Man and the Mask," *TLS*, 59:3051 (19 Aug 1960), 530.
4. T[homas] B[odkin], "A Study of W. B. Yeats," *Birmingham Post*, #26333 (15 Dec 1942), 2.
5. A. M. C., *U of Edinburgh J*, 12:2 (Summer 1943), 124-25.
6. M. D., *Dublin Mag*, 18:4 (Oct-Dec 1943), 59-60.
7. E. M. Forster, "An Indian on W. B. Yeats," *Listener*, 28:728 (24 Dec 1942), 824.
8. René Fréchet, "L'étude de Yeats: Textes, jugements et éclairisse-ments," *EA*, 14:1 (Jan-Mar 1961), 36-47.
9. P. J. Gannon, *Studies*, 32:125 (Mar 1943), 127-29.
10. R. G. Lienhardt, "Hopkins and Yeats," *Scrutiny*, 11:3 (Spring 1943), 220-24.
11. E. H. W. Meyerstein, "The Music of Death and Change," *English*, 4:23 (Summer 1943), 161-63.
12. George Orwell, "W. B. Yeats," *Horizon*, 7:37 (Jan 1943), 67-71; reprinted in *The Collected Essays, Journalism, and Letters*. Edited by Sonia Orwell and Ian Angus. London: Secker & Warburg, 1968. 4 v., 2:271-76. Orwell concerns himself mostly with Yeats's politics and fascist leanings. See also Menander, "Poetry and Prejudice," *TLS*, 42:2142 (20 Feb 1943), 87; correspondence by Orwell and Menander, :2144 (6 Mar 1943), 115.
13. ———, "The Way of a Poet," *Time and Tide*, 24:16 (17 Apr 1943), 325-26. A different review.
14. F. T. Prince, "Yeats," *Poetry London*, 2:10 (Dec 1944), 238-39.

1116. MISRA, BALA PRASAD: *William Butler Yeats*. Allahabad: Kitab Mahal,
1962. viii, 130 p. (Masters of English Literature. 3.)
Deals with the poetry and the plays only.

1117. MODERN DRAMA: [Yeats issue], *MD*, 7:3 (Dec 1964).
See the individual contributions by Ure (J3527), Lightfoot (3868),
Clark (3896), Scanlon (3831), Warschausky (3717), Moore (3335), Rose
(782), Vendler (3507), Murphy (2203), Fallon (646), Unterecker (3465),
Mercier (3324).

1118. MOKASHI-PUNEKAR, SHANKAR: *The Later Phase in the Development of
W. B. Yeats. (A Study in the Stream of Yeats's Later Thought and Creativ-
ity)*. Dharwar: Karnatak U, 1966. xv, 285 p. (Karnatak University Research
Studies. 8. [i.e., 9.])
Discusses *A Vision* as the crowning achievement of Yeats's quest for
Unity of Being. Deals with the love poetry; the motif of hatred and
the ancestry motif in the poetry; Yeats's aristocratic politics;
"Supernatural Songs"; and the influence of Shri Purohit Swami.
Reviews:
1. Prema Nandakumar, "The Aesthesis and Metaphysics of W. B. Yeats,"
Aryan Path, 39:10 (Oct 1968), 449-50.

1119. MULLIK, B. R.: *Yeats*. Delhi: Chand, 1961. iv, 61 p. (Studies in
Poets for M.A. and B.A. Students of English Literature in Indian Univer-
sities. 19.)
Consists almost entirely of quotations culled from other critics.
Practically worthless.

1120. O'DONNELL, FRANK HUGH: *The Stage Irishman of the Pseudo-Celtic
Drama*. London: Long, 1904. 47 p.
Invective against Yeats from an extreme nationalist and Catholic
point of view. See also O'Donnell's earlier *Souls for Gold* (J3642).

1121. OREL, HAROLD: *The Development of William Butler Yeats: 1885-1900*.
Lawrence: U of Kansas Publications, 1968. vii, 104 p. (Humanistic Studies.
39.)
Incorporates "Dramatic Values, Yeats, and *The Countess Cathleen*," *MD*,
2:1 (May 1959), 8-16. A plea for a new assessment of the early Yeats,
surveying his various activities of this period.
Reviews:
1. Joe Lee Davis, *Michigan QR*, 9:4 (Fall 1970), 280-81.
2. Edward Engelberg, *Victorian Poetry*, 8:4 (Winter 1970), 354-56.
3. Norman H. MacKenzie, "The Yeats Canon and Recent Scholarship," *QQ*,
78:3 (Autumn 1971), 462-64.
4. George Brandon Saul, *Éire-Ireland*, 4:1 (Spring 1969), 152-53.

1122. °PACK, ROBERT: *On William Butler Yeats*. NY: McGraw-Hill, 1962. 60
minutes.
Tape recording.

1123. PHOENIX: [Yeats centenary number], *Phoenix*, #10 (1965).
See the individual contributions by Empson (J3182), Jeffares (1102),
Fraser (4005), Tomlin (1661), Kim U-chang (2860), Kim Jong-gil (2719),
and Yi Ch'ang-pae (2808).

1124. POLLOCK, JOHN HACKETT: *William Butler Yeats*. London: Duckworth /
Dublin: Talbot Press, 1935. 112 p.
A personal but largely unprejudiced attempt to come to terms with
Yeats's works and their development (especially the stylistic develop-
ment). Remarkable for its sympathy with the earlier as well as the

later work. Pollock is, however, not attracted by Yeats's "metaphysical speculations," which he explains as a serious lack of humor, and is usually silent when faced with more complex questions. In the end, he finds Yeats "lacking in depth of human experience" and a "poet of frustration and isolation."
Reviews:
1. Anon., *TLS*, 34:1738 (23 May 1935), 332.
2. Karl Arns, *Englische Studien*, 71:2 (Dec 1936), 276-77.
3. G. Evans, *English Literary and Educational R*, 6:4 (Winter 1935 / 36), 133-37.
4. Desmond MacCarthy, "W. B. Yeats: His Seventieth Birthday," *Sunday Times*, #5855 (30 June 1935), 8.
5. P. S. O'H[egarty], *Dublin Mag*, 10:3 (July-Sept 1935), 82-83.
6. F[rancis] S[haw], *Studies*, 24:95 (Sept 1935), 492-93.

1125. PRITCHARD, WILLIAM H. (ed): *W. B. Yeats: A Critical Anthology*. Harmondsworth: Penguin, 1972. 390 p.
Contains 53 extracts from previously published criticism (not analyzed in this bibliography); some snippets from Yeats's own prose; two reviews of Yeats criticism by the editor (Early Criticism to 1940, pp. 17-28; Later Criticism after 1939, pp. 147-53); and a previously unpublished essay by Helen Vendler on the poetry, "Sacred and Profane Perfection in Yeats," 338-49, reprinted in *Southern R*, 9:1 (Jan 1973), 105-17.
Reviews:
1. John Bryson, "Unexpurgated Yeats," *Books and Bookmen*, 18:210 (Mar 1973), 52-53.
2. Robert Nye, "Yeats as a Bardic Poet," *Times*, #58678 (11 Jan 1973), 10.
3. Kathleen Raine, "Man behind the Magic," *Sunday Telegraph*, #620 (14 Jan 1973), 12.

1126. *RAJAN, BALACHANDRA: *W. B. Yeats: A Critical Introduction*. London: Hutchinson, 1965. 207 p.
Incorporates: "Yeats's 'Byzantium,'" *Osmania J of English Studies*, 5:1 (1965), 57-61; "The Reality Within," *Indian J of English Studies*, 6 (1965), 44-55. Perhaps the best short introduction to Yeats.
Reviews:
1. Anon., "A New Eye on Yeats," *TLS*, 64:3316 (16 Sept 1965), 802.
2. Charles Graves, "Consistency in Yeats," *Scotsman*, #38079 (12 June 1965), Weekend Mag, 2.
3. Giorgio Melchiori, *N&Q*, os 211 / ns 13:3 (Mar 1966), 114-17.
4. Harry T. Moore, "Time Pardons Him for Writing Well," *SatR*, 48:50 (11 Dec 1965), 39, 81.
5. Hermann Peschmann, *English*, 16:92 (Summer 1966), 67-69.
6. A. Ranganathan, *BA*, 41:1 (Winter 1967), 110.
7. Jon Stallworthy, *RES*, 17:67 (Aug 1966), 342-44.

1127. REID, BENJAMIN LAWRENCE: *William Butler Yeats: The Lyric of Tragedy*. Norman: U of Oklahoma Press, 1961. xiii, 282 p.
Based on "W. B. Yeats and Generic Tragedy," °Ph.D. thesis, U of Virginia, 1957. 376 p. (*DA*, 17:11 [Nov 1957], 2615.) Incorporates "Yeats and Tragedy," *Hudson R*, 11:3 (Autumn 1958), 391-410. On Yeats's theory of tragedy and on tragic themes in his poetry, not on the plays.
Reviews:
1. Patrick Cruttwell, "From Donne to Yeats," *Hudson R*, 15:3 (Autumn 1962), 451-54.

2. H. R. MacCallum, "W. B. Yeats: The Shape Changer and His Critics,"
   UTQ, 32:3 (Apr 1963), 307-13.
3. Francis Murphy, *BA*, 36:3 (Summer 1962), 319-20.

1128. REID, FORREST: *W. B. Yeats: A Critical Study*. Folcroft: Folcroft
Press, 1969 [1915]. 258 p.
   Incorporates "The Early Work of Mr. W. B. Yeats," *Irish R*, 1:11 (Jan
   1912), 529-36. Contains the following chapters: Early Poems; Poems,
   1890-1899; The Lyrical Dramas; Prose Tales and Sketches; Plays for
   an Irish Theatre; Collaboration [with Lady Gregory]; Philosophy; The
   Later Lyrics; Conclusion. Valuable as a document of the early Yeats
   reception, but otherwise somewhat dated.
   Reviews:
   1. Anon., *Athenaeum*, #4590 (16 Oct 1915), 259-60.
   2. Anon., *Irish Book Lover*, 7:6 (Jan 1916), 113-14.
   3. Anon., "Mr. Yeats's Poetry," *Nation* [London], 18:4 (23 Oct 1915),
      154, 156.
   4. Anon., "Living Authors as Seen by the Critic," *NYTBR*, [20:] (28
      Nov 1915), 478-79.
   5. Anon., "A Study of Mr. Yeats's Poetry," *Spectator*, 115:4555 (16
      Oct 1915), 510-11.
   6. Anon., "Mr. Yeats's Poetry," *TLS*, 14:715 (30 Sept 1915), 351.
   7. Lawrence Gilman, "The Last of the Poets," *NAR*, 202:719 (Oct 1915),
      592-97.
   8. P[hilip] L[ittell], "Books and Things," *New Republic*, 5:59 (18 Dec
      1915), 176.
   9. Crawford Neil, "W. B. Yeats," *New Ireland*, 2:32 (18 Dec 1915), 98-
      100.

1129. REVIEW OF ENGLISH LITERATURE: "W. B. Yeats Issue," *REL*, 4:3 (July
1963).
   A. N. J[effares]: "Editorial," 7-8. See the individual contributions
   by Yeats (J160 and 2204), Stallworthy (2440 and 5824), Stanford
   (4084), and Bushrui (3780).
   Reviews:
   1. Roger McHugh, "Yeats: A Phoenix among Hawks, Rooks and Sparrows,"
      Sunday Press, #705 (17 Nov 1963), 26.

1130. RISING GENERATION: "W. B. Yeats Centenary Number," *Rising Generation*, 111:11 (1 Nov 1965).
   Contains two articles on Yeats's poetry, one on his philosophy, two
   on his plays, and one on the Yeats Summer School, all in Japanese,
   pp. 722-34 (not analyzed in this bibliography); Frank Tuohy, "Yeats
   and Irish History" (reprinted from J1161, #1); Kenneth Gardiner,
   "Thoughts on Yeats and Mallarmé," 736-39; and eight general articles
   on Yeats in Japanese, 740-47 (not analyzed).

1131. SALVADORI, CORINNA: *Yeats and Castiglione: Poet and Courtier. A
Study of Some Fundamental Concepts of the Philosophy and Poetic Creed of
W. B. Yeats in the Light of Castiglione's "Il Libro del Cortegiano."*
Dublin: Figgis, 1965. x, 109 p.
   Based on an °M.A. thesis, University College, Dublin, 1961. Includes
   a discussion of the Yeats-Lady Gregory relationship.
   Reviews:
   1. Curtis Bradford, "A Yeats Gathering," *MLQ*, 28:1 (Mar 1967), 96-101.
   2. Timothy Brownlow, *Dublin Mag*, 5:1 (Spring 1966), 90-93.
   3. Michael P. Gallagher, *Studies*, 54:214-15 (Summer-Autumn 1965),
      284-88.

4. Harry T. Moore, "Time Pardons Him for Writing Well," *SatR*, 48:50
(11 Dec 1965), 39, 81.

1132. SCHAUP, SUSANNE MARGARETE: "William Butler Yeats in deutscher
Sicht," Dr. phil. thesis, U of Salzburg, [1968]. viii, 228 p.
On the reception of Yeats in Germany, Switzerland, and Austria, the
productions of his plays in these countries, and the German translations of his works. Includes a near-complete bibliography of German
translations and criticism. See also J1597.

1133. SCHMALENBECK, HILDEGARD: "The Early Career of W. B. Yeats," Ph.D.
thesis, U of Texas, 1957. ix, 414 p. (*DA*, 18:2 [Feb 1958], 593.)

1134. SEIDEN, MORTON IRVING: *William Butler Yeats: The Poet as Mythmaker,
1865-1939*. [East Lansing]: Michigan State UP, 1962. xiv, 397 p.
Based on "William Butler Yeats: His Poetry and Vision, 1914-1939,"
°Ph.D. thesis, Columbia U, 1952. 425 p. (*DA*, 12:4 [1952], 429). Incorporates: "Patterns of Belief: Myth in the Poetry of William Butler
Yeats," *American Imago*, 5:4 (Dec 1948), 258-300; "W. B. Yeats as a
Playwright," *WHR*, 13:1 (Winter 1959), 83-98.
   Sees *A Vision* as the center of Yeats's work and discusses the
influences and preliminary prose works leading up to it, the work
itself in its two versions and Yeats's own evaluation of it, and the
influence of the book on Yeats's poetry and plays.
Reviews:
1. Anon., "Thinking on Paper," *TLS*, 62:3187 (29 Mar 1963), 218.
2. Austin Clarke, "An Irish Chronicle," *Poetry*, 103:3 (Dec 1963),
185-87.
3. A. Norman Jeffares, "The Yeats Country," *MLQ*, 25:2 (June 1964),
218-22.
4. John B. Vickery, *WHR*, 18:2 (Spring 1964), 182-83.
5. John Unterecker, "Yeats: Seer and Dramatist," *Yale R*, 52:4 (June
1963), 585-88.

1135. SHENANDOAH: "Yeats and Ireland," *Shenandoah*, 16:4 (Summer 1965).
See the individual contributions by Hoffman (J5768), Unterecker
(827), Montague (2193), Clarke (611), Quinn (2722), and Murphy (6922).

1136. SKELTON, ROBIN, and ANN SADDLEMYER (eds): *The World of W. B. Yeats*.
Revised edition. Seattle: U of Washington Press, 1967. x, 231 p. (Washington Paperbacks. WP-23.)
   The first edition was entitled *The World of W. B. Yeats: Essays in
Perspective*. A symposium and catalogue on the occasion of the W. B.
Yeats Centenary Festival held at the University of Victoria, February
14 to March 16, 1965. Dublin: Dolmen Press, 1965. 278 p. The revised
edition does not contain the catalogue. Its documentation is rather
scrappy (unidentified quotations abound).
Contents: 1. Ann Saddlemyer: "The Cult of the Celt: Pan-Celticism in
the Nineties," 3-5. Too short to be of much help.
2. ————: "'The Noble and the Beggar-Man': Yeats and Literary Nationalism," 6-23. Particularly in the 1880s and 1890s.
3. Joan Coldwell: "'The Art of Happy Desire': Yeats and the Little
Magazine," 24-37. A rather superficial chronicle in which Yeats
occupies only an accidental and marginal place.
4. David R. Clark: "'Metaphors for Poetry': W. B. Yeats and the
Occult," 38-50.
5. Gwladys V. Downes: "W. B. Yeats and the Tarot," 51-53.
6. Ann Saddlemyer: "'The Heroic Discipline of the Looking Glass':
W. B. Yeats's Search for Dramatic Design," 57-73. Mostly on *The Player*

Queen and the influence of Gordon Craig and Ricketts.

7. ————: "'Worn Out with Dreams': Dublin's Abbey Theatre," 74-102.

8. Robin Skelton: "A Literary Theatre: A Note on English Poetic Drama in the Time of Yeats," 103-10. Davidson, Doughty, Phillips, Masefield, Gibson, Abercrombie, Sturge Moore, and Bottomley.

9. Liam Miller: "The Dun Emer and Cuala Press," 111-14, 127-33.

10. Joan Coldwell: "'Images That Yet Fresh Images Beget': A Note on Book-Covers," 134-39. The designs made by Althea Gyles, Sturge Moore, and Ricketts.

11. David R. Clark: "Vision and Revision: Yeats's *The Countess Cathleen*," 140-58.

12. Ann Saddlemyer: "Image-Maker for Ireland: Augusta, Lady Gregory," 161-68.

13. ————: "'All Art Is Collaboration'? George Moore and Edward Martyn," 169-88.

14. Robin Skelton: "Division and Unity: AE and W. B. Yeats," 189-98.

15. ————: "Aide to Immortality: The Satirical Writings of Susan L. Mitchell," 199-206.

16. Ann Saddlemyer: "'A Share in the Dignity of the World': J. M. Synge's Aesthetic Theory," 207-19.

17. Robin Skelton: "'Unarrangeable Reality': The Paintings and Writings of Jack B. Yeats," 220-31.

Reviews:

1. Curtis Bradford, "A Yeats Gathering," *MLQ*, 28:1 (Mar 1967), 96-101.

2. Ian Fletcher, *MLR*, 63:1 (Jan 1968), 228-29.

3. Hermann Peschmann, *English*, 16:92 (Summer 1966), 67-69.

4. Wulstan Phillipson, *Month*, os 221 / ns 35:1181 (Jan 1966), 60-61.

5. Hilary Pyle, *Dublin Mag*, 5:2 (Summer 1966), 94-95.

6. B. Rajan, "Conflict, More Conflict!" *UTQ*, 35:3 (Apr 1966), 315-20.

7. M. W. Steinberg, "Aspects of Yeats," *Canadian Literature*, #27 (Winter 1966), 67-69.

8. John Unterecker, *CE*, 27:7 (Apr 1966), 580-81.

1136a. SNUKAL, ROBERT MARTIN: *High Talk: The Philosophical Poetry of W. B. Yeats*. Cambridge: UP, 1973. viii, 270 p.

Based on °"Kantian and Neo-Kantian Elements in the Poetry of Yeats: A Study of the Controlling Metaphors of the Later Poetry," M.A. thesis, U. of Manitoba, 1968. Discusses Yeats's indebtedness to Kant, Hegel, Coleridge, Wordsworth, and Whitehead; his symbolism, romanticism, philosophy, and concept of history; and related poems, particularly "Among School Children," "At Algeciras," "Byzantium," "The Cold Heaven," "Colonus' Praise," "In Memory of Major Robert Gregory," "Lapis Lazuli," "The Second Coming," and "The Statues."

Reviews:

1. Anon., "Kant's Cousin Yeats," *TLS*, 72:3730 (31 Aug 1973), 996.

2. A. Norman Jeffares, "The Great Purple Butterfly," *Sewanee R*, 82:1 (Winter 1974), 108-18.

1137. SOUTHERN REVIEW: "Special Yeats Issue," *Southern R*, 7:3 (Winter 1941/42).

See the individual contributions by Blackmur (J2461), Knights (1709), Eliot (2512), Matthiessen (1480), Schwartz (1603), Gregory (2817), Davidson (1299), Ransom (2614), Burke (2742), Zabel (3987), Tate (1839), Mizener (2591), Warren (1830), Baker (3171), and Jarrell (1420). See also J1418.

Reviews:

1. Anon., *CE*, 3:3 (Mar 1942), 601-2.

2. M. D., *Dublin Mag*, 17:3 (July-Sept 1942), 54-55.

1138. —————: "W. B. Yeats: Critical Perspectives," *Southern R*, 5:3
(July 1969).
Contains a prefatory note by Donald E. Stanford, pp. 831-32, and
contributions by Henn (J1389), Frye (2702), Yeats (4089), Starkie
(1140), Parkinson (1538), and Fullwood (2117).

1139. °SPENDER, STEPHEN: *W. B. Yeats*. NY: McGraw-Hill, 1953. 49 minutes.
Tape recording. "The center of Yeats' vision is the inner life experience purged of the dross of actual living and transformed into a
symbol which possesses a life outside the poet's subjectivity"
(publisher's prospectus).

1140. STARKIE, WALTER, and ALEXANDER NORMAN JEFFARES: *Homage to Yeats*.
Papers read at a Clark Library Seminar, October 16, 1965. With an introduction by Majl Ewing. Los Angeles: William Andrews Clark Memorial
Library, 1966. vi, 78 p.
Starkie: "Yeats and the Abbey Theatre," 1-39; reprinted with slight
revisions in *Southern R*, 5:3 (July 1969), 886-921. Discusses the
development of Yeats's writing for, and interest in, the theater,
including some personal reminiscences.
Jeffares: "Women in Yeats's Poetry," 71-74; reprinted in J1102
(#5). Maud Gonne, "Diana Vernon" (whom Jeffares does not identify as
Olivia Shakespear), Lady Gregory, Iseult Gonne, and Mrs. Yeats.

1141. *STAUFFER, DONALD ALFRED: *The Golden Nightingale: Essays on Some
Principles of Poetry in the Lyrics of William Butler Yeats*. NY: Hafner,
1971 [1949]. vii, 165 p.
Incorporates: "Yeats and the Medium of Poetry," *ELH*, 15:3 (Sept 1948),
227-46; "The Reading of a Lyric Poem" ["The Wild Swans at Coole"],
Kenyon R, 11:3 (Summer 1949), 426-40. Particularly on *A Vision*,
Yeats's theory of the symbol, symbols in his poetry, the image of the
swan, and the development of his poetry.
Reviews:
1. Ray C. B. Brown, "The Song among the Reeds," *Voices*, #139 (Autumn
   1949), 35-39.
2. Mary Colum, "To a Yeatsian Urn," *SatR*, 33:4 (28 Jan 1950), 14-16.
3. Richard Ellmann, *MLN*, 66:5 (May 1951), 335-36.
4. John Farrelly, *New Republic*, 121:1810 (8 Aug 1949), 20.
5. Isabel Gamble, "Two Views of Yeats," *Hopkins R*, 3:2 (Winter 1950),
   52-54.
6. Robert Hillyer, "Explaining Yeats," *NYTBR*, 54:26 (26 June 1949),
   7, 16.
7. A. Norman Jeffares, *RES*, 2:7 (July 1951), 291-93.
8. Leo Kennedy, "Lyrical Approach to Yeats," *Chicago Sun-Times*, 2:167
   (15 Aug 1949), 39.
9. A. M. Klein, "The Masked Yeats," *Northern R*, 3:5 (June-July 1950),
   43-45.
10. R[oger] McH[ugh], *Studies*, 39:155 (Sept 1950), 345-46.
11. W. M. Parrish, *QJS*, 36:2 (Apr 1950), 263-64.
12. Henry W. Wells, "Intellectual Godfathers," *CE*, 11:5 (Feb 1950),
    294-96.
13. George Whalley, "Yeats's Mind," *Yale R*, 39:1 (Sept 1949), 165-67.
14. George F. Whicher, "The Lyricism of Yeats," *NYHTB*, 25:45 (26 June
    1949), 4.

1142. *STOCK, AMY GERALDINE: *W. B. Yeats: His Poetry and Thought*. Cambridge: UP, 1964 [1961]. xii, 255 p.

Incorporates: "W. B. Yeats: The Poet of Loneliness," *Modern R*, 86:
515 (Nov 1949), 405-7; "Art, Aristocracy and the Poetry of Yeats,"
Literary Criterion, 3:2 (Summer 1957), 131-40. Mostly on Yeats's
poetry and "ideas," with chapters on the Irish background, *The Countess Cathleen* and *The Land of Heart's Desire*, and *A Vision*.
Reviews:
1. Hazard Adams, *JEGP*, 61:2 (Apr 1962), 439-40.
2. H. H. Anniah Gowda, *Literary Half-Yearly*, 3:2 (July 1962), 80-82.
3. Anon., "Poet as Thinker," *Economist*, 200:6150 (8 July 1961), 146.
4. Anon., "A Dragonish Cloud," *TLS*, 60:3101 (4 Aug 1961), 480.
5. A[erol] A[rnold], *Personalist*, 43:2 (Spring 1962), 278-79.
6. Amalendu Bose, *Indian J of English Studies*, 3 (1962), 158-67.
7. V. L. O. Chittick, *MLQ*, 23:3 (Sept 1962), 272-73.
8. Austin Clarke, "Poet of Loneliness," *Irish Times*, #32979 (1 July
   1961), 8.
9. Gustav Cross, *AUMLA*, #17 (May 1962), 112-14.
10. David Daiches, "The Practical Visionary," *Encounter*, 19:3 (Sept
    1962), 71-74.
11. John Fraser, *Dalhousie R*, 42:1 (Spring 1962), 99-100.
12. René Fréchet, *EA*, 18:3 (July-Sept 1965), 321-22.
13. Brian Inglis, "'I, the Poet . . . ,'" *Spectator*, 206:6940 (30
    June 1961), 956.
14. A. Norman Jeffares, *MLR*, 57:2 (Apr 1962), 255-56.
15. H. R. MacCallum, "W. B. Yeats: The Shape Changer and His Critics,"
    UTQ, 32:3 (Apr 1963), 307-13.
16. George Brandon Saul, *Arizona Q*, 18:1 (Spring 1962), 95-96.
17. Irène Simon, *Revue des langues vivantes*, 31:4 (1965), 406-13.
18. Jon Stallworthy, *RES*, 13:52 (Nov 1962), 425-27.
19. Derek Stanford, *English*, 13:78 (Autumn 1961), 237-38.
20. John Unterecker, *CE*, 23:7 (Apr 1962), 605.
21. Peter Ure, *DUJ*, os 55 / ns 24:3 (June 1963), 155-56.

1143. *Terres celtiques: Ecole d'été de Dublin*. 12e voyage d'études (1965/
66). Lyon: Audin, [1966]. 83 p.
   Most of this issue is devoted to Yeats; it contains: 1. Claude
   Jandard: "Les voyages d'Oisin et la quête d'un poète," 39-43.
   2. Michel Christolhomme: "Enfance et jeunesse de Yeats," 44-46.
   3. Henri Carette: "Yeats poète irlandais," 47-51.
   4. Dominique Cesseux: "L'influence de Sligo, son pays natal, sur le
   poète William Butler Yeats," 52-53.
   5. Henri Carette: "La religion de Yeats," 54-59.
   6. Madeleine Revelin: "Magie et poésie populaire," 60-61.
   7. Renée Hougouvieux: "William Butler Yeats poète national," 62-64.
   8. René Fréchet: "Quelques étapes de l'oeuvre de Yeats," 65-74.
   9. Noël Pichon: "Yeats et les contes de fées," 75-78.

1144. *Terres celtiques: Ecole d'été de Dublin*. 13e voyage d'études (1966/
67). Lyon: Ecole d'été de Dublin, [1967]. 121 p.
   Most of this issue is devoted to Yeats; it contains translations of
   previously published material, which is more easily available elsewhere and therefore not listed separately in this bibliography.

1145. TEXAS QUARTERLY: [Yeats issue], *Texas Q*, 8:4 (Winter 1965).
   Contains a facsimile of Yeats's handprints, pp. 150-51, and contributions by Barker (J5729), Patmore (754), Mulvany (3084), and Raine
   (2154).

1146. THRESHOLD: "The Theatre of W. B. Yeats: Centenary 1965," *Threshold*, #19 (Autumn 1965). (Illustrated)
    See the individual contributions by McHugh (J3419), Clarke (3373), Jay (3537), Cohn (1944), Yeats (4193), O'Malley (3434), Warren (3513), and Oshima (2282).

1147. *TORCHIANA, DONALD THORNHILL: *W. B. Yeats & Georgian Ireland*. Evanston: Northwestern UP, 1966. xvi, 378 p.
    Based on "W. B. Yeats's Literary Use of Certain Anglo-Irish Augustans," °Ph.D. thesis, State U of Iowa, 1953. 289 p. (*DA*, 13:5 [1953], 815-16). Incorporates: "Senator Yeats, Burke, and Able Men," *Newberry Library Bulletin*, 5:8 (July 1961), 267-80; "W. B. Yeats, Jonathan Swift, and Liberty," *MP*, 61:1 (Aug 1963), 26-39.
    On the complex relationship between Yeats and Protestant Ireland, especially of the 18th century. A study based on an enormous amount of widely scattered material (uncollected essays and reviews, unpublished material, published interviews with Yeats, and reports of his speeches and lectures). Discusses the influence on, and importance for, Yeats of Trinity College Dublin, Lady Gregory, Robert Gregory, Sir Hugh Lane, John Shawe-Taylor, Swift (particularly on *The Words upon the Window-Pane*), Burke, Berkeley, and Goldsmith. The last two chapters are concerned with Yeats's treatment of the Georgian heritage in his poems, in *On the Boiler*, and in *Purgatory*.
    Reviews:
    1. Anon., "The Anglo-Irish Tradition," *Economist*, 221:6436 (31 Dec 1966), 1398.
    2. Denis Donoghue, "The Politics of Poetry," *NYRB*, 8:6 (6 Apr 1967), 22-25. David Levine's caricature of Yeats is not one of his best.
    3. David H. Greene, *MD*, 11:3 (Dec 1968), 336-38.
    4. Frank L. Kersnowski, *Éire-Ireland*, 1:4 (Winter 1966), 94-95.
    5. Richard J. Loftus, *JEGP*, 66:4 (Oct 1967), 613-14.
    6. Hugh B. Staples, *JJQ*, 3:4 (Summer 1966), 299-302.
    7. R. S. Thomas, *CQ*, 9:4 (Winter 1967), 380-83.
    8. Peter Ure, *N&Q*, os 213 / ns 15:2 (Feb 1968), 68-71.

1148. TRI-QUARTERLY: "W. B. Yeats Centenary," *Tri-Q*, #4 [Fall 1965]. (Illustrated)
    The lectures and discussions at the Yeats Festival of Northwestern University, Evanston, Illinois, in April 1965. Contents: Colton Johnson, "Editor's Foreword," 66-67; Donald T. Torchiana, "Some Dublin Afterthoughts," 138-43; and contributions by Fay (J1343), Colum (616), Ellmann (1874), Spender (1936), O'Brien (1101), Spender and others (1625), Prior (4183), Kelleher (1760), McHugh (3960), and Rajan (2665).

1149. UNIVERSITY REVIEW: "Special Yeats Edition," *University R* [Dublin], 3:8 [1966?].
    See the individual contributions by MacGreevy (J721), O'Meara (2284), Coffey (3279), O'Driscoll (994), Donoghue (1308), Liddy (1452), Burns (5738), O'Driscoll (6894), and Reynolds (5817).

1150. UNTERECKER, JOHN (ed): *Yeats: A Collection of Critical Essays*. Englewood Cliffs: Prentice-Hall, 1963. ix, 180 p. (Twentieth Century Views. S-TC-23.)
    Unterecker's introduction on Yeats as his own best interpreter (pp. 1-6) was first published in somewhat different form as "The Putting Together of W. B. Yeats," *Columbia U Forum*, 6:1 (Winter 1963), 41-44. The book contains 14 extracts from previously published criticism

(not analyzed in this bibliography).
Reviews:
1. Raymond Nelson, "Comments on Yeats," *Discourse*, 7:2 (Spring 1964), 203-7.
2. George Brandon Saul, *Arizona Q*, 20:4 (Winter 1964), 363-64.

1151. *URE, PETER: *Towards a Mythology: Studies in the Poetry of W. B. Yeats*. NY: Russell & Russell, 1967 [1946]. 123 p.

Defines myth as "a story, a framework of action and event, at once sufficiently firm to support passion and conflict, and sufficiently plastic for its meaning to be adapted to suit the personal poetic end" (p. 11). The poetic purpose is to translate the poet's inner landscape into poetry by means of the framework. Yeats's "stories" are those of Cuchulain, of his ancestors and friends, of *A Vision*, and of his fools, including Crazy Jane. Ure concludes that Yeats's framework was "a raft whose accommodation was severely limited to one" (p. 119). Yeats's poetry had little effect on his contemporaries.
Reviews:
1. Anon., "Yeats's Hero and Fool," *TLS*, 46:2345 (11 Jan 1947), 24.
2. Una Ellis-Fermor, *MLR*, 43:2 (Apr 1948), 267-69.
3. A. Norman Jeffares, *ES*, 30:1 (Feb 1949), 23-25.
4. J. B. Leishman, *RES*, 23:92 (Oct 1947), 372-74.

1152. *————: *Yeats*. Edinburgh: Oliver & Boyd, 1963. viii, 129 p. (Writers and Critics. 031.)

A good introduction to the poetry and the plays, less so to the prose. Includes a short survey of Yeats research (pp. 119-26). Does not attempt to see Yeats in any context, e.g., that of Irish tradition and history or of English literature, past or present.
Reviews:
1. Harry T. Moore, "Time Pardons Him for Writing Well," *SatR*, 48:50 (11 Dec 1965), 39, 81.
2. V. de S. Pinto, *CQ*, 6:2 (Summer 1964), 186-87.

1153. *VENDLER, HELEN HENNESSY: *Yeats's "Vision" and the Later Plays*. Cambridge, Mass.: Harvard UP, 1963. xiii, 286 p.

Based on "A Study of W. B. Yeats's *Vision* and the Plays Related to It," Ph.D. thesis, Radcliffe College, 1960. ii, 340 p. A patient analysis of *A Vision* and a rather prejudiced and unbalanced criticism of the following plays: *At the Hawk's Well, Calvary, The Death of Cuchulain, The Dreaming of the Bones, A Full Moon in March, The Herne's Egg, The King of the Great Clock Tower, The Only Jealousy of Emer, The Player Queen, Purgatory,* and *The Resurrection*. Includes extended notes on the following poems: "Byzantium," "Cuchulain Comforted," "Leda and the Swan" (pp. 105-8, not listed in the index), and "The Second Coming."
Reviews:
1. James L. Allen, *WHR*, 19:1 (Winter 1965), 90-92.
2. Anon., "Closed-Circuit," *TLS*, 62:3221 (21 Nov 1963), 945. Correspondence by Peter Ure, :3223 (5 Dec 1963), 1020.
3. Austin Clarke, "An Irish Chronicle," *Poetry*, 103:3 (Dec 1963), 185-87.
4. Padraic Fallon, "Documenting the Poet," *Irish Times*, #33645 (24 Aug 1963), 8.
5. David Fitzgerald, *Dubliner*, 3:1 (Spring 1964), 68-70.
6. Bernard Heringman, *MD*, 6:4 (Feb 1964), 464-65.
7. A Norman Jeffares, "The Yeats Country," *MLQ*, 25:2 (June 1964), 218-22.

8. Rolf Lass, *Kilkenny Mag*, #10 (Autumn-Winter 1963), 103-6.
9. E. L. Mayo, "Place of a Hot Potato," *SatR*, 46:24 (15 June 1963), 43.
10. Richard M. Ohmann, *Wisconsin Studies in Contemporary Literature*, 5:3 (Autumn 1964), 276-78.
11. V. de S. Pinto, *CQ*, 6:2 (Summer 1964), 186-87.
12. James Reaney, "How Not to Read Yeats," *Canadian Forum*, 43:513 (Oct 1963), 162-63.
13. Howard Sergeant, *English*, 14:84 (Autumn 1963), 243-44.
14. John Unterecker, "Yeats: Seer and Dramatist," *Yale R*, 52:4 (June 1963), 585-88.
15. Peter Ure, *RES*, 15:60 (Nov 1964), 444-47.
16. Sarah Youngblood, *Drama Survey*, 3:2 (Oct 1963), 319-20.

1154. °WEISS, THEODORE: *On William Butler Yeats*. NY: McGraw-Hill, 1966. 60 minutes.
  Tape recording.

1155. *WHITAKER, THOMAS RUSSELL: *Swan and Shadow: Yeats's Dialogue with History*. Chapel Hill: U of North Carolina Press, 1964. xi, 340 p.
  Based on "W. B. Yeats and His Concept of History," Ph.D. thesis, Yale U, 1953. i, 377 p. Incorporates: "W. B. Yeats: History and the Shaping Joy," *EIE*, 1959, 80-105; "The Dialectic of Yeats's Vision of History," *MP*, 57:2 (Nov 1959), 100-112; "The Early Yeats and the Pattern of History," *PMLA*, 75:2 (June 1960), 320-28; "Yeats's Alembic," *Sewanee R*, 68:4 (Oct-Dec 1960), 576-94; "Yeats's 'Dove or Swan,'" *PMLA*, 76:1 (Mar 1961), 121-32.
  This is not primarily a study of how history, past and contemporary, appears in Yeats's work, but rather the other way around: a discussion of Yeats's view of history as reflected in his work. As such, history appears in two principal perspectives: (1) as creative vision ("history is the landscape upon which the soul projects its image" [p. 8]) and (2) as dramatic experience "of existential immersion in history, where the anti-self may be . . . more disturbingly and dangerously confronted" (p. 9). Mainly on Yeats's poetry and related prose (especially *A Vision*). Chapters 7 and 9 discuss the Anglo-Irish background.
  Reviews:
  1. Hayden Carruth, "On Yeats and Others," *Poetry*, 107:3 (Dec 1965), 192-94.
  2. D. J. Gordon, *MLR*, 63:3 (July 1968), 693-94.
  3. Geoffrey Hartman, "Insiders and Outsiders," *Yale R*, 54:2 (Dec 1964), 270-73.
  4. John Montague, *CQ*, 8:4 (Winter 1966), 381-83.
  5. Timothy Rogers, *English*, 16:94 (Spring 1967), 152-54.
  6. Robert Scholes, "Yeats upon the Rood of Time," *American Scholar*, 34:1 (Winter 1964/65), 137-40.
  7. Helen Hennessy Vendler, "Assimilating Yeats," *MassR*, 7:3 (Summer 1966), 590-97.
  8. P[eter] W[olfe], *Prairie Schooner*, 39:1 (Spring 1965), 87-88.

1156. *WILSON, FRANCIS ALEXANDER CHARLES: *W. B. Yeats and Tradition*. London: Gollancz, 1958. 286 p.
  Incorporates "Patterns in Yeats's Imagery: *The Herne's Egg*," *MP*, 55: 1 (Aug 1957), 46-52. Part of the book was revised and submitted as a thesis: "W. B. Yeats: The Last Plays. A Commentary on Yeats's Sources for the Narrative, Symbolism and Philosophy of His Plays *The King of*

the *Great Clock Tower*, *A Full Moon in March*, *The Herne's Egg*, *Purgatory*, and *The Death of Cuchulain*," Ph.D. thesis, Cambridge U, 1959. ii, 282 p.

A controversial book. Besides the plays listed above, Wilson discusses *The Player Queen*, "Shepherd and Goatherd," "Chosen," "The Delphic Oracle upon Plotinus," "News for the Delphic Oracle," "The Black Tower," "Byzantium" (but see J3181), and "Cuchulain Comforted," by tracing their sources, usually Neo-Platonic and Irish. Wilson's readers were irritated by his claim that this "ulterior body of knowledge" is indispensable for a full understanding of the texts and by his failure to explain the texts as plays or poems. See also J1157.

Reviews:

1. Hazard Adams, *SAQ*, 58:3 (Summer 1959), 479-80.
2. Anon., *Listener*, 59:1507 (13 Feb 1958), 287.
3. Anon., "Plato in Sligo," *Times*, #54050 (16 Jan 1958), 13.
4. Anon., "Yeats's Use of Symbolism," *TLS*, 57:2917 (24 Jan 1958), 43.
5. Aerol Arnold, *Personalist*, 41:1 (Winter 1960), 115-16.
6. R. P. Blackmur, "Obscuris vera involvens," *Kenyon R*, 20:1 (Winter 1958), 160, 162-64, 166-68.
7. Christine Brooke-Rose, *London Mag*, 5:7 (July 1958), 77, 79, 81, 83.
8. Christopher Busby, "Yeats and His Beliefs," *Dublin R*, 232:476 (Summer 1958), 178-81.
9. Cyril Connolly, "Yeats's Use of Symbols," *Sunday Times*, #7026 (12 Jan 1958), 8.
10. Babette Deutsch, "The Poet and His Symbols," *NYHTB*, 35:38 (17 May 1959), 5.
11. Padraic Fallon, "Verse Chronicle," *Dublin Mag*, 33:2 (Apr-June 1958), 39-45 (pp. 39-41).
12. Hugh Fausset, "A Source-Book for Yeats," *Manchester Guardian*, #34723 (18 Feb 1958), 6.
13. Helen Gardner, "Symbolic Equations," *NSt*, 55:1403 (1 Feb 1958), 141-42. Correspondence by Kathleen Raine, "A Little Song about a Rose," :1404 (8 Feb 1958), 170; Helen Gardner, :1405 (15 Feb 1958), 202; F. A. C. Wilson, :1407 (1 Mar 1958), 273; Helen Gardner, :1408 (8 Mar 1958), 305.
14. John Edward Hardy, "After the New Criticism," *Yale R*, 48:3 (Mar 1959), 410-13.
15. Thomas Hogan, "Old Man's Anger," *Spectator*, 200:6760 (17 Jan 1958), 78.
16. G. F. Hudson, *Twentieth Century*, 163:975 (May 1958), 482-83.
17. A. Norman Jeffares, *MLR*, 54:2 (Apr 1959), 271-73.
18. Frank Kermode, "The Persecution of the Abstract," *Encounter*, 10:3 (Mar 1958), 77-78. Correspondence by T. R. Henn, "Studying Yeats," :5 (May 1958), 69-70; answer by Kermode, *ibid.*, 70-71; correspondence by F. A. C. Wilson, 11:1 (July 1958), 76.
19. Thomas P. McDonnell, *Catholic World*, 188:1128 (Mar 1959), 520-22.
20. Edwin Muir, "Ruthless Interpreter," *Observer*, #8689 (12 Jan 1958), 15.
21. Harold Orel, "Views of a Vision," *Prairie Schooner*, 33:3 (Fall 1959), 283-84.
22. Thomas Parkinson, "Two Books on Yeats," *Sewanee R*, 66:4 (Oct-Dec 1958), 678-87.
23. R. F. Rattray, *Hibbert J*, 56:222 (Apr 1958), 311-12.
24. George Brandon Saul, *Arizona Q*, 15:2 (Summer 1959), 177-78.
25. Eleanor M. Sickels, *Explicator*, 18:1 (Oct 1959), R1.

26. John Unterecker, *History of Ideas Newsletter*, 5:4 (Jan 1960), 80-82.

1157. *————: *Yeats's Iconography*. London: Gollancz, 1960. 349 p.
Written along the lines of the previous book (on which the author
comments on pp. 304-6). Discusses *At the Hawk's Well, The Only
Jealousy of Emer, The Cat and the Moon, Calvary, The Dreaming of the
Bones*, "The Two Trees," "He Thinks of His Past Greatness When a Part
of the Constellations of Heaven," "Towards Break of Day," "Meditations in Time of Civil War," "The Collar-Bone of a Hare," "The Wheel,"
"The Hour before Dawn," "Demon and Beast," "Solomon and the Witch,"
"At Algeciras," "Mohini Chatterjee," and "The Statues."
Reviews:
1. Anon., "The Man and the Masks," *TLS*, 59:3051 (19 Aug 1960), 530.
   Correspondence by Rupert and Helen Gleadow, :3055 (16 Sept 1960),
   593.
2. A[erol] A[rnold], *Personalist*, 43:2 (Spring 1962), 278-79.
3. Birgit Bramsbäck, *Studia Neophilologica*, 34:1 (1962), 168-70.
4. Austin Clarke, "Hither and Thither," *Irish Times*, #32702 (23 July
   1960), 6.
5. David Daiches, *Listener*, 64:1638 (18 Aug 1960), 269-70.
6. G. S. Fraser, "Hard Symbolic Bones," *NSt*, 60:1537 (27 Aug 1960),
   280.
7. W. R. Grey, *Focus*, 4:12 (Dec 1961), 289.
8. Frank Kermode, "A Bundle of Ideas," *Spectator*, 205:6893 (5 Aug
   1960), 220.
9. R. F. Rattray, *Hibbert J*, 59:232 (Oct 1960), 101-3.

1158. °WIMBISH, LELA ELLEN CLIFTON: "William Butler Yeats: His Mind and
Art," M.A. thesis, U of Texas, 1938 [i.e., 1941]. vii, 126 p.

1159. WRENN, CHARLES LESLIE: *W. B. Yeats: A Literary Study*. London:
Murby, 1920. 16 p.
Reprinted from *DUJ*, 22:3 (July 1919), 82-88; :4 (Nov 1919), 118-25.
A somewhat labored essay by a conservative critic who is out of
sympathy with Yeats's later development. Wrenn is, however, one of
the first critics to point to Neo-Platonic influences, but he does
not pursue the topic.

1160. YEATS ASSOCIATION [Dublin]: *Bulletin*.
#1 (Easter 1967): Contains news and notes and the constitution of
the Association.
#2 (Spring 1968): Contains news and notes and an article by Micheál
O hAodha (see J4180).
A third number is said to have been published in 1970. I have not
been able to trace it.

1161. YEATS SOCIETY OF JAPAN: *Annual Report*.
#1 (1966): News and notes; synopses of speeches made at the inaugura-
tion ceremony of the society; a congratulatory address by E. W. F.
Tomlin; an article by Frank Tuohy, "Yeats and Irish History," 6-9
(reprinted in J1130); and synopses of the following papers: Iwas
Mizuta, "W. B. Yeats and Zen Buddhism," 9-10; Yukio Oura, "On the
Wisdom of W. B. Yeats," 10-11; William Johnston, "On *Cathleen ni
Houlihan*," 11.
#2 (1967): News and notes; "Yeats and His Circle: A Series of Photo-
graphs for the Yeats Centenary . . . ," 5-8 (catalogue of 48 items);
"W. B. Yeats: Bibliography in Japan, 1966," 9; E. W. F. Tomlin, "The

Continuity of Yeats," 10-15 (also in J1162, #2; reprinted from J1661);
Shuji Yamamoto, "Yeats and Synge," 16-20 (see J2271).
#3 (1968-69): News and notes; Junzaburo Nishiwaki, "Yeats and Symbol-
ism," 3-4 (synopsis); Hisashi Furukawa, "Yeats and Noh," 5-6 (synopsis); Okifumi Komesu, "Brahman or Daimon: Yeats's Schooling in Eastern Thought," 7-18 (part 1, see J4019); Hiromi Itoh, "Yeats: Archetypal Religious Perception," 18-19; Shotaro Oshima, "Addresses Given
. . . before the Sligo Yeats Society and the Japan-Ireland Friendship
Society (August 1968)," 21-24.
#4 (1970): News and notes; James Kirkup, "The Stones of Yeats," 5-19
(see J2900); Okifumi Komesu, part 2 of his article (see J4019), 20-
26; Shotaro Oshima, "A Message to the People of Ireland," 27-28.
#5 (1970), combined with the society's *Bulletin*, #5: "Tributes in
Prose and Verse to Shotaro Oshima on the Occasion of His Seventieth
Birthday, Sept. 29, 1969," 1-26 (also published separately; see
J2443); James Kirkup, "The Stones of Yeats," 27-41 (reprinted from
the previous *Annual Report* [!]); Hiroshi Suzuki, "Shelley's Influence
on 'The Second Coming,'" 42-46 (see J3234); Ken'ichi Matsumura, "Fire
and Bird," 47-51 (see J2679); Shotaro Oshima, "Irish Notes," 52-57
(see J2391). All the preceding items are on the left-to-right pages.
The following articles are in Japanese, printed on the right-to-left
pages: Iwao Mizuta, "W. B. Yeats and Egan O'Rahilly," 1-9; Sachio
Oura, "The Theme of *At the Hawk's Well*," 10-15; Yushiro Takahashi,
"Allegory and Symbolism," 16-21; Tonaji Hoashi, "Donagh MacDonagh,"
22-27; Giichi Ouchi, "On Thomas Dermody," 28-33. Also some synopses.
#6 (1971): News and notes; Roger McHugh, "Ah, Sweet Dancer—W. B.
Yeats: Some Newly Discovered Letters and a New Poem," 4-14 (see
J2819); Shotaro Oshima, "Yeats and Michio Ito," 15-20 (see J3492);
Ken'ichi Matsumura, "A Tree Image of W. B. Yeats," 21-25 (see J2936).
#7 (1972): "The Seventh General Meeting of the Yeats Society of
Japan," 1-3; Frank Tuohy, "Yeats and Politics," 4-8 (see J2850);
Shotaro Oshima, "Yeats and the Noh," 9-18 (see J3567); Ken'ichi
Matsumura, "'Sailing to Byzantium': A Note," 19-23 (see J3192); mate-
rial on the visit of Michael and Grainne Yeats.
#8 (1973): Michael Yeats, "Words and Music," 7-18 (on Yeats's inter-
est in Irish folk music and ballads); news and notes.

1162. ———: *Bulletin*.
#1 (Apr 1966): Tetsuro Sano, "The Meaning of Yeats's 'Memory,'" 1-12;
Mariko Kai, "On Irish 'Mob Censorship,'" 13-19. Both articles are in
Japanese, right-to-left paging. News and notes and a list of the
society's members, pp. 32-19, partly in English, to be read left-to-
right but paged in reverse.
#2 (June 1967): E. W. F. Tomlin, "The Continuity of Yeats," 1-6 (see
J1161, #2). The following articles are in Japanese and printed and
paged right-to-left: Shūji Yamamoto, "Yeats and Synge," 1-6; Taketoshi Furomoto, "On the Repetition in Yeats's Poetry," 7-20; Yushiro
Takahashi, "Yeats and Mallarmé," 21-32; Saburo Onuki, "W. B. Yeats
and the Chicago Critic," 33-37 (the Cleanth Brooks—Elder Olson
approach); news and notes.
#3 (Dec 1968): All articles are in Japanese, right-to-left: Junzaburo
Nishiwaki, "Yeats and Symbolism," 1-2; Hisashi Furukawa, "Yeats and
the Noh," 3-4; Joji Mori, "'The Black Tower': On the Study of Literature," 5-15; Masao Igarashi, "Yeats: His Poetry and Drama," 16-20;
Tsunehiki Hoshino, "From *At the Hawk's Well* to *Takahime*," 21-28;
synopses, news, and notes.

#4 (Dec 1969): All articles are in Japanese, right-to-left: Taka-
michi Ninomiya, "Modernity of the Modern Poetry," 1-5; Giichi Ouchi,
"Songs about the Leprechaun," 7-11; Shirō Naitō, "Influence of Zen
upon 'The Statues,'" 12-20; Yasunari Shimizu, "W. B. Yeats's Anti-
Democracy Reconsidered," 21-28 (obviously concerned with Harrison,
J1380); Tonaji Hoashi, "In the Year 1891," 29-36; Shotaro Oshima,
"Dublin Notes: Mr. Michael Yeats and the Late Mrs. W. B. Yeats,"
37-39; synopses, news, and notes.
#5 (1970): See the society's Annual Report, #5 (J1161).
#6 (Oct 1971): All articles are in Japanese, right-to-left: Sadao
Sasakura, "The Disintegration of Images in Yeats's Poetry," 1-6;
Tatsuo Yamamoto, "Bernard Shaw and Ireland," 7-13; Minoru Hirooka,
"Yeats and Roethke," 14-17; synopses, news, and notes.
#7 (Dec 1972): All articles are in Japanese, right-to-left: Giichi
Ouchi, "On Carolan," 1-4; Akiko Suzue, "The Shadowy Waters: Dream,
Love, Reality," 5-10; Yoshiaki Inomata, "Yeats and Shakespeare,"
11-17; Toshiichiro Okazaki, "Poetic Imagination," 18-23; synopses,
news, and notes.
#8 (Dec 1973): All articles are in Japanese: Ken Mori, "W. B. Yeats
and French Symbolism (I)," 1-7; Shiro Naito, "From Cubism to Zen--
Yeats on the Eve of Fascism," 8-12; Hiroyuki Yamazaki, "Refrain in
Yeats's Poetry--On 'Poetry of Insight and Knowledge,'" 13-18; Akio
Matsuyama, "Yeats and Noh--On His The Dreaming of the Bones," 19-22;
news and notes.

1163. Yeats Studies: An International Journal.
#1 (Bealtaine 1971): "Yeats and the 1890s." Introduction by Lorna
Reynolds and Robert O'Driscoll. For individual contributions see
Murphy (J922), Beckson (2060), Fletcher (651), Harper (4009), Yeats
(171-74), and Harper (4010).
Reviews:
1. John Bryson, "Yeatsiana," Books and Bookmen, 17:199 (Apr 1972),
   24.
2. Norman H. MacKenzie, QQ, 78:4 (Winter 1971), 630-31.
3. Phillip L. Marcus, "Approaching W. B.," Irish Press, 41:229 (25
   Sept 1971), 12.
4. Augustine Martin, Studies, 61:241 (Spring 1972), 107-10.
#2 (Bealtaine 1972): "Theatre and the Visual Arts: A Centenary
Celebration of Jack Yeats and John Synge." For details see J7442.

1164. YOUNGBLOOD, SARAH HELEN: "William Butler Yeats: The Mature Style,"
Ph.D. thesis, U of Oklahoma, 1958. vi, 252 p. (DA, 19:7 [Jan 1959],
1764.)

1165. ZWERDLING, ALEX: Yeats and the Heroic Ideal. NY: New York UP, 1965.
ix, 196 p.
Based on a °Ph.D. thesis, Princeton U, 1960. 249 p. (DA, 21:8 [Feb
1961], 2301). Incorporates "W. B. Yeats: Variations on the Visionary
Quest," UTQ, 30:1 (Oct 1960), 72-85.
Zwerdling discusses the Irish hero, the aristocrat, the public
hero, and the visionary in Yeats's work. He does not offer extended
interpretations but is unfortunately content to assemble snippets
from various pieces and periods. He sees Yeats's conception "of
heroism as essentially nostalgic and anachronistic" (p. 134), which
I think is only one-half of the truth. Zwerdling does not answer the
obvious question of what Yeats thought to be heroic and whether he
believed that his convictions had a chance of realization or were
based on historically unassailable facts, or whether his convictions

developed or changed. Various minor inaccuracies suggest that
Zwerdling's scholarship is not of the highest standard, but I do not
think that he has written an entirely bad book. It is simply not good
enough and wastes its theme. See also Torchiana's review, below.
Reviews:
1. Curtis Bradford, "A Yeats Gathering," *MLQ*, 28:1 (Mar 1967), 96-101.
2. Brian John, "Hurt into Poetry: Some Recent Yeats Studies," *J of General Education*, 18:4 (Jan 1967), 299-306.
3. Harry T. Moore, "Time Pardons Him for Writing Well," *SatR*, 48:50 (11 Dec 1965), 39, 81.
4. B. Rajan, "Conflict, More Conflict!" *UTQ*, 35:3 (Apr 1966), 315-20.
5. Raney Stanford, *ELN*, 5:1 (Sept 1967), 67-68.
6. Donald T. Torchiana, "Three Books on Yeats," *PQ*, 46:4 (Oct 1967), 536-56.

See also J513, 514, 556, 3486.

CB   Articles and Parts of Books

1166. ACEVEDO, LUCIANO DE: "El poeta W. B. Yeats," *Cuba contemporánea*,
yr 12 / 34:136 (Apr 1924), 357-63.

1167. ADKINSON, R. V.: "Criticizing Yeats," *Revue des langues vivantes*,
33:5 (1967), 423-30.
Too many source studies and a "self-perpetuating process of re-
interpretation" have obscured the essential question of why Yeats
is worth reading and the position he occupies in his time.

1168. ALBERT, EDWARD: *A History of English Literature*. 3rd edition revised
by J. A. Stone. London: Harrap, 1960 [1923]. 624 p.
"William Butler Yeats," 482-86.

1168a. ALLEN, JAMES LOVIC: "The Road to Byzantium: Archetypal Criticism
and Yeats," *JAAC*, 32:1 (Fall 1973), 53-64.
Archetypal criticism based on Jung and Frye fails to explain Yeats
adequately; his own mythological views are much more akin to those
of Philip Wheelwright.

1168b. ————: "From Puzzle to Paradox: New Light on Yeats's Late Career,"
Sewanee R, 82:1 (Winter 1974), 81-92.
The paradox that Yeats accepted both the physical and the spiritual
world after about 1926 can be explained by reference to his belief
in the tenets of *A Vision* and his conviction that he must live according to his phase. Contains a note on the epitaph in "Under Ben Bulben."

1169. ANDERSON, GEORGE K., and EDA LOU WALTON (eds): *This Generation*.
Revised edition. Chicago: Scott, Foresman, 1949 [1939]. xvi, 1065 p.
"William Butler Yeats," 91-93.

1170. ANON.: "Some Younger Reputations: Mr. W. B. Yeats," *Academy*, 52:
1335 (4 Dec 1897), 488-89.
"To Mr. Yeats we look for a masterpiece, since his imagination is of
the highest quality, and his execution is not far beneath it."

1171. ANON.: "The Moderns: VII. William Butler Yeats," *America*, 30:740
(1 Dec 1923), 166.
"Of some of his work, there can be no word spoken in dispraise; but
in regard to other writings [i.e., those offensive to Catholics],
silence is charity."

1172. ANON.: Editorials, *Catholic Bulletin*, 13:12 (Dec 1923), 817-19; 14:
1 (Jan 1924), 5-7; :9 (Sept 1924), 745-50; :11 (Nov 1924), 929-38; 15:4
(Apr 1925), 291-94, 316-17; :7 (July 1925), 641-45; :9 (Sept 1925), 854-
57; 16:1 (Jan 1926), 4-10; :3 (Mar 1926), 242-52; :5 (May 1926), 456-57;
:6 (June 1926), 572-74; 18:7 (July 1928), 676-77; :10 (Oct 1928), 988-92.
    Hysterical anti-Yeats diatribes. See also other issues of the same
    period; in one of them (15:1 [Jan 1925], 1), the Ascendancy writers
    and politicians are called "The Cloacal Combine."

1173. ANON.: "Ireland and the Theatre," *Claidheamh Soluis*, 12:2 (19 Mar
1910), 7.
    Yeats and the Gaelic League.

1174. ANON.: "Setna rocznica urodzin Yeatsa" [Centenary of Yeats's birth],
Dialog, 10:8 (Aug 1965), 135-37.

1175. ANON.: "Centenary of the Birth of W. B. Yeats," *Eire-Ireland: Weekly
Bulletin of the Department of External Affairs*, #706 (15 June 1965), 1-16.

1176. ANON.: "Yeats: Sunday Next Will Be the Centenary of the Poet's
Birth," *Evening Herald*, 74:138 (11 June 1965), 6.

1177. ANON.: "A Dublin Literary Coterie Sketched by a Non-Pretentious
Observer," *Evening Telegraph*, ns #2583 (14 Jan 1888), [2].
    According to Monk Gibbon (J557, p. 58), Sappho is Katharine Tynan,
    O'Reilly is AE, and Augustus Fitzgibbon is Yeats.

1178. ANON.: "An Irish National Theatre," *Irish Daily Independent and
Daily Nation*, #3631 (8 Oct 1903), 4.
    Criticizes Yeats's "eccentricities," his "unwholesome products," and
    his advocacy of artistic freedom. See the report of a Yeats speech
    in which he replied to this article, "Mr. Yeats and Ourselves,"
    #3632 (9 Oct 1903), 6.

1179. ANON.: "William Butler Yeats: The Life and Labours of a Young Celtic
Poet," *Irish Emerald*, 6:4 (23 Jan 1897), 56.

1180. ANON.: "An Alchemist's Forge--Where Yeats Drew Out Crumbs of Gold,"
Irish Independent, 72:279 (22 Nov 1963), 14.
    Report of John Masefield's speech at the opening of the Yeats Room
    in the New Ambassador's Hotel, Woburn Place, London.

1181. ANON.: "These Characters Remain," *Irish Times*, #35145 (27 Aug 1968),
11.
    Editorial on the death of Mrs. Yeats. See also R. M. Fox, "Mrs. George
    Yeats: An Appreciation," #35156 (9 Sept 1968), 11; and J1185.

1181a. ANON.: [The Showing Up of Pensioner Yeats], *Leader*, 23:15 (25 Nov
1911), 348-49.
    Sneers; see also preceding and subsequent issues.

1182. ANON.: "Why Yeats Is a Nobel Prize Man," *Literary Digest*, 79:1755
(8 Dec 1923), 26-27.
    Extracts from press notices.

1182a. ANON.: "Mr. W. B. Yeats," *Literary Year-Book*, 1897, 174-75.
    A survey of his publications to date.

1183. ANON.: "Mr. Yeats's Nobel Prize," *Manchester Guardian*, #24102 (16
Nov 1923), 8.

1184. ANON.: "Mr. Yeats at Seventy," *NYT*, 84:28281 (30 June 1935), IV, 8.

1185. ANON.: "Georgina Yeats, Widow of Irish Poet, Dead at 75," *NYT*, 117: 40392 (26 Aug 1968), 39.
See also J1181.

1186. ANON.: "William Butler Yeats--Poezja i polityka," *Odgłosy*, 8:26 (4 July 1965), 9.

1187. ANON.: Note on Yeats in Croatian, *Radio Zagreb*, 8:1 (1952), 8.

1188. ANON.: "A Fine Poet: Mr. W. B. Yeats Visits Sheffield," *Sheffield Daily Telegraph*, #20015 (23 Nov 1922), 8.
Reprinted in J994.

1189. ANON.: "Mr. Yeats and the Chair," *Sinn Féin*, ns 4:170 (3 May 1913), 5.
See also J1194 and 1324.

1190. ANON.: "Personalities and Powers: William Butler Yeats," *Time and Tide*, 5:32 (8 Aug 1924), 762-64.

1191. ANON.: "Mr. W. B. Yeats: Award of Nobel Prize," *Times*, #43499 (15 Nov 1923), 12.

1192. ANON.: "Mr. W. B. Yeats: An Appreciation," *Times*, #48217 (31 Jan 1939), 17.
Correspondence by D[orothy] W[ellesley], #48225 (9 Feb 1939), 19.

1193. ANON.: "The Last Romantic," *Times*, #56346 (12 June 1965), 11.

1194. ANON.: "Vacant Trinity Professorships," *Times Educational Supplement*, 4:3 (6 May 1913), 74.
Discusses the prospects of Yeats's appointment as Professor of English Literature: "He has not of late given the world much verse; the delicate and sensitive quality of his poetic gift was hardly of a nature to last into middle life. But he is and will remain an excellent interpreter of poetry. He has not, indeed, published much regular criticism, but the occasional brief essays which have accompanied the play-bills of the Abbey Theatre show that he can write of the literary art with the tact and penetration of one who is familiar with its secrets. On the other hand, it is impossible to imagine Mr. Yeats facing the routine duties of a university professor; it would be, to say the least, incongruous to ask this poet of fairyland to set examination papers and add up columns of marks."
See also J1189 and 1324.

1195. ANON.: "Yeats's Inner Drama: A Poet of Two Reputations. Appeal of the Later Works," *TLS*, 38:1931 (4 Feb 1939), 72, 74.

1196. ANON.: "The Success of Yeats," *TLS*, 38:1931 (4 Feb 1939), 73.

1197. ANON.: "England Is Abroad," *TLS*, 57:2929 (18 Apr 1958), 201-2.
The development of Yeats attests "the diminished importance of England's contribution to English literature." Correspondence by Vivian Mercier, "Yeats and 'The Fisherman,'" :2936 (6 June 1958), 313.

1198. ANON.: "Under Ben Bulben," *TLS*, 64:3282 (21 Jan 1965), 47.
Correspondence by Robert O'Driscoll, :3286 (18 Feb 1965), 132.

1199. ANON.: "The Week's Work," *United Ireland*, 14:705 (9 Mar 1895), 4.
Editorial on Yeats's list of the thirty best Irish books, published in the *Dublin Daily Express*, 27 Feb 1895 (Wp. 346), and a note on Edward Dowden's reaction. Correspondence by D. F. Hannigan, :706 (16 Mar 1895), 3, and by Yeats, *ibid.* (Wp. 347).

1200. ANON.: "Mr. Yeats on Irish Literature," *United Ireland*, 15:728 (17 Aug 1895), 1.

Criticizes Yeats's articles on "Irish National Literature" in *Bookman* (Wp. 347).

1201. ANON.: "The Literary Movement in Ireland," *United Irishman*, 3:45 (6 Jan 1900), 2.

On Yeats's article "The Literary Movement in Ireland," in *NAR* (Wp. 357).

1202. ARCHER, WILLIAM: *Poets of the Younger Generation*. London: Lane, 1902. vii, 565 p.

"William Butler Yeats," 531-57. On the early poems and plays. Regards Yeats as "the quintessential spirit of Keltic eld," compares *The Countess Cathleen* with Maeterlinck's plays, and remarks in connection with the notes to *The Wind among the Reeds* that Yeats "is becoming more and more addicted to a petrified, fossilized symbolism, a system of hieroglyphs which may have had some inherent significance for their inventors, but which have now become matters of research, of speculation, of convention."

1202a. ARMSTRONG, ROBERT: *The Poetic Vision: Signposts and Landmarks in Poetry. Essays and Lectures*. London: Mitre Press, 1973. 133 p.

"W. B. Yeats: The Man and His Poetry," 79-85.

1203. ARNS, KARL: "Der Träger des Nobel-Preises," *Literatur*, 26:5 (Feb 1924), 261-65.

1204. ————: "William Butler Yeats," *Schöne Literatur*, 30:6 (June 1929), 248-56.

1205. ————: "W. B. Yeats: Zum 70. Geburtstag am 13. Juni," *Hamburger Fremdenblatt*, 107:161 (12 June 1935), 2.

1206. ASTALDI, MARIA LUISA: *Il poeta e la regina e altre letture inglesi*. Firenze: Sansoni, 1963. 284 p.

"Un grande poeta del novecento: W. B. Yeats," 107-10.

1207. ATKINS, JOHN: "Soul against the Intellect. W. B. Yeats: The Point of Balance," *Books and Bookmen*, 2:12 (Sept 1957), 11.

1208. ATKINSON, BROOKS: "Critic at Large: The Yeats Brothers Remain a Dominant Force in Ireland's Cultural Life," *NYT*, 112:38130 (14 Dec 1962), 5.

1209. ATKINSON, F. M.: "A Literary Causerie," *Dana*, #10 (Feb 1905), 314-17.

Criticizes Yeats's "synthetic Celticism" and the "twilight" limitation of his work: "where vigorous deedful life is required he can give nothing."

1210. AUDEN, W. H.: "The Private Life of a Public Man," *Mid-Century*, #4 (Oct 1959), 8-15.

A misnomer. Although intended to be a review of *Mythologies*(W211P/Q), this is Auden's assessment of a poet whom he admires in some respects (his workmanship, his adaptability) and confesses not to understand in others. Auden is especially critical of Yeats's "system," of his early work, and of his ninetyish background.

1211. A[YNARD], J[OSEPH]: "Le prix Nobel de littérature: W. B. Yeats," *Journal des débats politiques et littéraires*, 135:319 (17 Nov 1923), 1.

1212. ————: "W. B. Yeats: Lauréat du Prix Nobel," *Revue de Paris*, 31:1 (1 Jan 1924), 176–89.

1213. BACKER, FRANZ DE: "William Butler Yeats," *Dietsche Warande en Belfort*, 39:4 (Apr 1939), 249–68.

1214. BAGSHAW, WILLIAM: "W. B. Yeats," *Manchester Q*, 41:164 (Oct 1922), 227–48.

1215. BALL, PATRICIA M.: *The Central Self: A Study in Romantic and Victorian Imagination*. London: Athlone Press, 1968. x, 236 p.
Contains a note on Yeats, pp. 226–28, whose work constitutes "the apotheosis of the ego."

1215a. BARTOŠ, JOSEF: "William Butler Yeats," *Lumír*, 34:7 (17 May 1906), 327–31; :8 (16 June 1906), 372–75; :9 (17 July 1906), 423–26.

1216. BATES, KATHARINE LEE: "William Butler Yeats: The Irish Poet Who Is Now Visiting America," *BET*, 74:[] (11 Nov 1903), 16.
Subheadings: A sketch of his career and work and an estimate of their value—His great labors for the Celtic Revival—His ascetic devotion to his art—An important figure in literature. An extract was published as "The 'Standard-Bearer' of the Celtic Revival," *Literary Digest*, 27:710 (28 Nov 1903), 737–38.

1217. BÁTI, LÁSZLÓ, and ISTVÁN KRISTÓ-NAGY (eds): *Az angol irodalom a huszadik században*. Budapest: Gondolat, 1970. 2 v.
Ágnes Gergely: "William Butler Yeats," 1:103–21; 2:314–15.
Emil Koloszvári Grandpierre: "Sean O'Casey," 1:207–25; 2:301–2.

1218. BAUGH, ALBERT CROLL (ed): *A Literary History of England*. NY: Appleton-Century-Crofts, 1967 [1948]. 4 v. in 1.
Samuel C. Chew and Richard D. Altick: "The Irish Literary Renaissance," 1507–15; on Yeats, 1508–12.

1219. BAX, CLIFFORD: *Some I Knew Well*. London: Phoenix House, 1951. 192 p.
"W. B. Yeats: Chameleon of Genius," 97–103; and *passim* (see index).

1220. BAYLEY, JOHN: *The Romantic Survival: A Study in Poetic Evolution*. London: Constable, 1957. vii, 231 p.
"W. B. Yeats," 77–126. Yeats, Auden, and Dylan Thomas "found romanticism at low ebb, and its legacy rather a liability than an asset, but . . . were able to rediscover its original scope and richness" (p. 78). Comments on mask, conversation, and symbol in Yeats's poetry and includes a short comparison with Wilfred Owen.
Reviews:
1. Anon., "What Is Romantic Poetry?" *TLS*, 56:2875 (5 Apr 1957), 208.
2. Graham Hough, "Shrinking Poetry," *Spectator*, 198:6720 (12 Apr 1957), 490.
3. Peter Ure, "From Wordsworth to Yeats," *Listener*, 58:1478 (25 July 1957), 133–35.

1221. BENCE-JONES, MARK: *The Remarkable Irish: Chronicle of a Land, a Culture, a Mystique*. NY: McKay, 1966. xi, 243 p.
Yeats, *passim* (see index).

1221a. BERGONZI, BERNARD: *The Turn of a Century: Essays on Victorian and Modern English Literature*. London: Macmillan, 1973. x, 222 p.
"Fin de Siècle," 17–39; reprint of "Aspects of the *fin de siècle*," in Arthur Pollard (ed): *The Victorians*. London: Barrie & Jenkins, 1970. 436 p. (History of Literature in the English Language. 6.), pp. 364–

85. Comments *passim* on Yeats's attitude toward the nineties. "Modern Reactionaries," 177-82; a review of J1380.

1222. ———— (ed): *The Twentieth Century*. London: Barrie & Jenkins, 1970. 415 p. (History of Literature in the English Language. 7.)

Thomas Parkinson: "W. B. Yeats," 49-74; and *passim* (see index). Yeats was perhaps not the greatest modern poet but a great poet writing in the modern period.

1223. BERTI, LUIGI: *Boccaporto*. Firenze: Parenti, 1940. 293 p. (Collezione di Letteratura. Saggi e memorie. 35.)

"Memoria per Yeats," 87-95. Incorporates: "Epigrafe per Yeats," *Nazione*, 81:86 (11 Apr 1939), 5; "Memoria per Yeats," *Letteratura*, 3:12 (Oct 1939), 142-48.

1224. BICKLEY, FRANCIS: "The Development of William Butler Yeats," *Thrush*, 1:2 (Jan 1910), 147-51.

Reprinted in *Living Age*, 264:3429 (26 Mar 1910), 802-5.

1225. BING, JUST: *Verdens-litteraturhistorie: Grunnlinjer og hovedverker*. Oslo: Aschehoug, 1928-34. 3 v.

Yeats, 3:496-98.

1225a. BLACK, E. L. (ed): *Nine Modern Poets: An Anthology*. London: Macmillan, 1968 [1966]. x, 230 p.

"W. B. Yeats," 1-5.

1226. BLOEM, J. C.: "William Butler Yeats," *Nieuwe Rotterdamsche Courant*, 80:323 (17 Nov 1923), Lett. Bijbl., 1.

1227. BLOOM, HAROLD: *The Ringers in the Tower: Studies in Romantic Tradition*. Chicago: U of Chicago Press, 1971. xii, 352 p.

Numerous notes on Yeats, *passim* (see index).

1228. BOGAN, LOUISE: *Selected Criticism: Prose, Poetry*. NY: Noonday Press, 1955. x, 404 p.

"The Oxford Book of Modern Verse," 52-54. "William Butler Yeats," 86-104; reprinted from *Atlantic Monthly*, 161:5 (May 1938), 637-44. "On the Death of William Butler Yeats," 133-37; reprint of "The Cutting of an Agate," *Nation*, 148:9 (25 Feb 1939), 234-35. "The Later Poetry of William Butler Yeats," 202-6; combines "Verse," *New Yorker*, 16:16 (1 June 1940), 73-75 (a review of *Last Poems and Plays* [W203/204]), and "Poet and Mage," *New Republic*, 125:1920 (17 Sept 1951), 19-20 (a review of *Collected Poems* [W211/211A]).

The entire Yeats material is reprinted in *A Poet's Alphabet: Reflections on the Literary Art and Vocation*. Edited by Robert Phelps and Ruth Limmer. NY: McGraw-Hill, 1970. xvii, 474 p., pp. 446-68.

1228a. ————: *Selected Letters of Louise Bogan, 1920-1970*. Edited and with an introduction by Ruth Limmer. NY: Harcourt Brace Jovanovich, 1973. xiv, 401 p.

Numerous references to Yeats, *passim* (see index). Contains a parody of Yeats's poetic style, p. 152.

1229. BOLAND, EAVAN: "From Athens to Dublin," *Tablet*, 222:6669 (16 Mar 1968), 254.

Yeats gave Ireland "an image of herself."

1230. *Bol'shaîa sovetskaîa èntsiklopediîa*. Moskva: Gos. nauchno isd-vo "Bol'shaîa sovetskaîa èntsiklopediîa," 1948-58. 51 v.

Ĭits, 19:185.

1231. BORUM, POUL: *Poetisk modernisme; En kritisk introduktion.* København: Vendelkaers, 1966. 279 p.

Yeats, pp. 60-62 and *passim* (see index).

1232. BOURGEOIS, MAURICE: "William Butler Yeats," *Comoedia*, 17:4032 (1 Jan 1924), 4.

1233. BRADFORD, CURTIS B.: "Journeys to Byzantium," *VQR*, 25:2 (Spring 1949), 205-25.

"While Yeats saw the modern world as an ironic tragic spectacle and made sense of it, Eliot views it as a Christian mystic and makes less sense but still sense of it."

1234. BRADY, CHARLES A.: "Ireland and the Two Eternities," *America*, 64: 1637 (22 Mar 1941), 663-64.

"The three wraths of Ireland: the anger of St. Patrick; the rage of Swift; the defiance of Yeats."

1235. BRANCATI, VIVALDA: "William Butler Yeats, dal sogno alla realtà: Dopo aver guardato al mondo fittizio delle leggende e tradizioni irlandesi divenne il cantore della disillusione," *Persona*, 8:3 (1967), 12.

1236. BRASH, W. BARDSLEY: "W. B. Yeats, 1865-1939," *London Q and Holborn R*, 164 (ser 6 / 8):3 (July 1939), 320-33.

Discusses the early works only.

1237. BRÉGY, KATHERINE: "Yeats Revisited," *Catholic World*, 151:906 (Sept 1940), 677-86.

Written from a conservative Catholic point of view. Prefers the early work because the later is sexually too explicit.

1238. BRENNAN, CHRISTOPHER: *The Prose.* Edited by A. R. Chisholm and J. J. Quinn. Sydney: Angus & Robertson, 1962. ix, 461 p.

"Vision, Imagination and Reality," 19-39; reprinted from °*Australian Field*, 8 Mar 1902, 22 Mar 1902, 5 Apr 1902. On Yeats as one of the few poets "who had not merely the capacity of visionary perception, but further the capacity to examine and test their perceptions, and who had given proof of the latter capacity concurrently with the exercise of the former."

"Blake after Many Years," 248-52; reprinted from °*Bulletin*, 5 Feb 1925. Partly on Blake's influence on Yeats.

1239. BROCKHAUS: *Der Grosse Brockhaus.* 16th edition. Wiesbaden: Brockhaus, 1952-58. 13 v.

"Yeats," 12:625. Insufficient.

1240. BRONOWSKI, J.: "W. B. Yeats," *Cambridge R*, 54:1338 (8 June 1933), 475-76.

Yeats's poetry had sequence but not consequence. Yeats filled this gap between cause and effect by turning to mysticism.

1241. BROOKS, CLEANTH: *Modern Poetry and the Tradition.* NY: Oxford UP, 1965 [1939]. xxxiv, 253 p. (Galaxy Book. GB150.)

"Yeats: The Poet as Myth-Maker," 173-202; first published as "The Vision of William Butler Yeats," *Southern R*, 4:1 (Summer 1938), 116-42; reprinted in J1090. Discusses *A Vision* and the poems related to it. Other references to Yeats, *passim*, especially pp. 60-64, revised from "Three Revolutions in Poetry: III. Metaphysical Poetry and the Ivory Tower," *Southern R*, 1:3 (Winter 1935/36), 568-83; on "On a Picture of a Black Centaur" and "Byzantium."

1242. ————: "W. B. Yeats: An Introduction," *Yale Literary Mag*, 123:6 (May 1955), 18.

1243. ————: *A Shaping Joy: Studies in the Writer's Craft*. London: Methuen, 1971. xix, 393 p.
  "The Modern Writer and His Community," 17-36; incorporates *The Writer and His Community*. Glasgow: Jackson, 1968. 31 p. (W. P. Ker Memorial Lectures. 21.) Discusses Yeats's concept of unity of culture and unity of being in the context of 20th-century literature.
  "Poetry and Poeticality," 87-101. The choice of evil as a subject for poetry and Yeats's opinion on this matter.
  "W. B. Yeats as a Literary Critic," 102-25; reprinted from Peter Demetz, Thomas Greene, and Lowry Nelson (eds): *The Disciplines of Criticism: Essays on Literary Theory, Interpretation, and History* [Wellek Festschrift]. New Haven: Yale UP, 1968. x, 616 p., pp. 17-41. Yeats's views of poetry, the poet, and the cultural situation; specifically his views of Shelley, Shaw, Wilde, and Shakespeare. Frequent reference to "Ego Dominus Tuus."
  "The American 'Innocence' in James, Fitzgerald, and Faulkner," 181-97; contains a note on "A Prayer for My Daughter," 195-97.
  "The Unity of Marlowe's *Doctor Faustus*," 367-80; contains a note on *The Countess Cathleen*, 374-77.

1244. BROPHY, LIAM: "W. B. Yeats: That Hazy, Mixed-up Kid," *Friar*, 23:4 (Apr 1965), 13-19.

1245. BRUNIUS, AUGUST: *Modern engelsk litteratur*. Stockholm: Natur och Kultur, 1923. 142 p. (Natur och Kultur. 17.)
  Yeats, *passim* (see index).

1246. BUCHANAN, GEORGE: "Pages from a Journal," *Rann*, #15 (Spring 1952), 11-13.
  Includes some notes on Yeats.

1247. BURGESS, ANTHONY: *Urgent Copy: Literary Studies*. London: Cape, 1968. 272 p.
  "Enemy of Twilight," 58-62; on Synge.
  "Cast a Cold Eye: The Yeats Centenary," 62-67; reprinted from *Spectator*, 214:7125 (15 Jan 1965), 73. Appreciates Yeats's poetry and plays, but considers his prose "dangerous."

1248. CAHILL, PAUL [pseudonym]: "Cast a Cold Eye on Yeats," *Word*, June 1965, [7-10].

1249. CAMBON, GLAUCO: *La lotta con Proteo*. Milano: Bompiani, 1963. 318 p. (Portico Critica e Saggi. 40.)
  "Yeats e la lotta con Proteo," 69-111; reprinted from *Aut-Aut*, 7:37 (Jan 1957), 1-34.

1250. CAMERON, SUSAN ELIZABETH: "William Butler Yeats," *McGill U Mag*, 4:1 (Jan 1905), 94-105.

1251. Cattani [i.e., CATTAUI], GEORGES: "William Butler Yeats," *Journal des poètes*, 2:3 (29 Nov 1931), [3-4].

1252. ————: *Trois poètes: Hopkins, Yeats, Eliot*. Paris: Egloff, 1947. 171 p.
  "William Butler Yeats et le réveil celtique," 45-63. A rambling essay on Yeats as symbolist, Celtic dreamer, and adept of mysticism.

1253. ————: "W. B. Yeats: 'La mémoire de la nature elle-même,'" *Journal de Genève*, #134 (12-13 June 1965), I.

1254. CAZAMIAN, MADELEINE L.: "Un poète irlandais: W. B. Yeats," *Revue germanique*, 7:2 (Mar-Apr 1911), 129-54.

1255. ————: "Le poète de l'Irlande: W. B. Yeats," *Vie des peuples*, 12: 45 (Jan 1924), 102-32.
On the early works only.

1256. ————: *Le roman et les idées en Angleterre*. Paris: Belles Lettres, 1935-55. 3 v. (Publications de la Faculté des Lettres de l'Université de Strasbourg. 15. 73. 125.)
"Esthétisme et renaissance celtique," 2:326-68; contains the following subsections: "W. B. Yeats: Formation esthétique et mystique," 327-32; "W. B. Yeats, théoricien," 333-35; "W. B. Yeats: Le culte de la Rose," 335-45. See also vols. 2-3, *passim* (see index).

1257. ČERMÁK, FRANTIŠEK: "Baladický básník svobody," *Rudé pravo*, 45:182 (13 June 1965), [6].
"Ballad poet of liberty."

1258. *Chambers's Cyclopaedia of English Literature*. Edited by David Patrick, revised and expanded by J. Liddell Geddie and J. C. Smith. London: Chambers, 1938. 3 v.
Yeats, 3:709. There is a different article in an earlier edition, Philadelphia: Lippincott, 1902-4. 3 v., 3:711: Yeats is a good poet, but he deceives himself when he thinks he is an Irish poet.

1259. *Chambers's Encyclopaedia*. New revised edition. London: International Learning System, 1968. 15 v.
M[ichael] R[oberts]: Yeats, 14:764. Also in 1964 edition.

1260. CHAPPLE, J. A. V.: *Documentary and Imaginative Literature, 1880-1920*. London: Blandford Press, 1970. 395 p.
On Yeats, pp. 238-61 and *passim* (see index).

1261. CHASSÉ, CHARLES: "Le lauréat du Prix Nobel: W. B. Yeats, poète irlandais," *Figaro: Supplément littéraire*, ns #242 (24 Nov 1923), 1-2.

1262. CHATTERJEE, MANOJ KUMAR: "The Significance of the Later Works of Yeats," *Visva-Bharati Q*, 17:1 (May-July 1951), 19-28.
The significance lies in the "continual intellectual adventure."

1263. CHESTERTON, GILBERT KEITH: "Mr. Yeats and the Cosmic Moth," *America*, 15:380 (22 July 1916), 357-58.
Yeats should be saved from his idolators and be subjected to genuine criticism to bring out his considerable qualities. Discusses *The Shadowy Waters*.

1264. ————: *Irish Impressions*. NY: Lane, 1920 [1919]. 222 p.
Yeats, *passim*, especially 78 ("Mr. W. B. Yeats, in the very wildest vision of a loneliness remote and irresponsible, is careful to make it clear that he knows how many bean-rows make nine"), 139-40, 182-83.

1265. ————: *The Autobiography*. NY: Sheed & Ward, 1936. vii, 360 p.
Incorporates "Some Literary Celebrities," *SatR*, 14:20 (12 Sept 1936), 3-4, 13. Chesterton's estimate of Yeats appears on pp. 139-42, 146-50, and 293-94.

1266. CHIARI, JOSEPH: *The Aesthetics of Modernism*. London: Vision Press, 1970. 224 p.
Contains some rather general remarks on Yeats, *passim* (see index).

1267. CHURCH, RICHARD: *British Authors: A Twentieth-Century Gallery with 53 Portraits*. London: Longmans, Green, 1948 [1943]. 145 p.
"W. B. Yeats, 1865-1939," 40-42. Yeats's impact on the 20th century was indirect: he maintained high esthetic standards.

1267a. CLARK, DAVID: "Yeats on Hatred," *Pax*, 12:3 (Christmas 1957), 20-22.
Yeats was no pacifist, but his hatred was nonviolent.

1268. CLARKE, AUSTIN: "W. B. Yeats," *Dublin Mag*, 14:2 (Apr-June 1939), 6-10.

1269. ————: *The Celtic Twilight and the Nineties*. With an introduction by Roger McHugh. Dublin: Dolmen Press, 1969. 104 p. (Tower Series of Anglo-Irish Studies. 1.)
On the Celtic Twilight period of Yeats and AE, pp. 31-49; "Yeats's Early Plays," 74-91; "Yeats's Later Plays," 92-104. Rambling, gossipy, and at times somewhat uninformed, but nevertheless valuable for some firsthand information, e.g., concerning the productions of Yeats's plays.
Reviews:
1. Patrick Murray, "Yeats on Stage," *Irish Press*, 39:207 (30 Aug 1969), 10.
2. Eilean Ni Chuilleanain, "Twilight," *Irish Times*, #35549 (13 Sept 1969), 8.

1270. CLARKE, EGERTON: "William Butler Yeats," *Dublin R*, 204:409 (Apr-May-June 1939), 305-21.
Includes an untitled poem written in memory of Yeats.

1271. *Collier's Encyclopedia*. With bibliography and index. NY: Crowell-Collier, 1969. 24 v.
Russell K. Alspach, Yeats, 23:687-89. Also in 1963 edition.

1272. COLLINS, ARTHUR SIMONS: *English Literature of the Twentieth Century*. 4th edition. London: University Tutorial Press, 1965 [1951]. vii, 410 p.
"Yeats," 14-21, and *passim* (see index).

1273. COLUM, MARY M.: "The Later Yeats," *Poetry*, 7:5 (Feb 1916), 258-60.
The later Yeats is better than the earlier. Praises *The Green Helmet* as "his greatest dramatic work."

1274. ————: "Yeats and the Mysteries," *NYHTB*, [6:] (13 July 1930), 1, 6.

1275. COLUM, PADRAIC: "On the Centenary of William Butler Yeats." Introduced by Allan Nevins, *Proceedings of the American Academy of Arts and Letters. National Institute of Arts and Letters*, ser 2 / #16 (1966), 61-69.
Includes a poem "In Memory of William Butler Yeats," a reprint of "William Butler Yeats: The Arch Poet," *Programme for the Formal Opening of Thoor Ballylee on 20 June 1965*. [Dublin: Dolmen Press, 1965]. 4 p. The poem is also included in J616.

1276. COMBS, GEORGE HAMILTON: *These Amazing Moderns*. St. Louis: Bethany Press, 1933. 270 p.
"Moore, Synge, and Yeats--An Irish Stew," 220-47. Lectures of the minister of Country Club Christian Church, Kansas City, Missouri, sponsored by the young married people's class. Typical quotation: "His poems are delicately beautiful but not seldom lacking sufficient starch of an idea to stand up. . . . While he seems to have been a pretty poor Christian he was a real patriot."

1277. CONNOLLY, CYRIL: *The Modern Movement: One Hundred Key Books from England, France and America, 1880-1950.* NY: Atheneum, 1966. ix, 149 p.
  Yeats is represented by *Responsibilities, Later Poems* (1922), *The Tower*, and *The Winding Stair*.

1278. CONRAD, H. R.: "Englische Dichter der Neuzeit. I.: W. B. Yeats," *Neue Schweizer Rundschau*, ns 14:6 (Oct 1946), 360-68.
  Sees Yeats's work, especially his poetry, in the context of his time.

1279. COOKE, JOHN DANIEL, and LIONEL STEVENSON: *English Literature of the Victorian Period.* NY: Appleton-Century-Crofts, 1949. xiii, 438 p.
  Yeats, pp. 124-25, 132, 211-14.

1280. COOLE, T.: "The Poet—Clues to His Identity," *Claidheamh Soluis*, 12:1 (12 Mar 1910), 8-9.
  A reflection on the question "Can Mr. Yeats, as an Irishman, have the sincerity so necessary for the great poet?"

1281. COURTNEY, NEIL: "Triumphant Life of W. B. Yeats," *Age*, 12 June 1965, 21.

1282. COURTNEY, WINIFRED F. (ed): *The Reader's Adviser: A Guide to the Best in Literature.* 11th edition, revised and enlarged. NY: Bowker, 1968. 2 v.
  Yeats, 1:153-54, 935-36, 1024-25; Irish drama, 1:933-39. Not reliable.

1283. COUSINS, JAMES H.: "Yeats: The Occult Poet," *Herald of the Star*, 4:10 (11 Oct 1915), 443-45.
  By turning to theosophy and occultism Yeats transcended his Irish preoccupations.

1284. ————: "Yeats," *Madras Mail*, 56:274 (16 Nov 1923), 6.

1285. COUSTER, P. J.: "Un poète irlandais—W. B. Yeats," *Echanges et recherches*, 2:5 (Mar 1939), 296-99.

1286. COWLEY, MALCOLM: *Think Back on Us . . . . : A Contemporary Chronicle of the 1930's.* Edited with an introduction by Henry Dan Piper. Carbondale: Southern Illinois UP, 1967. xv, 400 p.
  "Yeats as Anthologist," 307-10; reprint of "A Poet's Anthology," *New Republic*, 89:1150 (16 Dec 1936), 221-22; a review of W250/251.
  "Yeats and the Baptism of the Gutter," 324-28; reprint of "Poet in Politics," *New Republic*, 96:1242 (21 Sept 1938), 191-92; a review of W198. Correspondence (not reprinted in book) by Delmore Schwartz and Malcolm Cowley, :1244 [i.e., 1244a] (12 Oct 1938), 272-73; James P. O'Donnell, 97:1253 (7 Dec 1938), 133-34.
  "Socialists and Symbolists," 328-32; reprinted from *New Republic*, 96:1243 (28 Sept 1938), 218-19; Yeats's example proves that a symbolic and not a realistic treatment of social problems produces better poetry.
  "Yeats and O'Faolain," 336-42; reprinted from *New Republic*, 98:1263 (15 Feb 1939), 49-50: On O'Faolain's essay, J2257.

1287. COX, AEDAN: "A Weaver of Symbols," *Hermes*, [1:1] (Feb 1907), 7-11.

1288. CRAIG, HARDIN (ed): *A History of English Literature.* NY: Oxford UP, 1950. xiii, 697 p.
  Joseph Warren Beach: "The Literature of the Nineteenth and the Early Twentieth Century, 1798 to the First World War," 463-618; includes "William Butler Yeats: The Celtic Mythos," 592-95 (also in J1090); "The Drama in Ireland," 599-601.

1289. CRONIN, ANTHONY: "A Question of Modernity," *X: A Quarterly Review*, 1:4 (Oct 1960), 283-92.
Yeats is mentioned *passim*.

1290. CROSS, GUSTAV: "'Unless Soul Clap Its Hands . . . ,'" *Sydney Morning Herald*, 135:39776 (12 June 1965), 14.

1291. Quiller, A., Jr. [i.e., CROWLEY, ALEISTER]: "The Shadowy Dill-Waters or Mr. Smudge the Medium," *Equinox*, 1:3 (Mar 1910), 327-31.
Crowley heaping ridicule on Yeats, whom he calls "Weary Willie," "Attis with a barren fig-leaf," and "Peer Gynt without his courage and light-heartedness, O onion with many a stinking sheath, and a worm at the heart."

1292. CUNLIFFE, JOHN WILLIAM, and ASHLEY HORACE THORNDIKE (eds): *The World's Best Literature*. NY: Warren Library, 1917. 30 v.
James Cobourg Hodgins: "William Butler Yeats," 26:16260a-h. Also contained in °John William Cunliffe and others (eds): *Columbia University Course in Literature Based on the World's Best Literature*. NY: Columbia UP, 1928-29 (vol. 8).

1293. CUNLIFFE, JOHN WILLIAM: *Leaders of the Victorian Revolution*. NY: Appleton-Century, 1934. viii, 343 p.
"William Butler Yeats," 305-11.

1294. CZERNIAWSKI, ADAM: Note on Yeats in Polish, *Kultura*, #10 (Oct 1965), 65.

1295. DAICHES, DAVID: *The Present Age after 1920*. London: Cresset Press, 1962 [1958]. x, 376 p. (Introductions to English Literature. 5.)
The American edition was published as *The Present Age in British Literature*. Bloomington: Indiana UP, 1962. x, 376 p. Yeats, pp. 30-39 and *passim* (see index). For the earlier version written by Edwin Muir see J2595.

1296. ———— (ed): *The Penguin Companion to Literature: Britain and the Commonwealth*. London: Lane / Penguin Press, 1971. 576 p.
G. S. F[raser] and J[ohn] K[elly]: "Yeats," 568-69.

1297. DALY, JAMES JEREMIAS: *A Cheerful Ascetic and Other Essays*. Freeport, N.Y.: Books for Libraries Press, 1968 [1931]. vii, 147 p.
"The Paganism of Mr. Yeats," 87-102; reprinted from *Catholic World*, 115:689 (Aug 1922), 595-605. Deplores Yeats's pagan ways, but is rather uninformed.

1298. DATTA, SUDHINDRANATH: *The World of Twilight: Essays and Poems*. Bombay: Oxford UP, 1970. xxiv, 292 p.
"W. B. Yeats and Art for Art's Sake," 185-203 (written in 1936).

1299. DAVIDSON, DONALD: *Still Rebels, Still Yankees and Other Essays*. [Baton Rouge]: Louisiana State UP, 1957. x, 284 p.
"Yeats and the Centaur," 23-30; reprinted from *Southern R*, 7:3 (Winter 1941/42), 510-16; and from J1090. In his early work, especially his poetry, Yeats drew heavily on popular Irish lore; it was only one of many themes in the later work, which had no visible impact on the popular imagination.

1300. DAVIS, ROBERT HOBART: *Man Makes His Own Mask: Text and Portraits*. Foreword by Benjamin de Casseres. NY: Huntington Press, 1932. viii, 239 p.
Note on Yeats and his portrait photograph, pp. 234-35. Says that "W. B. Yeats and W. Bird, whose drawings appear at interval in *Punch*, are one

and the same person," but this is not correct. W. Bird was a pseudonym
of Jack B. Yeats.

1301. DAVRAY, HENRY D.: "William Butler Yeats," *Ermitage*, 7:8 (Aug 1896),
88-96.

1302. DAY, MARTIN STEELE: *History of English Literature: 1837 to the
Present. A College Course Guide*. Garden City: Doubleday, 1964. xii, 442 p.
(Doubleday College Course Guides. U15.)
    Yeats, pp. 239-49.

1303. DAY LEWIS, C.: "W. B. Yeats," *New Masses*, 30:11 (7 Mar 1939), 22-23.

1304. DE BLACAM, AODH: "Yeats as I Knew Him," *Irish Monthly*, 67:789 (Mar
1939), 204-12.
    A misnomer. Not a biographical article but a condemnation of much of
the later work and a half-hearted appraisal of the earlier.

1305. ————: "Yeats Reconsidered," *Irish Monthly*, 71:839 (May 1943), 209-
17.
    "How richly the highest part of his genius would have been at home if
he had been reared in the Catholic culture!"

1305a. DE MAN, PAUL: *Blindness & Insight: Essays in the Rhetoric of Contemporary Criticism*. NY: Oxford UP, 1971. xiii, 189 p.
    Note on the concept of modernity in Yeats's introduction to the *Oxford
Book of Modern Verse* and on his idea of the soul, pp. 170-72.

1306. DEVANE, JAMES: "Is an Irish Culture Possible?" *Ireland To-day*, 1:5
(Oct 1936), 21-31.
    Includes some notes on Yeats's place in Irish culture.

1307. DICKINSON, ASA DON: *The Best Books of Our Time, 1901-1925*. Another
clue to the literary labyrinth consisting of a list of one thousand best
books published in the first quarter of the twentieth century selected by
the best authorities accompanied by critical descriptions. NY: Wilson,
1931 [1928]. xiv, 405 p.
    This is an interesting compilation. Yeats received 18 endorsements
(pp. 335-37), mainly for *Cathleen ni Houlihan*, *Reveries over Childhood
and Youth*, and *Selected Poems* (1921, especially *The Land of Heart's
Desire*). Yeats possesses, however, only a fraction of Galsworthy's
"quality" (197 endorsements, the winner of the contest); he is also
preceded by Wells (172), Bennett (137), Shaw (123), Synge (53), Moore
(45), Maeterlinck (33), James Stephens (24), and Lord Dunsany (20).
Less successful celebrities are Proust (7), Thomas Mann (6), Pirandello (6), Emily Dickinson (4), Hugo von Hofmannsthal (4), and Pound
(4). Another list was published in 1937 (*The Best Books of the Decade
1926-1935*). Yeats has 116 endorsements for his *Collected Poems*. The
winner is James Truslow Adams (733); Eliot gets 179 for his drama and
criticism; Pound has disappeared. Among 13 books of poetry, Yeats has
only tenth place, trailing Stephen Vincent Benét, Edna St. Vincent
Millay, Frost, Robinson, MacLeish, Sandburg, and Elinor Wylie; but he
is "better" than Sara Teasdale. In the 1936-45 list (published 1948),
Yeats collects 215 votes for his prose and poetry (but does not appear
in the list of 16 best books of poetry). Eliot gets 298 for his poetry
and plays; the winner is Van Wyck Brooks (1,711).

1308. DONOGHUE, DENIS: *The Ordinary Universe: Soundings in Modern Literature*. London: Faber & Faber, 1968. 320 p.
    "The Human Image in Yeats," 108-24; first published in *London Mag*, 1:9
(Dec 1961), 51-65, and in *University R* [Dublin], 3:8 [1956?], 56-70.

In most of Yeats's volumes of poetry, the human image is curiously
defective; it is either body or soul, rarely both, so that Yeats's
unity of being is never fully realized. The one great exception, and
hence his most splendid achievement, is the poems in *The Wild Swans at
Coole*.
"Yeats and the Living Voice," 125-45; first published in *Studies*, 55:
218 (Summer 1966), 147-65. Yeats was committed to an "oral culture."
Unlike the symbolists and Eliot, he wrote poems as a means of communication. This also explains "why Yeats resorted to the drama."

1309. DOORN, WILLEM VAN: "William Butler Yeats: A Lopsided Study," *ES*, 2:9
(June 1920), 65-77.
Reprinted as a pamphlet, °Amsterdam: Swets & Zeitlinger, 1920. 16 p.

1310. DOTTIN, PAUL: "W. B. Yeats, poète national de l'Irlande," *Revue de
France*, yr 3 / 6:3 (1 Dec 1923), 665-72.

1311. DOUGLAS, ALFRED, LORD: *Without Apology*. London: Secker, 1938. 316 p.
For Lord Alfred's Yeats complex see pp. 21-24 ("a minor Irish poet"),
46 (where Yeats advances to a "very minor poet"), 117, and 136.

1312. DOWDEN, EDWARD: *Letters of Edward Dowden and His Correspondents*.
London: Dent / NY: Dutton, 1914. xvi, 415 p.
Some references to Yeats (see index), especially pp. 350-51 in a
letter written in 1907, in which Dowden indicates that it would be
better for Yeats to stay out of the movement. In a preface (pp. xi-
xvi), John Eglinton defends Dowden's self-imposed isolation from the
Irish literary movement.

1313. The Editor [i.e., DOWNES, ROBERT PERCEVAL]: "Mr. W. B. Yeats," *Great
Thoughts*, ser 4 / vol 36 / pt 5 (Mar 1902), 356-58.
To Yeats, "romance is reality." Fortunately he does not belong to
that large part of the human world that is ruled by the "almighty
dollar."

1314. DOWNES, ROBERT P.: "William Butler Yeats," *Great Thoughts*, ser 7 /
8:1140 (30 Jan 1915), 214-16. (With an unknown photograph)

1315. DRĂGHICI, SIMONA: "Actualitatea lui William Butler Yeats" [The actuality of Yeats], *Secolul 20*, 5:12 (1965), 40-47.
General introduction to Yeats's life and work for Rumanian readers.
Claims that Yeats's philosophy implies the possibility of perceiving
an absolute truth, whereas his poetry does not. Yeats, not Auden and
others, wrote the best political poetry of his time, although he did
not propose any solutions to political problems. Discusses "Lapis
Lazuli" as very close to Yeats's idea of the ideal poem.

1315a. DUKES, ASHLEY: "The British Isles," *TAM*, 23:4 (Apr 1939), 252-56.
Contains a note on Yeats and the Abbey Theatre, pp. 252-53.

1316. D[UNCAN], E[LLEN] M.: "The Writings of Mr. W. B. Yeats," *Fortnightly
R*, os 91 / ns 85:506 (Feb 1909), 253-70.
A chronological survey. The author has sometimes been wrongly identi-
fied as Edward Dowden.

1317. DUNSANY, LORD [EDWARD JOHN MORETON DRAX PLUNKETT]: "Four Poets: AE,
Kipling, Yeats, Stephens," *Atlantic Monthly*, 201:4 (Apr 1958), 77-78, 80.

1318. DYBOSKI, ROMAN: *Sto lat literatury angielskiej*. Warszawa: Pax, 1957.
xx, 927 p.
"Wkład Irlandii" [The contribution of Ireland], 803-50 ("William Butler
Yeats . . . i George William Russell . . . ," 812-24).

1319. EARNSHAW, HERBERT GEOFFREY: *Modern Writers: A Guide to Twentieth-Century Literature in the English Language*. Edinburgh: Chambers, 1968. vi, 266 p.
"W. B. Yeats," 112-21.

1320. ECKHOFF, LORENTZ: *The Aesthetic Movement in English Literature*. Oslo: University Press, 1959. 34 p.
Based on "Den estetiske bevegelse," *Edda*, yr 34 / 47:2 (1947), 81-97. Yeats, *passim*.

1321. EDGAR, PELHAM: "William Butler Yeats and the Irish Movement," *Globe*, 60:17114 (17 Dec 1904), Mag Section, 7.

1322. ————: *Across My Path*. Edited by Northrop Frye. Toronto: Ryerson Press, 1952. xiv, 167 p.
"The Enigma of Yeats," 145-53; reprinted from *QQ*, 46:4 (Winter 1939), 411-22.

1323. EDWARDS, OLIVER: "W. B. Yeats and Ulster; and a Thought on the Future of the Anglo-Irish Tradition," *Northman*, 13:2 (Winter 1945), 16-21.
Discusses the reasons for Yeats's dislike of Ulster and says that true Anglo-Irish literature has a future only in Ulster, now that the Republic has a stifling censorship act.

1324. EDWARDS, PHILIP: "Yeats and the Trinity Chair," *Hermathena*, #101 (Autumn 1965), 5-12.
The professorship of English literature. See also J1189, 1194, and 1326.

1325. EGLINTON, JOHN: "National Ideals," *United Irishman*, 6:142 (16 Nov 1901), 3.
Answers Yeats's "John Eglinton" in the preceding number (Wp. 361).

1326. ————: "Life and Letters," *Irish Statesman*, 2:35 (21 Feb 1920), 181.
On Yeats's nonappointment to the Trinity Chair of English Literature.

1327. ————: *Irish Literary Portraits*. Freeport, N.Y.: Books for Libraries Press, 1967 [1935]. v, 158 p.
Contents: "Introductory," 3-14. Some general remarks on the Irish literary revival, pointing out that Yeats was its greatest poet but failed as its spiritual leader. Yeats's and the revival's enemy was Trinity College, not the Irish people.
"Yeats and His Story," 17-35; reprinted from *Dial*, 80:5 (May 1926), 357-66. On Yeats's life and work, especially in their relation to Ireland, including some reminiscences.
"A. E. and His Story," 39-61.
"Edward Dowden's Letters," 65-82.
"Recollections of George Moore," 85-111; another essay on Moore and two essays on Joyce.
Reviews:
1. Anon., "Literary Portraits," *TLS*, 34:1747 (25 July 1935), 474.
2. Karl Arns, *Englische Studien*, 71:2 (Dec 1936), 294-96.
3. Heinz Höpf'l, *Neuphilologische Monatsschrift*, 7:6 (June 1936), 252-55.
4. A. L. Morton, "The Ireland of W. B. Yeats," *New English Weekly*, 7:17 (5 Sept 1935), 330.
5. Horace Reynolds, "James Joyce and Other Irish Writers," *NYTBR*, 40:36 (8 Sept 1935), 3, 13.

1328. ————: *Confidential, or Take It or Leave It*. London: Fortune Press, 1951. 54 p.

"Apologia," 5-10. On Yeats and AE as leaders of the Irish literary revival.

1329. ELIOT, THOMAS STEARNS: *After Strange Gods: A Primer of Modern Heresy.* The Page-Barbour Lectures at the University of Virginia, 1933. [Folcroft, Pa.]: Folcroft Press, 1970 [1934]. 72 p.

Yeats, pp. 47-51. The supernatural world of the early Yeats was the wrong supernatural world: "It was not a world of spiritual signifi- cance, not a world of real Good and Evil, of holiness or sin, but a highly sophisticated lower mythology summoned, like a physician, to supply the fading pulse of poetry with some transient stimulant so that the dying patient may utter his last words."

1330. E[LIOT], T. S.: "A Commentary," *Criterion*, 14:57 (July 1935), 610-13.

A surprisingly generous tribute to Yeats on the occasion of his 70th birthday: With his literary Irish nationalism, Yeats "performed a great service to the English language" and to English poetry.

1330a. ELLMANN, RICHARD: "The Uses of Adversity," *American P.E.N.*, 4:1 (Winter 1972), 15-17.

Comparative affluence in later life may have influenced the quality of Yeats's works.

1331. EMBLER, WELLER: "Rage against Iniquity," *Arts in Society*, 6:1 (Spring/Summer 1969), 80-93.

On the nineties, with some references to Yeats.

1332. EMT.: "100-året for Yeats: Irland fejrer sin nationaldigter den 13. juni," *Jyllands Posten*, 4 June 1956, 19.

1333. *Enciclopedia cattolica.* Città del Vaticano: Enciclopedia cattolica, 1949-54. 12 v.

Augusto Guidi: Yeats, 12:1732-33.

1334. *Enciclopedia filosofica.* 2nd edition. Firenze: Sansoni, 1967. 6 v. A[lbino] Babolin: Yeats, 6:1180-81.

1335. *Enciclopedia italiana di scienze, lettere ed arti.* Roma: Istituto della Enciclopedia italiana (Treccani), 1929-39. 36 v.

M[ario] P[raz]: "W. B. Yeats," 35:833.

1336. *Encyclopaedia Britannica.* Chicago: Encyclopaedia Britannica, 1968. 24 v.

T. R. Henn: Yeats, 23:880-82. The 11th edition (1910-11) has an un- signed article on Yeats (28:909-10); the 1947 edition has an article by Lennox Robinson (23:882-83).

1337. *Encyclopedia Americana.* International edition. NY: Americana Corpor- ation, 1968. 30 v.

Richard Ellmann: Yeats, 29:659-60; Peter Kavanagh: Irish Literary Revival, 15:341-47.

1338. ERVINE, ST. JOHN GREER: "The Loneliest Poet: W. B. Yeats," *John o' London's Weekly*, 1:13 (5 July 1919), 375.

1339. *Essays in Memory of Barrett Wendell by His Assistants.* Cambridge, Mass.: Harvard UP, 1926. ix, 320 p.

Norreys Jephson O'Conor: "A Note on Yeats," 285-89. Yeats is a personal, not so much an Irish, poet.

1340. EVANS, BENJAMIN IFOR: *English Literature between the Wars.* London: Methuen, 1948. ix, 133 p.

"W. B. Yeats," 83-90. Yeats tried to discover "some formula through which the fragmentation of modern experience can be expressed."

1341. FARMER, ALBERT JOHN: *Le mouvement esthétique et "decadent" en Angle-terre (1873-1900)*. Paris: Champion, 1931. xvii, 413 p. (Bibliothèque de la Revue de la littérature comparée. 75.)
Several references to Yeats (see index), especially to his connection with the Rhymers' Club (pp. 261-75).

1342. FARREN, ROBERT: "Yeats: An Anniversary Tribute, 1941," *Irish Library Bulletin*, 9:[10] (Oct 1948), 161-63.

1343. FAY, WILLIAM P." "A Yeats Centenary," *Tri-Q*, #4 [Fall 1965], 68-70.
Yeats was "a great Irishman," says the Irish ambassador to the United States.

1344. FEHR, BERNHARD: *Die englische Literatur des 19. und 20. Jahrhunderts: Mit einer Einführung in die englische Frühromantik*. Berlin-Neubabelsberg: Akademische Verlagsgesellschaft Athenaion, 1923. iv, 524 p. (Handbuch der Literaturwissenschaft. [1].)
"Die keltische Renaissance," 452-61 (on Yeats, 454-57). "Das Drama der keltischen Renaissance," 497-506 (on Yeats, 500-503).

1345. ————: "William Butler Yeats, der Träger des Nobelpreises," *Neue Zürcher Zeitung*, 144:1605 (21 Nov 1923), 1-2.

1346. FLANAGAN, THOMAS: *The Irish Novelists, 1800-1850*. NY: Columbia UP, 1959. xiii, 362 p.
Scattered references to Yeats, *passim* (see index).

1347. FLEISCHMANN, WOLFGANG BERNARD (ed): *Encyclopedia of World Literature in the 20th Century in Three Volumes*. An enlarged and updated edition of the Herder *Lexikon der Weltliteratur im 20. Jahrhundert*. NY: Ungar, 1967-71. 3 v.
Melvin J. Friedman, "Irish Literature," 2:146-50; Richard Ellmann: "Yeats," 3:553-56. Both articles are also in the German edition, *Lexikon der Weltliteratur im 20. Jahrhundert* (Freiburg: Herder, 1960-61. 2 v.): Friedman, "Irische Literatur," 1:979-85; Ellmann, "Yeats," 2:1291-99.

1348. FLEMING, LIONEL: *Head or Harp*. London: Barrie and Rockliff, 1965. 187 p.
"The Synthesis," 149-56. Almost alone among the better-known 20th-century Irishmen, Yeats achieved a synthesis of heroic past and nationalistic present. Fleming, while on the staff of the *Irish Times*, met Yeats several times. On one occasion Yeats remarked: "It might surprise you to know what I am reading. It is Kipling. I dislike his work so much that I feel sure it must have something to teach me." "Cathleen ni Houlihan," 171-83; on George Moore.

1349. FLETCHER, IAN: "The 1890's: A Lost Decade," *VS*, 4:4 (June 1961), 345-54.
Yeats is mentioned *passim*.

1350. ———— (ed): *Romantic Mythologies*. London: Routledge & Kegan Paul, 1967. xiii, 297 p.
Ian Fletcher: "Bedford Park: Aesthete's Elysium?" 169-207. Yeats is mentioned *passim*.

1351. FORD, BORIS (ed): *The Modern Age*. Harmondsworth: Penguin Books, 1961. 560 p. (Pelican Guide to English Literature. 7.)

Yeats, *passim* (see index), especially in John Holloway: "The Literary Scene," 51-100; Graham Martin: "The Later Poetry of W. B. Yeats," 170-95; Grattan Freyer: "The Irish Contribution," 196-208.

1352. FORD, JULIA ELLSWORTH, and KATE V. THOMPSON: "The Neo-Celtic Poet—William Butler Yeats," *Poet Lore*, 15:4 (Winter 1904), 83-89.

1353. FOX, R. M.: "W. B. Yeats and the Abbey Theatre," *Irish Press*, 35: 145 (19 June 1965), 8.

1354. FRANULIC, LENKA: *Cien autores contemporaneos*. 3rd edition. Santiago de Chile: Ercilla, 1952. 997 p.
"William Butler Yeats," 975-83.

1355. FRASER, GEORGE SUTHERLAND: *The Modern Writer and His World*. London: Deutsch, 1964 [1953]. 427 p.
First published in Japan in °1950. Yeats, *passim* (see index).

1356. ————: *Vision and Rhetoric: Studies in Modern Poetry*. London: Faber & Faber, 1959. 285 p.
"The Romantic Tradition and Modern Poetry," 15-38; contains some remarks on Yeats's poetry.
"W. B. Yeats," 39-64; a reprint of J1085, q.v.
"Yeats and 'The New Criticism,'" 65-83; reprinted from *Colonnade*, 1:1 (Spring 1952), 6-12; :2 (Winter 1952), 14-21. Criticizes recent interpretations of "I Am of Ireland" by Walter E. Houghton (J2699) and of "Among School Children" by Delmore Schwartz (J1603).

1357. FRENCH, R. D. B.: "Yeats as Poet and Politician," *Glasgow Herald*, 183:118 (12 June 1965), 10.

1358. FRENZ, HORST (ed): *Nobel Lectures Including Presentation Speeches and Laureates' Biographies: Literature, 1901-1967*. Amsterdam: Elsevier, 1969. xxi, 630 p.
"William Butler Yeats," 193-212, includes "Presentation" by Per Hallström (see also J205 and 1378), Yeats's acceptance speech (apparently not published elsewhere), Yeats's lecture "The Irish Dramatic Movement" (see W144), and a short biography.

1359. FRIEDRICH, W. G.: "The Popularity of Yeats," *Cresset*, 28:8 (June 1965), 14-15.
"The main reason for Yeats' popularity is no doubt the fact that many of his best poems deal, not with esoteric matters, but with such universal things as love, friendship, youth, old age, and death . . . ."

1360. FROTHINGHAM, EUGENIA BROOKS: "An Irish Poet and His Work," *Critic*, 44:1 (Jan 1904), 26-31.

1361. FRYE, NORTHROP: *Anatomy of Criticism: Four Essays*. Princeton: Princeton UP, 1957. x, 383 p.
Scattered notes on Yeats, *passim* (see index).

1362. GANT, ROLAND: "Lights in the Darkness: No. 5: W. B. Yeats," *Opus*, #13 (New Year 1943), 25-28.

1363. GARBATY, THOMAS JAY: "*The Savoy* 1896: A Re-Edition of Representative Prose and Verse, with a Critical Introduction, and Biographical and Critical Notes," Ph.D. thesis, U of Pennsylvania, 1957. xxv, 719 p. (*DA*, 17:12 [Dec 1957], 3014-15.)
Yeats, *passim* (see index), especially pp. 81-92, 94-98, and 713-19.

1363a. GARGÀRO, F.: "Da William Butler Yeats," *Rassegna italiana*, #176 (Jan 1933), 1-2.

1364. GARNIER, CHARLES-MARIE: "W. B. Yeats: Fleurs de regrets et couronne de souvenirs," *Yggdrasill*, yr 4 / 3:35 (25 Mar 1939), 190–91.

1364a. GIBBON, MONK: "Personality: Determined or Determinable?" *Hibernia*, 37:6 (27 Apr 1973), 17.
Yeats's personality as seen through his correspondence with Katharine Tynan.

1364b. GIBBONS, TOM: *Rooms in the Darwin Hotel: Studies in English Literary Criticism and Ideas, 1880-1920.* Nedlands: U of Western Australia Press, 1973. xi, 164 p.
Mainly on Havelock Ellis, Symons, and Orage; Yeats is mentioned *passim* (see index).

1365. GLICKSBERG: CHARLES I.: "William Butler Yeats and the Role of the Poet," *Arizona Q*, 9:4 (Winter 1935), 293–307.
Yeats put the role of the poet above everything else and believed in it unswervingly.

1366. [GOGARTY, OLIVER ST. JOHN]: "Literature and Civilization," *Irish Statesman*, 1:11 (24 Nov 1923), 325–26.
Praises Yeats for having won the Nobel Prize.

1367. GORDON, DAVID: "The Twilight of the Celtic Twilight," *America*, 57: 1450 (24 July 1937), 379–80.
Lest it be forgot: "The true Gael is and must be a Catholic Christian." Yeats, however, poor man, has "drunk deep at the poisonous wells of Madame Blavatsky." He "bastardized" the Gaelic language.

1368. GRABOWSKI, ZBIGNIEW: "Życie umysłowe zagranicą: Ostatnie nagrody literackie," *Przegląd wspołczesny*, 3:[] (1924), 132–34.
"Cultural Life Abroad: Recent Literary Prizes."

1369. GREEN, MARTIN: *Yeats's Blessings on von Hügel: Essays on Literature and Religion.* London: Longmans, 1967. viii, 256 p.
Yeats, pp. 1–5, 24–29, 59–61, 121–26, and *passim* (see index). Unlike von Hügel, Yeats was not a liberal humanist. The relevant passage in "Vacillation" proves that he did not even understand von Hügel. I cannot help feeling, however, that Green mistakes Yeats for Richard Ellmann (consistently misspelled), who is another target of Green's attacks.

1370. GREGORY, HORACE: "W. B. Yeats: An Irish Traveler to Byzantium," *Griffin*, 8:8 (Sept 1959), 2–14.

1371. [GRIFFITH, ARTHUR]: "Ireland over All," *Sinn Féin*, os 4:179 / ns 1: 4 (19 Feb 1910), 4.
Comments on a Yeats lecture, "Ireland and the Arts," reported on p. 5 of the same issue. Correspondence by E. B. and P[atrick] MacCartan, 4:180 / 1:5 (26 Feb 1910), 4.

1372. GRIGSON, GEOFFREY, and CHARLES HARVARD GIBBS-SMITH (eds): *People: A Volume of the Good, Bad, Great & Eccentric Who Illustrate the Admirable Diversity of Man.* NY: Hawthorn, 1956. x, 470 p.
"Custom and Ceremony," 466–67.

1373. GRUBB, H. T. HUNT: "William Butler Yeats: His Plays, Poems and Sources of Inspiration," *Poetry R*, 26:5 (Sept/Oct 1935), 351–66; :6 (Nov/ Dec 1935), 455–65.

1374. GWYNN, STEPHEN: "Ebb and Flow," *Fortnightly R*, os 144 / ns 138:824 (Aug 1935), 229–38.

Contains sections on "Yeats's Poetry and Work," "A. E.," and "The Irish Theatre."

1375. HAERDTER, MICHAEL: "Den Deutschen unbekannt: 100. Geburtstag von William Butler Yeats," *FAZ*, #133 (11 June 1965), 32.

1376. HALL, DONALD: "Ezra Pound: An Interview," *Paris R*, 7:28 (Summer-Fall 1962), 22-51.
Pound on Yeats, pp. 29-30, 36.

1377. HALLSTRÖM, PER: "William Butler Yeats," *Edda*, 5:1 (1916), 22-39.

1378. ————: "The Nobel Prize in Literature for 1923," *Prix Nobel*, 1923, 61-65.
Reprinted in J1358.

1379. HARRISON, GEORGE BAGSHAWE (ed): *Major British Writers*. Enlarged edition. NY: Harcourt, Brace & World, 1959 [1954]. 2 v.
Reuben A. Brower: "William Butler Yeats, 1865-1939," 2:779-818.
Annotations to some poems and a general introduction.

1380. HARRISON, JOHN R.: *The Reactionaries: Yeats, Lewis, Pound, Eliot, Lawrence. A Study of the Anti-Democratic Intelligentsia*. Introduction by William Empson. NY: Schocken Books, 1967 [1966]. 224 p. (Schocken Paperback. SB205.)
Based on °"The Social and Political Ideas of W. B. Yeats, Wyndham Lewis, Ezra Pound, T. S. Eliot, and D. H. Lawrence," M.A. thesis, U of Sheffield, 1962.
"W. B. Yeats," 39-73; and *passim*. Yeats's view of democratic government, as expressed in poetry, prose, and letters, was that of "the election of those least able to govern by those least able to judge." His aristocratic view of political and sociological matters is clearly related to his literary style. Harrison admits, however, that Yeats "is probably the last poet who could legitimately reject our modern civilization without being guilty of intellectual and moral evasion." Generally, "Yeats, Lewis, Pound, and Eliot were really interested in society only in so far as it would allow the arts to flourish." Their hatred of democracy is unfounded because the evil phenomena that they detected in democracy are in reality not caused by it. The book has been criticized for its lack of substance and undue simplifications. See also J1162 (#4).
Reviews:
1. Bernard Bergonzi, *London Mag*, 6:8 (Nov 1966), 88, 91, 93-94; reprinted as "Modern Reactionaries," in J1221a, pp. 177-82.
2. Cyril Connolly, "Five Writers Accused," *Sunday Times*, #7474 (21 Aug 1966), 21.
3. Nigel Dennis, "Haters of the Herd," *Sunday Telegraph*, #289 (21 Aug 1966), 15.
4. D. J. Enright, "No Cheers for Democracy," *NSt*, 72:1854 (23 Sept 1966), 443-44; reprinted in *Man Is an Onion: Reviews and Essays*. London: Chatto & Windus, 1972. 222 p., pp. 163-69.
5. Irving Howe, "Beliefs of the Masters," *New Republic*, 157:2755 (16 Sept 1967), 19-20, 22-23, 26.
6. Graham Martin, "The Romantic Defence," *Listener*, 76:1957 (29 Sept 1966), 471-72.
7. Philip Rahv, "An Open Secret," *NYRB*, 8:10 (1 June 1967), 20-23; reprinted in *Literature and the Sixth Sense*. London: Faber & Faber, 1970. xv, 445 p., pp. 437-45.
8. David H. Stewart, *CE*, 31:3 (Dec 1969), 330-34.

9. Philip Toynbee, "Poetry and Fascism," *Observer*, #9138 (28 Aug 1966), 16.
10. Geoffrey Wolff, "Writers and Politics," *American Scholar*, 37:2 (Spring 1968), 356-62.

1381. HARTNETT, MICHAEL: "W. B. Yeats: Evolution of a Style," *Irish Times*, #35792 (23 Feb 1971), 10.

1382. HARVEY, SIR PAUL: *The Oxford Companion to English Literature*. 4th edition revised by Dorothy Eagle. Oxford: Clarendon Press, 1967 [1932]. x, 961 p.
    Yeats, pp. 903-4.

1383. HASSALL, CHRISTOPHER: *Edward Marsh: Patron of the Arts. A Biography*. London: Longmans, 1959. xvi, 732 p.
    Scattered references to Yeats, *passim* (see index), particularly pp. 95-96 (note on the genesis of *The Shadowy Waters*) and 383-84 (on the first performance of *At the Hawk's Well*).

1384. HEATH-STUBBS, JOHN: *The Darkling Plain: A Study of the Later Fortunes of Romanticism in English Poetry from George Darley to W. B. Yeats*. London: Eyre & Spottiswoode, 1950. 221 p.
    Yeats, pp. 203-11. Although Yeats's flirtation with fascism and his occult interests should not be overlooked, it can be argued that "no poetry which satisfies our intellect and our senses together will, on ultimate examination, prove false."

1385. HEISELER, BERNT VON: *Gesammelte Essays zur alten und neuen Literatur*. Stuttgart: Steinkopf, 1966-67. 2 v.
    "William B. Yeats," 1:264-75; reprinted from *Neue Rundschau*, yr 50 / 2:8 (Aug 1939), 142-49; *Sammlung*, 4 (1949), 257-63; and elsewhere. Rhapsodic praise, particularly of the early plays.

1385a. HELWIG, WERNER: "Letzter Besuch bei Frank O'Connor," *Neue Rundschau*, 82:1 (1971), 192, 194-96.
    O'Connor talks about Yeats.

1386. [HEMINGWAY, ERNEST]: "Learns to Commune with Fairies, Now Wins the $40,000 Nobel Prize: Yeats Also Elected Senator in the Irish Free State-- Hair Hangs Down in a Lank Sweep on One Side of His Celtic Face," *Toronto Star Weekly*, 14:[] (24 Nov 1923), 35.

1387. HENDERSON, PHILIP: *Literature and a Changing Civilisation*. London: Lane, 1935. xi, 180 p. (XXth Century Library. 15.)
    Yeats, pp. 95-98.

1388. HENN, T. R.: "Yeats and the Critical Pendulum," *Spectator*, 214:7146 (11 June 1965), 751.
    Argument similar to that of the next item.

1389. ————: "Towards the Values," *Southern R*, 5:3 (July 1969), 833-49.
    Those who criticize Yeats for his style, occultism, politics, and other matters usually overlook the very many and real values that his work contains.

1390. HENNECKE, HANS: *Englische Gedichte von Shakespeare bis W. B. Yeats: Einführungen, Urtexte und Übertragungen*. Berlin: Kiepenheuer, 1938. 160 p.
    "William Butler Yeats . . . ," 153-55. Also contained in *Gedichte von Shakespeare bis Ezra Pound: Einführungen, Urtexte und Übertragungen*. Wiesbaden: Limes, 1955. 352 p., pp. 163-65. Factually inaccurate.

1391. ———: *Dichtung und Dasein: Gesammelte Essays.* Berlin: Henssel, 1950. 274 p.
"William Butler Yeats und der europäische Symbolismus," 153-60 (reprinted from *Europäische Revue*, 15:3 [Mar 1939], 280-84), and *passim* (see index).

1392. ———: *Kritik: Gesammelte Essays zur modernen Literatur.* Gütersloh: Bertelsmann, 1958. 301 p.
"Dichtung—Philosophie—Gedicht: Zur Poetik von William Butler Yeats," 115-23; reprinted from *Jahresring*, [3] ([19]56/57), 52-55.

1393. ———: "Späte Wege zu William Butler Yeats," *Neue deutsche Hefte*, 18:4 (1971), 25-52.
A general assessment of Yeats's modernity and his reception in Germany by way of a review of *Werke*, vols. 1-2 (J223).

1394. HERLITSCHKA, HERBERT E.: Note on Yeats in German, *Merkur*, 9:12 (Dec 1955), 1134.

1395. HERTS, BENJAMIN RUSSELL: *Depreciations.* NY: Boni, 1914. 171 p.
"The Shadowy Mr. Yeats," 33-39; reprinted from *Forum*, 52:6 (Dec 1914), 911-14. Yeats's works are "comatose" and produce mostly "yawns."

1396. HICKS, GRANVILLE: *Figures of Transition: A Study of British Literature at the End of the Nineteenth Century.* NY: Macmillan, 1939. xvii, 326 p.
Yeats, *passim* (see index).

1397. HIGHET, GILBERT: *The Powers of Poetry.* NY: Oxford UP, 1960. xv, 356 p.
"The Old Wizard," 122-28; reprinted from *A Clerk of Oxenford: Essays on Literature and Life.* NY: Oxford UP, 1954. xii, 272 p., pp. 165-72.

1398. HOFFMAN, CHRISTINE B.: "William Butler Yeats and the Nobel Prize," *Personalist*, 49:1 (Winter 1968), 103-15.
Nobel's stipulation that the prize for literature should go to somebody whose work shows "an idealistic tendency" was inspired by his reading of Shelley. Yeats's idealism can be traced to the same source.

1399. HOGAN, J. J.: "W. B. Yeats," *Studies*, 28:109 (Mar 1939), 35-48.

1400. HOLROYD, STUART: *Emergence from Chaos.* London: Gollancz, 1957. 222 p.
"W. B. Yeats: The Divided Man," 113-37.

1401. HONE, J. M.: "W. B. Yeats: A Character Sketch," *Everyman*, 2:37 (27 June 1913), 328-29.

1402. HORTMANN, WILHELM: *Englische Literatur im 20. Jahrhundert.* Bern: Francke, 1965. 204 p. (Dalp-Taschenbücher. 379 G.)
"William Butler Yeats und die irische Renaissance," 27-35; "W. B. Yeats," 71-74; "Neue Stimmen im irischen Theater: O'Casey, Johnston," 92-96.

1403. HOUGH, GRAHAM: *Image and Experience: Studies in a Literary Revolution.* London: Duckworth, 1960. ix, 228 p.
The American edition was published as °*Reflections on a Literary Revolution.* Washington, D.C.: Catholic U of America Press, 1960. 127 p. Yeats, *passim* (see index).

1404. HOWARTH, HERBERT: "The Week of the Banquet," *London Mag*, 5:1 (Apr 1965), 36-45.

What Yeats did and probably thought in the week after his 70th birth-day. Includes an imagined conversation between Yeats, Gogarty, and Julian Bell.

1405. ———: "Yeats: The Variety of Greatness," *WHR*, 19:4 (Autumn 1965), 335-43.

1406. HUET, G. H. M. VAN: "Grootste moderne engels schrijvende dichter: William Butler Yeats," *Haagse Post*, 9 June 1956, 16.

1407. HÜTTEMANN, HERTA [i.e., GERTA]: "William Butler Yeats," *Germania*, "Das neue Ufer" supplement, #17 (1 June 1928), 1-2.

1408. HUGO, L. H.: "'The Last Romantic': The Poetry and Thought of W. B. Yeats," *Lantern*, 15:2 (Dec 1965), 24-37.

1409. HUMAYUN KABIR: *Poetry, Monads and Society.* Calcutta: U of Calcutta, 1941. xi, 203 p. (Sir George Stanley Lectures 1941.)
   "William Butler Yeats," 169-93. Yeats's work represents a synthesis of emotion and intellect and cannot be divided into different phases. A highly abstract essay almost devoid of illustrative quotations.

1410. HYMAN, STANLEY EDGAR: *The Armed Vision: A Study in the Methods of Modern Literary Criticism.* NY: Knopf, 1948. xv, 417, xxii p.
   Notes on what some of the modern critics thought of Yeats, *passim* (see index).

1411. I.: "Mr. W. B. Yeats," *To-day*, 42:547 (27 Apr 1904), 366.
   A sketch "from the life" by A. S. Forrest appears on p. 367.

1412. IMAAL: "A Rather Complex Personality," *Leader*, 7:5 (26 Sept 1903), 71-72.
   Mocks Yeats's "symbolical" inclinations. Correspondence by Stephen Gwynn, :7 (10 Oct 1903), 100; and Imaal, :8 (17 Oct 1903), 122.

1413. *Irlandskie teatral'nye miniatiūry.* Leningrad: Iskusstvo, 1961. 96 p.
   "Uil'îam Batler Eîts," 5-10; translation of *The Pot of Broth* by N. Rakhmanova, 11-20; also translations of, and short articles on, Synge, Lady Gregory, O'Casey, and Ervine.

1414. IZZO, CARLO: *Storia della letteratura inglese.* Milano: Nuova Accademia, 1961-63. 2 v.
   Yeats, 2:658-62 and *passim* (see index).

1415. [JACKSON, HOLBROOK]: "Men of To-day and To-morrow III: Mr. William Butler Yeats," *To-day*, 1:3 (May 1917), 93-97.
   Yeats withdraws more and more from the Irish literary movement that he helped to found.

1416. JACKSON, SCHUYLER: "William Butler Yeats," *London Mercury*, 11:64 (Feb 1925), 396-410.
   Yeats is the only poet of his time who has been consistent in follow-ing his imagination, but now he seems to betray a certain fragmenta-tion in his poetry and thought.

1417. JAECKLE, ERWIN: *Zirkelschlag der Lyrik.* Zürich: Fretz & Wasmuth, 1967. 302 p.
   "Flucht nach Byzanz: William Butler Yeats," 116-19. A rather one-sided sketch of Yeats's metaphysical leanings, written in a sometimes incom-prehensible style.

1418. JANSSENS, GERARDUS ANTONIUS MARIA: *The American Literary Review: A Critical History, 1920-1950.* The Hague: Mouton, 1968. 341 p. (Studies in

American Literature. 26.)
    Notes on the Yeats reception in American literary reviews, *passim*;
    see especially pp. 239-42 on the *Southern Review* Yeats issue (J1137).

1419. JARNES, BENJAMIN (ed): *Enciclopedia de la literatura*. México: Editora
central, [1946?]. 6 v.
    Yeats, 6:387-89.

1420. JARRELL, RANDALL: "The Development of Yeats's Sense of Reality,"
Southern R, 7:3 (Winter 1941/42), 653-66.
    The development of Yeats's thought and poetry falls into three phases:
    (1) neglect of reality (stereotyped poetry), (2) acknowledgment of
    reality (good poetry), (3) victory over reality (superb poetry). Yeats
    was driven to an acceptance of reality by his failure to create a
    unity of Irish culture in the early years of the century.

1421. JEFFARES, A. NORMAN: "W. B. Yeats: The Gift of Greatness," *Daily
Telegraph*, #34256 (12 June 1965), 8.

1422. JOHNSEN, WILLIAM ARNOLD: "Toward a Redefinition of the Modern,"
Ph.D. thesis, U of Illinois at Urbana-Champaign, 1970. iii, 210 p. (*DA*,
31:12 [June 1971], 6613A.)
    "W. B. Yeats," 87-102.

1423. JOHNSON, LOUIS: "Yeats Regained," *Numbers*, 1:4 (Oct 1955), 38-40.

1424. JONES, E. W.: Note on Yeats, *Sewanee R*, 34:4 (Oct-Dec 1926), 492-94.

1425. JURČINOVA, EVA: *Poutníci věčných cest: Essaye* [Pilgrims on eternal
paths]. Turnov: Muller, 1929. 117 p. (Edice sever a yýchod. 28.)
    "Před prahem století a na jeho prahu" [Before the threshold of the
    century and on the threshold], 9-24; contains a note on Yeats, 22-24.
    "Hlasy z irska" [The voices from Ireland], 25-52. A survey of the
    Irish literary revival and of the early works of Yeats and Synge.

1426. KAHN, DEREK: "The Morality of W. B. Yeats," *Left R*, 2:6 (Mar 1936),
252-58.
    A misnomer. Criticizes Yeats's "anti-democratic and anti-rational
    bias" and detects weak spots in his humanism. Concludes that Yeats
    "has written fine poetry, though he has not always taught good
    lessons."

1426a. KARRER, WOLFGANG, and EBERHARD KREUTZER: *Daten der englischen und
amerikanischen Literatur von 1890 bis zur Gegenwart*. Köln: Kiepenheuer &
Witsch, 1973. 301 p.
    Yeats, *passim* (see index).

1427. KAVANAGH, PATRICK: "On a Liberal Education," *X: A Quarterly Review*,
2:2 (Aug 1961), 112-19.
    Kavanagh's quarrel with Yeats and the Irish literary revival (it "was
    responsible for many lies").

1428. ————: *Collected Pruse*. London: McGibbon & Kee, 1967. 288 p.
    "William Butler Yeats," 254-56; reprinted from *Kilkenny Mag*, #6
    (Spring 1962), 25-28. "Yeats, you have much to answer for."

1429. ————: *Lapped Furrows: Correspondence 1933-1967 between Patrick
and Peter Kavanagh with Other Documents*. Edited by Peter Kavanagh. NY:
Peter Kavanagh Hand Press, 1969. vii, 307 p.
    Yeats, *passim* (see index).

1430. KELLNER, LEON: *Die englische Literatur im Zeitalter der Königin Viktoria*. Leipzig: Tauchnitz, 1909. xxx, 703 p.
"William Butler Yeats," 629-39. Insists on Yeats's otherworldliness, his lack of political interest, and his Celticism. The second edition of the book, *Die englische Literatur der neuesten Zeit von Dickens bis Shaw*. Leipzig: Tauchnitz, 1921. 402 p., although announced as radically revised, prints virtually the same material on Yeats (pp. 368-76).

1431. KELLY, BLANCHE MARY: *The Voice of the Irish*. NY: Sheed & Ward, 1952. xi, 340 p.
A compact literary history of Ireland, written from a conservative Catholic point of view. On Yeats, *passim* (see index), emphasizing and criticizing his theosophical and cabbalistic themes. Contains numerous errors of fact and judgment.

1432. KENNEDY, JOHN MURRAY: *English Literature, 1880-1905*. London: Swift, 1912. vi, 340 p.
On Yeats, pp. 280-89; he describes him as "a compound of Gaelic bard and William Blake," i.e., as one whose adoption of Irish subject matter is tempered by a thorough knowledge of English poetry. Also on George Moore, pp. 290-300, and AE, pp. 305-9.

1433. "Pat" [i.e., KENNY, PATRICK D.]: "Patriana . . . Lady Gregory, Mr. Yeats, and Irish Realities," *Irish Peasant*, 4:164 (3 Mar 1906), [4-5].
"Would it be too much to ask Mr. Yeats to come down to the ground, for just a little while, and to try something more directly and more obviously in touch with actual, human sympathies and imp[u]lses? I know my suggestion may appear a little vulgar, but Mr. Yeats is generous to critics, and after all, the theatre must have some more direct relation to national life."

1433a. KIDD, WALTER E. (ed): *British Winners of the Nobel Literary Prize*. Norman: U of Oklahoma Press, 1973. vii, 280 p.
James V. Baker: "William Butler Yeats," 44-82.

1434. KITCHIN, LAURENCE: "The Ditch and the Tower," *Listener*, 74:1907 (14 Oct 1965), 575-77.
Yeats's authority and modernity.

1435. KLEINSTÜCK, JOHANNES: "Im Kampf um Irlands Seele: Am 13. Juni vor hundert Jahren wurde W. B. Yeats geboren," *Welt*, #133 (11 June 1965), 7.

1436. KNOWER, E. T.: "A Modern Minstrel," *American R*, 3:4 (July-Aug 1925), 400-405.

1436a. K[OHL], N[IELS] V[ON]: "Irerens kaerlighed til det skjulte liv," *Kristeligt Dagblad*, 5 Aug 1965, 7.

1437. KRISTENSEN, SVEN MØLLER (ed): *Fremmede digtere i det 20. århundrede*. København: Gad, 1967-68. 3 v.
Peter P. Rohde: "William Butler Yeats," 1:69-85.

1438. KROJER, MAXIM: "Twintig jaar geleden overleed: William Butler Yeats," *Periscoop*, 9:4 (Feb 1959), 11.
A short overall assessment, mainly of the plays.

1439. K[UBIAK], Z[YGMUNT]: Note on Yeats in Polish, *Tygodnik Powszechny*, 20:21 (22 May 1966), 4.

1440. LAFFONT, [ROBERT], and [VALENTINO] BOMPIANI: *Dictionnaire des oeuvres de tous les temps et de tous les pays: Littérature, philosophie, musique, sciences.* Paris: S. E. D. E., 1968 [1953]. 5 v.

Contains synopses of *Cathleen ni Houlihan* (1:337), *The Countess Cathleen* (1:488), *Deirdre* (1:627), *The Land of Heart's Desire* (3:689),
Poems, 1895 (4:33), *The Tower* (4:579), and *The Wind among the Reeds*
(4:667) as Yeats's most memorable works.

1441. ───── (eds): *Dictionnaire biographique des auteurs.* Paris: S. E.
D. E., 1964 [1957]. 2 v.

Bernard Noël: "W. B. Yeats," 2:722-23.

1442. LANGBAUM, ROBERT: *The Modern Spirit: Essays on the Continuity of
Nineteenth- and Twentieth-Century Literature.* NY: Oxford UP, 1970. xiii,
221 p. (Galaxy Books. GB320.)

Yeats, *passim* (see index), especially in "The Mysteries of Identity:
A Theme in Modern Literature," 164-84; reprinted from *American
Scholar,* 34:4 (Autumn 1965), 569-86 (on myth, mask, and character in
Yeats's poetry).

1443. LAROUSSE: *Grand Larousse encyclopédique en dix volumes.* Paris:
Larousse, 1960-64. 10 v.

Yeats, 10:980.

1443a. LAUTERBACH, EDWARD S., and W. EUGENE DAVIS: *The Transitional Age
in British Literature, 1880-1920.* Troy, N.Y.: Whitston, 1973. xiii, 323 p.

A short survey of the period and selected checklists. On Yeats,
passim (see index); checklist, pp. 307-11 (insufficient).

1444. LENNARTZ, FRANZ: *Ausländische Dichter und Schriftsteller unserer
Zeit: Einzeldarstellungen zur schönen Literatur in fremden Sprachen.*
2nd edition. Stuttgart: Kröner, 1957 [1955]. vii, 749 p. (Kröners Taschenausgabe. 217.)

Yeats, pp. 737-45.

1445. LESTER, JOHN A.: *Journey through Despair, 1880-1914: Transformations
in British Literary Culture.* Princeton: Princeton UP, 1968. xxiii, 211 p.

On Yeats, *passim* (see index), especially on the concept of the mask.

1446. LEVIN, HARRY: *Contexts of Criticism.* Cambridge, Mass.: Harvard UP,
1957. xiii, 294 p. (Harvard Studies in Comparative Literature. 22.)

Scattered notes on Yeats, *passim* (see index).

1447. LEWIS, WYNDHAM: "W. B. Yeats," *New Verse,* ns 1:2 (May 1939), 45-46.

1448. ─────: *Rude Assignment: A Narrative of My Career Up-to-Date.*
London: Hutchinson, [1950]. 231 p.

Some notes on Yeats, *passim* (see index).

1449. LICHNEROWICZ, JEANNE: "Le dernier Prix Nobel de littérature: W.-B.
Yeats," *Revue bleue,* 61:23 (1 Dec 1923), 793-94.

An English summary was published as "The Latest Nobel Prize for
Literature: William Butler Yeats," *American R of Reviews,* 69:2 (Feb
1924), 205-6.

1450. ─────: "William Butler Yeats," *Europe,* 5:18 (15 June 1924), 162-74.

1451. LIDDY, JAMES, and ANTHONY CRONIN: "Two Offerings for W. B. Yeats,"
Arena, #4 (Spring 1965), 42-43.

1452. LIDDY, JAMES: "A Note on Yeats," *University R* [Dublin], 3:8 [1966?],
71.

Yeats's hallmark is his "arrogant will to stay an individual."

1453. hbl [i.e., LIISBERG, HENRIK BERING]: "W. B. Yeats," *Information*, 23: 182 (12 June 1965), 4.

1454. LYND, ROBERT: *Old and New Masters*. NY: Scribner's, [1919]. 249 p.
"W. B. Yeats," 156-70; reprinted in *Essays on Life and Literature*. London: Dent, 1951. xiv, 274 p. (Everyman's Library. 990.), pp. 160-72. An essay in two parts: "His Own Account of Himself" and "His Poetry." Also on "The Fame of J. M. Synge," 94-97, and "Lady Gregory," 178-83.

1455. ————: "Letters to Living Authors.—IV.: Mr. W. B. Yeats," *John o' London's Weekly*, 21:538 (10 Aug 1929), 608.
"I doubt whether the reading public . . . realizes yet what a good poet you are. . . ."

1456. ————: *Books and Writers*. With a foreword by Richard Church. London: Dent, 1952. xv, 331 p.
"William Butler Yeats," 76-84; incorporates "William Butler Yeats: A Great Poet Who Was a Missionary of Art," *John o' London's Weekly*, 40: 1035 (10 Feb 1939), 735-36.

1457. MCALINDON, T.: "Divine Unrest: The Development of William Butler Yeats," *Irish Monthly*, 83 [i.e., 82]:968 (Apr 1954), 152-59.

1458. MCAULEY, JAMES: "A Moment's Memory to That Laurelled Head," *Australian*, 12 June 1965, 9.

1459. MACCALLUM, THOMAS WATSON, and STEPHEN TAYLOR (eds): *The Nobel Prize-Winners and the Nobel Foundation, 1901-1937*. With an introduction by Gilbert Murray. Zürich: Central European Times Publishing Co., 1938. xi, 599 p.
"William Butler Yeats," 298-99.

1460. MACDONALD, QUENTIN: "William Butler Yeats and the 'Celtic Movement,'" *Book News Monthly*, 22:262 (June 1904), 1024-25.
Yeats belongs to the "Celtic Movement," not to the "Irish Literary Revival," but the difference is not explained.

1461. [MCGRATH, JOHN]: Answer to Yeats's letter on American and Irish literature, signed "A Student of Irish Literature," (Wp. 346), *United Ireland*, 14:690 (24 Nov 1894), 1.
See Yeats's reply, :691 (1 Dec 1894), 1. Yeats's letters are reprinted in Wade's edition, pp. 238-39, 241-42.

1462. MCHUGH, ROGER: "Yeats: The Era of the Celtic Twilight," *Irish Independent*, 74:139 (12 June 1965), 8.

1463. O'L., A. [i.e., MACKENNA, STEPHEN]: "Mr. W. B. Yeats: An Argument and an Appreciation (By an Admirer)," *Freeman's J*, 142:[] (2 Jan 1909), 5.

1464. MACLEOD, FIONA: *The Winged Destiny: Studies in the Spiritual History of the Gael*. London: Heinemann, 1925 [1904]. xiv, 393 p. (The Collected Works. 5.)
"The Shadowy Waters," 320-45; reprint of "The Later Work of Mr. W. B. Yeats," *NAR*, 175:551 (Oct 1902), 473-85. See also [Francis Thompson], "Fiona Macleod on Mr. W. B. Yeats," *Academy*, 63:1590 (25 Oct 1902), 444-45; reprinted in J4351.

1465. MACLIAMMÓIR, MICHEÁL: "W. B. Yeats: Poet and Patriot," *Ireland of the Welcomes*, 14:1 (May-June 1965), 14-20.

1466. MACM[ANUS], M. J.: "Yeats, Shaw and the New Ireland," *Irish Press*, 9:189 (10 Aug 1939), 8.
Yeats and Shaw are Irish, not English, writers.

1467. MCQUILLAND, LOUIS J.: "W. B. Yeats, Poseur and Poet," *Vanity Fair*, 79:2027 (4 Sept 1907), 311-12.
"Mr. Yeats is as great a poet as he is a *poseur*, which is saying much." Nevertheless, "he does often transcend the limits of allowable poetic absurdity."

1468. MAGILL, FRANK N. (ed): *Cyclopedia of World Authors*. NY: Harper & Row, 1958. xiii, 1200 p.
"William Butler Yeats," 1186-90.

1469. MAGUIRE, ALASTAIR: "Mr. W. B. Yeats, the True Interpreter of the Irish Mind," *National Student*, 1:5 (July 1911), 149-51.
Perhaps not to be taken too seriously.

1470. MAHON, A.: "The Man Who Was Yeats," *Irish Independent*, 74:137 (10 June 1965), 14, 17.

1471. MALONE, G. P.: "William Butler Yeats: A Centenary Tribute," *Contemporary R*, 207:1195 (Aug 1965), 96-99.

1472. MALVIL, ANDRÉ: "William Butler Yeats: Suivi de traductions inédites," *Monde nouveau*, 10:8 (15 Oct 1928), 548-57.
For the translations (pp. 553-57) see Wp. 439.

1473. MANNING, OLIVIA: *The Dreaming Shore*. London: Evans, 1950. 202 p.
"Yeats' Country," 149-63; essentially a description of Sligo and surroundings.

1474. MARBLE, ANNIE RUSSELL: *The Nobel Prize Winners in Literature*. NY: Appleton, 1925. xiii, 312 p.
"W. B. Yeats and His Part in the Celtic Revival," 253-63.

1475. MARSHALL, PERCY: *Masters of English Poetry*. London: Dobson, 1966. 242 p.
"William Butler Yeats (1865-1939)," 198-213. Rather naive and weak on facts.

1476. MARTINS, SOARES: "Introdução a W. B. Yeats," *Tempo presente*, #7 (Nov 1959), 31-36.

1477. MASON, EUGENE: *A Book of Preferences in Literature*. London: Wilson, 1915. 213 p.
"The Poet as Mystic: William Butler Yeats," 89-113.

1478. MASTERMAN, CHARLES FREDERICK GURNEY: *In Peril of Change: Essays Written in Time of Tranquillity*. NY: Huebsch, [1905]. xvi, 332 p.
"After the Reaction," 1-36; reprinted from *Contemporary R*, 86:468 (Dec 1904), 815-34, and *Living Age*, 244:3160 (28 Jan 1905), 193-208. After the imperialist reaction of late Victorianism, Yeats is one of the most promising representatives of a new literature of the golden age to come.

1479. MATTHEWS, HAROLD: "Yeats and the Irish Theatre," *Theatre World*, 61: 485 (June 1965), 35-36.

1480. MATTHIESSEN, FRANCIS OTTO: *The Responsibilities of the Critic: Essays and Reviews*. Selected by John Rackliffe. NY: Oxford UP, 1952. xvi, 282 p.

"Yeats: The Crooked Road," 25-40; reprinted from *Southern R*, 7:3 (Winter 1941/42), 455-70.

1481. MAUGHAM, WILLIAM SOMERSET: *W. Somerset Maugham's Introduction to Modern English and American Literature*. NY: New Home Library, 1943. xxi, 618 p.

Note on Yeats, pp. 600-601, where he is described as a pompous and vain but nevertheless great poet.

1482. MAYNARD, THEODORE: *Our Best Poets English and American*. NY: Holt, 1922. xxi, 233 p.

"W. B. Yeats: Fairies and Fog," 67-83. The later work is not as good as the earlier, because Yeats "has lost his sympathy for Ireland." But even the earlier verse "has not worn well."

1483. MENON, NARAYANA: "W. B. Yeats and the Irish Literary Revival," *Indian Literature*, 8:2 (1965), 12-22.

1484. MERCIER, VIVIAN: *The Irish Comic Tradition*. Oxford: Clarendon Press, 1962. xx, 258 p.

Notes on Yeats, *passim* (see index).

1485. MILLER, JOSEPH HILLIS: *Poets of Reality: Six Twentieth-Century Writers*. Cambridge, Mass.: Belknap Press of Harvard UP, 1965. xiii, 369 p.

"W. B. Yeats," 68-130; and *passim*. The book sketches a development from Romanticism through Nihilism to a New Realism, i.e., the redis-covery of God. The new realists are, in different ways, Conrad, Yeats, Eliot, Dylan Thomas, Stevens, and William Carlos Williams. Miller dis-cusses Yeats's thought in his prose and poetry and concludes that Yeats's "affirmation of the infinite richness of the finite moment" (p. 11) defines his kind of reality. I have three objections to Miller's argument. (1) It is sometimes hard to distinguish whether Miller or Yeats is speaking. (2) Miller uses quotations from Yeats's works, which are often chronologically wide apart, without giving appropriate indications. (Does he imply that there is an overall unity in Yeats's thought?) (3) Miller takes the poems to be direct statements of Yeats's thought—a rather dubious procedure without the necessary qualifications. See also the review by William H. Pritchard, "The Circus Animals' Desertion," *Mass R*, 7:2 (Spring 1966), 387-94.

1486. MIROIU, MIHAI: "William Butler Yeats, bardul irlandei moderne" [Poet of modern Ireland], *Studii de literaturǎ universalǎ*, 7 (1965), 195-215.

Includes a summary in English.

1487. MITCHELL, KEITH: "So Hard and Late: W. B. Yeats, 1865-1939," *Tablet*, 219:6525 (12 June 1965), 657-58.

Yeats was a good poet with an unacceptable mysticism and unsympathetic political views.

1488. MIX, KATHERINE LYON: *A Study in Yellow: The "Yellow Book" and Its Contributors*. Lawrence: U of Kansas Press, 1960. ix, 325 p.

Yeats, *passim* (see index).

1489. MOKAŚHI, S. R.: "Adam's Curse and Cussedness: W. B. Yeats's Rebellion against British English and Its Lesson to India," *Triveni*, 33:3 (Oct 1964), 35-41.

1489a. °MOKASHI-PUNEKAR, SHANKAR: *The Indo-Anglian Creed and Allied Essays*. Calcutta: Writers Workshop, 1972. 72 p.

Reported to contain material on Yeats.

1490. MOLUA [pseudonym]: "Purging the Pride of Pollexfen," *Catholic Bulletin*, 16:9 (Sept 1926), 937-43.
    Vitriolic.

1491. ————: "Pollexfen Pride and the People: An Anthology (1912-1925) with a Practical Result (1925-1927)," *Catholic Bulletin*, 17:8 (Aug 1927), 821-25.
    Yeats's contempt of Paudeen turned on him with a vengeance.

1492. MONAHAN, MICHAEL: *Nova Hibernia: Irish Poets and Dramatists of Today and Yesterday*. Freeport, N.Y.: Books for Libraries Press, 1967 [1914]. vii, 274 p.
    "Yeats and Synge," 13-37; reprinted from *Papyrus*, ser 3 / yr 9 / 3:2 (Dec 1911), 1-8.

1493. MONOD, SYLVÈRE: *Histoire de la littérature anglaise: De Victoria à Elizabeth II*. Paris: Colin, 1970. 392 p.
    "W. B. Yeats," 198-202; "J. M. Synge," 202-5.

1494. MONTGOMERY, K[ATHLEEN and] L[ETITIA]: "Some Writers of the Celtic Renaissance," *Fortnightly R*, os 96 / ns 90:537 (Sept 1911), 545-61.
    Mainly on Yeats.

1495. MOORE, ISABEL: "William Butler Yeats," *Bookman* [NY], 18:4 (Dec 1903), 360-63.

1496. MOORE, T. STURGE: "Yeats," *English*, 2:11 (Summer 1939), 273-78.

1497. MORAN, D. P.: "A Hundred Years of Irish Humbug," *Claidheamh Soluis*, 2:10 (19 May 1900), 149-51.
    Attacks the Irish literary revival, particularly Rolleston and Yeats: "I never knew a man who can, with such impunity, cast insults at his race and nation as Mr. W. B. Yeats." Correspondence by T. W. Rolleston, :12 (2 June 1900), 189.

1498. [———— (?)]: "At the Abbey Theatre," *Leader*, 9:20 (7 Jan 1905), 330-31.
    "Mr. Yeats does not interest us" and neither does the Abbey.

1499. MORAWSKI, STEFAN: "Kipling—Yeats—Auden," *Twórczość*, 5:6 (1949), 84-99.
    A Marxist approach.

1500. MORE, PAUL ELMER: *Shelburne Essays*. First series. NY: Putnam's, 1904. v, 253 p.
    "Two Poets of the Irish Movement," 177-92; reprinted from *Evening Post*, 102:[] (12 Dec 1903), Book Section, 1. Compares Yeats and Lionel Johnson to the latter's advantage. Yeats's poetry is one of "defeat"; compared to the healthy robustness of the Irish sagas, Yeats's works are feeble and decadent products.

1501. MORGAN, CHARLES: *The House of Macmillan (1843-1943)*. London: Macmillan, 1943. xii, 248 p.
    See pp. 220-24 for the relationship between Yeats and his publisher, particularly for two negative reader's reports by Mowbray Morris and John Morley. See also J1509.

1502. MORGAN, GERALD: "Cofio bardd: Canmlwyddiant geni W. B. Yeats" [Remembering the poet: The centenary of Yeats's birth], *Barn*, #33 (July 1965), 250-51.

1503. MORISSET, HENRI: "William Butler Yeats," *Esprit*, 7:84 (1 Sept 1939), 776-80.

1504. MORRALL, JOHN: "Personal Themes in the Public and Private Writings of W. B. Yeats," *University R* [Dublin], 1:9 (Summer 1956), 28-36.
Yeats as he appears from his letters and other writings.

1505. MORTON, J. B., and VIOLET CLIFTON: "William Butler Yeats: Two Appreciations," *Tablet*, 173:5152 (4 Feb 1939), 136-37.
Includes reminiscences.

1506. MOSES, MONTROSE J.: "W. B. Yeats and the Irish Players," *Metropolitan Mag*, 35:3 (Jan 1912), 23-25, 61-62.
After praising Yeats and the Abbey Players profusely, Moses offers some criticism: "There is perhaps one unfortunate factor in the movement: both dramatist and actor are self-conscious of their nationality. They never once allow you to forget that they are Irish and that they represent the Irish drama."

1507. MUDDIMAN, BERNARD: *The Men of the Nineties*. London: Danielson, 1920. iv, 146 p.
Yeats is mentioned *passim* (see index).

1508. MURPHY, SHEILA ANN: "William Butler Yeats: Enemy of the Irish People," *Literature & Ideology*, #8 (1971), 15-30.
The periodical is published by the Necessity for Change Institute of Ideological Studies, Dublin and Montreal, which favors the Chairman Mao approach. The article "expose[s] the fascist and anti-people character of imperialist cultural propaganda in Ireland represented by writers like Yeats, Lady Gregory, and many others." The Irish people, however, "refute and repudiate [Yeats] as part of their struggle against U.S. and British imperialism."

1509. MURRAY, T. C.: "The Casting Out of Shaw and Yeats," *Bell*, 12:4 (July 1946), 310-17.
Essentially a review of the Shaw and Yeats sections in Morgan's *The House of Macmillan*, J1501.

1509a. *Die Musik in Geschichte und Gegenwart: Allgemeine Enzyklopädie der Musik*. Kassel: Bärenreiter, 1949—.
Hans Ferdinand Redlich: Yeats, 14:932-33.

1510. NELSON, JAMES G.: *The Early Nineties: A View from the Bodley Head*. Cambridge, Mass.: Harvard UP, 1971. xv, 387 p.
Yeats, *passim* (see index), especially in connection with the Rhymers' Club.

1511. NEMEROV, HOWARD: *Reflexions on Poetry & Poetics*. New Brunswick: Rutgers UP, 1972. xii, 235 p.
"William Butler Yeats," 52-55; reprinted from Louis Kronenberger (ed): *Brief Lives: A Biographical Guide to the Arts*. London: Lane / Penguin Press, 1972. xxii, 900 p., pp. 894-97.

1512. *New Catholic Encyclopedia*. NY: McGraw-Hill, 1967. 15 v.
Stephen P. Ryan and John Montague: "Irish Poetry," 7:654-57.
Cleanth Brooks: "Yeats," 14:1067-68: "His poetry returns to Christianity the dimension of awe."

1513. NICHOLSON, NORMAN: *Man & Literature*. London: SCM Press, 1944 [1943]. 218 p.
"W. B. Yeats," 188-92. "It is a rather curiously Irish type of Natural Man that he presents to us."

1514. NIEMOJOWSKA, MARIA: "Iryjski głos" [The Irish voice], *Poezja*, 3:3 (Mar 1967), 69-77.

1515. NIST, JOHN: "In Defense of Yeats," *Arizona Q*, 18:1 (Spring 1962), 58-65.
Against Yvor Winters (J2445).

1516. *Nobel: The Man and His Prizes*. Edited by the Nobel Foundation. Norman: U of Oklahoma Press, 1951. 620 p.
Note by Anders Österling on the reasons for giving Yeats and not Hardy the prize for literature, pp. 119-20.

1517. *Nobel-díjas írók antológiája: Harmincnégy arcképpel* [Thirty-one portraits]. Budapest: Káldor könyvkiadóvállalat, 1935. xii, 583 p.
Dezső Kosztolányi: "William Butler Yeats," 403-5; translations of seven poems, 407-10.

1518. *Nobelprisen 50 år: Forskare, diktare, fredskämpar*. Stockholm: Sohlmans, 1950. 512 p.
Anders Österling: Yeats, pp. 109-10.

1519. OATES, JOYCE CAROL: "Speaking of Books: The Formidable W. B. Yeats," *NYTBR*, 7 Sept 1969, 2.
Correspondence by Dennis E. Smith, Fireman, Engine Co. 82, New York Fire Dept., 5 Oct 1969, 25.

1520. O'BRIEN, JAMES H.: "Yeats's Search for Unity of Being," *Personalist*, 48:3 (Summer 1967), 361-71.
Yeats's relevance to his age "lies in his continued pursuit of unity of being" and in his preservation of the self.

1521. O'CASEY, SEAN: *Blasts and Benedictions: Articles and Stories*. Selected and introduced by Ronald Ayling. London: Macmillan, 1967. xx, 314 p.
Yeats is mentioned *passim* (see index), especially in the following items:
1. "O'Casey on O'Casey: A Word before Curtain-Rise (1954)," 85-87; reprinted from the foreword to °*Selected Plays*. NY: Braziller, 1954.
2. "W. B. Yeats and *The Silver Tassie*," 99-102; reprinted from J2250, q.v.
3. "Literature in Ireland," 170-81; reprinted from *International Literature* [Moscow], #11 (Nov 1939), 104-8 [not Dec 1939, as stated by Ayling].
4. "Ireland's Silvery Shadow (1946)," 182-87; previously unpublished.
5. "John Millington Synge," 35-41; first published in Russian in °*Britanskii Soíuznik*, June 1946.
6. "On the Banks of the Ban (1963)," 146-49; reprinted from °*NYT*, 5 Jan 1964. On the Abbey Theatre.
7. "A Protestant Bridget (1946)," 205-12; reprinted from *Bell*, 13:5 (Feb 1947), 64-72. A review of *Lady Gregory's Journals* (J6704).
8. "A Sprig of Rosemary among the Laurel (1962)," 213-15; reprinted from the foreword to Lady Gregory's *Selected Plays* (J6949).

1522. O'CONNOR, FRANK: "The Plays and Poetry of W. B. Yeats: An Appreciation," *Listener*, 25:643 (8 May 1941), 675-76.

1523. O'DUFFY, EIMAR: "William Butler Yeats," *Flambeau*, 6:12 (31 Dec 1923), 549-52.

1524. O'FAOLÁIN, SEÁN: "W. B. Yeats," *English R*, 60:6 (June 1935), 680-88.
Yeats between romanticism and realism.

1525. [————]: "Fifty Years of Irish Literature," *Bell*, 3:5 (Feb 1942), 327-34.
An introduction to a collection of Yeats clippings ("The Wisdom of W. B. Yeats," 335-39), demonstrating how right Yeats was about certain Irish literary phenomena.

1526. The Editor [i.e., O'FAOLAIN, SEAN]: "Romance and Realism," *Bell*, 10:5 (Aug 1945), 373-82.
Yeats was a romantic, not a realist.

1527. O'FAOLAIN, SEAN: "W. B. Yeats Comes Back to Erin," *Sunday Times*, #6544 (12 Sept 1948), 2.

1528. ————: *Vive Moi! An Autobiography*. London: Hart-Davis, 1965. 288 p.
O'Faolain's opinion of Yeats and some anecdotes, pp. 272-83.

1529. O'GLASAIN, PADRAIC: "Yeats: Symbolist or Mystic?" *Ave Maria*, ns 54: 3 (19 July 1941), 71-74.
Since mystics can be only Catholic, Yeats was of necessity a symbolist.

1530. O'LEARY, JOHN: "The National Publishing Company," *Freeman's J*, 125: [] (8 Sept 1892), 5.
The Yeats—Sir Charles Gavan Duffy quarrel. For further letters and leaders by John O'Leary, John F. Taylor, Yeats, and others, see preceding and subsequent issues.

1531. OLIVERO, FEDERICO: *Correnti mistiche nella letteratura inglese moderna*. Torino: Bocca, 1932. 373 p.
Yeats, *passim* (see index), especially in chapter 6, "Il 'Celtic Twilight,'" which also discusses other figures of the revival.

1532. OLLES, HELMUT (ed): *Literaturlexikon 20. Jahrhundert*. Reinbek bei Hamburg: Rowohlt, 1971. 850 p.
J[ohannes] K[leinstück]: Yeats, pp. 840-42.

1533. O LOCHLAINN, COLM: "William Butler Yeats," *British Annual of Literature*, 2 (1939), 24-30.

1534. ORKNEY, MICHAEL: "William B. Yeats: A Character Sketch," *Irish Independent*, 17:69 (21 Mar 1908), 4.

1535. ORTENSI, ULISSE: "Letterati contemporanei: William Butler Yeats," *Emporium*, 21:124 (Apr 1905), 265-73.
With two unknown photographs.

1536. OSGOOD, CHARLES GROSVENOR: *The Voice of England: A History of English Literature*. 2nd edition with a chapter on English literature since 1910 by Thomas Riggs. NY: Harper, 1952 [1935]. xv, 671 p.
Yeats, *passim* (see index).

1537. PANHUIJSEN, JOS[EPH]: "Herzien, herdenken: William Butler Yeats," *Stem*, 19:3 (Mar 1939), 321-24.

1538. PARKINSON, THOMAS: "The Modernity of Yeats," *Southern R*, 5:3 (July 1969), 922-34.
"We should be grateful that Yeats was not trained in the designs of modern thought. . . . Yeats had another . . . important role in modern consciousness, to keep us aware of the obligations of the artist, to remind us of the kind of lonely courage that the poet has, perhaps above all men; and to hold before us a traditional ideal of artistic responsibility."

1539. PARROTT, THOMAS MARC, and WILLARD THORP (eds): *Poetry of the Transition, 1850-1914.* NY: Oxford UP, 1932. xli, 622 p.
"William Butler Yeats, 1865—," 290-93.

1540. PAUL, W. J. (ed): *Modern Irish Poets.* Belfast: Belfast Steam-Printing Co., 1894-97. 2 v.
"W. B. Yeats," 1:136-38.

1541. PAUL-DUBOIS, LOUIS: "M. Yeats et le mouvement poètique en Irlande," *Revue des deux mondes,* yr 99 / per 7 / 53:3 (1 Oct 1929), 558-83; :4 (15 Oct 1929), 824-46.

1542. PAYNE, BASIL: "Debunking Yeats," *Irish Times,* #33211 (31 Mar 1962), 9.
Yvor Winters is right: Yeats was not a great Irish poet. Correspondence by James Liddy, #33214 (4 Apr 1962), 7; Basil Payne and "Kathleen ni Houlihan," #33217 (7 Apr 1962), 7, 12.

1543. PESCHMANN, HERMANN: "Craftsmanship, Integrity and Passion," *Poetry Q,* 12:3 (Autumn 1950), 175-80.

1544. PFISTER, KURT: "Der irische Dichter William Yeats," *Frankfurter Zeitung,* 78:80 (14 Feb 1934), 1.

1545. PHELPS, ARTHUR L.: "William Butler Yeats," *Acta Victoriana,* 39:3 (Dec 1914), 153-54, 156-58, 160-62.

1546. PINTO, VIVIAN DE SOLA: *Crisis in English Poetry, 1880-1940.* NY: Harper & Row, 1966 [1951]. 228 p. (Harper Torchbooks. TB1260.)
Yeats, *passim* (see index), especially "Yeats and Synge," 85-111 (a general account of Yeats's life and work; almost nothing on Synge).

1547. PŁOŃSKI, JERZY: "Z nad Tamizy" [From the Thames], *Życie,* 2:8 (19 Feb 1898), 92-93.
A survey of Yeats's work to date.

1547a. PLUNKETT, JAMES: *The Gems She Wore: A Book of Irish Places.* London: Hutchinson, 1972. 208 p.
On Yeats, pp. 162-76 and *passim* (see index); also on Synge (pp. 78-82).

1548. POGGIOLI, RENATO: "Qualis Artifex Pereo! or Barbarism and Decadence," *Harvard Library Bulletin,* 13:1 (Winter 1959), 135-59.
Yeats was "able to see that the nemesis of decadence might turn into a catharsis transcending decadence itself." Includes a discussion of the two Byzantium poems.

1549. P[OORE], C[HARLES]: "Honors for Yeats, Now 70: 'The Re-Creator of Irish Literature' Will Revisit Dublin, the Scene Years Ago of His Picturesque Battles for a National Drama," *NYT,* 84:28260 (9 June 1935), VII, 14.

1550. PORTER, KATHERINE ANNE: *The Collected Essays and Occasional Writings.* NY: Delacorte Press, 1970. xiii, 496 p.
"From the Notebooks: Yeats, Joyce, Eliot, Pound," 298-300; reprinted from *Southern R,* 1:3 (July 1965), 570-73.

1551. POTEZ, HENRI: "W. B. Yeats et la renaissance poétique en Irlande," *Revue de Paris,* yr 11 / 4:3 (1 Aug 1904), 597-618; :4 (15 Aug 1904), 848-66.

1552. POURRAT, HENRI: "W. B. YEATS," *Nouvelle revue française,* ns yr 11 / 22:124 (1 Jan 1924), 124-28.

1553. PRAZ, MARIO: *Cronache letterarie anglosassoni.* Roma: Edizione di Storia e Letteratura, 1950-66. 4 v. (Letture di pensiero e d'arte. 16. 17. 41. 42.)

"Rivalutazione dei romantici," 1:123-28; reprinted from °*Tempo*, 31 Oct 1950; contains a note on Yeats.

"Due antologie di versi," 2:23-31; reprinted from °*Stampa*, 8 Dec 1936; contains a review of the *Oxford Book*(W250/251).

"Poeti maghi," 3:328-33; reprinted from °*Tempo*, 16 Apr 1965; on Blake and Yeats.

"L'usignolo d'oro," 4:70-76; on *A Vision.*

1554. PREMINGER, ALEX, FRANK J. WARNKE, and O. B. HARDISON (eds): *Ency-clopedia of Poetry and Poetics.* Princeton: Princeton UP, 1965. xxiv, 906 p.

Not indexed. The following contributions contain major references to Yeats:

R[ichard] H[arter] F[ogle]: "English Poetry," 236-37.
J[ames] B[aird]: "Exoticism," 265.
G[eorge] B[randon] S[aul]: "Irish Literary Renaissance," 403-4.
P[adraic] C[olum] and G. B. S[aul]: "Irish Poetry," 404-6.
E[arl] M[iner]: "Nō," 571.
N[orman] F[riedman]: "Symbol," 833-36.

1555. PRESS, JOHN: *The Chequer'd Shade: Reflections on Obscurity in Poetry.* London: Oxford UP, 1958. vii, 229 p.

References to Yeats, *passim* (see index).

1556. ————: *A Map of Modern English Verse.* London: Oxford UP, 1969. xii, 282 p.

"The Later Poetry of W. B. Yeats," 7-29, consists of an introduction (Yeats was neither a mystic nor a fanatic right-wing politician but a rather complex personality) and some samples from the poetry and criticism of Yeats and from Yeats criticism.

1557. QUILLER-COUCH, A. T.: "Sundry Poets—X.: Mr. Yeats," *Daily News,* #17815 (27 Apr 1903), 8; #17827 (11 May 1903), 8; #17833 (18 May 1903), 8.

This is really a bad joke. "Q" discusses Yeats only in the last paragraph of the last installment, where he labels Yeats's diction "foreign," i.e., not London English.

1558. QUINN, STEPHEN: "The Position of Yeats," *Catholic Bulletin,* 29:3 (Mar 1939), 183-84.

See also Quinn's "Further Placings for W. B. Yeats," :4 (Apr 1939), 241-44. Yeats was an English writer because he was an intolerable embarrassment to Ireland.

1559. QVAMME, BØRRE: "William Butler Yeats, 1865-1939," *Edda,* yr 30 / 43:2 (1943), 99-107.

1560. RAFROIDI, PATRICK: "W. B. Yeats: Sligo ou Byzance?" *Langues modernes,* 60:1 (Jan-Feb 1966), 45-54.

Not Sligo *or* Byzantium, but Sligo *and* Byzantium.

1561. RAINE, KATHLEEN, and MAX-POL FOUCHET (eds): *Aspects de la littéra-ture anglaise (1918-1945).* Paris: Fontaine, [1947]. 479 p.

Stephen Spender: "Quelques observations sur la poésie anglaise entre les deux guerres," 19-29; on Yeats, 25-26.

Edwin Muir: "W.-B. Yeats," 94-104; reprinted from *Fontaine*, 7:37-40 (Dec 1944), 105-14; translated by Austin and Madeleine Gill.

1562. RAIZISS, SONA: *The Metaphysical Passion: Seven Modern American Poets and Seventeenth-Century Tradition.* Philadelphia: U of Pennsylvania Press, 1952. xv, 327 p.
   Yeats is mentioned *passim* (see index).

1563. RAJAN, BALACHANDRA: "Now Days are Dragon-Ridden," *American Scholar*, 32:3 (Summer 1963), 407-14.
   "Reading Yeats in a time of crisis is a radical if not a liberal education. . . ."

1564. RAY, GORDON NORTON (ed): *Masters of British Literature.* 2nd edition. Boston: Houghton Mifflin, 1962 [1958]. 2 v.
   Richard Ellmann: Yeats, 2:823-31.

1565. READ, HERBERT: *Annals of Innocence and Experience.* London: Faber & Faber, 1946 [1940]. 236 p.
   Distrusts Yeats's Celtic Twilight phase (pp. 95-96) and comments on the exclusion of the war poets from the *Oxford Book of Modern Verse* (pp. 100-101).

1566. READE, ARTHUR ROBERT: *Main Currents in Modern Literature.* London: Nicholson & Watson, 1935. 223 p.
   "The Anglo-Irish and W. B. Yeats," 41-56. Discusses Yeats as a symbolist rather than as an Irish writer.

1567. REES, DAVID: "Another Troy," *Spectator*, 217:7225 (16 Dec 1966), 789-90.
   Yeats was "the great poet of our time."

1568. REES, LESLIE: "W. B. Yeats," *Australian English Association Bulletin*, 1:10 (Apr 1939); contained in *Union Recorder*, 13 Apr 1939, 43.

1569. REEVES, JAMES: "Yeats & Reeves," *NSt*, 68:1755 (30 Oct 1964), 651.
   Comments on the exclusion of Laura Riding and himself from the *Oxford Book of Modern Verse*.

1570. ————: *Commitment to Poetry.* NY: Barnes & Noble, 1969. vii, 295 p.
   Reeves does not like Yeats and his poetry and says so: "This perverse, despotic old man flogging his will to make himself a kind of pastiche of a great bardic figure" (pp. 6-7).

1571. ———— (ed): *The Poets and Their Critics: Arnold to Auden.* London: Hutchinson, 1969. 279 p. (Poets and Their Critics. 3.)
   "William Butler Yeats," 108-36; a short introduction and reprints of several snippets from various critics.

1572. RICHARDSON, KENNETH (ed): *Twentieth Century Writing: A Reader's Guide to Contemporary Literature.* London: Newnes, 1969. viii, 751 p.
   David L. Parkes: "Yeats," 668-70.

1573. RIFLER, PERCY STENT: "Men of the Times: VII.—Mr. W. B. Yeats," *Irish Truth*, 6:306 (14 Nov 1903), 3658.
   A satirical sketch.

1574. RIVOALLAN, A.: "William Butler Yeats, 1865-1939," *Langues modernes*, 37:2 (Mar 1939), 188-93.

1575. ROBINSON, NORMAN L.: "Poems of W. B. Yeats," *Central Literary Mag*, 28:5 (Jan 1928), 185-94.

1576. ROBSON, WILLIAM WALLACE: *Modern English Literature.* London: Oxford UP, 1970. xv, 172 p.
   Yeats, pp. 50-59 and *passim* (see index).

1577. ROHDE, PETER PREISLER: *Engelsk litteratur, 1900-1947*. København: Athenaeum, 1948. 351 p.
> Yeats, pp. 26-34, 35-38, 167-70, and *passim* (see index); "Den irske renaessance," 36-40.

1578. ROLAND HOLST, A.: "William Butler Yeats herdacht," *Verslagen en mededelingen van de Koninklijke Vlaamse Academie voor Taal en Letterkunde*, #1-2-3-4 (Jan-Feb-Mar-Apr 1964), 5-6.

1579. ROLLINS, RONALD G.: "Portraits of Four Irishmen as Artists: Verisimilitude and Vision," *Irish UR*, 1:2 (Spring 1971), 189-97.
> Verisimilitude and vision in the works of Synge, O'Casey, Yeats, and Joyce.

1580. ROLT, LIONEL THOMAS CASWELL: *High Horse Riderless*. London: Allen & Unwin, 1947. 172 p.
> An attack against "modernism," quoting with approval Yeats as a poet and thinker who "remained faithful to traditional form" and who "possessed a most profound perception of our social maladies" (pp. 101-4).

1581. ROONEY, PHILIP: "The Sligo of William Butler Yeats: Legendary Men Who Were Ancestors of the Poet," *Irish Press*, 31:189 (10 Aug 1961), 9.
> Continued as "Poet's Experiments in Telepathy," :190 (11 Aug 1961), 8-9; "A Tinkle of Water in Fleet Street—'Innisfree,'" :191 (12 Aug 1961), 9. Includes reminiscences.

1582. ROSATI, SALVATORE: Note on Yeats in Italian, *Nuova antologia*, ser 7 / yr 69 / 295:1491 (1 May 1934), 142-45.

1583. ROSENFELD, PAUL L.: "William Butler Yeats," *Yale Literary Mag*, 74:658 (Jan 1909), 146-53.

1584. ROSENTHAL, M. L.: "On Yeats and the Cultural Symbolism of Modern Poetry," *Yale R*, 49:4 (June 1960), 573-83.
> On the symbolic fusion of "man's day-to-day predicament" with "envisioned transformation" in Yeats's work.

1585. ROSSITER, FRANK: "Yeats—'Great Minor Poet,'" *Irish Press*, 37:201 (25 Aug 1967), 9.
> A depreciation. Correspondence by "Iconoclast," "Philosophy of Yeats," :203 (28 Aug 1967), 9; by "Celtic Codology," "Assessments of Yeats," :256 (28 Oct 1967), 10; and by Hugh Murphy, :278 (22 Nov 1967), 12.

1586. ROUTH, HAROLD VICTOR: *English Literature and Ideas in the Twentieth Century: An Inquiry into Present Difficulties and Future Prospects*. London: Methuen, 1950 [1946]. viii, 204 p.
> "William Butler Yeats," 63-68. Yeats "demonstrated that the most convincing and inexhaustible symbol is oneself." Weak on facts and figures.

1587. ROYAL HIBERNIAN ACADEMY AND METROPOLITAN SCHOOL OF ART, DUBLIN: *Report by Committee of Inquiry into the Work Carried On by the Royal Hibernian Academy and the Metropolitan School of Art* [. . .]. Dublin: HMSO, 1906. xxv, 98 p.
> For details see J83.

1588. [RUSSELL, GEORGE WILLIAM]: "Literature and Civilisation," *Irish Statesman*, 1:11 (24 Nov 1923), 325-26.
> Yeats's share in "creating" an Irish civilization.

1589. A. E. [i.e., RUSSELL, GEORGE WILLIAM]: *The Living Torch*. Edited by
Monk Gibbon with an introductory essay. London: Macmillan, 1937. xii,
382 p.
    A selection from AE's writings, including numerous paragraphs on
    Yeats, other figures of the Irish literary revival, and the Abbey
    Theatre (not analyzed in this bibliography).

1590. RYAN, WILLIAM PATRICK: *Literary London: Its Lights & Comedies*. London: Smithers, 1898. 167 p.
    "The Passing of the Poets," 109-28, contains some notes on Yeats: "If
    Mr. Yeats could go into Parliament, or edit *The Daily Chronicle*, or
    launch a newspaper syndicate, he would be a much larger figure to his
    age. But happily that is impossible."

1591. ———: "Celts in the Workshop," *Bookman*, 15:89 (Feb 1899), 136-37.
    Yeats's treatment of legendary material is "arbitrary and obscure."
    "A good deal of his late work . . . seems merely trite English. . . ."

1592. ———: *The Pope's Green Island*. London: Nisbet, 1912. vi, 325 p.
    "Materialism and Mysticism," 193-203: Yeats's "mysticism" is not
    accepted in Ireland.
    "Ireland at the Play," 299-307; on the Irish dramatic movement. Con-
    tends that the Abbey is much more enjoyable without Yeats's theories
    about it.

1593. S.: "Mr. Yeats and the British Association," *Sinn Féin*, 3:124 (19
Sept 1908), unpaged.
    Criticizes what he sees as Yeats's attempts to monopolize the Abbey
    Theatre. Correspondence by P. S. O hEigeartaigh, :125 (26 Sept 1908),
    1.

1593a. SALE, ROGER: *Modern Heroism: Essays on D. H. Lawrence, William
Empson, & J. R. R. Tolkien*. Berkeley: U of California Press, 1973. xi,
261 p.
    Contains some notes on Yeats, especially pp. 243-44.

1594. *Salmonsens Konversations Leksikon*. København: Schultz, 1915-30. 26 v.
    Yeats, 25:537.

1595. SAMPLEY, ARTHUR M.: "Quiet Voices, Unquiet Times," *Midwest Q*, 4:3
(Apr 1963), 247-56.
    Yeats is one of the 20th-century poets who have "developed a reasoned
    and thoughtful solution for the spiritual problem of modern man."

1596. SAVAGE, DEREK STANLEY: *The Personal Principle: Studies in Modern
Poetry*. Port Washington: Kennikat Press, 1969 [1944]. xiii, 196 p.
    "The Aestheticism of W. B. Yeats," 67-90; reprinted and revised from
    Kenyon R, 7:1 (Winter 1945), 118-34; also in J1090. See commentary
    by John Crowe Ransom, "The Severity of Mr. Savage," *Kenyon R*, 7:1
    (Winter 1945), 114-17.
    Savage claims that Yeats was an "aesthete," i.e., a watered-down
    symbolist, for all his life. Yeats lacked "inner dynamism, the
    religious impulse to grasp hold of life and make it surrender its
    meaning," and there is something "inhuman, or soulless," in his
    poetry.

1597. SCHAUP, SUSANNE: "W. B. Yeats: Image of a Poet in Germany," *Southern
Humanities R*, 2:3 (Summer 1968), 313-23.
    The sad case of an almost nonexistent Yeats reception in Germany (at
    least until recently) and some of the reasons for it. See also J1132.

1598. SCHIRMER, WALTER F.: "William Butler Yeats 70 Jahre," *Berliner Tageblatt*, #278 (14 June 1935), Beiblatt 1, unpaged.

1599. ————: *Geschichte der englischen und amerikanischen Literatur von den Anfängen bis zur Gegenwart.* 5th edition, written in collaboration with Arno Esch. Tübingen: Niemeyer, 1968 [1937]. xvi, 838 p.
"W. B. Yeats und die keltische Renaissance," 677-80; "Das irische Drama," 719-25.

1600. ————: "William Butler Yeats," *Tribüne: Halbmonatsschrift der Bühnen der Stadt Köln*, 25:9 (1955/56), 77-80.

1601. SCHMIELE, WALTER (ed): *Englische Geisteswelt von Bacon bis Eliot.* Darmstadt: Holle, 1953. 366 p.
Note on Yeats, pp. 227-28.

1602. SCHNEDITZ, WOLFGANG: "'. . . als ein Weg des Schicksals, als eine Stimme': Zum Werk des Iren W. B. Yeats und des Walisers Dylan Thomas," *Salzburger Nachrichten*, 4 Apr 1956, 3.

1603. SCHWARTZ, DELMORE: *Selected Essays.* Edited by Donald A. Dike and David H. Zucker. Chicago: U of Chicago Press, 1970. xxiv, 500 p.
"The Poet as Poet," 72-80; reprinted from *Partisan R*, 6:3 (Spring 1939), 52-59.
"An Unwritten Book," 81-101; reprinted from *Southern R*, 7:3 (Winter 1941/42), 471-91; and from J1090. Outline for a book that someone should write in the near future in order to show the real Yeats. The book should discuss the following topics: Yeats in Europe, Yeats in Ireland, Yeats in himself, and Yeats's lyric poems. See also J467 and 1356.

1604. SCOTT-JAMES, ROLFE ARNOLD: *Modernism and Romance.* London: Lane, 1908. xvi, 284 p.
"The Self-Conscious Poet," 189-213; on Yeats, 192-97: His criticism and plays have stifled the lyrical impulse of his poetry.

1605. ————: *The Day before Yesterday.* London: Muller, 1947. viii, 166 p.
"June 1935," 35-38; reprinted from *London Mercury*, 32:188 (June 1935), 105. On Yeats's 70th birthday.
"March 1939: The Farewell to Yeats," 160-65; reprinted from *London Mercury*, 39:233 (Mar 1939), 477-80. Includes some reminiscences.

1606. [————]: "The Defence of Culture," *Britain To-day*, #84 (Apr 1943), 1-4.
Is Yeats an Irish or an English poet?

1607. SELIGO, IRENE: "Ein Dichter des 20. Jahrhunderts: William Butler Yeats, gestorben 28. Januar 1939," *Frankfurter Zeitung*, 83:66 (5 Feb 1939), 1-2.
Comments on *Cathleen ni Houlihan*.

1608. SENA, VINOD: "W. B. Yeats and the Storm-Beaten Threshold," *Dublin Mag*, 8:4&5 (Summer/Autumn 1970), 56-75.
On Yeats and war poetry (and the influence of Arnold in this respect), on Yeats's view on suffering in tragedy, and on his theory of tragedy.

1609. SERGEANT, HOWARD: *Tradition in the Making of Modern Poetry.* Volume 1. London: Britannicus Liber, 1951. v, 122 p.
No other volume published. On Yeats's pre-1899 works, pp. 18-22, and *passim* (see index).

1609a. SEYMOUR-SMITH, MARTIN: *Guide to Modern World Literature*. London: Wolfe, 1973. xxi, 1206 p.

On Yeats, pp. 228-32, 262; mainly on the poetry.

1610. SHAPIRO, KARL: *In Defense of Ignorance*. NY: Random House, 1960. xi, 339 p.

"W. B. Yeats: Trial by Culture," 87-113. Yeats's idea of civilization was quite narrow.

1611. ————: *To Abolish Children and Other Essays*. Chicago: Quadrangle Books, 1968. 288 p.

"A *Malebolge* of Fourteen Hundred Books," 169-288: "Y/Yeats," 264-68; reprinted from *Carleton Miscellany*, 5:3 (Summer 1964), 110-14. "Yeats (unfortunately, from my philosophy) probably gave European poetry another millenium [sic] of life. In Yeats is summed up all the phoniness of the art of poetry and its practitioners and its adherents, its power and its meaninglessness."

1612. SIDGWICK, F.: "William Butler Yeats," *English Illustrated Mag*, 29:3 (June 1903), 286-88.

See also *Gael*, 22:8 (Aug 1903), 266-67.

1613. SINGH, GHAN SHYAM: "Il centenario di W. B. Yeats: Il poeta contro il tempo," *Mondo*, 17:52 (28 Dec 1965), 9.

1614. SKARTVEIT, ANDREAS (ed): *Fra skald til modernist: Dikterens rolle gjennom tidene*. Oslo: Dreyer, 1967. 116 p. (Perspektivbøkene. 26.)

Kristian Smidt: "Dikterens jeg eller verket for seg? Noen engelske modernister i speilet," 97-110; on Yeats, *passim*. Reprinted in Smidt, *Konstfuglen og nattergalen: Essays om diktning og kritikk*. Oslo: Gyldendal, 1972. 206 p. (pp. 75-85).

1615. SKOUMAL, ALOYS: "Wiliam [sic] Butler Yeats," *Kulturně politický kalendář*, 1965, 383.

1616. SMITH, A. J. M.: "A Poet Young and Old—W. B. Yeats," *UTQ*, 8:3 (Apr 1939), 255-63.

1617. SOMERVILLE, EDITH OENONE, and MARTIN ROSS: *Wheeltracks*. London: Longmans, 1923. x, 284 p.

For Martin Ross's estimate of Yeats see the letters on pp. 229-34 (Mr. X being Mr. Y). Includes comments on *Diarmuid and Grania* and *The King's Threshold*.

1618. SOMLYÓ, GYÖRGY: *Szélrózsa 2: Huszadik század*. Budapest: Magvető könyvkiadó, 1965. 588 p.

Note on Yeats, p. 515; translations of six Yeats poems, pp. 51-54.

1619. SPALDING, PHILIP ANTHONY: *In the Margin: Being Extracts from a Bookman's Notebook*. [London: Adam Books, 1959]. 84 p.

Reprinted from *Adam*, 25:262 (1957), 7-84. Yeats, *passim* (see index), especially pp. 39-42 (epigrams in praise of Yeats).

1620. SPEAIGHT, ROBERT: "Salute to Yeats," *Colosseum*, 5:21 (Apr-June 1939), 131-38.

An appreciation of Yeats's aristocratic mind.

1621. SPEARS, MONROE K.: *Dionysus and the City: Modernism in Twentieth-Century Poetry*. NY: Oxford UP, 1970. x, 278 p.

Yeats, *passim* (see index); partly on his poetry as an instance of modernism, more on his modern critics.

1622. SPENDER, STEPHEN: "The 'Egotistical Sublime' in W. B. Yeats," *Listener*, 21:527 (16 Feb 1939), 377-78.

1623. ————: "Movements and Influences in English Literature, 1927-1953," *BA*, 27:1 (Winter 1953), 5-32.
    Yeats, *passim*; Spender regards him as E. M. Forster's opposite in his preference for "things" and his contempt for "people."

1624. ————: *The Creative Element: A Study of Vision, Despair, and Orthodoxy among Some Modern Writers*. London: Hamilton, 1953. 199 p.
    Compares Arnold's "Dover Beach" and "The Second Coming," 33-34; discusses Yeats's and Rimbaud's use of "magic," 49-55; and deals with Yeats in "Hammered Gold and Gold Enamelling of Humanity," 108-24: "Where Yeats does convince us . . . is in his acceptance of the necessity of sacrifice in order that man may create the monuments of his own greatness." His insistence on the supernatural is less convincing. Compares Yeats and D. H. Lawrence.

1625. ————, W. D. SNODGRASS, THOMAS KINSELLA, and PATRICK KAVANAGH: "Poetry since Yeats: An Exchange of Views," *Tri-Q*, #4 [Fall 1965], 100-106, 108-11.
    After the rather academic efforts of the first three speakers, Kavanagh wrecked the discussion with some delightfully irreverent and irrelevant outbursts. The whole battle seems to have ended in chaos.

1626. SPENDER, STEPHEN: "Form and Pressure in Poetry," *TLS*, 69:3582 (23 Oct 1970), 1226-28.
    The effect of the "pressure of the modern time" on poetic form in Pound, Yeats, and others. Yeats is a poet of the "continuous tradition" who revised his subject matter almost organically like a plant "gradually adapting to meet new conditions," but who retained the formal standards of his early romanticism.

1627. SPICER-SIMSON, THEODORE: *Men of Letters of the British Isles: Portrait Medallions from the Life*. With critical essays by Stuart P. Sherman and a preface by G. F. Hill. NY: Rudge, 1924. 134 p.
    "W. B. Yeats," 131-33; medallion facing p. 131.

1628. SPINNER, KASPAR: "William Butler Yeats: Zum hundertsten Geburtstag (13. Juni)," *Neue Zürcher Zeitung*, 186:159 (12 June 1965), 20r-v.

1629. SQUIRE, J. C.: "The Nobel Prize Winner: Mr. W. B. Yeats," *Observer*, 132:6912 (18 Nov 1923), 4.

1630. STANFORD, DEREK (ed): *Poets of the 'Nineties: A Biographical Anthology*. London: Baker, 1965. 225 p.
    The introduction (pp. 17-45) quotes from Yeats, *passim*; "W. B. Yeats, 1865-1939," 168-76, comments on Yeats's early poetry, neglecting almost entirely its "Irish" elements.

1631. STARKIE, WALTER: "William Butler Yeats: Premio Nobel 1924 [*sic*]," *Nuova antologia*, ser 6 / yr 59 / 312:1249 (1 Apr 1924), 238-45.

1632. STEAD, CHRISTIAN KARLSON: *The New Poetic: Yeats to Eliot*. Harmondsworth: Penguin Books, 1967 [1964]. 201 p. (Pelican Book. A902.)
    "W. B. Yeats, 1865-1916," 17-45, and *passim* (see index). Investigates the triangle between the poet, the audience, and "that area of experience which we call variously 'Reality,' 'Truth,' or 'Nature'" (p. 11). Too much distance from the audience results in estheticism, too little in rhetoric. The perfect poem is one that exists "in an

equilateral triangle, each point pulling equally in a moment of perfect tension" (p. 12). Discusses "The Fisherman" and "Easter 1916"
as examples from Yeats's poetry.

1633. STEIN, ERNST: "Kulissen liebte ich und Spielerscharen: Der Dichter
William Butler Yeats, den Deutschland noch kaum zur Kenntnis genommen
hat," *Zeit*, 18:47 (22 Nov 1963), I.

1634. STEPHENS, JAMES: *James, Seumas & Jacques: Unpublished Writings*.
Chosen and edited with an introduction by Lloyd Frankenberg. London:
Macmillan, 1964. xxxii, 288 p.
    Mostly B.B.C. broadcasts. See particularly:
    1. Lloyd Frankenberg: "For Seumas," ix-xxx.
    2. "Reminiscences of J. M. Synge,: 54-60 (broadcast 15 Mar 1928); cf.
Radio Times, 18:234 (23 Mar 1928), 590, 611.
    3. "Some Irish Books I Like," 61-66 (16 June 1937), with notes on
Yeats's poetry.
    4. "W. B. Yeats," 67-72 (5 Jan 1942); excerpt in "Yeats and the Tele-
phone," *Listener*, 27:680 (22 Jan 1942), 106. Reminiscences.
    5. "Yeats as Dramatist," 73-76 (9 May 1943); reprint of "He Died
Younger Than He Was Born," *Listener*, 29:753 (17 June 1943), 728.
    6. "'Byzantium,'" 77-86 (28 Dec 1944 as "The Making of a Poem").
    7. "Yeats and Music," 87-88 (3 Oct 1947, excerpt).
    8. "Around and About Yeats," 89-95 (2 Jan 1948).
    9. "Yeats the Poet," 96-100 (9 Jan 1948). See Vernon Watkins, "The
Poetry of W. B. Yeats," *Listener*, 39:991 (22 Jan 1948), 143.
    10. "A. E.," 110-22 (27 Mar 1942 and 13 Jan 1948); reprinted from
Listener, 27:691 (9 Apr 1942), 467-68, and 39:991 (22 Jan 1948),
144-45. Includes reminiscences of Yeats.
    11. "Poets on Poetry," 168-75 (18 June 1946).
    12. A list of Stephens's broadcasts, 285-88.

1635. ————: "W. B. Yeats: A Tribute," *Observer*, 157:8208 (19 Sept 1948),
4.

1636. STEWART, JOHN INNES MACKINTOSH: *Eight Modern Writers*. Oxford:
Clarendon Press, 1963. ix, 704 p. (Oxford History of English Literature.
12.)
    "VII. Yeats," 294-421, 671-79. See the review by John Simon, "Unlucky
J. I. M.," *Partisan R*, 31:4 (Fall 1964), 632-37, 639 (quarrels with
Stewart's Yeats interpretations).

1637. °STOJANOVIĆ ZOROVAVELJ, VLADAN: "Tri barda," *Novosti*, 3:885 (5 Dec
1923), 885.

1638. STRONG, LEONARD ALFRED GEORGE: *Personal Remarks*. London: Nevill,
1953. 264 p.
    "William Butler Yeats," 13-33; revised from "W. B. Yeats: An Appreci-
ation," *Cornhill Mag*, 156:931 (July 1937), 14-29. Chapters on Synge
(pp. 34-62; reprint of *John Millington Synge*. London: Allen & Unwin,
1941, 44 p. [P.E.N. Books.]), Padraic Colum (79-85), and Seumas
O'Sullivan (86-91).

1639. ————: "W. B. Yeats," *Spectator*, 161:5760 (18 Nov 1938), 856-57.
Reprinted as "W. B. Yeats—Ireland's Grand Old Man," *Living Age*,
355:4468 (Jan 1939), 438-40.

1640. STUART, T. P.: "Mr. Yeats and the Irish Heart," *Leader*, 1:22 (26
Jan 1901), 352.

See the comments by the editor [D. P. Moran], *ibid.*; Stuart's rejoinder, :24 (9 Feb 1901), 387-88, and editor's comments, *ibid.* A discussion about whether Yeats is or is not an Irish poet.

1641. STURGEON, MARY C.: *Studies of Contemporary Poets*. Revised and enlarged. London: Harrap, 1920 [1916]. 440 p.
"An Irish Group," 137-80: Susan L. Mitchell, James H. Cousins, Joseph Campbell, and others.
"William Butler Yeats," 419-32.

1642. SÜHNEL, RUDOLF, and DIETER RIESNER (eds): *Englische Dichter der Moderne: Ihr Leben und Werk*. Berlin: Schmidt, 1971. viii, 598 p.
Werner Habicht: "John Millington Synge," 180-92; Johannes Kleinstück: "William Butler Yeats," 193-204; Thomas Metscher: "Sean O'Casey," 439-55.

1643. SULLIVAN, BARRY: "Der Turm von Ballylee: Über den irischen Dichter W. B. Yeats," *Englische Rundschau*, 8:13 (20 June 1958), 200.

1644. SURKOV, ALEKSEĬ ALEKSANDROVICH (ed): *Kratkaía literaturnaía entsiklopediía*. Moskva: Sovelskaía entsiklopediía, 1962—.
E. ÍA. Dombrovskaía: "Ĭits, Ĭets, Eĭts," 3:266-68.

1645. SUŠKO, MARIO: Note on Yeats, *Republika*, 22:5 (May 1966), 209.

1646. *Svensk Uppslagbok*. Malmö: Norden, 1954-63. 32 v.
[Harold] E[lovson]: "Yeats," 32:142-44.

1647. SWINNERTON, FRANK: *The Georgian Scene: A Literary Panorama*. NY: Farrar & Rinehart, 1934. x, 522 p.
"William Butler Yeats," 260-63. Also in *The Georgian Literary Scene: A Panorama*. London: Hutchinson, 1938 [1935]. xii, 532 p., pp. 271-73.

1648. SYMONS, ARTHUR: *Studies in Prose and Verse*. London: Dent, 1922 [1904]. ix, 292 p.
"Mr. W. B. Yeats," 230-41; reprint of "Mr. Yeats as a Lyric Poet," *Saturday R*, 87:2271 (6 May 1899), 553-54. A review of *Poems*, 1899 (W17), and *The Wind among the Reeds* (W27), including a general discussion of Yeats's poetry and plays.

1649. [TAGORE, RABINDRANATH]: "A Hindu on the Celtic Spirit," *American R of Reviews*, 49:1 (Jan 1914), 101-2.
Translated excerpts from an article on Yeats published in °*Prabashi*.

1650. °————: *Rabindra-Racanābali* [Rabindranath's works]. Calcutta: Visva-Bharati, 1964-66. 29 v.
"Kabi Ietsh" [Poet Yeats], 26:521-28.

1651. TALLQVIST, C. E.: "William Butler Yeats: En studie," *Finsk tidskrift*, 102:2 (1927), 119-41; :4 (1927), 281-307.

1652. TAYLOR, JOSEPH R.: "William Butler Yeats and the Revival of Gaelic Literature," *Methodist R*, 87:2 (Mar-Apr 1905), 189-202.
Yeats is quite outside the current revival of Gaelic language and literature. Although he is a good poet, he becomes increasingly obscure and thus less typically Irish.

1653. TEODORESCU, ANDA: "W. B. Yeats," *Contemporanul*, #999 (3 Dec 1965), 2.

1654. THAKUR, DAMODAR: *The Constant Pursuit: Studies in the Use of Myth and Language in Literature*. Patna: Novelty, 1964. ix, 206 p.

"The Personality of W. B. Yeats: Heritage and Achievement," 193-201. In Yeats, "the separation between the man who suffers and the mind that creates seems not to have occurred." A rather sketchy essay.

1655. THOMAS, EDWARD: *Letters from Edward Thomas to Gordon Bottomley.* Edited and introduced by R. George Thomas. London: Oxford UP, 1968. vi, 302 p.
Yeats is mentioned *passim* (see index).

1656. THOMPSON, FRANCIS: *The Letters.* Edited by John Evangelist Walsh. NY: Hawthorn Books, 1969. 272 p.
A few references to Yeats, *passim* (see index).

1657. THORNTON, ROBERT KELSEY ROUGHT: "The Poets of the Rhymers' Club," M.A. thesis, U of Manchester, 1961. iii, 269 p.
"William Butler Yeats," 230-57.

1658. THURLEY, GEOFFREY: "A Footnote on Yeats," *Icarus*, #47 (Dec 1965), 20-23.
A somewhat confused essay on the question "What does Yeats get to know . . . about the world in general?"

1659. TINDALL, WILLIAM YORK: *Forces in Modern British Literature, 1885-1956.* NY: Vintage Books, 1956 [1947]. xi, 316, xxi p. (Vintage Books. V35.)
Incorporates "The Symbolism of W. B. Yeats," *Accent*, 5:4 (Summer 1945), 203-12; also in J1090. On the Irish literary revival, pp. 63-82; on Yeats's symbolism, 265-74; and *passim* (see index).

1660. T[ITUS], E[WARD] W.: "Criticism à l'irlandaise," *This Quarter*, 3:4 (Apr-May-June 1931), 570-84.
Contains some notes on Yeats, especially in the section "Patriotism and Inspiration," 571-72.

1661. TOMLIN, E. W. F.: "The Continuity of Yeats," *Phoenix*, #10 (Summer 1965), 60-65.
Also in J1161 (#2). The difference between the early and the later Yeats is not as great as is usually thought.

1662. T[YNAN], K[ATHARINE]: "William Butler Yeats," *Magazine of Poetry*, 1:4 (Oct 1889), 454.

1663. TYNAN, KATHARINE: "W. B. Yeats," *Bookman*, 5:25 (Oct 1893), 13-14.
Summarized in *Bookman* [NY], 2:4 (Dec 1895), 258-60. "He is full of literary activity and plans, many of which are sure to be fulfilled, for with all his dreamy temperament he has a gift of energy and perseverance. There is not one of the younger men to whose career one looks with keener hope and faith."

1664. ——— (ed): *The Wild Harp: A Selection from Irish Poetry.* London: Sidgwick & Jackson, 1913. xxvi, 160 p.
"Introductory," ix-xv, praises Yeats for his immeasurable service to Irish literature, but criticizes him for having given up poetry in favor of drama.

1665. UNGVÁRI, TAMÁS: *Az eltűnt személyiség nyomában: Tanulmányok* [On the search for the lost personality: Essay]. Budapest: Szépirodalmi Könyvkiadó, 1966. 450 p.
"William Butler Yeats: Az ezoterikus forradalmár" [The esoteric revolutionary], 340-66.
"John Millington Synge: A népi komédiak költője" [The popular poet of comedy], 367-77.

1666. UNTERECKER, JOHN: "W. B. Yeats: On His Centennial," *NYTBR*, [70:] (13 June 1965), 7, 34-36.

1667. UNTERMEYER, LOUIS: *Makers of the Modern World: The Lives of Ninety-two Writers, Artists, Scientists, Statesmen, Inventors, Philosophers, Composers, and Other Creators Who Formed the Pattern of Our Century*. NY: Simon & Schuster, 1955. xx, 809 p.
"William Butler Yeats," 336-44.

1668. ————: *Lives of the Poets: The Story of One Thousand Years of English and American Poetry*. NY: Simon & Schuster, 1959. x, 758 p.
"William Butler Yeats," 615-22; a somewhat simplistic account of Yeats's development.

1669.————: *The Paths of Poetry: Twenty-five Poets and Their Poems*. NY: Delacorte Press, 1966. 251 p.
"Land of Heart's Desire," 218-22. For juvenile readers.

1670. URE, PETER: "The Integrity of Yeats," *Cambridge J*, 3:2 (Nov 1949), 80-93.
Defends Yeats against the charge that the later thought and work is different from the earlier and that his work lacks an awareness of ethical problems.

1671. USSHER, ARLAND: *Three Great Irishmen: Shaw, Yeats, Joyce*. London: Gollancz, 1952. 160 p.
Incorporates "The Magi," *Dublin Mag*, 20:2 (Apr-June 1945), 18-21.
On Yeats see "W. B. Yeats: Man into Bird," 63-113, and *passim*. Discusses Yeats as a thinker, his occult interests, his isolation, and his antidemocratic bias.
Reviews:
1. Anon., "Four Provocative Irishmen," *Times*, #52383 (6 Aug 1952), 6.
2. Anon., "Natives of Ireland," *TLS*, 51:2639 (29 Aug 1952), 560.
3. Thomas Bodkin, "Magi from the West," *Birmingham Post*, #29326 (12 Aug 1952), 3. This review contains what is perhaps the most malignant statement ever made about Yeats: "Yeats almost deserved the dishonouring tribute of condolence which Hitler's foreign office offered to his family on his death."
4. Padraic Colum, "A Gaelic Trill," *SatR*, 36:36 (5 Sept 1953), 11-12, 29.
5. Gerard Fay, "Three Irishmen," *Manchester Guardian*, #33024 (26 Aug 1952), 4. "Done in the manner of the Synge Street shopkeeper."
6. John Gassner, *TAM*, 38:8 (Aug 1954), 12.
7. Alfred Kazin, "The Talker," *New Yorker*, 29:51 (6 Feb 1954), 102, 105-6, 108.
8. Walter Kerr, "The Giants of the Irish Revival," *Commonweal*, 58:[] (7 Aug 1953), 446-47.
9. A. J. L[eventhal], *Dublin Mag*, 28:1 (Jan-Mar 1953), 72.
10. H. Marshall McLuhan, "Through Emerald Eyes," *Renascence*, 6:2 (Spring 1954), 157-58.
11. Raymond Mortimer, "Three Islanders," *Sunday Times*, #6747 (10 Aug 1952), 3.
12. Horace Reynolds, "A Triad of Literary Greatness," *NYTBR*, [58:] (26 July 1953), 3.
13. W. R. Rodgers, "The Flesh behind the Skeleton," *NSt*, 44:1125 (27 Sept 1952), 353.
14. Philip Toynbee, "An Irish Critic," *Observer*, #8409 (3 Aug 1952), 7.

1672. VALLARDI: *Grande enciclopedia Vallardi*. Milano: Vallardi, 1967-70. 16 v.
Yeats, 15:955-56.

1673. VENGEROVA, ZIN[AIDA ATHANAS'EVNA]: "Molodaia Angliia (Literaturnaia khronika)" [Young England: A literary chronicle], *Cosmopolis*, #15 (Mar 1897), 186-203.
On "Vill'iam Jets," 198-200.

1674. VIOLA, WILHELM: "Der Dichter des *Einhorns von den Sternen*," *Tribüne: Halbmonatsschrift der Bühnen der Stadt Köln*, 25:10 (1955/56), 98-99.

1675. WAIN, JOHN: "The Meaning of Yeats," *Observer*, #9076 (13 June 1965), 26.
He spoke for his age and the age spoke through him.

1676. WAKEFIELD, DAN: "Sailing to Byzantium: Yeats and the Young Mind," *Nation*, 182:25 (23 June 1956), 531-32.
"That cold, metallic world of abstraction described by William Butler Yeats in his poems 'Byzantium' and 'Sailing to Byzantium' seems to hold the climate most desired by the recently-graduated English majors."

1677. W[ALSH], E[RNEST]: "Senator William Butler Yeats and Miss Harriet Monroe," *This Quarter*, 1:2 [Autumn-Winter. 1926], 335-42.
A formidable and somewhat silly attack on Yeats and Miss Monroe. Has this to say about "No Second Troy," a poem that he dislikes particularly: ". . . lines of baldness . . . that no hair tonic on earth or in Mr. Yeats' heavens could grow even a charge of dandruff to dust over the smooth perfectly polished nothing of the crown."

1678. WALSH, THOMAS: "The Collected Yeats," *Commonweal*, 1:2 (19 Nov 1924), 39.
"We owe him many thanks, but little veneration."

1679. WALSH, WILLIAM: *A Human Idiom: Literature and Humanity*. London: Chatto & Windus, 1964. 212 p.
"Conclusion: To the Desert or the Cloister," 195-207. Yeats solved the problem of the relationship between the writer and his time by opting for the cloister.

1680. WARD, ALFRED CHARLES: *English Literature: Chaucer to Bernard Shaw*. London: Longmans, Green, 1958 [1953]. xxi, 781 p.
Yeats, pp. 725-28 and *passim* (see index).

1681. WARNER, OLIVER: *English Literature: A Portrait Gallery*. London: Chatto & Windus, 1964. xvii, 205 p.
Yeats, pp. 180-81.

1682. WATTS, HAROLD H.: "W. B. Yeats: Poetry and 'Solutions,'" *Poetry New York*, #1 (1949), 15-21.
As a poet, Yeats had the right answers to his problems; as a public man, however, he was a failure because he had no solutions for the political and social problems of his time. But the lack of solutions is a source of strength in his poetry.

1683. WEBB, W. L.: "Ireland's Tongue," *Guardian*, #36991 (12 June 1965), 7.

1684. WEBER, BROM (ed): *Sense and Sensibility in Twentieth-Century Writing: A Gathering in Memory of William Van O'Connor*. Carbondale: Southern Illinois UP, 1970. xvii, 174 p.
Earl Miner: "The Double Truth in Modern Poetic Criticism," 16-25; mentions Yeats *passim*.

1684a. WEBER, RICHARD: "About Him . . . and About . . . ," *Dublin Mag*, 10:
1 (Winter/Spring 1973), 21–28.
 Obiter dicta. Weber's attitude is best summed up in his poem "Envoy,"
 published in the same issue (p. 69):
>   Despite the Nineties, the art of art,
>   The arrogance, the magic and the looking back,
>   The Moon, the Saint, the Fool and Hunchback;
>   Despite the lot, how he hits the heart!

1685. WELLEK, RENÉ: "William Butler Yeats," *Literární noviny*, 7:17 (19
July 1935), 5.

1686. ———, and AUSTIN WARREN: *Theory of Literature*. NY: Harcourt, Brace,
[1959] [1949]. xii, 368 p. (Harvest Book. HB22.)
 Yeats, *passim* (see index).

1687. WELTMANN, LUTZ: "William Butler Yeats: Der mathematische Symbolist,"
Europa, 16:6 (June 1965), 62–63.

1688. WEST, PAUL: *The Wine of Absurdity: Essays on Literature and Consolation*. University Park: Pennsylvania State UP, 1966. xiv, 249 p.
 "W. B. Yeats," 5–18 [i.e., 3–18]. On the shaping of Yeats's thoughts
 in the nineties, particularly under the influence of Pater.

1689. WEYGANDT, CORNELIUS: *The Time of Yeats: English Poetry of To-day
against an American Background*. NY: Russell & Russell, 1969 [1937]. xiii,
460 p.
 "William Butler Yeats and the Irish Literary Renaissance," 167–251.
 Is mostly out of sympathy with Yeats's later work and regards his
 "spiritistic" leanings as pernicious to his poetry. Also on AE, Lionel
 Johnson, Katharine Tynan, Nora Hopper Chesson, Dora Sigerson Shorter,
 Stephens, Dunsany, Ledwidge, Gogarty, Clarke, Higgins, and others.
 Generally, the book's title is misleading; there are only sporadic
 attempts to link the English or Irish poets to the "American back-
 ground."

1690. WHITE, TERENCE DE VERE: *The Anglo-Irish*. London: Gollancz, 1972.
293 p.
 "Yeats as an Anglo-Irishman," 39–51, and *passim* (see index). Also on
 AE, Gogarty, Lady Gregory, Hyde, Martyn, Moore, and other figures of
 the revival. An informal sketch rather than a scholarly investigation;
 contains numerous small inaccuracies.

1691. WHITRIDGE, ARNOLD: "William Butler Yeats, 1865-1939," *Dalhousie R*,
19:1 (Apr 1939), 1–8.

1691a. WHITTEMORE, REED: *From Zero to the Absolute*. NY: Crown, 1967. xii,
210 p.
 See pp. 91-96: Yeats was "one of the great manipulators."

1692. WILEY, PAUL L., and HAROLD OREL (eds): *British Poetry, 1880-1920:
Edwardian Voices*. NY: Appleton-Century-Crofts, 1969. xliii, 681 p.
 "William Butler Yeats," 273-77; on the early works.

1693. WILPERT, GERO VON (ed): *Lexikon der Weltliteratur*. Stuttgart: Kröner,
1963-68. 2 v.
 Yeats, biographical entry, 1:1451-52; summaries and evaluations of
 some of his works by Johannes Kleinstück, 2:*passim* (see index).

1694. WILSON, COLIN: *The Strength to Dream: Literature and the Imagination*.
London: Gollancz, 1962. 224 p.

"W. B. Yeats," 29-35, and *passim* (see index). Yeats sees the world and art "in terms of a self-destructive pessimism." Like H. P. Lovecraft, Wilde, and Strindberg, he wages an escapist "assault on rationality."

1695. WILSON, EDMUND: "W. B. Yeats," *New Republic*, 42:541 (15 Apr 1925), Spring Book Section, 8-10.

1696. *————: *Axel's Castle: A Study in the Imaginative Literature of 1870-1930.* NY: Scribner's, 1963 [1931]. ix, 319 p.
"W. B. Yeats," 26-64; based on "William Butler Yeats," *New Republic*, 60:773 (25 Sept 1929), 141-48, and on "Yeats's Guide to the Soul," *New Republic*, 57:737 (16 Jan 1929), 249-51 (a review of *A Vision*, W149). Reprinted in J1090. The classical text for the discussion of Yeats as a symbolist; besides, one of the first intelligent attempts to come to terms with Yeats's unorthodoxies.

1697. WIMSATT, WILLIAM KURTZ: *Hateful Contraries: Studies in Literature and Criticism* [. . .]. [Lexington]: U of Kentucky Press, 1965. xix, 260 p.
A few scattered notes on Yeats, *passim* (see index).

1698. WINKLER PRINS: *Algemeene encyclopaedie.* 5th edition. Amsterdam: Elsevier, 1932-38. 16 v.
Willem van Doorn: "Yeats," 16:568.

1699. WINTERS, ARTHUR YVOR: "A Study of the Post-Romantic Reaction in Lyrical Verse and Incidentally in Certain Other Forms," Ph.D. thesis, Stanford U, 1933. vii, 401 p.
Yeats, *passim* (see index). Winters's dislike of Yeats was very pronounced even at this early stage. He accuses him of confusion and quotes as an example the last lines of "The Gift of Harun Al-Rashid." He has some praise for *The Only Jealousy of Emer*, but he is unwilling to specify the quality of the play. Since these are the only Yeats texts discussed at any length, the basis for the judgment that T. Sturge Moore is a far greater poet than Yeats is ridiculously small.

1699a. WOODWARD, A. G.: "The Artist and the Modern World," *ESA*, 16:1 (Mar 1973), 9-14.
Yeats combined estheticism and immediate experience.

1700. YEATS, W. B.: "A Postscript to a Forthcoming Book of Essays by Various Writers," *All Ireland R*, 1:48 (1 Dec 1900), 6.
See Wp. 359, W300, and J5918. Yeats's "Postscript" is followed by the comments of the editor [Standish O'Grady], who criticizes Yeats for having written his book for a London rather than a Dublin audience. Correspondence by Lady Gregory, :50 (15 Dec 1900), 5.

1701. ————: "The Irish National Theatre and Three Sorts of Ignorance," *United Irishman*, 10:243 (24 Oct 1903), 2.
See Wp. 367. Yeats's article is followed by the comments of the editor [Arthur Griffith ?].

1702. ————: Letter to the editor about the sources of Synge's *In the Shadow of the Glen, United Irishman*, 13:310 (4 Feb 1905), 1.
Wp. 368. Followed by a deprecatory reply of the editor [Arthur Griffith ?]. Correspondence by Yeats, Synge, and editor's comments, :311 (11 Feb 1905), 1. See also :309 (28 Jan 1905), 1.

1703. Z., O.: "From a Modern Irish Portrait Gallery: V.—W. B. Yeats," *New Ireland R*, 2:10 (Dec 1894), 647-59.

I suspect that the author, who seems to have some inside knowledge, is W. P. Ryan. Comments on the Yeats—Charles Gavan Duffy quarrel.

1704. Z[ABEL], M. D.: "Yeats at Thirty and Seventy," *Poetry*, 47:5 (Feb 1936), 268-77.

1705. ZADURA, BOHDAN: "W. B. Yeats: Dramat przezwyciężony" [The drama of overcoming], *Kultura*, 7:5 (2 Feb 1969), 3.

See also J385, 509, 596, 674a, 696, 697, 700, 719, 864, 915, 921, 959, 960, 3416, 4199, 4205, 4216, 4223, 4228, 4244, 4246, 4250, 4252, 4256, 4427-37, 4448-56, 5094-114, 5115-55 and note, 5555-64 and note, 5751, 5907, 5910, 5911, 5913, 5915, 5917-20, 5924, 5925, 5927, 5931, 5932, 5935, 5936, 5942, 5943, 5947, 5947a, 5948, 5951, 5952, 5963, 5971, 5973, 5974, 5982, 5982a, 5986, 5988, 5991, 5992, 6004, 6005, 6010, 6014, 6019, 6020, 6024, 6026, 6030a, 6035, 6038, 6041, 6052, 6054, 6057-59, 6063, 6073, 6080, 6081, 6085, 6088, 6094, 6097, 6099, 6101, 6103, 6106, 6108, 6115a, 6116, 6122, 6131, 6136, 6150, 6151, 6154, 6157, 6158, 6160, 6163, 6166, 6171, 6180, 6182, 6183, 6185, 6186, 6192, 6197, 6198, 6202, 6204-6, 6209, 6213-17, 6228, 6278, 6282, 6291, 6304, 6322, 6323, 6351, 6433, 6497, 6519, 6523a, 6577, 6599, 6632, 6646, 6667, 6672, 6683, 6705, 6724, 6729, 6742, 6744, 6754, 6766, 6780, 6804, 6814, 6820, 6821, 6871a, 6918, 6932, 6978, 6993a, 7059, 7071, 7178, 7227, 7233, 7239, 7272, 7276, 7311, 7362a, 7385, 7401, 7428, 7447-59.

CC Themes and Types

Because of frequent overlapping, no cross-references have been made *to* this section or to the corresponding sections DC and EC. The reader interested in certain aspects of Yeats's work is therefore advised to check the index of selected subjects, where references to more material will be found.

Anima Mundi

1706. CALLAN, EDWARD: "W. B. Yeats on the Coming of Age: From 'Homo Sapiens' to 'L'homme clairvoyant,'" *Dublin Mag*, 9:3 (Summer 1972), 34-46.
    Particularly on "Under Ben Bulben."

Aristocracy and the Aristocratic

1707. GILL, RICHARD: *Happy Rural Seat: The English Country House and the Literary Imagination*. New Haven: Yale UP, 1972. xix, 305 p.
    The "big house" in Yeats's works, pp. 168-75, and *passim* (see index).

1708. HARRIS, DANIEL ARTHUR: *Yeats: Coole Park & Ballylee*. Baltimore: Johns Hopkins UP, 1974. x, 262 p.
    Based on "The Spreading Laurel Tree: Yeats and the Aristocratic Tradition," °Ph.D. thesis, Yale U, 1968. 421 p. (*DA*, 30:5 [Nov 1969], 1982A). Essentially on the poetry that Yeats wrote about Lady Gregory's estate and his own tower. Discusses the indebtedness to Irish tradition and the influence of Castiglione and Ben Jonson.

1709. KNIGHTS, LIONEL CHARLES: *Explorations: Essays in Criticism Mainly on the Literature of the Seventeenth Century*. London: Chatto & Windus, 1951 [1946]. xii, 199 p.
    "Poetry and Social Criticism: The Work of W. B. Yeats," 170-85; first published as "W. B. Yeats: The Assertion of Values," *Southern R*, 7:3

(Winter 1941/42), 426-41. On the aristocratic concept and the idea of life in Yeats's poetry and thought.

1710. °MULKERN, JANE I.: "Yeats's Aristocratic Ideal," M.A. thesis, U of Hawaii, 1966.

1711. REID, BENJAMIN LAURENCE: *Tragic Occasions: Essays on Several Forms.* Port Washington, N.Y.: Kennikat Press, 1971. ix, 188 p.
"The House of Yeats," 163-88; reprinted from *Hudson R*, 18:3 (Autumn 1965), 331-50. Discusses "the meaning of nobility in the life and work of Yeats."

1712. °ROGERS, DOROTHY S.: "Yeats and Aristocracy," M.A. thesis, Columbia U, 1951. 67 p.

1713. STEIN, ARNOLD: "Yeats: A Study in Recklessness," *Sewanee R*, 57:4 (Oct-Dec 1949), 603-26.
"Sprezzatura" in Yeats's works and their indebtedness to Castiglione. Especially on "The Magi," "Leda and the Swan," "Nineteen Hundred and Nineteen," and "Easter 1916."

1714. °VINCENT, LYNNE ANN: "William Butler Yeats's Concept of Aristocracy," M.A. thesis, U of Colorado, 1964. 79 p.

Art(s) and Artists

1715. °FELDMAN, IRVING: "Yeats and the Artistic Vocation," M.A. thesis, Columbia U, 1953. 107 p.

1716. HENN, T. R.: "Yeats and the Picture Galleries," *Southern R*, 1:1 (Jan 1965), 57-75.
Painters and paintings in Yeats's poetry and plays.

Character

1716a. FOX, STEVEN JAMES: "Art and Personality: Browning, Rossetti, Pater, Wilde, and Yeats," °Ph.D. thesis, Yale U, 1972. 314 p. (*DA*, 33:2 [Aug 1972], 751A.)
Discusses Yeats's concept of character and personality.

Cuchulain

1717. °FOYE, THOMAS JAMES: "The Red Branch: A Study of the Cuchulain Legends in the Poems and Plays of W. B. Yeats," M.A. thesis, Columbia U, 1947.

1718. SAHA, PROSANTA KUMAR: "The Dialectics of the Cuchulain Theme in Yeats' Works," *Thought* [Delhi], 15:23 (8 June 1963), 12-14; :24 (15 June 1963), 12-14.

1719. ————: "Yeats's Cuchulain Works: Computer-Aided Analysis of Theme, Style, and Concordances," Ph.D. thesis, Western Reserve U, 1966. ix, 917 p. (*DA*, 28:2 [Aug 1967], 693A-94A.)

Daimon

1720. TAYLOR, RICHARD DEAN: "The Doctrine of the Daimon in the Works of AE (George W. Russell) and W. B. Yeats," M.A. thesis, U of Manchester, 1963. 175 p.

Dance and Dancer

1721. °PARKES, DOROTHY J.: "A Study of the Imagery of Dance and the Dancer in the Works of W. B. Yeats," M.A. thesis, Columbia U, 1959. 93 p.

Dream(s) and Dreamer

1722. HOWARD, M. F.: "A Poet of Dreamland: W. B. Yeats," *Quest* [London], 4:3 (Apr 1913), 484–93.
    The importance of dreams, originating in the great memory, in Yeats's works, particularly *The Shadowy Waters*.

1723. Entry canceled.

Estheticism

1724. O'CONNOR, WILLIAM VAN: "The Poet as Esthetician," *Quarterly R of Literature*, 4:3 (1948), 311–18.

Fairies

1725. CHESTERTON, GILBERT KEITH: *All Things Considered*. Henley-on-Thames: Darwen Finlayson, 1969 [1908]. 190 p.
    "Fairy Tales," 164–67. Yeats's ideas of the fairies are wrong.

1725a. DUFFY, MAUREEN: *The Erotic World of Faery*. London: Hodder & Stoughton, 1972. 352 p.
    Note on Yeats and the faeries, pp. 301–5.

1726. GRIERSON, H[ERBERT]: "Fairies—From Shakespeare to Mr. Yeats," *Dublin R*, 148:297 (Apr 1911), 271–84.
    Reprinted in *Living Age*, 269:3492 (10 June 1911), 651–58. Yeats's fairies no longer have the innocence that Shakespeare gave them; they know sorrow and age.

1727. HILL, DOUGLAS: "Yeats and the Invisible People of Ireland," *Brigham Young U Studies*, 7:1 (Autumn 1965), 61–67.
    Yeats's belief in the fairies was genuine and part of his peculiarly Irish outlook.

1728. PITCHFORD, MARY G.: "W. B. Yeats and the Commonwealth of Faery," M.A. thesis, U of Kansas, 1968. ii, 99 p.
    "The objective of this study is to trace the development and decline of Yeats's interest in and use of fairies and fairy tales in his early literary career" (p. 1).

1729. STACE, W. T.: "The Faery Poetry of Mr. W. B. Yeats," *British R*, 1:1 (Jan 1913), 117–30.
    Reprinted in *Living Age*, 276:3581 (22 Feb 1913), 483–90. Concentrates on *The Wanderings of Oisin* and *The Land of Heart's Desire*.

Fool

1730. °ANDERSON, WILLIAM JOSEPH: "The Fool in the Work of William Butler Yeats," M.A. thesis, Brown U, 1966. v, 112 p.

1731. BRODER, PEGGY FISHER: "Positive Folly: The Role of the Fool in the Works of W. B. Yeats," °Ph.D. thesis, Case Western Reserve U, 1969. 244 p. (*DA*, 30:9 [Mar 1970], 3902A.)

1731a. SMYTH, DONNA ELLEN: "The Figure of the Fool in the Works of W. B. Yeats, Samuel Beckett, and Patrick White," Ph.D. thesis, U of London,

1972. 465 p.
"W. B. Yeats," 22-111.

Hero and Heroic Literature

1732. BYARS, JOHN ARTHUR: "The Heroic Type in the Irish Legendary Dramas of W. B. Yeats, Lady Gregory, and J. M. Synge: 1903-1910," Ph.D. thesis, U of North Carolina, 1963. ii, 262 p. (*DA*, 24:8 [Feb 1964], 3333.)
    Discusses heroic types in Yeats's pre-1899 plays, poems, and prose, as well as *On Baile's Strand*, *The King's Threshold*, *Where There Is Nothing*, *Deirdre*, and *The Green Helmet*. Includes a chapter on "The Origin of the Heroic Type in the Context of the Irish Dramatic Movement."

1733. SWIFT, TERESA MAY: "The Significance of the Romantic Hero in the Work of W. B. Yeats," M.A. thesis, U of Manchester, 1950. v, 232 p.

Imagery

1734. ALEXANDER, JEAN: "Yeats and the Rhetoric of Defilement," *REL*, 6:3 (July 1965), 44-57.
    The use of images of defilement and corruption in Yeats and other writers.

1735. ALLEN, JAMES L.: "Miraculous Birds, Another and the Same: Yeats's Golden Image and the Phoenix," *ES*, 48:3 (June 1967), 215-26.
    Discusses the phoenix imagery.

1736. PIRKHOFER, A[NTON] M.: "Zur Bildersprache von Blake und Yeats," *Anglia*, 75:2 (1957), 224-33.
    Blake's influence on the imagery of Yeats's poetry and plays.

1737. UNTERECKER, JOHN EUGENE: "A Study of the Function of Bird and Tree Imagery in the Works of W. B. Yeats," Ph.D. thesis, Columbia U, 1956. x, 281 p. (*DA*, 17:3 [1957], 637-38.)

Imagination

1737a. WILNER, ELEANOR RAND: "The Eye of the Storm: An Inquiry into the Role of Imagination in Maintaining Human Order and Mediating Social and Personal Change," °Ph.D. thesis, Johns Hopkins U, 1973. 350 p. (*DA*, 34:6 [Dec 1973], 3362A-63A.)
    Contains a discussion of Yeats's apocalyptic and dualistic imagination.

Impersonality

1738. ROSE, ALAN: "The Impersonal Premise in Wordsworth, Keats, Yeats, and Eliot," °Ph.D. thesis, Brandeis U, 1969. 230 p. (*DA*, 30:6 [Dec 1969], 2547A-48A.)

Ireland

1739. BARZUN, JACQUES: *Race: A Study in Superstition*. Revised, with a new preface. NY: Harper & Row, 1965 [1937]. xxiv, 263 p.
    Note on whether Yeats was typically Irish, pp. 213-14.

1740. BOULGER, JAMES D.: "Yeats and Irish Identity," *Thought*, 42:165 (Summer 1967), 185-213.
    Yeats's increasing awareness of his Irish identity is shown in "Easter 1916." His later works (among others the Crazy Jane poems) demonstrate

"his spiritual identification with the racial majority" (p. 190).
Compares Yeats, Joyce, and O'Neill.

1741. FRIEDMAN, BARTON R.: "Yeats, Johnson, and Ireland's Heroic Dead:
Toward a Poetry of Politics," *Éire-Ireland*, 7:4 (Winter 1972), 32-47.
    Yeats's view of O'Leary, Parnell, and others, particularly in his
    poetry, compared with Lionel Johnson's.

1742. HENN, T. R.: "W. B. Yeats and the Irish Background," *Yale R*, 42:3
(Mar 1953), 351-64.

1743. KEE, ROBERT: *The Green Flag: A History of Irish Nationalism.* London:
Weidenfeld & Nicolson, 1972. xvi, 877 p.
    "Growth of National Consciousness," 426-37; on Yeats and the early
    days of the Irish literary revival.

1744. KIRBY, SHEELAH: *The Yeats Country: A Guide to Places in the West of
Ireland Associated with the Life and Writings of William Butler Yeats.*
Edited by Patrick Gallagher with drawings and maps by Ruth Brandt. Dublin:
Dolmen Press, 1962. 47 p.
    A collection of notes on Yeats's allusions to West of Ireland places
    (Sligo and surroundings, Thoor Ballylee, Coole Park, and surroundings).
    Reviews:
    1. Anon., "Poetic Haunts," *TLS*, 62:3178 (25 Jan 1963), 62.
    2. J[ames] D[elehanty], *Kilkenny Mag*, #8 (Autumn-Winter 1962), 56-58.
    3. Denis Donoghue, "Countries of the Mind," *Guardian*, #36241 (11 Jan
       1963), 5.
    4. T. R. Henn, *MLR*, 58:4 (Oct 1963), 627.
    5. A. Norman Jeffares, "The Yeats Country," *MLQ*, 25:2 (June 1964),
       218-22.

1745. MOKASHI, S. R.: "W. B. Yeats and Anglo-Phobia: A Lesson to India,"
Triveni, 30:2 (Oct 1960), 46-52.

1746. °MULLIGAN, MARY T.: "Yeats and His Relations with Ireland," M.A.
thesis, Columbia U, 1952. 51 p.

1747. O'BRIEN, CONOR CRUISE (ed): *The Shaping of Modern Ireland.* London:
Routledge & Kegan Paul, 1960. vi, 201 p.
    Deals mostly with political leaders. Of interest to this bibliography:
    Myles Dillon: "Douglas Hyde," 50-62.
    Donald Davie: "The Young Yeats," 140-51. Discusses Yeats's convictions
    concerning the relation between art and politics. Specifically on
    Yeats and the Young Irelanders, O'Leary, Parnell, the *Playboy* contro-
    versy, and the Lane pictures.
    J. J. Byrne: "AE and Sir Horace Plunkett," 152-63.

1748. PAUL, DAVID: "Yeats and the Irish Mind," *Twentieth Century*, 158:941
(July 1955), 66-75.
    Actually a review of *Autobiographies* (W211L).

1749. PEARCE, DONALD ROSS: "The Significance of Ireland in the Work of
W. B. Yeats," Ph.D. thesis, U of Michigan, 1948. iv, 373 p. (*Microfilm
Abstracts*, 9:1 [1949], 133-34.)

1750. SALVESEN, CHRISTOPHER: "Ireland and Its Dead Yeats," *New Society*,
5:141 (10 June 1965), 26-28.
    Yeats's Irish nationalism and contemporary Ireland's reaction to him.

1751. TUOHY, FRANK: "Yeats and Irish History," *Yeats Society of Japan.
Annual Report*, #1 (1966), 6-9.

"The cardinal point about Yeats's relationship with the history of his native land is one difficult for Irish critics to accept: he made use of Ireland for the purposes of his art, in the same way that he made use of the Noh plays and the history of Byzantium."

1752. WEST, REBECCA: *The Strange Necessity: Essays and Reviews*. London: Cape, 1928. 344 p.
    See pp. 152-71 for a discussion of Anglo-Irish writers, of whom Moore and Yeats are taken to be the only nonrevolutionaries. Is dismayed by Yeats's "magical view of the universe" and his use of Irish folklore, which, she says, merely serves to fill the gaps in his "system." Contains factual inaccuracies of a rather crude sort; e.g., Synge left Ireland to write his plays and promptly came under the influence of Villiers de l'Isle Adam (p. 153).

Irish Language

1753. Ó GLAISNE, RISTEÁRD: "Yeats agus an Ghaeilge," *Ultach*, 42:7 (July 1965), 3-5.

Irish Literature

1754. KEHOE, CONSTANCE DE MUZIO: "The Tradition of the Irish Poet in the Work of William Butler Yeats," Ph.D. thesis, Trinity College, Dublin, 1966. vi, 255 p.

1755. KENNELLY, BRENDAN: "Modern Irish Poets and the Irish Epic," Ph.D. thesis, Trinity College, Dublin, 1967. vi, 459 p.
    On Yeats, pp. 220-63 (*The Wanderings of Oisin*, *At the Hawk's Well*, *The Green Helmet*, *On Baile's Strand*, *The Only Jealousy of Emer*, and *Deirdre*); also on AE, Stephens, Clarke, Todhunter, and others.

1755a. O'BRIEN, FRANK: *Filíocht ghaeilge na linne seo: Staidéar criticiúil* [Contemporary Gaelic poetry: A critical study]. Baile Átha Cliath: An Clóchomhar Tta, 1968. xi, 347 p.
    Yeats is mentioned *passim* (see index).

Irish Nationalism, History, and Themes

1755b. °BROWN, R. M. C. S.: "Yeats's Early Approach to Nationalism," M.Litt. thesis, Trinity College, Dublin, 1970/71.

1756. EGERER, SISTER MARY ANNE MONICA: "The Rogueries of William Butler Yeats," Ph.D. thesis, Radcliffe College, 1962. iii, 609 p.
    Yeats's reading and writing on Irish subjects, 1885-1900.

1757. GWYNN, STEPHEN: "Ireland Week by Week: The Honour to Mr. Yeats [. . .]," *Observer*, 132:6912 (18 Nov 1923), 9.
    Yeats and Irish nationality.

1758. HOFFMAN, DANIEL: *Barbarous Knowledge: Myth in the Poetry of Yeats, Graves, and Muir*. NY: Oxford UP, 1967. xvi, 266 p.
    Irish myths in Yeats's works, particularly in the ballads, in "The Tower," and in the Cuchulain plays, which he treats as "Yeats's most successful version of an epic theme" (p. 87).
    Reviews:
    1. James D. Boulger, *Thought*, 43:168 (Spring 1968), 128-30.
    2. Patrick Cosgrave, "Barbarous Scholarship," *London Mag*, 7:5 (Aug 1967), 83-86. Correspondence by Hoffman and Cosgrave's reply, :10 (Jan 1968), 109-12.

3. Bruce Cutler, "Introductions and Conclusions," *Poetry*, 112:1 (Apr 1968), 52-56.
4. Denis Donoghue, *MLQ*, 29:1 (Mar 1968), 120-21.
5. Robert S. Kinsman, *Western Folklore*, 28:1 (Jan 1969), 63-64.
6. A. D. Nuttal, *RES*, 19:75 (Aug 1968), 349.
7. William Sylvester, *CE*, 29:1 (Oct 1967), 62-65.
8. R. S. Thomas, *CQ*, 9:4 (Winter 1967), 380-83.
9. Peter Ure, *MLR*, 65:1 (Jan 1970), 161-62.

1759. HONE, J. M.: "The Later Writings of Mr. Yeats," *NSt*, 5:107 (24 Apr 1915), 62-64.
Irish themes in the writings after the collected edition of 1908, with special reference to the influence of Synge.

1760. KELLEHER, JOHN V.: "Yeats's Use of Irish Materials," *Tri-Q*, #4 [Fall 1965], 115-25.
The expressions "lebeen-lone" in "The Three Beggars" and "Clooth-na-Bare" in "The Hosting of the Sidhe" and "Red Hanrahan's Song about Ireland," as well as the use of the Cuchulain myths.

1760a. LASS, ROLF HERMANN: "The Irish Ireland Myth: A Study of the Irish Idea of Nationality, Its Native and European Roots, and Its Bearing on the Work of W. B. Yeats," Ph.D. thesis, U of Cambridge, 1970. iii, 312 p.
Discusses Yeats's early prose, some poems (particularly "The Old Age of Queen Maeve," "The Two Kings," "The Grey Rock," "The Hour before Dawn," and "Under the Round Tower"), and some plays (particularly *The Player Queen, The King of the Great Clock Tower, A Full Moon in March,* and *The Herne's Egg*).

1761. °LEE, LENG KWONG: "W. B. Yeats and the 1916 Rebellion," M.A. thesis, U of New Brunswick, 1968.

1761a. LEWALD, H. ERNEST (ed): *The Cry of Home: Cultural Nationalism and the Modern Writer*. Knoxville: U of Tennessee Press, 1972. xii, 400 p.
Robert Tracy: "Ireland: The Patriot Game," 39-57; includes notes on Yeats and the relation between the Irish literary revival and politics.

1762. °MANN, JOHN ANTHONY: "W. B. Yeats and Nineteenth Century Irish Literary Nationalism," M.A. thesis, U of Toronto, 1969.

1763. MORISON, JOHN L.: "Modern Irish Literature: A Study in Nationalism," *QQ*, 30:1 (July-Aug-Sept 1922), 66-90.
"Irish folk-beliefs have found in Mr. Yeats their poet-laureate. For the rest, it is dangerous to take from so highly individualized a genius notable qualities and claim them as peculiarly Irish" (p. 83).

1764. O'HEGARTY, P. S.: "W. B. Yeats and Revolutionary Ireland of His Time," *Dublin Mag*, 14:3 (July-Sept 1939), 22-24.
Nationalism in Yeats's early works.

1765. PITTWOOD, ERNEST H.: "The Celtic Spirit in Literature," *Holborn R*, os 71 / ns 20:[4] (Oct 1929), 461-69.
The Celtic spirit of "wonder, reverence, faith" found in Yeats's works and elsewhere.

1766. REID, MARGARET J. C.: *The Arthurian Legend: Comparison of Treatment in Modern and Mediaeval Literature. A Study in the Literary Value of Myth and Legend*. London: Methuen, 1970 [1938]. viii, 277 p.
Note on Irish mythology in the works of Yeats and Lady Gregory, pp. 257-60.

1767. REYNOLDS, HORACE: "Yeats on Irish Wonders," *Tuftonian*, 2:2 (Jan 1942), 87-88.
 Introduction to Yeats's essay, "Irish Wonders," *ibid.* (Wp. 334).

1768. SHAW, FRANCIS: "The Celtic Twilight," *Studies*, 23:89 (Mar 1934), 25-41.
 A severe criticism of the term, of which "Twilight" may be correct but "Celtic" certainly isn't. As conceived by Yeats and others, "Celtic" does in no way describe Irish literature and culture. See also next item.

1769. ———: "The Celtic Twilight. Part II.—The Celtic Element in the Poetry of W. B. Yeats," *Studies*, 23:90 (June 1934), 260-78.
 The so-called Celtic works are neither Celtic nor Irish. They are simply romantic, whereas genuine Celtic tradition is realistic. Shaw admits, however, that to a certain extent Yeats's critics were more instrumental in creating the cliché than Yeats himself.

1770. °SLOAN, CORA MAE: "Irish Life in the Works of William Butler Yeats," M.A. thesis, U of Texas, 1937. vi, 134 p.

1771. °SPRINGER, ABRAHAM: "William Butler Yeats: Celtic Tradition and Nationalism," M.A. thesis, Columbia U, 1950.

1772. °TAKACS, DALMA S.: "The Relationship of Irish Christianity and Paganism as Reflected in the Works of W. B. Yeats and Lady Gregory," M.A. thesis, Columbia U, 1962. 74 p.

1772a. THUENTE, MARY HELEN ERNST: "W. B. Yeats and Nineteenth-Century Irish Literary Tradition," °Ph.D. thesis, U of Kansas, 1973. 244 p. (*DA*, 34:6 [Dec 1973], 3360A-61A.)
 "The major focus . . . is on the four anthologies of Irish folklore and nineteenth-century Irish fiction which Yeats edited between 1888 and 1892" (abstract).

Irish Poet (Yeats as)

1773. MACGREEVY, THOMAS: "The Gaelic and the Anglo-Irish Culture," *Irish Statesman*, 3:26 (7 Mar 1925), 816-17.
 A defense of Yeats as an Irish writer.

1774. QUIN, C. C. W.: "W. B. Yeats and Irish Tradition," *Hermathena*, #97 (1963), 3-19.
 Yeats was an "ignorant plunderer and raider in the field of Gaelic literature . . . but he shows his scholarship and artistry and his taste in the use he makes of [it]" (pp. 11-12).

Magic

1775. RAUCH, KARL: "William Butler Yeats und die magische Dichtung," *Deutsche Rundschau*, 81:8 (Aug 1955), 837-40.
 Visionary and magical elements in Yeats's work. Slight.

Mask

1776. °DRAWBAUGH, BETTY: "Ego Dominus Tuus: An Examination of the Doctrine of the Mask in the Works of William Butler Yeats," M.A. thesis, Columbia U, 1950.

1777. FARAG, FAHMY FAWZY: "W. B. Yeats's Antithetical Mask," *Annals of the Faculty of Arts* [Ain Shams U, Cairo], 7 (1962), 21-28.

1778. MAHON, CECIL MICHAEL: "The Fascination of What's Difficult: W. B. Yeats; the Mask as Esthetic and Discipline," Ph.D. thesis, U of California (Santa Barbara), 1966. viii, 226 p. (*DA*, 28:7 [Jan 1968], 2689A.)

1779. WATANABE, JUNKO: "The Symbolism of W. B. Yeats: His Doctrine of 'the Mask,'" *Kyoritsu Women's Junior College: Collected Essays by Members of the Faculty*, #11 (1968), 50-67.

1780. °WELLS, PATRICIA L.: "William Butler Yeats' Doctrine of the Mask in Poetic Theory and Practice," M.A. thesis, Columbia U, 1952. 133 p.

Metamorphosis

1781. QUINN, SISTER M. BERNETTA: *The Metamorphic Tradition in Modern Poetry: Essays on the Work of Ezra Pound, Wallace Stevens, William Carlos Williams, T. S. Eliot, Hart Crane, Randall Jarrell, and W. B. Yeats.* New Brunswick: Rutgers UP, 1955. xi, 263 p.
   "William Butler Yeats: The Road to Tír-na-n-Og," 207-36; on the metamorphosis motif in Yeats's works.
   Reviews:
   1. A. Norman Jeffares, *MLR*, 52:1 (Jan 1957), 108-10.

Moon

1782. EDWARDS, MICHAEL: "Yeats and the Moon," *Adam*, 34:334-36 (1969), 27-29.

Music

1783. °BORDOW, RITA LEE: "Yeats and Music," M.A. thesis, Columbia U, 1950.

1784. CLINTON-BADDELEY, VICTOR CLINTON: *Words for Music.* Cambridge: UP, 1941. xi, 168 p.
   "W. B. Yeats & the Art of Song," 149-64, and *passim* (see index). "Music for him was an aid to the performance of poetry and nothing more" (p. 151). "He was not so much interested in the art of song as in the art of the public presentation of poetry" (p. 155).

Mysticism

1785. B.-d. V., A.: "Moderne engelsche mystiek: William Butler Yeats," *Gulden winckel*, 11:12 (15 Dec 1912), 177-80.
   Explains the "mystical element" in Yeats as his desire to "bring mankind one step nearer to the earthly paradise." Thinks that Yeats is a Catholic.

1786. LINEHAN, MARY CLARE: "Mysticism and Some Irish Writers: An Examination of the Work of G. W. Russell (A. E.), William Butler Yeats, and John Eglinton," Ph.D. thesis, Pennsylvania State U, 1928. ii, 151 p.
   "William Butler Yeats," 69-125. "He is the poet whose sense of artistry is best served by the use of sensuous pictures dictated by a highly developed emotional imagination pursued through the labyrinth of the occult and the magical. But scarcely is he a mystic" (p. 125).

1787. MACHAC, LEOPOLD: "William Butler Yeats als Mystiker und Symbolist," Dr. phil. thesis, U of Wien, 1954. ix, 281 p.
   Misty.

Myth and Mythology

1788. ANGHINETTI, PAUL WILLIAM: "Alienation, Rebellion, and Myth: A Study of the Works of Nietzsche, Jung, Yeats, Camus, and Joyce," °Ph.D. thesis, Florida State U, 1969. 467 p. (*DA*, 30:5 [Nov 1969], 1974A-75A.)

1789. ARMYTAGE, WALTER HARRY GREEN: *Yesterday's Tomorrows: A Historical Survey of Future Societies*. London: Routledge & Kegan Paul, 1968. xi, 288 p.
"Yeats and the Dissociation of Myth and Fact," 109-11; reprint of "The Yeatsian Dialectic," *Riverside Q*, 3:1 (Aug 1967), 48-51.

1790. BUSH, DOUGLAS: *Mythology and the Romantic Tradition in English Poetry*. NY: Pageant Book Company, 1957 [1937]. xvi, 647 p.
Scattered notes on Yeats, *passim* (see index).

1791. CORNWELL, ETHEL FRAZIER: *The "Still Point": Theme and Variations in the Writings of T. S. Eliot, Coleridge, Yeats, Henry James, Virginia Woolf, and D. H. Lawrence*. New Brunswick: Rutgers UP, 1962. ix, 261 p.
Based on °"The 'Still Point' in Modern Literature," Ph.D. thesis, Tulane U, 1956. "Yeats and His System," 89-125, and *passim*. "His use of myth and his later development of a system was . . . Yeats's personal protest against the growing chaos of his world, and his personal solution to the problems of unity and coherence that so plague the modern artist" (p. 90).

1792. DAICHES, DAVID: *More Literary Essays*. Chicago: U of Chicago Press, 1968. vii, 274 p.
"Myth, Metaphor, and Poetry," 1-18; reprinted from *Essays by Divers Hands*, 33 (1965), 39-55. "The search for archetypal images, for the contents of Yeats's Great Memory . . . , is not always the surest way of accounting for the suggestion of myth. . . . One could use all the symbols in the book and still achieve no adequate poetic expression" (p. 12).
"Yeats's Earlier Poems: Some Themes and Patterns," 133-49; reprinted from J1101.

1793. FEDER, LILLIAN: *Ancient Myth in Modern Poetry*. Princeton: Princeton UP, 1971. xiv, 432 p.
"W. B. Yeats: Myth as Psychic Structure," 61-90. "W. B. Yeats: Prophecy and Control," 185-200 (part of a section entitled "Myth and Ritual"). "W. B. Yeats: History as Symbol," 277-93. Also *passim*, involving comparisons with Eliot, Pound, and Auden. Largely a psychoanalytical approach.

1794. °SALAND, ARNOLD GERSOW: "William Butler Yeats: Inspiration and Early Mythology," M.A. thesis, Columbia U, 1966. 119 p.

1795. STAUFFER, DONALD A.: "The Modern Myth of the Modern Myth," *EIE*, 1947, 23-49.
On Yeats, pp. 36-49; particularly on *A Vision*.

1796. WATTS, HAROLD HOLLIDAY: *Hound and Quarry*. London: Routledge & Kegan Paul, 1953. viii, 304 p.
"W. B. Yeats and Lapsed Mythology," 174-87; revised from *Renascence*, 3:2 (Spring 1951), 107-12. Yeats used myth, particularly Celtic myth, in order to erect a barrier between himself and the society in which he lived. The original users of the myth would not have understood him at all.

"W. B. Yeats: Theology Bitter and Gay," 188-208; revised from *SAQ*, 49:3 (July 1950), 359-77. Yeats's religious thinking was solipsistic. A difficult article to evaluate, since Watts does not use quotations to support his argument.

Opposites and Antinomies

1797. BOSE, ABINASH CHANDRA: "Yeat's [sic] View of Life as Conflict," *Shakti*, 3:8 (Aug 1966), 30-31.

1798. HOLLIS, JAMES RUSSELL: "Patterns of Opposition and Reconciliation in the Life and Work of W. B. Yeats," Ph.D. thesis, Drew U, 1967. iii, 453 p. (*DA*, 28:5 [Nov 1967], 1819A.)

1799. MIYOSHI, MASAO: *The Divided Self: A Perspective on the Literature of the Victorians*. NY: New York UP, 1969. xix, 348 p.
Contains some notes on the motif of the divided self in Yeats's early works (especially *John Sherman*), pp. 332-34 and *passim* (see index).

1800. MOORE, MARIANNE: "The Hawk and the Butterfly," *Westminster Mag*, 23:1 (Spring 1934), 63-66.
On the antinomies in Yeats's "system."

1801. NOON, WILLIAM: "Yeats and the Human Body," *Thought*, 30:117 (Summer 1955), 188-98.
The dichotomy of body and soul in Yeats's thought and poetry with references to *A Vision*.

1802. A. E. [i.e., RUSSELL, GEORGE WILLIAM]: *Song and Its Fountain*. London: Macmillan, 1932. vii, 133 p.
AE's opinion of Yeats's theory of self and anti-self and of *The Shadowy Waters*, pp. 9-12.

1803. SUŠKO, MARIO: "W. B. Yeats i ideja suprotnosti" [WBY and the idea of opposites], *Forum* [Zagreb], yr 8 / 18:10-11 (Oct-Nov 1969), 745-80.

1804. WEISNER, CLAUS JÜRGEN: "Dialektische Ästhetik und antithetische Struktur in W. B. Yeats' theoretischen Schriften und lyrischem Werk," Dr. phil. thesis, U of Freiburg, 1970. iii, 417 p.
Includes an English summary, pp. 412-15 (also in *English and American Studies in German*, 1970, #43). An ill-organized and cluttered attempt to discuss antithetical structures in Yeats's thought and poetry, particularly in the early work.

Pastoral

1804a. ESTOK, MICHAEL JOHN: "Elements of Pastoral and Satiric Tradition in W. B. Yeats," Ph.D. thesis, U of Toronto, 1971. 472 p. (*DA*, 33:9 [Mar 1973], 5120A.)

Perfection

1804b. BARNWELL, WILLIAM CURTIS: "W. B. Yeats: The Scheme of Perfection," °Ph.D. thesis, U of Florida, 1972. 129 p. (*DA*, 34:1 [July 1973], 303A-4A.)
Yeats "had a definite scheme of perfection" (abstract).

Persons in Yeats's Work

1805. BOULGER, JAMES D.: "Personality and Existence in Yeats," *Thought*, 39:155 (Winter 1964), 591-612.
Mythological, historical (especially Berkeley), and contemporary figures (especially Yeats himself) in the poetry and prose.

1806. BRADFORD, CURTIS: "Yeats and Maud Gonne," *TSLL*, 3:4 (Winter 1962), 452-74.
Maud Gonne in Yeats's life and poetry.

1807. BRIGGS, RICHARD STUART: "Michael Robartes and Owen Aherne: Two Voices of W. B. Yeats," B.A. Honors thesis, Harvard U, 1964. i, 41 p.

1807a. °CHIAMPI, RUBENS: "Yeats's View of Women," *ITA Humanidades*, 7 (1971), 137-45.

1808. °MILLER, DONALD W.: "Fathers and Sons in the Life and Works of William Butler Yeats," M.A. thesis, Columbia U, 1959. 74 p.

1809. OLNEY, JAMES: *Metaphors of Self: The Meaning of Autobiography*. Princeton: Princeton UP, 1972. xv, 342 p.
On autobiographical themes in Yeats's work, *passim* (see index).

1809a. RUNNELS, JAMES ALAN: "Mother, Wife, and Lover: Symbolic Women in the Work of W. B. Yeats," °Ph.D. thesis, Rutgers U, 1973. 277 p. (*DA*, 34: 1 [July 1973]. 336A.)

Phases

1810. BOSE, AMALENDU: "The Decade of Yeats's *In the Seven Woods*," *JJCL*, 8 (1968), 96-109.

1810a. CASSIDY, ROBERT LAWRENCE: "W. B. Yeats' Early Poetry and Prose: The Landscape of Art," °Ph.D. thesis, U of Western Ontario, 1971. (*DA*, 33:2 [Aug 1972], 748A.)
Discusses the work of the 1880s and 1890s.

1811. °HOLLAND, PATRICK JAMES: "Theme and Form in the Work of W. B. Yeats, 1935-1939," M.A. thesis, McMaster U, 1969.

Philosophy

1812. ROSSI, MARIO M.: "Yeats--and Philosophy," *Cronos*, 1:3 (Fall 1947), 19-24.
The philosophy in the poetry and plays, not in the "philosophical" works.

Psychoanalysis

1813. °SEIDEN, MORTON IRVING: "The Man Who Dreamed of Fairyland: A Psychoanalytical Study of William Butler Yeats," M.A. thesis, Columbia U, 1944.

1813a. WEBSTER, BRENDA ANN SCHWABACHER: *Yeats: A Psychoanalytical Study*. Stanford: Stanford UP, 1973. ix, 246 p.
Based on "Dream and the Dreamer in the Works of W. B. Yeats," Ph.D. thesis, U of California (Berkeley), 1967. iii, 374 p. (*DA*, 28:10 [Apr 1968], 4192A). Incorporates "Yeats' *The Shadowy Waters*: Oral Motifs and Identity in the Drafts," *American Imago*, 28:1 (Spring 1971), 3-16.
Discusses the relationship between Yeats's traumatic childhood experiences and the later work, particularly sexual fears, the non-existent relationship with his mother, Lady Gregory as mother figure, the island and escape motifs, the father-son theme, the relationship with Maud Gonne, the concept of the mask, and among others the following works: "Byzantium," *The Countess Cathleen*, "A Dialogue of Self and Soul," "The Double Vision of Michael Robartes," *A Full Moon in March*, *The Herne's Egg*, *The Island of Statues*, *John Sherman*, *The King of the Great Clock Tower*, *The King's Threshold*, *On Baile's Strand*,

"The Phases of the Moon," *The Player Queen*, *Purgatory*, "Rosa Alchemica," "Sailing to Byzantium," *The Shadowy Waters*, "Supernatural Songs," "The Tables of the Law," *The Unicorn from the Stars*, *A Vision*, *The Wanderings of Oisin*, and *Where There Is Nothing*.
Reviews:
1. A. Norman Jeffares, "The Great Purple Butterfly," *Sewanee R*, 82:1 (Winter 1974), 108-18.

Religion

1814. ALLT, G. D. P.: "W. B. Yeats," *Theology*, 42:248 (Feb 1941), 81-91.
Yeats was not a religious poet; in fact, some of his thoughts are very dangerous doctrines. But Christians should read him, because he was above all an honest poet.

1815. ———: "Yeats, Religion, and History," *Sewanee R*, 60:4 (Oct-Dec 1952), 624-58.
Discusses among other texts *Cathleen ni Houlihan*, *Calvary*, and *The Resurrection*.

1816. °ANDERSON, CAROL: "Christianity in the Poems and Plays of William Butler Yeats," M.A. thesis, Columbia U, 1963. 112 p.

1817. BROOKS, CLEANTH: *The Hidden God: Studies in Hemingway, Faulkner, Yeats, Eliot, and Warren*. New Haven: Yale UP, 1963. xi, 136 p.
"W. B. Yeats: Search for a New Myth," 44-67. Religion is very important to Yeats. Although he may explore it in rather strange contexts, he gives back to it a much-needed sense of urgency and a feeling of awe. Yeats's own beliefs are, however, difficult to determine.

1818. BRÜGGEMANN, THEODOR: "Das christliche Element in W. B. Yeats' dichterischer Symbolik," Dr. phil. thesis, U of Münster, 1954. 205 p.
Yeats's use of Christian symbolism is essentially that of a man outside Christianity who is equally distanced from and attracted by it. Christian symbolism provides points of orientation in Yeats's poetry and assists him in his search for truth. Discusses the poetry (especially "Vacillation," "Leda and the Swan," and "The Mother of God"), the plays (*Calvary*, *The Resurrection*), and the prose.

1819. DAICHES, DAVID: *Literary Essays*. Edinburgh: Oliver & Boyd, 1956. vii, 225 p.
"Religion, Poetry and the 'Dilemma' of the Modern Writer," 206-25. See also "Theodicy, Poetry, and Tradition," in Stanley Romaine Hopper (ed): *Spiritual Problems in Contemporary Literature*. NY: Harper, 1957 [1952]. xvii, 298 p. (Harper Torchbooks. TB21.), pp. 73-93. Yeats "needed a religious tradition to work with, but he could not accept any tradition specifically denominated as religious" (p. 218).

1820. EVERY, GEORGE: "Life. Life. Eternal Life." *Student World*, 31:2 (1938), 136-45.
On Yeats, religion, and "The Second Coming," 139-42.

1821. °FLACCUS, WILLIAM KIMBALL: "Occult Religions in the Work of William Butler Yeats," M.A. thesis, Columbia U, 1934.

1822. HEALY, J. V.: "Yeats and His Imagination," *Sewanee R*, 54:4 (Autumn 1946), 650-59.
On Yeats's religion and beliefs. Actually, less than half the article is concerned with Yeats.

1823. HOFFMAN, FREDERICK JOHN: *The Imagination's New Beginning: Theology and Modern Literature*. Notre Dame: U of Notre Dame Press, 1967. xiv, 105 p. (University of Notre Dame Ward-Phillips Lectures in English Language and Literature. 1.)
> On Yeats, pp. 10-15. "Despite his practice of shying away from Christianity, Yeats was fascinated by the metaphysical suggestiveness of Christ. The Incarnation remained a central attraction for him, though he preferred his own definition of it."

1824. HONE, J. M.: "A Letter from Ireland," *London Mercury*, 2:9 (July 1920), 341-43.
> Criticizes Yeats's views on religion.

1825. KREMEN, KATHRYN REBECCA: *The Imagination of the Resurrection: The Poetic Continuity of a Religious Motif in Donne, Blake, and Yeats*. Lewisburg, Pa.: Bucknell UP, 1972. 344 p.
> Based on a °Ph.D. thesis, Brandeis U, 1970. 444 p. (*DA*, 31:10 [Apr 1971], 5366A). On Yeats, *passim* (especially pp. 260-307).

1825a. NOON, WILLIAM T.: "The Lion and the Honeycomb: What Has Scripture Said. An Incarnational Perspective on Joyce and Yeats," *Newsletter of the Conference on Christianity and Literature*, 19:3 (Spring 1970), 18-24.
> Refers to "Vacillation" and von Hügel.

1826. °ORENT, JOEL: "Behold, My Servant: A Study of the Irish Poet, Yeats, Viewed against Some Basic Transformations in Western Religious Mood and Literary Theme," M.A. thesis, Columbia U, 1960. 162 p.

1827. PORTER, RAYMOND J.: "The Irish Messianic Tradition," *Emory UQ*, 22:1 (Spring 1966), 29-35.
> The theme of the deliverer in Yeats and in Irish literature.

1828. SCOTT, NATHAN ALEXANDER (ed): *The Climate of Faith in Modern Literature*. NY: Seabury Press, 1964. xvi, 239 p.
> E. Martin Browne: "The Christian Presence in the Contemporary Theater," 128-41; contains a note on *The Resurrection*, 130-31.
> Ralph J. Mills: "The Voice of the Poet in the Modern City," 142-76; comments on Yeats as an anti-Christian poet, 164-67.

1829. SHAPIRO, KARL: "Modern Poetry as Religion," *American Scholar*, 28:3 (Summer 1959), 297-305.
> Contains some notes on Yeats.

1830. WARREN, AUSTIN: *Rage for Order: Essays in Criticism*. Ann Arbor: U of Michigan Press, 1959 [1948]. vii, 165 p. (Ann Arbor Paperbacks. AA33.)
> "William Butler Yeats: The Religion of a Poet," 66-83; reprint of "Religio Poetae," *Southern R*, 7:3 (Winter 1941/42), 624-38; also in J1090. A discussion of Yeats's religious and quasi-religious convictions and their sources.

1831. WILLIAMS, MELVIN G.: "Yeats and Christ: A Study in Symbolism," *Renascence*, 20:4 (Summer 1968), 174-78, 222.
> The Christ figure in the poetry and plays.

1832. YEOMANS, W. EDWARD: "The Problem of Personal Religious Belief for W. B. Yeats," M.A. thesis, U of Toronto, 1957. ii, 102 p.

Revisions and Rewriting

1833. ALSPACH, RUSSELL K.: "'It Is Myself That I Remake,'" *JJQ*, 3:2 (Winter 1966), 95-108.

Part of the article was used as the introduction to *The Variorum Edition of the Plays* (W211FF).

Romantic and Romanticism

1834. HOUGH, GRAHAM: *The Last Romantics*. London: Duckworth, 1961 [1949]. xix, 284 p.
 "Yeats," 216-62; reprinted from *Cambridge J*, 2:5 (Feb 1949), 259-78; :6 (Mar 1949), 323-42. Subtitles: The Rejection of Rhetoric, The Search for a Mythology, The Mask and the Great Wheel, His Beliefs. "Conversation in Limbo," 263-74; between Yeats and H. G. Wells.
 Reviews:
 1. Austin Clarke, "The Last Ditch," *Irish Times*, #28791 (12 Nov 1949), 6.

1835. °JONES, WILLIAM L.: "William Butler Yeats and Romanticism," M.A. thesis, Mississippi State U, 1967.

1836. *KERMODE, FRANK: *Romantic Image*. NY: Vintage Books, 1964 [1957]. xi, 173 p. (Vintage Book. V260.)
 An essay on the troublesome relation between the artist and society. "Artists and contemplatives" have only two chances of escape from the world of action, "the making of Images and death" (p. 30). The reconciliation of action and contemplation in a poetic symbol is "the flowering of . . . the Romantic Image" (p. 43). Yeats is the prime example. Kermode concentrates on "In Memory of Major Robert Gregory" and Yeats's view of Gregory as the artist isolated from society, the image of the dancer and of Salome in Yeats's poetry, prose, and plays, and Yeats's use of the tree imagery that he learned from Blake. Discusses in connection with Yeats and the theory of the Image Pater, Wilde, Symons, Hulme's imagism, and Eliot's concept of the dissociation of sensibility.
 Reviews:
 1. Hazard Adams, *JAAC*, 17:4 (June 1959), 529-30.
 2. A. Alvarez, *Universities Q*, 12:2 (Feb 1958), 206, 208, 210, 212, 214, 216.
 3. Anon., "The Dancer and the Tree," *TLS*, 56:2881 (17 May 1957), 304.
 4. John Bayley, "Image and Intent," *Spectator*, 198:6730 (21 June 1957), 817.
 5. H. Marshall McLuhan, "Romanticism Reviewed," *Renascence*, 12:4 (Summer 1960), 207-9.
 6. Thomas Parkinson, "Two Books on Yeats," *Sewanee R*, 66:4 (Oct-Dec 1958), 678-85.
 7. Robert L. Peters, "By Way of Definition," *Victorian Newsletter*, #14 (Fall 1958), 18-19.
 8. Peter Ure, "From Wordsworth to Yeats," *Listener*, 58:1478 (25 July 1957), 133-35. Correspondence by Janice Bull, :1479 (1 Aug 1957), 174, and by Ure, :1480 (8 Aug 1957), 209.

1837. RIVOALLAN, ANATOLE: *Présence de Celtes*. Paris: Nouvelle Librairie Celtique, [1957]. iii, 444 p.
 "Le romantisme de W. B. Yeats," 200-203 (part of the section "Celtisme et romantisme"). "Les Celtes et le théâtre," 292-97 (on the Abbey Theatre). Also *passim* (see index).

1838. STEWART, ROBERT CALDWELL: "Those Masterful Images: A Study of Yeats's Symbols of Unity and Joy as Aspects of Romanticism," Ph.D. thesis, Yale U, 1969. v, 197 p. (*DA*, 29:11 [May 1969], 4021A-22A.)

1839. TATE, ALLEN: *Essays of Four Decades*. Chicago: Swallow Press, [1968]. xi, 640 p.

"Yeats's Romanticism: Notes and Suggestions," 299-309. Reprinted from *Southern R*, 7:3 (Winter 1941/42), 591-600, and various collections of Tate's essays. Also in J1090.

1839a. °WARDLE, JUDITH: "Myth and Image in Three Romantics: A Study of Blake, Shelley and Yeats," Ph.D. thesis, Queen's U, Belfast, 1971.

1840. °ZNEIMER, JOHN N.: "W. B. Yeats: A Study in Modern Romanticism," M.A. thesis, Columbia U, 1951.

Science

1841. ADAMS, HAZARD: "Yeatsian Art and Mathematic Form," *Centennial R*, 4:1 (Winter 1960), 70-88.

Mathematics in Yeats's poetry (especially "The Statues") and in *A Vision*.

1842. EVANS, SIR BENJAMIN IFOR: *Literature and Science*. London: Allen & Unwin, 1954. 114 p.

On Yeats, pp. 109-11.

1843. GLICKSBERG, CHARLES I.: "William Butler Yeats and the Hatred of Science," *Prairie Schooner*, 27:1 (Spring 1953), 29-36.

Yeats was opposed to science, education, democracy, and reason, and addicted to dreams, visions, ghosts, fairies, and the imagination.

1844. SRIGLEY, M. B.: "The Mathematical Muse," *Dublin Mag*, 31:3 (July-Sept 1956), 13-21.

The importance of mathematics for Yeats's poetry and thought, especially in *A Vision*.

Sexuality

1845. KANTAK, V. Y.: "Yeats's Meditation on 'the Bestial Floor,'" *JJCL*, 7 (1967), 64-84.

The sexual theme in Yeats's works and its indebtedness to Indian sources.

Society

1846. SZABO, ANDREW: "The Poet and Society: Problems of Communication with Special Reference to the Work of W. B. Yeats," M.A. thesis, U of Bristol, 1963. 377 p.

Style

1847. CLARK, JAMES MIDGLEY: *The Vocabulary of Anglo-Irish*. St. Gallen: Zollikofer, 1917. iii, 48 p. (Städtische Handelshochschule St. Gallen. Jahresbericht 17-18 [1915/16-1916/17]. Wissenschaftliche Beilage.)

Yeats, *passim*.

1848. TANIGUCHI, JIRO: *A Grammatical Analysis of Artistic Representation of Irish English with a Brief Discussion of Sounds and Spelling*. Tokyo: Shinozaki Shorin, [1955]. xxiv, 292 p.

Uses material from Yeats's plays and prose, *passim*.

C The Works (General Section)

Symbol and Symbolism

1849. ALLEN, JAMES LOVIC: "Bird Symbolism in the Work of William Butler Yeats," Ph.D. thesis, U of Florida, 1959. iii, 413 p. (*DA*, 20:8 [Feb 1960], 3288.)
Includes a long chapter on Yeats and Frazer (pp. 308-53) and an essay on the tower motif (363-90).

1850. BHALLA, M. M.: "A Ritual of a Lost Faith," *JJCL*, 7 (1967), 102-22. Reprinted in *Thought* [Delhi], 21:22 (24 May 1969), 14-16; :23 (31 May 1969), 14-16. A discussion of ritualism and symbolism in Yeats's poetry and prose.

1851. CAZAMIAN, LOUIS: *Symbolisme et poésie: L'example anglais.* Paris: Presse Française et Etrangère, 1947. 254 p.
See pp. 217-20 and 224-27 for a discussion of Yeats's symbolism in theory and practice (*The Wanderings of Oisin*).

1852. CHEADLE, B. D.: "Yeats and Symbolism" *ESA*, 12:2 (Sept 1969), 132-50. Symbolist tendencies in Yeats's poetry and thought, symbolism being understood both in a historical and a general sense. Points out that even the early Yeats at his most symbolic is usually tempered by matter-of-factness. Lengthy discussion of "Sailing to Byzantium."

1853. FRYE, NORTHROP: *Fables of Identity: Studies in Poetic Mythology.* NY: Harcourt, Brace & World, 1963. vi, 265 p.
"Yeats and the Language of Symbolism," 218-37; reprinted from *UTQ*, 17:1 (Oct 1947), 1-17.

1854. HAYDN, HIRAM: "The Last of the Romantics: An Introduction to the Symbolism of W. B. Yeats," *Sewanee R*, 55:2 (Apr-June 1947), 297-323.

1855. HÖNNIGHAUSEN, LOTHAR: *Präraphaeliten und Fin de Siècle: Symbolistische Tendenzen in der englischen Spätromantik.* München: Fink, 1971. 492 p. plus 46 illustrations.
Yeats, *passim* (see index).

1856. KLIMEK, THEODOR: *Symbol und Wirklichkeit bei W. B. Yeats.* Bonn: Bouvier, 1967. viii, 223 p. (Abhandlungen zur Kunst-, Musik- und Literaturwissenschaft. 45.)
Originally a Dr. phil. thesis, U of Hamburg, 1966. Discusses the concept of the symbol in Yeats's poetry and prose, not as a technical term but as a way of circumscribing poetical life and experience. Also on Yeats's use of the terms "image," "allegory," "metaphor," "emblem," and the relation "symbol-reality." Unfortunately the book does not contain an index.

1857. LIPSKI, W. DE: "Note sur le symbolisme de W. B. Yeats," *EA*, 4:1 (Jan-Mar 1940), 31-42.
Yeats's concept of symbolism as related to the subconscious.

1858. °MCGOVERN, MAIRE FLORENCE: "Symbolism in the Writings of Yeats," M.A. thesis, State U of Iowa, 1917.

1859. MORGAN, JOAN: "A Study of Symbolic Patterns in the Later Poetry and Plays of W. B. Yeats," B.Litt. thesis, Oxford U, 1953. i, 167 p.
On the basis of a discussion of *A Vision.*

1860. °PETTIT, MARVIN T.: "W. B. Yeats, Magician: The Movement toward a Symbolism in the Eighteen Nineties," M.A. thesis, Vanderbilt U, 1964.

1861. RAINE, KATHLEEN, "A Traditional Language of Symbols," *Listener*, 60:
1541 (9 Oct 1958), 559-60.
Platonic symbolism in Blake and Yeats.

1862. SEWELL, BARBARA: *The Symbolic Rose*. NY: Columbia UP, 1960. xi, 233 p.
"Yeats and Transition," 88-117; on the sources and function of the
rose symbol in Yeats's works.

1863. TILLYARD, EUSTACE MANDEVILLE WETENHALL: *Poetry Direct and Oblique*.
London: Chatto & Windus, 1945 [1934]. 116 p.
Note on Yeats's symbolism, pp. 62-68.

1864. TINDALL, WILLIAM YORK: *The Literary Symbol*. Bloomington: Indiana UP,
1962 [1955]. ix, 278 p.
On Yeats's symbolism, *passim* (see index). Especially on "Sailing to
Byzantium," pp. 247-53.

Syntax

1865. DAVIE, DONALD: *Articulate Energy: An Inquiry into the Syntax of
English Poetry*. London: Routledge & Kegan Paul, 1955. viii, 173 p.
Yeats's syntax, pp. 123-25, and *passim* (see index).

Tradition

1866. DONOGHUE, DENIS: "Tradition, Poetry, and W. B. Yeats," *Sewanee R*,
69:3 (Summer 1961), 476-84.
Yeats's idea of tradition, including a note on "Byzantium."

CD Influences, Parallels, and Contrast Studies

This section is subdivided into a general part and several more particu-
larized parts, which are arranged by country. Again, these may have a
general section and subsections arranged alphabetically by the writer or
poet with whom Yeats is compared. I have taken a few liberties with the
assignments to nationalities. Swift, Burke, and Berkeley are considered
to be Irish writers (because Yeats thought that they were); Wilde and
Shaw, however, are classified among the English authors. So are Samuel
Beckett, T. S. Eliot, and, for convenience, Madame Blavatsky. Hugo von
Hofmannsthal and C. G. Jung have been claimed for German literature. The
Japanese section looks somewhat thin, because the considerable amount of
material on the influence of the Nō has been relegated to a separate
section (ED).
Readers are advised to check the index of names for items *by* some of
the authors listed here and for some more casual references. The possibility that relevant material is missing in this section is greater than
elsewhere in this bibliography. There is a certain difficulty in guessing
which author or poet might serve as an occasion or excuse for comparison
with Yeats.

General Section

1867. BACHCHAN, HARBANS RAI: *W. B. Yeats and Occultism: A Study of His
Works in Relation to Indian Lore, the Cabbala, Swedenborg, Boehme, and
Theosophy*. Foreword by T. R. Henn. Delhi: Motilal Banarsidass, 1965. xxii,
296 p.
Based on a Ph.D. thesis, Cambridge U, 1954. xvi, 395 p. Indian lore
is represented by Mohini Chatterjee, Tagore, Purohit Swami, and the
Upanishads; theosophy by Madame Blavatsky. Contains a chapter on *The

Herne's Egg (pp. 185-206), as well as notes on the influence of Blake and MacGregor Mathers. Unfortunately, no Yeats criticism published after 1954 has been taken into account.

1868. °CARLTON, SYLVIA: "Philosophers Who Influenced the Works of William Butler Yeats," M.A. thesis, Columbia U, 1938.

1869. CARPENTER, WILLIAM MORTON: "W. B. Yeats's Literary Use of the Renaissance," Ph.D. thesis, U of Minnesota, 1967. i, 253 p. (*DA*, 28:12 [June 1968], 5010A-11A.)
Discusses Yeats's poetry and prose (especially *A Vision*).

1870. °CHANG, MING-CHU: "William Butler Yeats and the Orient," M.A. thesis, U of Colorado, 1949. v, 78 p.

1871. CHRISTY, ARTHUR EDWARD (ed): *The Asian Legacy and American Life.* NY: Day, 1945. xi, 276 p.
William York Tindall: "Transcendentalism in Contemporary Literature," 175-92; discusses Eastern influences on Yeats and his indebtedness to Madame Blavatsky.

1872. CRONIN, ANTHONY: "Some Aspects of Yeats and His Influence," *Bell*, 16:5 (Feb 1951), 52-58.
Although he was an important poet, Yeats exerted no influence on his generation and was essentially not a "contemporary figure."

1873. DUME, THOMAS LESLIE: "William Butler Yeats: A Survey of His Reading," Ph.D. thesis, Temple U, [1950]. iv, 378 p.
Does not trace influences but wants to establish precisely which books Yeats read; arranges his material as follows: works relating to Ireland and other Celtic material; magic, alchemy, mysticism, witchcraft; the East: theosophy, India, China, Japan, Arabia; psychical research; the ancient world: Greece, Rome, Egypt, Byzantium; science, history, philosophy; English literature; American literature; European literature. Valuable.

1874. ELLMANN, RICHARD. *Eminent Domain: Yeats among Wilde, Joyce, Pound, Eliot, and Auden.* NY: Oxford UP, 1967. vii, 159 p.
Incorporates: "Gazebos and Gashouses: Yeats and Auden," from J1097.
"Yeats & Eliot," *Encounter*, 25:1 (July 1965), 53-55; also as "Eliot's Conversion," *Tri-Q*, #4 [Fall 1965], 77-78, 80.
"Ez and Old Billyum," from J1896.
"Yeats and Joyce," from J1076 (#11).
Discusses the "poetic commerce" (mutual appropriations) between Yeats and the five poets, more precisely the biographical connections, and the esthetic, critical, poetic, and dramatic similarities. Valuable study, but not exhaustive.
Reviews:
1. Anon., "Yeats as Pickpocket," *TLS*, 67:3465 (25 July 1968), 787.
2. Bernard Benstock, *JJQ*, 5:3 (Spring 1968), 267-69.
3. Thomas W. Bergmann, "Getting Down to Cases," *NAR*, os 253 / ns 5:4 (July-Aug 1968), 39-40.
4. Bernard Bergonzi, *RES*, 20:78 (May 1969), 251.
5. Curtis Bradford, "Yeats and His Contemporaries," *Chicago Sun-Times Book Week*, 22 Oct 1967, 6-7.
6. Cyril Connolly, "A Choice of Critics," *Sunday Times*, #7553 (3 Mar 1968), 28.
7. Patrick Cruttwell, "How Many Ways of Looking at a Poem?" *Hudson R*, 21:1 (Spring 1968), 197-207 (pp. 199-201).

8. Denis Donoghue, "Clashing Symbols," *NYTBR*, [72:] (10 Dec 1967), 12, 14, 16.
9. Edward Engelberg, *VS*, 12:3 (Mar 1969), 387-89.
10. George Mills Harper, *SAQ*, 67:3 (Summer 1968), 564.
11. Daniel Hoffman, "Old Ez and Uncle William" *Reporter*, 37:7 (2 Nov 1967), 59-62.
12. K. P. S. Jochum, *Anglia*, 88:3 (1970), 418-19.
13. Robert Langbaum, "Literary Relations," *VQR*, 44:2 (Spring 1968), 333-37.
14. W. K. Rose, *American Literature*, 40:3 (Nov 1968), 415-16.
15. Kevin Sullivan, "Yeats and All That Crowd," *Nation*, 205:16 (13 Nov 1967), 501-2.
16. John Unterecker, "The Yeats Circle," *Contemporary Literature*, 10:1 (Winter 1969), 150-52.
17. Peter Ure, *ES*, 52:1 (Feb 1971), 84-85. Note by Kristian Smidt, "Eliot and Yeats," :4 (Aug 1971), 399.
18. H. L. Weatherby, "Knowledge and Forgiveness," *Sewanee R*, 77:1 (Jan-Mar 1969), 171-76.

1875. FARAG, FAHMY FAWZY: "Oriental Mysticism in W. B. Yeats," Ph.D. thesis, U of Edinburgh, 1959. ii, 261 p.
    The discussion centers on *A Vision* and the poems and plays related to it.

1876. GREGG, FREDERICK JAMES: "W. B. Yeats and Those He Has Influenced," *Vanity Fair* [NY], 5:2 (Oct 1915), 71.
    Slight.

1877. °ISLAM, SHAMSUL: "The Influence of Hindu, Buddhist and Muslim Thought on Yeats's Poetry," M.A. thesis, McGill U, 1966.

1878. ITO, H.: [in Japanese] "W. B. Yeats and the Buddhistic Philosophy," *J of Indian and Buddhist Studies*, 13:1 (1965), 180-82; 14:2 (1966), 770-75.

1879. JAMESON, GRACE EMILY: "Mysticism in AE and Yeats in Relation to Oriental and American Thought," Ph.D. thesis, Ohio State U, 1932. iii, 185 p.
    Contains chapters on Yeats and Ireland, the East, Plato, and Blake.

1880. °MULLEN, SISTER MARY: "The Origins of the 'Personal Utterance' of William Butler Yeats," M.A. thesis, Texas Woman's U, 1967.

1881. °PESCHEFSKY, HOWARD S.: "Oriental Philosophy in the Thought and Work of William Butler Yeats," M.A. thesis, Columbia U, 1957. 90 p.

1882. SANBORN, CLIFFORD EARLE: "W. B. Yeats and the Winds of Doctrine: The Literary Environments of His Early Life and Their Contribution to His Theory of Poetry," Ph.D. thesis, U of Toronto, 1959. ii, 306 p.
    Contains chapters on "Yeats and Young Ireland"; "The Celtic Twilight as a Moulder of Poetic Theory"; "Yeats, Symons, and the French Symbolists"; "Yeats and the Aesthetic Movement" [mainly on the Rhymers' Club]; "Yeats and Shelley"; and "The Occult and Poetic Theory in Yeats."

1883. SMITH, ELLEN ROSSER: "Yeats's Cultural Touchstone: The Period from Dante to Shakespeare," Ph.D. thesis, U of Michigan, 1968. vii, 209 p. (*DA*, 29:3 [Sept 1968], 914A.)
    Yeats's knowledge of the art and literature of the 13th through the 16th centuries and their influence on his work.

1884. °THOMPSON, THOMAS HAZZARD: "The Influences Affecting the Development of W. B. Yeats as a Poet," M.A. thesis, Louisiana State U, 1940.

See also J1097, 1156, 2417, 2767, 4100.

American Literature: General Section

See J1873, 1879, 2683.

American: Saul Bellow

1884a. MALONEY, STEPHEN R.: "Half-way to Byzantium: *Mr. Sammler's Planet* and the Modern Tradition," *South Carolina R*, 6:1 (Nov 1973), 31-40.
     Notes the indebtedness of the novel to "Sailing to Byzantium."

American: Robert Frost

1885. NITCHIE, GEORGE W.: *Human Values in the Poetry of Robert Frost: A Study of a Poet's Convictions*. Durham, N.C.: Duke UP, 1960. xiii, 242 p.
     Discusses Yeats's influence on Frost, pp. 203-13 and *passim* (see index).

American: Robert Hayden

1885a. O'SULLIVAN, MAURICE J.: "The Mask of Allusion in Robert Hayden's 'The Diver,'" *CLAJ*, 17:1 (Sept 1973), 85-92.
     Comments on Yeats's influence.

American: Henry James

See J1791, 4130.

American: Ira Levin

1885b. °MCMANIS, JO. A.: "*Rosemary's Baby*: A Unique Combination of Faust, Leda, and the Second Coming," *McNeese R*, 20 (1971-72), 33-36.

American: Henry Wadsworth Longfellow

See J3298.

American: Robert Lowell

1885c. COSGRAVE, PATRICK: *The Public Poetry of Robert Lowell*. London: Gollancz, 1970. 222 p.
     Compares Yeats and Lowell *passim* (see index).

See also J2490, 2894, 2895.

American: Stuart Merrill

1886. HENRY, MARJORIE LOUISE: *La contribution d'un américain au symbolisme français: Stuart Merrill*. Paris: Champion, 1927. x, 291 p. (Bibliothèque de la Revue de la littérature comparée. 34.)
     See pp. 109, 264.

American: Vladimir Nabokov

See J3976.

American: Eugene O'Neill

See J1740, 6469.

American: Sylvia Plath

See J2895.

American: Edgar Allan Poe

1887. KÜHNELT, HARRO HEINZ: *Die Bedeutung von Edgar Allan Poe für die englische Literatur: Eine Studie anlässlich des 100. Todestages des Dichters*. Innsbruck: Wagner, 1949. 320 p.
"William Butler Yeats," 301-2. Yeats's concept of poetry as a liberation from a bleak everyday world, his preoccupation with dreams and mysticism, and his distrust of the moral element in poetry have close parallels in Poe.

American: Ezra Pound

1888. AGOSTINO, NEMI D': "La fin de siècle inglese e il giovane Ezra Pound," *English Miscellany*, 6 (1955), 135-62.
Contains some notes on the WBY/EP relationship.

1889. BROOKE-ROSE, CHRISTINE: *A ZBC of Ezra Pound*. London: Faber & Faber, 1971. x, 297 p.
On Yeats and Pound, *passim* (see index); especially on Yeats allusions in the *Cantos*.

1890. DAVIE, DONALD: "Yeats and Pound," *Dublin Mag*, 30:4 (Oct-Dec 1955), 17-21.
Although both are prime examples of the "poet as sage," they are very different in other aspects. Yeats would have placed Pound in the subjective phase, opposite his own.

1891. ————: *Ezra Pound: Poet as Sculptor*. London: Routledge & Kegan Paul, 1965. viii, 261 p.
Passim (see index).

1892. EDWARDS, JOHN HAMILTON: "A Critical Biography of Ezra Pound: 1885-1922," Ph.D. thesis, U of California (Berkeley), 1952. vi, 319 p.
Passim, especially 97-102, 132-36.

1893. FRASER, GEORGE SUTHERLAND: *Ezra Pound*. Edinburgh: Oliver & Boyd, 1962 [1960]. vi, 118 p. (Writers and Critics. 001.)
See pp. 93-97.

1894. GOODWIN, KENNETH L.: *The Influence of Ezra Pound*. London: Oxford UP, 1966. xvi, 230 p.
"Pound and Yeats," 75-105. Pound's influence on Yeats's poetry and plays was not as pervasive as is usually believed.

1895. HÄUSERMANN, H. W.: "W. B. Yeats's Criticism of Ezra Pound," *ES*, 29:4 (Aug 1948), 97-109.
Also in *Sewanee R*, 57:3 (July-Sept 1949), 437-55. Especially on Yeats's treatment of Pound in *A Vision*.

1896. HESSE, EVA (ed): *New Approaches to Ezra Pound: A Co-ordinated Investigation of Pound's Poetry and Ideas*. London: Faber & Faber, 1969. 406 p.

Richard Ellmann: "Ez and Old Billyum," 55-85; reprinted from *Kenyon R*, 28:4 (Sept 1966), 470-95. Reprinted in J1874.
Other articles in the book comment on the Yeats-Pound relationship, *passim* (see index). The book is not identical with the following compilation by the same editor: *Ezra Pound: 22 Versuche über einen Dichter*. Frankfurt am Main: Athenäum, 1967. 456 p., which contains a German translation of Ellmann's article (pp. 17-44) and other material on the Yeats-Pound relationship, *passim* (see index).

1897. HUTCHINS, PATRICIA: "Yeats and Pound in England," *Texas Q*, 4:3 (Autumn 1961), 203-16.
Biographical connections.

1898. ————: *Ezra Pound's Kensington: An Exploration, 1885-1913*. London: Faber & Faber, 1965. 180 p.
Passim (see index).

1899. JACKSON, THOMAS H.: *The Early Poetry of Ezra Pound*. Cambridge, Mass.: Harvard UP, 1968. xvi, 261 p.
Compares the early poetry of Pound and Yeats, *passim* (see index), especially 47-60, 129-40, 152-53, and 191-94.

1900. KENNER, HUGH: *The Poetry of Ezra Pound*. Norfolk, Conn.: New Directions, [1951]. 342 p.
Scattered notes on the WBY/EP relationship, *passim* (see index).

1901. ————: *The Pound Era*. London: Faber & Faber, 1972. xiv, 606 p.
Passim (see index).

1902. MULLINS, EUSTACE: *This Difficult Individual, Ezra Pound*. NY: Fleet Publishing Corporation, 1961. 388 p.
See pp. 56-69 and *passim* for biographical connections.

1903. NAGY, NICOLAS CHRISTOPH DE: *The Poetry of Ezra Pound: The Pre-Imagist Stage*. Bern: Francke, 1960. 184 p. (Cooper Monographs. 4.)
See chapters 3, 4C, and 5, *passim*.

1904. NORMAN, CHARLES: *Ezra Pound*. Revised edition. London: Macdonald, 1969 [1960]. xvii, 493 p.
On Yeats, *passim*, especially "Pound and Yeats," 128-45, and "Pound and Yeats in Rapallo," 296-304. Discusses biographical connections.

1905. OLSON, CHARLES: *Human Universe and Other Essays*. Edited by Donald Allen. NY: Grove Press, 1967. v, 160 p.
"This Is Yeats Speaking," 99-102; reprinted from *Partisan R*, 13:1 (Winter 1946), 139-42. Olson defends Pound by speaking through an imagined Yeats.

1906. PARKINSON, THOMAS: "Yeats and Pound: The Illusion of Influence," *Comparative Literature*, 6:3 (Summer 1954), 256-64.
Pound's influence on Yeats was "minor and adventitious."

1907. POUND, EZRA: "On Criticism in General," *Criterion*, 1:2 (Jan 1923), 143-56.
Pound records his debt to Yeats in six lines (p. 144).

1908. ————: *Pound/Joyce: The Letters of Ezra Pound to James Joyce, with Pound's Essays on Joyce*. Edited and with commentary by Forrest Read. NY: New Directions, [1967]. vi, 314 p.
Numerous references to Yeats, *passim* (see index). Reprints Pound's "Le Prix Nobel," *Querschnitt*, 4:1 (Spring 1924), 41-44, which is actually not so much on Yeats as on British literary politics.

1909. READ, HERBERT: *The True Voice of Feeling: Studies in English Roman-tic Poetry.* London: Faber & Faber, 1953. 382 p.
"Ideas into Action: Ezra Pound," 116-38; contains notes on Pound's influence on Yeats.

1910. RECK, MICHAEL: *Ezra Pound: A Close-Up.* NY: McGraw-Hill, 1967. xiii, 205 p.
Passim (see index).

1911. RUTHVEN, K. K.: "Propertius, Wordsworth, Yeats, Pound and Hale," *N&Q*, os 213 / ns 15:2 (Feb 1968), 47-48.
On a supposed Yeats parody in Pound's "Homage to Sextus Propertius." Actually, I think that Pound does not parody, but only refers oblique-ly to, Yeats's "The Withering of the Boughs."

1912. SCHNEIDAU, HERBERT N.: "Pound and Yeats: The Question of Symbolism," *ELH*, 32:2 (June 1965), 220-37.
Yeats's influence on Pound.

1913. ————: *Ezra Pound: The Image and the Real.* Baton Rouge: Louisiana State UP, 1969. ix, 210 p.
Passim (see index).

1914. STOCK, NOEL: *The Life of Ezra Pound.* London: Routledge & Kegan Paul, 1970. xvii, 472 p.
Scattered notes (see index).

1915. °WAGGONER, MARCELINE S.: "The Reciprocal Influence of Ezra Pound and W. B. Yeats," M.A. thesis, Columbia U, 1960. 119 p.

1916. WILLIAMS, WILLIAM CARLOS: *The Selected Letters.* Edited with an introduction by John C. Thirlwall. NY: McDowell, Obolensky, 1957. xix, 348 p.
Some notes on the Yeats-Pound relationship, *passim* (see index).

1917. WITEMEYER, HUGH: *The Poetry of Ezra Pound: Forms and Renewal, 1908-1920.* Berkeley: U of California Press, 1969. xiv, 220 p.
Discusses Yeats's influence on Pound, Yeats allusions in Pound's poetry, and Yeats's concept of the mask in relation to Pound's per-sonae, *passim* (see index).

See also J671, 757, 1380, 1793, 1874, 1932, 1939, 2134, 2269, 2279, 2830, 2908a, 3151, 3395, 3557, 3570, 4100, 4133, 4137, 4723, 4737, 5814.

American: Theodore Roethke

1918. HEYEN, WILLIAM HELMUTH: "Essays on the Later Poetry of Theodore Roethke," Ph.D. thesis, Ohio U, 1967. iv, 132 p. (*DA*, 28:8 [Feb 1968], 3185A.)
"The Yeats Influence: Roethke's Formal Lyrics of the 1950's," 44-92.

1919. MALKOFF, KARL: *Theodore Roethke: An Introduction to the Poetry.* NY: Columbia UP, 1966. x, 246 p.
Passim (see index).

1920. MARTZ, LOUIS LOHR: *The Poem of the Mind: Essays on Poetry English and American.* NY: Oxford UP, 1966. xiii, 231 p.
Notes the influence of Yeats's "The Magi" on Roethke's "Frau Bauman, Frau Schmidt, and Frau Schwartze," pp. 175-76.

1920a. VANDERWERKEN, DAVID L.: "Roethke's 'Four for Sir John Davies' and 'The Dying Man,'" *Research Studies*, 41:2 (June 1973), 125-35.
Comments on Yeats's influence.

See also J1162 (#6).

American: Wallace Stevens

1921. KRIPKE, DANIEL FREDERICK: "Ideas of the 'World': Stevens, Yeats, and Lawrence," Honors thesis, Harvard U, 1961. i, 46 p.

See also J1072, 1485, 2862, 3013a, 3186, 4115.

American: Henry David Thoreau

1922. DUNCAN, MARGARET S.: "New England Dawn and Keltic Twilight (Notes on the Theosophy of Henry Thoreau and the Poems of W. B. Yeats)," *Theosophical R*, 27:157 (15 Sept 1900), 63-72.

1923. GLICK, WENDELL: "Yeats's Early Reading of *Walden*," *Boston Public Library Q*, 5:3 (July 1953), 164-66.
     Comments on the composition of "The Lake Isle of Innisfree."

1923a. °POGER, SIDNEY: "Yeats as Azad: A Possible Source in Thoreau," *Thoreau JQ*, 5:3 (1973), 13-15.

See also 3078, 3310.

American: Kurt Vonnegut

1923b. NELSON, JON ERIC: "Yeats and Vonnegut: The Artist as Mythmaker," *Lutheran Q*, 25:2 (May 1973), 124-35.

American: Walt Whitman

1924. *Comparative Literature: Proceedings of the Second Congress of the International Comparative Literature Association at the University of North Carolina, September 8-12, 1958*. Edited by Werner P. Friederich. Chapel Hill: U of North Carolina Press, 1959. 2 v. (U of North Carolina Studies in Comparative Literature. 23. 24.)
     Herbert Howarth: "Whitman and the Irish Writers," 2:479-88; reprinted as "Whitman among the Irish," *London Mag*, 7:1 (Jan 1960), 48-55.
     Whitman's influence on AE, Joyce, and Yeats.

American: Richard Wilbur

1924a. HERZMAN, RONALD B.: "A Yeatsian Parallel from Richard Wilbur's 'Merlin Enthralled,'" *Notes on Contemporary Literature*, 2:5 (1972), 10-11.
     A parallel from "Leda and the Swan."

American: Thornton Wilder

See J3566.

American: Tennessee Williams

1925. PRESLEY, DELMA E., and HARI SINGH: "Epigraphs to the Plays of Tennessee Williams," *Notes on Mississippi Writers*, 3:1 (Spring 1970), 2-12.
     Note on a quotation from "Sailing to Byzantium" in *The Milk Train Doesn't Stop Here Any More*, pp. 9-11.

American: William Carlos Williams

See J1485.

Arabic Literature

See J1101, 1873.

Australian Literature: Patrick White

See J1731a.

Belgian Literature: Maurice Maeterlinck

1926. DRAPER, JOHN W.: "Yeats and Maeterlinck: A Literary Parallel," *Colonnade*, 7:7 (Apr 1914), 240-45.
A comparison of their plays.

1927. HUYGELEN, PAUL: "Maeterlinck and England," Ph.D. thesis, U of London, [1954]. xiii, 498 p.
"W. B. Yeats," 383-87. "The extent of Maeterlinck's impact . . . remains till the present day still a matter of literary controversy."

1928. °WRIGHT, JUDY G.: "The Dramatic Principles of Maurice Maeterlinck and William Butler Yeats," M.A. thesis, Indiana U, 1967.

See also J1202, 3458, 4438.

Chinese Literature

See J1873.

Classical Literature

1929. DAVIS, DOROTHY ROSALIA: "Parallelism between Classical Tragedy and the Tragedy of William Butler Yeats," Ph.D. thesis, Boston U, 1937. x, 138 p.
Discusses parallels in subject and plot, the use of the chorus and of masks, and the devices of foreshadowing, irony, and peripety. Includes a chapter on the Aristotelian quality of Yeats's plays.

1930. INGALLS, JEREMY: "The Classics and New Poetry," *Classical J*, 40:2 (Nov 1944), 77-91.
Contains a note on some classical sources of Yeats's poetry, pp. 79-81.

1931. THOMSON, JAMES ALEXANDER KERR: *The Classical Background of English Literature.* London: Allen & Unwin, 1962 [1948]. 272 p.
See pp. 259-60: "Yeats had a somewhat false picture in his mind of classical antiquity, seeing it as it were through a veil of romantic mysticism."

See also J1873, 2150-55, 2284.

Danish Literature: Hans Christian Andersen

See J3199, 3205, 3306.

Egyptian Literature (Ancient)

See J1873.

English Literature: General Section

1932. *Approaches to the Study of Twentieth-Century Literature: Proceedings of the Conference in the Study of Twentieth-Century Literature.* Second session, May 3-5, 1962. East Lansing: Michigan State U, [1963?]. vi, 131 p.

David H. Greene: "Recent English and Irish Drama," 31-39, plus discussion about Yeats's influence on contemporary drama, 54-56. Greene maintains that Yeats exerted no influence.
John J. Espey on Pound and Yeats, 126-28.

1933. MCALINDON, T.: "Yeats and the English Renaissance," *PMLA*, 82:2 (May 1967), 157-69.
Yeats and Morris, Nietzsche, Shakespeare, Spenser, and Ben Jonson.

1934. OHMANN, RICHARD M.: *Shaw: The Style and the Man*. Middletown: Wesleyan UP, 1962. xv, 200 p.
"Appendix I," 169-85, offers a statistical comparison of the stylistic peculiarities in the prose of the following writers: Shaw, Yeats (*Per Amica Silentia Lunae*), Bertrand Russell, Sidney and Beatrice Webb, Chesterton, and Wilde.

1935. PRESS, JOHN: *Rule and Energy: Trends in British Poetry since the Second World War*. London: Oxford UP, 1963. xi, 245 p.
Notes on Yeats's influence on the poetry after 1945, *passim* (see index).

1936. SPENDER, STEPHEN: "The Influence of Yeats on Later English Poets," *Tri-Q*, #4 [Fall 1965], 82-89.
Yeats's volume *The Tower* had the greatest influence on the poets of Spender's generation, especially Auden. Yeats was admired for the "threefold responsibility" shown in his life and work: responsibility toward belief, toward political action, and toward art. Invokes frequent comparisons with Eliot.

1937. WALTON, GEOFFREY: "The Age of Yeats or the Age of Eliot? Notes on Recent Verse," *Scrutiny*, 12:4 (Autumn 1944), 310-21.

1938. WELLS, HENRY WILLIS: *New Poets from Old: A Study in Literary Genetics*. NY: Columbia UP, 1940. xi, 356 p.
See pp. 252-59 for a discussion of various influences on Yeats's poetry, notably the influence of Donne.

1939. WILDI, MAX: "The Influence and Poetic Development of W. B. Yeats," *ES*, 36:5 (Oct 1955), 246-53.
The mutual influence of Yeats-Symons, Yeats-T. Sturge Moore, Yeats-Pound, and others.

See also J1097, 1136, 1197, 1330, 1623, 1873, 2415, 2454, 5322-62.

English: Matthew Arnold

1940. MUSGROVE, S[IDNEY]: "Yeats and Arnold: A Common Rhythm," *Southerly*, 3:3 (Dec 1942), 25-26.
Yeats's irregular meters were anticipated in Arnold's "Haworth Churchyard." See A. W. V., "Voice and Verse," *N&Q*, 185:1 (3 July 1943), 20-21, who asks indignantly: "What sort of an ear can this Australian have?"

See also J1103, 1608, 1624, 2420, 2957, 3038, 6091.

English: W. H. Auden

1941. BLAIR, JOHN G.: *The Poetic Art of W. H. Auden*. Princeton: Princeton UP, 1965. ix, 210 p.
See pp. 91-95: Auden was influenced by Yeats's use of the occasional poem; in turn, Auden's prime achievement in this genre is his elegy on Yeats.

1941a. DAALDER, JOOST: "Yeats and Auden: Some Verbal Parallels," *N&Q*, os 218 / ns 20:9 (Sept 1973), 334-36.
  In the poetry.

See also J1097, 1108, 1220, 1499, 1793, 1874, 1936, 2784, 3469, 5940 (#1).

English: Jane Austen

See J2685.

English: George Barker

1941b. FODASKI, MARTHA: *George Barker*. NY: Twayne, 1969. 190 p. (Twayne's English Authors Series. 90.)
  Compares the poetry of Yeats and Barker, pp. 138-43 and *passim*.

English: Sir Arnold Bax

1942. BAX, SIR ARNOLD: *Farewell, My Youth*. London: Longmans, Green, 1943. 112 p.
  "Celtic," 41-48. Admits Yeats as the main influence on his own short stories, poems, and play, written under the pseudonym Dermot O'Byrne.

English: Aubrey Beardsley

1943. WEINTRAUB, STANLEY: *Beardsley: A Biography*. NY: Braziller, 1967. xvii, 285 p.
  Passim.

See also J3896.

English: Samuel Beckett

1944. COHN, RUBY: "The Plays of Yeats through Beckett Coloured-Glasses," *Threshold*, #19 (Autumn 1965), 41-47.
  Apart from a few Yeats echoes in Beckett's plays, both writers share a principal attitude, "a purgatorial view of earthly life."

1945. GADDIS, MARILYN: "The Purgatory Metaphor of Yeats and Beckett," *London Mag*, 7:5 (Aug 1967), 33-46.
  Parallels, parodies, and continuations of Yeatsian themes, types, and structures in *Waiting for Godot* and *Endgame*.

1945a. LONG, CAROL SUE: "Samuel Beckett, Irishman," °Ph.D. thesis, Northwestern U, 1972. 233 p. (*DA*, 33:6 [Dec 1972], 2939A.)
  Includes a discussion of the influence of Irish literature on Beckett and a comparison of the character of the fool in Yeats and Beckett.

1946. PARKIN, ANDREW: "Similarities in the Plays of Yeats and Beckett," *Ariel*, 1:3 (July 1970), 49-58.

See also J1731a, 3472, 3678.

English: Max Beerbohm

1947. FELSTINER, JOHN: *The Lies of Art: Max Beerbohm's Parody and Caricature*. London: Gollancz, 1973. xx, 283, xi p.
  Some notes on Beerbohm's view of Yeats, *passim* (see index).

English: Arnold Bennett

1948. MUNRO, JOHN M.: "'Byzantium' or the Imperial Palace? Ultimate Vision or Variable Compromise?" *Venture*, 5:2 (Apr 1969), 93-105.

The imperial palace is to Bennett what Byzantium is to Yeats.

English: William Blake

1949. ADAMS, HAZARD: *Blake and Yeats: The Contrary Vision*. NY: Russell &
Russell, 1968 [1955]. xxii, 328 p. (Cornell Studies in English. 40.)
 Based on "Structure of Myth in the Poetry of William Blake and W. B.
 Yeats," °Ph.D. thesis, U of Washington, 1953. 558 p. (*DA*, 14:1 [1954],
 105-6). Discusses "the obvious relationship and the question of influence . . . , Blake's aesthetic theory and . . . Yeats's interpretation of that theory . . . , the pattern of Blake's symbolism, with
 special emphasis upon those symbols Yeats later made his own . . . ,
 [and] Yeats's system" (pp. xiii-xiv).
 Reviews:
 1. Anon., *USQBR*, 12:2 (June 1956), 170-71.
 2. Anon., *Yale R*, 45:4 (June 1956), vi, viii.
 3. Sven Armens, "Suprarational Sources for Poetry," *Western R*, 21:1
    (Autumn 1956), 69-76.
 4. Peter F. Fisher, *QQ*, 64:1 (Spring 1957), 155-57.
 5. L. H., *Dublin Mag*, 31:3 (July-Sept 1956), 52-53.
 6. T. R. Henn, *MLR*, 52:2 (Apr 1957), 263-65.
 7. Nicholas Joost, *Renascence*, 9:3 (Spring 1957), 147-49.
 8. V. G. Kiernan, *Science and Society*, 21:2 (Spring 1957), 185-87.
 9. Calvin D. Linton, *American Scholar*, 25:3 (Summer 1956), 378.
 10. William Van O'Connor, *CE*, 18:2 (Nov 1956), 127.
 11. Thomas Parkinson, *MP*, 54:4 (May 1957), 281-84.
 12. William D. Templeman, *Personalist*, 40:1 (Winter 1959), 86-87.

1950. BENTLEY, GERALD EADES, and MARTIN K. NURMI: *A Blake Bibliography:
Annotated Lists of Works, Studies, and Blakeana*. Minneapolis: U of Minnesota Press, 1964. xix, 393 p.
 On the Yeats-Ellis edition, *passim*, especially pp. 19-20; it is
 described as remarkable and original, but very inaccurate and more
 characteristic of its compilers than of Blake.

1951. BLAKE, WILLIAM: *Vala or The Four Zoas*. A facsimile of the manuscript,
a transcript of the poems, and a study of its growth and significance by
G. E. Bentley. Oxford: Clarendon Press, 1963. xviii, 220 p., and illustrations.
 Some notes on the Yeats-Ellis edition, *passim* (see index).

1952. BOLDEREFF, FRANCES MOTZ: *A Blakean Translation of Joyce's "Circe."*
Woodward, Pa.: Classic Non-Fiction Library, 1965. xii, 178 p.
 Based on the Yeats-Ellis edition.

1953. CHISLETT, WILLIAM: *The Classical Influence in English Literature in
the Nineteenth Century and Other Essays and Notes*. Boston: Stratford Company, 1918. xvii, 150 p.
 "The Influence of William Blake on William Butler Yeats," 88-95.
 Blake influenced Yeats's critical theories, not so much his poetry
 and plays.

1954. CROMPTON, LOUIS WILLIAM: "Blake's Nineteenth-Century Critics," Ph.D.
thesis, U of Chicago, 1954. iv, 289 p.
 "Blake and Symbolism: William Butler Yeats," 235-78.

1955. DORFMAN, DEBORAH: *Blake in the Nineteenth Century: His Reputation
from Gilchrist to Yeats*. New Haven: Yale UP, 1969. xv, 314 p. (Yale
Studies in English. 170.)

"The Ellis-Yeats Edition," 190–226, and *passim* (see index). The edition, "albeit brilliant and revolutionary, must be one of the most idiosyncratic and poorly put-together among literary critiques. It does, however, still illuminate Blake despite dense, obscure, and dubious mystical doctrine" (p. 192).

1956. FITE, MONTE D.: "Yeats as an Editor of Blake: Interpretation and Emendation in *The Works of William Blake, Poetic, Symbolic, and Critical*," °Ph.D. thesis, U of North Carolina at Chapel Hill, 1968. 476 p. (*DA*, 31:1 [July 1970], 355A.)

1957. FLETCHER, IAN: "The Ellis-Yeats-Blake Manuscript Cluster," *Book Collector*, 21:1 (Spring 1972), 72–94.
  Description of the MSS. acquired by the University of Reading concerning the Yeats-Ellis edition, with quotations from unpublished Yeats material. A note indicates that the whole material is currently being edited for publication by Fletcher and Robert O'Driscoll.

1958. GARDNER, CHARLES: *Vision & Vesture: A Study of William Blake in Modern Thought*. Port Washington: Kennikat Press, 1966 [1916]. xi, 226 p.
  "W. B. Yeats," 156–65, and *passim* (see index).

1959. HÖNNIGHAUSEN, LOTHAR: "Aspekte des Blake-Verständnisses in der Ästhetik des neunzehnten Jahrhunderts," *Zeitschrift für Kunstgeschichte*, 33:1 (1970), 41–53.

1960. HOLMBERG, CAROL E.: "A Study of William Blake's Fourfold Perceptive Process as Interpreted by William Butler Yeats," °Ph.D. thesis, U of Minnesota, 1971. 271 p. (*DA*, 32:5 [Nov 1971], 2666A.)

1961. JAMESON, GRACE: "Irish Poets of To-day and Blake," *PMLA*, 53:2 (June 1938), 575–92.
  AE and Yeats.

1962. KEYNES, GEOFFREY: *A Bibliography of William Blake*. NY: Grolier Club, 1921. xvi, 516 p.
  Notes on Yeats's Blake editions, pp. 275–76.

1963. LISTER, RAYMOND: "W. B. Yeats as an Editor of William Blake," *Blake Studies*, 1:2 (Spring 1969), 123–38.
  As an editor, Yeats was a failure. His editorial comments on Blake's symbolism have some value, as has his and Ellis's insistence on Blake's sanity. The real value of the edition lies in what it meant to Yeats's poetry.

1964. QUINN, JOHN KERKER: "William Blake's Relation to Twentieth Century Poets," M.A. thesis, U of Illinois, 1936. iv, 134 p.
  "William Butler Yeats," 18–58. "Other Irish Poets," 59–76 (AE and James Stephens).

1965. ————: "Blake and the New Age," *VQR*, 13:2 (Spring 1937), 271–85.

1966. RAINE, KATHLEEN: *Defending Ancient Springs*. London: Oxford UP, 1967. vi, 198 p.
  "Yeats's Debt to William Blake," 66–87; reprinted from *Texas Q*, 8:4 (Winter 1965), 165–81, and from *Dublin Mag*, 5:2 (Summer 1966), 27–47. Also *passim* (see index). Places Yeats, Blake, and others in the tradition of the Perennial Philosophy, i.e., the Platonic and Neo-Platonic tradition of the myth and the beautiful.
  Reviews:
  1. Anon., "Unreasonable Gods," *TLS*, 67:3463 (11 July 1968), 717–19.

2. K. P. S. Jochum, *Anglia*, 89:1 (1971), 143–45.
3. Ants Oras, "Kathleen Raine: The Ancient Springs and Blake," *Sewanee R*, 80:1 (Jan–Mar 1972), 200–211.

1967. ————: *Blake and Tradition*. London: Routledge & Kegan Paul, 1969. 2 v. (A. W. Mellon Lectures in the Fine Arts. 11 [1962].) [(Bollingen Series. 35.)]
See 1:306–25 and *passim* (see index).

1968. RAY, WILLIAM ERNEST: "William Blake and the Critical Development of William Butler Yeats," °Ph.D. thesis, U of North Carolina at Chapel Hill, 1971. 290 p. (*DA*, 32:5 [Nov 1971], 2652A.)

1969. ROSENFELD, ALVIN H. (ed): *William Blake: Essays for S. Foster Damon*. Providence: Brown UP, 1969. xlvi, 498 p.
Hazard Adams: "Blake and the Postmodern," 3–17.

1970. RUDD, MARGARET ELIZABETH: *Divided Image: A Study of William Blake and W. B. Yeats*. London: Routledge & Kegan Paul, 1953. xv, 239 p.
Based on "William Blake and W. B. Yeats: A Study of Poetry and Mystical Vision," Ph.D. thesis, U of Reading, 1951. x, 340 p. Blake and Yeats are both "concerned with the drama of inner life" (p. 189). But where Blake identifies poetry with prophecy, Yeats equates it with magic. For Blake's belief Yeats substitutes vacillation. Comments on Yeats's "system" and on his poetry.
Reviews:
1. Anon., *Month*, 11:2 (Feb 1954), 126–27.
2. Anon., *NSt*, 45:1152 (4 Apr 1953), 407.
3. Anon., "Mysticism and Magic," *TLS*, 52:2665 (27 Feb 1953), 138.
4. T. R. Henn, *Cambridge R*, 74:1816 (6 June 1953), 579–80.
5. Edwin Muir, "Magician or Poet," *Observer*, #8438 (22 Feb 1953), 9.
6. Rex Warner, "Blake and Yeats," *Spectator*, 190:6510 (3 Apr 1953), 423.

1971. SCHORER, MARK: "Magic as an Instrumental Value: Blake and Yeats," *Hemispheres*, 2:5 (Spring 1945), 49–54.
The relations of both poets to the metaphysical were magical, not mystical. Neither was a visionary.

1972. ————: *William Blake: The Politics of Vision*. NY: Vintage Books, 1959 [1946]. xiv, 450, xxviii p.
Passim (see index).

1973. WALTER, JAKOB: *William Blakes Nachleben in der englischen Literatur des neunzehnten und zwanzigsten Jahrhunderts*. Schaffhausen: Bachmann, 1927. ix, 100 p.
A Dr. phil. thesis, U of Zürich, 1927. On Blake and Yeats see pp. 59–95.

See also J565, 1029, 1072, 1076 (#2, 8), 1088, 1112, 1238, 1553, 1736, 1825, 1836, 1839a, 1861, 1867, 1879, 2058, 2940, 2999, 3014, 3130, 4034, 4096, 4100, 4199, 5299–307, 5932, 7294.

English: Madame Blavatsky

See J1867, 1871, 2160, 2996, 3177, 4023.

English: Gordon Bottomley

1974. BOTTOMLEY, GORDON: *A Stage for Poetry: My Purposes with My Plays*. Kendal: Wilson, 1948. xvi, 78 p.

Bottomley acknowledges his indebtedness to Yeats's Nō experiments, pp. 9, 13, 20-21, 26. See also J1068.

See also J3552.

English: Robert Browning

1975. SHMIEFSKY, MARVEL: "Yeats and Browning: The Shock of Recognition," *SEL 1500-1900*, 10:4 (Autumn 1970), 701-21.
   Emphasizes the concept of unity of being.

1976. WOODARD, CHARLES R.: "Browning and Three Modern Poets: Pound, Yeats, and Eliot," Ph.D. thesis, U of Tennessee, 1953. iv, 288 p.
   "Browning and William Butler Yeats," 165-217. Although Yeats's indebtedness to Browning is less extensive than Pound's, it is nevertheless noticeable. Browning and Yeats share "prose precision" and the use of colloquialisms in poetic language, the concern with syntax, and "the preoccupation with the mask."

See also J1072, 1716a, 2983.

English: Edward Calvert

See J1076.

English: Thomas Carlyle

1977. JOHN, BRIAN: "Yeats and Carlyle," *N&Q*, os 215 / ns 17:12 (Dec 1970), 455.
   The description of Keats in "Ego Dominus Tuus" resembles Carlyle's objections to Keats.

See also J3984a.

English: George Chapman

1978. BRADFORD, CURTIS: "W. B. Yeats: A Quotation," *N&Q*, os 201 / ns 3:10 (Oct 1956), 455.
   Asks for identification of two lines of poetry in Yeats's "A General Introduction for My Work." Answer by Anthony W. Shipps, os 211 / ns 13:8 (Aug 1966), 306: the source is Chapman's *The Shadow of Night*.

English: Geoffrey Chaucer

1979. BLENNER-HASSETT, ROLAND: "Yeats' Use of Chaucer," *Anglia*, 72:4 (1955), 455-62.
   The concept of "Annus Mundus" or "Annus Magnus" in *A Vision* derives from Chaucer, not from Milton.

See also J2490, 2958.

English: G. K. Chesterton

See J1934.

English: S. T. Coleridge

1980. SCOUFFAS, GEORGE: "William Butler Yeats the Symbolist and Coleridge the Romantic: A Study of the Relationship of Romanticism and the Modern Irish Renaissance," M.A. thesis, U of Illinois, 1938. v, 114 p.

See also J1136a, 1791, 2154a, 2957, 2982, 3159, 3160.

English: Joseph Conrad

See J1485.

English: A. E. Coppard

1981. SAUL, GEORGE BRANDON: "Literary Parallels: Yeats and Coppard," *N&Q*, 168:18 (4 May 1935), 314.
Two Coppard quotations originate from a phrase in *Reveries over Childhood and Youth.*

English: Abraham Cowley

1982. COHANE, J. J.: "Cowley and Yeats," *TLS*, 56:2880 (10 May 1957), 289.
A stanzaic form used by Cowley reappears in several Yeats poems.

English: Edward Gordon Craig

1983. BABLET, DENIS: *Edward Gordon Craig.* Translated by Daphne Woodward. NY: Theatre Arts Books, 1966. ix, 207 p.
Translation of °*Edward Gordon Craig.* Paris: L'Arche, 1962. On Craig, Yeats, and the Abbey Theatre, pp. 128-30; other references to Yeats, *passim* (see index).

1984. TOMLINSON, ALAN: "W. B. Yeats and Gordon Craig," *Ariel*, 3:3 (July 1972), 48-57.
Craig's influence on Yeats's dramatic theories and his plays.

See also J503, 1136, 3325a, 3458, 3558, 6327.

English: John Davidson

1985. MACLEOD, ROBERT DUNCAN: *John Davidson: A Study in Personality.* Glasgow: Holmes, 1957. 35 p.
See pp. 14-16.

1986. TOWNSEND, JAMES BENJAMIN: *John Davidson: Poet of Armageddon.* New Haven: Yale UP, 1961. xvii, 555 p. (Yale Studies in English. 148.)
See pp. 141-50 and *passim* for a comparison of Davidson's and Yeats's characters and works.

English: C. Day Lewis

See J2049, 5940 (#1).

English: Walter de la Mare

1987. CLARKE, W. T.: "The Soul's Quest for Ideal Beauty in W. B. Yeats, Walter de la Mare, and John Masefield," *London QR*, 147 (ser 5 / 33):294 (Apr 1927), 165-73.
"W. B. Yeats voices the soul's dissatisfaction with present good and present beauty, while Walter de la Mare and John Masefield treat respectively of what may be distinguished as the poetic, and the more distinctively spiritual, realizations of the quest."

See also J2476.

English: John Donne

1988. DUNCAN, JOSEPH ELLIS: *The Revival of Metaphysical Poetry: The History of a Style, 1800 to the Present.* Minneapolis: U of Minnesota Press, 1959. ix, 227 p.

"Yeats, Donne and the Metaphysicals," 130-42. The affinities between Yeats's thought and the Metaphysicals, and the influence of Donne and Herbert on Yeats's poetry.

1989. °ELIAS, JOANNE MITCHELL: "Metaphor and Image: A Comparative Study of the 'Songs and Sonnets' of John Donne and 'Philosophical' Poetry (1917-1939) of William Butler Yeats," M.A. thesis, Mills College, 1955. 186 p.

1990. MARTZ, LOUIS LOHR: "Donne and the Meditative Tradition," *Thought*, 34:133 (Summer 1959), 269-78.
Notes some Donne-Yeats parallels.

1991. °PICOFF, GHITA M.: "The Mingling of Contraries: The Metaphysical Patterns in the Poetry of John Donne and William Butler Yeats," M.A. thesis, U of Vermont, 1967.

1992. STEIN, ARNOLD: *John Donne's Lyrics: The Eloquence of Action*. Minneapolis: U of Minnesota Press, 1962. ix, 244 p.
Some scattered notes (see index).

1993. WILLY, MARGARET: "The Poetry of Donne: Its Interest and Influence Today," *Essays & Studies*, 7 (1954), 78-104.

See also J1825, 1938, 2857, 4724.

English: Edward Dowden

1994. ELLIOTT, MAURICE: "Yeats and the Professors," *Ariel*, 3:3 (July 1972), 5-30.
The influence of, and relationship with, Dowden and Frederick York Powell.

1995. LUDWIGSON, KATHRYN MILLER: "Transcendentalism in Edward Dowden," Ph.D. thesis, Northwestern U, 1963. 234 p. (*DA*, 25:1 [July 1964], 479-80.)
On the Yeats-Dowden relationship and Dowden's rejection of the Irish literary revival, pp. 4-18, 174-218.

1995a.————: *Edward Dowden*. NY: Twayne, 1973. 170 p. (Twayne's English Authors Series. 148.)
Contains chapters on "Relation to the Yeatses and Irish Literature," 43-47, and "His [Dowden's] Aloofness from the Irish Literary Renaissance," 127-52. On Yeats, *passim* (see index).

English: Ernest Dowson

1996. GAWSWORTH: JOHN: "The Dowson Legend," *Essays by Divers Hands*, 17 (1938), 93-123.
Yeats's portrait of Dowson in *Autobiographies* is incorrect and based on rumor (pp. 101-2).

1997. GOLDFARB, RUSSELL M.: "The Dowson Legend Today," *SEL 1500-1900*, 4:4 (Autumn 1964), 653-62.
Yeats is one of those guilty of having invented and perpetuated falsehoods about Dowson.

1998. LONGAKER, MARK: *Ernest Dowson*. Philadelphia: U of Pennsylvania Press, 1967 [1945]. xv, 308 p.
References to Yeats, *passim* (see index); especially in "The Rhymers' Club," 80-110.

See also J2420.

English: John Dryden

1999. SPENCER, THEODORE: *Selected Essays*. Edited by Alan C. Purves. New Brunswick: Rutgers UP, 1966. xii, 368 p.
"Antaeus, or Poetic Language and the Actual World," 10-27; reprinted from *ELH*, 10:3 (Sept 1943), 173-92. Compares Dryden's and Yeats's use of language.
"William Butler Yeats," 308-20; reprinted from *Hound & Horn*, 7:1 (Oct-Dec 1933), 164-74. Originally a review of *Words for Music Perhaps* (W168), actually a defense of Yeats's poetry against the charges made by Yvor Winters (see J2043).

2000. SWAMINATHAN, S. R.: "Virgil, Dryden, and Yeats," *N&Q*, os 217 / ns 19:9 (Sept 1972), 328-30.
Mainly on Virgil/Dryden echoes in "Two Songs from a Play."

English: T. S. Eliot

2001. ALVAREZ, ALFRED: *The Shaping Spirit: Studies in Modern English and American Poets*. London: Chatto & Windus, 1958. 191 p.
The American edition was published as *Stewards of Excellence: Studies in Modern English and American Poets*. NY: Scribner's, 1958. 191 p.
"Eliot and Yeats: Orthodoxy and Tradition," 11-47; reprinted from *Twentieth Century*, 162:966 (Aug 1957), 149-63; :967 (Sept 1957), 224-34. "Eliot uses tradition, Yeats is in it." Eliot's poetry is intelligent, Yeats's emotional. Maintains that Yeats's poetry is good despite its mythological trappings and despite *A Vision*, that the early poetry is negligible, and that the prose of *Autobiographies* belongs to the 19th century, whereas the poetry written at the same time belongs to the 20th. Contains an extended discussion of "Sailing to Byzantium."

2002. BRAYBROOKE, NEVILLE (ed): *T. S. Eliot: A Symposium for His Seventieth Birthday*. London: Hart-Davis, 1958. 221 p.
G. S. Fraser, "W. B. Yeats and T. S. Eliot," 196-216.

2003. EAGLETON, TERRY: *Exiles and Emigrés: Studies in Modern Literature*. London: Chatto & Windus, 1970. 227 p.
Contrasts the use of myth in the poetry of Yeats and Eliot, pp. 174-77.

2003a. °HOSHINO, TŌRU: "Wheel Symbolism of T. S. Eliot and W. B. Yeats," *Ibaraki Daigaku Kyōyōbu Kiyō: Bulletin*, #3 (1971), 81-98.

2004. HOWARTH, HERBERT: *Notes on Some Figures behind T. S. Eliot*. Boston: Houghton Mifflin, 1964. xv, 396 p.
Some notes on Yeats and Eliot, *passim* (see index).

2005. JOHNSON, MAURICE: "The Ghost of Swift in *Four Quartets*," *MLN*, 64:4 (Apr 1949), 273.
A hidden allusion to Yeats and Swift in *Little Gidding*, confirmed by Eliot in a private letter.

2006. KERMODE, FRANK: "Eliot's Dream," *NSt*, 69:1771 (19 Feb 1965), 280-81.
Compares the later poetry of Yeats and Eliot.

2007. ———: *Continuities*. London: Routledge & Kegan Paul, 1968. viii, 238 p.
"A Babylonish Dialect," 67-77; reprinted from *Sewanee R*, 74:1 (Winter 1966), 225-37.

2008. KOHLI, DEVINDRA: "Yeats and Eliot: The Magnitude of Contrast?" *Quest* [Bombay], #58 (Monsoon 1968), 42-46.

The differences between the poets are great, yet they have one thing in common: their insistence on the individual's responsibility to remake his soul.

2009. KOLJEVIĆ, NIKOLA: "Jejts prema Eliotu: Delimično upoređenje" [Yeats and Eliot: A partial comparison], *Letopis matice srpske*, yr 141 / 396:1 (July 1965), 59-78.
Compares the poetry.

2010. LEAVIS, FRANK RAYMOND: *English Literature in Our Time & the University: The Clark Lectures, 1967.* London: Chatto & Windus, 1969. vii, 200 p.
See pp. 136-37, 148, where he compares Yeats and Eliot. Leavis thinks that Eliot is the greater poet and deplores the fact that the academic attention has gone to Yeats. On the basis of my own experience with Yeats and Eliot bibliographies, I would submit that the last statement is statistically wrong.

2011. LUCY, SEÁN: *T. S. Eliot and the Idea of Tradition.* London: Cohen & West, 1960. xiii, 222 p.
Passim (see index).

2012. MCCUTCHION, DAVID: "Yeats, Eliot and Personality," *Quest* [Bombay], #50 (Monsoon 1966), 13-24.
Yeats's and Eliot's personalities and their ideas of personality compared.

2013. Ó MUIRÍ, PÁDRAIG S.: "Filíocht agus reiligiún. Yeats agus Eliot: Comparáid" [Poetry and religion . . .], *Feasta*, 18:4 (July 1965), 7-9.

2014. SMIDT, KRISTIAN: "T. S. Eliot and W. B. Yeats," *Revue des langues vivantes*, 31:6 (1965), 555-67.
Both poets criticized each other; each objected to the other's style and philosophy. Discusses Yeats's influence on Eliot's poetry, plays, and criticism. A revised version of the article appears in Smidt, *The Importance of Recognition: Six Chapters on T. S. Eliot.* Tromsø: Norbye, 1973. 95 p. (pp. 81-95).

2015. SMITH, GROVER: *T. S. Eliot's Poetry and Plays: A Study in Sources and Meaning.* Chicago: U of Chicago Press, 1965 [1956]. xii, 342 p. (Phoenix Books. P54.)
Detects several Yeats echoes in Eliot's poetry (see index).

2016. UNGER, LEONARD: *T. S. Eliot: Moments and Patterns.* Minneapolis: U of Minnesota Press, 1966. vii, 196 p. (Minnesota Paperbacks. MP3.)
Some notes concerning Yeats's and Eliot's poetry, *passim* (see index).

2017. WATTS, HAROLD H.: "The Tragic Hero in Eliot and Yeats," *Centennial R*, 13:1 (Winter 1969), 84-100.
Discusses the "anti-anti-heroes" in Eliot's and Yeats's plays, who share an important quality: "They repudiate the world and its autocratic control over modern persons."

2017a. WHITE, GINA: "Modes of Being in Yeats and Eliot," *Modern Occasions*, 1:2 (Winter 1971), 227-37.
Sexuality and the self in the poetry of Yeats and Eliot.

See also J1097, 1108, 1233, 1308, 1380, 1485, 1738, 1791, 1793, 1836, 1874, 1936, 1937, 2111, 2165, 2279, 2415, 2830, 2862, 2877, 2894, 2895, 2906, 2926, 3096, 3115, 3125, 3231, 3438, 3469, 3578, 3588, 3678, 3798, 3868, 4112, 4129, 4133, 4158, 4161.

English: Ford Madox Ford

2018. Hueffer, Ford Madox [later FORD, FORD MADOX]: *Collected Poems*. London: Goschen, 1914. 227 p.
　　In the preface, Ford notes his indebtedness to Yeats and apologizes for having once thought that Yeats was merely a "literary" poet (pp. 25-27).

English: E. M. Forster

See J1623.

English: Sir James George Frazer

2019. VICKERY, JOHN B.: *The Literary Impact of "The Golden Bough."* Princeton: Princeton UP, 1973. ix, 435 p.
　　Incorporates "*The Golden Bough* and Modern Poetry," *JAAC*, 15:3 (Mar 1957), 271-88. "William Butler Yeats: The Tragic Hero as Dying God," 179-232, and *passim* (see index); particularly on the poetry.

See also J1849, 2678.

English: Edward Gibbon

See J3185.

English: Edmund Gosse

See J3984a.

English: R. B. Cunninghame Graham

2020. WATTS, C. T.: "A Letter from W. B. Yeats to R. B. Cunninghame Graham," *RES*, 18:71 (Aug 1967), 292-93.

English: Robert Graves

2021. WILSON, COLIN: "Some Notes on Graves's Prose," *Shenandoah*, 13:2 (Winter 1962), 55-62.
　　Largely on the question of why Graves doesn't like Yeats.

See also J1758, 3120.

English: Althea Gyles

See J651.

English: Arthur Hallam

See J4100.

English: Thomas Hardy

2022. DAVIE, DONALD: *Thomas Hardy and British Poetry*. London: Routledge & Kegan Paul, 1973. viii, 192 p.
　　Several notes comparing Hardy and Yeats, *passim* (see index). See also the anonymous review, "The Choice of Yeats or Hardy," *TLS*, 72:3723 (13 July 1973), 793-94, which refers to the influence of Yeats on Philip Larkin.

2023. Hueffer, Ford Maddox [sic, later FORD, FORD MADOX]: "The Poet's
Eye. III," New Freewoman, 1:7 (15 Sept 1913), 126-27.
Compares the poetry of Yeats and Hardy.

See also J2779.

English: William Ernest Henley

2023a. FLORA, JOSEPH M.: William Ernest Henley. NY: Twayne, 1970. 171 p.
(Twayne's English Authors Series. 107.)
Scattered notes on Yeats and Henley, passim (see index).

2023b. GUILLAUME, ANDRÉ: William Ernest Henley, 1849-1903, et son groupe.
Thesis, University of Paris III, 1972. xiii, 815 p.
Several notes on Yeats and Henley, passim (see index). Also published
as °William Ernest Henley et son groupe: Néo-romantisme et imperial-
isme à la fin du XIXe siècle. Paris: Klincksieck, 1973.

English: George Herbert

See J1988, 3049.

English: Gerard Manley Hopkins

2024. HOWARTH, R. G.: "Yeats and Hopkins," N&Q, 188:10 (19 May 1945),
202-4.
Yeats's indebtedness to Hopkins's "sprung rhythm."

See also J557, 2030, 2901.

English: W. T. Horton

See J2058.

English: A. E. Housman

See J1108, 5009.

English: T. E. Hulme

See J1836, 2874.

English: Aldous Huxley

See J2165, 3120.

English: Lionel Johnson

2025. °LHENRY-EVANS, ODETTE: "Lionel Johnson, 1867-1902: Etude biographique et critique," Doctorat de l'Université thesis (Lettres), U of Lille,
1964. 315 p.

2026. MILLAR, DAVID HASWELL: "Lionel Johnson, 1867-1902: A Biographical
and Critical Study," M.A. thesis, Queen's U, Belfast, 1947. iv, 228 p.
See pp. 47-82 and passim for a discussion of literary and biographical
relations between Johnson and Yeats (via the Rhymers' Club and the
Irish literary revival).

2027. PATRICK, ARTHUR W.: Lionel Johnson (1867-1902), poète et critique.
Paris: Rodstein, 1939. 254 p.
"La renaissance littéraire irlandaise," 53-64; on Johnson's involve-
ment in the Irish literary revival and Yeats's influence on him.

2028. ROGERS, JOHN ELTON: "Lionel Johnson: A Reassessment of His Work," M.A. thesis, U of Manchester, 1967. ii, 281 p.
   Contains a chapter on "Johnson, the Celt," 228-68, and numerous references to Yeats.

See also J1110, 1500, 1741, 2102, 2420, 4130, 5775.

English: Samuel Johnson

See J3185.

English: Ben Jonson

See J1708, 1933.

English: John Keats

2029. JONES, JAMES LAND: "Keats and Yeats: 'Artificers of the Great Moment,'" *XUS*, 4:2 (May 1965), 125-50.
   The early Yeats (before 1916) was closer to Shelley, the later closer to Keats.

2030. ————: "Keats and the Last Romantics: Hopkins and Yeats," °Ph.D. thesis, Tulane U, 1969. 301 p. (*DA*, 30:6 [Dec 1969], 2530A.)

2031. MAGAW, MALCOLM: "Yeats and Keats: The Poetics of Romanticism," *Bucknell R*, 13:3 (Dec 1965), 87-96.

See also J1088, 1112, 1738, 1977, 2086, 2420, 2694, 2982, 3180, 3205, 3286.

English: John Keble

See J3940a.

English: Rudyard Kipling

See J1499.

English: Charles Lamb

See J3185.

English: W. S. Landor

2032. LOGAN, JAMES V., JOHN E. JORDAN, and NORTHROP FRYE (eds): *Some British Romantics: A Collection of Essays*. Columbus: Ohio State UP, 1966. vii, 343 p.
   Vivian Mercier: "The Future of Landor Criticism," 41-85; on Yeats and Landor, pp. 45-47.

See also J3263.

English: Philip Larkin

2033. LARKIN, PHILIP: *The North Ship*. London: Faber & Faber, 1966 [1945]. 48 p.
   In the introduction, pp. 7-10 (not in the first edition), Larkin notes his indebtedness to Yeats.

2033a. WEATHERHEAD, A. KINGSLEY: "Philip Larkin of England," *ELH*, 38:4 (Dec 1971), 616-30.
   Contains notes on Yeats's influence on Larkin.

See also J2022.

English: D. H. Lawrence

2034. BRUNNER, KARL, HERBERT KOZIOL, and SIEGFRIED KORNINGER (eds):
*Anglistische Studien: Festschrift zum 70. Geburtstag von Professor Fried-
rich Wild*. Wien: Braumüller, 1958. x, 249 p. (Wiener Beiträge zur engli-
schen Philologie. 66.)
　　Franz Stanzel: "G. M. Hopkins, W. B. Yeats, D. H. Lawrence und die
　　Spontaneität der Dichtung," 179–93. Mythology and the theory of self
　　and anti-self helped Yeats to establish a distance between reality
　　and poetry. In this he differs from Lawrence's "expressionism."
　　Stanzel does not establish a meaningful relation between Yeats and
　　Hopkins.

2034a. GILBERT, SANDRA M.: *Acts of Attention: The Poems of D. H. Lawrence*.
Ithaca: Cornell UP, 1972. xv, 329 p.
　　Yeats is mentioned *passim* (see index).

2035. NEWMAN, PAUL B.: "The Natural Aristocrat in Letters," *UKCR*, 31:1
(Oct 1964), 23–31.
　　On Lawrence's *Women in Love*, frequently invoking Yeats in support of
　　the argument.

See also J1380, 1624, 1791, 1921, 2134a, 2618, 3231, 3591.

English: C. S. Lewis

2036. LEWIS, CLIVE STAPLES: *Narrative Poems*. Edited by Walter Hooper.
London: Bles, 1969. xiv, 178 p.
　　"Dymer," first published in 1926 under the pseudonym Clive Hamilton,
　　contains "Preface by the Author to the 1950 Edition," pp. 3–6, in
　　which Lewis admits certain debts to Yeats and explains that the
　　Magician in Canto VI owes something to the "physical appearance" of
　　Yeats.

English: Wyndham Lewis

See J1380, 4100.

English: John Locke

See J3048.

English: Hugh MacDiarmid

See J5274.

English: Arthur Machen

2036a. PETERSEN, KARL MARIUS: "Arthur Machen and the Celtic Renaissance in
Wales," °Ph.D. thesis, Louisiana State U, 1973. 222 p. (*DA*, 34:6 [Dec 1973],
3426A–27A.)
　　Discusses Yeats's influence on Machen.

English: Fiona Macleod

See J2912.

English: Louis MacNeice

2036b. SMITH, ELTON EDWARD: *Louis MacNeice*. NY: Twayne, 1970. 232 p. (Twayne's English Authors Series. 99.)
　　See pp. 97-104 and *passim* (see index).

See also J5940 (#1).

English: James Macpherson

See J2912.

English: John Masefield

2037. DREW, FRASER: "The Irish Allegiances of an English Laureate: John Masefield and Ireland," *Éire-Ireland*, 3:4 (Winter 1968), 24-34.
　　Masefield and Synge, Masefield and Yeats.

2038. MASEFIELD, JOHN: *So Long to Learn*. NY: Macmillan, 1952. iv, 181 p.
　　Yeats's influence on Masefield and some reminiscences, pp. 93-110.

See also J1987.

English: MacGregor Mathers

2038a. FENNELLY, LAURENCE WILLIAM: "S. L. Macgregor Mathers and the Fiction of W. B. Yeats," °Ph.D. thesis, Florida State U, 1973. 130 p. (*DA*, 34:6 [Dec 1973], 3389A.)
　　Discusses Yeats's occult interests, his involvement in the Golden Dawn, and the following texts: "Rosa Alchemica," *The Speckled Bird*, and *A Vision*.

See also J1867.

English: Metaphysical Poetry

See J1241, 1562, 1988, 2585, 2708, and individual metaphysical poets.

English: J. S. Mill

See J3984a.

English: John Milton

2039. UNGER, LEONARD: "Yeats and Milton," *SAQ*, 61:2 (Spring 1962), 197-212.
　　The influence of *Areopagitica* on Yeats's prose style and poetic theories; Miltonic imagery in Yeats's poetry, particularly in "The Second Coming."

See also J1088, 1102, 1979, 3117.

English: T. Sturge Moore

2040. EASTON, MALCOLM: "T. Sturge Moore and W. B. Yeats," *Apollo*, #92 (Oct 1970), 298-300.
　　Sturge Moore's covers for Yeats's books and Yeats's estimate of them.

2041. ———— (ed): *T. Sturge Moore (1870-1944): Contributions to the Art of the Book & Collaboration with Yeats*. Catalogue of an exhibition compiled and edited together with an introduction by Malcolm Easton. Hull: U of Hull, 1970. 55 p.

"Introduction: The Yeats Covers in Their Context," 7-13; discusses the Moore-Yeats relationship and Moore's book covers.

2042. EASTON, MALCOLM: "Thomas Sturge Moore: Wood-Engraver," *Private Library*, 4:1 (Spring 1971), 24-37.

2043. WINTERS, YVOR: "T. Sturge Moore," *Hound & Horn*, 6:3 (Apr-June 1933), 534-45.
Includes frequent comparisons with Yeats ("Mr. Moore is a greater poet than Mr. Yeats"). See answer by Theodore Spencer, J1999. Winters refers to the quarrel in his *In Defense of Reason* [. . .]. Denver: Swallow, 1947. vii, 611 p., pp. 490-92.

See also J677, 1699, 1939, 3111, 4005, 4113, 4214, 5456-69 and note.

English: Henry More

See J4109.

English: William Morris

2044. FAULKNER, PETER: *William Morris and W. B. Yeats*. Dublin: Dolmen Press, 1962. 31 p.
See also "W. B. Yeats and William Morris," *Threshold*, 4:1 (Spring-Summer 1960), 18-27; "Morris and Yeats," *J of the William Morris Society*, 1:3 (Summer 1963), 19-23. Discusses biographical connections; Morris's influence on Yeats as poet, "generous personality," and social critic; and Yeats's assessment of Morris's work.
Reviews:
1. Bruce Arnold, *Dubliner*, #5 (Sept-Oct 1962), 61-62.
2. Denis Donoghue, "Countries of the Mind," *Guardian*, #36241 (11 Jan 1963), 5.
3. Ian Fletcher, *MLR*, 58:4 (Oct 1963), 626.

2044a. GRENNAN, MARGARET R.: *William Morris: Medievalist and Revolutionary*. NY: Russell & Russell, 1970 [1945]. xi, 173 p.
See pp. 108-9, 118, 129, 151-52.

2045. HOARE, DOROTHY MACKENZIE: *The Works of Morris and of Yeats in Relation to Early Saga Literature*. NY: Russell & Russell, 1971 [1937]. x, 179 p.
Based on a Ph.D. thesis, Cambridge U, 1930. v, 180, cxvii p. Contains chapters on "The Irish Movement" (pp. 77-110, with sections "The Interest in the Past" [Moore, Martyn, Lady Gregory], "The Poetry of Yeats," "The Development of the Romantic Attitude to the Past--Fiona Macleod, Lady Gregory, Synge") and on "The Dreamer in Contact with Irish Saga" (pp. 111-39, with sections "Yeats," the *Deirdre* versions of AE, Yeats, Synge, and Stephens, and "James Stephens: The Corrective to the Romantic Attitude"). Concludes that for Morris and for the early Yeats the "sagas offered both liberation and escape." The escape was twofold: "First, from life to the sagas; and secondly, from the actuality which the sagas reveal to the dreaming and stilled refuge, with all harshness eliminated, which they made of them" (p. 143).
Reviews:
1. Anon., *N&Q*, 173:[] (24 July 1937), 72.
2. Edith C. Batho, *MLR*, 33:2 (Apr 1938), 289-90.
3. M. L. Cazamian, *EA*, 2:1 (Jan-Mar 1938), 58.
4. A[ustin] C[larke], *Dublin Mag*, 12:4 (Oct-Dec 1937), 64-65.

5. A[odh] DeB[lacam], "Yeats a 'Minor Poet'? . . . ," *Irish Press*, 7: 135 (8 June 1937), 7. Correspondence by Sean O Faolain, :136 (9 June 1937), 8.

6. I. K., "Morris and Yeats and Early Saga Literature," *Contemporary R*, 152:862 (Oct 1937), 508-9.

7. [C. S. Lewis], "The Sagas and Modern Life: Morris, Mr. Yeats, and the Originals," *TLS*, 36:1843 (29 May 1937), 409.

8. J. M. N., "Sagas and the Poets," *Time and Tide*, 18:39 (25 Sept 1937), 1271.

9. Margaret Schlauch, *MP*, 35:4 (May 1938), 469-70.

10. J. A. Smith, *Medium Aevum*, 8:3 (Oct 1939), 240-41.

2046. MCALINDON, T.: "The Idea of Byzantium in William Morris and W. B. Yeats," *MP*, 64:4 (May 1967), 307-19.
    Morris was one of the influences on Yeats's idea of Byzantium. Discusses Yeats's cultural theories (including *A Vision*), not so much the Byzantium poems.

2047. TALBOT, NORMAN: "Women and Goddesses in the Romances of William Morris," *Southern R* [Adelaide], 3:4 (1969), 339-57.

2048. THOMPSON, EDWARD PALMER: *William Morris: Romantic to Revolutionary*. London: Lawrence & Wishart, 1955. 908 p.
    See pp. 643-44 and *passim* (see index).

See also J1103, 1933, 2419, 2420, 4076a.

English: Edwin Muir

See J1758, 2926.

English: Alfred Noyes

2049. SAUL, GEORGE BRANDON: "Yeats, Noyes, and Day Lewis," *N&Q*, 195:12 (10 June 1950), 258.
    A Yeats echo in a Noyes poem and a Day Lewis echo in Yeats's "Vacillation." See correction by Alfred Noyes, :15 (22 July 1950), 309.

English: Arthur O'Shaughnessy

See J2983, 3048.

English: Wilfred Owen

2050. COHEN, JOSEPH: "In Memory of W. B. Yeats—and Wilfred Owen," *JEGP*, 58:4 (Oct 1959), 637-49.
    Author's correction, 59:1 (Jan 1960), 171. Yeats excluded Owen from the *Oxford Book of Modern Verse* because his work did not reflect "the joy of battle."

2051. JOHNSTON, JOHN HUBERT: *English Poetry of the First World War: A Study in the Evolution of Lyric and Narrative Form*. Princeton: Princeton UP, 1964. xvi, 354 p.
    Some notes on Yeats and Owen, *passim* (see index).

2052. PESCHMANN, HERMANN: "Yeats and the Poetry of War," *English*, 15:89 (Summer 1965), 181-84.
    When Yeats excluded Owen from the *Oxford Book of Modern Verse*, he betrayed a lack of insight into the "*raison d'être* of the new verse."

2053. STALLWORTHY, JON: "W. B. Yeats and Wilfred Owen," *CQ*, 11:3 (Autumn 1969), 199-214.
   On Yeats echoes in Owen's poetry and Yeats's failure to appreciate Owen's work. Maintains that Owen's work conforms in several important respects to Yeats's idea of poetry and implies that Yeats forsook his own convictions when he rejected it.

2053a. WHITE, GERTRUDE M.: *Wilfred Owen*. NY: Twayne, 1969. 156 p. (Twayne's English Authors Series. 86.)
   "Yeats and *The Oxford Book of Modern Verse*," 116-21, and *passim*.

See also J1220, 3230.

English: Samuel Palmer

See J1076.

English: Walter Pater

2054. FLETCHER, IAIN: "Leda and St. Anne," *Listener*, 57:1456 (21 Feb 1957), 305-7.
   Pater's influence on Yeats and Yeats's interpretation of Pater in the *Oxford Book of Modern Verse*.

2055. NATHAN, LEONARD P. [LEONARD E.?]: "W. B. Yeats's Experiments with an Influence," *VS*, 6:1 (Sept 1962), 66-74.
   Pater's influence on Yeats's view of literature.

See also J1072, 1101, 1688, 1716a, 1836, 2277, 4096, 4130.

English: Frederick York Powell

See J1994, 2277.

English: Pre-Raphaelitism

2056. COUGHLAN, SISTER JEREMY: "The Pre-Paphaelite Aesthetic and the Poetry of Christina Rossetti, William Morris, and William Butler Yeats," Ph.D. thesis, U of Minnesota, 1967. ii, 206 p. (*DA*, 28:2 [Aug 1967], 622A-23A.)
   "Pre-Raphaelitism in the Poetry of William Butler Yeats," 163-98.

2057. HUNT, JOHN DIXON: *The Pre-Raphaelite Imagination, 1848-1900*. Lincoln: U of Nebraska Press, 1968. xv, 262 p.
   Passim (see index).

2058. PETERS, ROBERT LOUIS: "The Poetry of the 1890's: Its Relation to the Several Arts," Ph.D. thesis, U of Wisconsin, 1952. ix, 516 p.
   Pre-Raphaelite elements in Yeats's poetry, pp. 56-62; the influence of Blake's and Horton's drawings on Yeats's poetry, pp. 115-31; note on "The Man Who Dreamed of Faeryland," pp. 155-58.

See also J1855.

English: James Reeves

2059. REEVES, JAMES: "Yeats and the Muses," *Time and Tide*, 39:20 (17 May 1958), 613.
   Quotes from two letters written by Yeats to Reeves, in which Yeats refuses the inclusion of his poems in the *Oxford Book of Modern Verse*.

English: Rhymers' Club

2060. BECKSON, KARL: "Yeats and the Rhymers' Club," *Yeats Studies*, #1
(Bealtaine 1971), 20–41.
    What the Rhymers' Club meant to Yeats and vice versa.

See also the index of institutions for further material.

English: Dorothy M. Richardson

2061. ROSE, SHIRLEY: "Dorothy Richardson Recalls Yeats," *Éire-Ireland*, 7:
1 (Spring 1972), 96–102.
    Discusses the material listed in J775.

English: Charles Ricketts

2062. FLETCHER, IFAN KYRLE: "Charles Ricketts and the Theatre," *Theatre
Notebook*, 22:1 (Autumn 1967), 6–23.
    Yeats was indirectly responsible for Ricketts's career as a stage
    designer. Ricketts designed three plays for him.

See also J1136.

English: Dante Gabriel Rossetti

See J1716a, 2420.

English: Margot Ruddock

See J118, 2819, 5532–41 and note.

English: Bertrand Russell

See J1934.

English: William Shakespeare

2063. DESAI, RUPIN WALTER: *Yeats's Shakespeare*. Evanston: Northwestern UP,
1971. xxiv, 280 p.
    Based on "Yeats and Shakespeare," Ph.D. thesis, Northwestern U, 1968.
    iv, 420 p. (*DA*, 29:7 [Jan 1969], 2255A–56A). Surveys Shakespeare pro-
    ductions that Yeats saw or may have seen and his Shakespeare criti-
    cism; discusses Shakespeare's place in *A Vision* and Shakespeare echoes
    in Yeats's plays. Valuable.

2064. RAM, ALUR JANKI: "Yeats on Shakespeare," *Phoenix* [Seoul], 11 (1967),
53–71.
    Incorporates "Yeats and Shakespeare's Tragic Vision," *English Miscel-
    lany* [Delhi], #3 (1965), 103–18, where the author's name is spelled
    Alur Janaki Ram. On Shakespeare in Yeats's theory of tragedy and
    Shakespearean echoes in Yeats's poetry.

2065. SEN, TARAKNATH (ed): *Shakespeare Commemoration Volume*. Calcutta:
Presidency College, Department of English, 1966. xii, 382 p.
    Gayatri Chakravorty [Spivak]: "Shakespeare in Yeats's *Last Poems*,"
    243–84.

2066. UNGER, LEONARD: "Yeats and *Hamlet*," *Southern R*, 6:3 (Summer 1970),
698–709.
    Hamlet as a source for "That the Night Come."

2067. URE, PETER: *W. B. Yeats and the Shakespearian Moment: On W. B. Yeats's Attitude towards Shakespeare as Revealed in His Criticism and in His Work for the Theatre*. A lecture delivered at Queen's University, Belfast, on 27 April 1966. Belfast: Institute of Irish Studies, 1969. 25 p.

Mainly on the concept of reverie as Yeats saw it in Shakespeare and as it appears in his own plays. Includes a discussion of Yeats's idea of unity of being.

Reviews:

1. Augustine Martin, *Studies*, 60:237 (Spring 1971), 98-102.

2067a. WEISS, THEODORE: *The Breath of Clowns and Kings: Shakespeare's Early Comedies and Histories*. London: Chatto & Windus, 1971. vii, 339 p.

See pp. 205-8 and *passim* (see index).

See also J1034, 1112, 1162 (#7), 1243, 1726, 1883, 1933, 2724, 2781, 3096, 3185, 3224, 3281a, 3585, 4175.

English: William Sharp (Fiona Macleod)

2068. ALAYA, FLAVIA: *William Sharp--"Fiona Macleod": 1855-1905*. Cambridge, Mass.: Harvard UP, 1970. xiv, 261 p.

Passim (see index).

2069. HALLORAN, WILLIAM F.: "W. B. Yeats and William Sharp: The Archer Vision," *ELN*, 6:4 (June 1969), 273-80.

Yeats's belief in psychic phenomena was undermined by a hoax perpetrated by William Sharp / Fiona Macleod.

See also J2912.

English: G. B. Shaw

2070. ADAMS, ELSIE BONITA: *Bernard Shaw and the Aesthetes*. Columbus: Ohio State UP, 1972. xxv, 193 p.

Notes on Yeats, *passim*, especially pp. 144-46 (a comparison of Shaw's *As Far as Thoughts Can Reach* with "Sailing to Byzantium").

2071. CARY, ELIZABETH LUTHER: "Apostles of the New Drama," *Lamp*, 27:6 (Jan 1904), 593-98.

Yeats and Shaw compared.

2072. CROMPTON, LOUIS: *Shaw the Dramatist*. Lincoln: U of Nebraska Press, 1969. xi, 261 p.

See pp. 29-44 for Shaw's reaction to Yeats and his use of *The Land of Heart's Desire* in *Candida*.

2072a. GIBBS, A. M.: "Yeats, Shaw, and Unity of Culture," *Southern R* [Adelaide], 6:3 (1973), 189-203.

2073. °SETHNA, K. D.: "Shaw and Yeats," *Mother India*, 2:11 (Nov 1950), 6-7.

2074. SIDNELL, MICHAEL J.: "John Bull's Other Island: Yeats and Shaw," *MD*, 11:3 (Dec 1968), 245-51.

2075. WILSON, COLIN: *Bernard Shaw: A Reassessment*. London: Hutchinson, 1969. xiv, 306 p.

On Shaw and Yeats, pp. 136-39 and *passim* (see index). Thinks that Marchbanks in *Candida* is modeled on Yeats.

2075a. WINSTEN, STEPHEN: *Shaw's Corner*. London: Hutchinson, 1952. 238 p.

Shaw on Yeats, pp. 167-68.

See also J561 (review #33), 947, 1018, 1243, 1934, 3446, 3884, 4177, 4179, 6321.

English: Percy Bysshe Shelley

2076. BERNSTEIN, HELMUT: "Shelleys Dichtung im Lichte der Kritik nach-viktorianischer Dichter," Dr. phil. thesis, U of Frankfurt, 1954. iii, 130 p.
"Symbolsistische [*sic*] Kritik: W. B. Yeats," 43-61. Negligible.

2077. BLOOM, HAROLD: *Shelley's Mythmaking.* New Haven: Yale UP, 1959. viii, 279 p. (Yale Studies in English. 141.)
Passim (see index).

2078. ————: *The Visionary Company: A Reading of English Romantic Poetry.* Garden City: Doubleday, 1961. xvii, 460 p.
See pp. 229-30, 322-26, and *passim.*

2079. BORNSTEIN, GEORGE JAY: *Yeats and Shelley.* Chicago: U of Chicago Press, 1970. xv, 239 p.
Based on "The Surfeited Alastor: William Butler Yeats's Changing Relation to Percy Bysshe Shelley," Ph.D. thesis, Princeton U, 1966. viii, 321 p. (*DA*, 27:11 [May 1967], 3832A-33A). A more balanced assessment than most of the items listed in this section.
Reviews:
1. Terence Brown, *Irish UR*, 1:2 (Spring 1971), 276-78.
2. Gerald L. Bruns, *Spirit*, 38:4 (Winter 1972), 41-45.
3. Richard J. Finneran, "Progress Report on the Yeats Industry," *JML*, 3:1 (Feb 1973), 129-33.
4. John S. Kelly, "Pathways," *Irish Press*, 40:278 (21 Nov 1970), 12.
5. Timothy Webb, *RES*, 22:87 (Aug 1971), 376-78.

2079a. BUTTER, PETER H.: *Shelley's Idols of the Cave.* Edinburgh: Edinburgh UP, 1954. vii, 228 p. (Edinburgh U Publications. Language & Literature. 7.)
Scattered notes, *passim* (see index).

2080. DALSIMER, ADELE MINTZ: "The Unappeasable Shadow: Shelley's Influence on Yeats," °Ph.D. thesis, Yale U, 1971. 270 p. (*DA*, 32:12 [June 1972], 6969A-70A.)

2080a. ————: "My Chief of Men: Yeats's Juvenilia and Shelley's *Alastor*," *Éire-Ireland*, 8:2 (Summer 1973), 71-90.
Discusses *The Island of Statues, The Seeker, Mosada,* and "The Two Titans."

2081. DUERKSEN, ROLAND A.: *Shelleyan Ideas in Victorian Literature.* The Hague: Mouton, 1966. 208 p. (Studies in English Literature. 12.)
See pp. 153-60, 200-201.

2082. GRIGSON, GEOFFREY (ed): *The Mint: A Miscellany of Literature, Art, and Criticism.* London: Routledge, 1946. xii, 220 p.
H. W. Häusermann: "W. B. Yeats's Idea of Shelley," 179-94.

2083. HOLLANDER, JOHN (ed): *Modern Poetry: Essays in Criticism.* London: Oxford UP, 1968. ix, 520 p.
Harold Bloom: "Yeats and the Romantics," 501-20.

2084. MERRITT, H. C.: "Shelley's Influence on Yeats," *Yearbook of English Studies*, 1 (1971), 175-84.
The development of Yeats's estimate of Shelley and the influence of Shelley's symbols on Yeats's poetry.

2085. NORMAN, SYLVA: "Twentieth-Century Theories of Shelley," *TSLL*, 9:2 (Summer 1967), 223-37.

2086. PEARCE, DONALD: "Yeats and the Romantics," *Shenandoah*, 8:2 (Spring 1957), 40-57.
 Shelley's skylark, Keats's nightingale, and Yeats's golden bird. Comments on both Byzantium poems and on "Coole Park 1929."

2087. °PURDY, STROTHER R.: "Yeats and Shelley," M.A. thesis, Columbia U, 1955. 118 p.

2088. SCHARFE, DONALD HOWARD: "W. B. Yeats' Interpretation of Shelley and Its Influence on His Writing," Honors thesis, Harvard U, 1961. i, 39 p.

See also J1072, 1088, 1102, 1161 (#5), 1243, 1398, 1839a, 1882, 2029, 2420, 2952, 2957, 2982, 2985, 3054, 3234, 3237, 3239, 3313, 4393.

English: Edith Sitwell

See J2111, 2747.

English: Stephen Spender

See J1936, 3588, 3591a, 3979, 5940 (#1).

English: Edmund Spenser

2089. REANEY, JAMES: "The Influence of Spenser on Yeats," Ph.D. thesis, U of Toronto, 1958. Abstract (6 p.) plus iii, 281 p.
 "The early influence of Spenser is . . . seen to be related to Yeats' failure to understand Spenser. As Yeats developed, certain things he says about Spenser after 1906 imply that he no longer regards the Elizabethan poet as having an imperfect, divided genius, but as a poet who successfully fused . . . aesthetics and morality into an imaginative synthesis. This thesis explores both these early and late attitudes to Spenser as well as the area between them" (abstract).

See also J1101, 1933, 2724, 5321.

English: Frank Pearce Sturm

See J814.

English: Algernon Charles Swinburne

See J3286.

English: Arthur Symons

2089a. ELLMANN, RICHARD: *Golden Codgers: Biographical Speculations*. London: Oxford UP, 1973. xi, 193 p.
 "Discovering Symbolism," 101-12; on Yeats and Symons. See also J2095.

2090. LHOMBREAUD, ROGER: *Arthur Symons: A Critical Biography*. London: Unicorn Press, 1963. xii, 333 p.
 Passim (see index).

2090a. MUNRO, JOHN M.: "Arthur Symons, 'The Symphony of Snakes,' and the Development of the Romantic Image," *ELT*, 7:3 (1964), 143-45.
 Notes Yeats's influence on Symons. Commentary by Edward Baugh and Munro, :4 (1964), 228-30.

2091. ————: "Arthur Symons and W. B. Yeats: The Quest for Compromise," *Dalhousie R*, 45:2 (Summer 1965), 137-52.

2092. ————: *Arthur Symons*. NY: Twayne, 1969. 174 p. (Twayne's English Authors Series. 76.)

Passim, especially pp. 56-81 on the mutual influence of Yeats-Symons. Concludes that Symons owes more to Yeats than vice versa. Prints a letter from Mrs. Rhoda Symons to Yeats, 153-54.

2093. STANFORD, DEREK: "Arthur Symons as a Literary Critic (1865-1945): A Centenary Assessment," *QQ*, 72:3 (Autumn 1965), 533-41.

Reprinted in *Contemporary R*, 207:1197 (Oct 1965), 210-16; :1198 (Nov 1965), 265-68; and as "Arthur Symons and Modern Poetics," *Southern R*, 2:2 (Spring 1966), 347-53. (Surely a waste of space.) "It sometimes appears as if they [Yeats and Symons] were co-authors of each other's books [of criticism]."

2094. STERN, CAROL SIMPSON: "Arthur Symons's Literary Relationships, 1882-1900: Some Origins of the Symbolist Movement," °Ph.D. thesis, Northwestern U, 1968. 271 p. (*DA*, 29:7 [Jan 1969], 2282A-83A.)

2095. SYMONS, ARTHUR: *The Symbolist Movement in Literature*. With an introduction by Richard Ellmann. NY: Dutton, 1958 [1899]. xxi, 164 p. (Dutton Paperback. D21.)

Ellmann's introduction (pp. vii-xvi) mentions Yeats *passim*. Symons dedicated the book to Yeats in a two-page appreciation.

2096. WILDI, MAX: *Arthur Symons als Kritiker der Literatur*. Heidelberg: Winter, 1929. 145 p. (Anglistische Forschungen. 67.)

Passim, especially pp. 51-60.

2097. WITT, MARION: "A Note on Yeats and Symons," *N&Q*, os 205 / ns 7:12 (Dec 1960), 467-69.

Symons echoes in several Yeats poems.

See also J1836, 1882, 1939, 2102, 2686, 4100, 4130.

English: Thomas Taylor

2098. TAYLOR, THOMAS: *Thomas Taylor the Platonist: Selected Writings*. Edited with introductions by Kathleen Raine and George Mills Harper. Princeton: Princeton UP, 1969. xiii, 544 p. (Bollingen Series. 88.)

Passim (see index).

English: Alfred Lord Tennyson

2099. GLASSER, MARVIN: "The Early Poetry of Tennyson and Yeats: A Comparative Study," Ph.D. thesis, New York U, 1962. v, 227 p. (*DA*, 24:10 [Apr 1964], 4174.)

See also J2420, 2425 (review #2), 2694, 2983, 2994.

English: Dylan Thomas

2099a. ASTLEY, RUSSELL: "Stations of the Breath: End Rhyme in the Verse of Dylan Thomas," *PMLA*, 84:6 (Oct 1969), 1595-605.

Involves frequent comparisons with Yeats.

See also J1220, 1485, 1602, 2951, 4169.

English: Francis Thompson

2100. DANCHIN, PIERRE: *Francis Thompson: La vie et l'oeuvre d'un poète*. Paris: Nizet, 1959. 554 p.

See pp. 433-34 and *passim* (see index).

English: W. J. Turner

2101. HÄUSERMANN, H. W.: "W. B. Yeats and W. J. Turner, 1935-1937 (With Unpublished Letters)," *ES*, 40:4 (Aug 1959), 233-41; 41:4 (Aug 1960), 241-53.
    Discusses the collaboration on the *Oxford Book of Modern Verse*, *The Ten Principal Upanishads*, the broadsides, and the poetry broadcasts.

English: Beatrice and Sidney Webb

See J1934.

English: Dorothy Wellesley

2101a. O'SHEA, EDWARD: "Yeats as Editor: Dorothy Wellesley's *Selections*," *ELN*, 11:2 (Dec 1973), 112-18.
    Yeats's MS. annotations to, and changes in, DW's *Poems of Ten Years*.

See also J1089, 2818, 4212, 5398-426 and note.

English: H. G. Wells

See J1834.

English: Alfred North Whitehead

See J1136a.

English: Oscar Wilde

2102. CHARLESWORTH, BARBARA: *Dark Passages: The Decadent Consciousness in Victorian Literature*. Madison: U of Wisconsin Press, 1965. xvi, 155 p.
    On Yeats and Wilde, Lionel Johnson, and Symons, *passim* (see index).

2103. KORNINGER, SIEGFRIED (ed): *Studies in English Language and Literature Presented to Professor Dr. Karl Brunner on the Occasion of His Seventieth Birthday*. Wien: Braumüller, 1957. x, 290 p. (Wiener Beiträge zur englischen Philologie. 65.)
    Rudolf Stamm: "W. B. Yeats und Oscar Wildes 'Ballad of Reading Gaol,'" 210-19. An English version of this article appears in J3248. Yeats's cuts in Wilde's poem (as printed in the *Oxford Book of Modern Verse*) improve it considerably, but then it is no longer a poem by Wilde.

2104. RHYNEHART, J. G.: "Wilde's Comments on Early Works of W. B. Yeats," *Irish Book*, 1:4 (Spring 1962), 102-4.

See also J1243, 1716a, 1836, 1874, 1934, 2277, 3248, 3730, 3779, 4576.

English: Charles Williams

See J2747.

English: Virginia Woolf

See J1791.

English: William Wordsworth

2105. PERKINS, DAVID: *The Quest for Permanence: The Symbolism of Wordsworth, Shelley, and Keats*. Cambridge, Mass.: Harvard UP, 1959. xi, 305 p.
    Scattered notes, *passim* (see index).

2106. ———: *Wordsworth and the Poetry of Sincerity*. Cambridge, Mass.: Harvard UP, 1964. xi, 285 p.

Scattered notes, *passim* (see index).

See also J1072, 1136a, 1738, 2691, 2957, 2982, 3003, 3984a.

European Literature

See J1873, 2107-34, 2135-49, 2276-80, 2285-88, 2291-95.

French Literature: General Section

2107. BALAKIAN, ANNA: *The Symbolist Movement: A Critical Appraisal*. NY: Random House, 1967. ix, 209 p. (Studies in Language and Literature. 11.)

On Yeats's "symbolist theater," pp. 148-55 (discusses *Deirdre* and *The Shadowy Waters*); on "Leda and the Swan," the "symbolist masterpiece constructed in the very spirit of Mallarmé's understanding of symbolist technique," 171-73; and *passim* (see index).

2108. BOWRA, CECIL MAURICE: *The Heritage of Symbolism*. London: Macmillan, 1951 [1943]. vii, 232 p.

"William Butler Yeats, 1865-1939," 180-218. On symbolism in Yeats's theory and practice and its indebtedness to French sources, particularly Mallarmé.

Reviews:

1. Anon., "W. B. Yeats and Symbolism," *Poetry R*, 34:2 (Mar-Apr 1943), 126-28.
2. Lawrence Leighton, "Criticism from Oxford," *Kenyon R*, 6:1 (Winter 1944), 146-50. Contends that the Yeats chapter is the weakest in the book.

2109. DAVIS, EDWARD: "A Study of Affinities between W. B. Yeats and French Symbolists," B.Litt. thesis, Oxford U, 1953. i, 196 p.

See also J2118.

2110. GRILL, RICHARD: "Der junge Yeats und der französische Symbolismus," Dr. phil. thesis, U of Freiburg, 1952. vii, 179 p.

Considers the influence of Mallarmé, Verlaine, and Villiers de l'Isle Adam on Yeats's early critical, dramatical, and poetical work.

2111. HASSAN, IHAB H.: "French Symbolism and Modern British Poetry: With Yeats, Eliot, and Edith Sitwell as Indices," Ph.D. thesis, U of Pennsylvania, 1953. vi, 533 p. (*DA*, 13:2 [1953], 232-33.)

"William Butler Yeats," 326-96, and *passim*.

2111a. °KEITNER, WENDY JOAN: "The Early Yeats and the French Symbolists: A Study of the Early Poetic Theory of W. B. Yeats and Its Relation to the French Symbolist Aesthetic," M.A. thesis, Queen's U (Kingston, Ont.), 1971.

2112. KILLEN, A. M.: "Some French Influences in the Works of W. B. Yeats at the End of the Nineteenth Century," *Comparative Literature Studies*, 2:8 (1942), 1-8.

The influence of Sâr Péladan, Villiers de l'Isle Adam, and Mallarmé.

2113. PAULY, MARIE-HÉLÈNE: "W. B. Yeats et les symbolistes français," *Revue de la littérature comparée*, 20:1 (Jan-Mar 1940), 13-33.

2114. STARKIE, ENID: *From Gautier to Eliot: The Influence of France on English Literature, 1851-1939*. London: Hutchinson, 1960. 236 p.

See pp. 115-28 and *passim*.

2115. TEMPLE, RUTH ZABRISKIE: *The Critic's Alchemy: A Study of the Introduction of French Symbolism into England.* New Haven: College and University Press, [1962] [1953]. 345 p.

Scattered notes, *passim* (see index).

See also J1161 (#3), 1162, 1882, 2118, 2131, 2284b, 2420, 4096, 4109, 4114.

French: Honoré de Balzac

2116. BENSON, CARL: "Yeats and Balzac's *Louis Lambert*," *MP*, 49:4 (May 1952), 242-47.

On Yeats's essay "Louis Lambert" (1934) and Balzac's influence on *A Vision*.

2117. FULLWOOD, DAPHNE: "Balzac and Yeats," *Southern R*, 5:3 (July 1969), 935-49.

French: Charles Baudelaire

2118. DAVIS, EDWARD: *Yeats's Early Contacts with French Poetry.* Pretoria: U of South Africa, 1961. 63 p. (Communications of the U of South Africa. C29.)

Neither "Irishness" nor the "mumbo-jumbo of the occultists" (p. 3) contributed significantly to Yeats's poetic development. He was profoundly influenced by Baudelaire, nevertheless highly original. See also J2109.

Reviews:

1. Peter Ure, *N&Q*, os 208 / ns 10:10 (Oct 1963), 400.

2119. °FITZSIMMONS, THOMAS: "Charles Baudelaire: Voyant, and William Butler Yeats: Seer," M.A. thesis, Columbia U, 1952. 64 p.

2120. GLENN, CHARLES LESLIE: "The Lonely Art: A Study of the Theme of Isolation in the Poetry of William Butler Yeats and Charles Baudelaire," Honors thesis, Harvard U, 1959. [45 p.]

French: Ferdinand Brunetière

2121. BARNET, SYLVAN: "W. B. Yeats and Brunetière on Drama," *N&Q*, os 214 / ns 16:7 (July 1969), 255-56.

Some of Yeats's ideas on farce and tragedy can also be found in Brunetière.

French: Albert Camus

See J1788.

French: Paul Claudel

See J2126, 3348.

French: Jean Cocteau

2122. ISKANDAR, FAYEZ: "Yeats and Cocteau: Two Anti-Romanticists," *Cairo Studies in English*, 1963/66, 119-35.

Yeats's solution of the problem of modern verse drama was "aesthetic perfection," whereas Cocteau presented "a 'coarsened' version of poetry where prosaicisms contribute as much to dramatic effect as poeticisms."

French: Gustave Flaubert

2123. BLOCK, HASKELL M.: "Flaubert, Yeats, and the National Library," *MLN*, 67:1 (Jan 1952), 55-56.
   Discusses Yeats's letter to the *Irish Times*, 8 Oct 1903 (Wp. 366).

French: Gérard de Nerval

2124. HUBERT, CLAIRE MARCOM: "The Still Point and the Turning World: A Comparison of the Myths of Gérard de Nerval and William Butler Yeats," Ph.D. thesis, Emory U, 1965. xxi, 337 p. (*DA*, 26:2 [Aug 1965], 1042-43.)

French: Joris-Karl Huysmans

See J3954.

French: Stéphane Mallarmé

2125. DE MAN, PAUL MICHAEL: "Mallarmé, Yeats, and the Post-Romantic Predicament," Ph.D. thesis, Harvard U, 1960. viii, 125, i, 191 p.

2126. FULLWOOD, DAPHNE: "The Influence on W. B. Yeats of Some French Poets (Mallarmé, Verlaine, Claudel)," *Southern R*, 6:2 (Apr 1970), 356-79.

2127. REVARD, STELLA: "Yeats, Mallarmé, and the Archetypal Feminine," *PLL*, 8:Supplement (Fall 1972), 112-27.
   The influence of *Hérodiade* on several poems and on *The Shadowy Waters*, *The King of the Great Clock Tower*, and *A Full Moon in March*.

2127a. SPIVAK, GAYATRI CHAKRAVORTY: "A Stylistic Contrast between Yeats and Mallarmé," *Language and Style*, 5:2 (Spring 1972), 100-107.
   Yeats and Mallarmé had a common theme but a different "stylistic tendency."

See also J801, 1130, 1162 (#2), 2107, 2108, 2110, 2112, 3678, 3730, 4095a, 4322.

French: Alfred de Musset

See J2758.

French: Sâr Joséphin Péladan

See J2112.

French: Marcel Proust

2128. WILSON, EDMUND: "Proust and Yeats," *New Republic*, 52:670 (5 Oct 1927), 176-77, 177a.
   Proust and Yeats as symbolists.

French: Arthur Rimbaud

See J1624.

French: Pierre de Ronsard

See J2781, 3292-96.

French: Denis de Rougemont

See J2731.

French: Jean-Paul Sartre

See J3976.

French: Stendhal (Henri Beyle)

See J2758.

French: Paul Valéry

2129. ALEXANDER, IAN W.: "Valéry and Yeats: The Rehabilitation of Time,"
Scottish Periodical, 1:1 (Summer 1947), 77-106.
    "Yeats's whole development may be described as the progressive dis-
    covery of concrete experience, and it is in this that he may best be
    brought into parallel with Valéry." This development ends "in a reha-
    bilitation of Time and Being." Valéry, unlike Yeats, however, is no
    idealist.

See also J2630, 2919a.

French: Paul Verlaine

See J2110, 2126, 3019.

French: Villiers de l'Isle Adam

2130. FRIEDMAN, MELVIN J.: "A Revaluation of *Axel*," *MD*, 1:4 (Feb 1959),
236-43.

2131. GOLDGAR, HARRY: "Deux dramaturges symbolistes: Villiers de l'Isle
Adam et William Butler Yeats," Doctorat d'Université thesis (Lettres),
U of Paris, 1948. vii, 410 p.
    Contains chapters on Yeats in Paris, the French influence on Yeats
    in general and of Villiers de l'Isle Adam in particular, "romantisme,"
    religion, mysticism, mythology, and symbolism in both poets, espe-
    cially in their plays.

2132. PARKS, LLOYD CLIFFORD: "The Influence of Villiers de L'Isle Adam
on W. B. Yeats," Ph.D. thesis, U of Washington, 1959. v, 215 p. (*DA*, 20:7
[Jan 1960], 2784-85.)

2133. ROSE, MARILYN GADDIS: "Yeats's Use of *Axel*," *Comparative Drama*, 4:4
(Winter 1970/71), 253-64.
    Particularly in *The Countess Cathleen*.

See also J2110, 2112, 3888, 4100.

French: François Villon

2134. BORNSTEIN, GEORGE J., and HUGH H. WITEMEYER: "From *Villain* to
Visionary: Pound and Yeats on Villon," *Comparative Literature*, 19:4 (Fall
1967), 308-20.
    Yeats's view of Villon was originally indebted to Pound, but changed
    later as his literary theory developed.

German Literature: General Section

2134a. HUMBLE, MALCOLM EDWARD: "German Contacts and Influences in the
Lives and Works of W. B. Yeats and D. H. Lawrence, with Special Reference
to Friedrich Nietzsche," Ph.D. thesis, U of Cambridge, 1969. xvii, 488 p.
    Discusses Yeats's acquaintance with Germans and German literature in
    general and with Goethe, Wagner, Boehme, Kant, Hegel, Spengler, and
    Nietzsche in particular.

See also J1132.

German: Jacob Boehme

2135. °SOUDERS, BRUCE C.: "The Reappearance of Jacob Boehme in the Work of William Law, William Blake, and William Butler Yeats," M.A. thesis, Columbia U, 1953. 188 p.

See also J1867, 2134a.

German: Bertolt Brecht

See J3027a, 3538, 3566.

German: Max Dauthendey

2136. LANGE, VICTOR, and HANS-GERT ROLOFF (eds): *Dichtung, Sprache, Gesellschaft.* Akten des IV. internationalen Germanisten-Kongresses 1970 in Princeton. Frankfurt am Main: Athenäum, 1971. x, 635 p. (Beihefte zum Jahrbuch für internationale Germanistik. 1.)
    O[liver] H. Edwards: "Dauthendey und Yeats: Ihre Begegnungen in den neunziger Jahren," 289-90. Summary of a lecture. See also J624.

German: Stefan George

See J4095a.

German: Johann Wolfgang Goethe

2137. EDWARDS, OLIVER: "Aspects of Goethe's Poetry," *Revue des langues vivantes*, 15:4 (Aug 1949), 210-21.
    Contains a section "Yeats and Goethe," 219-21.

2138. PERLOFF, MARJORIE: "Yeats and Goethe," *Comparative Literature*, 23:2 (Spring 1971), 125-40.

See also J2134a, 2758, 2953.

German: Gerhart Hauptmann

See J3832.

German: G. W. F. Hegel

See J1136a, 2134a.

German: Hugo von Hofmannsthal

2139. HAMBURGER, MICHAEL: *Hugo von Hofmannsthal: Zwei Studien.* Göttingen: Sachse & Pohl, 1964. 134 p. (Schriften zur Literatur. 6.)
    German translations of two introductions to English-language editions of Hofmannsthal's works. Includes frequent comparisons of Yeats's and Hofmannsthal's plays.

German: C. G. Jung

2139a. OLNEY, JAMES: "'A Powerful Emblem': The Towers of Yeats and Jung," *SAQ*, 72:4 (Autumn 1973), 494-515.
    The actual towers and their symbolical implications.

2140. WALL, RICHARD J., and ROGER FITZGERALD: "Yeats and Jung: An Ideological Comparison," *Literature and Psychology*, 13:2 (Spring 1963), 44-52.

Spiritus mundi, the mask, and opposites and antinomies and their Jungian counterparts.

See also J1168a, 1788, 2920.

German: Immanuel Kant

See J1136a, 2134a.

German: Thomas Mann

2141. CONVERSI, LEONARD: "Mann, Yeats and the Truth of Art," *Yale R*, 56:4 (June 1967), 506-23.
Opposites and antinomies in Mann and Yeats.

German: Karl Marx

See J2998.

German: Friedrich Nietzsche

2142. BRIDGWATER, PATRICK: *Nietzsche in Anglosaxony: A Study of Nietzsche's Impact on English and American Literature.* Leicester: Leicester UP, 1972. 236 p.
"'That Strong Enchanter' (W. B. Yeats)," 67-90; reprinted from R. W. Last (ed): *Affinities: Essays in German and English Literature Dedicated to the Memory of Oswald Wolff (1897-1968).* London: Wolff, 1971. x, 353 p., pp. 68-87. Also *passim* (see index). Quotes from Yeats's annotations to the Nietzsche edition in his possession.

2143. FRIEDRICH, CARL-JOACHIM, and BENNO REIFENBERG (eds): *Sprache und Politik: Festgabe für Dolf Sternberger zum sechzigsten Geburtstag.* Heidelberg: Schneider, 1968. 545 p.
Erich Heller: "Als der Dichter Yeats zum ersten Mal Nietzsche las," 116-31. See also Heller's "Yeats and Nietzsche: Reflections on a Poet's Marginal Notes," *Encounter*, 33:6 (Dec 1969), 64-72.

2143a. KEANE, PATRICK J.: "Yeats and Nietzsche: The 'Antithetical' Vision," °Ph.D. thesis, New York U, 1971. 439 p. (*DA*, 33:9 [Mar 1973], 5182A.)

2144. KNIGHT, GEORGE WILSON: *Christ and Nietzsche: An Essay in Poetic Wisdom.* London: Staples Press, 1948. 244 p.
Scattered notes, *passim* (see index).

2145. O'BRIEN, CONOR CRUISE: *The Suspecting Glance.* London: Faber & Faber, 1972. 91 p.
"Burke, Nietzsche, and Yeats," 67-91. The influence of Nietzsche prompted Yeats's withdrawal from popular Irish nationalism and his abandonment of a generally liberal attitude. Burke was important for a reconciliation of Yeats's liberal and fascist tendencies. Comments on several relevant poems.

2145a. REYNOLDS, LORNA: "Collective Intellect: Yeats, Synge and Nietzsche," *Essays and Studies*, 26 (1973), 83-98.
Poetry and philosophy as manifestations of unity of being in Yeats, Synge, and Nietzsche, and the influence of Nietzsche and Synge on Yeats in his efforts to formulate a "new syntax."

2146. THATCHER, DAVID S.: "A Misdated Yeats Letter on Nietzsche," *N&Q*, os 213 / ns 15:8 (Aug 1968), 286-87.

The letter to John Quinn, dated 26 Sept 1902 in *Letters* (p. 380), was presumably written between 27 Dec 1902 and 3 Jan 1903.

2147. ————: *Nietzsche in England, 1890–1914: The Growth of a Reputation.* Toronto: U of Toronto Press, 1970. xi, 331 p.
   "William Butler Yeats," 139–73, and *passim* (see index).

2147a. WESTERBECK, COLIN LESLIE: "The Dancer and the Statue: A Reading of the Poetry of Shelley, Keats, and Yeats in Terms of Friedrich Nietzsche's *The Birth of Tragedy*," °Ph.D. thesis, Columbia U, 1973. 261 p. (*DA*, 34:5 [Nov 1973], 2664A.)
   Discusses "The Song of the Happy Shepherd," "An Irish Airman Foresees His Death," "The Fisherman," "Among School Children," "Lapis Lazuli," "The Circus Animals' Desertion," and "Under Ben Bulben."

See also J1788, 1933, 2134a, 2599, 2804, 2863, 3884, 3932, 4100, 4169.

German: Rainer Maria Rilke

2148. MASON, EUDO COLECESTRA: *Rilke, Europe, and the English-Speaking World.* Cambridge: UP, 1961. xvi, 257 p.
   See pp. 111–13.

2149. ROSE, WILLIAM: "A Letter from W. B. Yeats on Rilke," *German Life and Letters*, 15:1 (Oct 1961), 68–70.

See also J1108, 2630, 2919a, 3110, 3114, 4978.

German: Oswald Spengler

See J2134a.

German: Richard Wagner

See J2134a.

Greek Literature: General Section

2150. GRAB, FREDERIC DANIEL: "William Butler Yeats and Greek Literature," Ph.D. thesis, U of California (Berkeley), 1965. ii, 327 p. (*DA*, 26:2 [Aug 1965], 1040–41.)

2151. °SUBLETTE, CYNTHIA A.: "Yeats' Use in His Major Works of the Greek Mystery Relgions," M.A. thesis, North Texas State U, 1967.

See also J1929–31, 3500, 3694, 3818.

Greek: Euripides

2152. MERRITT, ROBERT GRAY: "Euripides and Yeats: The Parallel Progression of Their Plays," Ph.D. thesis, Tulane U, 1963. ii, 181 p. (*DA*, 24:8 [Feb 1964], 3463.)
   Discusses *On Baile's Strand*, *The Shadowy Waters*, *At the Hawk's Well*, *Calvary*, *Purgatory*, and *The Resurrection*.

Greek: Heraclitus

See J1074.

Greek: Homer

2153. °ADAMS, STEPHEN JON: "Yeats and Homer," M.A. thesis, U of Toronto, 1967. 115 p.

Greek: Plato

2154. RAINE, KATHLEEN: "Yeats and Platonism," *Texas Q*, 10:4 (Winter 1964), 161-81.
    Reprinted in *Dublin Mag*, 7:1 (Spring 1968), 38-63.

See also J1074, 1156, 1879, 1966, 3196, 3999.

Greek: Plotinus

2154a. ESTERLY, JAMES DAVID: "Yeats, Plotinus, and Symbolic Perception," Ph.D. thesis, U of Cambridge, 1972. v, 281 p., with interleaved footnotes.
    Also on the influence of Coleridge; concentrates on Yeats's poetry with particular reference to "Sailing to Byzantium."

2154b. RITVO, ROSEMARY PUGLIA: "Plotinistic Elements in Yeats's Prose Works," °Ph.D. thesis, Fordham U, 1973. 214 p. (*DA*, 34:1 [July 1973], 334A.)
    In *A Vision* and *Per Amica Silentia Lunae*.

See also J3014.

Greek: Plutarch

See J2997.

Greek: Porphyry

See J2954, 3017.

Greek: Sophocles

2155. SOPHOCLES: *King Oedipus in the Translation by W. B. Yeats*. With selections from the *Poetics* of Aristotle, translated by G. M. A. Grube. Edited and with an introduction and notes by Balachandra Rajan. Toronto: Macmillan of Canada, 1969. vii, 99 p.
    Yeats's text and preface are on pp. 51-99; the introduction, pp. 1-12, comments on Yeats's interest in Sophocles.

See also J3557, 3769-70 and note, 3771-76, 3814, 3815, 3818, 4699-4700.

Indian Literature: General Section

2156. ARONSON, ALEX: "Yeats on India," *Aryan Path*, 16:4 (Apr 1945), 131-33.
    "And more than once he found in India what was so sadly lacking in the West: an intuitive approach to life, a religion born of an inner need, a challenge to materialism."

2157. BHARGAVA, HARSH VARDHAN: "Indian Philosophy in the Poetry of W. B. Yeats," M.A. thesis, Queen's U (Kingston, Ont.), 1964. vii, 68 p.
    Yeats's interest in Hindu philosophy, Mohini Chatterjee, and Tagore.

2158. BOSE, AMALENDU: "Yeats from a Personal Angle," *Bulletin of the Department of English, U of Calcutta*, 5:1 (1969-70), 62-69.

2159. °ELLYSON, GAIL C.: "Yeats' Genuflections to the East: A Study of Indian Influence upon His Thought and Poetry," M.A. thesis, U of Miami, 1967.

2160. GUHA, NARESH: "W. B. Yeats and India: The Story of a Relationship till the Advent of Tagore in the West," *JJCL*, 3 (1963), 41-79.
    The influence of Mohini Chatterjee and the influence through AE and Madame Blavatsky.

2161. ————: "The Upaniṣads, Patañjali, Apparitions, and W. B. Yeats (A New Approach to *A Vision*)," *JJCL*, 4 (1964), 104-24.

2162. ————: *W. B. Yeats: An Indian Approach*. Preface by Richard Ellmann. Calcutta: Jadavpur U, 1968. 170 p.
> Based on a Ph.D. thesis, Northwestern U, 1962. iii, 164 p. (*DA*, 23:12 [June 1963], 4684). Reprints J150 and 162.
> *Reviews:*
> 1. P. C. Chatterji, "A Poet's Captivations," *Thought* [Delhi], 21:51 (20 Dec 1969), 17-18.
> 2. C. N. Srinath, *Literary Criterion*, 8:4 (Summer 1969), 81-84.

2163. JAIN, SUSHIL KUMAR: "Indian Elements in the Poetry of Yeats: On Chatterji and Tagore," *CLS*, 7:1 (Mar 1970), 82-96.

2164. KANTAK, V. Y.: "Yeats's Indian Experience," *Indian J of English Studies*, 6 (1965), 80-101.
> Although some of Yeats's Indian sources were not reputable, his affinity with, and understanding of, Indian thought was closer than in most of his Western contemporaries.

2165. KHAN, S. M.: "Indian Elements in the Works of W. B. Yeats, T. S. Eliot, and Aldous Huxley," Ph.D. thesis, U of Nottingham, 1956. iv, 321 p.
> On Yeats, pp. 21-35, 65-131, and *passim*.

2166. KOMESU, OKIFUMI: "W. B. Yeats: Vision and Experience," Ph.D. thesis, Michigan State U, 1968. vii, 216 p. (*DA*, 29:6 [Dec 1968], 1900A.)
> "This study concerns itself with the question of whether W. B. Yeats was a visionary poet or not in the light of his Oriental interest" (abstract). Discusses Indian and Japanese influences, especially that of the Nō.

2167. °LING, MING-HUI CHANG: "Yeats and Indian Philosophy," M.A. thesis, U of Washington, 1952. 84 p.

2168. RAJAN, B.: "Yeats and Indian Philosophy," *Listener*, 38:971 (4 Sept 1947), 392-93.

2169. RAMAMRUTHAM, J. V.: "Indian Themes in the Poetry of W. B. Yeats," *Literary Half-Yearly*, 1:2 (July 1960), 43-48.

2170. RAO, K. BHASKARA: "The Impact of Theosophy on the Poetry of W. B. Yeats," *Aryan Path*, 26:12 (Dec 1955), 545-52.
> Particularly through Indian authors. Stresses the idea of incarnation as central to Yeats's "theosophical" poetry.

2171. °SHARMA, T. R. SRINIVASA: "Hindu Thought and Symbol in W. B. Yeats," M.A. thesis, U of Colorado, 1964. 89 p.

2172. VISWANATHAN, S.: "Yeats and the Swan: The Poet's Use of an Indian Tradition," *Aryan Path*, 39:8 (Aug 1968), 340-45.

See also J1845, 1867, 1873, 2736, 3744, 4100.

Indian: Mohini Chatterjee (or Chatterji)

2173. SENA, VINOD: "W. B. Yeats & the Indian Way of Wisdom," *Quest* [Bombay], 62 (July-Sept 1969), 76-77.

See also J1112, 1867, 2157, 2160, 2163.

Indian: Hamsa, bhagwan

See J3287.

Indian: Patañjali

See J2161.

Indian: Purohit, swami

2174. NAIK, M. K., S. K. DESAI, and S. T. KALLAPUR (eds): *The Image of India in Western Creative Writing*. Dharwar: Karnatak U / Madras: Macmillan, 1971. viii, 404 p.
Shankar Mokashi-Punekar: "Sri Purohit Swami and W. B. Yeats," 127-48.

See also J1118, 1867, 2189, 2190, 3743.

Indian: Rabindranath Tagore

2175. ANNIAH GOWDA, H. H.: "Ideas into Drama: Yeats and Tagore as Playwrights," *Literary Half-Yearly*, 2:1 (Jan 1961), 63-76.
"Yeats and Tagore express beautiful ideas, but their medium may be described as archaic and undramatic. They try to come to grips with the actualities of life but do not reduce the distance between the stage and the audience."

2175a. CHAUDHERY, SUMITA MITRA: "William Butler Yeats and Rabindranath Tagore: A Comparative Study," °Ph.D. thesis, U of Michigan, 1973. 226 p. (*DA*, 34:4 [Oct 1973], 1898A-99A.)

2176. DASGUPTA, PRANABENDU: "One or Two Aspects of the 'Subjective Tradition' in the Plays of W. B. Yeats and Rabindranath Tagore," *JJCL*, 4 (1964), 46-67.
The aspects are character and symbol.

2177. DASGUPTA, R. K. (ed): *Rabindranath Tagore and William Butler Yeats: The Story of a Literary Friendship*. A souvenir of the 100th anniversary of the birth of Yeats observed at the 104th anniversary of the birth of Tagore. Delhi: Department of Modern Indian Languages, U of Delhi, 1965. iv, 36 p.
Contents: 1. Tagore: "W. B. Yeats," 1-7; a translation of an essay originally written in Bengali and published in 1912. Tagore explains Yeats's achievement in modern English poetry as the "individual expression of his soul."
2. Yeats: Several pieces on Tagore, among others the introduction to W263, the preface to W267, and the letter from W318.
3. "W. B. Yeats on Tagore (Speech at a Reception to Tagore at the Trocadero Restaurant, London, 10 July 1912)," 13. Source not given; apparently not published elsewhere.
4. "Tagore's Reply," 13-14.
5. "Sri Aurobindo on W. B. Yeats," 15-17; four snippets from letters and various publications (1917-49).
6. Abinash Chandra Bose: "My Interview with W. B. Yeats," 18-24. The interview on 1 June 1937; for a fuller account see J595.
7. R. K. DasGupta: "Rabindranath Tagore and W. B. Yeats," 25-34.
8. "Rabindranath's Message on the Passing Away of Yeats," MS. facsimile opposite p. 34.
9. "Chronology of Rabindranath's Association with W. B. Yeats," 35-36. Rather sketchy.

2178. DATTA, HIRENDRANATH: "Tagore and Yeats," *Visva-Bharati Q*, 17:1 (May–July 1951), 29–34.

2179. FALLON, PADRAIC: "Poetic Labourers: Yeats and Tagore," *Irish Times*, #33288 (30 June 1962), 9.

2180. GUHA, NARESH: "Yeats and Rabindranath: A Study in Tradition and Modern Poetry," *Quest* [Bombay], #36 (Winter 1962-63), 9–19.
Revised as "Discovery of a Modern Poet," *Mahfil*, 3:1 (1966), 58–73. Reprinted in Aby Sayeed Ayyub and Amlan Datta (eds): *Ten Years of "Quest."* Bombay: Manaktalas, 1966. xi, 407 p., pp. 135–53.

2181. HURWITZ, HAROLD MARVIN: "Rabindranath Tagore and England," Ph.D. thesis, U of Illinois, 1959. iv, 223 p. (*DA*, 20:8 [Feb 1960], 3294–95.)
See pp. 76–88.

2182. ———: "Tagore's English Reputation," *WHR*, 16:1 (Winter 1962), 77–83.

2183. ———: "Yeats and Tagore," *Comparative Literature*, 16:1 (Winter 1964), 55–64.
Biographical connections and mutual interests.

2184. KRIPALANI, KRISHNA: *Rabindranath Tagore: A Biography*. London: Oxford UP, 1962. ix, 417 p.
Scattered references, *passim* (see index).

2185. LAGO, MARY M.: "The Parting of the Ways: A Comparative Study of Yeats and Tagore," *Indian Literature*, 6:2 (1963), 1–34.
Reprinted in *Mahfil*, 3:1 (1966), 32–57. "The similarities were in reality superficial. . . . by the age of seventy, Yeats and Tagore had moved steadily away from each other in opposite directions, Yeats going away from reality to a private world of myth, and Tagore coming closer to the world of men."

2185a. NARASIMHAIAH, C. D.: "The Reputation of English *Gitanjali*: Tagore and His Critics," *Literary Criterion*, 9:4 (Summer 1971), 1–22.
Yeats's introduction to *Gitanjali* "is in the nature of a literary scandal of the first magnitude and does little credit to Yeats's poetic, much less to his critical faculty."

2185b. °RANGANATHAN, SUDHA: "Rabindranath Tagore's *Malini* and W. B. Yeats's *The Countess Cathleen*: A Study in 'Hominisation,'" *Osmania J of English Studies*, 9:1 (1972), 51–54.

2186. SEN, NABANEETA DEV: "The Reception of Rabindranath Tagore in England, France, Germany, and the United States," Ph.D. thesis, Indiana U, 1964. vi, 167 p. (*DA*, 26:4 [Oct 1965], 2192–93.)
Yeats mentioned *passim*. Negligible.

2187. °*Tagore's Friend: Irish Poet, William Butler Yeats*. Lahore: Tagore Memorial Publications, [194-]. 15 p. (Tagore Pamphlets. First series.)

See also J785, 1012, 1015, 1016, 1089, 1867, 2157, 2163, 2865, 3379, 3743, 5379–81.

Indian: Upanishads

2188. DAVENPORT, A.: "Yeats and the Upanishads," *RES*, 3:9 (Jan 1952), 55–62.

2189. LAL, P. (trans): *The Isa Upaniṣad: With an Essay on "The Difficul-*
ties of Translation" (Based on a Study of the Yeats-Purohit Version of
the *Īśā-Upaniṣad).* Calcutta: Writer's Workshop, 1968. 16 p.
  Compares the Yeats-Purohit version with a literal translation and
concludes that the former is a mixture of successes and failures.

2190. MASSON, J.: "Yeats's *The Ten Principal Upanishads,*" *JJCL*, 9 [1971?],
24-31.
  "Nearly every passage is inaccurate, and what is more important, the
inaccuracies are never on the side of poetry." Moreover, many of the
most splendid passages are missing in the translations. The inference
is that Purohit Swami misinformed Yeats seriously.

See also J1867, 2161, 2525, 5363-72 and note.

Irish Literature (Anglo-Irish and Gaelic): General Section

2191. DONALDSON, ALLAN ROGERS: "The Influence of Irish Nationalism upon
the Early Development of W. B. Yeats," M.A. thesis, U of London, 1953
[i.e., 1954]. iii, 290 p.
  Discusses Yeats's work to 1914; contains chapters on "Irish Nationalism and Irish Nationalist Literature," "The Irish Literary Movement
and the Decadents," and "The Irish Theatre Movement."

2191a. GRANT, DAMIAN: "Body Poetic: The Function of a Metaphor in Three
Irish Poets," *Poetry Nation*, #1 (1973), 112-25.
  Personifications of Ireland in John Montague, Seamus Heaney, and Paul
Muldoon, with some references to Yeats's influence.

2192. HOLLOWAY, JOHN: "Yeats and the Penal Age," *CQ*, 8:1 (Spring 1966),
58-66.
  The influence of the Gaelic poetry of the 18th century on Yeats's
poetry and on *Cathleen ni Houlihan.*

2193. MONTAGUE, JOHN: "Under Ben Bulben," *Shenandoah*, 16:4 (Summer 1965),
21-24.
  Reprinted as "Living under Ben Bulben," *Kilkenny Mag*, #14 (Spring-
Summer 1966), 44-47. Maintains that Yeats's "direct influence on
Irish poetry has been disastrous."

2194. O'FAOLAIN, SEAN: "Ireland's Literature Now Yeats Is 70: Sean
O'Faolain Evaluates the Poet's Debt to Ireland and Her Debt to Him,"
NYTBR, 40:24 (16 June 1935), 2, 14.

2195. O'SULLIVAN, DONAL (ed): *Songs of the Irish: An Anthology of Irish*
Folk Music and Poetry with English Verse Translations. Dublin: Browne &
Nolan, 1960. xi, 199 p.
  "Introduction," 1-12; notes the influence of Irish folksong on Yeats.

2196. RAFROIDI, PATRICK: *L'Irlande et le romantisme: La littérature*
irlandaise-anglaise de 1789 à 1850 et sa place dans le mouvement occi-
dental. Paris: Editions universitaires, 1972. x, 787 p. (Etudes irlandaises. 1.)
  Notes on Yeats and the Irish romantics, *passim* (see index).

2196a. °SHERIDAN, MICHAEL: "W. B. Yeats: Irish Sources and Influences.,"
M.A. thesis, University College, Dublin, 1945.

2197. °SUTTON, DAVID: "W. B. Yeats and the Irish Ballad Tradition," M.A.
thesis, U of Leicester, 1972.

See also J1076, 1094, 1112, 1147, 1156, 1708, 1742, 1754, 1755, 1758, 1772a, 1774, 1873, 1879, 1882, 2045, 2671a, 2711, 3026, 3187, 3485, 3949a, 3961, 4100, 4235, 5910, 5929, 6018, 6149, 6245, 6246, 6269, 6272, 6322, 6851.

Irish: William Allingham

See J2420.

Irish: Brendan Behan

2197a. O'CONNOR, ULICK: *Brendan Behan.* London: Coronet Books, 1972 [1970]. 328 p.
  Yeats is mentioned *passim* (see index).

Irish: George Berkeley

2198. DAVIE, DONALD: "Yeats, Berkeley, and Romanticism," *Irish Writing,* #31 (Summer 1955), 36–41.
  Reprinted in S. P. Rosenbaum (ed): *English Literature and British Philosophy: A Collection of Essays.* Chicago: U of Chicago Press, 1971. vii, 365 p., pp. 278–84. Yeats based his rejection of romanticism in "Among School Children" on his reading of Berkeley.

2199. LUCE, ARTHUR ASTON: *Berkeley's Immaterialism: A Commentary on His "A Treatise concerning Principles of Human Understanding."* London: Nelson, 1950 [1945]. xii, 163 p.
  In the preface (pp. vii-ix), Luce refers to the Yeats-Berkeley relationship.

See also J1076, 1147, 1805, 2258, 2259.

Irish: Edmund Burke

See J1076, 1147, 2145, 2258, 2259.

Irish: William Byrne

2200. SWORDS, L. F. K.: "How to Read the Poems of William Byrne: W. B. Yeats and William Byrne," *Vexilla Regis,* 5 (1956), 104–10.
  Yeats is a good poet, but so is William Byrne. (I dissent; the two examples from Byrne are not very inspiring.)

Irish: Austin Clarke

See J2200a, 6866.

Irish: Michael Comyn

See J3284.

Irish: Thomas Davis

See J2420, 2711, 4054, 4067, 4228, 4235.

Irish: Lord Dunsany

See J6883.

Irish: Sir Samuel Ferguson

See J2420, 2711, 3080, 3284, 4228, 4235, 6891a.

Irish: George Fitzmaurice

2200a. GELDERMAN, CAROL: "Austin Clarke and Yeats's Alleged Jealousy of George Fitzmaurice," *Éire-Ireland*, 8:2 (Summer 1973), 62-70.
Clarke's allegation that Yeats was jealous of Fitzmaurice's achievement is without foundation.

See also J6896, 6897, 6906, 6907.

Irish: Oliver St. John Gogarty

2201. HUXLEY, D. J.: "Yeats and Dr. Gogarty," *Ariel*, 3:3 (July 1972), 31-47.
The influence of Gogarty's poetry on Yeats's.

See also J665, 1102, 5940 (#5, 8), 6909a, 6910.

Irish: Oliver Goldsmith

See J1147.

Irish: Lady Gregory

2202. CHISLETT, WILLIAM: *Moderns and Near-Moderns: Essays on Henry James, Stockton, Shaw, and Others.* NY: Grafton Press, 1928. 226 p.
"On the Influence of Lady Gregory on William Butler Yeats," 165-67.

2202a. FITZGERALD, MARY MARGARET. "The Dominant Partnership: W. B. Yeats and Lady Gregory in the Early Irish Theatre," °Ph.D. thesis, Princeton U, 1973. 275 p. (*DA*, 34:4 [Oct 1973], 2066A.)
Based on the unpublished Lady Gregory papers in the Berg Collection; discusses the efforts of Yeats and Lady Gregory to found and maintain a theater in Dublin and their collaboration in play writing.

2203. MURPHY, DANIEL J.: "Yeats and Lady Gregory: A Unique Dramatic Collaboration," *MD*, 7:3 (Dec 1964), 322-28.

2204. YEATS, W. B.: "Some New Letters from W. B. Yeats to Lady Gregory." Edited by Donald T. Torchiana and Glenn O'Malley, *REL*, 4:3 (July 1963), 9-47.

See also J172, 675, 1041, 1097, 1128, 1131, 1140, 1147, 1708, 1813a, 2810, 2825, 2827, 3142, 3520, 3607, 3673, 3971, 4100, 5390-97, 5940 (#3), 6938, 6940, 6942, 6948, 6951, 6953, 6964, 6969, 6971a.

Irish: Robert Gregory

See J1147.

Irish: Arthur Griffith

2205. Ó LÚING, SEÁN: *Art Ó Gríofa.* Dublin: Sáirséal agus Dill, 1953. 430 p.
"Art Ó Gríofa, J. M. Synge agus W. B. Yeats," 144-50, and *passim* on Griffith and Yeats (see index).

Irish: F. R. Higgins

2206. [O'FAOLAIN, SEAN]: "Frederick Robert Higgins (1897-1941)," *Bell*, 1:5 (Feb 1941), 53-55.
Higgins's poetry compared with Yeats's.

See also J6976.

Irish: Nora Hopper

See J1110.

Irish: Douglas Hyde

See J986, 1110, 3907, 4199, 5940 (#6).

Irish: James Joyce

2207. ATHERTON, JAMES S.: *The Books at the Wake: A Study of Literary Allusions in James Joyce's "Finnegans Wake."* London: Faber & Faber, 1959. 308 p.
    Note on Yeats allusions, p. 290, and *passim* (see index).

2208. °BASS, RICHARD K.: "Satiric Treatments of W. B. Yeats and His Circle in James Joyce's *Ulysses*," M.A. thesis, Columbia U, 1959. 56 p.

2208a. BATES, RONALD, and HARRY J. POLLOCK (eds): *Litters from.Aloft.* Papers delivered at the second Canadian James Joyce Seminar, McMaster University. Tulsa: U of Tulsa, 1971. ix, 111 p. (U of Tulsa Department of English Monograph Series. 13.)
    M. J. Sidnell: "A Daintical Pair of Accomplasses: Joyce and Yeats," 50-73. Mainly on parallel motives in *The Wanderings of Oisin* and *Finnegans Wake*.

2209. BOLDEREFF, FRANCES MOTZ: *Reading Finnegans Wake*. Woodward, Pa.: Classic Nonfiction Library, 1959. xxii, 210; x, 285 p.
    On Yeats's influence, especially that of *A Vision*: 1:59-60, 63-66, 69, 74-80, 82-83, 101-3, 108, 122, 126, 128, 130, 132-33, 135, 139, 141-47, 153, 162; 2:54, 74, 82, 247, 280. Somewhat eccentric.

2210. ————: *Hermes to His Son Thoth: Being Joyce's Use of Giordano Bruno in Finnegans Wake*. Woodward, Pa.: Classic Nonfiction Library, 1968. 289 p.
    Claims that Yeats preceded Joyce insofar as his "living delicate response to the times [he] lived in characterizes the genuinely creative spirit." Quotes in support Yeats's "The Adoration of the Magi" (pp. 232, 244-50).

2211. COLLINS, BEN L.: "Joyce's Use of Yeats and of Irish History: A Reading of 'A Mother,'" *Éire-Ireland*, 5:1 (Spring 1970), 45-66.
    Joyce uses *Cathleen ni Houlihan* satirically.

2212. DEMING, ROBERT H. (ed): *James Joyce: The Critical Heritage*. London: Routledge & Kegan Paul, 1970. 2 v.
    Reprinted items; Yeats is referred to *passim* (see index).

2213. DUNCAN, EDWARD: "James Joyce & the Primitive Celtic Church," *Alphabet*, #7 (Dec 1963), 17-38.
    On Yeats's *The Tables of the Law* and Joyce's *Stephen Hero*, pp. 21-25.

2214. ELLMANN, RICHARD: "Joyce and Yeats," *Kenyon R*, 12:4 (Autumn 1950), 618-38.

2215. FACKLER, HERBERT V.: "Stephen Dedalus Rejects Forgotten Beauty: A Yeats Allusion in *A Portrait of the Artist as a Young Man*," *CLAJ*, 12:2 (Dec 1968), 164-67.
    An allusion to Yeats's "He Remembers Forgotten Beauty," which serves to stress the difference between Joyce/Stephen and Yeats/Robartes in artistic and Irish matters.

2216. GECKLE, GEORGE L.: "Stephen Dedalus and W. B. Yeats: The Making of the Villanelle," *Modern Fiction Studies*, 15:1 (Spring 1969), 87–96.
    Stephen's villanelle is indebted to Yeats's "He Remembers Forgotten Beauty," his esthetic theory to Yeats's essay "The Symbolism of Poetry."

2217. GLASHEEN, ADALINE: *A Second Census of Finnegans Wake: An Index of the Characters and Their Roles*. Evanston: Northwestern UP, 1963. lxvi, 285 p.
    Index of Yeats in *Finnegans Wake*, pp. 283–84.

2218. ————: "Joyce and Yeats," *Wake Newslitter*, ns 4:1 (Feb 1967), 30.
    Explains six Yeats allusions in *Finnegans Wake*.

2218a. ————: "The Yeats Letters and FW," *Wake Newslitter*, ns 10:5 (Oct 1973), 76.
    Verbal parallels (some of them tenuous) between some Yeats letters and *Finnegans Wake*.

2219. HART, CLIVE: *Structure and Motif in "Finnegans Wake."* London: Faber & Faber, 1962. 271 p.
    Notes on Yeats's influence, particularly that of *A Vision*, *passim* (see index).

2220. JOYCE, JAMES: *Chamber Music*. Edited with an introduction and notes by William York Tindall. NY: Columbia UP, 1954. vii, 236 p.
    Passim (see index).

2221. ————: *The Critical Writings*. Edited by Ellsworth Mason and Richard Ellmann. NY: Viking Press, 1964 [1959]. 288 p. (Viking Compass Book. C145.)
    Passim (see index), especially in the following pieces:
    1. "The Day of the Rabblement," 68–72; first published in F. J. C. Skeffington and James A. Joyce: *Two Essays*. Dublin: Gerrard, [1901]. 8 p., pp. 7–8. Joyce's famous onslaught on the Irish Literary Theatre for surrendering to the "popular will."
    2. "The Holy Office," 149–52; reprinted from a °broadside published in 1904/5 (?). Contains a parody of "To Ireland in the Coming Times."

2222. ————: *A Portrait of the Artist as a Young Man*. Text, criticism, and notes edited by Chester G. Anderson. NY: Viking Press, 1968. vi, 570 p.
    See p. 541 for an index of the references to *The Countess Cathleen* and p. 549 for those to Michael Robartes.

2223. JOYCE, STANISLAUS: *My Brother's Keeper*. Edited with an introduction by Richard Ellmann, with a preface by T. S. Eliot. London: Faber & Faber, 1958. 258 p.
    On Yeats and Joyce, pp. 182–85, 206–7, and *passim* (see index).

2224. KENNER, HUGH: *Dublin's Joyce*. London: Chatto & Windus, 1955. xii, 372 p.
    Yeats, *passim*, especially "Yeats and *Chamber Music*," 39–41 (a comparison of Yeats's and Joyce's poetry); "Yeats as Tragic Hero," 45–46; "Yeats, Dedalus, and Mr. Duffy," 46–48 (Mr. Duffy of "A Painful Case"); pp. 158–61 (the influence of *The Tables of the Law* and *The Adoration of the Magi*).

2225. MCGREEVY, THOMAS: "James Joyce," *TLS*, 40:2034 (25 Jan 1941), 43–44.
    Denies, on the authority of both Yeats and Joyce, that Joyce said, "You are too old to be influenced by me."

2226. MOORE, JOHN REES: "Artifices for Eternity: Joyce and Yeats," *Éire-Ireland*, 3:4 (Winter 1968), 66-73.

2227. SCHOLES, ROBERT, and RICHARD M. KAIN (eds): *The Workshop of Daedalus: James Joyce and the Raw Materials for "A Portrait of the Artist as a Young Man."* Evanston: Northwestern UP, 1965. xiv, 287 p.
   On Yeats and other figures of the Irish literary revival, *passim* (see index).

2228. SULTAN, STANLEY: *The Argument of Ulysses.* Columbus: Ohio State UP, 1964. xv, 485 p.
   Notes on Yeats in *Ulysses*, *passim* (see index).

2229. THORNTON, WELDON: *Allusions in Ulysses: An Annotated List.* Chapel Hill: U of North Carolina Press, 1968. ix, 554 p.
   Index to Yeats allusions in *Ulysses*, p. 554.

2230. TINDALL, WILLIAM YORK: *James Joyce: His Way of Interpreting the Modern World.* NY: Scribner's, 1950. ix, 134 p.
   Scattered notes on Yeats and Joyce, *passim* (see index).

2231. ————: "James Joyce and the Hermetic Tradition," *J of the History of Ideas*, 15:1 (Jan 1954), 23-39.
   Comments on Yeats's occult interests and their influence on Joyce.

2232. ————: *A Reader's Guide to James Joyce.* NY: Noonday Press, 1959. xi, 304 p.
   On Yeats in Joyce's work (mostly interpreted as a father image), *passim* (see index).

2233. TRENCH, W. F.: "Dr. Yeats and Mr. Joyce," *Irish Statesman*, 2:25 (30 Aug 1924), 790.
   Horrified complaint that the poet of the beautiful sees in "foul-minded" Joyce a genius.

2234. WITT, MARION: "A Note on Joyce and Yeats," *MLN*, 63:8 (Dec 1948), 552-53.
   A Yeats allusion in *Ulysses*.

2235. WOLFF-WINDEGG, PHILIPP: "Auf der Suche nach dem Symbol—J. Joyce und W. B. Yeats," *Symbolon*, 5 (1966), 39-52.
   As Yeats's work matured, his symbolism became colder—glasslike and less obtrusive. Joyce is diametrically opposed; the symbolism of *Finnegans Wake* is enormously inflated, obscure, and finally a victim of the built-in mechanism. Contains extensive notes on *Purgatory*.

See also J1039, 1076, 1740, 1788, 1825a, 1874, 1952, 2279, 3959, 4112, 4133, 7000, 7001, 7002, 7006, 7008, 7011.

Irish: Patrick Kavanagh

2236. LIDDY, JAMES: "Open Letter to the Young about Patrick Kavanagh," *Lace Curtain*, #1 [1970?], 55-57.
   Why Kavanagh is a better poet and model than Yeats.

2236a. WARNER, ALAN: *Clay Is the Word: Patrick Kavanagh, 1904-1967.* Dublin: Dolmen Press, 1973. 144 p.
   Passim (see index).

Irish: Patrick Kennedy

2237. ALSPACH, RUSSELL K.: "The Use by Yeats and Other Irish Writers of the Folklore of Patrick Kennedy," *J of American Folklore*, 59:234 (Oct-Dec 1946), 404-12.
Yeats used Kennedy in "The Priest and the Fairy," "Baile and Ailinn," *The Wanderings of Oisin*, and *The King's Threshold*. The other Irish writers are Lady Gregory and James Stephens.

Irish: Charles Kickham

See J3284.

Irish: William Larminie

See J1110.

Irish: T. W. Lyster

2238. MACLOCHLAINN, ALF: "An Unrecorded Yeats Item," *Irish Book*, 1:3 (1960/61), 61-65.
Prints and comments upon Yeats's speech given at the ceremony of the unveiling of the memorial to T. W. Lyster. See W316A and Wp. 397.

Irish: Patrick McCartan

See J1076.

Irish: Thomas MacDonagh

2238a. JORDAN, JOHN: "MacDonagh and Yeats," *Hibernia*, 37:8 (25 May 1973), 22.
See also Jordan's "*The Irish Review*," :9 (8 June 1973), 12.

2239. RYAN, STEPHEN P.: "W. B. Yeats and Thomas MacDonagh," *MLN*, 76:8 (Dec 1961), 715-19.
The biographical connections.

See also J4510, 7019a, 7020.

Irish: Micheál MacLiammóir

2240. MACLIAMMÓIR, MICHEÁL: *An Oscar of No Importance: Being an Account of the Author's Adventures with His One-Man Show about Oscar Wilde, "The Importance of Being Oscar."* London: Heinemann, 1968. vi, 234 p.
Wilde fascinated, Yeats influenced MacLiammóir (p. 222). Several other references to Yeats, *passim* (see index).

See also J2344, 2380, 2408 for reviews of MacLiammóir's one-man Yeats show, "Talking about Yeats."

Irish: J. P. Mahaffy

2241. STANFORD, WILLIAM BEDELL, and ROBERT BRENDAN MCDOWELL: *Mahaffy: A Biography of an Anglo-Irishman.* London: Routledge & Kegan Paul, 1971. xiv, 281 p.
See pp. 113-15.

Irish: James Clarence Mangan

See J2711, 4228, 4235.

Irish: Edward Martyn

See J7030.

Irish: John Mitchel

See J1103.

Irish: George Moore

2242. BRUNIUS, AUGUST: *Engelska kåserier*. Stockholm: Bonniers, 1927. 227 p.
"Yeats och Moore: Två typer ur 'den irländska renässansen,'" 91–126;
reprinted from *Vår tid*, 8 (1923), 75–95.

2243. GILOMEN, WALTHER: "George Moore and His Friendship with W. B. Yeats,"
ES, 19:3 (June 1937), 116–20.
On the mutual treatment in the respective autobiographies.

2244. HENN, T. R.: "Moore and Yeats," *Dublin Mag*, 4:2 (Summer 1965), 63–
77.

2245. MICHIE, DONALD M.: "A Man of Genius and a Man of Talent," *TSLL*, 6:2
(Summer 1964), 148–54.
The Yeats-Moore collaboration in *Diarmuid and Grania* and its effect
on some other Yeats works.

See also J557, 974, 3707–11 and note, 3712–15 and note, 3933, 3974, 3975,
3983a, 4232b, 4908, 4920, 6537, 7047, 7050–52, 7058, 7060, 7062, 7064,
7066, 7073–75.

Irish: Thomas Moore

See J3060.

Irish: Sean O'Casey

2246. ANON.: "Mr. O'Casey's New Play: Why It Was Rejected. Mr. Yeats on
the Dramatist's Job. The War and the Stage," *Observer*, 137:7149 (3 June
1928), 19.
The letters concerning the *Silver Tassie* affair; reprinted in J2250,
q.v.

2247. BROMAGE, MARY C.: "The Yeats-O'Casey Quarrel," *Michigan Alumnus QR*,
64:14 (1 Mar 1958), 135–44.
About *The Silver Tassie*.

2248. FALLON, GABRIEL: "Sean O'Casey and W. B. Yeats vs. Canons of Dramatic
Art," *Leader*, 76:25 (27 Aug 1938), 586–87.
Yeats criticized *The Silver Tassie* because it betrays the author's
"opinions," but his own *Purgatory* is no better.

2249. KRAUSE, DAVID: "O'Casey and Yeats and the Druid (Some Reflections
Provoked by the Recent Publication of O'Casey's *Blasts and Benedictions*),"
MD, 11:3 (Dec 1968), 252–62.
The *Silver Tassie* quarrel and how and why O'Casey became reconciled
with Yeats.

2250. [O'CASEY, SEAN]: "The Abbey Directors and Mr. O'Casey," *Irish
Statesman*, 10:14 (9 June 1928), 268–72.
Letters about *The Silver Tassie* to and from O'Casey, Lennox Robinson,
Yeats, Lady Gregory, and Walter Starkie; reprinted in various publi-
cations about O'Casey (see section MA of this bibliography) and in
part in J1521. See also J1097 and 2246.

The book was subsequently reviewed by Y. O. (George William Russell),
10:20 (21 July 1928), 391-92; correspondence by O'Casey and Russell's
reply, :22 (4 Aug 1928), 430-31.

2251. O'FLAHERTY, LIAM: "The Plough and the Stars," *Irish Statesman*, 5:24
(20 Feb 1926), 739-40.
    Criticizes Yeats for defending O'Casey's play.

2252. SMITH, HUGH: "And Back Home," *NYT*, 84:28295 (14 July 1935), IX, 1.
    About the *Silver Tassie* affair. Correspondence by O'Casey, "Mr.
    O'Casey Dissents," :28323 (11 Aug 1935), IX, 1, defending Yeats as a
    great man and poet.

2253. YEATS, W. B.: "Sean O'Casey's Story," *Time and Tide*, 14:21 (27 May
1933), 640.
    Letter to the editor protesting the suppression of O'Casey's "I Wanna
    Woman" (Wp. 388). See the silly answers by John Gibbons and William
    Thomson, :22 (3 June 1933), 670, criticizing Yeats's position.

See also J743, 1051, 1052, 3978, 7092, 7093, 7097, 7103, 7104, 7107, 7110,
7111, 7113a, 7119, 7134, 7141, 7144, 7147-49, 7154, 7160, 7161, 7172,
7178, 7183, 7189, 7456.

Irish: Sean O'Faolain

See J1286, 7193.

Irish: Liam O'Flaherty

See J7196.

Irish: Standish O'Grady

See J1110, 2964, 4104, 7202.

Irish: John O'Leary

See J1103, 1741, 1747, 2849, 3962, 4054, 4076a, 4199, 4200, 7213.

Irish: Charles Stewart Parnell

See J1741, 1747, 4054, 4076a, 5922.

Irish: P. H. Pearse

2253a. JORDAN, JOHN: "Pearse and Yeats," *Hibernia*, 37:6 (27 Apr 1973), 12.
See also J5940, 7221.

Irish: Forrest Reid

2254. BURLINGHAM, RUSSELL: *Forrest Reid: A Portrait and a Study*. With an
introduction by Walter de la Mare. London: Faber & Faber, 1953. 259 p.
    See pp. 196-202 and *passim* for Reid's book on Yeats (J1128).

Irish: T. W. Rolleston

See J1110.

Irish: AE (George William Russell)

2255. MÖR, IAN: "W. B. Yeats and A. E. (George Russell)," *Theosophical R*,
37:218 (Oct 1905), 105-17.

Yeats's mysticism is magical: he wants an Ireland of artists. AE's mysticism is visionary: he wants an Ireland of saints.

2256. O'CONNOR, FRANK: "Two Friends: Yeats and A. E.," *Yale R*, 29:1 (Sept 1939), 60-88.

2257. O'FAOLAIN, SEAN: "AE and W. B.," *VQR*, 15:1 (Winter 1939), 41-57. A shorter version was published as "Yeats and the Younger Generation," *Horizon*, 5:25 (Jan 1942), 43-54. Discusses Yeats's and AE's occult interests and the conditions that made them possible; John Butler Yeats's influence on his son; WBY's gregariousness, which proves his affinity with the 18th century rather than with the romantics (although he writes like a hermit); and the development of his poetry. See also J1286.

See also J557, 788, 1110, 1136, 1720, 2160, 2865, 2873, 3091, 4034, 6213, 7243-46, 7250, 7251, 7255, 7257.

Irish: George Francis Savage-Armstrong

See J1110.

Irish: John Shawe-Taylor

See J1147.

Irish: James Stephens

See J1021, 2873, 7279, 7285.

Irish: Jonathan Swift

2258. ARCHIBALD, DOUGLAS NELSON: "W. B. Yeats's Encounters with Swift, Berkeley, and Burke," Ph.D. thesis, U of Michigan, 1966. xvii, 300 p. (*DA*, 28:1 [July 1967], 220A-21A.)
Includes an interpretation of "Lapis Lazuli," 278-94.

2259. ————: "Yeats's Encounters: Observations on Literary Influence and Literary History," *New Literary History*, 1:3 (Spring 1970), 439-70.
Yeats's "encounters with Swift, Berkeley, and Burke" as a basis for a general discussion of the problem of literary influence.

2260. DONOGHUE, DENIS: *Jonathan Swift: A Critical Introduction*. Cambridge: UP, 1969, viii, 235 p.
Swift and Yeats, *passim* (see index). Discusses parallels rather than influences.

2261. HONE, JOSEPH M.: "A Letter from Ireland," *Poetry*, 44:4 (July 1934), 215-20.

2262. JOHNSON, MAURICE: *The Sin of Wit: Jonathan Swift as a Poet*. Syracuse: Syracuse UP, 1950. xvii, 145 p.
"Eliot, Hardy, Joyce, Yeats, and the Ghost of Swift," 130-35.

2263. MCHUGH, ROGER, and PHILIP EDWARDS (eds): *Jonathan Swift, 1667-1967: A Dublin Tercentenary Tribute*. Dublin: Dolmen Press, 1967. xix, 231 p.
Louis A. Landa: "Jonathan Swift: 'Not the Greatest of Divines,'" 38-60, protests Yeats's image of Swift as fierce and brooding ("Blood and the Moon"); so does Austin Clarke, "The Poetry of Swift," 94-115, quoting *The Words upon the Window-Pane*.

2263a. RAWSON, CLAUDE JULIEN: *Gulliver and the Gentle Reader: Studies in Swift and Our Time.* London: Routledge & Kegan Paul, 1973. x, 190 p.
"'Tis Only Infinite Below: Swift, with Reflections on Yeats, Wallace Stevens and R. D. Laing," 60-83; reprinted from *Essays in Criticism,* 22:2 (Apr 1972), 161-81.

2264. SISSON, C. H.: "Yeats and Swift," *Agenda,* 9:4-10:1 (Autumn-Winter 1971/72), 34-38.
Yeats's understanding of Swift was very limited.

2264a. TRAUGOTT, JOHN: "Swift, Our Contemporary," *University R* [Dublin], 4:1 (Spring 1967), 11-34.
Reprinted with additions and corrections in Claude Julien Rawson (ed), *Focus: Swift.* London: Sphere, 1971. 270 p. (pp. 239-64).

2265. VOIGT, MILTON: *Swift and the Twentieth Century.* Detroit: Wayne State UP, 1964. vii, 205 p.
See pp. 131-33.

2265a. VOZAR, LEA BERTANI: "Yeats, Swift, Irish Patriotism, and 'Rationalistic Anti-Intellectualism,'" *Massachusetts Studies in English,* 3:4 (Fall 1972), 108-16.

2266. °WHITE, ROBERT O.: "William Butler Yeats and the Mask of Jonathan Swift," M.A. thesis, Columbia U, 1962. 151 p.

See also J1076, 1112, 1147, 2817, 2968, 3938-40 and note, 3941-48.

Irish: J. M. Synge

2267. °DAVENPORT, MARGUERITE: "Synge and Yeats: The Dramatist and His Critic," M.A. thesis, Trinity U (San Antonio, Tex.), 1965.

2268. EISENTHAL, SUSAN MITCHELL: "A Comparative Study of the Plays Written by William Butler Yeats and John Millington Synge during the Period of Their Association (1896-1909)," M.A. thesis, U of Kansas, 1965. ii, 127 p.

2269. FAULKNER, PETER: "Yeats, Ireland, and Ezra Pound," *Threshold,* #18 [1963?], 58-68.
When Yeats met Pound for the first time, he was already past the Symbolist stage in his esthetics. This was largely due to Synge's influence, which is therefore much more important than Pound's.

2270. HONE, J. M.: "A Memory of *The Playboy,*" *Saturday R,* 113:2956 (22 June 1912), 776-77.
Reprinted in *Irish Book Lover,* 4:1 (Aug 1912), 7-8. How Yeats defended the play.

2271. YAMAMOTO, SHUJI: "Yeats and Synge," *Yeats Society of Japan: Annual Report,* #2 (1967), 16-20.
The influence of Synge's poetry on Yeats.

See also J815, 947, 959, 1000, 1091, 1112, 1161 (#2), 1162 (#2), 1747, 1759, 2145a, 4096, 4100, 4159, 4462-65, 4701 and note, 7294, 7297, 7305, 7314, 7315, 7317, 7338, 7339, 7343, 7345, 7349, 7356, 7357, 7359, 7360, 7382, 7384, 7395, 7399, 7401, 7406, 7411, 7413, 7428, 7430, 7442.

Irish: John Todhunter

See J1110, 4199.

Irish: Katharine Tynan

See J177a, 690, 1110, 4201, 5094-114, 7446.

Irish: Jack B. Yeats

2272. ROSE, MARILYN GADDIS: "The Kindred Vistas of W. B. and Jack B. Yeats," *Éire-Ireland*, 5:1 (Spring 1970), 67-79.
   Spatial relations in WBY's poems and JBY's paintings.

2273. ————: *Jack B. Yeats: Painter and Poet*. Bern: Lang, 1972. 51 p. (European University Papers. Series 18. Vol. 3.)
   "Complementary Views: W. B. Yeats, Synge, Joyce, Beckett," 37-47.

Irish: John Butler Yeats

2274. MURPHY, WILLIAM M.: "Father and Son: The Early Education of W. B. Yeats," *REL*, 8:4 (Oct 1967), 75-96.
   Biographical connections and JBY's influence on WBY.

2275. °PATRICK, JEAN ELIZABETH D'OLIER: "John Butler Yeats and William Butler Yeats," M.A. thesis, McMaster U, 1969.

See also J556, 924, 1101, 1103, 2257, 4076a, 4100, 5439-55.

Italian Literature: General Section

2276. WILSON, ROGER SHADE: "W. B. Yeats's Myth of the Italian Renaissance," °Ph.D. thesis, U of Colorado, 1971. 220 p. (*DA*, 32:12 [June 1972], 7015A-16A.)

Italian: Giordano Bruno

2277. SCHRICKX, W.: "On Giordano Bruno, Wilde, and Yeats," *ES*, 45:Supplement presented to R. W. Zandvoort on the occasion of his 70th birthday (1964), 257-64.
   The concept of Anima Mundi traced from Bruno to Yeats via Pater, Wilde, and Frederick York Powell.

Italian: Baldassare Castiglione

See J1131, 1708, 1713.

Italian: Dante Alighieri

2278. MELCHIORI, GIORGIO: "Yeats and Dante," *English Miscellany*, #19 (1968), 153-79.

2279. VANCE, THOMAS: "Dante, Yeats, and Unity of Being," *Shenandoah*, 17:2 (Winter 1966), 73-85.
   Yeats's affinity of mind with Dante was greater than Eliot's, Pound's, or Joyce's. It rests on a common "visionary structure" that Yeats called Unity of Being. Comments on "Ego Dominus Tuus," "Cuchulain Comforted," and *A Vision*.

See also J1883, 2985.

Italian: Giambattista Vico

2280. °CARDEN, MARY: "The Few and the Many," M.A. thesis, University College, Dublin, 1967.
   On Vico, Synge, and Yeats.

Japanese Literature: General Section

2281. MINER, EARL: *The Japanese Tradition in British and American Literature*. Princeton: Princeton UP, 1958. xxi, 312 p.

"'An Aristocratic Form': Japan in the Thought and Writing of William Butler Yeats," 232-65; with subsections on Yeats's criticism, poetry, and plays.

2281a. NAITŌ, SHIRŌ: "Yeats and Zen Buddhism," *Eastern Buddhist*, 5:2 (Oct 1972), 171-78.

Refers specifically to "The Statues" and the influence on Yeats of Daisetz Suzuki.

2282. OSHIMA, SHOTARO: *W. B. Yeats and Japan*. Tokyo: Hokuseido Press, 1965. xiv, 198 p.

Incorporates: "A Recent Letter of Mr. W. B. Yeats and a New Version of the 'Youth and Age' etc.," *Studies in English Literature* [Tokyo], 9:3 (July 1929), 463-66; "W. B. Yeats and Japan in His Relation with the Zen Philosophy and the 'Noh,'" *Bulletin of the Graduate Division of Literature of Waseda U*, #9 (1963), 1-25; "The Poetry of Symbolic Tradition in the East and the West," *ibid.*, #10 (1964), 1-29; "Yeats and the Japanese Theatre," *Threshold*, #19 (Autumn 1965), 89-102.

Contents: 1. Letters from Yeats to Oshima, Hyde, Frederick Langbridge, Makoto Sangū, Yone Noguchi, Kazumi Yano; from Mrs. Yeats to Oshima; from Jack B. Yeats to Oshima; from Hyde to Oshima.
2. Four autograph poems sent to Oshima by Yeats.
3. "Yeats and the 'Noh' Plays"; the influence on Yeats's dramatic theory and practice.
4. "Yeats and the Zen Philosophy"; mostly in the poetry.
5. "'Meru'"; the Taoist influence.
6. "The Elements"; stone and water imagery in Japanese and Yeats's poetry.
7. "'Buddha's Emptiness'"; Buddhistic influence, particularly in "The Statues."
8. Interviews with Yeats, Jack B. Yeats, Elizabeth C. Yeats, and Junzo Sato.
9. Junzo Sato: "A Sketch of My Life."
10. "Books and Periodicals on Yeats in Japan"; a review of research.
11. "Bibliography of Yeats in Japan," primary and secondary. As explained in the introduction to this bibliography, I have excluded most of the items listed by Oshima with the exception of those written in English. Oshima's listing seems almost complete; the following item is missing: Hiroshi Fujiwara: "W. B. Yeats and the Irish Dramatic Movement," *Studies in English Literature*, 26:2 (Nov 1949), 239-60 (in Japanese, with an English summary, pp. 359-60).
12. 43 photographs.

Reviews:

1. Rachel Burrows, "Yeats's Debt to Japan," *Irish Times*, #34313 (17 Dec 1965), 9.
2. Rivers Carew, *Dublin Mag*, 5:1 (Spring 1966), 81.
3. James Kirkup, *Japan Q*, 12:4 (Oct-Dec 1965), 540-42.
4. Giorgio Melchiori, *N&Q*, os 211 / ns 13:3 (Mar 1966), 114-17.
5. William E. Naff, *Comparative Literature*, 19:1 (Winter 1967), 80-83.
6. Frank Tuohy, *Studies in English Literature*, 43:2 (Mar 1967), 284-86.
7. F. A. C. Wilson, *MLR*, 63:2 (Apr 1968), 469-70.

See also J1076, 1162, 1873, 2166, 3020, 3225a, 3550-76 and note, 3580a, 4137.

Japanese: Hagiwara

2283. TSUKIMURA, REIKO: "The Language of Symbolism in Yeats and Hagiwara," Ph.D. thesis, Indiana U, 1967. vii, 207 p. (*DA*, 28:9 [Mar 1968], 3689A.)
    Symbolism in Yeats's poetry.

Japanese: Komparu Zenchiku

2283a. KIM, MYUNG WHAN: "Zenchiku's Philosophy of Wheels and the Yeatsian Parallel," *Literature East & West*, 15:4-16:1-2 (Dec 1971, Mar 1972, June 1972), 647-61.
    Zenchiku's wheels and Yeats's gyres in *A Vision*.

Latin Literature: General Section

See J1929-31.

Latin: Augustinus, Aurelius, saint

See J3984a.

Latin: Catullus

2284. O'MEARA, JOHN J.: "Yeats, Catullus, and 'The Lake Isle of Innisfree,'" *University R* [Dublin], 3:8 [1966?], 15-24.
    Similarities in the poetry of Catullus and Yeats.

Latin: Lucretius

See J2958.

Latin: Virgil

See J2000.

Netherlands Literature: A. Roland Holst

2284a. BOSSAERT, HENRI: "De keltische en mythologische facetten in het werk van A. Roland Holst," *Vlaamse Gids*, 56:6 (June 1972), 7-12.
    Includes notes on Yeats's influence.

2284b. ————: "A. Roland Holst, W. B. Yeats en de kunstidealen van het franse symbolisme," *Nieuw Vlaams Tijdschrift*, 26:2 (Feb 1973), 155-76.

2285. SÖRENSEN, FREDDY: "Een vergelijking: Adiraan [*sic*] Roland Holst en William Butler Yeats," *Ruimten*, 3:12 (1964), 22-38.
    A detailed comparison of the poetry of both poets.

2286. STENFERT KROESE, WILLEM HERMAN: *De mythe van A. Roland Holst.* Amsterdam: De Bezige Bij, 1951. iii, 110 p.
    On the influence of Yeats on Roland Holst, pp. 6-33.

2287. VESTDIJK, S.: "Kroniek van de poezie: Nestoriaansche overpeinzingen," *Gids*, 119:3 (Mar 1956), 203-9.
    Compares the poetry of Yeats and Roland Holst and comments on Roland Holst's Yeats translations.

2288. WIJNGAARDS, N.: "*The Shadowy Waters* van W. B. Yeats en A. Roland Holst," *Spiegel der letteren*, 6:3 (1963), 197-209.

Nigerian Literature: Chinua Achebe

2288a. BROWN, LLOYD W.: "Cultural Norms and Modes of Perception in Achebe's Fiction," *Research in African Literatures*, 3:1 (Spring 1972), 21-35.
    Includes a note on Achebe's debt to Yeats.

2289. MELONE, THOMAS: "Architecture du monde: Chinua Achebe et W. B. Yeats," *Conch*, 2:1 (Mar 1970), 44-52.
    Unity of Being in Yeats and Unity of Humanity in Achebe.

2290. STOCK, A. G.: "Yeats and Achebe," *J of Commonwealth Literature*, #5 (July 1968), 105-11.
    Yeats's *A Vision* and Achebe's *Things Fall Apart*.

Norwegian Literature: Henrik Ibsen

2291. FOX, R. M.: "Ibsen and Yeats: Pioneers of National Drama," *Aryan Path*, 26:4 (Apr 1955), 154-58.
    Biographical parallels rather than influences.

See also J3446, 4155, 4159.

The Orient: General Studies

See J1870, 1871, 1873, 1875, 1877, 1879, 1881, 2166, 2747a, 3582a, 4019.

Portuguese Literature: Fernando Pessoa

2292. BIDERMAN, SOL: "Mount Abiegnos and the Masks: Occult Imagery in Yeats and Pessoa," *Luso-Brazilian R*, 5:1 (June 1968), 59-74.
    Mount Abiegnos, the rose, Rosicrucianism, initiation, and mask in the poetry of Yeats and Pessoa. The link seems to have been Annie Besant, who was read by both.

Spanish Literature: Juan Ramón Jiménez

2293. DEWEY, MARY LEWIS: "Juan Ramón Jiménez and William Butler Yeats," M.A. thesis, Stanford U, 1966. iv, 45 p.

2294. °PATTON, KATHRYN HART: "The Evolution of the Rose: From Form to Flame," *U of Mississippi Studies in English*, 12 (1971), 65-78.
    The rose symbol in Yeats and Jiménez.

See also J2973.

Swedish Literature: August Strindberg

2295. LAPISARDI, FREDERICK S.: "The Same Enemies: Notes on Certain Similarities between Yeats and Strindberg," *MD*, 12:2 (Sept 1969), 146-54.
    In dramatic theory and practice.

See also J4159.

Swedish: Emanuel Swedenborg

See J1867, 3014.

CE Less Important Material

The items in this section may be safely disregarded by most readers interested in Yeats. (Conversely, I do not imply that all the other items in this bibliography are required reading.) I include them because they are, after all, about Yeats. They are grouped in three subsections: The Burial in Drumcliff(e) Churchyard, the Yeats International Summer School in Sligo, and Other Material. I have made no attempt to trace and include the numerous newspaper reports about the first two events.

The Burial in Drumcliff(e) Churchyard

2296. ANON.: "The Burial of Poet Yeats," *Life*, 25:17 (25 Oct 1948), 146-50.

2297. ANON.: "In Drumcliffe Churchyard Yeats Is Laid . . . ," *Times Pictorial*, 74:3926 (25 Sept 1948), 1.

2298. COLLIS, MAURICE: *The Journey Up: Reminiscences, 1934-1968*. London: Faber & Faber, 1970. 222 p.
    Louis MacNeice insisted that the wrong body was interred (pp. 83-85).

2299. COLUM, PADRAIC: "A Poet Is Brought Home," *Commonweal*, 49:2 (22 Oct 1948), 33-36.

2300. HENN, T. R.: "The Return to the Valley," *Irish Library Bulletin*, 9:[10] (Oct 1948), 163-65.

2301. O'BRIEN, KATE: "Yeats Comes Home," *Spectator*, 181:6274 (24 Sept 1948), 394.
    Correspondence by St. John Ervine, "Yeats and Others," :6275 (1 Oct 1948), 432, questioning Yeats's "greatness."

2302. PUDNEY, JOHN: "A Poet Comes Home," *Illustrated*, 9 Oct 1948, 16-18.

2303. ROBINSON, LENNOX: "Journey's End," *Irish Library Bulletin*, 9:[10] (Oct 1948), 166.

2304. THOMAS, JOHN ORMOND: "W. B. Yeats Comes Home to Sligo," *Picture Post*, 41:2 (9 Oct 1948), 10-13.

Yeats International Summer School in Sligo

2305. ANON.: "Yeats's Work Takes on Added Grandeur for Students Visiting the Irish Poet's Sources of Inspiration [. . .]," *NYT*, 112:38568 (29 Aug 1963), 31.

2306. ANON.: "Interpreters of Yeats: Sligo Summer School," *Times Educational Supplement*, 53:2519 (20 Aug 1963), 235.

2307. ANON.: "Thoughts on Yeats: Ghosts and Computers," *Times Educational Supplement*, 54:2571 (28 Aug 1964), 277.

2308. BROWNLOW, TIMOTHY: "One Dear Perpetual Place," *Dublin Mag*, 4:3/4 (Autumn-Winter 1965), 94-96.

2309. CAREW, RIVERS: "Yeats: The Summer School in Sligo," *Hibernia*, 29:3 (Mar 1965), 26.

2310. ————: "The Yeats Summer School in Sligo: Successful Cultural Venture," *Hibernia*, 31:8 (Aug 1967), 7.

2311. COXHEAD, ELIZABETH: "The Dreaming of the Abbey," *Guardian*, #35793 (1 Aug 1961), 5.
    Also on Duras House.

2312. CURTAYNE, ALICE: "Ireland," *Critic*, 21:1 (Aug-Sept 1962), 48-50.

2313. DURYEE, MARY BALLARD: "William Butler Yeats in Modern Ireland,"
Recorder, 28 (Dec 1965), 7-9.

2314. EARLY, ELEANOR: "Ireland's Yeats Country," *NYT*, 115:39614 (10 July
1966), X, 29.

2315. FRIEND, ROBERT: "The Sixth Yeats International Summer School," *JJQ*,
3:2 (Winter 1966), 139-40.

2316. GIBBON, MONK: "The Yeats Country," *Ireland of the Welcomes*, 9:2
(July-Aug 1960), 12-14.

2317. HENN, T. R.: "Yeats Summer School," *TLS*, 59:3030 (25 Mar 1960), 193.

2318. RAFROIDI, PATRICK: "The First Yeats International Summer School,
Sligo, Eire (13-27 août 1960)," *EA*, 13:4 (Oct-Dec 1960), 502-3.

2319. SPEAIGHT, ROBERT: "A Centenary in Sligo: The Yeats Summer School,"
Tablet, 219:6536 (28 Aug 1965), 952-53.

2320. WARD, DAVID F.: "'Under Bare Ben Bulben's Head': The Yeats International Summer School," *JJQ*, 4:1 (Fall 1966), 46-49.

2321. WARD, HERMAN M.: "Thanne Longen Folk to Goon on Pilgrimages,"
English J, 51:4 (Apr 1962), 287-88.

See also J1130, 2391, 6074.

Other Material

2322. ADLARD, JOHN: "An Unnoticed Yeats Item," *N&Q*, os 214 / ns 16:7
(July 1969), 255.
  See J134.

2323. ANON.: Note on recent sales of the first edition of *Mosada*, *Book
Collector*, 12:4 (Winter 1963), 437-38.
  The highest price paid was $3,750.

2324. Entry canceled.

2325. ANON.: "The Visit of William Butler Yeats: Mr. Yeats Maintains
That Propaganda Cannot Take the Place of Art. Mr. Yeats's Activities
through George Moore's Eyes," *Current Opinion*, 56:4 (Apr 1914), 294-95.

2326. ANON.: "Poet's Tower to Be Restored: Plan for W. B. Yeats's Castle,"
Irish Times, #33698 (25 Oct 1963), 11.
  See also editorial on p. 9.

2327. ANON.: "Det keltiske element i literaturen," *Kringsjaa*, 12:1 (15
July 1898), 69-74.
  Summary of Yeats's "The Celtic Element in Literature" (Wp. 355).

2328. ANON.: "Irske hekse-doktere," *Kringsjaa*, 16:7 (15 Oct 1900), 489-93.
  Summary of Yeats's "Irish Witch Doctors" (Wp. 359).

2329. ANON.: "A Lille: Un hommage à Yeats," *Monde*, 22:6291 (6 Apr 1965),
12.
  Note on the Lille Yeats festival and exhibition, organized by the
  fifth Congrès de la Société des anglicistes de l'enseignement supérieur.

2330. ANON.: "Do We Deserve This Compliment?" *NYT*, 74:24351 (25 Sept
1924), 22.
  Yeats's favorable opinion of the Pennsylvania Railroad Station in New
  York.

2331. ANON.: "Changes in Oratory," *NYT*, 74:24685 (25 Aug 1925), 16.
Comments on Yeats's statement that "the day of oratory is past."

2332. ANON.: "Literary Gossip," *Outlook* [London], 1:11 (16 Apr 1898),
344-46.
Criticizes Yeats's "The Broken Gates of Death" for lack of factual
accuracy. See Yeats's reply, :12 (23 Apr 1898), 377 (Wp. 354), and
the answer by the "friendly paragraphist," *ibid.*

2333. ANON.: "The World in One Small Room . . . William Butler Yeats,"
Senior Scholastic, 47:5 (15 Oct 1945), 20.

2334. ANON.: "An Important Centenary," *Shavian*, 3:3 (Winter 1965), 34-35.

2335. ANON.: "T. P.'s Portrait Gallery—VI.," *T. P.'s Weekly*, 14:368 (26
Nov 1909), 703.
"He takes all beauty for his province, and lives in the Euston Road."

2336. ANON.: Warning to Yeats not to "pose" on his American lecture tour,
Theatre, 3:30 (Aug 1903), 186.

2337. ANON.: "Cast a Cold Eye," *Time*, 60:14 (6 Oct 1952), 41.
On the difficulties of erecting a Yeats memorial in Ireland.

2338. ANON.: "D. Litt. for Mr. W. B. Yeats," *Times*, #45833 (27 May 1931),
14.
The Oxford degree. See also J2395.

2339. ANON.: "A Tribute to W. B. Yeats," *Times*, #48344 (29 June 1939), 12.
Preview of a program at the Ellen Terry Barn Theatre with a note on
Purgatory.

2340. ARCHER, CHARLES: *William Archer: Life, Work and Friendships.* New
Haven: Yale UP, 1931. 451 p.
Gilbert Murray's enthusiasm for Yeats undergoes a change, p. 271.

2341. ARNOLD, BRUCE: "Moore's New Yeats Memorial Examined," *Sunday Independent*, 62:45 (5 Nov 1967), 25.
Henry Moore's memorial in St. Stephen's Green. See also J2410.

2342. ATKINSON, BROOKS: *Brief Chronicles.* NY: Coward-McCann, 1966. 255 p.
"The Yeats Boys," 44-46.

2343. BENCE-JONES, MARK: "A Yeats Pilgrim in Sligo," *Country Life*, 149:
3859 (27 May 1971), 1284-86.

2344. BILLINGTON, MICHAEL: "Welcome Partiality: Talking about Yeats,"
Times, #57984 (30 Sept 1970), 13.
MacLiammóir's one-man Yeats show.

2345. BLEI, FRANZ: *Zeitgenössische Bildnisse.* Amsterdam: De Lange, 1940.
345 p.
"William Butler Yeats," 162-63.

2346. BOEHRINGER, ERICH, and WILHELM HOFFMANN (eds): *Robert Boehringer:
Eine Freundesgabe.* Tübingen: Mohr, 1957. viii, 772 p.
W. M. Jablonski: "Bemerkenswertes aus dem Leben und der Gedankenwelt
des irischen Dichters William Butler Yeats," 325-29.

2347. BRADY, GERARD K.: "Yeats's Tower," *Irish Times*, #32749 (16 Sept
1960), 7.
The history of Thoor Ballylee before Yeats bought it. Correspondence
by Gabriel Fallon, #32750 (17 Sept 1960), 7, 9.

2348. CLEMENS, KATHARINE: "Some Reflections on William Butler Yeats," *Mark Twain Q*, 6:1 (Summer-Fall 1943), 17-18.
"Yeats' mental life had been mostly confusion."

2349. COLUM, PADRAIC: "A Dublin Letter," *SatR*, 13:16 (15 Feb 1936), 24.
Thoughts on Yeats's 70th birthday and a note on *The King of the Great Clock Tower*.

2350. [CRONE, J. S. (?)]: "Mr. Yeats' Confessions," *Irish Book Lover*, 15:2 (Apr 1925), 19-21.

2351. CRONIN, COLM: "A Visit to Thoor Ballylee," *Irish Press*, 36:184 (4 Aug 1966), 9.

2352. CROSLAND, THOMAS WILLIAM HODGSON: *The Wild Irishman*. London: Lane, 1905. 183 p.
"W. B. Yeats," 112-22. Silly.

2353. CUMBERLAND, GERALD: *Set Down in Malice: A Book of Reminiscences*. NY: Brentano's, 1919. 286 p.
"People I Would Like to Meet," 263-72; one of them Yeats, in order to find out why he is so self-deluded.

2354. CUNO, JOHN MARSHALL: "Irish TV Items," *CSM*, 57:87 (10 Mar 1965), 4.
A review of a CBS program that featured a reading and discussion of Yeats's love poems and a commentary by David Greene.

2355. DESMOND, SHAW: "Dunsany, Yeats, and Shaw: Trinity of Magic," *Bookman* [NY], 58:3 (Nov 1923), 260-66.

2356. DICKINSON, PATRIC: *The Good Minute: An Autobiographical Study*. London: Gollancz, 1965. 239 p.
Quotes from Yeats's poems *passim* for some sort of moral life support.

2357. DODD, LORING HOLMES: *Celebrities at Our Hearthside*. Boston: Dresser, Chapman & Grimes, 1959. ix, 402 p.
"An Irish Laureate: William Butler Yeats," 368-72.

2358. DOUGLAS, ALFRED, LORD: Text of the telegram sent to Yeats on the publication of the *Oxford Book of Modern Verse*, *Daily Express*, #11402 (30 Nov 1936), 6.
"Your omission of my work from the absurdly-named Oxford Book of Modern Verse is exactly typical of the attitude of the minor to the major poet. For example Thomas Moore, the Yeats of the 19th century, would undoubtedly have excluded Keats and Shelley from any anthology he had compiled. And why drag in Oxford? Would not shoneen Irish be a more correct description?" See note by William Hickey, #11404 (2 Dec 1936), 6, quoting Sir Arthur Quiller-Couch in support of Douglas.

2359. DUNCAN, RONALD: "Yeats," *Townsman*, 2:7 (Aug 1939), 19-21.

2360. EMERSON, DOROTHY: "William Butler Yeats," *Scholastic*, 28:6 (7 Mar 1936), 12.

2361. ENGLE, PAUL: "The Ireland of Yeats," *Saturday Evening Post*, 243:3 (Winter 1971), 91-93.
Saturday Eveningish.

2362. EVANS, OLIVE: "Topics: Centennial of a Poet," *NYT*, 114:39221 (12 June 1965), 30.

2363. FALLON, GABRIEL: "Dublin Letter," *America*, 98:2526 (12 Oct 1957), 46-47.
On the proposed Yeats memorial by Henry Moore.

2364. FOX, R. M.: "Yeats and His Circle," *Aryan Path*, 20:7 (July 1949), 306-9.

2365. FRÉCHET, RENÉ: "Le centenaire de Yeats," *EA*, 18:3 (July-Sept 1965), 225-27.

2365a. GRAHAM, RIGBY: "Thoor Ballylee: The Castle Home of W. B. Yeats," *American Book Collector*, 21:4 (1973), 11-13.
    See also "Letter from Dublin," *American N&Q*, 10:7 (Mar 1972), 107-8.

2366. HADEN-GUEST, ANTHONY: "Yeats Country," *Daily Telegraph: Weekend Telegraph*, #23 (26 Feb 1965), 18-23.

2367. HARLEY, E. S.: "A Note on a Yeats Quotation," *Bulletin of the Department of English, U of Calcutta*, 5:16&17 (1963), 1.
    Attempts to track down the source of "Think like a wise man but express yourself like the common people," reputedly said by Yeats to Lady Gregory.

2368. HEISELER, BERNT VON: "Erzählungen und Lyrik," *Deutsche Zeitschrift*, 47:9 (June 1934), 579-80.

2369. HENN, T. R.: *Address on the Occasion of the Gift of Duras House, Kinvara, to An Óige, Irish Youth Hostel Association, to Be Dedicated to the Memory of W. B. Yeats, Lady Gregory, Edward Martyn, and Florimond, Count de Basterot*. Kinvara, 20 August 1961. Dublin: Irish Times, 1961. 4 p.

2370. H[EWITT], J. H.: "William Butler Yeats, 1865-1939," *Belfast Municipal Museum and Art Gallery Q Notes*, #60 (Mar 1939), 6-7.
    On the H. M. Paget painting of Apr 1889.

2371. HODGART, M. J. C.: "Misquotation as Re-Creation," *Essays in Criticism*, 3:1 (Jan 1953), 28-38.
    On Yeats's misquotation of Burns's "Open the Door to Me, O" (in *Ideas of Good and Evil*), pp. 36-37.

2372. JACKSON, ROBERT WYSE: *A Memorial Sermon Preached at Drumcliffe on the Occasion of the Centenary of the Birth of William Butler Yeats*. Dublin: Dolmen Press / Sligo: Keohane, [1965]. 4 p.

2373. JOHNSON, COLTON: "Some Unnoticed Contributions to Periodicals by W. B. Yeats," *N&Q*, os 217 / ns 19:2 (Feb 1972), 48-52.
    Reprints, complete or in part, items J136, 137, and 930.

2374. KAIN, RICHARD M.: "The Yeats Centenary in Ireland," *JJQ*, 3:2 (Winter 1966), 130-38.

2375. KELLEHER, DANIEL LAWRENCE: *Ireland of the Welcomes*. 4th edition revised. Dublin: Irish Tourist Association, 1948 [1930]. 119 p.
    "W. B. Yeats at Lough Gill," 104-5.

2376. KINSELLA, THOMAS: "A Yeats Festival on the Shores of Lake Michigan," *Hibernia*, 29:6 (June 1965), 9.
    At Northwestern University. See also J1148.

2377. ————: "W. B. Yeats: The Last Romantic," *Daily Egyptian*, 47:89 (12 Feb 1966), 2.

2378. KIRSCH, HANS-CHRISTIAN: *Einladung nach Irland*. München: Langen-Müller, 1971. 240 p. (Einladung nach. . . . 13.)
    Thoor Ballylee and Yeats country, County Sligo, pp. 100-102, 130-34.

2379. LETTS, WINIFRED M.: "W. B. Yeats in Sligo," *Great Thoughts*, ser 11 / 8:2659 (Nov 1934), 75-76.

2380. LEWSEN, CHARLES: "Talking about Yeats," *Times*, #58298 (14 Oct 1971), 13.
MacLiammóir's one-man Yeats show.

2381. L[ITTELL], P[HILIP]: "Books and Things," *New Republic*, 21:272 (18 Feb 1920), 358.
Why one should like to meet Yeats in person.

2382. LONDREVILLE [i.e., LONDRAVILLE], RICHARD: "Jeanne Robert Foster," *Éire-Ireland*, 5:1 (Spring 1970), 38-44.
Preview of an edition of her papers that will include several unpublished Yeats items.

2383. LOWRY, HELEN BULLITT: "Another 'Contemptible Little Army': Minor Poets. Imaginative Account of What Happened When Yeats Told a Meeting of the Clan He Didn't Have Time to Read American Verse," *NYT*, 69:22667 (15 Feb 1920), IV, 7.

2384. MCAULEY, JAMES: "Driving through Kiltartan to the Yeats Tower," *Hibernia*, 29:10 (Oct 1965), 17.

2385. MCCUTCHION, DAVID: "Yeats Centenary Festival at Jadavpur," *JJCL*, 5 (1965), 117-21.

2386. MCGARRY, J. P.: "The Yeats Country," *Ireland of the Welcomes*, 6:2 (July-Aug 1957), 31-33.

2387. M[ONROE], H[ARRIET]: "Mr. Yeats and the Poetic Drama," *Poetry*, 16:1 (Apr 1920), 32-38.
Yeats's address at *Poetry*'s banquet, 3 Mar 1920 (see J729), as a starting point for a general discussion of the poetic drama. Not really on Yeats.

2388. MOULT, THOMAS: "The Bard of Houlihan," *Apple (of Beauty and Discord)*, 1:4 (1920), 220, 222, 224.

2389. NELSON, WALTER W.: *Oscar Wilde in Sweden and Other Essays*. Dublin: Dolmen Press, 1965. v, 84 p.
"Anglo-Irish and Scandinavian Authors Rewarded with the Nobel Prize in Literature," 38-50; contains a few vague remarks on the Yeats reception in Sweden.

2390. O'CONNOR, ULICK: "Let's Honour Yeats," *Sunday Independent*, 53:34 (24 Aug 1958), 8.
"Yeats, who so personifies our people, should have a statue in the middle of Dublin." Correspondence by C. F. N., :35 (31 Aug 1958), 11; by O'Connor, "Pearse Stood Up for Yeats," :38 (21 Sept 1958), 11; by C. F. N., :39 (28 Sept 1958), 15.

2391. OSHIMA, SHOTARO: "Irish Notes," *Yeats Society of Japan: Annual Report and Bulletin*, #5 (1970), 52-57.
In two parts: "Senator Michael B. Yeats and Mrs. Georgie Yeats"; "The Yeats International Summer School."

2392. *The Oxford Dictionary of Quotations*. 2nd edition. London: Oxford UP, 1959 [1941]. xx, 1003 p.
Yeats figures with 70 quotations (pp. 584-86), which is way behind Tennyson but much better than Eliot.

2393. POUND, EZRA: *ABC of Reading*. London: Faber & Faber, 1961. 206 p.
Two Yeats anecdotes, pp. 44, 197-98.

2394. POWELL, LAWRENCE CLARK: *Books in My Baggage: Adventures in Reading and Collecting*. Cleveland: World, 1960. 257 p.
"Ripeness Is All," 56-60: "To collect Yeats is . . . a joy."

2395. [POYNTON, ARTHUR BLACKBURNE]: Oration of the Public Orator in presenting the honorary degree of D.Litt. to W. B. Yeats on 26 May 1931, *Oxford U Gazette*, 61:1972 (3 June 1931), 628.

2396. PRICE, NANCY: *Into an Hour-Glass*. London: Museum Press, 1953. 245 p.
Praises Yeats as an inspiring man and poet, pp. 165-67.

2397. PURBECK, PETER: "Television: The Casual Discussion," *Listener*, 21:530 (9 Mar 1939), 543.
Review of a B.B.C. program in which Gogarty and Clinton-Baddeley chatted about Yeats.

2398. PYLES, THOMAS: "'Bollicky Naked,'" *American Speech*, 24:4 (Dec 1949), 255.
Explains this uninhibited phrase that appears in Yeats's letter to Olivia Shakespear of 26 Aug 1936 (printed in Hone's biography, p. 448 of the 1943 English edition, p. 480 of the 1943 American edition). In *Letters*, someone saw fit to alter the phrase to "she was without a stitch on her" (p. 861). "She" was Jean Forbes-Robertson.

2399. [ROBINSON, LENNOX]: *Augustus John: Yeats*. Address to be made at a presentation on November 23rd, 1955. [Dublin, 1955. 4 p.]
Mimeographed text about the presentation of a bust, copy in National Library of Ireland, P.2355.

2400. ROONEY, PHILIP: "Landmarks in the Yeats Country," *Ireland of the Welcomes*, 1:2 (July-Aug 1952), 5-8.

2401. RUTHERFORD, MALCOLM: "Thoor Ballylee," *Spectator*, 214:7148 (25 June 1965), 806.
The reopening ceremony.

2402. SADDLEMYER, ANN: "On 'Paragraphs from Samhain' and Some Additional Yeats Letters," *Irish Book*, 2:3/4 (Autumn 1963), 127-28.
Bibliographical note on letters to Winifred Letts (Wp. 394) and erroneous descriptions of the following:
(a) *Paragraphs from the Forthcoming Number of "Samhain"*: Miss Saddlemyer says that she describes National Library of Ireland MS. 1732, now W244A: actually part of her description is of W244B.
(b) *Paragraphs from Samhain*: This should be *Paragraphs from Samhain 1909*, listed under J71a, reprinted in J125 (q.v.). I owe this information to a query from Richard J. Finneran.

2403. SAHER, P. J.: *Symbole: Die magische Geheimsprache der Poesie (Zur Psycho-Kybernetik der logischen Begriffsformen im östlichen Denken und in der abendländischen Romantik)*. Ratingen: Henn, 1968. 328 p.
Some worthless and inaccurate notes on Yeats, pp. 184-86, 259.

2404. SCHUCHART, MAX: "Yeats in de Ierse legatie," *Vrij Nederland*, 12:14 (1 Dec 1951), 6.
Report of a recital of Yeats's poetry, mostly by A. Roland Holst, in the Irish embassy at The Hague.

2405. SHORTER, CLEMENT: Letter to the editor, *Daily News*, #18135 (4 May 1904), 4.

Complains about the use of the term "log-rolling" in connection with Yeats and Lady Gregory (cf. issue #18131 [29 Apr 1904], 4). Criticizes Yeats for declaring Lady Gregory's *Cuchulain of Muirthemne* to be "the best book that has come out of Ireland in my time." See Yeats's reply, #18141 (11 May 1904), 4 (Wp. 367), claiming that *Gods and Fighting Men* is an even better book. Incidentally, this last letter contains a statement that Yeats was later to repudiate: "Swift, Burke, and Goldsmith . . . hardly seem to me to have come out of Ireland at all. . . ."

2406. SIDNELL, M. J.: "Unicorn Territory?" *Canadian Forum*, 45:531 (Apr 1965), 2-3.
The Yeats centenary celebrations at the U of Victoria.

2407. TATE, SIR ROBERT WILLIAM: *Orationes et epistolae dublinenses (1914-40)*. Dublin: Hodges, Figgis, 1941. xix, 205 p.
"Comitia hiemalia, die vicesimo decembris, 1922, habita: Litt. D. Willelmus Butler Yeats," 51; at Trinity College, Dublin.

2408. TOBIN, TERENCE: "MacLiammoir vs. Yeats," *Drama Critique*, 9:1 (Winter 1966), 35-36.
The one-man Yeats show.

2409. TURNER, W. J.: "Words and Tones," *NSt*, 18:439 (22 July 1939), 141-42.
Review of a reading of Yeats's poetry at the Ellen Terry Barn Theatre, including some remarks on why Yeats loved folksongs.

2410. *W. B. Yeats, 1865-1939: A Tribute in Bronze by Henry Moore Erected by Admirers of the Poet October 1967*. [Dublin, 1967. 4 p.]
A pamphlet with a photograph of the sculpture. There is a copy in the National Library of Ireland (IR.92.p.85).

2411. WAGNER, LUDWIG: "William Butler Yeats," *30. Januar*, 1:12 (Feb 1934), 91-93.

2412. WHEELER, ETHEL: "The Fairyland of Heart's Desire," *Great Thoughts*, ser 4 / 8:948 (Oct 1901), 375-76.

2413. WILLIAMSON, CLAUDE CHARLES HORACE: *Writers of Three Centuries, 1789-1914*. London: Richards, 1920. 515 p.
"W. B. Yeats and the Irish School," 444-51.

DA   Books and Pamphlets Exclusively on Yeats

2414. ALBRIGHT, DANIEL FRANK: *The Myth against Myth: A Study of Yeats's Imagination in Old Age*. London: Oxford UP, 1972. ix, 195 p.

> Based on a °Ph.D. thesis, Yale U, 1970. 264 p. (*DA*, 31:6 [Dec 1970], 2903A). "This book is a study of Yeats's image of the human mind, his painstaking construction of his own personality by means of poetry" (p. 1). Concentrates on "The Circus Animals' Desertion," *The King of the Great Clock Tower*, "News for the Delphic Oracle," "The Tower," and *The Wanderings of Oisin*.
>
> *Reviews:*
> 1. Michael H. Begnal, *Éire-Ireland*, 8:3 (Autumn 1973), 114-15.
> 2. John Boland, "Poet's Self-Portrait," *Hibernia*, 37:3 (16 Feb 1973), 14.
> 3. Frederic S. Colwell, *QQ*, 80:4 (Winter 1973), 645-46.
> 4. Phillip L. Marcus, "Memoir and Myth," *Irish Press*, 43:18 (20 Jan 1973), 10.
> 5. Harold Orel, *JEGP*, 72:4 (Oct 1973), 578-80.
> 6. Roger N. Parisious, *Dublin Mag*, 10:1 (Winter/Spring 1973), 125-30.
> 7. Hermann Peschmann, *English*, 22:113 (Summer 1973), 83-84.

2415. BANKES, A. G. LIGHTFOOT: "W. B. Yeats and His Significance in the Development of Contemporary Poetry," M.A. thesis, U of Bristol, 1955. iii, 177 p.

> The comparison with contemporary poetry centers on Eliot.

2416. BEUM, ROBERT: *The Poetic Art of W. B. Yeats*. NY: Ungar, 1969. xvii, 161 p.

> Incorporates: "Yeats's Octaves," *TSLL*, 3:1 (Spring 1961), 89-96; "Yeats the Rhymer," *PELL*, 1:4 (Autumn 1965), 338-50; "Yeats's Idealized Speech," *Michigan QR*, 4:4 (Fall 1965), 227-33. A study of style, meter, and rhyme in the poems (particularly the later ones), including a short chapter on the drama.
>
> *Reviews:*
> 1. Terence Brown, *Irish UR*, 1:2 (Spring 1971), 276-78.
> 2. Edward Engelberg, *Contemporary Literature*, 11:2 (Spring 1970), 303-9.
> 3. Arra M. Garab, "The Legacy of Yeats," *JML*, 1:1 (1970), 137-40.
> 4. Richard M. Kain, *Éire-Ireland*, 4:3 (Autumn 1969), 123-27.

2417. CHATTERJEE, BHABATOSH: *The Poetry of W. B. Yeats*. Calcutta: Orient Longmans, 1962. xiii, 163 p.

> "This book is a study in certain aspects of Yeats' non-dramatic verse, seen against the background of the poet's life and the political, philosophical and literary influences that worked on him. The two chief aims of the book are to show the development of Yeats's mind and craft, and to examine the richness and complexity of his symbolism" (p. ix).
>
> *Reviews:*
> 1. Amalendu Bose, "W. B. Yeats: His Poetry and Thought," *Indian J of English Studies*, 3 (1962), 158-67.
> 2. A. Choudhuri, *Visva-Bharati Q*, 27:3&4 (1961/62), 285-87.
> 3. Frank Kermode, *RES*, 15:57 (Feb 1964), 119.
> 4. Peter Ure, *N&Q*, os 208 / ns 10:10 (Oct 1963), 400.
> 5. F. A. C. Wilson, *MLR*, 58:3 (July 1963), 468-69.

2418. COWELL, RAYMOND: *W. B. Yeats*. London: Evans, 1969. 160 p. (Literature in Perspective.)
A study of "Yeats's life, poetry and thought" (p. 37), aimed at the "ordinary reader" and neglecting almost entirely the prose and the plays.
Reviews:
1. Anon., *Teacher*, 13:11 (14 Mar 1969), 17.
2. Patrick Murray, "'W. B.' Plain," *Irish Press*, 39:40 (15 Feb 1969), 10.

2419. DENTON, MARILYN JEWELL: "The Form of Yeats' Lyric Poetry," Ph.D. thesis, U of Wisconsin, 1957. vii, 225 p. (*DA*, 17:12 [Dec 1957], 3012.)
"This dissertation suggests that Yeats gave far more attention to poetic form than is generally recognized. The writer consulted Yeats's MS notebooks and 'found passages illustrating his method of composing poems'; with Mrs. Yeats's assistance, transcribed those which illustrated Yeats's concern with form. She discusses in detail his indebtedness to certain poets, including William Morris. She lists Yeats's poems according to their verse forms. She discusses his scattered writings about poetic form. A noteworthy study" (from the evaluation in Slack, J456).

2420. *EDDINS, DWIGHT LYMAN: *Yeats: The Nineteenth Century Matrix*. University, Ala.: U of Alabama Press, 1971. x, 173 p.
Based on a Ph.D. thesis, Vanderbilt U, 1967. vii, 178 p. (*DA*, 28:10 [Apr 1968], 4123A). Discusses the development of the early poetry from a pictorial to a dramatic mode, seen against the influence, and compared with the poetry, of Keats, Shelley, Thomas Davis, Allingham, Ferguson, Tennyson, Rossetti, Morris, Lionel Johnson, Dowson, Arnold, the Golden Dawn and other arcana, and French symbolism.
Reviews:
1. Anon., "Yeats as Modern Master," *TLS*, 71:3655 (17 Mar 1972), 311.
2. Donna Gerstenberger, *Ohio R*, 14:1 (Fall 1972), 106-8.
3. T. R. Henn, *RES*, 23:90 (May 1972), 234-35.
4. Richard M. Kain, *Éire-Ireland*, 6:4 (Winter 1971), 134-36.

2421. FARRINGTON, BRIAN: *Malachi-Stilt-Jack: A Study of W. B. Yeats and His Work*. London: Connolly Publications, [1965?]. 12 p.
A lecture read to the Connolly Association and Irish Self-Determination League, London, June 1965. Attempts to bring Yeats's "good" poetry and "bad" politics into line, but does not go very deep.
Reviews:
1. Brendan Kennelly, *Hermathena*, #102 (Spring 1966), 96-97.

2422. GARAB, ARRA M.: *Beyond Byzantium: The Last Phase of Yeats's Career*. DeKalb: Northern Illinois UP, 1969. ix, 133 p.
Based on the more adequately titled "Beyond Byzantium: Studies in the Later Poetry of William Butler Yeats," °Ph.D. thesis, Columbia U, 1962. 200 p. (*DA*, 26:3 [Sept 1965], 1645-46). Incorporates: "Yeats's 'Dark betwixt the Polecat and the Owl,'" *ELN*, 2:3 (Mar 1965), 218-20; "Yeats and the Forged Casement Diaries," *ELN*, 2:4 (June 1965), 289-92; "Fabulous Artifice: Yeats's 'Three Bushes' Sequence," *Criticism*, 7:3 (Summer 1965), 235-49; "Times of Glory: Yeats's 'The Municipal Gallery Revisited,'" *Arizona Q*, 21:3 (Autumn 1965), 243-54.
Mainly concerned with the poems of the last decade, 1929-39. Discusses the time and escape theme, the Crazy Jane poems, the place of "The Gyres" in Yeats's poetry, "Lapis Lazuli," the Casement poems

(identifying Gilbert Murray as one of Yeats's villains), "The Municipal Gallery Revisited," and "The Three Bushes."
Reviews:
1. W. Bronzwaer, *Dutch QR*, 1:1 (1971), 42-43.
2. William M. Carpenter, *MP*, 68:4 (May 1971), 398-400.
3. Edward Engelberg, *Contemporary Literature*, 11:2 (Spring 1970),
   303-9.
4. George P. Mayhew, *BA*, 45:1 (Jan 1971), 129-30.
5. Charles Molesworth, "He Kept a Sword Upstairs," *Nation*, 212:2 (11
   Jan 1971), 58, 60.
6. Paul H. Stacy, "Yeats's Dualities: Two Restatements," *Hartford
   Studies in Literature*, 2:1 (1970), 68-69.
7. [F. A. C. Wilson], *West Coast R*, 5:3 (Jan 1971), 66.

2423. GREEN, HOWARD LEWIS: "The Poetry of W. B. Yeats: A Critical Evaluation," Ph.D. thesis, Stanford U, 1952. v, 510 p.
   On Yeats's theories of poetry and his poems. A thesis supervised by
   Yvor Winters and written along the lines of his criticism, but less
   hostile to Yeats.

2423a. HACKETT, VIRGINIA M.: "The Poetic Sequences of William Butler
Yeats," °Ph.D. thesis, New York U, 1973. 472 p. (*DA*, 34:3 [Sept 1973],
1279A.)
   Discusses "Upon a Dying Lady," "Meditations in Time of Civil War,"
   "A Man Young and Old," "Words for Music Perhaps," "A Woman Young and
   Old," "Supernatural Songs," "The Three Bushes," "Nineteen Hundred and
   Nineteen," and "Vacillation."

2424. JEFFARES, ALEXANDER NORMAN: *The Poetry of W. B. Yeats*. Great Neck,
N.Y.: Barron's Educational Series, 1961. 64 p. (Studies in English Literature. 4.)
   The English edition was published as °*W. B. Yeats: The Poems*. London:
   Arnold, 1961. The series attempts to give "close critical analyses
   and evaluations of individual works" and to present "studies of individual plays, novels and groups of poems and essays" (p. 5). In
   this sense, the booklet is a complete failure—the subject is much
   too large. On its own terms, however, it is a useful introduction to
   Yeats's poetry, enough to whet one's appetite but not more.
   Reviews:
   1. Birgit Bramsbäck, *Studia Neophilologica*, 34:1 (1962), 171-72.
   2. R. P. Draper, *CQ*, 3:3 (Autumn 1961), 274.

2425. *———: *A Commentary on the Collected Poems of W. B. Yeats*. Stanford: Stanford UP, 1968. xxxiv, 563 p.
   Explains, poem by poem, allusions, references, and obscurities, but
   does not interpret. Includes copious quotations from published and
   unpublished sources. The value of the book is indisputable, but some
   criticism has to be made: (1) More interpretations should have been
   cited, not just those dealing with biographical and background material. (2) Sometimes Jeffares belabors the obvious or quotes too copi-
   ously from material that is easily accessible elsewhere. (3) There
   is, regrettably, no index of names.
   Reviews:
   1. Anon., "Coughing in Ink: The Scholiast upon Yeats," *Human World*,
      #4 (Aug 1971), 73-86. An extremely hostile review.
   2. Anon., "Open Yeats," *TLS*, 68:3488 (2 Jan 1969), 7. The reviewer
      suggests that some lines in "Sailing to Byzantium" show similari-

ties to Marvell's "The Garden." See correspondence by Francis Noel Lees, :3491 (23 Jan 1969), 69, where the disputed lines are traced back to Tennyson; by the reviewer, *ibid.*; and by Morchard Bishop, :3492 (30 Jan 1969), 112.

3. Merlin Bowen, *MP*, 67:3 (Feb 1970), 294-95.
4. Edward Engelberg, *Victorian Poetry*, 8:4 (Winter 1970), 354-56.
5. Arra M. Garab, "The Legacy of Yeats," *JML*, 1:1 (1970), 137-40.
6. Geoffrey Grigson, "Use and Misuse of Folklore," *Country Life*, 145: 3748 (2 Jan 1969), 43.
7. George Mills Harper, "To Know All about Everything: Facts about Yeats," *CEA Critic*, 32:7 (Apr 1970), 14.
8. T. R. Henn, *Cambridge R*, 90:2186 (31 Jan 1969), 240-41.
9. Brendan Kennelly, "Yeats and Blake," *Hibernia*, 32:14 (29 Nov—12 Dec 1968), 14.
10. Heinz Kosok, *Neueren Sprachen*, 20:3 (Mar 1971), 167-68.
11. R. H. Lass, *Criticism*, 11:4 (Fall 1969), 391-93.
12. John Mosier, *New Orleans R*, 1:4 (Summer 1969), 387-88.
13. Hermann Peschmann, *English*, 19:103 (Spring 1970), 28-29.
14. Peter Ure, "About Yeats," *Guardian*, #38085 (20 Dec 1968), 7.
15. Stanley Weintraub, *BA*, 43:2 (Spring 1969), 266.

2426. ————: *W. B. Yeats*. London: Routledge & Kegan Paul, 1971. x, 118 p. (Profiles in Literature Series.)
An introduction to Yeats's poetry under various subject headings (Yeats as love poet, Yeats and *A Vision*, Yeats's own life, Yeats and classicism, Yeats and Ireland, Yeats and friendship, Yeats and heroic gesture).
Reviews:
1. Anon., "Coughing in Ink: The Scholiast upon Yeats," *Human World*, #4 (Aug 1971), 73-86.
2. Gulliver Boyle, "Beautiful Women v. the Furies," *Teacher*, 18:6 (6 Aug 1971), 7.
3. Anthony Cronin, "Yeats Seminar," *Irish Press*, 41:151 (26 June 1971), 12.
4. Michael Hartnett, "Handbook on Yeat's [*sic*]," *Irish Times*, #35867 (22 May 1971), 10.
5. John Jordan, "Introduction to Yeats' Poetry," *Irish Independent*, 80:109 (8 May 1971), 6.

2427. KOCH, VIVIENNE: *W. B. Yeats: The Tragic Phase. A Study of the Last Poems*. [Hamden, Conn.]: Archon Books, 1969 [1951]. 151 p.
Interpretations, with strong emphasis on the sexual theme, of the following poems: "The Wild Old Wicked Man," "An Acre of Grass," "The Statues," "A Bronze Head," "The Gyres," "The Man and the Echo," "The Three Bushes," "The Lady's First (Second and Third) Song," "The Lover's Song," "The Chambermaid's First (and Second) Song." See also J2898.
Reviews:
1. Anon., *Listener*, 45:1159 (17 May 1951), 807.
2. Anon., "Aspects of Yeats's Poetry," *TLS*, 50:2574 (1 June 1951), 339.
3. William Becker, *Dublin Mag*, 27:1 (Jan-Mar 1952), 46-48.
4. ————, "On the Margin of Yeats," *Poetry*, 81:5 (Feb 1953), 331-34.
5. Helen Bevington, *SAQ*, 52:1 (Jan 1953), 157.
6. M. C. Bradbrook, "La critique à la Robinson," *NSt*, 41:1057 (9 June 1951), 658-59. "The Robinson Crusoe method in criticism. . . ."

7. M.-L. Cazamian, "L'évolution de W. B. Yeats après ses dernières oeuvres," *EA*, 5:1 (Feb 1952), 50–54.
8. Stanley K. Coffman, *BA*, 27:3 (Summer 1953), 305.
9. Babette Deutsch, "Yeats Study," *NYHTB*, 29:2 (24 Aug 1952), 9.
10. Richard Eberhart, "New Looks at Yeats," *VQR*, 28:4 (Autumn 1952), 618–21.
11. Richard Ellmann, "Three Ways of Looking at a Triton," *Sewanee R*, 61:1 (Jan–Mar 1953), 149–56.
12. Kimon Friar, "Contrapuntal Serpent," *New Republic*, 126:1952 (28 Apr 1952), 17–18.
13. F. W. van Heerikhuizen, "Gedreven door angst," *Litterair paspoort*, 7:53 (Jan 1952), 10–11.
14. Roger McHugh, "Yeats, Synge and the Abbey Theatre," *Studies*, 41: 163–64 (Sept–Dec 1952), 333–40.
15. Ewart Milne, "The Glittering Eye," *Irish Writing*, #16 (Sept 1951), 54–58.
16. W. W. Robson, "Yeats's Last Poems," *Dublin R*, 225:453 (Third Quarter 1951), 83–86.
17. Grover Smith, *New Mexico Q*, 23:3 (Autumn 1953), 324–25.
18. Peter Ure, *Cambridge J*, 5:9 (June 1952), 571–72.
19. Earl R. Wasserman, *MLN*, 68:3 (Mar 1953), 185–90.

2428. LAL, D. K.: *W. B. Yeats: Selected Poems (A Study of Yeats's Important Poems)*. Bareilly: Prakash Book Depot, 1971. viii, 114 p.
Contains a general introduction and notes on 33 poems. Full of mistakes and misprints; negligible.

2429. LEVINE, BERNARD: *The Dissolving Image: The Spiritual-Esthetic Development of W. B. Yeats*. Detroit: Wayne State UP, 1970. 181 p.
Based on "The Dissolving Image: A Concentrative Analysis of Yeats' Poetry," Ph.D. thesis, Brown U, 1965. vi, 376 p. (*DA*, 26:6 [Dec 1965], 3341–42). Incorporates: "Yeats' Aesthetics and His Concept of Self," *Universitas* [Detroit], 4 (1966), 138–48; "'High Talk': A Concentrative Analysis of a Poem by Yeats," *JJQ*, 3:2 (Winter 1966), 124–29; "A Psychopoetic Analysis of Yeats's 'Leda and the Swan,'" *Bucknell R*, 17:1 (Mar 1969), 85–111.
Views Yeats's poetry "as external form dissolving toward its invisible center, the spiritual demesne of the speaker's self-transforming awareness" (pp. 9–10). Discusses in detail "The Lake Isle of Innisfree," "The Two Trees," "The Dedication to a Book of Stories Selected from the Irish Novelists," "The Lamentation of the Old Pensioner," "The Cap and Bells," "He Hears the Cry of the Sedge," "He Reproves the Curlew," *The Shadowy Waters*, "The Collar-Bone of a Hare," "Solomon to Sheba," "The Gift of Harun Al-Rashid," "The Second Coming," the "Helen of Troy" poems (especially "Leda and the Swan"), "Meditations in Time of Civil War," "Among School Children," "Byzantium," "Lapis Lazuli," "The Statues," "High Talk," and "The Circus Animals' Desertion."
Reviews:
1. Giles Gunn, *MP*, 69:1 (Aug 1971), 87–91.
2. T. R. Henn, *RES*, 23:89 (Feb 1972), 100–101.
3. Norman H. MacKenzie, "The Yeats Canon and Recent Scholarship," *QQ*, 78:3 (Autumn 1971), 462–64.

2429a. MORTON, RICHARD: *Notes on the Poetry of William Butler Yeats*. Toronto: Coles Publishing Co., 1971. iii, 80 p. (Coles Notes. 1119.)
Also published as *An Outline of the Poetry of William Butler Yeats*. Toronto: Forum House, 1971. iii, 80 p.

2430. MUNDRA, S. C.: *W. B. Yeats and His Poetry (With Critical Introduction and Exhaustive Notes)*. Bareilly: Prakash Book Depot, 1971. viii, 264 p.

Contains a general introduction to Yeats's life and work and notes on 25 poems. Somewhat elementary.

2431. *PARKINSON, THOMAS FRANCIS: *W. B. Yeats, Self-Critic: A Study of His Early Verse, and The Later Poetry*. Two vols. in one. Berkeley: U of California Press, 1971. xv, 196; xi, 260 p.

Part 1 was first published in 1951 and is based on °"Yeats as a Critic of His Early Verse," Ph.D. thesis, U of California (Berkeley), 1949. Incorporates "W. B. Yeats: A Poet's Stagecraft," *ELH*, 17:2 (June 1950), 136-61. Discusses the revisions of the early poems (1889-1901) up to 1933 and the interaction of dramatic and lyric writing during that period; also on *On Baile's Strand*, *The Shadowy Waters*, and Yeats's dramatic theories.

Part 2 was first published in 1964. Incorporates: "The Sun and the Moon in Yeats's Early Poetry," *MP*, 50:1 (Aug 1952), 50-58; "Intimate and Impersonal: An Aspect of Modern Poetics," *JAAC*, 16:3 (Mar 1958), 373-83; "Vestiges of Creation," *Sewanee R*, 69:1 (Winter 1961), 80-111. Discusses Yeats's iconography (swan, sun, and moon), prosody, and poetics as emerging from the poetry, as well as the revisions from MS. to printed version.

Reviews of Part 1:
1. Anon., *Listener*, 48:1220 (17 July 1952), 111, 113.
2. Anon., "A Poet's Revision," *TLS*, 51:2640 (5 Sept 1952), 582.
3. Anon., *USQBR*, 8:1 (Mar 1952), 28-29.
4. Richard Eberhart, "New Looks at Yeats," *VQR*, 28:4 (Autumn 1952), 618-21.
5. Richard Ellmann, "Three Ways of Looking at a Triton," *Sewanee R*, 61:1 (Jan-Mar 1953), 149-56.
6. Martin Price, "Three Critiques of Modern Poetry," *Yale R*, 41:3 (Mar 1952), 458-61.
Reviews of Part 2:
7. James L. Allen, *MP*, 62:4 (May 1965), 369-70.
8. ————, *WHR*, 19:1 (Winter 1965), 90-92.
9. Anon., *Quarterly R*, 303:643 (Jan 1965), 115-16.
10. Anon., "From Sligo to Byzantium," *TLS*, 64:3304 (24 June 1965), 529-30.
11. Harold Bloom, "Myth, Vision, Allegory," *Yale R*, 54:1 (Oct 1964), 143-49.
12. Donald Davie, "Bardolators and Blasphemers," *Guardian*, #36991 (12 June 1965), 7.
13. William Empson, "A Time of Troubles," *NSt*, 70:1793 (23 July 1965), 123-24.
14. Edward Engelberg, *Michigan QR*, 5:1 (Winter 1966), 65-66.
15. Peter Faulkner, *DUJ*, os 57 / ns 26:3 (June 1965), 180-81. "An unusually uneven book. . . ."
16. T. R. Henn, *MLR*, 60:3 (July 1965), 440-41.
17. John Montague, *CQ*, 8:4 (Winter 1966), 381-83.
18. Peter Ure, *RES*, 16:63 (Aug 1965), 328-31.
19. Thomas R. Whitaker, *ELN*, 2:2 (Dec 1964), 150-54.
20. George T. Wright, *JAAC*, 23:3 (Spring 1965), 392-93.
Reviews of the Combined Edition:
21. Donna Gerstenberger, *Ohio R*, 14:1 (Fall 1972), 106-8.
22. Irene Haugh, "Yeats at Work," *Irish Times*, #36246 (12 Aug 1972), 10.

2432. PERLOFF, MARJORIE GABRIELLE: *Rhyme and Meaning in the Poetry of Yeats.* The Hague: Mouton, 1970. 249 p. (De Proprietatibus Litterarum. Series Practica. 5.)

Based on a Ph.D. thesis, Catholic U of America, 1965. vi, 232 p. (*DA*, 26:11 [May 1966], 6721-22). Includes about a hundred pages of statistical tables.

Reviews:

1. Giles Gunn, *MP*, 69:1 (Aug 1971), 87-91.

2433. °PERRITT, M. E.: "Poetic Development of W. B. Yeats," M.A. thesis, Louisiana State College, 1967.

2434. RAI, VIKRAMADITYA: *The Poetry of W. B. Yeats.* Delhi: Doaba House, 1971. viii, 261 p.

Contains an introductory chapter on "The Making of the Poet" (nationalism, magic, various influences) and on "Yeats and the Romantic Tradition" (mask, symbolism, and "system"), followed by notes on some 80 poems and a chapter on the stylistic development.

2435. SEN, SRI CHANDRA: *Four Essays on the Poetry of Yeats.* Santiniketan: Visva-Bharati, 1968. v, 141 p.

Contents: 1. "The Irish Element in the Evolution of the Poetry of W. B. Yeats," 1-33; reprinted from *Bulletin of the Department of English, U of Calcutta,* 4:1&2 (1963), 13-25, :3&4 (1963), 1-13.
2. "The Love Lyrics of Yeats," 34-67; reprinted from the same periodical, 5:16&17 (1963), 13-38. Discusses the "island" theme, the "Maud Gonne Cycle," and the "Iseult [Gonne] Group of Poems."
3. "Time-Theme in the Poetry of Yeats," 68-108; reprinted from the same periodical, 5:18&19 (1964), 82-112.
4. "A Critical Study of Yeatsian Vocabulary," 109-41; reprinted from *Visva-Bharati Q,* 31:2 (1965-66), 133-69.

2436. °SENGUPTA, SUDHAYU KUMAR: "The Poetical Development of W. B. Yeats," Ph.D. thesis, U of Leeds, 1937.

2437. °SMITH, ARTHUR JAMES MARSHALL: "The Poetry of William Butler Yeats," M.A. thesis, McGill U, 1926.

2438. SPIVAK, GAYATRI CHAKRAVORTY: "The Great Wheel: Stages in the Personality of Yeats's Lyric Speaker," Ph.D. thesis, Cornell U, 1967. ix, 296 p. (*DA*, 28:10 [Apr 1968], 4188A.)

Investigates the relationship between the poetry and *A Vision* and claims that "the chronology of the Phases of the Moon is intimately linked to the successive periods of Yeats's poetry" (p. viii). Concentrates on "The Wild Swans at Coole," "The Tower," "The Black Tower," and "Cuchulain Comforted."

2439. *STALLWORTHY, JON HOWIE: *Between the Lines: Yeats's Poetry in the Making.* Oxford: Clarendon Press, 1965 [1963]. xi, 262 p.

Based on a B.Litt. thesis, Oxford U, 1960. iv, 312 p. Discusses Yeats's principles of revision in general and the following poems in particular: "The Second Coming" (but see J3233), "A Prayer for My Daughter," "The Sorrow of Love," "The Gift of Harun Al-Rashid," "Sailing to Byzantium," "Byzantium," "Chosen," "Parting," "In Memory of Eva Gore-Booth and Con Markiewicz," "Coole Park, 1929," "Memory," "Consolation," "After Long Silence," "The Nineteenth Century and After," "The Results of Thought," "An Acre of Grass," "A Bronze Head," and "The Black Tower."

Reviews:

1. Anon., "Thinking on Paper," *TLS*, 62:3187 (29 Mar 1963), 218.

2. Timothy Brownlow, *Dubliner*, 3:2 (Summer 1964), 71-73.
3. Robert Conquest, "Celtic Highlight," *Spectator*, 210:7036 (3 May 1963), 577-78.
4. Stephen Fanning, *Kilkenny Mag*, #10 (Autumn-Winter 1963), 127, 129, 131.
5. D. J. Gordon and Ian Fletcher, "Only a Magnifying Glass," *Review*, #9 (Oct 1963), 53-58. Criticizes the discussion of "In Memory of Eva Gore-Booth and Con Markiewicz" and "After Long Silence."
6. A. Norman Jeffares, "The Yeats Country," *MLQ*, 25:2 (June 1964), 218-22.
7. Louis MacNeice, "Yeats at Work," *Listener*, 69:1773 (21 Mar 1963), 521.
8. Horace Reynolds, "'It Is Myself That I Remake,'" *CSM*, 55:256 (26 Sept 1963), 13.
9. Howard Sergeant, *English*, 14:83 (Summer 1963), 203-5.
10. Peter Ure, *RES*, 15:60 (Nov 1964), 444-47.
11. Helen Hennessy Vendler, "Assimilating Yeats," *MassR*, 7:3 (Summer 1966), 590-97.

2440. ————: *Vision and Revision in Yeats's "Last Poems."* Oxford: Clarendon Press, 1969. xi, 182 p.
Incorporates: "Two of Yeats's Last Poems," *REL*, 4:3 (July 1963), 48-69; "W. B. Yeats and the Dynastic Thème," *CQ*, 7:3 (Autumn 1965), 247-65 (on the "concern with the ties of blood" in Yeats's poetry and in some other 20th-century poets, notably Robert Lowell, Anne Sexton, Philip Larkin, Anthony Thwaite, and Tony Connor [the paragraphs on Sexton, etc., have not been reprinted in the book]); "W. B. Yeats's 'Under Ben Bulben,'" *RES*, 17:65 (Feb 1966), 30-53.
Discusses and prints the early drafts of the following poems: "Lapis Lazuli," "The Man and the Echo," "The Three Bushes," "The Lady's First (Second and Third) Song," "The Lover's Song," "The Chambermaid's First (and Second) Song," "The Spur," "Long-legged Fly," "The Statues," and "Under Ben Bulben." The interpretations are prefaced by the shortened article from *CQ* and an essay on "The Prophetic Voice," both of which have very little to do with the main argument.
Reviews:
1. Curtis Bradford, *MLQ*, 31:1 (Mar 1970), 133-35.
2. Edward Engelberg, *Contemporary Literature*, 11:2 (Spring 1970), 303-9.
3. Roy Fuller, "Terrors of Fame," *Listener*, 81:2081 (13 Feb 1969), 212-13.
4. Giles Gunn, *MP*, 69:1 (Aug 1971), 87-91.
5. Edwin Honig, "On Knowing Yeats," *VQR*, 45:4 (Autumn 1969), 700-704.
6. A. Norman Jeffares, *RES*, 21:84 (Nov 1970), 532.
7. Thomas Kinsella, "Art and Labour," *Irish Press*, 39:76 (29 Mar 1969), 12.
8. Sean Lucy, "Yeats' Poems in the Making," *Irish Independent*, 78:99 (26 Apr 1969), 6.
9. J. R. Mulryne, *MLR*, 65:4 (Oct 1970), 893-94.
10. Hermann Peschmann, *English*, 19:103 (Spring 1970), 28-29.
11. R[obin] S[kelton], *Malahat R*, #11 (July 1969), 127-28.

2441. SUTTIS, EMMA LAURA: "Yeats: A Lyric Poet," M.A. thesis, U of Manitoba, 1927. iii, 42 p.

2442. TINDALL, WILLIAM YORK: *W. B. Yeats.* NY: Columbia UP, 1966. 48 p. (Columbia Essays on Modern Writers. 15.)

2443. *Tributes in Prose and Verse to Shotaro Oshima, President of the Yeats Society of Japan, on the Occasion of His Seventieth Birthday, September 29th 1969.* Tokyo: Hokuseido Press, 1970. iii, 30 p.

Also published in J1161 (#5). Partial contents:

1. A. Norman Jeffares: "Pallas Athene Gonne," 4-7; on the sources for the mythologizing treatment of Maud Gonne in Yeats's poems.

2. Brendan Kennelly: "Yeats and Unity," 8-9.

3. Sheelah Kirby: "The Importance of Place and Place-Names in the Poetry of W. B. Yeats," 10-12.

4. James Kirkup: "W. B. Yeats and the Dolls," 13-21; the doll symbol in Yeats's poetry.

5. Roger McHugh: "A Note on Some Later Poems of W. B. Yeats," 22-23.

6. Kathleen Raine: "Written with Yeats's Pen: For Shotaro Oshima, Aetat 70," 24. Poem.

7. Frank Tuohy: "W. B. Yeats: Some Thoughts in 1970," 28-30.

2444. *UNTERECKER, JOHN: *A Reader's Guide to William Butler Yeats.* NY: Noonday Press, 1963 [1959]. x, 310 p. (Noonday Paperback. 138.)

The book "is intended to supplement Yeats's *Collected Poems* by providing for the reader some of the basic information he will need in order to come to an intelligent evaluation of those poems" (p. vii).

Reviews:

1. René Fréchet, "L'étude de Yeats: Textes, jugements et éclairissements," *EA*, 14:1 (Jan-Mar 1961), 36-47.

2. T. R. Henn, *Listener*, 62:1597 (5 Nov 1959), 788, 791.

3. Thomas Hogan, "The Light Is Dark Enough," *Guardian*, #35274 (27 Nov 1959), 15.

4. F. J. K., "Guide to Yeats—Or Is It?" *Irish Independent*, 68:302 (19 Dec 1959), 8. It is not.

5. Thomas Parkinson, "The Respect of Monuments," *Sewanee R*, 68:1 (Jan-Mar 1960), 143-49.

6. Charles Poore, "Books of the Times," *NYT*, 108:37086 (8 Aug 1959), 15.

7. Martin Steinmann, *CE*, 22:6 (Mar 1961), 443-44.

2445. WINTERS, YVOR: *The Poetry of W. B. Yeats.* Denver: Swallow, 1960. 24 p. (Swallow Pamphlets. 10.)

Reprinted in *TCL*, 6:1 (Apr 1960), 3-24; *Dubliner*, #2 (Mar 1962), 7-33; and with slight revisions in *Forms of Discovery: Critical and Historical Essays on the Forms of the Short Poem in English.* [Denver]: Swallow, 1967. xxii, 377 p., pp. 204-34.

Extracts Yeats's "beliefs" from his poetry and finds that he does not like them. Hence Yeats's poetry is not "great." Dislikes Yeats's dramatizations of other people and thinks that the respective poems are inflated. See also J1515.

Reviews:

1. Anon., "Yeats in Winters's Grip," *TLS*, 64:3286 (18 Feb 1965), 126.

2. John B. Gleason, *Ramparts*, 2:1 (Mar 1963), 94-96.

3. John R. Moore, "Swan or Goose," *Sewanee R*, 71:1 (Jan-Mar 1963), 123-33.

See also J8, 550, 551, 553, 557, 1075, 1078, 1081, 1102a, 1109, 1127, 1141, 1142, 1708.

DB Articles and Parts of Books

2446. AAS, L.: "William Butler Yeats og hans verker lyrik, prosadiktning og kritik," *Ord och bild*, 36:3 (Mar 1927), 145-52.

Mainly on the poetry, not much on the prose. Relies to some extent on St. John Ervine's *Some Impressions of My Elders* (J641).

2447. ALDINGTON, RICHARD: *A. E. Housman & W. B. Yeats: Two Lectures*. Hurst, Berks.: Peacocks Press, 1955. 36 p.
"W. B. Yeats," 20-35; a rambling essay on Yeats's poetry together with some reminiscences.

2448. ALLEN, DON CAMERON (ed): *The Moment of Poetry*. Baltimore: Johns Hopkins Press, 1962. vii, 135 p. (Percy Graeme Turnbull Memorial Lectures on Poetry. 1961.)
Reprinted in Allen (ed): *A Celebration of Poets*. Baltimore: Johns Hopkins Press, 1967. xi, 241 p. References to Yeats's poetry in the essays by John Holmes and May Sarton (see index); Richard Wilbur, "Round About a Poem of Housman's," 73-98, criticizes "King and No King" for its obscurity (pp. 92-95).

2449. ANON.: "Living English Poets: William Butler Yeats," *Current Literature*, 31:2 (Aug 1901), 244-45.

2450. ANON.: "The Poetry of W. B. Yeats (1865-1939)," *English*, 15:89 (Summer 1965), 167-69.

2451. ANON.: "Poetry Album: William Butler Yeats," *Scholastic*, 39:12 (8-13 Dec 1941), 21.

2452. ANON.: "Poetry: The Quality of Recent Verse. Mr. Yeats as a Prophet," *Times*, #42248 (4 Nov 1919), 45.

2453. *Approaches to the Study of Twentieth-Century Literature: Proceedings of the Conference in the Study of Twentieth-Century Literature*. Third session, May 17-18, 1963. East Lansing: Michigan State U, [1964?]. vi, 186 p.
M. L. Rosenthal: "Alienation of Sensibility and 'Modernity,'" 49-59; repeatedly on Yeats's poetry, especially "Her Anxiety."

2454. AUDEN, W. H.: "Yeats as an Example," *Kenyon R*, 10:2 (Spring 1948), 187-95.
Reprinted in J1090. Yeats's influence on later poets has been great, but the "side summed up in the *Vision* . . . has left virtually no trace." Yeats's main legacies are the transformation of the occasional poem "into a serious reflective poem of at once personal and public interest" and the release of regular stanzaic poetry "from iambic monotony."

2455. BANERJEE, JAYGOPAL: "W. B. Yeats," *Calcutta R*, ser 3 / 26:3 (Mar 1928), 277-91; 27:1 (Apr 1928), 81-101; :2 (May 1928), 141-67; :3 (June 1928), 361-73; 28:1 (July 1928), 109-25; :2 (Aug 1928), 221-39; :3 (Sept 1928), 421-32; 29:1 (Oct 1928), 93-122.
A study of the development of Yeats's poetry, of his symbolism, and of his mysticism. Originally a series of lectures, hence somewhat elementary.

2456. BARNES, TERENCE ROBERT: *English Verse: Voice and Movement from Wyatt to Yeats*. Cambridge: UP, 1967. ix, 324 p.
See pp. 298-320. Yeats was not an esoteric or obscure but a public poet. Comments on "Sailing to Byzantium," "Byzantium," "Among School Children," "Coole Park and Ballylee 1931," and "The Circus Animals' Desertion."

2457. BEACH, JOSEPH WARREN: *The Concept of Nature in Nineteenth-Century English Poetry*. NY: Macmillan, 1936. xii, 618 p.
"Yeats and AE," 535-38.

2458. BERRY, FRANCIS: *Poetry and the Physical Voice*. NY: Oxford UP, 1962. x, 205 p.
On Yeats's method of recording his own poetry, pp. 180-82.

2459. BLACKBURN, THOMAS: *The Price of an Eye*. London: Longmans, 1961. 170 p.
"W. B. Yeats and the Contemporary Dream," 30-49; incorporates "The Contemporary Dream," *London Mag*, 6:1 (Jan 1959), 39-44. Yeats's poetry will endure because he was in touch with the deeper levels of the human being and of his age, which in turn speak through his poetry.

2460. BLACKMUR, RICHARD PALMER: *The Expense of Greatness*. Gloucester, Mass.: Smith, 1958 [1940]. v, 305 p.
"The Later Poetry of W. B. Yeats," 74-105; reprinted from *Southern R*, 2:2 (Autumn 1936), 339-62; reprinted in J1090, 2461, and 2462. The locus classicus for the discussion of "magic" in Yeats's poetry.

2461. ———: *Language as Gesture: Essays in Poetry*. London: Allen & Unwin, 1961 [1952]. vi, 440 p.
"The Later Poetry of W. B. Yeats," 80-104; reprinted from J2460, q.v.
"W. B. Yeats: Between Myth and Philosophy," 105-23; reprint of "Between Myth and Philosophy: Fragments of W. B. Yeats," *Southern R*, 7:3 (Winter 1941/42), 407-25; reprinted in J2462. "Yeats commonly hovered between myth and philosophy, except for transcending flashes, which is why he is not one of the greatest poets. . . . His curse was . . . that he could not create, except in fragments, the actuality of his age" (p. 122).
"Lord Tennyson's Scissors: 1912-1950," 422-40; reprinted from *Kenyon R*, 14:1 (Winter 1952), 1-20; reprinted in J2462. Yeats, Eliot, and Pound are the only 20th-century poets whose work will survive.
For a criticism of Blackmur's view of Yeats see John Wain: *Essays on Literature and Ideas*. London: Macmillan, 1964. xi, 270 p. ("R. P. Blackmur," 145-55).

2462. ———: *Form and Idea in Modern Poetry*. Garden City: Doubleday, 1957. vii, 388 p. (Doubleday Anchor Books. A96.)
See J2460 and 2461.

2463. ———: "The Key and the Hook," *Bennington R*, 2:1 (Winter 1968), 3-10.
A plea for the poetry as poetry.

2464. BLUMENFELD, JACOB P.: "Convention and Modern Poetry: A Study in the Development of Period Mannerisms," Ph.D. thesis, U of Tennessee, 1957. vii, 214 p. (*DA*, 18:4 [Apr 1958], 1427.)
Refers to some Yeats poems *passim*, but does not expand.

2465. BOLT, SYDNEY (ed): *Poetry of the 1920s: An Anthology*. London: Longmans, 1967. x, 272 p.
"W. B. Yeats (1865-1939)," 32-35. Particularly on "Among School Children." "It is . . . the function of style in the poetry of W. B. Yeats to prevent the reader from using his own judgment. The style takes him captive."

2466. BOURNIQUEL, CAMILLE: *Irlande*. Paris: Editions du Seuil, 1955. 192 p. (Collection Petite Planète. 5.)

English edition: *Ireland*. Translated by John Fisher. London: Vista Books, 1960. 192 p. (Vista Books. W8.). "Abbey Street," 157-63; on the Irish theater. "La mort d'Ossian," 165-69; on Yeats's poetry.

2467. BRADBROOK, H. L.: "The Development of Yeats's Poetry," *Contemporaries*, 2:1 (Summer 1935), 201-6.

2468. BRAUN, JOHN THEODORE: *The Apostrophic Gesture*. The Hague: Mouton, 1971. 217 p. (De Proprietatibus Litterarum. Series Maior. 17.)
Based on a Ph.D. thesis, U of Washington, 1967. vi, 338 p. (*DA*, 28:5 [Nov 1967], 1813A-14A). "The Apostrophic Gesture in the Poetry of Yeats," 99-208.

2469. BRENNER, RICA: *Poets of Our Time*. NY: Harcourt, Brace, 1941. xii, 411 p.
"William Butler Yeats," 357-411.

2470. BRKIĆ, SVETOZAR: "Vizantija kao pesnička inspiracija," *Književnost*, yr 24 / 49:9 (Sept 1969), 262-68.
Byzantium as poetic inspiration.

2471. BRONOWSKI, JACOB: *The Poet's Defence: The Concept of Poetry from Sidney to Yeats*. Cleveland: World, 1966 [1939]. xii, 258 p.
"William Butler Yeats," 229-52, and *passim* (see index). "Almost every poem he has written debates the same theme: the poet's place in the world. Far more pointedly than his criticism, Yeats's poems debate a theory of poetry."

2472. BROOKE, STOPFORD AUGUSTUS, and THOMAS WILLIAM ROLLESTON (eds): *A Treasury of Irish Poetry in the English Tongue*. Revised and enlarged. NY: Macmillan, 1932 [1900]. xlv, 610 p.
T. W. Rolleston: "W. B. Yeats," 492-98; written in 1899.

2473. BROWER, REUBEN ARTHUR (ed): *Twentieth-Century Literature in Retrospect*. Cambridge, Mass.: Harvard UP, 1971. vii, 363 p. (Harvard English Studies. 2.)
William H. Pritchard: "The Uses of Yeats's Poetry," 111-32; also in J1125.

2474. BROWN, HARRY, and JOHN MILSTEAD: *What the Poem Means: Summaries of 1000 Poems*. Glenview, Ill.: Scott, Foresman, 1970. v, 314 p.
See pp. 296-304 for short synopses of 25 Yeats poems. Undergraduate level and below.

2475. BUCKLEY, VINCENT: *Poetry and the Sacred*. London: Chatto & Windus, 1968. viii, 244 p.
"W. B. Yeats and the Sacred Company," 172-204; incorporates some material from J2688. "Yeats's concern with the past, racial or personal, gay or bitter, was at every stage religious in nature." This is especially true of the "dramatic" poems, those that celebrate Yeats's friends and, eventually, himself. Discusses among other poems "The Man and the Echo," "The Curse of Cromwell," "Easter 1916," and "Sailing to Byzantium."

2476. BULLOUGH, GEOFFREY: *The Trend of Modern Poetry*. Edinburgh: Oliver & Boyd, 1941 [1934]. vii, 191 p.
"W. B. Yeats and Walter de la Mare," 27-43. Both write "poetry of dream."

2477. ————: *Mirror of Minds: Changing Psychological Beliefs in English Poetry*. London: Athlone Press, 1962. viii, 271 p.

On Yeats as a representative of the "hermetic approach" in modern
poetry, pp. 242-44.

2478. BUNNELL, WILLIAM STANLEY: *Ten Twentieth-Century Poets*. Bath: Brodie,
[1963]. 89 p.
See pp. 64-74 for an introduction to Yeats's poetry on the freshman
level.

2478a. BURNSHAW, STANLEY: *The Seemless Web: Language-Thinking, Creature-
Knowledge, Art-Experience*. NY: Braziller, 1970. xv, 320 p.
Scattered notes on Yeats's poetry, *passim* (see index).

2479. BUSH, DOUGLAS: *English Poetry: The Main Currents from Chaucer to
the Present*. NY: Oxford UP, 1963 [1952]. 222 p. (Galaxy Book. GB93.)
See pp. 199-202 and *passim* (see index).

2480. BUSHRUI, SUHEIL BADI: "Shi'r Yaits" [Yeats's poetry], *Aswat*, 8
(1962), 6-27.

2481. ————: "Yaits wa-Tajdid Islub al-Shi'r" [Yeats and modern poetic
technique], *Shi'r*, 10:40 (Autumn 1968), 47-60.

2482. CHAKRAVARTY, AMIYA: *Modern Tendencies in English Literature*. Calcutta: Book Exchange, [1945?]. x, 74 p. (Greater India Series. 5.)
"Yeats and the Moderns," 1-9. When Yeats climbed the winding stair of
his tower, he became a modern poet.

2483. CHILMAN, ERIC: "W. B. Yeats," *Poetry R*, 4:2 (Feb 1914), 70-72.

2484. CHURCH, RICHARD: *Eight for Immortality*. London: Dent, 1941. ix,
113 p.
"The Later Yeats," 41-54; reprinted from *Fortnightly R*, os 154 / ns
148:884 (Aug 1940), 193-99. The kind of article in which poets "sing."

2485. CLINTON-BADDELEY, V. C.: "Reading Poetry with W. B. Yeats," *London
Mag*, 4:12 (Dec 1957), 47-53.
How Yeats wanted poetry, especially his own poetry, to be read.

2486. ————: "The Written and the Spoken Word," *Essays and Studies*, 18
(1965), 73-82.
Contains a note on the reciting and recording of Yeats's poems.

2487. COHEN, JOHN MICHAEL: *Poetry of This Age, 1908-1965*. 2nd impression,
revised. London: Hutchinson, 1966 [1960]. 256 p.
On Yeats, pp. 69-79 and *passim* (see index).

2488. COLLINS, H. P.: *Modern Poetry*. London: Cape, 1925. 224 p.
"Where We Stand," pp. 9-18; notes that Yeats is outside the tradition
of English poetry.

2489. COLUM, PADRAIC: "Yeats's Lyrical Poems," *Irish Writing*, #2 (June
1947), 78-85.

2490. COOPER, PHILIP: "Lyric Ambivalence: An Essay on the Poetry of
William Butler Yeats and Robert Lowell," Ph.D. thesis, U of Rochester,
1967. viii, 313 p. (*DA*, 28:6 [Dec 1967], 2241A.)
Discusses among other texts "The Two Trees," "Sailing to Byzantium,"
"Crazy Jane Talks with the Bishop," "Vacillation," *Purgatory* (which
is linked to Chaucer's *Pardoner's Tale*), and *A Vision*.

2491. COUSINS, JAMES H.: "William Butler Yeats: The Celtic Lyrist," *Poetry
R*, 1:4 (Apr 1912), 156-58.
"Yeats' poetry will long outlive the poet, though at present the poet
has outlived his poetry."

2492. COX, CHARLES BRIAN, and ANTHONY EDWARD DYSON (eds): *The Twentieth-Century Mind: History, Ideas, and Literature in Britain*. London: Oxford UP, 1972. 3 v.
Volume 1: *1900-1918*. xiii, 526 p. John Wain: "Poetry," 360-413 (*passim* on Yeats); D. J. Palmer: "Drama," 447-74 (on the Irish dramatic revival, 464-68); Graham Hough: "Criticism," 475-84 (on Yeats, 475-78). Volume 2: *1918-1945*. xi, 514 p. John Wain: "Poetry," 307-72 (on Yeats, 354-63).

2493. DAICHES, DAVID: *Poetry and the Modern World: A Study of Poetry in England between 1900 and 1939*. Chicago: U of Chicago Press, 1940. x, 247 p.
On Yeats, *passim*, especially pp. 128-89 (partly reprinted in J1090). Explains Yeats's poetic development as a search for a system that would enable the poet to symbolize experience completely. Eventually, in the last poems, the system conquered its creator.

2494. ———, and WILLIAM CHARVAT (eds): *Poems in English, 1530-1940*. Edited with critical and historical notes and essays. NY: Ronald Press, 1950. xli, 763 p.
Notes on some Yeats poems, pp. 731-36, especially on "To a Shade," "The Second Coming," "Byzantium," and "Long-legged Fly."

2495. DAICHES, DAVID: *A Critical History of English Literature*. London: Secker & Warburg, 1963 [1960]. viii, 1169 p. in 2 v.
On Yeats's plays, pp. 1109-10; on his poetry, 1117-23.

2496. DALE, PETER: "'Where All the Ladders Start . . . ,'" *Agenda*, 9:4-10:1 (Autumn-Winter 1971/72), 3-13.
Yeats's "ability to re-create a recognisable reality while endeavouring to see beyond it" is more important than "his do-it-yourself system."

2497. DAVISON, EDWARD: *Some Modern Poets and Other Critical Essays*. Freeport, N.Y.: Books for Libraries Press, 1968 [1928]. ix, 255 p.
"Three Irish Poets," 175-96; reprinted from *English J*, 15:5 (May 1926), 327-36. AE, Yeats, and James Stephens.

2498. DAY LEWIS, CECIL: *Notable Images of Virtue: Emily Brontë, George Meredith, W. B. Yeats*. Toronto: Ryerson Press, 1954. xiii, 77 p. (Chancellor Dunning Trust Lectures. 6.)
"W. B. Yeats and Human Dignity," 53-77. Dignity, aristocracy, and the ceremony of innocence in Yeats's poetry.

2499. ———: *The Lyric Impulse*. Cambridge, Mass.: Harvard UP, 1965. ix, 164 p. (Charles Eliot Norton Lectures. 1964-65.)
Notes on Yeats's poetry, *passim* (see index), especially on "Politics," pp. 136-37.

2500. DEUTSCH, BABETTE: *This Modern Poetry*. NY: Norton, 1935. 284 p.
Passim (see index).

2501. ———: *Poetry in Our Time: A Critical Survey of Poetry in the English-Speaking World, 1900-1960*. 2nd edition, revised and enlarged. NY: Doubleday, 1963 [1952]. xix, 457 p.
"A Vision of Reality," 287-320, and *passim* (see index).

2502. DOBRÉE, BONAMY: *The Broken Cistern*. London: Cohen & West, 1954. ix, 158 p. (Clark Lectures. 1952-53.)
Some notes on Yeats's poetry, *passim* (see index). The original title of the lectures was "Public Themes in English Poetry."

2503. DOORN, WILLEM VAN: "How It Strikes a Contemporary: A Pageant with Comments," *ES*, 5:6 (Dec 1923), 193–207.

2504. DOUGLAS, ALFRED, LORD: *The Principles of Poetry: An Address Delivered before the Royal Society of Literature on December 2nd, 1943.* [London: Richards Press, 1943]. 27 p.
Some disparaging remarks, pp. 22–23.

2505. DREW, ELIZABETH, and JOHN L. SWEENEY: *Directions in Modern Poetry.* NY: Norton, 1940. 296 p.
"W. B. Yeats," 148–71, and *passim* (see index).

2506. DREW, ELIZABETH: *Poetry: A Modern Guide to Its Understanding and Enjoyment.* NY: Norton, 1959. 288 p.
Yeats, *passim* (see index), especially on "Sailing to Byzantium" and "Leda and the Swan."

2507. ———, and GEORGE CONNOR: *Discovering Modern Poetry.* NY: Holt, Rinehart, & Winston, 1961. xix, 426 p.
Comments on several Yeats poems, *passim*.

2507a. DUNLOP, R. T.: "Yeats," *Teaching of English*, #20 (June 1971), 38–43.
Lecture on the continuity of the subject matter in Yeats's poetry.

2508. ĐUZEL, BOGOMIL: "Vilijam Batler Jejts--Poetot kako tvorec na mitovi" [Poet as creator of myth], *Razgledi*, ser 3 / 4:8 (1962), 754–62.

2509. EDFELT, JOHANNES: *Strövtag.* Stockholm: Bonniers, 1941. 179 p.
"En lyrikers väg," 94–101.

2510. EDGAR, PELHAM: "The Poetry of William Butler Yeats," *Globe*, 60:17120 (24 Dec 1904), Magazine Section, 5.

2511. ELIOT, THOMAS STEARNS: *The Use of Poetry and the Use of Criticism: Studies in the Relation of Criticism to Poetry in England.* London: Faber & Faber, 1964 [1933]. 156 p.
Eliot disapproves of Yeats's "mysticism" and praises the later, saner poetry, p. 140.

2512. ———: *On Poetry and Poets.* London: Faber & Faber, 1961 [1957]. 262 p.
"The Music of Poetry," 26–38; reprint of a pamphlet of the same title, Glasgow: Jackson, 1942. 28 p. (Glasgow University Publications. 57.) Contains a note on Yeats reading poetry aloud, pp. 31–32.
"Poetry and Drama," 72–88; reprint of a pamphlet of the same title, London: Faber & Faber, 1951. 35 p. Contains a note on *Purgatory*, p. 78.
"Yeats," 252–62; reprint of "The Poetry of W. B. Yeats," *Purpose*, 12: 3/4 (July-Dec 1940), 115–27; also in *Southern R*, 7:3 (Winter 1941/42), 442–54, and in J1090. A slightly revised extract appeared as "William Butler Yeats: A Tribute," *Ireland-American R*, #5 [1941?], 183–84. A praise of the later poetry and plays.

2513. ELLIOTT, GEORGE P.: *A Piece of Lettuce: Personal Essays on Books, Beliefs, American Places, and Growing Up in a Strange Country.* NY: Random House, 1964. xi, 271 p.
See pp. 36–42 for Elliott's struggles whether or not to like Yeats's poetry.

2514. ENRIGHT, DENIS JOSEPH: *Literature for Man's Sake: Critical Essays.* Tokyo: Kenkyusha, 1955. v, 209 p.
"The Poetic Development of W. B. Yeats," 129–44. From deathwish and dream (early poetry) to reality, precision, and life (later poetry).

2515. EVANS, BENJAMIN IFOR: "The Poetry of W. B. Yeats," *Fortnightly R*, os 151 / ns 145:867 (Mar 1939), 351-53.

2516. ———: *Tradition and Romanticism: Studies in English Poetry from Chaucer to W. B. Yeats*. London: Methuen, 1940. ix, 213 p.
"W. B. Yeats and the Continuance of Tradition," 201-8.

2517. O Faracháin, Riobárd [FARREN, ROBERT]: "Elements for a Credo," *Irish Monthly*, 64:761 (Nov 1936), 751-55; :762 (Dec 1936), 828-35; 65:763 (Jan 1937), 39-45; :764 (Feb 1937), 106-10; :765 (Mar 1937), 197-202; :766 (Apr 1937), 258-63.
Subtitles: The Conceptual in the Poetry of Yeats, The Image in Yeats, Rhythm in Yeats; also a note on Yeats's poetic theory.

2518. O'F., R. [———]: "Yeats the Poet," *RTV Guide*, 2:184 (11 June 1965), 6.
The same issue contains the program of the Yeats centenary productions, p. 6; Niall Sheridan, "Portrait of a Poet," 6; a note on *Deirdre* by Michael Garvey, p. 7; and Gabriel Fallon, "Yeats as a Dramatist," 7.

2518a. FAULKNER, PETER: "Yeats: Anti-Humanist?" *New Humanist*, 88:11 (Mar 1973), 455-56.
Yeats's poetry proves that he was, after all, a humanist.

2519. FIGGIS, DARRELL: *Studies and Appreciations*. London: Dent, 1912. vii, 258 p.
"Mr. W. B. Yeats' Poetry," 119-37; reprinted from *New Age*, 7:14 (4 Aug 1910), 325-28.

2520. FLETCHER, IAN: "The Vulnerable Yeats," *NSt*, 77:1998 (27 June 1969), 918.

2521. Hueffer, Ford Madox [later FORD, FORD MADOX]: "Impressionism: Some Speculations," *Poetry*, 2:6 (Sept 1913), 215-25.

2522. [———]: "Literary Portraits—XXXIX: Mr. W. B. Yeats and His New Poems," *Outlook* [London], 33:853 (6 June 1914), 783-84.
With *Responsibilities* (W110, reviewed here), Yeats is no longer grotesque and irritating. Of the earlier poems, "The Lake Isle of Innisfree" is particularly bad; Ford improves it as follows:
> At Innesfree [*sic*] there is a public-house;
> They board you well for ten and six a week.
> The mutton is not good, but you can eat
> Their honey. I am going there to take
> A week or so of holiday to-morrow.

2523. FRÉCHET, RENÉ: "Un poète en quête de sa vérité: W. B. Yeats," *Foi. Education*, 31:56 (July-Aug 1961), 49-56.

2524. FREER, ALLEN, and JOHN ANDREW (eds): *Cambridge Book of English Verse, 1900-1939*. Cambridge: UP, 1970. xi, 205 p.
"W. B. Yeats," 24-26; notes on several poems, 150-66.

2525. GALLAGHER, MICHAEL P.: "Yeats, Syntax, and the Self," *Arizona Q*, 26:1 (Spring 1970), 5-16.
The three stages in Yeats's development as poet and critic are described as the dominance of words, the substitution of syntax for words, and the discovery of the "self" or unity of being. Discusses "Among School Children" and the influence of the *Upanishads*.

2526. GERARD, MARTIN: "It Means What It Says," *X: A Quarterly Review*, 2:2 (Aug 1961), 100-107.
The problem of poetry and belief, with Yeats's poetry as object of demonstration.

2527. GIFFORD, HENRY: *Comparative Literature*. London: Routledge & Kegan Paul, 1969. xii, 99 p.
On Yeats as a writer of Irish poetry in the English language, pp. 21-24.

2528. GILBERT, KATHARINE: *Aesthetic Studies: Architecture & Poetry*. Durham, N.C.: Duke UP, 1952. vii, 145 p.
Some notes on Yeats's poetry in the chapters "Recent Poets on Man and His Place," 51-81, and "A Spatial Configuration in Five Recent Poets," 85-97.

2529. GILKES, MARTIN: *A Key to Modern English Poetry*. London: Blackie, 1937. vi, 178 p.
"William Butler Yeats," 153-65.

2530. GÖLLER, KARL HEINZ (ed): *Epochen der englischen Lyrik*. Düsseldorf: Bagel, 1970. 278 p.
Rudolf Haas: "Die moderne englische Lyrik," 209-35; on Yeats, pp. 220-22 and *passim*.

2531. GOLDGAR, HARRY: "Yeats and the Black Centaur in French," *Western R*, 15:2 (Winter 1951), 111-22.
On the difficulties of translating Yeats's poetry into French, with particular reference to "On a Picture of a Black Centaur by Edmund Dulac."

2532. ————: "Note sur la poésie de William Butler Yeats," *Bayou*, 22 [i.e., 21]:72 (Winter 1958), 547-52.

2533. GOMES, EUGENIO: *D. H. Lawrence e outros*. Pôrto Alegre: Edição da livraria do globo Barcellos, Bertaso, 1937. 329 p.
"W. B. Yeats," 79-110; on the early poetry and plays.

2534. GRAVES, ROBERT: *The Crowning Privilege: Collected Essays on Poetry*. Garden City: Doubleday, 1956. 311 p.
"These Be Your Gods, O Israel!" 119-42; reprinted from *Essays in Criticism*, 5:2 (Apr 1955), 129-50, and *New Republic*, 134:2153 (27 Feb 1956), 16-18; :2154 (5 Mar 1956), 17-18. Correspondence by Delmore Schwartz, :2156 (19 Mar 1956), 20-21; W. M. Laetsch, *ibid.*, 21-22; Karl Shapiro, :2158 (2 Apr 1956), 3, 23; and others.
A savage attack on Yeats's poetry; Graves accuses him of having nothing to say. See also Peter Ure, "Yeats and Mr. Graves," *TLS*, 58: 2989 (12 June 1959), 353.

2535. GRIERSON, HERBERT JOHN CLIFFORD, and J. C. SMITH: *A Critical History of English Poetry*. Revised edition. London: Chatto & Windus, 1950 [1944]. viii, 539 p.
See pp. 476-79.

2536. GRIGSON, GEOFFREY (ed): *The Arts To-day*. London: Lane / Bodley Head, 1935. xv, 301 p.
Louis MacNeice: "Poetry To-day," 25-67; Humphrey Jennings: "The Theatre To-day," 189-216.

2537. GROSS, HARVEY SEYMOUR: *Sound and Form in Modern Poetry: A Study of Prosody from Thomas Hardy to Robert Lowell*. Ann Arbor: U of Michigan Press,

1964. xii, 334 p.
"William Butler Yeats," 48-55.

2538. GRUBB, FREDERICK: *A Vision of Reality: A Study of Liberalism in Twentieth-Century Verse.* London: Chatto & Windus, 1965. 246 p.
"Tragic Joy: W. B. Yeats," 25-45, and *passim* (see index). This is an essay on some themes in Yeats's poetry. What they have to do with liberalism is not explained.

2539. GUPTA, N. DAS: *Literature of the Twentieth Century.* Gwalior: Kitab Ghar, 1967. 225, vii p.
"W. B. Yeats," 30-38; a survey of his poetry. On the Irish theater, pp. 104-8, 110-14.

2540. GUTNER, M. (ed): *Antologiĩa novoĩ angliĩskoĩ poezii.* Leningrad: Gosudarstvennoe izdatel'stvo "Khudozhestvennaĩa literatura," 1937. 455 p.
"Uil'ĩam Betler Eĩts," 245-54, 14 poems translated into Russian; note on the poems, pp. 437-38.

2541. HALDAR, S.: "The Poetry of William Butler Yeats," *Modern R*, 101:602 (Feb 1957), 139-47.

2542. HAMBURGER, MICHAEL: *The Truth of Poetry: Tensions in Modern Poetry from Baudelaire to the 1960s.* London: Weidenfeld & Nicolson, 1969. ix, 341 p.
See pp. 72-80, 86-90, and *passim* (see index). Mainly concerned with the "modernity" and the "politics" of Yeats's poetry.

2543. HART, JEFFREY: "Yeats: No Rootless Flower," *Triumph*, 5:3 (Mar 1970), 28-30.

2544. HENN, T. R.: "The Wisdom of W. B. Yeats," *Listener*, 44:1138 (21 Dec 1950), 790-91, 793.
Yeats's "philosophy," as shown in his poetry.

2545. HEXTER, GEORGE J.: "The Philosophy of William Butler Yeats," *Texas R*, 1:3 (Jan 1916), 192-200.
As contained in the poetry.

2546. °HIJAZI, TALAL: "Wilyam Batlar Yaits: Sha'ir al-Ru'ya" [The poet of vision], *Afkar*, 6 (Nov 1966).

2547. HILLYER, ROBERT: *In Pursuit of Poetry.* NY: McGraw-Hill, 1960. xiii, 231 p.
Yeats's poetry is too obscure for him; he prefers James Stephens, pp. 178-81.

2548. HODGSON, GERALDINE EMMA: *Criticism at a Venture.* London: Macdonald, 1919. vii, 215 p.
Scattered remarks, *passim* (see index).

2549. HUNGERLAND, ISABEL C.: *Poetic Discourse.* Berkeley: U of California Press, 1958. v, 177 p. (California U Publications in Philosophy. 33.)
References to Yeats's poetry, pp. 8-9, 12, 22, 25-26, 41, 92, 117-18, 129, 134.

2550. HUNTER, JIM (ed): *Modern Poets.* London: Faber & Faber, 1968. 4 v.
Notes on Yeats's poetry, 1:13-14, 44-50.

2551. IREMONGER, VALENTIN: "The Byzantine Poems of Yeats," *Bell*, 19:10 (Nov 1954), 36-44.
The Byzantium poems point to a general problem in Yeats's poetry: "Yeats's mind veered between the symbol and the reality but, lacking

sympathy with, or understanding of, ordinary life, failed to establish any connecting link between the two."

2551a. ISON, R.: "More Thoughts on W. B. Yeats," *Teaching of English*, #20
(June 1971), 60-64.
Personal concerns in Yeats's poetry.

2552. IZZO, CARLO (trans and ed): *Poesia inglese contemporanea da Thomas
Hardy agli apocalittici*. Introduzione, versione e note di Carlo Izzo.
Modena: Guanda, 1950. lxxxvii, 599 p.
Passim (see index).

2553. JEFFARES, A. NORMAN: "W. B. Yeats and His Methods of Writing Verse,"
Nineteenth Century and After, 139:829 (Mar 1946), 123-28.
Reprinted in J1090. Existing MSS. reveal that Yeats had two methods
of writing verse, spontaneous composition that underwent few changes
before it was published, and (more often) laborious writing and rewriting that he was careful to hide in the published version.

2554. ————: "Yeats as Modern Poet," *Mosaic*, 2:4 (Summer 1969), 53-58.
Yeats's poetry is popular with the young, because his subjects appeal
to them and because he cares for his audience.

2555. JONES, LLEWELLYN: *First Impressions: Essays on Poetry, Criticism,
and Prosody*. NY: Knopf, 1925. 249 p.
"The Later Poetry of W. B. Yeats," 137-48; reprinted from *NAR*, 219:
821 (Apr 1924), 499-506. Defends Yeats against Middleton Murry's
criticism (J4543).

2556. JUMPER, WILL C., LILLIAN SARA ROBINSON, and ELAINE SHOWALTER: Correspondence concerning an issue on "Women and the Profession" with supporting arguments taken from Yeats's poetry, *CE*, 33:2 (Nov 1971), 247-50.

2557. JURKIĆ-ŠUNJIĆ, MIRA: "Tragična ljepota u poeziji W. B. Yeatsa,"
Telegram, 7:311 (15 Apr 1966), 12.
Tragic beauty in the poetry of Yeats.

2558. KAPOOR, A. N.: *Modern English Poetry (1900-1920) (The Decline and
Fall of the Naturalistic Tradition)*. Allahabad: Kitab Mahal, 1962. vi,
169 p. (Masters of English Literature Series. 8.)
"William Butler Yeats," 112-24.

2558a. KAVANAGH, PATRICK: On Yeats's poems, *RTV Guide*, 2:164 (22 Jan
1965), 23.

2559. K[ELLER], T. G.: "The Poet of the Abbey Theatre: Evolution of Mr.
W. B. Yeats," *Northern Whig*, #31279 (3 Nov 1908), 5.
Surveys the poetical work and concludes: "The boughs of his lyrical
impulse have indeed withered."

2560. KELLY, T. J.: *The Focal Word: An Introduction to Poetry*. Brisbane:
Jacaranda Press, 1965. x, 317 p.
Notes on some Yeats poems, pp. 261-68.

2561. KENNER, HUGH: *Gnomon: Essays on Contemporary Literature*. NY: Obolen-
sky, 1958. vii, 301 p.
"The Sacred Book of the Arts," 9-29; reprinted from *Irish Writing*,
#31 (Summer 1955), 24-35, and *Sewanee R*, 64:4 (Oct-Dec 1956), 574-90.
Yeats wrote and composed *books* of poetry, in which the arrangement of
the poems is deliberate and meaningful.
"At the Hawk's Well," 198-214; a review of *Letters* (W211J/K).

2562. KING, RICHARD ASHE: "Mr. W. B. Yeats," *Bookman*, 12:72 (Sept 1897), 142-43.
   Yeats is a "distinctively Irish" poet.

2563. Forsman, Rafael [later KOSKIMIES, RAFAEL]: *Runoilijoita ja kiistamiehiä* [Poets and critics]. Porvoo: Söderström, 1926. 223 p.
   "Piirteitä W. B. Yeatsin runoudesta" [Extracts from Yeats's poetry], 155-70.

2564. KURATANI, NAOOMI: "Out of a Dead End--W. B. Yeats," *Mukogawa Women's U Bulletin*, #15 (1968), H99-117; #16 (1969), H127-42.

2565. LANGBAUM, ROBERT: *The Poetry of Experience: The Dramatic Monologue in Modern Literary Tradition*. London: Chatto & Windus, 1957. 246 p.
   Some notes, *passim* (see index).

2566. LEAVIS, FRANK RAYMOND: *New Bearings in English Poetry: A Study of the Contemporary Situation*. Ann Arbor: U of Michigan Press, 1960 [1932]. vii, 238 p. (Ann Arbor Paperbacks. AA36.)
   See pp. 27-50. Yeats's poetry has developed into "disillusion and waste" and is "little more than a marginal comment on the main activities of his life." Also in J1090.

2567. ———, and QUEENIE DOROTHY LEAVIS: *Lectures in America*. London: Chatto & Windus, 1969. vii, 152 p.
   F. R. L.: "Yeats: The Problem and the Challenge," 59-81. The problem is contained in the questions of what Yeats's achievement as a poet really was and how many of his poems are "great." The answers are (as far as I understand Leavis's somewhat redundant and idiosyncratic argument) that Yeats's work poses the continual question, "What *is* literary history?" and that he did not write many great poems. Most poems are not "closely enough organized and they haven't, as wholes, an intense enough life." Discusses the two Byzantium poems.
   Reviews:
   1. Anon., "Distillations from FRL and QDL," *TLS*, 68:3499 (20 Mar 1969), 297-98. The Yeats piece isn't up to the standard of the rest of the book.
   2. William H. Pritchard, "Discourses in America," *Essays in Criticism*, 19:3 (July 1969), 336-47.

2568. LEGRAS, CHARLES: *Chez nos contemporains d'Angleterre*. Paris: Ollendorff, 1901. iii, 332 p.
   "W. B. Yeats & William Watson," 207-19.

2569. LEHMANN, JOHN: *The Open Night*. London: Longmans Green, 1952. ix, 128 p.
   "The Man Who Learnt to Walk Naked," 15-22; reprinted from John Lehmann (ed): *Orpheus: A Symposium of the Arts*. London: Lehmann, 1948-49. 2 v. (1:96-102).

2570.——— (ed): *The Craft of Letters in England: A Symposium*. London: Cresset Press, 1956. vii, 248 p.
   Roy Fuller: "Poetry: Tradition and Belief," 74-97.

2571. LERNER, LAURENCE: "W. B. Yeats: Poet and Crank," *Proceedings of the British Academy*, 49 (1963), 49-67.
   Also issued separately as a pamphlet, °London: Oxford UP, 1964. Discusses "the relation between the value of a poem and the value of its subject matter," or more bluntly, "How is it that the greatest poet of the century, a poet of wisdom and understanding of the heart, a

sage as well as a singer--how is it that he expounded in his poems
such absurd, such eccentric, such utterly crackpot ideas?" Criticizes
A Vision.
Reviews:
1. Brendan Kennelly, *Hermathena*, #101 (Autumn 1965), 60.

2572. LESLIE, SHANE: "Wiliam [*sic*] Yeats," Translated by Georgette Camille,
Echanges, #5 (Dec 1931), 86-91.
I have not found a publication of the English original.

2573. LEVAL, ROGER DE: *5 essais sur la poésie anglaise contemporaine.*
Préface de Brand Whitlock. Paris: Editions gauloises, [1924]. 55 p.
"W.-B. Yeats: Prix Nobel 1923," 25-33. See also by the same author
°"W. B. Yeats," *Vie intellectuelle*, 10:11 (1 Jan 1924), 190-91.

2574. LEWIS, CLAUDE ELVIS: "Studies in Modern English Poetry," M.A. thesis,
U of Saskatchewan, 1925. Unpaged.
"The Poetry of William Butler Yeats," 19 negligible pages.

2575. LOMBARDO, AGOSTINO: *La poesia inglese dall estetismo al simbolismo.*
Roma: Edizione di Storia e letteratura, 1950. 303 p. (Letture di pensiero
e d'arte. 12.)
See pp. 67-68, 97-100, 249-88, and *passim* (see index), particularly
on the early poetry.

2576. MAC A'GHOBHAINN, IAIN: "Bardachd W. B. Yeats" [Yeats and the profession of the poet], *Gairm*, #64 (Autumn 1968), 363-69, 371-72.

2577. MACBETH, GEORGE (ed): *Poetry 1900 to 1965: An Anthology.* London:
Longman with Faber & Faber, 1967. xxiii, 343 p.
See pp. 1-2, 30-35.

2578. MACCARTHY, DESMOND: *Criticism.* London: Putnam, 1932. xiii, 311 p.
"Yeats," 81-88.

2579. MACKENNA, AILEEN (ed): *Ring of Verse.* Dublin: Fallon, 1968. 175 p.
A few negligible notes, pp. 11, 13, 15, 18, 20-21.

2580. MACLEISH, ARCHIBALD: *A Time to Speak: The Selected Prose.* Boston:
Houghton Mifflin, 1941. vii, 210 p.
"Public Speech and Private Speech in Poetry," 59-69; reprinted from
Yale R, 27:3 (Mar 1938), 536-47. There is no difference between Yeats
the man and Yeats the poet. He *is* a poet. Yeats himself read this and
approved of it (*Letters*, p. 908).

2581. ———: *Poetry and Experience.* Boston: Houghton Mifflin, 1961. ix,
204 p.
"The Public World: Poems of W. B. Yeats," 115-47.

2582. MACNEICE, LOUIS: "Subject in Modern Poetry," *Essays and Studies*, 22
(1937), 144-58.

2583. ———: *Modern Poetry: A Personal Essay.* 2nd edition with an introduction by Walter Allen. Oxford: Clarendon Press, 1968 [1938]. xxiii,
205 p.
Passim, especially pp. 23-25, 78, 80-83, 131, 143-44, 168-69, 194-95.

2584. MARSHALL, JOHN: "Some Aspects of Mr. Yeats' Lyric Poetry," *QQ*, 13:3
(Jan-Feb-Mar 1906), 241-45.

2584a. MARTIN, W. R.: "Yeats's 'Heaven Blazing into the Head,'" *ESA*, 15:2
(Sept 1972), 93-98.

Discusses the poems under the following aspect: "The persona begins in a certain drift of thought and feeling, then makes a discovery *in the course of the poem*; this brings an intense excitement and a deeper insight, and causes a different flow of thought and feeling, often a reversal of that of the beginning."

2585. MARTZ, LOUIS LOHR: *The Poetry of Meditation: A Study in English Religious Literature of the Seventeenth Century.* New Haven: Yale UP, 1955 [1954]. xv, 375 p. (Yale Studies in English. 125.)
   "'Unity of Being' and the Meditative Style," 321-30.

2586. [MAXWELL, IAN R.]: *Three Modern Poets: Selections from Gerard Manley Hopkins, William Butler Yeats, Thomas Stearns Eliot.* Melbourne: Department of English, U of Melbourne, 1947. 92 p.
   "Introduction," 9-25; "William Butler Yeats," 47-49.

2587. MAY, DERWENT: "Trzy wiersze W. B. Yeatsa—Przykład nowoczesnej krytyki angielskiej" [Three poems of WBY—An example of modern English criticism], *Zeszyty naukowe uniwersytetu łodzkiego. Seria I: Nauki humanistyczno-społeczne,* 25 (1962), 173-82.
   Contains interpretations of "Memory," "Crazy Jane on the Day of Judgment," and "Mad as the Mist and Snow."

2588. MAYNARD, THEODORE: "The Poems of William Butler Yeats," *America,* 24:580 (6 Nov 1920), 65-66.
   Qualified praise of the early poetry, crushing criticism of the later poetry ("he has not worn well . . . hopelessly lost his way," etc.).

2589. MÉGROZ, RODOLPHE LOUIS: *Modern English Poetry, 1882-1932.* London: Nicholson & Watson, 1933. ix, 267 p.
   See pp. 87-91, 120-23, and *passim* (see index).

2590. MILLS, JOHN GASCOIGNE: "Some Aspects of Poetic Creation," *Ochanomizu Joshi Daigaku Jimbun Kagaku Kiyō,* 10 (1957), 1-16.

2591. MIZENER, ARTHUR: "The Romanticism of W. B. Yeats," *Southern R,* 7:3 (Winter 1941/42), 601-23.
   Reprinted in J1090. Yeats's later poetry differs from the earlier not in its themes but in their realization. The early poetry is committed to fancy, the later to fact.

2592. MONRO, HAROLD: *Some Contemporary Poets.* London: Parsons, 1920. 224 p.
   Some scattered remarks, *passim* (see index).

2593. MOORE, JOHN R.: "Yeats as a Last Romantic," *VQR,* 37:3 (Summer 1961), 432-49.
   Misnomer; does not discuss Yeats's romanticism but rather the development of his thought as reflected in his poetry.

2593a. MORRIS, CHRISTOPHER D.: "World into Word: Tennyson, Ruskin, Hopkins, and the Nineteenth-Century Loss of Certainty," °Ph.D. thesis, State U of New York at Buffalo, 1972. 224 p. (*DA,* 33:8 [Feb 1973], 4427A.)
   Includes a discussion of Yeats's poetry.

2594. MORTIMER, ANTHONY: *Modern English Poets: Some Introductory Essays.* Toronto: Forum House, 1968. 159 p.
   "W. B. Yeats," 83-111.

2595. MUIR, EDWIN: *The Present Age from 1914.* London: Cresset Press, 1939. (Introductions to English Literature. 5.)
   For a second edition of the book see J1295. On Yeats, pp. 45-47, 52-61, and *passim.*

2596. ————: *The Estate of Poetry*. Cambridge, Mass.: Harvard UP, 1962. xix, 118 p. (Charles Eliot Norton Lectures. 1955-56.)
  "W. B. Yeats," 42-60. Yeats was a poet with a definite Irish audience for his poems.

2597. MULHOLLAND, ROSA: "Our Poets: No. 23—William B. Yeats," *Irish Monthly*, 17:193 (July 1889), 365-71.
  Reprinted from °*Melbourne Advocate*, 9 Mar 1889. Ireland has earned the right to have a famous poet and Yeats is a very likely candidate. Unfortunately his subject matter isn't all too Irish.

2598. NOGUCHI, YONE: *Through the Torii*. London: Mathews, 1914. xi, 208 p.
  "A Japanese Note on W. B. Yeats," 110-17; reprinted from *Academy*, 82: 2070 (6 Jan 1912), 22-23. The impression made by Yeats's poetry on an early Japanese visitor to England.

2599. OATES, JOYCE CAROL: *The Edge of Impossibility: Tragic Forms in Literature*. NY: Vanguard Press, 1972. xi, 259 p.
  "Yeats: Violence, Tragedy, Mutability," 139-61; reprinted from *Bucknell R*, 17:3 (Dec 1969), 1-17. In the poems and plays; comments on the influence of Nietzsche.
  "Tragic Rites in Yeats's *A Full Moon in March*," 163-87; reprinted from *Antioch R*, 29:4 (Winter 1969/70), 547-60.

2600. O'CONNOR, WILLIAM VAN: *Sense and Sensibility in Modern Poetry*, Chicago: U of Chicago Press, 1948. xii, 279 p.
  Scattered remarks on Yeats's poetry (see index).

2601. Ó HUANACHÁIN, MÍCHEÁL: "An snáthaid & an taipéis" [The needle and the carpet], *Comhar*, 24:7 (July 1965), 9-11.

2602. OLIVERO, FEDERICO: *Studi sul romanticismo inglese*. Bari: Laterza, 1914. iii, 335 p.
  "William Butler Yeats," 105-69 ("Le liriche," 107-19; "I drammi," 120-69).

2603. PARKINSON, THOMAS: "The Individuality of Yeats," *Pacific Spectator*, 6:4 (Autumn 1952), 488-99.

2604. PAVLOVIĆ, MIODRAG: "O poeziji V. B. Jetsa," *Književnost*, 10:11 (Nov 1955), 363-76.

2605. PEARCE, DONALD: "Flames Begotten of Flame," *Sewanee R*, 74:3 (July-Sept 1966), 649-68.
  Traditional elements in Yeats's poetry, particularly in the two Byzantium poems.

2606. PESCHMANN, HERMANN: "Yeats and His English Contemporaries," *English*, 9:51 (Autumn 1952), 88-93.
  Misnomer; a sketch of the development of Yeats's poetry with occasional glimpses of his contemporaries.

2607. PETERKIEWICZ, JERZY: *The Other Side of Silence: The Poet at the Limits of Language*. London: Oxford UP, 1970. viii, 128 p.
  See pp. 39-40.

2608. POUND, EZRA: "Status Rerum," *Poetry*, 1:4 (Jan 1913), 123-27.
  At present, Yeats is "the only poet worthy of serious study."

2609. PRESS, JOHN: *The Fire and the Fountain: An Essay on Poetry*. London: Methuen, 1966 [1955]. x, 256 p. (University Paperbacks. 159.)
  On Yeats, *passim* (see index).

2610. PRIESTLEY, JOHN BOYNTON: *Literature and Western Man.* London: Heinemann, 1960. xiii, 512 p.
On Yeats, pp. 398-404 and *passim* (see index).

2611. PUHALO, DUŠAN: "Poetske vrednosti jejtsove lirike" [The poetic values of Yeats's lyric work], *Letopis matice srpske,* yr 135 / 384:2-3 (Sept 1959), 144-58.

2612. RABONI, GIOVANNI: "Omaggio a Yeats: Variazioni su 'esperienza e astrazione,'" *Aut Aut,* 12:68 (Mar 1962), 172-76.
Not so much on Yeats but rather a general essay on experience and abstraction in 20th-century English poetry.

2613. RANSOM, JOHN CROWE: "Yeats and His Symbols," *Kenyon R,* 1:3 (Summer 1939), 309-22.
Reprinted in J1090. A defense of the later poetry at the expense of the earlier and a discussion of its symbols, which are taken to be not dependent on Yeats's esoteric speculations.

2614. ————: "The Irish, the Gaelic, the Byzantine," *Southern R,* 7:3 (Winter 1941/42), 517-46.
On the "naturalistic," "ontological," and "religionistic" aspects of Yeats's poetry.

2615. RAY, NIRENDRA NATH: "The Poetry of W. B. Yeats (1865-1939)," *Visva-Bharati Q,* 30:3 (1964-65), 177-96.

2616. READ, HERBERT: "Révolte et réaction dans la poésie anglaise moderne," *Présence,* 5:1 (Apr 1946), 49-64.
A revised version was published as "Poetry in My Time," *Texas Q,* 1:1 (Feb 1958), 87-100.

2617. ————: *The Tenth Muse: Essays in Criticism.* London: Routledge & Kegan Paul, 1957. xi, 331 p.
"The Image in Modern Poetry," 117-38.
"Sotto Voce: A Plea for Intimacy," 146-56; reprinted from *BBC Q,* 4:1 (Apr 1949), 1-6. Discusses Yeats's dramatic theories and suggests that he might have been a successful writer of radio plays.

2618. RICHARDS, IVOR ARMSTRONG: *Poetries and Sciences.* A reissue of *Science and Poetry* (1926, 1935) with commentary. NY: Norton, 1970. 123 p.
On Yeats's early poetry and D. H. Lawrence, pp. 70-75: "Mr. Yeats and D. H. Lawrence present two further ways of dodging those difficulties which come from being born into this generation rather than into some earlier age." The Yeats material is not included in the 1926 edition. It was first published as "A Background for Contemporary Poetry," *Criterion,* 3:12 (July 1925), 511-28.

2619. ————: *Coleridge on Imagination.* Bloomington: Indiana UP, 1965 [1934]. xxv, 237 p.
See pp. 207, 215, 217.

2620. RODMAN, SELDEN: "Poetry between the Wars," *CE,* 5:1 (Oct 1943), 1-8.

2621. ROSENTHAL, MACHA LOUIS: *The Modern Poets: A Critical Introduction.* NY: Oxford UP, 1960. xii, 288 p.
"Yeats and the Modern Mind," 28-48.

2622. RUSSELL, FRANCIS: "The Archpoet," *Horizon* [NY], 3:2 (Nov 1960), 66-69.
Subtitle: "As a young man, Yeats made old men's verses—he said so himself—but when he grew old, his verse became young."

2623. SANESI, ROBERTO (trans and ed): *Poeti inglesi del 900.* Testi, traduzioni e introduzione a cura di Roberto Sanesi. Milano: Bompiani, 1960. 564 p.
See pp. 25-34.

2624. SCHELLING, FELIX EMMANUEL: *The English Lyric.* Port Washington, N.Y.: Kennikat Press, 1967 [1913]. xi, 335 p.
Some notes (see index).

2625. SCHRICKX, W.: "William Butler Yeats, symbolist en visionair dichter," *Vlaamse gids,* 49:6 (June 1965), 380-96.

2626. SCHWARTZ, DELMORE: "Speaking of Books," *NYTBR,* [59:24] (13 June 1954), 2.
Yeats's preoccupation with the theater helped him to improve his lyrical style. The later poetry is utterly unlike the earlier.

2627. SERVOTTE, HERMAN: *Literatuur als levenskunst: Essays over hedendaagse engelse literatuur.* Antwerpen: Nederlandsche Boekhandel, 1966. 136 p.
"Van Innisfree naar Byzantium: W. B. Yeats (1865-1939)," 97-113; reprinted from *Dietsche Warande en Belfort,* 110:1 (1965), 13-27. The development of Yeats's poetry.

2628. SETHNA, K. D.: "W. B. Yeats—Poet of Two Phases," *Mother India,* 1:10 (25 June 1949), 4-5, 8.
Reprinted in *Mother India,* 18:8 (July 1966), 17-27. Yeats's early poetry was "his richest from the viewpoint of poetry proper," whereas the later poetry, especially that written in a more realistic style, is often an esthetic failure.

2629. SHAHANI, RANJEE G.: "Some Recent English Poets," *Asiatic R,* ns 31: 106 (Apr 1935), 379-89.

2630. SHAW, PRISCILLA WASHBURN: *Rilke, Valéry and Yeats: The Domain of the Self.* New Brunswick: Rutgers UP, 1964. xiv, 278 p.
Based on °"The Concept of Self in Rilke, Valéry and Yeats," Ph.D. thesis, Yale U, 1960. "William Butler Yeats: A Balance of Forces," 175-273; the balance of self and world in Yeats's poetry, particularly in "Leda and the Swan."
Reviews:
1. Robert M. Adams, "Critical Cases," *NYRB,* 3:5 (22 Oct 1964), 19-21.
2. Geoffrey Hartman, "Insiders and Outsiders," *Yale R,* 54:2 (Dec 1964), 270-73.
3. Joseph N. Riddel, *MLJ,* 49:3 (Mar 1965), 193-95.

2631. "SHELMALIER": "Plea for 'Bad Popular Poetry,'" *Phoblacht,* ns 9:26 (14 July 1934), 2, 7.
Yeats should also write it.

2632. SISSON, CHARLES HUBERT: *English Poetry, 1900-1950: An Assessment.* London: Hart-Davis, 1971. 267 p.
"W. B. Yeats," 155-79; slightly revised from *Ishmael,* 1:1 (Nov 1970), 38-59.

2633. SITWELL, EDITH: *Aspects of Modern Poetry.* London: Duckworth, 1934. 264 p.
"William Butler Yeats," 73-89. Yeats's poetry is not as escape from life, it *is* life.

2634. SITWELL, OSBERT, EDITH, and SACHEVERELL: *Trio: Dissertations on Some Aspects of National Genius*. Delivered as the Northcliffe Lectures at the University of London in 1937. London: Macmillan, 1938. viii, 248 p.
Edith Sitwell: "Three Eras of Modern Poetry," 95-187; on Yeats, pp. 114-21.

2635. SKELTON, ROBIN: "The Workshop of W. B. Yeats," *Concerning Poetry*, 1:2 (Fall 1968), 17-26.
The use of refrain in "The Apparitions," "Three Songs to the One Burden," and "What Then"; meter and sound in "The Municipal Gallery Revisited"; and some general remarks on Yeats's poetry.

2636. SOUTHWORTH, JAMES GRANVILLE: *Sowing the Spring: Studies in British Poetry from Hopkins to MacNeice*. Oxford: Blackwell, 1940. viii, 178 p.
"Age and William Butler Yeats," 33-45.

2637. SPALDING, P. A.: "The Last of the Romantics: An Appreciation of W. B. Yeats," *Congregational Q*, 17:3 (July 1939), 332-45.

2638. SPARROW, JOHN: *Sense and Poetry: Essays on the Place of Meaning in Contemporary Verse*. London: Constable, 1934. xxiv, 156 p.
See pp. 13-14, 35-36, 77-80, 85-87, and *passim*.

2639. ————: "Extracts from the Lecture on Tradition and Revolt in English Poetry," *British Institute of the U of Paris: The Bulletin*, #12 (Apr-May 1939), 15-23.

2640. SPENDER, STEPHEN: *The Destructive Element: A Study of Modern Writers and Beliefs*. Folcroft, Pa.: Folcroft Library Editions, 1970 [1935]. ii, 284 p.
"Yeats as a Realist," 115-31; reprinted from *Criterion*, 14:54 (Oct 1934), 17-26; also in J1090. There is realism in Yeats's later poetry, but not much awareness of contemporary issues (with the exception of "The Second Coming").

2641. ————: "A Double Debt to Yeats," *Listener*, 56:1436 (4 Oct 1956), 513, 515.

2642. ————: *The Struggle of the Modern*. London: Hamilton, 1963. xiii, 266 p.
See pp. 29-30, 41-42, 44-45, 48, 50, 91, 93, 113, 139, 162-64, 167, 215, 252-53, 259.

2643. SPIVAK, GAYATRI CHAKRAVORTY: "'Principles of the Mind': Continuity in Yeats's Poetry," *MLN*, 83:6 (Dec 1968), 882-99.
The Wind among the Reeds is important for an assessment of Yeats's poetry; it is the first collection to exhibit one of his persistent preoccupations, the dramatization of the lyric self in the guise of such characters as Michael Robartes and others.

2644. STAUFFER, DONALD ALFRED: *The Nature of Poetry*. NY: Norton, 1946. 291 p.
On Yeats's symbolism, pp. 168-75; on "Sailing to Byzantium," 243-46; and *passim* (see index).

2645. STEIN, FRANCIS PATIKY: "'And Time Runs On,' Cried She. 'Come Out of Charity, Come Dance with Me in Ireland,'" *Glamour*, 58:2 (Oct 1967), 144-57.
Perhaps the strangest thing that has ever happened to Yeats's poetry: quotations from his verse are used as caption titles for a collection of fashion photographs. Also honored are Joyce and MacNeice.

2646. SYMONS, ARTHUR: "Some Makers of Modern Verse," *Forum* [NY], 66:6 (Dec 1921), 476-88.
Yeats "is never quite human—life being the last thing he has learnt."

2647. THWAITE, ANTHONY: *Essays on Contemporary English Poetry: Hopkins to the Present Day*. Tokyo: Kenkyusha, 1957. ix, 222 p.
"W. B. Yeats," 30-47. Republished as *Contemporary English Poetry: An Introduction*. London: Heinemann, 1959. viii, 168 p., pp. 28-41.

2648. TOWNSHEND, GEORGE: *The Genius of Ireland and Other Essays*. Dublin: Talbot Press, [1930]. 120 p.
On the "idealistic" poetry of AE and Yeats, pp. 35-51.

2649. TURNER, W. J.: "Music and Words," *NSt*, 14:335 (24 July 1937), 146-47.
The relation between poetry and song, particularly in Yeats's poetry.

2650. UNTERMEYER, LOUIS (ed): *Modern American Poetry—Modern British Poetry*. NY: Harcourt, Brace, & World, 1962. xxvi, 701; xxiii, 541 p.
"William Butler Yeats," [2]:104-7.

2651. WAGNER, ROBERT DEAN: "The Last Illusion: Examples of Spiritual Life in Modern Literature," Ph.D. thesis, Columbia U, 1952. iii, 260 p. (*DA*, 12:5 [1952], 624-25.)
"Yeats and the Heresy of Paradox," 124-51.

2652. WALSH, WILLIAM: *The Use of Imagination: Educational Thought and the Literary Mind*. London: Chatto & Windus, 1959. 252 p.
"The Notion of Character in Education and Literature, and W. B. Yeats," 183-98; largely a reprint of "Columbia and Byzantium: The Notion of Character in Education and Literature," *Cambridge J*, 7:2 (Nov 1953), 101-13. Yeats's "universe of poetry" contains what pragmatical education lacks most: imagination.

2653. WALTON, JACOB: "The Poems of W. B. Yeats," *Primitive Methodist QR*, os 45 / ns 25:3 (July 1903), 472-80.

2654. WARNER, FRANCIS: "Explorations in Poetic Growth," *Western Mail*, 16 Jan 1965, 5.

2655. WARNER, REX: "Modern English Poetry," *International Literature*, #7 (July 1939), 80-85.
"One might demand from [Yeats] more political understanding: one cannot demand finer poetry."

2656. WARREN, CLARENCE HENRY: "William Butler Yeats," *Bookman*, 82:492 (Sept 1932), 284-86.

2657. ————: *Wise Reading*. London: Newnes, [1936]. 160 p.
Yeats's poems are included in the list of the world's best books, pp. 90-93.

2658. WATKINS, VERNON: "New Year 1965," *Listener*, 73:1867 (7 Jan 1965), 22-23.

2659. WHALLEY, GEORGE: *Poetic Process*. London: Routledge & Kegan Paul, 1953. xxxix, 256 p.
Notes on Yeats's poetry and criticism, *passim* (see index).

2660. W[HITE], H. O.: "Mr. W. B. Yeats: A Brief Study of His Poetry," *Sheffield Daily Telegraph*, #20015 (23 Nov 1922), 3.

2661. WHITELEY, ISABEL: "The Poetry of William Butler Yeats," *Catholic Reading Circle R*, 9:1 (Oct 1896), 12-15.

2662. WOLLMAN, MAURICE (ed): *Ten Twentieth-Century Poets*. London: Harrap, 1957. 224 p.

Notes on Yeats and some of his poems, pp. 145-47, 205-16.

2663. YEATS, W. B.: "A Critical Edition of Selected Lyrics of William Butler Yeats." Edited by Thomas Lee Watson, Editor's Ph.D. thesis, U of Texas, 1958. xii, 405 p. (*DA*, 19:5 [Nov 1958], 1080.)

Contains a long introduction (pp. 1-90) in which the editor discusses the continuity of Yeats's poetic production, and an altogether unsatisfactory "edition" of about 120 poems. The editorial work consists mostly of printing one or perhaps two texts of a poem and appending a few biographical notes.

2664. YEH, MAX WEI: "Poetry, Art, and the Structure of Thought," °Ph.D. thesis, U of Iowa, 1971. 314 p. (*DA*, 32:3 [Sept 1971], 1489A-90A.)

According to the abstract, on Yeats among others, particularly on "Among School Children."

See also J5, 402, 563, 587, 654, 676, 678, 736, 1035, 1036, 1037, 1040, 1042, 1043, 1055, 1076, 1077, 1088, 1125, 1140, 1241, 1308, 1351, 1379, 1442, 1454, 1555, 1556, 1575, 1603, 1609a, 1634, 1648, 1784, 1792, 1810a, 1869, 1875, 1877, 1884, 1894, 1899, 1930, 1941a, 1941b, 1949, 1963, 1970, 1989, 1991, 2001, 2003, 2006, 2009, 2019, 2023, 2039, 2045, 2056, 2058, 2064, 2065, 2084, 2097, 2099, 2110, 2120, 2127, 2145, 2145a, 2154a, 2169, 2170, 2192, 2201, 2206, 2224, 2257, 2272, 2281, 2282, 2283, 2284, 2285, 2287, 2292, 3176, 3318, 3511a, 3991, 3992, 4005, 4011a, 4016, 4027, 4033, 4034, 4050, 4061, 4076a, 4093, 4099, 4117, 4127, 4141, 4169, 4203, 4206, 4207, 4215, 4220, 4240, 4242, 4243, 4247, 4248, 4249, 4254, 4258-72, 4277-89, 4306-21, 4322-27 and note, 4328-36, 4337-38, 4354-65 and note, 4420-26 and note, 4451, 4457-61, 4475-76, 4481, 4482 and note, 4504-12 and note, 4513, 4532-45 and note, 4550-53, 4585-97 and note, 4625-33, 4666-67, 4668, 4672-98 and note, 4705-7, 4708-14, 4717-18 and note, 4719-55 and note, 4756-83 and note, 4845-55 and note, 4856-74, 4976-78, 4986-92 and note, 4996-5031 and note, 5037-67 and note, 5120, 5185-205, 5272-74, 5477, 5488, 5490-92, 5549-54, 5567, 5595, 5853, 5911, 5929, 5933, 5940 (#1, 11), 5944, 5946, 5949, 6087, 6219, 6223, 6226, 6227, 6230, 6231-33, 6242, 6243, 6249, 6251, 6253-56, 6259, 6260, 6262, 6265, 6266, 6269, 6269a, 6276, 6278, 6568, 6919, 6923, 6976, 7235, 7349.

DC Themes and Types

The omission of cross-references to this section is explained in the introductory remarks to section CC.

Absurd

2665. RAJAN, B.: "Yeats and the Absurd," *Tri-Q*, #4 [Fall 1965], 130-31, 133-37.

Discusses the absurd element in the poetry and the plays. Although Yeats had a sense of the absurd, he was no nihilist; the absurd was only one of many attitudes.

Animals

2666. STILZ, GERHARD: "Die Darstellung und Funktion des Tieres in der englischen Lyrik des 20. Jahrhunderts," Dr. phil. thesis, U of Tübingen, 1968. iv, 200 p.

Notes on animals in Yeats's poetry, *passim* (see index).

Art and Artist

2666a. °EVANS, VIRGINIA BETH: "The Figuration of the Artist in the Poetry of William Butler Yeats," M.A. thesis, Simon Fraser U, 1971.

2666b. FASS, BARBARA F.: "The Little Mermaid and the Artist's Quest for a Soul," *CLS*, 9:3 (Sept 1972), 291-302.
Contains a note on Yeats's poetry.

2667. MARSH, DERICK: "The Artist and the Tragic Vision: Themes in the Poetry of W. B. Yeats," *QQ*, 74:1 (Spring 1967), 104-18.
Particularly in "Long-legged Fly" and "Lapis Lazuli."

Ballad

2668. ALTIERI, CHARLES FRANCIS: "Yeats and the Tradition of the Literary Ballad," °Ph.D. thesis, U of North Carolina at Chapel Hill, 1969. 342 p. (*DA*, 31:1 [July 1970], 350A.)

2669. CASTEIN, HANNELORE: *Die anglo-irische Strassenballade*. München: Fink, 1971. 146 p. (Motive. 3.)
Abstract in *English and American Studies in German*, 1971, #40. Discusses the influence of street ballads on Yeats's poetry, pp. 94-102. Also on Lady Gregory and O'Casey.

2670. FRASER, G. S.: "Yeats and the Ballad Style," *Shenandoah*, 21:3 (Spring 1970), 177-94.

2671. FRIEDMAN, ALBERT B.: *The Ballad Revival: Studies in the Influence of Popular on Sophisticated Poetry*. Chicago: U of Chicago Press, 1961. vii, 376 p.
"Epilogue: The Ballad in Modern Verse," 327-56.

2671a. MEIR, COLIN: *The Ballads and Songs of W. B. Yeats: The Anglo-Irish Heritage in Subject and Style*. London: Macmillan, 1974. viii, 141 p.
Based on a °Ph.D. thesis, U of Essex, 1971/72. Contains chapters on "Popular Nationalism: 1885-1892," "Imaginative Nationalism," the influence of Gaelic material via Callanan, Ferguson, Walsh, Mangan, and Hyde, and the influence of the Anglo-Irish dialect. Discusses the various forms of Yeats's ballads, including the political ballads.

2672. TURNER, W. J.: "Broadside Songs," *NSt*, 10:250 (7 Dec 1935), 848-50.
Yeats's broadside songs have "the simplicity and directness of the old folk songs."

2673. YEATS, GRAINNE: "Some Unexpected Ballad Makers," *Ireland of the Welcomes*, 19:5 (Jan-Feb 1971), 11-14.

2674. YEATS, MICHAEL: "W. B. Yeats and Irish Folk Song," *Southern Folklore Q*, 31 [i.e., 30]:2 (June 1966), 153-78.
Discusses the influence of Irish folksong (particularly Gaelic folksong) on Yeats's poetry, Yeats's ballad poetry and the reasons for its failure to become popular, and his ideas about music and singing.

2675. ZIMMERMANN, GEORGES-DENIS: "Irish Political Street Ballads and Rebel Songs, 1780-1900," Docteur ès lettres thesis, U of Genève, 1965. 342 p. (Genève: La Sirène, 1966.)
Also published as °*Songs of the Irish Rebellion: Political Street Ballads and Rebel Songs, 1780-1900*. Hatboro, Pa.: Folklore Associates, 1967. 342 p. Scattered notes on Yeats, *passim* (see index).

2676. ————: "Yeats, the Popular Ballad and the Ballad-Singers," *ES*, 50:2 (Apr 1969), 185-97.

Beatitude

2677. °HORAN, DOLORES V.: "The Profane Perfection: Beatitude in *The Collected Poems* of William Butler Yeats," M.A. thesis, Columbia U, 1961. 95 p.

Bird

2678. ALLEN, JAMES L.: "The Golden Bird on *The Golden Bough*: An Archetypal Image in Yeats's Byzantium Poems," *Diliman R*, 11:2 (Apr 1963), 168-221.
 Yeats's indebtedness to Frazer, specifically in his use of the archer-star and the golden bird and bough symbolism. Discusses "Parnell's Funeral" and, in less detail, the two Byzantium poems.

2679. MATSUMURA, KEN'ICHI: "Fire and Bird," *Yeats Society of Japan Annual Report and Bulletin*, #5 (1970), 47-51.

2679a. MONTGOMERY, LINA LEE: "The Phoenix: Its Use as a Literary Device in English from the 17th Century to the 20th Century," *D. H. Lawrence R*, 5:3 (Fall 1972), 268-323.
 On Yeats's use of the image, pp. 307-10.

2680. SUŠKO, MARIO: "Ptice B. Miljkovića i W. B. Yeatsa" [The birds of Miljković and Yeats], *Telegram*, 6:290 (19 Nov 1965), 10.

Body and Soul

2681. ELEANOR, MOTHER MARY: "The Debate of the Body and the Soul," *Renascence*, 12:4 (Summer 1960), 192-97.

Carelessness

2682. SCHOLES, ROBERT (ed): *Learners and Discerners: A Newer Criticism. Discussions of Modern Literature.* Charlottesville: U Press of Virginia, 1964. ix, 177 p.
 John Frederick Nims: "Yeats and the Careless Muse," 29-60. The motif of carelessness in Yeats's poetry.

Ceremony

2683. BEACH, JOSEPH WARREN: *Obsessive Images: Symbolism in the Poetry of the 1930's and 1940's.* Edited by William Van O'Connor. Minneapolis: U of Minnesota Press, 1960. xv, 396 p.
 On Yeats's use of the word "ceremony" and its reverberations in American poetry, pp. 3-12.

Dance and Dancer

2684. CHITTICK, V. L. O.: "Yeats the Dancer," *Dalhousie R*, 39:3 (Autumn 1959), 333-48.

2685. DAICHES, DAVID: "Jane Austen, Karl Marx, and the Aristocratic Dance," *American Scholar*, 17:3 (Summer 1948), 289-96.
 The dance motif and the country house ideal in Jane Austen and in Yeats's poetry.

2686. FLETCHER, IAN: "Explorations and Recoveries--II: Symons, Yeats and the Demonic Dance," *London Mag*, 7:6 (June 1960), 46-60.

2687. °GODFREY, MICHAEL EDWARD: "The Development of the Symbol of the Dancer in the Poetry of William Butler Yeats," M.A. thesis, McGill U, 1966. 66 p.

2687a. NAPOLI, JOANNE LENORE: "The Meaning of the Dancer in the Poetry of William Butler Yeats," °Ph.D. thesis, U of Massachusetts, 1972. 153 p. (*DA*, 33:6 [Dec 1972], 2945A.)
    Discusses Yeats's occult sources and the concept of unity of being.

Dramatic Lyric

2688. BUCKLEY, VINCENT: "W. B. Yeats and the Dramatic Lyric," *Melbourne Critical R*, #2 (1959), 12-28.
    Partly reprinted in J2475.

2689. COX, JAMES BYRNE: "W. B. Yeats: The Dramatic Lyric. A Study of Yeats's Dramatic Use of Lyric Verse," Honors thesis, Harvard U, 1965. ii, 41 p.

2690. ROSE, PHYLLIS HOGE: "Yeats and the Dramatic Lyric," Ph.D. thesis, U of Wisconsin, 1958. v, 519 p. (*DA*, 18:6 [June 1958], 2130.)

Elegy

2690a. KINGSLEY, LAWRENCE WILSON: "The Modern Elegy: The Epistemology of Loss," °Ph.D. thesis, U of Wisconsin (Madison), 1973. 425 p. (*DA*, 34:2 [Aug 1973], 779A-80A.)

2691. POTTS, ABBIE FINDLAY: *The Elegiac Mode: Poetic Form in Wordsworth and Other Elegists*. Ithaca: Cornell UP, 1967. xii, 460 p.
    "Flute Song Yesterday: W. B. Yeats," 358-94, and *passim* (see index). On elegiac forms and themes in Yeats's poetry and plays and the classical and Wordsworthian influence behind them.

Epigram and Aphorism

2692. HUME, MARTHA HASKINS: "Yeats: Aphorist and Epigrammatist. A Study of *The Collected Poems*," °Ph.D. thesis, U of Colorado, 1969. v, 114 p. (*DA*, 30:10 [Apr 1970], 4454A.)

2693. QUIVEY, JAMES R.: "Yeats and the Epigram: A Study of Technique in the Four-Line Poems," *Discourse*, 13:1 (Winter 1970), 58-72.

Estheticism

2694. PRINCE, JEFFREY ROBERT: "Havens of Intensity: Aestheticism in the Poetry of Keats, Tennyson, and Yeats," °Ph.D. thesis, U of Virginia, 1971. 350 p. (*DA*, 32:8 [Feb 1972], 4629A-30A.)

Existentialism

2695. °CUFF, ELIZABETH L.: "Existential Themes in the Poetry of William Butler Yeats," M.A. thesis, Texas Christian U, 1965.

Fairies

2696. BRIGGS, KATHARINE MARY: *The Fairies in Tradition and Literature*. London: Routledge & Kegan Paul, 1967. x, 261 p.
    See pp. 172-73: "With Yeats' poetry a different note came into our literature, for he believed in the fairies."

2697. SCHWEISGUT, ELSBETH: *Yeats' Feendichtung*. Darmstadt: Bender, 1927. 61 p.
A Dr. phil. thesis, U of Giessen, 1927 [i.e., 1928].

Generosity

2698. NARASIMHAIAH, C. D.: "W. B. Yeats: Poetry as an Act of Generosity," *JJCL*, 8 (1968), 1-20.
The theme of generosity in "poems dealing with love, national politics, theatre business, and old age."

Hero and Heroic Literature

2699. HOUGHTON, WALTER E.: "Yeats and Crazy Jane: The Hero in Old Age," *MP*, 40:4 (May 1943), 316-29.
The heroic theme in Yeats's poetry and its final crystallization in *Words for Music Perhaps*. Reprinted in J1090. See also J1356.

2700. MCCUTCHION, DAVID: "The Heroic Mind of W. B. Yeats," *Visva-Bharati Q*, 27:1 (1961), 42-62.

Imagery

2701. BROOKE-ROSE, CHRISTINE: *A Grammar of Metaphor*. London: Secker & Warburg, 1958. xi, 343 p.
Passim on Yeats's metaphors.

2702. FRYE, NORTHROP: *The Stubborn Structure: Essays on Criticism and Society*. London: Methuen, 1970. xii, 316 p.
"The Top of the Tower: A Study of the Imagery of Yeats," 257-77; reprinted from *Southern R*, 5:3 (July 1969), 850-71.

2703. HAHN, SISTER M. NORMA: "W. B. Yeats's Search for Reality: A Study of the Imagery of His Later Poetry," Ph.D. thesis, Fordham U, 1960. iii, 204, 14 p.

2704. °MACCALLUM, HUGH REID: "Image and Pattern in the Poetry of W. B. Yeats," M.A. thesis, U of Toronto, 1954. 115 p.

2705. RAND, RICHARD ALDRICH: "The Conflict of Yeats's Imagery," Honors thesis, Harvard U, 1962. i, 37 p.

2706. RAYAN, KRISHNA: "When the Green Echoes or Doesn't," *Malahat R*, #14 (Apr 1970), 30-38.
Image and discourse in poetry, including some notes on Yeats.

2707. RUTLEDGE, ROBERT CLINTON: "The Development of the Poetry of William Butler Yeats as Reflected in His Metaphors," °Ph.D. thesis, George Washington U, 1966. 234 p. (*DA*, 27:6 [Dec 1967], 1836A.)

2708. TUVE, ROSEMOND: *Elizabethan and Metaphysical Imagery: Renaissance Poetics and Twentieth-Century Critics*. Chicago: U of Chicago Press, 1947. xiv, 442 p.
Notes on Yeats's imagery, *passim* (see index). See William Empson, "Donne and the Rhetorical Tradition," *Kenyon R*, 11:4 (Autumn 1949), 571-87; comments on the reading of "Byzantium," pp. 576-77.

Imagism

2709. BIANCHI, RUGGERO: *La poetica dell'imagismo*. Milano: Mursia, 1965. 243 p. (Civiltà letteraria del novecento. Sezione inglese-americana. 1.)
Several notes on Yeats and Imagism (see index), especially pp. 15-17.

Irish Literature, Yeats and

2710. ALSPACH, RUSSELL KING: *Irish Poetry from the English Invasion to 1798.* 2nd edition revised. Philadelphia: U of Pennsylvania Press, 1964 [1943]. xi, 146 p.
Some references, *passim.*

2711. CLARK, DAVID RIDGLEY: *Lyric Resonance: Glosses on Some Poems of Yeats, Frost, Crane, Cummings, & Others* [. . .]. Amherst: U of Massachusetts Press, 1972. ix, 274 p.
Incorporates: "Poussin and Yeats's 'News for the Delphic Oracle,'" *Wascana R,* 2:1 (1967), 33-44; °"Out of a People to a People," *Malahat R,* #22 (Apr 1972), 25-41.
"W. B. Yeats," 11-54, in three sections: "Out of a People to a People" (Yeats and the Anglo-Irish poetry of the 19th century, particularly Davis, Mangan, and Ferguson, and the reverberations in Yeats's own poetry); an interpretation of "He Bids His Beloved Be at Peace"; and an interpretation of "News for the Delphic Oracle" (commenting on the correspondences and differences between Yeats's poem and Poussin's painting "The Marriage of Peleus and Thetis," actually "Acis and Galatea").
"Some Irish Poems," 55-102. By Oscar Wilde, Gogarty, Seumas O'Sullivan, Joseph Campbell, and Thomas Kinsella. Yeats is mentioned *passim.*

2712. MACCATHMHAOIL, SEOSAMH [i.e., Joseph Campbell]: "A Plea for the Patriotic Ballad," *Nationist,* 1:2 (28 Sept 1905), 31-33.
Yeats is to blame (with his cry "Art for art's sake, not Ireland's") that there is no Irish patriotic poetry. Correspondence by Padraic Colum, "Nationality in Verse," :5 (19 Oct 1905), 77-78.

2713. NEWSON, RONALD: "W. B. Yeats and the Irish Movement," *Visva-Bharati Q,* 1:4 (Feb 1936), 18-28.
Misnomer; slight article on Irish themes in Yeats's poetry.

2714. STOCK, A. G.: "From the National to the Universal," *Dublin Mag,* 4:3-4 (Autumn-Winter 1965), 28-35.
Concentrates on "To Ireland in the Coming Times" and "Nineteen Hundred and Nineteen."

2715. °TELFER, GILES W. L.: "The Idea of the Gael in English Poetry, 1807-1914," D.Phil. thesis, Oxford U, 1967.

Irish Poet, Yeats as

2716. VENABLES, J. W.: "W. B. Yeats and His Poetry," *Holborn R,* os 62 / ns 11:4 (Oct 1920), 501-12.

Landscape

2717. DAVIE, DONALD: "Landscape as Poetic Focus," *Southern R,* 4:3 (Summer 1968), 685-91.

2718. *The Hidden Harmony: Essays in Honor of Philip Wheelwright.* NY: Odyssey Press, 1966. ix, 195 p.
Sister M. Bernetta Quinn: "Symbolic Landscape in Yeats: County Galway," 145-71. See also J2722.

2719. KIM JONG GIL: "The Topography of Yeats's Poetry," *Phoenix,* #10 (Summer 1965), 84-95.

2720. MALINS, EDWARD: "Coole Park," *Q Bulletin of the Irish Georgian Society*, 13:1 (Jan-Mar 1970), 20-28.
Coole Park in Yeats's poetry.

2721. PROSKY, MURRAY: "Landscapes in the Poetry of W. B. Yeats," Ph.D. thesis, U of Wisconsin, 1966. vi, 246 p. (*DA*, 28:2 [Aug 1967], 691A.)

2722. QUINN, SISTER M. BERNETTA: "Symbolic Landscape in Yeats: County Sligo," *Shenandoah*, 16:4 (Summer 1965), 37-62.

Long Poem

2723. YOUNGBLOOD, SARAH: "The Structure of Yeats's Long Poems," *Criticism*, 5:4 (Fall 1963), 323-35.
The long poems are fusions of the discursive and imagistic modes of poetry. Discusses "The Statues" and "Meditations in Time of Civil War."

Love Poetry

2724. BRADBROOK, MURIEL C.: "Yeats and Elizabethan Love Poetry," *Dublin Mag*, 4:2 (Summer 1965), 40-55.
The influence of Spenser and Shakespeare.

2725. BROADBENT, JOHN BARCLAY: *Poetic Love*. London: Chatto & Windus, 1964. x, 310 p.
Several notes on Yeats (see index), especially on "Among School Children" (pp. 4-7, 38).

2726. °DRAVES, ROBERT W.: "The Love Poetry of William Butler Yeats," M.A. thesis, U of Colorado, 1963. 86 p.

2727. ENSCOE, GERALD: *Eros and the Romantics: Sexual Love as Theme in Coleridge, Shelley and Keats*. The Hague: Mouton, 1967. 178 p. (Studies in English Literature. 45.)
See pp. 170-71.

2728. °HALLER, GLADYS L.: "A Man Young and Old: The Development of William Butler Yeats as a Love Poet," M.A. thesis, Columbia U, 1950.

2729. HOOPER, THOMAS BRADLEE: "Love and Time in Yeats," Honors thesis, Harvard U, 1958. i, 38 p.
The poems in *Words for Music Perhaps*.

2730. HÜHN, PETER: *Das Verhältnis von Mann und Frau im Werk von William Butler Yeats*. Bonn: Bouvier, 1971. vi, 243 p. (Studien zur englischen Literatur. 5.)
Originally a Dr. phil. thesis, U of Hamburg; abstract in *English and American Studies in German*, 1971, #66. Discusses the themes of love, time, and eternity in the poetry and in *The Shadowy Waters*, *The Only Jealousy of Emer*, *The King of the Great Clock Tower*, and *A Full Moon in March*. A somewhat one-sided intrinsic study that sees the female characters as either *femmes fatales* or images of perfection.

2731. JONG, MAX DE: "W. B. Yeats en Denis de Rougemont," *Criterium*, #9 (June 1946), 433-37.
Yeats's love poetry and its parallels in de Rougemont's *L'amour et l'occident*.

2732. KUIĆ, RANKA: "Jeitsova lubavna lirika" [Yeats's love poetry], *Književne novine*, 21:355 (7 June 1969), 3, 12.
Reprinted in *Mostovi*, 1:1 (Jan-Mar 1970), 30-38.

2733. PARKINSON, THOMAS: "Yeats and the Love Lyric," *JJQ*, 3:2 (Winter 1966), 109-23.

2734. PENNINGTON, BRUCE FRANKLIN: "The Personae of W. B. Yeats' *The Wind among the Reeds*: Love Poetry and Occultism," Honors thesis, Harvard U, 1968. ii, ? p. (the last pages of the copy in the Harvard Archives are wanting).

2735. PERLOFF, MARJORIE G.: "'Heart Mysteries': The Later Love Lyrics of W. B. Yeats," *Contemporary Literature*, 10:2 (Spring 1969), 266-83.
    Not all of Yeats's later love lyrics celebrate a sexual "mythology of earth." Discusses "Quarrel in Old Age," "The Results of Thought," and "A Bronze Head."

Mask

2736. MURSHID, K. S.: "Yeats and the Saint's Mask," *Dacca U Studies*, 10: pt 1 (June 1961), 79-96.
    Beggar, saint, and mask in Yeats's poetry, and the pertinent Indian influences.

Music

2737. ENGSBERG, RICHARD CARL: "Two by Two: Analogues of Form in Poetry and Music," °Ph.D. thesis, New York U, 1968. 450 p. (*DA*, 30:1 [July 1969], 278A.)
    According to the abstract, a discussion of Yeats's poetry is included.

2738. HOLLAND, PATRICK: "Yeats and the Musician's Art in *Last Poems*," *Éire-Ireland*, 6:4 (Winter 1971), 49-64.
    The music/song/ballad motif.

Myth (Poems Related to "A Vision")

2739. ADAMS, ROBERT MARTIN: "Now That My Ladder's Gone—Yeats without Myth," *Accent*, 13:3 (Summer 1953), 140-52.
    Particularly on "Byzantium."

2740. ALLEN, JAMES L.: "William Butler Yeats's One Myth," *Personalist*, 45:4 (Autumn 1964), 524-32.
    The one myth is a Platonic dualism; its central motif is the union of man and god.

2740a. BELL, MICHAEL: "The Assimilation of Doubt in Yeats's Visionary Poems," *QQ*, 80:3 (Autumn 1973), 383-97.
    Discusses "Lapis Lazuli," "The Second Coming," "The Gyres," and "Byzantium."

2741. BROWN, FORMAN G.: "Mr. Yeats and the Supernatural," *Sewanee R*, 33:3 (July 1925), 323-30.
    In the poetry and the plays.

2742. BURKE, KENNETH: "On Motivation in Yeats," *Southern R*, 7:3 (Winter 1941/42), 547-61.
    A Vision and some related poems. Reprinted in J1090.

2743. COUSINS, JAMES HENRY: *New Ways in English Literature*. Madras: Ganesh, 1919 [1917]. xv, 196 p.
    "William Butler Yeats, Poet and Occultist," 43-52; reprinted as "Yeats the Nobel Prizeman and His Poetry," *Visva-Bharati Q*, 2:2 (July 1924), 156-61. The most important sources of Yeats's poetry are theosophy and Neo-Platonism.

2743a. DEMERS, PIERRE E.: "Yeats' Great Wheel and the Use of Christian Myths and Symbols in His Poems," *Fu Jen Studies*, 2 (1969), 33-51.

2744. °DIETZ, JOHN J.: "The Influence of the Occult on Yeats' Early Poetry," M.A. thesis, Temple U, 1965.

2745. FLEMING, DAVID: "A Vision of History: Yeats's Mystical Pattern and Historical References in the Later Lyrics," *Delta Epsilon Sigma Bulletin*, 9:1 (Mar 1964), 18-29.
    The importance of *A Vision* for "Sailing to Byzantium," "Meditations in Time of Civil War," "Two Songs from a Play," "Leda and the Swan," and "Under Ben Bulben."

2746. GROSS, HARVEY SEYMOUR: *The Contrived Corridor: History and Fatality in Modern Literature*. Ann Arbor: U of Michigan Press, 1971. xiv, 202 p.
    Based on "The Contrived Corridor: A Study in Modern Poetry and the Meaning of History," Ph.D. thesis, U of Michigan, 1955. vii, 202 p. (*DA*, 15:4 [1955], 583). "W. B. Yeats," 74-99.

2747. °HEARD, G. T.: "A Study of the Influence of Occultism in Modern Poetry, with Particular Reference to the Works of W. B. Yeats, Charles Williams, and Edith Sitwell," M.A. thesis, U of Leeds, 1955.

2747a. ISLAM, SHAMSUL: "The Influence of Eastern Philosophy on Yeats's Later Poetry," *TCL*, 19:4 (Oct 1973), 283-90.
    Especially in "Supernatural Songs."

2748. KERANS, JAMES: "Relations between *A Vision* and the Later Poetry of William Butler Yeats," Honors thesis, Harvard U, 1948. i, 44 p.

2749. MACKINNON, KENNETH: "Yeats's Poetry and *A Vision*," M.A. thesis, Dalhousie U, 1962. iii, 219 p.
    Attempts to demonstrate that the later poems can be understood without the help of *A Vision*.

2750. °NAPOLI, JOANNE L.: "The Total Quest: Myth in the Poetry of Yeats," M.A. thesis, U of Vermont, 1965.

2751. SHEEHY, LEONARD MICHAEL: "Eternity Is Passion: A Study of the Function and Direction of Myth in the Poetry of William Butler Yeats," Honors thesis, Harvard U, 1960. i, 38 p.

2752. STURTEVANT, DONALD F.: "The Public and Private Minds of W. B. Yeats," *Thoth*, 4:2 (Spring 1963), 74-82.
    Largely concerned with the relationship between Yeats's system (particularly the concept of Anima Mundi) and his poetry.

2753. TSCHUMI, RAYMOND: *Thought in Twentieth-Century English Poetry*. London: Routledge & Kegan Paul, 1950. 299 p.
    A Docteur ès lettres thesis, U of Genève, 1950. "Yeats's Philosophical Poetry," 29-73; discusses *A Vision* and the poems related to it, including a section on "Yeats's Historical Vision" and on the two Byzantium poems. Includes a note on AE, pp. 252-56.

2754. WILSON, COLIN: *Poetry & Mysticism*. London: Hutchinson, 1970. 227 p.
    "W. B. Yeats," 125-60, and *passim*.

Opposites and Antinomies

2755. JACOBS, EDWARD CRANEY: "Yeats and the Artistic Epiphany," *Discourse*, 12:3 (Summer 1969), 292-305.

The reconciliation of opposites in Yeats's poetry is achieved in an epiphany, which emphasizes unity and separateness at the same time. Discusses "The Phases of the Moon," "The Double Vision of Michael Robartes," and "Byzantium."

2756. JENSEN, EJNER: "The Antinomical Vision of W. B. Yeats," *XUS*, 3:3 (Dec 1964), 127-45.
 The struggle of opposites in *A Vision*, *The Wanderings of Oisin*, "Ego Dominus Tuus," "Byzantium," "A Dialogue of Self and Soul," "Lapis Lazuli," and other poems.

2757. LERNER, LAURENCE DAVID: *The Truest Poetry: An Essay on the Question What Is Literature*. London: Hamilton, 1960. xi, 221 p.
 Note on the opposition of life and abstraction in Yeats's poetry, pp. 118-20; note on "The Second Coming," pp. 134-35.

2758. MCCUTCHION, DAVID: "Beast or Angel? Romantic Ambiguities in Goethe, Musset, Stendhal and Yeats," *JJCL*, 2 (1962), 31-67.
 Antinomies in Yeats's poetry, pp. 55-67.

Periods: Early Poetry

2759. BARNA, EDWARD ROBERT: "A Study of William Butler Yeats' Early Poetry: *The Wanderings of Oisin*, *Crossways*, and *The Rose*," Honors thesis, Harvard U, 1970. i, 44 p.

2760. BECKSON, KARL (ed): *Aesthetes and Decadents of the 1890's: An Anthology of British Poetry and Prose*. Edited with an introduction and notes by Karl Beckson. NY: Vintage Books, 1966. xli, 310 p. (Vintage Book. V342.)
 "Introduction," xvii-xl, *passim* on Yeats.

2761. BYRD, THOMAS L.: "The Early Poetry of W. B. Yeats: The Poetic Quest," Ph.D. thesis, U of Florida, 1968. iv, 174 p. (*DA*, 29:10 [Apr 1969], 3573A.)

2762. °EISOLD, KENNETH R.: "Symbols of Unity: The Early Poetry of William Butler Yeats," M.A. thesis, Columbia U, 1958. 103 p.

2763. °FEHLBERG, JOAN S.: "The Golden Chain: Relationships between the Early and Late Poetry of William Butler Yeats," M.A. thesis, Brigham Young U, 1965.

2764. FULLWOOD, DAPHNE: "The Early Poetry of W. B. Yeats," *Ariel*, 3:3 (July 1972), 80-90.

2765. GANNON, PATRICIO (ed): *Poets of the Rhymers' Club*. With a preface. Buenos Aires: Colombo, 1953. 75 p.
 "Preface," 11-21.

2766. GRIERSON, HERBERT JOHN CLIFFORD: *Lyrical Poetry from Blake to Hardy*. London: Hogarth Press, 1928. 159 p. (Hogarth Lectures on Literature. 5.)
 See pp. 148-52.

2767. GROSSMAN, ALLEN RICHARD: *Poetic Knowledge in the Early Yeats: A Study of "The Wind among the Reeds."* Charlottesville: U Press of Virginia, 1969. xxv, 240 p.
 Based on °"The Last Judgment of the Imagination: A Study of Yeats' *The Wind among the Reeds*," Ph.D. thesis, Brandeis U, 1960. An analysis more of the sources and the background than of the poems themselves, with particular emphasis on the occult tradition.
 Reviews:
 1. Arra M. Garab, "The Legacy of Yeats," *JML*, 1:1 (1970), 137-40.

2. Giles Gunn, *MP*, 69:1 (Aug 1971), 87-91.

3. Edwin Honig, "On Knowing Yeats," *VQR*, 45:4 (Autumn 1969), 700-704.

4. J. R. Mulryne, *MLR*, 66:3 (July 1971), 680-81.

5. Patrick Murray, *Studies*, 59:234 (Summer 1970), 215-18.

6. Marjorie Perloff, "Yeats as Gnostic," *Contemporary Literature*, 12: 4 (Autumn 1971), 554-61.

2768. GURD, PATTY: *The Early Poetry of William Butler Yeats*. Lancaster, Pa.: New Era Printing Company, 1916. iii, 101 p.
A Dr. phil. thesis, U of Zürich, 1916.

2769. HARRIS, WENDELL: "Innocent Decadence: The Poetry of *The Savoy*," *PMLA*, 77:5 (Dec 1962), 629-36.
Contains some remarks on Yeats, pp. 630-31.

2770. °HAZLEY, RICHARD A.: "From Innisfree to the Rag Shop of the Heart: Voyages of W. B. Yeats," M.A. thesis, Columbia U, 1959. 82 p.

2771. °KEEGAN, ELIZABETH: "The Early Poetry of W. B. Yeats," M.A. thesis, University College, Dublin, 1941.

2772. °KOLLARITSCH, MARTHA JANE MOORE: "A Study in Yeats's Early Verse," M.A. thesis, U of Texas, 1955. 125 p.

2773. °LAMBERG, WALTER: "Cultural Primitivism in the Early Poetry of William Butler Yeats," M.A. thesis, U of Houston, 1966.

2774. °MARTLAND, AGATHA M.: "A Study of the Transition in Subject Matter, Imagery, Rhythm, and Rhyme Reflected in the Poetry of W. B. Yeats between 1899-1914," M.A. thesis, New York U, 1955.

2775. MURPHY, FRANK HUGHES: "The Theme of Reconciliation in the Early Poetry of Yeats," °Ph.D. thesis, U of North Carolina, 1971. 200 p. (*DA*, 32:9 [Mar 1972], 5193A.)
From *Crossways* through *Michael Robartes and the Dancer*.

2776. ROBINSON, LENNOX: "Yeats: The Early Poems," *REL*, 6:3 (July 1965), 22-33.

2777. RUTENBERG, DANIEL: "A Study of Rhymers' Club Poetry," °Ph.D. thesis, U of Florida, 1967. 195 p. (*DA*, 31:1 [July 1970], 402A.)

2778. °SEQUEIRA, V. M.: "Prelude to Greatness: A Study of the Early Poetry of W. B. Yeats," M.A. thesis, University College, Dublin, 1957.

2779. *Victorian Poetry*. London: Arnold, 1972. 304 p. (Stratford-upon-Avon Studies. 15.)
Arnold Goldman: "The Oeuvre Takes Shape: Yeats's Early Poetry," 196-221. Lorna Sage: "Hardy, Yeats and Tradition," 254-75. Also *passim* (see index).

Periods: Poetry of the Middle Period

2780. AGOSTINO, NEMI D': "La poesia di William Butler Yeats: Il 'periodo del sole' (1900-1919)," *English Miscellany*, 5 (1954), 149-202.

2781. CARPENTER, WILLIAM M.: "The *Green Helmet* Poems and Yeats's Myth of the Renaissance," *MP*, 67:1 (Aug 1969), 50-59.
Traces the ideological and stylistic influence of what Yeats considered to be the main characteristic of the Renaissance: unity of intellect and emotion. Discusses various Ronsard and Shakespeare echoes in "At the Abbey Theatre" and "These Are the Clouds."

2782. CROSSAN, MARY ELIZABETH: "The Transition Period (1904-1919) in W. B. Yeats' Development as a Poet," M.A. thesis, U of Manchester, 1963. ii, 248 p.

2783. GORDAN, JOHN D.: "An Anniversary Exhibition: The Henry W. and Albert A. Berg Collection, 1940-1965. Part II," *BNYPL*, 69:9 (Nov 1965), 597-608.
"William Butler Yeats: The Holograph of *The Wild Swans at Coole*," 605.

2784. HAHN, HANS-JOACHIM: *Die Krisis des Lyrischen in den Gedichten von W. B. Yeats und W. H. Auden: Eine Untersuchung struktureller Wandlungen moderner Lyrik*. Göppingen: Kümmerle, 1971. xii, 245 p. (Göppinger akademische Beiträge. 31.)
Originally a Dr. phil. thesis, U of Tübingen, 1971; abstract in *English and American Studies in German*, 1971, #68. A largely unsuccessful attempt to explain the change in Yeats's poetic style in 1901-10.

2785. MACLEAN, MORA: "Four Lyric Books of William Butler Yeats," M.A. thesis, McGill U, 1961. iv, 106 p.
The Green Helmet and Other Poems, *Responsibilities*, *The Wild Swans at Coole*, and *Michael Robartes and the Dancer*.

2786. O'BRIEN, JAMES H.: "Yeats and the Sources of Morality," *University R* [Dublin], 3:10 [1966?], 48-60.
In *Responsibilities*.

2787. ————: "Yeats' Dark Night of Self and *The Tower*," *Bucknell R*, 15:2 (May 1967), 10-25.

2788. ————: "Overshadowers and Ideal Forms in Yeats's *Michael Robartes and the Dancer*," *Descant*, 11:4 (Summer 1967), 37-47.

2789. ————: "Yeats's Discoveries of Self in *The Wild Swans at Coole*," *Colby Library Q*, 8:1 (Mar 1968), 1-13.

2790. O'CASEY, SEAN: "Four Letters: Sean O'Casey to Oliver St. John Gogarty." Edited by James F. Carens, *JJQ*, 8:1 (Fall 1970), 111-18.
In two of the letters O'Casey ridicules Yeats's recent volume of poems, *The Tower*.

2791. °TUOHY, DERMOT A.: "W. B. Yeats: *The Wild Swans at Coole*. An Essay on the Interrelationship of Themes and Attitudes in the Book," M.A. thesis, University College, Dublin, 1958.

Periods: Late Poetry

2792. ACKLEY, RANDALL WILLIAM: "*The Winding Stair*: Variations on a Theme," *Research Studies*, 37:4 (Dec 1969), 313-19.
The theme of "life."

2793. BUNCH, DOROTHY: "The Later Poems of William Butler Yeats: Being Throughout a Comparison of His Earlier and Later Works," M.A. thesis, U of Kansas, 1933. iii, 75 p.

2794. DONOGHUE, DENIS: "The Vigour of Its Blood: Yeats's *Words for Music Perhaps*," *Kenyon R*, 21:3 (Summer 1959), 376-87.

2795. DURRANT, GEOFFREY: "Cast a Cold Eye," *Acorn*, #4 (Spring 1963), 9-15.
Reprinted from °*Trek*, 1945. Yeats's later poetry is better than the earlier "damp" romanticism.

2796. °GARAB, ARRA M.: "Sign of the Screaming Seraph: The Text and Testimony of William Butler Yeats' *Last Poems*," M.A. thesis, Columbia U, 1952. 154 p.

2797. °HANDY, JOHN L.: "The *Last Poems* of W. B. Yeats," M.A. thesis, Columbia U, 1951. 81 p.

2798. °HEMBEL, HENRY H.: "In Pursuit of Tragic Joy: The Influence of *A Vision* on the Later Poetry of W. B. Yeats," M.A. thesis, U of South Carolina, 1967.

2799. HENN, T. R.: "A Note on Yeats," *Cambridge R*, 60:1740 (10 Feb 1939), 225-27.
The outstanding quality of the later poetry (which is much better then the earlier) is "wisdom."

2800. O'BRIEN, JAMES H.: "Self vs. Soul in Yeats's *The Winding Stair*," *Éire-Ireland*, 3:1 (Spring 1968), 23-39.

2801. O'DONNELL, JAMES PRESTON: *Sailing to Byzantium: A Study in the Development of the Later Style and Symbolism in the Poetry of William Butler Yeats*. Cambridge, Mass.: Harvard UP, 1939. 95 p. (Harvard Honors Theses in English. 11.)
Reviews:
1. Anon., *Irish Times*, 82:25826 (20 Apr 1940), 5.

2802. ROTHFUSS, HEINRICH: "Wandlungen in der späten Lyrik William Butler Yeats'," Dr. phil. thesis, U of Tübingen, 1966. xi, 299 p.
A study of the "system" poems and of the revisions of Yeats's later poems in the light of his growing concern with philosophical "objectivity." Rothfuss fails to distinguish between different uses of the "system" and does not offer a convincing explanation of "objective." At times he becomes completely unintelligible. Numerous mistakes in both text and bibliography.

2803. STALLWORTHY, JON (ed): *Yeats: "Last Poems." A Casebook*. London: Macmillan, 1968. 280 p.
Contains "Introduction" (pp. 11-22), 20 previously published pieces, a set of "Questions," and an insufficient bibliography. The selection is rather one-sided.
Reviews:
1. Anon., "Devoted to Yeats," *TLS*, 67:3460 (20 June 1968), 641.

2804. °TUMMON, LAWRENCE STANLEY: "Nietzschean Elements in Yeats's Last Poems," M.A. thesis, Dalhousie U, 1970.

2805. °TURNER, RICHARD MERRILL: "Ideas and the Poetry of W. B. Yeats: With Special Reference to *The Winding Stair*," M.A. thesis, U of Colorado, 1961. 97 p.

2806. WILLIAMS, CHARLES: *Poetry at Present*, Oxford: Clarendon Press, 1930. xii, 216 p.
"William Butler Yeats," 56-69. Defends Yeats's later poetry, which he considers to be of Elizabethan magnitude. Includes an "End Piece," a poem on Yeats.

2807. WILSON, F. A. C.: "Yeats's Last Poems," *Moderna språk*, 54:1 (1960), 10-19.

2808. YI CH'ANG-PAE: [in Korean] "Yeats's Later Poetry," *Phoenix*, #10 (Summer 1965), 96-110.

Persons in Yeats's Poetry

2809. ADAMS, HAZARD: *The Contexts of Poetry*. Boston: Little, Brown, 1963. xiii, 200 p.
> On Yeats, *passim* (see index), especially pp. 72-74 (the revisions of "Leda and the Swan"), 159-62 (on "drama into character" in some poems), and 175-77 (on "The Symbolism of Poetry").

2810. ALLT, PETER: "Lady Gregory and Yeats's Cult of Aristocracy," *Irish Writing*, #31 (Summer 1955), 19-23.
> The aristocratic image of Lady Gregory in Yeats's poetry.

2811. ANTIPPAS, ANDY P.: "A Note on Yeats's 'Crazy Jane' Poems," *ES*, 49:6 (Dec 1968), 557-59.
> The relationship with *A Vision*.

2812. BOWEN, JAMES K.: "Consummation, Completeness, and Crazy Jane: Totality through Union," *Research Studies*, 39:2 (June 1971), 147-50.

2813. CORBIN, RICHARD JOHNSTONE: "An Interpretation of Yeats's 'Crazy Jane' Poems," M.A. thesis, Tulane U, 1960. ii, 50 p.

2814. DUGGAN, EILEEN: "Dedication, the Artist's Discipline," *America*, 61: 1548 (10 June 1939), 210-11.
> Constance Markievicz in Yeats's poetry.

2815. EGLESON, JANET FRANK: "Christ and Cuchulain: Interrelated Archetypes of Divinity and Heroism in Yeats," *Éire-Ireland*, 4:1 (Spring 1969), 76-85.
> Discusses the pertinent poems and plays.

2816. GREER, SAMMYE CRAWFORD: "Yeats's Lyric Personae," °Ph.D. thesis, U of Kentucky, 1970. 256 p. (*DA*, 31:10 [Apr 1971], 5401A-2A.)

2817. GREGORY, HORACE: *The Shield of Achilles: Essays on Beliefs in Poetry*. NY: Harcourt, Brace, 1944. xii, 211 p.
> "On William Butler Yeats and the Mask of Jonathan Swift," 136-55; on Swift in Yeats's poetry and in *The Words upon the Window-Pane*. First published in *Southern R*, 7:3 (Winter 1941/42), 492-509; reprinted in *Spirit of Time and Place: Collected Essays*. NY: Norton, 1973. xiii, 316 p. (pp. 122-35), which also includes J5188 (pp. 136-38).

2818. KOHLI, DEVINDRA: "Intelligence of Heart: Women in Yeats's Poetry," *Indian J of English Studies*, 8 (1967), 83-105.
> Maud Gonne, Lady Gregory, Iseult Gonne, Olivia Shakespear, and Dorothy Wellesley.

2819. MCHUGH, ROGER: "Ah Sweet Dancer--W. B. Yeats: Some Newly Discovered Letters and a New Poem," *Yeats Society of Japan Annual Report*, #6 (1971), 4-14.
> Margot Ruddock in "Sweet Dancer," "A Crazed Girl," "Beautiful Lofty Things," "The Man and the Echo," and "Margot."

2820. MACLEISH, ARCHIBALD: "Why Not?" *Amherst Literary Mag*, 10:2 (Summer 1964), 6-7.
> A note on Crazy Jane and on "Craze Jane on the King."

2821. MISE, RAYMOND: "Yeats' Crazy Jane Poems," *Paunch*, #25 (Feb 1966), 18-30.

2822. PACEY, DESMOND: "Children in the Poetry of Yeats," *Dalhousie R*, 50:2 (Summer 1970), 233-48.

2823. SLAVITT, DAVID: "The Significance of W. B. Yeats as a Modern Poet,"
Yale Literary Mag, 123:6 (May 1955), 19-24.
On the Crazy Jane poems.

2824. STANGE, G. ROBERT: "The Case of Hugh Lane's Paintings," *Texas Q*,
2:2 (Summer 1959), 180-87.
Hugh Lane in Yeats's poems.

2825. VANDERHAAR, MARGARET MARY: "Yeats's Relationships with Women and
Their Influence on His Poetry," Ph.D. thesis, Tulane U, 1966. ii, 154 p.
(*DA*, 27:5 [Nov 1966], 1387A.)
Mainly Maud Gonne, Lady Gregory, and Mrs. Yeats. The biographical
parts are derived from the standard publications and do not constitute
original research.

2826. WATSON-WILLIAMS, HELEN: "All the Olympians: W. B. Yeats and His
Friends," *English*, 14:83 (Summer 1963), 178-84.
Yeats's friends in his poetry.

2827. WITT, MARION: "William Butler Yeats," *EIE*, 1946, 74-101.
Yeats's biography in his poetry, notably his relationships with Maud
Gonne and Lady Gregory and his "supernatural" preoccupations (partic-
ularly in "Ego Dominus Tuus").

Poet, Figure of the

2828. BOLAND, EAVAN: "Precepts of Art in Yeats's Poetry," *Dublin Mag*, 4:1
(Spring 1965), 8-13.
Reflections on the poet's art in "Adam's Curse," "Sailing to Byzan-
tium," and "The Circus Animals' Desertion."

2829. SKELTON, ROBIN: "W. B. Yeats: The Poet as Synopsis," *Mosaic*, 1:1
(Oct 1967), 7-21.
The unifying force of the figure of the Master-Poet Yeats in his poems.

2830. WRIGHT, GEORGE THADDEUS: *The Poet in the Poem: The Personae of Eliot,
Yeats, and Pound*. Berkeley: U of California Press, 1962 [1960]. xiv, 167 p.
(California Paperback. CAL71.)
Based on °"Modern Poetry and the *Persona*: The Device and Its Aesthetic
Context, as Exhibited in the Work of Eliot, Yeats, and Pound," Ph.D.
thesis, U of California (Berkeley), 1956/57. The persona is the embodied representative of the poet in his work. With Eliot, Yeats, and
Pound, "it is the poem, not the speaker, through which the poet speaks,
and which therefore serves as his persona" (p. 59). "Yeats: The Tradition of Myself," pp. 88-123, discusses the mask and self in the poetry.
Reviews:
1. Donna Gerstenberger, *WHR*, 15:3 (Summer 1961), 285-86.
2. A. R. Jones, *MLR*, 56:4 (Oct 1961), 601-2.
3. Peter Ure, *RES*, 13:50 (May 1962), 214-15.

Politics

2831. BOWRA, CECIL MAURICE: *In General and Particular*. Cleveland: World,
1964. 248 p.
"The Prophetic Element," 223-40; reprint of a pamphlet of the same
title, London: Oxford UP, 1959. 19 p. (English Association Presiden-
tial Address, 1959.) Contains some remarks on prophecies in Yeats's
poetry.

2832. ————: *Poetry & Politics, 1900-1960*. Cambridge: UP, 1966. viii, 157 p.
See pp. 56-61, particularly on "The Black Tower."

2833. HARTMAN, GEOFFREY H.: *Beyond Formalism: Literary Essays, 1958-1970*. New Haven: Yale UP, 1970. xvi, 396 p.
"The Poet's Politics," 247-57. Yeats is also mentioned *passim* (see index).

2834. HENDERSON, PHILIP: *The Poet and Society*. London: Secker & Warburg, 1939. vii, 248 p.
"Politics and W. B. Yeats," 132-53.

2835. HENN, T. R.: "W. B. Yeats and the Poetry of War," *Proceedings of the British Academy*, 51 (1965), 301-19.
The Easter Rising and the Irish civil war in Yeats's poetry.

2836. HILL, GEOFFREY: "'The Conscious Mind's Intelligible Structure': A Debate," *Agenda*, 9:4-10:1 (Autumn-Winter 1971/72), 14-23.
Yeats's politics and poetry do not correlate in a "grammar of assent." Discusses "Easter 1916" and "The Second Coming."

2837. HONE, J. M.: "The Political Poems of Mr. Yeats," *Outlook* [London], 49:1253 (4 Feb 1922), 89-90.

2838. HOSKINS, KATHARINE BAIL: *Today the Struggle: Literature and Politics in England during the Spanish Civil War*. Austin: U of Texas Press, 1969. xvii, 294 p.
See pp. 28-31.

2839. LELYVELD, JOSEPH SALEM: "Yeats as a Public Poet," Honors thesis, Harvard U, 1958. i, 82 p.

2840. LOFTUS, RICHARD J.: "Yeats and the Easter Rising: A Study in Ritual," *Arizona Q*, 16:2 (Summer 1960), 168-77.

2841. MCHUGH, ROGER: "Yeats and Irish Politics," *University R* [Dublin], 2:13 [1961?], 24-36.
Reprinted in *Texas Q*, 5:3 (Autumn 1962), 90-100.

2842. MACMANUS, FRANCIS (ed): *The Years of the Great Test*. Cork: Mercier Press, 1967. 183 p.
Francis MacManus: "The Literature of the Period," 115-26. Anglo-Irish literature from 1925 to 1939; on Yeats, "this most political of genuine poets," pp. 123-26.

2843. MANSERGH, NICHOLAS: *The Irish Question, 1840-1921: A Commentary on Anglo-Irish Relations and on Social and Political Forces in Ireland in the Age of Reform and Revolution*. Toronto: U of Toronto Press, 1965. 316 p.
First published as °*Ireland in the Age of Reform and Revolution* [. . .]. London: Allen & Unwin, 1940. 272 p. On Irish politics in Yeats's poetry and his political convictions, pp. 245-66.

2844. MARTIN, GRAHAM: "Fine Manners, Liberal Speech: A Note on the Public Poetry of W. B. Yeats," *Essays in Criticism*, 11:1 (Jan 1961), 40-59.

2845. MILLS, JOHN GASCOIGNE: "On the Poetry and Politics of W. B. Yeats," *Ochanomizu Joshi Daigaku Jimbun Kagaku Kiyō*, 14 (1961), 1-6.

2846. MILNER, IAN: "Yeats and the Poetry of Violence," *Acta Universitatis Carolinae, Philologica*, #3 / *Prague Studies in English*, #13 (1969), 97-107.
Yeats's poems of anarchy and violence ("The Second Coming," "Nineteen Hundred and Nineteen") are effective because they use the mask of

traditional form. Formlessness would have made them unsuccessful.

2847. °OSBORNE, MARY J.: "Political and Social Themes Reflected in the Poetry of William Butler Yeats," M.A. thesis, Columbia U, 1952. 131 p.

2848. R[IDING], L[AURA], R[OBERT] G[RAVES], and H[ARRY] K[EMP]: "Politics and Poetry," *Epilogue*, #3 (Spring 1937), 6-51.
  Contains some critical asides on Yeats, "who believes in poems but not in poetry" (p. 46).

2849. THOMPSON, FRANCIS J.: "Poetry and Politics: W. B. Yeats," *Hopkins R*, 3:1 (Fall 1949), 3-17.
  Yeats did not stop being a political poet after he had outgrown his Celtic Twilight phase. Frequent reference to the influence of John O'Leary.

2850. TUOHY, FRANK: "Yeats and Politics," *Yeats Society of Japan Annual Report*, #7 (1972), 4-8.
  Negligible.

2851. WILLIAMS, DESMOND (ed): *The Irish Struggle, 1916-1926*. London: Routledge & Kegan Paul, 1966. vii, 193 p.
  Francis MacManus: "Imaginative Literature and the Revolution," 19-30.

Prosody

2852. FUSSELL, PAUL: *Poetic Meter and Poetic Form*. NY: Random House, 1965. xiii, 208 p. (Studies in Language and Literature. SLL3.)
  Passim (see index).

2853. °GOSE, ELLIOTT BICKLEY: "Technical Aspects of the Poetry of W. B. Yeats," M.A. thesis, U of Colorado, 1950. v, 97 p.

2854. O'CONNELL, ADELYN: "A Study of Rhythmic Structure in the Verse of William Butler Yeats," Ph.D. thesis, Catholic U of America, 1966. v, 163 p. (*DA*, 27:9 [Mar 1967], 3057A.)
  N.B.: This has now been published as a book with the same title but under the name Adelyn Dougherty. The Hague: Mouton, 1973. 136 p. (De Proprietatibus Litterarum. Series Practica. 38.)

2855. SCHRAMM, RICHARD: "The Line Unit: Studies in the Later Poetry of W. B. Yeats," *Ohio UR*, 3 (1961), 32-41.
  On "A Deep Sworn Vow," "After Long Silence," and "The Mother of God."

Psychoanalysis

2856. SEIDEN, MORTON IRVING: "A Psychoanalytic Essay on William Butler Yeats," *Accent*, 6:3 (Spring 1946), 178-90.
  A rather curious piece of literary criticism. Interprets *The Wanderings of Oisin* and "The Cap and Bells" as illustrations of the Oedipus complex, "made manifest in the artist's sense of psychic impotence."

Pun

2857. ALLEN, JAMES L.: "Yeats's Use of the Serious Pun," *Southern Q*, 1:2 (Jan 1963), 153-66.
  Also on the influence of Donne.

Rationality, Reason

2858. °GOTTSCHALK, HANS WALTER: "The Conflict of Sense and Spirit in the Life and Poetry of W. B. Yeats," M.A. thesis, New York U, 1943. i, 149 p.

2859. MANDL, OTTO WILLIAM: "Rational Elements in the Poetry of William Butler Yeats," Dr. phil. thesis, U of Wien, 1954. ii, 149 p.
    Yeats's poetry is intellectual rather than emotional.

Realism, Reality

2860. KIM U-CHANG: "The Embittered Sun: Reality in Yeats's Poetry," *Phoenix*, #10 (Summer 1965), 66-83.

Religion

2861. BABU, M. SATHYA: "Christian Themes and Symbols in the Later Poetry of W. B. Yeats," Ph.D. thesis, U of Wisconsin, 1968. vi, 259 p. (*DA*, 29:9 [Mar 1969], 3123A.)
    Includes chapters on "Statements on Religion in Yeats's Prose" and "Two Christian Plays" (*Calvary* and *The Resurrection*).

2862. BENZIGER, JAMES: *Images of Eternity: Studies in the Poetry of Religious Vision from Wordsworth to T. S. Eliot*. Carbondale: Southern Illinois UP, 1962. ix, 324 p.
    "Modern Instances: Yeats / Stevens / Eliot," 226-49.

2863. BODKIN, MAUD: *Studies of Type-Images in Poetry, Religion, and Philosophy*. London: Oxford UP, 1951. xii, 184 p.
    On Yeats, *passim* (see index), especially on "The Second Coming" (with reference to Nietzsche), "A Prayer for My Son," and "Sailing to Byzantium."

2864. BOKLUND, GUNNAR: "Time Must Have a Stop: Apocalyptic Thought and Expression in the Twentieth Century," *Denver Q*, 2:2 (Summer 1967), 69-98.
    See pp. 94-96 ("As an apocalyptic writer James Thurber is much preferable to William Butler Yeats").

2865. BOSE, ABINASH CHANDRA: *Three Mystic Poets: A Study of W. B. Yeats, A. E. and Rabindranath Tagore*. With an introduction by J. H. Cousins. Kolhapur: School & College Bookstall, 1945. xx, 156 p.
    Based on "Mysticism in Poetry: With an Illustrative Study of A. E., W. B. Yeats, and Rabindranath Tagore," Ph.D. thesis, Trinity College, Dublin, 1937. x, 406 p. "William Butler Yeats," 1-46. "Yeats belongs less to the class of mystics who also happen to be poets than to the class of poets who, owing to the special bent of their genius, come to be regarded as mystics. His mysticism is not . . . of the directly transcendental or religious type. . . . Yeats's poetic inspiration . . . is more purely aesthetic and humanistic" (p. 1).

2866. BUSH, DOUGLAS: *Pagan Myth and Christian Tradition in English Poetry*. Jayne Lectures for 1967. Philadelphia: American Philosophical Society, 1968. xvii, 112 p. (Memoirs of the American Philosophical Society. 72.)
    On Yeats, pp. 66-79 and *passim* (see index), especially on "Two Songs from a Play" and "Leda and the Swan."

2867. DEUTSCH, BABETTE: "Religious Elements in Poetry," *Menorah J*, 29:1 (Jan-Mar 1941), 21-48.
    See pp. 24-30.

2868. FAIRCHILD, HOXIE NEALE: *Religious Elements in English Poetry*. NY: Columbia UP, 1939-68. 6 v.
    On Yeats, 5:181-91, 539-50, and *passim* (see index); vol. 6, *passim* (see index).

2869. HAYES, R.: "W. B. Yeats, a Catholic Poet?" *Irish Monthly*, 56:658 (Apr 1928), 179-86.

2870. [JONES, LLEWELLYN]: "Poetry and Devotion--V: William Butler Yeats," *Christian Register Unitarian*, 118:7 (16 Feb 1939), 105-7.

2871. [MONAHAN, MICHAEL]: "A Poet of the Mystic," *Papyrus*, 1:6 (Dec 1903), 13.

2872. NOON, WILLIAM THOMAS: *Poetry and Prayer*. New Brunswick: Rutgers UP, 1967. xiv, 354 p.
"William Butler Yeats," 129-56, and *passim* (see index). Although Yeats separated poetry and religion sharply and opted for the former, he was always trying, unintentionally, to blur the distinction.

2873. O'BRIEN, JAMES HOWARD: "Theosophy and the Poetry of George Russell (AE), William Butler Yeats, and James Stephens," Ph.D. thesis, U of Washington, 1956. v, 367 p. (*DA*, 16:11 [1956], 2167-68.)
On Yeats see pp. 139-276 and *passim*.

2874. PHARE, ELSIE ELIZABETH: "Extract from an Essay on the Devotional Poetry of T. S. Eliot," *Experiment*, #6 (Oct 1930), 27-32.
Misnomer; mostly concerned with Christianity and Byzantinism in some of Yeats's poems and the influence of T. E. Hulme.

2875. SCOTT, NATHAN ALEXANDER: *The Broken Center: Studies in the Theological Horizon of Modern Literature*. New Haven: Yale UP, 1968 [1966]. xviii, 237 p.
See pp. 41-42.

2876. SPANOS, WILLIAM V.: "Sacramental Imagery in the Middle and Late Poetry of W. B. Yeats," *TSLL*, 4:2 (Summer 1962), 214-27.

2877. SPIVEY, TED R.: "The Apocalyptic Symbolism of W. B. Yeats and T. S. Eliot," *Costerus*, #4 (1972), 193-214.

2878. WATKINS, VERNON: "W. B. Yeats, poète religieux," *Critique*, 9:78 (Nov 1953), 913-30.
Also published as "W. B. Yeats--The Religious Poet," *TSLL*, 3:4 (Winter 1962), 473-88.

2879. WILDER, AMOS NIVEN: *The Spiritual Aspects of the New Poetry*. NY: Harper, 1940. xxiv, 262 p.
"W. B. Yeats and the Christian Option," 196-204, and *passim* (see index). Yeats's paganism and rejection of Christianity, as shown in his poetry, account for his "'numbness' to the intricacies of personal feeling."

2880. ————: *Modern Poetry and the Christian Tradition: A Study in the Relation of Christianity to Culture*. NY: Scribner's, 1952. xix, 287 p.
Passim (see index).

Revisions and Rewriting

2881. ALLT, G. D. P.: "Yeats and the Revision of His Early Verse," *Hermathena*, #64 (Nov 1944), 90-101; #65 (May 1945), 40-57.

2882. BARTLETT, PHYLLIS: *Poems in Process*. NY: Oxford UP, 1951. ix, 267 p.
Passim (see index).

2883. FRIEDMAN, ALAN HOWARD: "W. B. Yeats and the Passion for Completion," Honors thesis, Harvard U, 1948. i, 56 p.

2884. SULLIVAN, JOHN JOSEPH: "The Great Design: Yeats's Rearrangement of His Poems," Ph.D. thesis, U of Virginia, 1966. iv, 215 p. (*DA*, 27:12 [June 1967], 4266A-67A.)

2885. WITT, MARION: "A Competition for Eternity: Yeats's Revision of His Later Poems," *PMLA*, 64:1 (Mar 1949), 40-58.

Rhetoric

2885a. TARVIN, WILLIAM LESTER: "Yeats's Rhetorical Art: Dimensions of Rhetoric in the Non-Dramatic Poetry of William Butler Yeats," °Ph.D. thesis, U of Alabama, 1972. 199 p. (*DA*, 33:10 [Apr 1973], 5752A.)

Romanticism

2886. °BARKLEY, ROY REED: "Romantic Elements in the Poetry of Yeats," M.A. thesis, U of Texas, 1965. 254 p.

2887. HOLTON, ROSEMARY THERESE: "A Study of Romanticism in the Lyric Poetry of William Butler Yeats," Ph.D. thesis, U of Ottawa, 1951. ix, 251 p.
"Yeats was a Romantic in his poetry as in his life from first to last. The type of Romanticism changed from the languorous to the despairing to the passionate, but it was Romanticism throughout" (p. vi).

2888. SARAJAS, ANNAMARI: *Viimeiset romantikot: Kirjallisuuden aatteiden vaihtelua 1880-luvun jälkeen* [The last romantics: Thoughts on the literary revolution after 1880]. Porvoo-Helsinki: Söderström, 1962. 271 p.
"Yeatsin runouden kansallinen romantiikka" [Yeats: Folk romanticism in his poetry], 38-67.

2889. SUŠKO, MARIO: "O problemu romantičkog i simboličkog u poeziji W. B. Yeatsa," *Izraz*, yr 10 / 20:8-9 (Aug-Sept 1966), 234-57.

2890. WHALLEY, GEORGE: "Literary Romanticism," *QQ*, 72:2 (Summer 1965), 232-52.
Contains notes on "Coole Park and Ballylee, 1931," "Lapis Lazuli," and "The Second Coming."

Rose

2891. °ABRAMS, JEAN H.: "The Rose Symbol in the Poetry of Yeats," M.A. thesis, Columbia U, 1953. 89 p.

2892. °GRICE, DERMOT BERTRAND: "The Multifoliate Rose: A Study of the Rose Symbol in the Early Poetry of W. B. Yeats," M.A. thesis, U of Toronto, 1967. 109 p.

2893. RAY, ANN ALLEN: "A Study of Five Archetypal Symbols in the Poetry of W. B. Yeats," M.A. thesis, U of Texas, 1962. 116 p.
The symbols of rose, dance, tower, mask, and gyre.

Self

2894. BAGG, ROBERT ELY: "The Sword Upstairs: Essays on the Theory and Historical Development of Autobiographical Poetry," Ph.D. thesis, U of Connecticut, 1965. ix, 223 p. (*DA*, 26:9 [Mar 1966], 5408.)
"The Self vs. Impersonality in Yeats, Eliot and Lowell," 186-217.

2895. ———: "The Rise of Lady Lazarus," *Mosaic*, 2:4 (Summer 1969), 9-36.
Discusses "the context in which some exceptional modern poets discovered the self's various uses and its vulnerability." The poets

are Yeats, Eliot, and Lowell, who are seen as predecessors of Sylvia Plath.

2896. BERGER, HARRY: "Biography as Interpretation, Interpretation as Biography," *CE*, 28:2 (Nov 1966), 113-25.
   The "fictional or dramatic image of career and self" in Yeats's poetry.

2897. LEMIEUX, SISTER M. ST. AUGUSTINE: "Modes of the 'I': Yeats's Selves in *The Winding Stair and Other Poems*," Ph.D. thesis, U of Notre Dame, 1966. vii, 278 p. (*DA*, 27:4 [Oct 1966], 1059A-60A.)

2897a. SASAKURA, SADAO: "W. B. Yeats, an Eternal Wanderer," *Ibaraki Daigaku Kyōyōbu Kiyō. Bulletin*, #4 (1972), 109-34.
   In Japanese; English synopsis on pp. 109-11. Discusses the theme of self and anti-self in Yeats's poetry.

Sexuality

2898. HENN, T. R.: "The Accent of Yeats' *Last Poems*," *Essays and Studies*, 9 (1956), 56-72.
   The theme of sexuality is less prevalent than Vivienne Koch (J2427) thinks.

Stone

2899. BYRD, THOMAS L., and CAROLYN GLENN KARHU: "The Stone as a Symbol in the Lyric Poetry of W. B. Yeats," *XUS*, 8:3 (Nov 1969), 28-35.

2900. KIRKUP, JAMES: "The Stones of Yeats," *Yeats Society of Japan Annual Report*, #4 (1970), 5-19.
   Reprinted in #5 (1970), 27-41. Includes a "stony poem" of his own, "The Sacrifice at the Grave of Yeats."

Style

2901. BAKER, WILLIAM EDWIN: *Syntax in English Poetry, 1870-1930*. Berkeley: U of California Press, 1967. xii, 197 p. (Perspectives in Criticism. 18.)
   Passim (see index), especially pp. 84-94, where Hopkins's and Yeats's syntactical peculiarities are compared. It appears that Hopkins was far less orthodox than Yeats.

2902. BARTON, RUTH PENDERGRASS: "'The Natural Words in the Natural Order': A Study of W. B. Yeats' Verse Syntax," Ph.D. thesis, U of Wisconsin, 1969. v, 298 p. (*DA*, 30:12 [June 1970], 5438A.)

2903. COX, KENNETH: "The Poetry of Yeats and Its Place or Places between Vision and Action," *Agenda*, 9:4-10:1 (Autumn-Winter 1971/72), 46-55.
   Mainly on the vocabulary, syntax, and rhythm of Yeats's poetry.

2904. DAVID, PAUL: "Structure in Some Modern Poets," *New English Weekly*, 27:15 (26 July 1945), 131-32.
   Yeats had difficulties in writing poems "with a beginning, a middle and an ending."

2905. DAVIE, DONALD: *Purity of Diction in English Verse*. London: Routledge & Kegan Paul, 1969 [1952]. viii, 217 p.
   A few scattered notes on Yeats (see index).

2906. FRANKLIN, LAURA MABEL: "The Development of Yeats's Poetic Diction," Ph.D. thesis, Northwestern U, 1956. vii, 212 p. (*DA*, 16:12 [1956], 2456-57.)
   Includes statistical tables and a comparison with Eliot's diction.

2907. HALL, DONALD ANDREW: "Yeats' Stylistic Development as Seen through a Consideration of His Published Revisions of *The Rose*," Honors thesis, Harvard U, 1951. i, 50 p.

2908. °KÖNIG, DAGMAR: "Some Notes on the Syntax of W. B. Yeats' Poetry," M.A. thesis, University College, Dublin, 1963.

2908a. MACSWEEN, R. J.: "Yeats and His Language," *Antigonish R*, #14 (Summer 1973), 17-24.
The style of Yeats's poetry and Pound's influence on it.

2909. MILES, JOSEPHINE: *Major Adjectives in English Poetry from Wyatt to Auden*. Berkeley: U of California Press, 1946. v, pp. 305-426. (U of California Publications in English. 12:3.)
"Modern Quality," 389-407, contains a few notes on Yeats.

2910. ――――: *The Continuity of Poetic Language: Studies in English Poetry from the 1540's to the 1940's*. Berkeley: U of California Press, 1948-51. xiii, 542 p. in 3 parts. (U of California Publications in English. 19.)
Statistical investigation of the vocabulary; on Yeats, part 3.

2911. ――――: *Eras & Modes in English Poetry*. Berkeley: U of California Press, 1957. xi, 233 p.
"The Classical Mode of Yeats," 178-202; a study of Yeats's poetic vocabulary.

2912. SCHOCH, OLGA: "Macpherson, Fiona Macleod, Yeats (Ein Stilvergleich)," [Dr. phil. thesis, U of Wien, 1931]. v, 153 p.
A rather impressionistic study of "poetic style."

2913. SMITH, BARBARA HERRNSTEIN: *Poetic Closure: A Study of How Poems End*. Chicago: U of Chicago Press, 1968. xvi, 289 p.
Some notes on Yeats's poetry (see index).

2914. VEEDER, WILLIAM RICHARD: *W. B. Yeats: The Rhetoric of Repetition*. Berkeley: U of California Press, 1968. vii, 56 p. (U of California Publications. English Studies. 34.)
A study of the various forms of verbal repetition in Yeats's poetry.

Symbol and Symbolism

2915. BEATTY, RICHMOND C.: "The Heritage of Symbolism in Modern Poetry," *Yale R*, 36:3 (Mar 1947), 467-77.
Note on Yeats, pp. 473-75.

2916. BURNSHAW, STANLEY: "Three Revolutions in Modern Poetry," *Sewanee R*, 70:3 (Summer 1962), 418-50.
Note on Yeats, pp. 443-44.

2917. DURRELL, LAWRENCE: *A Key to Modern British Poetry*. Norman: U of Oklahoma Press, 1964 [1952]. xii, 209 p.
On symbolism and theosophy in Yeats's early poetry, pp. 104-10.

2918. GREEN, J. T.: "Symbolism in Yeats's Poetry," *Fort Hare Papers*, 4:3 (June 1969), 13-23.
"Through symbolism he discovered a medium to create an extremely lively and concrete poetry about himself." Also on Yeats's theory of symbolism.

2919. JAKOBITZ, ELLY: *Der Ausdruck des poetischen Empfindens in der modernen englischen Poesie*. Greifswald: Adler, 1935. 111 p.
A Dr. phil. thesis, U of Greifswald, 1935. On symbols in Yeats's poetry, pp. 88-96. Negligible.

2919a. LATIMER, DAN RAYMOND: "Problems in the Symbol: A Theory and the Application in the Poetry of Valéry, Rilke, and Yeats," °Ph.D. thesis, U of Michigan, 1972. 615 p. (*DA*, 33:11 [May 1973], 6316A.)

2920. RAWLINGS, ANN: "A Study of the Function of Symbolism in the Poetry of William Butler Yeats," M.A. thesis, U of Montreal, 1964. iv, 101 p.
The symbols of bird, egg, and sphere, including a comparison between Yeats and C. G. Jung.

2921. STOCK, A. G.: "Symbolism and Belief in the Poetry of W. B. Yeats," *Visva-Bharati Q*, 27:3-4 (1961-62), 181-96.

2922. SUŠKO, MARIO: "V. B. Jejts: Poezija simbola," *Život*, 16:1-2 (Jan-Feb 1967), 43-52.

2923. *Talks to Teachers of English*. Newcastle-upon-Tyne: Department of Education, King's College, 1959. 68 p.
Peter Butter: "The Symbolist Movement in Poetry and Drama," 27-52; on symbolism in Yeats's poetry, particularly in "A Dialogue of Self and Soul," pp. 40-45.

Textual Problems

2924. ALSPACH, RUSSELL K.: "Some Textual Problems in Yeats," *Studies in Bibliography*, 9 (1957), 51-67.

2925. SAUL, GEORGE BRANDON: "Yeats and His Poems," *TLS*, 49:2513 (31 Mar 1950), 208.
On the problem of dating Yeats's poems. Correspondence by Allan Wade, :2514 (7 Apr 1950), 215.

Time

2926. CASSIDY, JOHN: "The Concern in Modern Poetry with Unconventional Concepts of Time: With Special Reference to the Work of W. B. Yeats, Edwin Muir and T. S. Eliot," M.A. thesis, U of Manchester, 1953. iii, 194 p.
"W. B. Yeats," 20-77.

2927. DAICHES, DAVID: *Time and the Poet*. Cardiff: U of Wales Press, 1965. 30 p. (W. D. Thomas Memorial Lecture. 23 Feb 1965.)
Some notes on Yeats, pp. 28-30 and *passim*.

2928. GOMES, EUGENIO: *A neve e o girassol*. São Paulo: Conselho estadual de cultura: Comissão de literatura, 1967. 127 p. (Coleção ensaio. 46.)
"Yeats e a velhice" [Yeats and old age], 89-92.

2928a. METZ, GERALD MARVIN: "The Timeless Moment in the Poetry of W. B. Yeats," °Ph.D. thesis, U of Minnesota, 1972. 161 p. (*DA*, 33:10 [Apr 1973], 5736A.)

2929. °MURPHY, MURIEL J.: "Old Age and the Old Man Image in Selected Poems of W. B. Yeats," M.A. thesis, Columbia U, 1955. 96 p.

2930. RAINES, CHARLES A.: "Yeats' Metaphors of Permanence," *TCL*, 5:1 (Apr 1959), 12-20.

2931. WHALLEY, GEORGE: "Yeats' Quarrel with Old Age," *QQ*, 58:4 (Winter 1951/52), 497-507.

Tower

2932. KHANNA, URMILLA: "The Tower Symbol in the Poetry of Yeats," *English Miscellany* [Delhi], #3 (1965), 9-18.

2933. LAKIN, R. D.: "Unity and Strife in Yeats' Tower Symbol," *Midwest Q*, 1:4 (July 1960), 321-32.
>The symbol betrays dissonance, thus the poet's impotence, and points to the lack of final answers in Yeats's poetry.

2933a. WESTBROOK, EDWARD BRUCE: "The Tower Symbol in the Poetry of William Butler Yeats," °Ph.D. thesis, U of North Carolina at Chapel Hill, 1973. 184 p. (*DA*, 34:5 [Nov 1973], 2664A.)

Tragedy and the Tragic

2934. ALTIERI, CHARLES: "From a Comic to a Tragic Sense of Language in Yeats's Mature Poetry," *MLQ*, 33:2 (June 1972), 156-71.
>Particularly on "A Prayer for My Daughter" and "Coole Park and Ballylee, 1931."

2935. STANGE, GEORGE ROBERT: "W. B. Yeats and the Modern Spirit of Tragedy," Honors thesis, Harvard U, 1941. i, 53 p.
>On Yeats's "tragic poetry."

Tree

2936. MATSUMURA, KEN'ICHI: "A Tree Image of W. B. Yeats," *Yeats Society of Japan Annual Report*, #6 (1971), 21-25.
>Especially in "The Two Trees."

Unity of Being

2937. HUBANK, ROGER W. J.: "Unity of Being in the Poetry of W. B. Yeats," Ph.D. thesis, U of Nottingham, 1964. iii, 749, iv p.

Water

2938. LANDER, JEANNETTE [i.e., Seyppel, Jeannette]: *William Butler Yeats: Die Bildersprache seiner Lyrik*. Stuttgart: Kohlhammer, 1967. 168 p. (Sprache und Literatur. 41.)
>Based on the more adequately titled °"Wasserbilder in der Lyrik von W. B. Yeats," Dr. phil. thesis, Freie Universität Berlin, 1966.
>*Reviews:*
>1. Rosemarie Gläser, *ZAA*, 19:2 (1971), 195-97.
>2. Egon Werlich, *Praxis des neusprachlichen Unterrichts*, 15:2 (1968), 196-97.

2939. WILLIAMS, GWYN: "The Drowned Man in English Poetry," *Litera*, 8 (1965), 62-90.
>Note on Yeats, pp. 81-82.

DD Single Poems

The items listed in this section are not the only studies of Yeats's poems. I have not been able to analyze and cross-reference all the items listed in sections CA, CB, DA, DB, and DC, to which the reader is therefore referred for further material. It might also be advisable to check the subject index (NE) for entries such as Crazy Jane, Cuchulain, rose, tower, and so on, and the index of Yeats's works (ND) for poetry collections. Section DD serves as a complete index for studies of Yeats's poems listed in this bibliography with the restrictions explained above and with the exception of section AB. The titles of the poems are those used in the *Variorum Edition of the Poems*. Discussions of *The Shadowy Waters*,

The Island of Statues, *Mosada*, *The Seeker*, and *Time and the Witch Vivien* are listed in section EE.

"An Acre of Grass"

2940. NIMMO, D. C.: "Yeats' 'An Acre of Grass,'" *Explicator*, 29:6 (Feb 1971), #50.
   Yeats's use of Blake.

2941. PERRINE, LAURENCE: "Yeats' 'An Acre of Grass,'" *Explicator*, 22:8 (Apr 1964), #64.

2942. SPANOS, WILLIAM V.: "The Sexual Imagination in Yeats's Late Poetry: A Reading of 'An Acre of Grass,'" *CEA Critic*, 32:1 (Oct 1969), 16-18.

2943. TAUBE, MYRON: "Yeats' 'An Acre of Grass,' 10," *Explicator*, 26:5 (Jan 1968), #40.
   "The mill of the mind" refers to J. S. Mill.

See also J2427, 2439, 3080a.

"Adam's Curse"

2944. CIARDI, JOHN: *Dialogue with an Audience*. Philadelphia: Lippincott, 1963. 316 p.
   "The Morality of Poetry: Epilogue to an Avalanche," 105-15; reprinted from *SatR*, 40:13 (30 Mar 1957), 11-14, 34. The poem is an example of the poet's contempt of "counterfeit sentimentality."

2945. THEUMER, ERICH: "W. B. Yeats: 'Adam's Curse,'" *Neueren Sprachen*, 16:7 (July 1967), 305-11.

See also J2828.

"After Long Silence"

2946. MILLETT, FRED BENJAMIN: *The Rebirth of Liberal Education*. NY: Harcourt, Brace, 1945. xi, 179 p.
   Quotes two interpretations "from students of very high academic standing," one "false" and one "true," pp. 166-68.

2947. PARISH, JOHN E.: "The Tone of Yeats' 'After Long Silence,'" *WHR*, 16:4 (Summer 1962), 377-79.
   Criticizes the Brooks-Warren interpretation (J3016).

2947a. SUTHERLAND, RONALD: "Structural Linguistics and English Prosody," *CE*, 20:1 (Oct 1958), 12-17.
   Prosodic interpretation of the poem.

See also J2439 (main entry and review #5), 2855, 3016, 5711.

"Among School Children"

2948. BROOKS, CLEANTH: *The Well Wrought Urn: Studies in the Structure of Poetry*. NY: Harcourt, Brace, 1959 [1947]. xiv, 300 p. (Harvest Book.HB11.)
   "Yeats's Great Rooted Blossomer," 178-91; also on "Sailing to Byzantium."

2949. CHASE, RICHARD: "Myth as Literature," *EIE*, 1947, 3-22.
   Note on this poem and on "Leda and the Swan," 18-20.

2950. ———: *Quest for Myth*. Baton Rouge: Louisiana State UP, 1949. xi, 150 p.
   See pp. 120-21.

2950a. DAWSON, LEVEN MAGRUDER: "'Among School Children': 'Labour' and 'Play,'" *PQ*, 52:2 (Apr 1973), 286-95.
Relates the poem to 19th-century English socialism.

2950b. HANSON, CHRIS: "Yeats: 'Among School Children,'" *Critical Survey*, 6:1&2 (Summer 1973), 90-94.

2951. HOLBROOK, DAVID: *Dylan Thomas: The Code of Night*. London: Athlone Press, 1972. viii, 271 p.
See pp. 15-18.

2952. LINEBARGER, JAMES M.: "Yeats's 'Among School Children' and Shelley's 'Defence of Poetry,'" *N&Q*, os 208 / ns 10:10 (Oct 1963), 375-77.

2953. LUCAS, JOHN: "Yeats and Goethe," *TLS*, 67:3482 (21 Nov 1968), 1321.
Connects the last four lines of the poem with Goethe's *Wilhelm Meister* and *Werther*.

2954. ROSENBAUM, S. P.: "Yeats' 'Among School Children,' V," *Explicator*, 23:2 (Oct 1964), #14.
The Porphyry reference. See also Charles C. Walcutt, 26:9 (May 1968), #72.

2955. SCHIFFER, REINHOLD, and HERMANN J. WEIAND (eds): *Insight III: Analyses of English and American Poetry*. Frankfurt/Main: Hirschgraben, 1969. 366 p.
Reinhold Schiffer: "'Among School Children,'" 350-61; Peter H. Butter: "'The Wild Swans at Coole,'" 362-66.

2956. TERWILLIGER, PATRICIA J.: "A Re-Interpretation of Stanzas VII and VIII of W. B. Yeats's 'Among School Children,'" *Boston U Studies in English*, 5:1 (Spring 1961), 29-34.

2957. THOMPSON, WILLIAM IRWIN: "Collapsed Universe and Structured Poem: An Essay in Whiteheadian Criticism," *CE*, 28:1 (Oct 1966), 25-39.
The five-part structure of location, implication, association, crisis, and resolution in Coleridge ("Dejection: An Ode"), Wordsworth ("Tintern Abbey"), Shelley ("Ode to the West Wind"), Arnold ("Dover Beach"), and Yeats's poem.

2958. UTLEY, FRANCIS LEE: "Stylistic Ambivalence in Chaucer, Yeats and Lucretius—The Cresting Wave and Its Undertow," *UKCR*, 37:3 (Mar 1971), 174-98.
On Yeats's poem, pp. 192-98.

2959. VERHOEFF, ABRAHAM: *The Practice of Criticism: A Comparative Analysis of W. B. Yeats' "Among School Children."* Utrecht: Elinkwijk, [1966]. vii, 149 p.
A Dr. in de letteren thesis, U of Utrecht, 1966. A comparison of previous interpretations of the poem, which concludes that no ultimately satisfactory results have been achieved so far. Verhoeff's own interpretation attempts to show that the poem is a typical Yeats poem and in effect not a very good one. Its reputation is largely based on its inferior half.
Reviews:
1. Uta Janssens, *Neophilologus*, 52:3 (July 1968), 343-44.

2960. WAIN, JOHN (ed): *Interpretations: Essays on Twelve English Poems*. London: Routledge & Kegan Paul, 1955. xv, 237 p.
John Wain: "W. B. Yeats: 'Among School Children,'" 194-210.

2961. WALCUTT, CHARLES C.: "Yeats' 'Among School Children' and 'Sailing to Byzantium,'" *Explicator*, 8:6 (Apr 1950), #42.

See also J488, 1101, 1136a, 1356, 2147a, 2198, 2429, 2456, 2465, 2525, 2664, 2725, 3016, 3147, 3174, 3194a.

"The Apparitions"

See J740, 2635.

"At Algeciras—A Meditation upon Death"

See J1136a, 1157.

"At the Abbey Theatre"

See J2781, 5774.

"Baile and Aillinn"

2962. DUNSEATH, T. K.: "Yeats and the Genesis of Supernatural Song," *ELH*, 28:4 (Dec 1961), 399-416.
    Also on "Ribh at the Tomb of Baile and Aillinn" and "Supernatural Songs."

See also J2237, 5874.

"The Ballad of Earl Paul"

2963. H[AYES], R[ICHARD] [?]: "An Old Yeats Ballad," *Dublin Mag*, 2:2 (Apr-June 1927), 59-61.

"The Ballad of Father Gilligan"

See J3236.

"The Ballad of the Foxhunter"

See J5681.

"Beautiful Lofty Things"

See J2819.

"Before the World Was Made" (part 2 of "A Woman Young and Old")

See J3134.

"Beggar to Beggar Cried"

See J3503.

"The Black Tower"

2964. DISKIN, PATRICK: "A Source for Yeats's 'The Black Tower,'" *N&Q*, os 206 / ns 8:3 (Mar 1961), 107-8.
    Standish O'Grady's *Finn and His Companions*. See additional note by Diskin, os 210 / ns 12:7 (July 1965), 278-79.

2965. KEITH, W. J.: "Yeats's Arthurian Black Tower," *MLN*, 75:2 (Feb 1960), 119-23.

2966. MATTHEWS, SUSAN: "Defiance and Defeat in W. B. Yeats' 'The Black Tower,'" *Concerning Poetry*, 5:2 (Fall 1972), 22-26.

2967. SPIVAK, GAYATRI: "Allégorie et histoire de la poésie: Hypothèse de travail," *Poétique*, 2:8 (1971), 427-41.
Contains notes on the use of allegory in this poem.

See also J1156, 1162 (#7), 2438, 2439, 2832.

"Blood and the Moon"

2968. MEYERS, JEFFREY: "Yeats' 'Blood and the Moon,'" *Explicator*, 30:6 (Feb 1972), #50.
The Swift allusions.

See also J2263.

"A Bronze Head"

2969. DENHAM, ROBERT D.: "Yeats' ' A Bronze Head,'" *Explicator*, 29:2 (Oct 1970), #14.

2970. WILSON, F. A. C.: "Yeats's 'A Bronze Head': A Freudian Investigation," *Literature and Psychology*, 22:1 (1972), 5-12.
Also generally on the type of the masculine woman in Yeats's poetry (Maud Gonne and Dorothy Wellesley).

See also J2427, 2439, 2735.

"Brown Penny"

See J5607, 5688, 5694.

"Byzantium"

2970a. ALLEN, JAMES LOVIC: "Charts for the Voyage to Byzantium: An Annotated Bibliography of Scholarship and Criticism on Yeats's Byzantium Poems, 1935-1970," *BNYPL*, 77:1 (Autumn 1973), 28-50.
About 120 items.

2971. AUTY, R. A.: "'Byzantium,'" *TLS*, 49:2532 (11 Aug 1950), 501.
Is it "A starlit or a moonlit dome disdains" or "distains"?
See the following letters:
1. Gwendolen Murphy, :2534 (25 Aug 1950), 533: "distains."
2. Richard Murphy, :2535 (1 Sept 1950), 549: "disdains."
3. Maurice Craig, *ibid.*, points to difficulties in "The Municipal Gallery Revisited."
4. Peter Ure and Dennis Silk, :2536 (8 Sept 1950), 565, on other textual difficulties.
5. Gwendolen Murphy, :2537 (15 Sept 1950), 581: "distains."
6. John Crhistopherson, *ibid.*: "disdains."
7. Vernon Watkins and Bonamy Dobrée, :2538 (22 Sept 1950), 597: "disdains."
8. Gwendolen Murphy, :2544 (3 Nov 1950), 693, remains unconvinced.

2971a. BUNN, JAMES HARRY: "The Palace of Art: A Study of Form in Retrospective Poems about the Creative Process," °Ph.D. thesis, Emory U, 1969. 185 p. (*DA*, 30:10 [Apr 1970], 4400A.)
Includes interpretations of the two Byzantium poems.

2972. °BUTLER, JONE L.: "Yeats' Byzantium Poems: Some Versions of the Pastoral," M.A. thesis, Wichita State U, 1966.

2973. CERNUDA, LUIS: *Poesía y literatura*. Barcelona: Editorial Seix Barral, 1964. 2 v. (Biblioteca breve. 150. 205.)
"W. B. Yeats: 'Bizancio,'" 1:112-15; a translation plus some notes.
"Yeats," 2:163-83; reprinted from *Cultura universitaria*, #72-73 (July-Sept 1960), 45-55. A review of *Letters* (W211J/K).
"Jiménez y Yeats," 2:249-56; reprinted from *Palabra y el hombre*, 7:28 (Oct-Dec 1963), 591-94.

2974. ELVIN, LIONEL: *Introduction to the Study of Literature*. Volume 1: Poetry. London: Sylvan Press, 1949. 224 p.
No more published. See pp. 211-17.

2975. FRASER, G. S.: "Yeats's 'Byzantium,'" *CQ*, 2:3 (Autumn 1960), 253-61.
Correspondence by John Wain, :4 (Winter 1960), 372-73; by Joan Grundy, 3:2 (Summer 1961), 168-69.

2976. HAMARD, JEAN: "'Byzantium' de W. B. Yeats," *Langues modernes*, 60:1 (Jan-Feb 1966), 54-63.

2977. °HYMAN, VIRGINIA R.: "An Analysis of Yeats's 'Byzantium,'" M.A. thesis, Columbia U, 1961. 90 p.

2977a. ISER, WOLFGANG: "Manieristische Metaphorik in der englischen Dichtung," *GRM*, os 41 / ns 10:3 (1960), 266-87.
See especially pp. 278-84.

2978. JEFFARES, A. NORMAN: "The Byzantine Poems of W. B. Yeats," *RES*, 22: 85 (Jan 1946), 44-52.

2979. ————: "Yeats's Byzantine Poems and the Critics," *ESA*, 5:1 (Mar 1962), 11-28.

2980. ————: "Notes on Pattern in the Byzantine Poems of W. B. Yeats," *Revue des langues vivantes*, 31:4 (1965), 353-59.
Syntactical and rhetorical patterns.

2981. JERNIGAN, JAY: "The Phoenix as Thematic Symbol in Yeats's 'Byzantium,'" *Michigan Academician*, 1:3&4 (Spring 1969), 93-99.

2982. KNIGHT, GEORGE WILSON: *The Starlit Dome: Studies in the Poetry of Vision*. With an introduction by W. F. Jackson Knight and an appendix on "Spiritualism and Poetry." London: Methuen, 1959 [1941]. xiv, 330 p.
References to this poem on pp. 79, 93, 97, 175, 184, 202, 219, 225, 231, 233, 310-11; to "Sailing to Byzantium" on p. 310; in connection with a discussion of Wordsworth, Coleridge, Shelley, and Keats.

2983. ————: *Neglected Powers: Essays on Nineteenth and Twentieth Century Literature*. London: Routledge & Kegan Paul, 1971. 515 p.
"Poetry and the Arts: Tennyson, Browning, O'Shaughnessy, Yeats," 243-59; reprinted from *Essays and Studies*, 22 (1969), 88-104. See pp. 255-59 for a note on both Byzantium poems.

2984. KOSTELANETZ, ANNE: "Irony in Yeat's [*sic*] Byzantium Poems," *Tennessee Studies in Literature*, 9 (1964), 129-42.

2985. LEES, F. N.: "Yeats's 'Byzantium,' Dante, and Shelley," *N&Q*, os 202 / ns 4:7 (July 1957), 312-13.

2986. MCDOWELL, FREDERICK P. W. (ed): *The Poet as Critic*. Evanston: Northwestern UP, 1967. xiii, 114 p.
Murray Krieger: "*Ekphrasis* and the Still Movement of Poetry; or, *Laokoön* Revisited," 3-26; reprinted in Krieger: *The Play and Place of*

Criticism. Baltimore: Johns Hopkins Press, 1967. xiv, 256 p., pp. 105-28. Notes on both Byzantium poems, *passim*.

2987. MASSON, DAVID I.: "Word and Sound in Yeats' 'Byzantium,'" *ELH*, 20:2 (June 1953), 136-60.
See also Denis Davison, *Theoria*, #7 (1955), 111-14; correspondence by C. J. D. Harvey, #8 (1956), 66-67.

2988. ————: "The 'Musical Form' of Yeats's 'Byzantium,'" *N&Q*, 198:9 (Sept 1953), 400-401.

2988a. MITCHELL, JOAN TOWEY: "'Byzantium': Vision as Drama," *Concerning Poetry*, 6:2 (Fall 1973), 66-71.

2989. ROPPEN, GEORG, and RICHARD SOMMER: *Strangers and Pilgrims: An Essay on the Metaphor of Journey*. Bergen: Norwegian Universities Press, 1964. 388 p. (Norwegian Studies in English. 11.)
Roppen: "Yeats: To Byzantium," 337-52; an interpretation of both Byzantium poems.

2990. °SEN, S. C.: "'Byzantium,'" *Bulletin of the Department of English, U of Calcutta*, 1:3 (1960).

2991. WHITE, ALISON: "Yeats' 'Byzantium,' 20, and 'Sailing to Byzantium,' 30-32," *Explicator*, 13:2 (Nov 1954), #8.
The bird symbolism.

See also J1114, 1126, 1136a, 1153, 1156, 1241, 1548, 1634, 1676, 1813a, 1866, 2086, 2429, 2439, 2456, 2494, 2551, 2567, 2605, 2678, 2708, 2739, 2740a, 2753, 2755, 2756, 3150, 3169a, 3171, 3173, 3174, 3179, 3182-84, 3194, 3210, 3511a, 4006, 4115, 4116.

"The Cap and Bells"

2992. LONDRAVILLE, RICHARD: "The Manuscript of 'The Queen and the Jester,'" *Ariel*, 3:3 (July 1972), 67-68 and plates I-IV.
An early version of the poem.

2993. LOWDEN, SAMUEL MARION: *Understanding Great Poems*. Harrisburg: Handy Book Corporation, 1927. 340 p.
"'The Cap and Bells' by William Butler Yeats," 217-28.

2994. MILNE, FRED L.: "Yeats's 'The Cap and Bells': A Probable Indebtedness to Tennyson's 'Maud,'" *Ariel*, 3:3 (July 1972), 69-79.

2995. NATTERSTAD, J. H.: "Yeats' 'The Cap and Bells,'" *Explicator*, 25:9 (May 1967), #75.

See also J2429, 2856, 5859, 5887.

"The Cat and the Moon"

2996. BENSON, CARL: "Yeats's 'The Cat and the Moon,'" *MLN*, 68:4 (Apr 1953), 220-23.
A source in Madame Blavatsky.

2997. SMITH, GROVER: "Yeats, Minnaloushe, and the Moon," *Western R*, 11:4 (Summer 1947), 241-44.
The relationship with *A Vision* and a source of the poem in Demetrius. See Smith, "Yeats' 'The Cat and the Moon,'" *N&Q*, 195:2 (21 Jan 1950), 35, where the source is corrected to be Plutarch.

See also J3236, 3594 and note, 3595-98 and note.

"The Chambermaid's First (and Second) Song"

See J2427, 2440.

"Chosen" (part 6 of "A Woman Young and Old")

See J1156, 2439.

"The Circus Animals' Desertion"

2998. LAIDLAW, J. C. (ed): *The Future of the Modern Humanities*. The papers delivered at the Jubilee Congress of the Modern Humanities Research Association. Cambridge: MHRA, 1969. ix, 137 p. (Publications of the Modern Humanities Research Association. 1.)
  Conor Cruise O'Brien: "Imagination and Politics," 73-85; draws a parallel between the "rag and bone shop" and the thought of Karl Marx, pp. 73-75.

See also J1073, 2147a, 2414, 2429, 2456, 2828, 3150, 3202.

"The Cloak, the Boat, and the Shoes"

See J5615, 5700.

"A Coat"

2999. GLECKNER, ROBERT F.: "Blake and Yeats," *N&Q*, os 200 / ns 2:1 (Jan 1955), 38.
  A Blake echo in the poem.

See also J1084, 3080a, 5697.

"The Collar-Bone of a Hare"

3000. SAUL, GEORGE BRANDON: "Yeats's Hare," *TLS*, 46:2345 (11 Jan 1947), 23.
  The date of this poem and of "Two Songs of a Fool." Correspondence by Marion Witt, :2385 (18 Oct 1947), 535.

3001. WITT, MARION: "Yeats' 'The Collar-Bone of a Hare,'" *Explicator*, 7:3 (Dec 1948), #21.

See also J1157, 2429.

"Colonel Martin"

See J1004, 5722.

"Colonus' Praise"

See J1136a, 5605.

"Come Gather round Me, Parnellites"

3002. STERNFELD, FREDERICK W.: "Poetry and Music--Joyce's *Ulysses*," *EIE*, 1956, 16-54.
  Notes on the music of this poem and of "The Three Bushes," pp. 21-24, 28, 34.

See also J5722.

"Consolation"

See J2439.

"Coole Park and Ballylee, 1931"

3003. BROWER, REUBEN ARTHUR, and RICHARD POIRIER (eds): *In Defense of Reading: A Reader's Approach to Literary Criticism*. NY: Dutton, 1963 [1962]. x, 311 p. (Dutton Paperback. D113.)
Paul de Man: "Symbolic Landscape in Wordsworth and Yeats," 22-37; Yeats's poem compared with Wordsworth's "Composed by the Side of Grasmere Lake."

3004. CARNE-ROSS, D. S.: "A Commentary on Yeats' 'Coole [Park] and Bally-lee, 1931,'" *Nine*, 1:1 (Oct 1949), 21-24.
Comment by Ronald Bottrall, 2:1 (Jan 1950), 67.

3005. PERLOFF, MARJORIE: "'*Another* Emblem There': Theme and Convention in Yeats's 'Coole Park and Ballylee, 1931,'" *JEGP*, 69:2 (Apr 1970), 223-40.

3006. POLSKA AKADEMIA NAUK: INSTYTUT BADAŃ LITERACKICH: *Poetics. Poetyka. Poetika*. Warszawa: Państwowe wydawnictwo naukowe / 's Gravenhage: Mouton, 1961. xiii, 895 p. (First International Conference of Work-in-Progress Devoted to Problems of Poetics, Warsaw, August 18-27, 1960.)
Donald Davie: "The Relation between Syntax and Music in Some Modern Poems in English," 203-14.

See also J2456, 2890, 2934, 3202.

"Coole Park 1929"

See J2086, 2439.

"A Cradle Song"

See J5606, 5628, 5630, 5645, 5651, 5667, 5693, 5713, 5718, 7011.

"A Crazed Girl"

3007. FREYER, GRATTAN: "W. B. Yeats," *TLS*, 45:2307 (20 Apr 1946), 187.
Misprints in this poem and in "Three Marching Songs."

See also J2819.

"Crazy Jane and Jack the Journeyman"

3008. °PERRINE, LAURENCE: "Yeats's 'Crazy Jane and Jack the Journeyman,'" *CEA Critic*, 34:3 (Mar 1972), 22-23.

"Crazy Jane and (on) the King"

3009. YEATS, W. B.: "Crazy Jane on the King," *Amherst Literary Mag*, 10:2 (Summer 1964), 4-5.
With an introduction by Rolfe Humphries stating that he got the MS. of the poem in 1946. It was contained in the notebook of Oliver St. John Gogarty, who had set it down from memory. Humphries is unaware of Gogarty's previous publication (as "Crazy Jane and the King") in J91. The two texts differ somewhat.

See also J1081, 2820.

"Crazy Jane Grown Old Looks at the Dancers"

See J5598.

"Crazy Jane on the Day of Judgment"

See J2587, 5604.

"Crazy Jane Reproved"

3010. JOHN, BRIAN: "Yeats's 'Crazy Jane Reproved,'" *Éire-Ireland*, 4:4 (Winter 1969), 52-55.

3011. THOMPSON, J. B.: "The Tables Turned: An Analysis of Yeats's 'Crazy Jane Reproved,'" *ESA*, 11:2 (Sept 1968), 173-83.

"Crazy Jane Talks with the Bishop"

3012. ATKINS, ANSELM: "The Vedantic Logic of Yeats' 'Crazy Jane,'" *Renascence*, 19:1 (Fall 1966), 37-40.
    Jane's paradox echoes the Vedantic "logic of mutual exclusion."

3013. JOHNSON, W. R.: "Crazy Jane & Henry More," *Furioso*, 3:2 (Winter 1947), 50-53.
    A PFLA article ("PVBLICATIONS-OF-THE-FVRIOSO-LANGVAGE-ASSOCIATION"), hence somewhat facetious.

See also J2490, 5598.

"Cuchulain Comforted"

3013a. BLOOM, HAROLD: "Death and the Native Strain in American Poetry," *Social Research*, 39:3 (Autumn 1972), 449-62.
    Compares this poem with Stevens's "The Owl in the Sarcophagus."

3014. RAINE, KATHLEEN: "Life in Death and Death in Life: Yeats's 'Cuchulain Comforted' and 'News for the Delphic Oracle,'" *Southern R*, 9:3 (July 1973), 550-78.
    Also published as *Death-in-Life and Life-in-Death: "Cuchulain Comforted" and "News for the Delphic Oracle."* Dublin: Dolmen Press, 1974. 63 p. (Illustrated) (New Yeats Papers. 8.) Discusses the influence of Plotinus, Swedenborg, and Blake, and contains a note on *The Death of Cuchulain*.

See also J1071, 1153, 1156, 2279, 2438.

"Cuchulain's Fight with the Sea"

See J1071.

"The Curse of Cromwell"

See J2475, 5722.

"Death"

3015. COOMBES, HENRY: *Literature and Criticism*. Baltimore: Penguin Books, 1966 [1953]. 160 p.
    See pp. 75-77.

"The Dedication to a Book of Stories Selected from the Irish Novelists"

See J2429, 7011.

"A Deep-Sworn Vow"

3016. BROOKS, CLEANTH, and ROBERT PENN WARREN: *Understanding Poetry*. 3rd edition. NY: Holt, Rinehart & Winston, 1965 [1938], xxiv, 584 p.
    Comments on this poem, pp. 160-64; on "After Long Silence," 164-66 (see also J2947); on "Among School Children," 335-38; on "Two Songs from a Play," 403-9.

See also J2855, 5754.

"The Delphic Oracle upon Plotinus"

3017. PEARCE, DONALD: "Yeats's 'The Delphic Oracle upon Plotinus,'" *N&Q*, os 199 / ns 1:4 (Apr 1954), 175-76.
    A source in Porphyry. See note by Peter Ure, :8 (Aug 1954), 363.

See also J1156.

"Demon and Beast"

3018. URE, PETER: "Yeats's 'Demon and Beast,'" *Irish Writing*, #31 (Summer 1955), 42-50.

See also J1157.

"A Dialogue of Self and Soul"

3018a. FELDMAN, STEVE: "Four Short Prefaces to the 'Dialogue of Self and Soul' by W. B. Yeats," *Continental*, #4 (June 1949), 22-27.

3019. REVARD, STELLA: "Verlaine and Yeats's 'A Dialogue of Self and Soul,'" *PLL*, 7:3 (Summer 1971), 272-78.

3020. WITT, MARION: "Yeats' 'A Dialogue of Self and Soul,'" *Explicator*, 5:7 (May 1957), #48.
    Explains the Japanese background for the "emblems of the day."

See also J1813a, 2756, 2923, 3039, 3115, 3147, 3218, 5917a.

"The Dolls"

3021. BALLIET, CONRAD A.: "'The Dolls' of Yeats and the Cradle of Christ," *Research Studies*, 38:1 (Mar 1970), 54-57.
    The poem describes the birth of Christ.

3022. JOHNSON, RUSSELL I.: "The Vulgarity of His Death: Yeats and the Uncontrollable Mystery," *Spirit*, 38:1 (Spring 1971), 35-38.
    Also on "The Magi."

3023. SCHOLES, ROBERT: *Elements of Poetry*. NY: Oxford UP, 1969. ix, 86 p.
    Note on the symbolism of the poem, pp. 43-45.

See also J2443.

"The Double Vision of Michael Robartes"

3024. SHARMA, T. R. S.: "The Buddha as Symbol in W. B. Yeats: A Study of Two Poems," *Literary Criterion*, 7:4 (Summer 1967), 32-41.
    The other poem is "The Statues."

See also J1813a, 2755.

"Down by the Salley Gardens"

3025. HENDERSON, WILLIAM (ed): *Victorian Street Ballads: A Selection of Popular Ballads Sold in the Street in the Nineteenth Century.* London: Country Life, 1937. 160 p.
     Yeats's source was "The Rambling Boys of Pleasure," pp. 16-17.

3026. MOONEY, CANICE: "Yeats and 'The Salley Gardens,'" *Irish Book Lover*, 31:4 (Apr 1950), 86-87.
     The source of the poem is an 18th-century Irish MS. (Franciscan Library, Killiney, MS. A22). See also notes by P. S. O'H[egarty], :5 (Feb 1951), 105; A[ustin] C[larke], :6 (Nov 1951), 133-34.

3027. SHIELDS, H. E.: "Yeats and the 'Salley Gardens,'" *Hermathena*, #101 (Autumn 1965), 22-26.
     The source of the poem and the music written for it.

See also J5895, 5904, 6265, and many items listed in section IC (musical renderings of the poem, mostly arrangements of folksongs).

"A Dream of Death"

See J5620, 5648, 5686.

"A Drinking Song"

See J5678, 5713.

"Easter 1916"

3027a. BAXANDALL, LEE (ed): *Radical Perspectives in the Arts.* Harmondsworth: Penguin, 1972. 388 p.
     Meredith Tax: "Introductory: Culture Is Not Neutral, Whom Does It Serve?" 15-29, contains a note on revolutionary politics in this poem and Brecht's "An die Nachgeborenen," pp. 18-22.

3028. BRYSON, LYMAN, and others (eds): *Symbols and Values: An Initial Study.* NY: Cooper Square, 1964 1954]. xviii, 827 p. (Sumposium of the Conference on Science, Philosophy, and Religion. 13.)
     M. L. Rosenthal: "Cultural and Rhetorical Symbols in Contemporary American Poetry," 315-39; contains a note on this poem, pp. 315-18.

3029. COLLINS, BEN L.: "A Note on the Historicity of Yeats's Stanzaic Pattern in 'Easter 1916,'" *Éire-Ireland*, 3:1 (Spring 1968), 129.
     Easter Monday, 24 Apr [19]16, reappears in the poem in two 24-line stanzas, 4 stanzas in all, and two 16-line stanzas.

3030. COX, CHARLES BRIAN, and ANTHONY EDWARD DYSON: *Modern Poetry: Studies in Practical Criticism.* London: Arnold, 1963. 168 p.
     "'Easter 1916' by W. B. Yeats," 57-65.

3031. DYSON, A. E.: "Yeats's 'Easter 1916': An Analysis," *Critical Survey*, 1:1 (Autumn 1962), 28-32.

3032. EAGLETON, TERRY: "History and Myth in Yeats's 'Easter 1916,'" *Essays in Criticism*, 21:3 (July 1971), 248-60.

3033. EDWARDS, THOMAS R.: *Imagination and Power: A Study of Poetry on Public Themes.* London: Chatto & Windus, 1971. ix, 232 p.
     See pp. 185-97 and 200-212 for an interpretation of the poem against a background of Yeats's political and esthetic convictions.

3034. FRASER, G. S.: "A Yeats Borrowing," *TLS*, 64:3287 (25 Feb 1965), 156. "All changed, changed utterly" may have come from a similar phrase in M. I. Ebbutt's *Hero-Myths* (J3631).

3035. MCMULLAN, D. H.: "Yeats and O. Henry," *TLS*, 67:3483 (28 Nov 1968), 1339.
Yeats may have taken the phrase "A terrible beauty is born" from a short story by O. Henry. But see Austin Clarke, "Yeats and Le Fanu," :3485 (12 Dec 1968), 1409, where the line is traced to a poem by Le Fanu.

3036. MALONEY, STEPHEN: "Yeats's Meaningful Words: The Role of 'Easter 1916' in His Poetic Development," *English Record*, 22:2 (Winter 1971), 11-18.

3037. MAYHEW, GEORGE: "A Corrected Typescript of Yeats's 'Easter 1916,'" *HLQ*, 27:1 (Nov 1963), 53-71.

3038. PERLOFF, MARJORIE: "Yeats and the Occasional Poem: 'Easter 1916,'" *PLL*, 4:3 (Summer 1968), 308-28.
Includes a comparison with Arnold's "Haworth Churchyard."

See also J1632, 1713, 1740, 2475, 2836, 3202, 5748, 5940 (#1).

"Ego Dominus Tuus"

3039. CRONIN, ANTHONY: *A Question of Modernity*. London: Secker & Warburg, 1966. 130 p.
Note on the relationship between Yeats's mystical thought, this poem, and "A Dialogue of Self and Soul," pp. 43-44, 47-48.

See also J1243, 1977, 2279, 2756, 2827.

"The Empty Cup" (part 5 of "A Man Young and Old")

See J3128.

"Ephemera"

See J5652.

"The Everlasting Voices"

See J5697.

"A Faery Song"

See J5634, 5653.

"The Falling of the Leaves"

See J5607.

"The Fiddler of Dooney"

3040. COMBECHER, HANS: *Deutung englischer Gedichte: Interpretationen zur Sammlung "The Word Sublime."* Frankfurt/Main: Diesterweg, 1965. 2 v.
Notes on this poem and "The Lake Isle of Innisfree," 1:5-8.

See also J5625, 5633, 5651, 5659, 5666, 5681, 5694, 5712, 5863.

"The Fisherman"

3041. EDWARDS, OLIVER: "Yeats's 'The Fisherman,'" *Wales*, 7:25 (Spring 1947), 222-23.
    On the misleading punctuation of the poem and how it affects its meaning.

3042. LUCE, ARTHUR ASTON: *Fishing and Thinking*. London: Hodder & Stoughton, 1959. 191 p.
    See pp. 79-84.

3043. MERCIER, VIVIAN: "Yeats and 'The Fisherman,'" *TLS*, 57:2936 (6 June 1958), 313.
    On the punctuation of the poem.

See also J1197, 1632, 2147a, 3080a.

"The Folly of Being Comforted"

3044. DREW, ELIZABETH: *Discovering Poetry*. NY: Norton, 1933. 224 p.
    See pp. 108-11.

3045. MAIN, CHARLES FREDERICK, and PETER J. SENG (eds): *Poems: Wadsworth Handbook and Anthology*. San Francisco: Wadsworth, 1961. xxvii, 372 p.
    See pp. 264-66.

3046. MAIXNER, PAUL R.: "Yeats' 'The Folly of Being Comforted,'" *Explicator*, 13:1 (Oct 1954), #1.

3047. SENG, PETER J.: "Yeats' 'The Folly of Being Comforted,'" *Explicator*, 17:7 (Apr 1959), #48.

See also J5651.

"For Anne Gregory"

See J5632.

"Fragments"

3048. JEFFARES, A. NORMAN: "Notes on Yeats's 'Fragments,'" *N&Q*, 194:13 (25 June 1949), 279-80.
    Sources in John Locke and Arthur O'Shaughnessy.

"A Friend's Illness"

3049. LEACH, ELSIE: "Yeats's 'A Friend's Illness' and Herbert's 'Vertue,'" *N&Q*, os 207 / ns 9:6 (June 1962), 215.

"From *Oedipus at Colonnus*"

See J5711.

"From the *Antigone*" (part 11 of "A Woman Young and Old")

See J3316.

"The Gift of Harun Al-Rashid"

See J1101, 1699, 2429, 2439.

"Girl's Song"

See J5604.

"The Glove and the Cloak"

3050. WITT, MARION: "An Unknown Yeats Poem," *MLN*, 70:1 (Jan 1955), 26.
  Bibliographical note.

"The Grey Rock"

3051. ALSPACH, RUSSELL K.: "Yeats's 'The Grey Rock,'" *J of American Folklore*, 63:247 (Jan-Mar 1950), 57-71.
  The bibliography and sources of the poem.

See also J1760a.

"The Gyres"

3052. BALLIET, CONRAD A.: "Old Rocky Face in 'The Gyres' of W. B. Yeats," *N&Q*, os 215 / ns 17:12 (Dec 1970), 455-56.
  The rocky face is Ben Bulben's.

3053. BIERMAN, ROBERT: "Yeats' 'The Gyres,'" *Explicator*, 19:7 (Apr 1961), #44.

3054. JEFFARES, A. NORMAN: "Yeats's 'The Gyres': Sources and Symbolism," *HLQ*, 15:1 (Nov 1951), 87-97.
  The sources are in Yeats's own writings and in Shelley's *Hellas*.

3055. SICKELS, ELEANOR M.: "Yeats' 'The Gyres,' 6," *Explicator*, 15:9 (June 1957), #60.
  The function of Empedocles.

See also J1073, 2422, 2427, 2740a.

"The Happy Townland"

See J4195.

"The Harp of Aengus"

See J5703.

"He and She" (part 6 of "Supernatural Songs")

3056. RUBENSTEIN, JEROME S.: "Three Misprints in Yeats's Collected Poems," *MLN*, 70:3 (Mar 1955), 184-87.
  In this poem, "The Host of the Air," and "Whence Had They Come?"

"He Bids His Beloved Be at Peace"

See J2711, 5665.

"He Hears the Cry of the Sedge"

3056a. DOYLE, ESTHER M., and VIRGINIA HASTINGS FLOYD (eds): *Studies in Interpretation*. Amsterdam: Rodopi, 1972. x, 362 p.
  Chester C. Long: "The Poem's Text as a Technique of Performance in Public Group Readings of Poetry," 325-39.

See also J2429, 5709.

"He Remembers Forgotten Beauty"

3057. BRADY, FRANK, JOHN PALMER, and MARTIN PRICE (eds): *Literary Theory and Structure: Essays in Honor of William K. Wimsatt*. New Haven: Yale UP,

1973. viii, 429 p.
    Hugh Kenner: "Some Post-Symbolist Structures," 379–93.

See also J2215, 2216.

"He Reproves the Curlew"

See J727, 2429, 5649, 5663, 5709.

"He Tells of a Valley Full of Lovers"

See J5697.

"He Thinks of His Past Greatness [. . .]"

See J1157, 4195.

"He Thinks of Those Who Have Spoken Evil [. . .]"

See J5633.

"He Wishes for the Cloths of Heaven"

3058. RICKERT, EDITH: *New Methods for the Study of Literature*. Chicago:
U of Chicago Press, 1927. xiii, 275 p.
    Establishes a tone pattern of the poem, pp. 226–27.

See also J5599, 5614, 5620, 5633, 5643, 5656, 5663, 5696.

"He Wishes His Beloved Were Dead"

See J5637, 5643.

"The Heart of the Woman"

See J5637, 5647.

"Her Anxiety"

See J2453, 5602.

"Her Vision in the Wood" (part 8 of "A Woman Young and Old")

See J3207, 3314.

"The Hero, the Girl and the Fool"

3059. SAHA, P. K.: "A Linguistic Approach to Style," *Style*, 2:1 (Winter
1968), 7–31.
    See pp. 17–27.

"High Talk"

3060. JOHN, BRIAN: "Yeats' 'High Talk,'" *Explicator*, 29:3 (Nov 1970), #22.
    A source in Thomas Moore.

3061. REED, VICTOR: "Yeats' 'High Talk,' 9–11," *Explicator*, 26:6 (Feb 1968),
#52.
    An explanation of "Malachi Stilt-Jack."

See also J2429.

"Hills of Mourne"

See J547.

"His Confidence"

3062. BADER, ARNO LEHMAN (ed): *To the Young Writer*. Ann Arbor: U of Michigan Press, 1965. vii, 196 p. (Hopwood Lectures. 2.)
    Archibald MacLeish: "Why Can't They Say What They Mean?" 33-51; contains a note on the obscurity of this poem, pp. 35-38.

See also J5604.

"His Phoenix"

3063. CHESTERTON, GILBERT KEITH: *Christendom in Dublin*. London: Sheed & Ward, 1932. 72 p.
    Note on the phoenix symbol, pp. 51-52.

"The Host of the Air"

See J1073, 3056, 4195, 5633, 5681.

"The Hosting of the Sidhe"

See J1073, 1760, 5600, 5681.

"The Hour before Dawn"

See J1157, 1760a, 3503.

"How Ferenc Renyi Kept Silent"

3063a. GÁL, ISTVÁN: "Yeats magyar balladája," *Nagyvilág*, 16:11 (Nov 1971), 1729-30.

3064. SZERB, ANTAL: "Yeats magyar tárgyú költeménye" [A Yeats poem on a Hungarian subject], *Debreceni szemle*, 4:5 (May 1930), 255-56.

"I Am of Ireland"

3065. GROSS, MARTHA: "Yeats' 'I Am of Ireland,'" *Explicator*, 17:2 (Nov 1958), #15.

3066. SICKELS, ELEANOR M.: "Yeats' 'I Am of Ireland,'" *Explicator*, 15:2 (Nov 1956), #10.

See also J1356, 5598.

"I Saw a Shepherd Youth"

See J4, 129.

"In Church"

3067. DISHER, M. WILLSON: "A Yeats Poem?" *TLS*, 41:2108 (27 June 1942), 322.
    Correspondence by Seumas O'Sullivan, :2112 (25 July 1942), 367.

"In Memory of Alfred Pollexfen"

3068. MURPHY, WILLIAM M.: "'In Memory of Alfred Pollexfen': W. B. Yeats and the Theme of Family," *Irish UR*, 1:1 (Autumn 1970), 31-47.
    Explains the obscure references to the Pollexfen family background.

"In Memory of Eva Gore-Booth and Con Markiewicz"

3069. PERLOFF, MARJORIE: "Spatial Form in the Poetry of Yeats: The Two Lissadell Poems," *PMLA*, 82:5 (Oct 1967), 444-54.
The other poem is "On a Political Prisoner."

See also J1112, 1136a, 2439 (main entry and review #5).

"In Memory of Major Robert Gregory"

3070. BAGG, ROBERT: "The Electromagnet and the Shred of Platinum," *Arion*, 8:3 (Autumn 1969), 407-29.
Comments on Yeats's use of "John Synge," pp. 412-14.

3071. PERLOFF, MARJORIE: "The Consolation Theme in Yeats's 'In Memory of Major Robert Gregory,'" *MLQ*, 27:3 (Sept 1966), 306-22.

3072. WITT, MARION: "The Making of an Elegy: Yeats's 'In Memory of Major Robert Gregory,'" *MP*, 48:2 (Nov 1950), 112-21.

See also J1836.

"In the Seven Woods"

3073. HOWARTH, HERBERT: "Yeats' 'In the Seven Woods,' 6," *Explicator*, 17:2 (Nov 1958), #14.
The meaning of "Tara uprooted."

"Into the Twilight"

See J5621, 5624, 5891.

"An Irish Airman Foresees His Death"

3074. DRAPER, R. P.: "Style and Matter," *Revue des langues vivantes*, 27:1 (1961), 15-23.
Contains a rhetorical and stylistical analysis of the poem.

3075. VOGT, FRIEDRICH E.: "Übertragung eines fremdsprachigen Gedichts," *Deutschunterricht*, 2:3 (1950), 101-8.
How to translate the poem into German. The resulting "model version" is, to my mind, unsuccessful.

See also J2147a.

"Kanva on Himself"

See J3138.

"King and No King"

See J2448.

"The Lady's First (Second and Third) Song"

See J2427, 2440.

"The Lake Isle of Innisfree"

3076. CLEYMAET, R.: "Yeats's 'Lake Isle of Innisfree,'" *Revue des langues vivantes*, 9:5-6 (1943), 218-23.

3077. COOPER, CHARLES WILLIAM, and JOHN HOLMES: *Preface to Poetry.* NY: Harcourt, Brace, 1946. xxiii, 737 p.

On the rhythm and sound pattern of the poem, pp. 122-26.

3077a. °D'AVANZO, MARIO L.: "Yeats' 'The Lake Isle of Innisfree' and the Song of Solomon," *McNeese R*, 20 (1971-72), 15-18.

3078. FRANCIS, ROBERT: "Of Walden and Innisfree," *CSM*, 44:292 (6 Nov 1952), 12.

Why Thoreau left Walden and Yeats did not plant the nine bean rows.

3079. GRAVES, ROBERT: *The Common Asphodel: Collected Essays on Poetry, 1922-1949.* London: Hamilton, 1949. xi, 335 p.

Contains a savage attack on the poem, pp. 186-88 (revised from Laura Riding and Robert Graves: *A Pamphlet against Anthologies.* London: Cape, 1928. 192 p., pp. 95-102).

3080. "GULLIVER": "The Open Window," *Bell*, 5:4 (Jan 1943), 324-25.

The influence of Sir Samuel Ferguson.

3080a. HEDBERG, JOHANNES (ed): *Poets of Our Time--English Poetry from Yeats to Sylvia Plath.* Stockholm: Almqvist & Wiksell, 1970. 179 p.

"Yeats," 70-92, contains explanatory notes to the following poems: "The Lake Isle of Innisfree," "The Song of Wandering Aengus," "A Coat," "The Fisherman," "Sailing to Byzantium," and "An Acre of Grass."

3081. HOWARTH, R. G.: "Yeats's 'My Own Music,'" *N&Q*, 189:8 (20 Oct 1945), 167-68.

The rhythm of the poem is not Yeats's "own music"; it is indebted to numerous predecessors. See additional note by Howarth, 190:8 (20 Apr 1946), 175.

3082. KILGANNON, TADHG: *Sligo and Its Surroundings: A Descriptive and Pictorial Guide to the History, Scenery, Antiquities and Places of Interest in and around Sligo.* Sligo: Kilgannon, 1926. xxiv, 360 p.

"Inishfree Island," 179-82.

3083. KREUZER, JAMES R.: *Elements of Poetry.* NY: Macmillan, 1962. xiii, 256 p.

See pp. 117-19.

3084. MULVANY, TOM: "The Genesis of a Lyric: Yeats's 'The Lake Isle of Innisfree,'" *Texas Q*, 8:4 (Winter 1965), 160-64.

3085. O'GORDON, HANNAH JEAN: "As It Appears to Me," *English J*, 33:3 (Mar 1944), 157-58.

The "vivisection" of a "friendly lyric."

3086. PRITCHARD, FRANCIS HENRY: *Studies in Literature: An Aid to Literary Appreciation and Composition.* London: Harrap, 1919. 205 p.

See pp. 27-30.

3087. ROLA, DIONISIA: "On Yeats' 'The Lake Isle of Innisfree,'" *Diliman R*, 14:2 (Apr 1966), 133-34.

3088. STONOR, OLIVER: "Three Men of the West," *John o' London's Weekly*, 29:742 (1 July 1933), 469, 472.

A visit to the place to find out why it inspired the poem.

3089. THOMAS, GILBERT: *Builders and Makers: Occasional Studies.* London: Epworth Press, 1944. 219 p.

"Poets on Holiday," 202-5. Yeats never built the cabin in the bee-loud glade because he was better off with his imagination.

3090. TILLEKERATNE, NIHAL: "'The Lake Isle of Innisfree,'" *Community*, 3:1 (Apr 1959), 57-58.

See also J848, 1076, 1581, 1923, 2284, 2429, 2522, 3040, 3279, 4197, 5609, 5639, 5641, 5644, 5662, 5663, 5669, 5680, 5697, 5715, 5856, 5860, 5861, 5870, 5880, 5886, 5887, 5897, 5898.

"The Lamentation of the Old Pensioner"

3091. DANIELS, WILLIAM: "Yeats's 'Old Pensioner' and His 'Visionary': 1890-1925," *Irish UR*, 1:2 (Spring 1971), 178-88.
  On the revisions of this poem and of the related essay "An Irish Visionary." Comments on the role AE had in the writing and revision of both pieces.

See also J2429.

"Lapis Lazuli"

3092. BEATY, JEROME, and WILLIAM H. MATCHETT: *Poetry from Statement to Meaning*. NY: Oxford UP, 1965. xi, 353 p.
  See pp. 255-62; on "Sailing to Byzantium," pp. 245-46.

3093. CALARCO, NATALE JOSEPH: *Tragic Being: Apollo and Dionysus in Western Drama*. Minneapolis: U of Minnesota Press, 1968. ix, 202 p.
  See pp. 3-4, 14, 108, 183.

3094. GROSSMAN, ALLEN RICHARD: "William Butler Yeats' 'Lapis Lazuli': A Study of the Poem in Relation to Some Aspects of the Poet's Art and Thought," Honors thesis, Harvard U, 1955. ii, 52 p.

3095. JEFFARES, A. NORMAN: "Notes on Yeats's 'Lapis Lazuli,'" *MLN*, 65:7 (Nov 1950), 488-91.

3096. KING, S. K.: "Eliot, Yeats, and Shakespeare," *Theoria*, #5 (1953), 113-19.
  "The endurance of virtue" in "Marina," *The Winter's Tale*, and this poem.

3097. LABISTOUR, MARION: "'Lapis Lazuli,'" *Critical Survey*, 3:1 (Winter 1966), 13-16.

3098. MENDEL, SYDNEY: "Yeats' 'Lapis Lazuli,'" *Explicator*, 19:9 (June 1961), #64.

3099. SANESI, ROBERTO: "'Lapis Lazuli,'" *Osservatore politico letterario*, 7:10 (Oct 1961), 81-91.
  Reprinted in *Poesia e critica*, 1:2 [Dec 1961], 5-18.

3100. WARNER, JOHN M.: "'Lapis Lazuli': Structure through Analogy," *Concerning Poetry*, 3:2 (Fall 1970), 41-48.

See also J1112, 1136a, 1315, 2147a, 2258, 2422, 2429, 2440, 2667, 2740a, 2756, 2890, 4006, 4115, 5940 (#1).

"The Leaders of the Crowd"

3101. UTLEY, FRANCIS LEE: "Three Kinds of Honesty," *J of American Folklore*, 66:261 (July-Sept 1953), 189-99.
  Note on this poem and on "The Scholars," pp. 192-93.

"Leda and the Swan"

3102. ADAMS, JOHN F.: "'Leda and the Swan': The Aesthetics of Rape," *Bucknell R*, 12:3 (Dec 1964), 47-58.
An interpretation of the poem as an expression of "the sexual dream-myth."

3103. BERKELMAN, ROBERT: "The Poet, the Swan, and the Woman," *UKCR*, 28:3 (Mar 1962), 229-30.

3104. COLE, E. R.: "Three Cycle Poems of Yeats and His Mystico-Historical Thought," *Personalist*, 46:1 (Winter 1965), 73-80.
The other poems are "The Mother of God" and "The Magi."

3105. DEMETILLO, RICAREDO: *The Authentic Voice of Poetry*. Diliman, Quezon City: U of the Philippines, 1962. ix, 337 p.
Note on this poem, pp. 7-9; on "Sailing to Byzantium," pp. 10-11.

3106. DUTHIE, GEORGE IAN (ed): *English Studies Today*. 3rd series. Lectures and papers read at the fifth conference of the International Association of Professors of English held at Edinburgh and Glasgow, August 1962. Edinburgh: UP, 1964. 256 p.
M. A. K. Halliday: "Descriptive Linguistics in Literary Studies," 25-39; reprinted in Angus McIntosh and Michael Alexander Kirkwood Halliday: *Patterns of Language: Papers in General, Descriptive and Applied Linguistics*. London: Longmans, 1966. xi, 199 p., pp. 56-69. See also "The Linguistic Study of Literary Texts" in Horace G. Lunt (ed): *Proceedings of the Ninth International Congress of Linguists*, Cambridge, Mass., August 27-31, 1962. The Hague: Mouton, 1964. xxii, 1174 p. (Janua Linguarum. Series Maior. 12.), pp. 302-7.

3107. DUVALL, CECIL H., and JOHN B. HUMMA: "The Opening Phrase of Yeats' 'Leda and the Swan,'" *Research Studies*, 40:2 (June 1972), 131-32.
The sexual connotations of the word "blow."

3108. GREENFIELD, STANLEY B.: "Grammar and Meaning in Poetry," *PMLA*, 82:5 (Oct 1967), 377-87.

3109. KOCH, WALTER A.: "Einige Probleme der Textanalyse," *Lingua*, 16:4 (1966), 383-98.
Contains a linguistic analysis of the poem.

3110. LIND, L. R.: "Leda and the Swan: Yeats and Rilke," *Chicago R*, 7:2 (Spring 1953), 13-17.
Compares Yeats's poem with Rilke's "Leda."

3111. MADGE, CHARLES: "Leda and the Swan," *TLS*, 61:3151 (20 July 1962), 532.
Yeats's source may have been a bas-relief in the British Museum rather than a Michelangelo painting (illustrated). Correspondence by Giorgio Melchiori, :3153 (3 Aug 1962), 557, supporting Madge's thesis; by Hugh Ross Williamson, :3157 (31 Aug 1962), 657, asking for a pictorial source of "On a Picture of a Black Centaur by Edmund Dulac." See also the article by Charles B. Gullans, :3167 (9 Nov 1962), 864, who sees the source for "Leda" in a woodcut by T. Sturge Moore (illustrated), and a letter by Charles Madge, :3168 (16 Nov 1962), 873.

3112. MARGOLIS, JOSEPH: "Yeats' 'Leda and the Swan,'" *Explicator*, 13:6 (Apr 1955), #34.

3113. PRATT, JOHN CLARK: *The Meaning of Modern Poetry*. NY: Doubleday, 1962. xi, 400 p.

This is a weird anthology. The index lists a Yeats reference on p. 375; there one finds the text of the poem plus some comment, as well as a note to continue on p. 376. On p. 376 Pratt gives further comments and refers you to p. 369 (and from there to pp. 361, 377 ["When you have followed my suggestions and are either informed or thoroughly disgusted, return to page 369 and try again"], 380, and 382. Or you might continue from 376 to 371 and to 390 (where he refers you back to 369); 382 (remember that?) continues into 383 and then to 370 (and then to 381, 384, and 386), also to 378 (cf. 385, 387, 391, 392) and 388 (from there to 389 [and from there to 381, 384, and 386]). Help!

3114. REID, JANE DAVIDSON: "Leda, Twice Assaulted," *JAAC*, 11:4 (June 1953), 378-89.
    A comparison with Rilke's "Leda."

3115. ROSENTHAL, MACHA LOUIS, and ARTHUR JAMES MARSHALL SMITH (eds): *Exploring Poetry*. NY: Macmillan, 1967 [1955]. xli, 758 p.
    On this poem and "Sailing to Byzantium," pp. 576-82; a comparison of "A Dialogue of Self and Soul" with Eliot's "Little Gidding," 702-3.

3116. SKELTON, ROBIN: *Poetry*. London: English Universities Press, 1963. vii, 179 p. (Teach Yourself Books.)
    See pp. 137-39.

3117. STEIN, ARNOLD: "Milton and Metaphysical Art: An Exploration," *ELH*, 16:2 (June 1949), 120-34.
    See pp. 129-30.

3118. SUŠKO, MARIO: "Neki aspekti Yeatsove pjesme 'Leda i labud'" [Some aspects of Yeats's poem "Leda and the Swan"], *Republika*, 25:9 (Sept 1969), 494-95.

3119. TROWBRIDGE, HOYT: "'Leda and the Swan': A Longinian Analysis," *MP*, 51:2 (Nov 1953), 118-29.
    Reply by Leo Spitzer: "On Yeats's Poem 'Leda and the Swan,'" :4 (May 1954), 271-76; reprinted in Spitzer's *Essays on English and American Literature*, edited by Anna Hatcher. Princeton: Princeton UP, 1962. xvii, 290 p., pp. 3-13.

3120. VICKERY, JOHN B.: "Three Modes and a Myth," *WHR*, 12:4 (Autumn 1958), 371-78.
    The Leda myth and its treatment by Huxley, Graves, and Yeats.

See also J1114, 1153, 1713, 1818, 1924a, 2107, 2429, 2506, 2630, 2745, 2809, 2866, 2949, 3226, 3242, 5893, 5940 (#11).

"Long-legged Fly"

3121. CROSS, KENNETH GUSTAV WALTER, and DERICK R. C. MARSH (eds): *Poetry: Reading and Understanding. An Anthology with Commentaries and Questions*. Wellington: N.Z.: Reed, 1966. xvi, 245 p.
    See pp. 171-75.

3122. DYSON, A. E.: "An Analysis of Yeats's 'Long-legged Fly,'" *Critical Survey*, 2:2 (Summer 1965), 101-3.

3123. HODGES, ROBERT R.: "The Irony of Yeats's 'Long-legged Fly,'" *TCL*, 12:1 (Apr 1966), 27-30.

3124. SOUTHAM, B. C.: "Yeats: Life and the Creator in 'The Long Legged Fly [*sic*],'" *TCL*, 6:4 (Jan 1961), 175-79.

See James L. Allen: "Yeats' 'Long-legged Fly,'" *Explicator*, 21:6 (Feb 1963), #51; B. C. Southam, 22:9 (May 1964), #73.

See also J2440, 2494, 2667.

"The Lover Asks Forgiveness Because of His Many Moods"

See J1073.

"The Lover Pleads with His Friends [. . .]"

See J5887.

"The Lover's Song"

See J2427, 2440.

"Lullaby"

See J1073, 5705.

"Mad as the Mist and Snow"

See J2587, 5701.

"The Magi"

3125. JOSELYN, SISTER M.: "Twelfth Night Quartet: Four Magi Poems," *Renascence*, 16:2 (Winter 1964), 92-94.
    By Eliot, John Peale Bishop, Edgar Bowers, and Yeats.

3126. SANDERS, PAUL: "Yeats' 'The Magi,'" *Explicator*, 25:7 (Mar 1967), #53.

3126a. °TULLY, ROSEMARY FRANKLIN: "A Pictorial Source for Yeats's 'The Magi,'" *Éire-Ireland*, 8:4 (Winter 1973), 84-90.

See also J1713, 1920, 3022, 3104.

"Maid Quiet"

3127. ALSPACH, RUSSELL K.: "Yeats's 'Maid Quiet,'" *MLN*, 65:4 (Apr 1950), 252-53.
    A bibliographical note.

See also J5694.

"The Man and the Echo"

See J2427, 2440, 2475, 2819.

"The Man Who Dreamed of Faeryland"

See J2058, 5895.

"A Man Young and Old"

3128. KEITH, W. J.: "Yeats's 'The Empty Cup,'" *ELN*, 4:3 (Mar 1967), 206-10.

3129. SOMER, JOHN: "Unageing Monuments: A Study of W. B. Yeats' Poetry Sequence, 'A Man Young and Old,'" *Ball State U Forum*, 12:4 (Autumn 1971), 28-36.

See also J2423a.

"Margot"

See J118, 2819.

"A Meditation in Time of War"

3130. JEFFARES, A. NORMAN: "The Source of Yeats's 'A Meditation in Time of War,'" *N&Q*, 193:24 (27 Nov 1948), 522.
    Blake's poem "Time."

"Meditations in Time of Civil War"

3131. CURTIS, PENELOPE: "Yeats: The Tower in Time of Civil War," *Melbourne Critical R*, #6 (1963), 69-82.

3132. GLEN, HEATHER: "The Greatness of Yeats's 'Meditations,'" *Critical R*, #12 (1969), 29-44.

3133. GREER, SAMMYE CRAWFORD: "The Poet's Role in an Age of Emptiness and Chaos: A Reading of Yeats's 'Meditations in Time of Civil War,'" *Éire-Ireland*, 7:3 (Autumn 1972), 82-92.

3134. HENN, THOMAS RICE: *The Apple and the Spectroscope: Being Lectures on Poetry Designed (in the Main) for Science Students*. London: Methuen, 1951. xix, 166 p.
    "Two Poems by Yeats: 'The Stare's Nest by My Window' and 'Before the World Was Made' [part 2 of "A Woman Young and Old"]," 49-58.

3135. PLATER, ORMONDE: "Water Imagery in Yeats' 'Meditations in Time of Civil War,'" *Style*, 2:1 (Winter 1968), 59-72.

3136. SEYBOLT, STEPHEN: "A Reading of 'Meditations in Time of Civil War,'" *Massachusetts Studies in English*, 2:4 (Fall 1970), 107-16.

3137. THWAITE, ANTHONY: "Yeats and 'Sato's Ancient Blade,'" *Adam*, 25:261 (1957), 9.
    Montashigi is Yeats's version of Motoshige, who lived around 1330.

See also J1157, 2423a, 2429, 2723, 2745, 3145.

"Meeting" (part 10 of "A Woman Young and Old")

See J3315.

"Memory"

See J1162 (#1), 2439, 2587.

"Men Improve with the Years"

See J5711.

"Meru" (part 12 of "Supernatural Songs," q.v.)

See J2282.

"Mohini Chatterjee"

3138. WITT, MARION: "Yeats' 'Mohini Chatterjee,'" *Explicator*, 4:8 (June 1946), #60.
    Compared with "Kanva on Himself."

See also J1157.

"The Moods"

3139. WITT, MARION: "Yeats' 'The Moods,'" *Explicator*, 6:3 (Dec 1947), #15.

"The Mother of God"

3140. JENNINGS, MARGARET M.: "'The Mother of God': William Butler Yeats," *Spirit*, 38:4 (Winter 1972), 34-38.

See also J1073, 1818, 2855, 3104.

"The Municipal Gallery Revisited"

3141. *Yeats at the Municipal Gallery*. Dublin: Claremont House, 1959. [8 p.]
Contains an essay by Arland Ussher, "Yeats at the Municipal Gallery," [1-2], in which he comments on the paintings mentioned in the poem; the text of the poem; and black-and-white reproductions of the paintings.

See also J1064, 2422, 2635, 2971.

"The New Faces"

3142. JEFFARES, A. NORMAN: "'The New Faces': A New Explanation," *RES*, 23: 92 (Oct 1947), 349-53.
The references to Lady Gregory.

"News for the Delphic Oracle"

3143. OWER, JOHN: "Yeats' 'News for the Delphic Oracle,'" *Explicator*, 28:1 (Sept 1969), #7.

3144. WIND, EDGAR: "Raphael: The Dead Child on a Dolphin," *TLS*, 62:3217 (25 Oct 1963), 874.
The statue that served as pictorial source for the poem (illustrated).

See also J1156, 2414, 2711, 3014, 4006.

"Nineteen Hundred and Nineteen"

3145. GRAHAM, DESMOND: *Introduction to Poetry*. London: Oxford UP, 1968. vii, 168 p.
See pp. 80-85, 123-24; on "Meditations in Time of Civil War," part 6 ("The Stare's Nest by My Window"), pp. 111-18.

3146. LEHMAN, BENJAMIN HARRISON, and others: *The Image of the Work: Essays in Criticism*. Berkeley: U of California Press, 1955. ix, 265 p. (U of California Publications. English Studies. 11.)
Thomas Parkinson: "The World of Yeats' 'Nineteen Hundred and Nineteen,'" 209-27, 264.

3147. OPPEL, HORST (ed): *Die moderne englische Lyrik: Interpretationen*. Berlin: Schmidt, 1967. 342 p.
Willi Erzgräber on this poem, pp. 96-116; on "A Dialogue of Self and Soul," 164-84; Arno Esch on "Among School Children," 137-49.

See also J1073, 1713, 2423a, 2714, 2846, 3218, 4006.

"The Nineteenth Century and After"

See J2439.

"No Second Troy"

See J1677.

"O Do Not Love Too Long"

See J5711.

"The Old Age of Queen Maeve"

See J1760a.

"The Old Men Admiring Themselves in the Water"

3148. CHATMAN, SEYMOUR (ed): *Literary Style: A Symposium*. London: Oxford UP, 1971. xv, 427 p.
   Ruqaiya Hasan: "Rime and Reason in Literature," 299-329, contains a stylistic analysis of the poem.

See also J5711.

"On a Picture of a Black Centaur by Edmund Dulac"

3149. NIELSEN, MARGARET E.: "A Reading of W. B. Yeats's Poem 'On a Picture of a Black Centaur by Edmund Dulac,'" *Thoth*, 4:2 (Spring 1963), 67-73.

See also J1241, 2531, 3111.

"On a Political Prisoner"

3150. ROSOV, VICTOR: "Yeats and the Poetic Process: A Study of Three Poems," Honors thesis, Harvard U, 1967. iii, 42 p.
   The other two poems are "Byzantium" and "The Circus Animals' Desertion."

See also J3069.

"Parnell's Funeral"

3151. URE, PETER: "A Source of Yeats's 'Parnell's Funeral,'" *ES*, 39:6 (Dec 1958), 257-58.
   In Sordello di Goito via Ezra Pound.

3152. WILSON, F. A. C.: "Yeats' 'Parnell's Funeral,' II," *Explicator*, 27:9 (May 1969), #72.
   A source in Sordello.

See also J2678.

"Parting" (part 7 of "A Woman Young and Old")

See J2439.

"The Phases of the Moon"

See J1813a, 2755.

"The Pilgrim"

See J5722.

"The Pity of Love"

3153. WALSH, CHAD: *Doors into Poetry*. Englewood Cliffs: Prentice-Hall, 1962. xxvii, 292 p.

Note on this poem, pp. 32-33; on "Sailing to Byzantium," 54-56.
See also J5697.

"Politics"

See J2499.

"A Prayer for My Daughter"

3154. BECK, WARREN: "Boundaries of Poetry," *CE*, 4:6 (Mar 1943), 342-50.
See pp. 349-50.

3155. BROOKS, CLEANTH: "Yeats: His Poetry and Prose," *English*, 15:89 (Summer 1965), 177-80.
An extract from a lecture, made by a rather incompetent editor. The surviving snippet concerns itself largely with this poem.

3156. ————: "Metaphor, Paradox and Stereotype," *British J of Aesthetics*, 5:4 (Oct 1965), 315-28.
A note on metaphor and cliché in the poem, pp. 324-25.

3157. CLOTHIER, CAL: "Some Observations on Yeats' 'A Prayer for My Daughter,'" *Agenda*, 9:4-10:1 (Autumn-Winter 1971/72), 39-45.

3158. HARDY, JOHN EDWARD: *The Curious Frame: Seven Poems in Text and Context*. Notre Dame: U of Notre Dame Press, 1962. xiv, 196 p.
Based on "Some Problems in the Explication of Poetry," Ph.D. thesis, Johns Hopkins U, 1955. iii, 180 p. "Yeats' 'A Prayer for My Daughter': The Dimensions of the Nursery," 116-50.

3159. MARTIN, C. G.: "A Coleridge Reminiscence in Yeats's 'A Prayer for My Daughter,'" *N&Q*, os 210 / ns 12:7 (July 1965), 258-60.
The image of the tree in Coleridge's "Ver Perpetuum."

3160. ROWLAND, BERYL: "The Other Father in Yeats's 'A Prayer for My Daughter,'" *Orbis Litterarum*, 26:4 (1971), 284-90.
The other father is Coleridge.

See also J1243, 2439, 2934, 3218, 3303, 5570, 5597, 5741.

"A Prayer for My Son"

See J2863.

"The Priest and the Fairy"

See J2237.

"Quarrel in Old Age"

See J2735.

"The Queen and the Jester." See "The Cap and Bells"

"Red Hanrahan's Song about Ireland"

3161. ALSPACH, RUSSELL L.: "Two Songs of Yeats's," *MLN*, 61:6 (June 1946), 395-400.
Bibliographical note on this poem and on "The Song of Wandering Aengus."

3162. QUINN, SISTER M. BERNETTA: "Yeats and Ireland," *English J*, 54:5 (May 1965), 449-50.

See also J1760, 5631.

"Remembrance"

3163. JOCHUM, K. P. S.: "An Unknown Variant of an Early Yeats Poem," *N&Q*, os 216 / ns 18:11 (Nov 1971), 420-21.
A revised version of this poem, entitled "To ——," was found in the *New York Evening Post* of 31 Jan 1921 (see J143). Its authenticity is somewhat unclear.

"Reprisals"

3164. [EDWARDS, OLIVER]: "Note on the Publication of 'Reprisals,'" *Rann*, #2 (Autumn 1948), 1.

"The Results of Thought"

See J2439, 2735.

"Ribh at the Tomb of Baile and Aillinn" (part 1 of "Supernatural Songs," q.v.)

See J2962, 3257.

"Ribh Considers Christian Love Insufficient" (part 5 of "Supernatural Songs," q.v.)

See J1073.

"Ribh Denounces Patrick" (part 2 of "Supernatural Songs," q.v.)

See J3257.

"Ribh in Ecstasy" (part 3 of "Supernatural Songs," q.v.)

See J3257.

"Roger Casement"

3165. ANON.: "Poet Yeats and Poet Noyes," *Catholic Bulletin*, 27:3 (Mar 1937), 171-72.
"His bumptious and blundering parade of his bockety ballad. . . . this rheumatic rhapsody from the Pretentious Pensionary of Bull."

3166. NOYES, ALFRED: *Two Worlds for Memory*. London: Sheed & Ward, 1953, xi, 339 p.
"Sir Roger Casement," 123-37.

3167. YEATS, W. B.: "Irish Poet's Striking Challenge: Roger Casement (After Reading *The Forged Casement Diaries* by Dr. Maloney)," *Irish Press*, 7:28 (2 Feb 1937), 6.
The poem plus a short note by Yeats. See "Vindication of Casement [. . .]," :29 (3 Feb 1937), 9; tributes by Sean T. O'Kelly, Eoin Mac-Neill, and Liam Grogan in praise of Yeats's poem. Also the editorial, "A Poet's Vindication," *ibid.*, p. 8.
Muiris Ó Catháin: "Buidheachas," :30 (4 Feb 1937), 4, a poem on Yeats in Gaelic.
"Alfred Noyes Replies to W. B. Yeats," :37 (12 Feb 1937), 8-9; editorial, *ibid.*, p. 8.
W. B. Yeats: "Mr. Noyes' 'Noble Letter': Mr. Yeats Revises Song," :38 (13 Feb 1937), 8.

"The Rose Tree"

3168. BROWN, T. J.: "English Literary Autographs XLIX: William Butler Yeats, 1865-1939," *Book Collector*, 13:1 (Spring 1964), 53 (and illustration facing p. 53).

3169. SHUMAKER, WAYNE: *An Approach to Poetry*. Englewood Cliffs: Prentice-Hall, 1965. xxviii, 443 p.
See pp. 49-52.

See also J4138.

"Running to Paradise"

See J3503, 5702.

"The Sad Shepherd"

See J1069.

"Sailing to Byzantium"

3169a. ALLEN, JAMES LOVIC: "Yeats's Byzantium Poems and the Critics, Reconsidered," *Colby Library Q*, 10:2 (June 1973), 57-71.
A classified evaluation, especially of criticism published after 1962.

3170. ARNHEIM, RUDOLF, W. H. AUDEN, KARL SHAPIRO, and DONALD A. STAUFFER: *Poets at Work: Essays Based on the Modern Poetry Collection at the Lockwood Memorial Library, University of Buffalo*. Introduction by Charles D. Abbott. NY: Harcourt, Brace, 1948. x, 186 p.
Donald A. Stauffer: "Genesis, or The Poet as Maker," 37-82; notes allusions to "Sailing to Byzantium" in a poem by R. P. Blackmur, p. 47.

3171. BAKER, HOWARD: "Domes of Byzantium," *Southern R*, 7:3 (Winter 1941/ 42), 639-52.

3172. BEJA, MORRIS: "*2001*: Odyssey to Byzantium," *Extrapolation*, 10:2 (May 1969), 67-68.
Yeats's journey to Byzantium is analogous to the one undertaken by the astronaut in the film *2001*. See also °Robert Plank, "1001 Interpretations of *2001*," 11:1 (Dec 1969), 23-24.

3173. BRADFORD, CURTIS: "Yeats's Byzantium Poems: A Study of Their Development," *PMLA*, 75:1 (Mar 1960), 110-25.
Discusses the MS. drafts.

3174. BURKE, KENNETH: *A Grammar of Motives and A Rhetoric of Motives*. Cleveland: World, 1962 [1945, 1950]. xxv, 868 p.
Appendix A of *A Grammar* ("Symbolic Action in a Poem by Keats," 459-61) refers also to this poem and "Among School Children." Appendix B ("The Problem of the Intrinsic," 465-84) discusses Olson's article on "Sailing to Byzantium" (J3197). Part three of *A Rhetoric* contains a note on "Byzantium" and "Sailing to Byzantium," 840-41.

3175. CAMPBELL, HARRY MODEAN: "Yeats's 'Sailing to Byzantium,'" *MLN*, 70:8 (Dec 1955), 585-89.

3176. CRUMP, GEOFFREY: *Speaking Poetry*. London: Dobson, 1968 [1953]. viii, 231 p.
Note on this poem, pp. 41-42; on some other Yeats poems, *passim* (see index).

3177. DONALDSON, ALLAN: "A Note on W. B. Yeats's 'Sailing to Byzantium,'"
N&Q, os 199 / ns 1:1 (Jan 1954), 34-35.
A source in Madame Blavatsky and theosophy.

3178. DOUGLAS, WALLACE, ROY LAMSON, and HALLETT SMITH (eds): *The Critical
Reader: Poems, Stories, Essays*. NY: Norton, 1949. xiv, 785 p.
See pp. 115-18.

3179. DUME, THOMAS L.: "Yeats' Golden Tree and Birds in the Byzantium
Poems," *MLN*, 67:6 (June 1952), 404-7.

3180. EGGENSCHWILER, DAVID: "Nightingales and Byzantine Birds, Something
Less Than Kind," *ELN*, 8:3 (Mar 1971), 186-91.
Keats's nightingale and Yeats's golden bird represent two "radically
different ideals of art."

3181. EMPSON, WILLIAM: "Mr. Wilson on the Byzantium Poems," *REL*, 1:3 (July
1960), 51-56.
Criticizes F. A. C. Wilson's interpretations of both Byzantium poems
(J1156).

3182. ————: "The Variants for the Byzantium Poems," *Phoenix*, #10 (Summer
1965), 1-26.
Reprinted in Kumar Raj Kaul (ed): *Essays Presented to Amy G. Stock,
Professor of English, Rajasthan University, 1961-65*. Jaipur: Rajasthan
UP, 1965. viii, 195 p., pp. 111-36. Discusses the symbolism of the
poems and its sources.

3183. FINNERAN, RICHARD J. (ed): *William Butler Yeats: The Byzantium Poems*.
Columbus, Ohio: Merrill, 1970. v, 160 p. (Merrill Literary Casebook Series.)
Contains an introduction (pp. 1-10), the text of the two poems, other
relevant passages from Yeats's poetry and prose, and 17 items of previously published criticism.

3184. °FULTON, JOHN: "The Byzantine Paradox," M.A. thesis, Columbia U,
1949.

3185. GWYNN, FREDERICK L.: "Yeats's Byzantium and Its Sources," *PQ*, 32:1
(Jan 1953), 9-21.
Some of the sources are Shakespeare's *King Lear*, Lamb's essays on
Shakespeare's tragedies, and Gibbon's *Decline and Fall of the Roman
Empire*. See D. J. Greene: "Yeats's Byzantium and Johnson's Lichfield,"
33:4 (Oct 1954), 433-35.

3186. HAGOPIAN, JOHN V.: "Thirteen Ways of Looking at a Blackbird," *American N&Q*, 1:6 (Feb 1963), 84-85.
Stevens's poem is indebted to Yeats's.

3187. HOLLOWAY, JOHN: *Widening Horizons in English Verse*. Evanston: Northwestern UP, 1967. ix, 115 p.
Some notes on Yeats, the Nō, the 18th-century Irish "aisling," *Purgatory*, and this poem, pp. 92-102.

3188. KLEINSTÜCK, JOHANNES: "W. B. Yeats: 'Sailing to Byzantium,'" *Neueren
Sprachen*, 9:11 (Nov 1960), 527-39.

3189. KLIEWER, WARREN: "The Bruised Body," *Cresset*, 32:10 (Oct 1969), 8-12.
Stanislavskiĭ's method of beginning in the body and moving out into
the region of the soul resembles the plot of the poem.

3190. KOCH, WALTER A.: *Taxologie des Englischen: Versuch einer einheit-
lichen Beschreibung der englischen Grammatik und englischer Texte*. München:

Fink, 1971. 434 p. (Internationale Bibliothek für allgemeine Linguistik / International Library of General Linguistics. 5.)
See pp. 387-95 for an interpretation on the basis of information theory and advanced linguistics.

3191. LESSER, SIMON O.: "'Sailing to Byzantium'--Another Voyage, Another Reading," *CE*, 28:4 (Jan 1967), 291-310.
Against Olson's interpretation (J3197). Correspondence by D. C. Fowler, "Lesser on Yeats's 'Sailing to Byzantium,'" :8 (May 1967), 614; Frederic I. Carpenter, "A Lesser Byzantium," *ibid.*, 614-15; and Lesser's reply, *ibid.*, 615-17.

3192. MATSUMURA, KEN'ICHI: "'Sailing to Byzantium': A Note," *Yeats Society of Japan Annual Report*, #7 (1972), 19-23.
Yeats's use of "moment" and "memory."

3193. MELLER, HORST (ed): *Zeitgenössische englische Dichtung: Einführung in die englische Literaturbetrachtung mit Interpretationen.* I: Lyrik. Frankfurt/Main: Hirschgraben, 1966. 148 p.
Siegbert S. Prawer: "'Sailing to Byzantium': W. B. Yeats," 72-79.

3194. MURPHY, GWENDOLEN (ed): *The Modern Poet.* London: Sidgwick & Jackson, 1951 [1938]. xx, 208 p.
Note on both Byzantium poems, pp. 152-54.

3194a. MURRAY, PATRICK: *Herbert to Yeats.* Dublin: Educational Company, 1972. 64 p. (Inscapes. 1.)
"This series is designed specifically to meet the needs of students in Irish post-primary schools" (back cover). Contains a note on this poem, pp. 57-60, and on "Among School Children," 61-64.

3195. NOTOPOULOS, JAMES A.: "Sailing to Byzantium," *Classical J*, 41:2 (Nov 1945), 78-79.
The possible Byzantine sources of the golden bird image.

3196. ———: "Byzantine Platonism in Yeats," *Classical J*, 54:7 (Apr 1959), 315-21.
Platonic philosophy and Byzantine art in the poem.

3197. OLSON, ELDER: "'Sailing to Byzantium': Prolegomena to a Poetics of the Lyric," *UKCR*, 8:3 (Spring 1942), 209-19.
Reprinted in J1090 and 3218. See J3174 and 3191; also W. K. Wimsatt: "Comment on 'Two Essays in Practical Criticism,'" 9:2 (Winter 1942), 139-43; P. S. Sastri: "The Poetics of the Lyric and Olson's Approach," *Literary Criterion*, 9:1 (Winter 1969), 70-77.

3198. PARKS, L. C.: "The Hidden Aspect of 'Sailing to Byzantium,'" *EA*, 16:4 (Oct-Dec 1963), 333-44.
Rosicrucian influences.

3199. PHILLIPS, ROBERT S.: "Yeats' 'Sailing to Byzantium,' 25-32," *Explicator*, 22:2 (Oct 1963), #11.
Andersen's "The Emperor and the Nightingale" as source for the golden bird. Phillips does not seem to have noted Schanzer's earlier article on the same subject (J3205).

3200. PIGGOTT, JAN RICHARD: "The Context of Yeats's 'Sailing to Byzantium,'" °Ph.D. thesis, U of California (Davis), 1971. 350 p. (*DA*, 32:7 [Jan 1972], 3692A.)
A source study.

3201. RAYMOND, WILLIAM O.: "'The Mind's Internal Heaven' in Poetry," *UTQ*, 20:3 (Apr 1951), 215-32.

3202. *Le romantisme anglo-américaine: Mélanges offerts à Louis Bonnerot.* Paris: Didier, 1971. 421 p. (Etudes anglaises. 39.)
 Yves Bonnefoy: "Sailing to Byzantium," 307-16; a translation and a note.
 René Fréchet: "Trois poèmes de W. B. Yeats: 'Easter 1916,' 'Coole Park and Ballylee 1931,' 'The Circus Animals' Desertion,'" 317-30; translations and notes.

3203. ROSS, RALPH, JOHN BERRYMAN, and ALLEN TATE (eds): *The Arts of Reading.* NY: Crowell, 1960. xv, 488 p.
 See pp. 352-54.

3204. SAN JUAN, E.: "Yeats's 'Sailing to Byzantium' and the Limits of Modern Literary Criticism," *Revue des langues vivantes*, 38:5 (1972), 492-507.

3205. SCHANZER, ERNEST: "'Sailing to Byzantium,' Keats, and Andersen," *ES*, 41:6 (Dec 1960), 376-80.
 The "Ode to a Nightingale" and the Emperor's nightingale as influences.

3206. SCHMIDT-HIDDING, WOLFGANG: *Learning English: Book of English Verse. Interpretations.* Stuttgart: Klett, 1966. 96 p.
 Notes on this poem and "The Second Coming" (in German), *passim*.

3207. °SEN, S. C.: "'Her Vision in the Wood' and 'Sailing to Byzantium,'" *Bulletin of the Department of English, U of Calcutta*, 2:3&4 (1961).

3208. STAGEBERG, NORMAN C.: "Yeats' 'Sailing to Byzantium,'" *Explicator*, 6:2 (Nov 1947), #14.
 Explains "perne."

3208a. STUDING, RICHARD: "'That Is No Country for Old Men'--A Yeatsian Ambiguity?" *Research Studies*, 41:1 (Mar 1973), 60-61.
 "That" could be Byzantium itself.

3209. SULLIVAN, RUTH ELIZABETH: "Backward to Byzantium," *Literature and Psychology*, 17:1 (1967), 13-18.
 Beneath the poem's "conscious level, beneath the intellectual, spiritual, and aesthetic values . . . lies an unconscious wishful fantasy that moves . . . not forward toward some higher and superhuman state . . . but backward toward very early infancy."
  See comments by Aileen Ward, *ibid.*, pp. 30-33; Clare M. Murphy, 38-40; and Mrs. Sullivan, 43-46.

3210. THOMAS, WRIGHT, and STUART GERRY BROWN (eds): *Reading Poems: An Introduction to Critical Study.* NY: Oxford UP, 1941. xiv, 781 p.
 Notes on this poem, "Byzantium," and "The Second Coming," pp. 712-16.

3211. TRILLING, LIONEL (ed): *The Experience of Literature: A Reader with Commentaries.* NY: Holt, Rinehart & Winston, 1967. xxiv, 1320 p.
 Note on this poem, pp. 921-23; on *Purgatory*, 369-71.

3212. TRUCHLAR, LEO: *Zum Symbol des Schiffes in der englischsprachigen Lyrik.* Wien: Verband der österreichischen Neuphilologen, 1968. 31 p. (Moderne Sprachen. Schriftenreihe. 12.)
 Note on the ship symbol, pp. 27-29.

3213. VENTER, J. A.: "Phonic Patterning in 'Sailing to Byzantium,'" *ESA*, 10:1 (Mar 1967), 40-46.

3214. WALTON, GEOFFREY: "Yeats's 'Perne': Bobbin or Bird?" *Essays in Criticism*, 16:2 (Apr 1966), 255–58.

3215. WEBB, EUGENE: "Criticism and the Creative Process," *West Coast R*, 2:2 (Fall 1967), 13–20.
   Contains a note on the revisions of the poem.

3216. WERLICH, EGON: *Poetry Analysis: Great English Poems Interpreted.* With additional notes on the biographical, historical, and literary background. Dortmund: Lensing, 1967. 238 p.
   "William Butler Yeats: 'Sailing to Byzantium,'" 161–88.

3217. WHEELOCK, JOHN HALL: *What Is Poetry.* NY: Scribner's, 1963. 128 p.
   See pp. 81–86.

3218. WILLIAMS, OSCAR (ed): *Master Poems of the English Language: Over One Hundred Poems Together with Introductions by Leading Poets and Critics of the English-Speaking World.* NY: Washington Square Press, 1967 [1966]. xxiii, 1093 p. (Washington Square Press. W1446.)
   Elder Olson on this poem, pp. 875–80 (reprinted from J3197); Sarah Youngblood on "A Prayer for My Daughter," 883–87; Richard P. Blackmur on "The Second Coming," 888–92 (reprinted from J2461); Robin Skelton on "Nineteen Hundred and Nineteen," 896–900; Reed Whittemore on "A Dialogue of Self and Soul," 903–6.

3219. WILLIAMS, RAYMOND: *Reading and Criticism.* London: Muller, 1950. x, 142 p.
   See pp. 53–55.

3220. °YEATS, W. B.: *Sailing to Byzantium (with Discussion).* Kent, Ohio: Kent State U, National Tape Repository, [19—].
   Two reels, #L79–80; listed in J516. No further details available.

See also J1112, 1114, 1161 (#7), 1548, 1676, 1813a, 1852, 1864, 1884a, 1925, 2001, 2070, 2086, 2154a, 2425 (review #2), 2439, 2456, 2475, 2490, 2506, 2551, 2567, 2605, 2644, 2678, 2745, 2753, 2828, 2863, 2948, 2961, 2970a, 2971a, 2972, 2978–80, 2982–84, 2986, 2989, 2991, 3080a, 3092, 3105, 3115, 3153, 3300, 3307, 4006, 4115, 4116, 5711, 5885.

"The Scholars"

3221. INGLIS, FRED: *An Essential Discipline: An Introduction to Literary Criticism.* London: Methuen, 1968. xiv, 272 p.
   See pp. 90–92: The poem is bad, both in style and content.

See also J3101.

"The Second Coming"

3222. BLOOM, EDWARD A.: "Yeats' 'Second Coming': An Experiment in Analysis," *UKCR*, 21:2 (Winter 1954), 103–10.
   See also Edward Alan Bloom, Charles H. Philbrick, and Elmer M. Blistein: *The Order of Poetry: An Introduction.* NY: Odyssey Press, 1961. xv, 172 p. (pp. 43–52).

3223. DAVY, CHARLES: "Yeats and the Desert Titan," *TLS*, 59:3053 (2 Sept 1960), 561.
   Correspondence by A. Norman Jeffares and Rupert and Helen Gleadow, :3055 (16 Sept 1960), 593.

3224. GIBBS, A. M.: "The Rough Beasts of Yeats and Shakespeare," *N&Q*, os
215 / ns 17:2 (Feb 1970), 48-49.
A source in *The Rape of Lucrece*.

3225. HORRELL, JOE: "Some Notes on Conversion in Poetry," *Southern R*, 7:1
(Summer 1941), 117-31.
Analyzes the meaning of "beast," pp. 123-26.

3226. JEROME, JUDSON: *The Poet and the Poem*. Cincinnati: Writer's Digest,
1963. 227 p.
"Six Senses of the Poet," 20-33; reprinted from *Colorado Q*, 10:3
(Winter 1962), 225-40; discusses this poem.
"Man Bites Dog," 137-43; on "Leda and the Swan": "What is going on
here? Just what the poem says--a girl is being raped by a bird. That,
surely, is bigger news than that of man biting dog."

3227. ————: *Poetry: Premeditated Art*. Boston: Houghton Mifflin, 1968.
xxxiv, 542 p.
Note on the meter of the poem, pp. 100-103.

3228. KLEINSTÜCK, JOHANNES: "W. B. Yeats: 'The Second Coming.' Eine Studie
zur Interpretation und Kritik," *Neueren Sprachen*, 10:7 (July 1961), 301-13.

3229. MAZZARO, JEROME L.: "Yeats' 'The Second Coming,'" *Explicator*, 16:1
(Oct 1957), #6.
The falcon as related to the sphinx.

3230. SAVAGE, D. S.: "Two Prophetic Poems," *Adelphi*, 22:1 (Oct-Dec 1945),
25-32.
On Yeats's poem and Wilfred Owen's "Strange Meeting." Contends that
Yeats foresaw the advent of fascism and became a victim of his own
prophecy in later life. Refers to Owen's exclusion from the *Oxford
Book of Modern Verse*.

3231. SPENDER, STEPHEN: *Life and the Poet*. London: Secker & Warburg, 1942.
128 p. (Searchlight Books. 18.)
Note on the poem, pp. 96-102, involving a comparison with the poetry
of T. S. Eliot and D. H. Lawrence.

3232. ————: "La crise des symboles," *France libre*, 7:39 (15 Jan 1944),
206-10.
English version published as "The Crisis of Symbols," *Penguin New
Writing*, #19 (1944), 129-35.

3233. STALLWORTHY, JON: "'The Second Coming,'" *Agenda*, 9:4-10:1 (Autumn-
Winter 1971/72), 24-33.
A second attempt to decipher the MS. versions (for the first attempt
see J2439), plus an interpretation.

3234. SUZUKI, HIROSHI: "Shelley's Influence on 'The Second Coming,'" *Yeats
Society of Japan Annual Bulletin and Report*, #5 (1970), 42-46.
Shelley's "Ozymandias" as a source.

3235. UNGER, LEONARD, and WILLIAM VAN O'CONNOR: *Poems for Study*. NY: Rinehart, 1953. xxi, 743 p.
See pp. 582-86.

3236. VAN DOREN, MARK: *Introduction to Poetry*. NY: Sloane, 1951. xxix,
568 p.
Interpretation of this poem, pp. 80-85; of "The Cat and the Moon,"
85-89; of "The Ballad of Father Gilligan," 130-33.

3236a. WALSH, JOHN HERBERT: *Presenting Poetry: An Account of the Discussion Method with Twenty-two Examples*. London: Heinemann, 1973. viii, 112 p.
   See pp. 107-11.

3237. WEEKS, DONALD: "Image and Idea in Yeats' 'The Second Coming,'" *PMLA*, 63:1 (Mar 1948), 281-92.
   Comments on the influence of Shelley and the relationship with *A Vision*.

See also J1136a, 1153, 1161 (#5), 1624, 1820, 2039, 2429, 2439, 2494, 2640, 2740a, 2757, 2836, 2846, 2863, 2890, 3206, 3210, 3218, 5697, 5940 (#1).

"The Secrets of the Old"

See J5601.

"September 1913"

3238. ANON.: "The Art Gallery," *Irish Times*, 55:17533 (8 Sept 1913), 6.
   Editorial on the poem that appears on p. 7 as "Romance in Ireland."
   See also Lady Gregory's letter, p. 7.

See also J5780, 6308.

"Shepherd and Goatherd"

See J1156.

"Solomon and the Witch"

See J1157.

"Solomon to Sheba"

See J2429.

"A Song"

See J5711.

"The Song of the Happy Shepherd"

3239. STEMMLER, THEO: "W. B. Yeats' 'Song of the Happy Shepherd' and Shelley's *Defence of Poetry*," *Neophilologus*, 47:3 (July 1963), 221-25.

3240. WITT, MARION: "Yeats's 'The Song of the Happy Shepherd,'" *PQ*, 32:1 (Jan 1953), 1-8.
   The early MS. version compared with the printed version.

See also J1069, 2147a, 4138.

"The Song of the Old Mother"

See J4195, 5640, 5668.

"The Song of Wandering Aengus"

3241. GOLDZUNG, VALERIE J.: "Yeats's Tradition and 'The Song of Wandering Aengus,'" *Massachusetts Studies in English*, 1:1 (Spring 1967), 8-16.
   "Tradition" is defined as the union of literature, philosophy, and a belief in nationality.

3242. HALL, ROBERT: "Aengus and Leda," *LIT*, #2 (1958), 42-46.
The union of God and man, not possible in "The Song of Wandering
Aengus," is achieved in "Leda and the Swan."

3243. MAZZARO, JEROME L.: "Apple Imagery in Yeats' 'The Song of Wandering
Aengus,'" *MLN*, 72:5 (May 1957), 342-43.

3244. ROSENBERG, BRUCE A.: "Irish Folklore and 'The Song of Wandering
Aengus,'" *PQ*, 46:4 (Oct 1967), 527-35.

See also J3080a, 3161, 4195, 5708.

"Sonnet" ("I saw a shepherd youth")

See J4, 129.

"The Sorrow of Love"

3245. ANON.: "A Literary Foundling," *Douglas Library Notes*, 11:3 (Summer
1962), 13-16.
The history of the first printing of the poem, which involved the
assistance of Bliss Carman and Louise Imogen Guiney.

3246. MONTEIRO, GEORGE: "Unrecorded Variants in Two Yeats Poems," *PBSA*,
60:3 (1966), 367-68.
In this poem and in "When You Are Old." See also J131 and 132.

3247. NÉMETH, ANDOR: "Az 'újraköltött' vers" [The "repoeticized" poem],
Nyugat, 28:1 (Jan 1935), 63-64.
Compares the early and late versions of the poem.

3248. STAMM, RUDOLF: *The Shaping Powers at Work: Fifteen Essays on Poetic
Transmutation*. Heidelberg: Winter, 1967. 320 p.
"'The Sorrow of Love': A Poem by William Butler Yeats Revised by Him-
self," 198-209; reprinted from *ES*, 29:3 (June 1948), 79-87.
"William Butler Yeats and 'The Ballad of Reading Gaol' by Oscar Wilde,"
210-19; translation of the article in J2103.

See also J2439, 4777.

"The Spur"

3249. HENDERSON, HANFORD: "Yeats' 'The Spur,'" *Explicator*, 15:6 (Mar 1957),
#41.

See also J2440.

"The Stare's Nest by My Window" (part 6 of "Meditations in Time of Civil
War")

See J3134, 3145.

"The Statues"

3250. URE, PETER: "'The Statues': A Note on the Meaning of Yeats's Poem,"
RES, 25:99 (July 1949), 254-57.

3251. ZION, MATTHEW WILLIAM: "Yeats's 'The Statues': A Study of Form and
Thought," Honors thesis, Harvard U, 1962. ii, 17 p.

See also J1082, 1136a, 1157, 1162 (#4), 1841, 2281a, 2282, 2427, 2429,
2440, 2723, 3024.

"The Stolen Child"

3252. CASWELL, ROBERT W.: "Yeats' 'The Stolen Child,'" *Explicator*, 25:8 (Apr 1967), #64.

3253. LAGAN, PATRICK: "Was Yeats Referring to Donegal or Sligo Rosses?" *Irish Press*, 32:114 (14 May 1962), 8.

"Supernatural Songs"

3254. °KOBAYASHI, MANJI: "A Study of 'Supernatural Songs' of William Butler Yeats," M.A. thesis, Columbia U, 1966. 142 p.

3255. LANE, CHESTER TRAVIS: "A Gap in the Wall: 'Supernatural Songs' of W. B. Yeats," Honors thesis, Harvard U, 1969. ii, 42 p.

3256. °RUBENSTEIN, JEROME S.: "Yeats's 'Supernatural Songs': A Commentary," M.A. thesis, Columbia U, 1954. 206 p.

3257. URE, PETER: "Yeats's 'Supernatural Songs,'" *RES*, 7:25 (Jan 1956), 38-51.
    Discusses the first four songs, "Ribh at the Tomb of Baile and Aillinn," "Ribh Denounces Patrick," "Ribh in Ecstasy," and "There."

See also J1073, 1118, 1813a, 2282, 2423a, 2747a, 2962, 3056, 3287.

"Sweet Dancer"

See J2819.

"Symbols"

See J3299.

"That the Night Come"

3258. DEAN, H. L.: "Yeats' 'That the Night Come,'" *Explicator*, 31:6 (Feb 1973), #44.
    The function of Maud Gonne in the poem.

See also J2066, 3303, 5697.

"There" (part 4 of "Supernatural Songs," q.v.)

See J3257.

"There Are Seven That Pull the Thread"

See J5638.

"These Are the Clouds"

See J2781.

"Those Dancing Days Are Gone"

See J5598, 5711.

"The Three Beggars"

See J1760, 3503.

"The Three Bushes"

3259. PARTRIDGE, EDWARD B.: "Yeats's 'The Three Bushes'--Genesis and Structure," *Accent*, 17:2 (Spring 1957), 67-80.

See also J2422, 2423a, 2427, 2440, 3002, 5722.

"The Three Hermits"

See J3503.

"Three Marching Songs"

See J3007.

"Three Songs to the One Burden"

See J2635.

"Three Things"

3259a. PERRINE, LAURENCE: "Yeats' 'Three Things,'" *Explicator*, 32:1 (Sept 1973), #4.

See also J5598.

"To ——." See "Remembrance"

"To a Child in the Wind"

See J5697.

"To a Poet Who Would Have Me Praise Certain Bad Poets [. . .]"

3260. POUND, EZRA: "Un inedito Poundiano: A un poeta che voleva indurmi a dir bene di certi cattive poeti, emuli suoi e miei," *Almanacco del Pesce d'oro*, [1] (1960), 16.
    Italian translation plus note.

See also J5808.

"To a Shade"

See J2494.

"To a Squirrel at Kyle-na-no"

See J5713.

"To a Wealthy Man Who Promised a Second Subscription [. . .]"

3261. ANON.: "A Pensioner on Paudeen," *Sinn Féin*, ns 3:155 (18 Jan 1913), 1.
    Attacks the poem ("this rhymed schoolboy's prose"). Correspondence by Padraic Colum, "Mistaken Identity," :156 (25 Jan 1913), 1; and editor's comment, *ibid*.

3262. [HONE, JOSEPH]: "Art and Aristocracy," *Irish Times*, 55:17328 (11 Jan 1913), 6.
    See also p. 7 of the same issue. Correspondence by "Val d'Arno," :17329 (13 Jan 1913), 6; "Paudeen," *ibid*.; William M. Murphy, :17334 (18 Jan 1913), 8.

"To a Young Beauty"

3263. PERRINE, LAURENCE: "Yeats and Landor: 'To a Young Beauty,'" *N&Q*,
os 217 / ns 19:9 (Sept 1972), 330.
   A source in Landor's *Imaginary Conversations*.

"To an Isle in the Water"

See J5607, 5620, 5679, 5713, 5716.

"To His Heart, Bidding It Have No Fear"

3264. WITT, MARION: "Yeats' 'To His Heart, Bidding It Have No Fear,'"
Explicator, 9:5 (Mar 1951), #32.

See also J5663.

"To Ireland in the Coming Times"

See J2221, 2714.

"Towards Break of Day"

3265. KEITH, W. J.: "Yeats's Double Dream," *MLN*, 76:8 (Dec 1961), 710-15.

See also J1157, 3290.

"The Tower"

3266. °BICKAL, ROBERT RICHY: "'The Tower' of William Butler Yeats," M.A.
thesis, Columbia U, 1951.

3267. °CHATTERJI, B.: "'The Tower,'" *Bulletin of the Department of English,
U of Calcutta*, 1:2 (1960).

3268. SETURAMAN, V. S.: "'The Tower' by Yeats," *Mother India*, 17:10&11
(5 Dec 1965), 97-100.

3269. YOUNGBLOOD, SARAH: "A Reading of 'The Tower,'" *TCL*, 5:2 (July 1959),
74-84.

See also J1073, 1758, 2414, 2438, 4006.

"The Travail of Passion"

See J5697.

"The Two Kings"

3270. °MACKIMMIE, M. S.: "A Study of Yeats's 'The Two Kings,'" M.A. thesis,
U of Connecticut, 1951. 45 p.

See also J1760a.

"Two Songs from a Play"

3271. BRILLI, ATTILIO: "Dioniso, Cristo e il 'Fascio degli anni' in Yeats,"
Studi urbinati di storia, filosofia e letteratura, ns B / 43:2 (1969),
269-76.

3272. BROWER, REUBEN ARTHUR: *The Fields of Light: An Experiment in Critical
Reading*. NY: Oxford UP, 1951. xii, 218 p.
   See pp. 83-88.

3273. [POGER, SIDNEY]: "A Note on Yeats' 'Two Songs from a Play,'" *Éire-Ireland*, 6:1 (Spring 1971), 143-44.
The crow is traditionally associated with Apollo, the god of poetry.

3274. RAYAN, KRISHNA: *Suggestion and Statement in Poetry*. London: Athlone Press, 1972. ix, 182 p.
See pp. 91-93.

3275. URE, PETER: "Yeats and the Prophecy of Eunapius," *N&Q*, os 199 / ns 1:8 (Aug 1954), 358-59.
Neo-Platonic sources.

See also J2000, 2745, 2866, 3016, 3882-84 and note, 3885-87 and note, 4006.

"Two Songs of a Fool"

3276. JEFFARES, A. NORMAN: "'Two Songs of a Fool' and Their Explanation," *ES*, 26:6 (Dec 1945), 169-71.
Biographical explanation.

See also J3000.

"The Two Titans"

See J2080a, 3813.

"The Two Trees"

3277. MORTENSEN, ROBERT: "Yeats's *Vision* and 'The Two Trees,'" *Studies in Bibliography*, 17 (1964), 220-22.
Yeats revised the poem "with *A Vision* in mind."

3278. NILSEN, HELGE NORMANN: "'The Two Trees' by William Butler Yeats: The Symbolism of the Poem and Its Relation to Northrop Frye's Theory of Apocalyptic and Demonic Imagery," *Orbis Litterarum*, 24:1 (1969), 72-76.

See also J1157, 2429, 2490, 2936.

"Under Ben Bulben"

3279. COFFEY, BRIAN: "A Note on Rat Island," *University R* [Dublin], 3:8 [1966?], 25-28.
Actually a note on the word "trade" in this poem and its implications for the writing of poetry, including some remarks on "The Lake Isle of Innisfree."

3280. COMPRONE, JOSEPH J.: "Unity of Being and W. B. Yeats' 'Under Ben Bulben,'" *Ball State U Forum*, 11:3 (Summer 1970), 41-49.

3281. CRONE, G. R.: "Horseman, Pass By," *N&Q*, os 214 / ns 16:7 (July 1969), 256-57.
The epitaph may derive from vignettes on the *Mappa mundi* in Hereford Cathedral.

See also J1069, 1168b, 1706, 2147a, 2440, 2745, 5844, 5888, 6085.

"Under the Round Tower"

See J1760a, 3304.

"Upon a Dying Lady"

3282. FREEMAN, JOHN: "Decadence," *Root and Branch*, 2:3 (Mar 1918), 55-58.
Criticizes section 2 as "decadent" and "rigidly conventional."

3283. J.: "Yeats's 'Upon a Dying Lady,'" *Little R*, 4:5 (Sept 1917), 30-31.

See also J2423a.

"Vacillation"

See J1073, 1369, 1818, 1825a, 2049, 2423a, 2490.

The Wanderings of Oisin

3284. ALSPACH, RUSSELL K.: "Some Sources of Yeats's *The Wanderings of Oisin*," *PMLA*, 58:3 (Sept 1943), 849-66.
Michael Comyn's "The Lay of Oisin on the Land of Youth," other Ossianic material, Charles Kickham's *Knocknagow*, Sir Samuel Ferguson, and others.

3285. COSMAN, MADELEINE PELNER: "Mannered Passion: W. B. Yeats and the Ossianic Myths," *WHR*, 14:2 (Spring 1960), 163-71.
Purports to be a source study, but does not quote a single source as evidence. Besides that, rather weak on facts.

3286. FASS, BARBARA FRANCES: "La Belle Dame sans Merci and the Aesthetics of Romanticism," °Ph.D. thesis, New York U, 1969. 412 p. (*DA*, 31:3 [Sept 1970], 1226A.)
This has now been published under the same title (Detroit: Wayne State UP, 1974. 312 p.). See "Artist and Philistine," 224-46, a discussion of the influence of Keats and Swinburne on the poem.

See also J1069, 1076, 1143, 1729, 1755, 1813a, 1851, 2208a, 2237, 2414, 2756, 2759, 2856, 3890.

"What Magic Drum" (part 7 of "Supernatural Songs," q.v.)

3287. SMITH, DENIS E., and F. A. C. WILSON: "The Source of Yeats's 'What Magic Drum?'" *PLL*, 9:2 (Spring 1973), 197-201.
Bhagwan Shri Hamsa's *The Holy Mountain*.

"What Then"

3288. SKELTON, ROBIN: "The First Printing of W. B. Yeats's 'What Then?'" *Irish Book*, 2:3/4 (Autumn 1963), 129-30.
Includes some variants not recorded in the *Variorum Edition*.

See also J2635.

"The Wheel"

3289. SALERNO, NICHOLAS A.: "A Note on Yeats and Leonardo da Vinci," *TCL*, 5:4 (Jan 1960), 197-98.
The poem echoes a passage from Leonardo's notebooks.

3290. SAUL, GEORGE BRANDON: "Yeatsian Brevities," *N&Q*, os 199 / ns 1:12 (Dec 1954), 535-36.
A note on this poem and on "Towards Break of Day."

See also J1157.

"When You Are Old"

3291. BERGGREN, KERSTIN: Note on the poem in Swedish, *Studiekamraten*, 48:8 (1966), 150.

3292. BLUMENTHAL, MARIE LUISE: "Über zwei Gedichte von Ronsard und von W. B. Yeats," *Neuphilologische Zeitschrift*, 3:1 (1951), 11-15.
A comparison with Ronsard's "Quand vous serez bien vieille."

3293. CALLAN, NORMAN: *Poetry in Practice*. London: Drummond, 1938. xii, 189 p.
The poems of Yeats and Ronsard, pp. 174-76.

3294. JEUNE, SIMON: *Littérature générale et littérature comparée: Essai d'orientation*. Paris: Minard, 1968. 147 p. (Situation. 17.)
"Yeats, imitateur de Ronsard," 111-18.

3295. MACKEY, WILLIAM F.: "Yeats's Debt to Ronsard on a *Carpe Diem* Theme," *Comparative Literature Studies*, 5:19 (1946), 4-7.

3296. MACMANUS, FRANCIS: "Adventures of a Sonnet," *Irish Monthly*, 69:812 (Feb 1941), 85-90.
Yeats and Ronsard.

3297. MINTON, ARTHUR: "Yeats' 'When You Are Old,'" *Explicator*, 5:7 (May 1947), #49.
See also Marion Witt, 6:1 (Oct 1947), #6; and Elisabeth Schneider, :7 (May 1948), #50.

3298. SNOW, WILBERT: "A Yeats-Longfellow Parallel," *MLN*, 74:4 (Apr 1959), 302-3.
Yeats's poem and Longfellow's *Outre-Mer*.

See also J3246, 5608, 5611, 5694, 5695, 5883.

"Whence Had They Come" (part 8 of "Supernatural Songs," q.v.)
See J3056.

"Where My Books Go"
See J5617.

"The White Birds"

3299. DAICHES, DAVID: *The Place of Meaning in Poetry*. Edinburgh: Oliver & Boyd, 1935. v, 80 p.
Notes on the symbolism of this poem and of "Symbols," pp. 42-44.

"Who Goes with Fergus?"

3300. BRYSON, LYMAN, and others (eds): *Symbols and Society*. NY: Cooper Square, 1964 [1955]. xi, 611 p. (Symposium of the Conference on Science, Philosophy, and Religion. 14.)
William Y. Tindall: "The Literary Symbol," 337-67; contains a note on this poem, pp. 364-65.
William F. Lynch: "The Evocative Symbol," 427-52; contains a note on "Sailing to Byzantium," pp. 431-32.

3301. EMPSON, WILLIAM: *Seven Types of Ambiguity*. Harmondsworth: Penguin Books, 1965 [1930]. xiv, 256 p. (Peregrine Book. Y2.)
Note on the poem, pp. 187-91. See criticism by Andrew Rutherford, "Yeats' 'Who Goes with Fergus?'" *Explicator*, 13:7 (May 1955), #41.

"The Wild Old Wicked Man"

3302. GARDNER, C. O.: "An Analysis of Yeats's 'Wild Old Wicked Man,'"
Critical Survey, 2:2 (Summer 1965), 104-8.

See also J2427.

"The Wild Swans at Coole"

3303. BROOKS, CLEANTH, JOHN THIBAUT PURSER, and ROBERT PENN WARREN (eds):
*An Approach to Literature: A Collection of Prose and Verse with Analyses
and Discussions*. Alternate 4th edition. NY: Appleton-Century-Crofts, 1967
[1935]. xvii, 888 p.
Note on this poem, pp. 311-12; on "That the Night Come," 317-19; on
"A Prayer for My Daughter," 359-63.

3304. C., R. J.: "Yeats' 'The Wild Swans at Coole,'" *Explicator*, 2:4 (Jan
1944), Q20.
Asks for Yeats's pronunciation of rhyme words in this poem and in
"Under the Round Tower." Answer by T. O. Mabbott, 3:1 (Oct 1944), #5;
by Marion Witt, :2 (Nov 1944), #17.

3305. CASWELL, ROBERT W.: "Yeats's Odd Swan at Coole," *Éire-Ireland*, 4:2
(Summer 1969), 81-86.
There is a discrepancy between the 59 swans at the beginning of the
poem and the pairs of swans at the end. The odd swan is related to the
solitary poet on the shore.

3305a. CROFT, P. J. (ed): *Autograph Poetry in the English Language*. London:
Cassell, 1973. 2 v.
See J128e for details.

3306. DESAI, RUPIN W.: "Yeats's Swans and Andersen's Ugly Duckling," *Colby
Library Q*, 9:6 (June 1971), 330-35.

3307. GÖLLER, KARL HEINZ (ed): *Die englische Lyrik: Von der Renaissance
bis zur Gegenwart*. Düsseldorf: Bagel, 1968. 2 v.
Gisela and Gerhard Hoffmann: "William Butler Yeats: 'The Wild Swans at
Coole,'" 2:299-308.
Gisela Hoffmann: "William Butler Yeats: 'Sailing to Byzantium,'" 2:
309-20.

3308. HAHN, SISTER M. NORMA: "Yeats' 'The Wild Swans at Coole': Meaning
and Structure," *CE*, 22:6 (Mar 1961), 419-21.

3309. *National Poetry Festival Held in the Library of Congress October 22-
24, 1962: Proceedings*. Washington, D.C.: Library of Congress, General
Reference and Bibliography Division, 1964. ii, 367 p.
Léonie Adams: "The Problem of Form," 275-80; refers to this poem,
pp. 278-80.

3310. SHANLEY, J. LINDON: "Thoreau's Geese and Yeats's Swans," *American
Literature*, 30:3 (Nov 1958), 361-64.
The poem echoes the "Spring" chapter in *Walden*.

3311. SHAPIRO, KARL: "Prosody as the Meaning," *Poetry*, 73:6 (Mar 1949),
336-51.
Note on this poem, pp. 340-41.

3312. VOGEL, JOSEPH F.: "Yeats's 'Nine-and-Fifty' Swans," *ELN*, 5:4 (June
1968), 297-300.
The probable source for this unusual number is "Thomas Rymer."

See also J675, 1073, 1141, 2438, 2955.

"The Withering of the Boughs"

See J1911, 5709.

"A Woman Homer Sung"

3313. JEFFARES, A. NORMAN: "A Source for 'A Woman Homer Sung,'" *N&Q*, 195:5 (4 May 1950), 104.
　　In Shelley's *Hellas*.

"A Woman Young and Old"

3314. ALLEN, JAMES L.: "Yeats' 'Her Vision in the Wood,'" *Explicator*, 18:8 (May 1960), #45.

3315. FARREN, ROBERT: *Towards an Appreciation of Poetry*. Dublin: Metropolitan Publishing Co., 1947. 76 p.
　　Note on "Meeting," pp. 54-55.

3316. JUMPER, WILL C.: "Form *versus* Structure in a Poem of W. B. Yeats," *Iowa English Yearbook*, 7 (Fall 1962), 41-44.
　　On "From the *Antigone*."

See also J1156, 2423a, 2439, 3134, 3207.

"Words"

See J1073.

EA Books and Pamphlets Exclusively on Yeats

3317. BECKER, ARTHUR WILLIAM JOHN: "Yeats as a Playwright," D.Phil. thesis, Oxford U, 1953. viii, 538 p.
A detailed analysis of Yeats's dramatic theories and of the individual plays. The chapter on *The Player Queen* has been published separately (see J3839).

3318. BLOCH, DONALD ALAN: "The Reciprocal Relationship between W. B. Yeats's Plays and His Poems," Ph.D. thesis, Harvard U, 1970. i, 280 p.
Discusses *Deirdre*, *The Player Queen*, and *The King of the Great Clock Tower*, including their MS. versions, and the poems written at the same time.

3319. BRUCK, RUTH: "The Development of William Butler Yeats as a Dramatist," M.A. thesis, McGill U, 1956. iii, 220 p.

3320. BÜLOW, ISOLDE VON: *Der Tanz im Drama: Untersuchungen zu W. B. Yeats' dramatischer Theorie und Praxis.* Bonn: Bouvier, 1969. x, 205 p. (Studien zur englischen Literatur. 1.)
Originally a Dr. phil. thesis, U of Hamburg, 1968. Generally on Yeats's dramatic theories as well as on the theory and practice of the dance in his plays. Includes a discussion of the influence of the Nō. Besides numerous small inaccuracies, the thesis suffers from the author's lack of acquaintance with actual productions.
Reviews:
1. Gerhard Hoffmann, *Anglia*, 90:1/2 (1972), 266-70.
2. H[orst] O[ppel], *Neueren Sprachen*, 19:8 (Aug 1970), 421.

3321. BURGHARD, LORRAINE HALL: "The Snake and the Eagle: Modern Criticism and the Drama of W. B. Yeats. A Historical and Analytical Study of Modern Theory and a Dramatic Form," Ph.D. thesis, U of Chicago, 1968. ii, 366 p.

3322. BUSHRUI, SUHEIL BADI: *Yeats's Verse Plays: The Revisions, 1900-1910.* Oxford: Clarendon Press, 1965. xv, 240 p.
Based on °"Adam's Curse: A Study of Yeats's Revisions of His Verse Plays, 1900-1910," Ph.D. thesis, U of Southampton, 1962. Discusses *The Shadowy Waters*, *On Baile's Strand*, *The King's Threshold*, *Deirdre*, and *The Green Helmet*.
Reviews:
1. Anon., "Yeats's Variations," *TLS*, 66:3393 (9 Mar 1967), 187.
2. Curtis Bradford, "A Yeats Gathering," *MLQ*, 28:1 (Mar 1967), 96-101.
3. Denis Donoghue, "Between the Lines," *Guardian*, #37234 (25 Mar 1966), 8.
4. T. R. Henn, "New Angle on Yeats," *Irish Times*, #34260 (16 Oct 1965), 8.
5. K. P. S. Jochum, *Anglia*, 84:3/4 (1966), 494-97.
6. Peter Elvet Lewis, *DUJ*, os 58 / ns 27:3 (June 1966), 167-68.
7. Sean Lucy, "Yeatsiana: A Voice for the Stage," *Irish Independent*, 75:49 (26 Feb 1966), 10.
8. Thomas MacIntyre, "Joyce for the Multitude," *Irish Press*, 35:204 (6 Nov 1965), 6.
9. Donald T. Torchiana, "Three Books on Yeats," *PQ*, 46:4 (Oct 1967), 536-56.
10. Marion Witt, *MP*, 64:4 (May 1967), 377-79.

3323. °CHURCH, WILLIAM CHARLES: "The Evolution of the Drama of William Butler Yeats," M.A. thesis, Columbia U, 1950.

3324. *CLARK, DAVID RIDGLEY: *W. B. Yeats and the Theatre of Desolate Reality.* Dublin: Dolmen Press, 1965. 125 p.

Incorporates: "W. B. Yeats's *Deirdre*: The Rigour of Logic," *Dublin Mag*, 33:1 (Jan-Mar 1958), 13-21; "Yeats and the Modern Theatre," *Threshold*, 4:2 (Autumn-Winter 1960), 35-56; "W. B. Yeats and the Drama of Vision," *Arizona Q*, 20:2 (Summer 1964), 127-41; "*Nishikigi* and Yeats's *The Dreaming of the Bones*," *MD*, 7:2 (Sept 1964), 111-25. Besides the two plays mentioned, the book also discusses *The Words upon the Window-Pane* and *Purgatory*.

The book is an abridgment of "The Theatre of Desolate Reality: W. B. Yeats's Development as a Dramatist," Ph.D. thesis, Yale U, 1955. ii, 279 p., which is also concerned with *The Countess Cathleen*, all the plays from *Four Plays for Dancers* to *The Words upon the Window-Pane*, and *The Death of Cuchulain*.

Reviews:
1. Anon., "The Tragedy of Trust," *TLS*, 64:3305 (1 July 1965), 552.
2. Eavan Boland, *Dublin Mag*, 4:1 (Spring 1965), 71-72.
3. [John Jordan], "Yeats and the Theatre," *Hibernia*, 29:3 (Mar 1965), 27.
4. Thomas Kilroy, *Studies*, 55:220 (Winter 1966), 441-43.
5. Vivian Mercier, *MD*, 7:3 (Dec 1964), 357-58.
6. Hermann Peschmann, *English*, 16:92 (Summer 1966), 67-69.
7. John Unterecker, "Yeats as Dramatist," *MassR*, 6:2 (Winter-Spring 1965), 433-34.

3325. COARD, EDNA AGNES: "William Butler Yeats and the Theatre," M.A. thesis, U of Illinois, 1940. iv, 116 p.

3325a. DORN, KAREN: "Play, Set and Performance in the Theatre of W. B. Yeats," Ph.D. thesis, U of Cambridge, 1973. vi, 212 p. (Illustrated)

Discusses *Deirdre*, the collaboration with Craig, the influence of the Nō, performances of *The Player Queen*, *The Resurrection*, *King Oedipus*, and *Oedipus at Colonus*, and the dance in the last dance plays.

3326. EREMINA, I. K.: *Dramaturgiĭa U. B. Eĭtsa (Dramy ob Irlandii).* Avtoreferat dissertatsii na soiskanie uchenoĭ stepeni kandidata filologicheskikh nauk. Moskva: Moskovskiĭ oblastnoĭ pedagogicheskiĭ institut imeni N. K. Krupskoĭ, 1970. ii, 25 p.

A dissertation abstract; I have not seen the thesis itself.

3327. FLANNERY, JAMES WILLIAM: "W. B. Yeats and the Idea of a Theatre (The Early Abbey Theatre in Theory and Practice)," Ph.D. thesis, Trinity College, Dublin, 1970. xi, 572 p. (Illustrated)

Quotes from MS. letters to and from Yeats and to and from other figures in the dramatic revival, as well as from unpublished material in the Holloway notebooks and press cuttings. Includes chapters on the Fays and Miss Horniman. Valuable.

3328. HAERDTER, MICHAEL: "William Butler Yeats--Das theatralische Werk," Dr. phil. thesis, U of Wien, 1964. xiv, 443 p.

Explores the connections between Yeats the poet-dramatist and Yeats the man of the theater.

3329. HARRISON, DOROTHY GULBENKIAN: "W. B. Yeats's Plays: The Ritual of a Lost Faith," °Ph.D. thesis, State U of New York at Albany, 1971. 250 p. (*DA*, 32:4 [Oct 1971], 2091A.)

3330. °HEINEMAN, HARRY: "The Poetic Drama of William Butler Yeats and His Theory of Tragedy," M.A. thesis, Columbia U, 1950.

3331. JOCHUM, KLAUS PETER: *Die dramatische Struktur der Spiele von W. B. Yeats.* Frankfurt/Main: Athenäum, 1971. vii, 260 p. (Frankfurter Beiträge zur Anglistik und Amerikanistik. 2.)
   Originally a Dr. phil. thesis, U of Frankfurt, 1968. Contains an English summary, pp. 255-56; reprinted in *English and American Studies in German*, 1971, #67. A play-by-play analysis, including a chapter on the influence of the Nō.
   Reviews:
   1. Rudolf Halbritter, *Anglia*, 90:4 (1972), 548-50.
   2. R. Krohn, *Wissenschaftlicher Literaturanzeiger*, 11:4 (Sept 1972), 125.
   3. Klaus Peter Steiger, *Neueren Sprachen*, 22:10 (Oct 1973), 557-59.

3332. JONES, DAVID R.: "W. B. Yeats: The Poet in the Theatre," Ph.D. thesis, Princeton U, 1968. viii, 275 p. (*DA*, 29:12 [June 1969], 4489A-90A.)

3332a. KEYES, EVELYN CAMPBELL VINCENT: "A Theatre for Ideals: Yeats's Stagecraft in Context from *The Countess Kathleen* (1892) to *Cathleen ni Houlihan* (1902)," °Ph.D. thesis, U of Texas at Austin, 1972. 260 p. (*DA*, 33:7 [Jan 1973], 3651A.)
   Discusses *The Countess Cathleen*, *The Land of Heart's Desire*, *The Shadowy Waters*, *Cathleen ni Houlihan*, and *Diarmuid and Grania*.

3333. °KRICH, HELEN: "The Poet in the Theatre: A Study of W. B. Yeats as a Dramatist and Man of the Theatre," M.A. thesis, New York U, 1945. i, 134 p.

3334. °MCMAHON, DERMOT D.: "The Development of Yeats as a Dramatist," M.A. thesis, University College, Dublin, 1964.

3335. *MOORE, JOHN REES: *Masks of Love and Death: Yeats as Dramatist.* Ithaca: Cornell UP, 1971. xiv, 362 p.
   Based on "Evolution of Myth in the Plays of W. B. Yeats," Ph.D. thesis, Columbia U, 1957. viii, 252 p. (*DA*, 17:7 [July 1957], 1556-57). Incorporates: "Cold Passion: A Study of *The Herne's Egg*," *MD*, 7:3 (Dec 1964), 287-98; "The Janus Face: Yeats's *The Player Queen*," *Sewanee R*, 76:4 (Oct-Dec 1968), 608-30.
   Three introductory chapters on the concept of the mask, the characteristics of Yeats's drama, and the Cuchulain myth; followed by play-by-play analyses.
   Reviews:
   1. Anon., "Yeats's Attempts at Poetic Drama," *TLS*, 70:3626 (27 Aug 1971), 1020.
   2. Anon., *Yale R*, 61:1 (Autumn 1971), xii, xiv.
   3. Anthony Cronin, "Yeats Seminar," *Irish Press*, 41:151 (26 June 1971), 12.
   4. George M. Harper, *ELN*, 9:4 (June 1972), 316-17.
   5. D. E. S. Maxwell, *Dalhousie R*, 51:2 (Summer 1971), 290-91.
   6. Andrew Parkin, *MD*, 15:2 (Sept 1972), 211-12.
   7. Hilary Pyle, *RES*, 23:90 (May 1972), 249-50.
   8. August W. Staub, *QJS*, 58:4 (Dec 1972), 480-81.
   9. Stanley Weintraub, *BA*, 46:2 (Spring 1972), 307-8.

3336. *NATHAN, LEONARD EDWARD: *The Tragic Drama of William Butler Yeats: Figures in a Dance.* NY: Columbia UP, 1965. xii, 307 p.

Based on °"W. B. Yeats' Development as a Tragic Dramatist, 1884-1939,"
Ph.D. thesis, U of California (Berkeley), 1961. iii, 471 p. Discusses
almost all of Yeats's plays, especially *At the Hawk's Well*, *The Coun-
tess Cathleen* (first version), *The Death of Cuchulain*, *Deirdre*, *The
Dreaming of the Bones*, *The Island of Statues*, *The Land of Heart's
Desire*, *On Baile's Strand*, *The Only Jealousy of Emer*, *Purgatory*, *The
Resurrection*, *The Shadowy Waters*, *The Unicorn from the Stars*, *Where
There Is Nothing*, and *The Words upon the Window-Pane*. Also on the
influence of the Nō.
Reviews:
1. Anon., "Yeats as Dramatist," *TLS*, 64:3326 (25 Nov 1965), 1071.
2. Anne Dedio, *Anglia*, 85:3/4 (1967), 509-10.
3. D. J. Gordon, *MLR*, 63:3 (July 1968), 693-94.
4. T. R. Henn, *RES*, 17:68 (Nov 1966), 444-47.
5. Brian John, "Hurt into Poetry," *J of General Education*, 18:4 (Jan
   1967), 299-306.
6. Giorgio Melchiori, *N&Q*, os 211 / ns 13:11 (Nov 1966), 430-31.
7. M. K. Naik, *Indian J of English Studies*, 7 (1966), 125-28.
8. B. Rajan, "Conflict, More Conflict!" *UTQ*, 35:3 (Apr 1966), 315-20.
9. Ann Saddlemyer, *QQ*, 73:2 (Summer 1966), 296-97.

3337. °NOWELL, A. E.: "Yeats as a Poet Dramatist," M.A. thesis, U of North
Carolina, 1939.

3338. °O'GRADY, ANNE FRANCES: "Yeats's Ancestral Theatre," M.A. thesis, U
of Alberta, 1967.

3339. PARKIN, T. L.: "The Importance of Yeats's Drama," Ph.D. thesis, U of
Bristol, 1969. ix, 638 p.
    Discusses the following plays: *The King's Threshold*, *The Shadowy
Waters*, *On Baile's Strand*, *The Green Helmet*, *Deirdre*, *At the Hawk's
Well*, *The Only Jealousy of Emer*, *The Dreaming of the Bones*, *Calvary*,
A Full Moon in March, *Purgatory*, *The Death of Cuchulain*; also the
influence of the Nō. Especially interested in the possibilities of
staging the plays.

3340. SCHMITT, NATALIE SUE CROHN: "The Ritual of a Lost Faith: The Drama
of William Butler Yeats," Ph.D. thesis, Stanford U, 1968. iv, 473 p. (*DA*,
29:7 [Jan 1969], 2281A.)

3340a. SCHNEIDER, JOSEPH LEONDAR: "W. B. Yeats and the Theatre of Intellectual Reformation," Ph.D. thesis, Duke U, 1972. x, 266 p. (*DA*, 33:11
[May 1973], 6374A.)

3341. SIEGEL, SANDRA F.: "The Play of the Mind: The Theater of W. B.
Yeats," Ph.D. thesis, U of Chicago, 1968. iv, 115 p.

3342. °SOLEM, JANE R.: "Yeats as a Playwright: The Fascination of What's
Difficult," M.A. thesis, U of Miami, 1967.

3343. STRABEL, AUDREY LEE ELISE: "Yeats' Development of a Symbolic Drama,"
Ph.D. thesis, U of Wisconsin, 1953. vi, 409 p.

3344. TOMLINSON, ALAN: "Visual and Verbal Design in the Plays of W. B.
Yeats," M.Phil. thesis, U of London, 1969. 218 p.

3345. *URE, PETER: *Yeats the Playwright: A Commentary on Character and
Design in the Major Plays*. London: Routledge & Kegan Paul, 1963. vii,
182 p.
    Incorporates: "Yeats's Christian Mystery Plays," *RES*, 11:42 (May
1960), 171-82; "Yeats's Hero-Fool in *The Herne's Egg*," *HLQ*, 24:2

(Feb 1961), 125-36; "Yeats's *Deirdre*," *ES*, 42:4 (Aug 1961), 218-30; "The Evolution of Yeats's *The Countess Cathleen*," *MLR*, 57:1 (Jan 1962), 12-24.

The pioneer study. Discusses under various aspects (revisions and rewriting, dramatic theory and practice, irony, myth, realism) most of the plays with the following exceptions: the early uncollected attempts, *The Land of Heart's Desire*, *Cathleen ni Houlihan*, *The Hour Glass*, *The Pot of Broth*, *The Shadowy Waters*, *The Cat and the Moon*, and the Sophocles adaptations.
Reviews:
1. Anon., "Dramatic Treatment," *TLS*, 62:3179 (1 Feb 1963), 78.
2. Denis Donoghue, "Countries of the Mind," *Guardian*, #36241 (11 Jan 1963), 5.
3. Padraic Fallon, "Yeats and the Stage," *Irish Times*, #33466 (26 Jan 1963), 8.
4. G. S. Fraser, *Listener*, 69:1781 (16 May 1963), 843.
5. René Fréchet, *EA*, 18:4 (Oct-Dec 1965), 425-26.
6. Donna Gerstenberger, *MD*, 6:4 (Feb 1964), 463-64.
7. Keith Harrison, "Delicate Raddle," *Spectator*, 210:7026 (22 Feb 1963), 237.
8. Robert Hethmon, *ETJ*, 16:4 (Dec 1964), 381-82.
9. K. P. S. Jochum, *Neueren Sprachen*, 14:6 (June 1965), 297-99.
10. Rolf Lass, *Kilkenny Mag*, #10 (Autumn-Winter 1963), 103-6.
11. Patrick Murray, "Yeats on Stage," *Irish Press*, 39:207 (30 Aug 1969), 10.
12. Richard M. Ohmann, *Wisconsin Studies in Contemporary Literature*, 5:3 (Autumn 1964), 276-77.
13. V. de S. Pinto, *CQ*, 6:2 (Summer 1964), 186-87.
14. J. V. Ramamrutham, *Literary Half-Yearly*, 5:1 (Jan 1964), 78-80.
15. Jon Stallworthy, *RES*, 15:58 (May 1964), 215-17.
16. Rudolf Stamm, *ES*, 50:2 (Apr 1969), 218-21.
17. Sarah Youngblood, *Drama Survey*, 3:2 (Oct 1963), 319-20.

3346. °VAN DYKE, JOHN MARKHAM: "The Imagination of Yeats: A Study of Its Development through the Plays," English Honors paper, Yale U, 1964. 159 p.

3347. °WHITE, HELEN: "A Study of W. B. Yeats as a Dramatist, with Special Reference to His Treatment of Ideas Formulated in *A Vision*," M.A. thesis, U of Leeds, 1957.

3348. WIEDNER, ELSIE MARGARET: "The Use of the Theatre for the Presentation of Metaphysical Ideas: A Comparative Study of W. B. Yeats and Paul Claudel," Ph.D. thesis, Radcliffe College, 1961. iv, 301 p.
Describes Yeats's theater as one of "epiphany" and concentrates on the following plays: *The Countess Cathleen*, *The Shadowy Waters*, *At the Hawk's Well*, *The Cat and the Moon*, *The Player Queen*, *The Resurrection*, *The Herne's Egg*, *Purgatory*, and *The Death of Cuchulain*. Concludes that the theater of Yeats and Claudel remained "unique" and exerted no influence on later playwrights.

See also J9, 361, 552, 1117, 1146, 4161.

EB   Articles and Parts of Books

3349. AAS, L.: "William Butler Yeats og hans verker dramatikeren: Yeats og det irske teater," *Ord och bild*, 36:8 (Aug 1927), 461-68.
Discusses only the pre-1910 plays.

3350. ANNIAH GOWDA, H. H.: *The Revival of English Poetic Drama (In the Edwardian & Georgian Periods).* [Bangalore: Government Press], 1963. xvii, 322 p.
Based on °"English Verse Drama from 1890-1935," M.Litt. thesis, U of Durham, 1959. "The Influence of the Noh on Verse Drama," 221-55 (on Yeats, 225-36); "Yeats's Verse Plays," 283-309.

3350a. ————: *Dramatic Poetry from Mediaeval to Modern Times: A Philosophic Enquiry into the Nature of Poetic Drama in England, Ireland and the United States of America.* Madras: Macmillan, 1972. xiv, 406 p.
On Synge, O'Casey, and Yeats, pp. 272-93; on Yeats also *passim* (see index).

3351. ANON.: "Mr. Yeat's [*sic*] Irish Plays Charmingly Acted at the Carnegie Lyceum, New York," *Gael*, 22:7 (July 1903), 237-38.

3352. ANON.: Note on Yeats's plays, particularly on *Cathleen ni Houlihan, Theatre*, 3:29 (July 1903), 158-59.

3353. ANON.: "Ideas into Drama," *TLS*, 59:3051 (19 Aug 1960), 529.
The problematic relationship between ideas and dramatic effectiveness in Yeats's plays.

3354. AUGHTRY, CHARLES EDWARD (ed): *Landmarks in Modern Drama from Ibsen to Ionesco.* Boston: Houghton Mifflin, 1963. ix, 726 p.
"William Butler Yeats (1865-1939)," 386-89; a note on Yeats's place in the tradition of verse drama and on *On Baile's Strand*.

3355. BACKER, FRANZ DE: "William Butler Yeats," *Vandaag*, 1:1 (15 Feb 1929), [8-10].
A survey of the dramatic work.

3356. BEERS, HENRY A.: "The English Drama of To-day," *NAR*, 180:582 (May 1905), 746-57.
Contains a note on Yeats, especially on *The Land of Heart's Desire*, pp. 753-55.

3357. BENNETT, JAMES O'DONNELL: "Mr. Yeats as Missionary," *Chicago Record-Herald*, 23:225 (27 Jan 1904), 6.
Saw some performances of Yeats's plays (unspecified) and liked them, but was annoyed by Yeats's introductory speeches: "Mr. Yeats is the type of propagandist which [*sic*], possessing tremendous zeal in a good cause, seems determined to go the hardest way about forwarding that cause. Why not work from within and with the theater as it exists to-day rather than against it and aloof from it?"

3358. BENTLEY, ERIC: *The Playwright as Thinker: A Study of Drama in Modern Times.* NY: Reynal & Hitchcock, 1946. x, 382 p.
The English edition was published as *The Modern Theatre: A Study of Dramatists and the Drama.* London: Hale, 1950. xxv, 290 p. Yeats, *passim* (see index), especially pp. 222-26 (English edition, pp. 159-61); he was a "dramatist manqué," because the wrong kind of people sat in his theater.

3359. ————: *In Search of Theater.* NY: Knopf, 1953. xxiii, 411, ix p.
"Yeats's Plays," 315-26; reprinted from *Kenyon R*, 10:2 (Spring 1948), 196-208; also in J1090.
"Heroic Wantonness," 327-41; reprint of "Irish Theatre: Splendeurs et Misères," *Poetry*, 79:4 (Jan 1952), 216-32; a review of Peter Kavanagh's *The Story of the Abbey Theatre* (J6724).

3360. BERNARD, JEAN JACQUES, and others: *Le théâtre anglais d'hier et d'aujourd'hui*. Avec des textes de Wycherley, W.-B. Yeats [. . .]. Paris: Pavois, 1945. 228 p. (Théâtre. 2.)

"William-Butler Yeats," 136-42; largely translated excerpts from *The Pot of Broth* and *The Land of Heart's Desire*.

3361. BLAU, HERBERT: "Windlasses and Assays of Bias," *Encore*, 9:5 (Sept-Oct 1962), 24-40.

See pp. 33-35.

3362. BLOCK, HASKELL MAYER, and ROBERT GORDON SHEDD (eds): *Masters of Modern Drama*. With introductions and notes. NY: Random House, 1962. xii, 1199 p.

"William Butler Yeats (1865-1939)," 427-28; an introduction to Yeats's plays and to *At the Hawk's Well*.

3363. BOGARD, TRAVIS, and WILLIAM I. OLIVER (eds): *Modern Drama: Essays in Criticism*. NY: Oxford UP, 1965. vi, 393 p. (Galaxy Books. 138.)

Thomas Parkinson: "The Later Plays of W. B. Yeats," 385-93. Stresses the influence of the Nō and emphasizes the theatricality of the plays, but does not go very deep into the possibilities of an actual performance.

3364. BOYD, ERNEST A.: "Making the Drama Safe from Democracy," *Irish Commonwealth*, 1:2 (Apr 1919), 66-72.

Deplores Yeats's withdrawal from the popular theater: "Does he think that, in so doing, he escapes the duty which his genius owes to the contemporary theatre?"

3365. BRADBROOK, MURIEL CLARA: *English Dramatic Form: A History of Its Development*. London: Chatto & Windus, 1965. 205 p.

"Yeats and the Revival," 123-42. The revival of imagination in Yeats's plays.

3366. BROWNE, ELLIOTT MARTIN: *Verse in the Modern English Theatre*. The W. D. Thomas Memorial Lecture delivered at the University College at Swansea on 28 February, 1963. Cardiff: U of Wales Press, 1963. 32 p.

Note on Yeats's plays, particularly *Purgatory*, pp. 31-32.

3367. BULLOUGH, GEOFFREY: "Poetry in Modern English Drama," *Cairo Studies in English*, 1959, 26-42.

See pp. 26-28.

3368. BURTON, ERNEST JAMES: *A Student's Guide to British Theatre and Drama*. London: Jenkins, 1963. 191 p.

On the Irish theater, pp. 150-51; on Yeats's plays, 155-56.

3369. CHAMBERS, E. K.: "The Experiments of Mr. Yeats," *Academy*, 64:1618 (9 May 1903), 465-66.

Especially on *Cathleen ni Houlihan*, Yeats's dramatic theories, and his Speaking-to-the-Psaltery experiments.

3370. CHATURVEDI, B. N.: *English Poetic Drama of the Twentieth Century*. Gwalior: Kitab Ghar, 1967. x, 115 p.

"Revival of Poetic Drama and the Plays of W. B. Yeats," 7-30.

3371. CHESTERTON, GILBERT KEITH: *G. F. Watts*. London: Duckworth, 1906 [1904]. viii, 174 p.

"In Mr. Yeats' plays there is only one character: the hero who rules and kills all the others, and his name is Atmosphere" (see pp. 28-29).

3372. CHIARI, JOSEPH. *Landmarks of Contemporary Drama*. London: Jenkins, 1965. 223 p.
See pp. 83-85 and *passim* (see index).

3373. CLARKE, AUSTIN: "W. B. Yeats and Verse Drama," *Threshold*, #19 (Autumn 1965), 14-29.
This is a disappointing article, especially because it starts so well. Clarke argues that poetry today is largely a silent art and that this curtails the possibilities of a successful verse drama. He does not, however, pursue his argument in his discussion of Yeats's plays and does not show whether or why their poetry can be spoken and communicated.

3374. COLDWELL, JOAN: "Experiments in Form in Modern Symbolist Drama," M.A. thesis, U of London, 1960. 247 p.
"Yeats and the Theatre of Beauty," 219-31.

3375. COLUM, PADRAIC: "Poet's Progress: W. B. Yeats in the Theatre," *TAM*, 19:12 (Dec 1935), 936-43.
Reprinted in Rosamond Gilder and others (eds): *Theatre Arts Anthology: A Record and a Prophecy*. NY: Theatre Arts Books, [1950]. xvi, 687 p., pp. 143-51. A somewhat longer version of the article appeared as "A Poet's Progress in the Theatre," *Dublin Mag*, 11:2 (Apr-June 1936), 10-23.

3376. CORRIGAN, ROBERT WILLOUGHBY (ed): *The Modern Theatre*. NY: Macmillan, 1964. xxii, 1287 p.
See pp. 877-78.

3377. CRAIG, EDWARD GORDON: *The Theatre—Advancing*. Boston: Little, Brown, 1920 [i.e., 1919]. vii, 298 p.
"The Poet and Motion Pictures," 266-68: "His plays as they were at first are as well fitted for the modern stage as are Shakespeare's plays—that is to say, not at all."

3378. DALGARD, OLAV: *Teatret i det 20. hundreåret*. Oslo: Norske Samlaget, 1955. 308 p. (Teatret. 2.)
On Yeats, pp. 39-41 and *passim* (see index).

3379. DASGUPTA, PRANABENDU: "The 'Subjective' Tradition: A Comparative Analysis of the Dramatic Motives in the Plays of W. B. Yeats and Rabindranath Tagore," Ph.D. thesis, U of Minnesota, 1963. ii, 65 p. (*DA*, 27:12 [June 1967], 4245A.)

3380. DIETRICH, MARGARET: *Das moderne Drama: Strömungen, Gestalten, Motive*. Stuttgart: Kröner, 1963 [1961]. 714 p. (Kröner Taschenausgabe. 220.)
Contains some notes on Yeats's plays (see index). Unreliable.

3381. DOBRÉE, BONAMY: "Poetic Drama in England Today," *Southern R*, 4:3 (Winter 1938/39), 581-99.
Dismisses Yeats's plays as not being "solidly in the theatre."

3382. DONOGHUE, DENIS: *The Third Voice: Modern British and American Verse Drama*. Princeton: Princeton UP, 1959. vi, 286 p.
"Yeats and the Clean Outline," 32-61; reprinted from *Sewanee R*, 65:2 (Apr-June 1957), 202-25. Yeats's development as a verse dramatist, especially in *The Shadowy Waters*, *The Hour Glass*, *At the Hawk's Well*, and *A Full Moon in March*. Also *passim* (see index).

3383. DRIVER, TOM FAW: *Romantic Quest and Modern Query: A History of the Modern Theatre*. NY: Delacorte Press, 1970. xviii, 493 p.

On Yeats, *passim* (see index), especially pp. 131-36. Disappointing, because Yeats's plays are not related to the problem reflected in the book's title, and somewhat uninformed.

3384. EDWARDS, HILTON: *The Mantle of Harlequin.* Dublin: Progress House, 1958. xvi, 127 p.
On Yeats's plays, the Abbey, and the Gate Theatre, pp. 1-6. Photographs of Gate productions of *The King of the Great Clock Tower* and *The Countess Cathleen* between pp. 16 and 17, 80 and 81.

3385. EREMINA, I. K.: "Ranni͡ai͡a dramaturgii͡a Uil'i͡ama Batlera Ĭĭtsa" [The early drama of WBY], *Moskovskiĭ oblastnoĭ pedagogicheskiĭ institut imeni N. K. Krupskoĭ: Uchenye zapiski*, 175:10 (1967), 113-27.

3386. FARAG, F. F.: "Masrah Yaits: Thawrah 'ala wa-Waqi'iah" [Anti-realism in the theater of WBY], *Hiwar*, 2:2 (Jan-Feb 1964), 72-81.

3387. ————: "The Unpopular Theatre of W. B. Yeats," *Cairo Studies in English*, 1963/66, 97-108.
Particularly on *The Shadowy Waters, The Unicorn from the Stars*, and the influence of the Nō.

3388. FECHTER, PAUL: *Das europäische Drama: Geist und Kultur im Spiegel des Theaters.* Mannheim: Bibliographisches Institut, 1956-58. 3 v.
A survey of Yeats's plays, 2:169-79. Numerous names and dates are wrong.

3389. FEICHTNER, WALTER: "Das Wiederaufleben des englischen Versdramas im zwanzigsten Jahrhundert," Dr. phil. thesis, U of Wien, 1951. ii, 133 p.
On Yeats's theory of verse drama, pp. 16-18; on his plays, 33-37.

3390. FLANNERY, JAMES W.: "The Abbey Theatre: Dublin, Summer 1970," *ETJ*, 22:4 (Dec 1970), 414-15.
The public may yet come around and see the importance and quality of Yeats's plays.

3391. FOX, R. M.: "Yeats and Social Drama," *Irish Writing*, #9 (Oct 1949), 62-67.
Yeats's dislike of social drama was a mistake. There is enough social life in Ireland to provide subject matter for drama.

3392. FRICKER, ROBERT: *Das historische Drama in England von der Romantik bis zur Gegenwart.* Bern: Francke, 1940. vi, 363 p. (Schweizer anglistische Arbeiten / Swiss Studies in English. [8].)
See pp. 287-95, 312-15.

3393. ————: *Das moderne englische Drama.* Göttingen: Vandenhoeck & Ruprecht, 1964. 181 p. (Kleine Vandenhoeck-Reihe. 172. 173. 174.)
"William Butler Yeats," 32-45; "Synge, O'Casey und Johnston," 45-68.

3394. GAD, CARL: *Omkring kulturkrisen: Strejftog i moderne litteratur.* København: Schultz, 1929. 203 p.
"W. B. Yeats og den keltiske renaissance," 71-86. For an extended version see J6431.

3395. GAMBERINI, SPARTACO: "Il teatro di William Butler Yeats: L'Abbey Théâtre, Ezra Pound e i nô, le ultimo opere," *Rivista di studi teatrali*, 1:11-12 (July-Dec 1954), 47-89.

3396. GASKELL, RONALD: *Drama and Reality: The European Theatre since Ibsen.* London: Routledge & Kegan Paul, 1972. x, 171 p.
Notes on Yeats's plays, *passim* (see index).

3397. GASSNER, JOHN: *The Theatre in Our Times: A Survey of the Men, Materials and Movements in the Modern Theatre.* NY: Crown, 1963 [1954]. xiii, 609 p.
"Yeats: The Limits of Drama," 226-33; "John Millington Synge: Synthesis in Folk Drama," 217-24; "The Prodigality of Sean O'Casey," 240-48; "The Dublin Gate Theatre," 387-90.

3398. ————: *Directions in Modern Theatre and Drama.* An expanded version of *Form and Idea in Modern Theatre.* NY: Holt, Rinehart & Winston, 1965 [1956]. xvi, 457 p.
Scattered notes on Yeats's plays, especially *A Full Moon in March* (see index).

3399. ————, and RALPH GILMORE ALLEN (eds): *Theatre and Drama in the Making.* Boston: Houghton Mifflin, 1964. 2 v.
Scattered references to Yeats, *passim*, especially 2:784-86.

3400. GERSTENBERGER, DONNA LORINE: *The Complex Configuration: Modern Verse Drama.* Salzburg: Institut für Englische Sprache und Literatur, Universität Salzburg, 1973. vi, 178 p. (Salzburg Studies in English Literature. Poetic Drama. 5.)
Based on "Formal Experiments in Modern Verse Drama," Ph.D. thesis, U of Oklahoma, 1958. v, 195 p. (*DA*, 19:7 [Jan 1959], 1757-58). "W. B. Yeats: 'Everything Sublunary Must Change,'" 10-40; especially on *The Shadowy Waters, At the Hawk's Well, Calvary,* and *Purgatory.*

3401. GIROUX, ROGER: "William Butler Yeats (1865-1939)," *Cahiers de la Compagnie Madeleine Renaud—Jean-Louis Barrault,* #37 (1962), 69-70.

3402. GOSSE, EDMUND: "The Revival of Poetic Drama," *Atlantic Monthly,* 90: 538 (Aug 1902), 156-66.
Contains a note on Yeats, who "obtains new effects by plunging deeper than the dramatist has hitherto been expected to plunge into the agitations and exigencies of the soul." Unlike Stephen Phillips, however, he "separates himself from the common observation of mankind."

3403. GUERRERO ZAMORA, JUAN: *Historia de teatro contemporáneo.* Barcelona: Flors, 1961. 4 v.
"William Butler Yeats," 2:243-55.

3404. GWYNN, STEPHEN: "Poetry and the Stage," *Fortnightly R,* os 91 / ns 85:506 (Feb 1909), 337-51.
Reprinted in *Living Age,* 261:3378 (3 Apr 1909), 3-14.

3405. HAERDTER, MICHAEL: "William Butler Yeats--Irisches Theater zwischen Symbolismus und Expressionismus," *Maske und Kothurn,* 11:1 (1965), 30-42.
Mainly on *Deirdre, The Words upon the Window-Pane* and the influence of the Nō.

3406. HEISELER, HENRY VON: *Sämtliche Werke.* Heidelberg: Schneider, 1965. 799 p.
Note on Yeats's plays and his own translations of them, pp. 211-13.

3407. HOUGHTON, NORRIS: *The Exploding Stage: An Introduction to Twentieth Century Drama.* NY: Weybright & Talley, 1971. xv, 269 p.
On Yeats ("a sort of *fin-de-siècle* hippie"), pp. 110-12 and *passim* (see index).

3408. IREMONGER, VALENTIN: "Yeats as a Playwright," *Irish Writing,* #31 (Summer 1955), 51-56.

Yeats never had any interest in the theater "as we know it. . . . All his plays are, in fact, poems--or what poems also are, meditations-- but, within his self-imposed limits, they are highly dramatic."

3409. JAMESON, STORM: *Modern Drama in Europe.* London: Collins, 1920. xxvi, 280 p.

Yeats "represents the last state in symbolic imbecility"; his worst play is *The Land of Heart's Desire.* Yeats is defended by B[rinsley] M[acNamara], "Books and Their Writers," *Gael* [Dublin], 1:3 (14 Nov 1921), 18-19.

3410. JANKOVIĆ, MIRA: "Engleska poetska drama dvadesetog stoljeća" [English poetic drama of the 20th century], *Umjetnost riječi,* 1:2 (1957), 143- 55.

On Yeats, pp. 146-47, 153-54.

3411. KHAN, B. A.: *The English Poetic Drama.* Aligarh: Muslim U, 1962. xiv, 79 p. (Faculty of Arts Publication Series. 8.)

See pp. 28-32.

3412. KNIGHT, GEORGE WILSON: *The Golden Labyrinth: A Study of British Drama.* London: Phoenix House, 1962. xiv, 402 p.

On Martyn, Synge, and Yeats, pp. 322-28; on Yeats, *passim* (see index).

3413. KREYMBORG, ALFRED (ed): *Poetic Drama: An Anthology of Plays in Verse from the Ancient Greek to the Modern American.* NY: Modern Age Books, 1941. viii, 855 p.

On Yeats, pp. 33-34; on *The King's Threshold,* pp. 726-27.

3414. LENSON, DAVID ROLLAR: "Examples of Modern Tragedy," °Ph.D. thesis, Princeton U, 1971. 244 p. (*DA,* 32:11 [May 1972], 6433A-34A.)

Includes a discussion of some Yeats plays.

3415. °LOUGHLIN, MARIE THERESE: "Poetic Drama," M.A. thesis, U of Western Ontario, 1926. 87 p.

I do not know whether this thesis contains relevant material.

3416. LUCAS, FRANK LAURENCE: *The Drama of Chekhov, Synge, Yeats, and Pirandello.* London: Cassell, 1963. xii, 452 p.

"John Millington Synge," 147-237. "William Butler Yeats," 239-355, contains the following subsections: Introduction, Life and Personality, The Magician, Ideas (on *A Vision*), and a somewhat superficial discussion of most of the plays.

3417. MCBRIEN, PETER: "Dramatic Ideals of To-day," *Studies,* 11:42 (June 1922), 235-42.

"Mr. Yeats's drama is not great art, for great art is always humanly alive."

3417a. *McGraw-Hill Encyclopedia of World Drama.* NY: McGraw-Hill, 1972. 4 v.

See 4:439-45.

3418. MCGREEVY, THOMAS: "Mr. W. B. Yeats as a Dramatist," *Revue anglo- américaine,* 7:1 (Oct 1929), 19-36.

3419. MCHUGH, ROGER: "The Plays of W. B. Yeats," *Threshold,* #19 (Autumn 1965), 3-13.

3420. MACKAY, CONSTANCE D'ARCY: *The Little Theatre in the United States.* NY: Holt, 1917. viii, 277 p.

Lists Yeats's plays performed by American little theaters (see index).

3421. MCLEOD, STUART RAMSAY: *Modern Verse Drama*. Salzburg: Institut für
Englische Sprache und Literatur, Universität Salzburg, 1972. iv, 345 p.
(Salzburg Studies in English Literature. Poetic Drama. 2.)
Based on "Problems of Poetry and Dramaturgy in Modern Verse Drama,"
Ph.D. thesis, U of Florida, 1961. iv, 364 p. (*DA*, 29:3 [Sept 1968],
904A.) On Yeats, *passim*; concentrates on *The Herne's Egg*, *The Dreaming
of the Bones*, and *A Full Moon in March*.

3422. MACNEICE, LOUIS: "Some Notes on Mr. Yeats' Plays," *New Verse*, #18
(Dec 1935), 7-9.

3423. MADELIN, []: "William Butler Yeats," *Oeuvre*, époque 3 / fasc 70 /
#2 (Feb 1924), 50-53.

3424. MANDELBAUM, ALLEN: "Stasis and Dynamis: Two Modes of the Literary
Imagination," Ph.D. thesis, Columbia U, [1951]. v, 276 p. (*DA*, 12:4
[1952], 426.)
Note on Yeats as a "static dramatist," pp. 203-9.

3425. MATTHEWS, BACHE: *A History of the Birmingham Repertory Theatre*.
London: Chatto & Windus, 1924. xv, 250 p.
Some references to Yeats (see index). The appendices give the dates
of performances of Yeats plays by the Pilgrim Players and the Birmingham Repertory Theatre.

3426. MEACHAEN, PATRICK: "Two Irish Dramatists," *Library Assistant*, 20:
341 (June 1927), 123-34.
Yeats and O'Casey. Singles out *The Countess Cathleen*, *The Land of
Heart's Desire*, and *Cathleen ni Houlihan* as Yeats's best plays. "The
remainder . . . are in reality beautiful dramatic poems."

3427. MERCIER, VIVIAN: "In Defense of Yeats as a Dramatist," *MD*, 8:2
(Sept 1965), 161-66.
Mainly on *The Player Queen*, *Purgatory*, and *The Resurrection*.

3428. MERRILL, JOHN, and MARTHA FLEMING: *Play-Making and Plays: The
Dramatic Impulse and Its Educative Use in the Elementary and Secondary
School*. NY: Macmillan, 1930. xix, 579 p.
Contains synopses of several Yeats plays, pp. 541-42.

3428a. MOONEY, DONAL: "W. B. Yeats: No Dramatist He," *Hibernia*, 37:13 (24
Aug 1973), 19.
Refers to a London-based "Yeats Repertory Theatre Company" directed
by Niema Ash.

3429. MOORE, JOHN REES: "Cuchulain, Christ, and the Queen of Love: Aspects
of Yeatsian Drama," *TDR*, 6:3 (Mar 1962), 150-59.

3429a. NÜNNING, JOSEFA (ed): *Das englische Drama*. Darmstadt: Wissenschaft-
liche Buchgesellschaft, 1973. xiv, 538 p.
Paul Goetsch: "Yeats und Synge," 492-97; mainly on *The Dreaming of the
Bones*, *Purgatory*, and *Riders to the Sea*.

3430. OBERG, ARTHUR KENNETH: "Contemporary Verse and Poetic Drama," Ph.D.
thesis, Harvard U, 1965. iii, 303 p.
"Yeats as Poetic Dramatist," 158-218.

3431. O'CONNOR, FRANK, STEPHEN SPENDER, and EDITH EVANS: "Verse and Prose
in Drama: A Discussion," *Listener*, 25:631 (13 Feb 1941), 239-40.
Yeats is mentioned *passim*.

3432. O'CONNOR, FRANK: *The Art of the Theatre*. Dublin: Fridberg, 1947. 50 p.
　　See pp. 24-26.

3433. Ó h-É[igeartaigh] [O'HEGARTY], P. S.: "W. B. Yeats, Dramatist?" *Inis Fáil*, #30 (Mar 1907), 4-5.
　　"Mr. Yeats' genius is essentially lyrical, not dramatic."

3434. O'MALLEY, MARY: "The Dream Itself," *Threshold*, #19 (Autumn 1965), 58-63.
　　The Yeats productions of the Lyric Players Theatre, Belfast.

3435. PEACOCK, RONALD: *The Poet in the Theatre*. NY: Hill & Wang, 1960 [1946]. xiii, 198 p. (Dramabook. D23.)
　　"Synge," 105-16. "Yeats," 117-28 (one of the ablest defenses of Yeats the dramatist).

3436. ————: *The Art of Drama*. London: Routledge & Kegan Paul, 1960 [1957]. vi, 263 p.
　　Some scattered notes (see index).

3437. PELLIZZI, CAMILLO: *Il teatro inglese*. Milano: Treves, 1934. v, 434 p. (Il teatro del novecento. 3.)
　　See pp. 234-42. English edition: *English Drama: The Last Great Phase*, translated by Rowan Williams. London: Macmillan, 1935. ix, 306 p. (pp. 176-83).

3438. PHYTHYAN, BRIAN ARTHUR: "T. S. Eliot and the Contemporary Revival of Poetic Drama in England," M.A. thesis, U of Manchester, 1954. v, 323 p.
　　"W. B. Yeats," 219-50. Concentrates on *At the Hawk's Well* and connects Yeats's achievement with Eliot's later efforts.

3439. POEL, WILLIAM: "Poetry in Drama," *Contemporary R*, 104:575 (Nov 1913), 699-707.
　　Yeats's plays are too theoretical in nature.

3440. POPKIN, HENRY: "Yeats as Dramatist," *TDR*, 3:3 (Mar 1959), 73-82.

3441. PRIOR, MOODY ERASMUS: *The Language of Tragedy*. Bloomington: Indiana UP, 1966 [1947]. xi, 430 p. (Midland Book. MB86.)
　　The second edition incorporates "Poetic Drama: An Analysis and a Suggestion," *EIE*, 1949, 3-32. On Yeats's dramatic theory and practice (especially *Calvary* and *Purgatory*), pp. 326-40, and *passim* (see index).

3442. R.: "William Butler Yeats," *Dramma*, 22:10 (1 Apr 1946), 46-47.

3443. R., B., and E.: "Some Plays of W. B. Yeats," *Festival Theatre R*, 5:86 (28 Nov 1931), 1-3.

3444. REXROTH, KENNETH: *Bird in the Bush: Obvious Essays*. NY: New Directions, 1959. x, 246 p.
　　"The Plays of Yeats," 235-41.

3445. ROBINSON, MARION EVANGELINE: "Verse and Prose in Modern British Drama: A Study of the Literary Forms Developed by Four Representative British Playwrights--Shaw, Synge, Yeats and T. S. Eliot," M.A. thesis, U of Manchester, 1958. ii, 316 p.
　　"W. B. Yeats," 160-228.

3446. ROLL-HANSEN, DIDERIK: "W. B. Yeats som dramatiker," *Edda*, yr 52 / 65:3 (1965), 153-64.
　　Yeats's reaction to the plays of Ibsen and Shaw.

3447. ROOK, JEAN KATHLEEN: "The Impact of T. S. Eliot on the English Drama of His Time: A Study of the Years 1919-1955," M.A. thesis, U of London, 1956. viii, 462 p.
On Yeats's plays, pp. 32-39; not, however, in relation to Eliot's.

3448. ROY, EMIL: *British Drama since Shaw*. With a preface by Harry T. Moore. Carbondale: Southern Illinois UP, 1972. xv, 143 p.
On Yeats, *passim* (see index), particularly pp. 36-53 (concentrates on *The Player Queen*, *The Words upon the Window-Pane*, and *Purgatory*). Also on Synge (54-67) and O'Casey (68-82).

3449. RUBERTI, GUIDO: *Storia del teatro contemporaneo*. 2nd edition. Bologna: Cappelli, 1928 [1920-21]. 3 v.
"B. W. Yeats [*sic*]," 3:895-96.

3450. SANDBERG, ANNA: "The Anti-Theater of W. B. Yeats," *MD*, 4:2 (Sept 1961), 131-37.
Mainly on *At the Hawk's Well*. Uninformed.

3451. SARCAR, SUBHAS:•"Modern Poetic Drama," *Bulletin of the Department of English, U of Calcutta*, 4:3&4 (1963), 38-48.
"Yeats's greatest contribution to modern drama was that by upholding the urgency of passion and its articulation in beautiful words he paved the way for poetic drama."

3452. SCHILLER, SISTER MARY BEATRICE: "Trends in Modern Poetic Drama in English, 1900-1938," Ph.D. thesis, U of Illinois, 1939. xii, 416 p.
On Yeats's plays, pp. 102-10, 267-74, and *passim* (see index).

3453. °SENA, VINOD: "W. B. Yeats and English Poetic Drama," *English Miscellany* [Delhi], #2 (1963), 23-36.

3454. SHARP, WILLIAM L.: "W. B. Yeats: A Poet Not in the Theatre," *TDR*, 4:2 (Dec 1959), 67-82.
The plays (especially *At the Hawk's Well* and *Calvary*) fail, because they lack "individual speech."

3455. SNIDER, PEARL L.: "The Contributions of John Millington Synge and William Butler Yeats to the Irish Drama," M.A. thesis, U of Manitoba, 1923. i, 91 p.

3456. SPENDER, STEPHEN: "The Poetic Drama Today," *Listener*, 15:368 (30 Jan 1936), 224-26.
Yeats "has been defeated by blank verse."

3457. STAMM, RUDOLF: *Zwischen Vision und Wirklichkeit: Zehn Essays* [. . .]. Bern: Francke, 1964. 204 p.
"William Butler Yeats als Theaterdichter," 140-62; reprint of "William Butler Yeats und das Theater," *Neue Zürcher Zeitung*, 184:128 (11 May 1963), 22rv; :129 (12 May 1963), 4rv. Discusses *The Land of Heart's Desire*, *Deirdre*, and *Purgatory* as specimens of highly successful drama.

3458. STAUB, AUGUST W.: "The 'Unpopular Theatre' of W. B. Yeats," *QJS*, 47:4 (Dec 1961), 363-71.
Yeats's dramas fail because he had the wrong models: Maeterlinck, Gordon Craig, and the Nō.

3459. STORER, EDWARD: "Dramatists of To-day. VIII.—W. B. Yeats," *British R*, 5:3 (Mar 1914), 415-22.
Reprinted in *Living Age*, 281:3644 (9 May 1914), 329-32.

3460. THOULESS, PRISCILLA: *Modern Poetic Drama*. Oxford: Blackwell, 1934. vii, 204 p.
"W. B. Yeats," 136-62.

3461. TOMLINSON, ALAN: "W. B. Yeats the Playwright," *Gambit*, 4:15 (1970), 98-101.
Yeats's plays now get the attention they deserve; it is hoped that this will lead to more performances.

3462. TOWNSHEND, GEORGE: "Yeats' Dramatic Poems," *Drama*, [2]:5 (Feb 1912), 192-208.
"Aesthetic idealism" is the most powerful motive behind the plays, particularly *The Countess Cathleen*, *The Shadowy Waters*, *The Land of Heart's Desire*, and *Where There Is Nothing*.

3463. TUNBERG, JACQUELINE DUFFIÉ: "British and American Verse Drama, 1900-1965: A Survey of Style, Subject Matter, and Technique," Ph.D. thesis, U of Southern California, 1965. vi, 657 p. (*DA*, 26:4 [Oct 1965], 2226-27.)
"William Butler Yeats," 133-77.

3464. ULANOV, BARRY (ed): *Makers of the Modern Theater*. NY: McGraw-Hill, 1961. viii, 743 p.
"William Butler Yeats, 1865-1939," 213-15; includes comments on *On Baile's Strand* and *Purgatory*.

3465. UNTERECKER, JOHN: "The Shaping Force in Yeats's Plays," *MD*, 7:3 (Dec 1964), 345-56.
It would appear from this rather rambling essay that "action" is the shaping force, but no satisfactory definition of the term is provided. Mostly on *Purgatory*.

3466. URE, PETER: "The Hero on the World Tree: Yeats's Plays," *English*, 15:89 (Summer 1965), 169-72.
The reputation and reception of Yeats's plays.

3467. VÖLKER, KLAUS: *Irisches Theater I: William Butler Yeats, John Millington Synge*. Velber: Friedrich, 1967. 109 p. (Friedrichs Dramatiker des Welttheaters. 29.)
Totally inadequate.

3468. WARNER, FRANCIS (ed): *Studies in the Arts: Proceedings of the St. Peter's College Literary Society*. Oxford: Blackwell, 1968. viii, 180 p.
T. R. Henn: "Yeats and the Theatre," 62-81.

3469. WEST, WILLIAM CHANNING: "Concepts of Reality in the Poetic Drama of W. B. Yeats, W. H. Auden, and T. S. Eliot," Ph.D. thesis, Stanford U, 1964. iv, 244 p. (*DA*, 25:10 [Apr 1965], 6120-21.)
"William Butler Yeats," 8-81; on Yeats's dramatic theories, *Where There Is Nothing*, *The Unicorn from the Stars*, *The Hour Glass*, *The Player Queen*, and *Purgatory*.

3470. WHITEHEAD, J. V. ELIZABETH: "Twentieth Century Poetic Drama in English," M.A. thesis, McGill U, 1941. ii, 152 p.
"The Contribution of W. B. Yeats," 37-55.

3471. WILDE, PERCIVAL: *The Craftsmanship of the One-Act Play*. Boston: Little, Brown, 1923. xiv, 396 p.
Scattered notes (see index), particularly on *Cathleen ni Houlihan* (p. 65).

3472. WORTH, KATHARINE J.: "Yeats and the French Drama," *MD*, 8:4 (Feb 1966), 382-91.
Yeats as a precursor of Samuel Beckett.

3473. Z[ABEL], M. D.: "Poetry for the Theatre," *Poetry*, 45:3 (Dec 1934), 152-56.
Contains a few notes on Yeats's plays.

See also J360, 514, 563, 780, 1068 (#6, 9), 1076, 1078, 1089, 1112, 1140, 1269, 1344, 1385, 1438, 1634, 1732, 1758, 1875, 1894, 1926, 1929, 1944-46, 1984, 2017, 2063, 2067, 2071, 2107, 2110, 2122, 2131, 2139, 2152, 2175, 2176, 2202a, 2268, 2281, 2295, 2416, 2431, 2495, 2512, 2518, 2533, 2536, 2599, 2602, 2665, 2691, 2741, 2815, 4032, 4208, 4211, 4215, 4254, 4394, 4407-15 and note, 4416-17 and note, 4446-47, 4466-71, 4529-31 and note, 4598-99 and note, 4600-609, 4805-34 and note, 4835-44 and note, 4922-23, 4956-75 and note, 5068-88, 5473, 5483, 5484-87, 5489, 5548, 5573, 5578, 5911, 5933, 5940 (#3), 5944, 6028, 6046, 6095, 6165, 6191, 6219, 6294, 6301, 6302, 6306-8, 6315, 6316, 6320, 6322-24, 6327, 6328, 6330, 6333, 6336, 6352, 6353, 6364, 6366, 6369, 6371, 6375, 6380, 6384, 6385, 6392, 6393, 6409, 6410, 6417, 6431, 6435, 6438, 6441, 6443, 6444, 6450, 6451, 6453, 6466, 6469, 6471, 6474, 6476, 6479, 6495, 6499, 6502, 6505, 6508, 6514-16, 6524, 6527, 6530, 6531, 6534, 6549a, 6550, 6555, 6556, 6559, 6560, 6568, 6570, 6572, 6574, 6583, 6638, 6659, 6690, 6703, 6704, 6710, 6756, 6759, 6769, 6782, 6805, 6813, 6823, 6852, 6859-61, 6940, 6942, 7140, 7185, 7311, 7385, 7416, 7456.

EC   Themes and Types

The omission of cross-references to this section is explained in the introductory remarks to section CC.

Art and Artists

3474. MCCORMICK, JANE L.: "Drive That Man Away: The Theme of the Artist in Society in Celtic Drama, 1890-1950," *Susquehanna U Studies*, 8:3 (June 1969), 213-29.
In the plays of Yeats (*The Countess Cathleen*, *The King's Threshold*, *The Words upon the Window-Pane*), Synge, O'Casey, and Vernon Watkins (hence "Celtic"?).

3475. SUBOCZEWSKI, IRENE: "The Figure of the Artist in Modern Drama from Ibsen to Pirandello," °Ph.D. thesis, U of Maryland, 1970. 322 p. (*DA*, 31:11 [May 1971], 6074A.)
Includes a discussion of some Yeats plays.

Chance and Choice

3476. VOGT, KATHLEEN MARILYN: "Chance and Choice in the Drama of W. B. Yeats," °Ph.D. thesis, U of Massachusetts, 1970. 190 p. (*DA*, 31:5 [Nov 1970], 2406A.)

Chorus

3477. WENNEKER, JEROME SIDNEY: "The Chorus in Contemporary Drama," D.F.A. thesis, Yale U, 1961. iii, 439 p.
See pp. 244-49.

Cuchulain

3478. COHN, RUBY: Review of a performance of *Cuchulain*, *ETJ*, 21:2 (May 1969), 227.
A conflation of *At the Hawk's Well*, *On Baile's Strand*, *The Only Jealousy of Emer*, and *The Death of Cuchulain*, this was performed at the Little Theater, Stanford University, March 1969.

3479. COLTRANE, ROBERT: "From Legend to Literature: W. B. Yeats and the Cuchulain Cycle," *Lock Haven R*, 12 (1971), 24-46.

3479a. COURNOT, MICHEL: "Le cycle de Cuchulain," *Monde*, 30:8994 (15 Dec 1973), 31.
Review of a performance of four Cuchulain plays by the Théâtre oblique d'Henri Ronse. See also Robert Kanters, *Express*, #1172 (24-30 Dec 1973), 5.

3480. EDINBURGH FESTIVAL: IRISH FESTIVAL PLAYERS: *Cuchulain by W. B. Yeats*. [Edinburgh, 1958. 7 p.]
Programme of a performance of the five Cuchulain plays in the chrono-logical order of Cuchulain's life. Programme note by Meryl Gourley, pp. [6-7].

3481. FARRELLY, JAMES P.: "Cuchulain: Yeats' 'Mental Traveller,'" *Husson R*, 4:1 (Dec 1970), 32-41.
Analyzes *At the Hawk's Well*, *The Only Jealousy of Emer*, and *The Death of Cuchulain* as related to *A Vision*.

3481a. °GREENE, C. M.: "The Cuchulain Legend in the Plays of W. B. Yeats," M.A. thesis, U of Liverpool, 1970/71.

3482. KENNELLY, BRENDAN: "The Heroic Ideal in Yeats's Cuchulain Plays," *Hermathena*, #101 (Autumn 1965), 13-21.

3483. °KRAVETSKY, NAOMI ZENA: "The Significance of Defeat in W. B. Yeats's Cuchulain Plays," M.A. thesis, U of Manitoba, 1970.

3484. LINKE, HANSJÜRGEN: "Das Los des Menschen in den Cuchulain-Dramen: Zum 100. Geburtstag von W. B. Yeats," *Neueren Sprachen*, 14:6 (June 1965), 253-68.

3485. RUSSELL, BRENDA LEE: "The Influence of the Saga Tradition on the Irish Drama: 1900-1920," °Ph.D. thesis, U of Oregon, 1971. 248 p. (*DA*, 32:6 [Dec 1971], 3328A-29A.)
On Yeats's Cuchulain plays, AE, Synge, Lady Gregory, and Martyn.

3486. SKENE, REGINALD ROBERT: *The Cuchulain Plays by W. B. Yeats: A Study*. London: Macmillan, 1974. xiii, 278 p.
Based on °"The Unity in the Cuchulain Cycle of Plays by W. B. Yeats," M.A. thesis, U of Manitoba, 1967. Skene argues that each of the five plays corresponds to "an important phase on the great wheel of sym-bolic moon phases which is at the heart of the system of *A Vision*" and that "each play may be seen as a crisis point in the life of a single man" (p. 15). The plays are thus seen in the wider context of Yeats's life and thought. One of the general chapters deals with Yeats's concept of drama and staging. Unfortunately, Skene does not discuss the principles of staging that underlay his own productions of 1969, and he neglects much previous criticism.

Dance and Dancer

3487. °ASH, NIEMA: "Yeats's Use of the Dance Forms in His Drama," M.A. thesis, U of Montreal, 1968.

3488. °BANKERT, JERROLD P.: "A Study of the Dance Plays of Yeats," M.A. thesis, West Chester State College, 1966.

3489. HAYES, J. J.: "Mr. Yeats Plans an Experiment," *NYT*, 78:26146 (25 Aug 1929), VIII, 2.
    Dance and music in the plays for dancers, especially in *Fighting the Waves*. See also a review of a performance by M. G. Palmer in the same issue, II, 3.

3490. °IREY, CHARLOTTE ANN YORK: "The Dance in William Butler Yeats' Dance-Plays with Special Reference to *At the Hawk's Well* and *The Only Jealousy of Emer*," M.A. thesis, U of Colorado, 1965. 165 p.

3491. KIM, MYUNG WHAN: "Dance and Rhythm: Their Meaning in Yeats and the Noh," *MD*, 15:2 (Sept 1972), 195-208.
    Mainly on *The Cat and the Moon* and *The King of the Great Clock Tower*.

3492. OSHIMA, SHOTARO: "Yeats and Michio Ito," *Yeats Society of Japan Annual Report*, #6 (1971), 15-20.
    The importance of Ito's dance artistry for Yeats's plays.

3493. PINCISS, G. M.: "A Dancer for Mr. Yeats," *ETJ*, 21:4 (Dec 1969), 386-91.
    The function of the dance in Yeats's plays and its performance by the dancer Ninette de Valois.

3494. °QAMBER, AKHTAR: "Certain Noble Plays for Dancers by Yeats," M.A. thesis, Columbia U, 1950.

3495. SCHWABACHER, THOMAS KURT: "The Sacred Dance: Some Elements of Ritual in the Plays of William Butler Yeats," Honors thesis, Harvard U, 1958. i, 41 p.

Emotion

3496. °KELLY, DANIEL PATRICK: "The Aesthetic Use of Emotion in the Poetic Dramas of W. B. Yeats," M.A. thesis, U of Toronto, 1953. 89 p.

Fool

3497. PARKER, J. STEWART: "The Modern Poet as Dramatist: Some Aspects of Non-Realistic Drama, with Special Reference to Eliot, Yeats, and Cummings," M.A. thesis, Queen's U, Belfast, [1966]. v, 304 p.
    "W. B. Yeats as Dramatist," 93-171; on the character of the fool in *The Hour Glass*, *The Shadowy Waters*, *On Baile's Strand*, and *The Herne's Egg*.

Hero and Heroic Literature

3498. °BALLARD, CHARLES G.: "The Heroic Plays of William Butler Yeats," M.A. thesis, Oklahoma State U, 1966.

3499. BYARS, JOHN A.: "Yeats's Introduction of the Heroic Type," *MD*, 8:4 (Feb 1966), 409-18.
    In *The King's Threshold* and *On Baile's Strand*.

3500. JACQUET, KATHERINE MCGINN: "Greek Aspects of W. B. Yeats' Plays of the Irish Heroic Age," Ph.D. thesis, Arizona State U, 1967. v, 106 p. (*DA*, 28:4 [Oct 1967], 1397A-98A.)

> Discusses *On Baile's Strand*, *The Only Jealousy of Emer*, *The Death of Cuchulain*, *Deirdre*, and Yeats's use of the mask.

3501. KERSNOWSKI, FRANK L.: "Portrayal of the Hero in Yeats' Poetic Drama," *Renascence*, 18:1 (Autumn 1965), 9-15.

> Discusses *The Shadowy Waters*, *On Baile's Strand*, *Deirdre*, and *The Green Helmet*.

3502. RICHMAN, LARRY KERMIT: "The Theme of Self-Sacrifice in Yeats's Drama," °Ph.D. thesis, Duke U, 1970. 229 p. (*DA*, 31:10 [Apr 1971], 5422A.)

3503. SAGE, V. R. L.: "Representative Extra-Social Figures in Poetry and Poetic Drama, 1880-1920," M.A. thesis, U of Birmingham, 1966. vii, 367 p.

> "Synge: A Mythology of the Ditch," 207-42. "Yeats: Extra-Social Figures in the Earlier Plays," 243-73 (*The King's Threshold*, *At the Hawk's Well*, *On Baile's Strand*, *The Hour Glass*, *The Unicorn from the Stars*). "Yeats's Poetry: Men Escaped Out of Machinery," 274-302 (on "The Three Beggars," "The Three Hermits," "Beggar to Beggar Cried," "Running to Paradise," "The Hour before Dawn," and other poems).

3504. SUSS, IRVING DAVID: "Yeatsian Drama and the Dying Hero," *SAQ*, 54:3 (July 1955), 369-80.

Imagery

3505. PHELPS, WILLIAM LYON: "Crown of Gold, Dung of Swine: From a Language of Imagery to an Image in Language. A Study of the Verse Drama of William Butler Yeats," Honors thesis, Harvard U, 1951. iii, 79 p.

3506. REEVES, HALBERT ADAIR: "The Dramatic Effectiveness of Yeats's Imagery in the Later Plays," Ph.D. thesis, U of North Carolina at Chapel Hill, 1968. ii, 210 p. (*DA*, 29:12 [June 1969], 4467A.)

> Plays written after 1915.

3507. VENDLER, HELEN HENNESSY: "Yeats's Changing Metaphors for the Otherworld," *MD*, 7:3 (Dec 1964), 308-21.

> The relation otherworld-world suggests the relations art-life and imagination-experience.

Irish Nationalism, History, and Themes

3508. BRENNAN, SISTER MARY JEANNETTE: "Irish Folk History Drama," Ph.D. thesis, Niagara U, 1946. xxiv, 280 p.

> "William Butler Yeats," 16-38. Negligible.

3509. CAFFREY, JOHN GORDON: "A Glossary of Certain References to Native Mythology and Folk-lore in Irish Drama," M.A. thesis, U of Washington, 1948. vi, 144 p.

> On Yeats's plays, *passim*.

3510. KERSNOWSKI, FRANK LOUIS: "The Irish Scene in Yeats's Drama," Ph.D. thesis, U of Kansas, 1963. iii, 162 p. (*DA*, 24:12 [June 1964], 5409.)

3511. °LONG, MARY F.: "Irish Nationalism in the Plays of William Butler Yeats, Lady Augusta Gregory, and John Millington Synge," M.A. thesis, Baylor U, 1965.

Landscape

3511a. MACDONALD, EILEEN MARIE: "The Mask of Landscape: A Study of Inner Landscape in the Plays and Poetry of W. B. Yeats," °Ph.D. thesis, Bryn Mawr College, 1972. 248 p. (*DA*, 33:9 [Mar 1973], 5185A.)
  The Shadowy Waters, *The Dreaming of the Bones*, *Purgatory*, *At the Hawk's Well*, and "Byzantium."

Music

3512. HOFFMANN, GERHARD: "Die Funktion der Lieder in Yeats' Dramen," *Anglia*, 89:1 (1971), 87-116.
  The function of the songs in *The Countess Cathleen*, *The Land of Heart's Desire*, *Cathleen ni Houlihan*, *Deirdre*, *The Player Queen*, *At the Hawk's Well*, *The Only Jealousy of Emer*, *A Full Moon in March*, and *The Death of Cuchulain*.

3513. WARREN, RAYMOND: "An Idea of Music," *Threshold*, #19 (Autumn 1965), 64-73.
  Revised as "Music in the Plays of W. B. Yeats," *Composer*, #20 (Summer 1966), 18-19, 21, 23-24. "A composer who has written incidental music for a number of the plays of W. B. Yeats, reflects on the role of music in these plays, and on some of the problems he had to face."

Myth and Mythology

3514. °FAIRBAIRN, PATRICK WILLIAM: "Supernatural Themes in the Plays of Yeats," M.A. thesis, U of Toronto, 1966. 119 p.

3515. GOODMAN, HENRY: "The Plays of William Butler Yeats as Myth and Ritual," Ph.D. thesis, U of Minnesota, 1952. x, 542 p. (*DA*, 13:6 [1953], 1193-94.)

3516. JAECKLE, ERWIN: *Bürgen des Menschlichen*. Zürich: Atlantis, 1945. 224 p.
  "Yeats," 31-54; slightly extended version of "Yeats zum Gedächtnis," *Mass und Wert*, 2:5 (May-June 1939), 658-76. Discusses Celtic myths, sagas, and fairy tales and their repercussions in Yeats's plays. Jaeckle is, however, more concerned with the Celtic material than with the plays, which remain on the periphery of the essay.

3517. KIM, MYUNG WHAN: "Mythopoetic Elements in the Later Plays of W. B. Yeats and the Noh," °Ph.D. thesis, Indiana U, 1969. 237 p. (*DA*, 30:11 [May 1970], 4949A.)

3518. LEDERMAN, MARIE JEAN: "The Myth of the Dead and Resurrected God in Seven Plays of W. B. Yeats: A Psychoanalytic Interpretation," Ph.D. thesis, New York U, 1966. ix, 182 p. (*DA*, 27:4 [Oct 1966], 1059A.)
  The plays are *At the Hawk's Well*, *The Green Helmet*, *On Baile's Strand*, *The Only Jealousy of Emer*, *The Death of Cuchulain*, *Calvary*, and *The Resurrection*.

3519. SMITH, SISTER ROSE JOSEPHINE: "A Study of the Mythological and Legendary Material in Selected Plays of William Butler Yeats, Lady Augusta Gregory, and George William Russell (A. E.)," M.A. thesis, Catholic U of America, 1952. ii, 99 p.
  On *The Countess Cathleen*, *The Land of Heart's Desire*, and *The Shadowy Waters*.

3520. °SUTHERLAND, MARILYN VIRGINIA: "A Comparison of the Use of Celtic Legends in the Plays of W. B. Yeats and Lady Gregory," M.A. thesis, Queen's U (Kingston, Ont.), 1970.

3521. VERHULST, MARGARET MERCHANT: "Myth and Symbol in the Plays of William Butler Yeats," Ph.D. thesis, U of Texas at Austin, 1969. iii, 174 p. (*DA*, 30:7 [Jan 1970], 3028A.)

3522. °WOLFF, W. E.: "Legendary Materials in the Drama of the Irish Renaissance," M.A. thesis, U of North Carolina, 1942.

Phases: Last Plays

3523. °CALARCO, NATALE JOSEPH: "Unity of Action in the Later Plays of William Butler Yeats," M.A. thesis, Columbia U, 1962. 65 p.

3524. °TAYLOR, MARY A.: "An Approach to the Last Plays of William Butler Yeats," M.A. thesis, Columbia U, 1962. 76 p.

Politics

3525. °FARMILOE, DOROTHY: "The Unlucky Country: The Political Aspect of Yeats's Plays," M.A. thesis, U of Windsor, 1969.

Prose Plays

3526. POST, JULESTER SHRADY: "The Prose Plays of William Butler Yeats: Essay," M.A. thesis, Wesleyan U (Middletown, Conn.), 1958. i, 45 p.

3527. URE, PETER: "Yeats and the Two Harmonies," *MD*, 7:3 (Dec 1964), 237-55.
  Prose and verse in Yeats's plays.

Prosody

3528. STEINER, GEORGE: *The Death of Tragedy*. London: Faber & Faber, 1961. viii, 355, xii p.
  Note on Yeats's dramatic verse, pp. 316-18; also *passim* (see index).

Quest

3529. SMITH, BOBBY L.: "The Dimensions of Quest in *Four Plays for Dancers*," *Arizona Q*, 22:3 (Autumn 1966), 197-208.

Religion

3530. BRADBROOK, M. C.: "The Good Pagan's Achievement: The Religious Writing of W. B. Yeats," *Christian Drama*, 1:6 (June 1948), 1-6.
  "In those plays where he states more directly the problems of his own inner life, Yeats turned to the Christian stories and characters. . . . The good pagan runs no risk of handling such stories too lightly or easily. Precisely because they are so difficult for him to use, they are, when employed by a writer as powerful and scrupulous as Yeats, the only adequate vehicle of his deepest experiences."

3531. BROGUNIER, JOSEPH: "Expiation in Yeats's Late Plays," *Drama Survey*, 5:1 (Spring 1966), 24-38.
  In *The Dreaming of the Bones*, *The Words upon the Window-Pane*, and *Purgatory* the dead and the living expiate their sins.

3532. KOLB, EDUARD, and JÖRG HASLER (eds): *Festschrift Rudolf Stamm zu seinem sechzigsten Geburtstag am 12. April 1969*. Bern: Francke, 1969. 291 p.

Robert Fricker: "Das Kathedralenmotiv in der modernen englischen Dichtung," 225-38. *The King's Threshold*, *Calvary*, and *The Resurrection* are seen as examples of the "revival of the verse drama of Christian character," pp. 227-28.

3533. SPANOS, WILLIAM VAIOS: *The Christian Tradition in Modern British Verse Drama: The Poetics of Sacramental Time*. New Brunswick: Rutgers UP, 1967. xvi, 400 p.
    Contains a few references to Yeats's plays (see index).

Reverie

3534. GOLDMAN, MICHAEL PAUL: "The Point of Drama: The Concept of Reverie in the Plays of W. B. Yeats," Ph.D. thesis, Princeton U, 1962. vi, 196 p. (*DA*, 23:9 [Mar 1963], 3373-74.)

Society

3535. °REIMER, HOWARD JAMES: "The Poet and Society in Five Plays by W. B. Yeats," M.A. thesis, U of Manitoba, 1968.

Staging and Performance

3536. BENTLEY, ERIC: *What Is Theatre? Incorporating "The Dramatic Event" and Other Reviews, 1944-1967*. London: Methuen, 1969. xvi, 491 p.
    "On Staging Yeats," 94-97; reprinted from *New Republic*, 128:2011 (15 June 1953), 17-18. Thoughts on staging *The Player Queen* and *The Words upon the Window-Pane*.

3536a. ENO, R. D.: "Yeats' Theatre," *Dublin Mag*, 10:1 (Winter/Spring 1973), 9-17.
    The difficulties of staging Yeats's plays, particularly with regard to his stage directions, the dance, the music, the language, and the use of the open stage.

3537. JAY, JOHN: "What Stood in the Post Office?" *Threshold*, #19 (Autumn 1965), 30-40.
    The staging of the Cuchulain plays.

3538. JOHNSON, JOSEPHINE: "Yeats: What Methods? An Approach to the Performance of the Plays," *Carrell*, 10:2 (1969), 19-32.
    Reprinted in *QJS*, 57:1 (Feb 1971), 68-74. Includes a discussion of the influence of the Nō, a comparison with Brecht, and an interpretation of *Calvary*.

3539. PITKIN, WILLIAM: "Stage Designs, Masks and Costumes for Plays by W. B. Yeats." With introductory notes by Sherman Conrad, *Bard R*, 3:2 (Apr 1949), 93-110.
    The Herne's Egg, *The King of the Great Clock Tower*, *The Only Jealousy of Emer*, *At the Hawk's Well*, and *The Player Queen*.

3540. ROUYER, ANDRÉ: "In Quest of W. B. Yeats: Notes on the French Production of Three Plays." Translated by John Boyle, *Threshold*, 1:1 (Feb 1957), 22-30.
    The Land of Heart's Desire, *The Shadowy Waters*, and *The Only Jealousy of Emer*. See also J3812.

Symbols and Symbolism

3541. ALLEN, JAMES L.: "Yeats's Bird-Soul Symbolism," *TCL*, 6:3 (Oct 1960), 117-22.

3542. BHATNAGAR, K. C.: *The Symbolic Tendency in Irish Renaissance.*
Chandigarh: Panjab U, 1962. 18 p. (Research Bulletin [Arts] of the U of
the Panjab. 37.)
> Symbolic imagery in the plays of Yeats, Synge, Lord Dunsany, Martyn,
> Robinson, O'Casey, and others.

3543. GILL, STEPHEN M.: *Six Symbolist Plays of Yeats.* New Delhi: Chand,
[1971]. ix, 94 p.
> The plays are *The Countess Cathleen, On Baile's Strand, The Green
> Helmet, At the Hawk's Well, The Only Jealousy of Emer,* and *The Death
> of Cuchulain.* The discussion of their symbolism is inadequate; as a
> whole the book is rather naive.

3544. HETHMON, ROBERT HENRY: "The Theatre's Anti-Self: A Study of the
Symbolism of Yeats' Unpopular Plays," Ph.D. thesis, Stanford U, 1957. iv,
515 p. (*DA*, 17:4 [1957], 917.)

3544a. KENT, CONSTANCE KEMLER: "Stasis and Silence: A Study of Certain
Symbolist Tendencies in the Modern Theatre," °Ph.D. thesis, Columbia U,
1973. 282 p. (*DA*, 34:6 [Dec 1973], 3404A–5A.)
> Includes a chapter on *Four Plays for Dancers, The Cat and the Moon,*
> and *Purgatory.*

3545. KNAPP, JULIET LEE: "Symbolistic Drama of To-day," *Poet Lore,* 32:2
(Summer 1921), 201–33.
> Mentions Yeats *passim,* especially *The Land of Heart's Desire.*

3546. °MCMANUS, JUNE J.: "A Study of Symbols in the Myth Plays of William
Butler Yeats," M.A. thesis, Midwestern U, 1967.

3547. RYAN, SISTER M. ROSALIE: "Symbolic Elements in the Plays of William
Butler Yeats, 1892–1921," Ph.D. thesis, Catholic U of America, 1952. xxii,
203 p.

3548. WORTH, KATHARINE JOYCE: "Symbolism in Modern English Drama," Ph.D.
thesis, U of London, 1953. iii, 350 p.
> "Symbolism in Irish Drama," 149–212; on Yeats, 149–80.

Syntax

3549. VIGL, HARALD: "Studien zur Syntax der dramatischen Werke von Lady
Gregory, W. B. Yeats und J. M. Synge," Dr. phil. thesis, U of Innsbruck,
1954. iv, 149 p.
> See pp. 106–21 for a discussion of Anglo-Irish syntax ("Kiltartanese")
> in Yeats's plays.

Tragedy

3549a. °YOUNG, J. DUDLEY: "Yeats' Tragedy," M.Phil. thesis, U of Essex,
1970/71.

ED   Yeats and the Nō

3550. ARNOTT, PETER: *The Theatres of Japan.* London: Macmillan, 1969. 319 p.
> "Some English Imitations," 291–302; on Yeats, 291–98: "The Yeats
> adaptations remain one of the happiest instances of the transposition
> of styles: perhaps because of the striking similarities between the
> Japanese and Celtic temperaments; perhaps because, in Yeats, they
> found the rare combination of the mystic and practising dramatic poet."

3551. BAKSI, PRONOTI: "The Noh and the Yeatsian Synthesis," *REL*, 6:3 (July 1965), 34-43.

The Nō "embodied much of what had already found expression in different strands of his own work."

3552. BOTTOMLEY, GORDON: *Scenes and Plays*. London: Constable, 1929. vii, 123 p.

"Note," 120-23; on Yeats and the Nō, Bottomley's models.

3553. ERNST, EARLE: "The Influence of Japanese Theatrical Style on Western Theatre," *ETJ*, 21:2 (May 1969), 127-38.

3554. °FELTES, N. N.: "Memory and Prophecy: A Study of the Noh Plays of W. B. Yeats," M.A. thesis, University College, Dublin, 1957.

3555. GHOSH, PRABODH CHANDRA: *Poetry and Religion as Drama*. Calcutta: World Press, 1965. xiii, 213 p.

"Yeats and the Nō," 124-43, and *passim* (see index). Discusses Yeats's dramatic theories, *Calvary*, and *The Resurrection*.

3556. GUTIERREZ, DONALD: "Ghosts Benefic and Malign: The Influence of the Noh Theatre on the Three Dance Plays of Yeats," *Forum* [Houston], 9:2 (Summer 1971), 42-48.

At the Hawk's Well, *The Dreaming of the Bones*, and *Purgatory*.

3557. HUBBELL, LINDLEY WILLIAMS: "Yeats, Pound, and Nō Drama," *East-West R*, 1:1 (Spring 1964), 70-78.

Yeats "fell between the stools" of an aristocratic art for the few (the Nō) and a communal theater (the Sophocles translations).

3558. JACQUOT, JEAN (ed): *Les théâtres d'Asie*. Paris: Editions du Centre National de la Recherche Scientifique, 1961. 308 p. (Conférences du Théâtre des Nations [1958-59]. Journées d'Etudes de Royaumont [28 May— 1 June 1959].)

Jean Jacquot: "Craig, Yeats et le théâtre d'Orient," 271-83. Yeats's knowledge of Craig's ideas prepared him for the influence of the Nō.

3559. °KIM, MYUNG WHAN: "The Vision of the Spiritual World in Yeats's Plays and the Noh," *Phoenix*, #14 (1970), 39-79.

3560. LONDRAVILLE, RICHARD JOHN: "To Asia for a Stage Convention: W. B. Yeats and the *Noh*," °Ph.D. thesis, State U of New York at Albany, 1970. 244 p. (*DA*, 31:6 [Dec 1970], 2925A-26A.)

3561. MATSUBARA, HISAKO: "W. B. Yeats and the Japanese Noh Theater," M.A. thesis, Pennsylvania State U, 1960. v, 83 p.

Yeats saw only the surface and mistook it for the whole idea. "The true, essential phase of the original Noh remains unknown to him" (p. 81).

3562. MIDDLEBROOKS, JANE DANIELSON: "The Dance Plays of W. B. Yeats and the Noh Drama of Japan," M.A. thesis, U of Washington, 1968. ii, 99 p.

3563. MILLS, JOHN GASCOIGNE: "W. B. Yeats and Noh," *Japan Q*, 2:4 (Oct 1955), 496-500.

3564. MOORE, GERALD: "The *Nō* and the Dance Plays of W. B. Yeats," *Japan Q*, 7:2 (Apr-June 1960), 177-87.

3565. MURRAY, PETER: "Noh: The Japanese Theatre of Silence," *Icarus*, 4:15 (Feb 1955), 102-7.

3566. °NIEMOELLER, MARTHA: "The Influence of the Noh Drama on William Butler Yeats, Bertolt Brecht, and Thornton Niven Wilder," M.S. thesis, U of Wisconsin, 1961. vi, 184 p.

3567. OSHIMA, SHOTARO: "Yeats and the Noh," *Yeats Society of Japan Annual Report*, #7 (1972), 9-18.
Psychic phenomena in the Nō and in related plays by Yeats.

3568. PRONKO, LEONARD CABELL: *Theater East and West: Perspectives toward a Total Theater*. Berkeley: U of California Press, 1967. x, 230 p.
See pp. 71-73: Yeats did not understand the Nō.

3569. °SHAFFER, LAWRENCE E.: "Yeats and the 'No' Drama," M.A. thesis, Columbia U, 1948.

3570. THOMPSON, FRANCIS J.: "Ezra in Dublin," *UTQ*, 21:1 (Oct 1951), 64-77.
A survey of the plays written under the influence of the Nō and Ezra Pound. Includes a somewhat overingenious interpretation of the political implications of *At the Hawk's Well*.

3571. THWAITE, ANTHONY: "Yeats and the Noh," *Twentieth Century*, 162:967 (Sept 1957), 235-42.
The Nō, only imperfectly understood by Yeats, "did not act as his model but his justification."

3572. °TIRAPU, MARIA THERESA: "The Plays of W. B. Yeats Modelled on the Japanese Noh," M.A. thesis, University College, Dublin, 1962.

3573. TSUKIMURA, REIKO: "The Influence on Yeats of the Japanese Noh Plays," M.A. thesis, U of Saskatchewan, 1962. iii, 63 p.
Mainly on *At the Hawk's Well* and *The Dreaming of the Bones*.

3574. °UNRUH, K.: "The Influence of the Noh Plays of Japan on the Dramatic Art of W. B. Yeats," M.A. thesis, U of Manitoba, 1968.

3575. WELLS, HENRY WILLIS: *The Classical Drama of the Orient*. London: Asia Publishing House, 1965. viii, 348 p.
See pp. 307-20 and *passim*. Mainly on *At the Hawk's Well*, which is taken to bear the closest resemblance to the Nō; to a lesser extent on *The Only Jealousy of Emer*, *The Dreaming of the Bones*, *The Resurrection*, *The King of the Great Clock Tower*, and *A Full Moon in March*.

3576. °WONG, JEANNE: "The Influence of the Japanese Noh Drama on the Dramatic Development of William Butler Yeats," M.A. thesis, Mills College, 1959. viii, 78 p.

3576a. YUN, CHANG SIK: "The Tragic Theatre: The Nō and Yeats's Dance Plays," °Ph.D. thesis, Princeton U, 1972. 324 p. (*DA*, 33:7 [Jan 1973], 3608A-9A.)

See also J1076, 1161 (#3, 7), 1162 (#3), 1554, 1894, 1974, 2166, 2281, 2282, 3187, 3320, 3324, 3325a, 3331, 3336, 3339, 3350, 3363, 3387, 3395, 3405, 3458, 3487-95, 3517, 3538, 3580a, 3582a, 3584, 4156, 4163, 4176, 4184, 4190, 4558, 5382, 5911.

EE   Single Plays

As in section DD, the items listed here do not represent all the studies of Yeats's plays ever published. More discussions will be found in some of the unanalyzed items of sections CA, CB, CC, EA, EB, EC, and ED, to which the reader is therefore referred for further material. It is also advisable to consult the subject index (NE) for entries such as Cuchulain, dance, tragedy, and so on. Otherwise, section EE serves as a complete index for studies of Yeats's plays listed in this bibliography. It is arranged by plays in alphabetical order, with a subdivision for most plays into parts I and II; part I comprises general criticism, while part II lists selected reviews of performances, preferably first nights (including some German and Swiss productions).

Only a few records exist for the first private performance of *At the Hawk's Well* (see J1383); no date of a first performance seems to be ascertainable for *Calvary* and *A Full Moon in March*. The date given for *The Death of Cuchulain* in the *Variorum Edition of the Plays* (p. 1318) is wrong. The first night reviews of *The Resurrection* and *The King of the Great Clock Tower* could not be printed in Ireland because of a newspaper strike, so I had to rely on English and French material. I did locate three hitherto unrecorded first productions, that of *The Only Jealousy of Emer* in the Netherlands (see J3833), that of *The Herne's Egg* (see J3745a), and that of *The Death of Cuchulain* (see J3678a).

In spite of incredulous academics, some of Yeats's plays are still performed successfully, and not just in Ireland (see, e.g., J3478, 3480, 3586, 3834, 3835).

At the Hawk's Well I

3577. BABLER, OTTO F.: "A Speckled Shin," *N&Q*, 154:[] (30 June 1928), 461.
Asks for the origin of the phrase. See answer by Paul McPharlin, 155: [] (4 Aug 1928), 87; and a medical explanation by F. William Cock, (18 Aug 1928), 122.

3578. FLANAGAN, HALLIE: *Dynamo*. NY: Duell, Sloan and Pearce, 1943. x, 176 p.
Quotes, in its entirety, T. S. Eliot's letter to Mrs. Flanagan (dated 18 Mar 1933), in which he suggests a production of *Sweeney Agonistes* along the lines of Yeats's preface and notes to *At the Hawk's Well* (pp. 82-84).

3579. JOCHUM, K. P. S.: "W. B. Yeats's *At the Hawk's Well* and the Dialectic of Tragedy," *Visva-Bharati Q*, 31:1 (1965-66), 21-28.
An interpretation based on Kenneth Burke's theory of tragedy.

3580. KURDYS, DOUGLAS BELLAMY: *Form in the Modern Verse Drama*. Salzburg: Institut für Englische Sprache und Literatur, Universität Salzburg, 1972. iii, 419 p. (Salzburg Studies in English Literature. Poetic Drama. 17.)
Originally a Ph.D. thesis, Stanford U, 1968. iv, 419 p. (*DA*, 30:3 [Sept 1969], 1139A). "The Dance Plays and *Purgatory*, by W. B. Yeats," 18-70; mainly on *At the Hawk's Well*, *The Dreaming of the Bones*, *A Full Moon in March*, and *Purgatory*.

3580a. MENON, K. P. K., M. MANUEL, and K. AYYAPPA PANIKER (eds): *Literary Studies: Homage to Dr. A. Sivaramasubramonia Aiyer*. Trivandrum: St. Joseph's Press for the Dr. A. Sivaramasubramonia Aiyer Memorial Committee, 1973. vi, 258 p.
S. Ramaswamy: "*At the Hawk's Well* and the Noh," 211-15.

3581. NICOLL, ALLARDYCE: *Readings from British Drama: Extracts from British and Irish Plays*. London: Harrap, 1928. 446 p.
See pp. 384-87 for an extract from the play and a note.

3582. REEVES, HALBERT A.: "Dramatic Effectiveness of the Imagery in Yeats's *At the Hawk's Well*," *McNeese R*, 19 (1968), 27-35.

3582a. SHARONI, EDNA G.: "*At the Hawk's Well*: Yeats's Unresolved Conflict between Language and Silence," *Comparative Drama*, 7:2 (Summer 1973), 150-73.
Also on the influence of the Nō and Zen Buddhism.

3583. SPRINCHORN, EVERT (ed): *20th-Century Plays in Synopsis*. NY: Crowell, 1966. xii, 493 p.
Includes synopses of this play and of *The Only Jealousy of Emer*, *The Dreaming of the Bones*, *Calvary*, and *The Words upon the Window-Pane*, pp. 457-61.

3584. TSUKIMURA, REIKO: "A Comparison of Yeats's *At the Hawk's Well* and Its Noh Version *Taka no izumi*," *Literature East and West*, 11:4 (Dec 1967), 385-97.
Yeats's play, itself modeled on the Nō in a general way, was transformed into a Nō play by Mario Yokomichi. In the process, its meaning changed considerably.

3585. °TUTIAH, MARVIS CAMILLE: "The Relations between Music and Poetry in the Plays of Shakespeare and Yeats with Particular Reference to *Twelfth Night* and *At the Hawk's Well*," M.A. thesis, U of Manitoba, 1967.

See also J743, 1071, 1073, 1153, 1157, 1161 (#5), 1162 (#3), 1755, 2152, 3336, 3339, 3348, 3362, 3366, 3382, 3400, 3438, 3450, 3454, 3478-86, 3490, 3503, 3511a, 3512, 3518, 3537, 3539, 3543, 3556, 3570, 3573, 3575, 3594, 3644, 3798, 4245, 5579, 5719, 5876, 6498.

At the Hawk's Well II

3586. JONES, DAVID R.: Review of a performance of dance plays by the Chicago Circle Players, University of Illinois at Chicago Circle, November 1970, *ETJ*, 23:1 (Mar 1971), 90-91.
A performance of this play, *Purgatory*, *Calvary*, and *A Full Moon in March*.

3587. M[ITCHELL], S[USAN] L.: "*At the Hawk's Well*--An Impression," *Irish Statesman*, 2:5 (12 Apr 1924), 142.
A performance in Yeats's drawing room completely captivated Miss Mitchell.

3587a. RONSLEY, JOSEPH: Review of a performance of *At the Hawk's Well*, *A Full Moon in March*, and *The Cat and the Moon* by the English Theatre Company, University of Ottawa, directed by James Flannery, *ETJ*, 24:2 (May 1972), 199-200.

See also J663, 1393, 3834, 3941.

Calvary I

3588. GERSTENBERGER, DONNA: "The Saint and the Circle: The Dramatic Potential of an Image," *Criticism*, 2:4 (Fall 1960), 336-41.
Compares the use in this drama, Eliot's *Murder in the Cathedral*, and Spender's *Trial of a Judge*.

3589. GOSE, ELLIOTT B.: "The Lyric and the Philosophic in Yeats's *Calvary*," *MD*, 2:4 (Feb 1960), 370-76.

3590. GUERRERO ZAMORA, JUAN: *Uno de vosotros: Auto sacramental. Judas: Ensayos*. Barcelona: Flors, 1957. 224 p.
See pp. 187-89.

3591. ROSTON, MURRAY: *Biblical Drama in England: From the Middle Ages to the Present Day*. London: Faber & Faber, 1968. 335 p.
"W. B. Yeats and D. H. Lawrence," 264-79; on this play and on *The Resurrection*.

3591a. THOMPSON, LESLIE M.: "Spender's 'Judas Iscariot,'" *ELN*, 8:2 (Dec 1970), 126-30.
Compares Spender's poem with Yeats's play.

See also J1153, 1157, 1815, 1818, 2152, 2861, 3339, 3345, 3400, 3441, 3454, 3518, 3532, 3538, 3555, 3583, 4239, 4245, 6450.

Calvary II

3592. FLANNERY, JAMES W.: "Action and Reaction at the Dublin Theatre Festival," *Dublin Mag*, 5:3&4 (Autumn/Winter 1966), 26-36.
Reprinted in *ETJ*, 19:1 (Mar 1967), 72-80. Reviews his own productions of this play and of *The Resurrection* at Trinity College, Dublin, during the 1965 Theatre Festival and the discussions following the performances.

3592a. GUSSOW, MEL: "Theater: 3 'Visionary' Plays by Yeats: Jean Erdman Interprets His 'Moon Mysteries.' Dances, Music and Noh Blended with Mime," *NYT*, 122:41998 (18 Jan 1973), 47.
A performance by the Theater St. Clements, New York, of this play, *The Cat and the Moon*, and *A Full Moon in March*.

3593. JORDAN, JOHN: "Dublin Theatre Festival," *Hibernia*, 29:11 (Nov 1965), 17.
Reviews performances of this play, *The Resurrection*, and *Deirdre*.

See also J3586.

The Cat and the Moon I

3594. *Kindlers Literaturlexikon*. Zürich: Kindler, 1965-74. 8 v.
Contains notes by E[ckart] St[ein] on this play, 1:2239; *Cathleen ni Houlihan*, 1:2250-51; *The Countess Cathleen*, 2:298; *The Death of Cuchulain*, 2:631; *Deirdre*, 2:762; *The Hour Glass*, 3:2175-76; *The Land of Heart's Desire*, 4:983-84; by W[alter] K[luge] on *The Shadowy Waters*, 6:1262-63; *The Unicorn from the Stars*, 7:156-58; by J[ohann] N. S[chmidt] on *At the Hawk's Well*, 8:107-8.

See also J1157, 2996-97 and note, 3348, 3491, 3544a, 5572, 5578, 5579, 5692.

The Cat and the Moon II

3595. ANON.: "A Play by W. B. Yeats at the Abbey Theatre," *Irish Times*, 73:23215 (22 Sept 1931), 4.

3596. ANON.: "Abbey Theatre Dublin: New Play by W. B. Yeats," *Times*, #45936 (24 Sept 1931), 10.

3597. DAVIE, DONALD: "The Dublin Theatre Festival," *Twentieth Century*, 162:965 (July 1957), 71-73.

3598. M., M.: "New Play by Mr. W. B. Yeats," *Irish Independent*, 40:226 (22 Sept 1931), 8.

See also J3587a, 3592a, 3834.

Cathleen ni Houlihan I

3599. BRENNAN, ROBERT: *Allegiance*. Dublin: Browne & Nolan, 1950. x, 373 p.
The last line of the play was suggested by Arthur Griffith (pp. 202-3).

3600. GILL, W. W.: "Kathleen ni-Hoolihan," *N&Q*, 174:[] (2 Apr 1938), 248.
Answers a query by John Libis (12 Mar 1938), 188, concerning the meaning and origin of the name.

3601. HAMEL, A. G. VAN: "On Anglo-Irish Syntax," *Englische Studien*, 45:2
(Sept 1912), 272-92.
Most of the examples are drawn from this play and from *The Unicorn
from the Stars*.

3602. HOLT, EDGAR: *Protest in Arms: The Irish Troubles, 1916-1923*. London:
Putnam, 1960. 328 p.
The play was probably the most effective propaganda piece of the Irish
literary revival (pp. 21-22).

3603. MARKIEVICZ, CONSTANCE GORE-BOOTH: *Prison Letters of Countess Markie-
vicz (Constance Gore-Booth)*. Also poems and articles relating to Easter
Week by Eva Gore-Booth and a biographical sketch by Esther Roper. London:
Longmans Green, 1934. xix, 315 p.
The play was for both sisters "a sort of gospel" (pp. 63-64, 155).

3604. MILLETT, FRED BENJAMIN, and GERALD EADES BENTLEY: *The Art of the
Drama*. NY: Appleton-Century, 1935. viii, 253 p.
Note on the play, pp. 163-64.

3605. MILLETT, FRED BENJAMIN: *Reading Drama: A Method of Analysis with
Selections for Study*. NY: Harper, 1950. x, 252 p.
See pp. 115-17 and *passim* (see index).

3606. O NÉILL, SÉAMUS: "Did Yeats' Poem [*sic*] Inspire Easter Rising?"
Irish Press, 37:241 (11 Oct 1967), 9.
Perhaps, but it wasn't a good play. See correspondence by L[iam] S.
Cogan, :246 (17 Oct 1967), 9; O Néill, "Did Yeats Send Them Out to
Die?" :249 (20 Oct 1967), 11.

3607. RAMASWAMY, S.: "Two Faces of Cathleen," *Indian J of English Studies*,
10 (1969), 40-46.
Compares this play with Lady Gregory's *The Rising of the Moon*.

3608. WEISWEILER, JOSEF: *Heimat und Herrschaft: Wirkung und Ursprung eines
irischen Mythos*. Halle: Niemeyer, 1943. 149 p. (Schriftenreihe der
deutschen Gesellschaft für keltische Studien. 11.)
See pp. 25-27 and 86-89 for notes on the origin of the allegorical
protagonist.

See also J398, 693, 1161 (#1), 1307, 1440, 1607, 1815, 2192, 2211, 3332a,
3352, 3369, 3426, 3471, 3512, 3594, 4078, 4195, 5932, 5940 (#3), 5981,
6034, 6130, 6317, 6323, 6334, 6388, 6436, 6440, 6472, 6594, 6705, 6896,
7359.

Cathleen ni Houlihan II

3609. ANON.: "The Irish Players," *Academy*, 82:2092 (8 June 1912), 727-28.

3610. ANON.: "The Irish Players," *Athenaeum*, #4415 (8 June 1912), 663-64.

3611. ANON.: "Two Irish Plays by Mr. W. B. Yeats and A. E.: The Performance Last Night," *Freeman's J*, 135:[] (3 Apr 1902), 5.

3612. ANON.: "New Irish Plays Produced," *Gael*, 21:5 (May 1902), 166-67.
Includes a photograph of Maud Gonne.

3613. ANON.: "Maxine Elliott's--Irish Players," *NY Dramatic Mirror*, 66:
1720 (6 Dec 1911), 6.

3614. ANON.: "Mr. Yeats' New Play," *United Irishman*, 7:162 (5 Apr 1902), 5.

3615. FIRKINS, OSCAR W.: "Cathleen Ni Hoolihan at the Bramhall Playhouse,"
Weekly R, 3:62 (21 July 1920), 76.
"A divine play perfectly acted. . . ."

3616. GUEST, L. HADEN: "The Irish Theatre," *New Age*, ns 1:8 (20 June 1907),
124-25.
Reviews performances of this play and of *The Shadowy Waters*.

3617. MARTYN, EDWARD: Letter concerning the production of the play, *United
Irishman*, 7:164 (19 Apr 1902), [1].
Editor's reply, *ibid*.

3618. NEUNER, HEINRICH LUDWIG: "Giessener Stadttheater: *Die Tochter von
Houlihan*," *Giessener Anzeiger*, 189:242 (16 Oct 1939), [5].

3619. WEBER, LUDWIG: "Butler Yeats: *Tochter von Houlihan*," *Oberhessische
Tageszeitung*, #282 (16 Oct 1939), [5].

3620. Y[OUNG], E[LLA]: "The Irish Plays," *All Ireland R*, 3:7 (19 Apr 1902),
101.

See also J678, 3754, 3767, 3807-9, 3819, 3822, 6743, 6766.

The Countess Cathleen I

3621. ANON.: Note on *The Countess Cathleen* as an "un-Irish" play, *Claidheamh Soluis*, 1:8 (6 May 1899), 121.
See further notes in :9 (13 May 1899), 137; :10 (20 May 1899), 153
(on the un-Irishness of the Irish literary movement); and a letter by
P. H. Pearse, *ibid*., 157: "Against Mr. Yeats personally we have
nothing to object. He is a mere English poet of the third or fourth
rank, and as such he is harmless. But when he attempts to run an
'Irish' Literary Theatre it is time for him to be crushed."

3622. ANON.: Leader on *The Countess Cathleen*, *Daily Express*, #14615 / ns
#225 (8 May 1899), 4.

3623. ANON.: "Irish Literary Theatre," *Daily Express*, #14619 / ns #229
(12 May 1899), 5-6.
Long summary of a speech by T. P. Gill on this play, Yeats's answer,
plus related speeches by George Moore, J. F. Taylor, Standish O'Grady,
and others.

3624. ANON.: "*The Countess Cathleen*," *Daily Nation*, 3:108 (6 May 1899), 4.
An editorial protesting the proposed performance "in the names of
morality and religion." See also "Irish Literary Theatre," :109 (8 May
1899), 4; and letters by "Spectator," M. G. C., and "A Catholic Irishman," *ibid*., 5; a report of Yeats's speech, 5-6.
Further letters by "An Irish Catholic," :110 (9 May 1899), 3; a
review of the performance, 5-6; an editorial, "Cardinal Logue's Letter,"
:111 (10 May 1899), 4; the letter itself, 5; plus more letters by
"Catholic Students of the Royal University" (T. M. Kettle and others),
Myles O'Shea, "L.," and a telegram from F. Hugh O'Donnell, *ibid*.

See also :113 (12 May 1899), 5-6, for letters by T. W. Rolleston
and F. Hugh O'Donnell and a report of T. P. Gill's and the *Daily
Express*'s banquet for Yeats and of Yeats's speech, plus an editorial
on p. 4.

3625. ANON.: "The Irish Literary Theatre," *Gael*, 18:3 (June 1899), 78-79.
Endorses F. Hugh O'Donnell (J3642).

3626. ANON.: "All Ireland," *United Irishman*, [1]:9 (29 Apr 1899), 1.
Defends Yeats against O'Donnell. See also :11 (13 May 1899), 1; and
Frank Ryan's letter, "Mr. Yeats and His Critics," :12 (20 May 1899),
4.

3627. ARCHER, WILLIAM: "Mr. George Moore as a Dramatic Critic," *Daily
Chronicle*, #11508 (20 Jan 1899), 3.
Actually a review of Moore's introduction to Martyn's *The Heather
Field and Maeve* (J3640), in which Archer defends his view of Yeats's
plays, especially *The Countess Cathleen*, as beautiful poems but diffi-
cult to stage. See Moore's reply, #11512 (25 Jan 1899), 3: Archer's
reservations against a staging of *The Countess Cathleen* are unfounded.
See Archer, #11513 (26 Jan 1899), 3, and finally Yeats's letter, "Mr.
Moore, Mr. Archer, and the Literary Theatre," #11516 (30 Jan 1899),
3 (Wp. 356).

3627a. BAUER, GERO, FRANZ K. STANZEL, and FRANZ ZAIC (eds): *Festschrift
Prof. Dr. Herbert Koziol zum siebzigsten Geburtstag*. Wien: Braumüller,
1973. xi, 338 p. (Wiener Beiträge zur englischen Philologie. 75.)
Harro Heinz Kühnelt: "Oskar Kokoschka, Werner Egk und die *Irische
Legende* nach William Butler Yeats," 169-87. See also J3644a.

3628. CLARKE, AUSTIN: "The Cardinal and the Countess," *Ariel*, 3:3 (July
1972), 58-65.
Comments on the opposition to the play by F. Hugh O'Donnell and
Cardinal Logue.

3629. CLERY, ARTHUR E.: "A Roman Catholic Student on *Countess Cathleen*,"
Daily Express, #14618 (11 May 1899), 5.
Letter to the editor. The same page contains Cardinal Logue's letter.
Further correspondence by "Observer," #14619 (12 May 1899), 6; L. M.
Little, #14620 (13 May 1899), 3.

3630. *La comtesse Cathleen de William Butler Yeats*. [Paris]: Comédie de
Provence, [1961?]. [16 p.]
A theater program containing notes by Madeleine Gibert [p. 1] and
Michèle Dalmasso [2-6].

3631. EBBUTT, MAUDE ISABEL: *Hero-Myths & Legends of the British Race*.
London: Harrap, 1916 [1910]. xxix, 374 p.
"The Countess Cathleen," 156-83; a retelling based explicitly on
Yeats's play.

3632. EGK, WERNER: "Irische Legende," *Österreichische Musikzeitschrift*,
10:4 (Apr 1955), 125-30.
Archetypal characters and situations in Yeats's play prompted Egk to
write his opera, *Irische Legende* (J5636).

3633. ENGEL, EDUARD: Preface to his German translation of *The Countess
Cathleen*, *Bühne und Welt*, 6:2 (15 Oct 1903), 45.

3634. GILKES, MARTIN: "*Countess Cathleen* by the Avon," *English*, 3:16
(Spring 1941), 159-64.

Introduction to a performance by Randle Ayrton's Dramatic School at Stratford-upon-Avon.

3635. HADDON, ELIZABETH (ed): *Three Dramatic Legends*. London: Heinemann, 1964. ix, 196 p.
See pp. 131-38.

3636. HERLITSCHKA, HERBERTH E.: "Zur *Gräfin Katlin* und über ihren Dichter," *Bühnen der Stadt Köln: Programmblätter der Kammerspiele*, 7 Mar 1962, 2-4, 8-12.
Includes four photographs of the performance.

3637. H[EYNEN], H. G.: Note to his translation of *The Countess Cathleen*, *Roeping*, 8:10 (July 1930), 489.

3638. JOHNSON, LIONEL: "*The Countess Cathleen*," *Beltaine*, #1 (May 1899), 10-11.

3639. KETTLE, T. M., and others: "Mr. Yeats's *Countess Cathleen*: Letter from University Students," *Freeman's J*, 133:[] (10 May 1899), 6.
The same page contains a letter from T. W. Rolleston.

3639a. LINDEMANN, REINHOLD: "Das Religiöse bei W. B. Yeats," *Blätter der Städtischen Bühnen Frankfurt am Main*, 6:19 (1939), 225-28.
Mostly on religious themes in *The Countess Cathleen*.

3640. MARTYN, EDWARD: *The Heather Field and Maeve*. With an introduction by George Moore. London: Duckworth, 1899. xxviii, 129 p.
Moore's introduction contains praise of Yeats's play, pp. xx-xxii.
See also J3627.

3641. MEHL, DIETER (ed): *Das englische Drama: Vom Mittelalter bis zur Gegenwart*. Düsseldorf: Bagel, 1970. 2 v.
Heinz Bergner: "Yeats: *The Countess Cathleen*," 2:173-85, 369-71; "Synge: *The Playboy of the Western World*," 2:202-16, 373-75. Heinz Kosok: "O'Casey: *The Plough and the Stars*," 2:217-39, 375-77.

3642. [O'DONNELL, FRANK HUGH]: *Souls for Gold! Pseudo Celtic Drama in Dublin*. London: Nassau Press, 1899. 14 p.
Two vitriolic letters. The first, "Faith for Gold," was published as "Celtic Drama in Dublin: Mr. Frank Hugh O'Donnell Asks--Is This Celtic?" *Freeman's J*, 133:[] (1 Apr 1899), 6. The second letter, "Blasphemy and Degradation," was refused publication in *Freeman's J*. Both are reprinted in J6703.

3643. O'NEILL, GEORGE: "The Inauguration of the Irish Literary Theatre," *New Ireland R*, 11:4 (June 1899), 246-52.

3644. OPPEL, HORST (ed): *Das moderne englische Drama: Interpretationen*. Berlin: Schmidt, 1966 [1963]. 382 p.
Gerhard Stebner on this play, pp. 26-41; Rudolf Stamm on *Deirdre*, 60-84; Johannes Kleinstück on *At the Hawk's Well*. Also Willi Erzgräber on Synge and Robert Fricker on O'Casey.

3644a. PATSCH, SYLVIA: "*The Countess Cathleen*": *Sage--Drama--Oper--Illustration*. Innsbruck: Kommissionsverlag der österreichischen Kommissionsbuchhandlung, 1974. vii, 193 p. (Veröffentlichungen der Universität Innsbruck. 88.)
Based on a Dr. phil. thesis, U of Innsbruck, 1973. vi, 341 p. Discusses the play and its sources, Henry von Heiseler's German translation, the operatic version by Werner Egk (see J5636), and Oskar Kokoschka's illustrations to Egk's opera. See also J3627a.

3645. REISCHLE, HELMUT: "Die sieben Fassungen des Dramas *The Countess Cathleen* von W. B. Yeats: Ein Vergleich," Dr. phil. thesis, U of Tübingen, 1961. xvii, 325 p.
Maintains that Yeats's revisions improve the play step by step.

3646. SIDNELL, MICHAEL JOHN: "A Critical Study of the Evolution of W. B. Yeats's Play *The Countess Cathleen*, from Its Source to the Version of 1899," M.A. thesis, U of London, 1961. 266 p.

3647. ————: "Manuscript Versions of Yeats's *The Countess Cathleen*," *PBSA*, 56:1 (1962), 79–103.
"A description and chronological account of the manuscripts relating to *The Countess Cathleen*, deposited in the National Library of Ireland. . . ."

3648. THORPE, JAMES: "Writers at Work: The Creative Process and Our View of Art," *HLQ*, 30:3 (May 1967), 195–206.
On the revisions of this play, pp. 202-5.

3649. Entry canceled.

See also J398, 845, 1112, 1121, 1136, 1142, 1202, 1243, 1440, 1813a, 2133, 2185b, 2222, 3332a, 3336, 3345, 3348, 3426, 3462, 3474, 3512, 3519, 3543, 3594, 3965, 4076a, 4078, 4277–89, 4330, 4474, 5479, 5482, 5573, 5577, 5636, 5775, 5925, 5932, 6242, 6314, 6317, 6328, 6356, 6361, 6362, 6380, 6385, 6386, 6450, 6451, 6565, 6703, 6744.

The Countess Cathleen II

3650. ANON.: "Piękne słuchowisko o dobrej księżniczce" [Beautiful radio play on a good countess], *Antena*, 2:5 (1957), 30-31.
Review of a Polish radio version of the play.

3651. ANON.: "The Close of the Irish Season," *Athenaeum*, #4421 (20 July 1912), 71-72.

3652. ANON.: "Irish Literary Theatre: First Night of the *Countess Cathleen*," *Daily Express*, #14616 / ns #226 (9 May 1899), 5.
Positive reaction. See also the leader in the same issue, pp. 4-5.

3653. ANON.: "Irish Literary Theatre: First Night of the *Countess Cathleen*," *Dublin Evening Mail*, 76:[] (9 May 1899), 1.

3654. ANON.: "The Irish Literary Theatre: *The Countess Cathleen*. Production Last Night," *Freeman's J*, 133:[] (9 May 1899), 5.

3655. ANON.: "*The Countess Cathleen* at the Court," *Illustrated London News*, 141:3822 (20 July 1912), 88.

3656. ANON.: "Irish Literary Theatre: *The Countess Cathleen*," *Irish Daily Independent*, 8:110 (9 May 1899), 4.

3657. ANON.: "*The Countess Cathleen*," *Irish Times*, #27143 (19 July 1944), 3.
Review of a radio production.

3658. ANON.: "The Irish Players," *NY Dramatic Mirror*, 69:1784 (26 Feb 1913), 7.

3659. BAUMGARTEN, L. VON: Review of a German production in Frankfurt/Main, *Neue Literatur*, 35:5 (May 1934), 313.

3660. BEERBOHM, MAX: *More Theatres: 1898-1903.* With an introduction by
Rupert Hart-Davis. London: Hart-Davis, 1969. 624 p.
"In Dublin," 141-44; reprinted from *Saturday R*, 87:2272 (13 May 1899),
586-88, where it was signed "Max."

3661. COOPER, BRYAN: "Two Plays: A Criticism," *Irish R*, 1:11 (Jan 1912),
571-72.

3662. FINGALL, ELIZABETH MARY MARGARET BURKE PLUNKETT, COUNTESS OF:
Seventy Years Young: Memories Told to Pamela Hinkson. London: Collins,
1937. 441 p.
Reminiscences of a tableau of the play, directed by Yeats, in which
the countess made a lovely corpse, pp. 234-35.

3663. [GE]CK, [RUDOLF]: "Frankfurter Schauspielhaus: Ur-Aufführung von
Gräfin Chatleen [*sic*], Drama von W. B. Yeats," *Frankfurter Zeitung*, 78:
84 (16 Feb 1934), 1-2.

3664. GECK, R.: Review of the same performance as in J3663, *Literatur*,
36:8 (May 1934), 463-64.

3665. H[AYES], J. J.: "Poetry at the Lyric, Prose at the Abbey," *CSM*, 42:
95 (18 Mar 1950), Magazine Section, 5.

3666. HOGAN, THOMAS: "Theatre," *Envoy*, 2:4 [i.e., 5] (Apr 1950), 72-77.

3667. O., S.: "Yeats and the Irish Theatre," *English R*, 12:1 (Aug 1912),
146-48.
"The Abbey Theatre of Yeats and Lady Gregory must now be pronounced
to be not only the most interesting, but the best theatrical model in
these islands. . . ."

3668. RISCHBIETER, HENNING: "Yeats *Gräfin Katlin* in Köln," *Theater heute*,
3:4 (Apr 1962), 27.

3669. SCHULZE VELLINGHAUSEN, ALBERT: "Fern und schwierig--eine Vers-
legende: William Butler Yeats *Die Gräfin Cathleen* in Köln," *FAZ*, #62
(14 Mar 1962), 20.

3670. STEPHAN, HEINZ: "Zwischen Gut und Böse: *Die Gräfin Katlin* von W. B.
Yeats in Köln erstaufgeführt," *Kölnische Rundschau*, 17:58 (9 Mar 1962), 5.

3671. T[RAVERS], P[AMELA]: "The Ellen Terry Barn Theatre," *New English
Weekly and New Age*, 15:13 (13 July 1939), 207-8.
Performances of this play, *Purgatory*, and *The Resurrection*.

3672. UNGER, WILHELM: "Beweggrund oder Tat: W. B. Yeats' *Die Gräfin Katlin*
in den Kammerspielen," *Kölner Stadtanzeiger*, #58 (9 Mar 1962), 4.

See also J623, 3384, 3624, 6504, 6709.

Country of the Young

3673. ADAMS, HAZARD: "Yeats' *Country of the Young*," *PMLA*, 72:3 (June 1957),
510-19.
An unpublished play, a variant of Lady Gregory's *The Travelling Man*.
Adams examines both texts and discusses parallels and differences.

The Death of Cuchulain I

3674. FRIEDMAN, BARTON R.: "Reflections of a Son of Talma: A Reading of
The Death of Cuchulain," *Arizona Q*, 27:4 (Winter 1971), 308-20.
The Old Man as mouthpiece and image of the dying Yeats.

3675. JOCHUM, K. P. S.: "Yeats's Last Play," *JEGP*, 70:2 (Apr 1971), 220-29.

3676. MARCUS, PHILLIP L.: "Myth and Meaning in Yeats's *The Death of Cuchulain*," *Irish UR*, 2:2 (Autumn 1972), 133-48.

3677. RAMSEY, WARREN: "Some Twentieth Century Ideas of the Verse Theatre," *CLS*, Special Advance Issue (1963), 43-50.
Note on this play, pp. 48-49.

3678. SHARTAR, I. MARTIN: "The Theater of the Mind: An Analysis of Works by Mallarmé, Yeats, Eliot, and Beckett," Ph.D. thesis, Emory U, 1966. vii, 216 p. (*DA*, 27:7 [Jan 1967], 2161A.)
"Yeats's *The Death of Cuchulain*: Blackout--Heaven's Blaze in the Theater of the Mind," 64-103.

See also J1071, 1153, 1156, 3014, 3336, 3339, 3348, 3478-86, 3500, 3512, 3518, 3537, 3543, 3594, 3745, 4986-92 and note, 4996-5031 and note, 6321, 6450.

The Death of Cuchulain II

3678a. T., W.: "Theatre," *Irish Press*, 15:287 (3 Dec 1945), 7.
The performance by Austin Clarke's Lyric Theatre. There are no extensive reviews in the other Dublin papers.

See also J3823, 3834.

Deirdre I

3679. ANON.: "Experiments: *Deirdre*," *Festival Theatre (New Lease) Programme*, #13 (12 Feb 1934), 1-2.

3680. BICKLEY, FRANCIS: "Deirdre," *Irish R*, 2:17 (July 1912), 252-54.
Yeats's *Deirdre* is too beautiful for the stage.

3681. BRAMSBÄCK, BIRGIT: "The Musician's Knife in Yeats's *Deirdre*," *Studia Neophilologica*, 41:2 (1969), 359-66.

3682. COTTER, EILEEN MARY: "The Deirdre Theme in Anglo-Irish Literature," Ph.D. thesis, U of California (Los Angeles), 1967. x, 259 p. (*DA*, 28:5 [Nov 1967], 1815A.)
"W. B. Yeats's *Deirdre*," 150-73.

3683. °FACKLER, HERBERT VERN: "The Irish Legend of Deirdre: A Study of Its Adaptations by W. B. Yeats, J. M. Synge, and James Stephens," M.A. thesis, New Mexico Highlands U, 1965.

3684. ————: "W. B. Yeat's [*sic*] *Deirdre*: Intensity by Condensation," *Forum* [Houston], 6:3 (Summer 1968), 43-46.

3684a. ————: "The Deirdre Legend in Anglo-Irish Literature, 1834 to 1937," °Ph.D. thesis, U of North Carolina at Chapel Hill, 1972. 205 p. (*DA*, 33:3 [Sept 1972], 1166A.)

3685. HICKS, ALLENA: "A Comparison of the Modern Versions of the Deirdre Story," M.A. thesis, U of Kansas, 1936. iii, 106 p.
"*Deirdre* by Yeats," 19-28.

3686. °HOGAN, DOROTHY JUNE: "Deirdre: Two Plays and a Tragic Error," M.A. thesis, Columbia U, 1947.
I do not know whether this thesis includes a discussion of Yeats's play.

3687. KALDECK, WILHELM: "Die Deirdre-Sage und ihre Bearbeitungen," Dr. phil. thesis, U of Wien, 1924. iii, 124 p.
"William Butler Yeats," 76-87. Negligible.

3688. °KITTS, JUDITH: "The Deirdre Legend in Irish Drama," M.A. thesis, U of North Carolina at Chapel Hill, 1968.
Reported to be on AE, Synge, and Yeats.

3689. MAANEN, W. VAN: "Voorwoord [to his translation of the play]," *Onze eeuw*, v 24 / pt 3:3 (Sept 1924), 193-95.

3690. MACCABE, ZOA JANETTE: "The Deirdre Story," M.A. thesis, Acadia U, [1928]. iii, 26 p.
Worthless.

3691. MCHUGH, ROGER: "Literary Treatment of the Deirdre Story," *Threshold*, 1:1 (Feb 1957), 36-49.
By AE, Yeats, Synge, and Stephens.

3692. MILLER, MARCIA SCHUYLER KELLEY: "The Deirdre Legend in English Literature," Ph.D. thesis, U of Pennsylvania, 1950. iii, 293 p. (*DA*, 13:5 [1953], 798.)
"Yeats and Synge," 205-59.

3693. PEAUX, JOHA. R.: "Deirdre," *Nieuwe Rotterdamsche Courant*, 81:25 (26 Jan 1924), Avondblad A, gewijd aan de letterkunde, #114, 4-5.

3694. ROBERTS, ETHEL TERESA: "The Greek Tragic Chorus and Adaptations of It in Modern Drama in English," °Ph.D. thesis, Arizona State U, 1969 [i.e., 1968?]. 235 p. (*DA*, 29:7 [Jan 1969], 2276A-77A.)
Discusses this play, according to abstract.

3695. SALERNO, HENRY F. (ed): *English Drama in Transition, 1880-1920*. NY: Pegasus, 1968. 544 p.
See pp. 387-90.

3696. SLATTERY, SISTER MARGARET PATRICE: "*Deirdre*: The 'Mingling of Contraries' in Plot and Symbolism," *MD*, 11:4 (Feb 1969), 400-403.

3696a. VINALL, SHIRLEY W.: "Some Lines by W. B. Yeats in an Italian Magazine," *N&Q*, os 218 / ns 20:9 (Sept 1973), 327-29.
Reprints J137b and comments on it.

3697. WICKSTROM, GORDON MINTON: "The Deirdre Plays of AE, Yeats, and Synge: Patterns of Irish Exile," Ph.D. thesis, Stanford U, 1968. vi, 310 p. (*DA*, 29:11 [May 1969], 4027A.)

See also J600, 1440, 1732, 1755, 2045, 2107, 2518, 3318, 3322, 3324, 3325a, 3336, 3339, 3345, 3405, 3457, 3500, 3501, 3512, 3594, 3644, 3696a, 4195, 4438-40, 5573, 6026, 6498, 6510, 6538, 6553, 6690, 7314, 7442.

Deirdre II

3698. ANON.: Notes on Mrs. Patrick Campbell's performance in *Deirdre*, *Athenaeum*, #4232 (5 Dec 1908), 729-30.

3699. ANON.: "Irish Drama," *Athenaeum*, #4261 (26 June 1909), 767-68.

3700. ANON.: "The Abbey Theatre: Production of a New Play," *Daily Express*, #16956 (26 Nov 1906), 7.

3701. ANON.: "The Abbey Theatre: Mr. Yeats's New Play, *Deirdre*," *Irish Times*, 48:15416 (26 Nov 1906), 7.

3702. ANON.: "Abbey Theatre: Mrs. Patrick Campbell as Deirdre," *Irish Times*, 50:16026 (10 Nov 1908), 7.

3703. B.: "The Irish Players," *T. P.'s Weekly*, 17:449 (16 June 1911), 744.

3704. DONAGHY, LYLE: "The Staging of a Play," *Irish Statesman*, 6:3 (27 Mar 1926), 70-71.
   Reviews a "bad" production. Correspondence by Geoffrey Phibbs and C. H. Whitton, :4 (3 Apr 1926), 97; by Donaghy, :5 (10 Apr 1926), 125-26.

3705. O'B., K. M.: "Mrs. Patrick Campbell and the Abbey Theatre: Interesting Announcement," *Dublin Evening Mail*, #23405 (11 Nov 1908), 2.
   An interview about the play. A review of the performance by M. O'D. appears on the same page.

3706. TITTERTON, W. R.: "Drama," *New Age*, ns 4:7 (10 Dec 1908), 142-43.

See also J3593, 6585.

Diarmuid and Grania I

3707. CANDON, THOMAS HENRY: "The Legend of Diarmuid and Grania: Its History and Treatment by Modern Writers," Ph.D. thesis, Boston U, 1954. ii, 154 p.
   "George Moore and William Butler Yeats," 83-90.

3708. MACCOLGAN, SHAN: "*Diarmuid and Grania*--Another View," *United Irishman*, 6:140 (2 Nov 1901), 5.
   Correspondence by a disgusted Catholic "Parent," who believes everything the *Leader* tells him, :144 (30 Nov 1901), 6; by "Parent of Ten," :145 (7 Dec 1901), 3; and by "Willoughby Wallaby Wobbles," :146 (14 Dec 1901), 7, where the whole thing becomes rather ridiculous.

3709. NEWLIN, PAUL A.: "The Artful Failure of George Moore's Plays," *Éire-Ireland*, 8:1 (Spring 1973), 62-84.

3710. WEAVER, JACK WAYNE: "Some Notes on George Moore and Professor Watson," *ELT*, 6:3 (1963), 147-50.
   On Yeats, Moore, and the composition of the play.

3711. YEATS, W. B., and GEORGE MOORE: "A Critical Edition of *Diarmuid and Grania* by William Butler Yeats and George Moore." Edited by Ray Small. Editor's Ph.D. thesis, U of Texas, 1958. vi, 324 p. (*DA*, 19:5 [Nov 1958], 1073-74.)
   Contains an earlier typescript 1 and a later typescript 2 (the text used in the *Variorum Edition of the Plays*), an account of the Yeats-Moore collaboration, a critical analysis of the play, the sources of the legend, and a glossary.

See also J845, 1617, 2245, 3332a, 4211, 4232b, 5638, 5918, 5932, 6119, 6302 (#7, 9), 6314, 6327, 6439, 6544, 7050, 7060, 7062, 7064, 7074.

Diarmuid and Grania II

3712. ANON.: "The Irish Literary Theatre: *Diarm[u]id and Grania*," *Daily Express*, #15379 (22 Oct 1901), 5-6.

3713. ANON.: "The Irish Literary Theatre: Successful Performances Last Night. A Crowded and Enthusiastic Audience," *Freeman's J*, 135:[] (22 Oct 1901), 4.

3714. ANON.: "The Irish Theatre: *Diarmuid and Grania* [. . .]," *Irish Daily Independent and Daily Nation*, #3025 (22 Oct 1901), 5.

3715. ANON.: "An Irish Play and an English Afterpiece," *Leader*, 3:10 (2 Nov 1901), 155-56.

Correspondence by Mac an Chuill, "Diarmuid and Grainne," *ibid.*, 157-58; and Moore's defense, "On the Thoughtlessness of Critics," :11 (9 Nov 1901), 174-76, plus editorial, 176-77.

See also J591.

The Dreaming of the Bones I

3716. Q., J.: "Note on *The Dreaming of the Bones*," *Little R*, 5:9 (Jan 1919), 61-63.

3717. WARSCHAUSKY, SIDNEY: "Yeats's Purgatorial Plays," *MD*, 7:3 (Dec 1964), 278-86.

On this play, *The Words upon the Window-Pane*, and *Purgatory*.

See also J778, 1153, 1157, 1162, 3324, 3336, 3339, 3421, 3429a, 3511a, 3531, 3556, 3573, 3575, 3580, 3583, 3855, 5579, 5719, 6321, 6475, 7416.

The Dreaming of the Bones II

3718. ANON.: "Abbey Theatre Ballet: *The Dreaming of the Bones*," *Irish Times*, 73:23280 (7 Dec 1931), 5.

3719. ANON.: "The Abbey Theatre Dublin: A New Play by Mr. W. B. Yeats," *Times*, #46001 (9 Dec 1931), 10.

3720. S., D.: "*The Dreaming of the Bones*: Mr. Yeats's Dance Play," *Irish Independent*, 40:291 (7 Dec 1931), 11.

See also J3808, 3809.

Fighting the Waves I

See J398, 581, 1071, 3489, 5721.

Fighting the Waves II

3721. ANON.: "*Fighting the Waves*: Mr. Yeats's New Ballet Play," *Irish Times*, 71:22562 (14 Aug 1929), 6.

3722. ANON.: "*Fighting the Waves*: Mr. Yeats's New Ballet in Dublin," *Times*, #45282 (15 Aug 1929), 8.

3723. BELFOE, A.-E.: "*En combattant les vagues* par le sénateur W. B. Yeats: Matinée spéciale au Lyric Theatre Hammersmith [. . .]," *Figaro*, 105:173 (22 June 1930), 5.

3724. C[URRAN], C. P.: "*Fighting the Waves*," *Irish Statesman*, 12:24 (17 Aug 1929), 475-76.

Correspondence by "Stall," :25 (24 Aug 1929), 489-90.

3725. DE B[LACAM], A[ODH]: "The Theatre," *Spectator*, 143:5278 (24 Aug 1929), 243.

3726. G., J. W.: "Ballet Play by Mr. Yeats: New Experiment at the Abbey," *Irish Independent*, 38:193 (14 Aug 1929), 6.

3727. HAYES, J. J.: "A Ballet at the Abbey," *NYT*, 79:26174 (22 Sept 1929), IX, 4.

See also J3489, 6506, 6639.

Four Plays for Dancers

See J845, 3544a, 4554-75, and the individual entries of the four plays.

A Full Moon in March I

3728. BENSTON, ALICE NAOMI: "Theatricality in Contemporary Drama," Ph.D. thesis, Emory U, 1962. vii, 254 p. (*DA*, 24:5 [Nov 1963], 2026-27.)
   Note on this play and on *Purgatory*, pp. 205-11.

3729. BENTLEY, ERIC (ed): *From the Modern Repertoire*. Series one. Bloomington: Indiana UP, 1958 [1949]. 406 p.
   Sees Kenneth Burke's tragic rhythm in the play and suggests that it is a "dramatic meditation," pp. 404-6.

3730. ROSE, MARILYN GADDIS: "The Daughters of Herodias in *Hérodiade*, *Salomé*, and *A Full Moon in March*," *Comparative Drama*, 1:3 (Fall 1967), 172-81.

3730a. SCHMITT, NATALIE CROHN: "Dramatic Multitude and Mystical Experience: W. B. Yeats," *ETJ*, 24:2 (May 1972), 149-58.
   "Emotion of multitude" in this play and the dramatic structure that makes it possible.

See also J1073, 1153, 1156, 1760a, 1813a, 2127, 2599, 2730, 3339, 3382, 3398, 3421, 3512, 3575, 3580, 3989, 4856-74, 5660.

A Full Moon in March II

3731. FUNKE, LEWIS: "3 Plays by Yeats at the Living Theatre," *NYT*, 110: 37495 (20 Sept 1960), 48.
   This play, *Purgatory*, and *The Herne's Egg*.

See also J3586, 3587a, 3592a.

The Green Helmet (The Golden Helmet) I

See J1071, 1273, 1732, 1755, 3322, 3339, 3479, 3480, 3482-86, 3501, 3518, 3537, 3543, 4245, 4457-61, 4477.

The Green Helmet (The Golden Helmet) II

3732. ANON.: "Three New Plays at the Abbey Theatre," *Freeman's J*, 141:[] (20 Mar 1908), 10.

3733. ANON.: "Court Theatre," *Times*, #39306 (23 June 1910), 12.

3734. "CNO CÚIL": "More New Plays at the 'Abbey,'" *Peasant and Irish Ireland*, 2:60 (28 Mar 1908), [5].
   "As a satire on our national propensity to contention it is excellent."

3735. COLUM, PÁDRAIC: "A Topical Play by Mr. W. B. Yeats," *Manchester Guardian*, #19818 (14 Feb 1910), 12.

3736. COX, J. H.: "A Whole Range of History: New Plays at the Abbey," *Irish Independent*, 17:68 (20 Mar 1908), 5.

3737. ————: "The Story of a Helmet: Mr. Yeats's Versified Play," *Irish Independent*, 19:36 (11 Feb 1910), 8.

3737a. H[OWE], P. P.: "At the Theatre," *Justice*, 28:1381 (2 July 1910), 12.
   There are more articles on the Irish theater in the three preceding issues.

3738. R.: "Court: *The Green Helmet*. A Play in Ballad Metre by W. B. Yeats," *Sunday Times*, 89:4551 (26 June 1910), 6.

3739. TRENCH, HERBERT: "Dramatic Values and a Suggested Solution," *Saturday R*, 109:2852 (25 June 1910), 815–16.

3740. UAP., S.: "*The Green Helmet*," *Irish Nation*, 2:60 (19 Feb 1910), 5.

Heads or Harps

See J121.

The Herne's Egg I

3741. °CAMPION, THOMAS B.: "Symbol and Sexuality in *The Herne's Egg*," M.A. thesis, University College, Dublin, 1966.

3742. COLLINS, JAMES A.: "'Where All the Ladders Start' (The Dramatic Verse of W. B. Yeats's *The Herne's Egg*)," *Literary Half-Yearly*, 9:2 (1968), 105–14.

3743. GUHA, NARESH: "A New Interpretation of Yeats's *The Herne's Egg*," *JJCL*, 5 (1965), 105–16.
    Discusses the influence of Shri Purohit Swami and Tagore.

3744. MURSHID, K. S.: "Yeats, Woman and God," *Venture*, 1:2 (June 1960), 166–77.
    Sex, religion, and Indian influences.

3745. PEARCE, DONALD R.: "Yeats' Last Plays: An Interpretation," *ELH*, 18:1 (Mar 1951), 67–76.
    A political interpretation of this play, *Purgatory*, and *The Death of Cuchulain*.

See also J747, 1153, 1156, 1760a, 1813a, 1867, 3335, 3345, 3348, 3421, 3497, 3539, 4956–75 and note.

The Herne's Egg II

3745a. K.: "Two Lyric Plays in Abbey Theatre," *Irish Times*, #29089 (30 Oct 1950), 7.

3746. LEVENTHAL, A. J.: "Dramatic Commentary," *Dublin Mag*, 26:1 (Jan–Mar 1951), 49–51.
    "The audience appeared somewhat disturbed by the unusual theme and the Apuleian approach."

The Hour Glass I

3747. BARLEY, JOSEPH WAYNE: *The Morality Motive in Contemporary English Drama*. Mexico, Mo.: Missouri Printing and Publishing Co., 1912. 124 p. (Ph.D. thesis, U of Pennsylvania, 1911.)
    On this play, pp. 22–25; on *Where There Is Nothing*, 36–37.

3748. LEEPER, JANET: *Edward Gordon Craig: Designs for the Theatre*. Harmondsworth: Penguin Books, 1948. 48 p. and 40 illustrations. (King Penguin Books. 40.)
    Designs for this play (stage set and mask of the Fool) and for *On Baile's Strand* (mask of the Blind Man), illustrations 22–24; notes, pp. 46–47.

3749. PARKER, J. STEWART: "Yeats's *The Hour Glass*," *MD*, 10:4 (Feb 1968), 356-63.

3750. PHILLIPS, STEVEN R.: "W. B. Yeats' *The Hour-Glass* and the Faust Legend," *Research Studies*, 38:3 (Sept 1970), 240-41.

3751. REINERT, OTTO (ed): *Modern Drama: Alternate Edition.* Boston: Little, Brown, 1966. xxxvii, 630 p.
See pp. 351-54 for an expanded version of "Yeats' *The Hour-Glass*," *Explicator*, 15:3 (Dec 1956), #19.

See also J788, 1112, 3382, 3469, 3497, 3503, 3594, 3800, 4195, 6034, 6315, 6317, 6436, 6791.

The Hour Glass II

3752. ANON.: "The Morality Play Society: Mr. Yeats's *Hour Glass*," *Times*, #39818 (10 Feb 1912), 10.

3753. ANON.: "The Wise Fool: A Yeats Morality Broadcast," *Times*, #53017 (23 Aug 1954), 10.

3754. ARCHER, WILLIAM: "Irish Plays," *World*, #1506 (12 May 1903), 784-85.
This play and *Cathleen ni Houlihan*.

3755. F., C.: "3. Kammerspiel-Abend: Irische Einakter," *Arbeiterzeitung*, 15:43 (20 Feb 1935), 3.
A performance in Basel, Switzerland.

3756. GODING, LOLA: "A Play Producer's Notebook," *English J*, 12:3 (Mar 1923), 207-8.
"The *Hour Glass* by Samuel Butler Yeats, provides one of the best plays that I have ever tried for high-school production."

3757. H., W.: "Verträumte Spiele: Einakter aus Japan und Irland im Studio der Städtischen Bühnen Essen," *Essener Woche*, 9:21 (23-31 May 1959), 13.

3758. K.: "Stadttheater in Basel: Irische Einakter im Kammerspielzyklus," *Basler Nachrichten*, 91:50 (20 Feb 1935), 1. Beilage, [3].

3759. KL.: "Stadttheater: Irische Einakter von J. M. Synge and W. B. Yeats," *National-Zeitung*, 93:86 (20 Feb 1935), 6.
Same performance as in J3758.

3760. M'C., F.: "The Irish National Theatre Society," *Daily Express*, #15813 (16 Mar 1903), 6.

3761. ROBERTS, R. ELLIS: "W. B. Yeats, Dramatist," *NSt*, 10:245 (2 Nov 1935), 636-37.
Performance of this play, *The Pot of Broth*, and *The Player Queen*.

3762. S., H.: "Premiere war schwach besucht: Einakterabend im Bühnenstudio [. . .]," *Neue Ruhrzeitung*, 14:111 (14 May 1959), 10.
Same performance as in J3763.

3763. SCHÖN, GERHARD: "Lyrische Legende: Essen erinnert an William Butler Yeats," *Rheinische Post*, 14:114 (20 May 1959), 2.

3764. SCHRÖTER, WERNER H.: "Frömmigkeit gegen No-Artistik: Essener Studio [. . .]," *Mittag*, 40:125 (3 June 1959), 4.

3765. S[TREICHER], S[IEGFRIED]: "Basler Stadttheater," *Basler Volksblatt*, 63:43 (20 Feb 1935), [3].

3766. TAMMS, WERNER: "Die Szene als poetisches Gleichnis [. . .]," *West-deutsche Allgemeine Zeitung*, #111 (15 May 1959), 10.
    The performance in Essen.

3767. WALKLEY, ARTHUR BINGHAM: *Drama and Life*. London: Methuen, 1907. viii, 331 p.
    "The Irish National Theatre (May, 1903)," 309-15; reprinted from *TLS*, 2:69 (8 May 1903), 146, where it was published anonymously. Reviews this play and *Cathleen ni Houlihan*.

See also J592, 942, 3846, 6038, 6766.

The Island of Statues

3768. ALSPACH, RUSSELL K.: "Yeats's First Two Published Poems," *MLN*, 58:7 (Nov 1943), 555-57.
    A bibliographical note.

See also J1069, 1101 (#6-7), 1813a, 2080a, 3336.

King Oedipus I

3769. ANON.: "Sophocles, Yeats and Dr. Gogarty," *NYHT*, 92:31472 (15 Jan 1933), VII, 4.
    Report of a Gogarty lecture on Yeats's translation.

3770. GRAB, FREDERIC D.: "Yeats's *King Oedipus*," *JEGP*, 71:3 (July 1972), 336-54.
    Also generally on Yeats and Sophocles and on Yeats's dramatic theory.

See also J147, 968, 2155, 3325a, 4699-700, 5571, 5574, 5720.

King Oedipus II

3771. BENÉT, WILLIAM ROSE: "The Theatre," *SatR*, 9:28 (28 Jan 1933), 402.

3772. C[URRAN], C. P.: "Oedipus at the Abbey," *Irish Statesman*, 7:14 (11 Dec 1926), 326.

3773. DE CASSERES, BENJAMIN: "Yeats' *King Oedipus*," *Arts & Decoration*, 38:5 (Mar 1933), 58, 63.

3774. G., J. W.: "*Oedipus the King* Staged: Enthusiasm at Abbey," *Irish Independent*, 35:292 (8 Dec 1926), 6.

3775. GARLAND, ROBERT: "W. B. Yeats Tells All as Dublin Thespians Give *King Oedipus*: Translation and Adaptation of Sophocles' Melodrama More Lively in Its Pace Than Might Have Been Expected," *NY World Telegram*, 65: 166 (16 Jan 1933), 10.
    "All" means how and why he wrote the translation.

3776. HAYES, J. J.: "Oedipus in Dublin: The Theatre Rediscovers a Popular Success," *BET*, 98:18 (22 Jan 1927), pt 3, 6-7.

The King of the Great Clock Tower I

See J1153, 1156, 1760a, 1813a, 2127, 2349, 2414, 2730, 3318, 3491, 3539, 3575, 4845-55 and note, 4871, 5654.

The King of the Great Clock Tower II

3776a. ANON.: "Memorable 'First Night,'" *Sunday Times*, #5808 (5 Aug 1934), 5.

3777. DAVRAY, HENRY D.: Note on the performance of this play and *The Resurrection*, *Mercure de France*, yr 45 / 255:871 (1 Oct 1934), 197-98.

See also J3384, 3885.

The King's Threshold I

3778. BLOCK, HASKELL M.: "Yeats's *The King's Threshold*: The Poet and Society," *PQ*, 34:2 (Apr 1955), 206-18.

3779. BORNSTEIN, GEORGE: "A Borrowing from Wilde in Yeats's *The King's Threshold*," *N&Q*, os 216 / ns 18:11 (Nov 1971), 421-22.
A borrowing from *The Decay of Lying*.

3780. BUSHRUI, S. B.: "*The King's Threshold*: A Defence of Poetry," *REL*, 4:3 (July 1963), 81-94.

3781. FALLON, GABRIEL: "A Forgotten Prologue: When Did Yeats Write It?" *Irish Times*, #32746 (13 Sept 1960), 5.
Correspondence by Micheál Ó hAodha, #32747 (14 Sept 1960), 7; Corinna Salvadori, #32749 (16 Sept 1960), 7; Austin Clarke, #32750 (17 Sept 1960), 9; Gabriel Fallon, #32752 (20 Sept 1960), 7.

3782. FRIEDMAN, BARTON R.: "Under a Leprous Moon: Action and Image in *The King's Threshold*," *Arizona Q*, 26:1 (Spring 1970), 39-53.

3783. O'GRADY, STANDISH: "On *The King's Threshold*," *All Ireland R*, 4:32 (24 Oct 1903), 340.
A letter to Yeats expressing dissatisfaction with the play because it is "unreal," "unnatural," and "unhuman." See the defense of the play by T. W. Rolleston, "Mr. Yeats' Play," :33 (31 Oct 1903), 351-52, and O'Grady's reply, 352.

3784. OHDEDAR, ADITYA KUMAR: "*The King's Threshold*: A Significant Modern Poetic Drama," *Literary Criterion*, 3:2 (Summer 1957), 21-28.

See also J398, 1617, 1732, 1813a, 2237, 3322, 3339, 3413, 3474, 3499, 3503, 3532, 4195, 5726, 5882, 6034, 6498.

The King's Threshold II

3785. ANON.: "Irish National Theatre Society: Production of Two New Plays," *Freeman's J*, 136:[] (9 Oct 1903), 5-6.
Includes an account of Yeats's speech at the conclusion of the performance.

3786. ANON.: "Two New Plays—Irish National Theatre," *Irish Daily Independent and Daily Nation*, #3632 (9 Oct 1903), 6.

3787. ANON.: "Irish National Theatre," *Irish Times*, 45:14437 (9 Oct 1903), 8.

3788. ANON.: "*The King's Threshold*," *Sinn Féin*, ns 4:197 (8 Nov 1913), 1.

3789. ANON.: "The Irish National Theatre," *TLS*, 3:116 (1 Apr 1904), 102.

3790. ANON.: "All Ireland," *United Irishman*, 10:242 (17 Oct 1903), 1.
Reviews a performance of the play and comments generally on Yeats's work for the National Theatre Society.

3791. ARCHER, WILLIAM: "Irish Plays at the Royalty," *World*, #1552 (29 Mar 1904), 551.

3791a. "Chanel" [i.e., CLERY, ARTHUR EDWARD]: "Plays with Meanings," *Leader*, 7:8 (17 Oct 1903), 124-25.

3792. H., E.: "The Irish National Theatre," *Pilot*, 9:211 (2 Apr 1904), 309.
Review of this play and of *The Pot of Broth*.

3793. "IGNOTUS": "*The King's Threshold*," *United Irishman*, 10:243 (24 Oct 1903), 3.

3794. L[YND], R[OBERT] W[ILSON] [?]: "Ireland and the Play," *To-day*, 42: 544 (6 Apr 1904), 264.

3795. RYAN, HUBERT S.: "Some Irish Plays," *Outlook* [London], 13:322 (2 Apr 1904), 233-34.

See also J631, 4333, 5903, 6365, 6766.

The Land of Heart's Desire I

3796. ANON.: Note on *The Land of Heart's Desire*, *Bibelot*, 9:6 (June 1903), 4 unnumbered pages preceding p. 183.
". . . an outbreathing of that Celtic sorrowfulness over bright things faded. . . ."

3797. FARRELL, MICHAEL: "Plays for the Country Theatre," *Bell*, 2:1 (Apr 1941), 78-84.
See pp. 80-81.

3798. HIRSCH, FOSTER: "The Hearth and the Journey: The Mingling of Orders in the Drama of Yeats and Eliot," *Arizona Q*, 27:4 (Winter 1971), 293-307.
Discusses this play and *At the Hawk's Well*.

3799. REES, LESLIE (ed): *Modern Short Plays*. Sydney: Angus & Robertson, 1951. 276 p.
See pp. 259-60.

3800. SHIPLEY, JOSEPH TWADELL: *Guide to Great Plays*. Washington: Public Affairs Press, 1956. xi, 867 p.
The Land of Heart's Desire and *The Hour Glass* are Yeats's "great plays," pp. 837-39.

See also J398, 1142, 1307, 1440, 1729, 2072, 3336, 3356, 3360, 3409, 3426, 3457, 3462, 3512, 3519, 3540, 3545, 3594, 3824, 3855, 3965, 4195, 4196, 4300-4305, 4472-74, 5470-72, 5478, 5642, 5646, 5658, 5689, 5698, 6302 (#6), 6317, 6328, 6334, 6436, 6502, 6542, 6545, 6565, 6896, 7356.

The Land of Heart's Desire II

3801. ANON.: "Dr. Todhunter's New Play," *Daily Chronicle*, #10002 (30 Mar 1894), 6.

3802. ANON.: "Abbey Theatre: Mr. Yeats's *Land of Heart's Desire*," *Irish Times*, 53:16735 (17 Feb 1911), 5.
"In the days when he was still a true and natural poet, and a seer without affectation, Mr. W. B. Yeats wrote a little play called *The Land of Heart's Desire*."

3803. ANON.: "Present-Day Criticism," *New Age*, ns 11:1025 (2 May 1912), 10-11.
". . . this vague, pale, gaping drama. . . ." See correspondence by James Stephens, :1026 (9 May 1912), 46-47.

3804. A[RCHER], W[ILLIAM]: "The Theatre," *World*, #1031 (4 Apr 1894), 26-28.

3805. Dbd. [i.e., DIEBOLD, BERNHARD]: "Irische Einakter," *Frankfurter Zeitung*, 63:192 (12 Mar 1919), 1.
A performance in the Frankfurter Schauspielhaus.

3806. DITHMAR, EDWARD A.: "At the Theatres," *NYT*, 50:15851 (28 Oct 1900), 22.

3807. GILMAN, LAWRENCE: "The Neo-Celtic Drama in America," *Lamp*, 27:3 (Oct 1903), 231-33.
Performances of this play, *The Pot of Broth*, and *Cathleen ni Houlihan*.

3808. MCAVOCK, DESMOND: "Abbey Theatre: The Early Plays of Yeats," *Hibernia*, 29:3 (Mar 1965), 27-28.
Performances of this play, *Cathleen ni Houlihan*, and *The Dreaming of the Bones*.

3809. O'CONNOR, PATRICK: "Theatre," *Furrow*, 16:6 (June 1965), 374-76.
Same performances as in J3808.

3810. R.: "Two Irish Dramatists," *United Ireland*, 13:659 (21 Apr 1894), 1.

3811. SULLIVAN, MARGARET F.: "Triumph of the 'Literary Play,'" *Dial*, 30:360 (16 June 1901), 391-93.
A performance in Chicago.

3812. ZERAFFA, MICHEL: "Drames et poésie," *Europe*, 34:131-32 (Nov-Dec 1956), 225-29.
Contains a short note on Rouyer's production of this play, *The Only Jealousy of Emer*, and *The Shadowy Waters*. See J3540.

See also J624.

Mosada

3813. HOPKINS, GERARD MANLEY: *Further Letters of Gerard Manley Hopkins Including His Correspondence with Coventry Patmore*. Edited with notes and an introduction by Claude Colleer Abbott. London: Oxford UP, 1956 [1938]. xliii, 465 p.
In a letter to Patmore of 7 Nov 1886, Hopkins expresses his opinion of *Mosada*, which he hasn't read, and of "The Two Titans," which he has and doesn't like (pp. 373-74).

See also J2080a, 4257.

Oedipus at Colonus I

See J3325a.

Oedipus at Colonus II

3814. G., J. W.: "At the Abbey Theatre: Mr. Yeats's *Oedipus at Colonus*," *Irish Independent*, 36:218 (13 Sept 1927), 10.

3815. STARKIE, WALTER: "*Oedipus at Colonus* at the Abbey Theatre," *Irish Statesman*, 9:2 (17 Sept 1927), 40-41.
Correspondence by T. G. Keller and "Arcos," :3 (24 Sept 1927), 60: "What has come to Mr. Yeats that he permitted such demonstration of inartistry on the Abbey stage?"

On Baile's Strand I

3816. BARNET, SYLVAN, MORTON BERMAN, and WILLIAM BURTO (eds): *Eight Great Tragedies*. NY: New American Library, 1957. 443 p. (Mentor Book. MQ461.) See pp. 324-27.

3817. COLCORD, LINCOLN: "Imagined Drama," *New Republic*, 4:45 (11 Sept 1915), 157.

3818. SCHROETER, JAMES: "Yeats and the Tragic Tradition," *Southern R*, 1:4 (Oct 1965), 835-46.
On this play's paradoxical use of Greek tragedy and mythology: Although the pattern of action seems to conform to those of Sophocles and Aeschylus, Yeats nevertheless manages to steer the play's meaning into the opposite direction. Sophocles would never have consented to Yeats's contention that Cuchulain's mistake was his momentary surrender to reason and order.

See also J398, 1071, 1732, 1755, 1813a, 2152, 2431, 3322, 3336, 3339, 3354, 3464, 3478-80, 3482-86, 3497, 3499, 3500, 3501, 3503, 3518, 3537, 3543, 3748, 3842, 4162, 4167, 4195, 5570, 6046, 6381, 6450, 6510.

On Baile's Strand II

3819. ANON.: "The New Abbey Theatre: Opening Performance," *Daily Express*, #16371 (28 Dec 1904), 5.
This play and *Cathleen ni Houlihan*.

3820. ANON.: "A Mixed Programme," *Festival Theatre R*, [1]:6 (Jan 1927), 2-4.
A photograph of the performance appears in 3:47 (17 Nov 1928), 5.

3821. ANON.: "Irish National Theatre: Opening Night. New Play by Mr. Yeats [. . .]," *Freeman's J*, 137:[] (28 Dec 1904), 5-6.

3822. ANON.: "National Drama: The Abbey Theatre. Auspicious Inauguration," *Irish Daily Independent and Daily Nation*, #4013 (28 Dec 1904), 6.
See also the editorial, "Abbey Theatre," p. 4.

3823. CALTA, LOUIS: "Theatre: Yeats Cycle. Two Celtic Plays in One-Night Stand," *NYT*, 108:36969 (13 Apr 1959), 34.
Performances of this play and *The Death of Cuchulain* by the New York Theatre Society at the Beekman Tower Hotel Theatre.

3824. D., A.: "The Irish Players Again," *Academy*, 72:1833 (22 June 1907), 610-11.
The reviewer thinks this play inferior to *The Land of Heart's Desire*.

3825. GREIN, J. T.: "Two Irish Plays," *Sunday Times*, #4314 (10 Dec 1905), 13.
"We are spellbound by the poet, but we are not held by the dramatist."

3826. JOY, MAURICE: "The Irish National Theatre," *Speaker*, ns 11:[] (24 Dec 1904), 309-11.

3827. ————: "Mr. Yeats's New Play," *Speaker*, ns 11:[] (7 Jan 1905), 353.

3828. MASEFIELD, JOHN: "Irish Plays in Dublin: *On Baile's Strand* at the Abbey Theatre," *Daily News*, #18345 (4 Jan 1905), 6.

See also J936, 6755, 6766.

The Only Jealousy of Emer I

3829. COHN, RUBY, and BERNARD FRANK DUKORE (eds): *Twentieth Century Drama: England, Ireland, the United States*. NY: Random House, 1966. ix, 692 p.
    See pp. 147-50.

3830. KROP, HILDO: Photographs of the masks for Cuchulain, Eithne Inguba, Emer, Bricriu, and the Woman of the Sea, *Wendingen*, 7:2 (1925), 14-15.
    See also J3833.

3831. SCANLON, SISTER ALOYSE: "The Sustained Metaphor in *The Only Jealousy of Emer*," *MD*, 7:3 (Dec 1964), 273-77.

3832. WILSON, F. A. C.: "Yeats and Gerhart Hauptmann," *Southern R* [Adelaide], [1]:1 (1963), 69-73.
    Suggests that this play was influenced by Hauptmann's *Die versunkene Glocke*.

See also J1071, 1153, 1157, 1699, 1755, 2730, 3336, 3339, 3478-86, 3490, 3500, 3512, 3518, 3537, 3539, 3540, 3543, 3575, 3583, 5578, 5580, 5622, 5657, 6315, 6381.

The Only Jealousy of Emer II

3833. ANON.: "Maskerspel en maskerdans," *Nieuwe Rotterdamsche Courant*, 83:330 (28 Nov 1926), C1.
    Review of the Dutch performance: translation by Helene Swarth, production and leading part by Albert van Dalsum, masks by Hildo Krop. See also Anon., "Stadsschouwburg te Amsterdam," :331 (29 Nov 1926), C1; a long letter by W. B. Thieme, "Het maskerspel van Vrouwe Emer," *ibid.*, trying to make sense of the play; and J3830.

3834. ANON.: "Students Revive Plays by Yeats," *Times*, #56493 (1 Dec 1965), 15.
    The Bristol University Drama Studio productions of this play, *At the Hawk's Well*, *The Death of Cuchulain*, and *The Cat and the Moon*.

3835. BARNES, CLIVE: "Stage: Bright Twin Bill," *NYT*, 119:40968 (25 Mar 1970), 36.
    Performance by the La Mama Repertory Company at the Performing Garage. Music by Barbara Benary. See also Mel Gussow, *"Jealousy of Emer . . . ,"* 121:41639 (25 Jan 1972), 26, for a review of another performance by the La Mama group.

3836. KERR, WALTER: "Drama, Not Long Out of the Womb," *NYT*, 119:41000 (26 Apr 1970), II, 1, 5.
    Illustrated. The Performing Garage production.

3837. LEVENTHAL, A. J.: "Dramatic Commentary," *Dublin Mag*, 24:1 (Jan-Mar 1949), 38-41.

3837a. SAINER, ARTHUR: "Peering Down the Tunnel," *Village Voice*, 12 Feb 1970, 49.
    The La Mama performance.

See also J1097, 3812.

The Player Queen I

3838. ANON.: "Mr. Yeats and His New Play," *Irish Nation*, 2:81 (16 July 1910), 8.

Interview about the play, revealing that it was originally conceived as a puppet play.

3839. BECKER, WILLIAM: "The Mask Mocked: Or, Farce and the Dialectic of the Self (Notes on Yeats's *The Player Queen*)," *Sewanee R*, 61:1 (Jan-Mar 1953), 82-108.
An extract from J3317.

3840. HINDEN, MICHAEL: "Yeats's Symbolic Farce: *The Player Queen*," *MD*, 14:4 (Feb 1972), 441-48.

3841. NEWTON, NORMAN: "Yeats as a Dramatist: *The Player Queen*," *Essays in Criticism*, 8:3 (July 1958), 269-84.
A defense of Yeats's dramatic intelligence.

3842. S[ADDLEMYER], A[NN]: "Notes on the Plays," *Beltaine* [Victoria, B.C.], #1 (Mar 1965), [6-8].
Notes on this play and *On Baile's Strand*.

See also J159, 1069, 1114, 1136, 1153, 1156, 1760a, 1813a, 3318, 3325a, 3335, 3348, 3427, 3448, 3469, 3512, 3536, 3539, 5618, 5671, 6450, 6790.

The Player Queen II

3843. ANON.: "A Yeats Satire: First Production in the Abbey of *The Player Queen*," *Freeman's J*, 152:[] (10 Dec 1919), 2.

3844. ANON.: "The Abbey Theatre: New Play by Mr. W. B. Yeats," *Irish Times*, 61:19569 (10 Dec 1919), 6.

3845. ANON.: "The Stage Society," *Times*, #42111 (28 May 1919), 15.
". . . revealing a new gift in Mr. Yeats, the gift of writing thoroughly enjoyable nonsense."

3846. COOKMAN, A. V.: "The Theatre," *London Mercury*, 33:194 (Dec 1935), 191-92.
Performances of this play, *The Hour Glass*, and *The Pot of Broth*.

3847. HORN, EFFI: "Büchner-Theater: Partiegefühle beim Sandkasten," *Münchner Merkur*, #121 (23 May 1966), 4.

3848. J., G.: "Dilettanten-Mühen: Premiere im Büchner-Theater," *Süddeutsche Zeitung*, 22:122 (23 May 1966), 12.

3849. KTH.: "Von bösen Weibern," *Abendzeitung*, 19:122 (23 May 1966), 13.

3850. LEWISOHN, LUDWIG: "Drama: Importations," *Nation*, 117:3043 (31 Oct 1923), 495-96.
"Terribly overwritten and therefore terribly dull."

3851. "PRIOR": "*The Player Queen*," *Irish Statesman*, 1:25 (13 Dec 1919), 608-9.
"Most of the audience went to be mystified, and they came away disappointed, because they were not quite sure what they ought to be mystified about."

3852. S[TRACHEY], J[AMES]: "Swinburne and Mr. Yeats," *Athenaeum*, #4649 (6 June 1919), 438.
"The audience gasped. . . ."

3853. YOUNG, STARK: "At the Neighborhood," *New Republic*, 36:465 (31 Oct 1923), 257.
A performance at the Neighborhood Playhouse.

See also J3761, 6551.

The Pot of Broth I

3854. DRAVAINE, CLAUDE: Note on his translation of the play, *Jeux, tré-teaux et personnages*, 15:112 (Nov–Dec 1946), 276–78.

3855. GOURLEY, MERYL: "Four Plays by W. B. Yeats," *Icarus*, 5:17 (Nov 1955), 27–31.
     This play, *The Land of Heart's Desire*, *The Dreaming of the Bones*, and *Purgatory*.

3856. MÜLLER, MAX (ed): *Two English One-Act Plays by Modern Irish Authors*. Mit Einleitung und Anmerkungen herausgegeben von Max Müller. Frankfurt/Main: Diesterweg, 1928. iv, 47 p. (Diesterwegs Neusprachliche Schulausgaben mit deutschen Anmerkungen. 15.)
     Notes on this play and on Lady Gregory's *The Rising of the Moon*, pp. 6–9, 35–44.

See also J398, 1413, 3360, 4241, 5578, 6316, 6317.

The Pot of Broth II

3857. ANON.: "The Samhain Festival," *Freeman's J*, 135:[] (31 Oct 1902), 4.

3858. MACCARTHY, DESMOND: *The Court Theatre, 1904–1907: A Commentary and Criticism*. Edited with a foreword and additional material by Stanley Weintraub. Coral Gables: U of Miami Press, 1966 [1907]. xxvi, 182 p. (Books of the Theatre Series. 6.)
     See p. 116 for a list of performances of this play.

See also J3761, 3792, 3807, 3846.

Purgatory I

3859. ANON.: "Mr. Yeats Explains Play: Plot of *Purgatory* Is Its Meaning. Dramatist's Answer to U.S. Priest's Query," *Irish Independent*, 47:192 (13 Aug 1938), 9.
     Interview with Yeats about the Rev. Terence L. Connolly's questions.

3860. BARNET, SYLVAN, MORTON BERMAN, and WILLIAM BURTO (eds): *An Intro-duction to Literature: Fiction--Poetry--Drama*. 2nd edition. Boston: Little, Brown, 1963 [1961]. 611 p.
     See pp. 453–57.

3861. CALDERWOOD, JAMES L., and HAROLD E. TOLLIVER (eds): *Forms of Drama*. Englewood Cliffs: Prentice-Hall, 1969. v, 601 p.
     See pp. 192–93.

3862. COLLINS, JAMES A.: "The Dramatic Verse of W. B. Yeats in *Purgatory*," *Literary Half-Yearly*, 9:1 (Jan 1969), 91–98.

3863. FELSTINER, LOUIS JOHN: "*Purgatory*: Coda to the Life and Art of William Butler Yeats," Honors thesis, Harvard U, 1958. ii, 45 p.

3864. FREDRICKS, MARY VIRGINIA: "An Approach to the Teaching of Oral Interpretation in Terms of Dramatic Action," Ph.D. thesis, U of Minnesota, 1961. iii, 356 p. (*DA*, 22:4 [Oct 1961], 1300–1301.)
     Analysis of the play as a scene-role-gesture relationship, pp. 266–81.

3865. GASKELL, RONALD: "*Purgatory*," *MD*, 4:4 (Feb 1962), 397–401.

3866. KAWIN, BRUCE FREDERICK: *Telling It Again and Again: Repetition in Literature and Film*. Ithaca: Cornell UP, 1972. ix, 197 p.
   See pp. 72-84.

3867. LAPISARDI, FREDERICK S.: "A Most Conscious Craftsman: A Study of Yeat's [sic] *Purgatory* as the Culmination of His Expressed Dramatic Theories," *Eire-Ireland*, 2:4 (Winter 1967), 87-99.
   "If Yeats is ever generally accepted as a playwright, *Purgatory* will stand as his greatest dramatic achievement, for it is in this play that most of his expressed theories reach fruition." Most of the preceding plays are failures of one sort or another.

3868. LIGHTFOOT, MARJORIE J.: "*Purgatory* and *The Family Reunion*: In Pursuit of Prosodic Description," *MD*, 7:3 (Dec 1964), 256-66.

3869. LINEBARGER, JAMES MORRIS: "Yeats' Symbolist Method and the Play *Purgatory*," Ph.D. thesis, Emory U, 1963. viii, 172 p. (*DA*, 24:9 [Mar 1964], 3750-51.)

3870. MACLEISH, ARCHIBALD: "The Poet as Playwright," *Atlantic Monthly*, 195:2 (Feb 1955), 49-52.
   Contains a note on this play.

3871. MOORE, JOHN REES: "An Old Man's Tragedy--Yeats' *Purgatory*," *MD*, 5:4 (Feb 1963), 440-50.

3872. REINERT, OTTO (ed): *Drama: An Introductory Anthology*. Boston: Little, Brown, 1961. xi, 652 p.
   Note on this play, pp. 473-75; reprinted in Reinert's *Modern Drama: Nine Plays*. Boston: Little, Brown, 1962. xxvii, 491 p., pp. 311-13.

3873. RUBINSTEIN, HAROLD FREDERICK, and JOHN COURTENAY TREWIN (eds): *The Drama Bedside Book*. London: Gollancz, 1966. 544 p.
   The section "Darkest Hour" contains a complete reprint of the play plus an introductory note, pp. 395-403.

3873a. SCHMITT, NATALIE CROHN: "Curing Oneself of the Work of Time: W. B. Yeats's *Purgatory*," *Comparative Drama*, 7:4 (Winter 1973/74), 310-33.
   Discusses the play as religious drama and concentrates on rituals of rebirth and renewal.

See also J827, 1073, 1147, 1153, 1156, 1813a, 2152, 2235, 2248, 2339, 2490, 2512, 3187, 3324, 3336, 3339, 3348, 3400, 3427, 3429a, 3441, 3448, 3457, 3464, 3465, 3469, 3511a, 3531, 3544a, 3556, 3580, 3717, 3728, 3745, 3855, 3940, 3989, 4167, 4986-92 and note, 4996-5031 and note, 5578, 5623, 5714, 6450.

Purgatory II

3874. ANON.: "Mr. W. B. Yeats's New Play: Theatre Festival Production. 'His Own Beliefs,'" *Evening Mail*, #28500 (11 Aug 1938), 8.
   See also in the same issue "Yeats Play 'Not Understood': Enquirers Are 'Left Guessing,'" p. 9. The following issue contains an interview with Yeats, in which some of the problems are explained: "Puzzle of the New Play: Explanations by Mr. Yeats. 'The Dead Suffer,'" #28501 (12 Aug 1938), 12.

3875. ANON.: "Abbey Theatre Festival: Mr. Yeats's New Play," *Times*, #48074 (16 Aug 1938), 10.

3876. ANON.: "Poetic Play of Great Power: Yeats's *Purgatory*," *Times*, #53312 (30 Aug 1955), 5.
  A performance in Edinburgh.

3877. ANON.: "Irish Plays in Edinburgh: *Purgatory* Revived," *Times*, #53932 (29 Aug 1957), 3.

3878. C., L.: "New Yeats Play Given at Abbey," *Irish Press*, 8:190 (11 Aug 1938), 7.

3879. ELLIS-FERMOR, UNA: "The Abbey Theatre Festival (7-20 Aug 1938)," *English*, 2:9 (1938), 174-77.

3880. M[ALONE], A[NDREW] E.: "Abbey Theatre Festival: A New Yeats Play," *Irish Times*, 80:25298 (11 Aug 1938), 6.
  Correspondence by John Lucy, :25301 (15 Aug 1938), 5; Frank O'Connor, :25302 (16 Aug 1938), 8; Diarmuid Brennan, Mary Manning, and others, :25303 (17 Aug 1938), 5; and continued in the subsequent issues.

3881. S., D.: "Great Poet Has Warm Reception: New Yeats Play at the Abbey," *Irish Independent*, 47:190 (11 Aug 1938), 10.

See also J3586, 6775.

The Resurrection I

3882. BABU, M. SATHYA: "Treatment of Christianity in W. B. Yeats' *The Resurrection*," *Wisconsin Studies in Literature*, 5 (1968), 53-63.
  "The theme of the play has little to do with Christianity as an institutional religion."

3883. BAIRD, SISTER MARY JULIAN: "A Play on the Death of God: The Irony of Yeats's *The Resurrection*," *MD*, 10:1 (May 1967), 79-86.
  Written from an orthodox Catholic point of view.

3884. MORGAN, MARGERY M.: "Shaw, Yeats, Nietzsche, and the Religion of Art," *Komos*, 1:1 (Mar 1967), 24-34.
  The influence of Nietzsche and Shaw's *Major Barbara* on this play.

See also J1069, 1073, 1153, 1815, 1818, 1828, 2152, 2861, 3271-75 and note, 3325a, 3336, 3345, 3348, 3427, 3518, 3532, 3555, 3575, 3591, 5579, 5674.

The Resurrection II

3885. ANON.: "The Abbey Theatre: Two New Plays by W. B. Yeats," *Times*, #46820 (31 July 1934), 12.
  This play and *The King of the Great Clock Tower*.

3886. ANON.: "Dublin Festival Play on the Genesis of a Bully," *Times*, #56434 (23 Sept 1965), 8.

3887. ATKINSON, BROOKS: "Abbey Odds and Ends," *NYT*, 84:28059 (20 Nov 1934), 24.

See also J3592, 3593, 3776a, 3777.

The Seeker

See J2080a.

The Shadowy Waters I

3888. GOLDGAR, HARRY: "Axël de Villiers de l'Isle Adam et *The Shadowy Waters* de W. B. Yeats," *Revue de la littérature comparée*, 24:4 (Oct-Dec 1950), 563-74.

3889. °KAYLOR, MARY A.: "William Butler Yeats and the Shadowy Waters," M.A. thesis, Sacramento State College, 1966.

3890. OLIVERO, FEDERICO: *Studi su poeti e prosatori inglesi*. Torino: Bocca, 1925. vi, 394 p.
    "La leggenda di Ulisse nel Tennyson e in alcuni poeti irlandesi," 212-32; paraphrases this play and *The Wanderings of Oisin*.

3891. °SANDVOS, ANNIS: "A Study of *The Shadowy Waters* of William Butler Yeats: Its Sources and Symbolism," M.A. thesis, Columbia U, 1937.

3892. SIDNELL, MICHAEL JOHN: "A Critical Examination of W. B. Yeats's *The Shadowy Waters* with a Transcription and Collation of the Manuscript Versions," Ph.D. thesis, U of London, 1967. v, 548 p.
    See also J3896.

3893. ————: "Manuscript Versions of Yeats's *The Shadowy Waters*: An Abbreviated Description and Chronology of the Papers Relating to the Play in the National Library of Ireland," *PBSA*, 62:1 (1968), 39-57.
    See also Lola L. Szladits: "Addenda to Sidnell: Yeats's *The Shadowy Waters*," :4 (1968), 614-17 (additional material from the Lady Gregory Collection in the Berg Collection); and J3896.

3894. Entry canceled.

3895. YEATS, W. B.: *A Tower of Polished Black Stones: Early Versions of "The Shadowy Waters."* Arranged and edited by David Ridgley Clark and George Mayhew with five illustrations by Leonard Baskin and drawings by the poet. Dublin: Dolmen Press, 1971. xvi, 71 p. (Dolmen Editions. 11.)
    "Introduction," vii-xvi, comments on the early versions, which differ greatly from the published texts. Further commentary, *passim*. Prints the text from the National Library of Ireland MS. 8762 (#9, #2, #11 in part) and from Huntington MS. 474. See also J3896.

3896. ————: *Druid Craft: The Writing of "The Shadowy Waters."* Manuscripts of W. B. Yeats transcribed, edited, and with a commentary by Michael J. Sidnell, George P. Mayhew, David R. Clark. Amherst: U of Massachusetts Press, 1971. xxiii, 349 p. (Manuscripts of W. B. Yeats. 1.)
    This edition of MS. versions supersedes all previous editions, particularly Clark's "Aubrey Beardsley's Drawing of the 'Shadows' in W. B. Yeats's *The Shadowy Waters*," *MD*, 7:3 (Dec 1964), 267-72; J5948 (#3); J3892; J3893; J3895. Contains—apart from the transcriptions—chapters on structure, plot, mythical allusions, symbols, visions, and the published versions. For reviews of this book see J5516-20.

See also J1074, 1162 (#7), 1263, 1383, 1464, 1722, 1802, 1813a, 2107, 2127, 2152, 2288, 2429, 2431, 2730, 3322, 3332a, 3336, 3339, 3348, 3382, 3387, 3400, 3462, 3497, 3501, 3511a, 3519, 3540, 3594, 4195, 4366-79 and note, 5514-20, 5676, 5703, 5932, 5948, 7416.

The Shadowy Waters II

3897. ANON.: "The Abbey Theatre: Production of New Plays," *Daily Express*, #16967 (10 Dec 1906), 6.

3898. ANON.: "Irish National Theatre Society: Plays at the Molesworth Hall," *Freeman's J*, 137:[] (15 Jan 1904), 6.

3899. ANON.: Two photographs of, and some comments on, a performance of the play, *Illustrated London News*, 175:4714 (24 Aug 1929), 336.

3900. ANON.: "*The Shadowy Waters*: Theosophists and Mr. Yeats's Play," *Inis Fáil*, #11 (Aug 1905), 3.

3901. ANON.: "Irish National Theatre," *Irish Times*, 46:14520 (15 Jan 1904), 8.

3902. ANON.: "Abbey Theatre," *Irish Times*, 49:15428 (10 Dec 1906), 8.

3903. "Chanel" [i.e., CLERY, ARTHUR EDWARD]: "Plays That Are Not Plays," *Leader*, 7:23 (30 Jan 1904), 379-81.

See also J3616, 3812, 6766.

The Unicorn from the Stars I

3904. BRYAN, ROBERT A., and others (eds): . . . *All These to Teach: Essays in Honor of C. A. Robertson*. Gainesville: U of Florida Press, 1965. x, 248 p.
George M. Harper: "The Reconciliation of Paganism & Christianity in Yeats' *Unicorn from the Stars*," 224-36.

3905. HERING, GERHARD FRIEDRICH: *Der Ruf zur Leidenschaft: Improvisationen über das Theater*. Köln: Kiepenheuer & Witsch, 1959. 358 p.
"William Butler Yeats: *Das Einhorn von den Sternen*," 165-71.

3906. KENTER, HEINZ DIETRICH: "Irland und sein Dichter W. B. Yeats," *Landestheater Württemberg-Hohenzollern, Programm*, ser 7 (1959/60), 50-53.

3907. MERCIER, VIVIAN: "Douglas Hyde's 'Share' in *The Unicorn from the Stars*," *MD*, 7:4 (Feb 1965), 463-65.
Besides being responsible for some material in *Where There Is Nothing*, Hyde may or may not have had a hand in this play.

See also J121, 1114, 1813a, 3336, 3387, 3469, 3503, 3594, 3601, 3932, 3933, 4195, 4222, 6316, 6323, 6451, 6940, 7380.

The Unicorn from the Stars II

3908. ANON.: "New Plays at the Abbey Theatre: *The Unicorn from the Stars*," *Daily Express*, #19062 (22 Nov 1907), 6.
The reviewer suggests that the play was originally a "screaming farce" that got a mistakenly serious treatment by Yeats.

3909. ANON.: "*The Unicorn from the Stars* at the Chanticleer," *NSt*, 18: 459 (9 Dec 1939), 821.

3910. ANON.: "Chanticleer Theatre: *The Unicorn from the Stars*," *Times*, #48481 (6 Dec 1939), 6.

3911. A[TKINSON ?], F. M.: "The Abbey Theatre: *The Unicorn from the Stars*," *Dublin Evening Mail*, #23106 (22 Nov 1907), 2.
"There is neither incident nor character in the play. Not a vestige of drama."

3912. BAUKLOH, FRIEDHELM: "W. B. Yeats: *Das Einhorn von den Sternen*," *Echo der Zeit*, #37 (9 Sept 1956), 15.
The performance in Köln.

3913. BAYER, HANS: "Theater-Archäologie in Tübingen: Das Einhorn erwies sich als ziemlich versteinerter Fund," *Abendpost*, 13:10 (13 Jan 1960), [6].

3914. BUSCHKIEL, JÜRGEN: "Von den Nazis einst verboten: *Das Einhorn von den Sternen* von William Butler Yeats wieder aufgeführt," *Welt*, #11 (14 Jan 1960), 5.
    The Tübingen performance.

3915. COX, J. H.: "Unicorns and Much Mysticism at the Abbey Theatre," *Irish Independent*, 16:282 (22 Nov 1907), 4.

3916. -F.: "*Das Einhorn von den Sternen*: Tragisches Spiel von William Butler Yeats," *Reutlinger Generalanzeiger*, 74:4 (7 Jan 1960), unpaged.

3917. GATTER, LUDWIG: "Irischer Narr in Christo—Yeats-Premiere in Köln," *FAZ*, #16 (19 Jan 1956), 8.

3918. GZM.: "Rauchwolken über Irland: W. B. Yeats: *Das Einhorn von den Sternen* im Landestheater," *Reutlinger Nachrichten*, 16:5 (8 Jan 1960), unpaged.

3919. JEREMIAS, BRIGITTE: "Auch eine irische Legende: *Das Einhorn von den Sternen* von Yeats in den Kölner Kammerspielen," *Mittag*, #14 (17 Jan 1956), unpaged.

3920. KIN.: "Gedenkfeier für W. B. Yeats im Stadttheater: *Das Einhorn von den Sternen* in der Sonntagsmatinee," *Basler Nachrichten*, 95:118 (2 May 1939), 2. Beilage, [10].

3921. KOCH, WERNER: "Das Jenseits ist in uns: Anmerkung zu Yeats' tragischem Spiel *Das Einhorn von den Sternen*," *Tribüne: Halbmonatsschrift der Bühnen der Stadt Köln*, 25:9 (1955/56), 80-82.
    A program note for a performance. A sketch of the stage setting and a photograph of the performance are printed in 25:10, before p. 97.

3922. M., R.: "Irische Vision: Yeats' *Das Einhorn von den Sternen* in Tübingen," *Stuttgarter Zeitung*, 16:8 (12 Jan 1960), 11.

3923. P., H. T.: "A Strange Irish Play," *BET*, 84:91 (17 Apr 1913), pt 2, 13.

3924. Q., W.: "Heimatkunst aus Irland: Yeats-Premiere in Tübingen," *Stuttgarter Nachrichten*, 14:301 (30 Dec 1959), 6.

3925. -R-F.: "Die Verzückung, die zur Vernichtung führt," *Neue Basler Zeitung*, #101 (2 May 1939), 7.

3926. S[TREICHER], S[IEGFRIED]: "Stadttheater Basel," *Basler Volksblatt*, 67:101 (2 May 1939), 1.

3927. TG.: "Alles vergehe, die Seele bestehe! W. B. Yeats' *Einhorn von den Sternen* im Landestheater," *Schwäbisches Tagblatt*, #298 (28 Dec 1959), unpaged.

3928. WST., R.: "Stadttheater: *Das Einhorn von den Sternen* von Butler Yeats," *National-Zeitung*, 97:198 (2 May 1939), [5].

Where There Is Nothing I

3929. BULFIN, WILLIAM: *Rambles in Erinn*. Dublin: Gill, 1925 [1907]. xxiii, 456 p.
    On the impression the play made on a real (?) tinker: "It's all wrong" (pp. 296-98).

3930. GOLDMAN, EMMA: *The Social Significance of the Modern Drama*. Boston: Badger, 1914. 315 p.
   "The Irish Drama: William Butler Yeats," 250-60; enthusiastic praise of the anarchism preached in this play.

3931. MCFATE, PATRICIA ANN, and WILLIAM E. DOHERTY: "W. B. Yeats's *Where There Is Nothing*: Theme and Symbolism," *Irish UR*, 2:2 (Autumn 1972), 149-63.

3932. THATCHER, DAVID S.: "Yeats's *Where There Is Nothing*: A Critical Study," M.A. thesis, McMaster U, 1964. viii, 130 p.
   Compares this play with *The Unicorn from the Stars* and discusses the influence of Nietzsche.

3933. ————: "Yeats's Repudiation of *Where There Is Nothing*," *MD*, 14:2 (Sept 1971), 127-36.
   He repudiated the play (and preferred the biographically less interesting *The Unicorn from the Stars*) for moral reasons because it might offend George Moore.

See also J845, 1114, 1732, 1813a, 3336, 3462, 3469, 3747, 3907, 4383-89 and note, 6369, 6537, 6632, 7074.

Where There Is Nothing II

3934. A., L. F.: "Mr. Yeats' New Play: *Where There Is Nothing* by the Stage Society," *Daily Chronicle*, #13209 (28 June 1904), 3.
   "An exhilarating afternoon with five acts of pure hallucination."

3935. ANON.: "The Drama," *Academy*, 67:1678 (2 July 1904), 19-20.

3936. ANON.: "Court Theatre: *Where There Is Nothing*," *Times*, #37432 (28 June 1904), 11.

3937. CHESTERTON, G. K.: "Nothing," *Daily News*, #18186 (2 July 1904), 6.
   A good play with a detestable philosophy.

3937a. G[REIN], J. T.: "The Stage Society: *Where There Is Nothing*," *Sunday Times*, #4239 (3 July 1904), 4.
   ". . . misty . . . weird, and . . . indistinct."

The Words upon the Window-Pane I

3938. FLANAGAN, THOMAS: "A Discourse by Swift, a Play by Yeats," *University R* [Dublin], 5:1 (Spring 1968), 9-22.
   The influence of Swift's *Discourse of the Contests and Dissensions between the Nobles and the Commons in Athens and Rome*.

3939. MINER, EARL ROY: "A Poem by Swift and W. B. Yeats's *The Words upon the Window-Pane*," *MLN*, 72:4 (Apr 1957), 273-75.
   Swift's "Written upon Windows at Inns, in England," #6.

3940. PETELER, PATRICIA MARJORIE: "The Social and Symbolic Drama of the English-Language Theatre, 1929-1949," Ph.D. thesis, U of Utah, 1961. iv, 356 p. (*DA*, 22:12 [June 1962], 4441-42.)
   On this play and *Purgatory, passim*.

3940a. ROGAL, SAMUEL J.: "Keble's Hymn and Yeats's *The Words upon the Window-Pane*," *MD*, 16:1 (June 1973), 87-89.

See also J398, 1073, 1147, 2263, 2817, 3324, 3336, 3405, 3448, 3474, 3531, 3536, 3583, 3717, 3997, 4043a, 4179, 5578, 6317, 6364, 6382.

The Words upon the Window-Pane II

3941. ANON.: "A Contrast in Moods: Two Yeats Plays in Dublin," *Irish Times*, 72:22954 (18 Nov 1930), 4.
This play and *At the Hawk's Well*.

3942. ANON.: "No Bricks for Irish Players This Time," *Literary Digest*, 114:2222 (19 Nov 1932), 17-18.
"Only by stretching a point can it be called a play at all. . . ."

3943. ANON.: "Mr. W. B. Yeats's Play," *Times*, #47850 (24 Nov 1937), 20.
A broadcast version.

3944. ANON.: "Swift in Dublin," *Week-end R*, 2:38 (29 Nov 1930), 793-94.

3945. ATKINSON, BROOKS: "W. B. Yeats and J. Swift," *NYT*, 82:27307 (29 Oct 1932), 18.
"Since it is a mad little play altogether, it stimulates the imagination enormously. Only a poet would attempt anything so rash, and succeed so well. . . ."

3946. BROWN, JOHN MASON: "The Play: William Butler Yeats Speaks After the Irish Players Perform *The Words upon the Window-Pane*," *NY Evening Post*, 131:294 (29 Oct 1932), III, 4.
"His words of explanation were sadly needed."

3947. GOLDIE, GRACE WYNDHAM: "Blow, Ye Trumpets!" *Listener*, 18:464 (1 Dec 1937), 1206.
The broadcast version.

3948. S., D.: "*The Words upon the Window-Pane*: New Yeats Play at the Abbey," *Irish Independent*, 39:275 (18 Nov 1930), 12.

See also J6454, 6492.

YEATS, William Butler. . . . Pubns: . . .
"The Cuttings of an Agent"
—Thom's Irish Who's Who, 1923, p. 265

FA Prose Fiction and Prose in General

Yeats's prose fiction has not attracted many critics, as the following
list shows. Readers are advised, however, to check the important monographs in sections BA and CA for more material. Single works of prose
fiction are indexed in ND. What Thom's was actually referring to was of
course "The Cutting of an Agate."

3949. ALLEN, JAMES LOVIC, and M. M. LIBERMAN: "Transcriptions of Yeats's
Unpublished Prose in the Bradford Papers at Grinnell College," *Serif*, 10:1
(Spring 1973), 13-27.
    A description of Bradford's transcriptions of "what he considered to
    be the major items of Yeats's unpublished prose." They include (1)
    The Speckled Bird, (2) first drafts of *Autobiographies*, (3) journals,
    (4) works completed but never published, (5) extracts from the manu-
    script books, and (6) addresses. The article concentrates on the last
    three groups, which include items belonging to Yeats's political,
    occult, and literary interests. Due to late arrival of this article,
    I have not been able to inspect the Bradford collection and to compare
    the descriptions of addresses and lectures with the entries in section
    BG.

3949a. ANDREWS, C. E.: "One of W. B. Yeats's Sources," *MLN*, 28:3 (Mar
1913), 94-95.
    "The Crucifixion of the Outcast" is indebted to *The Vision of Mac
    Conglinne*.

3950. BEEBE, MAURICE: *Ivory Towers and Sacred Founts: The Artist as Hero
in Fiction from Goethe to Joyce*. NY: New York UP, 1964. xi, 323 p.
    Art as religion in the early stories, pp. 153-58.

3951. BROWN, STEPHEN JAMES: *Ireland in Fiction: A Guide to Irish Novels,
Tales, Romances, and Folk-lore*. Volume one, introduction by Desmond J.
Clarke. NY: Barnes & Noble, 1969 [1915]. xxviii, 362 p.
    See pp. 312-13. First published as °*Reader's Guide to Irish Fiction*
    (1910). A second volume is planned.

3952. FINNERAN, RICHARD J.: "Yeats's Revisions in *The Celtic Twilight*,
1912-1925," *Tulane Studies in English*, 20 (1972), 97-105.
    Important revisions that have been frequently overlooked.

3953. ————: "'Old Lecher with a Love on Every Wind': A Study of Yeats'
Stories of Red Hanrahan," *TSLL*, 14:2 (Summer 1972), 347-58.
    The sources and revisions and the meaning of the stories.

3953a. ————: *The Prose Fiction of W. B. Yeats: The Search for "Those
Simple Forms."* Dublin: Dolmen Press, 1973. 42 p. (New Yeats Papers. 4.)
    Includes a bibliographical note on the texts.

3954. FIXLER, MICHAEL: "The Affinities between J.-K. Huysmans and the
'Rosicrucian' Stories of W. B. Yeats," *PMLA*, 74:4 (Sept 1959), 464-69.
    Discusses "The Adoration of the Magi," "The Tables of the Law," and
    "Rosa Alchemica."

3955. GARVEY, JAMES JOSEPH: "W. B. Yeats's Prose: A Linguistic Description of 'Stylistic Competence,'" °Ph.D. thesis, U of Michigan, 1972. 269 p. (*DA*, 33:5 [Nov 1972], 2372A.)

3955a. GRANTHAM, SHELBY SMITH: "The Prose Fiction of William Butler Yeats," °Ph.D. thesis, U of Virginia, 1973. 352 p. (*DA*, 34:4 [Oct 1973], 1910A.)

3956. GUTIN, STANLEY SAMUEL: "*The Secret Rose*: A Study in the Early Prose Fiction of William Butler Yeats," °Ph.D. thesis, U of Pennsylvania, 1971. 371 p. (*DA*, 32:4 [Oct 1971], 2090A.)

3957. HARRIS, WENDELL V.: "English Short Fiction in the 19th Century," *Studies in Short Fiction*, 6:1 (Fall 1968), 1-93.
See pp. 41-44, 77, 79, 81-82.

3958. JEFFARES, A. NORMAN: "Prose Fed by Experience," *Western Mail*, 16 Jan 1965, 5.
Mainly on the style of Yeats's prose.

3958a. KEARNEY, RAYMOND WILLIAM: "Yeats, the Man of Letters," °Ph.D. thesis, Pennsylvania State U, 1972. 116 p. (*DA*, 33:12 [June 1973], 6915A-16A.)
On Yeats's prose works. "He is best seen as a man of letters in the European tradition" (abstract).

3959. LESTER, JOHN A.: "Joyce, Yeats, and the Short Story," *ELT*, 15:4 (1972), 305-14.

3960. MCHUGH, ROGER: "Yeats's Kind of Twilight," *TriQ*, #4 [Fall 1965], 126-29.
Discusses the short stories in *The Celtic Twilight* and *The Secret Rose*.

3961. MARCUS, PHILLIP L.: "Possible Sources for Yeats's 'Dhoya,'" *N&Q*, os 212 / ns 14:10 (Oct 1967), 383-84.
The sources are in *Leabhar na h-Uidhri* (*Book of Dun Cow*).

3962. ————: "A Fenian Allusion in Yeats," *University R* [Dublin], 4:3 (Winter 1967), 282.
An O'Leary quotation in "The Crucifixion of the Outcast."

3963. MARTIN, AUGUSTINE: "*The Secret Rose* and Yeats's Dialogue with History," *Ariel*, 3:3 (July 1972), 91-103.

3964. O'DONNELL, WILLIAM HUGH: "The Prose Fiction of W. B. Yeats: 1887-1905," °Ph.D. thesis, Princeton U, 1971. 344 p. (*DA*, 33:1 [July 1972], 321A.)
Includes a discussion of the unpublished *The Speckled Bird*.

3965. SCARBOROUGH, DOROTHY: *The Supernatural in Modern English Fiction*. NY: Octagon Books, 1967 [1917]. vii, 329 p.
Notes on the supernatural in Yeats's prose fiction and in *The Countess Cathleen* and *The Land of Heart's Desire*, *passim* (see index).

3966. YEATS, W. B.: "*The Speckled Bird*," *Bell*, 1:6 (Mar 1941), 23-30.
An extract from the concluding chapter of Book I, plus introductory remarks and a short summary of the remainder of the novel by J. M. Hone.

3967. ————: "*The Speckled Bird*: A Novel by W. B. Yeats." A section from the novel with a note by Curtis Bradford, *Irish Writing*, #31 (Summer 1955), 9-18.

3968. ————: "W. B. Yeats's Prose Contributions to Periodicals: 1900-1939." Edited by Charles Colton Johnson. Editor's Ph.D. thesis, Northwestern U, 1968. xxi, 622 p. (*DA*, 29:9 [Mar 1969], 3141A.)
> The editor provides a skimpy introduction (pp. v-xix) and some annotations.

3969. ————: "*The Tables of the Law*: A Critical Text." Edited by Robert O'Driscoll, *Yeats Studies*, #1 (Bealtaine 1971), 87-118.
> For details see J171.

3970. ————: "Versions of the Stories of Red Hanrahan." Edited by Michael J. Sidnell, *Yeats Studies*, #1 (Bealtaine 1971), 119-74.
> For details see J172.

3971. ————: "A Variorum Edition of W. B. Yeats's Stories of Red Hanrahan." Edited by Richard Louis Bonaccorso. Editor's °Ph.D. thesis, U of Connecticut, 1972. iii, 219 p. (*DA*, 33:6 [Dec 1972], 2922A.)
> Includes a discussion of the collaboration with Lady Gregory.

See also J1069, 1073, 1076, 1110, 1112, 1760a, 1799, 1810a, 1813a, 1934, 2038a, 2039, 2210, 2213, 2224, 2332, 2446, 3091, 3981, 4115, 4209, 4226, 4228, 4232a, 4254, 4273-76, 4290-99, 4339-53, 4380-82, 4418, 4419, 4478-80, 4625-33, 4669-71, 5206-20 and note, 5474-76, 5479-81, 5493-95, 5911, 5940 (#19), 6003, 6353, 6632.

FB   Autobiography

3972. B[ABLER], O[TTO] F.: "Queries from W. B. Yeats's Autobiographies," *N&Q*, 171:[] (12 Dec 1936), 421-22.
> Answers by W. W. G[ill], 172:[] (20 Feb 1937), 142.

3973. BUCKLEY, VINCENT: "Yeats: The Great Comedian," *Malahat R*, #5 (Jan 1968), 77-89.
> Humor and lack of humor in *Autobiographies*.

3974. CARY, MEREDITH RAY: "Novelistic Autobiography: A Special Genre," °Ph.D. thesis, U of Washington, 1968. 184 p. (*DA*, 29:7 [Jan 1969], 2207A-8A.)
> Includes a discussion of Moore's *Hail and Farewell* and Yeats's counterattack in *Autobiographies*.

3975. ————: "Yeats and Moore--An Autobiographical Conflict," *Éire-Ireland*, 4:3 (Autumn 1969), 94-109.
> Moore's description of Yeats in *Hail and Farewell* is much more successful than Yeats's description of Moore in *Dramatis Personae*, which is, in fact, an altogether inferior book.

3976. CULBERTSON, DIANA: "Twentieth Century Autobiography: Yeats, Sartre, Nabokov. Studies in Structure and Form," °Ph.D. thesis, U of North Carolina at Chapel Hill, 1971. 257 p. (*DA*, 32:12 [June 1972], 6968A.)

3977. DONOGHUE, DENIS, and FRANK KERMODE: "Jongsen," *TLS*, 71:3650 (11 Feb 1972), 157.
> Letter to the editor explaining that the mysterious painter Jongsen, mentioned in "The Tragic Generation," does not exist and may really be Cornelius van Ceulen Janssen.

3978. FIRTH, JOHN MIRKIL: "O'Casey and Autobiography," Ph.D. thesis, U of Virginia, 1965. v, 165 p. (*DA*, 26:10 [Apr 1966], 6039.)
> Contains some remarks on Yeats's *Autobiographies*, pp. 119-24.

3979. GORLIER, CLAUDIO: "Maschera e confessione: Da Yeats a Spender,"
Paragone, 7:76 (Apr 1956), 10-24.
Compares the autobiographies of Yeats and Spender.

3980. JOHNSTON, WALTER D.: "The Integral Self in Post-Romantic Autobiography," °Ph.D. thesis, U of Virginia, 1969. 209 p. (*DA*, 31:1 [July 1970],
391A-92A.)

3981. KÜNNE, WULF: *Konzeption und Stil von Yeats' "Autobiographies."* Bonn:
Bouvier, 1972. 247 p. (Studien zur englischen Literatur. 9.)
Originally a Dr. phil. thesis, U of Hamburg, 1971. A thorough analysis
of *Autobiographies* as an example of a literary genre as well as of its
language and style, including a general discussion of Yeats's prose
style. Contains an English summary, reprinted in *English and American
Studies in German*, 1972, 89-92.

3982. LEVIN, GERALD: "The Yeats of the Autobiographies: A Man of Phase 17,"
TSLL, 6:3 (Autumn 1964), 398-405.
The connections between *Autobiographies* and *A Vision*.

3983. °MAVEETY, STANLEY R.: "An Index to Some of the Autobiographical
Prose of William Butler Yeats," M.A. thesis, Columbia U, 1950.

3983a. O'BRIEN, KEVIN PATRICK: "Will and Reverie: The Personae of W. B.
Yeats' Autobiography," °Ph.D. thesis, Fordham U, 1972. 202 p. (*DA*, 33:7
[Jan 1973], 3662A.)
Includes a comparison with Moore's *Hail and Farewell*.

3984. PASCAL, ROY: *Design and Truth in Autobiography*. Cambridge, Mass.:
Harvard UP, 1960. ix, 202 p.
Passim (see index), especially pp. 136-39. In Yeats, the elements of
dream and reality "are curiously combined and curiously dissociated."

3984a. PIRRI, JOHN JOSEPH: "William Butler Yeats and Symbolic Autobiography," °Ph.D. thesis, U of Wisconsin, 1972. 280 p. (*DA*, 33:9 [Mar 1973],
5137A.)
Includes comparisons with Augustine's *Confessions*, Wordsworth's *Prelude*, Carlyle's *Sartor Resartus*, J. S. Mill's *Autobiography*, and
Gosse's *Father and Son*.

3985. *RONSLEY, JOSEPH: *Yeats's Autobiography: Life as Symbolic Pattern*.
Cambridge, Mass.: Harvard UP, 1968. xii, 172 p.
Based on "The Design of *The Autobiography* of W. B. Yeats," °Ph.D.
thesis, Northwestern U, 1966. 184 p. (*DA*, 28:1 [July 1967], 241A).
An attempt to discover "the design underlying Yeats's presentation
of events, people, and ideas" (p. 1), i.e., the fusion of life and
art, the establishment of Unity of Culture and Unity of Being, and
the blending of personal and Irish history. Contains numerous sidelights on *A Vision*.
Reviews:
1. Anon., "Single-Minded," *TLS*, 67:3480 (7 Nov 1968), 1249.
2. T. R. Henn, *RES*, 20:79 (Aug 1969), 373-75.
3. Richard Howard, "Masters and Friends," *Poetry*, 113:5 (Feb 1969),
   338-60 (pp. 356-58).
4. Brendan Kennelly, "Yeats and Blake," *Hibernia*, 32:14 (29 Nov—12
   Dec 1968), 14.
5. Augustine Martin, *Studies*, 60:237 (Spring 1971), 98-102.
6. J. R. Mulryne, *MLR*, 66:3 (July 1971), 680-81.
7. Hermann Peschmann, *English*, 19:103 (Spring 1970), 28-29.

8. August W. Staub, *QJS*, 55:1 (Feb 1969), 98–99.

9. Alex Zwerdling, *ELN*, 7:3 (Mar 1970), 236–38.

3986. *Schrijvers in eigen spiegel: Autobiografie, dagboek, brieven*. Zes belichtingen door J. M. M. Aler [etc.]. Lezingen gehouden gedurende het cursusjaar 1959/60 voor de School voor Taal- en Letterkunde to 's-Graven-hage. Den Haag: Servire, 1960. 152 p. (Servire Luxe-pockets. 36.)

M. D. E. de Leve: "Yeats," 107–22.

3986a. THORBURN, DAVID, and GEOFFREY HARTMAN (eds): *Romanticism: Vistas, Instances, Continuities*. Ithaca: Cornell UP, 1973. 284 p.

Yeats is mentioned *passim*, especially his *Autobiographies*, in Michael G. Cooke, "Modern Black Autobiography in the Tradition," 255–80 (pp. 267–70).

3987. ZABEL, MORTON DAUWEN: "The Thinking of the Body: Yeats in the Auto-biographies," *Southern R*, 7:3 (Winter 1941/42), 562–90.

Interpretation of *Autobiographies* along the lines of Yeats's poetic development.

See also J223 (#6), 567, 605, 624, 1073, 1078, 1101, 1996, 2001, 2243, 3949, 4209, 4232, 4255, 4483-503, 4576-84, 4639, 4640, 4641-65, 4701 and note, 4875-921 and note, 4979-85 and note, 5089-93, 5156-80 and note, 5511-13, 5521-30, 5564a.

FC   *A Vision* and Mystical, Occult, and Philosophical Writings and Activities

Although the number of cross-references to this section is rather high, it has not seemed feasible to introduce subsections according to subject matter. The reader is therefore referred to indexes NE (for entries such as Rosicrucianism and theosophy) and ND (for a complete list of references to *A Vision*).

3988. ADAMS, HAZARD: "Symbolism and Yeats's *A Vision*," *JAAC*, 22:4 (Summer 1964), 425–36.

Discusses the book as "a grammar of poetic symbolism" and as "a work of literary art of a kind for which we have had . . . no critical terminology." Stresses the various uses of irony in the book.

3989. ALEXANDER, WILLIAM RAYMOND HALL: "The Resurrection into Unity: A Consideration of William Butler Yeats's Metaphors of Judgment and Deliver-ance," Honors thesis, Harvard U, 1960. i, 49 p.

A study of *A Vision* and its influence on *A Full Moon in March* and *Purgatory*.

3989a. ALLEN, JAMES LOVIC: "Yeats's Phase in the System of *A Vision*," *Éire-Ireland*, 8:4 (Winter 1973), 91–117.

Yeats's phase was 13, not 17 as is commonly believed.

3990. *Approaches to the Study of Twentieth-Century Literature*. Proceedings of the Conference in the Study of Twentieth-Century Literature. First session, May 2–4, 1961. East Lansing: Michigan State U, [1962?]. vi, 169 p.

Quotes an unidentified query whether Yeats's view of history was dia-chronic or synchronic. Answer by Walter J. Ong: It was a modified syn-chronism (pp. 97-98).

3991. ARONSON, ALEX: "Myth and Modern Poetry. I: W. B. Yeats," *Visva-Bharati Q*, 17:1 (May-July 1951), 35–43.

The "myth" of *A Vision* replaces the Celtic mythology of Yeats's earlier phase. Without it, some of his poems cannot be understood. Eventually, however, "the myth, and the twenty-eight phases of the moon leave us cold, [and] we are persuaded by the poetry."

3991a. BARROW, CRAIG WALLACE: "Comprehensive Index to William Butler Yeats's *A Vision*," *BNYPL*, 77:1 (Autumn 1973), 51-62.
Indexes the second edition (NY, 1938).

3992. BENSON, CARL FREDERICK: "A Study of Yeats' *A Vision*," Ph.D. thesis, U of Illinois, 1948. iv, 257 p.
An analysis of both versions, of *Per Amica Silentia Lunae*, of their sources, and of their effect on Yeats's poetry.

3993. BUTLER, CHRISTOPHER: *Number Symbolism*. London: Routledge & Kegan Paul, 1970. xiii, 186 p.
Note on *A Vision*, pp. 162-64.

3993a. CALLAN, EDWARD: "Huddon and Duddon in Yeats's *A Vision*: The Folk Tale as Gateway to the Universal Mind," *Michigan Academician*, 6:1 (Summer 1973), 5-16.

3993b. °CHABRIA, R. G.: "Yeats and Theosophy," *Theosophist*, 92:11 (Aug 1971), 313-25.

3994. CHESTERTON, GILBERT KEITH: *Sidelights on New London and Newer York and Other Essays*. London: Sheed & Ward, 1932. 235 p.
"Magic and Fantasy in Fiction," 228-35, contains a note on Yeats's "cabalistic games and cryptograms," which Chesterton does not approve of (pp. 233-34).

3995. COMFORT, ALEX: *Darwin and the Naked Lady: Discursive Essays on Biology and Art*. NY: Braziller, 1962. xiii, 174 p.
On *A Vision* as an example of the "soft-centred approach" to generalization, pp. 13-21. ("The soft-centred approach is to state the regularity [in an observed sequence of events], call it a law, a truth, or a spiritual reality, and treat these names as if they were explanations" [p. 4].)

3996. [CROWLEY, ALEISTER]: "The Temple of Solomon the King," *Equinox*, 1:3 (Mar 1910), 133-280.
Contains an account of the revolt against MacGregor Mathers (called D. D. C. F.) with references to Yeats (D. E. D. I.) and Florence Farr (S. S. D. D.), pp. 253-54.

3997. CUMMINS, GERALDINE: "W. B. Yeats and Psychical Research," *Occult R*, 66:2 (Apr 1939), 132-33, 135, 137, 139.
Contains some reminiscences of Yeats at séances and a note on *The Words upon the Window-Pane*.

3998. DAVIDSON, CLIFFORD: "Yeats: The Active and Contemplative Modes of Life," *Renascence*, 23:4 (Summer 1971), 192-97.
Yeats's "religious quest" through occult studies and the Tarot.

3998a. DECKER, M. B.: "A Correction in Yeats's *A Vision*," *N&Q*, os 218 / ns 20:9 (Sept 1973), 329-30.

3999. DUPREY, JENELLE MANESS: "Hermetic and Platonic Elements in the Philosophy of William Butler Yeats," °M.A. thesis, American U, 1966. 131 p. (*Masters Abstracts*, 4:1 [Mar 1966], 13-14.)
Discusses *A Vision*.

4000. EBON, MARTIN: *They Knew the Unknown*. NY: World Publishing Co., 1971. xiii, 285 p.

"Yeats: A Poet's Lifetime Vision," 176–95; an account, but not an analysis, of Yeats's preoccupation with the supernatural and psychic phenomena.

4001. FARAG, FAHMY FAWZY: "W. B. Yeats's Daimon," *Cairo Studies in English*, 1961/62, 135–44.

Also on the concept of the mask.

4002. FISHWICK, MARSHALL: "Yeats and Cyclical History," *Shenandoah*, 1:2 (Summer 1950), 52–56.

Mainly on *A Vision*.

4003. FITZROY, CHRISTOPHER: "The Cult of Yeats," *Ireland's Catholic Standard*, 2:65 (2 Oct 1964), 5.

A polemic against Yeats's "cabbalistic" beliefs. Correspondence by John O'Riordan, :69 (30 Oct 1964), 5; K. McD., *ibid.*; R. Donnellan, :70 (6 Nov 1964), 5; FitzRoy and J. P. B., :71 (13 Nov 1964), 5; O'Riordan and Thomas O'Donnell, :72 (20 Nov 1964), 5; "Ben Bulben," :73 (27 Nov 1964), 5.

4004. FLETCHER, IAN: "History and Vision in the Work of W. B. Yeats," *Southern R*, 4:1 (Winter 1968), 105–26.

An omnibus review, discussing the problem of history in Yeats's work, the reception and interpretation of *A Vision*, and generally the state of Yeats scholarship.

4005. FRASER, G. S.: "Yeats as a Philosopher," *Phoenix* [Seoul], #10 (Summer 1965), 46–59.

On the Yeats—T. Sturge Moore letters and the relevance of Yeats's philosophy for his poetry.

4006. FRIAR, KIMON, and JOHN MALCOLM BRINNIN (eds): *Modern Poetry: American and British*. NY: Appleton-Century-Crofts, 1951. xix, 580 p.

Notes on *A Vision*, "News for the Delphic Oracle," "Lapis Lazuli," "Byzantium," "Sailing to Byzantium," "Two Songs from a Play," "The Tower," and "Nineteen Hundred and Nineteen," pp. 546–60.

4007. FULLER, JEAN OVERTON: *The Magical Dilemma of Victor Neuburg*. London: Allen, 1965. xv, 295 p.

On Yeats's association with the Golden Dawn, pp. 120–23, 126.

4008. °GORDER, CHARLES R.: "An Approach to the Vision of William Butler Yeats," M.A. thesis, Columbia U, 1953. 90 p.

4009. HARPER, GEORGE MILLS: "From Zelator to Theoricus: Yeats's 'Link with the Invisible Degrees,'" *Yeats Studies*, #1 (Bealtaine 1971), 80–86.

Yeats's promotion from Zelator Adeptus Minor to Theoricus Adeptus Minor in the Golden Dawn.

4010. ———: "'Meditations upon Unknown Thought': Yeats's Break with MacGregor Mathers," *Yeats Studies*, #1 (Bealtaine 1971), 175–202.

A long introduction to Yeats's Golden Dawn activities at the time of the break with Mathers, pp. 175–82, and the documents prepared by Yeats and Florence Farr in connection with the expulsion of Mathers from the London temple.

4011. ———: "Yeats on the Occult," *PMLA*, 86:3 (May 1971), 490.

Announces the following projects: "(1) a critical and historical study of Yeats's religion, (2) a critical edition with an extended introduction of *A Vision* (1925), and (3) an edition of selected letters to Yeats."

4011a. HIRSCHBERG, STUART: "*A Vision* and Yeats's Quest for a Unified Aesthetic Myth," Ph.D. thesis, New York U, 1972. ii, 337 p. (*DA*, 33:11 [May 1973], 6357A.)
    Discusses *A Vision*, *Per Amica Silentia Lunae*, and related poems.

4012. HOOD, WALTER KELLY: "A Study of *A Vision* by W. B. Yeats," Ph.D. thesis, U of North Carolina at Chapel Hill, 1968. iv, 245 p. (*DA*, 29:7 [Jan 1969], 2264A.)
    A book-by-book analysis, conceived by its author as "a philosophical study from a literary point of view" (p. iii).

4013. HOWE, ELLIC: *The Magicians of the Golden Dawn: A Documentary History of a Magical Order, 1887-1923*. With a foreword by Gerald Yorke. London: Routledge & Kegan Paul, 1972. xxviii, 306 p.
    On Yeats's Golden Dawn activities, *passim* (see index).

4014. Entry canceled.

4015. JACKSON, P. E.: "Recollections of the Old Dublin Lodge, Ely Place, in the Years 1891-2-3-4," *Theosophy in Ireland*, 17:3 (July-Sept 1938), 22-25; :4 (Oct-Dec 1938), 21-25; 19:1 (Jan-Mar 1940), 15-18; :2 (Mar-June 1940), 20-24.
    Yeats is mentioned *passim*.

4016. JOHN, BRIAN: "The Philosophical Ideas of W. B. Yeats," M.A. thesis, U of Wales, 1959. vi, 501 p.
    Author's summary of contents: (1) A review of the various esthetic alternatives open to the young poet at the end of the 19th century together with a brief introduction to and elucidation of Yeats's major philosophical terms. . . . (2) An analysis and evaluation of Yeats's poetry through the expression and interaction of his various poetic masks. (3) An examination of Yeats's philosophical ideas and their expression in the system, as appearing in the two editions of *A Vision*, in relation to his poetic achievement.

4017. KERMODE, FRANK: *The Sense of an Ending: Studies in the Theory of Fiction*. NY: Oxford UP, 1967. xi, 187 p. (Mary Flexner Lectures. 1965.)
    "The Modern Apocalypse," 93-124; first published as "The New Apocalyptists," *Partisan R*, 33:3 (Summer 1966), 339-61. Comments on Yeats's historical dialectics, *passim*.

4018. KING, FRANCIS: *Ritual Magic in England: 1887 to the Present Day*. London: Spearman, 1970. 224 p.
    Notes on Yeats's involvement in the Golden Dawn, pp. 73-78, 202, and *passim* (see index).

4019. KOMESU, OKIFUMI: "Brahman or Daimon: Yeats's Schooling in Eastern Thought," *Yeats Society of Japan Annual Report*, #3 (1968/69), 7-18; #4 (1970), 20-26.
    The monistic-experiential aspect of the saint and the dualistic-cognitive aspect of the artist in Yeats's thought and their Eastern sources.

4020. LASSETER, ROLLIN AMOS: "A Powerful Emblem: Epistemology in Yeats's Poetic Vision," °Ph.D. thesis, Yale U, 1970. 235 p. (*DA*, 31:6 [Dec 1970], 2924A.)

On *A Vision*.

4021. LEMONNIER, LEON: "Le symbolisme mystique de Yeats," *Nouvelle revue critique*, 22:4 (Summer 1938), 227-35.
Mainly concerned with *A Vision*.

4021a. MCCORMICK, JANE L.: "A Poet, Playwright, Essayist & Nobel Prize Winner Who Mixed in the *Paranormal*: William Butler Yeats & Psychic Phenomena," *Psychic*, 1:6 (May-June 1970), 19-23.
See also the same author's "Psychic Phenomena in Literature," 3:4 (Jan-Feb 1972), 40, 42-44.

4022. MULLER, HERBERT J.: "The New Criticism in Poetry," *Southern R*, 6:4 (Spring 1941), 811-39.
Criticizes Cleanth Brooks's treatment of *A Vision* (J1241). See J. V. Healy, "Scientific and Intuitable Language," 7:1 (Summer 1941), 214-16, who defends *A Vision* against Muller's critique.

4023. NETHERCOT, ARTHUR HOBART: *The First Five Lives of Annie Besant*. Chicago: U of Chicago Press, 1960. xii, 419 p.
Note on Yeats, Madame Blavatsky, Annie Besant, and theosophy, pp. 300-304.

4024. O'RAHILLY, ALFRED: "Mr. Yeats as Theologian," *Irish Tribune*, 1:7 (23 Apr 1926), 9-10.
Criticizes Yeats's "Our Need for Religious Sincerity" (first published as "The Need for Audacity of Thought," Wp. 383). Correspondence by Donald Attwater, :10 (14 May 1926), 16; O'Rahilly, :13 (4 June 1926), 19.

4025. PEARCE, DONALD: "Philosophy and Phantasy: Notes on the Growth of Yeats's 'System,'" *UKCR*, 18:3 (Spring 1952), 169-80.
A defense of *A Vision* as a book in its own right and as a dictionary of Yeats's symbols.

4026. PEMPLE, JOHN ALLAN BLAIR: "Three Modern Unities: An Oblique Approach to the 'Literature, Philosophy, and Nationality' of Yeats's *Vision*," Honors thesis, Harvard U, 1965. i, 37 p.

4027. RAINE, KATHLEEN: *Yeats, the Tarot and the Golden Dawn*. Dublin: Dolmen Press, 1972. 60 p. and 42 illustrations. (New Yeats Papers. 2.)
Incorporates "Yeats, the Tarot, and the Golden Dawn," *Sewanee R*, 77:1 (Jan-Mar 1969), 112-48. On the relationship between the Tarot symbols, the Golden Dawn magical practices, and the Platonic myth in Yeats's philosophy and poetry.
Reviews:
1. Anon., "Power Pack," *TLS*, 72:3717 (1 June 1973), 620.
2. William Empson, "Yeats and the Spirits," *NYRB*, 20:20 (13 Dec 1973), 43-45.
3. Mary Lappin, "Ritual and Magic," *Hibernia*, 36:18 (22 Sept 1972), 10.

4028. RAJAN, B.: "W. B. Yeats and the Unity of Being," *Nineteenth Century and After*, 146:871 (Sept 1949), 150-61.

4029. ———: "Yeats and the Renaissance," *Mosaic*, 5:4 (Summer 1972), 109-18.
Again on the concept of Unity of Being.

4030. REGARDIE, ISRAEL: *My Rosicrucian Adventure: A Contribution to a Recent Phase of the History of Magic, and a Study in the Technique of Theurgy*. Chicago: Engelke, 1936. 145 p.

Mentions Yeats twice (under his own name and under his pseudonym
D. E. D. I.) in connection with the Golden Dawn, pp. 52-53.

4031. °SANBORN, CLIFFORD EARLE: "W. B. Yeats: His View of History," M.A.
thesis, U of Toronto, 1951. 131 p.

4032. SCHMITT, NATALIE CROHN: "Ecstasy and Insight in Yeats," *British J of
Aesthetics*, 11:3 (Summer 1971), 257-67.
Yeats's faith postulated the unity of experience and the experienced,
perception and creation, ecstasy and insight. Truth is therefore "an
aesthetic matter." These observations are applied to a discussion of
the plays.

4033. SCHULER, ROBERT M.: "W. B. Yeats: Artist or Alchemist?" *RES*, 22:85
(Feb 1971), 37-53.
On Yeats's use of the symbols and doctrines of mystical alchemy in
"Rosa Alchemica" and some poems.

4034. SENIOR, JOHN: *The Way Down and Out: The Occult in Symbolist Literature.* Ithaca: Cornell UP, 1959. xxvii, 217 p.
"The Artifice of Eternity: Yeats," 145-69. Yeats's occult and visionary preoccupations are rather "empty" compared to those of Blake and
AE. Nevertheless, he wrote good poetry.

4035. SPENCE, LEWIS (ed): *An Encyclopaedia of Occultism: A Compendium of
Information on the Occult Sciences, Occult Personalities, Psychic Science,
Magic, Demonology, Spiritism, and Mysticism.* London: Routledge, 1920. xiv,
451 p.
W. G. B[laikie] M[urdoch]: "Yeats," 438.

4036. STOCK, A. G.: "*A Vision* (1925 and 1937)," *Indian J of English Studies*,
1:1 (1960), 38-47.

4037. SYMONDS, JOHN: *The Great Beast: The Life of Aleister Crowley.* London:
Rider, 1951. 316 p.
Note on Yeats's role in the Golden Dawn schism, pp. 32-33.

4038. THOMPSON, VANCE: "The Tame Ghosts of Yeats and the Sar Peladan,"
Criterion [NY], 22:521 (13 Jan 1900), 9-10.
Account of a séance with Yeats and Sâr Péladan in Paris.

4038a. THOMPSON, WILLIAM IRWIN: *At the Edge of History.* NY: Harper & Row,
1971. xi, 180 p.
Notes on Yeats's view of history, especially in *A Vision*, pp. 76-78,
166-67, and *passim.*

4039. [UPWARD, ALLEN]: *Some Personalities.* By 20/1631. Boston: Cornhill
Publication Co., 1922. xiii, 302 p.
Tried, sometime in the 1880s, to get into "telepathic communication"
with Yeats. The experiment failed (pp. 57-58).

4040. VICTOR, PIERRE: "Magie et sociétés secrètes: L'ordre hermétique de
la Golden Dawn," *Tour Saint-Jacques*, #2 (Jan-Feb 1956), 46-55; #3 (Mar-
Apr 1956), 39-47.
Notes on Yeats in #3, pp. 42-43, 45-46.

4041. °WAKEFIELD, H. C.: "William Butler Yeats and the Antithetical Philosophy," M.A. thesis, U of Melbourne, 1950.

4041a. WEBB, JAMES: *The Flight from Reason.* Volume 1 of *The Age of the
Irrational.* London: Macdonald, 1971. xiv, 305 p.
On Yeats's occult interests, pp. 208-13 and *passim* (see index).

4042. WESTON, JESSIE LAIDLAY: *From Ritual to Romance*. Garden City: Double-day, 1957 [1920]. xvii, 217 p. (Doubleday Anchor Book. A125.)
Quotes from a letter by Yeats in which he comments on the Tarot symbols, p. 79.

4043. WILSON, COLIN: *The Occult*. London: Hodder & Stoughton, 1971. 601 p.
On Yeats, pp. 102-9 and *passim* (see index).

4043a. YELLEN, SHERMAN: "The Psychic World of W. B. Yeats," *Tomorrow*, 10:1 (Winter 1962), 99-106.
A defense of Yeats, "the staunch advocate of psychic research," and a note on *The Words upon the Window-Pane* (the play is reprinted on pp. 107-22).

4044. YEOMANS, EDWARD: "W. B. Yeats and the 'Electric Motor Vision,'" *Alphabet*, #7 (Dec 1963), 44-48.
On *A Vision*. Once Yeats had started the motor that drives the great wheel, he was unable to switch it off.

See also J128b, 565, 633, 639, 655, 735, 797, 814, 1011, 1019, 1025, 1026, 1069, 1071, 1074, 1076, 1078, 1091, 1101, 1102, 1114, 1118, 1131, 1134, 1136, 1136a, 1141, 1142, 1147, 1151, 1153, 1155, 1156, 1168a, 1168b, 1240, 1241, 1252, 1256, 1329, 1487, 1553, 1581, 1671, 1696, 1720, 1737a, 1791, 1795, 1800, 1801, 1813a, 1841, 1843, 1844, 1859, 1867, 1869, 1873, 1875, 1882, 1949, 1970, 1979, 2038a, 2046, 2069, 2116, 2139a, 2140, 2145a, 2154a, 2154b, 2161, 2231, 2255, 2257, 2279, 2281a, 2283a, 2290, 2292, 2420, 2434, 2438, 2490, 2571, 2687a, 2739, 2740, 2742-45, 2747, 2747a, 2748, 2749, 2752-54, 2756, 2767, 2798, 2811, 2827, 2861, 2997, 3039, 3104, 3237, 3277, 3347, 3416, 3481, 3486, 3567, 3730a, 3873a, 3949, 3954, 3982, 3985, 4091, 4107a, 4113, 4141, 4214, 4233, 4514-28 and note, 4634-38 and note, 4702-4, 4712, 4715-16, 4924-53, 5181-84 and note, 5205a, 5206-20 and note, 5456-69 and note, 5547, 5932, 5940 (#8), 7252, 7416.

FD   Political Writings and Activities

> If a man don't occasionally sit in a senate
> how can he pierce the darrk mind of a
> senator?
>
> —EP, Canto LXXX

As in the preceding section, a further subdivision by subject matter here was not considered practical. The index to subjects (NE) is intended to take care of that. I feel that more material might have been found by a systematic search in the Irish daily press, particularly during the time of Yeats's senatorship, but I do not think that important material (as distinguished from items of transient interest) has been overlooked.

4045. ADAMS, HAZARD: "Criticism, Politics, and History: The Matter of Yeats," *Georgia R*, 24:2 (Summer 1970), 158-82.
A discussion of sociopolitical interpretations in general, their applicability to Yeats, and a review of previously published criticism of Yeats's politics.

4045a. ANON.: "Problem of Divorce: Dr. W. B. Yeats Replies to Bishops [. . .]," *Irish Times*, 67:21265 (12 June 1925), 7.
See also the editorial on p. 6, "Divorce in the Free State."

4046. ANON.: "Lively Exchanges," *Irish Times*, 68:21470 (8 Feb 1926), 6.
Patrick McCartan states that Yeats went to London to negotiate the abolition of the oath of allegiance. This is denied by Yeats and by

President Cosgrave's office, "Letter from Senator Yeats," :21471 (9 Feb 1926), 5.

4047. ANON.: "Thanks, Mr. Yeats," *Phoblacht*, ns 1:34 (30 July 1926), 1.
"In Mr. Yeats's own words, the horrors of the civil war were inflicted upon the Irish people so that Mr. Cosgrave and his friends might 'remain on the friendliest terms with royalty.'"

4047a. ANON.: "The Irish Scene 1925," *Round Table*, 15:60 (Sept 1925), 749-68.
Comments on Yeats's divorce speech, pp. 756-57.

4048. ANON.: "Mr. Yeats and St. Thomas," *Standard* [Dublin], 1:20 (29 Sept 1928), 12.
Criticizes Yeats's stand on the censorship bill.

4049. ARNOLD, CARROLL C.: "Oral Rhetoric, Rhetoric, and Literature," *Philosophy & Rhetoric*, 1:4 (Fall 1968), 191-210.
Discusses Yeats's undelivered speech on divorce as an example of oral rhetoric (as opposed to literary rhetoric).

4050. AUDEN, W. H.: "The Public v. the Late Mr. William Butler Yeats," *Partisan R*, 6:3 (Spring 1939), 46-51.
The public prosecutor: Yeats did not care for the social problems of his time. The council for the defense: "However false or undemocratic his ideas, his diction shows a continuous evolution towards what one might call the true poetic style." No verdict is given.

4051. AUSUBEL, HERMAN: *In Hard Times: Reformers among the Late Victorians*. NY: Columbia UP, 1960. xi, 403 p.
Some notes on Yeats's involvement in late 19th-century politics, *passim* (see index).

4052. BLANSHARD, PAUL: *The Irish and Catholic Power: An American Interpretation*. Boston: Beacon Press, 1953. viii, 375 p.
On Yeats's views of the relationship between the state and the Catholic church, pp. 25, 72-73, 89, 160-62. Written from an anti-Catholic point of view.

4053. BODKIN, THOMAS: *Hugh Lane and His Pictures*. Dublin: Stationery Office for An Chomhairle Ealaíon (The Arts Council), 1956 [1932]. xv, 96 p. and 51 plates.
Contains a few references to Yeats's defense of Lane's unwitnessed codicil.

4054. BROWN, MALCOLM: *The Politics of Irish Literature: From Thomas Davis to W. B. Yeats*. London: Allen & Unwin, 1972. xii, 431 p.
On Yeats, *passim*. See particularly "Enter: W. B. Yeats," 311-25 (Yeats's attitude toward the Irish/English problem and his connection with John O'Leary); "Poetry Defends the Gap: Yeats and Hyde," 348-70 (the Yeats-Sir Charles Gavan Duffy quarrel and Yeats's nationalism, which Brown mistakenly considers to be "noteworthy for his laughable alienation from the Irish nation, past or present"); "Literary Parnellism," 371-90 (mainly in Yeats, Lady Gregory, and Joyce. Again the Yeats picture is distorted: Brown sees an undue self-dramatization whenever Yeats speaks of Parnell and concludes: "Yeats's practice demonstrated with resounding finality the untruth of his theory that whatever is well said must be so.") I have two main objections to this book: (1) its sloppy style substitutes for precise argument at crucial places; (2) the documentation is poor, especially that of the early Irish opposition to Yeats.

Reviews:
1. Betty Abel, "Ireland in Literature," *Contemporary R*, 221:1280 (Sept 1972), 164-65.
2. Anon., "Political Characters and Literary Characters," *TLS*, 71:3671 (7 July 1972), 764.
3. Ian Fletcher, *N&Q*, os 219 / ns 21:1 (Jan 1974), 37-39.
4. Thomas Kinsella, "Literature and Politics in Ireland," *JML*, 3:1 (Feb 1973), 115-19.
5. M. A. Klug, *Dalhousie R*, 52:3 (Autumn 1972), 498-501.
6. Donal McCartney, "Politics Their Fuel . . . ?" *Irish Independent*, 81:114 (13 May 1972), 8.
7. Norman H. MacKenzie, *QQ*, 80:3 (Autumn 1973), 481-82.
8. John Mulcahy, "Romantic Ireland?" *Hibernia*, 36:8 (14 Apr 1972), 12.
9. Sean O'Faolain, "Genteel Dastards, Bellowing Slaves," *Guardian*, 25 May 1972, 16.
10. Robert W. Uphaus, *Éire-Ireland*, 8:3 (Autumn 1973), 151-53.

4055. BYRNE, JOSEPH: Rejoinder to Yeats's speech on divorce, *Catholic Bulletin*, 15:7 (July 1925), 685.

4056. CARDEN, MARY: "The Few and the Many: An Examination of W. B. Yeats's Politics," *Studies*, 58:229 (Spring 1969), 51-62.

4057. CROSS, GUSTAV: "'My Hundredth Year Is at an End': Reflections on the Yeats Centenary," *Quadrant*, 10:39 (Jan-Feb 1966), 62-69.
Yeats and fascism.

4058. CUANA: "Doctors Bodkin and Yeats in Their Animal Coinage Book," *Catholic Bulletin*, 21:4 (Apr 1931), 348-52.
Abusive.

4059. DONOGHUE, DENIS: "The Problem of Being Irish," *TLS*, 71:3655 (17 Mar 1972), 291-92.
Comments on Yeats's relationship with Irish literature and politics.

4060. [ELIOT, T. S.]: "The Censorship: And Ireland," *Criterion*, 8:31 (Dec 1928), 185-87.
Comments on Yeats's article "Irish Censorship" (Wp. 385).

4060a. FITZPATRICK, DAVID: "Yeats in the Senate," *Studia Hibernica*, 12 (1972), 7-26.

4061. FREYER, GRATTAN: "The Politics of W. B. Yeats," *Politics and Letters*, 1:1 (Summer 1947), 13-20.
Especially on Yeats's fascist leanings and some relevant poems.

4062. FRIAR, KIMON: "Politics and Some Poets," *New Republic*, 127:1962 (7 July 1952), 17-18.
Yeats and fascism.

4063. GRAVES, ALFRED PERCEVAL: "The State and the Child," *Irish Statesman*, 5:16 (26 Dec 1925), 491-92.
Comments on Yeats's article "The Child and the State" (Wp. 383).

4063a. HAMILTON, ALASTAIR: *The Appeal of Fascism: A Study of Intellectuals and Fascism, 1919-1945*. Foreword by Stephen Spender. London: Blond, 1971. xxiii, 312 p.
See pp. 278-80 and *passim* (see index).

4064. HARPER, GEORGE MILLS: "Yeats's Intellectual Nationalism," *Dublin Mag*, 4:2 (Summer 1965), 8-26.

Part of the article appeared as "Art and Propaganda in the Nationalism of William Butler Yeats," in *Actes du IVe Congrès de l'Association internationale de littérature comparée / Proceedings of the IVth Congress of the International Comparative Literature Association*. Fribourg, 1964. Edited by François Jost. The Hague: Mouton, 1966. 2 v. (1:245-53).

4064a. HASSAN, IHAB (ed): *Liberations: New Essays on the Humanities in the Revolution*. Middletown, Conn.: Wesleyan UP, 1971. xvi, 216 p.
David Daiches: "Politics and the Literary Imagination," 100-116; contains some notes on Yeats.

4065. °HILLS, FREDERIC WHEELER: "W. B. Yeats: The Politics of Culture," M.A. thesis, Stanford U, 1959. iii, 107 p.

4066. HONE, J. M.: "Yeats as Political Philosopher," *London Mercury*, 39: 233 (Mar 1939), 492-96.

4067. HORSLEY, LEE SONSTENG: "Song and Fatherland: W. B. Yeats and the Tradition of Thomas Davis, 1886-1905," M.Phil. thesis, U of Reading, 1967. iv, 233 p.
Discusses Yeats's early political and literary convictions.

4068. HOWLEY, JOHN: "Censorship and St. Thomas Aquinas," *Irish Statesman*, 11:5 (6 Oct 1928), 92-93.
Criticizes Yeats's article of that title (Wp. 385). Correspondence by A. E. F. Horniman, *ibid.*, 93; by Yeats, "Wagner and the Chapel of the Grail," :6 (13 Oct 1928), 112.

4069. "IRIAL": "Censorship and Independence," *United Irishman*, 6:143 (23 Nov 1901), 3.
Criticizes Yeats's views as expressed in "The Proposed Censorship" (Wp. 361). See Yeats's answer, "Literature and the Conscience," :145 (7 Dec 1901), 3; and again "Irial," :146 (14 Dec 1901), 5.

4069a. JORDAN, JOHN: "Senator Yeats and Civil Rights," *Hibernia*, 37:24 (14 Dec 1973), 16.
Yeats's defense of civil liberties was far ahead of his time, and it is only now that we begin to appreciate it.

4070. LYND, ROBERT: "Poets as Patriots," *British R*, 6:2 (May 1914), 264-80.
An article based on Yeats's contention (in *Ideas of Good and Evil*) that patriotism is something like "an impure desire in an artist."

4071. MCCARTAN, PATRICK: "William Butler Yeats—the Fenian," *Ireland-American R*, 1:3 [1940?], 412-20.
An expanded version of "Yeats—the Patriot," *National Student*, 29:5 (Mar 1939), 8-10. Reprinted in J1076 (#10). Yeats was never a sworn member of the Irish Republican Brotherhood, but he regarded himself as one. He was introduced into the IRB by John O'Leary, who had also entered it without being sworn in. The Fenians, in turn, always supported Yeats.

4072. MACCOLL, D. S.: "The National Gallery Bill, and Sir Hugh Lane's Bequest," *Nineteenth Century and After*, 81:480 (Feb 1917), 383-98.
Refutes Yeats's views about Lane's codicil.

4073. MARLOWE, N.: "The Silence of Mr. Yeats," *New Ireland*, 1:12 (31 July 1915), 187-89.
In political matters.

4074. MILLER, JACOB DAVID: "The Fate of a Vision: The Political Thought
and Activity of W. B. Yeats," Honors thesis, Harvard U, 1961. iv, 99 p.

4075. MOHR, MARTIN ALFRED: "The Political and Social Thought of William
Butler Yeats," Ph.D. thesis, State U of Iowa, 1964. iii, 302 p. (*DA*, 25:4
[Oct 1964], 2497-98.)

4076. MOORE, WILLIAM: Letter to the editor, *Irish Statesman*, 2:22 (9 Aug
1924), 690.
     About Yeats's dialogue "Compulsory Gaelic" (Wp. 382). Further corre-
     spondence by Hewson Cowen, :23 (16 Aug 1924), 724.

4076a. NAG, GOURIE: "W. B. Yeats and Politics: Some Approaches," Ph.D.
thesis, U of Edinburgh, 1969 [i.e., 1970]. xv, 413 p.
     Contains chapters on Yeats's relationship with his father, the Fenian
     identity (John O'Leary), aristocratic socialism (William Morris),
     Maud Gonne (including notes on *The Countess Cathleen* and Yeats's love
     poems), Parnell (with notes on relevant poems), and the fascist phase
     (Yeats and Kevin O'Higgins); also "Reference Outline of W. B. Yeats's
     Political Activities and Interests, 1885-1939."

4077. °NIMMO, DAVID CLARENCE: "Yeats and the Hugh Lane Controversy," M.A.
thesis, McMaster U, 1966.

4078. O'BRIEN, CONOR CRUISE: *States of Ireland*. London: Hutchinson, 1972.
336 p.
     "Songs of the Irish Race," 48-64; on Yeats's early political involve-
     ment and the reception of *The Countess Cathleen*. See also pp. 69-71
     (on *Cathleen ni Houlihan*) and *passim* (see index).

4079. O'REILLY, JAMES P.: "A Reply to Mr. Yeats," *Irish Statesman*, 4:3
(28 Mar 1925), 73-74.
     Criticizes Yeats's "An Undelivered Speech," on divorce (Wp. 383).

4080. O'SULLIVAN, DONAL: *The Irish Free State and Its Senate: A Study in
Contemporary Politics*. London: Faber & Faber, 1940. xxxi, 666 p.
     On Yeats's Senate activities, *passim* (see index), especially on his
     speech on divorce (pp. 167-68): "This extraordinary speech was happily
     unique in the history of the senate . . . it poisoned the atmosphere
     that surrounded the question of divorce. . . ."

4081. PRESS, JOHN: *The Lengthening Shadows*. London: Oxford UP, 1971. ix,
191 p.
     Defends Yeats against those critics who find his attitude toward 20th-
     century politics and social issues reactionary and pernicious, *passim*
     (see index).

4081a. RUTHVEN, K. K.: "On the So-Called Fascism of Some Modernist Writers,"
Southern R [Adelaide], 5:3 (Sept 1972), 225-30.
     Includes Yeats.

4082. SHEEHY, MICHAEL: *Is Ireland Dying? Culture and the Church in Modern
Ireland*. NY: Taplinger Publishing Co., 1968. 256 p.
     On Yeats, *passim* (see index), especially pp. 120-28. Maintains that
     Yeats's view of "paganism as earthy, potent, creative, and Christianity
     as lofty, transcendental but humanly negative" originated in the "anti-
     human policy" of the Catholic church in Ireland, which "specially con-
     tributed to Yeats's failure to achieve a unified system, since it was
     on Ireland his hopes were specially centred." Also on the Abbey
     Theatre's subjection to reactionary government and church politics,
     138-49.

4083. SPENDER, STEPHEN: "Writers and Politics," *Partisan R*, 34:3 (Summer 1967), 359-81.

Defends Yeats against those critics who accuse him of fascist leanings.

4084. STANFORD, W. B.: "Yeats in the Irish Senate," *REL*, 4:3 (July 1963), 71-80.

Criticizes Pearce's edition of *Senate Speeches* (W211R/S) and adds some thoughts on Yeats's politics.

4085. STENFERT KROESE, W. H.: "Yeats en het fascisme," *Litterair paspoort*, 6:52 (Dec 1951), 225-26.

4086. TIERNEY, MICHAEL (ed): *Daniel O'Connell: Nine Centenary Essays*. Dublin: Browne & Nolan, 1949. vii, 306 p.

John J. Horgan criticizes Yeats's view of O'Connell as expressed in the Senate speech of 11 June 1925 (pp. 275-76).

4087. TIERNEY, WILLIAM: "Irish Writers and the Spanish Civil War," *Éire-Ireland*, 7:3 (Autumn 1972), 36-55.

Contains a note on Yeats's attitude, pp. 50-51.

4088. WITT, MARION: "'Great Art Beaten Down': Yeats on Censorship," *CE*, 13:5 (Feb 1952), 248-58.

4089. YEATS, MICHAEL: "Yeats: The Public Man," *Southern R*, 5:3 (July 1969), 872-85.

More precisely, Yeats as an Irish nationalist.

4090. YEATS, W. B.: "The Irish Censorship," *Spectator*, 141:5231 (29 Sept 1928), 391-92.

Correspondence by William McCarthy, :5232 (6 Oct 1928), 435-36; Padraig Ua h'Eichthigheàrnan and H. Strachey, :5233 (13 Oct 1928), 488; Areopagitica, :5234 (20 Oct 1928), 528; Ezra Pound, :5240 (1 Dec 1928), 819.

See also J128b, 142a, 563, 634, 743, 792, 889, 930, 940, 941, 947, 955, 956, 963, 964, 972, 1001, 1004, 1013, 1015, 1031, 1038, 1049, 1050, 1056, 1057, 1076, 1097, 1101-3, 1108, 1115 (main entry and review #12), 1118, 1147, 1161 (#7), 1162 (#1, 4), 1186, 1286, 1315, 1357, 1380, 1384, 1426, 1487, 1508, 1580, 1671, 1682, 1741, 1743, 1747, 1755b, 1761, 1761a, 1843, 1936, 2044, 2145, 2265a, 2421, 2542, 2655, 2671a, 2698, 2824, 2831-51, 2950a, 2998, 3027a, 3033, 3230, 3525, 3570, 3745, 3949, 4204, 4212, 4993-95, 5120, 5221-35 and note, 5910, 5940 (#1), 5950, 5951, 6105, 6249, 6321, 6762a, 6787, 6978, 7459.

FE Theory of Poetry and Literature

4091. ADAMS, HAZARD: "Yeats, Dialectic, and Criticism," *Criticism*, 10:3 (Summer 1968), 185-99.

On the dialectic of subjectivity and objectivity in Yeats's thought and his ideas about the dichotomy of literature and science.

4092. ADAMS, J. DONALD: "Speaking of Books," *NYTBR*, [51:] (9 June 1946), 2.

Discusses Yeats's ideas on the moral element in literature.

4093. AGARWALA, D. C.: "Yeats's Concept of Image," *Triveni*, 36:2 (July 1967), 23-35.

Discusses Yeats's use of the term in his prose and poetry. For Yeats, images "form the content of which symbols are the only fitting and successful medium of communication." Yeats's "images" have very little in common with Imagism.

4094. BERWIND, SANDRA MURRAY: "The Origin of a Poet: A Study of the Critical Prose of W. B. Yeats, 1887-1907," Ph.D. thesis, Bryn Mawr College, 1968. iv, 247 p. (*DA*, 29:11 [May 1969], 3998A-99A.)

4095. BEYETTE, THOMAS KURT: "Symbolism and Victorian Literature," °Ph.D. thesis, U of Texas at Austin, 1969. 197 p. (*DA*, 30:12 [June 1970], 5440A.)
    Includes a discussion of Yeats's symbolist theories.

4095a. BLOCK, HASKELL M.: "Some Concepts of the Literary Elite at the Turn of the Century," *Mosaic*, 5:2 (Winter 1971/72), 57-64.
    Compares Yeats's concept of the literary elite with that of Mallarmé and George.

4096. DAVIS, ROBERT BERNARD: "The Shaping of an Agate: A Study of the Development of the Literary Theory of W. B. Yeats from 1885 to 1910," Ph.D. thesis, U of Chicago, 1956. iii, 239 p.
    Yeats's literary theory is based on the "belief that literature is the expression of the moods, or the emotional states which constitute reality, through symbols" (p. 6). Discusses among others this basic theory, the Irish element (folklore, legend, the literary revival, the Irish theater), estheticism and symbolism (the importance of Blake, the Rhymers' Club, Pater, and French symbolism, as well as the fin de siècle element), and Yeats's dramatic theories, including his defense of Synge.

4097. DE MAN, PAUL: "Lyric and Modernity," *Selected Papers from the English Institute*, 1969, 151-76.
    On Yeats's preface to the *Oxford Book of Modern Verse*, pp. 155-58.

4098. DION, SISTER CLARICE DE SAINTE MARIE: *The Idea of "Pure Poetry" in English Criticism, 1900-1945*. Washington, D.C.: Catholic U of America, 1948. iv, 137 p.
    On Yeats's criticism of "impurities" ("curiosities about politics, about science, about history, about religion") in relation to A. C. Bradley's idea of poetry for poetry's sake, pp. 15-16 and *passim* (see index).

4099. ESTERLY, JAMES DAVID: "Poetic Theory in the Prose and Verse of W. B. Yeats," Honors thesis, Harvard U, 1966. i, 42 p.

4099a. FALLIS, RICHARD CARTER: "The Poet as Critic: The Literary Criticism of W. B. Yeats," °Ph.D. thesis, Princeton U, 1972. 507 p. (*DA*, 33:8 [Feb 1973], 4410A-11A.)

4100. FAULKNER, PETER: "The Sources of the Literary Criticism of W. B. Yeats," [M.A. thesis, U of Birmingham, 1960?]. vi, 192, iv p.
    The sources are J. B. Yeats, the Romantic tradition, Irish nationalism, Blake, Arthur Hallam, Arthur Symons, Villiers de l'Isle Adam, Synge, Nietzsche, Lady Gregory, Pound, Wyndham Lewis, the Irish 18th century, and Indian mysticism.

4101. ————: "Yeats as Critic," *Criticism*, 4:4 (Fall 1962), 328-39.
    A survey of Yeats's criticism from the earliest reviews to 1934. Maintains that Yeats contradicted himself considerably at different times, but that there is always "the continuity of his concern with unity."

4102. ————: "Yeats as a Reviewer: *The Bookman*, 1892-1899," *Irish Book*, 2:3/4 (Autumn 1963), 115-21.

4103. °FELLOWS, JAY FRANKLIN: "W. B. Yeats and the Quest for Imaginative Equilibrium," M.A. thesis, Columbia U, 1964. 69 p.

4104. FINNERAN, RICHARD J.: "Yeats and the *Bookman*: Review of *The Chain of Gold*," *PLL*, 9:2 (Spring 1973), 194-97.
Prints and discusses the anonymous review of Standish O'Grady's book, attributed to Yeats (Wp. 348) but not reprinted in Frayne's edition of the uncollected prose (J61).

4104a. °GENET, NÉE VEYSSIE, JACQUELINE: "W. B. Yeats: Les fondements et l'evolution de la création poétique. Essai de psychologie littéraire," Doctorat d'Etat thesis, U of Paris III, 1973.

4105. °GOLDMAN, MARCUS A.: "Emotion of Multitude in William Butler Yeats," M.A. thesis, Columbia U, 1949.

4106. HEXTER, GEORGE JACOB: "The Aesthetic Philosophy of W. B. Yeats," M.A. thesis, U of Texas, 1919. iii, 290 p.

4107. °HIJIYA, YUKIHITO: "W. B. Yeats' Concept of Poetry as Religion," M.A. thesis, Wake Forest U, 1967.

4107a. HILL, JOHN EDWARD: "Dialectical Aestheticism: Essays on the Criticism of Swinburne, Pater, Wilde, James, Shaw, and Yeats," °Ph.D. thesis, U of Virginia, 1972. 147 p. (*DA*, 33:7 [Jan 1973], 3648A-49A.)

4108. HOFFMAN, DANIEL G., and SAMUEL HYNES (eds): *English Literary Criticism: Romantic and Victorian*. London: Owen, 1968 [1963]. xi, 322 p.
Note on Yeats and symbolism, pp. 312-13.

4109. HÜTTEMANN, GERTA: "Wesen der Dichtung und Aufgabe des Dichters bei William Butler Yeats," Dr. phil. thesis, U of Bonn, 1929. 88 p.
An essay on Yeats's esthetic theories and his concept of poetry. Considers the influence of the French symbolists and of Henry More.
Reviews:
1. Karl Arns, *Neueren Sprachen*, 40:7 (Oct 1932), 441.
2. C. Garnier, *Revue anglo-américaine*, 7:3 (Feb 1930), 271-72.
3. Helene Richter, *Beiblatt zur Anglia*, 42:2 (Feb 1931), 52-54.
4. Jakob Walter, *Deutsche Literaturzeitung*, 51:34 (23 Aug 1930), 1600-1602.

4110. °IRVINE, ESTELLA EUGENE: "W. B. Yeats's View of the Function of Poetry," M.A. thesis, Columbia U, 1948.

4111. JAGGI, SATYA DEV: *Coleridge's and Yeats' Theory of Poetry*. Delhi: Cosla, 1967. vi, 109 p.
Not, as one might expect, a comparison of both critics, but a collection of independent essays. The Yeats material (pp. 73-106) is subheaded "Poetry as Personal Utterance," "Poetry and the Buried Self," "Unity of Being and the Poet's World," "Art and Impersonality," "Poetry and Truth," "Theory of Symbolism," and "Poetry and Morality."

4112. °JOSEPHSON, CLIFFORD A.: "The Impersonal Aesthetics of T. S. Eliot, W. B. Yeats, and James Joyce," M.A. thesis, Columbia U, 1951.

4113. KHAN, JALILUDDIN AHMAD: "The Role of Intellect in Yeats's Imagination," *Venture*, 1:1 (Mar 1960), 58-69.
Includes a discussion of *A Vision* and of the Yeats-Sturge Moore correspondence.

4114. LEHMANN, ANDREW GEORGE: *The Symbolist Aesthetic in France, 1885-1895*. Oxford: Blackwell, 1950. viii, 328 p.
Yeats on symbolism, pp. 281-85 and *passim*.

4115. LENTRICCHIA, FRANK RICHARD: *The Gaiety of Language: An Essay on the Radical Poetics of W. B. Yeats and Wallace Stevens*. Berkeley: U of California Press, 1968. x, 213 p. (Perspectives in Criticism. 19.)
Based on "The Poetics of Will: Wallace Stevens, W. B. Yeats, and the Theoretic Inheritance," °Ph.D. thesis, Duke U, 1966. 225 p. (*DA*, 27:5 [Nov 1966], 1373A). Yeats rejected the romantic and symbolist theories of poetry and created a "poetics of will and impersonation" that is "framed in tragic awareness" (p. 62) and that prescribes the making of poetry as the poet's assertion of freedom. Comments on Yeats's early stories and several poems, particularly the Byzantium poems and "Lapis Lazuli."
Reviews:
1. Robert J. Bertholf, *Southern R* [Adelaide], 3:4 (1969), 378-80.
2. Philip Le Brun, *RES*, 21:82 (May 1970), 239-40.
3. Laurence Lieberman, "Poet-Critics and Scholar-Critics," *Poetry*, 115:5 (Feb 1970), 346-52 (pp. 350-51).
4. Joseph N. Riddel, *JEGP*, 68:4 (Oct 1969), 718-23.

4116. LUDOWYK, EVELYN FREDERICK CHARLES: *Marginal Comments*. Colombo: Ola Book Co., 1945. viii, 148, xxii p.
Comments on Yeats's theory of the symbol and the two Byzantium poems, pp. 58-69.

4117. MCBRIDE, JOHN DENNIS: "Primal and Bardic: The Role of Ireland in Yeats' Early Aesthetics," Ph.D. thesis, U of Illinois, 1967. v, 236 p. (*DA*, 28:12 [June 1968], 5062A.)
Claims that the struggle between permanence and flux, apparent in the later Yeats, is also important in the early work, where the retreat into the Irish fairyland signifies the futile search for permanence. Discusses Yeats's early criticism and poetry.

4117a. [M'GRATH, JOHN ?]: "North and South," *United Ireland*, 14:676 (18 Aug 1894), 1.
Re Yeats's "Some Irish National Books" (Wp. 345). Correspondence by Yeats, :678 (1 Sept 1894), 1 (Wp. 346).

4118. °MACLELLAN, FRANCES PRIMROSE: "W. B. Yeats as Critic, with Special Reference to the *Oxford Book of Modern Verse*," M.A. thesis, U of Toronto, 1939. 89 p.

4119. MADDEN, WILLIAM A.: "The Divided Tradition in English Criticism," *PMLA*, 73:1 (Mar 1958), 69-80.
Notes on Yeats and the relationship between poetry and religion, *passim*.

4120. [MATHER, FRANK JEWETT]: "Mute, Inglorious Literature," *Nation*, 83:2156 (25 Oct 1906), 344.
On Yeats's essay "Literature and the Living Voice" (Wp. 369).

4120a. Olkyrn, I. [i.e., MILLIGAN, ALICE]: "Literature and Politics," *United Ireland*, 13:641 (16 Dec 1893), 1.
Letter about a National Literary Society meeting with references to Yeats's views about Irish literature. Correspondence by Yeats, :642 (23 Dec 1893), 5; :643 (30 Dec 1893), 1 (Wp. 344).

4121. MONK, DONALD EDWARD: "Symbolist Tendencies in English Poetics (1885-1930)," Ph.D. thesis, U of Manchester, 1966. 466 p.
"W. B. Yeats," 190-250.

4122. MÜLLER, JOACHIM (ed): *Gestaltung Umgestaltung: Festschrift zum 75. Geburtstag von Hermann August Korff*. Leipzig: Koehler & Amelang, 1957. 291 p.

Wolfgang Kayser: "W. B. Yeats: Der dichterische Symbolismus, übersetzt und erläutert von Wolfgang Kayser," 239-48. A translation of "The Symbolism of Poetry," together with some explanatory notes.

4123. °PETRIE, ALLISON JUDITH: "The Evolution of W. B. Yeats's Aesthetic Theory," M.A. thesis, U of Toronto, 1966. 147 p.

4124. °PHILLIPS, ELIZABETH: "Analysis of Yeats's Auditory Theory of Poetry," M.A. thesis, Louisiana State U, 1966.

4125. POLLETTA, GREGORY THOMAS: "The Progress in W. B. Yeats's Theories on Poetry," Ph.D. thesis, Princeton U, 1961. vii, 576 p. (*DA*, 22:7 [Jan 1962], 2399-400.)

4125a. PRASAD, BAIDYA NATH: "Letters of W. B. Yeats to Katharine Tynan— A Study," *Indian J of English Studies*, 11 (1970), 87-98.
Mostly on Yeats's ideas about literature as expressed in these letters.

4125b. °————: *W. B. Yeats as Literary Critic and Other Essays*. Ranchi: Vishwamoham, 1971. xii, 134 p.
Reviews:
1. Anon., "Yeats and His Dialectics," *Literary Half-Yearly*, 14:2 (July 1973), 163-65.

4126. ROSENBLATT, LOUISE: *L'idée de l'art pour l'art dans la littérature anglaise pendant la période victorienne*. Paris: Champion, 1931. 328 p. (Bibliothèque de la littérature comparée. 70.)
Some references to Yeats, pp. 292-93 and *passim* (see index).

4126a. SENA, VINOD: "The Poet as Critic: W. B. Yeats on Poetry, Drama, and Tradition," Ph.D. thesis, Cambridge U, 1970. xi, 406 p.

4127. SHAW, IAN: "Yeats and the Oral Tradition," M.A. thesis, U of Toronto, 1963. ii, 118 p.
On the oral tradition in Yeats's poetic theory and practice. Concludes that Yeats's poetry is indebted to "the living language" and that he wrote "for the ear."

4128. SHMIEFSKY, MARVEL: *Sense at War with Soul: English Poetics (1865-1900)*. The Hague: Mouton, 1972. 172 p. (De Proprietatibus Litterarum. Series Major. 13.)
Based on "English Poetic Theory: 1864-1900," Ph.D. thesis, New York U, 1964. iii, 235 p. (*DA*, 27:5 [Nov 1966], 1345A-46A). "W. B. Yeats: Ideas of Good and Evil (1896-1903)," 131-44, and *passim* (see index).

4129. SINGH, BHIM: "W. B. Yeats on Modern Poetry," *Kurukshetra U Research J*, 2:1 (Dec 1967—Jan 1968), 23-29.
Particularly on Eliot.

4130. SINGH, BRIJRAJ: "A Study of the Concepts of Art, Life, and Morality in the Criticism of Five Writers from Pater to Yeats," °Ph.D. thesis, Yale U, 1971. 242 p. (*DA*, 32:6 [Dec 1971], 3331A-32A.)
On Pater, Lionel Johnson, Symons, Henry James, and Yeats.

4131. STANFORD, DEREK (ed): *Critics of the 'Nineties*. London: Baker, 1970. 244 p.
"W. B. Yeats, 1865-1939," 120-26: "Yeats's achievement, as a critic of the 'nineties, lies in two fields: his attempt to provide the Celtic Renaissance with a rough and ready working-body of ideas, as bearing on contemporary Irish letters, and his formulation of Symbolism—a French and Continental poetic—largely in terms of the Irish background and his occult studies."

4132. TAKAMATSU, YUICHI: [in Japanese] "The Situation of Yeats in 1906," *Studies in English Literature* [Tokyo], 43:2 (Mar 1967), 197-213. (English summary, pp. 295-96)
Discusses the concept of "oratory."

4133. THEALL, DONALD F.: "Communication Theories in Modern Poetry: Yeats, Pound, Eliot, and Joyce," Ph.D. thesis, U of Toronto, 1954. iii, 429 p.
"W. B. Yeats: Magic, Communication, and the *Anima Mundi*," 1-73.

4134. °THOMSON, GEORGE WILLIAM: "The Growth of Yeats's Ideas on the Poetic Process," M.A. thesis, U of Toronto, 1958. 139 p.

4135. TURNER, W. J.: "Yeats and Song-Writing," *NSt*, 17:426 (22 Apr 1939), 606-7.

4136. TUVESON, ERNEST LEE: *The Imagination as a Means of Grace: Locke and the Aesthetics of Romanticism.* Berkeley: U of California Press, 1960. v, 218 p.
Note on Yeats's concept of symbolism and estheticism, pp. 194-98.

4137. UEDA, MAKOTO: *Zeami, Bashō, Yeats, Pound: A Study in Japanese and English Poetics.* The Hague: Mouton, 1965. 165 p. (Studies in General and Comparative Literature. 1.)
Based on a °Ph.D. thesis, U of Washington, 1961. 179 p. (*DA*, 22:11 [May 1962], 4007-8). "W. B. Yeats: Imagination, Symbol, and the Mingling of Contraries," 65-89; an exposition of Yeats's thought that does not venture very far beyond paraphrase. The final chapter, "Toward a Definition of Poetry," 124-56, compares the four writers' theories.
Reviews:
1. Earl Miner, *Comparative Literature*, 18:2 (Spring 1966), 176-77.

4138. WALKER, JOYCE BRODBER: "W. B. Yeats' Poetic Theory, 1887-1915," M.A. thesis, U of Toronto, 1961. ii, 133 p.
Applies Yeats's theories to two of his poems: "The Song of the Happy Shepherd" and "The Rose Tree."

4139. WARSCHAUSKY, SIDNEY: "W. B. Yeats as Literary Critic," Ph.D. thesis, Columbia U, 1957. x, 314 p. (*DA*, 17:7 [1957], 1559-60.)
Includes a discussion of the Irish dramatic revival and of Yeats's theory of tragedy.

4140. WIEGNER, KATHLEEN KNAPP: "W. B. Yeats and the Ritual Imagination," Ph.D. thesis, U of Wisconsin, 1967. vi, 244 p. (*DA*, 28:12 [June 1968], 5077A-78A.)

4141. WIMSATT, WILLIAM KURTZ, and CLEANTH BROOKS: *Literary Criticism: A Short History.* London: Routledge & Kegan Paul, 1965 [1957]. xviii, 755, xxii p.
On Yeats, *passim* (see index), especially pp. 597-606. The discussion centers on the concepts of imagination and knowledge in Yeats's literary criticism, philosophy, and poetry.

4142. WITT, MARION: "Yeats on the Poet Laureatship," *MLN*, 66:6 (June 1951), 385-88.
On the unsigned "The Question of the Laureateship" (Wp. 340).

4142a. WOODCOCK, GEORGE: "Old and New Oxford Books: The Idea of an Anthology," *Sewanee R*, 82:1 (Winter 1974), 119-30.
Notes on Yeats's *Oxford Book of Modern Verse, passim.*

See also J651, 743, 948, 966, 993a, 994, 1001, 1004, 1009, 1039, 1082,
1102, 1110, 1141, 1243, 1256, 1772a, 1778, 1780, 1804, 1836, 1851, 1856,
1882, 1887, 1949, 1953, 1968, 2039, 2055, 2093, 2108, 2110, 2111a, 2134,
2145a, 2216, 2269, 2281, 2419, 2423, 2429, 2431, 2471, 2492, 2517, 2659,
2809, 2828, 2918, 3033, 3949, 3988, 4011a, 4067, 4199, 4210, 4212, 4228,
4391-406 and note, 4441-45, 4546-49, 4610-21 and note, 4622-24, 4784-804
and note, 4947, 4954-55, 5032-36, 5236-71 and note, 5277-86 and note,
5319, 5322-62, 5398-426 and note, 5496-510, 5546, 5933, 6290, 6291.

FF "Speaking to the Psaltery"

4143. ANON.: "Samhain," *Freeman's J*, 135:[] (3 Nov 1902), 6.
A review of a performance by Florence Farr and a report of a speech
by Yeats.

4144. ANON.: "'Speaking to the Psaltery': Mr. W. B. Yeats in Manchester,"
Manchester Guardian, #17713 (19 May 1903), 7.
A summary of Yeats's speech and a review of Florence Farr's perfor-
mance, followed by a favorable comment of the paper's music critic on
Yeats's conception of the relation between music and poetry.

4145. ANON.: "Words and Music," *Musical News*, 28:728 (11 Feb 1905), 129-30.
Criticizes Yeats's efforts as "archaic."

4146. ANON.: "Mr. Yeats's Method of Reciting," *Sphere*, 9:126 (21 June
1902), 278.

4147. BAUGHAN, E. A.: "The Chanting of Poems," *Outlook* [London], 15:364
(21 Jan 1905), 89-90.
Yeats's theory is shaky, Florence Farr's performance childish.

4148. CHESTERTON, G. K.: "Mr. Yeats and Popularity," *Daily News*, #17832
(16 May 1903), 8.
Yeats's speaking to the psaltery, which purports to revive a "popular
art," isn't popular at all but a "modern paradox of eccentric sanity."

4149. FARR, FLORENCE: *The Music of Speech, Containing the Words of Some
Poets, Thinkers and Music-Makers Regarding the Practice of the Bardic Art
Together with Fragments of Verse Set to Its Own Melody.* London: Mathews,
1909. ii, 27 p.
Dedicated to Yeats. Contains quotations from various articles and
reviews about herself, Yeats, and the recitals, extracts from her own
writings on the subject, and fragments of poems set to musical notes
(no Yeats poem included). See also J4195.

4150. HERFORD, C. H.: "Speaking to the Psaltery," *Manchester Guardian*,
#17705 (9 May 1903), 8.

4151. R[UNCIMAN], J. F.: "At the Alhambra and Elsewhere," *Saturday R*, 91:
2365 (23 Feb 1901), 236-37.
Includes an account of one of Yeats's "cantilating" recitals.

4152. S., H. A.: "The Art of the Chaunt," *Westminster Gazette*, 25:3675
(18 Jan 1905), 2.
The theory is "plausible enough," but the result was "sadly disappointing."

4153. SYMONS, ARTHUR: *Plays, Acting and Music: A Book of Theory.* London:
Constable, 1909 [1903]. xii, 323 p.
"The Speaking of Verse," 173-81, not contained in the 1903 edition,
reprinted from *Academy*, 62:1569 (31 May 1902), 559. On Yeats's theory

and Florence Farr's performance, which differed greatly from the theory. See Yeats's reply, :1570 (7 June 1902), 590–91 (Wp. 363; reprinted in *Letters*).

See also J931, 1076, 3369, 4124, 4127, 4169a, 4195, 5427–38, 5851, 6302 (#10), 7285.

FG   Theory of Drama and Tragedy

4154. *Academy Papers*. Addresses on the Evangeline Wilbour Blashfield Foundation of the American Academy of Arts and Letters. NY: Scribner's, 1925–51. 2 v.
George Pierce Baker: "Speech in Drama," 2:19–38; on Yeats, pp. 34–35.

4155. ARCHER, WILLIAM: "Study and Stage: 'Words That Sing and Shine,'" *Morning Leader*, #3946 (7 Jan 1905), 4.
Takes exception to Yeats's criticism that Ibsen has no "words that sing and shine" (in "The Play, the Player, and the Scene," Wp. 368), but agrees that more plays should be written that qualify in this respect.

4156. BAIRD, JAMES: *Ishmael*. Baltimore: Johns Hopkins Press, 1956. xxviii, 446 p.
Note on Yeats's thoughts about the Nō, pp. 70–71.

4157. BAKER, GEORGE PIERCE: "Rhythm in Recent Dramatic Dialogue," *Yale R*, 19:1 (Sept 1929), 116–33.
Contains some remarks about how Yeats wished a dialogue to be spoken.

4158. BAKSI, PRONOTI: "Yeats and Eliot as Theorists of Contemporary Drama: A Comparative Study," M.A. thesis, U of London, 1965 [i.e., 1966]. 286 p.

4159. BARNES, T. R.: "Yeats, Synge, Ibsen, and Strindberg," *Scrutiny*, 5:3 (Dec 1936), 257–62.
Yeats's dramatic ideals compared with those of Synge, Ibsen, and Strindberg.

4160. BLAKE, WARREN BARTON: "The Theater and Beauty," *Independent*, 77:3403 (23 Feb 1914), 271.
On Yeats's lecture "The Theatre of Beauty" (Wp. 373).

4161. BLAU, HERBERT: "W. B. Yeats and T. S. Eliot: Poetic Drama and Modern Poetry," Ph.D. thesis, Stanford U, 1954. vi, 671 p. (*DA*, 14:3 [1954], 523–24.)
Discusses Yeats's dramatic theories (which he finds surprisingly similar to Eliot's) and his plays, pp. 174–429.

4162. *Cahiers d'Aran*, #1 (Spring 1969), [17 p.]
A periodical issued by the Théâtre d'Aran (1, square Rocamadour, Paris 16e), directed by Isabelle Garma. The theater expressly derives its principles of staging and acting from Yeats and intends to produce several Yeats plays, among others *On Baile's Strand*, which is discussed on [p. 9]. No other issue of the periodical seems to have been published.

4163. CALENDOLI, GIOVANNI: "La polemica teatrale di W. Buttler [sic] Yeats: I limiti del realismo nell'arte dell'attore," *Fiera letteraria*, 17:45 (11 Nov 1962), 5.
Yeats's dramatic theory as influenced by the Nō.

4164. CHENEY, SHELDON: *The Art Theater: Its Character as Differentiated from the Commercial Theater; Its Ideals and Organization; and a Record of Certain European and American Examples.* NY: Knopf, 1925 [1917]. ix, 281 p.
Scattered references to Yeats's dramatic theories (see index).

4165. "Chanel" [i.e., CLERY, ARTHUR EDWARD]: "Mr. Yeats and Theatre Reform," *Leader*, 6:5 (28 Mar 1903), 72.

4166. ————: "The Philosophy of an Irish Theatre," *Leader*, 7:10 (31 Oct 1903), 154-55.

4167. °DOLAN, PAUL JOSEPH: "On Yeats's Conception of Tragedy and His *On Baile's Strand* and *Purgatory*," M.A. thesis, New York U, 1959.

4168. EGLINTON, JOHN: "Life and Letters," *Irish Statesman*, 2:51 (12 June 1920), 566.
A causerie on Yeats's theatrical aspirations.

4169. FAULK, CAROLYN SUE: "The Apollonian and Dionysian Modes in Lyric Poetry and Their Development in the Poetry of W. B. Yeats and Dylan Thomas," Ph.D. thesis, U of Illinois, 1963. iv, 372 p. (*DA*, 24:10 [Apr 1964], 4173-74.)
On Yeats's theory of tragedy and its indebtedness to Nietzsche, and on some related poems.

4169a. FLANNERY, J. W.: "W. B. Yeats and the Actor," *Studies*, 62:245 (Spring 1973), 1-17.
A "conspectus on Yeats's view of acting," including notes on the "Speaking to the Psaltery" experiments.

4170. °HETHMON, ROBERT HENRY: "The Dramatic Theory of William Butler Yeats," M.A. thesis, Cornell U, 1948.

4171. ————: "Total Theatre and Yeats," *Colorado Q*, 15:4 (Spring 1967), 361-77.
Yeats's dramatic theories and the modern world.

4172. JEFFARES, ALEXANDER NORMAN: *A Poet and a Theatre.* Inaugural lecture, May 21st, 1946. Groningen: Wolters, 1946. 20 p.
Answers the questions "how the Abbey Theatre was created . . . [and] why Yeats wanted a theatre" (p. 3).
Reviews:
1. R[udolf] St[amm], *ES*, 27:4 (Aug 1946), 128.

4173. KETTLE, THOMAS: "Mr. Yeats and the Freedom of the Theatre," *United Irishman*, 8:194 (15 Nov 1902), 3.
On Yeats's article "The Freedom of the Theatre" (Wp. 364). Correspondence by Fred Ryan, "The Artist as Teacher," :195 (22 Nov 1902), 3; M. C. Joy, "Mr. Yeats and the Freedom of the Theatre," :196 (29 Nov 1902), 3.

4174. MILLER, LIAM: "W. B. Yeats and Stage Design at the Abbey Theatre," *Malahat R*, #16 (Oct 1970), 50-64.
Includes 20 illustrations between pp. 64 and 85. On Yeats's ideas about stage design and how they worked in the Abbey Theatre.

4175. MÜNCH, WILHELM: "Gedanken eines Poeten in Shakespeares Stadt," *Shakespeare Jahrbuch*, 40 (1904), 204-12.
Discusses the dramatic theory expounded in "At Stratford-on-Avon" and Yeats's view of Shakespeare.

4176. NARANG, G. L.: "The Influences behind Yeats's Dramatic Theory,"
Kurukshetra U Research J, 1:2 (June-July 1967), 283-89.
The influences are Irish nationalism, his own subjective nature, and
the Nō.

4177. NORDELL, HANS RODERICK: "The Dramatic Theories of Yeats and Shaw,"
Honors thesis, Harvard U, 1948. iii, 81 p.

4178. °NORSE, HAROLD GEORGE: "Yeats and the Theatre: A Study of His Dramatic Principles," M.A. thesis, New York U, 1951.

4179. NYSZKIEWICZ, HEINZ (ed): *Zeitgenössische englische Dichtung: Ein-
führung in die englische Literaturbetrachtung mit Interpretationen. III.
Drama.* Frankfurt/Main: Hirschgraben, 1968. 233 p.
The Editor: "Zielsetzungen des modernen englischen Dramas: George
Bernard Shaw und William Butler Yeats," 15-27; on their dramatic
theories (see also pp. 27-74, *passim*).
Wolfgang Schlegelmilch: "*The Words upon the Window-Pane*: W. B. Yeats,"
99-115.

4180. O HAODHA, MICHEÁL: "Yeats and *The Voice of Ireland*," *Yeats Association Bulletin*, #2 (Spring 1968), [1-2].
On Yeats's article "The Irish Dramatic Movement" in W314A.

4181. OREL, HAROLD: "Yeats as a Young Man," *Books and Libraries at the U
of Kansas*, #25 (Feb 1961), 1-5.
Discusses Yeats's contributions to *Samhain* on drama and theater.

4182. [PEARSE, P. H. ?]: "Mr. Yeats on the Drama," *Claidheamh Soluis*, 6:47
(28 Jan 1905), 7.

4182a. PEYTON, ANN COLEMAN: "Unseen Reality: A Study of the Significance
of the Dramatic Theories of William Butler Yeats," Ph.D. thesis, Florida
State U, 1973. 253 p. (*DA*, 34:6 [Dec 1973], 3427A.)

4183. PRIOR, MOODY E.: "Yeats's Search for a Dramatic Form," *TriQ*, #4
[Fall 1965], 112-14.
Why the early Yeats turned away from the drama of his time and began
to write plays himself.

4184. SELLIN, ERIC: "The Oriental Influence in Modern Western Drama,"
France-Asie/Asia, 21:1 (1966), 85-93.
Discusses the influence of the Nō on Yeats's dramatic theory.

4185. SEN GUPTA, D. P.: "Yeats's Views on the Drama and the Stage," *Visva-
Bharati Q*, 30:3 (1964-65), 205-18.

4186. SENA, VINOD: "Yeats on the Possibility of an English Poetic Drama,"
MD, 9:2 (Sept 1966), 195-205.
A defense of Yeats's dramatic theories. See Rupin W. Desai, "A Note
on 'Yeats on the Possibility of an English Poetic Drama,'" *MD*, 11:4
(Feb 1969), 396-99: Yeats's failure to build up a successful Irish
dramatic movement does not imply that he felt he had failed as a
dramatist.

4187. SMITH, JEAN C.: "The Dramatic Theory of William Butler Yeats: The
Image of Loneliness," M.A. thesis, Catholic U of America, 1956. iv, 115 p.

4188. SNODDY, OLIVER: "Yeats and Irish in the Theatre," *Éire-Ireland*, 4:1
(Spring 1969), 39-45.
Collects some of Yeats's opinions on Gaelic plays and the necessity
of having good texts.

4189. STOLL, ELMER EDGAR: *From Shakespeare to Joyce: Authors and Critics; Literature and Life*. NY: Doubleday, Doran, 1944. xxi, 442 p.
"Poetry and the Passions: An Aftermath," 163-83; reprinted from *PMLA*, 55:5 (Dec 1940), 979-92. On Yeats's dramatic theories.

4190. STUCKI, YASUKO: "Yeats's Drama and the Nō: A Comparative Study in Dramatic Theories," *MD*, 9:1 (May 1966), 101-22.

4191. °WERBIN, MAY: "William Butler Yeats and the Irish National Theatre," M.A. thesis, Columbia U, 1950.

4192. YEATS, W. B.: "Seven Letters of W. B. Yeats." Edited by Ronald Ayling, *Theoria*, #20 (15 June 1963), 60-70.
For details see J159. On Abbey affairs.

4193. ————: "'Theatre Business, Management of Men': Six Letters by W. B. Yeats." Edited by Ronald Ayling, *Threshold*, #19 (Autumn 1965), 48-57.
Letters 1-3 and 5-7 from J4192; see J159 and Wp. 400.

4194. ————: "W. B. Yeats on Plays and Players." Edited by Ronald Ayling, *MD*, 9:1 (May 1966), 1-10.
Includes letters 5-7 from J4192; see J159 and Wp. 401.

See also J936, 940, 944, 952, 953, 967, 982, 996, 1004, 1006, 1014, 1022, 1023, 1034, 1054, 1077, 1082, 1127, 1136, 1608, 1928, 1984, 2063, 2064, 2067, 2121, 2282, 2295, 2431, 2617, 3317, 3320, 3327, 3330, 3345, 3369, 3389, 3441, 3469, 3486, 3555, 3558, 3770, 3867, 4096, 4126a, 4139, 4199, 4600-4609, 4805-34 and note, 5277-86 and note, 5319, 5320, 5382, 5530a, 5933, 6301, 6302, 6314, 6330, 6414, 6504, 6572, 6744, 6763, 7148.

The arrangement of this section is geared to Wade's bibliography, with the Wade numbers or pages preceding each entry. Items not listed by Wade can be found at the end of this section; they are arranged according to the numbers of this bibliography (section AB). Substantial items are cross-referenced to other relevant sections. For reviews of some of the items see part H.

4195. (W75-82) *The Collected Works in Verse and Prose*. Stratford-on-Avon: Shakespeare Head Press, 1908. 8 v.
> Volume 3 contains music by Florence Farr for *The King's Threshold*, *On Baile's Strand*, and *Deirdre* (225-30); by Sara Allgood for *Deirdre* (230); by Arthur Darley for *The Shadowy Waters* (231); traditional Irish airs for *The Unicorn from the Stars* and *The Hour Glass* (232); by Florence Farr for *Cathleen ni Houlihan* (233); and a note by Florence Farr on the speaking to the psaltery together with her notations for the following poems: Song from *The Land of Heart's Desire*, "The Happy Townland," and "He Thinks of His Past Greatness When a Part of the Constellations of Heaven." Also notations by Yeats for "The Song of Wandering Aengus" and "The Song of the Old Mother" and by A. H. Bullen for "The Host of the Air" (235-39).
> Volume 8 contains "A Bibliography of the Writings of William Butler Yeats" by Allan Wade and John Quinn (197-287).

4196. (W97) *The Land of Heart's Desire*. With a foreword by James S. Johnson. San Francisco: Windsor Press, 1926. 29 p.
> "Foreword," v-vii: The play is the essence of the genuinely Irish and national sentiment.

4197. (W143) *The Lake Isle of Innisfree*. With a facsimile of the poem in the poet's handwriting, also an appreciative note by George Sterling. Oakland: Mills College, Bender Collection, 1924. [8 p.]
> "A Note on 'The Lake Isle of Innisfree,'" [5-7]: Yeats's poem is a healthy antidote to technology and progress.

4198. (W155) *W. B. Yeats*. London: Benn, [1927]. 31 p. (The Augustan Book of English Poetry. Second series. 4.)
> Humbert Wolfe: "Introductory Note," iii [i.e., 3].

4199. (W173) *Letters to the New Island*. Edited with an introduction by Horace Reynolds. London: Oxford UP, 1970 [1934]. xii, 222 p.
> "Introduction," 3-66. Discusses Yeats's early preoccupation with Irish literature and theater and the relationship with and influence of John O'Leary, Blake, Hyde, Todhunter, the Rhymers' Club, Florence Farr, Maud Gonne, and others; also Yeats's role in the Irish literary revival.

4200. (W211F) *Some Letters from W. B. Yeats to John O'Leary and His Sister from Originals in the Berg Collection*. Edited by Allan Wade. NY: New York Public Library, 1953. 25 p.
> Introduction, pp. 3-5; notes, 19-25. Reprinted from *BNYPL*, 57:1 (Jan 1953), 11-22; :2 (Feb 1953), 76-87. Reprinted in *Letters* (W211J/K).

4201. (W211H/I) *Letters to Katharine Tynan*. Edited by Roger McHugh. Dublin: Clonmore & Reynolds / London: Burns, Oates & Washburn, 1953. 190 p.
> "Introduction," 11-22, on Yeats's early life and works and his relationship with Katharine Tynan; also headnotes to the individual sections and notes on pp. 152-84.

4202. (W211J/K) *The Letters*. Edited by Allan Wade. London: Hart-Davis, 1954. 938 p.

Wade's introductions to the six parts of the book and the notes provide a good, short biography.

4203. (W211N) *The Variorum Edition of the Poems*. Edited by Peter Allt and Russell K. Alspach. NY: Macmillan, 1957. xxxv, 884 p.

T. R. Henn: "George Daniel Peter Allt," xi-xiv; an obituary with comments on Allt's Yeats studies.

"Introduction," xv-xvi.

"Order and Placement of Poems," 858-63; the order and placement of poems in each of the individual volumes used for this edition.

4204. (W211R/S) *The Senate Speeches*. Edited by Donald R. Pearce. Bloomington: Indiana UP, 1960. 183 p.

"Introduction," 11-26, comments on Yeats's political career and discusses the relationship of imagination and politics in Yeats's speeches. The book also contains the congratulations for the Nobel Prize award, mainly by Oliver St. John Gogarty, pp. 153-55.

4205. (W211V) *The Celtic Twilight and a Selection of Early Poems*. Introduction by Walter Starkie. NY: New American Library, 1962. 222 p. (Signet Classic. CP120.)

"Introduction," ix-xxv [i.e., 9-25]; on the early biography and works.

4206. (W211W) *Selected Poems and Two Plays*. Edited and with an introduction by M. L. Rosenthal. NY: Macmillan, 1965 [1962]. xli, 236 p. (Macmillan Paperbacks. 93.)

"The Poetry of Yeats," xv-xxxix; "Notes," 210-22; "Glossary of Names and Places," 223-30.

4207. (W211X) *Selected Poetry*. Edited with an introduction and notes by A. Norman Jeffares. London: Macmillan, 1967 [1962]. xxi, 232 p. (Papermac. P97.)

"Introduction," xiii-xxi; "Notes," 209-20. See also J57a.

For W211AA see J553.

4208. (W211BB) *Selected Plays*. Edited with an introduction and notes by A. Norman Jeffares. London: Macmillan, 1964. v, 276 p.

"Introduction," 1-15; "Notes," 257-64. See also J57b.

4209. (W211CC) *Selected Prose*. Edited with an introduction and notes by A. Norman Jeffares. London: Macmillan, 1964. 286 p.

"Introduction," 9-18; "Notes," 263-86. The edition contains extracts from the autobiographical writings, some letters, essays, stories, and introductions.

4210. (W211DD) *Selected Criticism*. Edited with an introduction and notes by A. Norman Jeffares. London: Macmillan, 1970 [1964]. 295 p.

"Introduction," 7-16; "Notes," 273-92.

4211. (W211FF) *The Variorum Edition of the Plays*. Edited by Russell K. Alspach, assisted by Catharine C. Alspach. London: Macmillan, 1966. xxv, 1336 p.

Alspach contributes an introduction, pp. xi-xvi, in which he describes the editorial principles and difficulties; also a list of first performances (incomplete), an index of characters, and a general index. Includes William Becker's introductory note to *Diarmuid and Grania*, pp. 1169-71, reprinted from *Dublin Mag*, 26:2 (Apr-June 1951), 2-4.

4212. (W325/325A) *Letters on Poetry from W. B. Yeats to Dorothy Wellesley.*
With an introduction by Kathleen Raine. London: Oxford UP, 1964 [1940].
xiii, 202 p. (Oxford Paperback. 82.)
Includes letters from DW to WBY, two sections of comments and recorded
conversations, and an account of Yeats's last days. Kathleen Raine's
introduction (not in the 1940 edition) defends Yeats's more unpopular
views about poetry and politics (pp. ix-xiii).

4213. (W327/329) SHAW, GEORGE BERNARD, and W. B. YEATS: *Florence Farr,
Bernard Shaw, W. B. Yeats: Letters.* Edited by Clifford Bax. London: Home
& Van Thal, 1946 [1942]. x, 67 p.
Clifford Bax: "Prefatory Note," v-vii.
GBS: "An Explanatory Word from Mr. Shaw," viii-x.
George Yeats: "A Foreword to the Letters of W. B. Yeats," 33-35.

4214. (W340/341) YEATS, W. B., and THOMAS STURGE MOORE: *W. B. Yeats and
T. Sturge Moore: Their Correspondence, 1901-1937.* Edited by Ursula Bridge.
London: Routledge & Kegan Paul, 1953. xix, 214 p.
"Introduction," ix-xix. "Notes," 186-202. N.B.: The edition is not
complete; nine more letters may be found in the British Museum (Add.
MS. 45732, fols. 27, 29, 36, 37, 50, 54-57). They date from 1932 and
are concerned with Shri Purohit Swami.

4215. (Wp. 407) *Tragedie irlandesi.* Versione, proemio e note di Carlo
Linati. Milano: Studio Editoriale Lombardo, 1914. xlviii, 139 p.
"William Butler Yeats: Sua lirica, suoi drammi e la rinascenza celtico-
irlandese," ix-xxxix.

4216. (Wp. 408) *Erzählungen und Essays.* Übertragen und eingeleitet von
Friedrich Eckstein. Leipzig: Insel, 1916. 182 p.
"Einleitung des Übersetzers," 5-27, discusses Yeats as the exemplary
"Celtic" poet and the protagonist of the Irish literary revival.

4217. (Wp. 410) *Blaesten mellem sivene: Digte og skuespil.* Paa dansk ved
Valdemar Rørdam. København: Haase, 1924. xi, 226 p.
"Forord," vii-xi; notes, 223-26.

4218. (Wp. 414) *Irische Schaubühne.* Deutsch von Henry von Heiseler.
[München: Schmidberger], 1933. vi, 289 p.
The "Vorbemerkung des Herausgebers," [v-vi], quotes von Heiseler's
reasons for translating the plays.

4219. (Wp. 419) *Poems / Poesie.* Traduzione di Leone Traverso. Nota di
Margherita Guidacci. Milano: Cederna, 1949. 218 p.
"Nota," 201-6.

4220. (Wp. 422) *Poèmes choisis.* Traduction, préface et notes par Madeleine
L. Cazamian. Paris: Aubier, 1954. 383 p.
The introduction (pp. 7-96) provides the biographical background and
analyzes the poetry by grouping it according to themes. Notes on pp.
365-72.

4221. (Wp. 426) *Poèmes.* Traduits par Alliette Audra, préface de Edmond
Jaloux. Paris: Colombe, 1956. 95 p.
"Préface," 9-13; reprinted from *Temps*, 79:28346 (23 Apr 1939), 5.

4222. (Wp. 428) *Das Einhorn von den Sternen: Ein tragisches Spiel in drei
Akten.* Deutsch von Herberth E. Herlitschka. Emsdetten: Lechte, 1956. 89 p.
(Dramen der Zeit. 14.)
Artur Müller: "Vorwort," 5-10.

4223. (Wp. 428) *Poemas*. Selección, versión y prólogo de Jaime Ferran. Madrid: Rialp, 1957. 115 p. (Adonais. 140.)
   "Introducción a W. B. Yeats," 11-20.

4224. (J55) *A Selection of Poetry by W. B. Yeats (1865-1939)*. Cambridge: Metcalfe, 1951. 16 p. (*Oasis*, no. 4 [Nov 1951].)
   For details see J55.

4225. (J58) *Running to Paradise*. An introductory selection by Kevin Crossley-Holland, illustrated by Judith Valpy. NY: Macmillan, 1968. 94 p.
   "Introduction," 9-24; a rather simplified introduction to Yeats's life and works for juvenile readers.

4226. (J59) *John Sherman & Dhoya*. Edited with an introduction, collation of the texts, and notes by Richard J. Finneran. Detroit: Wayne State UP, 1969. 137 p.
   Based on "A Critical Edition of William Butler Yeats's *John Sherman and Dhoya*," editor's °Ph.D. thesis, U of North Carolina at Chapel Hill, 1968. 159 p. (*DA*, 30:1 [July 1969], 318A). "Introduction," 9-36; a commentary on composition and publication history, the sources, and the importance of the two stories for Yeats's later work, plus a short interpretation. "Explanatory Notes," 133-37.

4227. (J60) *The Poems*. Selected, edited and introduced by William York Tindall. Illustrated with drawings by Robin Jacques. NY: Printed at the Thistle Press for the Members of the Limited Editions Club, 1970. xviii, 135 p.
   "Introduction," v-xiii.

4228. (J61) *Uncollected Prose*. Collected and edited by John P. Frayne. NY: Columbia UP, 1970—. 2 v.
   Volume 1: *First Reviews and Articles, 1886-1896*. 437 p. Based on "The Early Critical Prose of W. B. Yeats: Forty-one Reviews." Edited with an introduction and notes by John Patrick Frayne, editor's °Ph.D. thesis, Columbia U, 1967. 440 p. (*DA*, 30:10 [Apr 1970], 4449A-50A). Frayne provides head- and footnotes as well as a useful three-part introduction: "Innisfree and Grub Street," 20-34, supplies the necessary biographical background; "Twilight Propaganda," 35-59, discusses Yeats's relationship with the Irish writers of the 1880s and 1890s (particularly Davis, Mangan, and Ferguson), his preoccupation with Irish subject matter, and his efforts to create the Irish literary revival; "Yeats as Critic-Reviewer," 60-77, explains the principles of literary criticism underlying the early prose.

4229. (J62) *Reflections*. Transcribed and edited by Curtis Bradford from the Journals. Dublin: Cuala Press, 1970. iii, 63 p.
   "Notes," 59-63.

For J63 and 64 see J3895 and 3896.

4230. (J65) DOMVILLE, ERIC: *A Concordance to the Plays of W. B. Yeats*. Based on *The Variorum Edition of the Plays*, edited by Russell K. Alspach. Ithaca: Cornell UP, 1972. xxi, 1559 p. in 2 v.
   "Preface," vii-xix.

4231. (J66) *W. B. Yeats and the Designing of Ireland's Coinage*. Texts by W. B. Yeats and others, edited with an introduction by Brian Cleeve. Dublin: Dolmen Press, 1972. 76 p. (New Yeats Papers. 3.)
   Contents: 1. Brian Cleeve: "The Yeats Coinage," 5-8.
   2. WBY: "What We Did or Tried to Do," 9-20.

3. J. J. McElligott: "Irish Coinage Past and Present," 21-24.
4. Leo T. McCauley: "From the Summary of the Proceedings of the Committee," 25-39.
5. Thomas Bodkin: "The Irish Coinage Designers. A lecture delivered at the Metropolitan School of Art, Dublin, 30th November, 1928," 40-54.
6. Thomas Bodkin: "Postscript to *Coinage of Saorstat Eireann*, 1928," 55-60.
7. Arthur E. J. Went: "The Coinage of Ireland, 1000 A.D. to the Present Day," 61-67.
8. Brian Cleeve: "Afterword," 68-75; short biographies of the competitors.

Items 2-4 and 6 are reprinted from *Coinage of Saorstat Eireann* (W317). For the Yeats scholar the book is of little interest, since Cleeve's introduction fails to discuss Yeats's work on the coinage committee in the context of his life and work.

4232. (J67) *Memoirs: Autobiography--First Draft. Journal.* Transcribed and edited by Denis Donoghue. London: Macmillan, 1972. 318 p.
"Introduction," 9-15.

4232a. (J67b) *The Speckled Bird.* Edited by William H. O'Donnell. Dublin: Cuala Press, 1973-74. 2 v.
For details see J67b.

4232b. (J67c) MOORE, GEORGE, and W. B. YEATS: *Diarmuid and Grania: A Three Act Tragedy.* Introduction by Anthony Farrow. Chicago: De Paul U, 1974. i, 59 p. (Irish Drama Series. 10.)
"Introduction," 1-18, comments on the Yeats-Moore collaboration.

4233. (J76a) *Fairy and Folk Tales of Ireland.* Edited by W. B. Yeats with a foreword by Kathleen Raine. Gerrards Cross: Smythe, 1973. xix, 389 p.
"Foreword," v-xvi, comments on Yeats's belief in fairies and psychic phenomena.

4234. (J118) YEATS, W. B., and MARGOT RUDDOCK: *Ah, Sweet Dancer: A Correspondence.* Edited by Roger McHugh. London: Macmillan, 1970. 142 p.
For details see J118.

4235. (J119) YEATS, W. B., and THOMAS KINSELLA: *Davis, Mangan, Ferguson? Tradition and the Irish Writer.* Dublin: Dolmen Press, 1970. 72 p. (Tower Series of Anglo-Irish Studies. 2.)
Roger McHugh: "Foreword," 7-11, discusses the influence of Davis, Mangan, and Ferguson on Yeats.
Thomas Kinsella: "The Irish Writer," 55-70; incorporates "The Irish Writer," *Éire-Ireland*, 2:2 (Summer 1967), 8-15, and "Irish Literature-- Continuity of the Tradition," *Poetry Ireland*, #7&8 (Spring 1968), 109- 16. Yeats's relationship with the past is essentially that of a broken tradition. Yeats is an isolated figure in 20th-century Irish literature. For a discussion of Kinsella's view see Micheál O hUanacháin, "Follow an Antique Drum," *Dublin Mag*, 8:6 (Winter 1970/71), 70-74.

4236. (J184) *Opowiadania o Hanrahanie rudym. Tajemnicza róża. Rosa alchemica.* Translated by Józef Birkenmajer. Lwów: Nakladem Wydawnictwa Polskiego, 1925. xx, 222 p. (Bibljoteka Laureatów Nobla. 41.)
"Slowo wstepne" [Foreword], ix-xx.

4237. (J186) *Tři hry (Temné vody. Na Bailové břehu. Deirdre).* Translated by Jaroslav Skalický, preface by Eva Jurčinová. Praha: Otto, 1928. 103 p. (Sborník Světové Poesie. 155.)
"Předmluva" [Preface], 5-7.

4238. (J199) *Gedichte*. Auswahl, Übertragung und Nachwort von H. E. Herlitschka. Zürich: Arche, 1958. 84 p. (Die kleinen Bücher der Arche. 222-
23.)
"Nachwort," 71-84; a short introduction to Yeats's life and work derived from various Yeats monographs.

4239. (J200) *Calvario*. A cura di Roberto Sanesi. Varese: Editrice Magenta,
1960. 55 p. (Oggetti e simbolo. 8.)
"Prefazione," 7-22, incorporates "Scheda al teatro di William Butler
Yeats," *Aut-Aut*, 5:26 (Mar 1955), 130-39. Reprinted in J4245.

4240. (J201) *Versek*. Edited with introduction and notes by Tamás Ungvári.
Budapest: Európa Könyvkiadó, 1960. 244 p.
"William Butler Yeats," 5-29; "Jegyzetek," 229-37.

4241. (J202) *A húsleves*. Budapest: Gondolat, 1961. 95 p. (Játékszín. 32.)
For details see J202.

4242. (J203) *Poesie*. Traduzione, introduzione e note di Roberto Sanesi.
Milano: Lerici, 1961. 513 p. (Poeti europei. 8.)
"Introduzione," 7-80; "Biografia," 81-86; "Note ai testi," 441-78;
"Bibliografia," 479-99.

4243. (J204) *Slova snad pro hudbu: Výbor z poesie*. Translated by Jiří
Valja, with a preface and explanatory notes by Jiří Levý. Praha: SNKLU,
1961. 144 p. (Světová četba. 265.)
"Poezie Williama Butlera Yeatse," 7-16.

4244. (J205) *Théâtre*. Translated by Madeleine Gibert, illustrated by Keogh.
Paris: Rombaldi, 1962. 277 p.
For details see J205.

4245. (J206) *Drammi celtici*. Introduzione di Roberto Sanesi, traduzione di
Francesco Vizioli. Parma: Guanda, 1963. xxxiii, 325 p. (Fenice. NS. Sezione
Poeti. 2.)
"Introduzione," ix-xxx; contains "Cuchulain nella terra desolata,"
reprinted from *Osservatore politico letterario*, 8:9 (Sept 1962), 93-
102 (on *At the Hawk's Well* and *The Green Helmet*); "Oltre il Calvario,"
reprinted from J4239.

4246. (J207) YEATS, W. B., GEORGE BERNARD SHAW, and EUGENE O'NEILL:
Gedichten / Toneel. Met inleidingen door W. H. Stenfert Kroese [etc.].
Haarlem: De Toorts, 1964. 419 p.
W. H. Stenfert Kroese: "W. B. Yeats," 9-23.

4247. (J210) *Quaranta poesie*. Prefazione e traduzione di Giorgio Melchiori.
Torino: Einaudi, 1965. 104 p. (Collezione di poesia. 15.)
[Prefazione], 5-8; "Nota bio-bibliografica," 9-10; "Note," 81-99.

4248. (J211) *Versuri*. Translated by Aurel Covaci. București: Editura
pentru literatură universală, 1965. 288 p.
Mihai Miroiu: "William Butler Yeats--Dialectica unei conştiinţe poetice"
[Dialectics of a poetic conscience], 5-28.

4249. (J212) *Runoja*. Translation, introduction and notes by Aale Tynni.
Porvoo, Helsinki: Söderström, 1966. 212 p.
"William Butler Yeats: Ihminen ja runoilija" [WBY: Man and poet], 11-
29; "Selityksiä" [Explanations], 201-12.

4250. (J213) *William Butler Yeats: Premio Nobel per la letteratura 1923*.
Milano: Fabbri, 1966. iii, 508 p. (Collana Premi Nobel di Letteratura. 24.)
For details see J213.

For J214 see J6316.

4251. (J215) MALORY, THOMAS, THOMAS SACKVILLE, and W. B. YEATS: *Testi*.
Roma: De Santis, [1967]. 239 p.
    For details see J215.

4252. (J219) *Le opere: Poesia, teatro, prosa*. Edited by Salvatore Rosati.
Torino: UTET, 1969. xxviii, 690 p.
    For details see J219.

4253. (J220) *Racconti, liriche*. Edited, translated and introduced by
Giuseppe Sardelli. Milano: Fabbri, 1969. 256 p. (I grandi della letteratura. 61.)
    Introduction, pp. 7-10.

4254. (J220a) *Shi'un min Yaits: Shi'r, nathir, masrah* [Poetry, prose,
drama]. Beirut: Matabi' Dar al-Nadwa, 1969. xix, 242 p.
    S. B. Bushrui: Introductions, pp. 1-36, 85-96, 143-77.

4255. (J221) *Le fremissement du voile*. Préface et traduction de Pierre
Leyris. Paris: Mercure de France, 1970. 301 p.
    "Préface du traducteur," 7-13.

4256. (J223) *Werke*. Edited by Werner Vordtriede. Neuwied: Luchterhand,
1970-73. 6 v.
    For details see J223.

As in the preceding part, the arrangement of the entries here is geared to Wade's bibliography and to my list of additions in section AB. Each group of reviews of an individual volume is headed by a W of J number, a short title, and the year of publication. It will be found that some minor publications received very few or no reviews at all. I am also aware of the possibility that more reviews are hidden in the daily and weekly press of England, Ireland, the United States, and other countries. Very short notices, as well as reviews that I have not been able to inspect personally, have been excluded.

Reviews of the following books in Wade's bibliography have not been included in this part: W211AA, 255, 261-62, 267-68, 270-90, 292-96, 298-311, 313-24, 326, 330-31, 333A-39, 342-66. (Some of these books plus reviews may be found elsewhere in this bibliography.) Reviews of items such as W252/253 have been included only when they are concerned with Yeats's contribution to the book in question.

The identifications of some of the authors of anonymous reviews are taken from other published works (such as letters) or from published indexes and bibliographies.

W1: Mosada (1886)

4257. T[YNAN], K[ATHARINE]: "Three Young Poets," *Irish Monthly*, 15:165 (Mar 1887), 166-68.
  "We are glad to welcome a new singer in Erin, one who will take high place among the world's future singers. . . ."

W2: The Wanderings of Oisin (1889)

4258. ANON.: "Notes on Books," *Atalanta*, 2:8 (May 1889), 551-52.
  "There is . . . an element of absolute genius in this poem. . . ."

4259. ANON.: *Dublin Evening Mail*, 66:[] (13 Feb 1889), [4].

4260. ANON.: "Some Recent Poetry," *Freeman's J*, 123:[] (1 Feb 1889), 2.
  "Mr. Yeats has yet to rid his mind of the delusion that obscurity is an acceptable substitute for strenuous thought and sound judgment."

4261. ANON.: *Irish Monthly*, 17:188 (Feb 1889), 109-10.
  Cross and Dunlop identify the author as Matthew Russell.

4262. ANON.: *Irish Times*, 31:9884 (4 Mar 1889), 6.

4263. ANON.: *Lucifer*, 4:19 (15 Mar 1889), 84-86.
  Cross and Dunlop identify the author as Carter Blake.

4264. ANON.: *Manchester Guardian*, #13248 (28 Jan 1889), 6.
  Detects much promise but also a certain roughness in the poetry. Yeats's music is not so much that of the "true lyre" as that of the "barrel organ."

4265. ANON.: "Recent Verse by Minor Poets," *St. James Budget*, 18:451 (16 Feb 1889), 15.

4266. ANON.: "Recent Verse," *Saturday R*, 67:1741 (9 Mar 1889), 292-93.

4267. ANON.: "A New Irish Poet," *Scots Observer*, 1:16 (9 Mar 1889), 446-47.
  Cross and Dunlop identify the author as W. E. Henley.

4268. ANON.: *Spectator*, 63:3187 (27 July 1889), 122.

"His volume is a refreshing change from the commonplace of much modern verse."

4269. ANON.: "New Poetry and Prose," *United Ireland*, 8:394 (23 Mar 1889), 6.

4270. THOMPSON, FRANCIS: *The Real Robert Louis Stevenson and Other Critical Essays*. Identified and edited by Terence L. Connolly, with a complete bibliography. NY: University Publishers, 1959. xiii, 409 p.
"W. B. Yeats," 201-3; reprint of an anonymous untitled review of W2 in *Weekly Register*, 82:2127 (27 Sept 1890), 407-8.
"Mr. Yeats's Poems," 203-9; reprint of an anonymous review of W17 and W27 from *Academy*, 56:1409 (6 May 1899), 501-2. See also "Mr. W. B. Yeats and *The Wind among the Reeds*," 58:1446 (20 Jan 1900), 63, an announcement of the award of 25 guineas, quoting extracts from the review.
"The Irish Literary Movement: Mr. Yeats as Shepherd," 210-15; reprint of an anonymous review of W225 from *Academy*, 58:1454 (17 Mar 1900), 235-36.

4271. TODHUNTER, JOHN: *Academy*, 35:882 (30 Mar 1889), 216-17.

4272. WILDE, OSCAR: *The Artist as Critic: Critical Writings*. Edited by Richard Ellmann. London: Allen, 1970. xviii, 446 p.
"[Yeats's *Fairy and Folk Tales*]," 130-35; reprint of The Editor: "Some Literary Notes," *Woman's World*, 2:16 (Feb 1889), 221-24, a review of W212 (221-22).
"Yeats's *The Wanderings of Oisin*," 150-51; reprinted from an anonymous review, "Three New Poets," *Pall Mall Gazette*, 49:7587 (12 July 1889), 3.
See also *A Critic in Pall Mall: Being Extracts from Reviews and Miscellanies*. Selected by E. V. Lucas. London: Methuen, 1919. vii, 218 p. This contains both of the above reviews (pp. 152-57, 160-62) and "Mr. W. B. Yeats," 158-60; a reprint of a different review of W2, first published in "Some Literary Notes," *Woman's World*, 2:17 (Mar 1889), 277-80.

W4/5: John Sherman and Dhoya (1891)

4273. A., L. F.: "A Causerie," *Illustrated London News*, 99:2744 (21 Nov 1891), 667.
"The author . . . is evidently a lady who does not believe in the 'mystery of the sex.'"

4274. ANON.: "Novels of the Week," *Athenaeum*, #3348 (26 Dec 1891), 858-59. The author "has a certain grace of style which atones in part for the extreme thinness of his matter."

4275. ANON.: "Two New Irish Books," *United Ireland*, 11:534 (28 Nov 1891), 5.

4276. ANON.: "Belles Lettres," *Westminster R*, yr 69 / 137:2 (Feb 1892), 221-27.
See pp. 224-25.

W6/7: The Countess Kathleen and Various Legends and Lyrics (1892)

4277. ANON.: "Recent Verse," *Athenaeum*, #3402 (7 Jan 1893), 14-16.

4278. ANON.: *Irish Monthly*, 20:232 (Oct 1892), 557-58.

4279. ANON.: "Lines Based on Irish Lore," *NYT*, 43:13143 (8 Oct 1893), 23.

4280. ANON.: "Recent Verse," *Saturday R*, 74:1930 (22 Oct 1892), 484-86.

4281. ANON.: "Dramatic and Other Verse," *Speaker*, 6:[] (12 Nov 1892), 598.

4282. [DAVIDSON, JOHN]: "A Minor," *Daily Chronicle*, #9509 (1 Sept 1892), 3.
> On the play: "The morality is excellent, but as an artistic achieve-
> ment the drama has much to lack." On the poems: "The verses have not
> enough beauty of diction or true lyrical quality to make up for their
> want of any other attraction."

4283. [HIGGINSON, THOMAS WENTWORTH]: "Recent Poetry," *Nation*, 55:1433 (15 Dec 1892), 452-54.
> "One of the most original and powerful of recent poetic volumes. . . ."

4284. JOHNSON, LIONEL: *Academy*, 42:1065 (1 Oct 1892), 278-79.

4285. LE GALLIENNE, RICHARD: *Retrospective Reviews: A Literary Log*. London: Lane / NY: Dodd, Mead, 1896. 2 v.
> "W. B. Yeats: *The Countess Cathleen*," 1:168-73; a reprint of the anon-
> ymous "Logroller's Literary Notes of the Week," *Star*, #1423 (1 Sept
> 1892), 2. Correspondence by John Augustus O'Shea, #1425 (3 Sept 1892),
> 4, pointing out that he supplied the source for the play.

4286. [M'CARTHY, JUSTIN HUNTLEY]: "Books and Book Gossip," *Sunday Sun*, 2:
69 (28 Aug 1892), 3.

4287. TRAILL, H. D.: *New R*, 7:43 (Dec 1892), 747-49.
> "No instance of such successful treatment of supernatural legend in
> poetic or dramatic form has come in my way for a long time past."
> But: "The general scheme of Mr. Yeats's blank verse leaves much to be
> desired. It is, to say the least of it, unfortunate that the very
> first line of the drama should be short by a foot. . . ."

4288. TYNAN, KATHARINE: "Mr. Yeats' New Book," *United Ireland*, 12:574
(3 Sept 1892), 5.
> See editorial note [by John M'Grath ?], "North and South," :575 (10
> Sept 1892), 1, commenting on Yeats's book and on his quarrel with
> Charles Gavan Duffy and including a letter by Yeats (Wp. 340).

4289. W., C.: "Mr. Yeats' New Book," *Bookman*, 3:13 (Oct 1892), 25-26.

W8/9: The Celtic Twilight (1893/1894)

4290. ANON.: *Athenaeum*, #3459 (10 Feb 1894), 173-74.
> "It reasserts the eternal reality of romance. . . ."

4291. ANON.: *Critic*, os 25 / ns 22:655 (8 Sept 1894), 156.

4292. ANON.: "Lights and Shadows of a Celtic Twilight," *Dial*, 17:195 (1
Aug 1894), 69-70.

4293. ANON.: *National Observer*, ns 11:276 (3 Mar 1894), 403-4.

4294. ANON.: *Saturday R*, 77:1993 (6 Jan 1894), 27.

4295. ANON.: "Two Aspects of 'Paganism,'" *Speaker*, 9:229 (19 May 1894),
562-63.

4296. G-Y.: *Bookman*, 5:29 (Feb 1894), 157-58.
> Sees in the book the signs for a new Celtic revival of English litera-
> ture.

4297. JONES, DORA M.: *"The Celtic Twilight*: The Poems of W. B. Yeats," *London QR*, os 94 / ns 4:1 (July 1900), 61-70.
   Enthusiastic review of W8, 17, and 27.

4298. M'GRATH, J.: *United Ireland*, 13:642 (23 Dec 1893), 5.

4299. RHYS, ERNEST: *Academy*, 45:1142 (24 Mar 1894), 244.

W10/11: The Land of Heart's Desire (1894)

4300. ANON.: "Poems by Irish Writers," *Critic*, os 25 / ns 22:646 (7 July 1894), 3-4.

4301. ANON.: "In Old, Old Ireland," *Daily Chronicle*, #10023 (24 Apr 1894), 3.
   "The quintessence of Celtic folk-lore."

4302. ANON.: "Recent English Poetry," *Nation*, 59:1534 (22 Nov 1894), 388-89.
   "Although disfigured and blighted in the publishing by one of Mr. Beardsley's ugliest and most meaningless frontispieces, the poem itself is as rare and unique as a witch-hazel blossom."

4303. ANON.: "Lines to Thank Ibsen For," *NYT*, 44:13473 (28 Oct 1892), 27.
   "At the best a childish groping after effects which are of no value when attained. . . . As long as we have Stevenson, Kipling, Conan Doyle, Stanley Weyman, William Morris, and a few minor writers like Bliss Carman, we need not fear that the epidemic will spread."

4304. G-Y.: *Bookman*, 6:33 (June 1894), 87.

4305. J., R. B.: *Cambridge R*, 15:384 (31 May 1894), 373.

W15/16: Poems (1895)

4306. ANON.: *Catholic World*, 62:370 (Jan 1896), 565.

4307. ANON.: "Two Voices of Today," *National Observer*, ns 15:369 (14 Dec 1895), 141-42.
   This review may be by W. E. Henley; cf. J926a, p. 28.

4308. ANON.: "Taste and Fancy in Them," *NYT*, 45:13893 (1 Mar 1896), 31.

4309. ANON.: "Recent Poetry and Verse," *Speaker*, 13:[] (4 Jan 1896), 22-23.

4310. ANON.: "Mr. Yeats's Poems," *Spectator*, 76:3526 (25 Jan 1896), 136-37.

4311. DAVRAY, HENRI-D.: *Mercure de France*, 19:1 (July 1896), 181-82.

4312. *Good Reading about Many Books Mostly by Their Authors*. London: Unwin, 1894-95. 264 p.
   Anon.: "Under the Moon," 197-98. Note about Yeats's forthcoming volume of poetry, to be entitled thus (published eventually as *Poems*, 1895). This note could be by Yeats himself.

4313. [HIGGINSON, THOMAS WENTWORTH]: "Recent Poetry," *Nation*, 61:1589 (12 Dec 1895), 429-31.

4314. [JOHNSON, LIONEL]: "A Poet," *Daily Chronicle*, #10506 (8 Nov 1895), 3.

4315. M[ACDONELL], A[NNIE]: "Mr. Yeats's Poems," *Bookman*, 9:51 (Dec 1895), 94-95.
   Reprinted anonymously in *Bookman* [NY], 2:5 (Jan 1896), 423-24.

4316. M'G[RATH], J[OHN]: "The Changing of *Oisin*," *United Ireland*, 15:745 (14 Dec 1895), 5.

4317. [MILLAR, JOHN HEPBURN]: "Recent Celtic Experiments in English Literature," *Blackwood's Edinburgh Magazine*, 159:967 (May 1896), 716-29.
See pp. 719-20.

4318. PAYNE, WILLIAM MORTON: "Recent Books of English Poetry," *Dial*, 20: 235 (1 Apr 1896), 205-11.
See p. 207.

4319. P[ORTER, CHARLOTTE ?]: "Recent British Verse," *Poet-Lore*, 8:1 ([Spring] 1896), 38-41.
See pp. 39-40.

4320. RHYS, ERNEST: *Academy*, 49:1242 (22 Feb 1896), 151-52.

4321. WAUGH, ARTHUR: "London Letter," *Critic*, os 27 / ns 24:715 (2 Nov 1895), 184-85.
See also the anonymous notice, :722 (21 Dec 1895), 426.

W17: Poems (1899)

4322. ANON.: *Athenaeum*, #3738 (17 June 1899), 747-48.
Compares Yeats and Mallarmé.

4323. ANON.: "Three Noteworthy Poets," *Literature*, 4:85 (3 June 1899), 565-66.

4324. ANON.: "A Revised Yeats," *Outlook* [London], 3:77 (22 July 1899), 810-11.
". . . poems to which we understand the final touches have yet to be given."

4325. FOWLER, J. H.: "Mr. Yeats's Poems," *Morning Leader*, #2200 (10 June 1899), Literary Supplement, 1.

4326. Entry canceled.

4327. [THOMPSON, FRANCIS]: "Yeats," *Daily Chronicle*, #11616 (26 May 1899), 3.

See also J1648, 4270, 4297.

W18: Poems (1901)

4328. ANON.: *Athenaeum*, #3880 (8 Mar 1902), 298-300.

4329. ANON.: *Cambridge R*, 22:564 (5 June 1901), 360.

4330. ANON.: "The Revised Poetry of Mr. Yeats," *Literature*, 8:188 (25 May 1901), 439-41.
Contains a long note on the revisions and sources of *The Countess Cathleen.*

4331. ANON.: "Mr. Yeats's Poems," *Spectator*, 86:3804 (25 May 1901), 773-74.

4332. E., F. Y.: "Plays and Lyrics of W. B. Yeats," *Speaker*, ns 4:[] (11 May 1901), 168-69.

4333. NEVINSON, HENRY WOODD: *Books and Personalities*. London: Lane, 1905. xiii, 317 p.
Reprinted reviews (I have not been able to identify the original publications of the first two items):

"The Poet of the Sidhe," 218-25; a review of W18.
"The Latter Oisin," 226-32; a review of W30.
"Irish Plays of 1904," 245-50, reprint of "The Irish Plays," *Speaker*,
ns 10:235 (2 Apr 1904), 12-13; reviews a performance of *The King's
Threshold*.

4334. [THOMPSON, FRANCIS]: "A Poet's Poet," *Daily Chronicle*, #12207 (16
Apr 1901), 3.

4335. [————]: "The Poet as Tinkerer," *Academy*, 60:1514 (11 May 1901),
409-10.
    Not all the revisions are to the better.

4336. T[HOMPSON], F[RANCIS]: "A Poet of the Inexpressible," *Illustrated
London News*, 119:3255 (7 Sept 1901), 331.

See also J6053.

W20: Poems (1908)

4337. ANON.: "A School of Irish Poetry," *Edinburgh R*, 209:427 (Jan 1909),
94-118.
    Reviews W20 and 64 and discusses AE, Moira O'Neill, and Padraic Colum.

4338. [O'CONNOR, T. P.]: "Mr. W. B. Yeats's Lyrics," *T. P.'s Weekly*, 12:
296 (10 July 1908), 40.

W21-23: The Secret Rose (1897/1905)

4339. ANON.: *Athenaeum*, #3630 (22 May 1897), 671.
    Discusses the positive and negative aspects of Yeats's stylistic
anachronisms.

4340. ANON.: *Critic*, os 31 / ns 28:823 (27 Nov 1897), 320.

4341. ANON.: "Mysteries of the Neo-Celtic Movement," *Dial*, 24:284 (16 Apr
1898), 266-67.

4342. ANON.: *New Ireland R*, 7:3 (May 1897), 182-83.

4343. ANON.: *Saturday R*, 83:2163 (10 Apr 1897), 365.

4344. ANON.: "A Poet's Prose," *Speaker*, 15:[] (8 May 1897), 524-25.
    "Few will deny to Mr. Yeats the possession of genius, yet it were
well that he should strive a little to make himself intelligible to
the plain people." Correspondence by Yeats, 22 May 1897 (Wp. 352).

4345. ANON.: *Spectator*, 79:3603 (17 July 1897), 82-83.

4346. ANON.: "Mr. Yeats's New Book," *United Ireland*, ns 16:31 (1 May
1897), 3.

4347. C., C.: *Nationist*, 1:9 (16 Nov 1905), 145.
    "We confess we are far from wholly understanding the drift of Mr.
Yeats' stories, and we are equally uncertain whether it is worth our
while to make the attempt. . . . After all, Mr. Yeats is over forty,
and we are entitled to look for a little maturity and fullness in
his thought."

4348. M[ACDONELL], A[NNIE]: *Bookman*, 12:68 (May 1897), 36-37.
    Reprinted in *Bookman* [NY], 6:2 (Oct 1897), 152-54.

4349. MOORE, GEORGE: "Mr. Yeats's New Book," *Daily Chronicle*, #10963 (24
Apr 1897), 3.

Compares Yeats and Stevenson and finds the former far better and the latter trivial. Correspondence by Vernon Blackburn, "Mr. George Moore on Stevenson," *Academy*, 51:1304 (1 May 1897), 476.

4350. S[HORTER], C. K.: "Notes on New Books," *Illustrated London News*, 110:3027 (24 Apr 1897), 569.

4351. THOMPSON, FRANCIS: *Literary Criticisms*. Newly discovered and collected by Terence L. Connolly, NY: Dutton, 1948. xv, 617 p.
   "A Schism in the Celtic Movement," 326-32. Reprint of an anonymous review of W297, *Academy*, 57:1417 (1 July 1899), 8-10.
   "William Butler Yeats," 370-73. Reprint of an anonymous review of W21, *Academy*, 51:1304 (1 May 1897), 467.
   "Fiona Macleod on Mr. W. B. Yeats," 373-76. See J1464.

W25: The Tables of the Law and The Adoration of the Magi (1904)

4352. THOMAS, EDWARD: "As the Wings of a Dove," *Week's Survey*, 3:149 (13 Aug 1904), 544-45.

4353. [————]: "Back into Other Years," *Daily Chronicle*, #13250 (15 Aug 1904), 3.

W27/28: The Wind among the Reeds (1899)

4354. ANON.: *Athenaeum*, #3742 (15 July 1899), 88.

4355. ANON.: "A Garland of Poets," *Critic*, os 35 / ns 32:867 (Sept 1899), 847-52.
   See pp. 850-51.

4356. ANON.: "The Gaelic Melancholy," *Literature*, 4:80 (29 Apr 1899), 439.

4357. ANON.: "Yeats's *Wind among the Reeds*," *NYTBR*, 4:[] (17 June 1899), 399.

4358. ANON.: "The Muse of Mr. Yeats," *Outlook* [London], 3:65 (29 Apr 1899), 423.

4359. ANON.: "Two Poets," *Spectator*, 83:3706 (8 July 1899), 54-55.
   Appreciates the beauty of the poems, but deplores the lack of "masterful and far-reaching ideas."

4360. DAVIDSON, JOHN: "A Spirit," *Speaker*, 19:[] (29 Apr 1899), 499.

4361. DAVRAY, HENRI-D.: *Mercure de France*, 31:115 (July 1899), 267-68.

4362. [HIGGINSON, THOMAS WENTWORTH]: "Recent Poetry," *Nation*, 68:1773 (22 June 1899), 479-81.

4363. LE GALLIENNE, RICHARD: "Mr. W. B. Yeats's New Poems," *Star*, #3487 (19 May 1899), 1.

4364. M[ACDONELL], A[NNIE]: *Bookman*, 16:92 (May 1899), 45-46.
   Reprinted in *Bookman* [NY], 9:6 (Aug 1899), 555.

4365. MACLEOD, FIONA: "Mr. Yeats' New Book," *Daily Express*, #14602 (22 Apr 1899), 3.

See also J1648, 4270, 4297, 4326.

W30/31: The Shadowy Waters (1900/1901)

4366. ANON.: "Mr. Yeats's New Play," *Academy*, 60:1499 (26 Jan 1901), 81-82.

4367. ANON.: "Two Celtic Poets," *Athenaeum*, #3820 (12 Jan 1901), 39-40.

4368. ANON.: *Bookman*, 19:114 (Mar 1901), 196.

4369. ANON.: "An Irish Symbolist," *Independent*, 53:2751 (22 Aug 1901), 1988-90.

4370. ANON.: *Literature*, 8:169 (12 Jan 1901), 34.

4371. ANON.: *Monthly R*, 3:7 (Apr 1901), 17-18.

4372. ANON.: "Poets from Ireland," *Outlook* [London], 6:154 (12 Jan 1901), 760-61.
    It is neither drama, nor Celtic, nor Irish, but "pretty English."

4373. ANON.: *Pilot*, 4:72 (13 July 1901), 46-47.

4374. ANON.: "Mr. Yeats' New Play," *Saturday R*, 90:2557 (29 Dec 1900), 824-25.
    Reading this review, it is interesting to note that even as early as 1900 Yeats's critics felt that his previous poetry was more elaborate and dreamlike, whereas the new work is "precise" and "simple."

4375. C[HESTERTON], G. K.: "The Shadowy Poet," *Speaker*, ns 3:[] (19 Jan 1901), 437-39.

4376. [GATES, LEWIS EDWARDS]: "Recent Verse," *Nation*, 73:1886 (22 Aug 1901), 152-55.

4377. GUTHRIE, WILLIAM NORMAN: "W. B. Yeats," *Sewanee R*, 9:3 (July 1901), 328-31.

4378. PAYNE, WILLIAM MORTON: "Recent Poetry," *Dial*, 31:367 (1 Oct 1901), 238-45.
    See pp. 238-39.

4379. [THOMPSON, FRANCIS]: "The Literary Week," *Academy*, 58:1464 (26 May 1900), 439-40.
    Reviews the *North American Review* version (Wp. 359).

See also J4333.

W35/36: The Celtic Twilight (1902)

4380. ANON.: "Mr. Yeats's Recent Writings," *Independent*, 55:2867 (12 Nov 1903), 2691-92.
    Also a review of W47. Both works, and the Irish literary revival, are criticized as "nothing after all but another form of decadence, no spontaneous movement but an abuse of spirit, like mysticism and symbolism. . . ."

4381. BOYNTON, H. W.: "Air and Earth," *Atlantic Monthly*, 92:552 (Oct 1903), 565-72.
    See pp. 565-69; also a review of W44/45, 46/47.

4382. [THOMAS, EDWARD]: "The Charm of Mr. Yeats," *Daily Chronicle*, #12595 (12 July 1902), 3.

W41: Where There Is Nothing (United Irishman, 1902)

4383. ANON.: *Academy*, 63:1597 (13 Dec 1902), 661-62.
    "Subversive and revolutionary enough to please the most advanced."

W44/45: Where There Is Nothing: Plays for an Irish Theatre I (1903)

4384. ANON.: "Drama," *Athenaeum*, #3995 (21 May 1904), 665-66.
Also a review of W53 and 56.

4385. ANON.: *Manchester Guardian*, #17733 (11 June 1903), 12.

4386. ANON.: "The Celtic Spirit," *Pilot*, 8:183 (19 Sept 1903), 289.
"Hardly anything published by him at any time has pleased us so ill."

4387. LYND, ROBERT: "Ibsenising Ireland," *To-day*, 39:503 (24 June 1903), 276-77.

4388. [THOMPSON, FRANCIS]: "A Drama of Revolt," *Academy*, 65:1626 (4 July 1903), 10.

4389. [WALKLEY, ARTHUR BINGHAM]: *TLS*, 2:76 (26 June 1903), 201-2.

4390. [WRIGHT, WILMER CAVE FRANCE]: *Nation*, 77:1985 (16 July 1903), 53.

See also J4381.

W46/47: Ideas of Good and Evil (1903)

4391. ANON.: "The State Called Reverie," *Academy*, 64:1623 (13 June 1903), 589-90.
Correspondence by Arthur Clutton-Brock, :1624 (20 June 1903), 617-19.

4392. ANON.: *Athenaeum*, #3948 (27 June 1903), 807-8.

4393. ANON.: "The Cave and the Tower," *British Weekly*, 34:864 (21 May 1903), 137-38.
Less a review than a discussion of the symbols of cave and tower in Christian tradition, prompted by Yeats's discussion of Shelley.

4394. ANON.: "Essays and Plays by an Irish Mystic," *Dial*, 36:430 (16 May 1904), 331-32.

4395. ANON.: *Monthly R*, 13:37 (Oct 1903), 95-96.

4396. ANON.: "The Ideas of Mr. Yeats," *Pilot*, 8:180 (29 Aug 1903), 205-6.

4397. ANON.: "On the Heels of the Symbol," *Saturday R*, 96:2498 (12 Sept 1903), 334-35.
Yeats fails to define the term "symbol."

4398. ANON.: "The Hidden Beauty," *Speaker*, ns 8:191 (30 May 1903), 213.

4399. ANON.: "The Essays of a Symbolist," *TLS*, 2:74 (12 June 1903), 184-85.

4400. CARY, ELISABETH LUTHER: "Ideas of Mr. Yeats: A New Volume of Striking Prose Essays by the Irish Poet," *NYTBR*, [8:] (11 July 1903), 477-78.

4401. EGLINTON, JOHN: *Anglo-Irish Essays*. Dublin: Talbot Press / London: Unwin, 1917. vi, 129 p.
"The Philosophy of the Celtic Movement," 41-46; a review of W46/47.
"Irish Books," 79-89; a complaint that the Irish literary revival has not yet produced "the Irish Book."

4402. P AND Q: "Pages in Waiting," *World*, #1509 (2 June 1903), 936-38.

4403. REYNOLDS, STEPHEN: *Weekly Critical R*, 1:26 (16 July 1903), 11; 2:27 (23 July 1903), 17-18.

4404. S[HORTER], C. K.: "A Literary Letter," *Sphere*, 13:176 (6 June 1903), 220.

4405. [VENGEROVA, Z.]: *Vestnik Evropy*, 38:8 (Aug 1903), 830-36.

4406. [WRIGHT, WILMER CAVE FRANCE]: *Nation*, 77:1985 (16 July 1903), 52-53.

See also J4380, 4381.

*W52/54: The Hour-Glass and Other Plays: Plays for an Irish Theatre II
    (1904/1905)*

4407. ANON.: "Dramatic Notes," *Academy*, 66:1665 (2 Apr 1904), 383-84.
    Also a review of W56. "If Mr. Yeats and his fellow workers desire to
    found a living Irish drama they must look to the life of to-day, not
    of yesterday, and must take for their characters human beings, not
    abstractions."

4408. ANON.: "Ireland in Drama," *Daily Chronicle*, #13192 (8 June 1904), 3.
    Also a review of W56.

4409. ANON.: "Three Fascinating Plays," *Daily News*, #18131 (29 Apr 1904),
    4.

4410. ANON.: "Mr. Yeats's Plays," *Spectator*, 92:3965 (25 June 1904), 989.
    Also a review of W56.

4411. ANON.: "Recent Books of Verse," *Standard* [London], #24901 (13 Apr
    1904), 8.

4412. [BOYNTON, H. W.]: "Three Dramatic Studies," *Atlantic Monthly*, 93:
    559 (May 1904), 712-14.

4413. P AND Q: *World*, #1560 (24 May 1904), 904.
    Also a review of W56.

4414. THOMAS, EDWARD: "The Music of Mr. Yeats," *Week's Survey*, 3:141 (18
    June 1904), 449.
    Also a review of W56.

4415. [WRIGHT, WILMER CAVE FRANCE]: *Nation*, 79:2042 (18 Aug 1904), 144.

See also J4384.

*W56: The King's Threshold and On Baile's Strand: Plays for an Irish
    Theatre III (1904)*

4416. ANON.: "Two Beautiful Plays," *Daily News*, #18102 (26 Mar 1904), 4.

4417. ANON.: *Monthly R*, 17:50 (Nov 1904), 157-60.

See also J4384, 4407, 4408, 4410, 4413, 4414.

W59: Stories of Red Hanrahan (1904)

4418. ANON.: *Athenaeum*, #4101 (2 June 1906), 667.
    "If Mr. Yeats had never published a line of verse, he might rest a
    claim of immortality on these *Stories*. . . ."

4419. [THOMAS, EDWARD]: *Academy*, 69:1733 (22 July 1905), 759.

W64: Poems, 1899-1905 (1906)

4420. ANON.: *Athenaeum*, #4129 (15 Dec 1906), 770.
    "The book suffers from its obvious connexion with the movement which
    is seeking--not always judiciously--to force a Gaelic literature into
    existence."

4421. ANON.: "Verse and Its Public," *Saturday R*, 103:2677 (16 Feb 1907), 206-7.

4422. ANON.: "Recent Verse," *Spectator*, 9:4093 (8 Dec 1906), 930-31.

4423. ANON.: "Mr. W. B. Yeats's Poems," *T. P.'s Weekly*, 8:208 (2 Nov 1906), 556.

4424. ANON.: "The Celtic Movement," *TLS*, 5:257 (14 Dec 1906), 414.

4425. BEECHING, H. C.: "Mr. Yeats's New Poems," *Bookman*, 31:182 (Nov 1906), 74-75.

4426. T[HOMAS], E[DWARD]: "Mr. Yeats Revises," *Daily Chronicle*, #13995 (1 Jan 1907), 3.

See also J4337.

W65/71/98: The Poetical Works I-II (1906/1907/1912)

4427. ANON.: "New Poems and Plays," *American R of Reviews*, 46:6 (Dec 1912), 750-52.

4428. ANON.: "Recent Verse," *Nation*, 84:2167 (10 Jan 1907), 34-35.

4429. ANON.: "Revised Yeats Plays," *NYTBR*, [18:] (6 Apr 1913), 196.

4430. ANON.: "Idle Notes by an Idle Reader," *Putnam's Monthly*, 2:1 (Apr 1907), 118-21.

4431. CARMAN, BLISS: "William Yeats and Alfred Noyes," *NYT Saturday R*, 12:5 (2 Feb 1907), 68.
"You may read many of Mr. Yeats's poems only to be borne away by a sense of rapt elation without exact meaning and without any definite idea of what he is trying to say. . . . With Mr. Noyes . . . the case is different. You will never be in any doubt about his meaning, but neither will you be carried out of yourself by any exaltation of words, any intensity of passion, any abandon of beauty."

4432. GREENSLET, FERRIS: "The Year on Parnassus," *Atlantic Monthly*, 100:6 (Dec 1907), 843-51.
See p. 850.

4433. JOHNSTON, CHARLES: "The Poems of W. B. Yeats," *NAR*, 187:629 (Apr 1908), 614-18.

4434. LUHRS, MARIE: "Gentle Poet," *Poetry*, 30:6 (Sept 1927), 346-49.

4435. RITTENHOUSE, JESSIE B.: "A Glance at Recent Poetry," *Putnam's Monthly*, 3:3 (Dec 1907), 362-67.
See pp. 363-64.

4436. [TOWSE, JOHN RANKEN]: *Nation*, 95:2468 (17 Oct 1912), 365.

4437. WILLCOX, LOUISE COLLIER: "The Poetic Drama," *NAR*, 186:622 (Sept 1907), 91-97.
See pp. 92-94.

W69: Deirdre: Plays for an Irish Theatre V (1907)

4438. ANON.: "Two Irish Plays," *Athenaeum*, #4171 (5 Oct 1907), 415-16.
Discusses the influence of Maeterlinck.

4439. [THOMAS, EDWARD]: "A Poet and Others," *Daily Chronicle*, #14227 (28 Sept 1907), 3.

4440. T[HOMAS], E[DWARD]: *Bookman*, 33:193 (Oct 1907), 47.

W72: Discoveries (1907)

4441. ANON.: *Academy*, 74:1873 (28 Mar 1908), 621.

4442. ANON.: *Athenaeum*, #4185 (11 Jan 1908), 41.

4443. ANON.: *Bookman*, 33:197 (Feb 1908), 216-17.

4444. ELTON, OLIVER: "Mr. W. B. Yeats's New Book," *Tribune*, #620 (7 Jan 1908), 2.

4445. THOMAS, EDWARD: "An Irish Poet," *Daily Chronicle*, #14426 (18 May 1908), 3.

W73: The Unicorn from the Stars and Other Plays (1908)

4446. ANON.: "More of the Irish Literary Drama," *Dial*, 45:536 (16 Oct 1908), 255-56.

4447. ANON.: *Nation*, 86:2241 (11 June 1908), 540.

W75-82: The Collected Works in Verse and Prose (1908)

4448. ANON.: "By the Waters of Babylon," *Nation* [London], 4:3 (17 Oct 1908), 122.

4449. ANON.: "Poetry and Neo-Kelticism," *Saturday R*, 106:2767 (7 Nov 1908), 577-78.

4450. ANON.: *Saturday R*, 107:2783 (27 Feb 1909), 280.

4451. BARING, MAURICE: *Punch and Judy & Other Essays*. London: Heinemann, 1924. x, 370 p.
"Mr. Yeats's Poems," 228-32; reprinted from an unidentified periodical.

4452. DE LA MARE, WALTER: "The Works of Mr. Yeats," *Bookman*, 35:208 (Jan 1909), 191-92.

4453. GARNETT, EDWARD: "The Work of W. B. Yeats," *English R*, 2:1 (Apr 1909), 148-52.

4454. [STRACHEY, LYTTON]: "Mr. Yeats's Poetry," *Spectator*, 101:4190 (17 Oct 1908), 588-89.

4455. TENNYSON, CHARLES: "Irish Plays and Playwrights," *Quarterly R*, 215:428 (July 1911), 219-43.
Also on Synge, Lady Gregory, Padraic Colum, and Douglas Hyde.

4456. THOMAS, EDWARD: "An Irish Poet," *Daily Chronicle*, #14677 (6 Mar 1909), 3.

See also J6071.

W84: The Green Helmet and Other Poems (1910)

4457. ANON.: "Mr. Yeats' New Book," *Academy*, 80:2035 (6 May 1911), 547.

4458. ANON.: "Verse," *Athenaeum*, #4347 (18 Feb 1911), 186.

4459. ANON.: "The Later Yeats," *Irish R*, 1:2 (Apr 1911), 100-101.
Notes an increasingly aristocratic and isolated attitude.

4460. ANON.: "Mr. Yeats's New Play," *Nation* [London], 8:14 (31 Dec 1910), 578, 580.

4461. DELATTRE, FLORIS: *Revue germanique*, 7:4 (July-Aug 1911), 449-50.

W88: Synge and the Ireland of His Time (1911)

4462. ANON.: *Academy*, 81:2058 (14 Oct 1911), 485-86.
Correspondence by M. P., "W. B. Yeats and J. M. Synge," :2059 (21 Oct 1911), 522-23.

4463. ANON.: *Athenaeum*, #4374 (26 Aug 1911), 240-41.

4464. ANON.: *English R*, 9:4 (Nov 1911), 719-20.

4465. ANON.: "An Irishman's Ireland," *NYTBR*, 16:37 (17 Sept 1911), 556.

W92: Plays for an Irish Theatre (1911)

4466. ANON.: *Athenaeum*, #4394 (13 Jan 1912), 51-52.

4467. ANON.: *English R*, 11:2 (May 1912), 330-31.

4468. ANON.: "Mr. Yeats's Plays," *TLS*, 10:520 (28 Dec 1911), 540.

4469. [CRAIG, GORDON ?]: *Mask*, 4:4 (Apr 1912), 342-43.

4470. FIGGIS, DARRELL: "The Theatre," *Bookman*, 41:246 (Mar 1912), 304-5.

4471. T[ENNYSON], C[HARLES ?]: "Mr. W. B. Yeats' Plays," *Contemporary R*, 101:558 (June 1912), 902-3.

W94: The Land of Heart's Desire (1912)

4472. CHESTERTON, G. K.: "Efficiency in Elfland," *Eye-Witness*, 3:1 (20 June 1912), 21-22.
Reprinted in *Living Age*, 274:3552 (3 Aug 1912), 317-19. This is a veritable Chestertonian paradox that nevertheless makes some sense. He argues that the play's vague fairyland world is really a fake. The play was written by an efficient, almost heartless poet. "There is only one thing wanting, one little flaw in the Land of Heart's Desire. The heart does not desire it."

4473. RUYSSEN, HENRI: *Revue germanique*, 9:3 (May-June 1913), 358-59.

W95: The Land of Heart's Desire. The Countess Cathleen (1925)

4474. ANON.: "Four Plays," *Nation & Athenaeum*, 37:11 (13 June 1925), 345-46.
". . . strangely out of date nowadays."

W99: Poems (1912)

4475: ANON.: "Mr. Yeats' Poems," *Academy*, 84:2122 (4 Jan 1913), 6-7.
"It is discomforting to see a poet, having won his way to a distinguished position, occupying his middle years with not much more than a careful revision of his early poems, just when we should expect him to display the maturity and strength of his powers."

4476. THOMAS, EDWARD: *Poetry and Drama*, 1:1 (Mar 1913), 53-56.
Discusses the revisions and approves of them. But: "He seems to have been revising in cold blood what was written in a mood now inaccessible. I cannot but be surprised that he has made the attempt, since it is one which he might find it necessary to renew indefinitely at intervals, should his energy remain unclaimed by creation."

W101: The Green Helmet and Other Poems (1912)

4477. ANON.: "Yeats and His Red Man," *American R of Reviews*, 47:3 (Mar 1913), 371-72.
   Also a review of W102.

W102: The Cutting of an Agate (1912)

See J4477, 7410, 7438.

W104/105: Stories of Red Hanrahan. The Secret Rose. Rosa Alchemica (1913/1914)

4478. ANON.: "Five Fiction Books of Quality," *American R of Reviews*, 50:1 (July 1914), 121-22.

4479. ANON.: "A Book of Celtic Tales by Mr. Yeats," *Dial*, 57:676 (16 Aug 1914), 110-11.

4480. [NEVINS, ALLAN]: *Nation*, 98:2548 (30 Apr 1914), 501-2.

W106: A Selection from the Love Poetry (1913)

4481. ANON.: "Mr. Yeats and Some Others," *Academy*, 85:2156 (30 Aug 1913), 262-63.

W110: Responsibilities: Poems and a Play (1914)

4482. POUND, EZRA: *Literary Essays*. Edited with an introduction by T. S. Eliot. London: Faber & Faber, 1954. 464 p.
   "The Later Yeats," 378-81; reprinted from *Poetry*, 4:2 (May 1914), 64-69.

See also J2522.

W111-13: Reveries over Childhood and Youth (1915/1916)

4483. ANON.: "Irish Memories," *American R of Reviews*, 53:6 (June 1916), 764-65.

4484. ANON.: "An English Parnassian--and Some Others," *Athenaeum*, #4611 (Nov 1916), 527-29.
   Also a review of W115.

4485. ANON.: "A Book of Memories and Musings," *Dial*, 61:722 (15 July 1916), 68.

4486. ANON.: "Mr. Yeats's Youth," *Independent*, 87:3529 (24 July 1916), 130.

4487. ANON.: *Irish Book Lover*, 8:5&6 (Dec & Jan 1916-17), 59-61.
   Also a review of W115.

4488. ANON.: "Mr. Yeats's Childhood and Youth," *Literary Digest*, 53:1377 (9 Sept 1916), 621.

4489. ANON.: "Mr. Yeats on Himself," *Nation* [London], 20:4 (28 Oct 1916), 150, 152.
   Also a review of W115.

4490. ANON.: *Nation*, 104:2688 (4 Jan 1917), 28.

4491. ANON.: "Looking Backward," *NSt*, 8:188 (11 Nov 1916), 139-40.
   Also a review of W115.

4492. ANON.: "William Butler Yeats," *NYTBR*, [21:] (20 Aug 1916), 328.

4493. ANON.: "Something That Never Happens," *Saturday R*, 122:3184 (4 Nov 1916), Supplement, v.

4494. ANON.: "Mr. Yeats in Middle Age," *TLS*, 15:770 (19 Oct 1916), 499.
Also a review of W115. "It is . . . improbable that he will 'wither into the truth.' He has more leaves and flowers yet to sway in the sun; and we, who have the earlier leaves and flowers to enjoy, need not be perturbed by any phrases about the 'lying days of my youth.'"

4495. BLAKE, BARTON: "Yeats and Youth," *Yale R*, 6:2 (Jan 1917), 410-12.

4496. DAVRAY, HENRY-D.: *Mercure de France*, 118:444 (16 Dec 1916), 719-20.
Also a review of W115.

4497. GILTINAN, CAROLINE: "William Butler Yeats," *Poetry R of America*, 1:3 (July 1916), 45-46.

4498. H., A. J.: *America*, 15:376 (24 June 1916), 263.
"He was never really normal at all."

4499. L[ESLIE], S[HANE]: "The Making of an Irish Poet: Mr. Yeats Looks Back on Childhood and Youth," *Ireland*, 1:24 (17 June 1916), 15-16.

4500. L[ITTELL], P[HILIP]: "Books and Things," *New Republic*, 7:86 (24 June 1916), 202.

4501. C., R. H. [i.e., ORAGE, A. R.]: "Readers and Writers," *New Age*, 20: 1260 (2 Nov 1916), 15-16.

4502. ROBINSON, LENNOX: "Memory Harbour," *NSt*, 7:180 (16 Sept 1916), 567-68.

4503. A. E. [i.e., RUSSELL, GEORGE WILLIAM]: *Imaginations and Reveries*. Dublin: Maunsel, 1921 [1915]. ix, 316 p.
"A Poet of Shadows," 34-38; reprinted from J5946, q.v.
"The Boyhood of a Poet," 39-42; reprinted from *New Ireland*, 3:6 (16 Dec 1916), 88-89. A review of W111.

W115/116: Responsibilities and Other Poems (1916)

4504. ANON.: "Verse and Verse-Makers," *American R of Reviews*, 54:6 (Dec 1916), 674-76.

4505. ANON.: "The Poetry of Mr. Yeats," *Saturday R*, 122:3185 (11 Nov 1916), 460-61.

4506. B., W. S.: "The Fragile Poetic Art of Mr. Yeats: His Latest Volume Reveals a Slackening of Poet's Energies during the Rapid Passing of the Years," *BET*, 87:288 (6 Dec 1916), pt 3, 4.

4507. FIRKINS, O. W.: "The Lyre in Britain," *Nation*, 105:2716 (19 July 1917), 66-68.

4508. L[ESLIE], S[HANE]: "Two Poets of the Time," *Ireland*, 1:51 (23 Dec 1916), 6-7.

4509. MAYNARD, THEODORE: "The Metamorphosis of Mr. Yeats," *Poetry R*, 10:4 (July-Aug 1919), 169-75.
Also a review of W120, 123, and 124.

4510. O'B., C.: "Poetry," *Studies*, 6:21 (Mar 1917), 154-57.
Compares Yeats and Thomas MacDonagh.

4511. P[OUND], E[ZRA]: "Mr. Yeats' New Book," *Poetry*, 9:3 (Dec 1916),150-51.

4512. ROBINSON, LENNOX: "Beauty Like a Tightened Bow," *New Ireland*, 3:6 (16 Dec 1916), 90-91.

See also J4484, 4487, 4489, 4491, 4494, 4496.

W118: The Wild Swans at Coole, Other Verses and a Play in Verse (1917)

4513. M[OORE], M[ARIANNE]: "Wild Swans," *Poetry*, 13:1 (Oct 1918), 42-44.

W120/121: Per Amica Silentia Lunae (1918)

4514. ANON.: "Ireland in Poetry," *American R of Reviews*, 57:5 (May 1918), 554-55.

4515. ANON.: "Black Magic," *Athenaeum*, #4628 (Apr 1918), 196-97.

4516. ANON.: "Yeats's Justification of the 'Dual Personality' of Artists: An Argument That Some of His Friends Regard as Subversive of Everything Good," *Current Opinion*, 64:5 (May 1918), 345-46.

4517. ANON.: "Mr. Yeats Theorizes," *Nation* [London], 22:20 (16 Feb 1918), 628, 630.

4518. ANON.: *Nation*, 106:2751 (21 Mar 1918), 326.

4519. ANON.: "Some Recent Books of Poetry," *NYTBR*, [23:] (19 May 1918), 236.

4520. ANON.: *Quest* [London], 9:3 (Apr 1918), 522-24.

4521. ANON.: "Poems [*sic*] by Yeats," *Springfield Sunday Republican*, 2 June 1918, 15A.

4522. ANON.: "Reality by Moonlight," *TLS*, 17:838 (7 Feb 1918), 66.
"Into that 'Celtic Twilight' we cannot follow him. . . . And yet, with it all, Mr. Yeats is a poet, as moonlight is beautiful. The beauty that we see is the only thing common between his mind and ours."

4523. BICKLEY, FRANCIS: "Anima Poetae," *Bookman*, 54:320 (May 1918), 74.

4524. [CRAIG, GORDON ?]: *Mask*, 8:10 (Nov 1918), 39-40.
"It is one of those profound little works which yawn before us like an abyss as we trip or stumble along our little path . . . and no amount of ribaldry can bring us to the brink."

4525. [ELIOT, T. S.]: *Egoist*, 5:6 (June-July 1918), 87.
Admits that he understands only half of the book.

4526. F[AUSSET], H. I'A.: *Cambridge R*, 39:980 (6 June 1918), 444.

4527. SHANKS, EDWARD: "Our London Letter," *Dial*, 64:763 (28 Mar 1918), 286-88.

4528. TYNAN, KATHARINE: *Studies*, 7:25 (Mar 1918), 188-89.
"This book is but a new stage on the road of mystery and magic which has slowly but surely taken away the poet from his poetry . . . it is painfully unlike the Yeats one remembers."

See also J4509.

W123: Two Plays for Dancers (1919)

4529. ANON.: "Mr. Yeats," *Nation* [London], 25:1 (5 Apr 1919), 20,22.
Also a review of W124.

4530. C[LARKE], A[USTIN]: "The World Lost for Love," *Irish Statesman*, 1:18
(25 Oct 1919), 438-39.

4531. SHANKS, EDWARD: *First Essays on Literature*. Freeport, N.Y.: Books
for Libraries Press, 1968 [1923]. ix, 267 p.
"The Later Poetry of Mr. W. B. Yeats," 238-44; reprint of an anonymous
review of W123 and 124, *NSt*, 12:312 (29 Mar 1919), 582.

See also J4509, 6637.

W124/125: The Wild Swans at Coole (1919)

4532. ANON.: "Criticisms of Modern Poetry: Yeats [. . .]," *American R of
Reviews*, 59:5 (May 1919), 556-57.

4533. ANON.: *Dial*, 67:795 (26 July 1919), 72.
"The Wild Swans at Coole beat upon the fancy with ineffectual wings."

4534. ANON.: "Recent Books of Poetry," *Nation*, 108:2814 (7 June 1919),
917-19.

4535. ANON.: "With Irish Bards Old and New," *NYTBR*, [24:] (21 Sept 1919),
477.

4536. ANON.: "The New W. B. Yeats and Others," *Poetry R*, 10:3 (May-June
1919), 152-53.

4537. ANON.: "Mr. Yeats," *Saturday R*, 127:3311 (12 Apr 1919), 353-54.

4538. ANON.: "New Yeats Volume: Disillusionment Uppermost [. . .]," *Springfield Daily Republican*, 76:[] (6 May 1919), 8.

4539. ANON.: "Tunes Old and New," *TLS*, 18:896 (20 Mar 1919), 149.

4540. B., W. S.: "The Poetry of William Butler Yeats: A New Book of His
Verse Which Maintains His Qualities of Subtle Workmanship and Symbolic
Imagery," *BET*, 90:86 (12 Apr 1919), pt 3, 9.

4541. FIRKINS, O. W.: "Mr. Yeats and Others," *Review* [NY], 1:7 (28 June
1919), 151-53.

4542. MACNAMARA, BRINSLEY: "Macnamara on Yeats," *Irish Commonwealth*, 1:3
(May 1919), 172-73.

4543. MURRY, JOHN MIDDLETON: *Aspects of Literature*. NY: Knopf, 1920. ix,
204 p.
"Mr. Yeats's Swan Song," 39-45; reprint of an anonymous review, *Athenaeum*, #4640 (4 Apr 1919), 136-37, and *Living Age*, 301:3905 (10 May
1919), 342-45. Reprinted in J1090; see also J2555.

4544. TOWNE, CHARLES HANSON: "The Vanished Yeats, the Never-Vanishing
Kipling, and Some Others," *Bookman* [NY], 49:5 (July 1919), 617-22.
"Yeats has died, artistically. . . ."

4545. TYNAN, KATHARINE: "A Strayed Poet," *Bookman*, 56:332 (May 1919), 78-
79.
"A plague upon what led him to those fountains of a fantastic and
muddling philosophy."

See also J4509, 4529, 4531.

W126: The Cutting of an Agate (1919)

4546. ANON.: "Mr. Yeats in Prose," *Nation* [London], 25:13 (28 June 1919), 395-96.

4547. BICKLEY, FRANCIS: "Mr. Yeats's Odyssey," *Bookman*, 56:335 (Aug 1919), 174.

4548. DE LA MARE, WALTER: *Private View*. With an introduction by Lord David Cecil. London: Faber & Faber, 1953. xvi, 256 p.
"A Lapidary," 90-94; reprint of an anonymous review, *TLS*, 18:902 (1 May 1919), 235.

4549. E[LIOT], T. S.: "A Foreign Mind," *Athenaeum*, #4653 (4 July 1919), 552-53.
"Mr. Yeats on any subject is a cause of bewilderment and distress."

W128: Selected Poems (1921)

4550. ANON.: *NAR*, 215:796 (Mar 1922), 426-27.

4551. COLUM, PADRAIC: "Mr. Yeats' Selected Poems," *Dial*, 71:4 (Oct 1921), 464-68.

4552. GORMAN, HERBERT S.: "The Later Mr. Yeats," *Outlook*, 130:16 (19 Apr 1922), 655-56.
Also a review of W129.

4553. WILKINSON, MARGUERITE: "The Lonely Poetry of Mr. Yeats," *NYTBR*, [26:] (14 Aug 1921), 14.

W129/130: Four Plays for Dancers (1921)

4554. ANON.: *Cambridge R*, 43:1059 (2 Dec 1921), 147.

4555. ANON.: "Poetic Drama," *Nation & Athenaeum*, 30:20 (11 Feb 1922), 730-32.
Correspondence by Robert N. D. Wilson, :22 (25 Feb 1922), 793.

4556. ANON.: "Moonlight Visions," *Observer*, 130:6808 (20 Nov 1921), 4.

4557. ANON.: "Plays in Verse," *Outlook* [London], 48:1248 (31 Dec 1921), 557-58.

4558. ANON.: "The Wizardry of Mr. Yeats," *Saturday R*, 132:3449 (3 Dec 1921), 643.
"We take the liberty to suggest that the art of Mr. Yeats would have developed in precisely the same direction had not the Noh plays been discovered to the Occident."

4559. ANON.: "Plays for Dancers: Mr. Yeats Employs a Japanese Model," *Springfield Daily Republican*, 78:278 (8 Mar 1922), 12.

4560. ANON.: "Plays for Dancers," *TLS*, 20:1039 (15 Dec 1921), 840.
"This sort of drama is in the straight line of descent from Mr. Yeats's previous plays."

4561. BISHOP, JOHN PEALE: "Decorative Plays," *Literary R*, 2:26 (4 Mar 1922), 465.

4562. BURROW, C. KENNETT: "Four Real Poets," *John o' London's Weekly*, 6:144 (7 Jan 1922), 461.

4563. COLUM, PADRAIC: "A New Dramatic Art," *Dial*, 72:3 (Mar 1922), 302-4.
In these plays, "Mr. Yeats makes a dramatic structure that admirably fits his art; in them he can be abstract and circumstantial, dramatic and lyrical, expressionistic and traditional. Above all, he can be ritualistic."

4564. D., B. H., and L. E. B.: *Quest* [London], 13:3 (Apr 1922), 422-24.

4565. FIRKINS, O. W.: "The Old Time in the New Drama," *Yale R*, 12:1 (Oct 1922), 193-94.

4566. GOSSE, EDMUND: "Plays in Verse," *Sunday Times*, 100:5148 (11 Dec 1921), 6.
The plays are "childish" and devoid of meaning.

4567. HEAD, CLOYD: "Mr. Yeats' Plays," *Poetry*, 19:5 (Feb 1922), 288-92.

4568. LYND, ROBERT: "Mr. W. B. Yeats's Experiments," *Daily News*, #23623 (2 Dec 1921), 8.
"Yeats's ideal spectators would be a queer sort of men and women, with uncivilised imaginations and civilised minds—let us say neo-Platonist South Sea Islanders."

4569. M[ACNAMARA], B[RINSLEY]: "Books and Their Writers," *Gael*, 1:9 (26 Dec 1921), 6-7.
"It is rather startling to realise suddenly that no one in Ireland nowadays thinks of attacking W. B. Yeats. . . . It should remain eternally as a reproach to us if other peoples were to exhibit a deeper acquaintance with his work than we ourselves."

4570. MOULT, THOMAS: "Poets and the Play," *Time and Tide*, 3:10 (10 Mar 1922), 226-27.

4571. OULD, HERMON: "Caviare," *English R*, 34:5 (May 1922), 447-53.

4572. R., W. L.: *Bookman*, 61:363 (Dec 1921), Christmas Supplement, 38, 40.

4573. WILSON, EDMUND: "The Poetry of Mr. W. B. Yeats," *Freeman*, 5:107 (29 Mar 1922), 68-69.

4574. [YOUNG, STARK]: *TAM*, 6:1 (Jan 1922), 79.

4575. Y[OUNG], S[TARK]: "Five Books of Plays," *New Republic*, 30:380 (15 Mar 1922), 83-84.

W131: Four Years (1921)

4576. ANON.: "Two Victorians at Close Range," *NYTBR*, [26:] (29 May 1921), 5.
On Yeats and Oscar Wilde.

4577. LE GALLIENNE, RICHARD: "A Moonbeam's Autobiography," *NYTBR*, [26:] (28 Aug 1921), 3, 24.
Reviews the *Dial* version (Wp. 381).

W133: The Trembling of the Veil (1922)

4578. ANON.: "Mr. Yeats Explains Himself," *Nation & Athenaeum*, 32:13 (30 Dec 1922), 520-22.
Also a review of W134 and 136.

4579. ANON.: "Mr. Yeats and the Nineties," *Observer*, 131:6859 (12 Nov 1922), 4.

4580. ANON.: "Mr. Yeats's Youth: Poet and Mystic," *Times*, #43218 (19 Dec 1922), 15.

4581. ANON.: "The Memories of Mr. Yeats," *TLS*, 21:1088 (23 Nov 1922), 761.

4582. BINYON, LAURENCE: "William Butler Yeats," *Bookman*, 63:376 (Jan 1923), 196-99.

4583. ELLIS, STEWART MARSH: *Mainly Victorian*. London: Hutchinson, [1925]. 403 p.
    "W. B. Yeats," 280-86; reprinted in part from "Current Literature,"
    Fortnightly R, os 119 / ns 113:676 (1 Apr 1923), 690-/02.

4584. O'H[EGARTY], P. S.: *Irish R*, 1:6 (6 Jan 1923), 70.

W134/135: Later Poems (1922/1924)

4585. ANON.: "William Butler Yeats," *BET*, 95:117 (17 May 1924), pt 6, 3.

4586. ANON.: *Outlook*, 137:14 (6 Aug 1924), 549.

4587. ANON.: "The Real Mr. Yeats," *Saturday R*, 135:3508 (20 Jan 1923), 82.
    Also a review of W136.

4588. ANON.: "Mr. Yeats's Dreams," *TLS*, 21:1092 (28 Dec 1922), 871.
    Also a review of W136.

4589. AUSLANDER, JOSEPH: *Atlantic Monthly*, 134:2 (Aug 1924), Atlantic's
Bookshelf section, 8.

4590. BOYD, ERNEST: "From the Yellow Nineties to the Nobel Prize," *Literary
Digest International Book R*, 3:26 (Jan 1925), 88-89.
    Also a review of W137.

4591. COLUM, PADRAIC: "Mr. Yeats's Plays and Later Poems," *Yale R*, 14:2
(Jan 1925), 381-85.
    Also a review of W137.

4592. FRENCH, CECIL: *Golden Hind*, 1:3 (Apr 1923), 28.
    "Mr. Yeats might be described as the spoiled child of letters. He
    does outrageous things; he affronts his readers, bewilders, exasper-
    ates them; but he is greatly loved."

4593. KOSZUL, A.: *Langues modernes*, 22:1 (Jan-Feb 1924), 81-82.

4594. Affable Hawk [i.e., MACCARTHY, DESMOND]: "Books in General," *NSt*,
20:508 (6 Jan 1923), 407.

4595. ————: "Books in General," *NSt*, 22:554 (24 Nov 1923), 212.
    Discusses Yeats as a love poet.

4596. O'CONOR, NORREYS JEPHSON: "A New Yeats Collection," *Bookman* [NY],
60:1 (Sept 1924), 91.
    Also a review of W137.

4597. SQUIRE, JOHN COLLINGS: *Essays on Poetry*. Freeport, N.Y.: Books for
Libraries Press, 1967 [1923]. viii, 228 p.
    "Mr. Yeats's Later Verse," 160-70; reprint of "Poetry," *London Mercury*,
    7:40 (Feb 1923), 431-32. See also "Mr. Yeats's Later Verse," *Observer*,
    131:6861 (26 Nov 1922), 4.

See also J4578.

W136/137: Plays in Prose and Verse (1922/1924)

4598. LEPPER, JOHN HERON: *New Witness*, 21:536 (16 Feb 1923), 109–10.

4599. MEREDITH, H. O.: "The Plays of W. B. Yeats," *NSt*, 20:511 (27 Jan 1923), 481–83.

See also J4578, 4587, 4588, 4590, 4591, 4596.

W139/140: Plays and Controversies (1923/1924)

4600. ANON.: "Mr. Yeats and His Theatre," *Spectator*, 132:4993 (8 Mar 1924), 373.

4601. ANON.: "Mr. Yeats's Theatre," *TLS*, 23:1147 (10 Jan 1924), 20.
    "Certainly one of the best books on the theatre published for several years." About the "Nō" plays: "Some day an influence from them will enter the modern, the popular theatre and be powerful there; but they themselves never will."

4602. GARNIER, CHARLES M.: *Revue anglo-américaine*, 1:6 (Aug 1924), 549–50.

4603. GIBBS, SIR PHILIP: "The Chance of a People's Theatre: W. B. Yeats and the Irish Drama," *John o' London's Weekly*, 10:248 (5 Jan 1924), 508.

4604. LUCAS, FRANK LAURENCE: *Authors Dead & Living*. NY: Macmillan, 1926. x, 297 p.
    "Sense and Sensibility," 241–44; reprinted from *NSt*, 22:568 (8 Mar 1924), 634–35.

4605. O'CONOR, NORREYS JEPHSON: "A Pioneer in Retrospect," *SatR*, 1:41 (9 May 1925), 738.
    Also a review of W142.

4606. RIVOALLAN, A.: *Langues modernes*, 23:3 (Apr 1925), 214–15.
    Also a review of W141.

4607. A. E. [i.e., RUSSELL, GEORGE WILLIAM]: *Irish Statesman*, 1:17 (5 Jan 1924), 534.

4608. RYAN, W. P.: *Bookman*, 65:390 (Mar 1924), 310.

4609. WINDER, BLANCHE: "Modern Poetic Drama," *Poetry R*, 15:2 (Mar–Apr 1924), 69–84.
    See pp. 74–77.

W141/142: Essays (1924)

4610. ANON.: "Poet's Prose," *Nation & Athenaeum*, 35:13 (28 June 1924), 416, 418.

4611. ANON.: "Mr. Yeats's Essays," *Saturday R*, 138:3584 (5 July 1924), 15.

4612. ANON.: "Mr. Yeats's Prose," *TLS*, 23:1166 (22 May 1924), 318.
    Yeats's prose has developed less radically than his verse. Correspondence by Henry Festing Jones, :1167 (29 May 1924), 340.

4613. C[OUSINS], J. H.: "Yeats as a Proseman," *Madras Mail*, 57:219 (12 Sept 1924), 10.

4614. FAUSSET, HUGH I'ANSON: "Mr. Yeats and the 'Nineties," *Spectator*, 132:5004 (24 May 1924), 844–45.

4615. GARNIER, CH. M.: *Revue anglo-américaine*, 2:5 (June 1925), 448–51.

4616. H[OLMES], J. F.: "Yeats' Essays," *NSt*, 23:586 (12 July 1924), 414, 416.

4617. HOOPS, J[OHANNES]: *Englische Studien*, 58:3 (1924), 454-55.

4618. KENDON, FRANK: "Belles Lettres," *London Mercury*, 11:64 (Feb 1925), 432-34.

4619. AE [i.e., RUSSELL, GEORGE WILLIAM]: "The Essays of W. B. Yeats," *Irish Statesman*, 2:13 (7 June 1924), 397-98.

4620. SAMPSON, GEORGE: "Two Ways of Criticism," *Bookman*, 66:394 (July 1924), 201-2.

4621. SONNENSCHEIN, HUGO: "In Quest of Poesy," *Literary R*, 5:15 (6 Dec 1924), 4.

See also J4605, 4606.

W146: The Bounty of Sweden (1925)

4622. GOSSE, EDMUND: "A Poet's Thanks," *Sunday Times*, 102:5337 (26 July 1925), 6.
Regards Yeats as an English poet and criticizes his insistence on Irish allegiances and unorthodox lore: "Will he never learn that he knows all there is to know about fairies and mahatmas, and nothing whatever about international polemics?" See the anonymous reply (presumably by AE) in *Irish Statesman*, 4:21 (1 Aug 1925), 645.

4623. Grieve, C. M. [real name of MACDIARMID, HUGH]: "Mannigfaltig: *The Dial*, Yeats, Strindberg, and Modern Swedish Literature," *New Age*, 35:1672 (25 Sept 1924), 260-61.
Review of the *Dial* version (Wp. 382).

4624. M[ITCHELL], S[USAN] L.: *Irish Statesman*, 4:21 (1 Aug 1925), 658, 660.

W147/148: Early Poems and Stories (1925)

4625. ANON.: *Cambridge R*, 47:1150 (6 Nov 1925), 74-75.

4626. ANON.: "Celtic Twilight," *Nation & Athenaeum*, 38:4 (24 Oct 1925), 156.

4627. ANON.: *Quarterly R*, 246:487 (Jan 1926), 217-18.
Never in his later work has Yeats "excelled those products of his unspoiled youth."

4628. ANON.: "Mr. Yeats in Transition," *TLS*, 24:1238 (8 Oct 1925), 652.

4629. GARNIER, CHARLES M.: *Revue anglo-américaine*, 3:5 (June 1926), 454-56.

4630. H[IGGINS], B[ERTRAM]: *Calendar of Modern Letters*, 2:9 (Nov 1925), 210-11.

4631. PRIESTLEY, J. B.: "The First Celt," *Saturday R*, 140:3649 (3 Oct 1925), 374.

4632. A. E. [i.e., RUSSELL, GEORGE WILLIAM]: "The Youth of a Poet," *Irish Statesman*, 5:6 (17 Oct 1925), 176-77.
Reprinted as "Yeats's Early Poems," *Living Age*, 327:4247 (28 Nov 1925), 464-66. This review elicited voluminous correspondence in the *Irish Statesman* on the question of whether Yeats is an Irish or an English

poet, which ran until 16 January 1926. Among the contributors were
Frank O'Connor and Sean O'Faolain.

4633. RYAN, W. P.: "The Youth of Mr. Yeats," *Bookman*, 69:414 (Mar 1926),
323-24.

W149: A Vision (1925)

4634. ANON.: *Adelphi*, 4:4 (Oct 1926), 266.

4635. ANON.: "The Visionary Yeats," *NSt*, 26:674 (27 Mar 1926), 749-50.

4636. ANON.: *Quest* [London], 18:1 (Oct 1926), 96-98.

4637. ANON.: "Mr. Yeats's Occultism," *TLS*, 25:1266 (22 Apr 1926), 296.
"His book, with its accomplishment, its genius of intuition, its
fleeting beauty, is tiresome because of the conviction it leaves with
us that he knows this as well as anyone and yet cannot detach himself
from the delights of dalliance."

4638. AE [i.e., RUSSELL, GEORGE WILLIAM]: *Irish Statesman*, 5:23 (13 Feb
1926), 714-16.
"Here I fall away from a mind I have followed, I think, with understanding, since I was a boy, and as he becomes remote in his thought
I wonder whether he has forgotten his own early wisdom. . . ."

See also J1696.

W150: Estrangement (1926)

4639. ANON.: *Dublin Mag*, ns 2:2 (Apr-June 1927), 72-73.

4640. AE [i.e., RUSSELL, GEORGE WILLIAM]: *Irish Statesman*, 6:26 (4 Sept
1926), 713-14.

W151/152: Autobiographies (1926/1927)

4641. ANON.: "The Tragic Generation: W. B. Yeats's Memories of the 'Eighties and 'Nineties," *John o' London's Weekly*, 16:405 (22 Jan 1927), 544-45.

4642. ANON.: *Outlook*, 145:12 (23 Mar 1927), 376-77.

4643. ANON.: *Quarterly R*, 248:492 (Apr 1927), 427.

4644. BICKLEY, FRANCIS: "Mr. Yeats and Himself," *Bookman*, 71:425 (Feb
1927), 282-83.

4645. CHURCH, RICHARD: "The Lifting of the Veil," *Spectator*, 137:5134
(20 Nov 1926), 912, 914.

4646. ————: "W. B. Yeats and the Creative Mask," *Calendar of Modern
Letters*, 3:4 (Jan 1927), 316-19.

4647. DAVIDSON, DONALD: *Nashville Tennessean*, 18:318 (27 Mar 1927), Magazine section, 7.

4648. DEUTSCH, BABETTE: "The Autobiographies of Yeats: This Eminent Poet,
If Mystic and Magician, Has Grappled Reality," *Literary R*, 7:35 (7 May
1927), 5.

4649. E[DSALL], R[ICHARD] L[INN]: *Catholic World*, 125:748 (July 1927),
566-67.

4650. EGLINTON, JOHN: "Mr. Yeats's Autobiographies," *Dial*, 83:2 (Aug 1927),
94-97.

4651. FORMAN, HENRY JAMES: "Yeats's Memories of His Youth: *Autobiographies* Is the Story of a Poet's Development," *NYTBR*, 32:20 (15 May 1927), 13.

4652. GARNIER, C.: *Revue anglo-américaine*, 7:3 (Feb 1930), 270-71.

4653. K[ELLER], T. G.: *Dublin Mag*, ns 2:2 (Apr-June 1927), 70.

4654. LUHRS, MARIE: "Gentle Poet," *Poetry*, 30:5 (Aug 1927), 279-83.

4655. LYND, ROBERT: "Men of Letters," *Observer*, 136:7073 (19 Dec 1926), 6.

4656. M[ACNEICE], F[REDERICK] L[OUIS]: *Cherwell*, 19:1 (29 Jan 1927), 28.
"When the rest of the world is sublimely vegetable, it is very ill-bred in Mr. Yeats still to be spiritual."

4657. MILES, HAMISH: *Monthly Criterion*, 5:3 (June 1927), 353-56.

4658. MINCHIN, H. C.: "Memory Harbour," *Sunday Times*, 105:5406 (21 Nov 1926), 8.

4659. PAYNE, L. W.: "The Inner Life of a Poet," *Southwest R*, 13:1 (Oct 1927), 123-25.

4660. RIVOALLAN, A.: "Quelques livres sur l'Irlande," *Langues modernes*, 26:8 (Nov-Dec 1928), 501-11.
See pp. 505-8; also a review of W158.

4661. AE [i.e., RUSSELL, GEORGE WILLIAM]: "The Memories of a Poet," *Irish Statesman*, 7:13 (4 Dec 1926), 302-3.

4662. VAN DOREN, MARK: "First Glance," *Nation*, 124:3219 (16 Mar 1927), 291.

4663. WALSH, THOMAS: *Commonweal*, 5:25 (27 Apr 1927), 696-97.
The book "contains uncertainties, wistfulness, suggestions, guesses, all the general penumbra of what possibly may be conceded to be Mr. Yeats's poetical state of mind. But it is far from the light in which reason and intellect make a pretense of figuring."

4664. WILSON, EDMUND: "Yeats's Memoirs," *New Republic*, 50:638 (23 Feb 1927), 22-23.

4665. WYLIE, ELINOR: "Path of the Chameleon," *NYHTB*, 3:22 (13 Feb 1927), 1, 6.
Includes a reproduction of Yeats's drawing of Maud Gonne.

W153: Poems (1927)

4666. ANON.: "Mr. Yeats's Afterthoughts," *NSt*, 29:729 (16 Apr 1927), 17.

4667. SEYMOUR, WILLIAM KEAN: "Mr. Yeats's Poetry," *G. K.'s Weekly*, 4:104 (12 Mar 1927), 289.
"It is . . . for the evocative phrase and music--not for profundity, that we turn to Mr. Yeats."

W156: October Blast (1927)

4668. AE [i.e., RUSSELL, GEORGE WILLIAM]: *Irish Statesman*, 8:25 (27 Aug 1927), 597-98.

W157: Stories of Red Hanrahan and The Secret Rose (1927)

4669. ANON.: "Red Hanrahan," *TLS*, 26:1349 (8 Dec 1927), 929.

4670. L[OBO], G[EORGE] E[DMUND]: "W. B. Yeats Illustrated," *Dublin Art Monthly*, 1:4 (Jan 1928), 20-21.
Praises Norah McGuinness's illustrations.

4671. Y. O. [i.e., RUSSELL, GEORGE WILLIAM]: *Irish Statesman*, 9:15 (17 Dec 1927), 354.
Actually on Norah McGuinness's illustrations, which are considered to be superfluous.

Wl58/159: The Tower (1928)

4672. ANON.: *Annual Register*, 170 (1928), II, 30.

4673. ANON.: *Living Age*, 334:4328 (15 Apr 1928), 747-48.
Reprinted from an unspecified issue of the *Morning Post*.

4674. ANON.: "Mr. W. B. Yeats," *NSt*, 30:780 (7 Apr 1928), 829-30.

4675. ANON.: "Mr. Yeats's New Poems," *TLS*, 27:1361 (1 Mar 1928), 146.

4676. B., A. F.: *Cambridge R*, 50:1220 (19 Oct 1928), 41.

4677. BRULÉ, A.: *Revue anglo-américaine*, 5:6 (Aug 1928), 570-71.

4678. CHURCH, RICHARD: "W. B. Yeats," *Spectator*, 140:5201 (3 Mar 1928), 324.

4679. DAVIDSON, DONALD: *Nashville Tennessean*, 23:65 (15 July 1928), Magazine section, 7.
Deplores the disappearance of Yeats's romanticism.

4680. DEM., S.: "Poems of Pessimism," *Contemporary R*, 134:755 (Nov 1928), 671-73.

4681. DEUTSCH, BABETTE: "The Making of a Soul," *NYHTB*, 4:46 (5 Aug 1928), 1-2.

4682. DRINKWATER, JOHN: *Daily Telegraph*, #22715 (28 Feb 1928), 17.

4683. EGLINTON, JOHN: "Mr. Yeats's Tower," *Dial*, 86:1 (Jan 1929), 62-65.

4684. FLETCHER, JOHN GOULD: *Criterion*, 8:30 (Sept 1928), 131-32.

4685. GREGORY, HORACE: "After a Half-Century," *Poetry*, 33:1 (Oct 1928), 41-44.

4686. GWYNN, STEPHEN: *Fortnightly R*, os 129 / ns 123:736 (Apr 1928), 561-63.

4687. H[IGGINS], F. R.: *Irish Statesman*, 10:6 (14 Apr 1928), 112-13.

4688. HILLYER, ROBERT: "A Poet Young and Old," *New Adelphi*, 3:1 (Sept-Nov 1929), 78-80.

4689. ÖSTERLING, ANDERS: *Horisonter*. Stockholm: Bonnier, 1939. 256 p.
"Den unge Yeats och den gamle," 205-21. Reprint of "Den unge Yeats," *Svenska Dagbladet*, #180 (7 July 1934), 7 (a review of Wl73), and "W. B. Yeats," *Svenska Dagbladet*, #11 (13 Jan 1934), 9-10 (a review of Wl58 and 169).

4690. O'FAOLAIN, SEAN: "Four Irish Generations," *Commonweal*, 9:26 (1 May 1929), 751.
Also a review of Wl62.

4691. R[ITCHIE], E[LIZA]: *Dalhousie R*, 8:4 (Jan 1929), 572.

4692. ROBERTS, R. ELLIS: *Bookman*, 74:439 (Apr 1928), 42-43.

4693. SPENCER, THEODORE: *New Republic*, 56:723 (10 Oct 1928), 219-20.

4694. STEWART, GEORGE R.: *U of California Chronicle*, 30:4 (Oct 1928), 484-85.

4695. TASKER, J. DANA: "A Philosophy of Faith," *Outlook*, 150:3 (19 Sept 1928), 831, 840.

4696. TWITCHETT, E. G.: "Poetry," *London Mercury*, 18:106 (Aug 1928), 433-36.

4697. WOLFE, HUMBERT: *Saturday R*, 145:3774 (25 Feb 1928), 225-26.

4698. [WOOLF, VIRGINIA]: "Mr. Yeats," *Nation & Athenaeum*, 43:3 (21 Apr 1928), 81.
   "Mr. Yeats has never written more exactly and more passionately."

See also J4660.

W160/161: Sophocles' King Oedipus (1928)

4699. ANON.: *Contemporary R*, 133:749 (May 1928), 673-75.
   ". . . very Irish, very effective, and, indeed, very Greek."

4700. ANON.: "Four Greek Poets," *TLS*, 27:1399 (22 Nov 1928), 876.

W162: The Death of Synge (1928)

4701. O'FAOLAIN, SEAN: "Yeats on Synge," *Irish Statesman*, 11:4 (29 Sept 1928), 71-72.
   "The fact is that Synge was by nature what Yeats has never been, and has always been trying to become by way of romance or mask or discipline." Correspondence by Arthur Lynch, :7 (20 Oct 1928), 131; Stephen MacKenna, :9 (3 Nov 1928), 169-70.

See also J4690.

W163: A Packet for Ezra Pound (1929)

4702. O'FAOLAIN, SEAN: "Mr. Yeats's Trivia," *Commonweal*, 10:20 (18 Sept 1929), 512-13.
   "This somewhat artificial connection with spirituality has not benefited Mr. Yeats's work, whether in prose or verse."

4703. ————: "Mr. Yeats's Kubla Khan," *Nation*, 129:3361 (4 Dec 1929), 681-82.

4704. AE [i.e., RUSSELL, GEORGE WILLIAM]: *Irish Statesman*, 13:1 (7 Sept 1929), 11-12.
   Reprinted in *Living Age*, 337:4347 (1 Oct 1929), 186-88.

W164: The Winding Stair (1929)

4705. ANON.: *TLS*, 29:1501 (6 Nov 1930), 910.

4706. MOORE, MARIANNE: "Words for Music Perhaps," *Poetry*, 42:1 (Apr 1933), 40-44.
   Also a review of W168.

4707. AE [i.e., RUSSELL, GEORGE WILLIAM]: *Irish Statesman*, 13:22 (1 Feb 1930), 436-37.

W165: Selected Poems Lyrical and Narrative (1929)

4708. BRULÉ, A.: *Revue anglo-américaine*, 8:3 (Feb 1931), 265-66.

4709. DAVRAY, HENRY D.: *Mercure de France*, yr 41 / 218:760 (15 Feb 1930), 227-28.

4710. GIBSON, WILFRID: "W. B. Yeats," *Bookman*, 77:460 (Jan 1930), 227-28.

4711. MACCARTHY, DESMOND: "The Poetry of Mr. Yeats," *Sunday Times*, 107: 5563 (24 Nov 1929), 8.
    Discusses Yeats as a love poet.

4712. O'FAOLAIN, SEAN: *Criterion*, 9:36 (Apr 1930), 523-28.
    Criticizes Yeats's revisions and his preoccupation with occultism.

4713. Y. O. [i.e., RUSSELL, GEORGE WILLIAM]: "The Reading of Poetry," *Irish Statesman*, 13:10 (9 Nov 1929), 191-92.

4714. S., B.: *Manchester Guardian*, #25972 (27 Nov 1929), 7.

W167: Stories of Michael Robartes and His Friends (1931)

4715. ANON.: *TLS*, 31:1573 (24 Mar 1932), 214.

4716. P[OWELL], C[HARLES]: "Mr. W. B. Yeats," *Manchester Guardian*, #26723 (2 May 1932), 5.

W168: Words for Music Perhaps and Other Poems (1932)

4717. BRADBROOK, M. C.: "Songs of Experience," *Scrutiny*, 2:1 (June 1933), 77-78.

4718. COLUM, PADRAIC: "Sailing to Byzantium," *Spectator*, 150:5476 (9 June 1933), 841.

See also J1999, 4706.

W169/170: The Winding Stair and Other Poems (1933)

4719. ANON.: *Church of Ireland Gazette*, 78:[ ] (10 Nov 1933), 648.

4720. ANON.: "W. B. Yeats," *Church Times*, 110:3688 (29 Sept 1933), 361.

4721. ANON.: "Mr. Yeats's Poems," *Irish Times*, 75:23857 (14 Oct 1933), 4.

4722. ANON.: *Life and Letters*, 9:51 (Dec 1933), 486-90.

4723. ANON.: "The New Poetry--and Poetry," *Modern Scot*, 4:3 (Oct 1933), 250-53.
    Compares Yeats and Pound and finds the latter lacking in universality.

4724. ANON.: "Donne and the Moderns: A New Volume by W. B. Yeats," *Scotsman*, #28186 (28 Sept 1933), 2.

4725. ANON.: "Mr. Yeats's New Poems," *TLS*, 32:1653 (5 Oct 1933), 666.

4726. ARNS, KARL: *Englische Studien*, 69:1 (July 1934), 145-46.

4727. BÄNNINGER, KONRAD: "W. B. Yeats' neue Gedichte," *Neue Zürcher Zeitung*, #663 (15 Apr 1934), Literarische Beilage, [8].

4728. BROWNE, WYNYARD: "Poetry," *London Mercury*, 28:168 (Oct 1933), 549-51.

4729. BRULÉ, A.: *Revue anglo-américaine*, 11:4 (Apr 1934), 360-61.

4730. CHURCH, RICHARD: "Yeats Re-Emerges," *NSt*, 6:138 (14 Oct 1933), Supplement, vi, viii.

4731. ———: *Fortnightly R*, os 140 / ns 134:803 (Nov 1933), 629-30.

4732. ———: "The Secret of Youth," *CSM*, 26:24 (23 Dec 1933), 9.

4733. E., C.: "Mr. Yeats's Latest 'Message,'" *Irish News*, #21609 (23 Sept 1933), 3.

4734. FALLON, PADRAIC: *Dublin Mag*, 9:2 (Apr-June 1934), 58-65.

4735. FAUSSET, HUGH I'ANSON: "Mr. Yeats and His Dark Tower: Poems of Protest and Regret," *Yorkshire Post*, #26914 (25 Oct 1933), 6.

4736. GREGORY, HORACE: "Yeats: Envoy of Two Worlds," *New Republic*, 77:993 (13 Dec 1933), 134-35.
Also a review of W171.

4737. GRIGSON, GEOFFREY: "Is Ezra Pound a Great Poet? The Testimony of Yeats," *Morning Post*, 161:50308 (15 Sept 1933), 4.
Involves a Yeats-Pound comparison.

4738. ———: "A Fanatic Heart," *New Verse*, #6 (Dec 1933), 24, 26.

4739. HONE, J. M.: "Mr. Yeats's Poems," *Week-end R*, 8:190A (21 Oct 1933), 414.

4740. ———: "Letter from Ireland," *Poetry*, 43:5 (Feb 1934), 274-79.
Includes a note on the Irish Academy of Letters.

4741. HUTCHINSON, PERCY: "The Poems of William Butler Yeats," *NYTBR*, 38:52 (24 Dec 1933), 2, 10.
Also a review of W171.

4742. LEAVIS, F. R.: "The Latest Yeats," *Scrutiny*, 2:3 (Dec 1933), 293-95.
The collection is not as good as *The Tower*; "the proud sardonic tension . . . is slackened."

4743. PARSONS, I. M.: "Port after Storm," *Spectator*, 151:5493 (6 Oct 1933), 452.

4744. PORTEUS, HUGH GORDON: *Criterion*, 13:51 (Jan 1934), 313-15.

4745. P[OWELL], C[HARLES]: "W. B. Yeats," *Manchester Guardian*, #27165 (2 Oct 1933), 5.

4746. POWELL, DILYS: "Mr. Yeats's New Poems: A Mind in Conflict," *Sunday Times*, #5771 (19 Nov 1933), 10.

4747. RIVOALLAN, A.: *Langues modernes*, 32:4 (June 1934), 308-9.

4748. SPENDER, STEPHEN: "Honour to Yeats," *Listener*, 10:248 (11 Oct 1933), Supplement, xi.

4749. STUART, FRANCIS: "Mr. Yeats' New Poems," *Irish Press*, 3:236 (3 Oct 1933), 6.

4750. SUNNE, RICHARD: "Men and Books," *Time and Tide*, 14:39 (30 Sept 1933), 1151-52.

4751. T., P. C.: *Irish Book Lover*, 22:3 (May-June 1934), 72-73.

4752. WALTON, EDA LOU: "Cast Out Remorse," *Nation*, 137:3571 (13 Dec 1933), 684-86.
Also a review of W171.

4753. WARREN, C. HENRY: "The New Yeats," *Bookman*, 85:507 (Dec 1933), 230, 232.

4754. WOLFE, HUMBERT: "Windy Halls of Heaven," *Observer*, 142:7427 (1 Oct 1933), 5.

4755. Z[ABEL], M. D.: "The Summers of Hesperides," *Poetry*, 43:5 (Feb 1934), 279-87.
 Also a review of W171.

See also J4689.

W171/172: The Collected Poems (1933)

4756. ANON.: *Annual Register*, 175 (1933), II, 29-30.

4757. ANON.: *Dublin Mag*, 9:3 (July-Sept 1934), 63-66.

4758. ANON.: *Listener*, 11:264 (31 Jan 1934), 213.

4759. ANON.: *Listener*, 15:388 (17 June 1936), 1175.

4760. ANON.: "Yeats's Collected Poems," *NSt*, 7:154 (3 Feb 1934), 160, 162.

4761. ARMSTRONG, MARTIN: "Daemonic Images," *Weekend R*, 8:200 (6 Jan 1934), 729-30.

4762. BENÉT, WILLIAM ROSE: "This Virtue," *SatR*, 10:22 (16 Dec 1933), 349-50.

4763. BLACKMUR, R. P.: "Under a Major Poet," *American Mercury*, 31:122 (Feb 1934), 244-46.

4764. B[REGY], K[ATHERINE]: *Catholic World*, 140:836 (Nov 1934), 241-42.

4765. COLUM, PADRAIC: "On Yeats," *Commonweal*, 20:3 (18 May 1934), 70-71.

4766. DEUTSCH, BABETTE: "Certain Good," *VQR*, 10:2 (Apr 1934), 298-302.
 "Hostile to the intellect, although marked by an acute and nimble intelligence, Yeats's genius is incapable of interpreting this age to itself."

4767. E., C.: "The Poems of Yeats: Little in Common with Ireland," *Irish News*, #21687 (23 Dec 1933), 3.

4768. FOX, ARTHUR W.: "Collected Poems of William Butler Yeats," *Papers of the Manchester Literary Club*, 61 (1935), 62-80.

4769. HAWKINS, DESMOND: "Recent Verse," *New English Weekly*, 4:19 (22 Feb 1934), 448-49.

4770. K[UNITZ], S. J.: "The Roving Eye: The Collected Poems of Yeats," *Wilson Bulletin for Librarians*, 8:6 (Feb 1934), 350-51.

4771. LAWRENCE, C. E.: "Poetry and Verse and Worse," *Quarterly R*, 262:520 (Apr 1934), 299-314.
 See pp. 308, 311-14.

4772. MACCARTHY, DESMOND: "A Note on the Poems of Yeats: The Forerunner," *Sunday Times*, #5782 (4 Feb 1934), 8.

4773. M[ACDONAGH], D[ONAGH]: "Re-Written Poems: Yeats' Collected Work," *Irish Press*, 4:1 (1 Jan 1934), 10.

4774. MATTHIESSEN, F. O.: "Yeats and Four American Poets," *Yale R*, 23:3 (Mar 1934), 611-17.

4775. PATERSON, ISABEL: "The Pure Flame of W. B. Yeats's Poetry: Such Sustained Intensity Suggests Stepping Out of Time into Eternity," *NYHTB*, 10: 13 (3 Dec 1933), 9.

4776. P[OWELL], C[HARLES]: "The Collected Yeats," *Manchester Guardian*, #27271 (5 Feb 1934), 5.

4777. READ, HERBERT: *A Coat of Many Colours*. London: Routledge & Kegan Paul, 1956 [1945]. x, 352 p.
  "The Later Yeats," 208-12; reprinted from *Criterion*, 13:52 (Apr 1934), 468-72. Discusses the revisions of "The Sorrow of Love."

4778. ROBERTS, R. ELLIS: "The Greatest Living Master in English," *News Chronicle*, #27381 (24 Jan 1934), 4.

4779. SCOVELL, E. J.: "W. B. Yeats," *Time and Tide*, 15:10 (10 Mar 1934), 322-23.

4780. SHANKS, EDWARD: "Prince of Our Poets," *John o' London's Weekly*, 30: 774 (10 Feb 1934), 721.

4781. SPENDER, STEPHEN: "Hammered Gold," *Spectator*, 152:5513 (23 Feb 1934), 284, 286.
  Criticizes Yeats's "incomplete approach to humanity."

4782. T., A. B.: "Collected Poems of William Butler Yeats: He Is Revealed as Distinctly More a Pagan Than He Was Twenty-five Years Ago," *BET*, 105:5 (6 Jan 1934), book section, 1.

4783. WEST, GEOFFREY: *Adelphi*, ns 8:3 (June 1934), 227-31.

See also J4736, 4741, 4752, 4755.

W173: Letters to the New Island (1934)

4784. ANON.: "The Man in the Youth," *Dublin Mag*, 9:3 (July-Sept 1934), 66-68.

4785. ANON.: "Literature and Nationality: Early Letters by Mr. Yeats," *Irish Times*, 76:24071 (23 June 1934), 5.

4786. ANON.: "W. B. Yeats and Ireland," *Springfield Daily Republican*, 90: 268 (3 Feb 1934), 8.

4787. ANON.: "Letters to America: Mr. Yeats as a Young Journalist," *Times*, #46721 (6 Apr 1934), 7.

4788. ANON.: "A Celt in London," *TLS*, 33:1680 (12 Apr 1934), 259.

4789. BOLAND, EAVAN: "Letters and Men of Letters," *Irish Times*, #35622 (1 Aug 1970), 10.

4790. CHURCH, RICHARD: "Yeats Forty Years Ago," *NSt*, 8:180 (4 Aug 1934), 157-58.

4791. COGHLAN, JOHN: *Bookman*, 86:515 (Aug 1934), 251.

4792. COLUM, PADRAIC: "The Man in the Youth," *SatR*, 10:46 (2 June 1934), 722-23.

4793. DEUTSCH, BABETTE: "The Poet as a Young Man," *Nation*, 138:3584 (14 Mar 1934), 309-10.

4794. G[REGORY], H[ORACE]: *New Republic*, 79:1019 (13 June 1934), 136.

4795. HERSEY, F. W. C.: *MLN*, 50:6 (June 1935), 411-12.

4796. MACCARTHY, DESMOND: "William Butler Yeats: The Journalism of a Poet," *Sunday Times*, #5801 (17 June 1934), 8.

4797. MONKHOUSE, ALLAN: "A Bookman's Notes: A Great Irishman," *Manchester Guardian*, #27376 (8 June 1934), 7.

4798. MURRAY, PATRICK: "What the Young Man Wrote," *Irish Independent*, 79:134 (6 June 1970), 10.

4799. P., R.: "Irish Renaissance Rehearsal," *CSM*, 26:179 (27 June 1934), Weekly Magazine section, 10.
> "One theme runs through all the articles . . . and that theme is the importance of nationalism to an author. . . . Such an intense aesthetic nationalism is all the easier for a poet when the country of his devotion is not a political reality, and indeed it is in the desire to develop the cultural unity of a people that we find the expression of a true national spirit as opposed to the blind, selfish nationalism so evident in the world today."

4800. QUINN, KERKER: "Memories Differ," *Yale R*, 26:1 (Sept 1936), 208-10. Also a review of W186.

4801. R., G. R. B.: "Letters from W. B. Yeats during His Earlier Years: He Was Even Then on His Way as the Guiding Spirit of the Irish Renaissance," *BET*, 105:64 (17 Mar 1934), book section, 1.

4802. STRONG, L. A. G.: "Letters to America," *Observer*, 143:7468 (15 July 1934), 5.

4803. SUNNE, RICHARD: "Men and Books," *Time and Tide*, 15:22 (2 June 1934), 702-3.

4804. WALTON, EDA LOU: "When William Butler Yeats Was Twenty-six," *NYTBR*, 39:14 (8 Apr 1934), 4.

See also J4689.

W175/176: Wheels and Butterflies (1934/1935)

4805. ANON.: *Dublin Mag*, 11:1 (Jan-Mar 1936), 70-72. Also a review of W177 and 179.

4806. ANON.: *Evening Mail*, #27348 (22 Nov 1934), 7.

4807. ANON.: "Mr. Yeats as Playwright," *Glasgow Herald*, 152:309 (27 Dec 1934), 2. Also a review of W177.

4808. ANON.: "Experiments in Dramatic Art: New Plays from Mr. Yeats," *Irish Independent*, 43:232 (4 Dec 1934), 5.

4809. ANON.: *Life and Letters*, 11:61 (Jan 1935), 483-86. Also a review of W177.

4810. ANON.: *Listener*, 13:316 (30 Jan 1935), 209. Also a review of W177.

4811. ANON.: "Yeats as a Dramatist," *Scotsman*, #28566 (17 Dec 1934), 15. Also a review of W177.

4812. ANON.: *TAM*, 19:8 (Aug 1935), 647.
> "The introductions . . . provide the richest fodder."

4813. ANON.: "New Poetic Drama," *TLS*, 34:1721 (24 Jan 1935), 37-38. Also a review of W177 and 179.

4814. BOGAN, LOUISE: "For Garrets and Cellars," *Poetry*, 46:2 (May 1935), 100-104.

4815. C., F.: *Granta*, 44:996 (23 Jan 1935), 198.

4816. CAZAMIAN, M.-L.: *Revue anglo-américaine*, 12:5 (June 1935), 450-51.

4817. CLARKE, AUSTIN: "The Poetic Drama of Mr. Yeats," *London Mercury*, 31:184 (Feb 1935), 391-92.
  Also a review of W177.

4818. F., E.: "Recent Plays," *Oxford Mag*, 53:17 (2 May 1935), 536-37.
  Also a review of W177.

4819. FLETCHER, JOHN GOULD: *Southern R*, 1:1 (Summer 1935), 199-203.

4820. GARRETT, JOHN: *Criterion*, 14:56 (Apr 1935), 488-91.
  Also a review of W177.

4821. GOLDRING, DOUGLAS: "Celtic Mists," *Liverpool Post and Mercury*, #24814 (15 Jan 1935), 5.

4822. GREGORY, HORACE: "Yeats: Last Spokesman," *New Republic*, 84:1085 (18 Sept 1935), 164-65.
  Also a review of W177 and 179.

4823. JOHNSTON, DENIS: "Mr. Yeats as Dramatist," *Spectator*, 153:5553 (30 Nov 1934), 843.

4824. MACCARTHY, DESMOND: "New Plays by W. B. Yeats: A Poet's Butterflies," *Sunday Times*, #5831 (13 Jan 1935), 8.

4825. M[ACDONAGH], D[ONAGH]: "Mr. Yeats' Symbolism," *Irish Press*, 4:245 (18 Dec 1934), 10.

4826. ÖSTERLING, ANDERS: "Små dramer av Yeats," *Svenska Dagbladet*, #39 (9 Feb 1935), 7.

4827. POORE, C. G.: "The Savor, the Splendor and the Eloquence of Yeats," *NYTBR*, 40:8 (24 Feb 1935), 3, 15.

4828. P[OWELL], C[HARLES]: "Plays by Mr. Yeats," *Manchester Guardian*, #27543 (20 Dec 1934), 5.

4829. REYNOLDS, HORACE: "Supernatural Plays," *SatR*, 11:34 (9 Mar 1935), 535.

4830. RICE, PHILIP BLAIR: "A Bell with Many Echoes," *Nation*, 140:3639 (3 Apr 1935), 397-98.

4831. RIVOALLAN, A.: *Langues modernes*, 34:3 (Mar 1936), 187-88.

4832. TAGGARD, GENEVIEVE: "The Mysteries of W. B. Yeats: Another Stage in the Irishman's Poetic Pilgrimage Finds Him in a Not Quite Mystic Reverie," *NYHTB*, 11:36 (12 May 1935), 2.

4833. WOLFE, HUMBERT: "Poets for All," *Observer*, 143:7488 (2 Dec 1934), 19.

4834. W[YATT], E[UPHEMIA] V[AN] R[ENSSELAER]: *Catholic World*, 141:846 (Sept 1935), 755.

See also J4845.

W177/178: The Collected Plays (1934/1935)

4835. ANON.: "W. B. Yeats and Dramatic Expression," *CSM*, 27:231 (28 Aug 1935), Weekly Magazine section, 11.

4836. BALL, ARTHUR: *Fortnightly R*, os 143 / ns 137:819 (Mar 1935), 380-81.

4837. B[ENEDEK], M[ARCELL]: "Költő, forradalom és heroizmus" [Poet, revolution, and heroism], *Nyugat*, 28:3 (Mar 1935), 259-60.

4838. COLM: *Irish Book Lover*, 23:2 (Mar-Apr 1935), 54.

4839. COLUM, MARY M.: "Worker in Dreams," *Forum and Century*, 94:5 (Nov 1935), 278-79.

4840. DEUTSCH, BABETTE: "Plays in a Living Language: The Dramatic Genius of W. B. Yeats Voiced in Symbolism, Folklore and Beauty," *NYHTB*, 11:52 (1 Sept 1935), 2.

4841. GREGORY, HORACE: "Poets in the Theatre," *Poetry*, 48:4 (July 1936), 221-28.
See pp. 226-27.

4842. REYNOLDS, HORACE: "That Dream-Made World of Yeats the Dramatist: In His *Collected Plays* We Have the Fruits of a Flaming Effort to Restore a Nation's Consciousness," *NYTBR*, 40:35 (1 Sept 1935), 2, 8.

4843. STRONG, L. A. G.: "The Plays of W. B. Yeats," *John o' London's Weekly*, 32:821 (5 Jan 1935), 550.

4844. VALLETTE, J.: *Langues modernes*, 33:7 (Dec 1935), 650-51.

See also J4805, 4807, 4809-11, 4813, 4817, 4818, 4820, 4822, 4845.

W179/A: The King of the Great Clock Tower, Commentaries and Poems (1934/ 1935)

4845. ANON.: "Poetry's Return to the Theatre: Three Books by W. B. Yeats," *Irish Times*, 77:24180 (5 Jan 1935), 7.
Also a review of W175 and 177.

4846. B., E.: "Return of Yeats: The Prose Dialogue of a Dance Play," *BET*, 106:134 (8 June 1935), book section, 4.

4847. BAKER, HOWARD: "Wallace Stevens and Other Poets," *Southern R*, 1:2 (Autumn 1935), 373-96.
See pp. 391-93: "Refusing to formulate experience, Yeats has really no means of telling the natural from the supernatural."

4848. BENET, WILLIAM ROSE: "Contemporary Poetry," *SatR*, 12:3 (18 May 1935), 20-21.

4849. DEUTSCH, BABETTE: "Yeats Is Not Too Old for Poetry: Nearing Seventy, He Wondered; but He Still Has the Power of Words," *NYHTB*, 11:49 (11 Aug 1935), 6.

4850. LYND, ROBERT: "A Great Poet Condemned," *News Chronicle*, #27698 (1 Feb 1935), 4.
The reference is to Pound's condemnation as recorded in Yeats's preface to his book.

4851. M[AYNARD], T[HEODORE]: *Catholic World*, 142:848 (Nov 1935), 254-55.

4852. PARSONS, I. M.: "The Winding Stair," *Spectator*, 154:5559 (11 Jan 1935), 57.

4853. P[OORE], C. G.: "Five-Finger Exercises of a Genius," *NYTBR*, 40:22 (2 June 1935), 2.

4854. REYNOLDS, HORACE: "New Poems by Yeats," *CSM*, 27:195 (17 July 1935), Weekly Magazine section, 11.

4855. Z[ABEL], M. D.: "For Saints and Patriots," *Poetry*, 46:2 (May 1935), 104-8.

See also J4805, 4813, 4822.

W182: A Full Moon in March (1935)

4856. ANON.: "New Poetry," *Dublin Mag*, 11:1 (Jan-Mar 1936), 72-75.

4857. ANON.: "*A Full Moon in March*: Mr. Yeats's New Book of Poems," *Irish Times*, 77:24473 (14 Dec 1935), 7.

4858. ANON.: *Listener*, 15:364 (1 Jan 1936), 41.

4859. ANON.: "Recent Poetry," *Scotsman*, #28883 (23 Dec 1935), 13.

4860. ANON.: "The Mind of Mr. Yeats in Verse," *TLS*, 34:1766 (7 Dec 1935), 833.

4861. C[AZAMIAN], M. L.: *Revue anglo-américaine*, 13:5 (June 1936), 445-46.

4862. CLARKE, AUSTIN: "Mr. Yeats--Contrasts in Verse and Prose," *London Mercury*, 33:195 (Jan 1936), 341-42.
   "Mr. Yeats proves himself master of that eloquence which he spent half a lifetime eradicating from his own literary movement."

4863. FAUSSET, HUGH I'A.: "Time and Mr. Yeats," *Yorkshire Post*, #27632 (19 Feb 1936), 6.

4864. GRIGSON, GEOFFREY: "W. B. Yeats in His Green Old Age: The Poet and His Emblems," *Morning Post*, 164:51059 (18 Feb 1936), 16.

4865. GRUBB, H. T. HUNT: *Poetry R*, 27:1 (Jan-Feb 1936), 62-63.

4866. M[ACDONAGH], D[ONAGH]: "Mr. Yeats' New Poems," *Irish Press*, 5:294 (10 Dec 1935), 11.

4867. M[ACNEICE], L[OUIS]: "The Newest Yeats," *New Verse*, #19 (Feb-Mar 1936), 16.

4868. POWELL, CHARLES: "Recent Poetry," *Manchester Guardian*, #27859 (30 Dec 1935), 5.

4869. RIVOALLAN, A.: *Langues modernes*, 34:10 (Dec 1936), 643.

4870. ROBERTS, MICHAEL: "The Moon and the Savage, Sunlit Heart," *Spectator*, 155:5609 (27 Dec 1935), 1078-79.

4871. S., D.: "A Variety of Plays: Two Poetic Versions of a Yeats Drama," *Irish Independent*, 45:24 (28 Jan 1936), 4.

4872. SMITH, JANET ADAM: *Criterion*, 15:60 (Apr 1936), 521-22.

4873. W., G.: *Granta*, 45:1023 (12 Feb 1936), 237.

4874. WAINEWRIGHT, RUTH M. D.: *English*, 1:3 (1936), 259-60.

W183: Dramatis Personae (1935)

4875. ANON.: *Dublin Mag*, 11:2 (Apr-June 1936), 67-68.

4876. CHURCH, RICHARD: "A Portrait in Vitriol," *NSt*, 11:264 (14 Mar 1936), 398.

W186/187: Dramatis Personae [. . .] *(1936)*

4877. ANON.: "Yeatsian Memories," *Commonweal*, 24:13 (24 July 1936), 332.

4878. ANON.: *Evening Mail*, #27811 (22 May 1936), 5.
See also "Jottings by a Man about Town," #27823 (5 June 1936), 6.

4879. ANON.: "The Irish Revival," *Outlook* [Glasgow], 1:4 (July 1936), 84-86.

4880. ANON.: *Quarterly R*, 267:529 (July 1936), 185.

4881. ANON.: "Prize Poet's Progress," *Time*, 27:20 (18 May 1936), 83.

4882. ANON.: "Mr. W. B. Yeats Looks Back: Varied Reminiscences," *Times*, #47381 (22 May 1936), 19.

4883. ANON.: "Mr. Yeats's Reminiscences: Years of Peace and the Age of Disillusion," *TLS*, 35:1790 (23 May 1936), 434.

4884. ATKINSON, BROOKS: "W. B. Yeats, Man of Letters," *NYT*, 85:28624 (7 June 1936), IX, 1.

4885. B., C. E.: "Books of the Day," *Illustrated London News*, 187:5070 (20 June 1936), 1126.

4886. BOSANQUET, THEODORA: "Men and Books," *Time and Tide*, 17:24 (13 June 1936), 849.

4887. BUCKRAM, ELIOT: "An Irish Poet," *Church of England Newspaper*, 43: 2207 (5 June 1936), 5.

4888. BURDETT, OSBERT: "W. B. Yeats's Memories: Stories of George Moore and a Visit to the Swedish Court," *John o' London's Weekly*, 35:897 (20 June 1936), 421.

4889. C.: "Yeats and His Literary Friends," *Irish News*, #21950 (17 June 1936), 4.

4890. CLARKE, AUSTIN: "Mr. Yeats and His Contemporaries," *London Mercury*, 34:200 (June 1936), 169-70.

4891. COLUM, PADRAIC: "Yeats Looks Back," *SatR*, 14:3 (16 May 1936), 7.

4892. CONLAY, IRIS: "Mirror to Man," *Catholic Herald*, #2631 (7 Aug 1936), 4.

4893. DAVRAY, HENRY D.: *Mercure de France*, 271:919 (1 Oct 1936), 184.

4894. DEUTSCH, BABETTE: "The Aristocratic Ideal Voiced by W. B. Yeats," *NYHTB*, 12:37 (17 May 1936), 6.

4895. EVANS, B. IFOR: "Mr. Yeats Looks Back," *Manchester Guardian*, #28000 (12 June 1936), 9.

4896. FLACCUS, KIMBALL: "Yeats as Dictator, the Man to Whom Pose Has Become a Second Self," *NY Sun*, 103:242 (15 June 1936), 24.

4897. GANNETT, LEWIS: "Books and Things," *NYHT*, 96:32685 (12 May 1936), 19.

4898. GILMORE, WILLIAM: "Yeats: Patriarch of the Irish Renaissance. He Stands as an Apostle of Aristocratic Values in a Democratized World," *Brooklyn Daily Eagle*, 95:199 (19 July 1936), Books, unpaged.

4899. GRIGSON, GEOFFREY: "Wisdom from Yeats," *Morning Post*, 164:51142 (26 May 1936), 16.

4900. GRUBB, H. T. HUNT: "A Poet's Friends," *Poetry R*, 27:4 (July-Aug 1936), 317-22.

4901. JEFFERS, UNA: "A Poet Remembers," *Pacific Weekly*, 5:3 (20 July 1936), 45.

4902. JENCKEN, EDWARD N.: "Yeats and Ireland," *Springfield Daily Republican*, 93:42 (16 May 1936), 6.

4903. MACDONAGH, DONAGH: "Yeats Never Forgets," *Ireland To-day*, 1:2 (July 1936), 75, 77.

4904. MCM[ANUS], M. J.: "W. B. Yeats Looks Back," *Irish Press*, 6:131 (2 June 1936), 6.

4905. MACNEICE, LOUIS: *Criterion*, 16:62 (Oct 1936), 120-22.

4906. M[ARTIN], C[HRISTOPHER]: *Catholic World*, 143:857 (Aug 1936), 626-27.

4907. MASON, H. A.: "Yeats and the Irish Movement," *Scrutiny*, ·5:3 (Dec 1936), 330-32.

4908. MORTIMER, RAYMOND: "Books in General," *NSt*, 11:275 (30 May 1936), 861.
     Discusses the Yeats-Moore relationship.

4909. MUIR, EDWIN: "A High Monologue: Autobiographical Papers by Mr. W. B. Yeats," *Scotsman*, #29017 (28 May 1936), 15.

4910. ÖSTERLING, ANDERS: "W. B. Yeats berättar bl. a. om Stockholmsbesöket 1923 da han hämtade Nobelpriset," *Stockholmstidningen*, 24 Aug 1936, 6.

4911. PRITCHETT, V. S.: "W. B. Yeats Speaking," *CSM*, 28:184 (1 July 1936), Weekly Magazine, 11.

4912. RASCOE, BURTON: *Esquire*, 6:2 (Aug 1936), 184-85.

4913. REYNOLDS, HORACE: "Yeats Continues His Memoirs: One of the Great Intellectual Autobiographies of Our Time," *NYTBR*, [41:] (17 May 1936), 1.

4914. SCHNELL, JONATHAN: "From a Poet's Notebook," *Forum and Century*, 95: 6 (June 1936), v.

4915. STARKIE, WALTER: "A Great Irish Poet Looks Back: Mr. Yeats Gives Us a Book of Memories," *Irish Independent*, 45:167 (14 July 1936), 6.

4916. STRONG, L. A. G.: "The Aristocratic Ideal," *Spectator*, 156:5631 (29 May 1936), 988.

4917. TROY, WILLIAM: "The Lesson of the Master," *Nation*, 142:3072 (17 June 1936), 780.

4918. VINES, SHERARD: "Mr. Yeats and the Irish Revival," *Listener*, 16: 390 (1 July 1936), 43.

4919. W., G.: *Granta*, 45:1034 (3 June 1936), 437-38.

4920. WOLFE, HUMBERT: "Yeats and George Moore: Great Writers at Cross Purposes," *Observer*, 145:7568 (14 June 1936), 8.

4921. YOUNG, GEORGE MALCOLM: *Daylight and Champaign: Essays*. London: Hart-Davis, 1948 [1937]. 296 p.
     "Magic and Mudlarks," 169-75; reprinted from *Sunday Times*, #5903 (31 May 1936), 8. A review of W186.

"Forty Years of Verse," 176-91; reprinted from *London Mercury*, 35:206 (Dec 1936), 112-22. A review of W250. Correspondence by A. C. Boyd, :207 (Jan 1937), 314 (not reprinted).

See also J4800.

W190: Nine One-Act Plays (1937)

4922. CAZAMIAN, M. L.: *EA*, 2:1 (Jan-Mar 1938), 65-66.

4923. M[URRAY], T. C.: "Yeats the Dramatist," *Irish Press*, 7:165 (13 July 1937), 8.

W191/192: A Vision (1937/1938)

4924. ANON.: *Church of Ireland Gazette*, 83:2840 (4 Feb 1938), 77.

4925. ANON.: *Listener*, 18:465 (8 Dec 1937), 1271.

4926. ANON.: *New English Weekly*, 12:15 (20 Jan 1938), 291-92.

4927. ANON.: *NSt*, 15:361 (22 Jan 1938), 140.

4928. B., C. E.: "Books of the Day," *Illustrated London News*, 192:5153 (22 Jan 1938), 126.

4929. BALD, R. C.: *Philosophical R*, 48:284 (Mar 1939), 239.

4930. BENÉT, WILLIAM ROSE: "Speculations of a Poet," *SatR*, 17:20 (12 Mar 1938), 19.

4931. BRONOWSKI, J.: "Yeats's Mysticism," *Cambridge R*, 59:1440 (19 Nov 1937), 113.

4932. CAZAMIAN, M. L.: *EA*, 2:3 (July-Sept 1938), 315.

4933. COLUM, MARY M.: "A Poet's Philosophy," *Forum and Century*, 99:4 (Apr 1938), 213-15.

4934. DEUTSCH, BABETTE: "Bones of a Poet's Vision," *NYHTB*, 14:36 (8 May 1938), 16.

4935. E., C.: "Mr. W. B. Yeats's Latest Book: 'The Shoemaker Should Stick to His Last,'" *Irish News*, #22385 (8 Nov 1937), 3.

4936. E[DWARDS], O[LIVER]: "Beyond the Normal," *Liverpool Daily Post*, #25689 (9 Nov 1937), 4.

4937. Ó F[arachâin], R[oibeârd] [FARREN, ROBERT]: "Invisible Beings Communicated with Mr. Yeats, He Says," *Irish Independent*, 46:261 (2 Nov 1937), 4.
". . . trivial and unprofitable."

4938. G[RIGSON], G[EOFFREY] E[DWARD]: "Thy Chase Had a Beast in View," *New Verse*, #29 (Mar 1938), 20-22.
Yeats is a quack and his chase after beauty is repulsive.

4939. GRUBB, H. T. HUNT: "A Poet's Dream," *Poetry R*, 29:2 (Mar-Apr 1938), 123-41.

4940. HOLMES, JOHN: "Poetry Now," *BET*, 109:95 (23 Apr 1938), pt 3, 2.

4941. MUIR, EDWIN: "Mr. Yeats's Vision: Messages of the 'Communicators,'" *Scotsman*, #29451 (18 Oct 1937), 13.

4942. O'FAOLAIN, SEAN: "Mr. Yeats's Metaphysical Man," *London Mercury*, 37:217 (Nov 1937), 69-70.

4943. PANHUYSEN, JOS[EPH]: "Het visioen van William Butler Yeats," *Boeken-schouw*, 31:7 (15 Nov 1937), 315-20.

4944. QUINN, KERKER: "Through Frenzy to Truth," *Yale R*, 27:4 (Summer 1938), 834-36.
  Also a review of W196.

4945. REYNOLDS, HORACE: "W. B. Yeats Expounds His 'Heavenly Geometry': In *A Vision* He Sets Forth a System of Enormous Complexity and Range," *NYTBR*, [43:] (13 Mar 1938), 2.
  "It is possible that it [the book] may some day be regarded as one of the great milestones of discovery on man's journey of exploration of the spirit world. . . . It reveals much of the man, among other things that either Yeats hasn't a stime of a sense of humor, or--a Gargantuan one."

4946. RIVOALLAN, A.: *Langues modernes*, 36:4 (May-June 1938), 384-85.

4947. ROBERTS, MICHAEL: "The Source of Poetry," *Spectator*, 159:5708 (19 Nov 1937), Supplement, 14, 16.
  "Mr. Yeats has written one of the simplest accounts of poetic composition that has ever appeared, but he has written it in his own language."

4948. SALKELD, CECIL FFRENCH: "Mummy Is Become Merchandise," *Ireland Today*, 2:11 (Nov 1937), 77-79.

4949. SPENDER, STEPHEN: *Criterion*, 17:68 (Apr 1938), 536-37.

4950. WALTON, EDA LOU: "Lend a Myth to God," *Nation*, 147:2 (9 July 1938), 51-52.
  Also a review of W196.

4951. WILLIAMS, CHARLES: "Staring at Miracle," *Time and Tide*, 18:49 (4 Dec 1937), 1674, 1676.

4952. WILLIAMS, MICHAEL: "Doom," *Commonweal*, 27:22 (25 Mar 1938), 611.

4953. WILSON, EDMUND: "Yeats's Vision," *New Republic*, 94:1220 (20 Apr 1938), 339.

W194: Essays 1931 to 1936 (1937)

4954. ANON.: "Yeatsian Fantasy," *TLS*, 37:1877 (22 Jan 1938), 56.
  Also a review of W195.

4955. O'FAOLAIN, SEAN: "More Ideas of Good and Evil," *London Mercury*, 37:220 (Feb 1938), 454-55.

W195/196: The Herne's Egg: A Stage Play / The Herne's Egg and Other Plays (1938)

4956. ANON.: "The Latest Egg of the Academy Auk," *Catholic Bulletin*, 28:3 (Mar 1938), 185-86.

4957. ANON.: *Listener*, 19:476 (23 Feb 1938), 431.

4958. ANON.: "Drama in Verse: A Yeats Fantasy," *Scotsman*, #29564 (28 Feb 1938), 13.

4959. BARKER, GEORGE: *Life and Letters To-day*, 18:11 (Spring 1938), 173.

4960. C., W. R.: *Dublin R*, 202:405 (Apr-June 1938), 387.

4961. C[AZAMIAN], M. L.: *EA*, 3:1 (Jan-Mar 1939), 66-67.

4962. CLARKE, AUSTIN: "Irish Poets," *NSt*, 15:362 (29 Jan 1938), 178, 180. "Mists of his own past have defeated Mr. Yeats at last."

4963. ————: "A Stage Fantasy," *London Mercury*, 37:221 (Mar 1938), 551-52.

4964. DEUTSCH, BABETTE: "Three New Gaelic Plays," *NYHTB*, 14:39 (29 May 1938), 9.

4965. FLETCHER, HELEN: "Leda in Eire," *Time and Tide*, 19:11 (12 Mar 1938), 355.

4966. GRUBB, H. T. HUNT: "A Rabelaisian Yeats [. . .]," *Poetry R*, 29:4 (July-Aug 1938), 327-30.

4967. LAWRENCE, C. E.: "Poetry and Otherwise," *Quarterly R*, 271:537 (July 1938), 153-73.
See pp. 163-64.

4968. Ó MEÁDHRA, SEÁN: *Ireland To-day*, 3:2 (Feb 1938), 183.

4969. POWELL, CHARLES: "Recent Verse," *Manchester Guardian*, #28532 (1 Mar 1938), 7.

4970. REYNOLDS, HORACE: "Three New Plays in Verse by Yeats," *NYTBR*, [43:] (29 May 1938), 8.

4971. ————: "Short Plays by Yeats," *CSM*, 30:168 (14 June 1938), 8.

4972. SMITH, JANET ADAM: "Recent Verse," *Criterion*, 17:68 (Apr 1938), 520-23.

4973. STRONG, L. A. G.: "A Violent Fable," *Spectator*, 160:5722 (25 Feb 1938), 330.

4974. WILSON, EDMUND: *New Republic*, 95:1230 (29 June 1938), 226.

4975. WYATT, EUPHEMIA VAN RENSSELAER: *Commonweal*, 28:6 (3 June 1938), 164.

See also J4944, 4950, 4954.

W197: New Poems (1938)

4976. BARNES, T. R.: "Yeats' New Poems," *Townsman*, 2:5 (Jan 1939), 25-26.

4977. SCOTT, WINFIELD TOWNLEY: "Yeats at 73," *Poetry*, 53:2 (Nov 1938), 84-88.

4978. ZABEL, MORTON DAUWEN: "Two Years of Poetry, 1937-1939," *Southern R*, 5:3 (Winter 1939/40), 568-608.
See pp. 605-8. Also a review of W200; compares Yeats and Rilke.

W198: The Autobiography (1938)

4979. ANON.: "Autobiography of William Butler Yeats," *Sign*, 18:3 (Oct 1938), 187-88.
"One closes the book toying with the intriguing speculation--what would Yeats not have become had he received the Faith!"

4980. C., R. J.: "William Butler Yeats Reviews 75 Years," *Springfield Sunday Union and Republican*, 18 Sept 1938, 7E.

4981. "AN CHRUIMH LEABHAR": *Celtic Digest*, 1:5 (Nov 1938), 27.

4982. COLUM, MARY M.: "The Conqueror Artist," *Forum and Century*, 100:5 (Nov 1938), 226-27.

4983. GREGORY, HORACE: "Personae and Masks," *Nation*, 148:6 (4 Feb 1939), 152-54.

4984. HOLMES, JOHN: "An Anglo-Irish Poet Looks into All His Years," *BET*, 109:218 (17 Sept 1938), Section 3, 1.

4985. TINKER, EDWARD LAROCQUE: "New Editions, Fine & Otherwise," *NYTBR*, [43:] (4 Sept 1938), 12.

See also J1286.

W200: Last Poems and Two Plays (1939)

4986. ANON.: *Listener*, 22:554 (23 Aug 1939), 394-95.

4987. ANON.: "W. B. Yeats: The Last Poems," *TLS*, 38:1955 (22 July 1939), 438.

4988. GWYNN, STEPHEN: "W. B. Yeats," *Fortnightly R*, os 152 / ns 146:874 (Oct 1939), 457-58.

4989. LEAVIS, F. R.: "The Great Yeats, and the Latest," *Scrutiny*, 8:4 (Mar 1940), 437-40.
    Finds the poems lacking in quality and inferior to those in *The Tower*; they do not possess what he calls "complex tension."

4990. MACCARTHY, DESMOND: "The Last Poems of Yeats," *Sunday Times*, #6070 (13 Aug 1939), 6.

4991. PROKOSCH, FREDERIC: "W. B. Yeats," *Spectator*, 163:5797 (4 Aug 1939), 190.

4992. ————: "Yeats's Testament," *Poetry*, 54:7 [i.e., 6] (Sept 1939), 338-42.
    "Spasmodic, fragmentary, horrible."

See also J4978.

W202: On the Boiler (1939)

4993. ANON.: *New Alliance*, 1:1 (Autumn 1939), 106.

4994. ANON.: "Yeats's 'Patter,'" *TLS*, 38:1968 (21 Oct 1939), 612.

4995. SPENDER, STEPHEN: "Honey-Bubblings of the Boilers," *NSt*, 18:455 (11 Nov 1939), 686-87.

W203/204: Last Poems & Plays (1940)

4996. AARONSON, L.: *Nineteenth Century and After*, 127:759 (May 1940), 634-36.

4997. ANON.: *Atlantic Monthly*, 166:2 (Aug 1940), Bookshelf.

4998. ANON.: "The Last Poems and Plays of W. B. Yeats," *Irish Times*, 82:25791 (9 Mar 1940), 5.

4999. ANON.: *Listener*, 23:584 (31 Mar 1940), 593-94.

5000. ANON.: "Irish Poetry and Plays: W. B. Yeats's Posthumous Collection," *Scotsman*, #30189 (29 Feb 1940), 9.

5001. ANON.: *TCD*, 46:806 (15 Feb 1940), 97-98.

5002. ANON.: "Shaw and Yeats," *TAM*, 24:8 (Aug 1940), 613.

5003. ANON.: "Poetry," *Time*, 35:23 (3 June 1940), 76, 78-79.
"The life of . . . Yeats . . . was a wild-goose chase after poetical wisdom—a chase that did not end before the goose was caught, cooked and eaten. How Yeats swallowed his bird—beak, bones and feathers—he has told in detail in his classic *Autobiography*. How the meal sat on his stomach is made plain in his motley, fearful, sometimes scabrous, more often superb *Last Poems & Plays*."

5004. ANON.: "Forty Years of Irish Drama: Yeats, Synge and Lady Gregory. From the Visionaries to the Realists," *TLS*, 39:1993 (13 Apr 1940), 182, 186.

5005. AUDEN, W. H.: "Yeats, Master of Diction," *SatR*, 22:7 (8 June 1940), 14.

5006. BLUNDEN, EDMUND: *Book Society News*, Mar 1940, 19.

5007. BROWN, IVOR: "The Irish Motley," *Observer*, 149:7761 (25 Feb 1940), 4.

5008. COLUM, MARY M.: "An Old Man's Eagle Mind," *Yale R*, 29:4 (Summer 1940), 806-8.

5009. ————: "Poets and Psychologists," *Forum*, 103:6 (June 1940), 322-24. Compares Housman and Yeats.

5010. DEUTSCH, BABETTE: "Sad, Proud and Tender Poems: W. B. Yeats, Facing Death, Wrote with Amazing Vitality," *NYHTB*, 16:40 (2 June 1940), 4.

5011. DUPEE, F. W.: "The Book of the Day: Last Poems of Yeats, Who Lived to Witness the Chaos of Post-War Europe," *NY Sun*, 107:231 (30 May 1940), 12.

5012. FORBES-BOYD, ERIC: "The Last Poems and Plays of W. B. Yeats," *CSM*, 32:117 (13 Apr 1940), Weekly Magazine, 13.

5013. GRUBB, H. T. HUNT: "The Curtain Falls," *Poetry R*, 31:3 (May-June 1940), 217-26.

5014. HEALY, J. V.: "The Final Poems of Yeats: His Last Collection Recapitulates All He Accomplished with His Art," *NYTBR*, [45:] (19 May 1940), 1, 16.

5015. H[OGAN], J. J.: *Studies*, 29:116 (Dec 1940), 650-53.

5016. HOLMES, JOHN: "Poems and Things," *BET*, 111:148 (24 June 1940), 11.

5017. HOULT, NORAH: "The Irish Theatre," *Life and Letters To-day*, 25:33 (May 1940), 158-62.

5018. K[NICKERBOCKER], F. W.: "Where Ladders Start," *Sewanee R*, 49:4 (Oct-Dec 1941), 568-69.

5019. KREYMBORG, ALFRED: "Hands Across the Sea," *Living Age*, 358:4485 (June 1940), 394-96.

5020. LEE, LAWRENCE: "The Extension of Poetry in Time," *VQR*, 16:3 (Summer 1940), 481-84.

5021. MACCARTHY, DESMOND: "W. B. Yeats on Poetry," *Sunday Times*, #6114 (16 June 1940), 4.
Also a review of W325.

5022. MACMANUS, FRANCIS: "Mr. Yeats' Last Poems," *Irish Press*, 10:56 (5 Mar 1940), 6.

5023. MACNEICE, LOUIS: "Yeats's Epitaph," *New Republic*, 102:1334 (24 June 1940), 862-63.

5024. R[ANSOM], J. C.: "Old Age of a Poet," *Kenyon R*, 2:3 (Summer 1940), 345-47.

5025. ROSENBERGER, COLEMAN: "Consuming Its Rag and Bone," *Accent*, 1:1 (Autumn 1940), 56-57.

5026. SHANKS, EDWARD: "Yeats the Symbolist: Why He Discarded His Romantic Epithets," *John o' London's Weekly*, 43:1095 (5 Apr 1940), 14.

5027. STRONG, L. A. G.: "The Eagle Mind," *Time and Tide*, 21:10 (9 Mar 1940), 251-52.

5028. T., P. C.: *Irish Book Lover*, 27:4 (July 1940), 238-39.

5029. WANNING, ANDREWS: "Criticism and Principles: Poetry of the Quarter," *Southern R*, 6:4 (Spring 1941), 792-810.
    See pp. 798-800.

5030. WILDER, AMOS N.: "Yeats' Final Flight," *Christian Century*, 57:28 (10 July 1940), 878.

5031. ZABEL, MORTON DAUWEN: "The Last of Yeats," *Nation*, 151:15 (12 Oct 1940), 333-35.
    Also a review of W325; reprinted with revisions in J1090.

See also J1228.

W205: If I Were Four-and-Twenty (1940)

5032. ANON.: *Listener*, 25:631 (13 Feb 1941), 242.

5033. ANON.: "W. B. Yeats," *TLS*, 39:2024 (16 Nov 1940), 580.

5034. CLARKE, AUSTIN: *Dublin Mag*, 16:1 (Jan-Mar 1941), 64.

5035. GIBBON, MONK: *Bell*, 1:2 (Nov 1940), 91, 93.

5036. SCOTT-JAMES, R. A.: "When Yeats Was Fifty-four," *Spectator*, 165:5860 (18 Oct 1940), 392, 394.

W211/A: The Collected Poems (1950/51)

5037. ANON.: *Adelphi*, 27:1 (Nov 1950), 80-81.

5038. ANON.: "The Finest of Modern Poets? . . . Bid for Yeats," *Newsweek*, 47:15 (9 Apr 1956), 120-22.
    Also a review of W211M.

5039. ANON.: "Lasting Songs," *Time*, 57:21 (21 May 1951), 128, 130.

5040. ANON.: "Yeats and His Critics," *TLS*, 49:2534 (25 Aug 1950), 525-26.

5041. AVISON, M.: *Canadian Forum*, 30:361 (Feb 1951), 261.

5042. BRÉGY, KATHERINE: *Catholic World*, 173:1036 (July 1951), 316-17.

5043. BREIT, HARVEY: "Repeat Performances," *NYTBR*, [56:] (3 June 1951), 23.

5044. BRYSON, JOHN: "An Old Man's Eagle Mind," *Time and Tide*, 31:39 (7 Oct 1950), 998-99.

5045. COLE, THOMAS: "W. B. Yeats's Complete Poems," *Voices*, #146 (Sept-Dec 1951), 48-50.

5046. DERLETH, AUGUST: "Clear Voices," *Voices*, #161 (Sept-Dec 1956), 44-46.

5047. DORN, NORMAN K.: "The Myriad World of Yeats . . . ," *San Francisco Chronicle*, 95:130 (10 May 1959), This World section, 27.

5048. [EDWARDS, OLIVER]: *Rann*, #9 (Summer 1950), 1-3.

5049. ELLMANN, RICHARD: "The Identity of Yeats," *Kenyon R*, 13:3 (Summer 1951), 512-15.

5050. FERLING, LAWRENCE: "The Second Volume of Poems by William Butler Yeats," *San Francisco Chronicle*, 174:133 (25 Nov 1951), Christmas book section, 15.

5051. GALLAGHER, JAMES: "Yeats Collective but Not Definitive," *Spirit*, 18:3 (July 1951), 92-93.

5052. GILLETT, ERIC: "Yeats Collected," *National and English R*, 135:811 (Sept 1950), 292-94.

5053. GUY, EARL F.: *Dalhousie R*, 30:4 (Jan 1951), 428-30.

5054. MCE[LDERRY], B. R.: *Personalist*, 38:3 (Summer 1957), 314-15.

5055. MACNEICE, LOUIS: "Great Riches," *Observer*, #8308 (27 Aug 1950), 7.

5056. MURPHY, ROBERT: "Books and Writers," *Spectator*, 185:6372 (11 Aug 1950), 183.

5057. POORE, CHARLES: "Books of the Times," *NYT*, 100:34074 (10 May 1951), 29.

5058. REMÉNYI, JÓZSEF: "Két költö" [Two poets], *Látóhatár*, 5:5 (1954), 305-7.

5059. ROSENTHAL, M. L.: "Sources in Myth and Magic," *Nation*, 182:25 (23 June 1956), 533-35.
Also a review of W211M.

5060. STAUFFER, DONALD A.: "A Half Century of the High Poetic Art of William Butler Yeats: Here Are the Lyrics and Dramatic Poems of the Great Irishman, That 'One-Man Renaissance,' Most Wanted to Endure," *NYHTB*, 27:38 (6 May 1951), 3.

5061. TINDALL, W. Y.: "Art Whose End Is Peace," *American Scholar*, 20:4 (Autumn 1951), 482, 484, 486.

5062. UNGER, LEONARD: "The New Collected Yeats," *Poetry*, 80:1 (Apr 1952), 43-51.

5063. VERY, ALICE: *Poet Lore*, 56:3 (Autumn 1951), 277-82.

5064. VIERECK, PETER: "Technique and Inspiration: A Year of Poetry," *Atlantic Monthly*, 189:1 (Jan 1952), 81-83.

5065. WARD, A. C.: *Litterair paspoort*, [5]:42 (Dec 1950), 236-37.

5066. WARNER, REX: "Books in General," *NSt*, 40:1020 (23 Sept 1950), 300-301.

5067. W[ATT], I[AN] P.: *Cambridge R*, 72:1747 (28 Oct 1950), 82.

See also J1228.

W211D/E: The Collected Plays (1952/1953)

5068. ANON.: "Master of Poetic Drama," *Church Times*, 135:4688 (12 Dec 1952), 900.

5069. ANON.: *Listener*, 49:1253 (5 Mar 1953), 397, 399.

5070. ANON.: "Yeats's Second String," *Nation*, 177:1 (4 July 1953), 16.

5071. BERTRAM, ANTHONY: "Reflection of Sunset," *Tablet*, 200:5875 (27 Dec 1952), 530-31.

5072. BUDDINGH', C[ORNELIS]: "Drama's van een dichter," *Critisch Bulletin*, 20:3 (Mar 1953), 135-38.

5073. CLARKE, AUSTIN: "Plays in Search of a Theatre," *Irish Times*, #29658 (18 Oct 1952), 8.

5074. DAVIES, ROBERTSON: "Observations on Yeats' Plays," *Saturday Night*, 68:17 (31 Jan 1953), 22.

5075. EATON, WALTER PRICHARD: "Great Lyric Poet's Plays," *NYHTB*, 29:44 (14 June 1953), 6.

5076. F[ERLING], L[AWRENCE]: *San Francisco Chronicle*, 178:60 (13 Sept 1953), This World section, 16.

5077. HABART, MICHEL: "W. B. Yeats et le théâtre aristocratique," *Critique* [Paris], 10:88 (Sept 1954), 739-53.

5078. MACDONAGH, DONAGH: "Folding and Unfolding of a Cloth," *Irish Press*, 22:234 (18 Nov 1952), 6.

5079. MCELDERRY, B. R.: *Personalist*, 35:4 (Autumn 1954), 427-28.

5080. MACNEICE, LOUIS: "Yeats's Plays," *Observer*, #8422 (2 Nov 1952), 8.

5081. MULKERNS, VAL: "Will Managers Please Take Note?" *Bell*, 18:7 (Dec 1952), 444, 446, 448.

5082. O'CONNOR, FRANK: "A Lyric Voice in the Irish Theatre: Yeats, the Poet, Says Frank O'Connor, Was the Magnificent Master of the One-Act Drama," *NYTBR*, 68:22 (31 May 1953), 1, 16.
    Reprinted in Francis Brown (ed): *Highlights of Modern Literature: A Permanent Collection of Memorable Essays from the New York Times Book Review*. NY: New American Library, 1954. 240 p. (Mentor Book. M104.), pp. 130-34. Includes personal reminiscences.

5083. [PRYCE-JONES, ALAN]: "Yeats as Dramatist," *TLS*, 51:2651 (21 Nov 1952), 760.
    Reprinted in *Griffin*, 2:5 (1953), 23-28.

5084. REYNOLDS, HORACE: "Yeats' Poetic Drama," *CSM*, 45:207 (30 July 1953), 11.

5085. RIDLER, ANNE: "The Passion in Drama," *Drama*, #37 (Summer 1955), 37-38.

5086. SALINGAR, LEO: "Yeats the Dramatist," *Highway*, 44 (Mar 1953), 222-25.

5087. WHITE, MARIE A. UPDIKE: *SAQ*, 53:1 (Jan 1954), 153-54.

5088. WOODCOCK, GEORGE: *Northern R*, 7:1 (Oct 1954), 43-46.

W211G; The Autobiography (1953)

5089. BEVINGTON, HELEN: *SAQ*, 53:2 (Apr 1954), 300-301.

5090. GREGORY, HORACE: "Yeats Revisited," *Poetry*, 84:3 (June 1954), 153-57.

5091. JACKINSON, ALEX: *American Poetry Mag*, 34:4 (1953), 8-9.

5092. PERRINE, CATHERINE: "Yeats and the Nineties," *Southwest R*, 39:1 (Winter 1954), 96.

5093. POORE, CHARLES: "Books of the Times," *NYT*, 103:35021 (12 Dec 1953), 17.

W211H/I: Letters to Katharine Tynan (1953)

5094. ANON.: *Listener*, 50:1277 (20 Aug 1953), 312.

5095. ANON.: *Quarterly R*, 291:598 (Oct 1953), 550-51.

5096. ANON.: "Letters of the Younger Yeats," *Sunday Independent*, 49:1 (3 Jan 1954), 6.
Correspondence by Pamela Hinkson, :6 (7 Feb 1954), 6.

5097. ANON.: "Yeats When Young," *TLS*, 52:2685 (17 July 1953), 462.

5098. BERRIGAN, DANIEL: *Thought*, 29:112 (Spring 1954), 143-44.

5099. BRÉGY, KATHERINE: *Catholic World*, 178:1063 (Oct 1953), 76.

5100. CLARKE, AUSTIN: "Between Friends," *Irish Times*, #29884 (11 July 1953), 6.

5101. CONNOLLY, TERENCE L.: "The Grass Is Greener," *Renascence*, 8:3 (Spring 1956), 167-68.

5102. DEUTSCH, BABETTE: "Yeats as Correspondent, in His Lonely Youth and His Rich Maturity," *NYHTB*, 30:18 (13 Dec 1953), 8.
Also a review of W340.

5103. FAY, GERARD: "Yeats's Letters," *Manchester Guardian*, #33276 (19 June 1953), 4.

5104. H., L.: *Dublin Mag*, 30 [i.e., 29]:1 (Jan-Mar 1954), 48-49.

5105. KIELY, BENEDICT: "Letters from Yeats to a Flamingo," *Irish Press*, 23:146 (20 June 1953), 4.
Flamingo was Francis Thompson's description of KT.

5106. MACNEICE, LOUIS: "A Poet's Progress," *Observer*, #8458 (12 July 1953), 7.

5107. O'DONOGHUE, FLORENCE: "Letters of Yeats," *Dublin R*, 228:463 (1954), 102-4.
Also a review of W340.

5108. O'H., T.: "Yeats's Letters to Katharine Tynan," *Irish Independent*, 62:194 (15 Aug 1953), 4.

5109. REYNOLDS, HORACE: "Absorbed in Poetry, Race and Vision," *NYTBR*, [58:] (27 Dec 1953), 4, 11.
Also a review of W340. Correspondence by R. L. Wilbur, "Letters and Discoveries," [59:4] (24 Jan 1954), 24.

5110. RODGERS, W. R.: "By the Waters of Babylon," *NSt*, 46:1167 (18 July 1953), 78, 80.

5111. SHACKLETON, EDITH: "Yeats as a Young Man," *Britain To-day*, #210 (Oct 1953), 44-45.

5112. V., J.: *San Francisco Chronicle*, 178:39 (23 Aug 1953), This World section, 15.

5113. WARNER, REX: "Yeats in His Youth," *Spectator*, 191:6526 (24 July 1953), 108.

5114. WHITE, TERENCE DE VERE: *Studies*, 42:[] (Winter 1953), 474-76.
   Also a review of W340.

W211J/K: The Letters (1954/1955)

5115. ADAMS, HAZARD: "Yeats the Stylist and Yeats the Irishman," *Accent*, 15:3 (Summer 1955), 234-37.

5116. ANON.: *CE*, 16:7 (Apr 1955), 466.

5117. ANON.: "Yeats in His Letters," *Nation*, 181:2 (9 July 1955), 29.

5118. ANON.: *Quarterly R*, 293:604 (Apr 1955), 279-80.

5119. ANON.: "Yeats as Letter Writer," *TLS*, 53:2750 (15 Oct 1954), 656.

5120. AUDEN, W. H.: "I Am of Ireland," *New Yorker*, 31:5 (19 Mar 1955), 142-46, 149-50.
   Includes lengthy comments on Yeats's poetry and on his political views.

5121. BRADFORD, CURTIS B.: "Yeats's Letters," *VQR*, 32:1 (Winter 1956), 157-60.

5122. BROOKS, CLEANTH: "Yeats's Letters," *Yale R*, 44:4 (June 1955), 618-20.

5123. CAZAMIAN, MADELEINE-L.: "La correspondance de W. B. Yeats," *EA*, 8:1 (Jan-Mar 1955), 50-60.

5124. COLUM, MARY: "In a Lifetime of Letters Yeats Spelled Out His Own Genius," *NYTBR*, 60:8 (20 Feb 1955), 7.

5125. CONNOLLY, CYRIL: *Previous Convictions*. London: Hamilton, 1963. xv, 414 p.
   "Yeats's Crucial Year," 252-54; reprinted from *Sunday Times*, #6873 (9 Jan 1955), 5.

5126. DAY LEWIS, C.: *London Mag*, 1:10 (Nov 1954), 85-88.

5127. DEUTSCH, BABETTE: "W. B. Yeats' Letters Are a Self-Portrait: They Reveal the Poet in All His Complexity and Grandeur," *NYHTB*, 31:30 (6 Mar 1955), 3.

5128. DOLBIER, MAURICE: "Letters of a Poet," *Harper's Mag*, 210:1259 (Apr 1955), 98.

5129. DUPEE, FREDERICK WILCOX: *"The King of Cats" and Other Remarks on Writers and Writing*. NY: Farrar, Straus & Giroux, 1965. x, 214 p.
   "The King of Cats," 42-48; reprint of "The Deeds and Dreams of Yeats," *Partisan R*, 23:1 (Winter 1956), 108-11.

5130. EDEL, LEON: "No More Opinions . . . No More Politics," *New Republic*, 132:2103 (14 Mar 1955), 21-22.

5131. ELLMANN, RICHARD: "Yeats without Panoply," *Sewanee R*, 64:1 (Jan-Mar 1956), 145-51.

5132. EVANS, ILLTUD: "A Poet to His Friends," *Tablet*, 205:5991 (19 Mar 1955), 279-80.

5133. FAY, GERARD: "Yeats in His Letters: Passion, Literary and Political," *Manchester Guardian*, #33669 (24 Sept 1954), 8-9.

5134. FERGUSON, DELANCEY: "Dreamer with His Dander Up," *SatR*, 38:20 (14 May 1955), 12, 44.

5135. HÄUSERMANN, H. W.: *ES*, 36:5 (Oct 1955), 284-86.

5136. HAMILTON, IAIN: "Truth Embodied," *Spectator*, 193:6588 (1 Oct 1954), 416, 418.

5137. JEFFARES, A. N.: "William Butler Yeats: A Mind Michael Angelo Knew," *Meanjin*, 14:4 (Summer 1955), 565-68.
Also a review of W211L.

5138. KENNER, HUGH: "Unpurged Images," *Hudson R*, 8:4 (Winter 1956), 609-17.

5139. LERMAN, LEO: "Collected Poets," *Mademoiselle*, 41:1 (May 1955), 125.

5140. M., W. P.: *Dublin Mag*, 31 [i.e., 30]:1 (Jan-Mar 1955), 52-53.

5141. MACKENZIE, COMPTON: "Sidelight," *Spectator*, 193:6588 (1 Oct 1954), 395.

5142. MCLUHAN, H. MARSHALL: "Yeats and Zane Grey," *Renascence*, 11:3 (Spring 1959), 166-68.

5143. MACNEICE, LOUIS: "Endless Old Things," *NSt*, 48:1230 (2 Oct 1954), 398.

5144. MANLEY, SEON: "The Yeats Letters: Cold Light on the Celtic Twilight," *New Leader*, 38:20 (16 May 1955), 21-22.

5145. MERCIER, VIVIAN: "Yeats' Lifelong Immersion in the Spirit of Ireland," *Commonweal*, 61:25 (25 Mar 1955), 660-61.

5146. MOORE, HARRY T.: "Rich, Intimate View of Poet W. B. Yeats," *Boston Sunday Herald*, 218:58 (27 Feb 1955), 48.

5147. O'NEILL, MICHAEL J.: *Thought*, 30:119 (Winter 1955/56), 618-19.

5148. P., P.: "Yeats as Seen in His Letters," *Irish Independent*, 63:235 (2 Oct 1954), 6.

5149. PHELPS, ROBERT: "Walking Naked," *Kenyon R*, 17:3 (Summer 1955), 495-500.

5150. READ, HERBERT: "W. B. Yeats," *Listener*, 52:1336 (7 Oct 1954), 582, 585.

5151. REYNOLDS, HORACE: "The Poet's Life in His Letters," *CSM*, 47:75 (24 Feb 1955), 11.

5152. ROBINSON, LENNOX: *I Sometimes Think*. Dublin: Talbot Press, 1956. 166 p.
Reprinted items from unspecified issues of *Irish Press*. "When Abbey Opposed Castle," 34-37; about the performance of Shaw's *The Shewing-Up of Blanco Posnet*. "W. B. Yeats," 101-4; a review of W211J. "Four Women," 118-21; on Lady Gregory, Miss Horniman, Sara Allgood, and Máire O'Neill.

5153. RODGERS, W. R.: "Facets of Yeats," *Observer*, #8540 (6 Feb 1955), 9.

5154. S[MITH], T[ERENCE]: *Irish Writing*, #28 (Sept 1954), 67-68.

5155. VOGLER, LEWIS: "Yeats's Letters Uncover the Roles He Played," *San Francisco Chronicle*, #32767 (10 Apr 1955), This World section, 21.

See also J2561, 2973, 5172.

W211L: Autobiographies (1955)

5156. ADAMS, HAZARD: "Where All Ladders Start," *Western R*, 19:3 (Winter 1955), 229-34.
    Also a review of W340.

5157. ANON.: "Voices of a Poet," *Church Times*, 138:4812 (29 Apr 1955), 4.

5158. ANON.: "Poet's Self-Portrait," *Economist*, 175:5827 (30 Apr 1955), Spring Books, 9.

5159. ANON.: *Quarterly R*, 293:606 (Oct 1955), 558.

5160. ANON.: "Yeats's Story: A Modern Fable," *Scotsman*, #34895 (31 Mar 1955), 11.

5161. ANON.: "Portrait of the Artist as a Young Man," *Times*, #53192 (17 Mar 1955), 9.

5162. ANON.: "Heroic Profiles," *TLS*, 54:2774 (29 Apr 1955), 201.

5163. BAILEY, ANTHONY: "The Close Companions," *Isis*, #1247 (27 Apr 1955), 24.

5164. BODKIN, THOMAS: "A Poet's Memories," *Birmingham Post*, #30135 (22 Mar 1955), 3.

5165. BRAYBROOKE, NEVILLE: "Poetry, Magic, Mysticism," *Catholic Herald*, #3620 (5 Aug 1955), 3.

5166. CLARKE, AUSTIN: "Cast a Cold Eye," *Irish Times*, #30418 (2 Apr 1955), 8.

5167. FALLON, GABRIEL: "A Handful of Sligo Soil," *Books of the Month*, 70:5 (May 1955), 15, 24.

5168. FAY, GERARD: "The Poet," *Manchester Guardian*, #33823 (25 Mar 1955), 10.

5169. FRASER, G. S.: "Platonic Tolerance," *NSt*, 49:1263 (21 May 1955), 723-24.

5170. MANGANELLI, GIORGIO: "Yeats autobiografo," *Mulino*, 4:10 (Oct 1955), 956-58.

5171. PHILLIPSON, WULSTAN: "W. B. Yeats," *Month*, 14:5 (Nov 1955), 309-10.

5172. POWELL, ANTHONY: "Celtic Mist," *Punch*, 228:5984 (18 May 1955), 620.
    Also a review of W211J.

5173. RAINE, KATHLEEN: "The Discipline of the Symbol," *Listener*, 53:1360 (24 Mar 1955), 540.
    Correspondence by Henry Lamb, :1361 (31 Mar 1955), 577.

5174. ROBINSON, LENNOX: "On *Autobiographies* by W. B. Yeats," *Library R*, #115 (Autumn 1955), 162, 164.

5175. SEYMOUR, WILLIAM KEAN: *St. Martin's R*, #770 (May 1955), 174.

5176. STRONG, L. A. G.: *London Mag*, 2:6 (June 1955), 83-86.

5177. TOYNBEE, PHILIP: "Good Books and Bad," *Observer*, #8547 (24 Apr 1955), 13.

5178. VALLETTE, JACQUES: "Souvenirs d'écrivains," *Mercure de France*, 325: 1105 (Sept 1955), 141-44.

5179. WADE, ALLAN: "A Poet Young and Old," *Time and Tide*, 36:13 (26 Mar 1955), 402-3.

5180. [WHITE, SEAN J.]: "Foreword" [to the Yeats issue], *Irish Writing*, #31 (Summer 1955), 7-8.

See also J1748, 5137.

W211M: A Vision (1956)

5181. DAVENPORT, WILLIAM H.: *Personalist*, 38:3 (Summer 1957), 315.

5182. DONOGHUE, DENIS: "Countries of the Mind," *Guardian*, #36241 (11 Jan 1963), 5.

5183. GALLAGHER, JAMES: "A Precis of a Myth," *Spirit*, 23:5 (Nov 1956), 154-55.

5184. WEBER, RICHARD: *Dubliner*, #6 (Jan-Feb 1963), 69-70.

See also J5038, 5059.

W211N: The Variorum Edition of the Poems (1957)

5185. ANON.: "Yeats in Youth and Maturity," *TLS*, 57:2923 (7 Mar 1958), 126. Correspondence by R. W. Chapman, :2926 (28 Mar 1958), 169; J. W. Bryce, :2929 (18 Apr 1958), 209; Katherine Haynes Gatch, :2934 (23 May 1958), 283.

5186. BRADFORD, CURTIS: "The Variorum Edition of Yeats's Poems," *Sewanee R*, 66:4 (Oct-Dec 1958), 668-78.

5187. FLETCHER, IAIN: *VS*, 2:1 (Sept 1958), 72-75.

5188. GREGORY, HORACE: "Like a Chambered Nautilus," *NYTBR*, [62:] (22 Dec 1957), 5, 18.
Includes reminiscences of a meeting with Yeats in 1934. Correspondence by Karl Beckson, [63:] (26 Jan 1958), 24. The review is reprinted in *Spirit of Time and Place* (J2817).

5189. HARVEY, W. J.: "Visions and Revisions: The Variorum Edition of Yeats," *Essays in Criticism*, 9:3 (July 1959), 287-99.

5190. HOOVER, ANDREW G.: *QJS*, 44:1 (Feb 1958), 90-91.

5191. JOHNSTON, GEORGE: "The Variorum Yeats," *Tamarack R*, #11 (Spring 1959), 97-102.

5192. KERMODE, FRANK: "Adam's Curse," *Encounter*, 10:6 (June 1958), 76-78.

5193. MACNEICE, LOUIS: *London Mag*, 5:12 (Dec 1958), 69, 71, 73, 75.

5194. MENON, NARAYANA: "The Poems of W. B. Yeats," *Cultural Forum*, 6:1 (Sept-Oct 1963), 37-43.

5195. MUIR, EDWIN: "Changing the Style," *Observer*, #8700 (30 Mar 1958), 16.

5196. PARKINSON, THOMAS: "Contesting a Will," *Kenyon R*, 20:1 (Winter 1958), 154-59.

5197. REANEY, JAMES: "The Variorum Yeats," *UTQ*, 28:2 (Jan 1959), 203-4.

5198. REEVE, F. D.: "The Variorum Yeats," *Voices*, #166 (May-Aug 1958), 35-37.

5199. REYNOLDS, HORACE: "How Yeats Wrote and Wrote Again," *CSM*, 49:286 (31 Oct 1957), 11.

5200. ROSENTHAL, M. L.: "Metamorphoses of Yeats," *Nation*, 186:14 (5 Apr 1958), 298-99.

5201. SAUL, GEORGE BRANDON: *Arizona Q*, 13:4 (Winter 1957), 373.

5202. SCHOECK, R. J.: "A Poet's Craft," *Spirit*, 25:2 (May 1958), 56-58.

5203. SCOTT, WINFIELD TOWNLEY: "The Remaking of an Artist," *SatR*, 40:49 (7 Dec 1957), 47-50.

5204. URE, PETER: *ES*, 41:4 (Aug 1960), 281-83.

5205. WITT, MARION: *Assembly*, 17:2 (Summer 1958), 23.

W211P/Q: Mythologies (1959)

5205a. ANGOFF, ALLAN: "Yeats' Poetic Sources," *Tomorrow*, 7:4 (Autumn 1959), 87-93.
   Discusses Yeats's "mystical life."

5206. ANON.: "Yeats," *Scotsman*, #36165 (25 Apr 1959), 13.

5207. BUCKLEY, VINCENT: *Quadrant*, 4:15 (Winter 1960), 90-91.

5208. COLUM, PADRAIC: "A Passion That Became Poetry," *SatR*, 42:31 (1 Aug 1959), 16-17.
   Includes some reminiscences.

5209. DEUTSCH, BABETTE: "W. B. Yeats," *NYHTB*, 36:3 (23 Aug 1959), 8.

5210. ELLMANN, RICHARD: "Imagination versus Reality," *Chicago Sunday Tribune*, 118:31 (2 Aug 1959), pt 4, 2.

5211. HENN, T. R.: "A Look into Darkness," *NSt*, 57:1465 (11 Apr 1959), 518-19.

5212. HEPPENSTALL, RAYNER: "The Alchemist," *Observer*, #8750 (15 Mar 1959), 22.

5213. HOFFMAN, DANIEL G.: *J of American Folklore*, 76:299 (Jan-Mar 1963), 83-86.

5214. HOGAN, WILLIAM: "The Celtic Myths of William Butler Yeats," *San Francisco Chronicle*, 95:211 (30 July 1959), 33.

5215. MERCIER, VIVIAN: "The Making of a Poet," *NYTBR*, [64:] (2 Apr 1959), 4.
   ". . . more pose than prose."

5216. O'BRIEN, CONOR CRUISE: *Writers and Politics*. NY: Pantheon Books, 1965. xxii, 259 p.
   "The Great Conger," 119-20; reprinted from *Spectator*, 202:6830 (22 May 1959), 736 (written under the pseudonym Donat O'Donnell).

5217. READY, WILLIAM B.: *Critic*, 18:2 (Oct-Nov 1959), 50-51.

5218. REANEY, JAMES: *Canadian Forum*, 39:461 (June 1959), 64-65.

5219. REEVES, JAMES: "Verbal Toughness," *Time and Tide*, 40:18 (2 May 1959), 508.

5220. SAUL, GEORGE BRANDON: *Arizona Q*, 16:1 (Spring 1960), 90-93.

See also J1210.

W211R/S: The Senate Speeches (1960/1961)

5221. ANON.: "Senator Yeats," *Times*, #55280 (4 Jan 1962), 11.

5222. ANON.: "Poet as Senator," *TLS*, 60:3121 (22 Dec 1961), 916.
"It is a triumphant irony that a man so often viewed by his contemporaries . . . as the weirdest of dreamers should have proved so splendidly the reverse when called upon to act as one of his country's statesmen."

5223. DAICHES, DAVID: "The Practical Visionary," *Encounter*, 19:3 (Sept 1962), 71-74.
Also a review of W211T/U.

5224. DAVIE, DONALD: "Poet in the Forum," *Guardian*, #35916 (22 Dec 1961), 8.

5225. DOBBS, KILDARE: "No Petty People," *Saturday Night*, 77:6 (17 Mar 1962), 35-36.

5226. ELLMANN, RICHARD: "Heard and Seen," *NSt*, 62:1604 (8 Dec 1961), 887-88.
Correspondence by William Empson, "A Question of Stock," :1607 (29 Dec 1961), 989; E. MacLysaght and Ellmann, "Taking Stock," 63:1619 (19 Jan 1962), 85.

5227. HENN, T. R.: *Listener*, 66:1708 (21 Dec 1961), 1084.

5228. MERCIER, VIVIAN: "To Pierce the Dark Mind," *Nation*, 191:20 (10 Dec 1960), 460-61.

5229. O'CONNOR, FRANK: "This Side of Innisfree," *Reporter*, 23:11 (22 Dec 1960), 44-45.

5230. Ó GLAISNE, RISTEÁRD: *Focus* [Dublin], 5:1 (Jan 1962), 17-18.

5231. O'ROURKE, JOSEPH: *QJS*, 47:3 (Oct 1961), 318.

5232. SANESI, ROBERTO: "William Butler Yeats uomo pubblico," *Aut-Aut*, 12:67 (Jan 1962), 69-71.
Reprinted in *Poesia e critica*, 1:3 [Dec 1962], 172-75.

5233. SPEAIGHT, ROBERT: "Poet and Prophet," *Tablet*, 215:6342 (9 Dec 1961), 1176, 1178.

5234. T., A.: ". . . But Not Yeats," *Irish Independent*, 71:30 (3 Feb 1962), 10.

5235. URE, PETER: *RES*, 14:54 (May 1963), 220-21.

See also J1102, 4084.

W211T/U: Essays and Introductions (1961)

5236. ANON.: "Irish Genius," *Church Times*, 144:5123 (21 Apr 1961), 4.

5237. ANON.: "The Poet's 'Powerful and Passionate Syntax,'" *Scotsman*, #36739 (25 Feb 1961), Weekend magazine, 2.

5238. ANON.: "Odd & Haunting Master," *Time*, 77:25 (16 June 1961), 88-90.

5239. ANON.: "Tame Swan at Coole," *TLS*, 60:3077 (17 Feb 1961), 97-98.

5240. BROADBENT, JOHN: "Speaking with His Own Tongue," *Time and Tide*, 42: [9] (2 Mar 1961), 335.

5241. BUSHRUI, S. B.: [Review of the book in Arabic], *Aswat*, #5 (1962), 99-103.

5242. CHURCH, RICHARD: "The Consistency of Genius," *John o' London's*, 4: 72 (16 Feb 1961), 176.

5243. CLARKE, AUSTIN: "The Prose of Yeats," *Irish Times*, #32872 (25 Feb 1961), 8.

5244. DEUTSCH, BABETTE: "A Poet's Credo Set Down in His Prose," *NYHTB*, 38:1 (6 Aug 1961), 4.

5245. DICKINSON, PETER: "The Magic of Criticism," *Punch*, 240:6293 (26 Apr 1961), 663.

5246. ELLMANN, RICHARD: "Three Ages of Yeats," *NSt*, 61:1580 (23 June 1961), 1011-12.

5247. GASKELL, RONALD: *London Mag*, ns 1:3 (June 1961), 89, 91, 93.

5248. HEALY, CAHIR: "Yeats in Many Moods," *Irish News*, #29117 (8 Apr 1961), 2.

5249. HOLLOWAY, DAVID: "Yeats on Poetry," *Daily Telegraph*, #32918 (17 Feb 1961), 19.

5250. IGOE, W. J.: "A Great Writer's Only Real Apologia: His Work," *Chicago Sunday Tribune*, 120:28 (9 July 1961), pt 4, 2.

5251. IREMONGER, VALENTIN: "The Remarkable Lady Gregory," *Catholic Herald*, #3925 (30 June 1961), 3.

5252. JEFFARES, A. NORMAN: *Stand*, 5:2 [1961?], 55-57.

5253. K., F. J.: "Yeats as Critic," *Irish Independent*, 70:95 (22 Apr 1961), 10.

5254. KENNER, HUGH: "Yeats's *Essays*," *Jubilee*, 9:10 (Feb 1962), 39-43.

5255. KERMODE, FRANK: "The Spider and the Bee," *Spectator*, 206:6927 (31 Mar 1961), 448-49.

5256. LANGBAUM, ROBERT: "The Symbolic Mode of Thought," *American Scholar*, 31:3 (Summer 1962), 454, 456, 458, 460.

5257. LID, RICHARD W.: "Nathanael West Reconsidered and Another Helping of Yeats," *San Francisco Chronicle*, 97:204 (23 July 1961), This World section, 20.

5258. MACCALLUM, H. R.: "W. B. Yeats: The Shape Changer and His Critics," *UTQ*, 32:3 (Apr 1963), 307-13.
      Also a review of W211Y/Z.

5259. MCCARTHY, PATRICK J.: *Arizona Q*, 19:3 (Autumn 1963), 277-79.

5260. MCHUGH, ROGER: "Yeats's Plenty," *Kilkenny Mag*, #4 (Summer 1961), 24-30.

5261. MORTIMER, RAYMOND: "Yeats on Himself and Others," *Sunday Times*, #7188 (19 Feb 1961), 26.

5262. MORTON, J. B.: "Yeats under the Microscope," *Tablet*, 215:6307 (8 Apr 1961), 330-31.

5263. NORMAN, SYLVA: *Aryan Path*, 32:7 (July 1961), 326-27.

5264. O'CONNOR, FRANK: "Conclusions Were Right," *NYTBR*, 66:27 (2 July 1961), 4-5.
   "Information usually wrong, arguments always wrong, Yeats still had the fairy gift of making his conclusions right."

5265. READ, HERBERT: "What Yeats Believed," *Listener*, 65:1667 (9 Mar 1961), 459.

5266. REYNOLDS, HORACE: "Yeats in His Collected Essays: A Poet's 'Structure of Thought,'" *CSM*, 53:176 (22 June 1961), 7.

5267. STEWART, J. I. M.: "Hankering after Magic," *Sunday Telegraph*, #5 (5 Mar 1961), 7.

5268. TOMLINSON, CHARLES: "Pull Down Thy Vanity," *Poetry*, 98:4 (July 1961), 263-66.

5269. UNTERECKER, JOHN: *MD*, 5:2 (Sept 1962), 249-50.

5270. WAIN, JOHN: "Poetry and the Past," *Observer*, #8853 (5 Mar 1961), 31.

5271. WATSON, GEORGE: "The Essays of Yeats," *Oxford Mag*, ns 1:18 (4 May 1961), 324.
   "To re-read these essays is to realize afresh how preposterously Yeats's own works are a mixture of feelings from everywhere under the sun, how uncritical and syncretic the whole caste [*sic*] of his intelligence was."

See also J5223.

W211W: Selected Poems (1962)

5272. GALLAGHER, JAMES: "A Valuable Paperback," *Spirit*, 29:2 (May 1962), 62-63.

5273. MOORE, JOHN R.: "Swan or Goose," *Sewanee R*, 71:1 (Jan-Mar 1963), 123-33.

5274. WELLS, HENRY W.: "Two Poets," *Voices*, #179 (Sept-Dec 1962), 54-56.
   Compares Yeats and Hugh MacDiarmid.

W211X: Selected Poetry (1962)

5275. BOSE, AMALENDU: "W. B. Yeats: His Poetry and Thought," *Indian J of English Studies*, 3 (1962), 158-67.

5276. HENN, T. R.: "Yeats Revisited," *Revue des langues vivantes*, 31:4 (1965), 404-5.
   Also a review of W211BB, 211CC, and 211DD.

W211Y/Z: Explorations (1962/1963)

5277. ANON.: "Collecting Yeats," *Times*, #55478 (23 Aug 1962), 11.

5278. ANON.: "A Poet's Prose," *TLS*, 61:3162 (5 Oct 1962), 778.
   Criticizes the unexplained and unjustified omission of important paragraphs.

5279. CONNOLLY, CYRIL: "Solitary Outlaw," *Sunday Times*, #7267 (26 Aug 1962), 21.

5280. CROSS, GUSTAV: "Yeats: Angry Old Poet," *Sydney Morning Herald*, 132:38975 (17 Nov 1962), 16.

5281. D[ELEHANTY], J[AMES]: *Kilkenny Mag*, #8 (Autumn-Winter 1962), 56-58.

5282. KERMODE, FRANK: "Dublin 1904," *NSt*, 64:1645 (21 Sept 1962), 366.

5283. MACALERNON, DON: "On the Yeats Shelf," *Focus* [Dublin], 6:1 (Jan 1963), 24.

5284. MACLIAMMÓIR, MICHEÁL: "Merlin in the Market-place," *Spectator*, 209: 7004 (21 Sept 1962), 403-4.

5285. MURPHY, RICHARD: "The Empty Tower at Ballylee," *Observer*, #8936 (7 Oct 1962), 29.

5286. REANEY, JAMES: "Yeats Unconquered," *Canadian Forum*, 42:504 (Jan 1963), 235-36.

See also J5258.

W211BB: Selected Plays (1964)

See J5276.

W211CC: Selected Prose (1964)

See J5276.

W211DD: Selected Criticism (1964)

See J5276.

W211EE/FF: The Variorum Edition of the Plays (1966)

5287. ANON.: "Yeats's Variations," *TLS*, 66:3393 (9 Mar 1967), 187.

5288. DONOGHUE, DENIS: "Between the Lines," *Guardian*, #37234 (25 Mar 1966), 8.

W212: Fairy and Folk Tales of the Irish Peasantry (1888)

5289. ANON.: *Athenaeum*, #3198 (9 Feb 1889), 174-75.

5290. ANON.: *Irish Monthly*, 16:185 (Nov 1888), 687-88.

5291. ANON.: "Irish Folk Lore," *Nation* [Dublin], 46:43 (27 Oct 1888), 4.

See also J4272.

W214: Stories from Carleton (1889)

5292. ANON.: *Nation* [Dublin], 48:52 (28 Dec 1889), 4.
  Correspondence by Yeats, "Carleton as an Irish Historian," 49:2 (11 Jan 1890), 5 (Wp. 333), and editor's reply, *ibid*.

W215: Representative Irish Tales (1891)

5293. ANON.: *Irish Monthly*, 19:217 (July 1891), 378-79.

5294. ANON.: *NYT*, 40:12363 (12 Apr 1891), 19.

5295. ANON.: *Saturday R*, 71:1857 (30 May 1891), 664-65.
  Very critical of Yeats's preface.

5296. ROLLESTON, T. W.: *Academy*, 40:1014 (10 Oct 1891), 306-7.
  "The selection and editing of these tales could hardly have been put into better hands than those of Mr. Yeats. . . ."

W216: Irish Fairy Tales (1892)

5297. ANON.: *Saturday R*, 73:1906 (7 May 1892), 551.

5298. ROLLESTON, T. W.: "The Fairy Tales of Ireland," *Library R*, 1:6 (Aug 1892), 342-45.

W218: The Works of William Blake (1893)

5299. ANON.: *Athenaeum*, #3453 (30 Dec 1893), 920-21.

5300. ANON.: *Saturday R*, 75:1945 (4 Feb 1893), 126-27.

5301. ANON.: "Two Mystics on Blake," *Speaker*, 7:[] (15 Apr 1893), 429-30.

5302. [JOHNSON, LIONEL]: "A Guide to Blake," *Westminster Gazette*, 1:15 (16 Feb 1893), 3.

5303. ————: *Post Liminium: Essays and Critical Papers*. Edited by Thomas Whittemore. London: Mathews, 1911. xiv, 307 p.
"William Blake," 81-90; reprinted from *Academy*, 44:1112 (26 Aug 1893), 163-65.

5304. M'G[RATH], J[OHN]: "North and South," *United Ireland*, 12:607 (22 Apr 1893), 1.

W219: The Poems of William Blake (1893)

5305. ANON.: "A New Blake," *Bookman*, 6:31 (Apr 1894), 22-23.

5306. ANON.: *Nation*, 58:1494 (15 Feb 1894), 123.

W221: Poems of William Blake (1905; reprinted 1969)

5307. JORDAN, JOHN: "William on William," *Irish Independent*, 78:195 (16 Aug 1969), 6.

W225: A Book of Irish Verse (1895)

5308. ANON.: "Four Irish Books," *Athenaeum*, #3519 (6 Apr 1895), 434-35.

5309. ANON.: *Daily Express*, #13348 (21 Mar 1895), 7.

5310. ANON.: "Irish Verse," *Saturday R*, 79:2056 (23 Mar 1895), 384-85.

5311. ANON.: "Some Recent Books of Verse," *Speaker*, 11:[] (20 Apr 1895), 443-44.

5312. ANON.: "Irish Verse," *Spectator*, 74:3485 (13 Apr 1895), 502-3.

5313. ANON.: *United Ireland*, 14:707 (23 Mar 1895), 1.
Correspondence by Hester Sigerson, :708 (30 Mar 1895), 1.

5314. ANON.: *United Irishman*, 3:54 (10 Mar 1900), 5.

5315. E., F. Y.: "The Prospects of Anglo-Irish Poetry," *Speaker*, ns 2:[] (28 Apr 1900), 111-12.

5316. ESTERRE-KEELING, ELSA D': "Four Irish Books," *Academy*, 47:1199 (27 Apr 1895), 349-51.

5317. JOHNSON, LIONEL: "Ireland in Verse," *Daily Chronicle*, #11916 (11 May 1900), 3.

5318. QUILL: "Books to Read," *Illustrated London News*, 116:3178 (17 Mar 1900), 372.

See also J4270.

W226: Beltaine (1899ff.)

5319. ANON.: "The Younger Generation," *Pilot*, 2:24 (11 Aug 1900), 185–86.
   Also a review of *Dome*, 6 (Apr 1900), which contains Yeats's "The Symbolism of Poetry" (Wp. 358). "We listen with pleasure, though with
   imperfect comprehension" to Yeats's discussion of symbolism. But:
   "There is a good deal of nonsense mixed up with the Irish literary
   movement."

W227: Samhain ([#1], 1901)

See J6053, 6302 (#8).

W230: Samhain (#4, 1904)

5320. ANON.: "The Drama: Mr. Yeats on the Irish Theatre," *TLS*, 4:156 (6
Jan 1905), 5.

W235: Poems of Spenser (1906)

5321. BAILEY, JOHN [CANN]: *Poets and Poetry: Being Articles Reprinted
from the Literary Supplement of "The Times."* Oxford: Clarendon Press,
1911. 217 p.
   "Spenser," 45–54; reprinted from *TLS*, 5:251 (2 Nov 1906), 365–66.
   Contains an extensive discussion of Yeats's introduction.

W250/251: The Oxford Book of Modern Verse (1936)

5322. ANON.: "A New Oxford Book of Verse," *National R*, 108:648 (Feb 1937),
261–62.

5323. ANON.: *N&Q*, 172:1 (2 Jan 1937), 16.

5324. ANON.: "Yeats's 'Modern' Anthology Keyed to Disillusionment,"
Springfield Sunday Republican, 50:20 (17 Jan 1937), 7E.

5325. ANON.: "Modern Verse: Mr. Yeats's Anthology," *Times*, #47537 (20 Nov
1936), 10.

5326. ARNS, KARL: *Englische Studien*, 72:1 (Oct 1937), 136–38.

5327. BINYON, LAURENCE: *English*, 1:4 (1937), 339–40.

5328. BULLETT, GERALD: "Poetry in Our Time: Mr. Yeats's Personal Anthology," *John o' London's Weekly*, 36:920 (27 Nov 1936), 357.

5329. CROWLEY, PAUL: "Mr. Yeats Selects," *Commonweal*, 25:6 (4 Dec 1936),
163–64.

5330. DAVRAY, HENRY D.: *Mercure de France*, 277:938 (15 July 1937), 420–21.

5331. DAY LEWIS, C.: "Poetry To-day," *Left R*, 2:16 (Jan 1937), 899–901.

5332. DEUTSCH, BABETTE: "The Personal Poetic Tastes of W. B. Yeats: His
Choices for This Anthology Are Surprising, He Likes the Irish and Omits
America," *NYHTB*, 13:15 (13 Dec 1936), 9.

5333. G., R.: "Moderner and Moderner," *Cambridge R*, 58:1420 (22 Jan 1937),
192–93.

5334. GWYNN, STEPHEN: "The Yeats Anthology: Some Omissions," *Fortnightly
R*, os 147 / ns 141:842 (Feb 1937), 237–39.

5335. H[AMPSHIRE], S[TUART] N.: *Oxford Mag*, 55:11 (4 Feb 1937), 343.

5336. HAWKINS, A. DESMOND: "Yeats as Anthologist," *New English Weekly*, 10: 22 (11 Mar 1937), 431-32.

5337. HAYWARD, JOHN: "Mr. Yeats's Book of Modern Verse," *Spectator*, 157: 5656 (20 Nov 1936), Supplement, 3.
    Criticizes the choice of poets, the introduction ("fragmentary . . . tantalising and unintegrated"), and the "slovenly proof-reading." Correspondence by W. J. Turner, "Mr. Yeats's Anthology," :5657 (27 Nov 1936), 950; by Yeats and I. M. Parsons, :5658 (4 Dec 1936), 995. Yeats's letter is not listed in Wade's bibliography; see J151.

5338. HILLYER, ROBERT: *Atlantic Monthly*, 159:3 (Mar 1937), Bookshelf.

5339. ————: *MLN*, 52:8 (Dec 1937), 618-19.
    "An amazingly bad compilation. . . ."

5340. HOGAN, J. J.: *Ireland To-day*, 2:1 (Jan 1937), 82-83.

5341. HOLMES, JOHN: "Modern Verse Selected by William Butler Yeats," *BET*, 107:302 (26 Dec 1936), pt 6, 2.
    An anthology "of first rank."

5342. HONE, JOSEPH: "A Letter from Ireland," *Poetry*, 49:6 (Mar 1937), 332-36.

5343. JAMES, TREVOR: "The Nineteenth Century and After," *Life and Letters To-day*, 16:7 (Spring 1937), 165-67.

5344. LYND, ROBERT: "Not a Subject for Poetry," *John o' London's Weekly*, 36:923 (18 Dec 1936), 508.
    Criticizes the exclusion of the War poets.

5345. MACM[ANUS], M. J.: "Modern Poetry: Mr. Yeats's Choice," *Irish Press*, 6:287 (1 Dec 1936), 6.

5346. MASON, H. A.: "Yeats and the English Tradition," *Scrutiny*, 5:4 (Mar 1937), 449-52.
    Yeats's taste in the selection is "merely eccentric," and the introduction is "perverse."

5347. MATTHIESSEN, F. O.: "W. B. Yeats and Others," *Southern R*, 2:4 (Spring 1937), 815-34.
    See pp. 815-27.

5348. NICHOLS, ROBERT: "Weimar and Wasteland," *Time and Tide*, 17:50 (12 Dec 1936), 1785-86.

5349. ÖSTERLING, ANDERS: "Poesi med nyckel," *Stockholmstidningen*, 4 Sept 1937, 6.

5350. PRESS, JOHN: "Anthologies," *REL*, 1:1 (Jan 1960), 62-70.
    See pp. 65-66.

5351. R[EILLY], J[OSEPH] J.: *Catholic World*, 145:865 (Apr 1937), 113-14.

5352. REYNOLDS, HORACE: "Yeats Assays a Poetic Era: The Oxford Book of Modern Verse Is 'More a Yeats Item Than an Anthology of Modern British and Irish Poetry' but It Reflects a Distinguished Literary Taste," *CSM*, 29:64 (10 Feb 1937), Weekly Magazine, 6.

5353. SELINCOURT, BASIL DE: "Bare Bones: Mr. Yeats and the Modern Poets," *Observer*, 145:7591 (22 Nov 1936), 5.

5354.————: "Modern Verse," *Manchester Guardian*, #28144 (27 Nov 1936), 7.
Introduction and selection are "whimsical"; too many poems are concerned with defeat, gloom, and the grave. Good as the selection sometimes is, a better one might have been made with poems not in Yeats's
anthology.

5355. [SPARROW, JOHN]: "Mr. Yeats Selects the Modern Poets: A Time of
Literary Confusion," *TLS*, 35:1816 (21 Nov 1936), 957.
An almost enthusiastic review that praises the eccentricity of the
selection as an original judgment.

5356. SPENDER, STEPHEN: "Modern Verse--Minus the Best of It," *Daily Worker*,
#2159 (16 Dec 1936), 7.
Complains that the War poets were omitted. Correspondence by R. B.
Marriott, #2162 (19 Dec 1936), 4; W. J. Turner, #2168 (29 Dec 1936),
4. This is presumably the review referred to in Yeats's letter to
Dorothy Wellesley, dated 23 Dec [1936] (*Letters*, p. 875).

5357. STONIER, G. W.: "Mr. Yeats Fumbles," *NSt*, 12:302 (5 Dec 1936), 940,
942.
"What the book suffers from most is not so much bad taste as an inco-
herent tactlessness. . . . The Introduction does not help. Apart from
its inadequacy as a historical sketch, it contains strange critical
blunders."

5358. VINES, SHERARD: "Mr. Yeats and Modern Poetry," *Listener*, 16:412 (2
Dec 1936), Supplement, iv.

5359. WALTON, EDA LOU: "From Stars to Bones," *Nation*, 143:23 (5 Dec 1936),
663, 665.

5360. WIDDEMER, MARGARET: "The Yeats Book of Modern Verse," *NYTBR*, 41:50
(13 Dec 1936), 2.

5361. WOOD, FREDERICK T.: *ES*, 19:4 (Aug 1937), 187-88.

5362. Z[ABEL], M. D.: "Poet as Anthologist," *Poetry*, 49:5 (Feb 1937), 273-
78.

For further references to the anthology see index ND.

W252/253: The Ten Principal Upanishads (1937)

5363. ANON.: "Poetry of Ancient India," *Church Times*, 117:3873 (16 Apr
1937), 472.

5364. ANON.: "Myths for the Poets," *TLS*, 36:1842 (22 May 1937), 393.

5365. D., M.: "The Hindu Search for God and Truth [. . .]," *Irish Independent*, 46:93 (20 Apr 1937), 4.

5366. KUNITZ, STANLEY J.: "May I Never Be Born Again," *Poetry*, 51:4 (Jan
1938), 216-18.

5367. M[AIRET], P[HILIP]: "Views and Reviews," *New English Weekly*, 11:10
(17 June 1937), 191-92.

5368. NICHOLS, ROBERT: "Upanishads for Everyman," *London Mercury*, 36:211
(May 1937), 76-77.

5369. REYNOLDS, HORACE: "The Upanishads and William B. Yeats," *NYTBR*,
[43:5] (30 Jan 1938), 3, 20.

5370. SELINCOURT, BASIL DE: "Interior Heaven: The Teaching of the Upanishads," *Observer*, 146:7613 (25 Apr 1937), 5.

5371. THOMAS, E. J.: "Old Light from the East," *Cambridge R*, 59:1437 (29 Oct 1937), 55.

5372. YEATS-BROWN, F.: "At the Feet of the Masters," *Listener*, 17:433 (28 Apr 1937), Supplement, vii.

See also J2188-90 and note.

W256/257: Lady Gregory: Cuchulain of Muirthemne (1902/1903)

5373. ANON.: *New Ireland R*, 17:4 (June 1902), 253-54.

5374. BOLAND, EAVAN: "Lady Gregory and the Anglo-Irish," *Irish Times*, #35556 (16 May 1970), 9.
   Also a review of W258.

5375. GARNETT, EDWARD: "Books Too Little Known: The Cuchullin Saga," *Academy*, 64:1606 (14 Feb 1903), 156-58.

5376. MACLEOD, FIONA: "The Four Winds of Eirinn," *Fortnightly R*, os 79 / ns 73:434 (1 Feb 1903), 340-54.

5377. [ROBINSON, FRED NORRIS]: "Lady Gregory's Cuchulain," *Nation*, 78:2026 (28 Apr 1904), 334-35.

See also J6053, 7428.

W258/259: Lady Gregory: Gods and Fighting Men (1904)

5378. BLUNT, WILFRID SCAWEN: *Speaker*, ns 9:[] (6 Feb 1904), 450-52.

See also J5374.

W263/266: Rabindranath Tagore: Gitanjali (1912/1919)

5379. ANON.: "East and West," *Westminster Gazette*, 40:6095 (7 Dec 1912), 5.

5380. [MORE, PAUL ELMER]: "Romance from Bengal," *Nation*, 96:2498 (15 May 1913), 500.

5381. ROLLESTON, T. W.: *Hibbert J*, 11:3 (Apr 1913), 692-94.

W269: Ernest Fenollosa and Ezra Pound: Certain Noble Plays of Japan (1916)

5382. ANON.: "The Japanese Masque," *Nation* [London], 20:2 (14 Oct 1916), 87.
   "We confess to preferring Mr. Yeats's highly-trained and eloquent introduction to all the material which has provoked it."

W291: The Book of the Rhymers' Club (1892)

5383. W., H.: *Irish Monthly*, 20:226 (Apr 1892), 212-16.

W297: John Eglinton, W. B. Yeats, AE, William Larminie: Literary Ideals in Ireland (1899)

5384. ANON.: "For Irish Poets," *Daily Chronicle*, #11671 (29 July 1899), 3.

5385. ANON.: "The Irish Literary Movement," *Literature*, 5:90 (8 July 1899), 9.

5386. GIBBON, MONK: "*Literary Ideals in Ireland*: A Comparison," *Irish Statesman*, 5:13 (5 Dec 1925), 399–400.

5387. JERROLD, LAURENCE: *Humanité nouvelle*, yr 4 / 6:35 (1900), 620–22.

5388. MACLEOD, FIONA: *Bookman*, 16:95 (Aug 1899), 136–37.

5389. Q[UILLER-] C[OUCH], A[RTHUR] T[HOMAS]: "A Literary Causerie: Irish Literary Ideals," *Speaker*, 19:494 (17 June 1899), 690–92.

See also J4351.

W312: Lady Gregory: Visions and Beliefs in the West of Ireland (1920)

5390. ANON.: "A Happy Collaboration," *NSt*, 15:390 (2 Oct 1920), 712.

5391. ANON.: "Spoof from Ireland," *Saturday R*, 130:3388 (2 Oct 1920), 280–81.

5392. ANON.: "Fairies and Discoveries," *TLS*, 19:975 (23 Sept 1920), 613.

5393. COLUM, PADRAIC: "Folk Seers," *Dial*, 69:3 (Sept 1920), 300–302.

5394. DE CASSERES, BENJAMIN: "West of Ireland in Vision and Belief," *NYTBR*, [25:] (23 May 1920), 270.

5395. MORRIS, LLOYD R.: "The Mood of the Irish Mind," *Outlook*, 125:[] (2 June 1920), 222–23.

5396. REID, FORREST: *Retrospective Adventures*. London: Faber & Faber, 1941. 286 p.
    "The Host of the Air," 156–60; reprinted from *Athenaeum*, #4721 (22 Oct 1920), 550.

5397. STEWART, HERBERT L.: "A Treasury of Folklore," *Weekly R* [NY], 3:74 (13 Oct 1920), 320–21.

See also J5936.

W325/A: Letters on Poetry from W. B. Yeats to Dorothy Wellesley (1940)

5398. ANON.: *Atlantic Monthly*, 166:6 (Dec 1940), Bookshelf.

5399. ANON.: *Listener*, 24:599 (4 July 1940), 29.

5400. ANON.: "Wise and Gay," *TLS*, 39:2001 (8 June 1940), 279.

5401. ANON.: "Hatred, Pity and Love: W. B. Yeats's Last Thoughts on His Vision," *TLS*, 39:2001 (8 June 1940), 282.

5402. BLACKMUR, RICHARD P.: "W. B. Yeats' Letters on Poetry," *Decision*, 1:2 (Feb 1941), 63–65.

5403. BOGAN, LOUISE: "Verse," *New Yorker*, 16:36 (19 Oct 1940), 87–89.

5404. BROOKS, CLEANTH: *MLN*, 57:4 (Apr 1942), 312–13.

5405. BROWNLOW, TIMOTHY: *Dublin Mag*, 4:1 (Spring 1965), 78–81.

5406. CLARKE, AUSTIN: *Dublin Mag*, 16:1 (Jan–Mar 1941), 65–66.

5407. CLAYBOROUGH, ARTHUR: *Moderna språk*, 59:4 (1965), 442.

5408. DAVIES, ROBERTSON: "Testament for Poets from W. B. Yeats," *Saturday Night*, 56:19 (18 Jan 1941), 20.

5409. DEUTSCH, BABETTE: "As One Poet to Another," *NYHTB*, 17:7 (13 Oct 1940), 20.

5410. FITTS, DUDLEY: "Yeats to Wellesley," *SatR*, 23:9 (21 Dec 1940), 20.

5411. Sister Mariella [GABLE, MARIELLA]: *Commonweal*, 32:26 (18 Oct 1940), 532-33.

5412. HOLMES, JOHN: "Poems and Things," *BET*, 111:266 (11 Nov 1940), 9.

5413. JACK, PETER MONRO: "Mr. Yeats on Poetry," *NYTBR*, [45:] (1 Dec 1940), 20.

5414. JENCKES, EDWARD N.: "Poets' Letters," *Springfield Republican*, 21 Sept 1940, 6.

5415. LYND, SYLVIA: *Book Society News*, June 1940, 16.

5416. MELLERS, W. H.: "Petulant Peacock," *Scrutiny*, 9:2 (Sept 1940), 197-99.

5417. MEYERSTEIN, E. H. W.: *English*, 3:15 (Autumn 1940), 136-38.

5418. POWELL, LAWRENCE CLARK: "Speaking of Books: Yeats-Wellesley Letters," *NYTBR*, [70:] (28 Mar 1965), 2.

5419. R[EYNOLDS], H[ORACE]: "Yeats Portrayed by Himself," *CSM*, 32:288 (2 Nov 1940), Weekly Magazine, 12.

5420. S., W.: *Clergy R*, ns 20:3 (Mar 1941), 273-75.
    "Yeats throughout all his periods appears chiefly as a literary man who always contrived to miss the truth about the things which most excited his interest--ballads, English prosody, Eastern thought, and so forth."

5421. SCOTT, WINFIELD TOWNLEY: "The Foolish, Passionate Man," *Accent*, 1:4 (Summer 1941), 247-50.

5422. SELINCOURT, BASIL DE: "Letters from Yeats," *Observer*, 149:7776 (9 June 1940), 4.

5423. ————: "Letters on Poetry," *Manchester Guardian*, #29251 (24 June 1940), 7.

5424. SIMON, IRÈNE: *Revue des langues vivantes*, 31:4 (1965), 410-13.

5425. TATE, ALLEN: "Yeats's Last Friendship," *New Republic*, 103:1356 (25 Nov 1940), 730, 732.

5426. UNTERMEYER, LOUIS: "Yeats and Others," *Yale R*, 30:2 (Dec 1940), 378-85.
    See pp. 378-80.

See also J5021, 5031.

W327/329: Florence Farr, Bernard Shaw, W. B. Yeats: Letters (1941/1946)

5427. ANON.: *NSt*, 23:569 (17 Jan 1942), 47.

5428. ANON.: "W. B. Yeats and G. B. Shaw Adored Her," *NYTBR*, [47:] (1 Mar 1942), 9.

5429. ANON.: "Florence Farr and Her Friends [. . .]," *TLS*, 41:2092 (7 Mar 1942), 118.

5430. EVANS, B. IFOR: "Letters from Shaw and Yeats," *Manchester Guardian*, #29751 (3 Feb 1942), 3.

5431. FAUSSET, H. I'A.: *Aryan Path*, 17:10 (Oct 1946), 395.

5432. GWYNN, STEPHEN: "Shaw, Yeats, and a Lady," *Observer*, 151:7859 (11 Jan 1942), 3.

5433. HONE, JOSEPH: "Shaw, Yeats and Florence Farr," *Bell*, 13:1 (Oct 1946), 80.

5434. JOHN, GWEN: *Dublin Mag*, 17:2 (Apr-June 1942), 53-54.

5435. REYNOLDS, HORACE: "Farr to Yeats to Shaw," *CSM*, 34:134 (2 May 1942), Weekly Magazine, 12.

5436. REYNOLDS, LORNA: *Dublin Mag*, 22:1 (Jan-Mar 1947), 52-53.

5437. ROBINSON, LENNOX: "Letters to an Amateur," *Irish Times*, #26361 (10 Jan 1942), 5.

5438. TURNER, W. J.: "Lively Letters," *Spectator*, 176:6156 (21 June 1946), 642.

W332/333: J. B. Yeats: Letters to His Son [. . .] *(1944/1946)*

5439. ANON.: *Listener*, 31:792 (16 Mar 1944), 305.

5440. ANON.: "Memorabilia," *N&Q*, 189:11 (1 Dec 1945), 221-22.

5441. ANON.: "Father and Son: Letters of J. B. to W. B. Yeats," *TLS*, 43: 2199 (25 Mar 1944), 152.

5442. BEAN, JACOB: "Engaging Contradiction," *Commonweal*, 45:4 (8 Nov 1946), 96-97.

5443. BODKIN, THOMAS: "Father of W. B. Yeats," *Birmingham Post*, #26700 (22 Feb 1944), 2.

5444. C., E.: *Connoisseur*, 113:492 (June 1944), 131-32.

5445. COLUM, MARY M.: "W. B. Yeats' Limberness and Grace," *SatR*, 29:45 (9 Nov 1946), 16-17.
    The title should probably read "J. B. Yeats' Limberness. . . ."

5446. COLUM, PADRAIC: "Good Conversation in the Form of Letters [. . .]," *NYHTB*, 23:8 (13 Oct 1946), 3.

5447. DEUTSCH, BABETTE: "Personality," *Poetry*, 69:5 (Feb 1947), 291-95.

5448. GOGARTY, OLIVER ST. JOHN: "From Father to Son," *NYTBR*, [51:] (20 Oct 1946), 34.

5449. HEERIKHUIZEN, F. W. VAN: "Brieven van een beminnelijk man," *Litterair paspoort*, 1:2 (Mar 1946), 6-7.

5450. HILLYER, ROBERT: *Atlantic Monthly*, 178:6 (Dec 1946), 182.

5451. LANDRETH, HELEN: *Catholic World*, 164:981 (Dec 1946), 276-77.

5452. [O'SULLIVAN, SEUMAS ?]: *Dublin Mag*, 19:2 (Apr-June 1944), 59-61.

5453. REYNOLDS, HORACE: "He Offered His Son the Poetry of Life," *NYTBR*, [49:] (18 June 1944), 25.

5454. ————: "The Successful Mr. Yeats: John Butler Yeats Was a Success as a Thinker, a Talker, a Letter Writer," *CSM*, 39:5 (30 Nov 1946), Weekly Magazine, 6.

5455. WORSLEY, T. C.: "A Poet's Father," *NSt*, 27:684 (1 Apr 1944), 229-30.

W340/341: W. B. Yeats and T. Sturge Moore: Their Correspondence (1953)

5456. ANON.: *Adelphi*, 30:2 (1954), 198-200.

5457. ANON.: "Collision of Ideas," *Nation*, 177:23 (5 Dec 1953), 472-73.

5458. ANON.: "Poets in Argument," *Times*, #52737 (26 Sept 1953), 9.

5459. ANON.: "Yeats and Sturge Moore," *TLS*, 52:2699 (23 Oct 1953), 681.

5460. ASKEW, MELVIN W.: *BA*, 28:3 (Summer 1954), 357.

5461. C[OHEN], J. M.: "Poets' Letters," *Observer*, #8471 (11 Oct 1953), 11.

5462. COLLINS, CLIFFORD: "Philosophy between Poets," *Spectator*, 191:6543 (20 Nov 1953), 598.

5463. C[ORMAN], C[ID]: *Black Mountain R*, #1 (Spring 1954), 48-51.

5464. HAWARD, LAWRENCE: "Two Poets," *Manchester Guardian*, #33372 (9 Oct 1953), 4.

5465. HENN, T. R.: "The Cat and the Moon," *NSt*, 46:1178 (3 Oct 1953), 386, 388.

5466. JONES, T. H.: "Letters of W. B. Yeats," *Month*, 11:3 (Mar 1954), 187-88.

5467. KENNER, HUGH: "Some Elders," *Poetry*, 83:6 (Mar 1954), 357-63, 366.

5468. SPENDER, STEPHEN: "Misery and Grandeur of Poets," *Listener*, 50:1284 (8 Oct 1953), 608.

5469. TAYLOR, GEOFFREY: "Letters between Yeats and Sturge Moore," *Time and Tide*, 34:42 (17 Oct 1953), 1352.

See also J5102, 5107, 5109, 5114, 5156.

Wp. 406: Das Land der Sehnsucht (1911)

5470. BRIE, FRIEDRICH: *Schöne Literatur*, 13:11 (18 May 1912), 201-2.

5471. HAEBLER, ROLF GUSTAF: *Schöne Literatur*, 13:14 (29 June 1912), 249-50.
    Yeats's name is consistently misspelled as Seats.

5472. NOLL, GUSTAV: *Beiblatt zur Anglia*, 22:12 (Dec 1911), 370-71.

Wp. 407: Tragedie irlandesi (1914)

5473. VINCIGUERRA, MARIO: "Rassegna inglese," *Conciliatore*, 2:2 (31 July 1915), 216-33.
    See pp. 216-29.

Wp. 408: Erzählungen und Essays (1916)

5474. EICHLER, ALBERT: *Beiblatt zur Anglia*, 28:10 (Oct 1917), 298-302.

5475. FRANCK, HANS: "William Butler Yeats: Der Gründer der 'Sinnfein'-Bewegung," *Tägliche Rundschau: Unterhaltungsbeilage*, 36:258 (2 Nov 1916), 1030-31.
    The strange title ("Yeats, the founder of Sinn Fein") has its origin in the erroneous assumption that "Samhain" is pronounced "Sinn Fein."

5476. STRUNZ, FRANZ: *Literarisches Zentralblatt für Deutschland*, 69:1 (5 Jan 1918), 38.

Wp. 410: Blaesten mellem sivene (1924)

5477. KRISTENSEN, TOM: *Den evige uro.* København: Gyldendal, 1958. 161 p. "W. B. Yeats: *Blaesten mellem sivene,*" 26-28; reprinted from *Tilskuer-en,* 42:3 (Mar 1925), 230-31.

Wp. 411: Längtans land (1924)

5478. ÖSTERLING, ANDERS: "Keltiska dramer," *Svenska dagbladet,* #86 (28 Mar 1924), 9.

Wp. 412: Gräfin Cathleen (1925)

5479. LOERKE, OSKAR: *Der Bücherkarren: Besprechungen im "Berliner Börsen-Courier,"* 1920-1928. Edited by Hermann Kasack and Reinhard Tgahrt. Heidelberg: Schneider, 1965. 447 p. (Veröffentlichungen der Deutschen Akademie für Sprache und Dichtung Darmstadt. 34.)
Review of *Gräfin Cathleen,* pp. 336-37; reprinted from °*Berliner Börsen-Courier,* #213 (9 May 1926).
Review of *Die chymische Rose,* pp. 392-93; reprinted from °*Berliner Börsen-Courier,* #449 (25 Sept 1927).

Wp. 412: Die chymische Rose (1927)

5480. ARNS, KARL: *Gral,* 22:7 (Apr 1928), 467.

5481. BEHLER-HAGEN, MALLY: *Schöne Literatur,* 29:2 (Feb 1928), 86.

See also J5479.

Wp. 413: Hraběnka Cathleenová (1929)

5482. VANĚK, F.: *Lidové noviny,* 37:288 (8 June 1929), 15.

Wp. 414: Země touhy (1929)

5483. VANĚK, F.: "Tři překlady z W. B. Yeatse," *Lidové noviny,* 37:202 (20 Apr 1929), 19.

Wp. 414: Irische Schaubühne (1933)

5484. ARNS, KARL: *Neue Literatur,* 36:2 (Feb 1935), 94.

5485. BÄNNINGER, KONRAD: "Heiselers Yeats-Übertragung," *Neue Schweizer Rundschau,* ns 3:6 (Oct 1935), 382-84.

5486. BRAUN, HANNS: "William Butler Yeats: Irische Schaubühne," *Deutsche Zeitschrift,* 47:9 (June 1934), 576-78.

5487. DRAWS-TYCHSEN, HELLMUT: "Die Dramen von William Butler Yeats," *Berliner Tageblatt,* 63:71 (11 Feb 1934), 1.

Wp. 415: Poesie (1939)

5488. ALTICHIERI, GILBERTO: *Letteratura,* 4:1 (Jan 1940), 154-55.

Wp. 422: Théâtre (1954)

5489. HABART, MICHEL: *Théâtre populaire,* #7 (May-June 1954), 93-94.

Wp. 422: Poèmes choisis (1954)

5490. FRÉCHET, RENÉ: *EA,* 9:2 (Apr-June 1956), 180-82.

Wp. 424: Verzen in vertaling (1955)

5491. RENS, LIEVEN: "Poeziekroniek," *Nieuwe Stemmen*, 11:7 (May 1955), 247-48.

J58: Running to Paradise (1968)

5492. ANON.: "Words," *TLS*, 66:3431 (30 Nov 1967), 1146.

J59: John Sherman & Dhoya (1969)

5493. FLETCHER, IAN: *N&Q*, os 216 / ns 18:7 (July 1971), 275-76.

5494. HENN, T. R.: *MLR*, 65:4 (Oct 1970), 891-93.

5495. SAUL, GEORGE BRANDON: *Arizona Q*, 26:2 (Summer 1970), 191-92.

J61: Uncollected Prose, I (1970)

5496. BRUNS, GERALD L.: *Spirit*, 38:4 (Winter 1972), 41-45.

5497. CAREW, RIVERS: "Marginalia," *Irish Press*, 40:182 (1 Aug 1970), 10.

5498. COLEMAN, ALEXANDER: *NYTBR*, 25 Oct 1970, 40.

5499. DONOGHUE, DENIS: "Golden Dawn," *Listener*, 84:2166 (1 Oct 1970), 457.
Also a review of J118.

5500. GELPI, BARBARA: "Misty Foreshadowings of W. B. Yeats," *CSM*, 62:231 (27 Aug 1970), 11.

5501. JEFFARES, A. NORMAN: *RES*, 22:87 (Aug 1971), 375-76.

5502. JORDAN, JOHN: "Early Nobility," *Hibernia*, 34:12 (12 June 1970), 12.

5503. KAIN, RICHARD M.: *Éire-Ireland*, 6:1 (Spring 1971), 133-36.

5504. LANGBAUM, ROBERT: "Growth of a Great Critic," *American Scholar*, 41:3 (Summer 1972), 460, 462, 464, 466.

5505. MAYHEW, GEORGE P.: *BA*, 45:3 (Summer 1971), 523.

5506. MOLESWORTH, CHARLES: "He Kept a Sword Upstairs," *Nation*, 212:2 (11 Jan 1971), 58, 60.

5507. MONTAGUE, JOHN: "The Young and the Old Campaigner," *Guardian*, 3 Sept 1970), 7.
Also a review of J119.

5508. MOORE, HARRY T.: *SatR*, 53:25 (20 June 1970), 37-39.

5509. SADDLEMYER, ANN: *JEGP*, 70:3 (July 1971), 567-69.

5509a. WEBB, TIMOTHY: *Studia Neophilologica*, 43:2 (1971), 594-96.

5510. WORDSWORTH, ANN: "Art Itself," *Spectator*, 224:7407 (13 June 1970), 790-92.

See also J6939, 6954.

J62: Reflections (1970)

5511. CRONIN, ANTHONY: "Poet above All," *Irish Press*, 41:56 (6 Mar 1971), 12.

5512. JORDAN, JOHN: "From Yeats's Journal," *Irish Independent*, 80:56 (6 Mar 1971), 6.

5513. WHITE, TERENCE DE VERE: "Inside the Factory of the Muse," *Irish Times*, #35796 (27 Feb 1971), 10.

J63: A Tower of Polished Black Stones (1971)

5514. ANON.: "Yeats as an Adolescent Dreamer," *TLS*, 71:3655 (17 Mar 1972), 311.

5515. FINNERAN, RICHARD J.: "Progress Report on the Yeats Industry," *JML*, 3:1 (Feb 1973), 129-33.
    Also a review of J64.

J64: Druid Craft (1971)

5516. ANON.: *Éire-Ireland*, 7:3 (Autumn 1972), 144-45.

5517. CLARKE, AUSTIN: "Deep Waters," *Irish Times*, #36180 (27 May 1972), 10.

5517a. LEAMON, WARREN: "Wasteland of the Imagination," *Hibernia*, 36:7 (31 Mar 1972), 10.

5518. PARKIN, ANDREW: *UTQ*, 41:4 (Summer 1972), 388-90.

5519. SAUL, GEORGE BRANDON: *MD*, 15:3 (Dec 1972), 343-44.

5520. SPIVAK, GAYATRI CHAKRAVORTY: *PQ*, 51:2 (Apr 1972), 493-95.

See also J5515.

J66: W. B. Yeats and the Designing of Ireland's Coinage (1972)

5520a. LAPPIN, MARY: "Ritual and Magic," *Hibernia*, 36:18 (22 Sept 1972), 10.

J67: Memoirs (1972)

5521. BOLAND, JOHN: "Poet's Self-Portrait," *Hibernia*, 37:3 (16 Feb 1973), 14.

5522. BRYSON, JOHN: "Unexpurgated Yeats," *Books and Bookmen*, 18:210 (Mar 1973), 52-53.

5523. ELLMANN, RICHARD: "The Confessions of W. B. Yeats," *Guardian*, 11 Jan 1973, 9.

5523a. EMPSON, WILLIAM: "Yeats and the Spirits," *NYRB*, 20:20 (13 Dec 1973), 43-45.

5523b. [FLETCHER, IAN]: "Yeats's Quest for Self-Transparency," *TLS*, 72: 3698 (19 Jan 1973), 53-55.
    A long review, discussing the *Autobiographies* in general and the rela-tion between draft and published product in particular. Correspondence by Denis Donoghue, :3700 (2 Feb 1973), 125.

5523c. HAMBURGER, MICHAEL: "Yeats: The Memoirs," *Poetry Nation*, #1 (1973), 130-32.

5524. HARDY, BARBARA: "The Memoirs of W. B. Yeats," *Spectator*, 230:7542 (13 Jan 1973), 42-43.

5524a. JEFFARES, A. NORMAN: "The Great Purple Butterfly," *Sewanee R*, 82:1 (Winter 1974), 108-18.
    Also a review of J76a.

5525. KERMODE, FRANK: "Scribbles and Revelations," *NSt*, 85:2182 (12 Jan 1973), 54-55.

5525a. LEHMANN-HAUPT, CHRISTOPHER: "Fragments of Yeats's Mask," *NYT*, 122: 42072 (2 Apr 1973), 33.

5525b. [MCSWEENEY, KERRY]: "Perfection of the Life or of the Work," *QQ*, 80:3 (Autumn 1973), 497-98.

5526. MARCUS, PHILLIP L.: "Memoir and Myth," *Irish Press*, 43:18 (20 Jan 1973), 10.

5526a. MURRAY, MICHELE: "Sure, Yeats Was a Crackpot--But Also a Great Poet," *National Observer*, 12:15 (14 Apr 1973), 23.

5526b. NYE, ROBERT: "Yeats as Bardic Poet," *Times*, #58678 (11 Jan 1973), 10.

5526c. O'HARA, J. D.: "'Before the Peacock Screamed,'" *Washington Post Book World*, 7:16 (22 Apr 1973), 13.

5527. PARKINSON, THOMAS: "Yeats Writing about Himself to Himself," *NYTBR*, 78:17 (29 Apr 1973), 2-3.

5528. PESCHMANN, HERMANN: *English*, 22:113 (Summer 1973), 83-84.

5528a. RAINE, KATHLEEN: "Man behind the Magic," *Sunday Telegraph*, #620 (14 Jan 1973), 12.

5529. TOYNBEE, PHILIP: "Behind the Yeats Mask," *Observer*, #9468 (14 Jan 1973), 34.

5530. WHITE, TERENCE DE VERE: "Closer to Yeats," *Irish Times*, #36368 (6 Jan 1973), 10.

J70/71: Beltaine/Samhain (1970)

5530a. SHARE, BERNARD: "First Principles," *Hibernia*, 36 [i.e., 35]:5 (5 Mar 1971), 20.

J76a: Fairy and Folk Tales of Ireland (1973)

5531. ANON.: "Leprechaunucopia," *TLS*, 72:3720 (22 June 1973), 726.

See also J5524a.

J118: W. B. Yeats and Margot Ruddock: Ah, Sweet Dancer (1970)

5532. ANDERSON, PATRICK: "Dance to Madness," *Sunday Telegraph*, #496 (16 Aug 1970), 8.

5533. BRONZWAER, R.: *Dutch QR*, 1:1 (1971), 42-43.

5534. FLANAGAN, THOMAS: "W. B. Yeats: The Opportunity to Love," *Hibernia*, 34:14 (7 Aug 1970), 10.

5535. KAIN, RICHARD M.: *Éire-Ireland*, 6:2 (Summer 1971), 171-74.

5536. MARTIN, AUGUSTINE: *Studies*, 60:237 (Spring 1971), 98-102.

5537. MILLAR, DAVID: "Late Love," *Irish Press*, 40:212 (5 Sept 1970), 12.

5538. RAYMOND, JOHN: "In Yeats' Shadow," *Sunday Times*, #7682 (23 Aug 1970), 26.

5539. SCOTT, PAUL: "Poet and Disciple," *Country Life*, 148:3824 (6 Aug 1970), 369.

5539a. SIMON, JOHN: "A Muse Driven Mad," *New Leader*, 54:15 (26 July 1971), 18-19.

5540. SNOW, C. P.: "Poet's Last Dance," *Financial Times*, #25208 (23 July 1970), 22.

5541. WHITE, TERENCE DE VERE: "St. Martin's Summer," *Irish Times*, #35622 (1 Aug 1970), 10.

See also J5499.

J119: W. B. Yeats and Thomas Kinsella: Davis, Mangan, Ferguson? (1970)

5542. CORRADINI FAVATI, GABRIELLA: "Tradizione e letteratura in Irlanda: Dal mito alla realtà," *Rivista di letteratura moderne e comparata*, 25:4 (Dec 1972), 273-78.

5543. GIBBON, MONK: "The Critical Balance," *Irish Independent*, 79:63 (14 Mar 1970), 10.

5544. MAXTON, HUGH: "Investigating Loss," *Hibernia*, 34:8 (17 Apr 1970), 23.

5545. WATTERS, EUGENE: "Link-Men," *Irish Press*, 40:74 (27 & 28 Mar 1970), 12.

See also J5507.

J179: Objevy (1920)

5546. Nk. [NOVÁK, BOHUMIL]: "Zapomenutá kniha" [A forgotten book], *Rozhledy*, 4:31 (7 Jan 1935), 247.

J183: Per Amica Silentia Lunae (1925)

5547. SKOUMAL, A.: *Tvar*, 3:[] (1929), 308-11.

J186: Tři hry (1928)

5548. -PA.-: *Zvon*, 29:3 (27 Oct 1928), 42-43.

See also J5483.

J199: Gedichte (1958)

5549. DRAWS-TYCHSEN, HELLMUT: "Bemühungen um Yeats," *Welt und Wort*, 14:6 (June 1959), 171-72.

J201: Versek (1960)

5550. RONAY, GYÖRGY: "Yeats versei," *Élet és irodalom*, 4:43 (21 Oct 1960), 6.

J203: Poesie (1961)

5551. PEROSA, SERGIO: *Verri*, 7:3 (Aug 1962), 90-93.

J210: Quaranta poesie (1965)

5552. BALDI, SERGIO: "Poesie di Yeats," *Approdo letterario*, 11:32 (Oct-Dec 1965), 108-9.

5553. SERPIERI, ALESSANDRO: "Poesia anglo-americana," *Ponte*, 21:10 (Oct 1965), 1316-24.
   See pp. 1322-23.

J212: Runoja (1966)

5554. TUURNA, MARJA-LEENA: "Irlannin suuri runoilija" [Ireland's great poet], *Valvoja*, 87:1 (1967), 42-44.

J223: Werke (1970-73)

5555. BLÖCKER, GÜNTER: "Die Maske eines anderen Lebens anlegen!" *FAZ*, #216 (18 Sept 1971), Literaturblatt.

5556. HELWIG, WERNER: "Yeats auf Deutsch," *Darmstädter Echo*, 28:7 (10 Jan 1972), 22.

5557. ———: "William Butler Yeats--Mystiker und Senator," *Merkur*, 26:5 (May 1972), 490-93.

5558. KLEINSTÜCK, JOHANNES: "W. B. Yeats, der letzte Romantiker," *Welt der Literatur*, 8:18 (3 Sept 1971), 5.

5559. KRAMBERG, K. H.: "Wie eine langbeinige Fliege: Ausgewählte Gedichte als Auftakt zur deutschen Yeats-Ausgabe," *Süddeutsche Zeitung*, 27:170 (17/ 18 July 1971), [117].

5560. ———: "Wovon träumen die Toten? Vision und Maske in Yeats' erzählender Prosa," *Süddeutsche Zeitung*, 27:275 (17 Nov 1971), Weihnachts-Literatur-Beilage, 5.

5561. KROHN, R[ÜDIGER]: *Wissenschaftlicher Literaturanzeiger*, 11:3 (June 1972), 84.

5562. LICHTWITZ, MANUEL: "Eine Chance für Yeats," *Frankfurter Rundschau*, #150 (3 July 1971), Zeit und Bild, VI.

5563. WALLMANN, JÜRGEN P.: "Von der Stimmung zur Rechenschaft," *Tat*, 37: 154 (3 July 1971), 33.

5564. ———: "Yeats wird entdeckt," *Darmstädter Echo*, 27:228 (2 Oct 1971), 55.

5564a. ———: "William Butler Yeats' Werke: 'Ich weiss sehr wenig von mir.' Zur Autobiographie des irischen Dichters," *Deutsche Zeitung*, #48 (30 Nov 1973), 12.

See also J1393.

IA Recordings

Entries in this section are restricted to those records that contain a
substantial amount of Yeats material, not just one or two poems. Individual poems are not cross-referenced in this bibliography, but individual
plays are. In an appendix to this section, I list some reviews and similar
material.

5565. *The Caedmon Treasury of Modern Poets Reading Their Own Poetry*. Caedmon, TC 2006, [195-]. 2 12" long-play records.
> Yeats reads "The Song of the Old Mother," "The Lake Isle of Innisfree,"
> and extracts from "Coole Park and Ballylee" (side 2).

5566. °DE MOTT, BENJAMIN: *Beyond Dailiness: Yeats*. NY: McGraw-Hill, 1968.
45 minutes.
> A tape recording made live at the Poetry Center of the Young Men's
> and Young Women's Hebrew Association, New York.

5567. MCKENNA, SIOBHAN: *Siobhan McKenna Reading Irish Poetry*. Spoken Arts,
707, [1956]. 1 12" long-play record.
> Includes 16 Yeats poems; cover note by Padraic Colum.

5568. °MACLIAMMOIR, MICHAEL: *Michael MacLiammoir in Revolutionary Speeches
and Poems of Ireland*. Spoken Arts, 749, [1959]. 1 12" long-play record.
> Includes a Yeats selection.

5569. °MASSEY, RAYMOND (ed): *Helen Hayes, Raymond Massey, Thomas Mitchell*.
RCA Victor, LM 1812-13, [1955]. 2 12" long-play records.
> Includes some Yeats poems.

5570. O'CONNOR, FRANK: *The Irish Tradition*. Folkways, FL 9825, 1958. 1 12"
long-play record.
> O'Connor lectures on Irish literature, with special emphasis on the
> revival period, and reads and comments upon the recognition scene in
> *On Baile's Strand* and "A Prayer for My Daughter." The text of the
> lecture accompanies the record. See also J5590.

5571. PARTCH, HARRY: *Sophocles' King Oedipus*. Based on the version by
William Butler Yeats. San Francisco: Wolfe, [1952?]. 1 16" record.
> A musical drama performed at Mills College, Oakland, California, in
> Mar 1952; the record is in the Mills College Library. I have been
> unable to locate a printed score. For a review see Wilford Leach,
> "Music for Words Perhaps," *TAM*, 37:1 (Jan 1953), 65-68.

5572. PUTSCHÉ, THOMAS: *The Cat and the Moon*. Opera in one act, based on a
play by W. B. Yeats. Composers Recordings, Inc., CRI SD 245, [196-]. 1 12"
long-play record.
> Composed in 1957; performed by the Contemporary Chamber Players, Uni-
> versity of Chicago (three singers), conducted by Ralph Shapey. For
> the unpublished score see J5692.

5573. ROBINSON, LENNOX: *Lennox Robinson Presents William Butler Yeats*.
Spoken Arts, 751-52, [1958?]. 2 12" long-play records.
> On the first record Robinson reads his own reminiscences of Yeats,
> together with some poems; on the second record he reads an essay on
> Yeats as a playwright and some passages from *The Countess Cathleen*
> and *Deirdre*. See also J5589 and 5590.
>
> I do not know whether this recording is identical with °*W. B. Yeats:
> Poems and Memories*. Read by Lennox Robinson. HEAR (Home Educational
> Art Records, Ltd.), 751.

5574. SOPHOCLES: *Oedipus Rex*. The William Butler Yeats translation, chorus music by Thorpe Davies, additional dialogue by E. V. Watling, directed by Tyrone Guthrie. Caedmon, TC 2012, [1957]. 2 12" long-play records.
From the sound track of the motion picture starring Douglas Campbell with the members of the Stratford, Ontario, Shakespearean Festival Players.

5575. THOMAS, DYLAN: *An Evening with Dylan Thomas Reading His Own Poetry and Other Poems*. Caedmon, TC 1157, 1963. 1 12" long-play record.
Reads three Yeats poems: "In Tara's Halls," "The Three Bushes," and "Lapis Lazuli." Recorded at the University of California, 10 Apr 1950.

5576. °———: *Dylan Thomas Reads the Poetry of William Butler Yeats and Others*. Caedmon, TC 1353, [1971]. 1 12" long-play record.

5577. YEATS, W. B.: *The Countess Cathleen*. Incidental music composed by Robert M. Abramson, performed by Siobhán McKenna, John Neville, and others, directed by Tom Clancy. Tradition Recording, TLP 501, [1957?]. 1 12" long-play record.
Notes on slipcase by Padraic Colum.

5578. ———: *Five One Act Plays*. Caedmon, TRS 315, [1966]. 3 12" long-play records.
Contains *The Cat and the Moon*, *The Only Jealousy of Emer*, *The Pot of Broth*, *Purgatory*, and *The Words upon the Window-Pane*; directed by Howard Sackler. A 31-page booklet is included, containing the texts and an article by Walter Starkie, "The Irish Dramatic Movement," 3-4, and by Cyril Cusack, "From Behind the Mask," 5-6.

5579. ———: *Noh Plays*. Directed by Barry Cassin and Noel MacMahon, music composed and directed by Gerard Victory. Argo, RG 468-69, 1965. 2 12" long-play records.
Contains *At the Hawk's Well*, *The Dreaming of the Bones*, *The Cat and the Moon*, and *The Resurrection*; cover note by Noel MacMahon. Reviewed by Charles Acton, "Four Plays by Yeats," *Irish Times*, #34363 (16 Feb 1966), 10.

5580. ———: *The Only Jealousy of Emer*. Counterpoint/Esoteric, 5506, [195-]. 1 12" long-play record.
Directed by Bonnie Bird, music by Lou Harrison, cover note by Barry Ulanov. The recording is based on a performance "given by students and instructors in the Summer Workshop in Dance and Drama at Reed College in Oregon in the summer of 1949."

5581. °———: *Poems*. Read by Mary O'Farrell and C. Day Lewis. Columbia [London], DX 1637-38, [19--]. 2 78rpm records.

5582. °———: *Poems*. Read by Robert Speaight. Harvard Vocarium Records, L 1012-13, 1941. 1 78rpm record (12").

5583. °———: *Poems*. Spoken according to his own directions by V. C. Clinton-Baddeley, Marjorie Westbury, and Jill Balcon. Jupiter, jur OOB2, [19--]. 1 10" long-play record.
See also J5590.

5584. ———: *The Poems of William Butler Yeats*. Read by Yeats, Siobhan McKenna, and Michael MacLiammoir. Spoken Arts, 753, [1959?]. 1 12" long-play record.
Also on °Argo, R 182, [19--]. See J5588-90.

5585. ————: *The Poetry of Yeats*. Read by Siobhan McKenna and Cyril Cusack. Caedmon, TC 1081, 1958. 1 12" long-play record.
See also J5588 and 5590.

5586. °————: *W. B. Yeats, June 13, 1865: A Centenary Record*. Jupiter, JEP OC38, [1965]. 1 7" record.
Read by Gabriel Woolf, V. C. Clinton-Baddeley, and Michael Gwynn.

5587. ————: *Yeats*. Read by Chris Curran, Jim Norton, Arthur O'Sullivan, Sheila Manahan. Argo, RG 449, [1966]. 1 12" long-play record.
Thirty-five poems from all periods.

Appendix to Section IA

5588. ANON.: "Verse on the Record," *TLS*, 60:3098 (4 July 1961), 434.
Review of J5584 and 5585.

5589. GREENE, DAVID: "Recordings of William Butler Yeats," *Evergreen R*, 2:8 (Spring 1959), 200-201.
Review of J5573 and 5584.

5590. ROACH, HELEN: *Spoken Records*. NY: Scarecrow Press, 1963. 213 p.
Reviews of J5584 (pp. 46-47), 5585 (pp. 69-70), 5583 (pp. 127-28), 5570 (pp. 150-51), and 5573 (pp. 155-56).

5591. SLOCOMBE, MARIE: "Cultural Documents," *TLS*, 69:3568 (16 July 1970), 774.
Letter to the editor referring to the recordings that Yeats made for the B.B.C.

See also J12, 516, 529.

IB Films

5592. °*Cradle of Genius*. Dublin: Plough Productions, 1961. 16mm black and white film, 33 minutes.
Director: Paul Rotha; commentary: Frank O'Connor; music: Gerard Victory; cast: Siobhan McKenna, Sean Barlow, Maureen Delaney, May Craig, Cyril Cusack.
Summary: A tribute to the poets, playwrights, and actors who contributed to the fame of the Abbey Theatre from 1930 to 1950. Presents dialogues and soliloquies performed by well-known Irish actors who reminisce about Yeats, Synge, Lady Gregory, F. J. McCormick, and the Fay brothers. Includes an interview between Sean O'Casey and Barry Fitzgerald. Filmed in the ruins of the old Abbey Theatre. (Description adapted from the entry in the National Union Catalog of Motion Pictures and Film Strips, 1963-67.) See also J6617.

5593. *Horseman, Pass By! The Story of a Poet: W. B. Yeats (1865-1939)*. Film script. [London]: B.B.C. Television, [1965?]. ii, 25 p.
Narrated by Frank O'Connor and Brendan Kennelly, special music composed by Gerard Victory, directed and produced by Malcolm Brown. Broadcast on 23 Jan 1966. (I have not seen the film; the script is in the National Library of Ireland, P2478.)
For a review of the film see "Notes on Broadcasting," *Times*, #56542 (29 Jan 1966), 5. An edited version of Frank O'Connor's contribution was published as "'A Gambler's Throw': On W. B. Yeats," *Listener*, 75: 1925 (17 Feb 1966), 237-39.

5594. °*W. B. Yeats--A Tribute.* Dublin: National Film Institute, 1950.
16mm black and white film, 23 minutes.
    Directed and written by John D. Sheridan, narrated by Cyril Cusack,
poetry reading by Siobhan McKenna and Micheal MacLiammoir, music by
Eamonn Gallchobhair. Traces the career of the poet Yeats by combining
scenes of places that played an important part in his life--Sligo
County, Dublin, and London. Relevant quotations from his poems are
read to create an impression of the man and his work. (Description
adapted from the entry in the National Union Catalog, 1953-57, 28:
905.)

5595. *Yeats Country.* Dublin: Department of External Affairs of Ireland,
1965. 16mm color film, 18 minutes.
    Producers: Joe Mendoza, Patrick Carey; director and photographer:
Patrick Carey; literary advisers: T. R. Henn, Liam Miller; commenta-
tor: Tom St. John Berry; music: Brian Boydell; editor: Ann Chegwidden.
The film visually re-creates the moods and impressions of the poetry
of Yeats with scenes of mountains, lakes, rivers, and buildings of
Ireland. Recounts some of the legends from which Yeats drew his
material. Discusses his poetry in relation to his life and social
environment and the literary movement of the early 20th century.
(Description adapted from the entry in the National Union Catalog of
Motion Pictures and Film Strips, Apr-June 1968, p. 55.)
    Reviewed by Liam Miller, "Patrick Carey and the Making of *Yeats
Country*," *Ireland of the Welcomes*, 17:3 (Sept-Oct 1968), 19-30 (illus-
trated).

5596. °*Young Cassidy.* London: Sextant Films, released in the United States
by Metro-Goldwin-Mayer, 1965. Color film, 108 minutes.
    Producers: Robert D. Graff, Robert Emmett Ginna; director: Jack Card-
iff; screenplay: John Whiting; music: Sean O Riada; director of pho-
tography: Ted Sciafe; editor: Anne V. Coates; cast: Rod Taylor, Julie
Christie, Michael Redgrave, Edith Evans, Flora Robson, Maggie Smith.
Based on O'Casey's autobiography. A biographical drama about the
literary rebel Sean O'Casey and his life in Dublin in 1911, during
the troubled times of opposition to the British. (Description adapted
from the National Union Catalog of Motion Pictures and Film Strips,
1963-67.)
    One of the characters in the film is Yeats; cf. Eileen O'Casey,
Sean (J7160), pp. 283, 287.

See also J7178.

IC Musical Renderings

It is amazing to see how many Yeats poems and plays have been set to music,
although it has to be admitted that more than 25 of the 125 or so entries
in this section record the various arrangements of folk tunes made for
"Down by the Salley Gardens." Yeats himself was less than happy with the
compositions; Robert Frost relates that Yeats once "said that nothing he
hated more than having his poems set to music--it stole the show" (Cleanth
Brooks and Robert Penn Warren: *Conversations on the Craft of Poetry*, NY:
Holt, Rinehart & Winston, 1961. P. 13). Ethel Mannin reports a similar
opinion (J727).
    Entries are arranged alphabetically by composer with the exception of
the music contained in Yeats's own books, which are listed under Yeats.
Apart from "Down by the Salley Gardens," all entries are cross-referenced
to the poems and plays that were set to music (see sections DD and EE). A

great many compositions are unpublished, but have been deposited in public libraries. These are cited by composer, title, MS., year, and the library (DLC: Library of Congress; ICN: Newberry Library, Chicago; IU: University of Illinois Library at Urbana-Champaign; NN: New York Public Library).

I include a few items on the authority of Grove (J432), although I have not been able to locate a printed or MS. score. I also suspect that with the help of better bibliographical tools many more items could be found. For literature on Yeats and music the reader is referred to index NE and to section FF ("Speaking to the Psaltery").

5597. °ALTER, MARTHA: "A Prayer for My Daughter," MS., 1962 (DLC).

5598. ASTON, PETER: *Five Songs of Crazy Jane*. For unaccompanied soprano. London: Novello, 1964.
These songs are "I Am of Ireland," "Crazy Jane Grown Old Looks at the Dancers," "Those Dancing Days Are Gone," "Crazy Jane Talks with the Bishop," and "Three Things."

5599. °AUSTIN, FREDERIC: *Love's Pilgrimage*. Three songs for medium voice and piano forte. London: Enoch, 1920.
Contains "He Wishes for the Cloths of Heaven."

5600. °BANTOCK, GRANVILLE: *The Hosting of the Sidhe*. Part-song for unaccompanied double chorus of mixed voices. London: Williams, 1930.

5601. BARBER, SAMUEL: *Collected Songs for High Voice*. NY: Schirmer, 1955.
"The Secrets of the Old, op. 13, no. 2," 34-37. Composed in 1941.

5602. °BARON, STEVE: "Her Anxiety," MS., 1966 (DLC).

5603. °BEATSON, THOMAS JEFFERSON: *Down by the Salley Gardens*. For male chorus a capella. NY: Flammer, 1951.

5604. BERGER, ARTHUR VICTOR: *Three Poems of Yeats from "Words for Music, Perhaps."* NY: New Music, 1950. (*New Music: A Quarterly*, 24:1 [Oct 1950].)
"Crazy Jane on the Day of Judgment," "His Confidence," and "Girl's Song."

5605. BERKELEY, LENNOX: *Colonus' Praise*. For chorus and orchestra, op. 31. [London, before 1951].
Copy in IU.

5606. BESLEY, MAURICE: *The Angels Are Stooping: Song*. London: Enoch, 1923.
"A Cradle Song."

5607. BLANK, ALLAN: "Eight Songs for Voice and Piano," MS., 1957 (DLC).
Contains "Down by the Salley Gardens," "To an Isle in the Water," "The Falling of the Leaves," and "Brown Penny."

5608. °BOOTH, THOMAS: "When You Are Old," MS., 1968 (DLC).

5609. BRAUN, RUTH FISHER: "The Lake Isle of Innisfree," MS., n.d. (NN).

5610. °BRIAN, HAVERGAL: "Songs." Words by W. B. Yeats. Grove, 1:932. Further details not available.

5611. °BRIDGE, FRANK: *When You Are Old*. London: Chappell, 1920.

5612. °BRIGGS, ALICE: "Down by the Salley Gardens," MS., 1961 (DLC).

5613. BRITTEN, BENJAMIN: *Folk-Song Arrangements for Voice and Piano*. London: Boosey & Hawkes, 1943-61. 6 v.
"The Salley Gardens," 1:1-3.

5614. °BRUMBY, COLIN: *The Cloths of Heaven*. Song for female voices. London: Boosey, 1961.

5615. °BRYSON, ERNEST: "The Cloak, the Boat, and the Shoes." For chorus and orchestra. Grove, 1:990. Further details not available.

5616. °CAHN, RICHARD: "Down by the Salley Gardens," MS., 1970 (DLC).

5617. CAMPBELL-TIPTON, [LOUIS]: *All the Words That I Gather*. Song with piano accompaniment. NY: Schirmer, 1911.
"Where My Books Go."

5618. CARPENTER, JOHN ALDEN: *The Player Queen*. Song from an unfinished play by W. B. Yeats. NY: Schirmer, 1915.

5619. CHANDLER, LEN H.: "I Made My Song a Coat," *Broadside*, #65 (15 Dec 1965), [8].

5620. CLARKE, REBECCA: *Songs*. London: Rogers, 1928.
Includes "The Cloths of Heaven," "Down by the Salley Gardens," "Shy One" ["To an Isle in the Water"], and "A Dream [of Death]."

5621. COERNE, LOUIS ADOLPHE: *Three Songs for High Voice with Piano Accompaniment*. NY: Schirmer, 1919.
Includes "Into the Twilight."

5622. °COHN, JAMES MYRON: "Music for *The Only Jealousy of Emer*," MS., 1955 (DLC).

5623. CROSSE, GORDON: *Purgatory*. Opera in 1 act, op. 18. German translation by Ernst Roth. London: Oxford UP, 1968.
Commissioned by B.B.C. 2 Television and first performed at the Cheltenham Festival, 7 July 1966.

5624. °CROSSLEY-HOLLAND, PETER: "Two Mystical Songs for Baritone and Orchestra," 1945. Grove, 2:544.
One of the songs is "Into the Twilight." No further details available.

5625. CURRY, ARTHUR MANSFIELD: *The Fiddler of Dooney*. Song for bass or baritone. Boston: Thompson, 1909.

5626. °DEALE, EDGAR MARTIN: *Down by the Salley Gardens*. London: Elkin, 1957.

5627. °DE BEER, ALAN: *Down by the Salley Gardens: Song*. London: Chester, 1935.

5628. DEL RIEGO, TERESA: *How Shall I Miss You (Cradle Song)*. NY: Chappell, 1914.

5629. °DONOVAN, RICHARD: *Down by the Salley Gardens*. Air: The Maids of Mourne Shore, arranged for soprano 1 and 2 and alto. NY: Galaxy Music, 1931.

5630. DOUTY, NICHOLAS: *Two Songs for a Medium Voice with Piano Accompaniment*. NY: Schirmer, 1913.
Includes "A Cradle Song."

5631. °DROSTE, DOREEN: *Red Hanrahan's Song about Ireland*. For four-part chorus of mixed voices with piano accompaniment. NY: Associated Music Publishers, 1966.

5632. DUKE, JOHN WOODS: *Yellow Hair*. Song for medium voice and piano accompaniment. Boston: Row Music Co., 1953.
"For Anne Gregory."

5633. DUNHILL, THOMAS FREDERICK: *The Wind among the Reeds.* A cycle of four songs for tenor voice and orchestra, op. 30. London: Stainer & Bell, 1911.
"To Dectora" (reprinted from *Dome*, ns 5:3 [Jan 1900], 231-33; now "He Thinks of Those Who Have Spoken Evil of His Beloved"), "The Host of the Air," "The Cloths of Heaven," and "The Fiddler of Dooney."

5634. DUNN, JAMES P.: *Album of New Songs.* Volume one for high voice. NY: Fischer, 1917.
"A Faery Song" (#5).

5635. °DYER-BENNET, RICHARD: "The Salley Gardens," MS., 1966 (DLC).

5636. EGK, WERNER: *Musik--Wort--Bild: Texte und Anmerkungen, Betrachtungen und Gedanken.* München: Langen-Müller, 1960. 314 p.
"Irische Legende: Oper in fünf Bildern," 113-82. Reprint of *Irische Legende: Text zu einer Oper.* Freiburg i. B.: Klemm-Seemann, [1955]. 48 p. An opera based on *The Countess Cathleen.*
"Ausbruch aus der Hoffnungslosigkeit: Ein Briefwechsel zur Oper *Irische Legende* anlässlich der Uraufführung bei den Salzburger Festspielen 1955," 183-96; reprinted from *Frankfurter Hefte*, 10:5 (May 1955), 318-25. An exchange of letters between Egk and Reinhold Kreile.
"Rundfunkeinrichtung zur *Irischen Legende*," 197-200. The changes made for the radio version.
See also J3632 and 3644a.

5637. EICHHEIM, HENRY: *Seven Songs.* Boston: Boston Music Co., 1910.
"The Heart of the Woman" (#1) and "Aedh Wishes His Beloved Were Dead" ["He Wishes His Beloved Were Dead"] (#7).

5638. ELGAR, SIR EDWARD: *Incidental Music and Funeral March, "Grania and Diarmid"* [*sic*] *(George Moore and W. B. Yeats)* [op. 42]. London: Novello, 1902.
Includes a rendering of "There Are Seven That Pull the Thread."

5639. FAIRCHILD, BLAIR: *Three Songs with Pianoforte Accompaniment.* Boston: Thompson, 1909.
"The Lake Isle of Innisfree" (#1).

5640. °FAY, VERNON: *The Song of the Old Mother.* For male voices. Charlotte, N.C.: Brodt Music Co., 1966.

5641. FIELDEN, THOMAS PERCEVAL: *The Lake Isle of Innisfree.* London: Breitkopf & Härtel, 1911.

5642. FLORES, BERNAL: "The Land of Heart's Desire (A Chamber Opera)," °Ph.D. thesis, U of Rochester, 1964. 226 p. (*DA*, 28:2 [Aug 1967], 707A.)
"The whole play, word by word, is used as a libretto in the opera. . . . The style of the music is atonal . . ." (abstract).

5643. FOGEL, CLYDE VAN NUYS: *Two Poems by William Butler Yeats.* For solo voice with piano accompaniment. NY: Schirmer, 1911.
"He Wishes for the Cloths of Heaven" and "He Wishes His Beloved Were Dead."

5644. FOOTE, ARTHUR: *The Lake Isle of Innisfree.* For soprano or tenor. Boston: Schmidt, 1921.

5645. GANZ, RUDOLPH: *The Angels Are Stooping.* A song with piano accompaniment. NY: Schirmer, 1917.
"A Cradle Song."

5646. GILBERT, HENRY F.: *Faery Song*. Newton Center, Mass.: Wa-Wan Press, 1905.
"The wind blows out of the gates of day . . ." from *The Land of Heart's Desire*.

5647. GILMAN, LAWRENCE: "The Heart of the Woman (For Contralto Voice),"
Wa-Wan Series of American Compositions, 2:1 (Sept 1903), 12-14.

5648. ————: "A Dream of Death: Recitation, with Piano Accompaniment,"
Wa-Wan Series of American Compositions, 2:2 (Sept 1903), 1-3.

5649. ————: "The Curlew: Recitation, with Piano Accompaniment," *Wa-Wan Series of American Compositions*, 3:1 (July 1904), 1-2.

5650. GRAVES, ALFRED PERCEVAL (ed): *The Irish Song Book with Original Irish Airs*. London: Unwin, 1895 [1894]. xxiv, 188 p.
"Down by the Salley Gardens." Air--The Maids of Mourne Shore, p. 55.

5651. GURNEY, IVOR: *Twenty* [i.e., Forty] *Songs*. London: Oxford UP, 1938-59. 4 v.
Contains "Down by the Salley Gardens" and "Cathleen ni Houlihan" (°vol. 1), "The Folly of Being Comforted" (°vol. 2), and "A Cradle Song" and "The Fiddler of Dooney" (vol. 4).

5652. °HADLEY, PATRICK: "Ephemera for Tenor (or Soprano) and Chamber Orchestra," 1924. Grove, 4:10. Further details not available.

5653. ————: *A Faery Song Sung by the People of Faery over Diarmuid and Grania, in Their Bridal Sleep under a Cromlech*. For female chorus and orchestra. London: Oxford UP, 1927.

5654. °HAENSELMAN, CARL FERDINAND: "Three Chamber Orchestra Scores for Modern Dance," M.A. thesis, U of Colorado, 1950.
One of them is based on *The King of the Great Clock Tower*.

5655. °HALL, ARTHUR E.: *Down by the Salley Gardens*. Arranged for male chorus unaccompanied. Air: The Maids of Mourne Shore. NY: Galaxy Music, 1933.

5656. °HARRIS, EDWARD: *Cloths of Dreams*. Words by W. B. Yeats. NY: Boosey & Hawkes, 1950.
Presumably "He Wishes for the Cloths of Heaven."

5657. °HARRISON, LOU: "The Only Jealousy of Emer: Opera," 1949. Grove, 4:116: "after a story of W. B. Yeats."
See also J5580.

5658. °HART, FRITZ: "The Land of Heart's Desire: Opera in 1 Act, Op. 18," 1914. Grove, 4:121. Further details not available.

5659. °HARTY, HAMILTON: *The Fiddler of Dooney: Song*. London: Boosey, 1938.

5560. °HARVEY, JONATHAN: "A Full Moon in March: Opera," 1967.
I do not know whether this has been published. See the announcement in the *Times*, #56861 (8 Feb 1967), 6, that the opera would be performed at the Southampton University Arts Festival.

5661. °HENDERSON, RAY: *Down by the Salley Gardens*. Arranged on an Irish folk tune. N.p.: Kjos, 1957.

5662. °HERBERT, MURIEL: *The Lake Isle of Innisfree*. Arranged by Basil Ramsey. London: Elkin, 1963.

5663. °HILL, MABEL WOOD: "To the Poet Who Claims That His Rhythms Are Lost in Song--Quintette of Oboe, Violin, Viola, Piano, and Voice Reciting with Rhythms and Meaning of the Poems of W. B. Yeats," MS., before 1941 (DLC).
> Contains "Be You Still" ["To His Heart, Bidding It Have No Fear"], "Cloths of Heaven," "Innisfree," and "The Curlew" ["He Reproves the Curlew"].

5664. °HINCHCLIFFE, IRVIN: *Down by the Salley Gardens*. In G. London: Murdoch, 1931.

5665. HOMER, SIDNEY: *Four Songs with Piano Accompaniment, op. 17*. NY: Schirmer, 1906.
> "Michael Robartes Bids His Beloved Be at Peace" (#1) ["He Bids His Beloved Be at Peace"].

5666. ————: *The Fiddler of Dooney*. Song with piano accompaniment, op. 20. NY: Schirmer, 1909.

5667. °HOUSMAN, ROSALIE: "The Angels Are Stooping," MS., 1935 (NN).
> "A Cradle Song."

5668. °————: "[The] Song of the Old Mother," MS., n.d. (NN).

5669. HOWE, MARY: *Songs*. Volume 3: Baritone songs. NY: Galaxy Music, 1959.
> Includes "The Lake Isle of Innisfree."

5670. HUGHES, HERBERT: *Irish Country Songs*. Edited, arranged, and for the most part collected by Herbert Hughes. London: Boosey, 1909-36. 4 v.
> "Down by the Salley Gardens," 1:37-39. Set to the air of The Maids of Mourne Shore, for voice and piano.

5671. °HUGHES, SPIKE: "Incidental Music for *The Player Queen*," 1927. Grove, 4:400. Further details not available.

5672. IRELAND, JOHN: *Songs Sacred and Profane*. With piano accompaniment. London: Schott, 1934.
> "The Salley Gardens," #4.

5673. °JOHNSON, REGINALD THOMAS: *Down by the Salley Gardens*. Part-song for men's voices, unaccompanied. London: Curwen, 1952.

5674. °JOUBERT, JOHN: *Incantation*. For unaccompanied chorus and soprano solo. Words from the play *The Resurrection* by W. B. Yeats. London: Novello, 1957.

5675. °KAHN, RACHAEL: "A Collection of English, American, and Irish Verse Set to Music." Arranged by Murray Ross, MS., 1961 (DLC).
> Volume 2 contains one or more Yeats poems; details not available.

5676. °KALOMIRIS, MANOLIS: *The Shadowy Waters*. London: British Broadcasting Corporation, [1953].
> "A musical dramatic poem in one Act with a Prologue based on the poem of W. B. Yeats translated into Greek by Veta Pezopoulos. Retranslated into English by Geoffrey Dunn who has used, wherever possible, Yeats's own wording" ([1]). Performed on the B.B.C. Third Programme, 23 and 26 Oct 1953.

5677. °KASTLE, LEONARD: "Two Songs of Love," MS., 1957 (DLC).
> One of them with words by Yeats; details not available.

5678. °KEATS, DONALD: *A Drinking Song*. For four-part chorus of men's voices a cappella. NY: Schirmer, 1965.

5679. °LE FLEMING, CHRISTOPHER: *To an Isle in the Water*. London: Chester, 1931.

5680. LEHMANN, LIZA: *The Lake Isle of Innisfree: Song*. NY: Boosey, 1911.

5681. LOEFFLER, CHARLES MARTIN: *Five Irish Fantasies for Voice and Orchestra or Piano*. NY: Schirmer, 1934 [1908]. 5 v.
Contains "The Hosting of the Sidhe," "The Host of the Air," "The Fiddler of Dooney," and "The Ballad of the Foxhunter."

5682. °MACONCHY, ELIZABETH: "Six Settings of Yeats Poems for Three-Part Women's Chorus, with Harp, Clarinet and 2 Horns," 1951 [?]. Grove, 5:483. Further details not available.

5683. °MANHEIM, ERNEST: "Down by the Salley Gardens," MS., 1948 (DLC).

5684. °MISHKIN, HENRY GEORGE: *Down by the Salley Gardens*. For four-part chorus of men's voices, a cappella. Old Irish air from The Maids of Mourne Shore. Boston: Schirmer, 1951.

5685. °MITCHELL, HELEN I.: *Down by the Salley Gardens*. Waterloo, Ont.: Waterloo Music, 1957.

5686. °MOERAN, ERNEST JOHN: *A Dream of Death*, London: Oxford UP, 1925.

5687. MOFFAT, ALFRED: *The Minstrelsy of Ireland: 200 Songs Adapted to Their Traditional Airs* [. . .]. London: Augener, 1897. x, 346 p.
"Down by the Salley Gardens," 47. For voice and piano, adapted from the air Far beyond Yon Mountains.

5688. °NABOKOV, NICOLAS: *Brown Penny*. For women's voices. NY: Associated Music Publishers, 1957.

5689. °NELSON, HAVELOCK: *The Lonely of Heart (Land of Heart's Desire)*. London: Curwen, 1968.

5690. °PARKER, ALICE, and ROBERT SHAW: *Down by the Salley Gardens*. For four-part chorus of men's voices a cappella, set on a traditional Irish air. [NY]: Lawson-Gould Music, 1961.

5691. °PLUMSTEAD, MARY: *Down by the Salley Gardens*. London: Curwen, 1951.

5692. °PUTSCHÉ, THOMAS: "The Cat and the Moon." An opera in 1 act based upon the play of W. B. Yeats, MS., 1969 (DLC).
See also J5572.

5693. RICCI, VITTORIO: *Three Musical Ideas*. London: Williams, 1909.
Contains "A Cradle Song" for voice and piano.

5694. RIETI, VITTORIO: *Two Songs between Two Waltzes*. NY: General Music / London: Novello, 1964.
"The Fiddler of Dooney (A Waltz)," "When You Are Old (A Barcarolle)," "Maid Quiet (A Madrigal)," and "Brown Penny (Another Waltz)."

5695. °ROBBINS, REGINALD C.: *When You Are Old*. Songs for bass or baritone, no. 74. Paris: Senart, 1929.

5696. °ROBERTSON, HUGH S.: *The Cloths of Heaven*. Song, arranged by Maurice Jacobson. London: Curwen, 1961.

5697. SCHÖNTHAL, RUTH: "Works," MS., 1949-52 (ICN).
Contains "9 Lyric-Dramatic Songs for Mezzo Soprano & Piano by D. B. Yeats [*sic*]": "The Lake Isle of Innisfree," "The Pity of Love," "The Everlasting Voices," "To a Child in the Wind," "He Tells of a Valley

Full of Lovers," "A Coat," "The Travail of Passion," "That the Night Come," and "The Second Coming."

5698. SHAW, MARTIN: *The Land of Heart's Desire*. London: Curwen, 1917. Musical rendering of "The wind blows out of the gates of the day."

5699. ————: *Down by the Salley Gardens*. London: Curwen, 1919.

5700. °SKUTA, RONALD GEORGE: "The Cloak, the Boat and the Shoes," MS., 1970 (DLC).

5701. °————: "Mad as the Mist and Snow," MS., 1970 (DLC).

5702. °STEVENS, BERNARD: *Running to Paradise*. London: Novello, 1968.

5703. °SWAIN, FREDA: "Unpublished Operatic Setting for *The Shadowy Waters*," n.d. / "The Harp of Aengus after W. B. Yeats." For violin and orchestra, 1924. Grove, 8:199.

5704. °TAYLOR, STANLEY: *Down by the Salley Gardens*. Set for voice and piano (or harp) with ad lib recorder. London: Curwen, 1963.

5705. °TIPPETT, MICHAEL: *Lullaby*. For six voices, words by W. B. Yeats. London: Schott, 1960.

5706. °TOBIN, JOHN: *Down by the Salley Gardens*. Song for voice and piano. London: Elkins, 1938.

5707. °VINE, JOHN: *Down by the Salley Gardens*. Arranged on an Irish air for tenor solo and male voices. London: Oxford UP, 1948.

5708. °WALTER, DAVID: "[The] Song of Wandering Aengus," MS., 1969 (DLC).

5709. WARLOCK, PETER: *The Curlew*. For tenor voice, flute, English horn, and string quartet. London: Stainer & Bell, 1924.
   Contains the following poems: "He Reproves the Curlew," "The Lover Mourns for the Loss of Love," "The Withering of the Boughs," and "He Hears the Cry of the Sedge." Yeats did not like the music; see J727.

5710. °WARREN, RAYMOND: *Elegy: The Lover Mourns for the Loss of Love*. Part-song, unaccompanied. London: Novello, 1964.

5711. ————: *Songs of Old Age*. A song cycle for voice and piano, words by W. B. Yeats. Sevenoaks: Novello, 1971.
   "Men Improve with the Years," "The Old Men Admiring Themselves in the Water," "O Do Not Love Too Long," "A Song," "From Oedipus at Colonnus," "After Long Silence," "Those Dancing Days Are Gone," and "Sailing to Byzantium."

5712. °WEBBER, LLOYD: *The Fiddler of Dooney*. Two-part song. London: Ascherberg, Hopwood & Crew, 1964.

5713. WEIGEL, EUGENE: *Four Songs for Women's Voices*. South Hadley, Mass.: Valley Music Press, 1950.
   "To an Isle in the Water," "A Drinking Song," "A Cradle Song," and "To a Squirrel at Kyle-na-no."

5714. WEISGALL, HUGO: *Purgatory*. Opera in 1 act. Bryn Mawr, Pa.: Merion Music, 1959.

5715. °WERTHER, R. T.: *The Lake Isle of Innisfree*. Sydney: Chappell, 1966.

5716. WHITHORNE, EMERSON: *Shy One*. A song for medium voice with piano accompaniment, op. 31, no. 2. NY: Schirmer, 1916.
   "To an Isle in the Water."

5717. °WOODGATE, LESLIE: *Down by the Salley Gardens*. Irish air for 2 treble voices and piano. London: Oxford UP, 1950.

5718. WORDEN, MAGDALEN: *Cradle-Song*. Song for solo voice with piano accompaniment. NY: Schirmer, 1912.

5719. YEATS, W. B.: *Four Plays for Dancers*. London: Macmillan, 1921. xi, 138 p.
    Edmond [*sic*] Dulac: "Music for *At the Hawk's Well*," 89-101; includes a note on the instruments.
    Walter Morse Rummel: "Music for *The Dreaming of the Bones*," 107-25; includes notes on instruments and performance.

5720. ───────: *Sophocles' King Oedipus: A Version for the Modern Stage*. London: Macmillan, 1928. vi, 61 p.
    Music for the chorus and a note, signed L[ennox] R[obinson], pp. 55-61.

5721. ───────: *Wheels and Butterflies*. NY: Macmillan, 1935. ix, 163 p.
    George Antheil: "Music for *Fighting the Waves*," 141-63.

5722. ───────: *New Poems*. Dublin: Cuala Press, 1938. iv, 47 p.
    Edmund Dulac's music for the following poems appears on pp. 41-45: "The Three Bushes," traditional Irish airs for "The Curse of Cromwell," "Come Gather round Me Parnellites," "The Pilgrim," and "Colonel Martin."

See also J4195, 5571.

JA Poems

Some of the most dreary or most exhilarating Yeatsiana (depending on the reader's attitude) may be found among the poems written about Yeats, many of which are, regrettably, quite worthless. The subject proves to be an irresistible attraction, not only among young Irish poets from the 1940s onward who try to digest their literary past. Easily the best poem among the lot is Auden's elegy; three quotations from others may serve to illustrate my point (authors will remain mercifully unidentified):

> And, through the mists of Innisfree
> in undiluted glory--See!
> The feckless fairies of the isles are dancing round his tomb.

> Yeats would have it so;
> Truth without device,
> Every word a blow,
> None struck twice.
> Yet the magic is
> That the music sings:
> A naked Goddess his,
> But sheathed in wings.

> A son of Sligo now careers sublime,
> The truest, sweltest poet of our time,
> Whose fame in every cultured nation rings,
> In cots of peasants, palaces of kings,
> Whose mystic call allures us to explore
> Enchanting fields we never saw before.
> Immortal Yeats! long may thy course aspire;
> Long may thy adept fingers tune the lyre;
> Long may the lustre of thy mind aspire,
> The brightest flame cast from the muse's fire.

As in the case of the preceding section and for the same reasons, I am aware that I have not picked up all the relevant material; much of it was found accidentally. I am grateful for additions; perhaps one day an undaunted enthusiast will collect these gems and publish them.

5723. ALLOTT, KENNETH: *The Ventriloquist's Doll*. London: Cresset Press, [1943]. 64 p.
"The Memory of Yeats," 41-43; reprinted from *Poetry London*, 2:8 (Nov-Dec 1942), 66-67.

5724. AUDEN, WYSTAN HUGH, and LOUIS MACNEICE: *Letters from Iceland*. London: Faber & Faber, 1937. 268 p.
See p. 242.

5725. AUDEN, W. H.: "In Memory of W. B. Yeats," *New Republic*, 98:1266 (8 Mar 1939), 123.
This version does not include the section beginning "You were silly like us." See the version published in *London Mercury*, 39:234 (Apr 1939), 578-80, which includes the omitted section but lacks line 30 of the *New Republic* version. Both versions have been reprinted in various collections.

5726. B., B.: "To Eithne Magee in *The King's Threshold*," *T. C. D.*, 20:364 (16 Dec 1914), 183.

5727. BAKER, PETER: "W. B. Yeats," *Poetry Q*, 2:4 (Winter 1940), 100.

5728. BARKER, GEORGE: *Collected Poems, 1930-1965*. NY: October House, 1965. xii, 273 p.
"The Death of Yeats," 53-54; reprinted from *Poetry London*, 1:2 (Apr 1939), [1].

5729. ————: "More News for the Delphic Oracle," *Texas Q*, 8:4 (Winter 1965), 149.

5730. "BATES, WILLIAM CUTLER": "On Seeing a Man Get Ill in the Abbey Theatre on Thursday Last," *Sinn Féin*, ns 3:156 (25 Jan 1913), 7.

5731. BERRYMAN, JOHN: *His Toy, His Dream, His Rest: 308 Dream Songs*. NY: Farrar, Straus & Giroux, 1969. xxi, 317 p.
Several songs are concerned with Yeats, particularly #331 (p. 263) and #334 (p. 266).

5732. BOLAND, EAVAN: "Yeats in Civil War," *Dublin Mag*, 5:2 (Summer 1966), 26.

5733. BOTTOMLEY, GORDON: *Lyric Plays*. London: Constable, 1932. xii, 166 p.
Dedicatory poem, "To W. B. Yeats," v-vi.

5734. BRIGGS, ERNEST: *The Merciless Beauty: A Poetry Sequence*. Brisbane: Meanjin Press, 1943. i, 29 p. (Folios of Australian Poetry. [1.])
"William Butler Yeats," 21-27.

5735. BROWN, HARRY: *The End of a Decade*. Norfolk, Conn.: New Directions, 1940. [32 p.] (Poet of the Month. 1:2.)
"On the Death of Yeats," [12]; reprint of "Elegy on the Death of Yeats," *Twentieth Century Verse*, #17 (Apr/May 1939), 12.

5736. BROWNLOW, TIMOTHY, and RIVERS CAREW: *Figures Out of Mist*. Dublin: New Square Publications, 1966. 47 p.
Rivers Carew: "Sligo 1965 (In Memory of W. B. Yeats)," 44-45; reprinted from *Dublin Mag*, 4:2 (Summer 1965), 27.

5737. BROWNLOW, TIMOTHY: *The Hurdle Ford*. Dublin: New Square Publications, 1964. 28 p.
"Dublin," 7-10.

5738. BURNS, RICHARD: "Three Verse Pieces for W. B. Yeats," *University R* [Dublin], 3:8 [1966?], 72.

5739. BYRNE, J. PATRICK: "Yeats," *UKCR*, 9:3 (Spring 1943), 204.

5740. CAMPBELL, ROY: *The Collected Poems*. London: Bodley Head, 1949-57. 2 v.
"Félibre (To Frédéric Mistral, Neveu)," 2:111-12, contains the following lines on Yeats:
Yeats on his intellect could pull the blinds
Rapping up spooks. He fell for freaks and phoneys.
Weird blue-stockings with damp, flatfooted minds,
Theosophists and fakirs, were his cronies.

5741. CARRUTH, HAYDEN: *Nothing for Tigers: Poems, 1959-1964*. NY: Macmillan, 1965. viii, 85 p.
"A Pseudo-Prayer," 44-47. According to Carruth, this is modeled on Yeats's "A Prayer for My Daughter" (see "How Not to Rate a Poet," *SatR*, 49:7 [12 Feb 1966], 21, 43-44).

5742. CLARKE, AUSTIN: *Flight to Africa and Other Poems*. Dublin: Dolmen Press, 1963. 128 p.
 "The Abbey Theatre Fire," 16-17. A different poem, "Abbey Theatre Fire," appears on p. 8 of Clarke's *Too Great a Vine: Poems and Satires. Second Series*. Templeogue, County Dublin: Bridge Press, 1957. 29 p.

5743. ————: *The Echo at Coole & Other Poems*. Dublin: Dolmen Press, 1968. 78 p.
 "A Centenary Tribute: W. B. Yeats," 9-10. "In the Savile Club," 11-13. "The Echo at Coole," 13-14.

5744. COATES, FLORENCE EARLE: *Mine and Thine*. Boston: Houghton, Mifflin, 1904. xv, 175 p.
 "To William Butler Yeats," 52-53.

5745. CRONIN, ANTHONY: "The Great Poetry Boom, 1970's," *Dublin Mag*, 8:8 (Summer 1971), 116-17.
 Partly concerned with Yeats. Contains the remarkable lines "Yeats, Yeats, Yeats, Yeats, / Fart, fart, fart, fart."

5746. CUMBERLEGE, MARCUS: "Coole Park and Ballylee, Winter: For Michael Mulkhere," *Dublin Mag*, 8:8 (Summer 1971), 8-9.

5747. CURLE, J. J.: "Homage to Yeats," *Poetry R*, 42:6 (Nov-Dec 1952), 328.

5748. DANIELS, EARL: "On a Line of William Butler Yeats," *Spirit*, 7:3 (July 1940), 81.
 A line from "Easter 1916."

5749. DOLLARD, JAMES BERNARD: *Irish Lyrics and Ballads*. Toronto: McClelland, Goodchild & Stewart, 1917. viii, 131 p.
 "To William Butler Yeats," 40; reprinted from *Ireland* [NY], 1:25 (24 June 1916), 6.
 "William Butler Yeats," 51.

5750. DOYLE, LIAM: "W. B. Yeats," *Leader*, 77:22 (4 Feb 1939), 572.

5751. DURYEE, MARY BALLARD: *Words Alone Are Certain Good: William Butler Yeats. Himself, the Poet, His Ghost*. Dublin: Dolmen Press, 1961. 45 p.
 Fourteen poems plus annotations indicating their relation to Yeats's life and work.
 Reviews:
 1. Anon., *TLS*, 62:3201 (5 July 1963), 498-99. (". . . a touch of banality. . . .")
 2. John Hewitt, "Three Americans," *Threshold*, 5:2 (Autumn-Winter 1961/ 62), 81-84.

5752. FALLON, PADRAIC: "Yeats's Tower at Ballylee," *Dublin Mag*, 26:4 (Oct-Dec 1951), 1-5.

5753. FERLINGHETTI, LAWRENCE: *A Coney Island of the Mind: Poems*. NY: New Directions, 1958. 93 p. (New Directions Paperbook. 74.)
 "Reading Yeats I Do Not Think," 90-91; reprinted from °*Pictures of the Gone World*. San Francisco: City Lights Pocket Bookshop, 1955. [42 p.].

5754. FLINT, ERIC: "On Reading Yeats' 'A Deep Sworn Vow,'" *WHR*, 21:2 (Spring 1967), 163.

5755. FORSSELL, LARS: *Ändå: Dikter*. Stockholm: Bonnier, 1968. 126 p.
 "Tolv variationer till minne av W. B. Yeats," 27-56.

5756. FRASER, GEORGE SUTHERLAND: *Leaves without a Tree*. Tokyo: Hokuseido Press, 1953. ix, 71 p.
"For Yeats," 2-4.

5757. GAWSWORTH, JOHN: "The Return (W. B. Y. Reinterred)," *Literary Digest*, 3:4 (Winter 1948), 30.

5758. GIBBON, MONK: *This Insubstantial Pageant*. NY: Devin-Adair, 1951. 190 p.
"Yeats's Earlier Poems," 24; reprinted from *Irish Statesman*, 14:4 (29 Mar 1930), 67.
"The Heroic Mind," 105.

5759. GIBSON, WILFRID: *Solway Ford and Other Poems*. A selection made by Charles Williams. London: Faber & Faber, 1945. 74 p.
"The Three Poets," 73-74; first published as "The Three Poets: A Reminiscence," *English*, 5:27 (Autumn 1944), 81-82. On T. Sturge Moore, Laurence Binyon, and Yeats.

5760. GOGARTY, OLIVER ST. JOHN: *The Collected Poems*. London: Constable, 1951. xxvii, 212 p.
A. E.: "The Poetry of My Friend," ix-xiii.
Horace Reynolds: "Gogarty in the Flesh," xv-xxvii; contains some Yeats anecdotes.
"To the Lady—," 24-25 (the poet referred to is Yeats).
"To W. B. Yeats Who Says That His Castle of Ballylee Is His Monument," 25.
"To the Poet W. B. Yeats, Winner of the Nobel Prize 1924 [*sic*]. (To Build a Fountain to Commemorate His Victory)," 30-31; reprinted from *Irish Statesman*, 1:14 (15 Dec 1923), 427.
"Elegy on the Archpoet William Butler Yeats Lately Dead," 200-206; reprinted from *Contemporary Poetry*, [1:3] (Autumn 1941), 3-7.

5761. H., E.: "To a Celtic Poet," *Outlook* [London], 6:140 (6 Oct 1900), 304.
Presumably addressed to Yeats, since it repeats many of his early poetic clichés.

5762. HALL, JOHN CLIVE: *The Burning Hare*. London: Chatto & Windus / Hogarth Press, 1966. 50 p.
"The Wood," 12. "The Vigil," 17.

5763. HAMMOND, MAC: "Of What Is Past or Passing or to Come: A Mosaic for W. B. Yeats," *Audience*, 4:2 [Oct? 1956], 10.

5764. HARGADON, MICHAEL A.: *A Lovely Home*. Dublin: Maunsel, 1915. viii, 75 p.
"William Butler Yeats," 7.

5765. HARRIS, MICHAEL: *Poems*. With an introduction by Sir Compton Mackenzie. Dublin: Dolmen Press, 1965. 28 p.
"Coole 1960: In Memoriam Yeats, Lady Gregory, Synge, Douglas Hyde," 9.

5766. HAYES, JOAN: "Sligo Holy Well: Tribute to W. B. Yeats," *Everyman*, #2 (1969), 109.

5767. HENN, T. R.: "The Tower Revisited (18 August 1959)," *Acorn*, #3 (Autumn 1962), 15.

5768. HOFFMAN, DANIEL: "Instructions to a Medium to Be Transmitted to the Shade of W. B. Yeats, the Latter Having Responded in a Seance Held on 13 June 1965, Its Hundredth Birthday," *Shenandoah*, 16:4 (Summer 1965), 5-6.

5769. HOFFMANN, DIETER (ed): *Personen: Lyrische Porträts von der Jahr-hundertwende bis zur Gegenwart.* Frankfurt am Main: Societäts-Verlag, 1966. 288 p.
Karl Alfred Wolken: "Yeats, nach einem späten Bild," 244-45.

5770. HOPE, ALEC DERWENT: *Collected Poems, 1930-1965.* NY: Viking Press, 1966. xiii, 214 p.
"William Butler Yeats," 72. Written in 1948 (cf. p. xi). Reprinted in J1101.

5771. ————: *New Poems, 1965-1969.* Sydney: Angus & Robertson, 1969. viii, 76 p.
"The Apotelesm of W. B. Yeats," 18; reprinted from *Poetry*, 114:3 (June 1969), 174, and *Quadrant*, 13:60 (July-Aug 1969), 9.

5772. HOUSTON, RALPH: "On First Reading W. B. Yeats," *Poetry Ireland*, #14 (July 1951), 17-18.

5773. HURLEY, DORAN: "For Maud Conne [sic] MacBride and William Butler Yeats: A Literary Romance of Modern Ireland. And God Stands Winding His Lonely Horn," *Ireland-American R*, [1]:4 [1940?], 73-74.

5774. An Craoibhinn Aoibhinn [HYDE, DOUGLAS]: "An Answer to Mr. Yeats' Poem 'In [sic] the Abbey Theatre,'" *Irish R*, 2:23 (Jan 1913), 561.
In reply to Yeats's "At the Abbey Theatre," :22 (Dec 1912), 505.

5775. JOHNSON, LIONEL: *The Complete Poems.* Edited by Iain Fletcher. London: Unicorn Press, 1953. xlviii, 395 p.
"A Cornish Night: To William Butler Yeats," 25-29. Written in 1888.
"To Samuel Smith with a Copy of W. B. Yeats' *The Celtic Twilight*," 251-52. Written in 1895.
"Prologue," 259-60; reprinted from *Beltaine*, #1 (May 1899), 5. According to a note on p. 1 of the same issue, the prologue was spoken at the first performance of *The Countess Cathleen.* Reprinted in J6703.
"In a Copy of Yeats's Poems. To Edmund Gosse," 273. Written in 1895.
Fletcher mentions Yeats *passim* in "Introduction," xi-xliv, and in "Textual Notes," 325-95.

5776. KAVANAGH, PATRICK: "Yeats," *Holy Door*, #3 (Spring 1966), 1.
Perhaps Kavanagh's best diatribe against Yeats.

5777. KENNEDY, M. J.: "At Drumcliffe (For the Birthday of W. B. Yeats)," *Irish Independent*, 74:133 (5 June 1965), 12.

5778. KENNELLY, BRENDAN: "Yeats," *Icarus*, #31 (June 1960), 2.

5779. KERNAN, PLOWDEN: *Hawthorn Time in Ireland and Other Poems.* Los Angeles: Ward Ritchie Press, 1939. xii, 81 p.
"W. B. Yeats," 49.

5780. KILMER, JOYCE: *Main Street and Other Poems.* NY: Doran, 1917. 78 p.
"Easter Week," 66-67. An answer to Yeats's "September 1913."

5781. KINSELLA, THOMAS: "Tara: A Poem for Yeats," *Guardian*, #36991 (12 June 1965), 7.

5782. LERNER, LAURENCE: "Yeats I Brought to You . . . ," *CQ*, 3:3 (Autumn 1961), 238.

5783. LESLIE, SHANE: "In Memoriam--W. B. Yeats," *Irish Library Bulletin*, 9:[10] (Oct 1948), 159-60.

5784. ─────: "The Wake of Willie Yeats," *Irish Library Bulletin*, 9:[10] (Oct 1948), 166.

5785. LYNCH, BRIAN: "West from Ballylee," *University R* [Dublin], 3:8 [1966?], 72.

5786. "MAC": "To Certain Anglo-Irish Writers," *Phoblacht*, ns 1:47 (18 Mar 1927), 2.
"For what ye are we know you all, / With words so big and minds so small."

5787. MCCRACKEN, D. J.: "After Re-Reading Yeats," *Acorn*, #4 (Spring 1963), 7.

5788. MACDIARMID, HUGH: *Poetry Like the Hawthorn from "In Memoriam James Joyce."* Hemel Hempstead: Glen, 1962. 7 p.
A poem on the death of Yeats, reprinted from *Wales*, #11 (Winter 1939-40), 296-97. Also in *In Memorian James Joyce: From a Vision of World Language.* Glasgow: MacLellan, 1955. 150 p. (pp. 35-36).

5789. MACDONNELL, RANDAL: "'Abbey' Epitaphs," *Leader*, 17:4 (12 Sept 1908), 81.
The customary *Leader* sneers.

5790. MCFADDEN, ROY: *The Garryowen.* London: Chatto & Windus / Hogarth Press, 1971. 40 p.
"In Drumcliffe Churchyard," 39; reprinted from *Irish Writing*, #8 (July 1949), 57.

5791. MCGLAUN, RITHIA: "Safe in Byzantium," *Contempora*, 1:1 (Mar 1970), 5.

5792. MACGLOIN, TOMMY: "Yeats," *Icarus*, 5:16 (May 1955), 26.

5793. MACKEY, THOMASINA: "Centenary," *Irish Independent*, 74:184 (14 Oct 1965), 13.

5794. MACKINLAY, JAMES: "Thoughts on Yeats," *Lagan*, [#2 (1944)], 79.

5795. MACLEISH, ARCHIBALD: *"The Wild Old Wicked Man" & Other Poems.* London: Allen, 1969. ix, 45 p.
"The Wild Old Wicked Man," 44-45.

5796. MANDER, JOHN: "William Morris and William Yeats," *Delta*, [#1 (1953), 11].

5797. MANSFIELD, RICHARD: "Yeat's [sic] Grave," *Focus* [Dublin], 5:6 (June 1962), 134.

5798. MARSZAŁEK, JAN: "Spotkanie z W. B. Yeatsem" [A meeting with WBY], *Odra*, 10:3 (1970), 75-76.

5799. MASEFIELD, JOHN: "Old 18, Woburn Buildings, or The Generosities of Life," MS., Bodleian Library, Oxford (Ms. Eng. Poet. d. 195, fol. 117).
A poem "Remembering November the 5th, 1900." I do not know whether it is identical with one of those poems contained in J564.

5800. MEDDAUGH, DAVID H.: "To William B. Yeats," *Four Winds*, 1:1 (Summer 1952), 28-29.

5801. MERRILL, JAMES: "Flying from Byzantium," *Salmagundi*, 1:3 (1966), 61.

5802. MILNE, EWART: *Boding Day: Poems.* London: Muller, 1947. 32 p.
"Christmas Eve, 1945," 24.

5803. MOORE, MARIANNE: *Poems*. London: Egoist Press, 1921. 24 p.
"To William Butler Yeats on Tagore," 8; reprinted from *Egoist*, 2:5
(1 May 1915), 77.

5804. NELSON, LAWRENCE G.: "Two Sonnets: Requiem for a Keltic Gyravague,"
CEA Critic, 33:3 (Mar 1971), 28.

5805. O BROIN, PADRAIG: "Yeats," *Laurel R*, 5:2 (Fall 1965), 2.

5806. O'CONNOR, FRANK: "Directions for *My* Funeral (Written after the
Burial of W. B. Yeats)," *Atlantic Monthly*, 223:2 (Feb 1969), 120.

5807. OSHIMA, SHOTARO: *Poems*. Tokyo: Hokuseido Press, 1973. x, 109 p.
"Thoor Ballylee: On Its Being Repaired on the Centenary of Yeats
1965," 51.
"To the Land of the Ever-Living: A Tribute to W. B. Yeats," 59-60.
Also in *Poems: Journeys and Scenes*. Tokyo: Hokuseido Press, 1968. 16
p. (pp. 1-2).

5808. O'SULLIVAN, SEUMAS: *Collected Poems*. Dublin: Orwell Press, 1940.
226 p.
"To a Poet," 58. The answer to Yeats's "To a Poet, Who Would Have Me
Praise Certain Bad Poets, Imitators of His and Mine."

5809. PAYNE, BASIL: "Remembering Yeats," *Kilkenny Mag*, #15 (Spring-Summer
1967), 135.

5810. PAYNE, ELIZABETH: "W. B. Yeats," *Circle*, [1:1] (Dec 1941), 35.

5811. POLLARD, MARGUERITE: "In Memoriam: W. B. Yeats," *Poetry R*, 30:3
(Mar-Apr 1939), 151.

5812. POTTS, PAUL: "William Butler Yeats, 1865-1939," *Poetry Q*, 8:1
(Spring 1946), 38.

5813. POULIN, A.: "Sailing from Byzantium," *Concerning Poetry*, 5:1 (Spring
1972), 24.

5814. POUND, EZRA: *The Cantos*. NY: New Directions, 1970. v, 802 p.
References to Yeats are contained in canto 41 (p. 205), 74 (433), 76
(453), 77 (473), 79 (487), 80 (496, 504, 505, 507, 508, 511), 82 (524-
25), 83 (528, 529, 533-34). See John Hamilton Edwards and William W.
Vasse: *Annotated Index to the Cantos of Ezra Pound: Cantos I-LXXXIV*.
Berkeley: U of California Press, 1959. xvii, 332 p.
Further Yeats references are in canto 93 (p. 632), 95 (645), 96
(661), 97 (676), 98 (685, 686), 101 (725), 102 (728, 729), 113 (789),
114 (793).

5815. PURDY, ALFRED: *The Cariboo Horses*. Toronto: McClelland & Stewart,
1965. 112 p.
"Malachi Stilt-Jack Am I," 51-52.

5816. REILLY, ROBERT: "To William B. Yeats, Author of 'The Wanderings of
Oisin,'" *Irish Monthly*, 17:191 (May 1889), 277.

5817. REYNOLDS, LORNA: "Thoor Ballylee, June 1965," *University R* [Dublin],
3:8 [1966?], 101.

5818. ROETHKE, THEODORE: *The Collected Verse: Words for the Wind*. Garden
City: Doubleday, 1958. 212 p.
Part 1 of "Four for Sir John Davies," entitled "The Dance" (p. 120),
is expressly indebted to Yeats ("I take this cadence from a man named
Yeats").
"The Dying Man: In Memoriam W. B. Yeats," 185-90.

5818a. ROSEN, STANLEY: "Yeats I" and "Yeats II," *Sewanee R*, 82:1 (Winter 1974), 79-80.

5819. SACKETT, S. J.: "An Open Letter to W. B. Yeats," *Antioch R*, 20:3 (Fall 1966), 293.

5820. SALOMON, I. L.: "Thoor Ballylee," *Dublin Mag*, 8:4&5 (Summer/Autumn 1970), 81.

5821. SCHEVILL, JAMES: "For the Old Yeats," *American Scholar*, 33:2 (Spring 1964), 236.

5822. SHAPIRO, KARL: *Essay on Rime*. NY: Random House, 1945. vii, 72 p.
A long poem. The following lines pertain to Yeats: 493-504, 1393-401, 1788-93.

5823. SMITH, ARTHUR JAMES MARSHALL: *Collected Poems*. Toronto: Oxford UP, 1962. Unpaged.
"Ode: On the Death of William Butler Yeats," #9.

5824. STALLWORTHY, JON: "From W. B. Yeats to His Friend Maud Gonne," *REL*, 4:3 (July 1963), 70.

5825. ————: "On Being Asked for a Centenary Poem," *English*, 15:89 (Summer 1965), 169.

5826. STEEN, SHIELA: *The Honeysuckle Hedge*. London: Oxford UP, 1943. v, 48 p.
"W. B. Yeats, Died Roquebrune, Cap Martin, 28 Jan. 1939," 18-19; first published under the name S. M. Tusting, *English*, 2:10 (1939), 228-29.

5827. SWAN, JON C.: "Sonnet to W. B. Yeats," *Personalist*, 39:4 (Autumn 1958), 372.

5828. TATE, ALLEN: *Poems*. NY: Scribner's, 1960. xii, 224 p.
"Winter Mask: To the Memory of W. B. Yeats," 62-65; first published in *Chimera*, 1:4 (Spring 1943), 2-3.

5829. TATE, JAMES: "The Whole World's Sadly Talking to Itself--W. B. Yeats," *Poetry*, 110:4 (July 1967), 239.

5830. THOMAS, RONALD STUART: *The Stones of the Field*. Carmarthen: Druid Press, 1946. 49 p.
"Memories of Yeats Whilst Travelling to Holyhead," 22; reprinted from *Poetry London*, 2:10 (Dec 1944), 176.

5831. TURNER, WALTER JAMES: *Fossils of a Future Time?* London: Oxford UP, 1946. xiii, 143 p.
"W. B. Yeats," 24-26; first published as "Ode (In Memory of W. B. Yeats)," *NSt*, 17:417 (18 Feb 1939), 243.

5832. UNTERECKER, JOHN: "Abelard Perhaps and Perhaps Heloise--Variations on a Theme by W. B. Yeats," *Poetry Ireland*, #7&8 (Spring 1968), 94-95.

5833. W., A. M.: "The Ideal Beauty Show," *Leader*, 26:7 (29 Mar 1913), 153.
Poem, scene: "A hall filled with long-haired bards, bounders and other intensely cultured persons. Pensioner Yeats comes forward to chant, and is received with a tremulous outburst of rhymthical [*sic*] cheering, followed by an opal hush." See also another bad poem by the same versifier, "The Opal Hush Bungery," :8 (5 Apr 1913), 177.

5834. WAKE, GABRIEL: *Earthquake: A Vision of Ireland*. N.p., 1924. [4 p.]
A satiric poem with a section on Yeats.

5835. WATKINS, VERNON: *Selected Poems*. Norfolk, Conn.: New Directions, 1948. vii, 92 p.
"Yeats' Tower," 24; reprinted from *Wales*, #3 (Autumn 1937), 86-87.

5836. ————: *The Lamp and the Veil: Poems*. London: Faber & Faber, 1945. 61 p.
"Yeats in Dublin," 7-19; first published in *Life and Letters Today*, 21:20 (Apr 1939), 67-78; also in *Poetry Ireland*, #11 (Oct 1950), 3-12, and *Dublin Mag*, 6:1 (Spring 1967), 19-29.

5837. ————: "The Last Poems of Yeats," *Life and Letters Today*, 23:28 (Nov 1939), 312-13.

5838. WATSON, WILLIAM: *The Muse in Exile: Poems*. London: Jenkins, 1913. 116 p.
"A Chance Meeting," 95. This epigram is quoted, or rather misquoted, by Gogarty (J558, p. 21), who says that Watson alluded to Yeats.

5839. WEBER, RICHARD: *Lady & Gentleman*. Dublin: Dolmen Press, 1963. 30 p.
"Yeats in London," 23; reprinted from *TLS*, 61:3150 (13 July 1962), 508.

5840. WELLESLEY, DOROTHY: *Early Light: The Collected Poems*. London: Hart-Davis, 1955. 255 p.
"To Yeats," 253.

5841. WHEATCROFT, JOHN: "Reading Yeats on the Beach," *Dalhousie R*, 46:3 (Autumn 1966), 318.

5842. WILKINSON, MARGUERITE O. B.: "To William Butler Yeats," *Little R*, 1:4 (Apr 1914), 52.

5842a. WILSON, GRAEME: "Yeats," *Denver Q*, 6:4 (Winter 1972), 33-34.

5843. WILSON, PATRICK: *Staying at Ballisodare*. Northwood, Middlesex: Scorpion Press, 1960. 23 p.
A long poem concerned with Yeats *passim*.

5844. WILSON, R. N. D.: "Postscript to an Epitaph," *Dublin Mag*, 24:3 (July-Sept 1949), 1-2.
Yeats's epitaph in "Under Ben Bulben."

5845. WINN, G. HOWARD: "Thoor Ballylee 1969," *Barat R*, 5:2 (Autumn 1970), 104.

5846. WYMAN, LINDA: "Concerning the Relevance of Falconers," *CEA Critic*, 33:3 (Mar 1971), 35.

See also J557, 564, 616, 729, 1097 (#17), 1101 (#5, 10, 13, 16), 1102a, 1112 (#2, 3, 19), 1270, 1275, 1684a, 2005, 2036, 2443, 2806, 2900, 3167, 6241.

JB Novels, Stories, and Plays

5847. °BUFANO, ROCCO, and JOHN DUFFY: "Horseman, Pass By: Musical," 1969.
I do not know whether this has been published. The musical was performed at the Fortune Theater, 62 East 4th Street, New York (see "A Yeats Musical: *Horseman, Pass By* Bows Off Broadway," *NYT*, 118:40535 [16 Jan 1969], 46). It was based on the writings of Yeats and had the following characters: Intellect, Political Man, Imagination, Spirit, Sensuality, Vanity, Timidity, and The Voice; a sort of morality, it appears.

5848. [CROWLEY, ALEISTER]: "At the Fork of the Road," *Equinox*, 1:1 (Mar 1909), 101-8.

A short story. According to Crowley, it is a "true account of an episode of [the late 1890s]." He identifies some of its characters: Will Bute = Yeats; Hypatia Gay = Althea Gyles; Publisher = Leonard Smithers; and adds: "The identification is conjectural, depending solely on the admission of Miss Gyles" (see J622, 1:259)--which is quite probably an infernal lie. Virginia Moore (J565, p. 210) identifies the main character, Count Swanoff, as Crowley himself. The sickening story deals with the hellish machinations of Will Bute, who sends Hypatia Gay to seduce Swanoff. After a near success, Hypatia is punished severely through counter-magic. See also J639.

5849. ————: *Moonchild: A Prologue*. London: Mandrake Press, 1929. 335 p.

A novel in which Yeats appears as Gates (see J4018). The first appearance is on p. 152.

5850. MARTYN, EDWARD: "Romulus & Remus: Or, The Makers of Delights. A Symbolist Extravaganza in One Act," *Irish People*, 7:333 (21 Dec 1907), Supplement, 1-2.

A satire on Yeats, who appears as Remus Delaney, hairdresser, and on Moore, Lady Gregory, and Martyn himself. Somewhat dull, but contains one really good line: "As for living Miss Hoolihan at least can do that for me."

5851. ————: *The Dream Physician: Play in Five Acts*. Dublin: Talbot Press / London: Unwin, [1917?]. vi, 87 p.

George Augustus Moon = George Moore; Beau Brummell = Yeats (he appears with a banjo; presumably a comment on Yeats's "Speaking to the Psaltery" experiments); Otho = James Joyce (he says to Brummell: "I see you are too old to influence me," p. 67).

5852. MOORE, GEORGE: *Evelyn Innes*. London: Unwin, 1898. v, 480 p.

A novel in which the character of Ulick Dean is modeled on Yeats. See his description in chapter 14 (p. 182).

5853. ROSMAN, ELEANOR M.: "'A Vision': A Dance Based on Two Symbols from the Poetry of W. B. Yeats," M.A. thesis, New York U, 1970. iv, 75 p.

The two symbols are "Gyre" and "Golden Bird." A performance took place on 19 and 20 Dec 1969 at New York University; the author was the choreographer.

5854. °SHYRE, PAUL: "Yeats and Company," N.p., [1965?]. Typescript, 1 v., various pagings.

A play produced by The Theatre Group at the University of Southern California, Los Angeles, 23 Oct 1965. According to the National Union Catalog, the New York Public Library owns a copy.

5854a. STUART, FRANCIS: *Black List / Section H*. With a preface and post-script by Harry T. Moore. Carbondale: Southern Illinois UP, 1971. ix, 442 p.

A largely autobiographical novel in which Yeats, Maud and Iseult Gonne, and other figures of the time appear under their own names.

See also J775, 5867, 6896, 7255.

JC Parodies

5855. *The Abbey Row NOT Edited by W. B. Yeats*. Dublin: Maunsel, 1907. 12 p.

The authors of this skit on the first production of *The Playboy* are
generally thought to have been Page Lawrence Dickinson, Frank Sparrow,
Richard Caulfield Orpen, William Orpen, Joseph Hone, and Susan L.
Mitchell. Yeats is mentioned *passim*.

5856. ANON.: "Competition No. 573," *Spectator*, 223:7374 (25 Oct 1969),
574.
    Conditions: To write two stanzas of a poem modeled on "The Lake Isle
    of Innisfree," "celebrating the attractions of a dream island for
    hippies, Liberal MPs or any other minority groups." Five parodies are
    printed.

5857. ANON.: "Next Week's Programme at the Abbey Theatre: *The College
Playboy*. A Tragedy in Two Acts by Post and Neo Synge," *T. C. D.*, 22:386
(8 Mar 1916), 226-28.

5858. AUDEN, WYSTAN HUGH: *Homage to Clio*. NY: Random House, 1960. viii,
93 p.
    Contains a limerick on Yeats, p. 90.

5859. B.: "Cap and Bells Up-to-Date," *T. C. D.*, 23:398 (28 Feb 1917), 97.

5860. BRADBY, GODFREY FOX: *Parody and Dust-Shot*. London: Oxford UP, 1931.
viii, 42 p.
    "What Really Happens (After W. B. Yeats)," 18; a parody of "The Lake
    Isle of Innisfree."

5861. BRAHMS, CARYL: "A Parody: The Lamentable Effect of a Sea-Fever upon
the Muse of Mr. Yeats," *Time and Tide*, 8:41 (14 Oct 1927), 903.
    A parody of "The Lake Isle of Innisfree."

5862. CHESTERTON, GILBERT KEITH: *Collected Poems*. NY: Dodd, Mead, 1966.
vii, 391 p.
    "Variations on an Air: Composed on Having to Appear in a Pageant as
    Old King Cole," 43-46; includes a variation "After W. B. Yeats," p. 44.

5863. COMPTON-RICKETT, ARTHUR: *Our Poets at School and Other Fancies in
Prose and Verse*. Bournemouth: Cooper, 1921. 72 p.
    Contains a Yeats parody loosely modeled on "The Fiddler of Dooney,"
    p. 31.

5864. DEANE, ANTHONY CHARLES: *New Rhymes for Old and Other Verses*. London:
Lane, 1901. 96 p.
    "The Cult of the Celtic (An Experiment, Dedicated with Apologies to
    Fiona Macleod, W. B. Yeats, and Others)," 61-63.

5865. FELTON, JOHN: "Contemporary Caricatures," *Egoist*, 1:15 (1 Aug 1914),
296-97.
    No. 2 concerns Mr. W****** B***** Y****.

5866. FRENCH, PERCY: *Prose, Poems, and Parodies*. Edited by his sister
Mrs. De Burgh Daly with a foreword by Alfred Perceval Graves. Dublin:
Talbot Press, [1930]. xix, 204 p.
    "The Queen's After-Dinner Speech," 55-58, alludes to Maud Gonne and
    Yeats, containing the famous lines
        "An' I think there's a slate," sez she,
        "Off Willie Yeats," sez she.
        "He should be at home," sez she,
        "French polishin' a pome," sez she. . . .

5867. [GALE, NORMAN ROWLAND]: *All Expenses Paid*. Westminster: Constable,
1895. vi, 113 p.

A short comic novel describing the journey to Parnassus of a couple of "minor poets," headed by Yeats. The journey has been paid by one Mr. Patterson, formerly a pork butcher, now a modern Maecenas.

5868. GOGARTY, OLIVER ST. JOHN: "He Accounts for the Skyscrapers," *American Spectator*, 1:5 (Mar 1933), 2.

5869. HARRISON, R.: "An Interview with Mr. Y--ts," *New Age*, 20:1271 (18 Jan 1917), 286.

5870. HOLLIS, CHRISTOPHER: "The Innisfree Report," *Spectator*, 214:7148 (25 June 1965), 806.

5871. HOWE, MARTYN: "The Long Road: A Symbolistic Drama (This Play May Be Performed at the Abbey Theatre without Fee or Licence)," *T. C. D.*, 21:377 (10 Nov 1915), 127.

5872. ————: "Epigrams (In the Style of W. B. Yeats)," *T. C. D.*, 23:397 (21 Feb 1917), 87.

5873. "IMAAL": "A Conversation between William Shakespeare and Mr. Yeats (Without Apologies to W. S. Landor)," *Leader*, 7:15 (5 Dec 1903), 239-41.

5874. JOYCE, JAMES: *Ulysses*. NY: Modern Library, 1934. xvii, 768 p.
Buck Mulligan's parody of "Baile and Ailinn," stanza 1, may be found at the end of the library scene (p. 213). Other references to Yeats, *passim* (see J2229).

5875. "Evoe" [KNOX, EDMUND GEORGE VALPY]: *Parodies Regained*. Illustrated by George Morrow. London: Methuen, 1921. x, 114 p.
"The Deirdrenought (Mr. W. B. Yeats Presents Dramatically His Views on the Battleship of the Future)," 59-63.

5876. LEWIS, DOMINIC BEVAN WYNDHAM: *At the Sign of the Blue Moon*. London: Melrose, 1924. 316 p.
"Celtic Twilight," 50-56; a parody of *At the Hawk's Well*, here called *At the Pump*.

5877. ————: "Synge-Song," *John o' London's Weekly*, 11:283 (6 Sept 1924), 750.
"Extract from *The Tinker's Aunt*, a one-act peasant play by an unknown author, here printed for the first time, and evidently owing some of its inspiration to the dramatic works of J. M. Synge and the Abbey Theatre, Dublin, generally."

5878. MACMANUS, FRANCIS: "Frivolous Encounters: Signor Alighieri Meets Mr. Yeats," *Irish Monthly*, 67:793 (July 1939), 492-97.

5879. MACMANUS, MICHAEL JOSEPH: *A Green Jackdaw: Adventures in Parody*. Dublin: Talbot Press, [1925]. 73 p.
Contains two Yeats parodies, "The Dreamer," and "The End of Heart's Desire," 33-34, and a play, "Gregorian Chant: A Kiltartanese Comedy (Potted)," 48-52.

5880. ————: *So This Is Dublin!* Dublin: Talbot Press, 1927. 123 p.
"The New Kiltartan History," 77-79, contains a paragraph on "The Poet Yeats."
Professor Jonathan P. Hoggenheim, Lecturer in Poetry and Scientific Salesmanship at Winkinville University, Oskoosh, Massachusetts, re-writes "The Lake Isle of Innisfree" in the American style, pp. 90-91. "Poets in Collaboration" features "The Lake Isle of Innisfree (Written by Mr. W. B. Y—ts; rewritten by Mr. J—s St—ph—ns)," 120-21. See also "A Misunderstanding," 123.

5880a. MACNEICE, LOUIS: *I Crossed the Minch*. London: Longmans, Green, 1938. ix, 248 p.
Contains a parody of Yeats's prose style, pp. 181-83.

5881. Mac [MACNIE, ISA]: *The Celebrity Zoo (First Visit): Some Desultory Rhymes and Caricatures*. Dublin: Browne & Nolan, 1925. Unpaged.
On show: Yeats, Hyde, AE, Lennox Robinson, James Stephens, and others.

5882. MARRIOTT, ERNEST: "The Shadow of the Wind (After W. B. Yeats)," *Manchester Q*, 29:113 (Jan 1910), 87-92.
A parody of *The King's Threshold*.

5883. MITCHELL, SUSAN LANGSTAFF: *Aids to the Immortality of Certain Persons in Ireland Charitably Administered*. A new edition with poems added. Dublin: Maunsel, 1913 [1908]. xvii, 89 p.
Yeats is mentioned or satirized in the following pieces:
"Prologue to Some Who Are Mentioned in This Book," xvii (a parody of "When You Are Old").
"George Moore Comes to Ireland," 1-5.
"The Voice of One," 6-15; a play whose dramatis personae are Bates, Barton, and M'Clure (Yeats, Martyn, and Moore).
"The Ballad of Shawe-Taylor and Hugh Lane," 23-26.
"George Moore Becomes High Sheriff of Mayo," 33-35.

5884. Moore, Edward [i.e., MUIR, EDWIN]: "Epigrams," *New Age*, 18:23 (6 Apr 1916), 544.
Contains one "To W. B. Yeats" and one "To James Stephens." See Stephens' reply, :24 (13 Apr 1916), 562, and Muir's rejoinder, :25 (20 Apr 1916), 595.

5885. Ó BROIN, PÁDRAIG: *No Casual Trespass*. Toronto: Cló Chluain Tairbh, 1967. ix, 113 p.
"Railing at Byzantium (On Reading Certain Anthologized Younger 'Poets')," 4-5.

5886. O'HIGGINS, BRIAN: *The Voice of Banba: Songs, Ballads and Satires*. Dublin: Hearthstone, [1931]. 114 p.
"The Isle of Innisfree," 94.

5887. POUND, EZRA: *Personae: Collected Shorter Poems*. London: Faber & Faber, 1952. 287 p.
"Au Jardin," 67; first published as "Und Drang," in *Canzoni*, London: Mathews, 1911. viii, 52 p. (pp. 51-52). A parody of "The Cap and Bells."
"Amitiés," 110-12; reprinted from *Poetry*, 4:5 (Aug 1914), 173-74. A parody of "The Lover Pleads with His Friends. . . ."
"The Lake Isle," 128; reprinted from *Poetry*, 8:16 (Sept 1916), 277.

5888. ————: *Pavannes and Divagations*. Norfolk, Conn.: New Directions, 1958. xi, 243 p.
"Neath Ben Bulben's Buttoks Lies," 228.

5889. POWELL, CHARLES: *The Poets in the Nursery*. With an introduction by John Drinkwater. London: Lane, 1920. 80 p.
"Little Boy Blue: William Butler Yeats," 35-37.

5890. PRIESTLEY, JOHN BOYNTON: *Brief Diversions: Being Tales, Travesties, and Epigrams*. Cambridge: Bowes & Bowes, 1922. vii, 60 p.
"The Later Manner of Mr. W. B. Yeats," 48. "The Poetry of Mr. W. B. Yeats," 57.

5891. READ, HERBERT: *Naked Warriors*. London: Arts & Letters, 1919. 60 p.
"Parody of a Forgotten Beauty," 3; parodies "Into the Twilight."

5892. ROSS, ROBERT: *Masques & Phases*. London: Humphreys, 1909. xii, 315 p.
"Swinblake: A Prophetic Book, with Zarathrusts," 91-102; an imaginary
conversation with several poets, among them Yeats.

5893. SEALY, DOUGLAS: "Aids to Immortality: Seven Parodies," *Dubliner*, 2:
2 (Summer 1963), 29-34.
These are parodies on the subject of Leda and the Swan, written in
the manner of contemporary Irish poets. A postscript by Rudi Holzapfel
(pp. 34-35) answers Yeats's question "Did she put on his knowledge
with his power?"

5894. *Secret Springs of Dublin Song*. Dublin: Talbot Press / London: Unwin,
1918. xi, 51 p.
This collection of anonymous parodies was edited by either Susan L.
Mitchell, who signed the preface and is credited with the editing by
Alan Denson (J7238, p. 113), or by Ernest A. Boyd, who says so in his
own copy, now in the Houghton Library at Harvard. Contains the follow-
ing Yeats parodies (authors supplied by Denson and corroborated in
some cases by Boyd):
Seumas O'Sullivan: "The Wild Dog Compares Himself to a Swan," 14.
AE: "Ideal Poems: (2) Y...s," 26.
Oliver St. John Gogarty: "From *The Queen's Threshold*," 27; "The Old
Man Refreshing Himself in the Morning," 28; "A Lament for George
Moore," 47-48.

5895. SMILES, SAM: Competition no. 814, *NSt*, 30:761 (22 Sept 1945), 202-3.
Conditions: "The Tate Gallery has reopened. Competitors are invited
to write 16 lines, welcoming the pictures back to London, in the style
of *Don Juan* or of W. B. Yeats." Answers by Thomas Bodkin (parody of
"Down by the Salley Gardens"), Terence Melican (in Yeats's later
ballad style), and L. E. J. (parody of "The Man Who Dreamed of Faeryland").

5896. SQUIRE, JOHN COLLINGS: *Collected Parodies*. London: Hodder & Stoughton, [1921]. vii, 238 p.
"How They Do It: No. 6. Numerous Celts," 64; reprinted from *NSt*, 1:7
(24 May 1913), 212.

5897. ———— (ed): *Apes and Parrots: An Anthology of Parodies*. London:
Jenkins, 1928. 309 p.
Harry Graham: "The Cockney of the North," 239-40; a parody of "The
Lake Isle of Innisfree."

5898. STODART-WALKER, ARCHIBALD: *The Moxford Book of English Verse, 1340-
1913*. London: Nash, 1913. 192 p.
"W. B. Y**ts," 188; a parody of "The Lake Isle of Innisfree."

5899. T[HOMAS], D[YLAN] M[ARLAIS]: "In Borrowed Plumes," *Swansea Grammar
School Magazine*, 27:1 (Apr 1930), 25-26.
Parodies on the theme of Miss Muffett in the manner of Ella Wheeler
Wilcox and Yeats.

5900. UNTERMEYER, LOUIS: *Collected Parodies*. NY: Harcourt, Brace, 1926.
xiv, 324 p.
"William Butler Yeats Gives a Symbolically Keltic Version of 'Three
Wise Men of Gotham,'" 12; reprinted from "———— *and Other Poets*,"
NY: Holt, 1916. 121 p. (pp. 20-21).

5901. VILLON, FRANÇOIS: *The Legacy and Other Poems*. Translated by Peter Dale. London: Agenda Editions, 1971. 27 p. (Agenda Editions. 1.)
   "Ballade: A Modern Version," 20, is a pastiche of Yeats phrases.

5902. W., A. M.: "Shadows of the Celtic Night (With Apologies to W. B. Mystic Symbol)," *Leader*, 7:10 (31 Oct 1903), 150-51.

5903. ———: "On the King's Threshold," *Leader*, 8:7 (9 Apr 1904), 102-4.

5903a. ———: "The Artful Dodger," *Leader*, 23:17 (9 Dec 1911), 415-16.
   A somewhat silly attack on Yeats in form of a play scene ("Scene-- Outside the Abbey. Time--The Celtic Twilight. Enter Constable Yeats of the Art Division, D. M. P.").

5903b. ———: "A Talk between Yeats and Goldsmith," *Leader*, 24:7 (30 Mar 1912), 155.
   Satirical skit ("'Tis Bill the Pensioner, I know, / The man who runs the Wild West Show").

5904. WILLIAMS, WILLIAM CARLOS: "Lillian," *American Prefaces*, 8:4 (Summer 1943), 296.
   A parody of "Down by the Salley Gardens."

5905. WOLFE, HUMBERT: *Lampoons*. London: Benn, 1925. 109 p.
   "'W. B. Yeats' by W. H. Davies," 89. "'W. H. Davies' by W. B. Yeats," 91.

5905a. X., O.: "Kleinbier, the Poet: A Literary Portrait," *New Ireland R*, 2:12 (Feb 1895), 803-7.
   A satirical sketch of Yeats, who appears as W. B. Kleinbier.

See also J566, 1228a, 1291, 1945, 2221, 2522, 6085, 6308, 6646, 7359.

Users of this and the following two parts L and M are advised that I have
not included anything by Yeats himself because of the sheer bulk of the
material. Instead the reader is referred to Allan Wade's bibliography
(J12) and to section AB in this bibliography. The most important material
will be found in the collections of Yeats's prose, *Autobiographies*, *Essays
and Introductions*, *Explorations*, *Uncollected Prose*, and in the several
editions of his letters. I have made one exception, though, by cross-
referencing the relevant items in sections BF and BG (interviews, speeches,
and lectures). Those items in parts K-M that deal with Yeats are cross-
referenced in the appropriate sections A-J and are included in the subject index.

I make no attempt to define the term "Irish Literary and Dramatic
Revival." For the purposes of this compilation I have assumed that the
description covers, more or less, the literature written by Irish writers,
conscious of their Irish themes and background, in the English language
from the 1880s to 1939, that is, during the time of Yeats's activities.

I do not include material on the Gaelic Revival, the Gaelic League,
and similar movements and organizations, except when it touches on the
(Anglo-) Irish Revival.

KA   Books and Pamphlets Exclusively on the Irish
Literary Revival (General Studies)

5906. ABERDEEN, ISHBEL, COUNTESS OF: *The Irish Literary Revival*. A lecture
delivered at the request of the Catholic Young Ladies' Association at the
Massey Hall, Toronto, May 31, 1895. [Toronto, 1895]. 32 p.

5907. ALLT, GEORGE DANIEL PETER: "The Anglo-Irish Literary Movement in
Relation to Its Antecedents," Ph.D. thesis, Cambridge U, 1953. iv, 207 p.
(bibliographical references on opposite blank pages).
    Deals with the life and works of Molyneux, Swift, Grattan, the Edge-
    worths, Thomas Moore, Mangan, Mitchel, Yeats, and Joyce. See particu-
    larly "Yeats, Religion, Ireland, and History," 132-73; presumably
    written along the same lines as Allt's published essay "Yeats, Reli-
    gion, and History" (J1815).

5908. AMERICAN COMMITTEE FOR IRISH STUDIES: *Newsletter*. Milwaukee: Department of English, U of Wisconsin.
    Four issues to be published yearly, but I have seen only the following:
    #1 (Dec 1971): News and notes; "Current Books of Irish Interests"
    (compiled by Jim Ford).
    #2 (Feb 1972): News, notes, and short reviews.

5909. ARNOLD, SIDNEY: *Irish Literature and Its Influence*. A lecture delivered extempore on September 20th, 1953, at the Irish Club, 82, Eaton
Square, London, S.W.1. South Chingford, Essex: Candlelight Press, [1953].
11 p.
    Mainly on AE.

5910. BESSAI, DIANE ELIZABETH: "Sovereignty of Erin: A Study of Mythological Motif in the Irish Literary Revival," Ph.D. thesis, U of London,
1971. 531 p.
    Nationalism and the national literary heritage, particularly in Yeats.

5911. BOYD, ERNEST: *Ireland's Literary Renaissance*. Dublin: Figgis, 1968 [1916]. 456 p.

Contains three chapters on Yeats (Poems, Plays, Prose) that are still interesting (pp. 122-87). Grants that Yeats's poems are symbolical, but not mystical and not intellectual, and thereby underrates Yeats's wide, if eclectic, reading. Deplores Yeats's experiments with the Nō. The prose impresses by its beauty, not so much by intellectual power. Also on O'Grady, Hyde, Sigerson, Todhunter, Katharine Tynan, Rolleston, Larminie, Nora Hopper, Ethna Carberry, AE, Eglinton, Seumas O'Sullivan, Colum, Stephens, Campbell, Clarke, MacDonagh, Martyn, Moore, Synge, Corkery, Joyce, Dunsany, Lady Gregory, Rutherford Mayne, and others. Contains chapters on the dramatic revival, the Abbey Theatre, the Ulster Literary Theatre, and the narrative prose of the revival.
Reviews:
1. Anon., "The Anglo-Irishman," *Nation* [London], 20:10 (9 Dec 1916), 362, 364.
2. Anon., "The Irish Renaissance," *NSt*, 21:539 (11 Aug 1923), 528-29.
3. Anon., *NAR*, 217:806 (Jan 1923), 138-40.
4. Anon., "The New Irish Literature," *TLS*, 16:783 (18 Jan 1917), 31.
5. J. W. Cunliffe, "Recent Irish Literature," *Literary R*, 3:23 (10 Feb 1923), 451.
6. John Eglinton, "Anglo-Irish Literature," *Dial*, 74:4 (Apr 1923), 395-98.
7. St. John Ervine, "Ireland's Literary Renaissance," *Observer*, 125: 6555 (7 Jan 1917), 4.
8. Sean Lucy, "Yeats' Poems in the Making," *Irish Independent*, 78:99 (26 Apr 1969), 6.
9. D. L. M., "Literary Men of Ireland," *BET*, 88:20 (24 Jan 1917), pt 2, 8.
10. Augustine Martin, "Classic Survey," *Hibernia*, 33:6 (14-27 Mar 1969), 20.
11. Susan L. Mitchell, "Ireland's Literary Renaissance," *New Ireland*, 3:6 (16 Dec 1916), 92-93.
12. John C. Reville, "The Irish Revival," *America*, 16:397 (18 Nov 1916), 137-38.
13. W. P. Ryan, *Bookman*, 51:306 (Mar 1917), 187-88.
14. Solomon Eagle [i.e., J. C. Squire], "Books in General," *NSt*, 8: 193 (6 Dec 1916), 257.
15. Philip Tillinghast, *Publisher's Weekly*, 90:2328 (16 Sept 1916), 848-49.
16. Katharine Tynan, *Studies*, 6:21 (Mar 1917), 164-65.

5912. BROWNE, RAY BROADUS, WILLIAM JOHN ROSCELLI, and RICHARD LOFTUS (eds): *The Celtic Cross: Studies in Irish Culture and Literature*. [West Lafayette, Ind.]: Purdue U Studies, 1964. 155 p.

Papers read at the first conference of the American Committee for Irish Studies (1963). Contains among others the following essays: Edward Brandabur: "Stephen's Aesthetic in *A Portrait of the Artist*," and a comment by Maurice Beebe; George Brandon Saul: "The Poetry of Austin Clarke"; Maurice Harmon: "The Later Poetry of Austin Clarke"; W. J. Roscelli: "The Private Pilgrimage of Austin Clarke"; MacEdward Leach: "Matthew Arnold and 'Celtic Magic'"; Vivian Mercier: "The Irish Short Story and Irish Tradition."

5913. BRUGSMA, REBECCA PAULINE CHRISTINE: *The Beginnings of the Irish Revival*. Part 1. Groningen: Noordhoff, [1933]. vii, 108 p. (Doctor's thesis, U of Amsterdam, 1933.)

Discusses the following aspects: "The Origin of the Irish Revival,"
"W. B. Yeats and the Irish Revival," and "W. B. Yeats and the Irish
Dramatic Movement." No more published.

5914. C[AMPBELL], J[OSEPH], E[DWARD] J[OHN] K[AVANAGH], and J[AMES]
E[DWARD] T[OBIN] (eds): *Irish Culture.* An announcement of the School of
Irish Studies in Fordham University. NY: Fordham UP, 1928. 48 p.
A description of the aims and accomplishments of the school.

5915. COXHEAD, ELIZABETH: *Daughters of Erin: Five Women of the Irish
Renascence.* London: Secker & Warburg, 1965. 236 p.
Short biographies of Maud Gonne, Constance Markievicz, Sarah Purser,
Sara Allgood, and Maire O'Neill. Numerous references to Yeats, *passim.*

5916. DUFFY, SIR CHARLES GAVAN, GEORGE SIGERSON, and DOUGLAS HYDE: *The
Revival of Irish Literature.* London: Unwin, [1894]. 161 p.
Contains: Duffy's "What Irishmen May Do for Irish Literature" and
"Books for the Irish People" (addresses delivered to the Irish Liter-
ary Society, London); Sigerson's "Irish Literature: Its Origin,
Environment, and Influence"; and Hyde's "The Necessity for De-Angli-
cising Ireland."

5917. EGLINTON, JOHN, W. B. YEATS, A. E., and WILLIAM LARMINIE: *Literary
Ideals in Ireland.* London: Unwin, [1899]. i, 88 p.
Articles reprinted from the *Daily Express* [Dublin]:
1. Eglinton: "What Should Be the Subjects of a National Drama?" 9-13
(*Daily Express*, #14414 [10 Sept 1898], 3).
2. Yeats: "A Note on National Drama," 17-20 (#14426 [24 Sept 1898],
3).
3. Eglinton: "National Drama and Contemporary Life?" 23-27 (#14438
[8 Oct 1898], 3).
4. Yeats: "John Eglinton and Spiritual Art," 31-37 (#14453 [29 Oct
1898], 3).
5. Eglinton: "Mr. Yeats and Popular Poetry," 41-46 (#14456 [5 Nov
1898], 3).
6. A. E.: "Literary Ideals in Ireland," 49-54 (#14463 [12 Nov 1898],
3).
7. Larminie: "Legends as Material for Literature," 57-65 (#14469 [19
Nov 1898], 3).
8. Yeats: "The Autumn of the Flesh," 69-75 (#14486 [3 Dec 1898], 3).
9. A. E.: "Nationality and Cosmopolitanism in Literature," 79-88
(#14491 [10 Dec 1898], 3); reprinted in J5946.
For reviews see J5384-89 and note.

5917a. *Etudes irlandaises: Bulletin de liaison des spécialistes franco-
phones d'histoire, civilisation et littérature de l'Irlande.* Lille:
C.E.R.I.U.L., 1972—.
#1 (Nov 1972). vii, 40 p.: News and notes.
#2 (Nov 1973). vii, 58 p.: News and notes.
#3 (Nov 1974). 141 p.: Jacques Chuto: "Yeats's 'A Dialogue of Self
and Soul,'" 33-37 (in French); Patrick Rafroidi: "The Year's Work in
Anglo-Irish Literature," 41-56; Marie-Jocelyne Deboulonne: "Thèses
françaises sur l'Irlande," 101-14; news and notes.

5918. GREGORY, LADY ISABELLA AUGUSTA (ed): *Ideals in Ireland.* London: At
the Unicorn, 1901. 107 p.
Contains: 1. Editor's note, pp. 9-11.
2. D. P. Moran: "The Battle of Two Civilizations," 25-41; reprinted
from *New Ireland R*, 13:6 (Aug 1900), 323-36; also in J6129.

3. George Moore: "Literature and the Irish Language," 45-51; reprint of "The Irish Literary Renaissance and the Irish Language: An Address [delivered at the meeting of the promoters of the Irish Literary Theatre]," *New Ireland R*, 13:2 (Apr 1900), 65-72. Contains some remarks on *Diarmuid and Grania*.
4. Douglas Hyde: "What Ireland Is Asking For & 'The Return of the Fenians,'" 55-73.
5. Standish O'Grady: "The Great Enchantment," 77-83; reprinted from *All Ireland R*, 1:38 (22 Sept 1900), 4-5. See also J136.
6. W. B. Yeats: "The Literary Movement in Ireland" and "Postscript," 87-107; see W300, Wp. 359, and J1700.
Reviews:
1. Anon., "A Manifesto," *Academy*, 60:1510 (13 Apr 1901), 320-21. Contends that Moore is entirely misplaced in the Irish literary revival and does not belong to it.
2. Anon., *Pilot*, 3:57 (30 Mar 1901), 408-9. Mainly on Moore's contribution.

5919. GWYNN, STEPHEN: *Irish Literature and Drama in the English Language: A Short History.* London: Nelson, 1936. ix, 240 p.
See especially "Beginnings of the Irish Drama," 145-64; "Development of Prose Fiction," 165-82; "James Stephens, Joyce, and the Ulster Writers," 183-206; "After the Revolution," 207-31; and "Appendix," 232-36 (on the Irish Academy of Letters). On Yeats, *passim* (see index)--surprisingly little on the poetry.
Reviews:
1. Anon., "The Irish Revival," *Outlook* [Glasgow], 1:4 (July 1936), 84-86.
2. Padraic Fallon, *Dublin Mag*, 11:3 (July-Sept 1936), 66-68.
3. H. T. Hunt Grubb, "A Poet's Friends," *Poetry R*, 27:4 (July-Aug 1936), 317-22.
4. Francis MacManus, "Ireland with the English Mouth," *Irish Monthly*, 64:761 (Nov 1936), 744-50.
5. Sean Moran, "A Survey of the Sham Irish: Mr. Stephen Gwynn's Review of Some English Writers," *Catholic Bulletin*, 26:8 (Aug 1936), 657-61.

5920. °HARMON, MAURICE: *Modern Irish Literature.* NY: McGraw-Hill, 1968. 25 minutes.
A tape recording: "Covers the growth of Irish writing from 1800 to the present. Discusses and illustrates the main periods and the principal writers, including the leading figures of the Irish Literary Revival" (publisher's prospectus).

5921. HOLLAND, MIGNONETTE: "Irish Saga Material and the Irish Literary Revival," M.A. thesis, U of Washington, 1951. i, 122 p.

5922. *HOWARTH, HERBERT: *The Irish Writers, 1880-1940: Literature under Parnell's Star.* London: Rockliff, 1958. x, 318 p.
Two general chapters and one each on George Moore, Lady Gregory, Yeats, AE, Synge, and Joyce. The Yeats chapter (pp. 110-64) discusses Irish themes and allegiances.
Reviews:
1. Anon., "Dubliners," *TLS*, 58:2971 (6 Feb 1959), 72.
2. René Fréchet, "Les écrivains irlandais et la réalité: Note brève," *EA*, 12:4 (Oct-Dec 1959), 338-44.
3. Monk Gibbon, *London Mag*, 6:8 (Aug 1959), 73, 75-77.

4. John Hewitt, *MLR*, 54:4 (Oct 1959), 631.

5. J. Mitchell Morse, *Comparative Literature*, 12:4 (Fall 1960), 374–76.

5923. IRISH LITERARY SOCIETY, LONDON: *Souvenir Programme of the Coming of Age of the Irish Literary Society of London, 1898–1913*. [London, 1913?]. 44 p.

Contains a history of the society by E[leanor] H[ull].

5924. KAIN, RICHARD MORGAN: *Dublin in the Age of William Butler Yeats and James Joyce*. Norman: U of Oklahoma Press, 1962. xi, 216 p. (Centers of Civilization Series. 7.)

Reprinted °Newton Abbott: David & Charles, 1972. The intelligent reader's Baedeker to Irish literature and literary Dublin; informative but chatty and not particularly deep. Documentation practically nil.
Reviews:

1. Anon., "The Glow Lingers On," *TLS*, 71:3655 (17 Mar 1972), 302.

2. Austin Clarke, "Literary Revivalists," *Irish Times*, #36091 (12 Feb 1972), 8.

3. Denis Donoghue, "Dear Shadows," *Nation*, 195:10 (6 Oct 1962), 203–4.

5925. KELLY, JOHN STEPHEN: "The Political, Intellectual, and Social Background to the Irish Literary Revival to 1901," Ph.D. thesis, Cambridge U, 1971. vi, 392, vii, xv p.

Contains individual chapters on O'Grady, Hyde, Yeats, and the Irish National Theatre, including an account of the *Countess Cathleen* row. Lacks a table of contents.

5926. KLUGH, CONSTANCE MERCER: "The Sinn Fein Spirit in the Irish Renaissance," M.A. thesis, Columbia U, 1933. iii, 68 p.

5927. LAW, HUGH ALEXANDER: *Anglo-Irish Literature*. With a foreword by A. E. London: Longmans Green, 1926. xviii, 302 p.

A defense of Anglo-Irish literature as distinct from English and Irish literature. Discusses the 17th- and 18th-century origins; Goldsmith, Sheridan, and Burke; the orators; the poets from Moore to Ferguson; early 19th-century novelists; "The Spirit of *The Nation*"; the historians; the dramatic revival; and Anglo-Irish literature from 1900 to 1920. On Yeats, *passim* (see index).
Reviews:

1. Anon., "Modern Irish Literature," *NSt*, 28:720 (12 Feb 1927), 542.

2. Karl Arns, *Englische Studien*, 64:1 (1929), 150–52.

3. Shan F. Bullock, *Bookman*, 72:428 (May 1927), 148.

4. J. M. Hone, "A Letter from Ireland," *London Mercury*, 16:94 (Aug 1927), 424–26.

5. AE [George William Russell], *Irish Statesman*, 7:20 (22 Jan 1927), 477–78.

5928. °MCBAIN, MARY NORMILE: "The Myths and Legends of the Heroic Cycle and Their Use in Anglo-Irish Literature," M.A. thesis, McGill U, 1921.

5929. MACDONAGH, THOMAS: *Literature in Ireland: Studies Irish and Anglo-Irish*. Dublin: Talbot Press, 1916. xiii, 248 p.

On Yeats's poetry, *passim*; particularly on his use of Gaelic names and on his prosody.

5930. MCILHONE, JOHN T.: "The Anglo-Irish Renaissance in Literature and Its Influence on the National Character of Ireland," M.A. thesis, U of Montreal, 1939. 2 v.

Worthless.

5931. MALYE, JEAN: *La littérature irlandaise contemporaine.* Paris: Sansot, 1913. 70 p.
    Based on a series of articles in *Entretiens idéalistes*, "La renaissance celtique en Irlande," yr 5 / 8:51 (25 Dec 1910), 281-91; yr 6 / 9:54 (25 Mar 1911), 113-26; :55 (25 Apr 1911), 198-209; °:56 (25 May 1911). On Yeats, pp. 53-70.

5931a. °MANNSAKER, F. M.: "The Literature of Anglo-Irish, 1757-1914," Ph.D. thesis, U of Nottingham, 1971/72.

5932. MOORE, GEORGE: *Hail and Farewell!* London: Heinemann, 1920-21 [1911-14]. 3 v.
    The individual volumes are subtitled *Ave, Salve,* and *Vale.* Part of volume 3, section vii, was published as "Yeats, Lady Gregory, and Synge," *English R,* 16:2 (Jan 1914), 167-80; :3 (Feb 1914), 350-64.
    George Moore's none-too-objective autobiographical reminiscences of the early years of the Irish literary revival, in the form of a loosely organized novelistic first-person narrative. Edward Martyn ("Dear Edward") figures *passim.*
Selective contents: Volume 1, section i, pp. 40-68: Early meetings with WBY, his early works and interest in Blake, and his involvement in the Golden Dawn (here called Golden Door).
1, ii, 69-103: Rehearsal and first performance of *The Countess Cathleen.*
1, iii, 103-34: Further meetings with WBY, notes on the Irish Literary Theatre, and the reception of *The Countess Cathleen*; also on T. P. Gill.
1, iv, 134-64: Other celebrities of the revival: O'Grady, Rolleston, Gill, Hyde, AE, Eglinton, and again WBY.
1, ix, 241-51: GM revises an early version of *The Shadowy Waters.*
1, x, 268-76: WBY at Lady Gregory's.
1, xi, 276-88: How WBY treated "dear Edward"; also on *The Shadowy Waters.*
1, xiv-xv, 342-62: The writing of *Diarmuid and Grania.*
2, i, 10-21: On AE and Hyde.
2, ii-v, 26-87: Again AE; note on WBY, 82-85.
2, vi, 101-8: The writing of *Diarmuid and Grania.*
2, vii, 127-43: The first performance of AE's *Deirdre* and WBY's *Cathleen ni Houlihan*; also on W. G. Fay and further impressions of WBY.
2, xix, 318-43: AE and John Eglinton.
3, vii, 164-204: WBY ridiculed by GM for denouncing the middle classes; on Lady Gregory, her collaboration with WBY, and her Kiltartanese prose style (criticized severely); also on Synge's being persuaded by WBY to go to Aran, on the reception of the *Playboy,* and the impression it made on dear Edward.
3, viii, 204-10: The plays of Synge and Lady Gregory.
3, x, 234-53: Further reminiscences of AE, WBY, James Stephens, Eglinton, and Hyde.

5933. MORRIS, LLOYD REGINALD: *The Celtic Dawn: A Survey of the Renascence in Ireland, 1889-1916.* NY: Cooper Square, 1970 [1917]. xix, 251 p.
    The "Irish renascence" is not only a literary movement, but also "the expression of a social synthesis, having its foundations in political and social history, concerned as much with intellectual emancipation and economic progress as it is with the art by which it is most widely known" (p. 1). Discusses the literary theories, the poetry, the drama, the novel, the folklore, and the political, social, and economic

importance of the movement. On Yeats's poetry and poetic theories, pp. 38-60; on his plays and dramatic theories, pp. 94-112; and *passim*.

5934. NATIONAL LITERARY SOCIETY OF IRELAND: *Journal of the National Literary Society of Ireland*. Dublin, 1 (1900)—2:1 (1916).

Although the *Journal* does not contain any article of immediate relevance to this bibliography, the whole publication as such is indicative of the reactivated interest in things literary and Irish.

5935. O'CONNOR, FRANK: *The Backward Look: A Survey of Irish Literature*. London: Macmillan, 1967. viii, 264 p.

The American edition was published as °*A Short History of Irish Literature: A Backward Look*. NY: Putnam, 1967. Incorporates: "Willie Is So Silly," *Vogue*, 145:2135 (1 Mar 1965), 122, 189-91, 193-95; "All the Olympians," *SatR*, 49:50 (10 Dec 1966), 30-32, 99; "W. B. Yeats," *Critic*, 25:3 (Dec 1966—Jan 1967), 50-59; "Bring In the Whiskey Now, Mary," *New Yorker*, 43:25 (12 Aug 1967), 36-40, 42, 45, 48, 50, 55-56, 58, 60, 63-64, 66, 68, 70-71.

Based on lectures, rambling rather than scholarly. On Yeats, including reminiscences, *passim*, especially pp. 163-82. Also on Lady Gregory, Joyce, O'Casey, Stephens, Synge, and others.
Reviews:
1. Vivian Mercier, "Irish Literature and a Cross-Fertilized Culture," *Commonweal*, 87:17 (2 Feb 1968), 541-42.
2. Raymond Rosenthal, "What the Old Man Said," *New Leader*, 50:15 (17 July 1967), 16-17.

5936. O'CONOR, NORREYS JEPHSON: *Changing Ireland: Literary Backgrounds of the Irish Free State, 1889-1922*. Cambridge, Mass.: Harvard UP, 1924. xii, 259 p.

A somewhat sketchy book. The parallel between literature and politics, suggested by the title, is not pursued very far. Of interest: "The Gaelic Background of Ireland's Literary Revival," 20-44; "Yeats and His Vision," 72-82 (the dream of restoring Ireland's "ancient spiritual dignity"); "Modern Anglo-Irish Poetry," 94-120; "A Dramatist of Changing Ireland," 157-71 (Lennox Robinson); and "Lady Gregory: Folklorist," 192-96, reprint of "Visions of the Celtic World as Seen by Lady Gregory in the West of Ireland," *BET*, 91:141 [i.e., 140] (16 June 1920), pt 2, 6 (a review of W312).

5937. °O'NEILL, MICHAEL JOSEPH: "The Diaries of a Dublin Playgoer as a Mirror of the Irish Literary Revival," Ph.D. thesis, University College, Dublin, 1952.

The Holloway diaries; see also J6307-8.

5938. O Suilleabhain, Pronnseas Eoghan [O'SULLIVAN, FRANCIS EUGENE]: "The Forerunners of the Irish Literary Revival," Dr. phil. thesis, U of Freiburg, [1925]. xii, 152 p.

A study of Callanan, Edward Walsh, Mangan, Ferguson, O'Grady, Sigerson, Hyde, and others.

5939. °PHELAN, FRANCIS J.: "Aspects of a National Literature in the *United Irishman* and Other Periodicals of the Anglo-Irish Literary Revival, 1899-1906," Ph.D. thesis, University College, Dublin, 1966.

5940. PORTER, RAYMOND J., and JAMES D. BROPHY (eds): *Modern Irish Literature: Essays in Honor of William York Tindall*. [New Rochelle, N.Y.]: Iona College Press / NY: Twayne, 1972. ix, 357 p. (Library of Irish Studies. 1.)

Contents: 1. Samuel Hynes: "Yeats and the Poets of the Thirties," 1-22; on Yeats's political poetry, particularly "The Second Coming," "Easter 1916," and "Lapis Lazuli," and his influence on Auden, Mac-Neice, Day Lewis, and Spender.
2. John Unterecker: "Interview with Liam Miller," 23-41; on the Dolmen Press and what it did for Irish literature; also on the Cuala Press.
3. Daniel J. Murphy: "Lady Gregory, Co-Author and Sometimes Author of the Plays of W. B. Yeats," 43-52. Lady Gregory was the coauthor of almost every early Yeats play; *Cathleen ni Houlihan* seems to be entirely hers.
4. Eileen Kennedy: "Design in George Moore's *The Lake*," 53-66.
5. James F. Carens: "Gogarty and Yeats," 67-93.
6. Lester Conner: "The Importance of Douglas Hyde to the Irish Literary Renaissance," 95-114; on Hyde and Yeats, *passim*.
7. Maurice Wohlgelernter: "Mother and Father and Son: Frank O'Connor's Portrait of the Artist as an Only Child," 115-28.
8. Grover Smith: "Yeats, Gogarty, and the Leap Castle Ghost," 129-41. The ghost occurs in *A Vision* (1937), Book 3, Section 5; it is indebted to Gogarty and others.
9. Mabel Worthington: "Maundy Thursday, Good Friday, the Sorrowing Mother, and the Day of Judgment," 143-51; on Joyce's use of Catholic liturgical hymns.
10. James D. Brophy: "John Montague's 'Restive Sally-Switch,'" 153-69.
11. E[dmund] L. Epstein: "Yeats' Experiments with Syntax in the Treatment of Time," 171-84. Static syntax and kinetic content in Yeats's poetry, especially in "Leda and the Swan."
12. Marvin Magalaner: "James Joyce and Marie Corelli," 185-93.
13. Raymond J. Porter: "Language and Literature in Revival Ireland: The Views of P. H. Pearse," 195-214. Includes a discussion of what Pearse thought of Yeats and the dramatic revival.
14. John P. Frayne: "Brian Moore's Wandering Irishman--The Not-So-Wild Colonial Boy," 215-34.
15. Chester G. Anderson: "On the Sublime and Its Anal-Urethral Sources in Pope, Eliot, and Joyce," 235-49.
16. Sighle Kennedy: "'The Devil and Holy Water'--Samuel Beckett's *Murphy* and Flann O'Brien's *At Swim-Two-Birds*," 251-60.
17. Rubin Rabinovitz: "*Watt* from Descartes to Schopenhauer," 261-87.
18. Kathleen McGrory: "Medieval Aspects of Modern Irish Writing: Austin Clarke," 289-99.
19. David H. Greene: "Yeats's Prose Style: Some Observations," 301-14.
20. Kevin Sullivan: "*The House by the Churchyard*: James Joyce and Sheridan Le Fanu," 315-34.
21. Thomas S. W. Lewis: "Some New Letters of John Butler Yeats," 335-54. Five letters (1920) to his cousin Frank Yeats, mostly concerned with the Yeats family.
Reviews:
1. Edward Brandabur, *Éire-Ireland*, 8:3 (Autumn 1973), 109-14.

5941. RANDALL, ETHEL CLAIRE: "The Celtic Movement: The Awakening of the Fires," M.A. thesis, U of Chicago, 1906. Various pagings.
    Worthless.

5942. REED, GERTRUDE HUMMEL: "The Restoration of the Irish Spirit in Anglo-Irish Literature from 1880 to 1930," M.A. thesis, U of Pittsburgh, 1932. iv, 114 p.

The restoration started with O'Grady, the prime mover was Yeats, and the highlight was Synge.

5943. REYNOLDS, HORACE: *A Providence Episode in the Irish Literary Renaissance*. Providence: Study Hill Club, 1929. 41 p. (Study Hill Club Publication. 1.)

The contributions of some writers of the revival (among them Yeats) to the *Providence Sunday Journal*.

5944. RIVOALLAN, ANATOLE: *Littérature irlandaise contemporaine*. Paris: Hachette, 1939. ix, 203 p.

On Yeats's early plays, pp. 16-20; on the early poetry, pp. 45-55; on the later poetry, pp. 104-13; and *passim* (see index). Also on Lady Gregory, Joyce, Moore, O'Casey, O'Connor, AE, and Synge.
Reviews:

1. Austin Clarke, *Dublin Mag*, 15:2 (Apr-June 1940), 70-71.
2. Ch.-M. Garnier, *Langues modernes*, 38:1 (Jan-Mar 1940), 67-69.
3. Armand Rébillon, *Annales de Bretagne*, 47 (1940), 267-70.

5945. RODGERS, WILLIAM ROBERT: *Irish Literary Portraits* [. . .]: *W. R. Rodgers's Broadcast Conversations with Those Who Knew Them*. London: British Broadcasting Corporation, 1972. xix, 236 p.

Contents: 1. Conor Cruise O'Brien: "Introduction," vii-x.
2. "Preface," xi-xix.
3. "W. B. Yeats," 1-21 (broadcast June 1949); reprinted from J1101 (q.v.). Yeats is also mentioned in the other programs.
4. "James Joyce," 22-74 (Feb 1950). Some of the participants: George Roberts, R. I. Best, Gogarty, Eglinton, Udolphus Wright, C. P. Curran, Stanislaus Joyce, James Stephens, and Austin Clarke.
5. "George Moore," 75-93 (Apr 1952): Best, Seumas O'Sullivan, Gogarty, Brinsley Macnamara, O'Connor, Robinson, Stephens, Monk Gibbon, and Clarke.
6. "J. M. Synge," 94-115 (May 1952): Edward Millington Stephens, O'Sullivan, Best, Gogarty, Roberts, and Wright.
7. "George Bernard Shaw," 116-41 (Sept 1954): O'Casey, Ervine, Denis Johnston, O'Connor, Thomas Bodkin, Clarke, and Gogarty.
8. "Oliver St. John Gogarty," 142-68 (Apr 1961): Colum, Johnston, Clarke, Macnamara, Gibbon, and Bodkin.
9. "F. R. Higgins," 169-84 (Feb 1964): O'Connor, Gibbon, Colum, and Clarke.
10. "AE (George Russell)," 185-203 (Jan 1965): Gibbon, O'Connor, Colum, and Patrick Kavanagh.
11. "Old Ireland Free," 204-29 (Apr 1966); reminiscences of the Easter 1916 Rising.
12. Harden Jay: "Biographical Notes on Some of the Contributors," 230-36; virtually worthless.
Reviews:
1. Anon., "Literary Lore," *TLS*, 71:3682 (29 Sept 1972), 1148.

5946. A. E. [RUSSELL, GEORGE WILLIAM]: *Some Irish Essays*. Dublin: Maunsel, 1906. 39 p. (Tower Press Booklets. 1.)

"Nationality and Cosmopolitanism in Art," 9-20; reprinted from J5917.
"The Dramatic Treatment of Heroic Literature," 21-27; reprinted from *United Irishman*, 7:166 (3 May 1902), 3, and *Samhain*, [#2] (Oct 1902), 11-13.
"On an Irish Hill," 28-34; reprinted from an unspecified issue of *Kilkenny Moderator* (not traced).

"The Poet of Shadows," 35-39; reprinted from *Reader*, 2:3 (Aug 1903), 249-50; reprinted in J4503. On Yeats's poetry.

5947. RYAN, WILLIAM PATRICK: *The Irish Literary Revival: Its History, Pioneers and Possibilities*. London: The Author, 1894. vii, 184 p.

On Yeats, *passim*, especially pp. 29-30, 36, 50-51, 53-60, 66-68, 70, 75, 125-29, 132-36. He receives high praise as the most imaginative of the Irish writers.

5947a. SARUKHANĨAN, ALLA PAVLOVNA: *Sovremennaĩa irlandskaĩa literatura* [Contemporary Irish literature]. Moskva: Izdatel'stvo Nauka, 1973. 319 p.

Contains chapters on the Easter Rising and its literature, the turning point in the Irish literary revival (i.e., after 1916), the development of realism in the twenties and thirties, Irish literature during World War II and in the first decade after the war, and the literature of discussion and protest in the sixties. Concentrates on Behan, Lady Gregory, Johnston, Yeats (pp. 28-30, 52-66, 84-86, 90-119, and *passim*), Kinsella, Clarke, Colum, Kavanagh, Carroll, MacDonagh, Macken, Milne, Peadar O'Donnell, O'Casey, O'Connor, O'Faolain, O'Flaherty, Pearse, Plunkett, AE, Synge, Stephens, Darrell Figgis, F. R. Higgins, John Hewitt, and George Shiels.

5948. SKELTON, ROBIN, and DAVID RIDGLEY CLARK (eds): *Irish Renaissance: A Gathering of Essays, Memoirs, and Letters from "The Massachusetts Review."* Dublin: Dolmen Press, 1965. 167 p.

Contents: 1. "Preface," 11.

2. W. B. Yeats: "Modern Ireland: An Address to American Audiences, 1932-1933," 13-25. Transcribed from the MS. and edited by Curtis Bradford. (*MassR*, 5:2 [Winter 1964], 256-68.)

3. David R. Clark: "W. B. Yeats: *The Shadowy Waters* (MS. Version): Half the Characters Had Eagles' Faces," 26-55. (*MassR*, 6:1 [Autumn-Winter 1964], 151-80.) Now in J3896.

4. John Butler Yeats: "John Butler Yeats to Lady Gregory: New Letters," 56-64. Eight letters written between 18 June 1898 and 23 Sept 1907, edited by Glenn O'Malley and Donald T. Torchiana. (*MassR*, 5:2, 269-77.)

5. J. M. Synge: "Synge to MacKenna: The Mature Years," 65-79. Edited by Ann Saddlemyer. The letters contain some critical remarks on the Abbey and on Yeats's plays, especially *The Shadowy Waters*. (*MassR*, 5:2, 279-95.)

6. W. B. Yeats: "Discoveries: Second Series," 80-89. Transcribed from the MS. and edited by Curtis Bradford. (*MassR*, 5:2, 297-306.)

7. Austin Clarke: "A Centenary Celebration," 90-93. An account of the meeting held at the Thomas Davis Centenary in the Antient Concert Rooms on 20 Nov 1914. Yeats made a speech on this occasion. (*MassR*, 5:2, 307-10.)

8. George Bernard Shaw: "The Roger Casement Trial: An Unpublished Statement," 94-97. (*MassR*, 5:2, 311-14.)

9. W. B. Yeats: "A Fair Chance of a Disturbed Ireland: W. B. Yeats to Mrs. J. Duncan," 98-105. Edited by John Unterecker. Eleven letters written in 1918; Mrs. James Duncan seems to be the same as Ellen M. Duncan, who wrote occasionally on Yeats (see index of names). (*MassR*, 5:2, 315-22.)

10. Richard M. Kain: "James Joyce's Shakespeare Chronology," 106-19. (*MassR*, 5:2, 342-55.)

11. Denis Johnston: "Clarify Begins At: The Non-Information of *Finnegans Wake*," 120-27. (*MassR*, 5:2, 357-64.)

12. Sean O'Casey: "Sean O'Casey Concerning James Joyce," 128-29. (*MassR*, 5:2, 335-36.)
13. Seymour Rudin: "Playwright to Critic: Sean O'Casey's Letters to George Jean Nathan," 130-38. (*MassR*, 5:2, 326-34.)
14. David Krause: "Sean O'Casey: 1880-1964," 139-57. Quotes some of O'Casey's remarks on Yeats. (*MassR*, 6:2 [Winter-Spring 1965], 233-51.)
15. Robin Skelton: "Twentieth-Century Irish Literature and the Private Press Tradition: Dun Emer, Cuala, & Dolmen Presses, 1902-1963," 158-67. (*MassR*, 5:2, 368-77.)
Reviews:
1. Anon., "Mad Ireland," *TLS*, 65:3382 (22 Dec 1966), 1190.
2. Harold Orel, *MD*, 9:4 (Feb 1967), 466.

5948a. °TAFT, M. H.: "The Influence of Parnell on Irish Imaginative Literature," M.Litt. thesis, Trinity College, Dublin, 1971/72.

5949. TÉRY, SIMONE: *L'île des bardes: Notes sur la littérature irlandaise contemporaine*. Paris: Flammarion, 1925. 249 p.
"W. B. Yeats," 57-98; based on "W. B. Yeats, poète irlandais: Lauréat du Prix Nobel," *Grande revue*, yr 27 / 113:12 (Dec 1923), 259-72. Includes some personal reminiscences. Also chapters on Synge (based on "J. M. Synge et son oeuvre," *Revue anglo-américaine*, 2:3 [Feb 1925], 204-16), AE, Stephens, Moore, and Joyce.
Reviews:
1. C. P. Curran, "French Critics and Irish Literature," *Irish Statesman*, 4:23 (15 Aug 1925), 723-24.
2. André Maurois, "La littérature irlandaise contemporaine," *Candide*, 12:74 (13 Aug 1925), 3.

5950. THOMPSON, FRANCIS JOHN: "Fenianism and the Celtic Renaissance," Ph.D. thesis, New York U, 1940 (for 1941). xxxv, 1281 p.
On Yeats, *passim*.

5951. THOMPSON, WILLIAM IRWIN: *The Imagination of an Insurrection: Dublin, Easter 1916. A Study of an Ideological Movement*. NY: Oxford UP, 1967. xiii, 262 p.
Based on "Easter 1916: A Study of Literature and Revolution," °Ph.D. thesis, Cornell U, 1966. 250 p. (*DA*, 26:12 [June 1966], 7302). Discusses the historical and literary conditions that led to the Easter Rising, its poet-martyrs Pearse, MacDonagh, and Plunkett, and the aftermath in the works of Yeats, AE, and O'Casey. See also Conor Cruise O'Brien, "Two-faced Cathleen," *NYRB*, 8:12 (29 June 1967), 19-21.

5951a. °WELCH, ROBERT A.: "Aspects of Translation from the Irish in Anglo-Irish Literature," M.A. thesis, University College, Cork, 1970/71.

5952. WITTIG, KURT: "Die Nationalliteratur Irlands in englischer Sprache von 1889 bis 1939: Motive--Probleme--Charaktere," Habilitationsschrift, U of Halle, [1945]. i, 340 p.
A general survey rather than a critical account. On Yeats, pp. 12-25 and *passim*.

See also J377-405, 1105, 1110, 1269, 1327, 1690, 1755, 1760a, 4054, 6307, 6308, 6321.

KB   Articles and Parts of Books (General Studies)

5953. ÅBERG, ALF: *Irlands historia*. Stockholm: Natur och Kultur, 1961. 190 p.
"Den keltiska renässansen," 121-29.

5954. ALEXANDER, CALVERT: *The Catholic Literary Revival: Three Phases in Its Development from 1845 to the Present*. Milwaukee: Bruce, 1939 [1935]. xv, 399 p.
"The Celtic Dawn," 175-200. Assesses the Catholic contribution to early 20th-century Irish literature but overrates it greatly. Admits that the revival was not a "predominantly Catholic manifestation," but closes with the dubious statement that "the long literary dictatorship of the Ascendancy [the "Yeats-Russell group"] . . . is now definitely at an end."

5955. AMICO, MASOLINO D': "Scrittori irlandesi," *Mondo*, 17:25 (22 June 1965), 9-10.

5956. ANON.: "The Old and New in Ireland," *Academy*, 63:1583 (6 Sept 1902), 238-39.
The prospects for a harmonious relationship between the revival and the Gaelic League.

5957. ANON.: "The Irish Literary Renaissance," *Athenaeum*, #4505 (28 Feb 1914), 303-4.

5958. ANON.: Commentary on Yeats's letter concerning a proposed National Literary Society, *Daily Express*, #12490 (2 June 1892), 4.
See J130.

5959. ANON.: "The Irish Literary Movement," *Daily Express*, #13330 (28 Feb 1895), 5.
Report of a debate on the motion "That the movement for the revival of Irish literature deserves our support." One of the participants was Edward Dowden.

5960. ANON.: "The Irish Literary Revival," *Harper's Weekly*, 47:2424 (6 June 1903), 958.

5961. ANON.: "Ireland: Writers. A Floating Conundrum," *Illustrated London News*, 248:6612 (23 Apr 1966), 22-23.
Irish literature of the 1960s as a continuation of the revival.

5962. ANON.: "Talking to H. O. White," *Irish Times*, #33217 (7 Apr 1962), 8.
White's reminiscences of Yeats, Lady Gregory, AE, and others.

5962a. ANON.: "How Ireland Turned from Politics to Playwriting: Lady Gregory Traces the New Literary Movement to the Political Break-up That Followed the Death of Parnell--She Tells of the 'Western World' Where Every Poet Is a Peasant," *NYT*, 61:19671 (3 Dec 1911), pt V, 5.
Interview.

5963. ANON.: "A New Literary Impulse," *Speaker*, 7:[] (11 Mar 1893), 276-77.
On the founding of the Irish Literary Society, London. "From Mr. Yeats, with his exquisite feeling for form, much is to be expected in the future, especially if he can emancipate himself from the little 'sheeogue' and 'luricaun' way of looking at everything. . . ." Correspondence by T. W. Rolleston, (18 Mar 1893), 312.

5964. ANON.: "Modern Literature: Ulster's Share in the Revival," *Times*, #43206 (5 Dec 1922), Northern Ireland supplement, xviii.

5965. ANON.: "Irish Tradition and Transition," *TLS*, 51:2639 (29 Aug 1952), xxxii.
Part of the supplement "Fresh Minds at Work: Reflections on the Practice of Letters among the Younger Generation at Home and Abroad."

5966. ANON.: "Writing in the Republic of Ireland," *TLS*, 54:2788 (5 Aug 1955), viii.

5967. ANON.: "Eire Looks Outward," *TLS*, 56:2894 (16 Aug 1957), xxxii-xxxiii.
Part of the supplement "A Sense of Direction: Being an Examination of the Efforts of Writers to Keep or Regain Contact with the Everyday Realities of Life in Terms of Modern Literature."

5968. ANON.: "The Irish Literary Movement," *United Ireland*, 12:616 (24 June 1893), 4.

5969. ARNS, KARL: "Alte und neue irische Renaissance," *Gral*, 26:12 (Sept 1932), 928-33.

5970. ————: *Literatur und Leben im heutigen England*. Leipzig: Rohmkopf, 1933. 128 p.
"Alte und junge Anglo-Iren," 111-23; a survey of Anglo-Irish literature of the twenties and early thirties, based on a mistaken nationalistic typology: all Englishmen are Shylocks, etc.

5971. ————: *Grundriss der Geschichte der englischen Literatur von 1832 bis zur Gegenwart*. Paderborn: Schöningh, 1941. 235 p.
"Die keltische Renaissance und die neuen Anglo-Iren," 205-24; on Yeats, pp. 207-11.

5972. BEHAN, MERRILL BERNARD: "Anglo-Irish Literature," M.A. thesis, U of Montréal, [1939]. i, 76 p.
Negligible.

5973. BIRMINGHAM, GEORGE A.: "The Literary Movement in Ireland," *Fortnightly R*, os 88 / ns 82:492 (Dec 1907), 947-57.
Reprinted in *Living Age*, 256:3316 (25 Jan 1908), 235-43. On Yeats, *passim*.

5974. ————: *An Irishman Looks at His World*. London: Hodder & Stoughton, 1919. 307 p.
"--And Scholars--Ireland's Culture," 102-22. "Ireland, in spite of its springtime of promise, has failed to create a national kind of literature because Ireland does not want literature of any kind, national or other." Yeats is included among the unwanted.

5975. BOYD, ERNEST A.: "The Drift of Anglo-Irish Literature," *Irish Commonwealth*, 1:1 (St. Patrick's Day 1919), 19-28.

5976. ————: "Books That Ireland Is Reading To-day," *Literary Digest International Book R*, 1:4 (Mar 1923), 25-26, 62.

5977. BROMAGE, MARY COGAN: "Literature of Ireland Today," *SAQ*, 42:1 (Jan 1943), 27-37.

5978. BROOKS, VAN WYCK: "Ireland, 1916," *Dial*, 61:730 (30 Nov 1916), 458-60.
An omnibus review.

5979. ————: *From the Shadow of the Mountain: My Post-Meridian Years*. NY:
Dutton, 1961. ix, 202 p.
"Impressions of Ireland," 138-61; a visit to some of the survivors of
the revival in 1951.

5980. BROWN, STEPHEN J.: "Gaelic and Anglo-Irish Literature--Contacts and
Quality," *Irish Statesman*, 13:12 (23 Nov 1929), 232-33; :13 (30 Nov 1929),
252-54.

5981. BRYANT, SOPHIE: *The Genius of the Gael: A Study of Celtic Psychology
and Its Manifestations*. London: Unwin, 1913. 292 p.
"The Gael in Literature," 183-218; contains some high praise of *Cathleen ni Houlihan*.

5982. CADENHEAD, I. E. (ed): *Literature and History*. Tulsa: U of Tulsa,
1970. vii, 102 p. (U of Tulsa [Department of English] Monograph Series.
9.)
James H. Matthews: "History to Literature: Alternatives to History in
Modern Irish Literature," 73-87. Mainly on Irish poetry after 1940
(Clarke and Kavanagh), including some notes on Yeats.

5982a. CAHILL, SUSAN and THOMAS: *A Literary Guide to Ireland*. NY: Scribner's, 1973. xvii, 333 p.
Extended passages on Coole Park, Lady Gregory, Joyce, O'Casey,
O'Connor, Sligo, Synge, Thoor Ballylee, and Yeats (especially pp. 101-
15, 167-86).

5983. CANADIAN ASSOCIATION FOR IRISH STUDIES: *Newsletter*. Kingston, Ont. /
Hamilton, Ont.
#1 (22 Feb 1973); #2 (June 1973); #3 (Nov 1973).

5984. CANBY, HENRY SEIDEL: *Education by Violence: Essays on the War and
the Future*. NY: Macmillan, 1919. xi, 233 p.
"On Irish Literature," 55-56.

5985. CIARLANTINI, FRANCO: "L'anima d'Irlanda," *Augustea*, 6:16 (31 Aug
1930), 487-89.

5986. CLARK, JAMES M.: "The Irish Literary Movement," *Englische Studien*,
49:1 (July 1915), 50-98.
On Yeats, *passim*; also on Synge, Lady Gregory, and Moore.

5987. COHEN-PORTHEIM, PAUL: "Irische Literatur," *Berliner Tageblatt*, 19:
100 (28 Feb 1930), Beiblatt 1, [1-2].

5988. COLBY, ELBRIDGE: "Irish Literary Patriotism," *Catholic World*, 99:
591 (June 1914), 361-66.
The works of Seumas MacManus are more representative of the Irish
people than are those of Yeats.

5989. COLLES, RAMSAY: *In Castle and Courthouse: Being Reminiscences of
30 Years in Ireland*. London: Laurie, [1911]. 320 p.
"The Irish Literary Movement," 19-27.

5990. COLUM, MARY MAGUIRE: "Letter from Ireland," *SatR*, 1:12 (18 Oct
1924), 214.
There is no vitality in the present literary life of Dublin.

5991. ————: *From These Roots: The Ideas That Have Made Modern Literature*. Port Washington, N.Y.: Kennikat Press, 1967 [1937]. xiii, 386 p.
"The Outside Literatures in English: The Irish and the American,"
260-311; on Irish literature, pp. 260-69, with some remarks on Yeats.

5992. COLUM, PADRAIC: "The Irish Literary Movement," *Forum*, 53:1 (Jan 1915), 133-48.
On Yeats, Hyde, AE, and the dramatic revival.

5993. ———: "Youngest Ireland," *Seven Arts*, 2:11 (Sept 1917), 608-23.

5994. ———: "The Promise of Irish Letters," *Nation*, 117:3040 (10 Oct 1923), 396-97.

5995. ———: *The Road round Ireland*. NY: Macmillan, 1926. xvii, 492 p.
"Dublin through the Abbey Theatre," 260-338; a series of sketches of Dublin literary life in the early years of the 20th century.

5996. CONACHER, W. M.: "The Irish Literary Movement," *QQ*, 45:1 (Spring 1938), 56-65.
Mainly a somewhat misguided attack on Synge.

5997. COULTER, GEOFFREY: "Litir o Éirinn," *Transatlantic R*, 1:5 (May 1924), 345-49.
In English.

5998. ———: "Litir o Eirinn," *Transatlantic R*, 2:5 [1924], 537-46.
In English. See also J144.

5999. COUSINS, JAMES HENRY, and MARGARET E. COUSINS: *We Two Together*. Madras: Ganesh, 1950. xvii, 784 p.
See especially "Renaissance Personal and National," 39-50; "Irish Drama Arrives," 55-78; and "State and Rostrum," 91-103. Includes an account of a visit to Les Mouettes to see Maud Gonne and Yeats, whom Cousins overheard "composing" poetry (pp. 158-63).

6000. COUSINS, JAMES H.: "Culture and National Renaissance: The Irish Example," *Visva-Bharati Q*, 17:3 (Nov 1951-Jan 1952), 179-90.

6001. CRONIN, JOHN: "The Funnel and the Tundish: Irish Writers and the English Language," *Wascana R*, 3:1 (1968), 80-88.

6002. CROSLAND, MARGARET (ed): *A Guide to Literary Europe*. Philadelphia: Chilton Books, 1966. 3 v. in 1.
Patrick Byrne: "Ireland," 2:77-96.

6003. CROWLEY, MARY: "The Norman Tradition in Anglo-Irish Literature," *Irish Statesman*, 13:18 (4 Jan 1930), 354-56.
Especially in the prose style, including Yeats's.

6004. CUNLIFFE, JOHN WILLIAM: *English Literature during the Last Half Century*. NY: Macmillan, 1919. viii, 315 p.
"The Irish Movement," 223-43; on Yeats, pp. 225-31.

6005. ———: *English Literature in the Twentieth Century*. NY: Macmillan, 1933. vii, 341 p.
"The Irish Renaissance," 100-124; includes sections on Yeats (pp. 101-5), Synge, Moore, Dunsany, and O'Casey.

6006. CURTAYNE, ALICE: *The Irish Story: A Survey of Irish History and Culture*. Dublin: Clonmore & Reynolds / London: Burns & Oates, 1962. 176 p.
"Literature in Twentieth Century Ireland," 154-63.

6007. CURTIS, LEWIS PERRY: *Anglo-Saxons and Celts: A Study of Anti-Irish Prejudice in Victorian England*. Bridgeport, Conn.: Conference on British Studies at the U of Bridgeport, 1968. xi, 162 p. (Studies in British History and Culture. 2.)
"Celticism: The Irish Response," 108-16.

6008. ———: "The Anglo-Irish Predicament," *Twentieth-Century Studies*, #4 (Nov 1970), 37-63.
A social and political survey with occasional remarks on literature.

6009. CURTIS, W. O'LEARY: "The National Literary Society," *Catholic Bulletin*, 2:8 (Aug 1912), 569-75.

6010. DANAHER, KEVIN: "Folk Tradition and Literature," *J of Irish Literature*, 1:2 (May 1972), 63-76.
Includes notes on Synge, Lady Gregory, and Yeats (who is said to have never understood the Irish folk tradition).

6011. DAVRAY, HENRY-D.: "La jeune Irlande," *Mercure de France*, yr 16 / 54: 185 (1 Mar 1905), 19-32.

6012. DEAN-SMITH, MARGARET: "Celtic Twilight," *N&Q*, os 207 / ns 9:1 (Jan 1962), 30.
Attempts a lexical definition.

6012a. DEANE, SEAMUS: "The Position of the Irish Intellectual," *Cambridge R*, 94:2213 (18 May 1973), 134-36, 138.
Deplores the lack of a school of Irish literary criticism.

6013. DE BLACAM, AODH: "The Irish Literary Prospect," *Dublin R*, 173:347 (Oct-Nov-Dec 1923), 235-42.

6014. ———: *A First Book of Irish Literature: Hiberno-Latin, Gaelic, Anglo-Irish. From the Earliest Times to the Present Day.* Dublin: Talbot Press, [1934]. xii, 236 p.
"Renascent Ireland," 211-28; a survey and short author sketches from a conservative, Catholic, and nationalistic point of view. See his opinion of Yeats: "His idiosyncratic temperament has withdrawn him from the great central themes on which high literature must rest."

6015. DE LURY, A. T.: "Literature in Ireland," *Canadian Bookman*, 20:3 (Aug-Sept 1938), 25-29.

6016. DESMOND, SHAW: "The Irish Renaissance," *Outlook*, 138:7 (15 Oct 1924), 247-49.

6017. DONNELLY, FRANCIS P.: "Literary Renaissance and Nationality," *America*, 29:726 (25 Aug 1923), 448-49.
See also Donnelly's "Ireland's Literary Renaissance," :729 (15 Sept 1923), 520-21. The movement is not particularly Celtic, i.e., it does not correspond to the sweet innocent picture of Catholic Ireland that *America* maintains is the true one. Abuses Joyce ("load of sawdust").

6018. DONOGHUE, DENIS: "Irische Literatur nach Yeats und Joyce," *Dokumente*, 14:3 (June 1958), 233-35.
The Irish writers of today have not really assimilated the literary work of Joyce and Yeats.

6019. DORSON, RICHARD MERCER: *The British Folklorists: A History.* London: Routledge & Kegan Paul, 1968. x, 518 p.
"Ireland," 431-39; mostly on Hyde, with notes on Yeats and Lady Gregory.

6020. "DUBLINENSIS": "The Soothsayers: To Captain Stephen Gwynn," *Catholic Bulletin*, 21:7 (July 1931), 684-99.
A denunciation of the writers of the revival, including Yeats.

6021. DUFF, CHARLES: *Ireland and the Irish*. NY: Putnam's, 1954 [1953]. 288 p.
  "Renaissance," 130–35.

6022. DUNN, JOSEPH, and PATRICK JOSEPH LENNOX (eds): *The Glories of Ireland*. Washington, D.C.: Phoenix, 1914. ix, 357 p.
  Joseph Holloway: "The Irish Theatre," 304–9. Horatio S. Krans: "The Irish Literary Revival," 317–25.

6023. DUNSANY, LORD: "Some Irish Writers Whom I Have Known," *Irish Writing*, #20–21 (Nov 1952), 78–82.
  See also "Irish Writers I Have Known," *Atlantic Monthly*, 192:3 (Sept 1953), 66–68. Particularly AE and James Stephens.

6024. EDWARDS, OWEN DUDLEY (ed): *Conor Cruise O'Brien Introduces Ireland*. London: Deutsch, 1969. 240 p.
  Máire Cruise O'Brien: "The Two Languages," 43–60; contains some remarks on the Gaelic influence on the revival.
  Kevin Sullivan: "Literature in Modern Ireland," 135–47: Between the extremes of Yeats and Joyce lies the whole body of modern Irish literature.
  Benedict Kiely: "The Whores on the Half-Doors; or, An Image of the Irish Writer," 148–61; only marginally connected with the revival.
  Seamus Kelly: "The Theatre," 162–69.
  James Plunkett: "Dublin Streets: Broad and Narrow," 189–94; contains some reminiscences of Yeats (p. 193).

6025. ELLIS, AMANDA MAE: *The Literature of England*. Boston: Little, Brown, 1937. xv, 478 p.
  See pp. 372–87.

6026. ELTON, OLIVER: *Modern Studies*. London: Arnold, 1907. viii, 342 p.
  "Living Irish Literature," 285–320. On Yeats, pp. 299–307 (particularly on *Deirdre*); also on the Abbey Theatre, Synge, and AE.

6027. *Encyclopaedia of Ireland*. Dublin: Figgis / NY: McGraw-Hill, 1968. 463 p.
  Eavan Boland: "The Literary Revival," 354–58; Brendan Kennelly: "Modern Writing," 358–61; Anon.: "Theatre," 372–79.

6028. ENRIGHT, D. J.: "A Note on Irish Literature and the Irish Tradition," *Scrutiny*, 10:3 (Jan 1942), 247–55.
  The problem of writing Irish literature in the English language, with some disparaging remarks on Yeats's plays.

6028a. ENRIGHT, TIM: "The Celtic Revival: Lilting Cadence and Earthy Wit," *Daily Worker*, #9561 (28 June 1962), 2.

6029. F., M.: "Irische Literatur–Renaissance," *Frankfurter Zeitung*, 63: 186 (10 Mar 1919), 1–2.
  Summarizes a lecture by Ernst Leopold Stahl.

6030. FARRELL, JAMES T.: "The Irish Cultural Rennaissance [*sic*] in the Last Century," *Irish Writing*, #25 (Dec 1953), 50–53.
  Scrappy and uninformed.

6030a. FAUCHEREAU, SERGE: "Introduction," "Quelques aînés," "La génération d'après-guerre," *Lettres nouvelles*, #1 (Mar 1973), 6–12, 19–28, 97–104.
  Introductions to a special number, "Ecrivains irlandais d'aujourd'hui." Yeats is mentioned *passim*.

6031. FAVERTY, FREDERIC E.: *Matthew Arnold the Ethnologist*. NY: AMS Press, 1968 [1951]. vii, 241 p. (Humanities Series. 27.)
"The Celt," 111-61; on Arnold's influence on the revival.

6032. FAY, WILLIAM P.: "Dublin, capitale littéraire," *Revue des deux mondes*, #23 (1 Dec 1960), 403-16.

6033. °FEENEY, WILLIAM JACKSON: "The Informer in Irish History and Literature," Ph.D. thesis, U of Oregon, 1956. 675 p.

6034. FILON, AUGUSTIN: "Le réveil de l'âme celtique," *Journal des débats politiques et littéraires*, 117:108 (19 Apr 1905), 1.
Includes comments on *The Hour Glass*, *The King's Threshold*, and *Cathleen ni Houlihan*.

6035. FORD, MARY K.: "Is the Celtic Revival Really Irish?" *NAR*, 183:601 (19 Oct 1906), 771-75.
No, it is not--at least not in the works of Yeats, Lady Gregory, and AE, which are altogether inferior to those of Ethna Carberry and Moira O'Neill.

6036. FOX, RICHARD MICHAEL: *Green Banners: The Story of the Irish Struggle*. London: Secker & Warburg, 1938. 352 p.
"Emerging Ireland," 16-24; "Celtic Renaissance," 25-32.

6037. F[RANCIA], E[NNIO]: "Letteratura irlandese contemporanea," *Osservatore romano*, 70:23525 (20 Oct 1937), 3.

6038. FREUDENTHAL, M[ARIE]: "Von irischer Art und Kunst," *Bühne und Welt*, yr 11 / 21:6 (Dec 1908), 245-49.
On Yeats, pp. 245-47; includes two photographs of a performance of *The Hour Glass*.

6039. FREYER, GRATTAN: "A Letter from Ireland," *Scrutiny*, 6:4 (Mar 1938), 376-85.
Some impressions of the cultural scene.

6040. FREYER, MICHAEL G.: "The Dolmen Press: A Talk Given to the Bibliographical Society of Ireland," *Private Library*, 3:2 (Apr 1960), 10-14.

6041. FRIIS-MØLLER, KAI (ed): *Irland*. København: Branner, 1918. vii, 183 p.
K. Friis-Møller: "Irlands harpe," 161-73; contains some notes on Yeats.

6042. GHEORGHIU, MIHNEA: *Dionysos: Eseuri lirice*. București: Editura Pentru Literatură, 1969. 307 p.
"Eriniile lui Erin," 162-68; a description of literary Dublin.

6043. GLENAVY, LADY BEATRICE: *"Today We Will Only Gossip."* London: Constable, 1964. 206 p.
Memories of some figures of the revival, *passim*.

6044. GOBLET, YANN-M.: "Le mouvement littéraire en Irlande," *Vie des peuples*, yr 4 / 12:48 (Apr 1924), 1103-14.

6045. ————: "Le mouvement littéraire en Irlande," *Comoedia*, 17:434 (25 July 1924), 3, 5.

6046. GOGARTY, OLIVER: "The Irish Literary Revival: Present Poetry and Drama in Dublin," *Dublin Evening Mail*, #21254 (4 Mar 1905), 2.
Criticizes Yeats's plays, particularly *On Baile's Strand*, because they tend "to lilliputianize our legends."

6047. GOGARTY, OLIVER ST. JOHN: *A Week End in the Middle of the Week and Other Essays on the Bias.* NY: Doubleday, 1958. 285 p.
"The Big House at Coole," 139-43.

6048. [GOLDRING, DOUGLAS]: *Dublin: Explorations and Reflections by an Englishman.* Dublin: Maunsel, 1917. vii, 271 p.
"The Intellectuals," 165-91; "Literature in Dublin," 192-239; "The Theatre in Dublin," 240-57.

6049. GRABISCH, JOSEF: "Die heutige irische Dichtung," *Deutsche Allgemeine Zeitung*, 70:153-54 (8 Apr 1931), Beilage Das Unterhaltungsblatt, unpaged.
Worthless.

6050. GRAVES, ALFRED PERCEVAL: *To Return to All That: An Autobiography.* London: Cape, 1930. 350 p.
On the activities of the Irish Literary Society, London, pp. 261-70.

6051. GREENE, DAVID / Ó hUaithne, Daithí: *Writing in Irish Today / Nua-litríocht na Gaeilge.* Cork: Mercier Press, 1972. iv, 60 p. (Irish Life and Culture. 18.)
Contains frequent references to the revival.

6051a. GREVER, GLENN ALBERT: "The Poetic Achievement of Patrick Kavanagh," °Ph.D. thesis, U of Illinois at Urbana-Champaign, 1973. 377 p. (*DA*, 34:1 [July 1973], 314A-15A.)

6052. GRZEBIENIOWSKI, TADEUSZ: "Irlandja współczesna: Stan literatury" [Contemporary Ireland: The literary situation], *Droga* [:] (1935), 250-68.
On Yeats, *passim*.

6053. GWYNN, STEPHEN: *To-day and To-morrow in Ireland: Essays on Irish Subjects.* Dublin: Hodges Figgis / London: Macmillan, 1903. xix, 223 p.
"The Gaelic Revival in Literature," 1-37; an omnibus review, among others of W18 and 227. First published anonymously in *Quarterly R*, 195:390 (Apr 1902), 423-49.
"Celtic Sagas Retold," 38-58; reprint of "Celtic Sagas," *Macmillan's Mag*, 87:517 (Nov 1902), 95-104. A review of W256.
"The Gaelic League and the Irish Theatre," 87-96.

6054. ———: *Irish Books and Irish People.* Dublin: Talbot Press / London: Unwin, [1920]. vii, 120 p.
"Introduction," 1-6: "Yeats and Synge have showed how completely it is possible to be Irish while using the English language."

6055. ———: *Ireland.* With an introduction by H. A. Fisher. London: Benn, 1924. 252 p. (The Modern World: A Survey of Historical Forces. 1.)
"The Two Cultures," 109-26.

6056. HARMON, MAURICE: "The Era of Inhibitions: Irish Literature, 1920-60," *Emory UQ*, 22:1 (Spring 1966), 18-28.

6057. HEALY, THOMAS: "A. E. Talks of Irish Letters," *Commonweal*, 6:26 (2 Nov 1927), 632-34.
Interview. Yeats, in AE's words, "belongs to what we call 'the literature of dream.'"

6058. HEINEY, DONALD W.: *Essentials of Contemporary Literature.* Great Neck, N.Y.: Barron's Educational Series, 1954. xviii, 555 p.
"The Irish Renaissance," 308-23; on Yeats, pp. 310-13. To be used with caution.

6059. HERHOLTZ, FRITZ: "Die neuirische Literaturbewegung (The Irish Literary Revival)," *Xenien*, 7:[7] (July 1914), 412–16.
Contains notes on the works of Yeats and Moore.

6060. HIERONIMI, MARTIN: "Die irische Dichtung," *Bewegung*, 9:8 (25 Feb 1941), 10.
Nazi point of view.

6061. HILL, DEREK, and VIVIAN MERCIER: "Letters from Ireland," *Horizon*, 13:76 (Apr 1946), 268–85.

6062. HILL, DOUGLAS: "The Other Presences in Irish Life and Literature," *Brigham Young U Studies*, 6:1 (Autumn 1964), 35–39.
On "mythological thinking" among the writers of the revival.

6063. HOLM, INGVAR: *Fran Baudelaire till första världskriget*. Stockholm: Bonnier, 1964. 267 p. (Bonniers allmänna litteratur-historia. 6.)
"Irländskt," 126–36; on Yeats, pp. 131–36.

6064. HONE, JOSEPH M.: "Literature and the Drama: Modern Tendencies. Influences of the War. Future of the Literary Movement," *Times*, #42248 (4 Nov 1919), 45.

6065. ———: "A Letter from Ireland," *London Mercury*, 2:12 (Oct 1920), 732–34.
The plays of Synge, Robinson, and others in the context of the revival.

6066. ———: "A Letter from Ireland," *London Mercury*, 4:23 (Sept 1921), 524–26.
The influence of the revival on Irish historical studies.

6067. ———: "A Letter from Ireland," *London Mercury*, 5:29 (Mar 1922), 531–33.
The places of Darrell Figgis and John B. Yeats in the revival.

6068. ———: "A Letter from Ireland," *London Mercury*, 7:42 (Apr 1923), 646–48.
The prospects of writing a history of modern Irish literature.

6069. ———: "A Letter from Ireland," *London Mercury*, 8:48 (Oct 1923), 646–48.
Ulster and the revival.

6070. ———: "A Letter from Ireland," *Poetry*, 45:6 (Mar 1935), 332–36.

6071. HUNEKER, JAMES GIBBONS: *The Pathos of Distance: A Book of a Thousand and One Moments*. NY: Scribner's, 1913. viii, 394 p.
"The Celtic Awakening," 219–44; a rapturous praise, consisting of "Ireland," "John M. Synge," and "A Poet of Visions," which was first published anonymously as "Yeats, the Poet of Vision," *NY Sun*, 76:328 (25 July 1909), III, 2 (a review of W75–82).

6072. HUNTRESS, KEITH GIBSON: "Thomas Bird Mosher: A Biographical and Literary Study," Ph.D. thesis, U of Illinois, 1942. iv, 212 p.
On Mosher's interest in the revival as seen through relevant items in his periodical, the *Bibelot*, pp. 58–67.

6073. HURLEY, MICHAEL (ed): *Irish Anglicanism, 1869–1969*. Essays on the role of Anglicanism in Irish life presented to the Church of Ireland on the occasion of the centenary of its disestablishment by a group of Methodist, Presbyterian, Quaker, and Roman Catholic scholars. Dublin: Figgis, 1970. xi, 236 p.

Thomas P. O'Neill: "Political Life: 1870-1921," 101-9; contains a note on Yeats and the revival, 107-8.
Augustine Martin: "Anglo-Irish Literature," 120-32; on Yeats, *passim*.

6074. IASAIL (INTERNATIONAL ASSOCIATION FOR THE STUDY OF ANGLO-IRISH LITERATURE): *Newsletter*. Dublin.
#1 (Spring/Summer 1971): Contains material on the Synge centenary, pp. 2-3.
#2 (Autumn/Winter 1971): Contains a report on the Yeats International Summer School by Declan Kiberd, pp. 7-8.
#3 (Spring/Summer 1972): Contains a review of J6331 by Christopher Murray, pp. 5-6.
#4 (Autumn/Winter 1972/73): News and notes.
#5 (Summer 1973): News and notes.
#6 (Autumn/Winter 1973): News and notes and reports of national IASAIL representatives.

6075. IRELAND, DENIS: "Fog in the Irish Sea: Some Afterthoughts on Anglo-Irish Literature," *Threshold*, 5:2 (Autumn-Winter 1961/62), 59-74.

6076. *The Ireland of To-day*. Reprinted with some additions from the London *Times*. Boston: Small, Maynard, 1915. xiii, 419 p.
Based in part on the Irish number of the *Times*, #40161 (17 Mar 1913). "The Irish Literary Spirit," 121-24; "The Modern Irish Poets," 125-30; "The Abbey Theatre," 131-37.

6077. *Ireland's Hope: A Call to Service*. London: Irish Inter-Collegiate Christian Union, Student Christian Movement, 1913. viii, 232 p.
E. Margaret Cunningham: "Some Modern Irish Movements," 137-51.

6078. *Irlanda*. Con cartina geografica e molte illustrazioni in tavole fuori testo. Roma: Edizioni Roma, 1940. 160 p.
Serafino Riva: "Profilo della letteratura irlandese," 33-53.
Renato Simoni: "Carattere del teatro irlandese," 55-69.

6079. ÍUR'EVA, LIDIÍA M. (ed): *Zarubezhnaîa literatura: 30-e gody XX veka*. Moskva: Izdatel'stvo "Nauka," 1969. 400 p.
A. P. Sarukhanîan: "Tema naîsional'no-osvoboditel'nogo dvizheniîa v irlandskoĭ literature 30-kh godov" [The theme of the national and liberation movement in the Irish literature of the thirties], 269-92. Mainly on O'Faolain, O'Flaherty, and O'Casey.

6080. JACKSON, HOLBROOK: *The Eighteen Nineties: A Review of Art and Ideas at the Close of the Nineteenth Century*. London: Cape, 1931 [1913]. 304 p. (Life & Letters Series. 17.)
"The Discovery of the Celt," 147-56; on Yeats, pp. 152-56.

6081. JEFFARES, A. NORMAN: "The Anglo-Irish Temper," *Essays by Divers Hands*, 36 (1970), 84-112.
A survey of Anglo-Irish literature from the end of the 17th century to the present day. Three elements combine to produce the Anglo-Irish temper: the classical and English literary convention, the native Irish tradition, particularly oral literature, and the urge to write for a national audience. On Yeats, *passim*.

6081a. JOANNON, PIERRE: *Histoire de l'Irlande*. Paris: Plon, 1973. 503 p.
"L'affirmation de soi dans la sphère culturelle," 172-78.

6082. JOHN, IRMGARD VON: "Vorschläge zu einer Arbeitsgemeinschaft über irische Literatur," *Mädchenbildung auf christlicher Grundlage*, 24:20 (20 Oct 1928), 675-78.

Naive and with curious mistakes (Yeats is consistently misspelled Jeats).

6083. JOHNSTON, CHARLES, and CARITA SPENCER: *Ireland's Story*. New edition with an additional chapter 1904-22. Boston: Houghton Mifflin, 1923 [1905]. xv, 442 p.
> "The Irish Literary Revival," 370-79.

6084. KAIN, RICHARD M.: "Irish Periodical Literature, an Untilled Field," *Éire-Ireland*, 7:3 (Autumn 1972), 93-99.
> The importance of periodicals for the early years of the revival.

6085. KAVANAGH, PATRICK: "Diary: Being Some Reflections on the 50th Anniversary of Irish Literature," *Envoy*, 1:1 (Dec 1949), 86-90.
> Continued in subsequent issues; Yeats is mentioned *passim*. In one installment (3:10 [Sept 1950], 84-85), Kavanagh includes a parody of "Under Ben Bulben."

6086. KELLEHER, JOHN V.: "Irish Literature Today," *Atlantic Monthly*, 175:3 (Mar 1945), 70-76.
> Reprinted in *Bell*, 10:4 (July 1945), 337-53.

6086a. "Pat" [KENNY, PATRICK D.]: "The Irish Mind in Modern Print," *Saturday R*, 107:2787 (27 Mar 1909), 396-97.

6087. LALOU, RENÉ: *Panorama de la littérature anglaise contemporaine*. Paris: Kra, 1927. 251 p.
> "La renaissance irlandaise," 171-205; includes "Yeats et la poésie," 182-89.

6088. LEGOUIS, EMILE, LOUIS CAZAMIAN, and RAYMOND LAS VERGNAS: *A History of English Literature*. Revised edition. London: Dent, 1971 [1926]. xxiii, 1488 p.
> "The Celtic Revival," 1281-91; on Yeats, *passim*.

6089. LESLIE, SHANE: *The Irish Tangle for English Readers*. London: Macdonald, 1946. 254 p.
> "The Literary Revival," 134-39.

6090. LETTS, WINIFRED M.: "Old Dublin Days," *Commonweal*, 27:21 (18 Mar 1938), 570-72.
> Reminiscences.

6091. LEVIN, HARRY (ed): *Perspectives of Criticism*. Cambridge, Mass.: Harvard UP, 1950. xvii, 248 p. (Harvard Studies in Comparative Literature. 20.)
> John V. Kelleher: "Matthew Arnold and the Celtic Revival," 197-221. Includes a few notes on Yeats.

6092. LIDDELL, M. F.: "The Irish Literary Renaissance," *Contemporary R*, 120:672 (Dec 1921), 811-16.

6093. ————: "Literatur und Geistesleben im irischen Freistaat der Gegenwart," *Zeitschrift für neusprachlichen Unterricht*, 35:4 (July 1936), 209-17.

6094. LIEBERSON, GODDARD (producer): *The Irish Uprising, 1916-22*. With a foreword by Eamon de Valera. NY: Macmillan, 1966. xvi, 164 p. (CBS Legacy Book.)
> Thomas P. O'Neill: "The Springs of 1916," 1, 4, 6, 8, 12, 18, 24; one of them the literary revival, which, Yeats notwithstanding, was political in nature.

Benedict Kiely: "A Terrible Beauty," 117, 121, 129, 132, 138, 144, 147, 158, 160; on the literary aspects of the rising.

6095. LILJEGREN, STEN BODVAR: *Irish Studies in Sweden*. Upsala: Lundequist, 1961. 40 p. (Irish Essays and Studies. 6.)
  A highly personal record of Liljegren's attempts to promote the study of Irish language and literature in Sweden and elsewhere. Contains an abstract of an unpublished essay on the Irish background of Yeats's plays, pp. 22-24. No documentation whatsoever.

6096. LINATI, CARLO: *Scrittori anglo-americani d'oggi*. 2nd edition. Milano: Corticelli, 1944 [1932]. 319 p.
  "Voci della nuova Irlanda," 37-46.

6097. LONGAKER, MARK, and EDWIN COURTLANDT BOLLES: *Contemporary English Literature*. NY: Appleton, 1953. xvii, 526 p.
  "The Celtic Renaissance," 34-66; on Yeats, pp. 35-43.

6098. LONGLEY, MICHAEL (ed): *Causeway: The Arts in Ulster*. Belfast: Arts Council of Northern Ireland, 1971. 181 p.
  John Cronin: "Prose," 71-82. Sam Hanna Bell: "Theatre," 83-94. Michael Longley: "Poetry," 95-109.

6099. LUCEY, CHARLES: *Ireland and the Irish: Cathleen ni Houlihan Is Alive and Well*. Garden City: Doubleday, 1970. viii, 256 p.
  "Where Poets Walk Proudly," 123-40; on Yeats, *passim*.

6100. LÜTH, RUDOLF: "Lektüreausgaben über Irland," *Zeitschrift für neusprachlichen Unterricht*, 35:4 (July 1936), 265-74.
  An omnibus review of German high school texts of Irish literature and history.

6100a. LYMAN, W. W.: "Ella Young: A Memoir," *Éire-Ireland*, 8:3 (Autumn 1973), 65-69.
  Miss Young's role in the revival and her contacts with some of the protagonists.

6101. LYNCH, ARTHUR: *Our Poets!* London: Remington, 1894. viii, 92 p.
  "Contemporary Irish Literature," 56-59; contains a note on Yeats, who is considered promising but derivative.

6102. L[YND], R[OBERT] W. [?]: "The Nation and the Man of Letters," *Dana*, #12 (Apr 1905), 371-76.
  The prospects for an Irish national literature, with particular emphasis on Synge.

6103. LYND, ROBERT: *Home Life in Ireland*. London: Mills & Boon, 1910 [1909]. xvi, 317 p.
  "Literature and Music," 305-17; on Yeats, pp. 305-9.

6104. ———: *Ireland a Nation*. NY: Dodd, Mead, 1920. ix, 299 p.
  "The Witness of the Poets," 176-88. "A Note on Irish Literature," 187-217, includes an interview with Yeats "on the prospects and functions of an Irish theatre," 211-17; reprinted from *Daily News*, #20041 (6 June 1910), 4.

6105. LYONS, FRANCIS STEWART LELAND: *Ireland since the Famine: 1850 to the Present*. London: Weidenfeld and Nicolson, 1971. xiii, 852 p.
  "The Battle of Two Civilisations," 219-42; on Yeats's role in Irish politics, pp. 229-42, and *passim* (see index).

6106. M., T.: "The Irish Literary Renascence," *Weekly Sun*, 4:102 (16 Dec 1894), Literary Supplement, 14.

A new Irish literature is on its way with Yeats as one of its most notable figures, but his work "is richer in promise than in performance."

6107. MCBRIEN, PETER: "The Renascence of Ireland," *Studies*, 8:29 (Mar 1919), 46-58.

In literature and politics.

6108. ———: "Those Irish Pagans!" *Dublin R*, 177:355 (Oct-Nov-Dec 1925), 179-92.

Diatribe against the "Liffey School of English Literature [which] was born with chronic anaemia": Dunsany, AE, Robinson, Stephens, and Yeats.

6109. MCCAFFREY, LAWRENCE J.: "Trends in Post-Revolutionary Irish Literature," *CE*, 18:1 (Oct 1956), 26-30.

6110. MCCARTHY, JOE, and the Editors of LIFE: *Ireland*. NY: Time, 1964. 160 p.

"Masters of Language," 89-97.

6111. MACDONALD, J. F.: "The Irish Renascence," *QQ*, 19:1 (July-Aug-Sept 1911), 39-46.

6112. MACDONELL, A[NNIE]: "The New Young Irelanders," *Bookman*, 27:160 (Jan 1905), 159-64.

6113. MCDONOUGH, ROBERT: "Portrait of the Artist as Celtophile," *America*, 51:1281 (21 Apr 1934), 41-42.

6114. MACGREEVY, THOMAS: "Count Your Blessings," *Irish Bookman*, 1:1 (Aug 1946), 43-52.

On the present literary situation in Ireland as compared with the time of the revival.

6115. MCHUGH, ROGER: "Irish Myths and Irish Writing," *Blackfriars*, 32:371 (Feb 1951), 61-64.

6115a. °MCLEAN, W. I.: "*The Savoy* (1896): Its Genesis and History, and Its Significance as an Organ of the Celtic Revival," Ph.D. thesis, U of Hull, 1970/71.

6116. MACLEOD, FIONA: "A Group of Celtic Writers," *Fortnightly R*, os 71 / ns 65:385 (1 Jan 1899), 34-53.

Mainly on Yeats; also on AE, Hyde, and others.

6117. MCMAHON, SEÁN: "Backgrounds for the Study of Irish Literature," *Éire-Ireland*, 1:1 (Spring 1966), 77-88.

6118. MACMANUS, L. [CHARLOTTE ELIZABETH]: "The Irish Literary Revival," *Academy*, 66:1664 (26 Mar 1904), 355-56.

The Irish literary revival is concerned with literature and should not be confused with the Irish revival, which is concerned with the Irish (Gaelic) language. Reprinted in *Living Age*, 241:3119 (16 Apr 1904), 189-90.

6119. ———: *White Light and Flame: Memories of the Irish Literary Revival and the Anglo-Irish War*. Dublin: Talbot Press, 1929. viii, 228 p.

"Memories of the Irish Literary Revival," 1-73; actually more on the Gaelic revival. Reminiscences of Yeats, pp. 15-16; notes on *Diarmuid and Grania*, pp. 46-48.

6120. MACMANUS, MICHAEL JOSEPH: *Adventures of an Irish Bookman: A Selection from the Writings*. Edited by Francis MacManus. Dublin: Talbot Press, 1952. xvi, 192 p.
  "How the Irish Literary Revival Began," 117-21. It began with *Poems and Ballads of Young Ireland* (1888).
  "The Playboy of the Literary Revival," 122-26; on Susan L. Mitchell's portrait of George Moore.
  "The Big House at Coole," 127-31; slight piece about Yeats and Lady Gregory at Coole.

6120a. MANLEY, SEON, and SUSAN BELCHER: *O, Those Extraordinary Women! Or the Joys of Literary Lib*. Philadelphia: Chilton Book Co., 1972. xii, 331 p.
  "The High Style of Cathleen ni Houlihan," 261-82; on Constance Markievicz, Maud Gonne, and Lady Gregory. Yeats is mentioned *passim*.

6121. MARTIN, AUGUSTINE: "Inherited Dissent: The Dilemma of the Irish Writer," *Studies*, 54:213 (Spring 1965), 1-20.
  The Irish writer and society.

6122. Brother Leo [MEEHAN, FRANCIS JOSEPH GALLAGHER]: *English Literature: A Survey and a Commentary*. Boston: Ginn, 1928. xiii, 738 p.
  "The Irish Literary Revival," 624-40; on Yeats, *passim*: "Much of what he has written is of no permanent worth, and more is incomprehensible to the generality of his countrymen, but . . . he has had a pronounced effect on the development of literature in Ireland. . . ."

6123. MERCIER, VIVIAN: "The Arts in Ireland," *Commonweal*, 46:8 (6 June 1947), 183-85.

6124. ———: "Speech after Long Silence," *Irish Writing*, #6 (Nov 1948), 76-81.

6125. ———, and DAVID HERBERT GREENE (eds): *1000 Years of Irish Prose. Part I: The Literary Revival*. NY: Devin-Adair, 1953 [1952]. xxix, 607 p.
  "Introduction," ix-xxix.

6126. MILLER, JOSEPH DANA: "The Celtic Renaissance," *Era Mag*, 12:5 (Nov 1903), 415-19.

6127. MILLER, LIAM: "The Heirs of Saint Columba: Publishing in Ireland," *TLS*, 71:3655 (17 Mar 1972), 315-16.
  Including the publishing of works of the Irish literary revival.

6128. MOFFAT, W. D.: "The Open Letter," *Mentor*, 9:218 (Apr 1921), 40.
  Note on the importance of the Irish literary revival.

6129. MORAN, DAVID P.: *The Philosophy of Irish Ireland*. Dublin: Duffy, [1905]. v, 114 p.
  "The Battle of Two Civilisations," 94-114; reprinted from J5918.

6130. "NÉALL": "The Irish Literary Movement," *Irish Monthly*, 48:566 (Aug 1920), 397-402; :567 (Sept 1920), 453-61; :568 (Oct 1920), 524-32.
  Includes a discussion of *Cathleen ni Houlihan*, pp. 457-61.

6131. NOWLAN, KEVIN B., and T. DESMOND WILLIAMS (eds): *Ireland in the War Years and After, 1939-51*. Dublin: Gill and Macmillan, 1969. ix, 216 p.
  Augustine Martin: "Literature and Society, 1938-51," 167-84; mentions Yeats *passim*.

6131a. O'BRIEN, KATE: *My Ireland*. London: Batsford, 1962. 199 p.
  On Coole Park and Lady Gregory, pp. 46-50; on the Abbey Theatre, pp. 116-19; scattered notes on other writers of the revival, *passim*.

6132. °O'BRIEN, MARGARET THERESA: "The Influence of Irish Folk-Songs and Folk-Lore on English Literature," M.A. thesis, McGill U, 1928.
I do not know whether this item is of any relevance.

6133. O'CONNOR, FRANK: "The Future of Irish Literature," *Horizon*, 5:25 (Jan 1942), 55-63.

6134. O'CONOR, NORREYS JEPHSON: "The Trend of Anglo-Irish Literature," *Bookman*, 86:515 (Aug 1934), 233-34.

6135. O'DONOGHUE, D. J.: "The Present Irish Literary Movement," *United Ireland*, 14:728 (27 July 1895), 1.

6136. O'DONOVAN, J.: "The Celtic Revival of Today," *Irish Ecclesiastical Record*, ser 4 / yr 32 / 5:375 (Mar 1899), 238-56.
"What is it which is flooding so many masterminds, which is gradually seeking its way through the land in tiny rivulets, soon to join into a mighty river in which the men of Ireland are to bathe and arise with hearts and minds re-vivified? It is the revival of the Celt." One of these purifying streams is Yeats, who is pronounced thoroughly Celtic in spirit.

6137. O'FAOLAIN, SEAN: "Provincialism and Literature," *Motley*, 1:3 (Aug 1932), 3-4.

6138. ———: "The Emancipation of Irish Writers," *Yale R*, 23:3 (Mar 1934), 485-503.

6139. ———: "Irish Letters: To-day and To-morrow," *Fortnightly R*, os 144 / ns 138:825 (Sept 1935), 369-71.

6140. ———: "The Literary Scene in Ireland," *NYTBR*, 41:1 (5 Jan 1936), 8, 19.

6141. ———: "The Literary Scene in Ireland," *NYTBR*, [41:] (16 Aug 1936), 8, 18.
"Drama and poetry are clearly in their dog-days for the present."

6142. ———: "The Raw Material of Irish Literature," *Tablet*, 168:5039 (5 Dec 1936), 769-70; :5040 (12 Dec 1936), 827-28.

6143. ———: "The Literary Scene in Ireland," *NYTBR*, [42:] (30 May 1937), 8, 16.

6144. ———: "The Literary Scene in Ireland," *NYTBR*, [43:] (14 Aug 1938), 8, 16.

6145. ———: "The Case of the Young Irish Writer," *Commonweal*, 38:16 (6 Aug 1943), 392-93.

6146. ———: "An Unhappy Report from Ireland by an Irish Novelist," *NYTBR*, [53:] (10 Oct 1948), 3.
The movement is almost dead.

6147. ———: *The Irish: A Character Study.* NY: Devin-Adair, 1949. x, 180 p.
"The Writers," 156-80.

6148. ———: "The Dilemma of Irish Letters," *Month*, 2:6 (Dec 1949), 366-79.

6149. ———: "Ireland after Yeats," *BA*, 26:4 (Autumn 1952), 325-33.
Reprinted in *Bell*, 18:11 (Summer 1953), 37-48.

6150. ————: "Fifty Years of Irish Writing," *Studies*, 51:201 (Spring 1962), 93-105.
Yeats is referred to *passim*.

6151. O'NEILL, GEORGE: "Some Aspects of Our Anglo-Irish Poets: The Irish Literary Theatre. Foreign Inspiration of Alleged Irish Plays," *Irish Catholic*, 24:51 (23 Dec 1911), 5.
Attacks Yeats.

6152. ORAGE, ALFRED RICHARD: *Selected Essays and Critical Writings*. Edited by Herbert Read and Denis Saurat. London: Nott, 1935. v, 216 p.
"Ireland: Diagnoses," 54-56; "An Irish National Literature," 56-65, reprinted from *New Age*, 20:1269 (4 Jan 1917), 229-30, :1270 (11 Jan 1917), 254, :1271 (18 Jan 1917), 278, where it was published as "Readers and Writers" over the initials R. H. C. Mostly concerned with Boyd's *Ireland's Literary Renaissance* (J5911). Correspondence by E. A. Boyd, :1272 (25 Jan 1917), 309-10; answer by R. H. C., :1273 (1 Feb 1917), 326-27.

6153. OSHIMA, SHOTARO: "Modern Irish Literature: A Study," *Japanese Science R*, 9 (1958), 43-46.
A summary of the author's book on the same subject in Japanese (°Tokyo: Hokuseido-shoten, 1956).

6154. O'SULLIVAN, SEAN (ed): *Folktales of Ireland*. Foreword by Richard M. Dorson. London: Routledge & Kegan Paul, 1969 [1966]. xliii, 321 p.
The foreword discusses the contributions of some writers of the Irish literary revival (Yeats, Synge, Lady Gregory, Hyde, and Larminie) to the exploration of Irish folklore.

6155. Ó TUAMA, SEÁN (ed): *The Gaelic League Idea*. Cork: Mercier Press, 1972. 109 p. (Thomas Davis Lectures. 1968-69.)
See especially Earnán De Blaghd [Ernest Blythe]: "Hyde in Conflict," 31-40; Kevin B. Nowlan: "The Gaelic League and Other National Movements," 41-51 (especially the Irish literary revival).

6156. PAUL-DUBOIS, LOUIS: *L'Irlande contemporaine et la question irlandaise*. Paris: Perrin, 1907. viii, 516 p.
See pp. 406-8. Translated into English (probably by T. P. Gill) as *Contemporary Ireland*, with an introduction by T. M. Kettle. Dublin: Maunsel, 1908. xv, 536 p. (pp. 423-26).

6157. ————: "Le mystère d'une renaissance littéraire: La littérature irlandaise contemporaine," *Revue des deux mondes*, per 8 / yr 107 / 41:1 (1 Sept 1937), 176-97.
Mainly on James Stephens; Yeats is mentioned *passim*.

6158. [PEARSE, P. H.]: "Some Thoughts," *Claidheamh Soluis*, 7:48 (10 Feb 1906), 7.
"Do Mr. Yeats and his fellows hold a place in the intellectual present of Ireland . . . ?" Answer: No.

6159. PETRIE, SIR CHARLES: *Scenes of Edwardian Life*. London: Eyre & Spottiswoode, 1965. xii, 244 p.
Note on the revival and Lady Gregory, pp. 166-70.

6160. PHELPS, WILLIAM LYON: *The Advance of English Poetry in the Twentieth Century*. NY: Dodd, Mead, 1933 [1918]. xv, 343 p.
"The Irish Poets," 157-93; a revised version of "The Advance of English Poetry in the Twentieth Century, Part VI," *Bookman* [NY], 47:1 (Mar 1918), 58-72. On Yeats, pp. 163-71.

6161. PICKERING, ERNEST: *A Brief Survey of English Literature from Its Beginnings to the Present Day*. With chapters on the Irish literary movement and American literature. London: Harrap, 1932. 254 p.
"The Irish Literary Movement," 221-26.

6162. POUND, EZRA: "The Non-Existence of Ireland," *New Age*, ns 16:17 (25 Feb 1915), 451-53.

6163. POWER, PATRICK C.: *A Literary History of Ireland*. Cork: Mercier Press, 1969. 191 p.
Mostly concerned with Gaelic literature. On the Irish literary revival, pp. 159-80, with a few remarks on Yeats, *passim* (see index). Written on an elementary and introductory level.

6163a. PRESSLEY, STUART: "The Archives of the *Dublin Magazine*, 1923-58," *Long Room*, #7 (Spring 1973), 27-32.

6164. RAFROIDI, PATRICK: "La scène littéraire irlandaise contemporaine," *Langues modernes*, 61:2 (Mar-Apr 1967), 212-17.

6165. ———: *L'Irlande: 2. Littérature*. Paris: Colin, 1970. 239 p. (Collection U2. 124.)
See especially "Un phénix renaissant," 37-58; "Aspects du théâtre irlandais-anglais," 59-107 (on Yeats, pp. 80-84). Includes select bibliographies and a chronological table of Irish history and literature since 1690.

6165a. ———: "The Uses of Irish Myth in the Nineteenth Century," *Studies*, 67:247/248 (Autumn/Winter 1973), 251-61.

6166. REBORA, PIERO: *La letteratura inglese del novecento*. Firenze: Edizione le lingue estere, 1950. 227 p.
"La rinascita irlandese," 61-72; on Yeats, pp. 64-67.

6167. REDDIN, KENNETH SHEILS: *Somewhere to the Sea*. Boston: Houghton, Mifflin, 1936. vi, 344 p.
Published in England (London: Nelson, 1936) under the pseudonym Kenneth Sarr. A novel set in Ireland in 1920, with some figures of the revival playing minor parts under their own names. Yeats, however, is not included.

6168. REDMOND-HOWARD, LOUIS G.: *The New Birth of Ireland*. London: Collins, [1914]. 264 p.
"Literature--Art--Life," 214-36.

6169. REYNOLDS, LORNA: "Thirty Years of Irish Letters," *Studies*, 40:160 (Dec 1951), 457-68.

6170. RIVOALLAN, A.: "Autour de l'Irlande," *Langues modernes*, 28:3 (Apr 1930), 246-53.

6171. ———: *L'Irlande*. Paris: Colin, 1950 [1934]. iv, 220 p. (Collection Armand Colin. 170.)
"La littérature irlandaise," 117-34; on Yeats, pp. 128-34.

6172. ROBERTS, GEORGE: "Memoirs of George Roberts," *Irish Times*, #30504 (13 July 1955), 5.
A meeting with AE. Continued in #30505 (14 July 1955), 5 (on the National Theatre Society); #30509 (19 July 1955), 5 (George Moore in Dublin); #30520 (1 Aug 1955), 5 (the emergence of Synge); #30521 (2 Aug 1955), 5 (the plays of Synge). Reminiscences of Yeats, *passim*.

6173. ROLLESTON, T. W.: "Twenty-one Years of Irish Art and Thought," *Celtic R*, 9:[3] (Jan 1914), 226-47.
A lecture delivered "on the occasion of the celebration by the Irish Literary Society, London, of the twenty-first year of the life and work of the society. Mr. W. B. Yeats occupied the Chair." A survey of the Irish cultural revival from Gaelic football to poetry. Emphasizes the role of the theater as the most significant instrument in creating a national consciousness.

6174. Y. O. [RUSSELL, GEORGE WILLIAM]: "Heredity in Literature," *Irish Statesman*, 8:13 (4 June 1927), 304, 306.

6175. RUSSELL, GEORGE WILLIAM: Address given at the 30th annual dinner of the American Irish Historical Society, *J of the American Irish Historical Society*, 27 (1928), 368-80.
A rambling sketch of the history of the revival.

6176. A. E. [————]: "Twenty-five Years of Irish Nationality," *Foreign Affairs*, 7:2 (Jan 1929), 204-20.

6177. RYAN, STEPHEN P.: "Literary Life in Dublin," *Commonweal*, 71:12 (18 Dec 1959), 347-49.

6178. ————: "Ireland and Its Writers," *Catholic World*, 192:1149 (Dec 1960), 149-55.
Subtitle: "What has become of the Emerald Isle's once promising literary revival?" Answer: Not much.

6179. R[YAN], W. P.: "That Irish Renaissance," *Outlook* [London], 2:27 (6 Aug 1898), 20-22.

6179a. SADKOWSKI, WACŁAW: *Kręgi wspołnoty: Skice literackie*. Warszawa: Państwowy Instytut Wydawniczy, 1972. 312 p.
"Przebudzenie" [The reawakening], 84-95.

6180. SAMPSON, GEORGE: *The Concise History of English Literature*. 3rd edition. Cambridge: UP, 1970 [1941]. xiii, 976 p.
"Anglo-Irish Literature and the Irish Literary Revival in the Age of Synge and Yeats," 716-33. On Yeats, pp. 723-25 and *passim* (see index).

6181. SAORSTÁT EIREANN, IRISH FREE STATE: *Official Handbook*. Dublin: Talbot Press, 1932. 324 p.
Robert Lynd: "Anglo-Irish Literature," 279-80, 283-85.

6182. SARRAZIN, GREGOR: "Keltische Renaissance in der neuesten englischen Literatur," *Internationale Monatsschrift für Wissenschaft, Kunst und Technik*, 7:8 (May 1913), 967-86.
Contains notes on Moore, AE, and Yeats.

6183. SAUL, GEORGE BRANDON (ed): *Age of Yeats: Irish Literature*. NY: Dell, 1964. 382 p. (Laurel Masterpieces of World Literature. Dell Books. 0049.)
"The Irish Renaissance," 13-25; "Concise Notes on Authors Included," 363-82. On Yeats, pp. 378-81.

6184. SCHMIDT, WOLFGANG (ed): *Englische Kultur in sprachwissenschaftlicher Deutung. Max Deutschbein zum 60. Geburtstage*. Leipzig: Quelle & Meyer, 1936. xvi, 237 p.
Herbert Huscher: "Das Anglo-Irische und seine Bedeutung als sprachkünstlerisches Ausdrucksmittel," 40-59. A linguistic survey of the Anglo-Irish idiom and its use in some works of the revival.

6185. SCOTT-JAMES, ROLFE ARNOLD: *Fifty Years of English Literature, 1900-1950. With a Postscript, 1950 to 1955.* London: Longmans Green, 1956 [1950]. xi, 282 p.

"The Irish Literary Movement," 89-98; on Yeats, pp. 94-98.

6186. SENA, JORGE DE: *A literatura inglêsa: Ensaia de interpretação e de história.* São Paulo: Editôra Cultrix, 1963. 469 p. (Roteira das grandes literaturas. 7.)

On the "Celtic Revival," pp. 340-44; on Yeats, pp. 341-43.

6187. SHERIDAN, JOHN D.: "Irish Writing Today," *Books on Trial*, 10:8 (May 1952), 308-9, 335.

Heavy Catholic bias.

6188. SHUSTER, GEORGE NAUMAN: *The Catholic Spirit in Modern English Literature.* NY: Macmillan, 1922. xiii, 365 p.

"The Voice of Ireland," 268-93; on the Catholic writers of the revival.

6189. SINKO, GRZEGORZ: "Irlandia--daleka i bliska" [Ireland--far and near], *Dialog*, 6:10 (Oct 1961), 106-17.

Particularly on O'Casey.

6190. SJOESTEDT, MARIE-LOUISE: *Marie-Louise Sjoestedt (1900-1940) in memoriam; suivi de Essai sur une littérature nationale: La littérature irlandaise contemporaine.* Paris: Droz, 1941. 78 p.

"Essai sur une littérature nationale: La littérature irlandaise contemporaine," 53-78; from a MS. dated 21 Mar 1937.

6191. STAHL, ERNST LEOPOLD: "Die irische Wiedergeburt: Umriss einer nationalpolitischen Literaturbewegung," *Deutsche Kultur im Leben der Völker*, 14:1 (Mar 1939), 10-27.

6192. STANDOP, EWALD, and EDGAR MERTNER: *Englische Literaturgeschichte.* Heidelberg: Quelle & Meyer, 1967. 679 p.

"Die irische Renaissance," 591-602; on Yeats, pp. 592-97.

6193. STARKIE, WALTER: *Scholars and Gipsies: An Autobiography.* London: Murray, 1963. xi, 324 p.

Reminiscences of the Abbey Theatre and some of the celebrities of the revival, including Yeats, *passim* (see index).

6194. STENFERT KROESE, W. H.: "Problemen van de Ierse literatur: Gesprek met Sean O'Faolain," *Litterair paspoort*, 7:57 (May 1952), 97-99.

6195. STURM, F. P.: "The Irish Literary Movement," *Aberdeen Free Press*, #11667 (9 June 1906), 5.

A very long article, not in J814.

6196. [SUTTON, DENYS]: "Editorial: The Heroic Energy of Cuchulain," *Apollo*, 84:56 (Oct 1966), 256-59.

The connections between the revival and painting.

6197. TRAUSIL, HANS (ed and trans): *Ein Zweig vom Schlehdorn: Irische Dichtungen.* Mit einer Einleitung von Padraic Colum. München-Pasing: Roland, 1923. 134 p.

"Einleitung," 7-15: Yeats, AE, and Hyde are the main representatives of the revival.

6198. TRÉDANT, PAUL: "La littérature irlandaise devant la nouvelle Europe," *Comoedia*, ns 2:38 (14 Mar 1942), 5.

6199. TUCKER, WILLIAM JOHN: "The Celt in Contemporary Literature," *Catholic World*, 146:876 (Mar 1938), 650-57.
On Yeats's early works (despite the title of the article), *passim*.

6200. TURNER, EDWARD RAYMOND: *Ireland and England in the Past and at Present*. NY: Century, 1919. xii, 504 p.
"Irish Language and Literature and the Irish Revival," 315-48.

6201. TYNAN HINKSON, KATHARINE: "The Literary Revival in Ireland," *Outlook*, 49:26 (30 June 1894), 1189-91.

6202. TYNAN, KATHARINE: "Neglect of Irish Writers," *Catholic World*, 87:517 (Apr 1908), 83-92.
The Irish neglect their best writers, Yeats included.

6203. URNOV, M.: "Literaturnyĭ Dublin (Zametki)" [Literary Dublin (Notes)], *Inostrannaĭa literatura*, #12 (Dec 1967), 247-50.

6204. USSHER, ARLAND: "Literaturbrief aus Irland," *Neue deutsche Literatur*, 13:11 (Nov 1965), 151-65.
A short sketch of the revival; on Yeats, *passim*.

6205. ———: "Irish Literature," *ZAA*, 14:1 (1966), 30-55.
Another brief survey of the history of Irish literature; on Yeats as a model escapist writer, pp. 48-52.

6206. VAN DOREN, CARL, and MARK VAN DOREN: *American and British Literature since 1890*. NY: Century, 1925. xi, 350 p.
"Irish Literature," 273-309; on Yeats, pp. 275-79, 288-91, 307-8, and *passim* (see index).

6207. VINES, SHERARD: *100 Years of English Literature*. London: Duckworth, 1950. 316 p.
"Anglo-Irish Writers," 206-19.

6208. W., C.: "A Literary Causerie: The Dublin School," *Academy*, 68:1720 (22 Apr 1905), 447-48.
Reprinted in *Living Age*, 245:3180 (17 June 1905), 753-57.

6209. WAIS, KURT (ed): *Die Gegenwartsdichtung der europäischen Völker*. Berlin: Junker & Dünnhaupt, 1939. xix, 567 p.
Hans Galinsky: "Die irische Dichtung in englischer Sprache," 150-60; on Yeats, pp. 152-53 and *passim*.

6210. WALLER, BOLTON CHARLES: *Hibernia, or The Future of Ireland*. London: Kegan Paul, 1928. 96 p.
See pp. 58-65.

6211. WALSH, MICHAEL: "Dublin Literary Memories," *Bonaventura*, 2:3 (Winter 1938), 199-208.

6212. WALSH, THOMAS: "The Neo-Celts," *America*, 13:333 (28 Aug 1915), 497-98.
Criticizes the "Neo-Celts" because they are neither Neo nor Celts, but does not define them any further. The targets, however, seem clear enough.

6213. WELLS, WARRE BRADLEY: *Irish Indiscretions*. London: Allen & Unwin, [1923]. 230 p.
See pp. 188-222 for discussions of George Moore and John Butler Yeats, as well as for a comparison between AE and WBY. Also notes on the genesis of *If I Were Four-and-Twenty*, of which Wells was a witness,

on the Abbey Theatre and WBY's dissatisfaction with its peasant plays, and on the prose writers of the revival.

6214. *Die Weltliteratur: Biographisches, literarhistorisches und biblio-graphisches Lexikon in Übersichten und Stichwörtern.* Wien: Hollinek, 1951-53. 3 v.
  "Anglo-irische Literatur," 1:58-59; "Irische Literatur," 2:812-16; "Yeats," 3:1948-49.

6215. WEYGANDT, CORNELIUS: "The Irish Literary Revival," *Sewanee R*, 12:4 (Oct 1904), 420-31.
  On Yeats, *passim*.

6216. ———: "Literary Workers in Ireland To-day: The Irish Renaissance and What It Has Accomplished," *Book News Monthly*, 25:9 (May 1907), 575-89.
  Contains sections on Yeats, AE, Lionel Johnson, Nora Hopper Chesson, Synge, Padriac MacCormac Colm [*sic*, i.e., Padraic Colum], Lady Gregory, Hyde, and others.

6217. WILLIAMS, HAROLD: *Modern English Writers: Being a Study of Imaginative Literature, 1890-1914.* London: Sidgwick & Jackson, 1925. xii, 532 p.
  "Irish Poets and Playwrights," 173-240; on Yeats, pp. 183-93 and *passim*.
  First published as *Outlines of Modern English Literature.* London: Sidgwick & Jackson, 1920. 268 p. "Irish Poets and Playwrights," 145-84; on Yeats, pp. 151-57, 172-74.

6218. WOLFF, PHILIPP: "Irlands Dichtung in der Unabhängigkeit," *Schweizer Rundschau*, 54:11-12 (Feb-Mar 1955), 657-62.
  Post-1922 literature.

See also J557, 587, 611, 614, 618, 623, 627, 644, 665, 676, 679, 743, 756, 768, 840, 926, 928, 957, 960, 980, 980a, 984, 985, 992, 1060, 1200, 1201, 1216, 1218, 1256, 1318, 1321, 1323, 1328, 1337, 1344, 1347, 1351, 1402, 1415, 1425, 1427, 1460, 1483, 1494, 1497, 1521, 1525, 1531, 1541, 1551, 1554, 1577, 1589, 1599, 1659, 1689, 1743, 1752, 1761a, 1768, 1847, 1945a, 1980, 1995, 1995a, 2026-28, 2045, 2191, 2227, 2671a, 2842, 2851, 3621, 3682, 4059, 4096, 4117a, 4120a, 4131, 4199, 4215, 4216, 4228, 4235, 4380, 4401, 4784-804 and note, 5319, 5330a, 5384-89 and note, 5542-45 and note, 5570, 6721, 6783, 6795, 6873, 6894, 7324, 7428.

KC   The Poetry of the Irish Literary Revival

6219. ALSPACH, RUSSELL KING: "A Consideration of the Poets of the Literary Revival in Ireland, 1889-1929," Ph.D. thesis, U of Pennsylvania, 1942. iii, 122 p.
  "This dissertation attempts to do two things: (1) to estimate the worth of the poetic contribution of the following poets of the Irish Literary Revival: William Butler Yeats, Katharine Tynan Hinkson, A. E. [. . .], Lionel Johnson, Padraic Colum, and James Stephens; (2) to present, in rather compact form, a study of Irish literature from the end of the eighteenth century to the years immediately preceding the revival" (p. iii).
  "William Butler Yeats (1865-1939)," 50-74, presents an enthusiastic account of Yeats's development up to *The Tower*. The section described under (2) has been published separately (Philadelphia: College Offset Press, 1942. ii, 48 p.).

6220. ANON.: "The Poetry of Ireland," *Church QR*, 72:144 (July 1911), 406-21.
      Reprinted in *Living Age*, 271:3509 (7 Oct 1911), 15-24.

6221. ANON.: "The Celtic Muse," *Outlook* [London], 4:79 (5 Aug 1899), 22-23.

6222. ANON.: "Modern Irish Poets: Irish Literature and English Influences," *Times*, #40161 (17 Mar 1913), 15.

6223. ARNS, KARL (ed): *Jüngstes England: Anthologie und Einführung.* Leipzig: Kuner, 1925. vii, 322 p.
      "Die Iren," 275-87; on Yeats, pp. 278-81.

6224. Belis, Andrew [i.e., BECKETT, SAMUEL]: "Recent Irish Poetry," *Bookman*, 86:515 (Aug 1934), 235-36.

6225. CLARKE, AUSTIN: "Irish Poetry To-day," *Dublin Mag*, 10:1 (Jan-Mar 1935), 26-32.

6226. ————: "Poetry in Ireland To-day," *Bell*, 13:2 (Nov 1946), 155-61.
      Contains some references to Yeats.

6227. ————: *Poetry in Modern Ireland.* With illustrations by Louis Le Brocquy. Cork: Mercier Press for the Cultural Relations Committee of Ireland, [1961?] [1951]. 77 p. (Irish Life and Culture. 2.)
      Discusses the indebtedness to Irish mythology, the Celtic Twilight phase, the "folk phase," political and patriotic verse, Gaelic influences, the development of Yeats's poetry (pp. 47-52), and the poets of the late 1940s and early 1950s.

6228. COLUM, PADRAIC: "Irish Poetry," *Bookman* [NY], 54:2 (Oct 1921), 109-15.
      Yeats's contribution to the revival was the idea "of a culture that would be personal and aristocratic."

6229. ———— (ed): *An Anthology of Irish Verse: The Poetry of Ireland from Mythological Times to the Present.* NY: Liveright, 1948 [1922]. xiv, 425 p.
      "Introduction," 3-20.

6230. COUSINS, JAMES HENRY: *Modern English Poetry: Its Characteristics and Tendencies.* Madras: Ganesh, [1921]. xiii, 214, ii p. (Keiogijuku U, Tokyo, Public Lectures in Literature, Autumn 1919.)
      "Poets of the Irish Literary Revival," 85-116; on Yeats, *passim.*

6231. DAVIDSON, DONALD (ed): *British Poetry of the Eighteen-Nineties.* Garden City: Doubleday, Doran, 1937. lxxii, 420 p.
      "The Celtic Renaissance," xliii-xlvii; "William Butler Yeats," 244-46.

6231a. °DISKIN, PATRICK: "The Gaelic Background to Anglo-Irish Poetry," *Topic*, 12:24 (Fall 1972), 37-51.

6232. ERSKINE, JOHN: *The Delight of Great Books.* London: Nash & Grayson, 1928. 312 p.
      "Modern Irish Poetry," 295-312; on Yeats, pp. 303-5.

6233. FARREN, ROBERT: *The Course of Irish Verse in English.* London: Sheed & Ward, 1948. xii, 171 p.
      From Goldsmith to Austin Clarke. Discusses the following poets of the revival: Larminie, Hyde, Yeats (pp. 64-78), AE, Seumas O'Sullivan, Campbell, Colum, Stephens, Ledwidge, Pearse, Synge, Higgins, and Clarke.

6234. GERARD, PAUL: "Poetry in Ireland, 1930-1950," *Envoy*, 3:8 (July 1950), 65-74.

6235. GOLDING, WILLIAM: "Party of One: Exile, Poverty, Homecoming. The Haunting Themes of Irish Poetry," *Holiday*, 33:4 (Apr 1963), 10, 16-19.

6236. GONNE, MAUD: "La poésie irlandaise," *Magazine international*, #6 (May 1896), 156-58.

6237. GRUBB, H. T. HUNT: "The Ancient Celtic Muse and Its Effects upon English Poetry," *Poetry R*, 29:3 (May-June 1938), 219-31.

6238. GWYNN, STEPHEN: "Irish Nationalist Poetry," *Pilot*, 1:12 (19 May 1900), 351-52.

6239. HARMON, MAURICE (ed): *Fenians and Fenianism: Centenary Essays*. Dublin: Scepter Books, 1968. 89 p.
> Based on a special issue of *University R* [Dublin], 4:3 (Winter 1967). Malcolm Brown: "Fenianism and Irish Poetry," 49-57 (*University R*, pp. 241-49); particularly on John O'Leary.

6240. HEWITT, JOHN: "Irish Poets, Learn Your Trade," *Threshold*, 2:3 (Autumn 1958), 62-71.

6241. HOAGLAND, KATHLEEN (ed): *1000 Years of Irish Poetry: The Gaelic and Anglo-Irish Poets from Pagan Times to the Present*. NY: Devin-Adair, 1947. liv, 830 p.
> "Anglo-Irish Poetry," xli-liv. Patrick MacDonough: "Bring Home the Poet," 629; a poem on Yeats.

6242. HODGSON, GERALDINE E.: "Some Irish Poetry," *Contemporary R*, 98:[537] (Sept 1910), 323-40.
> Reprinted in *Living Age*, 267:3460 (29 Oct 1910), 282-93. On Yeats's poetry, *passim*; on *The Countess Cathleen*, pp. 332-37; also on AE, Campbell, and others.

6243. —————: "Three Candles: III. Ireland," *Quest* [London], 19:4 (July 1928), 400-413.
> Dream, vision, and escape in modern Anglo-Irish poetry, including Yeats's.

6244. JASPERT, WILLEM: *Irland*. Berlin: Siegismund, 1938. 232 p.
> "Die Dichtung Irlands," 163-82; reprinted from *Geist der Zeit*, 15:8 (Aug 1937), 602-11. Negligible.

6245. KENNELLY, BRENDAN: "The Rebirth of Irish Poetry," *Hibernia*, 33:16 (29 Aug—11 Sept 1969), 13.
> After Yeats had "said it all and said it splendidly," there was a twenty-year silence in Irish poetry. But in the last few years "poetry in Ireland has become alive again."

6246. ————— (ed): *The Penguin Book of Irish Verse*. Harmondsworth: Penguin Books, 1970. 428 p.
> "Introduction," 29-42; stresses Yeats's role as a unifying force and powerful influence.

6247. KILMER, JOYCE: "Poets Marched in the Van of Irish Revolt," *NYT*, 65: 21288 (7 May 1916), V, 4.
> Interview with Padraic Colum about the 1916 poets.

6248. KIRTLAN, SAIDÉE: "Irish Poets and Poetry," *London QR*, 122:244 (Oct 1914), 259-67.

6249. LOFTUS, RICHARD JOSEPH: *Nationalism in Modern Anglo-Irish Poetry.*
Madison: U of Wisconsin Press, 1964. xi, 362 p.

> Based on a °Ph.D. thesis, U of Wisconsin, 1962. 543 p. (*DA*, 23:3
> [Sept 1962], 1021). Contains individual chapters on Yeats (pp. 38-96),
> AE, Pearse, MacDonagh, Plunkett, Colum, Stephens, Higgins, Clarke.
> Yeats emerges from the book as the only poet of truly nationalist
> stature, because he was able to withstand the pressures that the mid-
> dle class brought to bear on the Irish writers. A controversial con-
> ception of nationalism that provoked some rather hostile reviews as
> well as considerable praise.
>
> *Reviews:*
> 1. David H. Greene, *CE*, 27:4 (Jan 1966), 337.
> 2. T. R. Henn, *MLR*, 60:4 (Oct 1965), 604-5.
> 3. Manly Johnson, *JJQ*, 2:3 (Spring 1965), 230-31.
> 4. John Jordan, "The Irish Thing under Review," *Hibernia*, 29:1 (Jan
>   1965), 14-15.
> 5. Eoin McKiernan, *American N&Q*, 3:8 (Apr 1965), 126-28.
> 6. Harold Orel, *JEGP*, 64:3 (July 1965), 598-600.
> 7. George Brandon Saul, *Arizona Q*, 22:2 (Summer 1966), 174.
> 8. Kaspar Spinner, *Anglia*, 86:1/2 (1968), 253-56.
> 9. Peter Ure, *N&Q*, os 211 / ns 13:3 (Mar 1966), 118-19.

6250. ————: "The Poetry of the Easter Rising," *Éire-Ireland*, 2:3 (Autumn
1967), 111-21.

> Particularly on Pearse, MacDonagh, and Plunkett.

6251. LUCY, SEÁN (ed): *Irish Poets in English: The Thomas Davis Lectures
in Anglo-Irish Poetry.* Cork: Mercier Press, 1973. 238 p.

> Séan [*sic*] Lucy: "What Is Anglo-Irish Poetry," 13-29.
> Austin Clarke: "Gaelic Ireland Rediscovered: The Early Period," 30-43.
> Eiléan Ní Chuilleanáin: "Gaelic Ireland Rediscovered: Courtly and
> Country Poetry," 44-59.
> Bryan MacMahon: "Place and People into Poetry," 60-74.
> Roger McHugh: "Anglo-Irish Poetry, 1700-1850," 75-90.
> Lorna Reynolds: "Irish Romantic Poets, 1850-1900," 91-104.
> A. Norman Jeffares: "Yeats," 105-17.
> Benedict Kiely: "The Poets and the Prosemen," 118-30.
> Robert Farren: "The Gaelic Voice in Anglo-Irish Poetry," 131-43.
> John Montague: "The Impact of International Modern Poetry on Irish
> Writing," 144-58.
> Brendan Kennelly: "Patrick Kavanagh," 159-84.
> Maurice Harmon: "New Voices in the Fifties," 185-207.
> Thomas Kinsella: "The Divided Mind," 208-18 (Irish/Anglo-Irish).
> Yeats is mentioned *passim* (see index).

6252. MACDONAGH, DONAGH, and LENNOX ROBINSON (eds): *The Oxford Book of
Irish Verse: XVIIth Century—XXth Century.* Oxford: Clarendon Press, 1958.
xxxviii, 343 p.

> "Introduction," xi-xxiv (by MacDonagh). See also the reviews by Monk
> Gibbon, *London Mag*, 6:8 (Aug 1959), 73, 75-77; and Donat O'Donnell
> [i.e., Conor Cruise O'Brien], "Irishness," *NSt*, 57:1453 (17 Jan 1959),
> 78-79.

6253. MACDONAGH, MICHAEL: "Irish National Poetry," *Time* [London], ns 1:[6]
(June 1890), 603-9.

> One of the promising young poets is a W. B. Yates.

6254. ————: "A Bunch of Anglo-Irish Verse," *Irish Ecclesiastical Record*, ser 5 / yr 66 / 35:748 (Apr 1930), 373-88.
On Yeats, pp. 379-80.

6255. MCGILL, ANNA BLANCHE: "Concerning a Few Anglo-Celtic Poets," *Catholic World*, 75:450 (Sept 1902), 775-85.
Naively enthusiastic about Yeats's poetry.

6256. MACLEOD, FIONA: "The Irish Muse," *NAR*, 179:576 (Nov 1904), 685-97; :577 (Dec 1904), 900-912.
Contains some remarks on Yeats's poetry.

6257. MAHON, DEREK (ed): *Modern Irish Poetry*. London: Sphere, 1972. 250 p.
"Introduction," 11-15.

6258. MARCUS, DAVID: "Contemporary Irish Poetry (1939-1950)," *Meanjin*, 11:2 (Winter 1952), 169-71.

6259. MARTIN, AUGUSTINE: "To Make a Right Rose Tree: Reflections on the Poetry of 1916," *Studies*, 55:217 (Spring 1966), 38-49.
Mainly on Pearse, Plunkett, MacDonagh, Stephens, and Yeats.

6260. MAXWELL, J. R. N.: "Some Real Irish Poets," *Columbia*, 10:4 (Nov 1930), 16, 33.
The real Ireland is not in the poetry of AE and Yeats, whose Ireland is one "of false philosophies, of weary melancholy and worn-out mythology"; it is rather in the poems of Catholics like Joseph Campbell and Padraic Colum.

6261. MONTAGUE, JOHN: "Order in Donnybrook Fair," *TLS*, 71:3655 (17 Mar 1972), 313.

6262. MORTON, DAVID: *The Renaissance of Irish Poetry, 1880-1930*. NY: Washburn, 1929. 256 p.
More enthusiasm and quotation than discrimination and interpretation. Only a few scattered remarks on Yeats's poetry.
Reviews:
1. Austin Clarke, *Dublin Mag*, 5:1 (Jan-Mar 1930), 56-61.
2. Y. O. [George William Russell], *Irish Statesman*, 13:17 (28 Dec 1929), 337-38.

6263. O'D., S.: "Poetry of the Irish Renaissance," *Irisleabhar Muighe Nuadhad*, 1919, 23-27.

6264. O'FAOLAIN, SEAN: "Irish Poetry since the War," *London Mercury*, 31:186 (Apr 1935), 545-52.

6265. O'LOCHLAINN, COLM: *Anglo-Irish Song Writers since Moore*. Dublin: At the Sign of the Three Candles, [1950]. 23 p. ([Bibliographical Society of Ireland Publications, 6:1.])
Yeats's only real song is "Down by the Salley Gardens," his other "songs" being "rather too delicate and precious ever to get into the pedlar's pack, or the balladmonger's sheaf."

6266. PALMER, HERBERT: *Post-Victorian Poetry*. London: Dent, 1938. xiii, 378 p.
"The Irish School of Poets," 96-122; Yeats, *passim* (see index), is treated rather cursorily.

6267. PÉRON, ALFRED R.: "La jeune poésie irlandaise," *Revue anglo-américaine*, 5:6 (Aug 1928), 540-56; 6:2 (Dec 1928), 155-69.
Mainly on Seumas O'Sullivan, Stephens, Joyce, and Clarke.

6268. *Poets of the Insurrection.* Dublin: Maunsel, 1918. 60 p.
Contains appreciations of Padraic H. Pearse by Cathaoir O'Braonain, Thomas MacDonagh by George O'Neill, Joseph M. Plunkett by Peter McBrien, John Francis MacEntee [Sean McEntee] by Padraic Gregory, and a general chapter by Arthur E. Clery. Reprinted from various issues of *Studies.*

6269. POWER, PATRICK E. C.: *The Story of Anglo-Irish Poetry (1800-1922).* Cork: Mercier Press, 1967. 187 p.
Based on °"Gaelic Influence on Anglo-Irish Poetry, 1800-1922," M.A. thesis, University College, Galway, 1965. "This . . . study . . . is an attempt to discover just how far the principal poets of the time were influenced by Gaelic literature and folklore" (p. 7). See particularly "Style--Poets of the Revival," 152-71; on Yeats, *passim* (see index).

6269a. °————: "The Countryside and Anglo-Irish Poets (1885-1947)," Ph.D. thesis, University College, Galway, 1970/71.

6270. R., V.: "Novyie irlandskie poetyi," *Sovremennyi zapad,* 1 (1922), 148-49.

6271. SMITH, MICHAEL: "Irish Poetry since Yeats: Notes towards a Corrected History," *Denver Q,* 5:4 (Winter 1971), 1-26.

6272. TORCHIANA, DONALD T.: "Contemporary Irish Poetry," *Chicago R,* 17:2-3 (1964), 152-68.
"Contemporary Irish poetry written in English can show nothing comparable to the poetry of Yeats. . . ."

6273. TURNER, WILLIAM JOHN: "Literary Aspects of Ireland," *Catholic World,* 150:900 (Mar 1940), 652-59.
Notes on the poetry of Thomas Moore, Mangan, Katharine Tynan, MacDonagh, and Plunkett.

6274. TYNAN, KATHARINE: "Recent Irish Poetry," *Studies,* 6:22 (June 1917), 200-211.

6275. URBACH, OTTO: "Irische Dichtung der Gegenwart," *Neues Wiener Tagblatt,* 73:207 (30 July 1939), 13.

6276. WILD, FRIEDRICH: *Die englische Literatur der Gegenwart seit 1870: Versdichtungen.* Leipzig: Dioskuren Verlag, 1931. 299 p.
"Keltische Renaissance und Mystik," 155-67; on Yeats, pp. 157-60.

6277. WILLIAMS, IOLO ANEURIN: *Poetry To-day.* London: Jenkins, 1927. 138 p.
See pp. 43-48.

6278. WILLIAMS, JOHN ELLIS CAERWYN (ed): *Literature in Celtic Countries: Taliesin Congress Lectures.* Cardiff: U of Wales Press, 1971. 218 p.
"Introduction," 5-19; contains some notes on Yeats and Synge.
Austin Clarke: "Anglo-Irish Poetry," 153-74; on Yeats, *passim.*

6279. WITTIG, KURT: "Die Nachkriegsliteratur Irlands. II. Versdichtung," *Archiv,* yr 95 / 178 (ns 78):3&4 (Feb 1941), 79-89.
A survey of Anglo-Irish poetry since 1918.

See also J1512, 1554, 1641, 1689, 4337, 5911, 5933, 5936, 6076, 6098, 6459.

KD   The Prose of the Irish Literary Revival

Prose Fiction

6280. °BRENNAN, BRIGID M. T.: "The Short Story in Ireland," M.A. thesis, University College, Galway, 1968.

6281. DOCKRELL-GRÜNBERG, SUSANNE: "Studien zur Struktur moderner anglo-irischer Short Stories," Dr. phil. thesis, U of Tübingen, 1967. vi, 218 p.
     Particularly on Michael McLaverty, Liam O'Flaherty, Mary Lavin, Frank O'Connor, Bryan MacMahon, and Sean O'Faolain.

6282. KIELY, BENEDICT: *Modern Irish Fiction: A Critique.* Dublin: Golden Eagle Books, 1950. xv, 179 p.
     Mentions Yeats *passim* (see index), but not his prose fiction.

6283. KILROY, THOMAS: "Teller of Tales," *TLS*, 71:3655 (17 Mar 1972), 301-2.

6283a. MARCUS, DAVID (ed): *Modern Irish Stories.* London: Sphere Books, 1972. 265 p.
     "Introduction," 5-14.

6283b. °MARTIN, T. A.: "Versions of Form in the Irish Short Story," Ph.D. thesis, University College, Dublin, 1971/72.

6284. MERCIER, VIVIAN: "Realism in Anglo-Irish Fiction, 1916-1940," Ph.D. thesis, Trinity College, Dublin, 1945. 391 p.
     Particularly on Corkery, Seumas O'Kelly, O'Flaherty, Peadar O'Donnell, Kate O'Brien, and O'Connor.

6285. O'FAOLAIN, SEAN: "Letter from a Novelist to an Idealist," *Motley*, 2:7 (Nov 1933), 3-5.

6286. ————: "Ah, Wisha! The Irish Novel," *VQR*, 17:2 (Spring 1941), 265-74.
     The difficulties awaiting the Irish novelist, especially if he happens to be a realist.

6287. SAUL, GEORGE BRANDON: *Rushlight Heritage: Reflections on Selected Irish Short-Story Writers of the Yeatsian Era.* Philadelphia: Walton Press, 1969. vi, 140 p.
     A collection of essays on the short prose fiction of Yeats (pp. 9-13; reprinted from J1076), Moore, Dunsany, Ella Young, Stephens, Joyce, Corkery, Seumas O'Kelly, Elizabeth Bowen, O'Flaherty, O'Connor, O'Faolain, and others. Incorporates "Minor Irish Miscellany," *BNYPL*, 68:5 (May 1964), 331-38; on Shan F. Bullock, AE, Stephen Gwynn, Ervine, George A. Birmingham, Forrest Reid, and others. No attempt is made to discuss the prose fiction of the revival systematically. The individual essays are often fairly superficial.

6287a. °SCOTT, A. C.: "The Conflict between the Individual and Society in the Modern Anglo-Irish Novel, 1920-1960," Ph.D. thesis, National U of Ireland, 1971/72.

6288. WADE, JENNIFER ANNE: "Irish Fiction and Its Background after 1922 with Special Reference to the Work of Liam O'Flaherty, Sean O'Faolain, Frank O'Connor and Flann O'Brien," M.A. thesis, U of London, 1964. iii, 185 p.

See also J5911, 5912, 5919, 5933, 6003, 6213, 6251, 6573.

Literary Criticism

6289. FENNELL, DESMOND: "Irish Literary Criticism," *Hibernia*, 32:4 (Apr 1968), 12.
   It is largely nonexistent.

6290. MADDEN, REGINA DOROTHY: "The Literary Criticism of the Irish Renaissance," Ph.D. thesis, Boston U, 1938. ii, 297 p.
   Discusses among others O'Grady, Hyde, Stopford A. Brooke, Yeats (pp. 44-79), AE, Larminie, Eglinton, Todhunter, Rolleston, Lionel Johnson, Moore, Lady Gregory, Synge, Colum, Dunsany, Ervine, Joyce, MacDonagh, Stephens, O'Casey, Corkery, Forrest Reid, and O'Faolain.

6291. TAYLOR, ESTELLA RUTH: *The Modern Irish Writers: Cross Currents of Criticism*. NY: Greenwood Press, 1969 [1954]. ix, 176 p.
   Based on °"Mutual Criticism in the Modern Irish School of Literature," Ph.D. thesis, Northwestern U, 1946. A study of the literary criticism that the poets and writers of the revival wrote about their colleagues and about themselves, arranged thematically (e.g., "The Expatriate Considered," "The Irish Mind and Character," "The Attitude toward the English," "The Language Problem"). Mainly on Colum, Dunsany, Eglinton, Ervine, Gogarty, Lady Gregory, Joyce, Moore, AE, Synge, and Yeats.

See also J5933, 6012a, 6301, 6302, 6330. ·

L THE IRISH LITERARY AND DRAMATIC REVIVAL II

This part of the bibliography supersedes the compilation made by E. H. Mikhail (J396), which is, in my opinion, of only limited usefulness. A few items listed by Mikhail are not included here, either because they are irrelevant or because I have been unable to see them.

LA Books and Pamphlets Exclusively on the Irish Dramatic Revival

6292. *Beltaine: An Occasional Publication. The Organ of the Irish Literary Theatre*. Edited by W. B. Yeats. London: At the Sign of the Unicorn, 1899–1900.
#1 (May 1899); #2 (Feb 1900); #3 (Apr 1900). No more published. For a reprint see J70; for articles listed individually see the index of periodicals (NF).

6293. [BLACK, HESTER MARY]: *The Theatre in Ireland: An Introductory Essay.* Exhibition of books and mss. in Trinity College Library. [Dublin: Dolmen Press, 1957. 8 p.]
Sketches the history from 1700 to 1936.

6294. BOYD, ERNEST AUGUSTUS: *The Contemporary Drama of Ireland*. Dublin: Talbot Press / London: Unwin, 1918. vii, 228 p.
Contains chapters on Martyn, the beginnings of the Irish National Theatre, Yeats (pp. 47-87), Synge, Colum, Lady Gregory, William Boyle, George Fitzmaurice, Seumas O'Kelly, Dunsany, and the Ulster Literary Theatre (Rutherford Mayne and St. John Ervine).
"Yeats imposed a new standard which was at once literary and national, and out of its adoption there grew that poetic flowering which constituted the chief distinction of the Celtic Renaissance" (pp. 48-49). Discusses the plays to 1910 and concludes that Yeats "is an isolated figure in the repertory of the Abbey Theatre." His plays, however, put him among "the first of the poetic dramatists of to-day" in western Europe (p. 86).
Reviews:
1. Anon., "The Irish Stage," *Nation* [London], 23:22 (31 Aug 1918), 576, 578.
2. Anon., "The Irish Theatre," *Spectator*, 121:4720 (14 Dec 1918), 697-98; reprinted in *Living Age*, 300:3888 (11 Jan 1919), 119-21.
3. Anon., "The Irish Drama," *TLS*, 17:857 (20 June 1918), 287.
4. John Louis Haney, *MLN*, 32:8 (Dec 1917), 494-96.
5. R. H. C. [i.e., A. R. Orage], "Readers and Writers," *New Age*, 23:1350 (25 July 1918), 201.
6. J. Ranken Towse, "The Drama of Ireland," *Nation*, 105:2733 (15 Nov 1917), 546-47.
7. Katharine Tynan, "The Irish Theatre," *Bookman*, 54:324 (Sept 1918), 184-85.

6295. °ÇAPAN, CEVAT: *İrlanda tiyatrosunda gerçekçilik* [Irish dramatic realism]. İstanbul: İstanbul Matbaası, 1966. 160 p. (İstanbul Üniversitesi Edebiyat Fakültesi yayınları. 1194.)
Mainly on Synge and O'Casey.

6296. CARLSON, AVIS DUNGAN: "Realism in the New Irish Drama," M.A. thesis, U of Illinois, 1922. iii, 132 p.

6297. COLE, ALAN: "Stagecraft in the Modern Dublin Theatre," Ph.D. thesis, Trinity College, Dublin, 1954. i, 99 p.

See especially the first five chapters: "Crisis," "The Buildings," "From Literary to National Theatre," "Acting at the Abbey," and "Abbey Sets." Also on the Gate Theatre and similar companies of the early 20th century. Valuable.

6298. COLEMAN, SISTER ANNE GERTRUDE: "Social and Political Satire in Irish Drama," Ph.D. thesis, Fordham U, 1954. xxxvi, 261 p., abstract (7 p.).

Discusses Synge, Lady Gregory, Boyle, Fitzmaurice, O'Casey, Robinson, Johnston, Norreys Connell, Paul Vincent Carroll, and others.

6299. COOPER, MABEL: "The Irish Theatre, Its History and Its Dramatists," M.A. thesis, U of Manitoba, 1931. 33 p.

6300. DRAMA LEAGUE OF AMERICA: *Courses Recommended by the National Committee on Drama Study. The New Irish Drama: Yeats, Synge, Lady Gregory and Others.* Chicago: Drama League of America, 1911. 16 p. (Course E.)

Biographical and bibliographical data, as well as abstracts from published criticism, presumably compiled by Katharine Lee Bates.

6301. *ELLIS-FERMOR, UNA: *The Irish Dramatic Movement.* London: Methuen, 1964 [1939]. xvii, 241 p.

Still a very good book. Contains the following chapters: "The Origins and Significance of the Irish Dramatic Movement," "The English Theatre in the Nineties," "The Early History of the Movement," "Ideals in the Workshop," and individual chapters on the plays of Yeats (pp. 91-116), Martyn, Moore, Lady Gregory, and Synge. A conclusion discusses the lesser playwrights and O'Casey. In appendices the author provides "Chronological Table of the Main Events in the Early Years of the Movement" (up to 1904), "Materials" (bibliographical note on out-of-the-way pamphlets), "The Main Dates Connected with the Spread of Ibsen's Work and Thought in England" (up to 1892), "A List of Plays Produced in London between 1890-9," and "Index to the Critical Opinions of Lady Gregory and W. B. Yeats."

Reviews:

1. Anon., "The Rise of the Irish Drama," *Irish Times*, 81:25726 (23 Dec 1939), 5.
2. Anon., "Ireland's Dramatic Renaissance: Poetic Faith and Works," *TLS*, 38:1975 (9 Dec 1939), 714.
3. F. S. Boas, *English*, 3:14 (Summer 1940), 86-87.
4. Austin Clarke, *Dublin Mag*, 15:2 (Apr-June 1940), 70-71.
5. Denis Donoghue, *Studies*, 44:[] (Spring 1955), 121-22.
6. Gabriel Fallon, "Amazing Theatres," *Irish Monthly*, 68:799 (Jan 1940), 30-37.
7. J. J. H[ogan], *Studies*, 28:112 (Dec 1939), 692-94.

6302. FAY, FRANK J.: *Towards a National Theatre: The Dramatic Criticism.* Edited and with an introduction by Robert Hogan. Dublin: Dolmen Press, 1970. 111 p. (Irish Theatre Series. 1.)

With one exception reprints from *United Irishman* between 1 July 1899 and 15 Nov 1902, i.e., the period in which the Irish National Theatre grew from idea to reality. Of particular interest:

1. "Introduction," 7-12.
2. "Mr. Yeats and the Stage," 50-53 (*United Irishman*, 5:114 [4 May 1901], 6); exhorts Yeats to be less polished, less oratorical, and more vigorous: "The plays which Mr. Yeats wishes to see on the stage . . . remind me of exquisitely beautiful corpses."

3. "The Irish Literary Theatre," 53-55 (5:114 [4 May 1901], 6).
4. "An Irish National Theatre," 55-58 (5:115 [11 May 1901], 6).
5. "An Irish National Theatre--II," 60-63 (5:116 [18 May 1901], 8).
6. *"The Land of Heart's Desire,"* 69-71 (6:126 [27 July 1901], 3); on
the success of the play in America.
7. "The Irish Literary Theatre," 71-73 (6:139 [26 Oct 1901], 2); on
Diarmuid and Grania.
8. *"Samhain,"* 74-77 (6:139 [26 Oct 1901], 2); on Yeats's periodical
(W227).
9. "The Irish Literary Theatre," 77-79 (6:140 [2 Nov 1901], 2); on
Diarmuid and Grania and Joyce's *The Day of the Rabblement.*
10. "Mr. Yeats' Lecture on the Psaltery," 95-97 (8:193 [8 Nov 1902],
3). Correspondence by X. Y. Z., :195 (22 Nov 1902), 3; not reprinted.
11. "The Irish Literary Theatre," 83-86 (originally "The Irish Literary Theatre--And After," 6:143 [23 Nov 1901], 3).
12. "Some Account of the Early Days of the Irish National Theatre
Society," 101-7; a lecture held in NY in 1908.
    See also the review by Patrick Murray, "Fay the Critic," *Irish
Independent*, 79:104 (2 May 1970), 6.

6303. °HARVEY, J. L.: "The Development of Irish Drama," M.A. thesis, U of
Melbourne, 1947.

6304. HICKEY, DES, and GUS SMITH: *A Paler Shade of Green.* London: Frewin,
1972. 253 p.
    American edition: °*Flight from the Celtic Twilight.* Indianapolis:
Bobbs-Merrill, 1973. 253 p. Interviews with Irish dramatists and
actors, among them with or about Padraic Colum, Cyril Cusack, F. J.
MacCormick, Denis Johnston, Hilton Edwards, Micheál MacLiammóir, and
Sean O'Casey. Yeats and the Abbey are mentioned *passim.*

6305. °HIGGINS, PAUL VINCENT: "Religious Themes in the Irish Drama of the
Twentieth Century," M.A. thesis, New York U, 1948. ii, 71 p.

6306. HOGAN, ROBERT. *After the Irish Renaissance: A Critical History of
the Irish Drama since "The Plough and the Stars."* Minneapolis: U of Minnesota Press, 1967. xii, 282 p.
    Main emphasis on Paul Vincent Carroll, Michael Molloy, Denis Johnston,
George Fitzmaurice, Brendan Behan, John B. Keans, and the later
O'Casey. On Yeats, *passim* (see index), especially pp. 147-51, where
Hogan admits playing the devil's advocate and makes the following
dubious statements: (1) Yeats's plays have never been successful in
the theater; (2) Yeats's later plays are private statements; (3) most
of Yeats's plays are undramatic; and (4) Yeats was never interested
in the theater and knew little about it.
    Reviews:
    1. William Angus, *QQ*, 75:3 (Autumn 1968), 543-46.
    2. Anon., "Stage-Door Gossip," *TLS*, 67:3464 (18 July 1968), 746.

6307. HOLLOWAY, JOSEPH: *Joseph Holloway's Abbey Theatre: A Selection from
His Unpublished Journal "Impressions of a Dublin Playgoer."* Edited by
Robert Hogan and Michael J. O'Neill, with a preface by Harry T. Moore.
Carbondale: Southern Illinois UP, 1967. xxiii, 296 p.
    The introduction appeared in somewhat different form as "An Introduc-
tion to Joseph Holloway," *Dubliner*, 3:4 (Winter 1964), 6-16. The
excerpts from the diary are concerned mainly with the years 1899-1926;
they include reminiscences of Yeats and notes on his plays and lectures, as well as on other figures of the revival. See also J107 and
6308.

Reviews:

1. Anon., "Dublin First-Nighter," *TLS*, 66:3396 (30 Mar 1967), 263.
2. Eavan Boland, *Hermathena*, 105 (Autumn 1967), 104-5.
3. V. C. Clinton-Baddeley, *Theatre Notebook*, 22:1 (Autumn 1967), 46-47.
4. Brendan Kennelly, *Irish Historical Studies*, 16:61 (Mar 1968), 98-99.
5. Benedict Kiely, "Joe the Post: or a Portrait of the Irishman as a Mole," *Northwest R*, 9:2 (Fall-Winter 1962 [i.e., 1967]-1968), 110-16; reprinted in *Kilkenny Mag*, #16-17 (Spring 1969), 64-72.
6. John W. Robinson, "On Drama," *Prairie Schooner*, 41:3 (Fall 1967), 349-50.
7. August W. Staub, *QJS*, 53:3 (Oct 1967), 305.

6308. ———: *Joseph Holloway's Irish Theatre*. Edited by Robert Hogan and Michael J. O'Neill. Dixon, Calif.: Proscenium Press, 1968-70. 3 v. (88, 85, 110 p.)

A sequel to J6307; covers the periods 1926-31, 1932-37, 1938-44. Reminiscences of and anecdotes about Yeats, as well as notes about his plays, appear *passim* (see index). Contains a parody of "September 1913" by John Burke, entitled "September ?," 3:78-79.

6309. ——— (comp): A collection of 57 copybooks containing news cuttings relating to the Irish Literary Theatre, the Irish National Theatre Society, and the Abbey Theatre. Arranged chronologically by Joseph Holloway. 1899-1916.

In the National Library of Ireland, MSS. 4374-430.

6310. ——— (comp): News cuttings relating mainly to the Irish theater. 1920-34. 1 v.

In the National Library of Ireland, MS. 4433.

6311. °HUSSEY, MARY E.: "The Peasant in Modern Irish Drama," M.A. thesis, Columbia U, 1926.

6312. *Irish Plays: By Mr. W. B. Yeats, Mr. J. M. Synge, Mr. Wm. Boyle, and Lady Gregory*. Toured under the direction of Alfred Wareing, Summer 1906. [NY?, 1906]. 12 p.

Obviously a theater programme, which contains a short history and an appreciation of the Irish dramatic revival. The National Library of Ireland owns a copy (IR. 82189. N. 15).

6313. °KROCHALIS, JEANNE BROWN: "The Development of the Irish National Theatre Movement," M.A. thesis, Wesleyan U, Middletown, Conn., 1946. ix, 161 p.

6314. LUNARI, GIGI: *Il movimento drammatico irlandese (1899-1922)*. Bologna: Cappelli, 1960. 175 p. (Documenti di teatro. 13.)

On Yeats see especially "William B. Yeats e l'idea di un teatro," 41-62; "Il Teatro Letterario Irlandese e la prima fase sperimentale (1899 - 1901)," containing notes on *The Countess Cathleen* and *Diarmuid and Grania*; and *passim* (no index).

6315. ——— (ed): *Teatro irlandese*. Milano: Nuova Accademia, 1961. 320 p. (Thesaurus Litterarum, sezione terza: Teatro di tutto il mondo. 29.)

"Panorama del teatro irlandese," 9-36; on Yeats, pp. 14-19, also pp. 39-43. Contains Italian translations of *The Hour Glass* and *The Only Jealousy of Emer*. Also introductions to Lady Gregory, Synge, Robinson, O'Casey, and Maurice Meldon.

6316. ——— (ed): *Teatro irlandese moderno*. Roma: Casini, 1967. 96 p. (Tutto il teatro. 18.)

Contains: Gigi Lunari: "Storia di un teatro poetico," 5-11; on the Abbey Theatre and its most famous playwrights.
G. Mazzotti and L. Chiavarelli: "Altri drammaturghi irlandesi," 12-14.
"Le rappresentazioni in Italia," 15-16.
Various photographs, 17-32.
W. B. Yeats: "La pietra del miracolo: Atto unico" and "L'unicorno dalle stelle: Commedia in tre atti," 33-58, translated by Lidia Locatelli.
Translations of Synge's *Riders to the Sea* and *The Playboy*.

6317. LYMAN, KENNETH COX: "Critical Reaction to Irish Drama on the New York Stage: 1900-1958," Ph.D. thesis, U of Wisconsin, 1960. ix, 834 p. (*DA*, 21:3 [Sept 1960], 699.)
Includes discussions of the following Yeats plays: *The Land of Heart's Desire*, *Cathleen ni Houlihan*, *The Hour Glass*, *The Pot of Broth*, *The Countess Cathleen*, and *The Words upon the Window-Pane*.

6318. MCGUIRE, JAMES BRADY: "Realism in Irish Drama," [Ph.D. thesis, Trinity College, Dublin, 1941]. iii, 575, 10, 23 p.
Mainly on Moore, Martyn, Lady Gregory, Synge, Colum, Fitzmaurice, Robinson, and O'Casey.

6319. MACLIAMMÓIR, MICHEÁL: *Theatre in Ireland*. Dublin: At the Three Candles for the Cultural Relations Committee of Ireland, 1964 [1950]. 83 p. (Irish Life and Culture. 1.)

6320. MALONE, ANDREW E.: *The Irish Drama*. NY: Blom, 1965 [1929]. vii, 351 p.
On Yeats (pp. 42-52, 129-46, and *passim*), Colum, Dunsany, Fitzmaurice, Lady Gregory, Brinsley Macnamara, Martyn, Moore, T. C. Murray, O'Casey, Seumas O'Kelly, Robinson, George Shiels, and Synge. Malone was a regular theater-goer and professional critic whose taste was essentially conservative. Yeats's later plays are beyond his comprehension, and of the earlier ones he says: "Two or three of his plays are dramatic in the ordinary meaning of the word, but all the others depend upon something which is strictly not necessary to the theatre. . . . He is not the greatest of the symbolists, in fact it is doubtful if he be a profound thinker at all. Surfaces and emotions have attracted him more than logic and thought . . ." (p. 145).
Reviews:
1. Anon., *Dublin Mag*, 4:3 (July-Sept 1929), 73-75.
2. Anon., "The Theatre in Dublin," *Nation & Athenaeum*, 45:11 (15 June 1929), 369-70.
3. Anon., "Irish Drama," *Saturday R*, 147:3842 (15 June 1929), 802.
4. Anon., "The Irishman's Stage," *Spectator*, 143:5277 (17 Aug 1929), 226.
5. Anon., *TAM*, 14:3 (Mar 1930), 269-70.
6. Anon., "The Irish Drama," *TLS*, 28:1425 (23 May 1929), 417.
7. Ralph Sargent Bailey, *Theatre*, 50:343 (Oct 1929), 6.
8. W[illiam] D[awson], *Studies*, 18:70 (June 1929), 353-54.
9. M. R. N., *Irish Statesman*, 12:17 (29 June 1929), 333-34.
   See the furious letter by St. John Ervine complaining about undeservedly scanty treatment, :23 (10 Aug 1929), 449-50; further correspondence by "Ballymacarett," :24 (17 Aug 1929), 470-71; Gerald Enright, :26 (31 Aug 1929), 509-10.
10. M. P., "'Irlandskaîa' dramaturgiîa," *Vestnik inostrannoĭ literatury*, #5 (1930), 175-76.
11. W. P. Ryan, "Drama and Democracy," *Bookman*, 76:455 (Aug 1929), 271.

6321. O'DRISCOLL, ROBERT (ed): *Theatre and Nationalism in Twentieth-Century Ireland.* Toronto: U of Toronto Press, 1971. 216 p.
Contents: 1. "Introduction," 9-20.
2. Ann Saddlemyer: "Stars of the Abbey Ascendancy," 21-39; on the foundations and early history.
3. George Mills Harper: "'Intellectual Hatred' and 'Intellectual Nationalism': The Paradox of Passionate Politics," 40-65; mainly on Yeats.
4. W. B. Yeats: "Two Lectures on the Irish Theatre," edited by Robert O'Driscoll, 66-88. First printing of a lecture written in 1913 and reprint of "The Irish Dramatic Movement" from *The Voice of Ireland* (W314A).
5. Thomas MacAnna: "Nationalism from the Abbey Stage," 89-101.
6. Roger McHugh: "The Rising," 102-13.
7. David Krause: "Sean O'Casey and the Higher Nationalism: The Desecration of Ireland's Household Gods," 114-33.
8. David R. Clark: "Yeats, Theatre, and Nationalism," 134-55; particularly on *The Death of Cuchulain* and *The Dreaming of the Bones.*
9. M. J. Sidnell: "Hic and Ille: Shaw and Yeats," 156-78; includes seven previously unpublished letters from WBY to GBS, 1901-32.
10. Francis Warner: "The Absence of Nationalism in the Work of Samuel Beckett," 179-204.
Four photographs from a performance of *The Death of Cuchulain.*
Reviews:
1. Anon., "Abbey Ascendant," *TLS*, 71:3648 (28 Jan 1972), 100.
2. Gabriel Fallon, "Soul and Soil," *Irish Press*, 41:244 (16 Oct 1971), 12.
3. T. R. Henn, *MLR*, 67:4 (Oct 1972), 879-80.
4. Denis Johnston, "National Theatre," *Hibernia*, [36:] (3 Mar 1972), 11.
5. Tomas [*sic*] MacAnna, "An Irish Theatre?" *Irish Times*, #36010 (6 Nov 1971), 9.
6. Norman H. MacKenzie, *Dalhousie R*, 51:3 (Autumn 1971), 433-35.
7. Brian F. Tyson, *MD*, 14:4 (Feb 1972), 480-81.

6322. Ó HAODHA, MICHEÁL: *Theatre in Ireland.* Oxford: Blackwell, 1974. xiv, 160 p.
Includes chapters on "The Founders of the National Theatre" (Yeats, Martyn, the Fay brothers), "Synge and the Abbey Plays," "Synge's Successors" (Lady Gregory, Colum, Fitzmaurice, Murray), "The Abbey Style and Its Influence" (particularly on other Irish companies), "Poetry on the Fringe" (Yeats's plays and their influence), "O'Casey and After," "The Gate Theatre and Some Actors" (on Denis Johnston and others).

6323. OLSSON, JAN OLOF, and MARGARETA SJÖGREN: *Plogen och stjärnorna: Irländsk dramatik i verkligheten och på scenen. En krönika skriven för Radioteaterns huvudserie 1968/69 "Det irländska dramat."* Stockholm: Sverige's Radios Förlag, 1968. 208 p.
On Yeats's work in general, pp. 62-102 and *passim* (see index). Also on Synge, Joyce, Lady Gregory, and O'Casey. In the course of the program, *Cathleen ni Houlihan* and *The Unicorn from the Stars* were broadcast.
See also the review by Clas Zilliacus, *Éire-Ireland*, 4:2 (Summer 1969), 150-52.

6324. O'MAHONY, MATHEW: *Progress Guide to Anglo-Irish Plays*. Dublin: Progress House, 1960. xx, 182 p.

> Author and title indexes, as well as plot outlines. Yeats's plays are annotated *passim*.

6325. OPPEN, GENEVIEVE LUCILE: "The Irish Players in America," M.A. thesis, U of Washington, 1943. vi, 220 p.

6326. [QUINN, JOHN (ed)]: *Theodore Roosevelt: "A Note on the Irish Theatre"* & *G. B. Shaw: "An 'Interview' on the Irish Players in America."* NY: Kennerly, 1912. 26 p.

> Introductory note by Quinn, pp. 5-7. Roosevelt's article is reprinted from *Outlook*, 99:16 (16 Dec 1911), 915, and reprinted in J6703. The spurious Shaw interview is from the °*Evening Sun* [NY], 9 Dec 1911, and is reprinted in J6703 and 6547.

6327. RAFROIDI, PATRICK, RAYMONDE POPOT, and WILLIAM PARKER (eds): *Aspects of the Irish Theatre*. Lille: P. U. L. / Paris: Editions universitaires, [1972]. 300 p. (Cahiers irlandais. 1.)

> A somewhat mediocre collection, of which the following items belong in this bibliography:
> Patrick Rafroidi: "Plays for Ireland," 67-73.
> Jeanne Lezon: "The Easter Riding Seen from the Tenements," 75-95; on O'Casey.
> Bernard Mathelin: "From the Shadow of War to the Broken Tassie," 97-105; again on O'Casey.
> Patrick Rafroidi: "Nation of Myth-Makers," 151-62.
> Pascale Mathelin: "Irish Myths in the Theatre of W. B. Yeats," 163-71.
> Raymonde Popot: "The Hero's Light," 173-212; Irish playwrights and the Cuchulain myth; on Yeats see especially pp. 194-205.
> Mireille Schodet: "The Theme of Diarmuid and Grainne," 213-23; on the Yeats-Moore production, pp. 216-19.
> Robert Hogan: "Where Have All the Shamrocks Gone?" 261-71; the Irishness of Irish drama is fast becoming extinct.
> Christiane Thilliez: "From One Theatrical Reformer to Another: W. B. Yeats's Unpublished Letters to Gordon Craig," 275-86; includes quotations from the letters that are now in the Bibliothèque Nationale, Paris. The most interesting article of the collection.
> See also the review by Andrew T. L. Parkin, *Éire-Ireland*, 8:2 (Summer 1973), 137-44.

6328. ROBINSON, LENNOX (ed): *The Irish Theatre*. Lectures delivered during the Abbey Theatre Festival held in Dublin in August 1938. London: Macmillan, 1939. xiii, 229 p.

> Contents: 1. "Foreword," vii-xiii.
> 2. Andrew E. Malone: "The Early History of the Abbey Theatre," 1-28.
> 3. Frank O'Connor: "Synge," 29-52; mainly concerned with refuting Corkery's opinions (J7324).
> 4. Lennox Robinson: "Lady Gregory," 53-64.
> 5. F. R. Higgins: "Yeats and Poetic Drama in Ireland," 65-88. Yeats is the only poetic dramatist in Ireland; he has no predecessors and no successors.
> 6. Andrew E. Malone: "The Rise of the Realistic Movement," 89-115. On William Boyle, W. F. Casey, Padraic Colum, George Fitzmaurice, Lennox Robinson, and T. C. Murray.
> 7. T. C. Murray: "George Shiels, Brinsley Macnamara, etc.," 117-46.
> 8. Walter Starkie: "Sean O'Casey," 147-76. Comments on the *Silver Tassie* affair.

9. Ernest Blythe: "Gaelic Drama," 177-97.
10. Michael MacLiammoir: "Problem Plays," 199-227; i.e., plays that deal with Irish problems, among them *The Countess Cathleen* and *The Land of Heart's Desire*.
11. "Programme" of the Abbey Theatre Festival, 228-29.
Reviews:
1. Anon., "Irish Poetry and Plays [. . .]," *Scotsman*, #30189 (29 Feb 1940), 9.
2. Anon., *TAM*, 24:4 (Apr 1940), 299-300.
3. Anon., "Forty Years of Irish Drama," *TLS*, 39:1993 (13 Apr 1940), 182, 186.
4. Anon., "Vital Drama," *TLS*, 39:1993 (13 Apr 1940), 183.
5. Benjamin Gilbert Brooks, "The Irish Theatre," *Nineteenth Century and After*, 128:762 (Aug 1940), 196-200.
6. Ivor Brown, "The Irish Motley," *Observer*, 149:7761 (25 Feb 1940), 4.
7. Austin Clarke, "The Abbey," *NSt*, 19:476 (6 Apr 1940), 472, 474.
8. Norah Hoult, "The Irish Theatre," *Life and Letters To-day*, 25:33 (May 1940), 158-62.
9. L. A. G. Strong, "The Eagle Mind," *Time and Tide*, 21:10 (9 Mar 1940), 251-52.

6329. RUST, ADOLF: *Beiträge zu einer Geschichte der neu-keltischen Renaissance*. Bückeburg: Grimme, 1922. viii, 87 p. (Dr. phil. thesis, U of Münster, 1919 [i.e., 1922].)
   Not, as promised, a history of the Neo-Celtic renaissance, but a rather slight sketch of the Irish Literary Theatre and the Abbey Theatre, together with an appreciation of Synge's life and work.

6330. SADDLEMYER, ELEANOR ANN: "A Study of the Dramatic Theory Developed by the Founders of the Irish Literary Theatre and the Attempt to Apply This Theory in the Abbey Theatre, with Particular Reference to the Achievements of the Major Figures during the First Two Decades of the Movement," Ph.D. thesis, U of London, 1961. 661 p. (Illustrated)
   Especially on Yeats, Lady Gregory, and Synge; also on Martyn, Moore, AE, Alice Milligan, Cousins, Colum, Robinson, Boyle, and Fitzmaurice.

6331. SAHAL, N.: *Sixty Years of Realistic Irish Drama (1900-1960)*. Bombay: Macmillan, 1971. xii, 220 p.
   Mainly on Lady Gregory, Synge, Colum, Boyle, W. F. Casey, Murray, R. J. Ray, Robinson, Ervine, O'Casey, Shiels, Teresa Deevy, and Carroll. Written before 1960, not brought up to date. Of limited value only because too elementary; see also the review in J6074.

6332. *Samhain: An Occasional Review*. Dublin: Sealy, Bryers & Walker [#5ff., Dublin: Maunsel] / London: Unwin, 1901-8.
   [#1], Oct 1901; [#2], Oct 1902; [#3], Sept 1903; [#4], Dec 1904 ; [#5], Nov 1905; #6, Dec 1906; #7, Nov 1908. No more published; but see J71 and 6703. For individual articles see index NF; for a reprint see J71; for some reviews see J5320 and note.

6333. SCHMITZ-MAYR-HARTING, ELISABETH: "The Irish National Theatre: From Edward Martyn to Sean O'Casey," Dr. phil. thesis, U of Wien, 1956 [i.e., 1961]. ii, 296 p.
   On Martyn, Moore, Yeats (pp. 149-203), Lady Gregory, Synge, and O'Casey. Not very illuminating.

6334. SMYTH, DOROTHY PEARL: "The Playwrights of the Irish Literary Renaissance," M.A. thesis, Acadia U, 1936. 50 p.

Mainly a discussion of Yeats's *The Land of Heart's Desire* and *Cathleen ni Houlihan*, Synge, Colum, and Dunsany. Negligible.

6335. SUSS, IRVING DAVID: "The Decline and Fall of Irish Drama," Ph.D. thesis, Columbia U, 1951. 213 p. (*Microfilm Abstracts*, 11:4 [1951], 841–42.)

6336. WEYGANDT, CORNELIUS: *Irish Plays and Playwrights*. Port Washington: Kennikat Press, 1966 [1913]. xi, 314 p.
Contains individual chapters on Yeats (pp. 37–71), Martyn, Moore, Lady Gregory, Synge, and the younger dramatists (Colum, Boyle, Murray, Robinson, Rutherford Mayne, Norreys Connell, Ervine, and Joseph Campbell). Also on William Sharp (Fiona Macleod).
Reviews:
1. F. L. B., "The Celtic Renaissance," *Cambridge R*, 34:859 (22 May 1913), 479–81. Criticizes Yeats because he has led the movement astray into mysticism.
2. Warren Barton Blake, "Irish Plays and Players," *Independent*, 74: 3353 (6 Mar 1913), 515–19.
3. Edith Kellogg Dunton, "Irish Plays and Players," *Dial*, 54:644 (16 Apr 1913), 335–37.
4. Frank Swinnerton, "General Literature," *Blue R*, 1:3 (July 1913), 194–99.
5. [John Ranken Towse], *Nation*, 96:2494 (17 Apr 1913), 398–99.

6337. WIECZOREK, HUBERT: *Irische Lebenshaltung im Neuen Irischen Drama*. Breslau: Priebatsch, 1937. vi, 104 p. (Sprache und Kultur der germanischen und romanischen Völker. A. Anglistische Reihe. 26.) (Dr. phil. thesis, U of Breslau, 1937.)
Tries to extract the typically Irish way of life from some plays of the revival.

6337a. WINTERGERST, MARIANNE: "Die Selbstdarstellung der Iren: Eine Untersuchung zum modernen anglo-irischen Drama," Dr. phil. thesis, U of München, [1973]. ii, 203 p.
The Irish as seen by themselves in the Irish drama of the 20th century. Mainly on Johnston, Carroll, Behan, Shiels, Robinson, and O'Casey.

6338. °YAMAMOTO, SHŪJI: *Airurando engeki kenkyū* [A story of Irish drama]. Kyoto: Aporon-sha, 1968. iii, 206 p.

See also J377–405, 1120, 3522, 6703.

LB   Articles and Parts of Books

6339. ADAMS, J. DONALD: "The Irish Dramatic Movement," *Harvard Monthly*, 53:2 (Nov 1911), 44–48.

6340. ALLEN, JOHN: *Great Moments in the Theatre*. Illustrated by Joanna Riley. London: Phoenix House, 1958. 127 p.
"Celtic Twilight," 95–105; juvenile literature. Contains a rather silly drawing of Yeats prowling "round the dress circle with his long black cloak sweeping from his shoulders."

6341. ANDREWS, CHARLTON: *The Drama of To-day*. Philadelphia: Lippincott, 1913. 236 p.
See pp. 160–68.

6342. ANDREWS, IRENE DWEN: "The Irish Literary Theatre," *Poet Lore*, 39: [1] (Spring 1928), 94–100.

6343. ANON.: "The Irish Theatre as an Exponent of the Irish People," *American R of Reviews*, 45:3 (Mar 1912), 356-57.

6344. ANON.: "The Irish Dramatic Renaissance," *American R of Reviews*, 47:5 (May 1913), 633-34.

6345. ANON.: "The Irish Theater in America," *American R of Reviews*, 51:2 (Feb 1915), 244-45.
On Padraic Colum's lecture "The Irish Theater, Its Tendencies and Ideals."

6346. ANON.: "The Irish Plays," *Cambridge R*, 32:810 (7 June 1911), 502-3.

6347. ANON.: "Le théâtre en Irlande," *Courrier dramatique de l'Ouest*, #39 (Jan 1961), 10-16.
Based on MacLiammoir's *Theatre in Ireland* (J6319). The same issue contains a five-page article on O'Casey by Philippe Kellerson (unnumbered pages preceding p. 1).

6348. ANON.: "Irish Home Rule in the Drama," *Current Literature*, 50:1 (Jan 1911), 81-84.

6349. ANON.: "The Irish Literary Theatre: Interview with Miss Florence Farr," *Daily Express*, #14587 (5 Apr 1899), 5.

6350. ANON.: "The Irish Literary Theatre," *Daily Express*, #14611 (3 May 1899), 5.

6351. ANON.: "The Irish Literary Theatre: Interview with Mr. George Moore. He Wants the Censorship of the Church," *Freeman's J*, 135:[] (13 Nov 1901), 5-6.
Yeats is mentioned *passim*.

6352. ANON.: "Dramatic Movement in Ireland: Paper by Mr. Sheehy-Skeffington, M.A. Speeches of Mr. T. M. Kettle, M.P., and Others," *Freeman's J*, 140:[] (25 Mar 1907), 5.
Includes a letter from W. B. Yeats to John O'Byrne (J138). On Yeats's plays, *passim*.

6353. ANON.: "The New Irish Peasant," *Gentleman's Mag*, 300:2103 (Mar 1906), 143-50.
Reprinted in *Living Age*, 249:3226 (5 May 1906), 301-5. Nostalgic reminiscences of the lovable Irish peasant of old, who has disappeared in the new Abbey plays but is still to be found in Yeats's plays and stories.

6354. ANON.: "The Early Days of the Irish National Theatre. With Personal Recollections of Synge, Yeats, Moore, Lady Gregory, and Others. An Interview with P. J. Kelly [. . .]," *NYT*, 68:22408 (1 June 1919), IV, 2.

6355. ANON.: "Those Who Write the Irish Drama: Another Recounting of a Historic Theatrical Movement Which Again Finds Representation Here," *NYT*, 77:25509 (27 Nov 1927), IX, 2.

6356. ANON.: "Billy Kelly and the Irish Literary Theatre," *Outlook* [London], 3:68 (20 May 1899), 519-20.
Largely on the reception of *The Countess Cathleen*: "How things wint . . . whin Misther Yeats brought the fairies to the footlights."

6357. ANON.: "The Irish Play of To-day," *Outlook* [NY], 99:10 (4 Nov 1911), 561-63.

6358. ANON.: "The Irish National Theatre," *Samhain*, [#3] (Sept 1903), 34-36.
This was not written by Yeats.

6359. ANON.: "Po teatram mira: Irlandiîa" [World theater: Ireland], *Teatr*, 18:5 (May 1957), 181-83.

6360. ARCHER, WILLIAM: *The Old Drama and the New: An Essay in Re-valuation*. Boston: Small, Maynard, 1923. viii, 396 p.
On the Irish theater, pp. 369-74; apart from Synge, Lennox Robinson is its greatest genius.

6361. ARMSTRONG, WILLIAM ARTHUR (ed): *Classic Irish Drama*. Harmondsworth: Penguin, 1964. 224 p. (Penguin Play. PL54.)
"Introduction: The Irish Dramatic Movement," 7-15. "*The Countess Cathleen*," 17-19.

6362. ASHLEY, LEONARD R. N. (ed): *Nineteenth-Century British Drama: An Anthology of Representative Plays*. Glenview, Ill.: Scott, Foresman, 1967. 700 p.
"*The Countess Cathleen*," 438-41; generally on the Irish theater, less on this play.

6363. BACKER, FRANZ DE: "Hedendaagsche engelsche tooneelliteratuur," *Dietsche Warande en Belfort*, 32:1 (Jan 1932), 20-44.
"Decentralisatie: De Ieren," 25-29.

6364. BARNET, SYLVAN, MORTON BERMAN, and WILLIAM BURTO (eds): *The Genius of the Irish Theater*. NY: New American Library, 1960. 366 p. (Mentor Book. MT315.)
"The Irish Theater: An Introduction," 7-11. Also short notes on Shaw, Lady Gregory, Synge, Yeats and *The Words upon the Window-Pane* (pp. 194-97), Jack B. Yeats, O'Connor, and O'Casey.

6365. BEERBOHM, MAX: *Around Theatres*. London: Hart-Davis, 1953 [1924]. xvi, 583 p.
"Some Irish Plays and Players," 314-19; reprinted from *Saturday R*, 97:2528 (9 Apr 1904), 455-57. The Irish theater is an oasis in the sandy desert of contemporary English drama. Reviews a performance of *The King's Threshold*.

6366. BERGHOLZ, HARRY: *Die Neugestaltung des modernen englischen Theaters, 1870-1930*. Berlin: Bergholz, 1933. xv, 314 p.
Originally °"Die Neugestaltung des modernen englischen Theaterwesens und ihre Bedeutung für den Spielplan," Dr. phil. thesis, U of Berlin, 1933. On the Irish theater, pp. 82-90, 155-60. Contains a list of productions of English repertory theaters, some of which performed plays by Yeats (see index).

6367. BERGSTRÖM, LASSE: "Det irländska dramat," *Teatern*, 21:1 (Jan 1954), 4-5.

6367a. BERROW, J. H.: "The Stage Irishman, 1800-1910," M.A. thesis, U of Wales (Swansea), 1966 [i.e., 1967?]. 245 p.
See especially "The Irish Character in the Early Twentieth Century Irish Theatre," 140-57.

6368. BLUNT, JERRY: *Stage Dialects*. Scranton, Pa.: Chandler Publishing Co., 1967. xi, 156 p.
"Irish," 75-90; the phonetics of the Irish stage dialect with examples from the dramatists of the revival.

6369. BORSA, MARIO: *The English Stage of To-day*. Translated from the original Italian and edited with a prefatory note by Selwyn Brinton. London: Lane, 1908. xi, 317 p.

Originally °*Il teatro inglese contemporaneo*. Milano: Treves, 1906. "The Irish National Theatre," 286-314; on Yeats's plays, particularly *Where There Is Nothing*, pp. 301-14.

6370. BOUCICAULT, DION: *The Dolmen Boucicault*. Edited by David Krause, with an essay by the editor on the theatre of Dion Boucicault [. . .]. Dublin: Dolmen Press, 1964. 253 p.

"The Theatre of Dion Boucicault: A Short View of His Life and Art," 9-47; refers repeatedly to Boucicault as one of the forefathers of the revival.

6371. BOYD, ERNEST A.: "Le théâtre irlandais," *Revue de Paris*, yr 20 / 5: 17 (1 Sept 1913), 191-205.

Mainly on Synge, with a few notes on Yeats's plays.

6372. ————: "The Work of the Irish Theatre," *Irish Monthly*, 47:548 (Feb 1919), 71-76.

6373. BRAWLEY, BENJAMIN: *A Short View of the English Drama*. NY: Harcourt, Brace, 1921. ix, 260 p.

See pp. 230-34.

6374. BRERETON-BARRY, R.: "The Need for a State Theatre," *Irish Statesman*, 3:7 (25 Oct 1924), 210, 212.

Correspondence by "An Old Back Number" [Miss Horniman], :8 (1 Nov 1924), 238; Francis Birrell, :9 (8 Nov 1924), 270; R. Brereton-Barry, :10 (15 Nov 1924), 301.

6375. BROCKETT, OSCAR GROSS, and ROBERT R. FINDLAY: *Century of Innovation: A History of European and American Theatre and Drama since 1870*. Englewood Cliffs: Prentice-Hall, 1973. xv, 826 p.

On the Irish theater, pp. 160-70, 479-84; on Yeats's plays, pp. 161-65.

6376. BROOK, DONALD: *The Romance of the English Theatre*. London: Rockliff, 1952 [1947]. 222 p.

"Irish Creation and Provincial Awakening," 166-77.

6377. BRUN, LIAM DE: "Random Musings on Plays and the Theatre," *Shannonside Annual*, 1:2 (1957), 85-88.

6378. BURKE, MICHAEL: "The Irish Theatre: Forty Years After--An Outline," *New Alliance*, 1:1 (Autumn 1939), 70-77.

6379. C.: "The Irish Literary Theatre--1900," *New Ireland R*, 13:1 (Mar 1900), 49-53.

6380. CAMPBELL, JOHN: "The Rise of the Drama in Ireland," *New Liberal R*, 7:39 (Apr 1904), 291-307.

Comments on Yeats's part in the revival and the plays he wrote for it, especially *The Countess Cathleen*.

6381. CANFIELD, CURTIS (ed): *Plays of the Irish Renaissance, 1880-1930*. With an introduction and notes. NY: Washburn, 1938 [1929]. 436 p.

"Plays Based on Ancient Gaelic Legends and Mythology," 15-26; includes notes on *On Baile's Strand* and *The Only Jealousy of Emer*.

6382. ――――― (ed): *Plays of Changing Ireland*. With introductions and notes. NY: Macmillan, 1936. xv, 481 p.

"Introduction," xi-xv; "Note on *The Words upon the Window-Pane*," 3-7.

6383. CARROLL, DONALD: "Contemporary Irish Theatre," *Drama*, #66 (Autumn 1962), 34-36.

"The present Irish theatrical impotence derives from the people for whom the theatre exists, the playgoers and the playwrights."

6384. CHANDLER, FRANK WADLEIGH: *Aspects of Modern Drama*. NY: Macmillan, 1939 [1914]. ix, 494 p.

"Irish Plays of Mysticism and Folk History," 233-56; "Irish Plays of the Peasantry," 257-76; on Yeats's pre-1910 plays, pp. 239-47 and *passim* (see index).

6385. CLARK, BARRETT HARPER: *The British and American Drama of To-day: Outlines for Their Study*. Suggestions, questions, biographies and bibliographies for use in connection with the study of the more important plays. Cincinnati: Stewart & Kidd, 1921 [1915]. xiii, 317 p.

"The Irish Drama," 179-90; notes on Yeats and *The Countess Cathleen*, pp. 181-87.

6386. ――――――: *A Study of the Modern Drama*. A handbook for the study and appreciation of typical plays, European, English, and American, of the last three-quarters of a century. NY: Appleton-Century, 1938 [1925]. xv, 534 p.

"The Irish Drama," 331-57; the Yeats section (pp. 331-36) is again concerned with *The Countess Cathleen*.

6387. ――――――, and GEORGE FREEDLEY: *A History of Modern Drama*. NY: Appleton-Century, 1947. xiii, 832 p.

George Freedley: "Irish Drama," 216-32; the section on Yeats (pp. 217-18) is worthless.

6388. COLBY, ELBRIDGE: "Some Irish Plays and Social Sketches," *SAQ*, 13:3 (July 1914), 248-59.

Mainly on Seumas MacManus, who is considered to be a better writer and truer representative of the Irish people than either Yeats or Synge. Proves his point by misreading *Cathleen ni Houlihan*.

6389. COLUM, PADRAIC: "Early Days of the Irish Theatre," *Dublin Mag*, 24:4 (Oct-Dec 1949), 11-17; 25:5 [i.e., 1] (Jan-Mar 1950), 18-25.

6390. ――――――: *Three Plays*. Dublin: Figgis, 1963. iv, 188 p. (An Chomhairle Ealaíon Series of Irish Authors. 3.)

"Preface," 1-8; contains Colum's very personal history of the dramatic revival plus some notes on his own plays.

6391. CONNOLLY, JAMES: "National Drama," *United Irishman*, 10:243 (24 Oct 1903), 2.

6392. *Contemporary Theatre*. London: Arnold, 1962. 208 p. (Stratford-upon-Avon Studies. 4.)

Kenneth Muir: "Verse and Prose," 97-115; contains some notes on Yeats's plays.

John Jordan: "The Irish Theatre: Retrospect and Premonition," 165-83. Synge, O'Casey, and Johnston are the only outstanding dramatists produced by the Irish theater. The Abbey Theatre was a very provincial enterprise, out of touch with contemporary Irish reality and with not enough quality in it to earn a European reputation. Its future does not look promising.

6393. CORRIGAN, ROBERT WILLOUGHBY (ed): *Masterpieces of the Modern Irish Theatre*. NY: Collier Books, 1967. 319 p.
"The Irish Dramatic Flair," 6-8; note on Yeats's plays, p. 32.

6394. CUNLIFFE, JOHN WILLIAM: *Modern English Playwrights: A Short History of the English Drama from 1825*. NY: Harper, 1927. xi, 260 p.
"The Irish Drama and J. M. Synge (1871-1909)," 131-42.

6395. CUSACK, CYRIL: "In Terms of Theatre," *Iris Hibernia*, 4:3 (1960), 20-26.
"In Ireland, despite its scattered flights of dramatic glory and its extraordinary output of plays over the past half-century, appreciation of theatre, both before and behind our footlights, awaits its coming of age."

6396. DE BLACAM, AODH: "Dublin--The Drama," *Capuchin Annual*, 1 (1930), 53-56.

6397. DE LURY, A. T.: "The Irish Drama: Once More the Soul of Eire Throbs in Tara's Tragic Muse," *Celtic Forum*, 1:2 (Mar 1935), 10-11.

6398. DE SMET, ROBERT: "La littérature dramatique en Irlande," *Revue de Paris*, yr 49 / 50:20 (15 Oct 1937), 903-19.

6399. DICKINSON, THOMAS HERBERT: *An Outline of Contemporary Drama*. Boston: Houghton Mifflin, 1927. ix, 299 p.
"The Irish National Theater," 225-28.

6400. DIGGES, DUDLEY: "The Actors' Part in the Irish Theatre," *Recorder*, 10:2 (1 July 1939), 15-18.

6401. DONNE, MAURICE: "Irish Drama," *Irish Statesman*, 4:5 (11 Apr 1925), 141-42.
Correspondence by J. Bernard MacCarthy, :9 (9 May 1925), 269.

6402. DUDGEON, PATRICK ORPEN, and MIGUEL ALFREDO OLIVERA: *Teatro ingles del siglo XX*. Buenos Aires: Ediciones Losange, 1958. 117 p.
See pp. 25-38.

6403. DUKES, ASHLEY: "The Irish Scene: Dublin Plays and Playhouses," *TAM*, 14:5 (May 1930), 378-85.

6404. [DUMUR, GUY (ed)]: *Histoire des spectacles*. Paris: Gallimard, 1965. xxi, 2010 p. (Encyclopédie de la Pleiade. 19.)
Michel Habart: "Irlande," 1196-205.

6405. D[UNCAN], E[LLEN] M.: "Literary Drama in Dublin," *Athenaeum*, #4126 (24 Nov 1906), 665-66.

6406. D[UNTON], E[DITH] K[ELLOGG]: "The Irish Theatre Society," *Dial*, 51: 612 (16 Dec 1911), 521.

6407. EATON, WALTER PRICHARD: *The Drama in English*. NY: Scribner's, 1930. xv, 365 p.
"Local Drama and the Irish Revival--Synge and O'Casey," 287-91.

6408. ELLEHAUGE, MARTIN: "Nogle hovedtyper indenfor det moderne irske drama," *Edda*, yr 16 / 29:4 (1929), 456-64.

6409. *Enciclopedia dello spettacolo*. Roma: Casa Editrice le Maschere, 1954-66. 10 v.
S[ybil] Ro[senfeld]: "Dublino," 4:1041-47.
M[alcolm] Mo[rley]: "Irlanda," 6:606-12.
W[illiam] A. Ar[mstrong]: "Yeats," 9:2045-48.

6410. EREMINA, I. K.: "Irlandskaĩa dramaturgiĩa kont͡sa XIX-nachala XX vv.,"
Moskovskiĩ oblastnoĩ pedagogicheskiĩ institut imeni N. K. Krupskoĩ. Uchen-
ye zapiski, 152:9-10 (1964), 81-100.
Contains sections on Yeats (pp. 83-85), Lady Gregory, Synge (pp. 87-
96, the longest section), Martyn, and others.

6411. ERVINE, ST. JOHN G.: "The Irish Dramatist and the Irish People,"
Forum, 51:6 (June 1914), 940-48.

6412. EVANS, SIR BENJAMIN IFOR: *A Short History of English Drama.* Boston:
Houghton Mifflin, 1965 [1948]. 216 p. (Riverside Studies in Literature.
L9.)
See pp. 178-82.

6413. FALLON, GABRIEL: "The Future of the Irish Theatre," *Studies*, 44:[]
(Spring 1955), 92-100.

6414. ———: "Theatre," *Month*, 17:3 (Mar 1957), 206-8.
Argues for the necessity of sticking to Yeats's principles in order
to restore a genuine Irish theater of quality.

6415. FAY, W. G.: "Yeats and the Irish Drama: Part of a Broadcast," *Lis-*
tener, 21:529 (2 Mar 1939), 484.
More on the Irish drama than on Yeats.

6416. FITZGERALD, MAURICE: "The Future of the Peasant Play," *Sinn Féin*,
ns 4:163 (15 Mar 1913), 6-7.
Mainly on Synge and Lady Gregory.

6417. FITZGERALD, WILLIAM GEORGE (ed): *The Voice of Ireland (Glór na*
h-Éireann): A Survey of the Race and Nation from All Angles by the Fore-
most Leaders at Home and Abroad. [Revised edition]. Dublin: Virtue, [1924]
[1923]. xx, 612 p.
Theodore Roosevelt: "The Irish Theatre as an American Model (A Tribute to Lady Augusta Gregory)," 255-56.
T. C. Murray: "Church and Stage in the New Day: A Defence and a Plea
for Co-operation," 278-81: "These writers [among them Yeats] are what
they are not because of their Protestantism, but in spite of it. In
studying the work of W. B. Yeats, whether in verse or in prose drama,
the most casual student will observe that he reaches his highest
moments only when his mind is absorbed in Catholic ways of thought."
William J. Flynn: "The Irish Literary Theatre," 466-70.

6418. FITZ-SIMON, CHRISTOPHER: "The Theater in Dublin," *MD*, 2:3 (Dec 1959),
289-94.

6419. *Five Great Modern Irish Plays.* With a foreword by George Jean Nathan.
NY: Modern Library, 1941. xiii, 352 p. (Modern Library. 30.)
"Foreword," ix-xiii.

6420. FLORENCE, JEAN: "Le theatre irlandais (J.-M. Synge, Lady Gregory),"
Phalange, yr 6 / 10:55 (20 Jan 1911), 52-61.

6421. FOX, R. M.: "Realism in Irish Drama," *Irish Statesman*, 10:16 (23
June 1928), 310-12.

6422. ———: "Modern Irish Drama," *TAM*, 24:1 (Jan 1940), 22-25.

6423. ———: "The Theatre Goes On: In Ireland," *TAM*, 24:11 (Nov 1940),
783-86.

6424. ———: "Ups and Downs in the Irish Theatre," *TAM*, 25:5 (May 1941),
253-58.

6425. ———: "Irish Drama in War and Peace," *TAM*, 30:4 (Apr 1946), 231-35.

6426. ———: "Irish Drama Knocks at the Door," *Life and Letters*, 61:140 (Apr 1949), 16-21.

6427. ———: "Social Criticism in the Irish Theatre," *Aryan Path*, 38:4 (Apr 1967), 179-81.

6428. FRANK, ANDRÉ: "Georges Pitoëff et le baptême parisien du théâtre d'Irlande . . . ," *Cahiers de la Compagnie Madeleine Renaud--Jean-Louis Barrault*, #37 (1962), 102-6.
Pitoëff's productions of plays by Irish playwrights, notably Synge, Lady Gregory, and Shaw.

6429. FREEDLEY, GEORGE, and JOHN A. REEVES: *A History of the Theatre*. Newly revised with a supplementary section. NY: Crown, 1955 [1941]. xvi, 784 p.
"The Irish National Theatre (1899-1940)," 481-94; "Ireland," 670-71.

6430. FRIEL, BRIAN: "Plays Peasant and Unpeasant," *TLS*, 71:3655 (17 Mar 1972), 305-6.

6431. GAD, CARL: "Moderne irsk theater," *Ugens tilskuer*, 6:299 (23 June 1916), 313-15; :301 (7 July 1916), 329-31; :309 (1 Sept 1916), 391-94.
The third installment is mostly on Yeats's plays. For a shorter version see J3394.

6432. GAYNOR, ARTHUR: "Ireland & the Theatre," *Banba*, 3:2 (June 1922), 106-12.

6433. GILL, MICHAEL J.: "Neo-Paganism and the Stage," *New Ireland R*, 27:3 (May 1907), 179-87.
Anti-Synge, anti-Yeats.

6434. GONNE MACBRIDE, MAUD: "A National Theatre," *United Irishman*, 10:243 (24 Oct 1903), 2-3.
Correspondence by J. B. Yeats and editor's comment, :244 (31 Oct 1903), 7. About Synge's *In the Shadow of the Glen*. Refers to WBY *passim*.

6435. GRZEBIENIOWSKI, TADEUSZ: "Teatr i dramat w Irlandii jako czynniki odradzającej się kultury narodowej" [Theater and drama in Ireland as an element of revival of its national culture], *Kultura i spoleczeństwo*, 2:4 (1958), 190-200.
On Yeats's plays, *passim*.

6436. GUNNELL, DORIS: "Le nouveau théâtre irlandais," *Revue*, ser 6 / yr 23 / 94:1 (1 Jan 1912), 91-106.
On the plays of Yeats (especially *The Land of Heart's Desire*, *The Hour Glass*, and *Cathleen ni Houlihan*), Synge, and Lady Gregory.

6437. GUTHRIE, TYRONE: *A Life in the Theatre*. London: Hamilton, 1960. vii, 320 p.
"Ireland," 258-71.

6438. GVOZDEV, A.: "Irlandskiǐ teatr," *Iskusstvo i zhizn*, #6 (June 1940), 10-13.
Mainly on Yeats and Synge.

6439. GWYNN, STEPHEN: "The Irish Literary Theatre and Its Affinities," *Fortnightly R*, os 76 / ns 70:420 (1 Dec 1901), 1050-62.
Mainly on *Diarmuid and Grania* and Douglas Hyde.

6440. ————: "An Uncommercial Theatre," *Fortnightly R*, os 78 / ns 72:432 (1 Dec 1902), 1044-54.
Includes a long note on *Cathleen ni Houlihan*.

6441. HABART, MICHEL: "Le théâtre irlandais," *Théâtre populaire*, #9 (Sept-Oct 1954), 24-43.
On Yeats's plays, *passim*; also on Synge, Lady Gregory, and O'Casey.

6442. HANIGHEN, FRANK C.: "The Irish Players Present--," *Commonweal*, 17:9 (28 Dec 1932), 237-38.

6443. HARTMANN, ALFONS: *Der moderne englische Einakter*. Leipzig: Noske, 1936. 181 p. (Aus Schrifttum und Sprache der Angelsachsen. 6.) (Dr. phil. thesis, U of Tübingen.)
"Der irische Einakter," 36-67; contains notes on Yeats's one-act plays.

6444. HARTNOLL, PHYLLIS (ed): *The Oxford Companion to the Theatre*. 3rd edition. London: Oxford UP, 1967 [1951]. xv, 1088 p.
"Abbey Theatre," 1-2. Una Ellis-Fermor and Dan O'Connell: "Ireland," 472-77. Una Ellis-Fermor: "Yeats," 1020-21.

6445. HAYES, J. J.: "The Little Theatre Movement in Ireland," *Drama* [Chicago], 16:7 (Apr 1926), 201-2.
Also in *Little Theatre Monthly*, 2:7 (Apr 1926), 261-62.

6446. ————: "The Irish Scene," *TAM*, 16:11 (Nov 1932), 922-26.

6447. ————: "The Theater in Ireland," *CSM*, 39:92 (15 Mar 1947), Weekly Magazine, 19.

6448. HEIDE, HERMINE: "Das moderne irische Drama," *Münchener Neueste Nachrichten*, 72:322 (14 Aug 1919), 1.

6449. HENDERSON, WILLIAM A.: "The Irish Theatre Movement," *Sunday Independent*, 17:8 (17 Sept 1922), 6.

6450. HENN, THOMAS RICE: *The Harvest of Tragedy*. London: Methuen, 1966 [1956]. xvi, 304 p. (University Paperbacks. UP177.)
"The Irish Tragedy (Synge, Yeats, O'Casey)," 197-216. On Yeats's plays, pp. 205-12 (particularly *The Countess Cathleen*, *On Baile's Strand*, *The Player Queen*, *Calvary*, *Purgatory*, and *The Death of Cuchulain*) and *passim* (see index).

6451. HENSEL, GEORG: *Spielplan: Schauspielführer von der Antike bis zur Gegenwart*. Berlin: Propyläen, 1966. 2 v.
"Das Sprechzimmer der Seelenkenner oder: Dramatiker, die man Naturalisten nennt," 2, xii; contains an Irish section (pp. 786-804) with notes, somewhat incongruously, on Yeats's plays, especially *The Countess Cathleen* and *The Unicorn from the Stars* (pp. 789-92).

6452. HOARE, JOHN EDWARD: "Ireland's National Drama," *NAR*, 194:671 (Oct 1911), 566-75.
Mainly on the plays of Lady Gregory and Synge.

6453. HOGAN, ROBERT (ed): *Seven Irish Plays, 1946-1964*. With an introduction. Minneapolis: U of Minnesota Press, 1967. v, 472 p.
"Pull Back the Green Curtains," 3-27: "No, the Irish dramatic renaissance is definitely not with Yeats in his grave. Indeed, perhaps it was never with Yeats at all."

6454. ————: "Dublin: The Summer Season and the Theatre Festival, 1967," *Drama Survey*, 6:3 (Spring 1968), 315-23.
Includes a reivew of a performance of *The Words upon the Window-Pane*.

6455. ————, and JAMES KILROY (eds): *Lost Plays of the Irish Renaissance.* [Dixon, Calif.]: Proscenium Press, 1970. 84 p.

"Introduction," 9–16. Contains the following plays: P. T. McGinley, *Lizzie and the Tinker*; Fred Ryan, *The Laying of the Foundation* (see also J7264); James H. Cousins, *The Racing Lug*; Lady Gregory, *Twenty-five*; Padraic Colum, *The Saxon Shillin'*; and Maud Gonne, *Dawn* (see also J6922).
Reviews:
1. Anon., "Abbey Prelude," *TLS*, 71:3655 (17 Mar 1972), 306.

6456. HUBBELL, JAY BROADUS, and JOHN OWEN BEATY (eds): *An Introduction to Drama.* Corrected 1st edition, with index. NY: Macmillan, 1944 [1927]. xiii, 849 p.

"Irish Dramatists," 522–24.

6457. HUDSON, LYNTON: *The Twentieth-Century Drama.* London: Harrap, 1946. 220 p.

"The Irish Movement," 37–44.

6458. "IRIAL": "Has the Irish Literary Theatre Failed?" *United Irishman*, 6:141 (9 Nov 1901), 3.

6459. *Irish Art Handbook.* Dublin: Cahill, 1943. viii, 163 p.

Lord Longford: "Irish Drama To-day," 81–83. Michael MacLiammoir: "We Start a Theatre," 85–92 (the Gate Theatre). W. B. Stanford: "Recent Irish Poetry," 103–6.

6460. JOHNSTON, DENIS: "The Theatre in Ireland," *One Act Play Mag & Radio Drama R*, 1:6 (Oct 1937), 557–59.

6461. ————: "What Has Happened to the Irish?" *TAM*, 43:7 (July 1959), 11–12, 72.

Since Yeats's death the Irish theater is declining.

6462. KASCHNER, GERHARD: "Nationale Dichtung in Irland: Ein Querschnitt durch zeitgenössisches irisches Bühnenschaffen," *Rheinisch-Westfälische Zeitung*, #281 (5 June 1935), 9.

6463. KAVANAGH, PETER: "The History of Gaelic Drama," *Bell*, 14:1 (Apr 1947), 56–61.

The importance of the Irish Literary Theatre for the revival of 20th-century Gaelic drama.

6464. KELLER, T. G.: "The Irish Theatre Movement—Some Early Memories," *Sunday Independent*, 24:1 (6 Jan 1929), 7.

Includes reminiscences of Yeats.

6465. KILROY, THOMAS: "Groundwork for an Irish Theatre," *Studies*, 48:190 (Summer 1959), 192–98.

There is no creativity in the present Irish theater. See reply by Gabriel Fallon, "All This and the Abbey Too," :192 (Winter 1959), 434–42.

6466. KINDERMANN, HEINZ: *Theatergeschichte Europas.* Salzburg: Müller, 1961–. v.

"Die Sonderentwicklung des irischen Theaters," 9:491–514; on Yeats's plays, *passim*.

6467. KIRWAN, H. N.: "Irish Theatre," *Inisfail*, 1:1 (Mar 1933), 35–37.

6468. KRAFT, IRMA: *Plays, Players, Playhouses: International Drama of Today*. NY: Dobsevage, 1928. xix, 265 p.
  "Ireland--The Rebellions," 146-51.

6469. KRAJEWSKA, WANDA: "Irlandskość Eugene'a O'Neill," *Przegląd humanistyczny*, 10:4 (1966), 51-66.
  The influence of the Irish theater, especially of the plays of Yeats, Synge, and O'Casey, on O'Neill, and Irish themes and materials in his plays.

6470. [KUTTNER, ALFRED B.]: "Notes on the Irish Movement," *International*, 5:2 (Jan 1912), 23-24.

6471. LAMM, MARTIN: *Det moderna dramat*. Stockholm: Bonnier, 1948. v, 363 p.
  "Irländskt drama," 299-319. English edition: *Modern Drama*. Translated by Karin Elliott. Oxford: Blackwell, 1952. xx, 359 p. "Irish Drama," 293-314; on Yeats, pp. 295-302 (prefers the pre-1910 plays).

6472. LEAL, RINE (ed): *Teatro irlandès: Yeats / Lady Gregory / O'Casey / Synge / Carroll / Behan*. Selección, prólogo y notas de Rine Leal. Habana: Consejo Nacional de Cultura, 1966. 479 p.
  "A manera de homenaje," 7-24; note on Yeats, pp. 25-26. Includes a translation of *Cathleen ni Houlihan*.

6473. LECLERCQ, R.: "La situation du théâtre en Irlande," *Comoedia*, 23: 6068 (27 Aug 1929), 5.

6474. LÉOPOLD-LACOUR, [ ]: "Le théâtre en Irlande," *Comoedia*, 18:4341 (10 Nov 1924), 2.
  An interview with Maurice Bourgeois, mostly on Yeats and Synge. Although this is marked "à suivre," I have not been able to find any continuation.

6475. LEWIS, SAUNDERS: "Recent Anglo-Celtic Drama," *Welsh Outlook*, 9:99 (Mar 1922), 63-65.
  Praises *The Dreaming of the Bones*.

6476. LEWISOHN, LUDWIG: *The Modern Drama: An Essay in Interpretation*. NY: Viking Press, 1928 [1915]. xii, 340 p.
  On the Irish "neo-romantic drama," pp. 267-74. Yeats's "art is based upon a vision of things which is not only unreal but, if one must be frank, puerile." Does not seem to know any of Yeats's plays written after 1903.

6477. LUMLEY, FREDERICK (ed): *Theatre in Review*. Edinburgh: Paterson, 1956. xvi, 201 p.
  Gerard Fay: "The Irish Theatre: A Decline and Perhaps, in the End, a Fall," 80-89. Wanted: A new O'Casey.

6478. LUNARI, GIGI: "Dublino: Due grandi tabù locali: Religione e nazionalismo," *Dramma*, 35:273 (June 1959), 69-71.

6479. MCBRIEN, PETER F.: *Higher English Drama: How to Know Good Drama, and to Say Why It Is Good*. A textbook of literary appreciation and an anthology from the best plays in English, including Anglo-Irish drama, for intermediate, civil service, university, and other students. Dublin: Intermediate & University College, [1931]. 269 p.
  Anglo-Irish examples, *passim*, especially from Yeats and T. C. Murray.

6480. MACCARTHY, DESMOND: "The Irish Plays," *Speaker*, ns 13:[] (9 Dec 1905), 251-52.

6481. MCCARTHY, JUSTIN (ed): *Irish Literature.* Chicago: DeBower-Elliott, 1904. 10 v.
Stephen Gwynn: "The Irish Drama," 10:xiii-xxv.

6481a. °MCDERMOTT, HUBERT: "The Background to Anglo-Irish Drama," *Topic,* 12:24 (Fall 1972), 69-76.

6482. MACDONAGH, JOHN: "Acting in Dublin," *Commonweal,* 10:7 (19 June 1929), 185-86.

6483. MACGOWAN, KENNETH, and WILLIAM MELNITZ: *The Living Stage: A History of the World Theater.* Englewood Cliffs: Prentice-Hall, 1955. xiii, 543 p.
See pp. 419-23.

6484. MCHUGH, ROGER: "Towards a National Theatre," *Irish Library Bulletin,* 12:[9-10] (Sept-Oct 1951), 131-34.

6485. ———: "Tradition and the Future of Irish Drama," *Studies,* 40:160 (Dec 1951), 469-74.

6486. ———: "Drama in Ireland To-day," *Iris Hibernia,* 4:3 (1960), 40-42.

6486a. MCKENNA, T. P.: "A View on the Irish Theatre," *Labour Monthly,* 49:4 (Apr 1967), 185-87.
The decline of the Irish theater is due to tensions between the Anglo-Irish and Gaelic cultures.

6487. °MACMILLAN, W. D.: "Certain Recent Dramatizations of Ancient Irish Legends," M.A. thesis, U of North Carolina, 1920.

6488. °MALEH, GHASSAN: "al-Harakah al-Masrahiyah al-Irlandiyah" [The Irish dramatic movement], *al-Ma'rifah,* 3:34 (Dec 1964), 376-84.

6489. MALONE, ANDREW E.: "The Decline of the Irish Drama," *Dublin Mag,* os 1:8 (Mar 1924), 706-14.
Reprinted with slight revisions in *Nineteenth Century,* 97:578 (Apr 1925), 578-88.

6490. ———: "The Late Development of Irish Drama," *Edinburgh R,* 245:500 (Apr 1927), 364-74.
Reprinted in *Dublin Mag,* ns 3:3 (July-Sept 1928), 16-30; and as "The Tardy Irish Drama," *English J,* 17:6 (June 1928), 469-80. Sketches the development up to Yeats.

6491. ———: "The Coming of Age of the Irish Drama," *Dublin R,* 181:362 (July 1927), 101-14.

6492. ———: "The Irish Theatre in 1930," *Dublin Mag,* 6:2 (Apr-June 1931), 1-11.
Includes a review of a performance of *The Words upon the Window-Pane,* pp. 6-7.

6493. ———: "The Irish Theatre in 1935," *Dublin Mag,* 11:1 (Jan-Mar 1936), 48-59.
"It would seem as if the Irish drama has almost reached its end, or that it is on the verge of a new departure. . . ."

6494. [MANNING, MARY ?]: "The Present Position of Irish Drama," *Motley,* 1:6 (Nov 1932), 2-3.

6495. MARRIOTT, JAMES WILLIAM: *Modern Drama.* London: Nelson, [1934]. vi, 327 p.
"Irish Dramatists," 190-203; contains some uninformed remarks about Yeats (e.g., Marriott makes a doctor of law out of him).

6496. MARTYN, EDWARD: "A Plea for a National Theatre in Ireland," *Samhain*, [#1] (Oct 1901), 14-15.
See also J7034.

6497. ————: "A Plea for the Revival of the Irish Literary Theatre," *Irish R*, 4:38 (Apr 1914), 79-84.
See also J7034. Martyn's characterization of Yeats is interesting: "A fine poet and subtle literary critic, he has, above all[,] a weird appearance, which is triumphant with middle-aged masculine women, and a dictatorial manner which is irresistible with the considerable bevy of female and male mediocritics interested in intellectual things. In this way he practically dictates to the critics who reproduce his opinions."

6498. MASON, RUPERT: *Robes of Thespis: Costume Design by Modern Artists*. Edited for Rupert Mason by George Sheringham and R. Boyd Morrison. London: Benn, 1928. xv, 143 p., 109 plates.
"Irish Dramatic Costume," 33-62; contains among other things the following: Lennox Robinson, "Irish Dramatic Costume," 35-39; Gerald Macnamara, "Irish Costume and the Theatre," 41-48; and several plates with costumes, e.g., Charles Ricketts for *The King's Threshold*, Norah McGuinness for *Deirdre*, and Laurence Bradshaw for *At the Hawk's Well*.

6499. MATLAW, MYRON: *Modern World Drama: An Encyclopedia*. London: Secker & Warburg, 1972. xxiii, 960 p.
Contains paragraphs on Carroll, Colum, Ervine, Fitzmaurice, Lady Gregory, Hyde, Ireland, Johnston, Macnamara, Martyn, Murray, O'Casey, Robinson, Shiels, Synge, and Yeats (pp. 842-44). Plays cited by Matlaw in small caps are summarized in alphabetical order, *passim*.

6500. MATTHEWS, BRANDER: *The Principles of Playmaking and Other Discussions of the Drama*. NY: Scribner's, 1925 [1919]. vii, 306 p.
"Irish Plays and Playwrights," 196-213; reprinted from *Scribner's Mag*, 61:1 (Jan 1917), 85-90; mainly on the theater and drama before the revival.

6501. MERCIER, VIVIAN: "The Dublin Tradition," *New Republic*, 135:2175 (6 Aug 1956), 21-22.

6502. MILLER, NELLIE BURGET: *The Living Drama: Historical Development and Modern Movements Visualized. A Drama of the Drama*. NY: Century, 1924. xx, 437 p.
"The New Theater of Ireland," 330-53; on Yeats's plays, pp. 331-35. Discusses *The Land of Heart's Desire* "as an example of the best of Mr. Yeats's work, with its mysticism, its twilight moods, and its formless yearning. . . ."

6503. M[ONTAGUE], C. E.: "The Irish Theatre," *Manchester Guardian*, #18622 (16 Apr 1906), 10.

6504. MOORE, GEORGE: "The Irish Literary Theatre," *Samhain*, [#1] (Oct 1901), 11-13.
Contains some carefully worded criticism of a performance of *The Countess Cathleen* and of its author's dramatic theories.

6505. MORGAN, ARTHUR EUSTACE: *Tendencies of Modern English Drama*. London: Constable, 1924. vii, 320 p.
"The Irish Pioneers," 139-57; Yeats, Martyn, and Lady Gregory. "Synge," 158-73. "Irish Dramatists," 198-221; Colum and Robinson. "More Irish Dramatists," 222-46; Murray and Ervine.

6506. MORTON, DAVID: "A Letter from Dublin: Immediate and Retrospective," *Drama* [Chicago], 20:4 (Jan 1930), 106, 108.
Includes a review of a performance of *Fighting the Waves*.

6507. MOSELEY, VIRGINIA: "A Week in Dublin (February 20-26, 1961)," *MD*, 4:2 (Sept 1961), 164-71.
Report of a panel discussion among Brendan Behan, John B. Keane, Ray MacAnally, and Seamus Kelley on "Modern or Begorrah (Whither Irish Theatre)."

6508. MOSES, MONTROSE JONAS (ed): *Representative British Dramas Victorian and Modern*. Revised edition with introductions and bibliographies. Boston: Heath, 1931 [1918]. xvi, 996 p.
"The Irish School of Playwrights," 889-97; "William Butler Yeats," 901-5.

6509. MUSEK, KAREL: "Irské literární divadlo" [The Irish literary theater], *Divadelní list máje*, 3:2 (2 Nov 1906), 17-19.

6510. °NARDIN, FRANCES LOUISE: "A Study of Tragic Situation and Character in English Drama, 1900-1912," Ph.D. thesis, U of Missouri, 1914. 168 p.
According to information kindly supplied by the U of Missouri Library, the thesis contains a section on "Dramas Using Themes from Irish Legends," pp. 112-24, which touches on *Deirdre* and *On Baile's Strand*.

6511. NATHAN, GEORGE JEAN: *Encyclopaedia of the Theatre*. NY: Knopf, 1940. ix, 449 p.
"Erin Go Blah," 120-21; reprinted from *Newsweek*, 10:26 (27 Dec 1937), 25. "Irish Drama," 199-201.

6512. ————: *The Entertainment of a Nation or Three-Sheets in the Wind*. NY: Knopf, 1942. vi, 290 p.
"The Contribution of the Irish," 68-75: ". . . the quondam rich vein appears to have run dry."

6513. "NIAMH": "Our National Drama," *J of the Ivernian Society*, 2:6 (Jan 1910), 105-10.

6514. NICOLL, ALLARDYCE: *British Drama: An Historical Survey from the Beginnings to the Present Time*. 4th edition revised. London: Harrap, 1951 [1925]. vii, 533 p.
"Irish Dramatists," 391-99; mostly on Robinson, Murray, and Colum. On Yeats's early plays, pp. 405-10. "J. M. Synge and the Irish School of Imaginative Dramatists," 410-21; also on Martyn and Dunsany. "J. M. Synge and the Irish School [of Comedy]," 432-35.

6515. ————: *World Drama from Aeschylus to Anouilh*. London: Harrap, 1951 [1949]. iv, 1000 p.
"The Irish School," 689-98; on Yeats, pp. 729-31 and *passim* (see index).

6516. ————: *English Drama, 1900-1930: The Beginnings of the Modern Period*. Cambridge: UP, 1973. x, 1083 p.
See pp. 248-60; notes on Yeats's plays, *passim* (see index).

6517. NOWACZYŃSKI, ADOLF: *Szkice literackie*. Poznań: Nakładem spółki wydawniczej ostoja, 1918. 222 p.
"Teatr irlandzki," 59-70.

6518. O'DONNELL, FRANK J. HUGH: "The Irish Theatre: Its Inception and Progress," *Red Hand Mag*, 1:2 (Oct 1920), 51-54.

6519. Ó DROIGHNEÁIN, MUIRIS: *Taighde i gComhair stair litridheachta na nua-Ghaedhilge ó 1882 annas.* Baile Átha Cliath: Oifig díolta foillseacháin rialtais, 1936. 266 p.
  A history of the literature of the Gaelic literary revival; contains "An 'Irish Literary Theatre,'" 94-97, and some remarks on Yeats (see index).

6520. O'HAGAN, THOMAS: *Essays on Catholic Life.* Freeport, N.Y.: Books for Libraries, 1965 [1916]. 166 p.
  "The Irish Dramatic Movement," 57-73. Mainly on Synge, whose "pagan" outlook is considered distasteful. The author admits, however, that without the "pagan" writers there would have been no revival.

6521. O hEigeartaigh [O'HEGARTY], P. S.: "About Drama," *Inis Fáil,* #46 (Aug 1908), 5-6.
  The dramatic movement in Ireland is not progressing.

6522. OLIVER, D. E.: *The English Stage: Its Origin and Modern Developments. A Critical and Historical Study.* London: Ouseley, [1912]. xv, 152 p.
  See pp. 118-21.

6523. O'MAHONY, D. D.: "Samhain--1904," *Blarney Magazine,* #14 (Summer 1958), 17-19.
  Blarney.

6523a. O'MANGAIN, H. C.: "The National Drama," *Evening Telegraph,* ns #7953 (4 Feb 1907), 4.
  Subheading: "Mr. Henry Mangan discusses Mr. Yeats, Mr. Synge, Mr. Boyle, and Lady Gregory." The same issue carries letters by Boyle, Alice Milligan, and others commenting on Yeats's position in the *Playboy* affair.

6524. O'NEILL, GEORGE: "Recent Irish Drama and Its Critics," *New Ireland R,* 25:1 (Mar 1906), 29-36.
  Detects a certain "mystico-pagan cant" in the plays of Yeats and Synge and does not like it.

6525. PALMER, JOHN: *The Future of the Theatre.* London: Bell, 1913. xi, 196 p.
  See pp. 167-72.

6526. PASSEUR, STÈVE: "Le théâtre irlandais," *Oeuvre,* epoch 4 / yr 32 / #75 (Spring-Summer 1925), 81-85.

6527. PAUL-DUBOIS, LOUIS: "Le théâtre irlandais," *Revue des deux mondes,* per 8 / yr 105 / 27:3 (1 June 1935), 631-57.
  Mainly on Synge and O'Casey; Yeats is mentioned *passim.*

6528. RAY, MOIRA L.: "Birth of Ireland's National Drama," *Theatre,* 3:29 (July 1903), 167-68.

6529. REES, LESLIE: "Irish Drama," *New English Weekly,* 2:17 (9 Feb 1933), 397-98.

6530. REST, JAIME: *El teatro inglés.* Buenos Aires: Centro Editor de América Latina, 1968. 104 p. (Enciclopedia de teatro historia. 7.)
  "El teatro irlandés," 72-82; on Yeats's plays, pp. 74-76.

6531. REYNOLDS, ERNEST: *Modern English Drama: A Survey of the Theatre from 1900.* With a foreword by Allardyce Nicoll. Norman: U of Oklahoma Press, 1951 [1949]. 240 p.
  "Yeats, Synge, and the Irish School," 87-97.

6532. RICE, ELMER: *The Living Theatre*. London: Heinemann, 1960. xiii, 306 p.
See pp. 75-78.

6533. RIVOALLAN, A.: "Dublin au théâtre," *Mercure de France*, yr 48 / 275: 932 (15 Apr 1937), 299-307.

6534. ROBINSON, LENNOX: "Recipe for a National Theatre," *Realist*, 1:3 (June 1929), 130-41.
On Yeats's plays, *passim*.

6535. AE [RUSSELL, GEORGE WILLIAM]: "The Dramatic Treatment of Heroic Literature," *Samhain*, [#2] (Oct 1902), 11-13.
Refutes O'Grady's opinion that "the Red Branch ought not to be staged."

6536. ————: "The Irish Players in London," *Vanity Fair*, 74:1934 (23 Nov 1905), 662.

6537. RUTTLEDGE, PAUL: "Stage Management in the Irish National Theatre," *Dana*, #5 (Sept 1904), 150-52.
See also the correction in a note by the editor [John Eglinton], #8 (Dec 1904), 256. Mainly on W. G. Fay. "Paul Ruttledge" has been iden-tified as George Moore; see Jack Wayne Weaver: "'Stage Management in the Irish National Theatre': An Unknown Article by George Moore," *ELT*, 9:1 (1966), 12-17. Weaver argues that Moore disguised his identity by adopting as a pseudonym the name of the hero in *Where There Is Nothing*, a bone of contention between himself and Yeats.

6538. RUYSSEN, HENRI: "Le théâtre irlandais," *Revue germanique*, 5:1 (Jan-Feb 1909), 123-25.
Mainly on Yeats's *Deirdre*.

6539. ————: "Le théâtre irlandais," *Revue germanique*, 7:1 (Jan-Feb 1911), 69-70.

6540. ————: "Le théâtre irlandais," *Vie des peuples*, 6:23 (10 Mar 1922), 554-70.

6541. S., A. J.: "I've Been to Coole Park," *CSM*, 31:84 (6 Mar 1939), 8.

6542. S., W. T.: "The Past and Future of Our Drama--VII.," *Academy*, 67: 1687 (3 Sept 1904), 168-69.
Praises the work of the National Theatre Society with specific refer-ence to *The Land of Heart's Desire*. Correspondence by "Dublin," "The Irish National Theatre Society," :1689 (17 Sept 1904), 202: The society does not deserve the name Irish because Yeats has a "pecu-liarly un-Irish imagination."

6542a. SALVAT, RICARD: *Teatre contemporani*. Barcelona: Ediciones 62, 1966. 2 v. (Col·lecció a l'abast. 39. 40.)
"El teatre poètic a Irlanda," 1:278-81; "Synge," 1:281-83.

6543. SAMACHSON, DOROTHY, and JOSEPH SAMACHSON: *The Dramatic Story of the Theatre*. London: Abelard-Schuman, 1955. viii, 168 p.
"Dublin, 1907," 128-34.

6544. SAMPSON, MARTIN W.: "The Irish Literary Theatre," *Nation*, 73:1899 (21 Nov 1901), 395-96.
Contains notes on *Diarmuid and Grania*.

6545. SCHAFF, HARRISON HALE (ed): *Three Irish Plays*. Boston: International Pocket Library, 1936. 64 p. (International Pocket Library. 15.)
"Introduction," 5-10. Includes *The Land of Heart's Desire*.

6546. SCUDDER, VIDA D.: "The Irish Literary Drama," *Poet Lore*, 16:1 (Spring 1905), 40-53.

6547. SHAW, [GEORGE] BERNARD: *The Matter with Ireland*. Edited by David H. Greene and Dan H. Laurence. NY: Hill & Wang, 1962. xviii, 309 p.
  "The Irish Players," 61-68: "An 'interview,' written entirely by Shaw, in *The Evening Sun*, New York, 9 December 1911." See also J6326.

6548. SHORT, ERNEST: *Sixty Years of Theatre*. London: Eyre & Spottiswoode, 1958. 402 p.
  See pp. 374-78.

6549. Sil-Vara [i.e., SILBERER, GEORG]: "Irisches Theater," *Neue Freie Presse*, #17595 (17 Aug 1913), 31-32.
  Mainly on Synge.

6549a. SIMONS, LEO: *Het drama en het tooneel in hun ontwikkeling*. [Amsterdam]: Wereldbibliotheek, 1932. 699 p. (Nederlandsche Bibliotheek. [585.])
  "De vlucht uit de werkelijkheid . . . in Engeland en Ierland," 551-69; on Yeats, *passim*.

6550. SINKO, GRZEGORZ, and TADEUSZ GRZEBIENIOWSKI: *Teatr krajów zachodniej Europy XIX i początku XX wieku* [The theater of the west European countries in the 19th and early 20th centuries]. Vol. 1: *Kraje anglosakie*. Warszawa: Państwowe Wydawnictwo Naukowe, 1954. 210 p. (Skrypty dla szkół wyższych państwowy instytut sztuki. Materiały do nauki historii teatru. 11.)
  "Teatr i dramat irlandzki na przelomie XIX i XX wieku" [Irish theater and drama at the turn of the 19th and 20th century]. 126-43; mainly on the plays of Yeats and Synge.

6551. SMITH, HESTER TRAVERS: "Drama in Ireland, 1919-1920," *Drama* [Chicago], 10:9 (June 1920), 308-9.
  "Perhaps the most important dramatic event . . . was the production of *The Player Queen*. . . ."

6552. STAHL, ERNST LEOPOLD: "Von dem modernen irischen Drama [. . .]," *Masken: Wochenschrift des Düsseldorfer Schauspielhauses*, 6:11 (14 Nov 1910), 165-66.

6553. STAMM, RUDOLF (ed): *Three Anglo-Irish Plays*. Bern: Francke, 1943. iii, 114 p. (Bibliotheca Anglicana. 5.)
  "Introduction," 3-18; with notes on Yeats's *Deirdre*.

6554. ———: "Die neu-irische Theaterbewegung und wir," *Schweizer Annalen*, 1:3 (May 1944), 156-66.
  What the Swiss theater could learn from the Irish dramatic revival.

6555. ———: "Von Theaterkrisen und ihrer Überwindung: Der Beitrag eines Anglisten zur deutsch-schweizerischen Berufsbühnenfrage," *Jahrbuch der Gesellschaft für schweizerische Theaterkultur*, 16 (1946), 1-102.
  See "Neues poetisches Drama," 51-70, on the Irish dramatic revival and the plays of Yeats and Synge.

6556. ———: *Geschichte des englischen Theaters*. Bern: Francke, 1951. 484 p.
  On the Irish theater and the plays of Yeats, pp. 388-93, 404-9.

6557. °STOKES, J. A. A.: "The Non-Commercial Theatres in London and Paris in the Late Nineteenth Century and the Origins of the Irish Literary Theatre and Its Successors," Ph.D. thesis, U of Reading, 1968.

6558. "The Story of the Irish Players from Various Intimate and Authoritative Sources," *Sunday Record Herald*, 31:39 (4 Feb 1912), pt 7, 1.
  Consists of a short introduction, some pictures, and the following articles: George Moore, "From the Beginning"; Sara Allgood, "Not for Money"; T. W. Rolleston, "Thanking God for Synge"; Augusta Gregory, "Our Trials and Triumphs"; and W. B. Yeats, "What We Try to Do" (Wp. 373).

6559. *Teatral'naiͣa entsiklopediiͣa*. Moskva: Gosudarstvennoe nauchnoe izdatel'stvo "Sovetskaiͣa entsiklopediiͣa," 1961—. v.
  El[ena Viͣacheslavovna] K[ornilova]: "Irlandskiĭ literaturnyĭ teatr," 2:903; "Irlandskiĭ teatr i dramaturgiiͣa," 2:903-4; "Ĭits, Eĭts," 2:1013.

6560. TOBIN, MICHAEL: "The Ponderings of a Playgoer," *Iris Hibernia*, 4:3 (1960), 27-39.
  Includes a note on Yeats's plays, pp. 32-35.

6561. TREBITSCH-STEIN, MARIANNE: "Ein Beitrag zur Geschichte des irischen Theaters," *Neue Freie Presse*, #17470 (13 Apr 1913), 31-34.

6562. UA FUARÁIN, EOGHAN: "National Drama in Ireland," *Irisleabhar Muighe Nuadhad*, 1909, 22-29.

6563. ————: "The Anglo-Irish Dramatic Movement," *Irisleabhar Muighe Nuadhad*, 1910, 6.

6564. VERNON, GRENVILLE: "The Irish Players," *Commonweal*, 21:5 (30 Nov 1934), 149.

6565. VINCIGUERRA, MARIO: *Romantici e decadenti inglesi*. Foligno: Campitelli, 1926. 208 p.
  "Il teatro irlandese," 179-98; contains notes on *The Countess Cathleen* and *The Land of Heart's Desire*.

6566. WALBROOK, H. M.: "Irish Dramatists and Their Countrymen," *Fortnightly R*, os 100 / ns 94:563 (1 Nov 1913), 957-61.
  Reprinted in *Living Age*, 279:3625 (27 Dec 1913), 789-93. "It will be admitted that, whatever else the modern dramatists of Ireland are doing, they are not flattering the constituency to which they appeal."

6567. WALKLEY, A. D. [i.e., A. B.]: "L'année théâtrale en Angleterre," translated from the English by R. P., *Temps*, 44:15743 (25 July 1904), 1-2.
  Contains a flattering note on the Irish dramatic movement.

6568. WARD, ALFRED CHARLES: *Twentieth-Century Literature, 1901-1950*. London: Methuen, 1956. viii, 248 p.
  "The Irish Theatre," 110-18, contains some critical remarks on Yeats's early plays. On Yeats's early poetry, pp. 150-53. Virtually nothing on his later work.

6569. WAUCHOPE, GEORGE ARMSTRONG: "The New Irish Drama," *Bulletin of the U of South Carolina*, #168 (1 Oct 1925), 1-11.
  Reprinted from °*Division for Women Series*, #1 (Oct 1919). This is an annotated reading list prepared "for the use of Women's Literary Clubs."

6570. WILD, FRIEDRICH: *Die englische Literatur der Gegenwart seit 1870: Drama und Roman*. Wiesbaden: Dioskuren-Verlag, 1928. iv, 403 p.
  "Anglo-irisches Drama," 82-106; on Yeats's plays, pp. 83-89 and *passim* (see index).

6571. WILDHABER, R[OBERT]: "The Drama of the Irish Renaissance," *Jahrbuch des Vereins schweizerischer Gymnasiallehrer*, 68 (1940), 105-23.
Worthless.

6572. WILLIAMS, RAYMOND: *Drama from Ibsen to Brecht*. London: Chatto & Windus, 1968. 352 p.
Revised version of *Drama from Ibsen to Eliot*. London: Chatto & Windus, 1954. 283 p. Part of the Yeats material was first published in "Criticism into Drama, 1898-1950," *Essays in Criticism*, 1:2 (Apr 1951), 120-38.
"The Irish Dramatists," 113-53, contains sections on Yeats, Synge, Joyce, and O'Casey. The Yeats and Synge sections are revised versions of similar sections in the 1954 edition; the other two are new. Connects Yeats's dramatic theories, especially their escapist character, with his dramatic output, but the chapter attempts to do too much in too little space. Documentation is practically nil.

6573. WITTIG, KURT: "Die Nachkriegsliteratur Irlands. I: Die Prosa," *Archiv*, yr 94 / 176:1-4 (Nov 1939), 12-28.
A survey of Anglo-Irish prose drama and fiction after 1918.

6574. WOOD, J. BERTRAM: "The Irish Drama," *Humberside*, 6:2 (Oct 1938), 99-116.
Concentrates on Yeats, Lady Gregory, Synge, and O'Casey.

6575. WOODBRIDGE, HOMER E.: "A Group of Irish Plays," *Dial*, 61:730 (30 Nov 1916), 462-63.
Especially plays by Colum and Ervine.

6576. [WRIGHT, WILMER CAVE FRANCE]: Note on the Irish theater, *Nation*, 79:2043 (25 Aug 1904), 162-63.

6577. YOUNG, CECILIA MARY: *Ring Up the Curtain*. St. Paul: Library Service Guild, 1941. 279 p.
"The Irish Theatre," 134-52. All the old nonsense again: Only Catholic playwrights understand the Irish; Synge's plays are filthy, and so are O'Casey's; Yeats's belief in "Art for Art's sake . . . in a pagan sense" was a "stumbling block"; and so on.

6578. ZUCKER, IRVING: *Le "Court Theatre" (1904-1914) et l'évolution du théâtre anglais contemporain*. Reims: Presses modernes, 1931. 282 p.
"Le répertoire irlandais au 'Court Theatre,'" 182-214.

See also J778, 941, 945, 981-84, 987, 988, 1004, 1006-8, 1010, 1028, 1110, 1178, 1282, 1288, 1344, 1374, 1479, 1592, 1599, 1732, 2191, 2202a, 2221, 2282 (#11), 2291, 2466, 2492, 2539, 3349, 3368, 3455, 3508, 3509, 3542, 3548, 3623, 3624, 3737a, 3790, 4096, 4139, 4166, 4186, 4455, 5320, 5578, 5911, 5913, 5917, 5925, 5932, 5933, 5940 (#13), 5992, 6022, 6024, 6027, 6046, 6048, 6053, 6078, 6098, 6104, 6151, 6165, 6172, 6173, 7294, 7317, 7395, 7435.

LC   The Abbey Theatre

The Abbey Theatre was and continues to be a very real presence on the Irish cultural and political scene. From 1904 onward, the Irish daily and weekly papers contain an enormous amount of material on the Abbey, its playwrights and staff, its plans, policies, and performances, its impact or lack of impact on Irish life. Add to this the many "opinions" in letters to the editor, the periodic outbreaks of doubts and misgivings

about the standard of the plays or of the acting or about the whole enterprise, and you will end up with a bibliography of several thousand titles
in this area alone. The material listed below is therefore highly selective, but I think that very little of lasting value has been omitted. I
have concentrated on the Abbey's revival phase, i.e., on its activities
in Yeats's lifetime; I include, however, several items about more recent
developments (such as the new Abbey building). I have made no attempt to
subdivide the entries.

It should be noted that the cross-references appended to this section
are also only selective; many other items in sections KA, KB, LA, LB, and
MA contain relevant material.

6579. The Abbey Theatre: A collection of news cuttings, letters, etc.,
relating to the theatrical careers of the brothers Fay and to the Abbey
Theatre, including letters to Yeats. 5 v.
   In the National Library of Ireland (IR. 3919. n. 3). The library also
   possesses two files of Abbey Theatre programmes: (1) 1902-8, 1913,
   1934-36 (391941. a. 1); (2) up to 1906 (3919. t. 2).

6580. Abbey Theatre: Programmes, 1904-54. 75 parts.
   In the British Museum (P. 901/26).

6581. *Abbey Theatre, Dublin, Twenty-first Birthday Anniversary Performance, 27th December 1925 at 8.15.* Dublin: Corrigan & Wilson, [1925].
[12 p.]
   Contains "The Abbey Theatre," [5], a short historical sketch, and
   "List of plays produced by the National Theatre Society, Limited, in
   the Abbey Theatre, with dates of their first productions there,"
   [7-9].

6582. *Abbey Theatre Dramatic Festival of Plays and Lectures, Dublin Aug.
6th—20th, 1938: Official Souvenir.* Dublin: Cahill, [1938]. ii, 36 p.
   Lennox Robinson: "The Irish National Theatre," 7, 9-11; abridged in
   Irish Digest, 1:3 (Sept 1938), 40-43. Also portraits of some Abbey
   playwrights and "The Irish Drama: A Select Bibliography," 25, 27.

6583. ABOOD, EDWARD F.: "The Reception of the Abbey Theatre in America,
1911-1914," Ph.D. thesis, U of Chicago, 1962. ii, 218 p.
   Presents a wealth of material, taken mostly from newspaper reviews of
   the performances. For the reception of Yeats's plays, see pp. 49-57
   and 133-42. I have not included these reviews in my bibliography.

6584. ALLGOOD, SARA: "The National Theatre: An Autobiographical Sketch,"
Weekly Freeman, 93:4808 (20 Mar 1909), 11.

6585. ANON.: "The Court Theatre: The Irish Players," *Academy*, 80:2040 (10
June 1911), 723-24; :2041 (17 June 1911), 746-47; :2042 (24 June 1911),
785-86.
   Includes a review of a performance of *Deirdre*, p. 746.

6586. ANON.: "New Abbey Theatre, Dublin," *Architect & Building News*, 230:9
(31 Aug 1966), 371-74.

6587. ANON.: "Rebuilding the Abbey Theatre in Dublin," *Architects' J*,
129:3338 (19 Feb 1959), 305-8.

6588. ANON.: "Abbey Theatre, Dublin," *Building*, 211:6436 (23 Sept 1966),
81-88.

6589. ANON.: "The Stormy Debut of the Irish Players," *Current Literature*, 51:6 (Dec 1911), 675-76.
Mostly concerned with Synge's *Playboy*.

6590. ANON.: "The Abbey Theatre: Its Objects and Aspirations," *Daily Express*, #16360 (15 Dec 1904), 6.

6591. ANON.: "Irisches Nationaltheater," *Dresdner Neueste Nachrichten*, 20:200 (26 July 1912), 1.

6592. ANON.: "The Abbey Festival," *Dublin Evening Mail*, #28496 (6 Aug 1938), 6, 9.
See also the following issues for further reports.

6593. ANON.: "The Irish Players," *Everybody's Mag*, 26:2 (Feb 1912), 231-33, 238, 240.

6594. ANON.: "New Dublin Theatre: Application of Letters Patent. Wealthy English Lady's Help for Irish Drama. The Future of the National Drama," *Freeman's J*, 137:[] (5 Aug 1904), 2.
Long report of the legal proceedings of Miss Horniman's application, including Yeats's evidence with reference to *Cathleen ni Houlihan*.
See also the issue of 9 Aug, p. 2.

6595. ANON.: "A New Thing in the Theater: Some Impressions of the Much-Discussed 'Irish Players,'" *Harper's Weekly*, 55:2868 (9 Dec 1911), 19.

6596. ANON.: "Problems That Confront the New Abbey Theatre," *Irish Digest*, 78:4 (Oct 1963), 79-82.
Condensed from an unspecified issue of the *Irish Times*.

6597. ANON.: "The Irish National Theatre," *Irish Times*, 45:14435 (7 Oct 1903), 7.
A preview.

6598. ANON.: "Irish Players in America: Company Arrested. Publicans and Morality," *Irish Times*, 54:17023 (20 Jan 1912), 8.
Includes "Statement by Mr. W. B. Yeats." See also the editorial, p. 6.

6599. ANON.: "The Abbey Theatre," *Irish Times*, 61:19354 (1 Apr 1919), 4.
Praise of its work but criticism of the directors' reluctance to test the public's opinion as to what they want to see. Yeats is not "a sound judge of the Irish public's taste in drama."

6600. ANON.: "The Abbey," *Irish Times*, 80:25299 (12 Aug 1938), 6.
Editorial. This issue and the preceding and following issues carry reports of the speeches and lectures made at the Abbey Theatre Festival. Correspondence by Louis N. LeRoux, :25302 (16 Aug 1938), 8; continued in following issues.

6601. ANON.: "The Abbey," *Irish Times*, #33487 (20 Feb 1963), 7.
Editorial on the disgraceful state of affairs.

6602. ANON.: "'I Will Not Attack the Abbey Theatre'--MacLiammoir," *Irish Times*, #33488 (21 Feb 1963), 1.
Report of a lecture on "The Abbey Theatre To-day."

6603. ANON.: "Hollywood's Abbey Veterans," *Irish Times*, #33510 (19 Mar 1963), 8.
The reminiscences of Arthur Shields and F. J. McCormick.

6604. ANON.: "President [de Valera] Lays Abbey Foundation Stone," *Irish Times*, #33654 (4 Sept 1963), 1.

In the same issue: "President Recalls His Only Appearance on the Abbey Stage," 8. See also "The New Abbey and the Old," #33653 (3 Sept 1963), 8 (photographs).

6605. ANON.: "What Ireland Now Offers Us," *Literary Digest*, 43:1121 (14 Oct 1911), 632-33.

6606. ANON.: "Abbey Theater Subsidy," *Literary Digest*, 86:1847 (12 Sept 1925), 29-30.

6607. ANON.: "Abbey's New Policy: Famous Theater at Dublin to Import Plays from Continent," *Literary Digest*, 119:[] (1 June 1935), 24.

6608. ANON.: Leading article on the Irish National Theatre, *Manchester Guardian*, #18094 (6 Aug 1904), 6.

6609. ANON.: "The Abbey Theatre: What Is Wrong with the Drama," *Manchester Guardian Weekly*, 32:16 (19 Apr 1935), 318.
On Yeats's plans to produce more foreign plays because there are not enough Irish ones of quality.

6610. ANON.: "The Decline of the Irish Players," *New Weekly*, 2:19 (25 July 1914), 169-70.
"The Irish Players . . . have lost the simplicity of artless actors, but they have not gained the artistry of actors who have made their work perfect."

6611. ANON.: "Dublin's Abbey Players Set for Coast-to-Coast Tour," *Newsweek*, 4:21 (24 Nov 1934), 25.

6612. ANON.: "The Irish National Literary Theatre," *Observer*, #5928 (1 Jan 1905), 4.

6613. ANON.: "Irish Plays and Players," *Outlook*, 98:13 (29 July 1911), 704.

6614. ANON.: "The Irish Players in New York," *Outlook*, 99:14 (2 Dec 1911), 801.

6615. ANON.: "The Abbey Players and Censorship," *Panorama*, #9 (June 1934), 6.

6616. Entry canceled.

6617. ANON.: "Au Revoir to the Abbey Theatre," *Sunday Times*, #7080 (25 Jan 1959), 9.
"To preserve a record of the Abbey Theatre, Dublin, before it is pulled down for rebuilding, some of its former illustrious members recently revisited it to make a film." This was probably *Cradle of Genius*; see J5592.

6618. ANON.: "The Irish Players," *Theatre*, 14:128 (Oct 1911), xvi.

6619. ANON.: "The Abbey Theatre: Its Origin and Accomplishments," *Times*, #40161 (17 Mar 1913), 15.

6620. ANON.: "Two Actors Relive Great Days at the Abbey Theatre," *Times*, #55610 (28 Jan 1963), 5.
Some memories of Arthur Shields and J. M. Kerrigan.

6621. ANON.: "The Future of the Abbey Theatre," *Times*, #55808 (17 Sept 1963), 16.

6622. ANON.: "Helping Hands for Abbey Theatre," *Times*, #56249 (18 Feb 1965), 16.

Names the new shareholders. See also "New Directors for Abbey Theatre," #56219 (14 Jan 1965), 5.

6623. ANON.: "Ireland's Most Famous Theatre Reopens," *Times*, #56687 (19 July 1966), 14.
Includes a review of Walter Macken's revue *Recall the Years*.

6624. ANON.: "Stage Workshop," *TLS*, 58:3000 (28 Aug 1959), 495.
The outlook for the new Abbey.

6625. ARCHER, WILLIAM: "Things in General: The Irish Theatre," *Morning Leader*, #5170 (5 Dec 1908), 4.
A description of the building.

6626. ARNOLD, SIDNEY: "The Abbey Theatre," *Arts and Philosophy*, #1 (Summer 1950), 25-30.

6627. *The Arrow*. Edited by W. B. Yeats. Dublin, 1906-9.
#1 (20 Oct 1906); #2 (24 Nov 1906); #3 (23 Feb 1907); #4 (1 June 1907); #5 (25 Aug 1909). No more published, but see J1068.

6628. "AVIS": "The Shabby Theatre," *Leader*, 20:24 (30 July 1910), 561-62.
"They must give us more matter with less Art, or else the Shabby Theatre will wax shabbier and shabbier, until it reverts to its first use as a morgue, and becomes the scene of an inquest on itself."

6629. B., F. L.: "The Irish Players," *Cambridge R*, 35:883 (27 May 1914), 474-75.

6630. THE BELLMAN: "Meet Mr. Blythe," *Bell*, 3:1 (Oct 1941), 49-56.
Imaginary (?) interview with Ernest Blythe about the Abbey.

6630a. Tonson, Jacob [i.e., BENNETT, ARNOLD]: "Books and Persons," *New Age*, ns 9:16 (17 Aug 1911), 374-75.
On the Abbey Theatre. Correspondence by "An Irish Playgoer," :18 (31 Aug 1911), 431; Sidheog Ní Annáin, :19 (7 Sept 1911), 454.

6631. BESSEY, MABEL A.: "There Are No Stars: How 'Team Work' Has Made the Abbey Theatre and the Irish Players a National Institution," *Scholastic*, 26:6 (9 Mar 1935), 8-9, 14.

6632. BEWLEY, CHARLES: "The Irish National Theatre," *Dublin R*, 152:304 (Jan 1913), 132-44.
Reprinted in *Living Age*, 276:3580 (15 Feb 1913), 410-18. Criticizes the "paganism" of Synge and Yeats, especially in *Where There Is Nothing* and "The Crucifixion of the Outcast," and finds a "saner and more wholesome outlook" in William Boyle.

6633. De Blaghd, Earnan [i.e., BLYTHE, ERNEST]: "The Abbey Theatre and the Irish Language," *Threshold*, 2:2 (Summer 1958), 26-33.
Defense of the policy of sponsoring plays in Irish and of promoting and hiring Irish-speaking actors, which in the view of many almost wrecked the theater.

6634. BLYTHE, ERNEST: *The Abbey Theatre*. Dublin: National Theatre Society, [1963?]. [32 p.]
A history and a commentary.

6635. BOYD, ERNEST A.: "The Irish National Theatre: A Criticism," *Irish Times*, 54:17315 (27 Dec 1912), 5.
Correspondence by Ellen Duncan, :17316 (28 Dec 1912), 9; E. A. Boyd and E. J. Finlan, :17317 (30 Dec 1912), 9; Lennox Robinson and Constance de Markievicz, 55:17319 (1 Jan 1913), 9.

6636. ———: "The Abbey Theatre," *Irish R*, 2:24 (Feb 1913), 628-34.
The theater will come to a sad end if it continues to present melo-
dramas to fashionable audiences.

6637. ———: "The Irish Renaissance--Renascent," *Dial*, 67:795 (26 July
1919), 53-55.
On the Abbey Theatre and a review of W123.

6638. BRODZKY, LEON: "The Irish National Theatre," *Lone Hand*, 1 May 1908,
105-10.
Mostly on the plays of Yeats, Synge, and Lady Gregory.

6639. BROSNAN, GERALD: "Dublin's Abbey--The Immortal Theatre," *TAM*, 35:10
(Oct 1951), 36-37.
Anecdotes, including one of a typical Dubliner's reaction to a perfor-
mance of *Fighting the Waves*.

6640 °BUTLER, HENRY J.: "The Abbey Theatre and the Principal Writers
Connected Therewith," M.A. thesis, University College, Dublin, 1925.

6641. BYRNE, DAWSON: *The Story of Ireland's National Theatre: The Abbey
Theatre, Dublin*. Dublin: Talbot Press, 1929. ix, 196 p.
An arrogant and worthless book that concludes quite correctly: "I
realize that I have fallen short in my attempt to give an accurate
account of the Abbey Theatre, its Plays and Players" (p. 157). For
a review see "The Abbey Theatre," *TLS*, 28:1455 (19 Dec 1929), 1077.

6642. C., P.: "The Irish Theatre," *Vanity Fair*, 71:1849 (7 Apr 1904), 450-
51.

6643. CAPIN, JEAN, and ESTHER ALCALAY: "Ce théâtre au milieu d'un peuple
. . . ," *Cahiers de la Compagnie Madeleine Renaud--Jean-Louis Barrault*,
#37 (1962), 42-51.

6644. CARROLL, PAUL VINCENT: "Can the Abbey Theatre Be Restored?" *TAM*,
36:1 (Jan 1952), 18-19, 79.

6645. CASWELL, ROBERT W.: "Unity and the Irish Theatre," *Studies*, 49:193
(Spring 1960), 63-67.
Petty quarrels have ruined what the Abbey has achieved.

6646. Chanel [i.e., CLERY, ARTHUR EDWARD]: *The Idea of a Nation*. Dublin:
Duffy, 1907. v, 76 p.
Essays, reprinted mostly from the *Leader*. Of interest: "After the
Abbey Is Over," 17-19, a parody of the plays of Yeats and Lady Greg-
ory; and "The Philosophy of an Irish Theatre," 48-51, which criticizes
Yeats's view that an Abbey dramatist need not be confined to the
accepted standards of morality.

6647. COHEN, HELEN LOUISE: "The Irish National Theatre," *Scholastic*, 24:7
(17 Mar 1934), 7-8.

6648. C[OLDWELL], J[OAN]: "The Abbey Theatre and Its Bulletins," *Beltaine*
[Victoria, B.C.], #1 (Mar 1965), [1-2].

6649. COLE, ALAN: "Acting at the Abbey," *University R* [Dublin], 2:13
[1961], 37-52.

6650. COLUM, PADRAIC: "The Abbey Theatre Comes of Age," *TAM*, 10:9 (Sept
1926), 580-84.

6651. CONNERY, DONALD S.: *The Irish*. NY: Simon & Schuster, 1968. 304 p.
See pp. 234-38 and *passim*.

6652. CORRY, PERCY: "Ireland's National Theatre," *Tabs*, 24:3 (Sept 1966), 6-12.
Description of the new theater building, especially its lighting equipment.

6653. CRAWFORD, MARY CAROLINE: "The Irish Players," *Theatre*, 14:129 (Nov 1911), 157-58, ix.

6654. DE BLACAM, AODH: "What Do We Owe the Abbey?" *Irish Monthly*, 63:741 (Mar 1935), 191-200.
"Both happiness in youth and a great advance in the cultivation of letters."

6655. DOLPH, WERNER: "Irisches im irischsten Theater," *Zeit*, 26:42 (15 Oct 1971), 20.

6656. DONN, BRIAN: "The Dublin Actors in London," *Inis Fáil*, #34 (July 1907), 9.
The Abbey Theatre is not nationalistic enough.

6657. DONOGHUE, DENIS: "Dublin Letter," *Hudson R*, 13:4 (Winter 1960-61), 579-85.
On the Abbey Theatre and the Lyric Theatre, Belfast.

6658. DOWLING, JOHN: "The Abbey Theatre Attacked I," *Ireland To-day*, 2:1 (Jan 1937), 35-43.
Continued by Mervyn Wall, "The Abbey Theatre Attacked II," *ibid.*, pp. 43-47. See also Sean O Meadhra, "Sack of the Abbey," :2 (Feb 1937), 25-32; and Pat [Patrick D. Kenny], "Neo-Druidic Despotism," :3 (Mar 1937), 76-77.

6659. DOWNER, ALAN SEYMOUR: *The British Drama: A Handbook and Brief Chronicle*. NY: Appleton-Century-Crofts, 1950. xi, 397 p.
"The Abbey Theatre Dramatists," 320-26; on Yeats's plays, pp. 326-28.

6660. DUNCAN, ELLEN: "The Irish National Theatre," *Speaker*, ns 15:[] (26 Jan 1907), 496-97.

6661. DUNCAN, GEORGE A.: *The Abbey Theatre in Pictures*. Dublin: National Press Service of Ireland, 1962. 47 p.

6661a. DUNSANY, LORD [EDWARD JOHN MORETON DRAX PLUNKETT, BARON]: *My Ireland*. Leipzig: Tauchnitz, 1938 [1937]. 251 p.
"Dublin," 226-36; on the Abbey. There are also short chapters on AE (pp. 7-14) and Francis Ledwidge (pp. 45-48).

6662. EGLINTON, JOHN: "Irish Letter," *Dial*, 81:6 (Dec 1926), 496-99.

6663. ERVINE, ST. JOHN: *The Organized Theatre: A Plea in Civics*. NY: Macmillan, 1924. 213 p.
Some references to the Abbey Theatre, pp. 82-86, 145, 149.

6664. ————: *The Theatre in My Time*. London: Rich & Cowan, 1933. 253 p.
Scattered references to the Abbey Theatre.

6665. ————: "The Abbey--Past, Present, and Future," *Observer*, 144:7529 (15 Sept 1935), 15; :7530 (22 Sept 1935), 17.

6666. FALLON, GABRIEL: "Abbey Interlude: Being Passages from a Pastiche in Progress," *Capuchin Annual*, 8 (1937), 95-102.

6667. ————: "Drama of Lost Leaders," *Irish Monthly*, 65:773 (Nov 1937), 769-76.
Strong criticism of a dictatorial "Director Yeats."

6668. ————: "The Ageing Abbey," *Irish Monthly*, 66:778 (Apr 1938), 265-72; :779 (May 1938), 339-44.
Defends the Fays and criticizes the directors. The decline of the theater began when the Fays walked out.

6669. ————: "Subsidies, Cinemas and Theatre Festivals," *Irish Monthly*, 66:782 (Aug 1938), 553-58.

6670. ————: "And Now This Abbey Theatre," *Leader*, 76:24 (20 Aug 1938), 562-64.
Is or isn't it a national theater? Correspondence by Patrick K. Lynch, :26 (3 Sept 1938), 610, and continued in the following issues.

6671. ————: "Festival Fanfare," *Hibernia*, 2:9 (Sept 1938), 11, 19-20.
A collection of snippets and pronouncements concerning the Abbey Theatre Festival.

6672. ————: "Words on a National Theatre," *Irish Monthly*, 66:783 (Sept 1938), 631-38.
Yeats is not the founder of Ireland's national theater; in fact, there is no Irish national theater. "An Irish National Theatre will come in time, despite Abbey Theatre Festivals and the 'perverseness' of Mr. Yeats. But that time will be Ireland's time. And not before."

6673. ————: "That After-Festival Feeling," *Irish Monthly*, 66:784 (Oct 1938), 698-704.
A big hangover.

6674. ————: "The Abbey Theatre Speaks," *Irish Monthly*, 76:896 (Feb 1948), 88-92.

6675. ————: "Abbey Theatre Today," *America*, 88:2264 (4 Oct 1952), 14-16.
Reprinted in *Tablet*, 200:5864 (11 Oct 1952), 302-3.

6676. ————: "The Abbey Theatre To-day," *Threshold*, 3:4 (Winter 1959-60), 24-32.
Reprinted in *Iris Hibernia*, 4:3 (1960), 46-54.

6677. ———— (ed): *Abbey Theatre--Dublin, 1904-1966.* [Dublin: Sackville Press, 1966. 33 p.]
A souvenir to mark the opening of the new theater.

6678. FAUGHNAN, LESLIE: "The Future of the Abbey Theatre: Towards a New Dynamic," *Studies*, 55:219 (Autumn 1966), 236-46.

6679. FAY, F. J.: "The Irish Players," *Saturday R*, 112:2905 (1 July 1911), 17.
On the origin and management of the Abbey Theatre.

6680. F[AY], G[ERARD]: "The Abbey Theatre's Growth: Irish Players for Irish Plays," *Manchester Guardian Weekly*, 39:7 (12 Aug 1938), 139.

6681. FAY, GERARD: "The Abbey Theatre and the One Act Play," *One Act Play Mag & Radio Drama R*, 2:4 (Aug-Sept 1938), 323-26.
Mainly on Synge.

6682. ————: "At the Abbey," *Spectator*, 193:6600 (24 Dec 1954), 802, 804.

6683. ————: *The Abbey Theatre: Cradle of Genius.* Dublin: Clonmore & Reynolds, 1958. 190 p.
A personal and selective rather than comprehensive history of the Abbey. Quotes much unpublished material, but documentation is virtually nonexistent. On Yeats, *passim*.

Reviews:
1. Anon., "Theatre Story," *TLS*, 57:2961 (28 Nov 1958), 684.
2. W. Bridges-Adams, "A National Theatre," *Drama*, #51 (Winter 1958), 27-30.
3. William C. Burto, *ETJ*, 11:3 (Oct 1959), 247-48.
4. Brian Inglis, "Sixpenny Passport," *Spectator*, 201:6802 (7 Nov 1958), 622.
5. B. Iden Payne, *Theatre Notebook*, 13:2 (Winter 1958/59), 68-69.
6. Edwin Burr Pettet, *QJS*, 45:2 (Apr 1959), 212-13.

6684. ————: "Dandy Cockadoodle," *Guardian*, #36442 (4 Sept 1963), 7. The laying of the foundation stone for the new theater.

6685. ————: *Fay's Third Book*. London: Hutchinson, 1964. 288 p. "Me at the Abbey," 265-73; critical thoughts on the future of the theater.

6686. ————: "The Abbey Theatre," *Ireland of the Welcomes*, 15:2 (July-Aug 1966), 28-32.

6687. ————: "Theatre Built on Sand," *Hibernia*, 30:8 (Aug 1966), 9. Review of Walter Macken's revue *Recall the Years*.

6688. ————: "The Abbey Theatre--Past, Present and Future," *Hibernia*, 31:3 (Mar 1967), 11.

6689. ————: "The Irish Theatre," *Drama*, #84 (Spring 1967), 33-35. Sees a new lease on life for the theater.

6690. FAY, WILLIAM GEORGE, and CATHERINE CARSWELL: *The Fays of the Abbey Theatre: An Autobiographical Record*. With a foreword by James Bridie. NY: Harcourt, Brace, 1935. xv, 314 p.
In Fay's view, the Abbey "was first and foremost a theatrical, not a literary movement" (p. 106). Contains scattered comments on Yeats's plays, especially *Deirdre* (pp. 207-10). The Fays found that Yeats's dramatic verse was "as easy to speak as any play of Shakespeare's" (p. 112).
Reviews:
1. Anon., "The Fays of the Abbey Theatre," *TLS*, 34:1752 (29 Aug 1935), 535.
2. Austen Clark [presumably Austin Clarke], "The Abbey Theatre," *NSt*, 10:237 (7 Sept 1935), 310.
3. Padraic Colum, "Behind the Irish Theatre," *New Republic*, 87:1129 (22 July 1936), 330.
4. Walter Prichard Eaton, "Wars in the Dublin Theatre," *NYHTB*, 12:19 (12 Jan 1936), 6.
5. Norah Hoult, "The Old Days at the Abbey Theatre," *Time and Tide*, 16:36 (7 Sept 1935), 1279-80.
6. T. G. K[eller], *Dublin Mag*, 10:4 (Oct-Dec 1935), 89-90.
7. Allan Monkhouse, "A Great Adventure," *Manchester Guardian*, #27757 (30 Aug 1935), 5.
8. Edwin Muir, "The Fays: A Famous Theatrical Movement," *Scotsman*, #28784 (29 Aug 1935), 11.
9. Horace Reynolds, "The Actors Who Trouped in the Abbey Theatre," *NYTBR*, 40:47 (24 Nov 1935), 4.
10. Andrew Stewart, *Scottish Bookman*, 1:2 (Oct 1935), 85-87.
11. L. A. G. Strong, "The Abbey Theatre," *Spectator*, 155:5591 (23 Aug 1935), 295.

6991. FAY, W. G.: "How We Began the Abbey," *Irish Digest*, 28:4 (Nov 1947), 30-32.

6692. FAY, WILLIAM P.: "Le théâtre national irlandais ou les débuts de l'Abbey Theatre," *Revue des deux mondes*, #17 (1 Sept 1959), 93-103.

6693. "FIACH": "Abbey Theatre Subsidy," *Phoblacht*, 1:12 (4 Sept 1925), 2.

6694. FLACCUS, KIMBALL: "Irish Ambassadors of Culture: Abbey Players Again Bring Celtic Theatre to Broadway," *Scholastic*, 31:6 (23 Oct 1937), 17-18.

6695. FLANAGAN, HALLIE: *Shifting Scenes of the Modern European Theatre*. London: Harrap, 1929. viii, 280 p.
   "Erin," 19-43; impressions of the Abbey Theatre, AE, Frank Fay, and Lady Gregory.

6696. FLANNERY, JAMES W.: *Miss Annie F. Horniman and the Abbey Theatre*. Dublin: Dolmen Press, 1970. 40 p. (Irish Theatre Series. 3.)
   Miss Horniman's interest in the Abbey was doubly motivated—by her emotional attachment to Yeats and by her desire to have "an instrument for the expression of her personal artistic ambitions" (p. 14). Flannery comments on her relations with Willie Fay, on her aversion to everything Irish (which did considerable damage to the Abbey), but also on the theater's achievements, which her subsidy made possible.
   Reviews:
   1. Anon., "The Angel of the Abbey," *TLS*, 70:3632 (8 Oct 1971), 1222.

6697. Hueffer, Ford Madox [later FORD, FORD MADOX]: "The Irish Theatre," *Daily News*, #20053 (20 June 1910), 10.
   Letter to the editor supporting Lady Gregory and Yeats's appeal on behalf of the Irish National Theatre.

6698. FOX, R. M.: ". . . Same Program . . . Fifty Years Later," *American Mercury*, 81:378 (July 1955), 43-44.

6699. ————: "Foundations of the Abbey," *Aryan Path*, 35:1 (Jan 1964), 14-16.

6700. ————: "Abbey Theatre," *Aryan Path*, 36:5 (May 1965), 225-27.

6701. GAFFNEY, SYLVESTER: *The Burning of the Abbey Theatre (or The Lament for the Queen's)*. Dublin: Walton, 1951.
   Ballad set to music (allegro con fuoco).

6702. GRAY, TONY: *The Irish Answer: An Anatomy of Modern Ireland*. London: Heinemann, 1966. x, 411 p.
   Contains a critical note on the "dreary but comfortable routine" at the Abbey Theatre, pp. 255-56.

6703. GREGORY, LADY ISABELLA AUGUSTA: *Our Irish Theatre: A Chapter of Autobiography*. With a foreword by Roger McHugh. Gerrards Cross: Smythe, 1972. 279 p. (Illustrated) (Coole Edition of the Works of Lady Gregory. 4.)
   The first edition was published in 1913; there is also an edition with an introduction by Daniel J. Murphy, NY: Capricorn Books, 1965. xxi, 319 p. (Capricorn Books. CAP114.)
   A personal rather than objective history. Includes letters to Yeats, Lionel Johnson's prologue to *The Countess Cathleen* (see J5775), notes on Yeats's plays, and a chapter on Synge, which is not that of the original 1913 edition but a reprint of "Synge," *English R*, 13:4 (Mar 1913), 556-66. Also two chapters on the *Playboy* riots in Ireland and

America, one chapter on the controversy over Shaw's *The Shewing-Up of Blanco Posnet*, a list of "Plays produced by the Abbey Theatre Co.," and the following appendices (not contained in the 1913 edition): "The Irish Theatre and the Irish People," reprinted from *Yale R*, 1:2 (Jan 1912), 188–91; a short account of the history of the Abbey Theatre.

"The Coming of the Irish Players," reprinted from *Collier's*, 48:5 (21 Oct 1911), 15, 24; a sketch of the early years of the Irish dramatic revival.

Interviews with Lady Gregory on the Abbey's American tours, reprinted from various newspapers.

"Last Year," reprinted from *Beltaine*, #2 (Feb 1900), 25–28; a sampling of press reactions to performances of *The Countess Cathleen* and Martyn's *The Heather Field*.

"An Explanation," reprinted from *Arrow*, #4 (1 June 1907); about Synge's *Playboy*.

"Paragraphs from *Samhain*, 1909"; see J125.

"The Irish National Theatre: Its Work and Its Need"; see J17.

A letter from Lady Gregory to Synge.

John Quinn's pamphlet; see J6326.

F. Hugh O'Donnell's *Souls for Gold*; see J3642.

Reviews:

1. Anon., *Athenaeum*, #4505 (28 Feb 1914), 324.
2. Anon., "The Modern Irish Theater," *Independent*, 78:3411 (20 Apr 1914), 140.
3. Anon., "Mr. Yeats's Theatre," *Nation* [London], 14:19 (7 Feb 1914), 799–800.
4. Anon., "The Irish Theatre," *NSt*, 2:45 (14 Feb 1914), 601.
5. Anon., "Lady Gregory's Irish Theatre," *Outlook* [London], 33:843 (28 Mar 1914), 425.
6. Anon., "In the Abbey," *TLS*, 72:3708 (30 Mar 1973), 354; comments on Yeats's *The Countess Cathleen*.
7. Padraic Colum, "Irish Plays and Irish Poets," *New Witness*, 3:72 (19 Mar 1914), 632–33.
8. Hildegarde Hawthorne, "Lady Gregory: Her Account of the Irish Theatre Movement," *NYTBR*, [18:] (28 Dec 1913), 765.
9. W. P. R[yan], "The Irish Theatre," *Bookman*, 45:269 (Feb 1914), 269–70.
10. [John Ranken Towse], *Nation*, 98:2536 (5 Feb 1914), 140–41.
11. James W. Tupper, "Synge and the Irish Theatre," *Dial*, 56:665 (1 Mar 1914), 177–79.
12. Sir Frederick Wedmore, *Certain Comments*. London: Selwyn & Blount, 1925. 95 p. (pp. 61–65, reprinted from an unidentified periodical).

6704. ────: *Lady Gregory's Journals, 1916–1930*. Edited by Lennox Robinson. London: Putnam, 1946. 344 p.

On the Abbey Theatre and some of Yeats's plays, pp. 51–126; reminiscences of Yeats, pp. 259–66 and *passim* (the index is unreliable).

Reviews:

1. Alwyn Andrew, *Life and Letters*, 53:[3] (June 1947), 229–31.
2. Anon., "Lady Gregory Organizes," *TLS*, 46:2348 (1 Feb 1947), 66.
3. Thomas Bodkin, "An Irish Chronicle," *Tablet*, 189:5567 (18 Jan 1947), 40–41.
4. Francis X. Connolly, "American Opinion on Lady Gregory's Journal," *Irish Bookman*, 2:1 (Sept 1947), 71–74.
5. M. D., *Dublin Mag*, 22:3 (July–Sept 1947), 61–63.

6. Gabriel Fallon, "Some Aspects of Irish Theatre," *Studies*, 36:143 (Sept 1947), 296-306.
7. R. F. Grady, *Thought*, 22:87 (Dec 1947), 703-4.
8. Horace Gregory, "Plain Statement, Courage, Honesty," *NYTBR*, 52:13 (30 Mar 1947), 3.
9. Edward F. Kenrick, *Catholic Historical R*, 34:1 (Apr 1948), 58-60.
10. Desmond MacCarthy, "Living Records," *Sunday Times*, #6460 (2 Feb 1947), 4.
11. Sean O'Casey, "A Protestant Bridget," *Bell*, 13:5 (Feb 1947), 64-72; reprinted in J1521.
12. Sean O'Faolain, "Personalities in the Abbey Theatre," *Yale R*, 37:1 (Sept 1947), 165-66.
13. George Orwell, "The Final Years of Lady Gregory," *New Yorker*, 23:9 (19 Apr 1947), 92, 94, 97.
14. Horace Reynolds, "Greatest Irishwoman of Her Time," *CSM*, 39:163 (7 June 1947), Weekly Magazine, 9.
15. Edith Shackleton, "Lady Gregory," *Britain To-day*, #133 (May 1947), 41-42.
16. Desmond Shawe-Taylor, "Lady Gregory," *NSt*, 33:832 (1 Feb 1947), 98.
17. James Stephens, "Abbey Theatre Echoes," *Spectator*, 178:6186 (10 Jan 1947), 49.

6705. [GRIFFITH, ARTHUR]: "The Origin of the Abbey Theatre," *Sinn Féin*, ns 5:201 (14 Feb 1914), 1.
Yeats did not build the National Theatre; he ruined it. Says that he suggested the end to *Cathleen ni Houlihan*.

6706. GUNNING, G. HAMILTON: "The Decline of the Abbey Theatre Drama," *Irish R*, 1:12 (Feb 1912), 606-9.
The plays of Robinson, Irvine [sic], and Murray are responsible for the decline.

6707. GWYNN, STEPHEN: *Dublin Old and New*. NY: Macmillan, 1938. xii, 244 p.
See pp. 49-53.

6708. HAMILTON, CLAYTON: *Studies in Stagecraft*. NY: Holt, 1914. vii, 298 p.
"The Irish National Theatre," 123-44; reprinted from *Bookman* [NY], 34:5 (Jan 1912), 508-16.

6709. ———: "New Irish Plays," *Everybody's Mag*, 28:5 (May 1913), 678-80.
Reviews performances by the Abbey Theatre Players, including one of *The Countess Cathleen*.

6710. HEWITT, BARNARD: *History of the Theatre from 1800 to the Present*. NY: Random House, 1970. viii, 210 p.
Note on the Abbey, pp. 66-70; on Yeats's plays, pp. 76-77, 160.

6711. HORNIMAN, A. E. F.: "Miss Horniman's Offer of Theatre and the Society's Acceptance," *Samhain*, [#4] (Dec 1904), 53-54.
Two letters.

6711a. ———: "The Abbey Theatre: Letter from Patentee. Her Defence of *The Playboy*," *Irish Independent*, 16:38 (13 Feb 1907), 4.
Also published in various other Dublin papers.

6712. ———: "The Manchester Players," *Poet Lore*, 25:2 (Spring 1914), 210-14.
Includes some remarks on the Abbey Theatre.

6713. ———: "The Origin of the Abbey Theatre," *John o' London's Weekly*, 27:697 (20 Aug 1932), 741.

6714. HOULT, NORAH: "The Abbey Theatre," *Life and Letters To-day*, 14:3 (Spring 1936), 40–47.

6715. HOWE, PERCIVAL PRESLAND: *The Repertory Theatre: A Record & a Criticism.* London: Secker, 1910. 242 p.
   See pp. 43–51, 231–33, 238–40.

6716. ISAACS, EDITH J. R.: "Without Benefit of Ingenue: Broadway in Review," *TAM*, 19:1 (Jan 1935), 9–20.
   On the Abbey Players, pp. 10–11.

6717. J.: "The Abbey Theatre," *NSt*, 6:150 (19 Feb 1916), 472.
   On St. John Ervine's management.

6718. JACKSON, HOLBROOK: "The Irish National Theatre," *International*, 1:4 (Mar 1908), 345–49.

6719. JONES, ROBERT EDMOND: *The Dramatic Imagination: Reflections and Speculations on the Art of the Theatre.* NY: Theatre Art Books, [1956] [1941]. 157 p.
   Reminiscences of seeing the Abbey Players, pp. 29–30; of their stage sets, p. 75.

6720. JORDAN, JOHN: "Much Ado about the Abbey," *Hibernia*, 24:46 (5 Aug 1960), 6.
   The present Abbey is bad on all counts.

6721. JOY, MAURICE: "The Irish Literary Revival: Some Limitations and Possibilities," *New Ireland R*, 23:5 (July 1905), 257–66.
   "I do not understand what conception of honesty justifies Mr. Yeats in assuming the greatest Irish name it could bear [Irish National Theatre] for a theatre which is, at present, obnoxious to all but a handful of the Irish people."

6722. [KAVANAGH, PATRICK]: "Abbey Theatre," *Kavanagh's Weekly*, 1:8 (31 May 1952), 2.
   "The Abbey is far more a Pre-Raphaelite creation than an Irish, and it should long since have been allowed to die its natural death."

6723. KAVANAGH, PETER: *The Irish Theatre: Being a History of the Drama in Ireland from the Earliest Period up to the Present Day.* Tralee: Kerryman, 1946. xiii, 489 p.
   "The Abbey Theatre," 436–38; "The Gate Theatre," 439–41.

6724. ————: *The Story of the Abbey Theatre: From Its Origins in 1899 to the Present.* NY: Devin-Adair, 1950. xi, 243 p.
   Concentrates on the share Yeats had in the creation of the theater. Emphasizes the many quarrels between the directors, the actors, and the audience, and claims that Yeats and Lady Gregory's role was dictatorial and that Yeats annoyed everybody until the theater was solely his. The book is rather superficial at times, lacks adequate documentation at various places, and contains several errors.
   Reviews:
   1. Eric Bentley, "Irish Theatre: Splendeurs et Misères," *Poetry*, 79:4 (Jan 1952), 216–32; reprinted as "Heroic Wantonness" in J3359.
   2. Walter Prichard Eaton, "Drama Born of Tensions," *NYHTB*, 27:13 (12 Nov 1950), 32.
   3. Gabriel Fallon, "Dr. Kavanagh's 'Abbey Theatre,'" *Irish Monthly*, 79:935 (May 1950), 208–12, 240.
   4. Thomas Hogan, "The Abbey," *Irish Times*, #29223 (7 Apr 1951), 6.

5. Roger McHugh, *Envoy*, 4:16 (Mar 1951), 74-77.
6. Sean O'Casey, "The Tumult and the Pathos," *NYTBR*, [55:] (15 Oct 1950), 6, 30.
7. E. B. P[ettet], *ETJ*, 3:4 (Dec 1951), 356-58.
8. Henry Popkin, *TAM*, 34:12 (Dec 1950), 5-6, 90.
9. Francis J. Thompson, "Yeats' Theatre," *Hopkins R*, 4:2 (Winter 1951), 73-75.
10. Allys Dwyer Vergara, *Renascence*, 3:2 (Spring 1951), 168-70.

6725. KELLY, SEAMUS: "Where Motley Is Worn," *Spectator*, 196:6669 (20 Apr 1956), 538, 540.
The Abbey is declining; part of the blame goes to Ernest Blythe.

6726. ──────: "Bridgehead Revisited," *Spectator*, 204:6879 (29 Apr 1960), 626-27.
Another attack on Ernest Blythe.

6727. KELSON, JOHN HOFSTAD: "Nationalism in the Theater: The Ole Bull Theater in Norway and the Abbey Theater in Ireland: A Comparative Study," Ph.D. thesis, U of Kansas, 1963. xiii, 288 p. (*DA*, 24:12 [June 1964], 5387.)

6728. KENNEDY, MAURICE: "Shining in Its Infancy," *Sunday Press*, #93 (10 June 1951), 9.
Continued as "Those Early Days: Guilding the Prom," #94 (17 June 1951), 9.

6729. KENNY, M.: "The 'Irish' Players and Playwrights," *America*, 5:129 (30 Sept 1911), 581-82.
Hostile Irish-American Catholic reaction. For further amusing specimens see:
Anon., "Irish Opinion on 'The Irish Players,'" :130 (7 Oct 1911), 614-15.
Anon., "Further Opinion of the Irish Players," 6:131 (14 Oct 1911), 11-12.
Henry A. Brann, "The Modern Literary Conscience," :132 (21 Oct 1911), 30-31.
M. Kenny, "The Irish Pagans," :132 (21 Oct 1911), 31-32; and "The Plays of the 'Irish' Players," :134 (4 Nov 1911), 78-79: "Yeats is more dangerous than Synge. . . ."
Anon., "Careless Editing," :134 (4 Nov 1911), 87-88; deplores the scandal created by some Catholic publications that supported the Irish players.
Anon., "Plays That May Not Be Patronized," :137 (25 Nov 1911), 159-60.

6730. KEOHLER, THOMAS: "The Irish National Theatre," *Dana*, #10 (Feb 1905), 319-20.

6731. KIPPHOFF, PETRA: "Ein sehr irisches Theater," *Zeit*, 21:34 (19 Aug 1966), 16.

6732. LALEC: "The Scandaleers: A G[i]lbertian Opera, Dedicated Respectfully to the Directors of the Abbey Theatre," *T. C. D.*, 45:794 (18 May 1939), 159-61.
Dramatis personae: Robinson, Starkie, Blythe, O'Connor, and O'Faolain.

6733. L[AWRENCE], W. J.: "The First Subsidised Playhouse in Our Islands: The New Irish Theatre in Dublin," *Tatler*, 15:189 (8 Feb 1905), 224.

6734. LAWRENCE, W. J.: "The Abbey Theatre: Its History and Mystery," *Weekly Freeman*, 96:5002 (7 Dec 1912), 11-12.

6735. LAWSON, ROBB: "The Irish Players," *Girl's Realm*, 15:179 (Sept 1913), 813-16.

6736. LEONARD, HUGH, HILTON EDWARDS, MAURICE KENNEDY, and PHYLLIS RYAN: "What's Wrong with the Abbey?" *Plays and Players*, 10:5 (Feb 1963), 22-24.

6737. LETTS, WINIFRED M.: *Songs from Leinster*. London: Smith, Elder, 1914. x, 114 p.
> "For Sixpence," 40-41; a poem commemorating "the old days when the pit seats at the Abbey Theatre . . . cost sixpence at matinées."

6738. ————: "Young Days at the Abbey Theatre," *Irish Writing*, #16 (Sept 1951), 43-46.

6739. ————: "When the Abbey Was Young," *Ireland of the Welcomes*, 1:2 (July-Aug 1952), 9-11.

6740. LEVENTHAL, A. J.: "The Abbey Theatre and After," *Dublin Mag*, 26:4 (Oct-Dec 1951), 47-49.

6741. LEWIS, THEOPHILUS: "The Play's the Thing on the Stage or in the Page," The Abbey Theatre Reviewed in Peace and Comfort," *America*, 59:1505 (13 Aug 1938), 442-43.
> Sympathetic review. But see correspondence by M. G., :1510 (17 Sept 1938), 570; and M. K., :1511 (24 Sept 1938), 593: ". . . infused with the dregs of their Protestant prejudice. . . ."

6742. L[YND], R[OBERT] W[ILSON]: "The Inspiration of Dublin," *To-day*, 45: 583 (4 Jan 1905), 275-76.
> Mostly on the Abbey and Yeats's work for it.

6743. M., D. L.: "In Aid of the Abbey Theatre," *Nation & Athenaeum*, 29:3 (16 Apr 1921), 104, 106.
> Includes a review of a performance of *Cathleen ni Houlihan*. Correspondence by Lennox Robinson, :4 (23 Apr 1921), 128-29.

6744. MCCANN, SEAN (ed): *The Story of the Abbey Theatre*. London: New English Library, 1967. 157 p. (Four Square Books. 1774.)
> Contents: 1. Sean McCann, "The Beginnings," 7-17.
> 2. Anthony Butler: "The Guardians," 18-52; curious, gossipy, and some-times revolting, up-valuing Moore, Martyn, AE, Lady Gregory, and the Fays, and debunking Yeats, whom Butler prefers to call "Wobbly Wily Willie the Wonder Wire Walker." Although Butler may be right in insisting that Yeats's adulators have glossed over the less admirable aspects of his character and actions, many of his own statements are plainly wrong, malicious, or lacking documentary proof.
> 3. Sean McCann: "The Theatre Itself," 53-68; on the old Abbey build-ing, its anecdotes, and its ghosts.
> 4. Catherine Rynne: "The Playwrights," 69-100; a chronicle, 1904-66.
> 5. Gabriel Fallon: "The Abbey Theatre Acting Tradition," 101-25. Dis-cusses the importance of the Fays, the influence of Antoine, Stanis-lavsky, and Coquelin, F. J. Cormick and Barry Fitzgerald, and "Yeats and the Actor."
> 6. Donal Dorcey: "The Big Occasions," 126-57; on the performances of controversial plays and the reactions of press and public. Particu-larly on the rows about *The Countess Cathleen*, *The Shadow of the Glen*, *The Playboy*, *The Shewing-Up of Blanco Posnet*, *The Plough and the Stars*, and *The Silver Tassie*.
> *Reviews:*
> 1. Patrick Funge, "Introduction to the Abbey," *Hibernia*, 31:4 (Apr 1967), 19.

6745. MACCARTHY, DESMOND: "The Irish National Theatre," *Saturday R*, 109: 2851 (18 June 1910), 782-83.

6746. MACDONAGH, DONAGH: "The Death-Watch Beetle," *Drama*, #12 (Feb 1949), 4-7.
"The Abbey was Yeats. When he lived it lived, too, and when he died it died with him."

6747. MCHUGH, ROGER J.: "The Abbey Theatre Controversy," *Irish Library Bulletin*, 9:[1] (Jan 1948), 9-13.

6748. MCINTOSH, DECOURCY EYRE: "The Abbey Theatre, 1898-1912: The National Theme," Honors thesis, Harvard U, 1965. vi, 36 p.

6749. MACNAMARA, BRINSLEY: *Abbey Plays, 1899-1948, Including the Productions of the Irish Literary Theatre. With a Commentary and an Index of Playwrights.* Dublin: At the Sign of the Three Candles, [1949]. 84 p.
"Commentary," 7-24.

6750. "MAHON, CHRISTOPHER": "Ochone, Ochone Agus Ochone!" *National Observer*, 1:10 (Apr 1959), 4-5.
On the current Abbey malaise. See comment by J. F. Reynolds, *ibid.*, p. 5.

6751. MALONE, ANDREW E.: "The Abbey Theatre, Dublin: Its Plays, Playwrights, and Players," *Millgate Monthly*, 21:250 (July 1926), 522-25.

6752. ————: "The Abbey Theatre Season," *Dublin Mag*, 2:4 (Oct-Dec 1927), 30-38.

6753. ————: "The Irish Theatre in 1933," *Dublin Mag*, 9:3 (July-Sept 1934), 45-64.
"The Abbey Theatre is apparently outmoded--for the moment."

6754. "MALVOLIO": "Those Whom the 'Gods' Love," *Outlook* [Cork], 1:5 (18 Nov 1911), 10-11; :6 (25 Nov 1911), 2-3.
A diatribe against the Abbey Olympians, particularly Synge and Yeats. Correspondence by J. O'M., Seamus O'Brien, "A Graduate," Frank Thompson, and "Playgoer," :7 (2 Dec 1911), 6-7; by "Malvolio," :8 (9 Dec 1911), 3-4.

6755. [MASEFIELD, JOHN]: "The Irish National Theatre," *Manchester Guardian*, #18218 (29 Dec 1904), 4 (includes a review of a performance of *On Baile's Strand*); #18221 (2 Jan 1905), 3.

6756. MENNLOCH, WALTER: "Dramatic Values," *Irish R*, 1:7 (Sept 1911), 325-29.
The Abbey Theatre has become a fixture; its playwrights develop mannerisms. Yeats's plays do not seem capable of further development.

6757. MILLER, ANNA IRENE: *The Independent Theatre in Europe: 1887 to the Present.* NY: Long & Smith, 1931. xv, 435 p.
"The National Theatre of Ireland," 255-310.

6758. MILLER, LIAM: "Across the River: New Abbey Theatre Will Provide Chance to Improve Irish Drama," *Hibernia*, 30:7 (July 1966), 3.

6758a. M[ITCHELL], S[USAN] L.: "Dramatic Rivalry," *Sinn Féin*, 4:157 (8 May 1909), 1.
Berates Yeats for letting go Maire Nic Shiubhlaigh.

6759. MOORE, GEORGE: "George Moore on the Irish Theatre: The Intimate and Reminiscent Impressions of the Noted Writer," *BET*, 82:223 (23 Sept 1911), pt 3, 8.

Moore on the Abbey, Yeats, Synge, and others.

6760. MORIN, JEAN-HENRY: "La lutte de l'Irlande pour l'indépendence: Le théâtre de l'Abbey berceau du Sinn-Fein," *Liberté*, 56:21235 (2 Sept 1921), 2.

6761. MORONEY, HELEN: "The Most Exciting Day of My Life," *Irish Statesman*, 4:2 (21 Mar 1925), 42-43.
The day included a visit to the Abbey. Correspondence by A. E. F. Horniman, :5 (11 Apr 1925), 143.

6762. MORTISHED, R. J. P.: "What Is Wrong with the Abbey Theatre?" *Irish Statesman*, 2:1 (15 Mar 1924), 13.
Argues for a municipal subsidy, more foreign plays, occasional films, more pit seats than stalls, and a substitute for "the atrocious gong."

6762a. MURPHY, SHEILA ANN: "A Political History of the Abbey Theatre," *Literature & Ideology*, #16 (1973), 53-60.
An article with a doctrinaire left-wing point of view and a ridiculously pretentious title. "By watching plays on themes of spiritual power, Yeats and the Unionists had hoped, the Irish might lull themselves to a sleep that lasts for seven hundred years. This imperialist dream of putting people to an apolitical slumber . . . ."

6763. MURRAY, THOMAS C.: "Two Abbey Dramatists," *Ireland-American R*, 1:2 [1938-40 ?], 172-87.
A short history of the Abbey, Murray's views on the ideas of the founders, and an appreciation of the work of George Shiels and Brinsley Macnamara.

6764. N., P.: "The Abbey Theatre's Success," *Mask*, 3:4 (Apr 1911), 190-91.
I.e., Gordon Craig's success.

6765. NATIONAL THEATRE SOCIETY: *Rules of the National Theatre Society Limited*. Dublin: Cahill, [1903]. 19 p.
See J82.

6766. NIC SHIUBHLAIGH, MAIRE: *The Splendid Years: Recollections as Told to Edward Kenny*. With appendices and lists of Irish theatre plays, 1899-1916. Foreword by Padraic Colum. Dublin: Duffy, 1955. xix, 207 p.
On the early years of the Abbey, which the author left in 1905, and the Theatre of Ireland, which she joined in 1906. She returned to the Abbey for a brief spell and for the American tour of 1911/12, which is described in some detail. On Yeats see pp. 14-16, 19-20 (first performance of *Cathleen ni Houlihan*), 33-34 (*The Hour Glass*), 49-50 (*The King's Threshold*), 52-53 (*The Shadowy Waters*), and 59-60 (*On Baile's Strand*).

6767. O'Donnell, Donat [i.e., O'BRIEN, CONOR CRUISE]: "The Abbey: Phoenix Infrequent," *Commonweal*, 57:17 (30 Jan 1953), 423-24.

6768. O'BRIEN, ERNST: "Teatro d'Irlanda: L'Abbey sotto la cenere," *Dramma*, 28:160 (1 July 1952), 40-41.

6769. O'CONNOR, FRANK: "The Unicorn from the Stars," *Irish Times*, 81:25724 (21 Dec 1939), 2.
Complains that the Abbey does not produce Yeats's plays or a Yeats memorial program.

6770. ———: "Public Opinion," *Bell*, 2:3 (June 1941), 61-67.

6771. ————: "The New Abbey Will Be a Vested Interest When It Should Be Free," *Sunday Independent*, 58:36 (8 Sept 1963), 10.

6772. O'CONNOR, ULICK: "Dublin's Dilemma," *TAM*, 40:7 (July 1956), 64-65, 96.
The present Abbey standard is below that of the peak years but still high enough.

6773. ————: "Abbey Memories," *Everyman*, #2 (1969), 46-47.
The memories of actors Arthur Shields and J. M. Kerrigan.

6774. O'FAOLAIN, SEAN: *She Had to Do Something: A Comedy in Three Acts*. London: Cape, 1938. 156 p.
In his preface, pp. 7-24, O'Faolain sums up his thoughts on the Abbey.

6775. ————: "The Abbey Festival," *NSt*, 16:391 (20 Aug 1938), 281-82.
With a note on the reception of *Purgatory*.

6776. Ó hÉigeartaigh [O'HEGARTY], P. S.: "Art and the Nation," *Irish Freedom*, #16 (Feb 1912), 8; #17 (Mar 1912), 2; #18 (Apr 1912), 7; #19 (May 1912), 2.
A defense of the Abbey.

6777. O'LAOGHAIRE, LIAM: "Producing at the Abbey," *Bell*, 15:4 (Jan 1948), 27-39.
Sharp criticism by a former Gaelic producer.

6778. O'MAHONY, T. P.: "Theatre in Ireland," *Éire-Ireland*, 4:2 (Summer 1969), 93-100.
The Abbey is now recovering from the stifling Yeats influence.

6779. O'NEILL, DAVID: "The Abbey—Mother Playhouse," *Columbia*, 32:8 (Mar 1953), 5, 21-22.

6780. O'NEILL, GEORGE: "Irish Drama and Irish Views," *American Catholic QR*, 37:146 (Apr 1912), 322-32.
Reprinted as "Abbey Theatre Libels," *Irish Catholic*, 25:33 (31 Aug 1912), 6; :34 (7 Sept 1912), 6. Attacks Yeats, *passim*.

6781. OREL, HAROLD: "Playbills of the Abbey Theatre, 1904-1941," *Books and Libraries at the U of Kansas*, #17 (Feb 1958), 11-15.
Description of the P. S. O'Hegarty Collection. See J528.

6782. O'RYAN, AGNES: "The Drama of the Abbey Theatre," *Irish Educational R*, 6:3 (Dec 1912), 154-63.
On the plays of Yeats, Synge, Colum, Lady Gregory, Robinson, and Boyle ("the finest writer of the Abbey Theatre").

6783. O'SULLIVAN, SEUMAS: *The Rose and Bottle and Other Essays*. Dublin: Talbot Press, 1946. vii, 126 p.
"The Irish National Theatre," 116-26; other reminiscences of the Irish literary revival, *passim*.

6784. P., E. J., and ST. JOHN ERVINE: "After the Abbey?" *New Ireland*, 2:42 (4 Mar 1916), 276-78.

6785. PAGE, SEAN: "The Abbey Theatre," *Dublin Mag*, 5:3&4 (Autumn/Winter 1966), 6-14.
What the new Abbey should (but of course doesn't) do to become a truly national theater.

6786. PALMER, JOHN: "The Success of the Irish Players," *Saturday R*, 114: 2959 (13 July 1912), 42-43.

6787. °PEAKE, DONALD JAMES: "The Influence of the Abbey Theatre on Irish Political Opinion, 1899-1924," M.A. thesis, Southern Illinois U, 1964. 149 p.

6788. PETTET, EDWIN BURR: "Report on the Irish Theatre," *ETJ*, 8:2 (May 1956), 109-14.
The Gate and the Abbey are boring. "Seanchan has simply walked away from the King's Threshold."

6789. PHILLIPSON, WULSTAN: "An Irish Occasion," *Month*, 26:6 (Dec 1961), 356-62.
At the opening of Duras House as a youth hostel, a plaque was unveiled with the following inscription: "It was in this house, then the property of Florimond Alfred Jacques, Count de Basterot, that Augusta, Lady Gregory of Coole Park, in the summer of 1898, met William Butler Yeats at the request of her neighbour, Edward Martyn, and there began between them the conversation which led to the founding of the Abbey Theatre."

6790. PLUNKETT, GRACE: *Twelve Nights at the Abbey Theatre: A Book of Drawings*. Dublin: At the Sign of the Three Candles, 1929. [27 p.]
One of the drawings is a sketch of Abbey celebrities, Yeats included, another of a performance of *The Player Queen*.

6791. ————: *Doctors Recommend It: An Abbey Theatre Tonic in 12 Doses*. Dublin: At the Sign of the Three Candles, 1930. [27 p.]
Includes a drawing of a scene from *The Hour Glass*.

6792. POGSON, REX: *Miss Horniman and the Gaiety Theatre, Manchester*. Foreword by St. John Ervine. London: Rockliff, 1952. xvi, 216 p.
On Miss Horniman's association with the Abbey, pp. 8-13.

6793. P[ORTER], C[HARLOTTE]: "The Irish Players in Philadelphia," *Poet Lore*, 23:2 (Spring 1912), 159-60.
Account of their arrest and trial.

6794. POST, JULESTER SHRADY: "The Dear Old Morgue," *Capuchin Annual*, 31 (1964), 376-79.

6795. POTTER, GEORGE WILLIAM: *An Irish Pilgrimage*. A series of 17 articles published in the *Providence Journal and Evening Bulletin* on people, life and culture in contemporary Ireland. Together with an appendix of original writings by William Butler Yeats, Douglas Hyde, and John Todhunter, first published in the *Providence Sunday Journal*. Sketches by Paule Loring. Providence: Providence Journal Co., 1950. viii, 94 p.
"Stagestruck Ireland and the Abbey," 62-65.
Francis MacManus: "A Friend Came from Rhode Island," 72-74; reprinted from °*Irish Press*, 22 Sept 1949; on the role that Alfred M. Williams played in the Irish literary revival.
The Yeats contribution is "A Legend of the Phantom Ship" (Wp. 331).

6796. PRILIPP, BEDA: "Irlands Nationaltheater und seine Dichter," *Hamburger Nachrichten*, #39 (28 Aug 1913), unpaged.

6797. ————: "Vom irischen Nationaltheater," *Irische Blätter*, 2:2 (Mar 1918), 107-16.

6798. R., J.: "The Irish Plays," *Aberdeen Daily J*, 159:16039 (13 June 1906), 4.
Correspondence by H. J. C. Grierson, *ibid*.

6799. REID, ALEC: "Dublin's Abbey Theatre Today," *Drama Survey*, 3:4 (Spring-Fall 1964), 507-19.
Not what it used to be.

6800. ROBINSON, LENNOX: *A Young Man from the South*. Dublin: Maunsel, 1917. vii, 213 p.
A novel about a fictitious young Abbey playwright, Willie Powell. No actual persons are mentioned.

6801. ————: "The Abbey Theatre: Reflecting the National Life," *Times*, #42248 (4 Nov 1919), 45.

6802. ————: "The Abbey Theatre," *Observer*, 133:6923 (3 Feb 1924), 11; :6924 (10 Feb 1924), 11.

6803. ————: *Ireland's Abbey Theater*. NY: French, [193-]. 19 p.

6804. ————: "The Birth of a Nation's Theater," *Emerson Q*, 13:2 (Jan 1933), 3-4, 16-18, 20.

6805. ————: *Ireland's Abbey Theatre: A History, 1899-1951*. Port Washington: Kennikat Press, 1968 [1951]. xiv, 224 p.
Includes *Pictures in a Theatre: A Conversation Piece*. Dublin: Abbey Theatre, [1947]. 24 p. (conversations on the paintings hanging in the Abbey Theatre, compiled from a series of articles published in the *Leader*).
According to the author, the book is neither an "appreciation" nor a "criticism," but a "history," i.e., a compilation of the bare facts. Reminiscences of Yeats and comments on his plays, *passim* (see index).
Reviews:
1. William Becker, "Shades of the Abbey," *New Republic*, 127:1964 (21 July 1952), 22.
2. John Bryson, "The Abbey," *NSt*, 43:1097 (15 Mar 1952), 316.
3. Joseph Carroll, "The Abbey Theatre: A Riotous History Tamely Told," *TAM*, 36:10 (Oct 1952), 6-7.
4. Austin Clarke, "The Truth about the Abbey Theatre," *John o' London's Weekly*, 61:1437 (25 Jan 1952), 75.
5. René Fréchet, *EA*, 6:1 (Feb 1953), 78-79.
6. K. H., *Spectator*, 188:6450 (8 Feb 1952), 188.
7. Desmond MacCarthy, "At the Abbey," *Sunday Times*, #6715 (30 Dec 1951), 3.
8. Roger McHugh, "Yeats, Synge and the Abbey Theatre," *Studies*, 41: 163-64 (Sept-Dec 1952), 333-40.
9. Edith Shackleton, "The Abbey Theatre," *Britain To-day*, #192 (Apr 1952), 42-43.
10. T[erence] S[mith], *Irish Writing*, #18 (Mar 1952), 53-54.

6806. RUSHE, DESMOND: "When the Wind Blows . . . ," *Éire-Ireland*, 5:4 (Winter 1970), 84-87.
The Abbey in 1969-70: disappointing.

6807. ————: "The Abbey's New Policies," *Éire-Ireland*, 7:4 (Winter 1972), 32-47.

6808. AE [RUSSELL, G. W.]: "The Coming of Age of the Abbey," *Irish Statesman*, 5:17 (2 Jan 1926), 517-19.
"Frankly we wish, for the sake of the Abbey itself, that it shall continue to live in that exasperating atmosphere in which it grew up. Nothing can be worse for an intellectual movement than a chorus of approval."

6809. R[YAN], F[RED]: "The Abbey Theatre [. . .] and the Abbey Peasant: A Curious Development and Its Inner History," *Evening Telegraph*, ns #9289 (13 May 1911), 5.

Correspondence by Padraic Col[u]m, "The Irish Peasant in Abbey Theatre Plays [. . .]," #9295 (20 May 1911), 5; Fred Ryan, "The Irish Peasant and the Abbey Dramatists: Is He a Moral Freak?" #9307 (3 June 1911), 4.

6810. SCOTT, MICHAEL, and PIERRE SONREL: "The New Abbey Theatre, Dublin," *Builder*, 195:6034 (21 Nov 1958), 856-59.

6811. SMITH, PAUL: "Dublin's Lusty Theater," *Holiday*, 33:4 (Apr 1963), 119-20, 123, 156-59, 161.

6812. *Stage Design at the Abbey Theatre: An Exhibition of Drawings and Models*. Dublin: Peacock Theatre, 1967. 22 p.

With an introductory note by Liam Miller, pp. 3-5.

6813. STARKIE, WALTER: "Den irländska nationalteatern," translated from the author's MS. by A. L. W., *Ord och bild*, 38:10 (Oct 1929), 529-48; :11 (Nov 1929), 593-608.

On Yeats (pp. 532-36), Synge, Lady Gregory, Colum, Murray, Robinson, and O'Casey.

6814. ————: "Ireland To-day," *Quarterly R*, 271:538 (Oct 1938), 343-60.

On the Abbey Theatre and Yeats, *passim*.

6815. STEPHENSON, P. J.: "The Abbey Theatre," *Dublin Historical Record*, 13:1 (Mar-May 1952), 22-29.

See also note by T. S. C. Dagg, 15:2 (Apr 1959 for Oct 1956), 62. A history of the buildings in which the Irish Literary Theatre and its successors played.

6816. STEWART, ANDREW J.: "The Acting of the Abbey Theatre," *TAM*, 17:3 (Mar 1933), 243-45.

6817. STRONG, LEONARD ALFRED GEORGE: *The Body's Imperfection: The Collected Poems*. London: Methuen, 1957. 164 p.

Contains the poem "An Old Woman outside the Abbey Theatre," 20; originally in *Dublin Days*, Oxford: Blackwell, 1921. 31 p. (p. 9).

6818. SUTTON, GRAHAM: "For the Abbey Theatre," *Bookman*, 60:356 (May 1921), 116.

6819. ————: "The Abbey Theatre," *Irish Monthly*, 49:580 (Oct 1921), 416-18.

6820. "TAXPAYER": "A National Theatre: Does 'The Abbey' Need Reform to Merit This Description? 'The Irish' and 'The Natives.' Plea for New Directorate and Larger State Subsidy," *Star* [Dublin], 1:5 (2 Feb 1929), 2.

Yeats, described as "fitted . . . with the natural attributes of an Armenian colporteur of Persian carpets," would not qualify for the new directorate.

6821. TENNYSON, CHARLES: "The Rise of the Irish Theatre," *Contemporary R*, 100:548 (Aug 1911), 240-47.

Yeats's "scheme" has developed away from him.

6822. "THEATREGOER" and others: "The Abbey Theatre," *Irish Times*, #27148 (25 July 1944), 3.

See also the following issues for more letters on the Abbey crisis, particularly one by P. S. O'Hegarty, #27185 (6 Sept 1944), 3.

6823. TREWIN, JOHN COURTENAY: *The Theatre since 1900*. London: Dakers, 1951. 339 p.
"The Abbey," 46-48; "Yeats and Synge," 48-52.

6824. VALOIS, NINETTE DE: Talk about the Abbey Theatre and W. B. Yeats, *Trinity News*, 11:10 (13 Feb 1964), 5.

6825. VERNON, GRENVILLE: "The Abbey Theatre Players," *Commonweal*, 27:1 (29 Oct 1937), 20.

6826. [WALKER, RICHARD JOHNSON ?]: "The Abbey Theatre," *Oxford and Cambridge R*, #25 (Nov 1912), 12-16.

6827. WALL, MERVYN: "Some Thoughts on the Abbey Theatre," *Ireland To-day*, 1:4 (Sept 1936), 59-62.

6828. WALSH, LOUIS J.: "The Defiance of 'The Abbey,'" *Irish Rosary*, 39:9 (Sept 1935), 650-54.
"Unless steps can be taken to ensure that the Theatre is not going to be allowed to trample all our ideas of morality and all our national ideals under foot, then it is the clear duty of the Government to withdraw its subsidy. . . ."

6829. ————: "A Catholic Theatre for Dublin," *Irish Rosary*, 39:10 (Oct 1935), 749-54.
Because the Abbey is unsuited for a Catholic audience.

6830. WATKINS, ANN: "The Irish Players in America: Their Purpose and Their Art," *Craftsman*, 21:4 (Jan 1912), 352-63.

6831. WEBBER, JOHN E.: "The Irish Players and Other Theatrical Attractions of the Season," *Canadian Mag*, 38:5 (Mar 1912), 471-80.

6832. WHITE, MATTHEW: "Those Worth-while Irish Players," *Munsey's Mag*, 46:4 (Jan 1912), 588-90.

6833. WILLIAMS, HERSCHEL: "Mid-Channel: Broadway in Review," *TAM*, 17:1 (Jan 1933), 12-24.
On the Abbey company's visit, pp. 12-14.

6834. WINKLER-BETZENDAHL, MADELINE: "Gedenkt der Jahre: Das neue Abbey Theatre rekapituliert seine Geschichte," *Theater heute*, 7:11 (Nov 1966), 36.
A review of Walter Macken's *Recall the Years*.

6835. X.: "The Abbey Theatre and the English Censor of Plays," *Sinn Féin*, 4:17 (21 Aug 1909), [3].
The controversial performance of Shaw's *The Shewing-Up of Blanco Posnet*. See also the editorial in the same issue, "The Castle and the Theatre," [2].

See also J387, 389, 403, 523, 531, 533, 538, 547, 563, 610, 611, 614, 627, 646, 658, 662, 699, 725, 742, 743, 746, 747, 749, 760, 764, 779, 780, 791, 807, 813, 815, 828, 849, 935, 936, 942-44, 946, 951, 975, 977, 993, 1008, 1033, 1041, 1047, 1051, 1053, 1054, 1096 (#6, 7), 1097, 1136, 1140, 1315a, 1353, 1433, 1498, 1506, 1521, 1589, 1592, 1593, 1701, 1837, 1983, 2202a, 3327, 3359, 3384, 3390, 3395, 3667, 3822, 3879, 4082, 4172, 4174, 4191-94, 5152, 5592, 5730, 5742, 5855, 5871, 5877, 5911, 5948, 5995, 5999, 6026, 6076, 6131a, 6193, 6213, 6297, 6301, 6304, 6306-9, 6316, 6320-22, 6328, 6330, 6392, 6464, 6465, 6842, 6849, 6851, 6940, 6942, 6948, 6951, 6971, 6993a, 7101, 7121, 7142, 7223, 7224, 7267, 7328, 7345, 7377, 7385, 7400.

LD   The Gate Theatre and Other Dramatic Companies

Dublin Drama League

6836. FALLON, GABRIEL: "Thanks to the Dublin Drama League," *Irish Monthly*, 68:806 (Aug 1940), 444-49.
Its place in Dublin theatrical life from 1919 onward; largely due to the initiative of Lennox Robinson.

Gate Theatre

6837. COLE, ALAN: "The Gate Influence on Dublin Theatre," *Dublin Mag*, 29 [i.e., 28]:3 (July-Sept 1953), 6-14.

6838. *Did You Know That the Gate. . . .* Dublin: Corrigan & Wilson, [1940]. 12 p.
Pamphlet of self-advertisement.

6839. GASSNER, JOHN: "The Theatre Arts," *Forum*, 109:4 (Apr 1948), 212-14.

6839a. HENDERSON, GORDON: "An Interview with Hilton Edwards and Micheál MacLiammóir," *J of Irish Literature*, 2:2&3 (May-Sept 1973), 79-97.

6840. HOBSON, BULMER (ed): *The Gate Theatre, Dublin.* Dublin: Gate Theatre, 1934. 140 p.

6841. KNOWLES, ROBERT L.: "The Dublin Gate Theatre, 1928-1948," M.A. thesis, U of Florida, 1950. iv, 141 p.
Contains an extensive bibliography of Gate production criticism and an appendix listing most of the plays produced by the Gate company between 1928 and 1948.

6842. MACARDLE, DOROTHY: "Experiment in Ireland," *TAM*, 18:2 (Feb 1934), 124-32.
The Gate has taken over where the Abbey failed.

6843. *Motley: The Dublin Gate Theatre Magazine.* Dublin, 1932-34.
Vol. 1, #1 (Mar 1932)—vol. 3, #4 (May 1934). No more published. For individual entries see index NF.

6844. POWELL, SISTER MARIAN RITA: "A History of the Dublin Gate Theater, 1927-1943," M.S. thesis, Catholic U of America, 1959. iii, 50 p.

6845. PYLADES: "The Dublin Gate Theatre," *Inisfail*, 1:1 (Mar 1933), 18-19.

6846. SEARS, WILLIAM P.: "New Dublin Players' Group Challenges Abbey Theater," *Literary Digest*, 117:23 (9 June 1934), 26.

See also J725, 3384, 3397, 6297, 6322, 6459, 6723, 6788, 6849, 6993a.

Edward Martyn's Irish Theatre (Theatre of Ireland)

6847. MACDONAGH, JOHN: "Enterprise at the Irish Theatre," *New Ireland*, 3:18 (10 Mar 1917), 293-95.

6848. PLUNKETT, JOSEPH: "The Irish Theatre," *Irish R*, 4:41 (Sept-Nov 1914), 337-38.
The aims of the theater that was founded by Martyn, Thomas MacDonagh, and Plunkett.

See also J6766, 7028-40.

Pike Theatre

6849. SIMPSON, ALAN: *Beckett and Behan and a Theatre in Dublin*. London: Routledge & Kegan Paul, 1962. xiv, 193 p.
    Frequent references to the Abbey and the Gate.

Ulster (General Section)

6850. ALLEN, PERCY: "The Theatre in Ulster," *Living Age*, 329:4273 (29 May 1926), 467-69.
    Reprinted from °*Daily Telegraph*, 25 Mar 1926.

6851. BELL, SAM HANNA, NESCA ADELINE ROBB, and JOHN HEWITT (eds): *The Arts in Ulster: A Symposium*. London: Harrap, 1951. 173 p.
    David Kennedy: "The Drama in Ulster," 47-68; contains notes on Yeats and the Abbey's influence on the Ulster theater.

6852. BELL, SAM HANNA: *The Theatre in Ulster: A Survey of the Dramatic Movement in Ulster from 1902 until the Present Day*. Dublin: Gill & Macmillan, 1972. xi, 147 p.
    Notes on Yeats's plays, *passim*, especially in "The Lyric Players Theatre," 114-24.

6853. MCHENRY, MARGARET: "The Ulster Theatre in Ireland," Ph.D. thesis, U of Pennsylvania, 1931. 109 p.

See also index NE under "Ulster."

Ulster Literary Theatre

6854. DE PAOR, SEOSAMH: "The Ulster Literary Theatre," *Uladh*, 1:4 (Sept 1905), 5-10.

6854a. KANE, WHITFORD: *Are We All Met?* London: Mathews & Marrot, 1931. 294 p.
    See pp. 107-16.

6855. MACNAMARA, GERALD: "The Rise of the Ulster Players," *Crystal*, 1:10 (Nov-Dec 1926), 296-97, 318-19.

6856. MAYNE, RUTHERFORD: "The Ulster Literary Theatre," *Dublin Mag*, 31 [i.e., 30]:2 (Apr-June 1955), 15-21.

6857. REID, FORREST: "Eighteen Years' Work: The Ulster Players," *Times*, #43206 (5 Dec 1922), Northern Ireland supplement, xviii.

6858. W., J.: "The Ulster Literary Theatre," *Uladh*, 1:2 (Feb 1905), 4-8.

See also J5911, 6294.

Lyric Players Theatre, Belfast

6859. *Lyric Theatre, 1951-1968*. [Belfast, 1968. 69 p.]
    Souvenir of the opening of the new theater; the company specializes in the production of Yeats's plays.

6860. O'MALLEY, MARY: "Theatre in Belfast," *Iris Hibernia*, 4:3 (1960), 55-57.

6861. ———: "Irish Theatre Letter," *MassR*, 6:1 (Autumn-Winter 1964-65), 181-86.
    Includes notes on the theater's Yeats productions.

See also J3434, 6657, 6852.

MA   Individual Poets, Playwrights, Novelists, Essayists, and Actors

The problem of deciding who does and who does not belong to the Irish literary revival has never been resolved satisfactorily. By most standards, Shaw, Joyce, Dunsany, and some others should be out and Austin Clarke in. But there is some material on the first three writers in connection with the revival and not very much on the last. And then what about the status of Somerville and Ross and the 1916 poets Pearse, Plunkett, and MacDonagh? Do they belong to the revival, which has often been regarded as national-istic *and* Ascendancy? Other doubtful cases are Gogarty (who was often ironically aloof) and O'Flaherty (who scorned the whole movement). All of these writers are at least partially represented in this bibliography. On the other hand, a case might be made for Beckett, Behan, Patrick Kavanagh, and W. R. Rodgers, whom I have not included. Lionel Johnson, however, definitely belongs to English literature and not to the Irish literary revival.

   Items written by those included here and material on some little-known persons who figure only with one or two cross-references will be found with the help of the index of names (NA).

   In view of my intention to provide a bibliography of criticism of Yeats and the Irish literary revival, the material on individual figures is restricted to those items that discuss the respective poet/playwright/actor/etc. in this context. I do not list straightforward interpretations and reviews. Some of this material can be found by consulting the bibliog-raphies listed below or cited in part A. Items concerning members of the Yeats family, especially John B. Yeats and Jack Yeats, can be found in section BE.

Sara Allgood

See J5915, 6584.

Elizabeth Bowen

See J6287, 7194.

William Boyle

See J6294, 6298, 6328, 6330, 6331, 6336, 6523a, 6632, 6782, 7359, 7385.

Joseph Campbell

6862. COLUM, PADRAIC: "Recent Irish Poetry," *Nation*, 108:2812 (24 May 1919), 832-34.
   On Campbell, Seumas O'Sullivan, and Florence M. Wilson.

See also J1641, 2711, 5911, 6233, 6242, 6260, 6336.

Ethna Carberry

See J5911, 6035.

Paul Vincent Carroll

6863. CONWAY, JOHN DENNIS: "The Plays of Paul Vincent Carroll," °Ph.D. thesis, U of Connecticut, 1971. 129 p. (*DA*, 32:11 [May 1972], 6419A.)

6863a. ———: "Paul Vincent Carroll's Major Dramatic Triumphs," *Connect-icut R*, 6:2 (Apr 1973), 61-69.

6864. DOYLE, PAUL A.: *Paul Vincent Carroll*. Lewisburg, Pa.: Bucknell UP, 1971. 115 p.

6865. °JOURNAL OF IRISH LITERATURE: Paul Vincent Carroll Number, *J of Irish Literature*, 1:1 (Jan 1972).

See also J5947a, 6298, 6306, 6331, 6337a, 6472, 6499, 7338.

Austin Clarke

6866. ANON.: "The Irelands of Austin Clarke," *TLS*, 71:3691 (1 Dec 1972), 1459-60.
    Compares Yeats and Clarke.

6866a. FARIS, BERNARD GEORGE: "Journey to Apostasy: The Work of Austin Clarke from 1929 to 1968," °Ph.D. thesis, New York U, 1972. 303 p. (*DA*, 33:6 [Dec 1972], 2929A-30A.)

6866b. GARRATT, ROBERT FRANCIS: "The Poetry of Austin Clarke," °Ph.D. thesis, U of Oregon, 1972. 186 p. (*DA*, 33:10 [Apr 1973], 5721A-22A.)

6867. HIRSHFELD, SUSAN EVE: "Austin Clarke: His Life and Works," °Ph.D. thesis, City U of New York, 1972. 251 p. (*DA*, 33:3 [Sept 1972], 1170A.)

6867a. IRISH UNIVERSITY REVIEW: Austin Clarke Special Issue, *Irish UR*, 4:1 (Spring 1974).
    Partial contents: Maurice Harmon: "Notes Towards a Biography," 13-25.
    Brendan Kennelly: "Austin Clarke and the Epic Poem," 26-40.
    Robert Welch: "Austin Clarke and Gaelic Poetic Tradition," 41-51.
    Roger McHugh: "The Plays of Austin Clarke," 52-64.
    Tina Hunt Mahony: "The Dublin Verse-Speaking Society and the Lyric Theatre Company," 65-73 (a checklist of performances).
    Vivian Mercier: "Mortal Anguish, Mortal Pride: Austin Clarke's Religious Lyrics," 91-99.
    Robert F. Garratt: "Austin Clarke in Transition," 100-116.
    Martin Dodsworth: "'Jingle-go-Jangle': Feeling and Expression in Austin Clarke's Later Poetry," 117-27.
    Thomas Kinsella: "The Poetic Career of Austin Clarke," 128-36.
    Gerard Lyne: "Austin Clarke—A Bibliography," 137-55. Primary and secondary; selective.

6868. °KALISTER, FREDERICK A.: "The Poetry and Drama of Austin Clarke," M.A. thesis, University College, Dublin, 1964.

6868a. MARTIN, AUGUSTINE: "The Rediscovery of Austin Clarke," *Studies*, 54:216 (Winter 1965), 408-34.

6869. MOORE, JOHN REES: "Now Yeats Has Gone: Three Irish Poets," *Hollins Critic*, 3:2 (Apr 1966), 6-12.
    Clarke, Patrick Kavanagh, and Denis Devlin.

See also J370, 547, 676, 1689, 1755, 2200a, 5911, 5912, 5940 (#18), 5947a, 5982, 6233, 6249, 6267.

Padraic Colum

6870. BOWEN, ZACK: *Padraic Colum: A Biographical-Critical Introduction*. With a preface by Harry T. Moore. Carbondale: Southern Illinois UP, 1970. xiii, 162 p.

6871. ————: "Padraic Colum and Irish Drama," *Éire-Ireland*, 5:4 (Winter 1970), 71-82.

6871a. ————: *Annotated Catalogue and Bibliography for the Colum Collection of the Library at State University of New York at Binghamton*. Binghamton: State U of New York, 1970. iv, 45 p.
   Includes material on Yeats in items 53, 55, 56, 78, 81, 91, 160.

6872. BOYD, ERNEST A.: "An Irish Folk-Dramatist: Padraic Colum," *Irish Monthly*, 45:533 (Nov 1917), 718-25.

6873. JOURNAL OF IRISH LITERATURE: A Padraic Colum Number, *J of Irish Literature*, 2:1 (Jan 1973).
   Partial contents: Zack Bowen and Gordon Henderson: "Introduction: Padraic Colum, 1881-1972," 3-8.
   Zack Bowen: "Ninety Years in Retrospect: Excerpts from Interviews with Padraic Colum," 14-34. Colum reminisces about Yeats and other figures of the revival.
   Charles Burgess: "A Playwright and His Work," 40-58.

6874. °KINSELLA, PATRICIA: "Padraic Colum," M.A. thesis, University College, Dublin, 1949.

6875. MORRIS, LLOYD R.: "Four Irish Poets," *Columbia UQ*, 18:4 (Sept 1916), 332-44.
   AE, Synge, Colum, and Stephens.

See also J676, 742, 1638, 4337, 4455, 5911, 5947a, 6216, 6219, 6233, 6250, 6260, 6290, 6291, 6294, 6304, 6318, 6320, 6322, 6328, 6330, 6331, 6334, 6336, 6499, 6505, 6514, 6575, 6782, 6813, 7385.

Norreys Connell (Conal O'Riordan)

See J676, 1002, 6298, 6336.

Daniel Corkery

6876. LARKIN, EMMET: "A Reconsideration: Daniel Corkery and His Ideas on Cultural Nationalism," *Éire-Ireland*, 8:1 (Spring 1973), 42-51.

6877. MCCAFFREY, LAWRENCE J.: "Daniel Corkery and Irish Cultural Nationalism," *Éire-Ireland*, 8:1 (Spring 1973), 35-41.

6877a. SAUL, GEORGE BRANDON: *Daniel Corkery*. Lewisburg, Pa.: Bucknell UP, 1973. 69 p.

See also J5911, 6284, 6287, 6290, 6328, 6961, 7324 (reviews).

James H. Cousins

6878. COUSINS, JAMES: *The Sleep of the King: A One Act Poetic Drama; and The Sword of Dermot: A Three Act Tragedy*. Introduction by William A. Dumbleton. Chicago: DePaul U, 1973. i, 38 p. (Irish Drama Series. 8.)
   "Introduction," 1-9.

6879. DENSON, ALAN: *James H. Cousins (1873-1956) and Margaret E. Cousins (1878-1954): A Bio-Bibliographical Survey*. Family reminiscences and an autobiographical note by William D. Cousins, foreword by Padraic Colum. Kendal: Denson, 1967. ii, 350 p.
   With appendices to the AE (J7238) and Thomas Bodkin (J429) bibliographies, and appendices to these appendices, and appendices to these. . . . All in all a very useful book, but a terrible jumble, larded

with frequent outbursts against publishers, critics, and the detractors of Cousins, AE, and Monk Gibbon, as well as with some embarrass-
ing self-advertisement.

6880. °DUMBLETON, WILLIAM A.: "James H. Cousins and the Irish Literary
Movement," M.A. thesis, University College, Dublin, 1971.

See also J1641, 6330, 6455.

C. P. Curran

6881. BODKIN, MATHIAS: "Constantine P. Curran, 1886-1972," *Studies*, 61:242
(Summer 1972), 171-74.

See also J526, 623.

Theresa (or Teresa) Deevy

6882. JORDAN, JOHN: "Theresa Deevy: An Introduction," *University R* [Dub-
lin], 1:8 (Spring 1956), 13-26.
   A dramatist unduly neglected by the Abbey.

See also J6331.

Lord Dunsany

6883. AMORY, MARK: *Biography of Lord Dunsany*. London: Collins, 1972.
288 p.
   On the uneasy Yeats-Dunsany relationship, pp. 61-78 and *passim* (see
   index).

6884. BLACK, H. M.: "A Check-list of First Editions of Works by Lord
Dunsany and Sean O'Casey," *Friends of the Library of Trinity College,
Dublin, Annual Review*, 1957, 4-9.

6884a. CLARKE, AUSTIN: "Dunsany, Diehard of the Celtic Twilight," *Hibernia*,
36:12 (9 June 1972), 10.

See also J1689, 5911, 6005, 6108, 6287, 6290, 6291, 6294, 6320, 6334,
6514, 7198.

John Eglinton

6885. °BRYSON, MARY ELIZABETH: "John Eglinton: Irish Critic," M.A. thesis,
University College, Dublin, 1967.

6886. CLARKE, AUSTIN: "John Eglinton," *Irish Writing*, #20-21 (Nov 1952),
74-77.

6887. HONE, J. M.: "A Letter from Ireland," *London Mercury*, 7:38 (Dec
1922), 197-98.

See also J789, 1110, 1786, 5911, 5932, 6290, 6291, 7012, 7073, 7198, 7255.

St. John Ervine

6888. °SCOFIELD, J. M.: "The Dramatic Work of Mr. St. John Ervine," M.A.
thesis, U of Wales, 1952.

See also J1413, 6287, 6290, 6291, 6294, 6331, 6336, 6499, 6505, 6575,
6706, 6717.

Frank J. Fay and William George Fay

6889. FALLON, GABRIEL: "Tribute to the Fays," *Irish Monthly*, 73:[859] (Jan 1945), 18-23.

6890. ————: "The Genius of W. G. Fay," *Irish Monthly*, 75:894 (Dec 1947), 505-8.

6891. LETTS, WINIFRED: "The Fays at the Abbey Theatre," *Fortnightly R*, os 169 / ns 163:978 (June 1948), 420-23.
   Includes reminiscences of Yeats.

See also J389, 3327, 5592, 5932, 6302, 6322, 6537, 6579, 6668, 6690, 6695, 6696, 6744.

Sir Samuel Ferguson

6891a. BROWN, MALCOLM: *Sir Samuel Ferguson*. Lewisburg, Pa.: Bucknell UP, 1973. 101 p.
   Contains some references to Yeats, *passim*.

6892. °CASEY, PATRICK JOSEPH: "Ferguson and Anglo-Irish Literature," M.A. thesis, University College, Dublin, 1946.
   See also the same author's °"Sir Samuel Ferguson: His Life and Work," Ph.D. thesis, University College, Dublin, 1947.

6893. °O'DRISCOLL, PATRICK ROBERT: "A Critical Study of the Works of Samuel Ferguson," Ph.D. thesis, U of London, 1964.

6894. O'DRISCOLL, ROBERT: "Two Voices: One Beginning," *University R* [Dublin], 3:8 [1966?], 88-100.
   Ferguson's influence on the Irish literary revival.

See also J3080, 4228, 5927, 5938.

George Fitzmaurice (Bibliography)

6895. HENDERSON, JOANNE L.: "Checklist of Four Kerry Writers: George Fitzmaurice, Maurice Walsh, Bryan MacMahon, and John B. Keane," *J of Irish Literature*, 1:2 (May 1972), 101-19.

George Fitzmaurice (Criticism)

6896. CLARKE, AUSTIN: "A Spark of Genius . . . Smothered by Yeats and Lady Gregory," *Irish Press*, 33:121 (22 May 1963), 8.
   Fitzmaurice told Clarke that his play *The Linnaun Shee* (i.e., "The Fairy Lover") was a satire on Yeats. If this is the case, the satire is weak; the play seems to allude to both *The Land of Heart's Desire* and *Cathleen ni Houlihan*. The play is available in J6898, 1:39-55.

6897. CONBERE, JOHN P.: "The Obscurity of George Fitzmaurice," *Éire-Ireland*, 6:1 (Spring 1971), 17-26.
   Yeats rejected Fitzmaurice's play *The Dandy Dolls* either because it did not fit his own concept of what Irish drama should be or because he felt that Fitzmaurice satirized his heroic mode.

6898. FITZMAURICE, GEORGE: *The Plays*. With introductions by Austin Clarke (volume 1) and Howard K. Slaughter (volumes 2-3). Dublin: Dolmen Press, 1967-70. 3 v.
   "Introduction," 1:vii-xv; 2:vii-xx; 3:vii-xviii.

6899. GELDERMAN, CAROL WETTLAUFER: "In Defense of George Fitzmaurice," °Ph.D. thesis, Northwestern U, 1972. 235 p. (*DA*, 33:10 [Apr 1973], 5722A.)

6900. HOGAN, ROBERT: "The Genius of George Fitzmaurice," *Drama Survey*, 5:3 (Winter 1966/67), 199-212.

6900a. KELLEY, NORA M.: "George Fitzmaurice, 1877-1963: A Biographical and Critical Study," °Ph.D. thesis, New York U, 1973. 229 p. (*DA*, 34:3 [Sept 1973], 1284A-85A.)

6901. KENNEDY, MAURICE: "George Fitzmaurice: Sketch for a Portrait," *Irish Writing*, #15 (June 1951), 38-46.

6902. MILLER, LIAM: "Fitzmaurice Country," *J of Irish Literature*, 1:2 (May 1972), 77-89.

6903. O HAODHA, MICHEAL: "George Fitzmaurice and the Pie Dish," *J of Irish Literature*, 1:2 (May 1972), 90-94.

6904. RILEY, J. D.: "The Plays of George Fitzmaurice," *Dublin Mag*, 31 [i.e., 30]:1 (Jan-Mar 1955), 5-19.

6905. SLAUGHTER, HOWARD KEY: "A Biographical Study of Irish Dramatist George Fitzmaurice, Together with Critical Editions of His Folk and Realistic Plays," Ph.D. thesis, U of Pittsburgh, 1966. iv, 409 p. (*DA*, 27:11 [May 1967], 3975A-76A.)

6906. ————: "Fitzmaurice and the Abbey," *ETJ*, 22:2 (May 1970), 146-54.
    Comments on Yeats's unjustly low opinion of Fitzmaurice's work.

6907. ————: *George Fitzmaurice and His Enchanted Land*. Dublin: Dolmen Press, 1972. 62 p. (Irish Theatre Series. 2.)
    Comments on the Yeats-Fitzmaurice relationship.

6908. WARDLE, IRVING: "George Fitzmaurice," *London Mag*, 4:11 (Feb 1965), 68-74.

See also J2200a, 6294, 6298, 6306, 6318, 6320, 6322, 6328, 6330, 6499, 7362a.

Oliver St. John Gogarty

6909. GOGARTY, OLIVER ST. JOHN: *The Plays*. With an introduction by James F. Carens. Newark, Del.: Proscenium Press, 1971. 103 p.
    "Introduction," 9-13.

6909a. HUXLEY, DAVID JOSEPH: "A Study of the Works of Oliver St. John Gogarty," M.A. thesis, U of Sheffield, 1969. xii, 290 p.
    Contains chapters on Gogarty's biography, "The Dublin Wit," the poetry (including a discussion of Yeats's estimate of Gogarty's work), and "The Yeats Connexion."

6910. O'CONNOR, ULICK: *The Times I've Seen: Oliver St. John Gogarty. A Biography*. NY: Obolensky, 1963. xiii, 365 p.
    English edition: *Oliver St. John Gogarty: A Poet and His Times*. London: Cape, 1964. 316 p. Yeats is mentioned *passim* (see index).

6911. WILSON, T. G.: "Oliver St. John Gogarty, MD, FRCSI: Otolaryngologist, Statesman, Author, and Poet," *Archives of Otolaryngology*, 90:2 (Aug 1969), 235-43.

See also J370, 634, 663, 665, 676, 1102, 1689, 1690, 2201, 2711, 5760, 5940 (#5, 8), 5945, 6291.

Maud Gonne

6912. ANON.: "The Phoenix," *Time*, 50:22 (1 Dec 1947), 34.

6913. ANON.: "Death of a Patriot," *Time*, 61:19 (11 May 1953), 37–38.

6914. FINLAY, ROBERT: "Lady on a White Horse: Some Recollections of Madame Maud Gonne MacBride, Irish Revolutionary," *American Mercury*, 77:6 (Dec 1953), 47–48.

6914a. FOX, RICHARD MICHAEL: *Rebel Irishwomen*. Dublin: Talbot Press, 1935. 204 p.
   Contains chapters on Maud Gonne, Constance Markievicz, and Eva Gore-Booth.

6915. ————: "Madame Gonne-MacBride: The Prisoners' Friend," *Aryan Path*, 25:5 (May 1954), 210–13.

6916. ————: "Maud Gonne: Her Place in Irish History and Drama," *Aryan Path*, 37:12 (Dec 1966), 552–54.

6917. HEALY, CHRIS: *Confessions of a Journalist*. London: Chatto & Windus, 1904. xv, 383 p.
   "Maud Gonne," 227–36.

6918. JOCHUM, K. P. S.: "Maud Gonne on Synge," *Éire-Ireland*, 6:4 (Winter 1971), 65–70.
   English translation of J7340 plus comments on Maud Gonne, Synge, and Yeats.

6919. MACGREEVY, THOMAS: "Maud Gonne MacBride," *Father Mathew Record*, 46:6 (June 1953), 1–3.
   Includes a note on Maud Gonne in Yeats's poetry.

6920. MACLIAMMÓIR, MICHEÁL: "Maud Gonne," *Harper's Bazaar*, 88:2908 (Mar 1954), 124.

6921. MACMANUS, FRANCIS: "The Delicate High Head: A Portrait of a Great Lady," *Capuchin Annual*, 27 (1960), 127–32.

6922. MURPHY, DANIEL: "Maud Gonne's *Dawn!*," *Shenandoah*, 16:4 (Summer 1965), 63–77.
   The text of the play and an introduction. See also J6455.

6922a. °NÍ ÉIREAMHOIN, EIBHLIN: *Two Great Irishwomen: Maud Gonne MacBride, Constance Markievicz*. Dublin: Fallons, 1971. 78 p.
   The National Union Catalog classifies this as juvenile literature.

6923. STOCK, A. G.: "The World of Maud Gonne," *Indian J of English Studies*, 6 (1965), 56–79.
   Includes some comments on Yeats's attitude toward her and his treatment of her in his poetry.

6924. STRIKER, HERTHE: "Ireland's Joan of Arc," *Coronet*, 36:215 (Sept 1954), 30–34.

See also J389, 514, 557, 584, 611, 670, 691, 716, 718, 1101 (#9), 1140, 1806, 2825, 4076a, 4199, 5915, 5999, 6120a, 7255.

Eva Gore-Booth

6925. FOX, R. M.: "Eva Gore-Booth," *Aryan Path*, 24:11 (Nov 1953), 489–92.

See also J514, 1112 (#8), 3603, 6914a, 7026, 7027.

Alice Stopford Green

6926. MCDOWELL, ROBERT BRENDAN: *Alice Stopford Green: A Passionate Historian*. Dublin: Figgis, 1967. iv, 116 p.

Lady Gregory (Bibliography)

6927. MIKHAIL, EDWARD HALIM: "The Theatre of Lady Gregory," *Bulletin of Bibliography*, 27:1 (Jan-Mar 1970), 10, 9.
    Lists 60 items without annotation.

See also J363, 366a, 389, 512, 533, 546, 547.

Lady Gregory (Criticism)

6928. ADAMS, HAZARD: *Lady Gregory*. Lewisburg, Pa.: Bucknell UP, 1973. 106 p.

6929. ANON.: "'Charwoman' of the Abbey Theater," *Literary Digest*, 113: 2199 (11 June 1932), 17.

6930. ANON.: "Lady Gregory," *Nation*, 134:3492 (8 June 1932), 640.

6931. ANON.: "Personalities and Powers: Lady Gregory," *Time and Tide*, 5:30 (25 July 1924), 714-15.

6932. ANON.: "Lady Gregory, the Abbey, Yeats, Moore, Synge," *TLS*, 69:3568 (16 July 1970), 761-62.
    A sympathetic assessment of her achievement; not much on Yeats, less on Moore, nothing on Synge.

6933. AYLING, RONALD: "Charwoman of the Abbey," *Shaw R*, 4:3 (Sept 1961), 7-15.

6934. °BENSON, BRIAN: "An Examination of the Contributions of Lady Augusta Persse Gregory to the Development of the Irish National Theatre," M.A. thesis, U of North Carolina at Greensboro, 1967.

6935. °BOWEN, ANNE: "Lady Gregory's Use of Folk-Lore in Her Plays," M.A. thesis, U of North Carolina, 1939.

6936. ————: "Lady Gregory's Use of Proverbs in Her Plays," *Southern Folklore Q*, 3:4 (Dec 1939), 231-43.

6937. BRÉGY, KATHERINE: "Lady Gregory and the Lore of Ireland," *Forum*, 48:4 (Oct 1912), 465-72.

6938. BUIDIN, CLAUDINE: *The Dramatic Works of Lady Gregory (1852-1932)*. Bruxelles: Presses universitaires de Bruxelles, [1964]. viii, 162 p.
    This is not a printed book but a bound carbon-copy MS. Contains a chapter on "Collaboration, Yeats-Lady Gregory," 134-45. Rather weak on facts.

6939. CONNOLLY, CYRIL: "Gael Force," *Sunday Times*, #7668 (17 May 1970), 31.
    Includes a review of J61.

6940. COXHEAD, ELIZABETH: *Lady Gregory: A Literary Portrait*. 2nd edition, revised and enlarged. London: Secker & Warburg, 1966 [1961]. xii, 227 p.
    Several chapters are devoted to Lady Gregory's involvement in the Irish literary revival and the Abbey Theatre. Chapter 7, "Collaboration—Yeats," 98-107, attempts to disprove two attacks on Lady Gregory's reputation: "that she interfered with and spoilt Yeats's plays, and that he really wrote the best of hers." The one play that was

certainly written by both, *The Unicorn from the Stars*, has its best parts in what must be credited to her. Criticizes Yeats for not doing Lady Gregory justice in his *Dramatis Personae*.

Reviews:
1. Walter Allen, "The Lady of Coole," *NSt*, 61:1560 (3 Feb 1961), 186.
2. Anon., "Tame Swan at Coole," *TLS*, 60:3077 (17 Feb 1961), 97-98.
3. R. F. Ayling, "That Laurelled Head [. . .]," *ESA*, 4:2 (Sept 1961), 162-73.
4. Ernest Blythe, *Studia Hibernica*, #2 (1962), 249-53.
5. Donna Gerstenberger, *WHR*, 17:2 (Spring 1963), 193.
6. Valentin Iremonger, "The Remarkable Lady Gregory," *Catholic Herald*, #3925 (30 June 1961), 3.
7. Frank Kermode, "The Spider and the Bee," *Spectator*, 206:6927 (31 Mar 1961), 448-49.
8. Sir Shane Leslie, "Ireland's Boadicea," *National R*, 11:20 (18 Nov 1961), 344-45.
9. Augustine Martin, *Studies*, 51:203 (Autumn 1962), 438-40.
10. Harry T. Moore, "Revival in Eire," *SatR*, 44:38 (23 Sept 1961), 20.
11. Raymond Mortimer, "Patriot Grande Dame of Galway," *Sunday Times*, #7186 (5 Feb 1961), 26.
12. Anne O'Neill-Barna, "Dublin's Great Lady of the Theatre," *NYTBR*, 66:39 (24 Sept 1961), 6.
13. Edwin Rhodes, "Sailing from Byzantium," *Acorn*, 1:1 (Winter 1961), 20-22.
14. W. R. Rodgers, *Listener*, 65:1666 (2 Mar 1961), 401.
15. Kevin Sullivan, "Portrait of Lady Gregory," *Nation*, 193:12 (14 Oct 1961), 253-54.

6941. ———: "New York Public Library," *TLS*, 66:3389 (9 Feb 1967), 112. Refers to the Lady Gregory papers in the Berg Collection.

6942. DEDIO, ANNE: *Das dramatische Werk von Lady Gregory*. Bern: Francke, 1967. 135 p. (Cooper Monographs. 13.)
Contains some material on the Abbey Theatre and Yeats's theatrical activities, a note on parallels between Lady Gregory's and Yeats's plays, and several unpublished letters from Lady Gregory, mostly to George Roberts.

6943. °DONOVAN, D. C.: "Lady Gregory and the Abbey Theatre," M.A. thesis, National U of Ireland, 1951.
I do not know where this thesis was written; it is not listed in the University College, Dublin, catalogue.

6944. GATLIN, DANA: "Lady Gregory," *American Mag*, 73:5 (Mar 1912), 550, 553.

6945. G[EDDIE], J. L.: "Lady Gregory and the Irish Theatre," *Everyman*, 3:73 (6 Mar 1914), 686-87.

6946. °GIBSON, KATHERINE R.: "A New View of Lady Gregory," M.A. thesis, Wagner College, 1966.

6947. GREGORY, LADY ISABELLA AUGUSTA: *The Coole Edition of the Works of Lady Gregory*. Gerrards Cross: Smythe, 1970—.
18 volumes are planned. Published so far:
1. *Visions and Beliefs in the West of Ireland* [. . .]. With a foreword by Elizabeth Coxhead. 1970. 365 p. (See also J84.)
2. *Cuchulain of Muirthemne* [. . .]. With a preface by W. B. Yeats and a foreword by Daniel Murphy. 1970. 272 p. (See also J77.)

3. *Gods and Fighting Men* [. . .]. With a preface by W. B. Yeats and a foreword by Daniel Murphy. 1970. 367 p. (See also J78.)

4. *Our Irish Theatre* [. . .]. With a foreword by Roger McHugh. 1972. 279 p. (For details see J6703.)

5. *The Comedies, Being the First Volume of the Collected Plays.* Edited and with a foreword by Ann Saddlemyer. 1970. xviii, 304 p.

6. *The Tragedies and Tragiccomedies,* [sic] *Being the Second Volume of the Collected Plays.* Edited and with a foreword by Ann Saddlemyer. 1970. xvii, 361 p.

7. *The Wonder and Supernatural Plays, Being the Third Volume of the Collected Plays.* Edited and with a foreword by Ann Saddlemyer. 1970. xviii, 434 p. (See also J120.)

8. *The Translations and Adaptations and Her Collaborations with Douglas Hyde and W. B. Yeats, Being the Fourth Volume of the Collected Plays.* Edited and with a foreword by Ann Saddlemyer. 1970. xix, 376 p. (See also J121.)

9. *The Kiltartan Books, Comprising the Kiltartan Poetry, History and Wonder Books.* Illustrated by Robert and Margaret Gregory, with a foreword by Padraic Colum. 1971. 213 p.

10. *Sir Hugh Lane: His Life and Legacy.* With a foreword by James White. 1973. 324 p. Yeats is mentioned *passim*. For details see J128b.

11. Not yet published.

12. *A Book of Saints and Wonders.* Put down here by Lady Gregory according to the old writings and the memory of the people of Ireland. With illustrations by Margaret Gregory and a foreword by Edward Malins. 1971. 116 p.

6947a. ————: "Unveröffentlichte Briefe der Lady Isabella A. Gregory," edited by Hans Marcus, *Archiv*, yr 90 / 167:3&4 (June 1935), 216–22.
　　Introductory note by, and ten letters to, the editor.

6948. ————: "The Letters of Lady Gregory to John Quinn." Edited by Daniel Joseph Murphy. Editor's Ph.D. thesis, Columbia U, 1961. vii, 237 p. (*DA*, 22:9 [Mar 1962], 3204.)
　　Letters written between 1906 and 1924, dealing with Yeats, the Abbey, the Lane pictures, and Irish questions.

6949. ————: *Selected Plays.* Chosen and introduced by Elizabeth Coxhead, foreword by Sean O'Casey. London: Putnam, 1962. 269 p.
　　"Foreword," 7–9; reprinted in J1521. "Introduction," 11–15.

6950. ————: "The Lady Gregory Letters to Sean O'Casey," edited by A. C. Edwards, *MD*, 8:1 (May 1965), 95–111.
　　23 letters, of which 4 are only paraphrased.

6951. ————: "Letters from Lady Gregory: A Record of Her Friendship with T. J. Kiernan," edited by Daniel Murphy, *BNYPL*, 71:10 (Dec 1967), 621–61; 72:1 (Jan 1968), 19–63; :2 (Feb 1968), 123–31.
　　Letters written between 1924 and 1932, some of them concerning Yeats and Abbey affairs.

6952. ————: "The Lady Gregory Letters to G. B. Shaw," edited by Daniel J. Murphy, *MD*, 10:4 (Feb 1968), 331–45.

6953. GREGORY, VERE RICHARD TRENCH: *The House of Gregory.* Dublin: Browne & Nolan, 1943. xv, 210 p.
　　Quotes Yeats's "Gregory poems," pp. 136–41, and comments briefly on them. On Lady Gregory, *passim*, especially pp. 88–105 and 120–33.

6954. HOLLOWAY, DAVID: "Remarkable Lady of Coole," *Daily Telegraph*, #35775 (7 May 1970), 6.
Includes a review of J61.

6955. KLENZE, HILDA VON: *Lady Gregorys Leben und Werk*. Bochum-Langendreer: Pöppinghaus, 1940. vi, 92 p. (Kölner anglistische Arbeiten. 37.)

6956. KUNITZ, STANLEY JASSPON (ed): *Authors Today and Yesterday*. NY: Wilson, 1934. vii, 726 p.
"Lady Gregory," 281-83; "Lennox Robinson," 574-77; "J. M. Synge," 641-45.

6957. LAWRENCE, C. E.: "Lady Gregory," *Bookman*, 59:390 (Nov 1920), 72-75.

6958. °MCSTEA, ELIZABETH MARY: "Lady Gregory and the Gaelic Revival," M.A. thesis, New York U, 1935. 105 p.

6959. MALONE, ANDREW E.: "The Plays of Lady Gregory," *Studies*, 13:50 (June 1924), 247-58.
Also in *Yale R*, 14:3 (Spring 1925), 540-51.

6960. ————: "Lady Gregory: 1852-1932," *Dublin Mag*, 8:1 (Jan-Mar 1932), 37-47.

6961. MARCUS, HANS: "Besuche bei irischen Dichtern," *Archiv*, yr 81 / 150: 3&4 (Aug 1926), 203-8.
Visited Corkery, Lady Gregory, and AE.

6961a. MULLET, OLIVE GALE: "The War with Women and Words: Lady Gregory's Destructive, Celtic Folklore Woman," °Ph.D. thesis, U of Wisconsin, 1973. 277 p. (*DA*, 34:6 [Dec 1973], 3351A.)

6962. NEWELL, MARY O'CONNOR: "The First Lady of Ireland," *Sunday Record Herald*, 31:39 (4 Feb 1912), Woman's section, 1.

6963. PELLIZZI, CAMILLO: "Lady Gregory," *Scenario*, 1:6 (July 1932), 9-12.

6964. PICK, MARIANNE: "The Work of Lady Gregory: Her Contribution to the Irish Dramatic and Literary Revival," [M.A. thesis, U of London, 1940]. vi, 193 p.
Contains a chapter on "Lady Gregory and W. B. Yeats," 156-73.

6965. POUND, EZRA: "Books Current," *Future*, 2:12 (Dec 1918), 311-12.
Finds her "rather smothered by dialect."

6966. ROBINSON, LENNOX: "Lady Gregory," *Ireland To-day*, 1:2 (July 1936), 49-51.

6967. ROSSI, MARIO MANLIO: *Viaggio in Irlanda*. Milano: Doxa Editrice, 1932. 189 p.
Mainly on Lady Gregory; on Yeats, *passim*, especially pp. 140-44. An abridged version appeared as *Pilgrimage in the West*. Translated by J. M. Hone. Dublin: Cuala Press, 1933. viii, 53 p.

6968. SACKVILLE, LADY MARGARET: "Lady Gregory," *Aylesford R*, 4:5 (Winter 1961/62), 192-95.

6969. SADDLEMYER, ANN: *In Defence of Lady Gregory, Playwright*. Dublin: Dolmen Press, 1966. 131 p.
Includes notes on the Yeats-Lady Gregory relationship.

6970. SEXTON, HELENA ITA: "A Critical Assessment of Lady Gregory's Achievement as a Dramatist," M.A. thesis, U of Manchester, 1963. iv, 259 p.

6971. °SMITH, MILBURN D.: "The Contribution of Lady Gregory to the Abbey Theatre, with Emphasis on Her Plays," M.A. thesis, Columbia U, 1958. 137 p.

6971a. SMYTHE, COLIN: *A Guide to Coole Park, Co. Galway, Home of Lady Gregory*. Foreword by Maurice Craig. Gerrards Cross: Smythe, 1973. 48 p. (Illustrated)
> Contains some notes on Yeats.

6972. TANNER, WILLIAM EDWARD: "A Study of Lady Gregory's Translations of Molière," °Ph.D. thesis, U of Tulsa, 1972. 152 p. (*DA*, 33:2 [Aug 1972], 734A.)

6973. TOKSVIG, SIGNE: "A Visit to Lady Gregory," *NAR*, 214:789 (Aug 1921), 190-200.

6974. VAN VORIS, WILLIAM H.: "Lady Gregory at Smith," *Smith Alumnae Q*, 59:3 (Apr 1968), 10-11.

6975. YOUNG, LORNA D.: "The Plays of Lady Gregory," Ph.D. thesis, Trinity College, Dublin, 1958. xi, 671 p.

See also J514, 545, 614, 625, 646, 653, 674, 675, 702, 706, 725, 743, 746, 764, 794, 796, 849, 1041, 1136, 1147, 1413, 1454, 1521 (#7, 8), 1690, 1708, 1732, 1766, 1772, 2045, 2202, 2202a, 2203, 2204, 2237, 2669, 2818, 2825, 3485, 3511, 3519, 3520, 3549, 3673, 4054, 4455, 5152, 5373-78, 5390- 97, 5592, 5850, 5879, 5911, 5922, 5932, 5935, 5936, 5940 (#3), 5944, 5947a, 5948, 5962, 5982a, 5986, 6010, 6019, 6035, 6053, 6120, 6120a, 6131a, 6154, 6159, 6216, 6290, 6291, 6294, 6298, 6301, 6315, 6318, 6320, 6322, 6323, 6328, 6330, 6331, 6336, 6354, 6364, 6410, 6416, 6417, 6420, 6428, 6436, 6441, 6452, 6472, 6499, 6505, 6523a, 6574, 6616, 6638, 6646, 6695, 6703, 6704, 6724, 6744, 6782, 6813, 7073, 7156, 7178, 7317, 7327, 7370, 7385, 7416.

F. R. Higgins

6976. BYRNE, J. PATRICK: "Manager of the Abbey: The Late F. R. Higgins," *Accent*, 2:2 (Winter 1942), 92-94.
> Suggests that Yeats's later ballads were influenced by Higgins.

6976a. REDSHAW, THOMAS DILLON: "Atavistic Salvages," *Hibernia*, 36 [i.e., 35]:14 (16 July 1971), 12.

See also J370, 1689, 5945, 5947a, 6233, 6249.

Joseph Holloway

See J5937, 7007, 7111, 7266, 7389.

Nora Hopper Chesson

See J1110, 1689, 5911, 6216.

Douglas Hyde

6977. COFFEY, DIARMID: *Douglas Hyde: President of Ireland*. Dublin: Talbot Press, 1938. 152 p.
> Based on an earlier study published under the name Diarmid O Cobhthaigh: *Douglas Hyde: An Craoibhín Aoibhinn*. Dublin: Maunsel, 1917. xi, 131 p.

6978. DALY, DOMINICK PATRICK JOSEPH: *The Young Douglas Hyde: The Dawn of the Irish Revolution and Renaissance, 1874-1893.* Foreword by Erskine Childers. Dublin: Irish UP, 1974. xix, 232 p.

Based on "The Political and Cultural Formation of Douglas Hyde, 1874-1893," Ph.D. thesis, U of Cambridge, 1972. ii, 282 p. Quotes extensively from Hyde's unpublished journals, which contain frequent references to Yeats.

6979. *Douglas Hyde and the Revival of the Irish Language.* N.p., n.d. 24 p.

A copy of this is in the U of Illinois Library at Urbana-Champaign.

6980. FRANKE, WILHELM: "Douglas Hyde," *Neuphilologische Zeitschrift*, 1:4 (1949), 44-56.

6981. GREGORY, LADY ISABELLA AUGUSTA: *Poets and Dreamers: Studies and Translations from the Irish.* Dublin: Hodges Figgis / London: Murray, 1903. vii, 254 p.

"An Craoibhin's Plays," 196-99.

6982. °HEFFERNAN, GRACE MARIE: "Douglas Hyde: With Some Consideration of His Connection with the Irish Literary Renaissance," M.A. thesis, Columbia U, 1930.

6983. HYDE, DOUGLAS: *Abhráin Grádh Chúige Connacht. Love Songs of Connacht. Being the Fourth Chapter of the Songs of Connacht.* Introduction by Mícheál Ó hAodha. Shannon: Irish UP, 1969 [1893]. x, viii, 158 p.

The introduction comments on the influence of the book on the Irish literary revival.

6984. ————: *A Literary History of Ireland from the Earliest Times to the Present Day.* New edition with introduction by Brian Ó Cuív. London: Benn / NY: Barnes & Noble, 1967 [1899]. xliii, 654 p.

The introduction discusses the importance of Hyde and of this book for modern Irish and Anglo-Irish literature. The book itself does not discuss Anglo-Irish literature.

6985. KELEHER, JULIA: "Douglas Hyde and the Irish Renaissance," *New Mexico Q*, 8:4 (Nov 1938), 219-27.

6986. MADDEN, REGINA: "Douglas Hyde: Savior of Gaelic Ireland," *Catholic World*, 147:881 (Aug 1938), 543-47.

6987. MURPHY, GERALD: "Douglas Hyde, 1860-1949," *Studies*, 38:151 (Sept 1949), 275-81.

6988. Ó LÚING, SEÁN: "Douglas Hyde and the Gaelic League," *Studies*, 62:246 (Summer 1973), 123-38.

6989. REYNOLDS, HORACE: "From the Little Branch to the New Island," *Dublin Mag*, 13:4 (Oct-Dec 1938), 9-29.

6990. RYAN, DESMOND: *The Sword of Light: From the Four Masters to Douglas Hyde, 1638-1938.* London: Barker, 1939. vii, 256 p.

Mostly on the Irish language revival.

See also J389, 572, 764, 986, 1110, 1690, 1747, 3907, 4054, 4199, 4455, 5881, 5911, 5925, 5932, 5938, 5940 (#6), 5992, 6019, 6116, 6154, 6155, 6197, 6216, 6233, 6290, 6439, 6499, 6947 (#8), 7048, 7073.

Denis Johnston

6991. °COBEY, PATRICIA M.: "The Plays of Denis Johnston," M.A. thesis, University College, Dublin, 1962.

6992. COLLIS, J. S.: "The Irish Drama and Denis Johnston," *New English Weekly*, 7:12 (4 July 1935), 232.

6993. FERRAR, HAROLD: *Denis Johnston's Irish Theatre*. Dublin: Dolmen Press, 1973. 144 p. (Irish Theatre Series. 5.)
    Based on "Denis Johnston and the Irish Theatre," Ph.D. thesis, Columbia U, 1968. vi, 308 p. (*DA*, 29:9 [Mar 1969], 3134A.)

6993a. HENDERSON, GORDON: "An Interview with Denis Johnston," *J of Irish Literature*, 2:2&3 (May–Sept 1973), 31–44.
    Johnston on his own plays, the Gate, the Abbey, and Yeats.

6994. HOGAN, THOMAS: "Denis Johnston: Last of the Anglo-Irish," *Envoy*, 3:9 (Aug 1950), 33–46.

6995. LEE, DEREK: "The Plays of Denis Johnston: An Expository and Critical Study," Ph.D. thesis, U of London, 1972. 691 p.

6996. °WEST, F. W.: "The Life and Works of Denis Johnston," Ph.D. thesis, U of Leeds, 1966/67.

See also J370, 725, 1402, 3393, 5947a, 6298, 6306, 6322, 6337a, 6392, 6499, 7232.

James Joyce (Bibliography)

6997. DEMING, ROBERT H.: *A Bibliography of James Joyce Studies*. Lawrence: U of Kansas Libraries, 1964. viii, 180 p. (U of Kansas Publications. Library Series. 18.)
    Continued in the bibliographies published regularly in *JJQ*.

6998. SLOCUM, JOHN J., and HERBERT CAHOON: *A Bibliography of James Joyce, 1882–1941*. London: Hart-Davis, 1957. ix, 195 p. (Soho Bibliographies. 5.)

James Joyce (Criticism)

6999. BOYD, ERNEST: "Joyce and the New Irish Writers," *Current History*, 39:6 (Mar 1934), 699–704.

7000. CURRAN, CONSTANTINE PETER: *James Joyce Remembered*. [Foreword by Padraic Colum]. NY: Oxford UP, 1968. x, 129 p.
    On Joyce and Yeats and on Joyce and the revival, *passim*.

7001. ELLMANN, RICHARD: *James Joyce*. NY: Oxford UP, 1965 [1959]. xvi, 842 p. (Galaxy Book. GB149.)
    On Yeats and Joyce, *passim* (see index). See also J97.

7002. ———: *Ulysses on the Liffey*. London: Faber & Faber, 1972. xviii, 208 p.
    Yeats is mentioned *passim* (see index).

7003. FÜGER, WILHELM (ed): *James Joyces "Portrait": Das "Jugendbildnis" im Lichte neuerer deutscher Forschung*. München: Goldmann, 1972. 233 p. (Wissenschaftliche Taschenbuch. GE15.)
    Ortwin Kuhn: "Zur Rolle des Nationalismus im Frühwerk von James Joyce," 102–64; contains a section on "Joyce und die irische Literaturrenaissance," 157–60.

7004. GRIGORESCU, DAN: "Joyce irlandezul" [Joyce the Irishman], *Secolul 20*, 5:2 (1965), 107–16.

7005. HENNING, JOHN: "A Footnote to James Joyce," *Bell*, 11:2 (Nov 1945), 704–9.

7006. LYONS, F. S. L.: "James Joyce's Dublin," *Twentieth-Century Studies*, #4 (Nov 1970), 6-25.
The literary, social, and political Irish background of Joyce's early career. Yeats is mentioned *passim*.

7007. MAGALANER, MARVIN (ed): *A James Joyce Miscellany*. 2nd series. Carbondale: Southern Illinois UP, 1959. xvi, 233 p.
Michael J. O'Neill: "The Joyces in the Holloway Diaries," 103-10.

7008. MAGALANER, MARVIN, and RICHARD MORGAN KAIN: *Joyce: The Man, the Work, the Reputation*. NY: New York UP, 1956. xiv, 377 p.
On Yeats and Joyce, pp. 68-70 and *passim* (see index).

7009. MIRSKY, D. S.: "Joyce and Irish Literature," *New Masses*, 11:1 (3 Apr 1934), 31-34.

7010. MURPHY, MAURICE: "James Joyce and Ireland," *Nation*, 129:3354 (16 Oct 1929), 426.

7011. SCHOLES, ROBERT: "James Joyce, Irish Poet," *JJQ*, 2:4 (Summer 1965), 255-70.
Compares Joyce's poems "Tilly" and "Ecce Puer" with Yeats's "The Dedication to a Book of Stories Selected from the Irish Novelists" and "A Cradle Song," respectively.

7012. SCHUTTE, WILLIAM METCALF: *Joyce and Shakespeare: A Study in the Meaning of "Ulysses."* New Haven: Yale UP, 1957. xiv, 197 p. (Yale Studies in English. 134.)
Includes discussions of Joyce's relationship with the Irish literary revival, especially with AE and John Eglinton.

See also J676, 2207-35 and note, 4054, 5907, 5911, 5912, 5919, 5922, 5935, 5940, 5944, 5945, 5948, 5949, 5982a, 6203, 6267, 6287, 6290, 6291, 6302, 6323, 6572, 7038, 7397.

Patrick Weston Joyce and Robert Dwyer Joyce

7013. HÖBARTH, ELFRIEDE: "P. W. Joyce und R. D. Joyce: Ihr Leben, ihre Werke und ihre Bedeutung für die anglo-irische Literatur," Dr. phil. thesis, U of Wien, 1938. iv, 143 p.

William Larminie

7014. EGLINTON, JOHN: "William Larminie," *Dublin Mag*, 19:2 (Apr-June 1944), 12-16.

See also J1110, 5384-89 and note, 5911, 5917, 6154, 6233, 6290.

Emily Lawless

7015. LINN, WILLIAM J.: "The Life and Works of the Hon. Emily Lawless, First Novelist of the Irish Literary Revival," °Ph.D. thesis, New York U, 1971. 228 p. (*DA*, 32:7 [Jan 1972], 4007A.)

Francis Ledwidge

7016. CURTAYNE, ALICE: *Francis Ledwidge: A Life of the Poet (1887-1917)*. London: Brian & O'Keeffe, 1972. 209 p.

See also J1689, 6233, 6661a.

F. J. McCormick

7017. "F. J. McCormick (Peter C. Judge): A Symposium of Tributes,"
Capuchin Annual, 18 (1948), 149-225.

7018. FALLON, GABRIEL: "F. J. McCormick: An Appreciation," *Studies*, 36:
142 (June 1947), 181-86.

7019. LANE, YOTI: *The Psychology of the Actor.* With a foreword by W.
Bridges-Adams. London: Secker & Warburg, 1959. 208 p.
   On F. J. McCormack [sic] as the example of an actor who by instinc-
tively avoiding publicity "may do himself a tragic injustice," pp.
126-28.

See also J5592, 6304, 6603, 6744.

Thomas MacDonagh

7019a. MACDONAGH, THOMAS: *When the Dawn Is Come: A Tragedy in Three Acts.*
Introduction by Chester Garrison, textual commentary by Johann Norstedt.
Chicago: De Paul U, 1973. i, 52 p. (Irish Drama Series. 9.)
   "Introduction," 1-13; "Textual Commentary," 44-51. On Yeats and Mac-
Donagh, *passim.*

7019b. °NORSTEDT, JOHN A.: "Thomas MacDonagh: A Biography," Ph.D. thesis,
University College, Dublin, 1971/72.

7020. PARKS, EDD WINFIELD, and AILEEN WELLS PARKS: *Thomas MacDonagh: The
Man, the Patriot, the Writer.* Athens: U of Georgia Press, 1967. xiv, 151
p.
   On Yeats and MacDonagh, *passim.*

See also J370, 1161 (#5), 2238a, 5911, 5947a, 5951, 6249, 6250, 6259,
6268, 6273, 6290, 7219.

Stephen MacKenna

7021. ROSENBLATT, ROGER: "Stephen MacKenna and the Irish Literary Revival,"
Ph.D. thesis, Harvard U, 1968. i, 234 p.

See also J5948, 7442.

Seumas MacManus

7022. MACMANUS, SEUMAS: *The Townland of Tamney: A One Act Comedy* [and]
Edward Martyn: *The Dream Physician: A Five Act Comedy.* Chicago: De Paul U,
1972. i, 73 p. (Irish Drama Series. 7.)
   William J. Feeney: "Introduction [to MacManus]," 1-6; Patricia McFate:
"Introduction [to Martyn]," 15-27.

See also J5988, 6388.

Brinsley Macnamara (also MacNamara, McNamara)

7023. DONOVAN, JUDY L.: "A Study of Brinsley MacNamara," M.A. thesis, U of
Kansas, 1965. iii, 106 p.

7024. MALONE, ANDREW E.: "Brinsley MacNamara: An Appreciation," *Dublin Mag*,
4:3 (July-Sept 1929), 46-56.

7025. O SAOTHRAI, SEAMAS: "Brinsley Macnamara (1890-1963)," *Irish Booklore*,
2:1 (Spring 1972), 75-81.

See also J370, 547, 6320, 6328, 6499, 6763.

Constance Markievicz

7026. MARRECO, ANNE: *The Rebel Countess: The Life and Times of Constance Markievicz*. Philadelphia: Chilton Books, 1967. xiii, 330 p.
On Yeats, *passim* (see index).

7027. VAN VORIS, JACQUELINE: *Constance de Markievicz in the Cause of Ireland*. Amherst: U of Massachusetts Press, 1967. 384 p.
Yeats's connections with the countess and the Gore-Booth family are referred to *passim* (see index).

See also J514, 1112 (#8), 3603, 5915, 6120a, 6914a, 6922a.

Edward Martyn

7028. COURTNEY, SISTER MARIE-THÉRÈSE: *Edward Martyn and the Irish Theatre*. NY: Vantage Press, 1956. 188 p.

7029. GWYNN, DENIS: "Edward Martyn," *Studies*, 19:74 (June 1930), 227-39.

7030. ———: *Edward Martyn and the Irish Revival*. London: Cape, 1930. 349 p.
"The Irish Literary Theatre," 113-70; corrects some statements made about Martyn by Yeats and Lady Gregory.

7031. MACGREEVY, THOMAS: "Edward Martyn: An Irish Catholic Eccentric," *Father Mathew Record*, 37:4 (Apr 1943), 2.

7032. MARTYN, EDWARD: *The Heather Field: A Play in Three Acts*. Chicago: DePaul U, 1966. i, 67 p. (Irish Drama Series. 1.)
[William J. Feeney]: Introduction to Martyn, pp. 1-15.

7033. ———: *Maeve: A Psychological Drama in Two Acts* [and] Alice Milligan: *The Last Feast of the Fianna: A Dramatic Legend*. Chicago: DePaul U, 1967. i, 60 p. (Irish Drama Series. 2.)
[William J. Feeney]: Introduction to Martyn, pp. 1-11; introduction to Alice Milligan, pp. 40-46.

7034. MILLER, LIAM: "Unpublished Revisions to an Edward Martyn Essay," *Irish Book*, 2:3/4 (Autumn 1963), 130-32.
Revisions to J6496 and 6497. See also the note by Ann Saddlemyer, *ibid.*, pp. 132-33.

7035. AE [RUSSELL, GEORGE WILLIAM]: "The Irish Literary Drama," *Daily Express*, #14530 (28 Jan 1899), 3.

7036. °RYAN, STEPHEN P.: "Edward Martyn, Playwright and Man of the Theatre: A Survey, Chiefly Historical, of His Work in the Irish Dramatic Movement," Ph.D. thesis, University College, Dublin, 1956.

7037. ———: "Edward Martyn's Last Play," *Studies*, 47:[] (Summer 1958), 192-99.

7038. ———: "James Joyce and Edward Martyn," *XUS*, 1:5 (Spring 1961-62), 200-205.

7039. SETTERQUIST, JAN: *Ibsen and the Beginnings of Anglo-Irish Drama. II. Edward Martyn*. Upsala: Lundequist, 1960. 115 p. (Upsala Irish Studies. 5.)
For volume 1 see J7408.

7040. WILDE, MARTHA HEDWIG: "Edward Martyn, seine Dramen und deren Beziehung zur irischen Renaissance," Dr. phil thesis, U of Wien, [1931]. iv, 137 p.
Negligible.

See also J363, 389, 1136, 1690, 2045, 3412, 3485, 5850, 5883, 5911, 5932, 6294, 6301, 6318, 6320, 6322, 6330, 6333, 6336, 6410, 6499, 6505, 6514, 6703, 6744, 6847-48 and note, 7022, 7056, 7058, 7073, 7083.

Rutherford Mayne

See J5911, 6294, 6336, 6850-58.

Alice Milligan

See J6330, 7033.

Susan L. Mitchell

7041. KAIN, RICHARD MORGAN: *Susan L. Mitchell*. Lewisburg, Pa.: Bucknell UP, 1972. 103 p.

7042. O'SULLIVAN, SEUMAS: *Essays and Recollections*. Dublin: Talbot Press, 1944. 143 p.
"Seumas O'Kelly," 118-22; "Susan Mitchell," 123-28.

See also J1136, 1641, 6120.

George Moore (Bibliography)

7043. GERBER, HELMUT E.: "George Moore: An Annotated Bibliography of Writings about Him," *English Fiction in Transition*, 2:2 (Summer-Fall 1959), 1-91.
Supplement I, 3:2 (1960), 34-46; Supplement II, 4:2 (1961), 30-42; and continued in subsequent issues (beginning with volume 6 [1963], the periodical changed its name to *ELT*).

7044. GILCHER, EDWIN: *A Bibliography of George Moore*. DeKalb: Northern Illinois UP, 1970. xiv, 274 p.

See also J366a, 389, 512.

George Moore (Criticism)

7045. ADAMS, MILDRED DAVIS: "The Apprenticeship of George Moore: His Response to Cultural Influences," Ph.D. thesis, Columbia U, 1960. vii, 223 p. (*DA*, 21:7 [Jan 1961], 1935.)
"Ireland: Rebirth," 174-212: In "Ireland's renaissance, Moore experienced one of his own."

7046. ARCHER, WILLIAM: *Real Conversations*. London: Heinemann, 1904. xiii, 254 p.
A conversation with Moore in May 1901 touches on Irish and Anglo-Irish literature, pp. 85-106.

7047. BROWN, MALCOLM: *George Moore: A Reconsideration*. Seattle: U of Washington Press, 1955. xix, 235 p.
On Yeats and Moore, *passim* (see index).

7048. DUNLEAVY, GARETH W., and JANET EGLESON DUNLEAVY: "Editor Moore to Playwright Hyde: On the Making of *The Tinker and the Fairy*," *Irish UR*, 3:1 (Spring 1973), 17-30.

7048a. DUNLEAVY, JANET EGLESON: *George Moore: The Artist's Vision, the Storyteller's Art*. Lewisburg, Pa.: Bucknell UP, 1973. 156 p.

7049. FIRTH, JOHN: "George Moore and Modern Irish Autobiography," *Wisconsin Studies in Literature*, #5 (1968), 64-72.

7050. FREEMAN, JOHN: *A Portrait of George Moore in a Study of His Work.* London: Laurie, 1922. xi, 283 p.
On Moore's involvement in the Irish literary revival, pp. 125-66; on the making of *Diarmuid and Grania*, pp. 141-45.

7051. HONE, JOSEPH: *The Life of George Moore* [. . .]. NY: Macmillan, 1936. 515 p.
Yeats is mentioned *passim* (see index).

7052. HUGHES, DOUGLAS A. (ed): *The Man of Wax: Critical Essays on George Moore.* NY: New York UP, 1971. xxvi, 364 p.
Reprinted essays; references to Yeats, *passim* (see index).

7053. JEFFARES, ALEXANDER NORMAN: *George Moore.* London: Longmans, 1965. 43 p. (Writers and Their Work. 180.)

7054. KENNEDY, SISTER EILEEN: "Circling Back: The Influence of Ireland on George Moore," °Ph.D. thesis, Columbia U, 1968. 269 p. (*DA*, 30:2 [Aug 1969], 727A.)

7055. KRÜGER, FRITZ: "George Moore und die irische Renaissance," *Neuphilologische Monatsschrift*, 6:7/8 (July/Aug 1935), 333-36.
Moore belongs only partially to the revival; he is best thought of as its chronicler.

7056. LYONS, F. S. L.: "George Moore and Edward Martyn," *Hermathena*, 98 (Spring 1964), 9-32.

7057. °MACDONNCHA, SEAMUS: "George Moore: Some Irish Aspects," M.A. thesis, University College, Galway, 1969.

7058. MCFATE, PATRICIA: "*The Bending of the Bough* and *The Heather Field*: Two Portraits of the Artists," *Éire-Ireland*, 8:1 (Spring 1973), 52-61.
Includes comments on Martyn and the Yeats-Moore relationship.

7058a. °MCGUNIGLE, BRIAN E.: "George Moore and Ireland, 1898-1914: Toward a Definitive Critical Biography," M.A. thesis, University College, Dublin, 1970/71.

7059. MACY, JOHN: *The Critical Game.* NY: Boni & Liveright, 1922. 335 p.
"George Moore and Other Irish Writers," 305-14; contains some general remarks on Yeats.

7060. MITCHELL, SUSAN LANGSTAFF: *George Moore.* Dublin: Maunsel, 1916. 149 p. ([Irishmen of To-day. 4.])
On Yeats, *passim*, especially pp. 100-103 on the genesis of *Diarmuid and Grania*.

7061. MOORE, GEORGE: *Letters from George Moore to Ed. Dujardin, 1886-1922.* NY: Gaige, 1929, 118 p.
In "Introduction," John Eglinton recalls Moore's Dublin years and his interest in the revival, pp. 5-17.

7062. ————: *George Moore in Transition: Letters to T. Fisher Unwin and Lena Milman, 1894-1910.* Edited with a commentary by Helmut E. Gerber. Detroit: Wayne State UP, 1968. 343 p.
On Yeats, *passim* (see index); on *Diarmuid and Grania*, pp. 224-26.

7063. ————: *The Bending of the Bough: A Play in Five Acts.* Chicago: DePaul U, 1969. i, 87 p. (Irish Drama Series. 3.)
[William J. Feeney]: "Introduction," 1-21.

7064. NOËL, JEAN C.: *George Moore: L'homme et l'oeuvre (1852-1933)*. Paris: Didier, 1966. xiv, 706 p. (Etudes anglaises. 24.)
   Numerous references to Yeats, especially in "Pour le Théâtre litté-raire irlandais: *Diarmuid and Grania* (1901)," 304-10.

7065. °O'SULLIVAN, M. E.: "George Moore and Ireland," M.A. thesis, University College, Dublin, 1956.

7066. OWENS, GRAHAM (ed): *George Moore's Mind and Art: Essays*. Edinburgh: Oliver & Boyd, 1968. xi, 182 p. (Essays Old and New. 2.)
   On Moore and Yeats, *passim* (see index), especially in the following articles: William F. Blissett: "George Moore and Literary Wagnerism," 53-76; and Herbert Howarth: "Dublin, 1899-1911: The Enthusiasms of a Prodigal," 77-98.

7067. PAUL-DUBOIS, L.: "George Moore, irlandais," *Correspondant*, 297:1705 (10 Oct 1933), 3-25.

7068. POTTER, WINIFRED IRENE NELSON: "A Roving Mind: A Review and Appraisal of George Moore's Pronouncements on Literature, Painting, and Music," Ph.D. thesis, Bryn Mawr College, 1950. v, 214 p. (*DA*, 13:5 [1953], 799-800.)

7069. PRILIPP, BEDA: "Die irische Renaissance und George Moore," *Grenzboten*, 72 (pt II):14 (1913), 34-39.
   Moore did not really belong to it.

7070. ———: "George Moore und die irische Renaissance," *Irische Blätter*, 2:6 (Oct 1918), 549-58.

7071. SHERMAN, STUART PRATT: *On Contemporary Literature*. NY: Holt, 1917. vii, 312 p.
   "The Aesthetic Naturalism of George Moore," 120-68; "The Exoticism of John Synge," 190-210. Both essays contain remarks on Yeats.

7072. SHUMAKER, WAYNE: *English Autobiography: Its Emergence, Materials, and Form*. Berkeley: U of California Press, 1954. xiii, 262 p. (U of California Publications. English Studies. 8.)
   "The Narrative Mode: Moore's *Hail and Farewell*," 185-213.

7073. WEAVER, JACK WAYNE: "A Story-Teller's Holiday: George Moore's Irish Renaissance, 1897 to 1911," Ph.D. thesis, U of North Carolina at Chapel Hill, 1966. xiv, 214 p. (*DA*, 27:9 [Mar 1967], 3067A-68A.)
   Discusses the relationships between Moore and Martyn, Lady Gregory, Yeats, AE, John Eglinton, Hyde, some minor figures, and the Irish theater in general.

7074. ———: "An Exile Returned: Moore and Yeats in Ireland," *Éire-Ireland*, 3:1 (Spring 1968), 40-47.
   Moore's involvement in the revival and his collaboration and quarrel with Yeats. Comments on *Diarmuid and Grania* and *Where There Is Nothing*.

7075. WHITE, CLYDE PATRICK: "George Moore: From Naturalism to Pure Art," °Ph.D. thesis, U of Virginia, 1970. 258 p. (*DA*, 31:9 [Mar 1971], 4800A.)
   Discusses the Yeats-Moore relationship.

7076. WOLFE, HUMBERT: *George Moore*. London: Butterworth, 1933 [1931]. xxiii, 135 p.
   See especially "Ireland," 46-78.

7077. ZIRKER, HERBERT: *George Moore: Realismus und autobiographische Fiktion. Versuch zur Form der Autobiographie*. Köln: Böhlau, 1968. vi, 264 p. (Anglistische Studien. 5.)

See also J611, 614, 729a, 845, 974, 1136, 1327, 1348, 1432, 1690, 1752, 2045, 2242-45, 3707-11 and note, 3712-15 and note, 4232b, 5850, 5851, 5883, 5894, 5911, 5918 (reviews #1, 2), 5922, 5932, 5940 (#4), 5944, 5945, 5949, 5986, 6005, 6059, 6120, 6172, 6182, 6213, 6287, 6290, 6291, 6301, 6318, 6320, 6330, 6333, 6336, 6354, 6537, 6744, 6932, 7255.

T. C. Murray

7078. °CONLIN, MATTHEW T.: "T. C. Murray: A Critical Study of His Dramatic Works," Ph.D. thesis, University College, Dublin, 1952.

7079. ————: "T. C. Murray: Ireland on the Stage," *Renascence*, 13:3 (Spring 1961), 125-31.

7080. HOGAN, J. J.: "Thomas Cornelius Murray," *Studies*, 38:150 (June 1949), 194-96.

7081. HOGAN, THOMAS: "T. C. Murray," *Envoy*, 3:12 (Nov 1950), 38-48.
    "If the Abbey ever justified itself as an Irish theatre, it did so by T. C. Murray."

7081a. JORDAN, JOHN: "Courage and Realism," *Hibernia*, 37:3 (2 Feb 1973), 11.

7082. Ó HAODHA, MICHEÁL: "T. C. Murray and Some Critics," *Studies*, 47:[] (Summer 1958), 185-91.

7083. ————: *Plays and Places*. Dublin: Progress House, 1961. vi, 128 p.
    "T. C. Murray--Dramatist (1873-1939)," 18-30; "Edward Martyn and His Ideals (1859-1923)," 82-91.

7084. °WALSH, RAYMOND: "The Permanence of T. C. Murray," M.A. thesis, University College, Dublin, 1963.

See also J363, 6320, 6322, 6328, 6331, 6336, 6479, 6499, 6505, 6514, 6706, 6813.

Sean O'Casey (Bibliography)

7085. BRANDSTÄDTER, OTTO: "Eine O'Casey-Bibliographie," *ZAA*, 2:2 (1954), 240-54.

7086. CARPENTER, CHARLES A.: "Sean O'Casey Studies through 1964," *MD*, 10:1 (May 1967), 17-23.

7087. [LEVIDOVA, I. M., and B. M. PARCHEVSKAIA]: *Shon O'Keĭsi: Biobibliograficheskiĭ ukazatel'*. Moskva: Izdatel'stvo "Kniga," 1964. 100 p.
    E. Kornilova: "Shon O'Keĭsi," 5-20. "Bibliografiia proizvedeniĭ Shona O'Keĭsi i literatury o nem," 27-80.

7088. MIKHAIL, EDWARD HALIM: *Sean O'Casey: A Bibliography of Criticism*. With an introduction by Ronald Ayling. London: Macmillan, 1972. xi, 152 p.

See also J363, 364, 366a, 370, 533, 547, 6884, 7147, 7188. N.B.: There is as yet no good primary O'Casey bibliography.

Sean O'Casey (Criticism)

7089. ANON.: "O'Casey Papers Acquired," *BNYPL*, 73:6 (June 1969), 356-58.

7090. ANON.: "The World of Sean O'Casey: Dublin Today Mirrors a Great Playwright's Past," *Life*, 37:4 (26 July 1954), 68-77, 79-80.
    Twenty photographs by Gjon Mili and some text.

7091. ANON.: "Ireland's New Playwright," *Literary Digest*, 89:1878 (17 Apr 1926), 27-28.

7092. ANON.: "A Dublin Tempest," *Literary Digest*, 98:1998 (4 Aug 1928), 24-25.
The *Silver Tassie* row.

7093. ANON.: "Ploughing the Star," *Manchester Guardian*, #25511 (4 June 1928), 8.
The *Silver Tassie* row. Correspondence by O'Casey, #25518 (12 June 1928), 22; on Yeats's actions in this affair.

7094. ARMSTRONG, WILLIAM ARTHUR: *Sean O'Casey*. London: Longmans, Green, 1967. 39 p. (Writers and Their Work. 198.)

7095. AYLING, RONALD: "Feathers Finely Aflutther," *MD*, 7:2 (Sept 1964), 135-47.

7096. ———: "Sean O'Casey & His Critics," *New Theatre Mag*, 8:1 (Autumn 1968), 5-19.

7097. ——— (ed): *Sean O'Casey: Modern Judgments*. London: Macmillan, 1969. 274 p.
On Yeats, *passim* (see index), especially in the following two contributions:
William A. Armstrong: "Sean O'Casey, W. B. Yeats and the Dance of Life," 131-42. On O'Casey's use and implied criticism of Yeats in his description of Mild Millie in *Drums under the Window* and in *Red Roses for Me*. O'Casey did not approve of Yeats's romantic conception of Cathleen ni Houlihan and of his later pessimistic view of Irish society.
David Krause: "A Self Portrait of the Artist as a Man," 235-51; abridged from J7149.

7098. ———: "A Note on Sean O'Casey's Manuscripts and His Working Methods," *BNYPL*, 73:6 (June 1969), 359-67.

7099. ———: "History and Artistry in Sean O'Casey's Dublin Trilogy," *Theoria*, #37 (1970), 1-13.

7100. ———: "Sean O'Casey, 1880-1964: A Retrospective Survey," *Research Studies*, 39:4 (Dec 1971), 259-70.

7101. ———: "Sean O'Casey and the Abbey Theatre, Dublin," *Dalhousie R*, 52:1 (Spring 1972), 21-33.
Reprinted in *ESA*, 15:2 (Sept 1972), 71-80; slightly revised as "Sean O'Casey and the Abbey Theatre Company," *Irish UR*, 3:1 (Spring 1973), 5-16.

7102. ———: "Popular Tradition and Individual Talent in Sean O'Casey's Dublin Trilogy," *JML*, 2:4 (Nov 1972), 491-504.

7103. BENSTOCK, BERNARD: *Sean O'Casey*. Lewisburg, Pa.: Bucknell UP, 1970. 123 p.
Yeats is mentioned *passim*.

7104. BERGHOLZ, HARRY: "Sean O'Casey," *Englische Studien*, 65:1 (1930), 49-67.
Comments on the Yeats-O'Casey quarrel about *The Silver Tassie*.

7105. BLÖCKER, GÜNTER: "Irische Rhapsodie: Sean O'Casey--Träumer und Rebell," *Merkur*, 26:5 (May 1972), 483-90.

7106. BRUGÈRE, RAYMOND: "Sean O'Casey et le théâtre irlandais," *Revue anglo-américaine*, 3:3 (Feb 1926), 206-21.

7107. BRULÉ, A.: "Sean O'Casey et le théâtre moderne," *Revue anglo-américaine*, 6:1 (Oct 1928), 53-57.
On the *Silver Tassie* row.

7108. CASWELL, ROBERT W.: "Sean O'Casey as a Poetic Dramatist," Ph.D. thesis, Trinity College, Dublin, 1960. v, 558 p.

7109. COLUM, PADRAIC: "Sean O'Casey," *TAM*, 9:6 (June 1925), 396-404.

7110. COWASJEE, SAROS: *Sean O'Casey: The Man behind the Plays*. Edinburgh: Oliver & Boyd, 1963. xv, 265 p. (Biography and Criticism. 2.)
Yeats is mentioned *passim*. Contains a long chapter on the *Silver Tassie* row.

7111. ————: "O'Casey Seen through Holloway's Diary," *REL*, 6:3 (July 1965), 58-69.
Contains some notes on the Yeats-O'Casey relationship.

7112. ————: *O'Casey*. Edinburgh: Oliver & Boyd, 1966. viii, 120 p. (Writers and Critics. 51.)

7113. DARIN, DORIS DEPODESTA: "Influence on the Dramas of Sean O'Casey: 'Past Experiences--The Molds in Which Myself Was Made,'" °Ph.D. thesis, New York U, 1969. 318 p. (*DA*, 30:6 [Dec 1969], 2523A-24A.)

7113a. DEANE, SEAMUS: "Irish Politics and O'Casey's Theatre," *Threshold*, #24 (Spring 1973), 5-16.
"In fact . . . in Yeats['s] drama . . . modern Irish drama finds its greatest possibilities, not among the saved women of O'Casey. . . . It is O'Casey, not Yeats, who is guilty of literary gestures."

7114. °DRUZINA, MARINA VALERIEVNA: *Shon O'Keĭsi--dramaturg*. Moskva: Znanie, 1963. 29 p. (Novoe v zhizni, nauke, tekhnike. Ser 6: Literatura i iskusstvo. 6.)

7115. ELIZAROVA, MARIĬA EVGEN'EVNA, and N. P. MIKHAL'SKAĬA: *Kurs lektsiĭ po istorii zarubezhnoĭ literatury XX veka*. Moskva: Isdatel'stvo Vysshaĭa Shkola, 1965. 803 p.
"Shon O'Keĭsi," 321-35.

7116. ESSLINGER, PATRICIA MOORE: "The Dublin Materia Poetica of Sean O'Casey," Ph.D. thesis, Tulane U, 1960. ii, 302 p. (*DA*, 21:8 [Feb 1961], 2291-92.)

7117. ————: "The Irish Alienation of Sean O'Casey," *Éire-Ireland*, 1:1 (Spring 1966), 18-25.

7118. FALLON, GABRIEL: "Pathway of a Dramatist," *TAM*, 34:1 (Jan 1950), 36-39.

7119. ————: *Sean O'Casey: The Man I Knew*. London: Routledge & Kegan Paul, 1965. x, 213 p.
Reminiscences of Yeats defending *The Plough and the Stars*, pp. 91-93; on the *Silver Tassie* row, pp. 108-16.

7120. FEENEY, WILLIAM J.: "Sean O'Casey and the Abbey Theatre," M.A. thesis, U of Kansas, 1948. v, 216 p.

7121. FLYNN, SISTER MARY AURELIA: "A Study of the Relationship between Sean O'Casey's Plays and the Abbey Theatre," M.A. thesis, Catholic U of America, 1955. iv, 72 p.

7122. GEROLD, BERTHILD: "Sean O'Casey as a Dramatist," Dr. phil. thesis, U of Innsbruck, [1953]. vi, 156 p.

7123. GHEORGHIU, MIHNEA: "O'Casey: Menestrel al irlandei eroice" [O'Casey: Singer of heroic Ireland], Secolul 20, 1:4 (1961), 144-50.

7124. ———: "Sean O'Casey: Trandafiri fără pîine" [Sean O'Casey: Roses without bread]. Secolul 20, 4:12 (1964), 92-103.

7125. GOLDSTONE, HERBERT: In Search of a Community: The Achievement of Sean O'Casey. Cork: Mercier Press, 1972. vi, 225 p.

7126. GOOD, J. W.: "A New Irish Dramatist," NSt, 22:571 (29 Mar 1924), 731.

7127. GOZENPUD, ABRAM AKIMOVICH: Puti i pereput'ia: Angliĭskaia i fran-t͡suzskaia dramaturgiia XX veka. Leningrad: Iskusstvo, 1967. 328 p.
"Shon O'Keĭsi," 139-53.

7128. GRAZHDANSKAIA, ZOIA TIKHONOVNA (ed): Istoriia zarubezhnoĭ literatury dvadt͡sogo veka. Moskva: Gosuchebno-pedagog. izd-vo, 1963. 855 p.
"Irlandskaia literatura: Shon O'Kejsi," 540-47.

7129. GREGORY, LADY [ISABELLA AUGUSTA]: "How Great Plays Are Born: The Coming of Mr. O'Casey," Daily News, #24961 (27 Mar 1926), 6.

7130. HABART, MICHEL: "Introduction à Sean O'Casey," Théâtre populaire, #34 (Second trimester 1959), 5-37.

7131. ———: "Le théâtre irlandais et Sean O'Casey," Bref, #43 (Feb 1961), 4-5.

7132. ———: "Sean O'Casey: Théâtre et réalité," Nouvelle critique, #127 (June 1961), 71-82.

7133. ———: "Une mère et deux fils," Cahiers de la Compagnie Madeleine Renaud--Jean-Louis Barrault, #37 (1962), 17-31.
O'Casey and Shaw.

7134. HOGAN, ROBERT: The Experiments of Sean O'Casey. NY: St. Martin's Press, 1960. viii, 215 p.
Contains an appendix on the Silver Tassie row, pp. 184-206.

7135. ———: "O'Casey's Dramatic Apprenticeship," MD, 4:3 (Dec 1961), 243-53.

7136. HONE, J. M.: "A Letter from Ireland," London Mercury, 14:80 (June 1926), 189-91.

7137. Istoriia angliĭskoĭ literatury. Tom III. Moskva: Izdatel'stvo Akademii Nauk SSSR, 1958, 732 p.
[P. S. Balashov]: "O'Keĭsi," 627-46.

7138. IVASHEVA, VALENTINA VASIL'EVNA: Angliĭskaia literatura XX vek. Moskva: Izdatel'stvo "Prosvechnie," 1967. 476 p.
See pp. 93-98, 114-17.

7139. JACOBY, GORDON ABRAHAM: "The Construction and Testing of a Self-Instructional, Audiolingual Program of the Irish-English Dialect for the Stage," Ph.D. thesis, Ohio State U, 1967. xiv, 301 p. (DA, 28:9 [Mar 1968], 3808A-9A.)
Draws on O'Casey's Juno and the Paycock, Synge's Playboy, and other texts.

7140. JACQUOT, JEAN (ed): Le théâtre moderne: Hommes et tendances. Paris: Editions du Centre national de la recherche scientifique, 1958. 372 p.

René Fréchet: "Sean O'Casey: Un épisode de la vie du théâtre anglais," 321-36. Includes notes on Yeats's plays.

7141. JOHNSTON, DENIS: "Joxer in Totnes: A Study in Sean O'Casey," *Irish Writing*, #13 (Dec 1950), 50-53.
O'Casey & Johnston vs. Ireland & Yeats.

7142. KERR, ANTHONY PETTUS: "Sean O'Casey: The New Spirit of the Abbey Theatre," M.A. thesis, Louisiana State U, 1935. vi, 134 p.

7143. KIRWAN, H. N.: "Sean O'Casey: The Man and the Dramatist," *Crystal*, 1:1 (Feb 1926), 5, 20.
An amusing photograph of O'Casey's wedding appears in 2:10 (Oct 1927), 291.

7144. KOPELEV, LEV ZALMANOVICH (ed): *Sovremennaı͡a zarubezhnaı͡a drama*. Moskva: Akademiı͡a Nauk SSSR, 1962. 383 p.
E. Kornilova: "Dramaturgiı͡a Shona O'Keĭsi," 63-131. Contains some references to Yeats.

7145. KORNILOVA, E.: "Vsegda s irlandieĭ, vsegda s narodom . . ." [Always with Ireland, always with the people], *Teatr*, #5 (May 1959), 167-78.

7146. KOSOK, HEINZ: "Sean O'Casey: 1880-1964," *Neueren Sprachen*, 13:10 (Oct 1964), 453-68.

7147. ———: *Sean O'Casey: Das dramatische Werk*. Berlin: Schmidt, 1972. 419 p.
On Yeats and O'Casey, *passim*, especially pp. 372-75. The bibliography contains several items overlooked by Mikhail (J7088).

7148. KRAUSE, DAVID: *Sean O'Casey: The Man and the Work*. London: MacGibbon & Kee, 1960. xi, 340 p.
Includes "The Playwright's Not for Burning," *VQR*, 34:1 (Winter 1958), 60-76 (on the *Silver Tassie* row). Discusses the Yeats-O'Casey relationship, including a comparison of their dramatic theories, *passim*, especially pp. 94-109, 122-31.

7149. ———: *A Self-Portrait of the Artist as a Man: Sean O'Casey's Letters*. Dublin: Dolmen Press, 1968. 39 p. (New Dolmen Chapbook. 6.)
Includes remarks on the Yeats-O'Casey relationship. See also J7097.

7150. LENNON, MICHAEL J.: "Sean O'Casey and His Plays," *Catholic World*, 130:777 (Dec 1929), 294-301; :778 (Jan 1930), 452-61.

7151. LEWIS, ALLAN: *The Contemporary Theatre: The Significant Playwrights of Our Time*. NY: Crown, 1962. viii, 312 p.
"Irish Romantic Realism—Sean O'Casey," 169-91.

7152. LOCKLIN, MAE: "Sean O'Casey: A Critical Study," M.A. thesis, Queen's U, 1932. ii, 136 p.

7153. °MCALEVEY, JOAN G.: "Sean O'Casey: Three Decades of Criticism," M.A. thesis, Columbia U, 1956. 173 p.

7154. MCCANN, SEAN (ed): *The World of Sean O'Casey*. London: New English Library, 1966. 252 p. (Four Square Books. 1610.)
On O'Casey, the Abbey, and Yeats, *passim*, especially in: Donal Dorcey: "The Great Occasions," 50-72; mostly on the reception of *The Plough and the Stars*.
Anthony Butler: "The Abbey Daze," 92-105. On the *Silver Tassie* affair. Speculates about the reasons for Yeats's behavior and concludes that he was jealous.
David Krause: "Towards the End," 137-57; reprinted from J5948.

7155. MCHUGH, ROGER: "The Legacy of Sean O'Casey," *Texas Q*, 8:1 (Spring 1965), 123-37.

7156. ———: "Sean O'Casey and Lady Gregory," *JJQ*, 8:1 (Fall 1970), 119-23.

7157. MARGULIES, MARTIN B.: *The Early Life of Sean O'Casey*. Dublin: Dolmen Press, 1970. 87 p.

7158. MAROLDO, WILLIAM JOHN: "Sean O'Casey and the Art of Autobiography: Form and Content in the Irish Books," Ph.D. thesis, Columbia U, 1964. xii, 526 p. (*DA*, 26:3 [Sept 1965], 1649-50.)

7159. METSCHER, THOMAS: *Sean O'Caseys dramatischer Stil*. Braunschweig: Westermann, 1968. 214 p. (Archiv für das Studium der neueren Sprachen und Literaturen. Beiheft 3.)
   Includes a discussion of O'Casey's use of the Anglo-Irish dialect.

7160. O'CASEY, EILEEN: *Sean*. Edited with an introduction by J. C. Trewin. London: Macmillan, 1971. 318 p.
   On the *Silver Tassie* row, pp. 83-103.

7160a. O'Keĭsi, Shon [O'CASEY, SEAN]: *Za teatral'nym zanavesom: Sbornik stateĭ* [Behind the theater curtain: A collection of articles]. Moskva: Izdatel'stvo "Progress," 1971. 288 p.
   G. Zlobin: "Privety i poritsaniĭa Shona O'Keĭsi" [O'Casey's benedictions and blasts], 3-15.

7161. O'FAOLAIN, SEAN: "The Case of Sean O'Casey," *Commonweal*, 22:24 (11 Oct 1935), 577-78.
   The *Silver Tassie* affair.

7162. O'HEGARTY, P. S.: "A Dramatist of New Born Ireland," *NAR*, 224:835 (June 1927), 315-22.

7163. O'RILEY, MARGARET CATHERINE: "The Dramaturgy of Sean O'Casey," Ph.D. thesis, U of Wisconsin, 1955. vii, 473 p. (*DA*, 16:2 [1956], 340.)

7164. O'RIORDAN, JOHN: "O'Casey's Dublin Critics," *Library R*, 21:2 (Summer 1967), 59-63.

7165. ———: "Sean O'Casey: Colourful Quixote of the Drama," *Library R*, 22:5 (Spring 1970), 235-42.

7166. PEINERT, DIETRICH: "Sean O'Casey," *Praxis des neusprachlichen Unterrichts*, 15:2 (1968), 182-86.
   In English.

7167. PELLEGRINI, ALESSANDRA: "Della tragedia irlandese e di Sean O'Casey," *Convegno*, 17:9-10 (29 Oct 1936), 329-42.

7168. RAFROIDI, PATRICK: "Dramaturges irlandais d'hier et d'avant-hier," *Langues modernes*, 60:3 (May-June 1966), 320-24.

7169. RAMSEY, ROGER: "The Making of an Angry Old Playwright," *English Record*, 22:2 (Winter 1971), 19-25.

7170. REID, ALEC: "The Legend of the Green Crow: Observations on Recent Work by and about O'Casey," *Drama Survey*, 3:1 (May 1963), 155-64.

7171. °REST, JAIME: "O'Casey: Adios al Teatro de la Abadia," *Teatro XX*, #6 (1964), pages unknown.

7172. REYNOLDS, HORACE: "Riot in the Abbey," *American Spectator*, 3:26 (Dec 1934), 14-15.

The controversial production of *The Plough and the Stars* and Yeats's speech of defense.

7172a. ROLLINS, RONALD GENE: "Sean O'Casey: The Man with Two Faces," °Ph.D. thesis, U of Cincinnati, 1960. 280 p. (*DA*, 21:9 [Mar 1961], 2721.)

7173. ————: "O'Casey and Synge: The Irish Hero as Playboy and Gunman," *Arizona Q*, 22:3 (Autumn 1966), 216-22.

7174. RÜHLE, JÜRGEN: *Literatur und Revolution: Die Schriftsteller und der Kommunismus*. Köln: Kiepenheuer & Witsch, 1960. 616 p.
    See pp. 417-21.

7175. SARUKHANÍAN, ALLA PAVLOVNA: *Tvorchestvo Shona O'Keĭsi* [The work of Sean O'Casey]. Moskva: Nauka, 1965. 219 p.

7176. SAUREL, RENÉE: "Un dramaturge inconfortable . . . ," *Temps modernes*, 17:193 (June 1962), 1938-44.

7177. SCHOEN, ERNST: "Sean O'Casey--ein Dramatiker unserer Zeit," *Theater der Zeit*, 15:3 (Mar 1960), 53-64.

7178. °*Sean O'Casey*. [London]: National Broadcasting Co., released by Encyclopaedia Britannica Films, 1958. Black-and-white film, 28 minutes.
    "Dramatist Sean O'Casey visits with a young American friend at his home on the Devon coast in England, surrounded by his family and his books. He tells of the poverty of his youth, discusses great playwrights whom he has known and admired--including Shaw, Yeats, and Lady Gregory, and speaks of the great hope he has for the world" (from the description in the National Union Catalog).

7179. SELZ, JEAN: "Sean O'Casey," *Lettres nouvelles*, #31 (Nov 1959), 15-17.

7180. SNOWDEN, J. H.: "Dialect in the Plays of Sean O'Casey," *MD*, 14:4 (Feb 1972), 387-91.

7181. STARKIE, WALTER: "The Plays of Sean O'Casey," *Nineteenth Century and After*, 104:618 (Aug 1928), 225-36.
    Mostly concerned with the rejection of *The Silver Tassie*. See O'Casey's scathing reply, :619 (Sept 1928), 399-402.

7182. *Sŭvremenni angliĭski pisateli*. Sofiĭa: Nauka i izkustvo, 1965. 300 p.
    L. Sarieva: "Shon O'Keĭsi," 218-44.

7183. TABORSKI, BOLESŁAW: *Nowy teatr elżbietański*. Kraków: Wydawnictwo literackie, 1967. 520 p.
    ". . . A dla mnie bukiet czerwonych roz: O dramaturgii Seana O'Caseya" [Red roses for me: On Sean O'Casey's dramatic art], 55-98. Contains notes on Yeats.

7184. *Terres celtiques: Ecole d'été de Dublin*. 11e voyage d'études (1964/65). Lyon: Audin, 1965. 71 p.
    An O'Casey issue. Contains:
    Patrick O'Connor: "Sean O'Casey," 21-24; translated by J.-B. de Villeneuve-Bargemon.
    F. de Rocquois: "Le prêtre et l'homme," 25-33.
    Françoise Hanriot: "Le communisme de O'Casey," 35-36.
    Gisèle Bissuel: "La muse tragi-comique," 37-38.
    Roland Ronzière: "*Juno et le paon*: Sean O'Casey et la tragédie des H. L. M.," 39-48.
    Jean-Claude Rolland: "*Les tambours du Père Ned*," 49-51.
    Monique Payrand: "Le trivial et le sublime," 53-54.

7185. TREWIN, JOHN COURTENAY: *Dramatists of Today*. London: Staples Press, 1953. 239 p.
Contains a note on Yeats and Synge, p. 23, and a chapter on O'Casey, pp. 56-66.

7186. VILAÇA, MARIO: "Sean O'Casey e o movimento dramático irlandès," *Vertice*, 11:94 (June 1951), 293-99; :95 (July 1951), 369-72; :96 (Aug 1951), 399-406; :97 (Sept 1951), 479-83; :98 (Oct 1951), 553-56.

7187. VÖLKER, KLAUS: *Irisches Theater II: Sean O'Casey*. Velber: Friedrich, 1968. 126 p. (Friedrichs Dramatiker des Welttheaters. 55.)
Negligible.

7188. WILLIAMSON, WARD: "An Analytical History of American Criticism of the Works of Sean O'Casey, 1924-1958," Ph.D. thesis, State U of Iowa, 1962. ii, 304 p. (*DA*, 23:5 [Nov 1962], 1713.)

7189. WITTIG, KURT: *Sean O'Casey als Dramatiker: Ein Beitrag zum Nachkriegsdrama Irlands*. Leipzig: Scherf, 1937. 90 p. (Dr. phil. thesis, U of Halle, 1937.)

See also J674, 676, 743, 1051, 1052, 1097, 1217, 1402, 1413, 1521, 1642, 2246-53, 2669, 3350a, 3393, 3397, 3426, 3448, 3474, 3641, 3644, 3978, 5596, 5935, 5944, 5947a, 5948, 5951, 5982a, 6005, 6079, 6189, 6203, 6290, 6295, 6298, 6301, 6304, 6306, 6315, 6318, 6320-23, 6327, 6328, 6331, 6333, 6337a, 6347, 6364, 6392, 6407, 6441, 6450, 6469, 6472, 6477, 6499, 6527, 6572, 6574, 6577, 6744, 6813, 6950, 7232, 7338, 7358, 7362, 7373, 7378, 7419.

Frank O'Connor

7190. SHEEHY, MAURICE (ed): *Michael-Frank: Studies on Frank O'Connor with a Bibliography of His Writings*. Dublin: Gill & Macmillan / London: Macmillan, 1969. viii, 203 p.
See especially Roger McHugh: "Frank O'Connor and the Irish Theatre," 64-76; reprinted from *Éire-Ireland*, 4:2 (Summer 1969), 52-63.
Thomas Flanagan: "The Irish Writer," 148-64.
"Towards a Bibliography of Frank O'Connor's Writings," 168-99.

See also J749, 1385a, 5940 (#7), 5944, 5947a, 5982a, 6281, 6284, 6287, 6288, 6364, 7194, 7255.

Sean O'Faolain

7191. DOYLE, PAUL A.: *Sean O'Faolain*. NY: Twayne, 1968. 156 p. (Twayne's English Authors Series. 70.)

7192. °HARMON, MAURICE: "Seán O'Faoláin," Ph.D. thesis, University College, Dublin, 1961.

7193. ————: *Sean O'Faolain: A Critical Introduction*. Notre Dame: U of Notre Dame Press, 1966. xix, 221 p.
On O'Faolain's indebtedness to Yeats, especially regarding the concept of unity of being and the romantic-heroic tradition, *passim* (see index).

See also J1286, 5947a, 6079, 6281, 6287, 6288, 6290, 7194.

Liam O'Flaherty

7194. DAVENPORT, GARY TOLLESON: "Four Irish Writers in Time of Civil War: Liam O'Flaherty, Frank O'Connor, Sean O'Faolain, and Elizabeth Bowen,"

°Ph.D. thesis, U of South Carolina, 1971. 238 p. (*DA*, 32:10 [Apr 1972], 5780A-81A.)

7194a. DOYLE, PAUL A.: "A Liam O'Flaherty Checklist," *TCL*, 13:1 (Apr 1967), 49-51.
   See also Angeline A. Hampton: "Liam O'Flaherty: Additions to the Checklist," *Éire-Ireland*, 6:4 (Winter 1971), 87-94; and Doyle's *Liam O'Flaherty: An Annotated Bibliography*. Troy, N.Y.: Whitston, 1972. vii, 68 p.

7195. ———: *Liam O'Flaherty*. NY: Twayne, 1971. 154 p. (Twayne's English Authors Series. 108.)

7195a. O'BRIEN, JAMES H.: *Liam O'Flaherty*. Lewisburg, Pa.: Bucknell UP, 1973. 124 p.

7196. ZNEIMER, JOHN N.: *The Literary Vision of Liam O'Flaherty*. Syracuse: Syracuse UP, 1971. xiii, 207 p.
   Contains some comments on the Yeats-O'Flaherty relationship, pp. 10-13, 15-20.

See also J676, 5947a, 6079, 6281, 6284, 6287, 6288.

Standish O'Grady

7197. ANON.: "Bibliographies of Irish Authors. No. 2: Standish O'Grady," *Dublin Mag*, 4 [i.e., 5]:2 (Apr-June 1930), 49-56.

7198. BOYD, ERNEST AUGUSTUS: *Appreciations and Depreciations: Irish Literary Studies*. Dublin: Talbot Press / London: Unwin, 1917. viii, 162 p.
   Essays on O'Grady, AE, Eglinton, Dunsany, Shaw, and Dowden.

7199. CLARKE, AUSTIN: "Standish O'Grady," *Dublin Mag*, 22:1 (Jan-Mar 1947), 36-40.

7200. GWYNN, DENIS: "Standish O'Grady," *Old Kilkenny R*, #22 (1970), 11-14.

7201. MCKENNA, JOHN R.: "The Standish O'Grady Collection at Colby College: A Checklist," *Colby Library Q*, 4:16 (Nov 1958), 291-303.

7202. MARCUS, PHILLIP LEDUC: *Standish O'Grady*. Lewisburg, Pa.: Bucknell UP, 1970. 92 p.
   Refers repeatedly to O'Grady's influence on Yeats.

7203. MERCIER, VIVIAN: "Standish James O'Grady," *Colby Library Q*, 4:16 (Nov 1958), 285-90.

7204. O'GRADY, HUGH ART: *Standish James O'Grady: The Man and the Writer. A Memoir by His Son*. With a foreword by Alfred Perceval Graves and contributions by A. E. and others [i.e., Alice L. Milligan and David Morton]. Dublin: Talbot Press, 1929. 84 p.

7205. SULLIVAN, DANIEL J.: "Standish James O'Grady's *All Ireland Review*," *Studia Hibernica*, 9 (1969), 125-36.

7206. TÉRY, SIMONE: "Standish O'Grady: Précurseur de la renaissance littéraire irlandaise," *Nouvelles littéraires*, 3:86 (7 June 1924), 6.

7207. °WHITE, SEAN J.: "Standish James O'Grady and the Irish Literary Movement," M.A. thesis, University College, Dublin, [1952?].

7208. WHITE, S[EAN] J.: "Standish O'Grady," *Kilkenny Mag*, #2 (Autumn 1960), 10-26.
   "The father of the revival."

See also J1110, 5911, 5925, 5932, 5938, 5942, 6290.

Seumas O'Kelly

7209. MALONE, ANDREW E.: "Seumas O'Kelly," *Dublin Mag*, 4 [i.e., 5]:3 (July-Sept 1930), 39-46.

7210. °O'HANLON, AIDEN: "Seumas O'Kelly (1880-1918)," M.A. thesis, University College, Dublin, 1946.

7211. O'KELLY, SEUMAS: *The Shuiler's Child: A Tragedy in Two Acts*. Introduction by George Brandon Saul. Chicago: DePaul U, 1971. i, 46 p. (Irish Drama Series. 5.)
     "Introduction," 1-4.

7212. SAUL, GEORGE BRANDON: *Seumas O'Kelly*. Lewisburg, Pa.: Bucknell UP, 1971. 101 p.

See also J6284, 6287, 6294, 6320, 7042.

John O'Leary

7213. BOURKE, MARCUS: *John O'Leary: A Study in Irish Separatism*. Athens: U of Georgia Press, 1967. xi, 251 p.
     Refers to O'Leary's influence on Yeats, *passim* (see index).

See also J514, 620, 722, 1103, 1747, 2849, 4054, 4071, 4076a, 4199, 4200, 6239.

Maire O'Neill (Molly Allgood)

See J815, 5152, 5915, 7436.

Moira O'Neill

See J4337, 6035.

Seumas O'Sullivan

7214. COLUM, PADRAIC: "Irishry," *Nation*, 107:2777 (21 Sept 1918), 317-19.
     On O'Sullivan, Robinson, and Pearse.

7215. DENSON, ALAN: *Seumas O'Sullivan (James Sullivan Starkey), 1879-1958: A Check-list of His Publications*. Foreword by Padraic Colum. Kendal: The Author, 1969. 27 p.
     Reprinted, with additions, from *Dublin Mag*, 7:2-4 (Autumn-Winter 1968). Lists only books and some "periodicals to which he contributed."

7216. HÖPF'L, HEINZ: "Seumas O'Sullivan," *Neuphilologische Monatsschrift*, 8:4 (Apr 1937), 155-70.

7217. MACMANUS, M. J.: "Bibliographies of Irish Authors. No. 3: Seumas O'Sullivan," *Dublin Mag*, 5:3 (July-Sept 1930), 47-50.

7218. MILLER, LIAM (ed): *Retrospect: The Work of Seumas O'Sullivan, 1879-1958, & Estella F. Solomons, 1882-1968*. Dublin: Dolmen Press, 1973. 104 p. (Dolmen Editions. 17.)
     Partial contents: A. J. Leventhal: "Seumas O'Sullivan," 7-20; Padraic Colum: "Introduction," 50-55, to O'Sullivan's poetry, written in 1923.

See also J370, 1638, 2711, 5911, 6233, 6267, 6862.

P. H. Pearse

7219. COLUM, PADRAIC: "Poets under Arms," *Phoenix* [Dublin], 1:5 (6 Jan 1917), 37-38.
Pearse, MacDonagh, and Plunkett.

7220. DALMASSO, MICHÈLE: "Padraic H. Pearse: Patriote et poète irlandais (1879-1916)," *Annales de la Faculté des Lettres et Sciences Humaines d'Aix*, 45 (1968), 39-50.

7221. LEROUX, LOUIS N.: *Patrick H. Pearse*. Adapted from the French and revised by the author; translated into English by Desmond Ryan. Dublin: Talbot Press, 1932. xiii, 440 p.
The French edition was published as °*L'Irlande militante: La vie de Patrice Pearse*. Rennes: Imprimerie commerciale de Bretagne, 1932. 336 p. On Yeats and Pearse, pp. 47, 133-34, 152, 155, 224.

7221a. °MCCAY, HEDLEY: *Padraic Pearse: A New Biography*. Cork: Mercier Press, 1966. 95 p.

7222. PORTER, RAYMOND JAMES: *P. H. Pearse*. NY: Twayne, 1973. 168 p. (Twayne's English Authors Series. 154.)
Based on "P. H. Pearse: A Study of His Writings," °Ph.D. thesis, Columbia U, 1970. 252 p. (*DA*, 33:7 [Jan 1973], 3665A.)

See also J614, 2253a, 5940 (#13), 5947a, 5951, 6233, 6249, 6250, 6259, 6268, 7214, 7439.

Joseph Mary Plunkett

See J5947a, 5951, 6249, 6250, 6259, 6268, 6273, 7219.

Forrest Reid

See J769, 2254, 6287, 6290.

Lennox Robinson

7223. EVERSON, IDA G.: "Young Lennox Robinson and the Abbey Theatre's First American Tour (1911-1912)," *MD*, 9:1 (May 1966), 74-89.
Includes a list of places and dates of performances.

7224. GILLIS, HERBERT RUSSELL: "Lennox Robinson: Some of His Production and Direction Problems at the Abbey Theatre, Dublin, Ireland," M.A. thesis, Kent State U, 1949. vii, 104 p.

7225. O'CONOR, NORREYS JEPHSON: "A Dramatist of Changing Ireland," *Sewanee R*, 30:3 (July 1922), 277-85.

7226. °O'NEILL, MICHAEL JOSEPH: "Lennox Robinson: Playwright of a Changing Ireland," M.A. thesis, University College, Dublin, 1950.

7227. ————: *Lennox Robinson*. NY: Twayne, 1964. 192 p. (Twayne's English Authors Series. 9.)
Yeats is mentioned *passim*.

7228. PEAKE, DONALD JAMES: "Selected Plays of Lennox Robinson: A Mirror of the Anglo-Irish Ascendancy," °Ph.D. thesis, Southern Illinois U, 1972. 243 p. (*DA*, 33:9 [Mar 1973], 5340A.)

7229. PHILLIPSON, WULSTAN: "Lennox Robinson," *Downside R*, 77:249 (Summer 1959), 266-70.

7230. ROBINSON, LENNOX: *The Whiteheaded Boy: A Comedy in Three Acts*. With an introduction by Ernest Boyd. NY: Putnam's, 1921. xviii, 169 p.
"Introduction," vii-xviii; discusses Robinson's contributions to the Irish theater.

7231. SMITH, CHARLES B.: "Unity in Diversity: A Critical Study of the Drama of Lennox Robinson," Ph.D. thesis, Trinity College, Dublin, 1960. viii, 410 p.

7232. SPINNER, KASPAR: *Die alte Dame sagt: Nein! Drei irische Dramatiker: Lennox Robinson, Sean O'Casey, Denis Johnston*. Bern: Francke, 1961. vi, 210 p. (Schweizer anglistische Arbeiten. 52.)

7233. STARKIE, WALTER: "Lennox Robinson, 1886-1958," *Theatre Annual*, 16 (1959), 7-19.

See also J389, 547, 706, 5881, 5936, 6065, 6108, 6298, 6315, 6318, 6320, 6328, 6330, 6331, 6336, 6337a, 6360, 6499, 6505, 6514, 6706, 6782, 6813, 6836, 6956, 7214, 7333, 7385.

T. W. Rolleston

7234. °BEGLEY, PATRICK: "T. W. Rolleston," M.A. thesis, University College, Dublin, 1966.

7235. ROLLESTON, CHARLES HENRY: *Portrait of an Irishman: A Biographical Sketch of T. W. Rolleston*. London: Methuen, 1939. xv, 189 p.
Biographical references to Yeats, *passim* (see index). Reprints an article from an unidentified issue of *Irish Weekly Independent*, 1896, in which Rolleston comments on Yeats's poetry (pp. 20-21).

See also J1110, 1497, 5911, 5932, 6290.

AE (George William Russell) (Bibliography)

7236. ANON.: "Bibliographies of Irish Authors. No. 1: 'AE' (George W. Russell)," *Dublin Mag*, 5:1 (Jan-Mar 1930), 44-52.

7237. BLACK, HESTER M.: "A Check-list of First Editions of Works by John Millington Synge and George William Russell," *Friends of the Library of Trinity College, Dublin, Annual Bulletin*, 1956, 4-9.

7238. DENSON, ALAN: *Printed Writings of George W. Russell (AE): A Bibliography*. With some notes on his pictures and portraits. Foreword by Padraic Colum. Reminiscences of AE by M. J. Bonn. A note on AE and painting by Thomas Bodkin. Evanston: Northwestern UP, 1961. 255 p.
See also J6879.

7239. KINDILIEN, CARLIN T.: "The George Russell Collection at Colby College: A Check List," *Colby Library Q*, 4:2 (May 1955), 31-55.
Colby College possesses several (unpublished?) letters dealing with Yeats.

See also J389, 512.

AE (George William Russell) (Criticism)

7240. BIENS, FRIEDRICH: *"A. E.": George William Russell. Sein Leben und Werk im Lichte seiner theosophischen Weltanschauung*. Greifswald: Dallmeyer, 1934. 96 p. (Greifswalder Beiträge zur Literatur- und Stilforschung. 6.)

7241. COLUM, PADRAIC: "From Old Ireland Comes AE, Her Sage," *NYT*, 77:25565 (22 Jan 1928), V, 6-7, 20.

7242. CURRAN, CONSTANTINE P.: "George Russell (A. E.), 1867-1935," *Studies*, 24:95 (Sept 1935), 366-78.

7243. DANIELS, WILLIAM LAWS: "AE: 1867-1967," *University R* [Dublin], 4:2 (Summer 1967), 107-20.
    Contains numerous references to Yeats.

7244. ————: "The Early AE: Prose, Poetry, Life, 1867-1905," Ph.D. thesis, Harvard U, 1968. 3 v.
    On Yeats, *passim*. Quotes copiously from MS. sources.

7245. EGLINTON, JOHN: *A Memoir of AE: George William Russell*. London: Macmillan, 1937. vii, 291 p.
    On Yeats and AE, *passim*.

7246. FIGGIS, DARRELL: *AE (George W. Russell): A Study of a Man and a Nation*. Dublin: Maunsel, 1916. vii, 159 p.
    On Yeats, pp. 26-29, 133-38. "What was called the 'Irish Literary Revival' was truly an English Literary Revival conducted by Irishmen. In this W. B. Yeats had a conscious part; but AE was rather caught into it from his own separate world" (pp. 27-28).

7247. FORD, JULIA ELLSWORTH: "'A. E.,' the Neo-Celtic Mystic," *Poet-Lore*, 16:4 (Winter 1905), 82-86.

7248. °FRÉCHET, JACQUES-RENÉ: "Images and Imagination in A. E. (George Russell)," Thèse de lettres complémentaire, U of Paris, 1951.

7249. FRÉCHET, RENÉ: "A propos d'A. E., l'irlandais libre et fidèle," *EA*, 15:4 (Oct-Dec 1962), 365-74.

7250. GIBBON, MONK: "The Early Years of George Russell (AE) and His Connection with the Theosophical Movement," Ph.D. thesis, Trinity College, Dublin, 1947/48. iv, 399 p.
    "Correspondence with Yeats," 301-13.

7251. ————: "AE: The Years of Mystery," *Dublin Mag*, 31:1 (Jan-Mar 1956), 8-21.
    Includes some references to Yeats.

7252. ————: "AE and the Early Days of Theosophy in Dublin," *Dublin Mag*, 32:3 (July-Sept 1957), 25-37.
    Some references to Yeats's theosophical interests.

7253. HÖPF'L, HEINZ: *A. E. (George William Russell): Dichtung und Mystik. Versuch einer Deutung von A. E.'s mystischer Weltanschauung*. Bonn: Hanstein, 1935. 77 p. (Bonner Studien zur englischen Philologie. 23.)

7254. ————: "A. E. (George William Russell): Dichter und Mystiker," *Neuphilologische Monatsschrift*, 7:1 (Jan 1936), 39-45.

7255. MCFATE, PATRICIA ANN: "AE's Portraits of the Artists: A Study of *The Avatars*," *Éire-Ireland*, 6:4 (Winter 1971), 38-48.
    Some of the figures of the revival and their (supposed) disguises in AE's novel: Eglinton, Yeats, Moore, Maud Gonne, Katharine Tynan, Mrs. Yeats, Stephens, O'Connor, and AE himself.

7256. MERCHANT, FRANCIS JOHN: *A. E.: An Irish Promethean. A Study of the Contribution of George William Russell to World Culture*. Columbia, S.C.: Benedict College Press, 1954. iii, 242 p.

Based on "The Place of AE in Irish Culture," °Ph.D. thesis, New York U, 1951. iii, 564 p. (*DA*, 12:2 [1952], 188-89.)

7257. O'BRIEN, JAMES H.: "A. E. and the Self," *Arizona Q*, 22:3 (Autumn 1966), 258-68.
Includes frequent comparisons with Yeats.

7258. O FAOLAIN, SEAN: "The Humanity of AE," *Inisfail*, 1:1 (Mar 1933), 38-43.

7259. PELLIZZI, CAMILLO: "Literary Men of Ireland—The Poet AE," translated by Phyllis Bury, *Motley*, 3:4 (May 1934), 3-6.

7260. RUSSELL, DIARMUID: "'AE' (George William Russell)," *Atlantic Monthly*, 171:2 (Feb 1943), 51-57.

7261. RUSSELL, GEORGE WILLIAM: *Deirdre: A Legend in Three Acts*. Introduction by Herbert V. Fackler. Chicago: DePaul U, 1970. i, 34 p. (Irish Drama Series. 4.)
"Introduction," 1-7.

7262. SUMMERFIELD, HENRY: "A Mystic in the Modern World," *Iliff R*, 26:3 (Fall 1969), 13-21.

7263. TIERNEY, MICHAEL: "A Prophet of Mystic Nationalism—A. E.," *Studies*, 26:104 (Dec 1937), 568-80.

See also J453, 557, 611, 614, 617, 634, 669, 681, 729a, 743, 769, 788, 789, 839, 847, 1110, 1136, 1177, 1269, 1317, 1318, 1327, 1328, 1374, 1432, 1589, 1634, 1689, 1690, 1720, 1747, 1755, 1786, 1879, 1924, 1961, 1964, 2045, 2255-57, 2457, 2497, 2648, 2753, 2865, 2873, 3091, 3485, 3519, 3684a, 3688, 3691, 3697, 4337, 5881, 5909, 5911, 5922, 5932, 5944, 5945, 5947a, 5949, 5951, 5962, 5992, 6023, 6026, 6035, 6057, 6108, 6116, 6172, 6182, 6197, 6213, 6216, 6219, 6233, 6242, 6249, 6260, 6287, 6290, 6291, 6330, 6661a, 6695, 6744, 6875, 6961, 7012, 7073, 7198, 7272, 7401, 7442.

Fred Ryan

7264. KELLY, JOHN: "A Lost Abbey Play: Frederick Ryan's *The Laying of the Foundations*," *Ariel*, 1:3 (July 1970), 29-48.
See also J6455.

G. B. Shaw

7265. ANON.: "The Blanco Posnet Controversy," *Shaw Bulletin*, [1]:7 (Jan 1955), 1-9.
Includes statements by Shaw, Yeats, and Lady Gregory and Joyce's review.

7266. O'NEILL, MICHAEL J.: "Some Shavian Links with Dublin as Recorded in the Holloway Diaries," *Shaw R*, 2:8 (May 1959), 2-7.

See also J676, 1466, 5945, 6364, 6428, 6703, 6744, 6835, 7133, 7198.

Arthur Shields

7267. SWANDER, HOMER D.: "Shields at the Abbey: A Friend of Cathleen," *Éire-Ireland*, 5:2 (Summer 1970), 25-41.

See also J6603, 6619, 6773.

George Shiels

7268. °KELLY, J. J.: "George Shiels as an Exponent of Modern Irish Comedy," M.A. thesis, University College, Dublin, 1950.

See also J5947a, 6320, 6328, 6331, 6337a, 6499, 6763.

Dora Sigerson Shorter

7269. SMITH, SISTER MARIE EMILY: "A Biographical and Critical Study of Dora Sigerson Shorter (1866-1918)," Ph.D. thesis, U of Pennsylvania, 1954. xxii, 152 p. (*DA*, 14:6 [1954], 978.)

See also J1689.

George Sigerson

See J5911, 5938.

Somerville and Ross

7270. COLLIS, MAURICE: *Somerville and Ross: A Biography*. London: Faber & Faber, 1968. 286 p.
   For Martin Ross's unflattering impressions of Yeats see pp. 128-31.

7271. CRONIN, JOHN: *Somerville and Ross*. Lewisburg, Pa.: Bucknell UP, 1972. 111 p.

7272. CUMMINS, GERALDINE: *Dr. E. OE. Somerville: A Biography*. Being the first biography of the leading member of the famous literary partnership of E. OE. Somerville and Martin Ross, with a new bibliography of first editions compiled by Robert Vaughan and a preface by Lennox Robinson, Litt.D. London: Dakers, 1952. xv, 271 p.
   Contains a negligible chapter on "Some Literary Celebrities (AE., Yeats, G. B. S., The Founding of the Irish Academy of Letters)," 70-82.

7273. FEHLMANN, GUY: *Somerville et Ross: Témoins de l'Irlande d'hier*. Caen: Association des publications de la Faculté des Lettres et Sciences Humaines de l'Université de Caen, 1970. x, 516 p.

7274. FLANAGAN, THOMAS: "The Big House of Ross-Drishane," *Kenyon R*, 28:1 (Jan 1966), 54-78.

7275. LYONS, F. S. L.: "The Twilight of the Big House," *Ariel*, 1:3 (July 1970), 110-22.

7276. POWELL, VIOLET: *The Irish Cousins: The Books and Background of Somerville and Ross*. London: Heinemann, 1970. x, 214 p.
   Yeats is mentioned *passim* (see index). There is a nice story, by Saki, of a lady "notorious for unconventional manners" who was said to have "slept in a hammock and understood Yeats' poems. Her family denied both stories" (p. 117).

James Stephens

7277. ANON.: "The James Stephens Papers: A Catalogue," *Serif*, 2:2 (June 1965), 29-32.
   Lists the holdings of the Kent State U Library.

7278. BOYD, ERNEST A.: "A New Phase of the Irish Literary Revival: James Stephens," *New Ireland*, 2:44 (18 May 1916), 304-6.

7279. BRAMSBÄCK, BIRGIT: *James Stephens: A Literary and Bibliographical Study*. Upsala: Lundequist, 1959. 209 p. (Upsala Irish Studies. 4.)
"Introductory Chapter on James Stephens: A Literary Study," 13-54; mentions Yeats *passim* (see index). The bibliography (pp. 57-195) lists MSS. and printed material.

7280. CARY, RICHARD: "James Stephens at Colby College," *Colby Library Q*, 5:9 (Mar 1961), 224-52.

7281. CONRAD, GRACE: "L'Irlande et les irlandais dans les oeuvres de James Stephens," Doctorat d'Université thesis, U of Paris, 1955. ii, 342 p.

7282. FRIEDMAN, BARTON R.: "Returning to Ireland's Fountains: Nationalism and James Stephens," *Arizona Q*, 22:3 (Autumn 1966), 232-52.

7283. °MULHOLLAND, EILEEN: "James Stephens: An Appreciation," M.A. thesis, Columbia U, 1928.

7284. POEPPING, HILDE: *James Stephens: Eine Untersuchung über die irische Erneuerungsbewegung in der Zeit von 1900-1930*. Halle: Niemeyer, 1940. iii, 101 p. (Schriftenreihe der Deutschen Gesellschaft für keltische Studien. 4.)

7285. PYLE, HILARY: *James Stephens: His Work and an Account of His Life*. London: Routledge & Kegan Paul, 1965. xi, 196 p.
On Yeats and Stephens, *passim* (see index), especially pp. 56-57 and 80-83 (their methods of reciting verse).

7285a. TYNAN, KATHARINE: "The Poetry of James Stephens," *J of English Studies*, 1:2 (Sept 1912—Jan 1913), 92-107.

See also J366a, 370, 512, 611, 634, 676, 729a, 1021, 1317, 1634, 1689, 1755, 1964, 2045, 2237, 2497, 2873, 3683, 3684a, 3691, 5880, 5881, 5884, 5911, 5919, 5932, 5935, 5947a, 5949, 6023, 6108, 6157, 6219, 6233, 6250, 6259, 6267, 6287, 6290, 6875, 7255, 7416.

J. M. Synge (Bibliography)

7286. DYSINGER, ROBERT E.: "The John Millington Synge Collection at Colby College: A Checklist," *Colby Library Q*, 4:9 (Feb 1957), 166-72; :11 (Aug 1957), 192-94.

7287. LEVITT, PAUL M.: *John Millington Synge: A Bibliography of Published Criticism*. Dublin: Irish UP, 1974. ix, 224 p.
The introduction, pp. 1-8, sketches the history of Synge criticism; the bibliography seems to be fairly complete. It is arranged as follows: bibliographies, biography, general dramatic criticism, general literary criticism, criticism of single works, less important material, and material published in daily and weekly papers (mostly on the *Playboy* riots). Due to the late arrival of the book, I was unable to incorporate some Yeats interviews and statements listed by Levitt.

7288. MACMANUS, M. J.: "Bibliographies of Irish Authors. No. 4: John Millington Synge," *Dublin Mag*, 5:4 (Oct-Dec 1930), 47-51.

7289. [MACPHAIL, IAN]: *John Millington Synge, 1871-1909*. A catalogue of an exhibition held at Trinity College Library, Dublin, on the occasion of the fiftieth anniversary of his death. Dublin: Dolmen Press for the Friends of the Library of Trinity College, Dublin, 1959. 40 p.

7290. ————: "John Millington Synge: Some Bibliographical Notes," *Irish Book*, 1:1 (Spring 1959), 3-10.

7291. MIKHAIL, EDWARD HALIM: "Sixty Years of Synge Criticism, 1907-1967: A Selective Bibliography," *Bulletin of Bibliography*, 27:1 (Jan-Mar 1970), 11-13; :2 (Apr-June 1970), 53-56.
   328 items, not annotated.

7292. MULCAHY, BRIGID MARY: "A Bibliography of J. M. Synge," [typewritten bibliography submitted in part requirement for the diploma in librarianship of the U of London, 1951. 47 p.].

7293. SADDLEMYER, ANN: "'Infinite Riches in a Little Room'--The Manuscripts of John Millington Synge," *Long Room*, #3 (Spring 1971), 23-31.
   Description of the Trinity College, Dublin, collection. See also next item.

7294. *The Synge Manuscripts in the Library of Trinity College, Dublin.*
A catalogue prepared on the occasion of the Synge centenary exhibition, 1971. Dublin: Dolmen Press, 1971. 55 p.
   The following items are of interest: an article, "The Dramatic Movement in Ireland" (MS. 4347); a collection of documents relating to theater business including press opinions of Abbey plays (MS. 4355); notes on Yeats's Blake edition (MS. 4378); and some letters from Yeats and other celebrities of the revival (MSS. 4424-29).

See also J363, 364, 366a, 371, 389, 533, 7237, 7317.

J. M. Synge (Criticism)

7295. °ADELMAN, GARY S.: "Synge and the Irish Audience of His Time," M.A. thesis, Columbia U, 1958. 83 p.

7296. ALLEN, BEVERLY S.: "John Synge: A Problem of His Genius," *Colonnade*, 11:1 (Jan 1916), 5-15.

7297. ANDERSON, PATRICK: "Down among the Nuts," *Spectator*, 221:7311 (9 Aug 1968), 196-97.
   Includes some remarks on the mutual Yeats-Synge influence.

7298. ANON.: "John Millington Synge (1871-1909)," *Eire-Ireland* [Dublin], #836 (15 Apr 1971), 1-14.

7299. ANON.: Editorial on the death of Synge, *Irish Times*, 51:16141 (25 Mar 1909), 6.
   See also the obituary on p. 8.

7300. ANON.: "J. M. Synge: His Work and Genius," *Irish Times*, 53:16713 (23 Jan 1911), 7.

7301. ANON.: "Mr. J. M. Synge," *Manchester Guardian*, #19540 (25 Mar 1909), 7.
   Obituary; see also the editorial on p. 6.

7302. ANON.: "A Playboy of the Western World," *Pall Mall Gazette*, #24268 (16 Jan 1911), 4.

7303. ANON.: "The 'Ascendancy' Writer," *TLS*, 70:3618 (2 July 1971), 749-50.

7303a. ANON.: "Mr. Yeats and Some Others," *Weekly Sun*, #723 (15 June 1907), 3.

Yeats was right to call the police because *The Playboy*, although a "ridiculous play," deserves to be seen in its entirety.

7304. AUFHAUSER, ANNEMARIE: *Sind die Dramen von John Millington Synge durch französische Vorbilder beeinflusst?* Würzburg: Mayr, 1935. vii, 63 p. (Dr. phil. thesis, U of München, 1935.)
No, they are not. Synge is the Irish dramatist incarnate.

7305. BAŁUTOWA, BRONISŁAWA: "Wpływ kultury ludowej na odrodzenie irlandzkiego (John Millington Synge)" [The influence of folk culture on the renaissance of the Irish theater], *Prace Polonistyczne*, 9 (1951), 281-305.
Yeats is mentioned *passim*.

7306. BATEMAN, REGINALD: *Reginald Bateman, Teacher and Soldier: A Memorial Volume of Selections from His Lectures and Other Writings*. London: Sotheran for the U of Saskatchewan, 1922. xi, 147 p.
"Synge," 85-91; incomplete notes of an address to a study club.

7307. BAUMAN, RICHARD: "John Millington Synge and Irish Folklore," *Southern Folklore Q*, 27:4 (Dec 1963), 267-79.

7308. BENNETT, CHARLES A.: "The Plays of John M. Synge," *Yale R*, 1:2 (Jan 1912), 192-205.

7309. BESSAI, DIANE E.: "Little Hound in Mayo: Synge's Playboy and the Comic Tradition in Irish Literature," *Dalhousie R*, 48:3 (Autumn 1968), 372-83.

7310. BICKLEY, FRANCIS: "Synge and the Drama," *New Q*, 3:9 (Feb 1910), 73-84.

7311. ————: *J. M. Synge and the Irish Dramatic Movement*. London: Constable / Boston: Houghton Mifflin, 1912. 97 p.
Reprinted °NY: Russell & Russell, 1968. On Yeats, *passim*, especially in "Yeats and the Movement," 49-66 (on the early work); and "The Irish Theatre," 67-85 (on Yeats's plays). Reviewed by F. L. B., "The Celtic Renaissance," *Cambridge R*, 34:859 (22 May 1913), 479-81.

7312. BLAKE, WARREN BARTON: "John Synge and His Plays," *Dial*, 50:590 (16 Jan 1911), 37-41.

7313. ————: "A Great Irish Playwright: John M. Synge," *Theatre*, 13:124 (June 1911), 202, 204.

7314. BOURGEOIS, MAURICE: *John Millington Synge and the Irish Theatre*. London: Constable, 1913. xvi, 338 p.
Reprinted °NY: Blom, 1965. Contains numerous references to Yeats, especially to *Deirdre* (see index).
Reviews:
1. Anon., "The Modern Irish Theater," *Independent*, 78:3411 (20 Apr 1914), 140.
2. Anon., "Mr. Yeats's Theatre," *Nation* [London], 14:19 (7 Feb 1914), 799-800.
3. W. P. Ryan, "Synge and the Irish Theatre," *Bookman*, 45:267 (Dec 1913), 170-71.
4. James W. Tupper, "Synge and the Irish Theatre," *Dial*, 56:665 (1 Mar 1914), 177-79.
5. Sir Frederick Wedmore, *Certain Comments*. London: Selwyn & Blount, 1925. 95 p.: "The Irish Theatre," 61-65.

7315. BROOKS, SYDNEY: "The Irish Peasant as a Dramatic Issue," *Harper's Weekly*, 51:2620 (9 May 1907), 344.
Comments on the *Playboy* row and Yeats's involvement in it.

7316. BROPHY, G. M.: "J. M. Synge and the Revival of the Irish Drama," *Everyman*, 1:1 (18 Oct 1912), 8.

7317. BUSHRUI, SUHEIL BADI (ed): *Sunshine and the Moon's Delight: A Centenary Tribute to John Millington Synge, 1871-1909*. With a foreword by A. Norman Jeffares. Gerrards Cross: Smythe / Beirut: American U of Beirut, 1972. 356 p.
Contents: 1. A. Norman Jeffares: "Foreword," 9-15.
2. Marcus Smith: "Centennial Poem," 19.
3. Jean Alexander: "Synge's Play of Choice: *The Shadow of the Glen*," 21-31.
4. T. R. Henn, "*Riders to the Sea*: A Note," 38-39.
5. David R. Clark: "Synge's 'Perpetual "Last Day"'": Remarks on *Riders to the Sea*," 41-51.
6. M. J. Sidnell: "*The Well of the Saints* and the Light of This World," 53-59.
7. Augustine Martin: "Christy Mahon and the Apotheosis of Loneliness," 61-73.
8. Vivian Mercier: "*The Tinker's Wedding*," 75-89.
9. John Rees Moore: "Synge's *Deirdre* and the Sorrows of Mortality," 91-105.
10. Ann Saddlemyer: "Art, Nature, and 'The Prepared Rationality': A Reading of *The Aran Islands* and Related Writings," 107-20.
11. Lanto M. Synge: "The Autobiography of J. M. Synge," 121-40.
12. Francis Warner: "A Note on the Poems of J. M. Synge," 141-52.
13. Elizabeth Coxhead: "Synge and Lady Gregory," 153-58.
14. Robert O'Driscoll: "Yeats's Conception of Synge," 159-71.
15. Richard M. Kain: "The *Playboy* Riots," 173-88.
16. Suheil Badi Bushrui: "Synge and Yeats," 189-203.
17. Douglas Duncan: "Synge and Jonson (with a Parenthesis on Ronsard)," 205-18.
18. John Munro: "Synge and the Drama of the Late Nineteenth Century," 219-30.
19. Robert Hogan: "The Influence of Synge in Modern Irish Drama," 231-44.
20. Ghassan Maleh: "Synge in the Arab World," 245-52.
21. Shotaro Oshima: "Synge in Japan," 253-63. See also J80.
22. Gérard Leblanc: "Synge in France," 265-70.
23. Johannes Kleinstück: "Synge in Germany," 271-77.
24. Alan Price: "A Survey of Recent Work on J. M. Synge," 279-95.
25. Alan Bliss: "A Synge Glossary," 297-316.
26. "A Select Bibliography," 317-38 (works by and about Synge).
Reviews:
1. Anon., "Up for Judgment," *TLS*, 71:3667 (9 June 1972), 662.

7318. CANBY, HENRY SEIDEL: On Synge, *Yale R*, 2:4 (July 1913), 767-72.

7318a. CASEY, HELEN: "Synge's Use of the Anglo-Irish Idiom," *English J (College Edition)*, 27:9 (Nov 1938), 773-76.

7319. CAZAMIAN, MADELEINE: "Le théâtre de J. M. Synge," *Revue du mois*, yr 6 / 12:70 (10 Oct 1911), 456-68.

7320. CHICA SALAS, SUSANA: "Synge y García Lorca: Aproximacíon de dos mundos poéticos," *Revista hispanica moderna*, 27:2 (Apr 1961), 128-37.

7321. CLARK, DAVID RIDGLEY (ed): *John Millington Synge: "Riders to the Sea."* Columbus, Ohio: Merrill, 1970. v, 137 p.

Introduction, text of the play, and previously published criticism.

7322. CLEMENT, KATHARINE ELIZABETH: "John Millington Synge," M.A. thesis, U of Colorado, 1927. ii, 97 p.

7322a. COLUM, PADRAIC: "Letter from Mr. Padraic Colum, Author of *The Land*," *Evening Telegraph*, ns #7950 (31 Jan 1907), 2.

About *The Playboy*. The same page carries a report of the disturbances and two letters commenting on Yeats's views.

7323. CONNELL, F. NORREYS: "John Millington Synge," *English R*, 2:3 (June 1909), 609-13.

7324. CORKERY, DANIEL: *Synge and Anglo-Irish Literature.* Cork: Mercier Press, 1966 [1931]. vi, 247 p.

A controversial book. Corkery contends that the so-called Anglo-Irish literature is not rooted in Ireland at all, but is part of the Ascendancy. Although this literature treats Irish themes, it is written for foreign markets, which in turn impose the rules of treatment and selection on the writer. A true Anglo-Irish literature should deal with "The Religious Consciousness of the People," "Irish Nationalism," and "The Land" (p. 19). Synge was the one great exception of an Ascendancy writer who "went into the huts of the people and lived with them" (p. 27). See also J6328 (#3).

Reviews:

1. Anon., "A Provincial Irishman," *Modern Scot*, 2:3 (Oct 1931), 240-43.
2. Anon., "Synge and Irish Life," *TLS*, 30:1538 (23 July 1931), 578.
3. Austin Clarke, "Synge and Ireland," *NSt*, 2:27 (29 Aug 1931), 258-59.
4. Hugh De Blacam, "A New School in Ireland," *Spectator*, 147:5377 (18 July 1931), 89.
5. Sean O'Faolain, *Criterion*, 11:42 (Oct 1931), 140-42.
6. P. S. O'Hegarty, *Dublin Mag*, 7:1 (Jan-Mar 1932), 51-56.

7325. CORNIER, SIDSEL: *John Millington Synge et Arne Garborg. L'homme et son milieu naturel: Aggressivité, passivité et harmonie.* Caen: Association des Publications de la Faculté des Lettres et Sciences Humaines de l'Université de Caen, 1971. 200 p.

7325a. Ó Cuisín, Seumas [COUSINS, JAMES H.]: "J. M. Synge: His Art and Message," *Sinn Féin*, 4:166 (17 July 1909), 1.

7326. COUSTEAU, JACQUES: "Synge, vagabond solitaire et passioné," *Cahiers de la Compagnie Madeleine Renaud--Jean-Louis Barrault*, #37 (1962), 37-41.

7327. COXHEAD, ELIZABETH: *J. M. Synge and Lady Gregory.* London: Longmans Green, 1962. 35 p. (Writers and Their Work. 149.)

7328. CUSACK, CYRIL: "A Player's Reflections on *Playboy*," *MD*, 4:3 (Dec 1961), 300-305.

Includes comments on the Abbey Theatre.

7328a. CZÁSZÁR, EDE: "*The Playboy of the Western World*," *Angol és amerikai filológiai tanulmányok*, 1 (1971), 196-207.

7329. DALY, LORNA M.: "John Millington Synge," *Blarney Mag*, #14 (Summer 1958), 13-16.

7330. DEANE, SEAMUS: "Synge's Poetic Use of Language," *Mosaic*, 5:1 (Fall 1971), 27-36.

As distinct from "Synge's use of poetic language." See also J7349 (#9).

7331. ELLEHAUGE, MARTIN: *Striking Figures among Modern English Dramatists* [. . .]. Copenhagen: Levin & Munksgaard, 1931. 151 p.
   "J. M. Synge," 16-29.

7332. ESTILL, ADELAIDE DUNCAN: "The Sources of Synge," Ph.D. thesis, U of Pennsylvania, 1939. iii, 51 p.

7333. EVERSON, IDA G.: "Lennox Robinson and Synge's *Playboy* (1911-1930): Two Decades of American Cultural Growth," *New England Q*, 44:1 (Mar 1971), 3-21.
   Discusses Robinson's efforts to present the play to American audiences, especially at Amherst, Massachusetts.

7334. FERRIS, WILLIAM R.: "Folklore and Folklife in the Works of J. M. Synge," *NY Folklore Q*, 27:4 (Dec 1971), 339-56.

7335. FIGGIS, DARRELL: "J. M. Synge," *Bookman*, 40:235 (Apr 1911), 30-33.

7336. FLETCHER, D.: "The Plays of Synge," *Transactions of the Rochdale Literary & Scientific Society*, 11 (1912-13), 99-104.

7337. FLORENCE, JEAN: "John Millington Synge," *Phalange*, yr 8 ·/ 15:89 (20 Nov 1913), 463-68.

7337a. FREYER, GRATTAN: "The Little World of J. M. Synge," *Politics and Letters*, 1:4 (Summer 1948), 5-12.

7338. GASSNER, JOHN: *Masters of the Drama*. NY: Random House, 1940. xvii, 804 p.
   "John Millington Synge and the Irish Muse," 524-74; includes notes on Yeats, O'Casey, and Paul Vincent Carroll.

7339. GERSTENBERGER, DONNA: *John Millington Synge*. NY: Twayne, 1964. 157 p. (Twayne's English Authors Series. 12.)
   On Yeats and Synge, *passim* (see index).

7339a. °GIBBS, J. M.: "Nationalism and Drama: An Examination of the Inter-action of National Mood and National Traditions with the Playwright in the Early Work of Henrik Ibsen, John M. Synge and Wole Soyinka," M.Litt. thesis, U of Bristol, 1971/72.

7340. GONNE, MAUD: "A propos de J. M. Synge," *Entretiens idéalistes*, yr 9 / 15:88 (Jan 1914), 31-33.
   See also J6918.

7341. GOSSE, EDMUND: "The Playwright of the Western Wild," *Morning Post*, 139:43271 (26 Jan 1911), 2.

7342. GREENE, DAVID HERBERT: "The Drama of J. M. Synge: A Critical Study," Ph.D. thesis, Harvard U, 1942. ii, 380 p.

7343. ————: "Synge's Unfinished *Deirdre*," *PMLA*, 63:4 (Dec 1948), 1314-21.
   Yeats is mentioned *passim*.

7344. ————: "Synge and the Irish," *Colby Library Q*, 4:9 (Feb 1957), 158-66.

7345. ————, and EDWARD MILLINGTON STEPHENS: *J. M. Synge, 1871-1909*. NY: Macmillan, 1959. xiii, 321 p.
   The standard biography; Yeats and the Abbey Theatre are referred to *passim* (see index).

Reviews:
1. Anon., "Tinkers and Bully Boys," *Newsweek*, 53:16 (20 Apr 1959), 119.
2. Anon., "Farewell to Irish Fairies but Not to Playboys," *Times*, #54478 (4 June 1959), 15.
3. Anon., "Playboy of the Irish Stage," *TLS*, 58:2990 (19 June 1959), 370.
4. DeLancey Ferguson, "John Millington Synge and the Great Period of the Irish Renaissance," *NYHTB*, 19 Apr 1959, 5.
5. Russell A. Fraser, "Ireland Made Him," *Nation*, 190:8 (20 Feb 1960), 171-73.
6. Donna Gerstenberger, *WHR*, 17:2 (Spring 1963), 193.
7. Monk Gibbon, *Studies*, 48:[] (Autumn 1959), 359-61.
8. John Hewitt, *Listener*, 62:1593 (8 Oct 1959), 590.
9. Ellen Douglass Leyburn, *MD*, 3:1 (May 1960), 93-95.
10. Louis MacNeice, *London Mag*, 7:8 (Aug 1960), 70-73.
11. Vivian Mercier, "How Did the Miracle Come About?" *NYTBR*, 64:16 (19 Apr 1959), 5, 20.
12. Donat O'Donnell [Conor Cruise O'Brien], "Mother's Tongue," *Spectator*, 203:6842 (14 Aug 1959), 201.
13. Walter Starkie, "Everything Irish Was Sacred," *SatR*, 42:16 (18 Apr 1959), 19-20.

7346. GREENE, DAVID HERBERT: "Synge and the Celtic Revival," *MD*, 4:3 (Dec 1961), 292-99.

7347. ————: "Synge in the West of Ireland," *Mosaic*, 5:1 (Fall 1971), 1-8.

7347a. GRENE, NICHOLAS: "A Critical Study of the Comedies of J. M. Synge: Their Relation to the Irish Background and to the Context of European Drama," Ph.D. thesis, U of Cambridge, 1973. iii, 323 p.

7348. GRIGSON, GEOFFREY: "Synge," *NSt*, 64:1649 (19 Oct 1962), 528-29.

7349. HARMON, MAURICE (ed): *J. M. Synge: Centenary Papers, 1971*. Dublin: Dolmen Press, 1972. xv, 202 p.
   Contents: 1. Roger McHugh: "Preface," ix-xiii.
   2. Seán Ó Tuama: "Synge and the Idea of a National Literature," 1-17.
   3. Seán Ó Súilleabháin: "Synge's Use of Irish Folklore," 18-34.
   4. Alan J. Bliss: "The Language of Synge," 35-62.
   5. Hugh Hunt: "Synge and the Actor--A Consideration of Style," 63-74.
   6. Hilary Berrow: "Eight Nights in the Abbey," 75-87; on the *Playboy* riots.
   7. Ann Saddlemyer: *"Deirdre of the Sorrows*: Literature First--Drama Afterwards," 88-107.
   8. T. R. Henn: "The Prose of John Millington Synge," 108-26.
   9. Seamus Deane: "Synge's Poetic Use of Language," 127-44; see also J7330.
   10. Jon Stallworthy: "The Poetry of Synge and Yeats," 145-66.
   11. Thomas Kilroy: "Synge and Modernism," 167-79.
   12. David H. Greene: "J. M. Synge--A Centenary Appraisal," 180-96; reprinted from *Éire-Ireland*, 6:4 (Winter 1971), 71-86, with footnotes added.
   Reviews:
   1. Anon., "The Pagan Roots," *TLS*, 71:3681 (22 Sept 1972), 1112.

7349a. HENN, T. R.: "The Solitary Man," *Hibernia*, 36 [i.e., 35]:9 (30 Apr 1971), 14-15.

7350. ————: "John Millington Synge: A Reconsideration," *Hermathena*, #112 (Autumn 1971), 5-21.

7351. HOARE, J. E.: "John Synge," *University Mag* [Montreal], 10:1 (Feb 1911), 91-109.

7351a. HOLLOWAY, JOSEPH: "John Millington Synge as Critic of Boucicaultian Irish Drama," *Evening Herald*, 22:165 (10 July 1913), 2.

7352. HONE, J. M.: "J. M. Synge," *Everyman*, 2:44 (15 Aug 1913), 555.

7353. HOWE, PERCIVAL PRESLAND: *J. M. Synge: A Critical Study*. London: Secker, 1912. 216 p.
   Interprets Synge's works without attempting to see them in the context of the Irish literary revival or the development of 20th-century Anglo-Irish drama.

7354. JACKSON, HOLBROOK: "The Plays of J. M. Synge," *Book-Lover's Mag*, 8:2 (1908), 53-57.

7355. ————: *All Manner of Folk: Interpretations and Studies*. London: Richards, 1912. 206 p.
   "John M. Synge," 61-77.

7356. JOHNSTON, DENIS: *John Millington Synge*. NY: Columbia UP, 1965. 48 p. (Columbia Essays on Modern Writers. 12.)
   Compares Yeats and Synge briefly, especially *The Land of Heart's Desire* and *In the Shadow of the Glen*, p. 14.

7356a. JORDAN, JOHN: "Synge," *Hibernia*, 36 [i.e., 35]:7 (2 Apr 1971), 9; :10 (14 May 1971), 8.

7357. KAIN, RICHARD M.: "A Scrapbook of the '*Playboy* Riots,'" *Emory UQ*, 22:1 (Spring 1966), 5-17.
   Includes notes on Yeats's involvement.

7358. °KENNELLY, BRENDAN: "The Two Irelands of Synge and O'Casey," *New Knowledge*, 6:1 (1966), 961-65.

7359. KILROY, JAMES (ed): *The "Playboy" Riots*. Dublin: Dolmen Press, 1971. 101 p. (Irish Theatre Series. 4.)
   Reprints numerous contemporary reviews and articles from newspapers and periodicals. The following items show Yeats's involvement:
   "Abbey Theatre Scenes [. . .]: Mr. Yeats' Appeal for a Fair Hearing," 25-31; from *Freeman's J*, 140:[] (30 Jan 1907), 7.
   "Interview with Mr. W. B. Yeats [. . .]," 31-34; from *ibid.*
   "Police Prosecutions [. . .]: Mr. W. B. Yeats Examined [. . .]," 47-51; from *Freeman's J*, 140:[] (31 Jan 1907), 8 (the Piaras Beaslai case).
   "The Poet Is Pleased: Interview with Mr. Yeats," 64-65; from *Irish Independent*, 16:28 (1 Feb 1907), 5.
   Part of an interview with Yeats about William Boyle's defection from the Abbey, pp. 80-81; from *Freeman's J*, 140:[] (4 Feb 1907), 4.
   "Parricide and Public: Discussion at the Abbey Theatre," 81-88; from *Freeman's J*, 140:[] (5 Feb 1907), 6-7. Includes Yeats's contributions.
   Criticism of Yeats's defense of the play, pp. 89-91; partial reprint of "The Playboy of the West: The Freedom of the Theatre [. . .]," *Sinn Féin*, 2:41 (9 Feb 1907), 2.
   "Brittania Rule-the-Wave: A Comedy (In One Act and in Prose)," 91-94; reprinted from *Sinn Féin*, same issue, 3. A parody of *Cathleen ni Houlihan*, attributed to AE; also in *Nationality*, 1:3 (29 Jan 1916), 5-6.

7360. KILROY, THOMAS: "Synge the Dramatist," *Mosaic*, 5:1 (Fall 1971), 9–16.
Includes a note on the Yeats–Synge relationship.

7361. KOSTIĆ, VESELIN: "Džon Milington Sing dramatičar irske obnove,"
Savremenik, yr 7 / 13:2 (Feb 1961), 189–203.

7362. KRAUSE, DAVID: "'The Rageous Ossean': Patron–Hero of Synge and
O'Casey," *MD*, 4:3 (Dec 1961), 268–91.

7362a. ————: "The Barbarous Sympathies of Antic Irish Comedy," *Malahat R*,
#22 (Apr 1972), 99–117.
Mainly on Synge and Fitzmaurice with a note on Yeats.

7363. KRIEGER, HANS: *John Millington Synge, ein Dichter der "keltischen
Renaissance."* Marburg: Elwert, 1916. 152 p. (Dr. phil. thesis, U of
Marburg, 1916.)

7364. KRONENBERGER, LOUIS: *The Thread of Laughter: Chapters on English
Stage Comedy from Jonson to Maugham*. NY: Knopf, 1952. x, 298, vi p.
"Synge," 279–88.

7365. KRUTCH, JOSEPH WOOD: *"Modernism" in Modern Drama*. NY: Russell &
Russell, 1962 [1953]. xiii, 138 p.
"Synge and the Irish Protest," 88–103.

7366. °LAWSON, JONATHAN M.: "John M. Synge: Regional Dramatist," M.A.
thesis, Texas Christian U, 1966.

7366a. LEECH, CLIFFORD: "John Synge and the Drama of His Time," *MD*, 16:3/4
(Dec 1973), 223–37.

7367. LERNER, LAURENCE: "Homage to Synge," *Encounter*, 38:1 (Jan 1972),
62–67.

7368. LOWTHER, GEORGE: "J. M. Synge and the Irish Revival," *Oxford and
Cambridge R*, #25 (Nov 1912), 43–59.

7369. LYDON, J. F.: "John Millington Synge: The Man and His Background,"
Mosaic, 5:1 (Fall 1971), 17–26.

7370. MacCarten [MCCARTAN], PATRICK: "Lady Gregory, the Language, and the
Abbey Plays," *Irish Freedom*, #15 (Jan 1912), 7.
Actually on the *Playboy* riots.

7371. M[ACDONAGH], T[HOMAS]: "J. M. Synge: Irish Dramatist, Writer, Poet,"
T. P.'s Weekly, 13:335 (9 Apr 1909), 469.

7372. °MAHER, WILLIAM: "John M. Synge," M.A. thesis, University College,
Dublin, 1948.

7373. MALONE, ANDREW E.: "Synge and O'Casey," *Tribune* [Cork], 1:1 (12 Mar
1926), 17–19.

7374. MASEFIELD, JOHN: *John M. Synge: A Few Personal Recollections with
Biographical Notes*. NY: Macmillan, 1915. 35 p.
Part of the material was first published in *Contemporary R*, 99:544
(Apr 1911), 470–78. Reprinted in *Recent Prose*. NY: Macmillan, 1933.
ix, 294 p. (pp. 163–87).

7375. MEYERFELD, MAX: "Letters of J. M. Synge," *Yale R*, 13:4 (July 1924),
690–706.

7376. MICHIE, DONALD M.: "Synge and His Critics," *MD*, 15:4 (Mar 1973),
427–31.

7377. MONTAGUE, CHARLES EDWARD: *Dramatic Values*. London: Methuen, 1911. ix, 276 p.
"The Plays of J. M. Synge," 1-15; on the acting at the Abbey, pp. 52-57.

7378. °MOONEY, MARY GENEVIEVE A.: "A Folkal Habitation and a Game: Some Characteristics of the Irish 'National Mood' in the Drama of Synge and the Early O'Casey," M.A. thesis, University College, Dublin, 1967.

7379. MURPHY, DANIEL J.: "The Reception of Synge's *Playboy* in Ireland and America: 1907-1912," *BNYPL*, 64:10 (Oct 1960), 515-33.

7380. NEWLIN, NICHOLAS: "The Language of Synge's Plays: The Irish Element," Ph.D. thesis, U of Pennsylvania, 1949. xii, 187 p.
Includes a discussion of *The Unicorn from the Stars*.

7380a. NORDMAN, C. A.: "J. M. Synge, dramatikern," *Finsk tidskrift*, 79 (July-Dec 1915), 26-70.

7381. O'CONNOR, ANTONY CYRIL: "Synge and National Drama," *Unitas*, 27:2 (Apr-June 1954), 294-346; :3 (July-Sept 1954), 430-64.

7382. O'CONNOR, FRANK: "A Classic One-Act Play," *Radio Times*, 94:1214 (3 Jan 1947), 4.
Riders to the Sea. Compares Yeats and Synge.

7383. O'DONOGHUE, D. J.: "John M. Synge: A Personal Appreciation," *Irish Independent*, 18:73 (26 Mar 1909), 4.

7384. ————: "The Synge Boom: Foreign Influences," *Irish Independent*, 20:198 (21 Aug 1911), 4.
Comments on Yeats's ideas about Synge. Further correspondence in subsequent issues.

7385. Ó h-Éigeartaigh [O'HEGARTY], P. S.: "Irish Dramatic Impressions. I. --Synge," *Irish Nation*, 2:81 (16 July 1910), 1.
Continued in the following issues: II.--Robinson, :82 (23 July 1910), 1; III.--Colum, :83 (30 July 1910), 1; IV.--Lady Gregory, :84 (6 Aug 1910), 1; V.--Poetical Drama and the Pilgrim Players, :85 (13 Aug 1910), 1 (on Yeats's plays); VI.--Boyle, :90 (17 Sept 1910), 1; VII. --Yeats, :91 (24 Sept 1910), 1; IX.--The [Abbey] Players, :92 (1 Oct 1910), 1.

7386. Ó MARCAIGH, CAOIMHÍN: *The Playboy of the Western World*. Dublin: Educational Company, 1972. 45 p. (Inscapes. 3.)

7387. O'NEILL, MICHAEL J.: "Holloway on Synge's Last Days," *MD*, 6:2 (Sept 1963), 126-30.

7388. ORBÓK, ATTILA: "John Millington Synge," *Nagyvilág*, 4:4 (Apr 1959), 577-82.

7389. Ó SAOTHRAÍ, SÉAMUS: *Díolaim inseora* [The diary of a journalist]. Dublin: Foilseacháin Náisiúnta Teoranta, 1970. viii, 220 p.
"Synge agus Ghaeilge," 83-85.

7390. O SÍOCHÁIN, P. A.: *Aran: Islands of Legend*. Dublin: Foilsiúcháin Éireann, 1962. viii, 192 p.
"Synge and the Aran Island," 159-66; "Synge's Life on the Islands," 167-76; "The Islands Yesterday and Today," 177-87.

7391. P., A.: "John Millington Synge," *Evening Standard*, #27006 (24 Jan 1911), 5.

7392. [PEARSE, P. H.]: "The Passing of Anglo-Irish Drama," *Claidheamh Soluis*, 8:48 (9 Feb 1907), 7.
Mostly on the *Playboy* affair.

7393. PITTWOOD, ERNEST H.: "John Millington Synge," *Holborn R*, os 55 / ns 4:[3] (July 1913), 488-501.

7394. POUPEYE, CAMILLE: "Le théâtre irlandais: J. M. Synge," *Renaissance d'Occident*, yr 4 / 8:6 (Dec 1923), 1559-80.

7395. PRICE, ALAN: *Synge and Anglo-Irish Drama*. London: Methuen, 1961. xi, 236 p.
Includes a survey of Synge criticism and a chapter on "Yeats and Synge," 51-68.
Reviews:
1. J. R. Brown, *MLR*, 57:3 (July 1962), 434-35.
2. Herbert Huscher, *Anglia*, 80:1/2 (1962), 226-31.
3. Edwin Rhodes, "Sailing from Byzantium," *Acorn*, 1:1 (Winter 1961), 20-22.

7396. ――――: "Synge's Prose Writings: A First View of the Whole," *MD*, 11:3 (Dec 1968), 221-26.

7397. PRITCHETT, VICTOR SAWDON: *In My Good Books*. London: Chatto & Windus, 1942. 192 p.
"The End of the Gael," 155-60; on Synge and Joyce.

7398. QUINN, OWEN: "No Garland for John Synge," *Envoy*, 3:11 (Oct 1950), 44-51.

7399. R.: "Synge a Yeats" [Synge and Yeats], *Jeviště*, 2:43 (27 Oct 1921), 638-40.
More on Synge than on Yeats.

7400. RAHILLY, SEAN O'MAHONY: "Synge and the Early Days of the Abbey," *Irish Press*, 19:94 (21 Apr 1949), 4.
Interview with Maire O'Neill.

7401. RIVA, SERAFINO: *La traduzione celtica e la moderna letteratura irlandese. I. John Millington Synge*. Roma: "Religio," 1937. v, 319 p.
Contains "La triade crepuscolare: John M. Synge, W. B. Yeats, George W. Russell (AE)," 148-56; and "William Butler Yeats," 162-68. No more published.

7402. ROBERTS, GEORGE: "A National Dramatist," *Shanachie*, #3 (Mar 1907), 57-60.

7402a. ROLLESTON, T. W.: "The *Playboy* as a Book," *Irish Independent*, 16: 56 (6 Mar 1907), 7.

7403. ROY, JAMES A.: "J. M. Synge and the Irish Literary Movement," *Anglia*, os 37 / ns 25:[] (June 1913), 129-45.

7404. RYAN, W. P.: "A Singer 'o' the Green,'" *Daily Chronicle*, #15277 (4 Feb 1911), 6.

7405. SADDLEMYER, ANN: "Rabelais versus a Kempis: The Art of J. M. Synge," *Komos*, 1:3 (Oct 1967), 85-96.

7406. ――――: *J. M. Synge and Modern Comedy*. Dublin: Dolmen Press, 1968. 32 p.
Comments on Yeats's inadequate understanding of Synge: "In seeing Synge only through Yeats's glass darkly, not only the man but to an

important extent the plays--and certainly the audience's reaction to them--remain incomplete."

7407. ———: "John Millington Synge: Poet and Playwright of the Western World," *Ireland of the Welcomes*, 19:6 (Mar-Apr 1971), 6-12.
The same issue, dedicated to Synge, contains other material about him, especially illustrations.

7408. SETTERQUIST, JAN: *Ibsen and the Beginnings of Anglo-Irish Drama. I. John Millington Synge*. Upsala: Lundequist, 1951. 94 p. (Upsala Irish Studies. 2.)
For part II see J7039.

7409. SHARP, MARTHA MARTIN: "J. M. Synge and the Theatre," M.A. thesis, Louisiana State U, 1955. v, 86 p.

7410. SHERMAN, STUART P.: "John Synge," *Nation*, 95:2478 (26 Dec 1912), 608-11.
Includes a review of W102.

7411. SIDNELL, MICHAEL J.: "Synge's Playboy and the Champion of Ulster," *Dalhousie R*, 45:1 (Spring 1965), 51-59.
The sources of the play in the Cuchulain saga and some comparisons with Yeats.

7412. SKELTON, ROBIN: *J. M. Synge and His World*. London: Thames & Hudson, 1971. 144 p.
Numerous references to Yeats (see index).

7413. ———: *The Writings of J. M. Synge*. London: Thames & Hudson, 1971. 190 p.
Yeats is mentioned *passim* (see index).
Reviews:
1. Alan J. Bliss, "Two Books on Synge," *Hibernia*, 36 [i.e., 35]:9 (30 Apr 1971), 15.
2. William Hart, "Synge and the Christian Ethos," *Studies*, 61:241 (Spring 1972), 85-96.
3. Milton Levin, *Éire-Ireland*, 8:1 (Spring 1973), 156-58.
4. Hilary Pyle, *RES.* 23:90 (May 1972), 235-36.

7414. ———: "J. M. Synge," *Essays by Divers Hands*, 37 (1972), 95-107.

7415. ———: *J. M. Synge*. Lewisburg, Pa.: Bucknell UP, 1972. 89 p.

7416. SOCIÉTÉ DES ANGLICISTES DE L'ENSEIGNEMENT SUPÉRIEUR: *La raison et l'imaginaire*. Actes du Congrès de Rennes (1970). Paris: Didier, [1973]. 223 p. (Études anglaises. 45.)
Gérard Leblanc: "*Le baladin du monde occidental* ou les délices de l'imaginaire," 177-87; on Synge.
Michèle Dalmasso: "Littérature anglo-irlandaise et imagination verbale: Synge et Lady Gregory (Quelques notations pour un très vaste sujet)," 189-97.
Raymonde Popot: "Aspects de l'imaginaire dans deux oeuvres de James Stephens, *The Crock of Gold* et *The Demi-Gods*," 199-212.
André Chapois: "Note sur l'imaginaire dans le théâtre du Yeats," 213-22; on occultism in Yeats's plays, especially in *The Shadowy Waters* and *The Dreaming of the Bones*.

7416a. STEWART, IAN: "A Wanderer in the Western World: J. M. Synge and the Irish Scene," *Country Life*, 152:3923 (24 Aug 1972), 462-63.

7417. STORK, UWE: "Der sprachliche Rhythmus in den Bühnenstücken John Millington Synges," Dr. phil. thesis, U of Freiburg, 1969. iv, 121 p.
Summary in *English and American Studies in German*, 1969, #37.

7418. STRONG, L. A. G.: "John Millington Synge," *Bookman* [NY], 73:2 (Apr 1931), 125-35.
See also *Dublin Mag*, 7:2 (Apr-June 1932), 12-32.

7419. STYAN, JOHN LOUIS: *The Dark Comedy: The Development of Modern Comic Tragedy.* 2nd edition. Cambridge: UP, 1968 [1962]. viii, 310 p.
"Synge and O'Casey," 130-36.

7420. SUSS, IRVING D.: "The *Playboy* Riots," *Irish Writing*, #18 (Mar 1952), 39-42.

7421. SUTTON, GRAHAM: "John Millington Synge," *Bookman*, 69:414 (Mar 1926), 299-301.

7421a. Sing, Dzhon [SYNGE, JOHN]: *Dramy*. Translated by V. D. Metal'nikov. Leningrad: Gosudarstvennoe izdatel'stvo "Khudozhestvennaîa literatura," 1937. 300 p.
M. Gutner: "Dramy Singa," 3-28.

7422. SYNGE, JOHN MILLINGTON: *Plays, Poems, and Prose.* London: Dent, 1941. xiii, 301 p. (Everyman's Library. 968.)
Ernest Rhys: "Introduction," vii-x.

7423. ————: *The Playboy of the Western World.* With an introduction and notes by T. R. Henn. London: Methuen, 1968 [1961]. 111 p.
"Introduction," 7-37.

7424. ————: *Plays, Poems, and Prose.* Introduction by Micheál MacLiammóir. London: Dent, 1961. xiii, 301 p. (Everyman's Library. 968.)
"Introduction," v-x.

7425. ————: *Riders to the Sea & The Playboy of the Western World.* With introduction and notes by F. R. Wood. London: Heinemann, 1961. xxiv, 85 p.
"Introduction," vii-xxiv.

7426. ————: *Riders to the Sea and In the Shadow of the Glen.* With an introduction and notes by T. R. Henn. London: Methuen, 1961. 111 p.
"Introduction," 9-23; also pp. 71-85.

7427. ————: *The Aran Islands and Other Writings.* Edited with an introduction and notes by Robert Tracy. NY: Vintage Books, 1962. xxiii, 415 p. (Vintage Original. V53.)
"General Introduction," vii-xx.

7428. ————: *Collected Works.* London: Oxford UP, 1962—. 4 v. to date.
1. *Poems.* Edited by Robin Skelton (1962). Contains an introduction by Skelton, pp. xi-xxix, and Yeats's preface to the first edition, pp. xxx-xxxv (reprinted from W243).
2. *Prose.* Edited by Alan Price (1966). Contains an introduction by Price, pp. x-xvi, and among others the following items:
   a. "An Epic of Ulster," 367-70; reprinted from *Speaker*, ns 6:[] (7 June 1902), 284-85; a review of W256.
   b. "Le mouvement intellectuel irlandais," 378-82; reprinted from °*Européen*, 2:[] (31 May 1902), 12-13.
   c. "The Old and New in Ireland," 383-86; reprinted with the addition of a discarded passage from *Academy*, 63:1583 (6 Sept 1902), 238-39, where it was published anonymously. On Yeats, *passim*.

3. *Plays: Book I*. Edited by Ann Saddlemyer (1968). Contains the editor's introduction, pp. xi-xxxi, and Yeats's preface to the first edition of *The Well of the Saints*, pp. 63-68 (from W262).
4. *Plays: Book II*. Edited by Ann Saddlemyer (1968). Contains the editor's introduction, pp. xi-xxxiii (on Synge and Yeats, *passim*), and Yeats's preface to the first edition of *Deirdre of the Sorrows*, pp. 179-80 (reprinted from W245).
5. Not yet published; will contain a bibliography.

7429. ———: *Four Plays and The Aran Islands*. Edited with an introduction by Robin Skelton. London: Oxford UP, 1962. xix, 327 p. (World's Classics. 585.)
   "Introduction," vii-xiv.

7430. ———: *The Plays and Poems*. Edited with an introduction and notes by T. R. Henn. London: Methuen, 1963. xi, 363 p.
   "General Introduction," 1-21; "Introduction to the Plays," 22-78; "Introduction to the Poems and Translations," 274-86; "Synge and Yeats," 308-11; "Notes [. . .]," 321-63.

7430a. Sing, Dzhon Millington [SYNGE, JOHN MILLINGTON]: *Dramy*. Translated by V. Metal'nikov. Leningrad: "Iskusstvo," 1964. 287 p.
   ÎU. Kovalev: "Dramaturgiîa Dzhona Singa," 5-33. N. Sitnikova: "Primechaniîa" [Notes], 277-85.

7431. SYNGE, JOHN MILLINGTON: *Emerald Apex: A Selection from J. M. Synge's Studies of Irish People and Places*. Edited with an introduction, notes and exercises by Alan Price. Glasgow: Blackie, 1966. xxii, 130 p.
   "Introduction," vii-xx.

7432. ———: *Die Aran-Inseln*. Frankfurt am Main: Suhrkamp, 1972. 219 p. (Bibliothek Suhrkamp. 319.)
   Christian Grote: "Nachwort des Übersetzers," 211-19.

7433. TAKÁCS, DALMA SAROLTA: "J. M. Synge as a Dramatist," °Ph.D. thesis, Columbia U, 1969. 229 p. (*DA*, 32:11 [May 1972], 6457A.)

7434. *Terres celtiques: Ecole d'été de Dublin*. 15e voyage d'études (1968/69). Lyon: Audin, [1969]. 83 p.
   Monique Burlet: "Introduction à John Millington Synge," 23-27.
   René Fréchet: "Le thème de la parole dans le théâtre de J. M. Synge," 28-42. Omnibus review of recent books by and about Synge, pp. 42-49.
   Augustine Martin: "*The Playboy of the Western World*: Etude sur ce qui est essentiel dans cette pièce," 50-55.
   Réginald de Rocquois: "Le baladin du monde occidental," 56-60.

7435. TOWNSHEND, GEORGE: "The Irish Drama. I. The Irish National Theatre Society," *Drama*, [1]:3 (Aug 1911), 93-104.
   Mainly on Synge.

7436. TRIESCH, MANFRED: "Some Unpublished J. M. Synge Papers," *ELN*, 4:1 (Sept 1966), 49-51.
   The University of Texas has acquired 32 letters from Synge and four letters from Yeats to Maire O'Neill, as well as other Synge papers.

7437. TRIVIDIC, C.: "John Millington Synge devant l'opinion irlandaise," *EA*, 7:2 (Apr 1954), 185-89.

7438. TUPPER, JAMES W.: "J. M. Synge and His Work," *Dial*, 54:642 (16 Mar 1913), 233-35.
   Includes a review of W102.

7439. °WALSH, MARJORIE: "Synge and Pearse: Contrasting Exponents of the Celtic Renaissance," M.A. thesis, Columbia U, 1933.

7439a. WHITAKER, THOMAS RUSSELL (ed): *Twentieth Century Interpretations of "The Playboy of the Western World": A Collection of Critical Essays.* Englewood Cliffs: Prentice-Hall, 1969. iii, 122 p.
   A long introduction and 11 reprinted pieces.

7440. WOODS, ANTHONY S.: "Synge Stayed at Home by the Fireside," *Catholic World*, 141:841 (Apr 1935), 46-52.
   Of the Ascendancy writers, Synge is the one who comes closest to the spirit of the Irish people.

7440a. YEATS, JACK B.: "Jack Yeats's Memories of Synge," *Irish Nation and the Peasant*, 1:33 (14 Aug 1909), 7.

7440b. YEATS, JOHN BUTLER: "Ireland Out of the Dock," *United Irishman*, 10:241 (10 Oct 1903), 2.

7441. ————: *Essays Irish and American.* With an appreciation by AE. Dublin: Talbot Press / London: Unwin, 1918. 95 p.
   "Synge and the Irish," 51-61; reprint of "Synge and the Irish: Random Reflections on a Much-Discussed Dramatist from the Standpoint of a Fellow-Countryman," *Harper's Weekly*, 55:2866 (25 Nov 1911), 17.

7442. YEATS STUDIES: "Theatre and the Visual Arts: A Centenary Celebration of Jack Yeats and John Synge." Edited by Robert O'Driscoll and Lorna Reynolds. *Yeats Studies*, #2 (Bealtaine 1972).
   1. Anne Yeats: "Jack Yeats," 1-5.
   2. Kenneth Clark: "Jack Yeats: Introduction to the Catalogue for the Exhibition of Jack Yeats Paintings, University of Toronto, 11-27 February 1971," 6-8.
   3. James White: "Memory Harbour: Jack Yeats's Painting Process," 9-17.
   4. Ann Saddlemyer: "Synge and Some Companions, with a Note Concerning a Walk through Connemara with Jack Yeats," 18-34; the companions are WBY, Stephen MacKenna, Masefield, and Jack Yeats.
   5. William Hart: "Synge's Ideas on Life and Art: Design and Theory in *The Playboy of the Western World*," 35-51.
   6. Lorna Reynolds: "The Rhythms of Synge's Dramatic Prose," 52-65.
   7. Balachandra Rajan: "Yeats, Synge and the Tragic Understanding," 66-79; a comparison of the Deirdre plays of AE, Yeats, and Synge.
   8. Alec Reid: "Comedy in Synge and Beckett," 80-90.
   9. Walter Starkie: "Memories of John Synge and Jack Yeats," 91-99.
   10. Robin Skelton: "Themes and Attitudes in the Later Drama of Jack B. Yeats," 100-120.
   11. Patricia Hutchins: "Jack Yeats and His Publisher," 121-26; the publisher was Elkin Mathews.
   12. "Theatre and the Visual Arts: A Panel Discussion," 127-38; an interesting discussion between Auden, McLuhan, Buckminster Fuller, and Jack MacGowran, chaired by A. N. Jeffares, but quite out of place in this volume because it relates neither to Yeats nor to Synge.

7443. Z[ABEL], M. D.: "Synge and the Irish," *Poetry*, 42:2 (May 1933), 101-6.

7444. ZYDLER, TOMASZ: "John Millington Synge and the Irish Theatre," *Kwartalnik neofilologiczny*, 18:4 (1971), 383-96.

See also J137c, 514, 623, 706, 716, 743, 764, 794, 815, 841a, 849, 938, 945a, 945b, 1000, 1136, 1247, 1413, 1425, 1454, 1492, 1493, 1521, 1547a,

1634, 1638, 1642, 1665, 1702, 1732, 2045, 2267-71, 3350a, 3393, 3397,
3412, 3416, 3429a, 3435, 3445, 3448, 3455, 3467, 3474, 3485, 3503, 3511,
3549, 3641, 3644, 3683, 3684a, 3688, 3691, 3692, 3697, 4455, 4462-65,
4701 and note, 5592, 5855, 5857, 5877, 5911, 5922, 5932, 5935, 5942,
5944, 5947a, 5948, 5949, 5982a, 5986, 5996, 6005, 6010, 6026, 6054, 6065,
6071, 6074, 6102, 6154, 6172, 6216, 6233, 6278, 6290, 6291, 6294, 6295,
6298, 6301, 6315, 6316, 6318, 6320, 6322, 6323, 6328, 6330, 6331, 6333,
6334, 6336, 6354, 6360, 6364, 6371, 6388, 6392, 6394, 6407, 6410, 6416,
6420, 6428, 6433, 6434, 6436, 6438, 6441, 6450, 6452, 6469, 6472, 6474,
6499, 6505, 6514, 6520, 6523a, 6524, 6527, 6531, 6542a, 6549, 6550, 6555,
6558, 6572, 6574, 6577, 6589, 6632, 6638, 6681, 6703, 6711, 6744, 6754,
6759, 6782, 6813, 6823, 6875, 6918, 6956, 6965, 7071, 7139, 7173, 7185.

John Todhunter

7445. °MACDERMOTT, BRIGID J. P.: "John Todhunter, M.D.: A Minor Figure in
Anglo-Irish Literature," M.A. thesis, University College, Dublin, 1968.

See also J1110, 1755, 4199, 5911, 6290.

Katharine Tynan

7446. MOLONEY, SISTER FRANCIS INÉS: "Katharine Tynan Hinkson: A Study of
Her Poetry," Ph.D. thesis, U of Pennsylvania, 1952. iii, 158 p. (*DA*, 14:
10 [1954], 1726-27.)
   On Yeats and Katharine Tynan, *passim*, especially pp. 48-58. The
   author claims on the authority of letters written to her by KT's
   nephew that KT and WBY contemplated marriage at one time.

See also J389, 1110, 1177, 1689, 4201, 5094-114, 5911, 6219, 6273, 7255.

MB   The Irish Academy of Letters

7447. ANON.: "The Pollexfen Peacock Parade: Dismal Drip from Westmoreland
Street," *Catholic Bulletin*, 22:10 (Oct 1932), 773-75.
   See also "Shaw and Yeats and Their Tribe," 23:9 (Sept 1933), 693-96
   (". . . parade of putridity . . .").

7448. ANON.: "Academy of Immorality [. . .]: A Real Insult to Ireland,"
Catholic Mind, 3:11 (Nov 1932), 247-48.

7449. ANON.: "Irish Academy of Letters: Names of Those Selected. Mr. Yeats
Expects Refusals. The Creation of Modern Ireland," *Irish Times*, 74:23524
(19 Sept 1932), 7.
   See also the editorial on p. 6.

7450. ANON.: "An Academy for Irish Letters," *Literary Digest*, 114:2218
(22 Oct 1932), 16.

7451. ANON.: "An Academy of Absentees," *Tablet*, 160:4820 (24 Sept 1932),
394-95.
   "An impudent usurpation. . . ."

7452. ANON.: "An Irish Academy of Letters: Mr. W. B. Yeats's Proposal,"
Times, #46098 (4 Apr 1939), 9.

7453. BOYD, ERNEST: "An Unacademic Academy," *Nation*, 135:3519 (14 Dec
1932), 590.
   Defends the project.

7454. GWYNN, STEPHEN: "The Irish Academy of Letters," *Fortnightly R*, os 138 / ns 132:791 (Nov 1932), 653-54.

7455. [MANNING, MARY ?]: "Processional," *Motley*, 1:5 (Oct 1932), 6-7.

7456. O'CASEY, SEAN: "Laurel Leaves and Silver Trumpets," *American Spectator*, 1:2 (Dec 1932), 4.

> O'Casey's unfavorable opinion of the academy and of Yeats's "Noh" plays. But he does not "hate" Yeats as has been frequently alleged: "I myself have gone about, arm in arm with him a thousand times, and sincerely hope to renew these delightful experiences. . . ."

7457. O'HEGARTY, P. S.: "About the Academy of Letters," *Motley*, 2:2 (Feb 1933), 10-12.

> Wants to see some members replaced because of lack of merit—Gogarty, Higgins, O'Faolain, O'Flaherty, and others. See also "More about the Academy," :3 (Mar 1933), 4-7.

7458. T., O.: "The New Academy: To Throw Bad Eggs at Mrs. Grundy? Mr. Yeats' History," *United Irishman*, 1:19 (24 Sept 1932), 5.

7459. TALBOT, FRANCIS: "The Irish Academy of Literature," *America*, 48:1211 (10 Dec 1932), 240-41.

> Vicious attack on Yeats's project and on his attempts to abolish censorship.

See also J844, 970, 1059, 1076, 4740, 5919, 7272.

MC   The Cuala and Dun Emer Press

7460. ANON.: "Cuala Industries," *Irish Life*, 20:5 (23 Feb 1917), 259-61.

7461. CAVE, RODERICK: *The Private Press*. London: Faber & Faber, 1971. 376 p.

> See pp. 199-200 and frontispiece.

7462. DURKAN, MICHAEL J.: "The Dun Emer and the Cuala Press," *Wesleyan Library Notes*, #4 (Spring 1970), 7-18.

7463. FOX, R. M.: "She's Printer to the Poets," *British Printer*, [65:4] (Jan-Feb 1953), 33-35.

> On Mrs. Yeats.

7464. ————: "The Name on the Knocker Is Yeats," *Ireland of the Welcomes*, 14:1 (May-June 1965), 21-22.

7465. GIBBON, MONK: "At the Cuala Press," *Irish Times*, #35562 (29 Sept 1969), 12.

7466. °GOODWIN, AILEEN M.: *The Cuala Press in Ireland: A Woman's Contribution to Fine Printing*. [Dublin: Cuala Press, ca. 1925]. 8 p.

7467. HAAS, IRVIN: "Miss Elizabeth Yeats and the Cuala Press with a List of Books Printed at the Cuala Press," *American Book Collector*, 4:9/10 (Sept-Oct 1933), 133-38.

7468. HORWILL, HERBERT W.: "Yeats as a Printer," *NYTBR*, [31:] (24 Oct 1926), 13.

7469. KIERNAN, T. J.: "Fifty Years of the Cuala Press," *Biblionews*, 7:8 (July 1954), 27-29.

7469a. °*A List of Books Published by the Dun Emer Press and the Cuala Press Founded in Nineteen Hundred and Three by Elizabeth Corbet Yeats.* With a preface by Liam Miller. Dublin: Cuala Press, 1972. xvi p.

7470. MACGLYNN, LOCHLINN: "In the Golden Land of Yeats," *Irish Press*, 16:122 (23 May 1946), 7.

7471. MARRINER, ERNEST C.: "Fifty Years of the Cuala Press," *Colby Library Q*, 3:11 (Aug 1953), 171-83.

7472. [MAXWELL, WILLIAM]: *The Dun Emer Press, Churchtown, Dundrum, July 1903-September 1907. The Cuala Press, Churchtown, Dundrum, October 1908- July 1923; Merrion Square Dublin, October 1923-October 1924; Lower Baggot Street Dublin, from May 1925.* A complete list of the books, pamphlets, leaflets, and broadsides printed by Miss Yeats, with some notes by the compiler. [Edinburgh]: Privately printed, 1932. 67 p.

7473. MILLER, LIAM: "The Dun Emer Press," *Irish Book*, 2:2 (Spring 1963), 43-52; :3/4 (Autumn 1963), 81-90.

7474. [————]: *A Brief Account of the Cuala Press, Formerly the Dun Emer Press Founded by Elizabeth Corbet Yeats in MCMIII.* Dublin: Cuala Press, 1971. [8 p.]

7475. ————: *The Dun Emer Press, Later the Cuala Press.* With a preface by Michael B. Yeats. Dublin: Dolmen Press, 1973. 131 p. (New Yeats Papers. 7.)
References to WBY's involvement in the affairs of the press, *passim*.

7476. MURDOCH, W. G. BLAIKIE: "The Cuala Press," *Bookman's J and Print Collector*, 6:10 (July 1922), 107-11.

7477. O'SULLIVAN, PHILIP: "Hand-Printing Press Revived," *Irish Independent*, 78:238 (6 Oct 1969), 6.

7478. QUIDNUNC: "An Irishman's Diary," *Irish Times*, #29939 (14 Sept 1953), 5.
Correspondence by Katherine MacCormack, #29941 (16 Sept 1953), 5.

7479. RANSOM, WILL: *Private Presses and Their Books.* NY: Bowker, 1929. 493 p.
Contains some notes on the press and a checklist (see index).

7480. TICKELL, ADELINE HILL: "The Dun Emer Press," *Book-Lover's Mag*, 8:1 (1908), 6-14.

7481. TOMKINSON, GEOFFREY STEWART: *A Select Bibliography of the Principal Modern Presses Public and Private in Great Britain and Ireland.* With an introduction by B. H. Newdigate. London: First Edition Club, 1928. xxv, 238 p.
"The Cuala Press," 32-38.

7482. TURNER, G. W.: "The Cuala Industries," *Lady's Pictorial*, 72:1853 (2 Sept 1916), 301-2.

7483. YEATS, LILY: *Elizabeth Corbet Yeats. Born March 11th. 1868. Died January 16th. 1940.* [Dublin: Cuala Press, 1940. 4 p.]

See also J12, 1076, 1136, 5940 (#2), 5948.

NA Index of Names

Brown, R. M. C. S., 1755b
Brown, Ray C. B., 1141
Brown, Stephen James, 380, 381,
  3951, 5980
Brown, Stuart Gerry, 3210
Brown, T. J., 3168
Brown, Terence, 1102, 2079, 2416
Browne, Elliott Martin, 1828, 3366
Browne, Maurice, 604
Browne, Ray Broadus, 5912
Browne, Wynyard, 4728
Browning, Robert, 1072, 1716a,
  1975, 1976, 2983
Brownlow, Timothy, 1112, 1131,
  2308, 2439, 5405, 5736, 5737
Bruck, Ruth, 3319
Brüggemann, Theodor, 1818
Brugère, Raymond, 7106
Brugsma, Rebecca Pauline Christine,
  5913
Brulé, André, 4677, 4708, 4729, 7107
Brumby, Colin, 5614
Brun, Liam de, 6377
Brunetière, Ferdinand, 2121
Brunius, August, 1245, 2242
Brunner, Karl, 2034, 2103
Bruno, Giordano, 2210, 2277
Bruns, Gerald L., 1072, 2079, 5496
Bryan, Robert A., 3904
Bryant, Sophie, 5981
Bryce, J. W., 5185
Bryson, Ernest, 5615
Bryson, John, 359, 1125, 1163,
  5044, 5522, 6805
Bryson, Lyman, 3028, 3300
Bryson, Mary Elizabeth, 6885
Buchanan, George, 1246
Buckley, Tom, 604a
Buckley, Vincent, 2475, 2688, 3973,
  5207
Buckram, Eliot, 4887
Bucur, Alexandru, 336
Buddingh', Cornelis, 5072
Bülow, Isolde von, 3320
Bufano, Rocco, 5847
Buhler, C. Walter, 537
Buidin, Claudine, 6938
Bulfin, William, 3929
Bull, Janice, 1836
Bullen, A. H., 532, 4195
Bullett, Gerald, 5328
Bullock, Shan F. (i.e., John
  Williams), 5927, 6287
Bullough, Geoffrey, 2476, 2477, 3367
Bunch, Dorothy, 2793
Bunn, James Harry, 2971a

Bunnell, William Stanley, 2478
Burch, Vacher, 605
Burdett, Osbert, 4888
Burgess, Anthony (i.e., John Anthony
  Burgess Wilson), 1247
Burgess, Charles, 6873
Burghard, Lorraine Hall, 3321
Burgoyne, F. J. P., 382
Burke, Edmund, 1076, 1147, 2145,
  2258, 2259, 2405, 5927
Burke, John, 6308
Burke, Kenneth, 1090, 1137, 2742,
  3174, 3579, 3729
Burke, Michael, 6378
Burkhart, Charles Joseph, 845
Burlet, Monique, 7434
Burlingham, Russell, 2254
Burnham, James, 1089, 1108
Burns, Richard, 1149, 5738
Burns, Robert, 2371
Burnshaw, Stanley, 2478a, 2916
Burrow, C. Kennett, 4562
Burrows, Rachel, 1097, 2282
Burto, William C., 9, 3816, 3860,
  6364, 6683
Burton, Ernest James, 3368
Bury, Phyllis, 7259
Busby, Christopher, 1156
Buschkiel, Jürgen, 3914
Bush, Douglas, 1790, 2479, 2866
Bushee, Ralph, 506
Bushrui, Suheil Badi, 80, 220a,
  554, 1101, 1112, 1129, 2480,
  2481, 3322, 3780, 4254, 5241,
  7317
Butenschön, Andrea, 225
Butler, Anthony, 6744, 7154
Butler, Christopher, 3993
Butler, Henry J., 6640
Butler, Jone L., 2972
Butter, Peter H., 2079e, 2923,
  2955
Byars, John Arthur, 1732, 3499
Byrd, Thomas L., 2761, 2899
Byrne, Dawson, 6641
Byrne, J. J., 1747
Byrne, J. Patrick, 5739, 6976
Byrne, Joseph, 4055
Byrne, Lawrence P. *See* Malone,
  Andrew E.
Byrne, Patrick, 6002
Byrne, William, 2200

C., 4889, 6379
C., A. M., 1115

Conway, John Dennis, 6863, 6863a
Cooke, John Daniel, 1279
Cooke, Michael G., 3986a
Cookman, A. V., 3846
Coole, T., 1280
Coombes, Henry, 3015
Cooper, Bryan, 1038, 3661
Cooper, Charles William, 3077
Cooper, Edith Emma. *See* Field, Michael
Cooper, Mabel, 6299
Cooper, Philip, 2490
Copeland, Tom W., 551
Coppard, A. E., 1981
Coquelin, Benoît-Constant, 6744
Corbin, Richard Johnstone, 2813
Corelli, Marie, 5940
Corkery, Daniel, 5911, 6284, 6287, 6290, 6328, 6876-77a, 6961, 7324
Corman, Cid, 5463
Cornier, Sidsel, 7325
Cornwell, Edith Frazier, 1791
Corradini Favati, Gabriella, 5542
Corrigan, Robert Willoughby, 3376, 6393
Corry, Percy, 6652
Cosgrave, Patrick, 1101, 1758, 1885a
Cosgrave, William T., 4046, 4047
Cosman, Madeleine Pelner, 3285
Cotter, Eileen Mary, 3682
Coughlan, Sister Jeremy, 2056
Coulter, Geoffrey, 144, 5997, 5998
Courcy, J. de, 514
Cournos, John, 556
Cournot, Michel, 3479a
Courtney, Sister Marie-Thérèse, 7028
Courtney, Neil, 1281
Courtney, Winifred F., 1282
Cousins, James Henry, 885, 1283, 1284, 1641, 2491, 2743, 2865, 4613, 5999, 6000, 6230, 6330, 6455, 6878-80, 7325a
Cousins, Margaret E., 5999, 6879
Cousins, William D., 6879
Cousteau, Jacques, 7326
Couster, P. J., 258, 1285
Covaci, Aurel, 211, 329, 330, 336, 4248
Cowasjee, Saros, 7110-12
Cowell, Raymond, 1075, 2418
Cowen, Hewson, 4076
Cowley, Abraham, 1982
Cowley, Malcolm, 561, 603, 886, 1286
Cox, Aedan, 1287
Cox, Charles Brian, 2492, 3030
Cox, E. M. H., 507

Cox, J. H., 3736, 3737, 3915
Cox, James Byrne, 2689
Cox, Kenneth, 1065, 2903
Coxhead, Elizabeth, 84, 1097, 2311, 5915, 6940, 6941, 6947, 6949, 7317, 7327
Craig, Edward Gordon, 92, 503, 942, 943, 949, 950, 1136, 1983, 1984, 3325a, 3377, 3458, 3558, 3748, 4469, 4524, 6327, 6764
Craig, Hardin, 1288
Craig, Maurice, 2971, 6971a
Craig, Maurice James, 1108
Craig, May, 1097, 5592
Crane, Hart, 1781
An Craoibhin Aoibhinn. *See* Hyde, Douglas
Crawford, Mary Caroline, 6653
Crişan, Constantin, 353
Croft, P. J., 128e, 3305a
Crompton, Louis William, 1954, 2072
Crone, G. R., 3281
Crone, John S., 619, 620, 2350
Cronin, Anthony, 1079, 1101, 1110, 1289, 1451, 1872, 2426, 3039, 3335, 5511, 5745
Cronin, Colm, 621, 2351
Cronin, John, 6001, 6098, 7271
Crosland, Margaret, 6002
Crosland, Thomas William Hodgson, 1094, 2352
Cross, Kenneth Gustav Walter, 103, 359, 561, 1101, 1142, 1290, 3121, 4057, 5280
Crossan, Mary Elizabeth, 2782
Crosse, Gordon, 217, 5623
Crossley-Holland, Kevin, 58, 4225
Crossley-Holland, Peter, 5624
Crowley, Aleister, 111a, 622, 639, 1291, 3996, 4037, 5848, 5849
Crowley, Jeananne, 1079
Crowley, Mary, 6003
Crowley, Paul, 5329
Crump, Geoffrey, 3176
Cruttwell, Patrick, 1127, 1874
Cuana, 4058
Cuff, Elizabeth L., 2695
Culbertson, Diana, 3976
Cumberland, Gerald (i.e., Charles Frederick Kenyon), 961, 2353
Cumberlege, Marcus, 5746
Cummings, Edward Estlin, 3497
Cummins, Geraldine, 3997, 7272
Cunard, Nancy, 845
Cunliffe, John William 1292, 1293, 5911, 6004, 6005, 6394

2126, 2764
Fulton, John, 3184
Funge, Patrick, 6744
Funke, Lewis, 3731
Furomoto, Taketoshi (or Taketosh),
   177b, 1162
Furukawa, Hisahi, 1161, 1162
Fussell, Paul, 2852
Fylyppovski, A., 188

G., J. W., 3726, 3774, 3814
G., M., 6741
G., R., 5333
Gable, Mariella, 5411
Gad, Carl, 3394, 6431
Gaddis, Marilyn, 1945. See also
   Rose, Marilyn Gaddis
Gaffney, Sylvester, 6701
Gál, István, 3063a
Gale, Norman Rowland, 5867
Galinsky, Hans, 6209
Gallagher, James, 1090, 5051, 5183,
   5272
Gallagher, Michael P., 1101, 1131,
   2525
Gallagher, Patrick, 1744
Gallchobhair, Eamonn, 5594
Galsworthy, John, 1307
Gamberini, Spartaco, 3395
Gamble, Isabel, 1090, 1100, 1141
Gannett, Lewis, 4897
Gannon, P. J., 561, 1115
Gannon, Patricio, 2765
Gant, Roland, 1362
Ganz, Rudolph, 5645
Garab, Arra M., 2416, 2422, 2425,
   2767, 2796
Garbaty, Thomas Jay, 1363
Garborg, Arne, 7325
García Lorca, Federico, 7320
García Terres, Jaime, 328
Gardiner, Kenneth, 1130
Gardner, C. O., 3302
Gardner, Charles, 1958
Gardner, Dame Helen, 1156
Gargàro, F., 190, 251a, 1363a
Garland, Robert, 3775
Garma, Isabelle, 4162
Garnett, David, 844, 889
Garnett, Edward, 61, 4453, 5375
Garnier, Charles-Marie, 1364, 4109,
   4602, 4615, 4629, 4652, 5944
Garratt, Robert Francis, 6866b,
   6867a
Garrett, Eileen J., 655

Garrett, John, 4820
Garrison, Chester, 7019a
Garvey, James Joseph, 3955
Garvey, Michael, 2518
Gaskell, Ronald, 3396, 3865, 5247
Gassner, John, 1671, 3397-99, 6839,
   7338
Gatch, Katherine Haynes, 5185
Gates, Lewis Edwards, 4376
Gatlin, Dana, 6944
Gatter, Ludwig, 3917
Gawsworth, John (i.e., Terence Ian
   Fytton Armstrong), 1996, 5757
Gaynor, Arthur, 6432
Geck, Rudolf, 3663, 3664
Geckle, George L., 2216
Geddie, J. Liddell, 1258, 6945
Gelderman, Carol Wettlaufer, 2200a,
   6899
Gelpi, Barbara, 5500
Gelsted, Otto, 196
Genet, née Veyssie, Jacqueline,
   4104a
Gentile, Giovanni, 1101
George, Stefan, 4095a
Georges-Bazile, Cecil, 236
Gerard, Martin, 2526
Gerard, Paul, 6234
Gérard de Nerval (Gérard Labrunie),
   2124
Gerber, Helmut E., 7043, 7062
Gergely, Ágnes, 358a, 1217
Gerold, Berthild, 7122
Gerstenberger, Donna Lorine, 360,
   1112, 2420, 2431, 2830, 3345,
   3400, 3588, 6940, 7339, 7345
Gheorghiu, Mihnea, 6042, 7123,
   7124
Ghose, Aurobindo, 784, 2177
Ghosh, Prabodh Chandra, 3555
Gibbon, Edward, 3185
Gibbon, Monk, 557, 563, 656, 788,
   1177, 1364a, 1589, 2316, 5035,
   5386, 5543, 5758, 5922, 5945,
   6252, 6879, 7250-52, 7345, 7465
Gibbons, John, 2253
Gibbons, Tom, 1364b
Gibbs, A. M., 2072a, 3224
Gibbs, J. M., 7339a
Gibbs, Sir Philip, 657, 4603
Gibbs-Smith, Charles Harvard, 1372
Gibert, Madeleine, 205, 3630, 4244
Gibson, Katherine R., 6946
Gibson, Wilfrid W., 1136, 4710,
   5759

Lalec, 6732
Lalou, René, 6087
Lamb, Charles, 3185
Lamb, Henry, 5173
Lamberg, Walter, 2773
Lamm, Martin, 6471
Lamson, Roy, 3178
Landa, Louis A., 2263
Lander, Jeannette (i.e., Jeannette
 Seyppel), 2938
Landor, Walter Savage, 2032, 3263,
 5873
Landreth, Helen, 5451
Lane, Chester Travis, 3255
Lane, Sir Hugh, 128b, 955, 1056,
 1057, 1063, 1064, 1147, 1747,
 2824, 4053, 4072, 4077, 5883,
 6947, 6948
Lane, Yoti, 7019
Langbaum, Robert, 1442, 1874, 2565,
 5256, 5504
Langbridge, Frederick, 2282
Lange, Victor, 2136
Lapisardi, Frederick S., 2295, 3867
Lappin, Mary, 562, 923, 4027, 5520a
Larkin, Emmet, 6876
Larkin, Jim, 100
Larkin, Philip, 2022, 2033, 2033a,
 2440
Larminie, William, 1110, 5384-89
 and note, 5911, 5917, 6154, 6233,
 6290, 7014
Lass, Rolf Hermann, 1153, 1760a,
 2425, 3345
Lasseter, Rollin Amos, 4020
Last, R. W., 2142
Las Vergnas, Raymond, 6088
Latimer, Dan Raymond, 2919a
Laurence, Dan H., 128, 796, 6547
Lauterbach, Edward S., 1443a
Lavin, Mary, 6281
Law, Hugh Alexander, 5927
Law, William, 2135
Lawless, Emily, 7015
Lawrence, Sir Alexander, 707
Lawrence, Arnold Walter, 98
Lawrence, C. E., 4771, 4967, 6957
Lawrence, David Herbert, 1108, 1380,
 1593a, 1624, 1791, 1921, 2034,
 2035, 2134a, 2618, 3231, 3591
Lawrence, Thomas Edward, 98, 844
Lawrence, W. J., 6733, 6734
Lawson, Jonathan, 7366
Lawson, Robb, 6735
Lázaro Ros, Amando, 197

Leach, Elsie, 3049
Leach, MacEdward, 5912
Leach, Wilford, 5571
Leacock, Stephen, 708
Leal, Rine, 6472
Leamon, Warren, 5517a
Leamy, Edward, 756
Leary, Lewis, 477, 561
Leavis, Frank Raymond, 1090, 2010,
 2566, 2567, 4742, 4989
Leavis, Queenie Dorothy, 2567
Léblanc, Gerard, 7317, 7416
Le Brocquy, Louis, 6227
Le Brun, Philip, 4115
Leclercq, R., 6473
Lederman, Marie Jean, 3518
Ledwidge, Francis, 1689, 6233,
 6661a, 7016
Lee, Derek, 6995
Lee, Lawrence, 5020
Lee, Leng Kwong, 1761
Leech, Clifford, 7366a
Leeming, A. Emid, 709
Leeper, Janet, 3748
Lees, Francis Noel, 2425, 2985
Le Fanu, Elizabeth. *See* Maconchy,
 Elizabeth
Le Fanu, Joseph Sheridan, 3035,
 5940
Le Fleming, Christopher, 5679
Le Gallienne, Richard, 833, 4285,
 4363, 4577
Legg, L. G. Wickham, 628
Legge, J. G., 710
Legge, M. Dominica, 710
Legouis, Emile, 6088
Legras, Charles, 2568
Lehman, Benjamin Harrison, 3146
Lehmann, Andrew George, 4114
Lehmann, John, 799, 1100, 2569,
 2570
Lehmann, Liza, 5680
Lehmann-Haupt, Christopher, 1079,
 5525a
Leibniz, Gottfried Wilhelm, 1081
 (review #3)
Leighton, Lawrence, 2108
Leishman, J. B., 1100, 1151
Lelyveld, Joseph Salem, 2839
Lemieux, Sister M. St. Augustin,
 2897
Lemonnier, Léon, 4021
Lengold, Saša, 310
Lennartz, Franz, 1444
Lennon, Michael J., 7150

Nordell, Hans Roderick, 4177
Nordman, C. A., 7380a
Norman, Charles, 1904
Norman, Sylva, 2085, 5263
Norse, Harold George, 4178
Norstedt, Johann (John A.), 7019a, 7019b
Norton, Clara Mulliken, 371
Norton, Jim, 5587
Notopoulos, James A., 3195, 3196
Novák, Bohumil, 5546
Nowaczyński, Adolf, 6517
Nowell, A. E., 3337
Nowell-Smith, Simon, 106, 741
Nowlan, Kevin B., 6131, 6155
Noyes, Alfred, 2049, 3165-67, 4431
Noyes, Henry, 901
Nünning, Josefa, 3429a
Nurmi, Martin K., 1950
Nuttal, A. D., 1758
Nye, Robert, 1125, 5526b
Nyszkiewicz, Heinz, 4179

O., S., 3667
O., Y. *See* Russell, George William
Oates, Joyce Carol, 1519, 2599
O'B., C., 4510
O'B., F. C., 950
O'B., K. M., 3705
Oberg, Arthur Kenneth, 3430
O'Braonain, Cathaoir, 6268
O'Brien, Conor Cruise, 557, 1097, 1101, 1148, 1747, 2145, 2998, 4078, 5216, 5945, 5951, 6024, 6252, 6767, 7345
O'Brien, Ernst, 6768
O'Brien, Flann (i.e., Brian O'Nolan), 5940, 6288
O'Brien, Frank, 1755a
O'Brien, James Howard, 1520, 2786-89, 2800, 2873, 7195a, 7257
O'Brien, Kate, 561, 2301, 6131a, 6284
O'Brien, Kevin Patrick, 3983a
O'Brien, Máire Cruise, 6024
O'Brien, Margaret Theresa, 6132
O'Brien, Maurice Neill, 398
O'Brien, Seamus, 6754
O'Brien, Seumas, 742
O'Broin, Padraig, 5805, 5885
O'Byrne, Dermot. *See* Bax, Sir Arnold
O'Byrne, John, 138, 6352
O'Casey, Eileen, 5596, 7160
O'Casey, Sean, 363, 364, 366a, 370, 533, 547, 674, 676, 743, 1051,

1052, 1097, 1217, 1402, 1413, 1521, 1579, 1642, 2246-53, 2669, 2790, 3350a, 3393, 3397, 3426, 3448, 3474, 3542, 3641, 3978, 5592, 5596, 5935, 5944, 5945, 5948, 5951, 5982a, 6005, 6079, 6189, 6290, 6295, 6298, 6301, 6304, 6306, 6315, 6318, 6320-23, 6327, 6328, 6331, 6333, 6337a, 6347, 6364, 6392, 6407, 6441, 6450, 6469, 6472, 6477, 6499, 6527, 6572, 6574, 6577, 6704, 6724, 6744, 6813, 6884, 6949, 6950, 7085-189, 7232, 7338, 7358, 7362, 7373, 7378, 7419, 7456
O Catháin, Muiris, 3167
O Cobhthaigh, Diarmid. *See* Coffey, Diarmid
O'Connell, Adelyn, 2854. *See also* Dougherty, Adelyn
O'Connell, Dan, 6444
O'Connell, Daniel, 4086
O'Connor, Antony Cyril, 7381
O'Connor, Frank (i.e., Michael O'Donovan), 557, 744-49, 975, 1101, 1385a, 1522, 2256, 3431, 3432, 3880, 4632, 5082, 5229, 5264, 5570, 5592, 5593, 5806, 5935, 5940, 5944, 5945, 5947a, 5982a, 6133, 6281, 6284, 6287, 6288, 6328, 6364, 6732, 6769-71, 7190, 7194, 7255, 7382
O'Connor, Patrick, 3809, 7184
O'Connor, T. P., 750, 4338
O'Connor, Ulick, 557, 2197a, 2390, 6772, 6773, 6910
O'Connor, William Van, 1684, 1724, 1949, 2600, 2683, 3235
O'Conor, Norreys Jephson, 1339, 4596, 4605, 5936, 6134, 7225
Ó Cuisín, Seumas. *See* Cousins, James H.
O'D., M., 3705
O'D., S., 6263
O'Donnell, Donat. *See* O'Brien, Conor Cruise
O'Donnell, Frank Hugh, 980a, 1120, 3624-26, 3628, 3642, 6703
O'Donnell, Frank J. Hugh, 6518
O'Donnell, James Preston, 1286, 2801
O'Donnell, Peadar, 5947a, 6284
O'Donnell, Thomas, 4003
O'Donnell, William Hugh, 67b, 3964, 4232a

Ramsey, Warren, 3677
Rand, Richard Aldrich, 2705
Randall, Ethel Claire, 5941
Ranganathan, A., 1126
Ranganathan, Sudha, 2185b
Ransom, John Crowe, 1090, 1137, 1596, 2613, 2614, 5024
Ransom, Will, 36, 7479
Rao, K. Bhaskara, 2170
Raphael, 3144
Rascoe, Burton, 765, 766, 924, 4912
Rattray, Robert Fleming, 605, 767, 1114, 1156, 1157
Rauch, Karl, 1775
Rawlings, Ann, 2920
Rawson, Claude Julien, 2263a, 2264a
Ray, Ann Allen, 2893
Ray, Gordon Norton, 1564
Ray, Moira L., 6528
Ray, Nirendra Nath, 2615
Ray, R. J. (i.e., R. J. Brophy), 6331
Ray, William Ernest, 1968
Rayan, Krishna, 2706, 3274
Raymond, John, 1072, 5538
Raymond, William O., 3201
Read, Forrest, 106a, 1908
Read, Sir Herbert, 1081, 1565, 1909, 2616, 2617, 4777, 5150, 5265, 5891, 6152
Reade, Arthur Robert, 1566
Ready, William B., 5217
Reaney, James, 561, 1153, 2089, 5197, 5218, 5286
Rébillon, Armand, 5944
Rebora, Piero, 6166
Reck, Michael, 1910
Reddin, Kenneth Sheils (Kenneth Sarr), 6167
Reddin, Norman, 1053, 1054
Redgrave, Michael, 5596
Redlich, Hans Ferdinand, 1509a
Redmond, John, 142
Redmond, Liam, 529
Redmond-Howard, Louis G., 6168
Redshaw, Thomas Dillon, 6976a
Reed, Gertrude Hummel, 5942
Reed, Victor, 3061
Rees, David, 1567
Rees, Leslie, 1568, 3799, 6529
Reeve, F. D., 5198
Reeves, Halbert Adair, 3506, 3582
Reeves, James, 1569-71, 2059, 5219
Reeves, John A., 6429
Regardie, Israel, 4030

Reid, Alec, 6799, 7170, 7442
Reid, Benjamin Lawrence, 111a, 768, 1127, 1711
Reid, Forrest, 769, 1128, 2254, 5396, 6287, 6290, 6857
Reid, Jane Davidson, 3114
Reid, Margaret J. C., 1766
Reifenberg, Benno, 2143
Reilly, Joseph J., 5351
Reilly, Robert, 5816
Reimer, Howard James, 3535
Reinert, Otto, 3751, 3872
Reischle, Helmut, 3645
Reményi, József, 283, 5058
Rens, Lieven, 5491
Rest, Jaime, 6530, 7171
Revard, Stella, 2127, 3019
Revelin, Madeleine, 1143
Reville, John C., 5911
Rexroth, Kenneth, 3444
Reynek, Bohuslav, 179a
Reynolds, Ernest, 6531
Reynolds, Horace, 42, 61, 485, 556, 564, 1100, 1327, 1671, 1767, 2439, 4199, 4829, 4842, 4854, 4913, 4945, 4970, 4971, 5084, 5109, 5151, 5199, 5266, 5352, 5369, 5419, 5435, 5453, 5454, 5760, 5943, 6690, 6704, 6989, 7172
Reynolds, J. F., 6750
Reynolds, Lorna, 556, 1149, 1163, 2145a, 5436, 5817, 6169, 6251, 7442
Reynolds, Reginald, 770
Reynolds, Stephen, 4403
-r-f., 3925
Rhodes, Edwin, 6940, 7395
Rhodes, Raymond Crompton, 951
Rhynehart, J. G., 2104
Rhys, Ernest, 771-74, 4299, 4320, 7422
Ricci, Vittorio, 5693
Rice, Elmer, 6532
Rice, Philip Blair, 4830
Richards, Ivor Armstrong, 2618, 2619
Richardson, Dorothy Miller, 775, 2061
Richardson, Kenneth, 1572
Richman, Larry Kermit, 3502
Richter, Helene, 4109
Rickert, Edith, 369, 3058
Ricketts, Charles, 776, 1136 (#6, 10), 2062, 6498

1602, 2099a, 2951, 4169, 5575,
5576, 5899
Thomas, E. J., 5371
Thomas, Edward, 1655, 4352, 4353,
4382, 4414, 4419, 4426, 4439,
4440, 4445, 4456, 4476
Thomas, Gilbert, 3089
Thomas, John Ormond, 2304
Thomas, R. George, 1655
Thomas, Ronald Stuart, 1147, 1758,
5830
Thomas, Wright, 3210
Thompson, Edward Palmer, 2048
Thompson, Francis, 1464, 1656,
2100, 4270, 4327, 4334-36, 4351,
4379, 4388, 5105
Thompson, Francis John, 2849, 3570,
5950, 6724
Thompson, Frank, 6754
Thompson, J. B., 3011
Thompson, Kate V., 1352
Thompson, Lawrance, 654, 817
Thompson, Leslie M., 3591a
Thompson, Thomas Hazzard, 1884
Thompson, Vance, 4038
Thompson, William Irwin, 2957,
4038a, 5951
Thomson, George William, 4134
Thomson, James Alexander Kerr, 1931
Thomson, William, 2253
Thorburn, David, 3986a
Thoreau, Henry David, 1922-23a,
3078, 3310
Thorndike, Ashley Horace, 1292
Thornton, Robert Kelsey Rought, 790,
1657
Thornton, Weldon, 2229
Thorp, Willard, 1539
Thorpe, James, 3648
Thouless, Priscilla, 3460
Thuente, Mary Helen Ernst, 1772a
Thurber, James, 2864
Thurley, Geoffrey, 1658
Thwaite, Anthony, 2440, 2647, 3137,
3571
Tickell, Adeline Hill, 7480
Tierney, Michael, 4086, 7263
Tierney, William 4087
Tietjens, Eunice, 818
Tillekeratne, Nihal, 3090
Tillinghast, Philip, 5911
Tillyard, Eustace Mandeville Weten-
hall, 1863
Tindall, William York, 60, 1090,
1659, 1864, 1871, 2220, 2230-32,

2442, 3300, 4227, 5061, 5940
Tinker, Edward Larocque, 4985
Tippett, Michael, 5705
Tirapu, Maria Theresa, 3572
Titlestad, V. K., 1078
Titterton, W. R., 3706
Titus, Edward W., 1660
Tobin, James Edward, 5914
Tobin, John, 5706
Tobin, Michael, 6560
Tobin, Richard Montgomery, 819
Tobin, Terence, 2408
Todhunter, John, 1110, 1755, 3801,
4199, 4271, 5911, 6290, 6795,
7445
Toksvig, Signe, 6973
Tolkien, J. R. R., 1593a
Toller, Ernst, 727
Tolliver, Harold E., 3861
Tomkinson, Geoffrey Stewart, 7481
Tomlin, E. W. F., 1123, 1161, 1162,
1661
Tomlinson, Alan, 1067, 1984, 3344,
3461
Tomlinson, Charles, 1078, 5268
Tonson, Jacob. *See* Bennett, Arnold
Torchiana, Donald Thornhill, 1072,
1073, 1101, 1147, 1148, 1165,
2204, 3322, 5948, 6272
Tovar, Juan, 338
Towne, Charles Hanson, 4544
Townsend, James Benjamin, 1986
Townshend, George, 2648, 3462,
7435
Towse, John Ranken, 4436, 6294,
6336, 6703
Toynbee, Philip, 1380, 1671, 5177,
5529
Tracy, Robert, 1761a, 7427
Traill, H. D., 4287
Trausil, Hans, 6197
Travers, Pamela, 3671
Traverso, Leone, 257, 273, 277,
4219
Trebitsch-Stein, Marianne, 6561
Trédant, Paul, 6198
Trench, Herbert, 3739
Trench, W. F., 2233
Trewin, John Courtenay, 3873, 6823,
7160, 7185
Triesch, Manfred, 7436
Trilling, Lionel, 3211
Trividic, C., 7437
Trowbridge, Hoyt, 3119
Troy, William, 556, 4917

NB   Index of Institutions

NC   Index of Titles

This section comprises only books published or edited anonymously, as well
as anthologies, collections, and encyclopedias with or without editor. I
do not list the titles of all monographs referred to in this bibliography.

ND   Index of Yeats's Works

This section does not include the titles of Yeats's poems and plays. For
these two groups the reader is referred to sections DD and EE. I have
also omitted references to section IA.

"A tada?" [. . .], 287
"A un poeta che voleva indurmi a

dir bene di certi cattive poeti,
emuli suoi e miei," 309

NE   Index of Selected Subjects

This index is, of course, incomplete. Further discussions of the subjects
listed below may be found in the standard monographs that could not be
analyzed in this bibliography.

2372
Dublin, 5924
Duras House, 2311, 2369, 6789

Easter Rising 1916, 142a, 1076,
    1761, 2835, 2840, 3028-38 and
    note, 3606, 5945, 5947a, 5951,
    6094, 6247, 6250, 6259, 6268,
    6321, 6327
Eden, 1076, 1101
education, 1101, 1843, 2274, 2652,
    4063
egg, 2920. See also bird(s)
egotism, 1622. See also self
Egyptian literature, 1873
elegy, 2690a, 2691, 3072
elitism, 4095a
emblem, 1856, 3005
emotion, 3496
emotion of multitude, 3730a, 4105
England, 1745
English language, 1489, 6001, 6028,
    6054
English literature, 1932-2106 and
    note
epigram, 2692, 2693
epiphany, 2755, 3348
epistemology, 4020
eroticism. See sexuality
escape, escapism, 1813a, 2422, 2618,
    6205, 6243, 6572
estheticism, 1256, 1320, 1341, 1350,
    1596, 1632, 1699a, 1724, 1882,
    2575, 2694, 2760, 3462, 4096,
    4136
ethics, 1670. See also morality
Europe, Yeats in, 1603, 1611
European literature, 1873, 2107-34,
    2135-49, 2276-80, 2285-88, 2291-
    95
evil, 1243
exile, 560, 3697
existentialism, 2695
exoticism, 1554
experience, 1699a
expiation, 3531
expressionism, 3405

fairies, 707, 709, 978, 979, 991,
    1143, 1162, 1725-29, 1843, 2696,
    2697, 4233
farce, 2121, 3839, 3840
fascism, 1101, 1115, 1380, 1384,
    1426, 1508, 1671, 2145, 3230,
    4057, 4061, 4062, 4063a, 4076a,

4081a, 4083, 4085
fathers and sons, 1808, 1813a
Faust legend, 3750
Fenianism, 792, 1076, 3962, 4071,
    4076a, 5950, 6239. See also Sinn
    Fein
fin de siècle, 1221a, 1855, 4096.
    See also nineties
fire, 2679
folklore, 1161, 1772a, 2237, 3244,
    3509, 3993a, 4096, 6010, 6019,
    6154
folksong, 784, 2195, 2409, 2669,
    2674-76
fool, 1074, 1151, 1730-31a, 1945a,
    3345, 3497
French literature, 2107-34 and notes
friendship, 803, 2426, 2826

Gaelic language. See Irish language
Gaelic literature and culture, 1002a,
    1076, 1112, 1652, 1755a, 2192,
    2671a, 4188, 5936, 5980, 6024,
    6051, 6231a, 6251, 6269, 6463,
    6519. See also Irish literature
Galway, 2718
generosity, 2698
German literature, 2134a-49 and
    notes
ghosts, 658, 711, 1019, 1020, 1025,
    1026, 1843, 3556, 5940. See also
    psychic experiments
Golden Age, 1076
Golden Dawn. See index NB
Greek literature, 2150-55 and note
gyre, 1102, 2283a, 2893, 3052-55
    and note, 5853

hatred, 1118, 1267a
Helen of Troy, 1114, 2429
Hereford Cathedral, 3281
hermetism, 2477, 3999. See also
    obscurity; symbolism
hero and heroic literature, 997,
    1074, 1151, 1165, 1348, 1732,
    1733, 1741, 2017, 2019, 2426,
    2699, 2700, 2815, 3345, 3482,
    3498-504, 7193
Hinduism, 1877, 2157, 2171, 3012
history, 1136a, 1155, 1751, 1793,
    1815, 1873, 2745, 2746, 2753,
    3032, 3104, 3963, 3990, 4002,
    4004, 4017, 4031, 4038a, 5907
human image, 1308, 1801
humanism, 1624, 2518a

NF   Index of Periodicals and Selected Series

2855

Old Kilkenny Review (place of
publication not ascertainable),
7200

Omladinska riječ (Yugoslavia), 288

One Act Play Magazine & Radio Drama
Review (Boston), 6460, 6681

Ontmoeting (Baarn), 320

Onze eeuw (Haarlem), 3689

Opus (Tring, Herts.), 1362

Orbis Litterarum (København), 3160,
3278

Ord och bild (Stockholm), 2446,
3349, 6813

Ordre (Paris), 887

Oriel Review (NY), 819

Osmania Journal of English Studies
(Hyderabad), 1126, 2185b

Osservatore politico letterario
(Roma), 3099, 4245

Osservatore romano (Città del
Vaticano), 6037

Outlook (Cork), 6754

Outlook (Glasgow), 4879, 5919

Outlook (London), 1105, 2332, 2522,
2837, 3795, 4147, 4324, 4358,
4372, 4557, 5761, 6179, 6221,
6356, 6703

Outlook (NY), 764, 945, 1105, 4552,
4586, 4642, 4695, 5395, 6016,
6201, 6326, 6357, 6613, 6614

Oxford and Cambridge Review (London), 6826, 7368

Oxford Magazine (Oxford), 4818,
5271, 5335

Oxford University Gazette, 2395

Pacific Spectator (Stanford, Calif.),
2603

Pacific Weekly (Carmel, Calif.),
4901

Palabra y el hombre (Veracruz), 338,
2973

Pall Mall Gazette (London), 140,
934, 943, 4272, 7302

Panorama (Boston), 6615

Papers of the Bibliographical
Society of America (PBSA; NY),
12, 3246, 3647, 3893

Papers of the Manchester Literary
Club, 4768

Papers on Language and Literature
(PLL; Edwardsville, Ill.; formerly
Papers on English Language and
Literature [PELL]), 2127, 2416,

3019, 3038, 3287, 4104

Papyrus (Mount Vernon, N.Y.),
1492, 2871

Paragone (Firenze), 1114, 3979

Paris Review (Paris), 1376

Partisan Review (NY), 556, 561,
639, 1072, 1603, 1636, 1905,
4017, 4050, 4083, 5129

Paunch (Buffalo, N.Y.), 2821

Pax: The Journal of the Irish
Pacifist Movement (Dublin),
1267a

Peasant and Irish Ireland (Dublin),
3734

Penguin New Writing (London), 3232

Periscoop (Brussel), 1438

Persona (Roma), 349, 1235

Personalist (Los Angeles), 557,
564, 565, 1090, 1091, 1114,
1142, 1156, 1157, 1398, 1520,
1949, 2740, 3104, 5054, 5079,
5181, 5827

15 [Petnaest] dana (Zagreb), 325,
326

Phalange (Paris), 6420, 7337

Philological Quarterly (PQ; Iowa
City), 1073, 1165, 2950a, 3185,
3240, 3244, 3322, 3778, 5520

Philosophical Review (Boston),
4929

Philosophy & Rhetoric (University
Park, Pa.), 4049

Phoblacht (Dublin), 2631, 4047,
5786, 6693

Phoenix (Dublin), 7219

Phoenix (Seoul), 1102, 1123, 1661,
2064, 2719, 2808, 2860, 3182,
3559, 4005

Picture Post (London), 2304

Pilot (London), 3792, 4373, 4386,
4396, 5918, 6238

Plays and Players (London), 6736

PMLA (Publications of the Modern
Language Association of America)
(NY), 497, 1155, 1933, 1961,
2099a, 2769, 2885, 3069, 3108,
3173, 3237, 3284, 3673, 3954,
4011, 4119, 4189, 7343

Poesia (Milano), 137b

Poesia e critica (Milano), 3099,
5232

Poet Lore (Philadelphia), 696,
1076, 1352, 3545, 4319, 5063,
6342, 6546, 6712, 6793, 7247

Poétique (Paris), 2967

Reader (NY), 5946

Reader's Guide to Periodical Literature (NY), 450

Reading and Collecting (Chicago), 570

Realist (London), 6534

Recorder (NY), 2313, 6400

Red Hand Magazine (Glasgow), 6518

Regional Language Studies (St. John's, Newfoundland), 376a

Renaissance d'Occident (Bruxelles), 7394

Renascence (St. Mary-in-the-Woods, Ind.), 1671, 1796, 1831, 1836, 1949, 2681, 3012, 3125, 3501, 3998, 5101, 5142, 6724, 7079

Repertorio americano (San José, Costa Rica), 250

Reporter (NY), 1874, 5229

Republika (Zagreb), 340, 1645, 3118

Research in African Literatures (Austin, Tex.), 2288a

Research Studies (Pullman, Wash.), 1920a, 2792, 2812, 3021, 3107, 3208a, 3750, 7100

Reutlinger Generalanzeiger (Reutlingen), 3916

Reutlinger Nachrichten, 3918

Review (London), 2439

Review (NY), 4541

Review of English Literature (*REL*; London), 160, 948, 1013, 1018, 1114, 1129, 1734, 2204, 2274, 2440, 2776, 3181, 3551, 3780, 4084, 5350, 5824, 7111

Review of English Studies (*RES*; London), 8, 165, 553, 561, 1071-73, 1076, 1078, 1100-1102, 1126, 1141, 1142, 1151, 1153, 1758, 1874, 2020, 2079, 2188, 2417, 2420, 2429, 2431, 2439, 2440, 2830, 2978, 3142, 3250, 3257, 3335, 3336, 3345, 3985, 4033, 4115, 5235, 5501, 7413

Review of Review Index (London), 451

Revista de bellas artes (México), 331

Revista de la Universidad de México, 328

Revista hispanica moderna (NY), 7320

Revue (Paris; title varies), 6436

Revue anglo-américaine (Paris), 3418, 4109, 4602, 4615, 4629, 4652, 4677, 4708, 4729, 4816,

4861, 5949, 6267, 7106, 7107

Revue belge (Bruxelles), 242

Revue bleue (Paris), 1449

Revue critique des idées et des livres (Paris), 239

Revue de France (Paris), 1310

Revue de Genève (Genève), 240

Revue de la littérature comparée (Paris), 2113, 3888

Revue de la Société d'histoire du théâtre (Paris), 452

Revue de Paris, 1212, 1551, 6371, 6398

Revue des deux mondes (Paris), 890, 1541, 6032, 6157, 6527, 6692

Revue des langues vivantes (Bruxelles), 1142, 1167, 2014, 2137, 2980, 3074, 3076, 3204, 5276, 5424

Revue du mois (Paris), 7319

Revue du siècle (Paris), 246

Revue européenne (Paris), 237, 245, 248

Revue germanique (Paris), 1254, 4461, 4473, 6538, 6539

Rheinisch-Westfälische Zeitung (Essen), 6462

Rheinische Post (Düsseldorf), 3763

Rising Generation (Tokyo), 1130

Riverside Quarterly (Saskatoon, Sask.), 1789

Rivista di letteratura moderne e comparata (Firenze; title varies), 5542

Rivista di studi teatrali (Milano), 3395

Roeping (Tilburg), 280, 3637

Romans i Powieść (supplement to Świat; Warszawa), 232d

Root and Branch (Bognor, Sussex), 3282

Round Table (London), 871, 4047a

Rozhledy (Praha), 5546

RTV Guide (Dublin), 2518, 2558a

Rudé právo (Praha), 1257

Ruimten (Hoboken), 2285

St. James Budget (London), 4265

St. Martin's Review (London), 5175

St. Pancras Journal (London), 775, 798

Salmagundi (Saratoga Springs, N.Y.), 5801

Salzburger Nachrichten (Salzburg),

NG   Index of Provenance

This index represents the geographical distribution of the items contained in this bibliography, including reviews. Listed below are the countries of publication other than Ireland, England, the United States, and Canada. I do not record the nationalities of authors. Some international periodicals (e.g., *English Studies*, published in Amsterdam) and the books published by firms like Mouton are not included because this would have resulted in serious misrepresentations. Mouton, for instance, publishes more American than Dutch authors. The number of Japanese contributions is in fact only a fraction of those actually published; as explained in the preface, I do not duplicate the list given by Oshima (J2282). I do not differentiate between the various governments of countries such as Germany; pre-1945 Germany and the two post-1945 German states are all listed together. References to sections AB and AF are omitted.

Italy, 464, 715, 906, 1100, 1101,
1114, 1206, 1223, 1235, 1249,
1334, 1335, 1363a, 1414, 1531,
1535, 1553, 1582, 1613, 1631,
1672, 1888, 2278, 2552, 2575,
2602, 2612, 2623, 2709, 2780,
3099, 3260, 3271, 3395, 3437,
3442, 3449, 3890, 3979, 4163,
4215, 4219, 4239, 4242, 4245,
4247, 4250-53, 5170, 5232, 5473,
5488, 5542, 5551-53, 5955, 5985,
6078, 6096, 6166, 6314-16, 6369,
6409, 6478, 6565, 6768, 6963,
6967, 7167, 7401
Japan, 549, 1130, 1161, 1162, 1355,
1751, 1779, 1848, 1878, 2003a,
2271, 2281a, 2282, 2391, 2443,
2514, 2564, 2590, 2647, 2679,
2819, 2845, 2850, 2897a, 2900,
2936, 3192, 3234, 3492, 3557,
3563, 3564, 3567, 4019, 4132,
5756, 5807, 6153, 6230, 6338
Korea, 1102, 1123, 1661, 2064, 2719,
2808, 2860, 3182, 3559, 4005
Lebanon, 554, 2481, 3386, 4254,
7317
Mexico, 1419, 2973
Netherlands, 473, 556, 1071, 1072,
1100, 1108, 1213, 1226, 1309,
1406, 1418, 1537, 1698, 1785,
2286, 2287, 2345, 2404, 2422,
2427, 2627, 2731, 2959, 3239,
3637, 3689, 3693, 3830, 3833,
3986, 4085, 4172, 4246, 4943,
5065, 5072, 5449, 5533, 5913,
6194, 6363, 6549a
New Zealand, 1142, 1423, 3121
Norway, 372, 1225, 1320, 1377, 1559,
1614, 2014, 2327, 2328, 2989,
3378, 3446, 6408
Pakistan, 1948, 2736, 3744, 4113
Philippines, 2678, 3087, 3105, 7381
Poland, 481, 1174, 1186, 1318, 1368,
1439, 1499, 1514, 1547, 1705,
2587, 3006, 3650, 4236, 5798,

6052, 6179a, 6189, 6435, 6469,
6517, 6550, 7183, 7305, 7444
Portugal, 1476, 7186
Rumania, 1315, 1486, 1653, 4248,
6042, 7004, 7123, 7124
South Africa, 1078, 1408, 1699a,
1852, 2118, 2584a, 2795, 2918,
2979, 2987, 3011, 3096, 3213,
4192, 6940, 7099, 7101
Spain, 2973, 3403, 3590, 4223,
6542a, 7320
Sweden, 463, 1071, 1081, 1245,
1378, 1518, 1646, 2242, 2424,
2446, 2509, 2807, 3080a, 3291,
3349, 3681, 4689, 4826, 4910,
5349, 5407, 5478, 5509a, 5755,
5953, 6063, 6095, 6323, 6367,
6471, 6813, 7039, 7279, 7408
Switzerland, 492, 698a, 909, 1104,
1253, 1278, 1345, 1402, 1417,
1628, 1847, 1903, 1973, 2235,
2616, 2675, 2753, 2768, 3392,
3457, 3516, 3532, 3594, 3755,
3758, 3759, 3765, 3920, 3925,
3926, 3928, 4238, 4727, 5485,
5563, 6218, 6395, 6486, 6553-
56, 6560, 6571, 6676, 6860,
6942, 7232
Syria, 6488
Taiwan, 2743a
Turkey, 2939, 6295
USSR, 1230, 1413, 1521, 1644, 1673,
2540, 2655, 3326, 3385, 4405,
5947a, 6079, 6203, 6270, 6320,
6359, 6410, 6438, 6559, 7087,
7114, 7115, 7127, 7128, 7137,
7138, 7144, 7145, 7160a, 7175,
7421a, 7430a
Vatican City, 1333, 6037
Venezuela, 2973
Vietnam, 4184
Yugoslavia, 1187, 1637, 1645, 1803,
2009, 2470, 2508, 2557, 2604,
2680, 2732, 2889, 2922, 3118,
3410, 7361

NH   Index of Asterisked Items

As explained in the introduction, items marked with an asterisk (*) are,
in my opinion, essential reading for any extended research on Yeats.

12, 389, 390, 514, 556, 561, 923, 1072, 1073, 1076, 1078, 1079, 1081, 1082,
1090, 1091, 1101, 1108, 1112, 1114, 1126, 1141, 1142, 1147, 1151-53, 1155-
57, 1696, 1836, 2420, 2425, 2431, 2439, 2444, 3324, 3335, 3336, 3345, 3985,
4228, 5922, 6301

K. P. S. JOCHUM teaches in the English department
of the University of Freiburg, Germany. He has
published *W. B. Yeats's Plays: An Annotated
Checklist of Criticism* and *Die dramatische Struktur der Spiele von W. B. Yeats* and has completed
a book on informational strategies in English
Renaissance drama. Jochum earned a doctor of
philosophy degree in 1968 at Johann Wolfgang
Goethe-Universität, Frankfurt am Main, Germany.